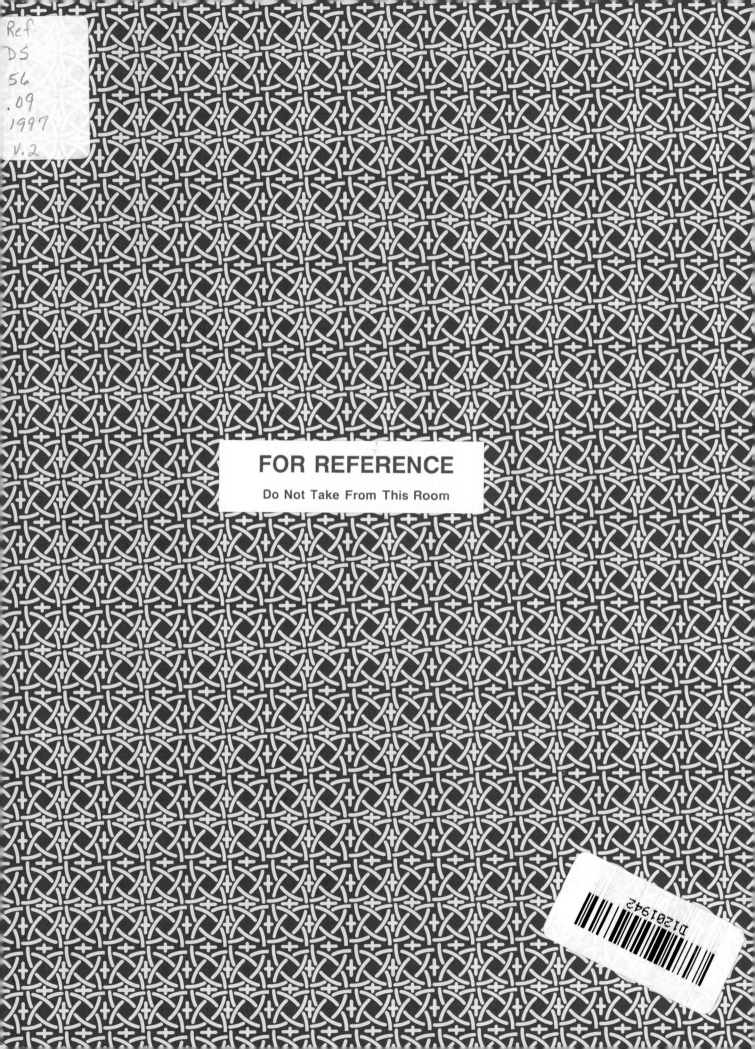

THE OXFORD
ENCYCLOPEDIA OF
ARCHAEOLOGY
IN THE NEAR EAST

PREPARED UNDER THE AUSPICES OF THE

AMERICAN SCHOOLS OF ORIENTAL RESEARCH

Eric M. Meyers

EDITOR IN CHIEF

VOLUME 2

New York   Oxford
OXFORD UNIVERSITY PRESS
1997

Oxford University Press

Oxford   New York
Athens   Auckland   Bangkok   Bogotá
Bombay   Buenos Aires   Calcutta   Cape Town
Dar es Salaam   Delhi   Florence   Hong Kong   Istanbul
Karachi   Kuala Lumpur   Madras   Madrid   Melbourne
Mexico City   Nairobi   Paris   Singapore
Taipei   Tokyo   Toronto

and associated companies in
Berlin   Ibadan

Published by Oxford University Press, Inc.,
198 Madison Avenue, New York, New York 10016

Oxford is a registered trademark of Oxford University Press

Library of Congress Cataloging-in-Publication Data
The Oxford encyclopedia of archaeology in the Near East / prepared
under the auspices of the American Schools of Oriental Research;
Eric M. Meyers, editor in chief.
p.   cm.
Includes bibliographical references (p.   ) and index.
1. Middle East—Antiquities—Encyclopedias. 2. Africa, North—Antiquities—
Encyclopedias. I. Meyers, Eric M. II. American Schools of Oriental Research.
DS56.09   1996   96-17152   939′.4—dc20   CIP

ISBN 0-19-506512-3 (set)
ISBN 0-19-511216-4 (vol. 2)

*Many photographs and line drawings used herein were supplied by contributors to the work. Others
were drawn from the archives of the American Schools of Oriental Research, from commercial
photographic archives, and from the holdings of major museums and cultural institutions.
The publisher has made every effort to ascertain that necessary permissions to reprint
materials have been secured. Sources of all photographs and line drawings
are given in the captions to illustrations.*

Printing (last digit): 9   8   7   6   5   4   3   2   1

Printed in the United States of America on acid-free paper

ABBREVIATIONS AND SYMBOLS

ACOR	American Center of Oriental Research
AD	*anno Domini,* in the year of the (our) Lord
AH	*anno Hegirae,* in the year of the Hijrah
AIA	Archaeological Institute of America
AIAR	(W. F.) Albright Institute of Archaeological Research
AJA	*American Journal of Archaeology*
Akk.	Akkadian
Am.	*Amos*
ANEP	J. B. Pritchard, ed., *Ancient Near East in Pictures*
ANET	J. B. Pritchard, ed., *Ancient Near Eastern Texts*
AOS	American Oriental Society
APES	American Palestine Exploration Society
Ar.	Arabic
'Arakh.	*'Arakhin*
Aram.	Aramaic
ASOR	American Schools of Oriental Research
Assyr.	Assyrian
A.Z.	*'Avodah Zarah*
b.	born
B.A.	Bachelor of Arts
Bab.	Babylonian
BASOR	*Bulletin of the American Schools of Oriental Research*
B.B.	*Bava' Batra'*
BC	before Christ
BCE	before the common era
Bekh.	*Bekhorot*
Ber.	*Berakhot*
Bik.	*Bikkurim*
BP	before the present
BSAE	British School of Archaeology in Egypt
BSAI	British School of Archaeology in Iraq
BSAJ	British School of Archaeology in Jerusalem
B.T.	Babylonian Talmud
c.	*circa,* about, approximately
CAARI	Cyprus American Archaeological Research Institute
CAD	computer-aided design/drafting
CAORC	Council of American Overseas Research Centers
CE	of the common era
cf.	*confer,* compare
chap., chaps.	chapter, chapters
1 Chr.	*1 Chronicles*
2 Chr.	*2 Chronicles*
CIG	*Corpus Inscriptionum Graecarum*
CIS	*Corpus Inscriptionum Semiticarum*
cm	centimeters
CNRS	Centre National de la Recherche Scientifique
col., cols.	column, columns
Col.	*Colossians*
1 Cor.	*1 Corinthians*
2 Cor.	*2 Corinthians*
CTA	A. Herdner, *Corpus des tablettes en cunéiformes alphabétiques*
cu	cubic
d.	died
DAI	Deutsches Archäologisches Institut
diss.	dissertation
Dn.	*Daniel*
DOG	Deutche Orient-Gesellschaft
D.Sc.	Doctor of Science
Dt.	*Deuteronomy*
EB	Early Bronze
Eccl.	*Ecclesiastes*
ed., eds.	editor, editors; edition
ED	Early Dynastic
EEF	Egyptian Exploration Fund
e.g.	*exempli gratia,* for example
Egyp.	Egyptian
Elam.	Elamite
En.	*Enoch*
Eng.	English
enl.	enlarged
esp.	especially
et al.	*et alii,* and others
etc.	*et cetera,* and so forth
Eth.	Ethiopic
et seq.	*et sequens,* and the following
Ex.	*Exodus*
exp.	expanded
Ez.	*Ezekiel*
Ezr.	*Ezra*
fasc.	fascicle
fem.	feminine
ff.	and following
fig.	figure
fl.	*floruit,* flourished
ft.	feet
frag., frags.	fragment, fragments
gal., gals.	gallon, gallons
Geog.	Ptolemy, *Geographica*
Ger.	German
GIS	Geographic Information Systems
Gk.	Greek
Gn.	*Genesis*
ha	hectares
Heb.	Hebrew
Hg.	*Haggai*
Hist.	Herodotus, *History*
Hitt.	Hittite
Hos.	*Hosea*
Hur.	Hurrian
IAA	Israel Antiquities Authority
ibid.	*ibidem,* in the same place (as the one immediately preceding)
IDA(M)	Israel Department of Antiquities (and Museums)
i.e.	*id est,* that is

IEJ	*Israel Exploration Journal*	*Meg.*	*Megillah*	*SEG*	*Supplementum Epigraphicum Graecum*
IES	Israel Exploration Society	mi.	miles	ser.	series
IFAPO	Institut Français d'Archéologie du Proche-Orient	*Mk.*	*Mark*	sg.	singular
Is.	*Isaiah*	mm	millimeter	*Sg.*	*Song of Songs*
IsMEO	Istituto Italiano per il Medio ed Estremo Oriente	mod.	modern	*Shab.*	*Shabbath*
Jb.	*Job*	*Mt.*	Mount	S.J.	Societas Jesu, Society of Jesus (Jesuits)
Jer.	*Jeremiah*	*Mt.*	*Matthew*	*1 Sm.*	*1 Samuel*
Jgs.	*Judges*	n.	note	*2 Sm.*	*2 Samuel*
Jn.	*John*	NAA	Neutron Activation Analysis	sq	square
Jon.	*Jonah*	*Nat. Hist.*	Pliny, *Naturalis Historia* (Natural History)	St., Sts.	Saint, Saints
Jos.	*Joshua*	n.b.	*nota bene*, note well	Sum.	Sumerian
JPOS	*Journal of the Palestine Oriental Society*	n.d.	no date	supp.	supplement
JRA	*Journal of Roman Archaeology*	*Nm.*	*Numbers*	Syr.	Syriac
J.T.	Jerusalem Talmud	no., nos.	number, numbers	*Ta'an.*	*Ta'anit*
KAI	H. Donner and W. Röllig, *Kanaanäische und aramäische Inschriften*	n.p.	no place	Th.D.	Theologicae Doctor, Doctor of Theology
Kel.	*Kelim*	n.s.	new series	*Ti.*	*Titus*
Ket.	*Ketubbot*	O.P.	Ordo Praedicatorum, Order of Preachers (Dominicans)	Tk.	Turkish
kg	kilogram	p., pp.	page, pages	*1 Tm.*	*1 Timothy*
1 Kgs.	*1 Kings*	para.	paragraph	*2 Tm.*	*2 Timothy*
2 Kgs.	*2 Kings*	PEF	Palestine Exploration Fund	trans.	translated by
km	kilometers	Pers.	Persian	Ugar.	Ugaritic
KTU	M. Dietrich and O. Lorentz, *Die keilalphabetischen Texte aus Ugarit*	Ph.D.	Philosophiae Doctor, Doctor of Philosophy	v.	verse
l	liter	*Phil.*	*Philippians*	viz.	*videlicet*, namely
l., ll.	line, lines	pl.	plate; plural	vol., vols.	volume, volumes
Lat.	Latin	PN	Pottery Neolithic	vs.	versus
lb.	pounds	ppm	parts per million	*Yad.*	*Yadayim*
LB	Late Bronze	PPN	Pre-Pottery Neolithic	*ZDPV*	*Zeitschrift des Deutschen Palästina-Vereins*
lit.	literally	*Prv.*	*Proverbs*	*Zec.*	*Zechariah*
Lk.	*Luke*	*Ps.*	*Psalms*	★	hypothetical; in bibliographic citations, English language pages in Hebrew journals
LM	Late Minoan	pt., pts.	part, parts	?	uncertain; possibly; perhaps
Lv.	*Leviticus*	*1 Pt.*	*1 Peter*	°	degrees
m	meters	*2 Pt.*	*2 Peter*	′	minutes; feet
M.A.	Master of Arts	r.	reigned, ruled	″	seconds; inches
masc.	masculine	*RCEA*	*Répertoire chronologique d'epigraphie arabe*	+	plus
Mal.	*Malachi*	*Rev.*	*Revelations*	−	minus
MB	Middle Bronze	rev.	revised	±	plus or minus
Mc.	*Maccabees*	*Ru.*	*Ruth*	=	equals; is equivalent to
M.Div.	Master of Divinity	SBF	Studium Biblicum Franciscanum	×	by
		SBL	Society of Biblical Literature	→	yields

C

CHURCHES. The earliest Christians called their communities *ekklesiai,* "gatherings," "congregations," "assemblies." *Ecclesia* was used throughout the period of Late Antiquity to denote both the local community of Christians gathered in a specific place and the worldwide Christian community, the church universal. The early fourth-century adoption of the Greek term *kyriakon* ("place" or "house" or "temple belonging to the Lord") to denote the place where Christians gathered to worship is a sign of the heightened awareness of physical place that characterized Christianity at the end of the pre-Constantinian period. From the early fourth century onward, *kyriakon* and *ecclesia* came to be used interchangeably (and with some frequency) to denote Christian places of worship.

Before Constantine. In the *Acts of the Apostles,* Christians are said to have gathered in private houses in Jerusalem, Caesarea, Jaffa, Damascus, Paphos, Ephesus, Colossae, Philippi, Thessalonike, Corinth and Kenchreai, Alexandria in the Troad, and Rome (Finney, 1984, pp. 208, 209). During the period of his missionary activity in western Turkey, Paul aimed his message at heads of households, and it is primarily on this basis that the existence is inferred of mid-first-century communities of Christians or *ekklesiai* gathered in private houses. Archaeology cannot identify the specific buildings used as meeting places within the Pauline missionary territory because they were left intact. As structural types, it would be impossible to distinguish them from the local residential vernacular.

The oldest surviving house that can be given a positive identification as a building that served a small community of mid-third-century Christians is in Syria, at Dura-Europos, a Roman trading city on the west bank of the Middle Euphrates River. Shortly before the mid-third century, the Christian building at Dura was extensively remodeled on the ground-floor level. Thereafter it no longer served as a residence. Instead, the first-floor space was given over to community-related activities, although the arrangement and assignment of space on the second floor are not known. One of the first-floor rooms was converted into a baptistery; another—a large, rectangular room created by the consolidation of two previously small spaces—probably functioned as the worship room. A celebrating priest would have stood on a raised platform (bema) at the east end and presided in the reading of Scripture and perhaps in a community eucharistic meal.

As argued elsewhere (Finney, 1984, p. 224), once the secular functions of the Durene first-floor space were replaced, the community had to readjust its symbolic associations with its place of worship. The way was opened for a new set of symbolic associations centering on the sacral character of the place and its architectural embodiment.

There are other examples of pre-Constantinian structures (residential, commercial, and possibly municipal) remodeled and retrofitted to make way for an emerging ecclesia, but none is so clear or so dramatic as the Christian building at Dura. Most of the material parallels are found in the West (Rome, Aquileia, Parentium-Poreč, Lullingstone in Kent, England), but there is at least one relatively clear Near Eastern example, the so-called Julianos basilica (cf. Piccirillo, 1981, pp. 54–55) at Umm el-Jimal (Butler, 1919, 2.A.3; Corbett, 1957) 18 km (11 mi.) southwest of Bosra. [*See* Umm el-Jimal.]

Although surviving literary/documentary sources, together with bits and pieces of material evidence, favor the view that pre-Constantinian Christians gathered for worship mainly in residential buildings and over time adapted and converted those structures into church buildings, it is also true that this pattern alone does not exhaust the totality of the pre-Constantinian evidence. Other kinds of spaces were needed from time to time, particularly where the size of Christian congregations exceeded imposed space limitations. This became a pressing issue late in the tetrarchy (293–312 CE), as urban churches were increasing their numbers on a dramatic scale. It is in the time frame of the late third century that some Christian communities evidently turned to nonresidential architecture (warehouses and rectangular municipal halls) to solve the problem. L. Michael White calls this a transitional phase, sandwiched between the so-called house church *(domus ecclesiae)* period of Christian worship and the basilical architectural settings that came in the wake of Constantine's building program (White, 1990, pp. 127–139). Two examples of early fourth-century hall-like rectangular structures that fit White's typology were designed and constructed de novo as church buildings: the

Roman Church of San Crisogono in Trastevere and the church at Qirk Bize, one of the so-called Dead Cities west of Aleppo (and west of Jebel ʿAla) in northern Syria (Tchalenko, 1953–1958, pp. 319–332; Donceel-Voûte, 1988, pp. 259–260; also Georges Tate, "Qirk Bizah," in *Encyclopedia of Early Christian Art and Archaeology* [hereafter *EECAA*]).

Geographic Setting. The geographic extent of the evidence in the Near East is impressive. Church buildings and church-related structures (e.g., baptisteries and martyria) that predate the seventh century survive either intact or in fragments over a broad area. [*See* Martyrion.] In the north and northwest, churches are found in the Caucasus Mountains (e.g., Georgia [see Kleinbauer, no. 375] and Armenia [see R. Edwards, "Armenia," *EECAA*]) and in central and eastern Turkey, including the Pontic region (Kleinbauer, 1992, no. 207), Cappadocia (Restle, 1971–), and Cilicia (Hild et al., 1971–). At the other end of the Near East, in Africa to the far south, Early Christian architectural remains are attested in the Nile Delta and on both banks of the Nile River, south to Syene/Aswan (Grossmann, 1991, pp. 552–553; Grossmann, "Egypt," *EECAA*) In Nubian territory, from Aswan south to the confluence of the White and Blue Niles, there is little or no material that predates the seventh century and can be positively identified as Christian (Adams, 1991), but east of Khartoum, on Ethiopian soil (M. E. Heldman, "Ethiopia," *EECAA*), Early Christian architectural remains of church buildings appear at several sites, the most important being Adulis, Axum, and Maṭara. Across the Gulf of Suez in the southern Sinai (Wadi Feiran and the region of Jebel Musa), there are monastic churches and chapels from Late Antiquity (Tsafrir, 1993, pp. 315–350). For the territories opposite Nubia and Ethiopia across the Red Sea—namely Saudi Arabia, Yemen (especially Najran), southern Yemen, and the island of Socotra (at the eastern end of the Gulf of Aden)—literary traditions and selected epigraphic evidence attest the presence of Christians from the late-fourth century onward but no church architecture (Trimingham, 1979).

Within the central Near East—Cyprus, the Syro-Palestinian littoral (and the adjacent inland territories), Lebanon, Israel, Syria, Jordan, Iraq, and the western third of Iran—there is extensive evidence of Early church buildings. The evidence is greatest in roughly the western quarter, from the Mediterranean coastline east for approximately 300 km, or 186 mi.: in Lebanon (Donceel-Voûte, 1988); Israel (Tsafrir, 1993); and Cyprus (Kleinbauer, 1992). There is considerable evidence of pre-seventh-century church buildings on Cyprus. From the late fifth century onward, Cypriot church architecture was substantially influenced by Constantinopolitan models; hence, for the period from about 450 to 650, Cyprus must be studied with particular attention to its Greek progenitors (Megaw, 1974; Papageorghiou, 1986).

Inland from the Syro-Palestinian littoral, the western third of Jordan, from the Gulf of ʿAqaba north to the Jordanian/

Syrian border, also contains numerous early Christian church buildings (Piccirillo, 1981, 1993). This distribution pattern continues northward, also within roughly the western third of Syria (Butler, 1919–1920) from Bosra (Bostra; Butler, 1919, 2.A.4; Dentzer-Feydy 1985) at the southern end of the so-called lava lands (the Hauran; Dentzer-Feydy, 1985) to Jebal Arab (also known as Jebel Druze and Jebel Hauran) in the south to Ḥalab (Aleppo) in the north and to the architecturally extraordinary territory west of Aleppo, the region of the so-called Dead Cities. The region is one of the richest centers of Early Christian architecture in the ancient world. It is there, for example, that the great monastery-church of St. Simeon Stylites is located (at Qalʿat Simʿan; J.-P. Sodini, "Qalʿat Semaʿan," *EECAA*). [*See* Qalʿat Simʿan.] Across the Syrian/Turkish border, in southeastern Anatolia (Osrhoene, fourth–seventh centuries), stretching from Urfa/Edessa to Mardin, Nusaybin, and Cizre on the Tigris River, are remains of numerous church buildings from Late Antiquity (Wiessner, 1981–1993). There are also important Early Christian remains along the Syrian Euphrates River: at Membij/Hierapolis, Rusafa/Sergiopolis (T. Ulbert, "Rusafa," *EECAA*), Halabiyya/Zenobia, and, of course, at as-Salihiyeh/Dura-Europos (Kraeling, 1967). [*See* Rusafa; Dura-Europos.] Both Iraq and Iran, within roughly the western third of the Sasanian Empire (226–651), once contained an extensive Early Christian material culture—church buildings, chapels, baptisteries, monasteries—but the surviving remains are meager (Lerner, 1982–).

The most important urban centers for church architecture in the Near East before the seventh century were Jerusalem and Syrian Antioch (now located in the province of Hatay, Turkey). Alexandria was also an important city for Early Christian culture (Epiphanius and Eusebius; Pearson, 1992) It housed numerous church buildings, but almost no material evidence survives (for a twelfth-century list of Alexandrian churches, many of them alleged to be pre-seventh century, cf. Atiya, 1991). Jerusalem, more firmly rooted (than Constantinople) in tradition, was arguably the most important center of church architecture from the fourth through sixth centuries. Constantine built two churches there, the Holy Sepulcher (now within the city's Christian Quarter; see figure 1) and the Eleona Church on the Mt. of Olives. Each commemorates events in the life of Jesus, and hence both served martyrial purposes. At Antioch, Constantine also became a church builder, of an eight-sided church with a gilded roof, of which nothing survives (Kleinbauer, 1992, no. 2064). In general, direct material evidence of Early Christian church buildings in Syrian Antioch is slight (excluding the martyrion of St. Babylas outside the city in suburban Kaoussie; Kleinbauer, 1992, no. 1894a).

Fourth Century. The fourth century was a watershed for church design and construction; it was a period of invention, innovation, diversity and creativity. The architectural legacy of Constantine I the Great cast a long shadow beyond his death in 337 (Krautheimer, 1967). Beginning as early as 305, the emperor and his architects had set about creating a tradition of Christian church architecture, in both halves of the empire, but especially in the Byzantine Levant. The degree to which the emperor was directly involved in design is a matter for debate (Krautheimer, 1967), but he provided financial and logistical support and there can be no question about his commitment and determination to see church buildings in virtually all major urban centers: Bishop Paulinus's church in Tyre; the Holy Sepulcher (Church of the Anastasis) and the Eleona Church on the Mt. of Olives (over a cave associated by tradition with the Ascension of Jesus) in Jerusalem (Taylor, 1993, pp. 143–156); the Church of the Nativity in Bethlehem (Taylor, 1993, pp. 86–95); the basilica built at the sacred oak tree in Mamre/Ramat el-Khalil, where God spoke to Abraham; the Hagia Sophia and the Church (or Martyrium) of the Holy Apostles in Constantinople; and the palace church, called the Golden Octagon, in Antioch.

The growth of Christian communities in the fourth century necessitated large interior spaces to accommodate the faithful. Architectural precedents were lacking within pagan tradition, so builders looked to secular spatial and architectonic paradigms that could be adapted. The best solutions were the imperial halls *(aulae)* and assembly rooms spread throughout the empire that had been designed as indoor markets, law courts, and audience rooms—large interior spaces that served the interests of bureaucrats seeking to govern Rome's subjects.

The Constantinian church building came to be known by the epithet *basilica,* understood as the building belonging to the *basileus,* or "king." The formal architectural precedents of the rectangular building that came to typify it have long been debated (Ward-Perkins, 1954). It is now understood that the term denotes a rectangular building, with two long sides and two short sides, oriented on liturgical and symbolic grounds toward one of the short ends (usually on the east), with or without aisles, with a sanctuary and often an apse (or apses) at one end, and with a gabled roof (often faced with terra-cotta tiles) supported by wooden trusses (Orlandos, 1952–1956). However, for the Constantinian period there was no equivalency between the term *basilica* and these architectural elements. The Holy Sepulcher, the Church of the Nativity, the Hagia Sophia, the Church of the Holy Apostles, and the Golden Octagon are all centrally planned spaces, dominated both spatially and visually by large domes sitting on circular or polygonal perimeters; the domed spaces interrupt the longitudinal flow of space from nave to apse and instead proclaim a rather different symbolic hierarchy. In short, the term *basilica* does not denote a fixed architectural form until the late fourth century—and even at that late date there is still considerable variation in architectural detail.

From the beginning of the Constantinian architectural program, there was a strong pull toward assimilating two distinct functions: community worship and other veneration and/or commemoration of a sacred person, place, thing or event. The Holy Sepulcher was constructed over places where Jesus was thought to have been crucified, buried, and risen, and the octagonal domed structure at the east end of the Church of the Nativity was constructed over a cave that

CHURCHES. Figure 1. *Church of the Holy Sepulcher, Jerusalem.* (Courtesy Pictorial Archive)

came to be identified in one tradition as the place where Mary had given birth. In both, the church building functioned at once as a place for liturgical worship and veneration of the hero of the Christian story.

In the second half of the fourth century, a church building was assimilated to a martyrium (begun perhaps early in the reign of Theodosius I, 379–395) and dedicated to St. Babylas at Kaoussie (Donceel-Voûte, 1988, pp. 21–31). Constructed on the model of a Greek cross, this building contained the buried remains of the saint at the center of the cruciform plan; in the same emplacement aboveground was an altar for celebrating the Eucharist.

Fifth–Sixth Centuries. Architecturally, the fifth century was a period of consolidation and standarization. The Constantinian architectural types were replicated across the Near East. The two basic spatial concepts that animated Early Christian architecture—rectangular, longitudinally oriented, hall-like space and open, centrally planned, domical vertical space—continued to dominate. Fifth-century remains are extensive. Within the Anatolian realm is the remarkable cluster of churches called Bin Bir Kilisse ("the Thousand and One Churches") in southeastern Lycaonia, approximately 80 km (50 mi.) southeast of Konya/Iconium. The Anatolian churches include a few centrally planned structures, but the majority are longitudinally oriented on a rectagonal grid with an apse at one of the short ends. Northeast of Bin Bir Kilisse, across the Cappadocian highlands (Aksaray, Nevşehir, Kayseri) to the Anti-Taurus range, and then south toward the Cilician coast, and east again across Osrhoene, are numerous remains of church buildings from the late fifth and early sixth centuries.

For centrally planned structures and a common architectural matrix for eastern Anatolia (including Armenia) and the adjacent Levantine territories, especially northern Syria, a fifth-/sixth-century example is the octagonal building (now destroyed) at Sivasa, northeast of Aksaray (Rott, 1908, pp. 249–54). A roofless apse projected from the eastern perimeter of this octagon, reproducing the same plan found in the so-called Church of the House of Peter (Virgilio Corbo in Tsafrir, 1993, pp. 71–76; Taylor, 1993, pp. 268–288) at Capernaum in Galilee and the Church of Mary Theotokos (Yitzhak Magen in Tsafrir, 1993, pp. 83–89) on Mt. Gerizim in Samaria.

As in the fourth century, the sixth was a period of innovation dominated by a powerful patron, Emperor Justinian (482–565). Justinian was more directly involved in the design and execution of church buildings than was Constantine. The result was a building type (centrally planned, vaulted, and domed) that appears throughout the sixth century, especially in the Near East. The paradigm is the centrally planned Hagia Sophia built in 532–537 (Mainstone, 1988). Along with domed and centrally planned buildings, longitudinally planned churches continued to be built throughout the Near East in the sixth century.

[*See also* Baptisteries; Basilicas; House Churches; Martyrion; *and* Monasteries. *In addition to the sites individually cross-referenced above, many other sites mentioned are the subject of independent entries.*]

BIBLIOGRAPHY

Adams, William Y. "Nubia." In *The Coptic Encyclopedia*, vol. 6, pp. 1800–1801. New York, 1991.

Atiya, A. S. "Alexandria, Historic Churches." In *The Coptic Encyclopedia*, vol. 1, pp. 92–95. New York, 1991.

Bell, Gertrude Lowthian. *The Churches and Monasteries of the Ṭūr ʿAbdīn.* Edited by Marlia M. Mango. London, 1982.

Butler, Howard Crosby. *Publications of the Princeton University Archaeological Expeditions to Syria in 1904–1905 and 1909.* Division II, Section A (Southern Syria) Section B (Northern Syria). Leiden, 1919–1920. Valuable for its maps, plans, photos, and line-drawn reconstructions.

Corbett, G. U. S. "Investigations at the 'Julianos' Church' at Umm-el-Jemal." *Papers of the British School at Rome* 25 (1957): 39–65.

Dentzer-Feydy, Jacqueline. "Décor architectural et développement du Hauran du Ier siècle avant J.-C. au VIIe siècle après J.-C." In *Hauran I*, edited by Jean-Marie Dentzer, pp. 261–310. Bibliothèque Archéologique et Historique, vol. 124. Paris, 1985.

Dölger, Franz Joseph. "'Kirche' als Name für den christlichen Kultbau." *Antike und Christentum* 6 (1950): 161–195. Constructive remarks on the terminology of church buildings based on fourth-century literary evidence.

Donceel-Voûte, Pauline. *Les pavements des églises byzantines de Syrie et du Liban: Décor, archéologie et liturgie.* 2 vols. Louvain-la-Neuve, 1988. Mosaic inventory, useful also as a handbook of Early Christian churches in Syria and Lebanon, with important observations on the liturgical uses of church buildings.

Encyclopedia of Early Christian Art and Archaeology (EECAA). Grand Rapids, forthcoming.

Finney, Paul Corby. "TOPOS HIEROS und christlicher Sakralbau in vorkonstantinischer Überlieferung." *Boreas* 7 (1984): 193–225. Survey of pre-Constantinian literary evidence for Christian practices and attitudes toward sacred place and sacred space.

Gerster, Georg. *Churches in Rock: Early Christian Art in Ethiopia.* London, 1970. Well-illustrated book of medieval Ethiopian monuments, with a brief but useful bibliography.

Grossmann, Peter. "Church Architecture in Egypt." In *The Coptic Encyclopedia*, vol. 2, pp. 552–555. New York, 1991.

Heldman, Marilyn E. *African Zion.* New Haven, 1993. Catalog of an exhibition on Ethiopian art, primarily concerned with the pictorial arts but including a brief discussion of architecture and a valuable bibliography.

Hild, Friedrich, et al. "Kommagene-Kilikein-Isaurien." In *Reallexikon zur byzantinischen Kunst*, vol. 4, cols. 182–355. Stuttgart, 1971–.

Hirschfeld, Yizhar. *The Judean Desert Monasteries in the Byzantine Period.* New Haven, 1992.

Kleinbauer, W. Eugene. *Early Christian and Byzantine Architecture: An Annotated Bibliography and Historiography.* Boston, 1992. Now the indispensable lexical tool for the study of Early Christian architecture; immensely informative.

Kraeling, Carl H. *The Christian Building.* The Excavations at Dura-Europos, Final Report 8, part 2. New Haven, 1967.

Krautheimer, Richard. "The Constantinian Basilica." *Dumbarton Oaks Papers* 21 (1967): 115–140.

Krautheimer, Richard, and Slobodan Curcic. *Early Christian and Byzantine Architecture.* 4th ed. New Haven, 1986. Concise introduction to Early Christian architecture.

Lerner, Judith. "Christianity in Pre-Islamic Persia: Material Remains." *Encyclopaedia Iranica*, vol. 5, pp. 528–530. London, 1982–.

Mainstone, Rowland J. *Hagia Sophia: Architecture, Structure, and Liturgy of Justinian's Great Church.* New York, 1988.

Mathews, Thomas F. *The Early Churches of Constantinople: Architecture and Liturgy.* University Park, Pa., 1971. Description and interpretation of nine churches (see Müller-Wiener, below, excluding the church of St. Menas), with a brief evaluation of St. John in Hebdomon, outside Istanbul.

Megaw, A. H. S. "Byzantine Architecture and Decoration in Cyprus: Metropolitan or Provincial?" *Dumbarton Oaks Papers* 28 (1974): 57–88. An informative survey of church buildings dated before the mid-seventh century.

Müller-Wiener, Wolfgang. "Kirchen." In *Bildlexikon zur Topographie Istanbuls,* pp. 72–215. Tübingen, 1977. Description with photographs and bibliography of nine Constantinopolitan churches (unnamed buildings in Beyazit and Topkapı Sarayı, Theotokos in Chalkoprateia, St. Sophia, St. Eirene, St. Euphemia, St. John Studios, SS. Peter and Paul/Sergius and Bacchos, St. Polyeuktos), dating to Late Antiquity. A tenth church, by tradition attributed to St. Menas, is perhaps better identified with the lost church of SS. Karpos and Polykarp, a possible early (c. 400) copy of the Holy Sepulcher.

Munro-Hay, Stuart. *Aksum: An African Civilisation of Late Antiquity.* Edinburgh, 1991.

Orlandos, Anastasios K. *He xylostegos palaiochristianike Basilike tes mesogeiakes lekanes.* 3 vols. Athens, 1952–1956. Wooden-roofed Early Christian basilica in the Mediterranean basin.

Papageorghiou, Athanasios. "Foreign Influences on the Early Christian Architecture of Cyprus." In *Acts of the International Archaeological Symposium, "Cyprus between the Orient and the Occident," 8–14 September 1985,* edited by Vassos Karageorghis et al., pp. 489–504. Nicosia, 1986.

Pearson, Birger A. "Alexandria." In *The Anchor Bible Dictionary,* vol. 1, p. 152. New York, 1992.

Piccirillo, Michele. *Chiese e mosaici della giordania settentrionale.* Jerusalem, 1981. Inventory of floor mosaics, also informative as a listing (and in parts a description) of Early Christian church buildings.

Piccirillo, Michele. *The Mosaics of Jordan.* Amman, 1993. More tessellated floors. An exemplary publication, with splendid photographs, plans of churches, an informative introduction with notes and descriptions of individual monuments, and a good bibliography.

Ponomarew, Wladimir. "Georgien." In *Reallexikon zur byzantinischen Kunst,* vol. 2, cols. 662–734. Stuttgart, 1971–.

Restle, Marcell. "Höhlenkirchen." In *Reallexikon zur byzantinischen Kunst,* vol. 3, cols. 247–252. Stuttgart, 1971–.

Restle, Marcell. "Kappadokien." In *Reallexikon zur byzantinischen Kunst,* vol. 3, cols. 975–1116. Stuttgart, 1971–. Informative survey of Cappadocian churches, including selected cave churches.

Rott, Hans. *Kleinasiatische Denkmäler aus Pisidien, Pamphylien, Kapodokien und Lykien.* Leipzig, 1908.

Taylor, J. E. *Christians and the Holy Places: The Myth of Jewish-Christian Origins.* Oxford, 1993. Informative and careful study of the pre-Constantinian cults and religious traditions associated with the sites that came to be venerated as Christian in the fourth century. Highly critical of the theory that Christian material continuity can be traced from the apostolic to Constantinian periods.

Tchalenko, Georges. *Villages antiques de la Syrie du Nord: Le massif du Bélus à l'époque romaine.* 3 vols. Bibliothèque Archéologique et Historique, vol. 50. Paris, 1953–1958.

Thierry, Jean-Michel. *Les arts armeniens.* Paris, 1987.

Thierry, Michel. *Répertoire des monastères arméniens.* Turnhout, 1993. List of Armenian monastic establishments (with churches), most of them medieval.

Trimingham, J. Spencer. *Christianity among the Arabs in Pre-Islamic Times.* London, 1979. Brief, popular introduction based on literary and epigraphic sources, with a useful historical survey and bibliography.

Tsafrir, Yoram, ed. *Ancient Churches Revealed.* Jerusalem, 1993. Brief descriptions and interpretations with a bibliography of churches, most of them pre-Islamic and most (except monuments in southern Sinai) in Israel.

Ward-Perkins, J. B. "Constantine and the Origins of the Christian Basilica." *Papers of the British School at Rome* 22 (1954): 69–90. Intelligent survey of putative architectural models.

White, L. Michael. *Building God's House in the Roman World: Architectural Adaptation among Pagans, Jews, and Christians.* Baltimore, 1990. Informative discussion of the pre-Constantinian period. Advances earlier scholarship by isolating several socioevolutionary stages that set the framework for the gradual development of architectural types.

Wiessner, Gernot. *Nordmesopotamische Ruinenstätten.* Göttinger Orientforschungen, II. Reihe: Studien zur spätantiken und frühchristlichen Kunst, vol. 2. Wiesbaden, 1980. Environs of Diyarbakir/Mardin: two fortresses and two Early Christian churches.

Wiessner, Gernot. *Christliche Kultbauten im Ṭur ʿAbdin.* Göttinger Orientforschungen, II. Reihe: Studien zur spätantiken und frühchristlichen Kunst, vol. 4.1–4.8 vols. Wiesbaden, 1981–1993. Careful survey of churches with longitudinal and transverse naves (some of the latter are cave churches) within the region of Mardin Dağları/Ṭūr ʿAbdin east to Dicle; includes a bibliography.

PAUL CORBY FINNEY

CHURCH INSCRIPTIONS.

CHURCH INSCRIPTIONS. Epigraphic sources constitute a major contribution to what is known of the historical development of a local or regional church, its specific organization, and its beliefs. Inscriptions from the early centuries of Christianity have been discovered by the thousands and continue to be recovered and published. Only the character and contents of church inscriptions written in Greek, the language most commonly used by Christians in Byzantine lands, are considered here. Relevant epigraphy exists in other languages, such as Syriac, Armenian, Georgian and Coptic. [*See* Syriac; Armenian; Coptic.]

Although methodical studies on church epigraphy exist, there is no general corpus. However, besides those appearing in the *Corpus Inscriptionum Graecarum* (4 vols., Berlin, 1828–1877), inscriptions are published as they are discovered in the region: in Syria (Jalabert and Mouterde, 1929–1959; Moab (Canova, 1954); the Negev desert (Alt, 1921; Negev, 1981); Jordan (Gatier, 1986; Piccirillo, 1993); Israel (Meimaris, 1986); Madaba (Piccirillo, 1989); and others. Monographs may concentrate on a particular subject, such as magical formulas on the lintels of Christian homes in Syria (see William K. Prentice, *American Journal of Archaeogy* 10 [1906]: 137–150) or on a heretical expression typical of Asia Minor (Gibson, 1978). Inscriptions are found in all areas of religious buildings, but especially on the floors of churches and chapels, on liturgic furniture, on column capitals, and on chancel screens; tombstones; lintels of private houses; and objects of daily use. They may also differ from one another in style and content. In general, however, they tend to be formulaic and do not deviate from the tradition.

Dedicatory Inscriptions. The immediate aim of the dedicatory inscription is to keep a public record of the names and titles of those who contributed in one way or another to the construction, embellishement, or renewal of a religious place or a part of it. This material is of reliable historical value, as much as it records also some information about an inscription's date and circumstances. By way of example, recent excavations of churches in Israel have yielded information about Byzantine emperors as promoters of church construction, such as Justinian I in Jerusalem, or merely as dating references, such as Mauritius Tiberius in Kursi and Tiberius Constantinus in Nessana. References to donors of rank, such as an ex-assessor of the city of Emesa/Homs in such a remote place as Nessana in the Negev (Meimaris, 1986, p. 227), are significant because they reflect the degree of involvement of secular authorities in church life. The names of numerous donors (lit., "fruit bearers" in Greek), however, remain anonymous, even though they are usually the relatives of the person "for whose salvation" a building or some small part of it had been offered.

The main contribution of dedicatory inscriptions is in the field of church organization, as by their nature they refer to local clergy, recording their full titles and epithets, from the highest dignitaries to the lowest ecclesiastical orders. Meimaris's monograph on the church of Palestine lists the following titles: patriarch, metropolitan, archbishop, bishop, country bishop (chorepiscopus), archpresbyter (only two cases), presbyter, assistant presbyter, archdeacon, deacon, deaconess, subdeacon, lector, doorkeeper, *periodeutes*, oeconomus, and *paramonarius* (Meimaris, 1986, pp. 165–226).

Epigraphic references to church officials, who often otherwise would not be known to have existed, thus essentially help in the drawing up of the episcopal lists of a given diocese in periods for which no literary proofs exist. A case in point is the Madaba region in Transjordan, where a number of recently discovered inscriptions unexpectedly attest to the vitality and organization of that diocese during the 'Abbasid period (Piccirillo, 1989, pp. 322–324). An interesting feature of the dedicatory inscriptions appearing on mosaic floors is the occasional reference to the people who worked on the mosaic, suggesting art schools or mosaic workshops. The mosaists appear to add their own names to the list of dignataries and donors, almost as a prayer: "In the time of . . . this mosaic was completed . . . for the (eternal) rest of Basilides and the salvation of Elias son of Elias the mosaist." Other inscriptions start by mentioning the artisan: "This is the work of mosaists Nahum, Cyriakos, and Thomas. . . ."

Funerary Inscriptions. Mortuary epigraphy is an indispensable complement to the historic relevance of dedications. Inscriptions are found on funerary stelae in open cemeteries as well as on the floors of churches. Tomb slabs are often seen in the nave, aisles, presbytery, diaconicum, annexed chapels, and baptisteries. Not all of these tombs have identifying inscriptions, but those that do attest to the presence of clergy, monks, and lay people—men and women—probably of a certain position and particularly related to that specific church or to its patron saint. [*See* Burial Techniques; Churches; Baptisteries.]

The style and formulas of Christian funerary inscriptions may vary from one region to another, but they are always important inasmuch as they include historical data about the members of a specific community, its hierarchy, and its religious culture. Anthropomorphic funerary stelae found at Khueinat in North Sinai, although Christian in intention (they display crosses), include such pagan formulae as "Be courageous. . . . Nobody is immortal!" In other regions they

CHURCH INSCRIPTIONS. *Dedicatory inscription from the Nea Church in Jerusalem.* Dated to the reign of Justinian, sixth century CE. (Courtesy Israel Antiquities Authority)

consist of a nicely planned text including the full names and titles of the deceased and the exact date of the death and/or the burial. An epitaph from Oboda/Avdat gives even the exact hours of the death and burial, as well as the day, according to the two calendars, for better clarity (Negev, 1981, p. 33). So much precision is an exception, but it exemplifies the kind of historic contribution of such records.

The name of the deceased in many cases may reveal ethnic origin (e.g., Arab). The frequency of certain Christian and biblical names helps in developing demographic and church statistics (e.g., the number and kind of clergy serving in a specific church) and in comparisons of the distinctive features of certain communities in different periods, such as before and after the Muslim conquest in the seventh century. Unfortunately, this cannot be done for most regions. Where, however, later building activity has not disturbed a site, such as in the cemeteries in the Moab region in Transjordan (Canova, 1954) and the Negev towns (Alt, 1921; Negev, 1981), interesting results can be achieved. For example, statistics are available for the monastic element in towns of regions for which no literary records are available.

Monastic functions as well as honorary titles and epitaphs have been gathered from the funerary epigraphy in Palestine: superior (hegumenos), archimandrite, mother superior *(hegumene), abbas,* our father, monk (monachos, *monazon),* nun (monacha), recluse, old man *(geron),* cell dweller *(kel-*

CHURCH INSCRIPTIONS. *Tomb inscription from Byzantine Beersheba.* The inscription contains the name "Stephan son of Regimus." Dated to the sixth century CE. (Courtesy Israel Antiquities Authority)

liotes, only in inscriptions from Deir Koziba in Wadi Qelt, probably recent), brother, and sister. [*See* Monasteries.] A deaconess is described as "Christ's servant and bride" (Meimaris, 1986, p. 51), an expression certainly meaning "consecrated virgin," rather than the epithet *parthenos,* "virgin," sometimes also occurring on tomb inscriptions. Actually, one of the most important contributions of such inscriptions concerns women's roles, responsibilities, and general involvement in the life of the Christian communities in the East. The title of deaconess, often occurring in inscriptions, has not existed in the church since the Middle Ages. The deaconess was ordained by a bishop to perform full ecclesiastical functions among women. In the sixth century, the mother superior *(hegumene)* of a monastery, who could also be a deaconess, became totally independent from an appointed father superior, as had been the norm (Meimaris, 1986, p. 240). Hundreds of names in inscriptions refer either to women considered deserving of burial inside the church premises, or to prominent women donors, benefactors, and even founders of churches and monasteries. A case in point is the reference to Lady Maria in a monastery at Scythopolis (Beth-Shean), and the names of two women represented as offering gifts in the mosaic inscription of a monastery church at Kissufim near Gaza (Tsafrir, 1993, p. 280).

Devotional Inscriptions. Both dedicatory and funerary inscriptions expressed religious beliefs and theological credos. They were an appropriate means to proclaim faith and apologetics. There are also, however, thousands of purely devotional epigraphs in the form of spontaneous invocations and short personal prayers in graffito, rather than in inscriptions, that recount popular faith and devotion. On the walls of shrines, martyria, and monastic cells, pilgrims and monks wrote or carved personal prayers and invocations addressing the local patron saints, otherwise unknown, that help to identify certain sites. Short invocations such as "Oh Lord, help!" are frequently found on religious structures along pilgrim routes, such as those leading to Sinai, sometimes accompanied by the name of the patron saint of the place and/ or the name of the writer.

Archaeological and epigraphic evidence for the presence of the early Jewish Christians, their veneration of the holy places, and their theology, has been claimed by some scholars (see, in particular, Emmanuele Testa, *Il simbolismo dei giudeo-cristiani,* Jerusalem, 1962), but there is so far no consensus of scholarly opinion, as the risk inherent in misdating and interpreting devotional graffiti is great. On the other hand, recent epigraphic support for the presence of Jewish Christian groups in ancient villages in the Golan is claimed by Claudine Dauphin ("Encore des Judéo-Chrétiens au Golan?," in *Early Christianity in Context: Monuments and Documents. Essays in Honour of Father E. Testa,* edited by F. Manns and E. Alliata, pp. 69–84, Jerusalem, 1993).

Other interesting graffiti include a fourth-century ship drawn in charcoal accompanied by the Latin words *"Domine ivimus*" (cf. *Ps.* 122:1) on a wall in the Church of the Holy Sepulcher in Jerusalem (Figueras, 1989, p. 1780). There are several instances of the acrostic ICHTHYS, known in inscriptions and graffiti since the late second century CE in Asia Minor and at Dura-Europos on the eastern border of the Roman Empire. [*See* Jerusalem; Dura-Europos.] From the Holy Land shrines, as well as from known martyr's tombs, such as St. Menas in Egypt, ancient pilgrims took home as *eulogiae,* or "blessed souvenirs," oil lamps and water or oil in small pottery, glass, or silver bottles decorated with designs and inscriptions referring to the holy place of origin. Even a piece of the rock of Golgotha was identified by inscription (Bellarmino Bagatti, *The Church from the Gentiles in Palestine,* Jerusalem, 1971, p. 232, fig. 130).

Implicit references to the Old and the New Testaments are numerous in all kinds of inscriptions, though their textual importance is relative (Gabba, 1958). References to the House of the Lord and its holiness (*Ps.* 63:5; Meimaris, 1986, p. 31) and to the Gate of the Lord, where the "righteous will enter" (*Ps.* 117:19–20), are found in churches. Biblical saints, and particularly the patriarchs Abraham, Isaac, and Jacob, are mentioned, either as examples of virtue or of God's fulfilled promises. One tombstone recounts that the deceased has "completed his race in the Lord" (*2 Tm.* 4:7) and another that a deaconess is simply called the second Phoebe (*Rom.* 16:1; Meimaris, 1986, p. 177).

The fragmentary mosaic known as the Madaba map, although replete with biblical references, is of greater value as a sixth-century geographic document for Palestine, with no fewer than 157 extant toponyms (Piccirillo, 1989, pp. 82–86). On another church floor, at Umm er-Rasas in Jordan, Palestinian, Arabian, and Egyptian cities are illustrated and labeled. Although its geographic value is questionable, it is a witness to the life and organization of the local community in 785 CE, a late date (Piccirillo, 1989, pp. 292–301).

[*See also* Inscriptions, *article on* Inscriptions of the Hellenistic and Roman Periods; *and* Synagogue Inscriptions. *In addition, many of the sites mentioned are the subject of independent entries.*]

BIBLIOGRAPHY

The periodical publication *Supplementum Epigraphicum Graecum* updates epigraphy in general and epigraphy for the ancient Near East in particular. All texts appearing in scholarly publications are being republished and partly commented there by an excellent group of specialists.

Alt, Albrecht. *Die griechischen Inschriften der Palaestina Tertia westlich der 'Araba.* Berlin and Leipzig, 1921. Includes materials from all former publications; complemented by later collections such as the one by Negev (below).

Canova, Reginetta. *Iscrizioni e monumenti protocristiani del paese de Moab.* The Vatican, 1954. The particular feature of these texts is their provenance from the simplest layers of the Christian population along the ancient limits of empire in Transjordan.

Figueras, Pau. "Découvertes récentes d'épigraphie chrétienne en Is-

raël." In *Actes du XIe congrès international d'archéologie chrétienne, Lyon, Vienne, Grenoble, Genève et Aoste, 21–28 septembre 1986,* edited by Noel Duval et al., pp. 1771–1785. Rome, 1989. Revision of all the Byzantine Palestinian epigraphy discovered from one of its most fruitful periods.

Gabba, Emilio. *Iscrizioni greche latine per lo studio della Bibbia.* Turin, 1958. The author endeavors to make the best use of ancient epigraphy to study the Bible; should be complemented by Denis Feissal, "La Bible dans les inscriptions grecques," in *Bible de tous les temps,* vol. 1, *Le monde grec ancien et al Bible,* pp. 223–231 (Paris, 1984).

Gatier, Pierre-Louis. *Inscriptions de la Jordanie,* vol. 2, *Région centrale (Amman, Hesban, Madaba, Maʿin, Dhiban).* Paris, 1986. Promising collection to be completed by the results of more recent excavations by the Franciscan school (see Piccirillo, 1989).

Gibson, Elsa. *The "Christians for Christians" Inscriptions at Phyrgia.* Missoula, 1978. Excellent example of the difficulty in correctly interpreting certain epigraphic expressions.

Grégoire, Henri. *Recueil des inscriptions grecques chrétiennes d'Asie Mineure.* Paris, 1922. The best collection to date of Christian inscriptions from Asia Minor.

Jalabert, Louis, and René Mouterde. *Inscriptions grecques et latines de la Syrie.* 5 vols. Paris, 1929–1959. This result of extended field research complements the better-known collections by W. H. Waddington (1870) and E. D. Littman et al. (1907–1921).

Lefèbvre, Gustave. *Recueil des inscriptions grecques chrétiennes d'Égypte.* Cairo, 1907. The only collection of Christian Greek epigraphy from Egypt published to date.

Meimaris, Yiannis E. *Sacred Names, Saints, Martyrs, and Church Officials in the Greek Inscriptions and Papyri Pertaining to the Christian Church of Palestine.* Athens, 1986. The best study to date on the subject; indispensable for further research on Palestinian epigraphy up to the Middle Ages.

Negev, Avraham. *The Greek Inscriptions from the Negev.* Jerusalem, 1981. Systematic collection of all the inscriptions found in the Byzantine cities of Sobota (Subeita), Mampsis, and Avdat.

Piccirillo, Michele. *Chiese e mosaici di Madaba.* Jerusalem, 1989. All the new inscriptions in the mosaic pavements in and around Madaba, including unpublished fragments of the map.

Piccirillo, Michele. *The Mosaics of Jordan.* Amman, 1993. The most comprehensive treatment of Jordanian churches and their inscriptions.

Tsafrir, Yoram, ed. *Ancient Churches Revealed.* Jerusalem, 1993. Collection of articles on recent Christian archaeology of the Holy Land, mostly translated from the Hebrew originals, including important epigraphic material.

PAU FIGUERAS

CILICIA. A geographic region in southern Turkey, Cilicia is circumscribed by the Taurus Mountains on the north and west, by the Amanus Mountains on the east, and the Mediterranean on the south. [*See* Taurus Mountains.] Western Cilicia (Cilicia Aspera) occupies the rough, hilly country between Mersin and Silifke (Seleucia on the Calycadnos) at the mouth of the Göksu Valley. The fertile alluvial plains of eastern Cilicia (Cilicia Campestris) are broken by three major rivers that drain into the Mediterranean from their headwaters in the Taurus range: Ceyhan (Pyramus), Seyhan (Sarus), and Tarsus (Cydnus). Although none is currently navigable, the rock relief of the Hittite king Muwatalli overlooking the Ceyhan River at Sirkili, and the report of Cleopatra arriving at Tarsus on a boat suggest that in antiquity the rivers served as north–south communication routes as well as water sources.

The road from east to west follows the base of the foothills above the marshy and fertile plains but below the rocky terrain of the Taurus Mountains. At the junction of river and road lay the major settlements of the region: Adana (the modern capital), Misis (Mopsuestia), and Tarsus. Tarsus sits at the juncture of the east–west road and the route north through the Gates of Cilicia and on to the Anatolian plateau. Four other major sites are near good harbors: Silifke, Mersin, Karatepe, and Iskanderun. The combination of Cilicia's fertile agricultural land and excellent harbors, roads, and passes made it an important crossroads throughout antiquity (Ramsay, 1903).

Neolithic and Chalcolithic Periods (6300–4500 BCE). No Aceramic Neolithic sites have been securely identified in Cilicia. Early Pottery Neolithic occurs at the water-table level at Mersin (Garstang, 1953) and at Tarsus (Goldman, 1956). [*See the biographies of Garstang and Goldman.*] M. V. Seton-Williams (1954) and others collected surface materials from a number of other sites. The few excavated remains represent settled villages with a mixed agricultural economy and fairly simple level of social organization. In style and manufacture, the ceramic vessel and chipped-stone industries have links with the 'Amuq plain and coastal Syria rather than the Anatolian plateau. [*See* 'Amuq.] Obsidian, however, originated on the plateau and reveals some level of trade. For the Chalcolithic period, excavated remains illustrate more complex forms of architecture and political structure. The level XVI settlement at Mersin is fortified by a double-wide common rear wall for the radiating ring of two-room houses (Garstang, 1953, fig. 79). The architecture indicates both community cooperation and the need for security. Cilicia's local pottery and stone-tool tradition continued to develop in form and technique through the Chalcolithic period. Machteld Mellink (1962) discusses the international connections visible in the pottery with Tell Halaf and Ubaid affinities at Mersin and Tarsus.

Early Bronze Age (3400–2000 BCE). Early Bronze Age levels were excavated at Mersin and Tarsus. The survey noted above collected material from this period from a few sites. The EB I levels at Tarsus are contemporary with 'Amuq F in the North Syria sequence but show more evidence of interaction in the ceramic repertoire with the southern Anatolian plateau. This includes the first beak-spouted vessels. The small percentage of wheel-made wares is more in line with the north Syrian tradition of ceramic manufacture. Evidence for architecture exists in wall fragments lining the EB I street, however full architectural units were not recovered until EB II levels. Two-room mud-brick houses with party walls were built, modified, destroyed by fire, and replaced with a town wall. Ceramics in the EB II levels shows increasing contact with northern Syria and Cyprus.

The sequence testifies both to internal community cooperation and external regional conflict, probably the result of the rise of complex society during this period. In EB III, contact with western Anatolian is illustrated by the bell-shaped two-handled drinking cup (Gk., *depas*), known from the site of Troy (Mellink, 1986).

Middle Bronze Age (1900–1600 BCE). The early part of the Middle Bronze Age is documented only in the excavations at Mersin and Tarsus and the survey material collected by Seton-Williams (1954). At the end of the Middle Bronze Age, texts from Boğazköy, the Hittite capital in central Anatolia, and from Alalakh, a town in northern Syria, testify to Cilicia's increasing importance on the international scene (Kümmel, 1980). [*See* Boğazköy; Hittites; Alalakh.] The ceramic sequence for the early part of the Middle Bronze Age at Tarsus shows a general correspondence with level IV or levels III–Ib in the Assyrian trading colony at Kültepe/ Kaneš. [*See* Kaneš.] Bowls, jugs and jars painted with parallel lines, triglyph and metope designs, and solid or hatched triangles called Syro-Cilician painted ware can also be found in the 'Amuq and at Ebla in central Syria. [*See* Ebla.] The architectural tradition at Tarsus also shows continuity from the Early Bronze through the middle of the Middle Bronze. Known as Kizzuwatna (Götze, 1940), Cilicia was at various times an independent state and the vassal of the Mitanni Empire. [*See* Mitanni.] Cultural and linguistic ties to North Syria correspond to political alliance with the Mitanni (Beal, 1986). The break in architectural tradition at Tarsus is accompanied by some new ceramic forms and a cuneiform document that suggest a date in the Hittite Old Kingdom. The historical document is a land deed sealed with the seal of *tabarna*, a title taken by the Hittite rulers. The presence of a royal land deed suggests that Kizzuwatna had been brought under control of the Anatolian plateau. It is probably this level in which the local king, Išpuhtahšu, concluded a parity treaty found in the Hittite royal archives in Boğazköy. Išpuhtahšu's title is known also from a seal impression found at Tarsus naming him "Great King" of Kizzuwatna.

Late Bronze Age (1600–1200 BCE). The existence of Cilicia as a semi-independent state ended in the mid-thirteenth century BCE with Šuppiluliuma I, who established his son as the high priest of Kizzuwatna and incorporated the territory into his empire. In the thirteenth century BCE the Hittite king Hattušili III married Puduhepa, a Kizzuwatnan princess. During her tenure as queen she gained considerable political power and took an unprecedented interest in foreign relations. The LB archaeology of Cilicia demonstrates the incorporation of Hittite material culture into a strong local tradition. This is particularly evident in the Hittite fortress at Mersin (Garstang, 1953, fig. 151) and the Hittite temple or administrative building at Tarsus (Goldman, 1956, plan 22). The ceramic assemblage contains some handmade items in the local tradition, although the most of the repertoire is inspired by the Hittite bowl and jar sequence. In the early part of the Late Bronze Age, the Hittites probably used Kizzuwatna as a staging area for military incursions into Syria. After the limits of the Hittite Empire had been secured, Hittite interest in Kizzuwatna was as a source of taxable agricultural products and as an outlet to the profitable sea trade with the Levant, Egypt, and Cyprus. The merchants of Ura, against whom the king of Ugarit protested in a letter to the Hittite king Ḫattušili III, are thought to come from this area. The disruption of the society and economy brought about by the collapse of the Hittite Empire and the movements of the Sea Peoples are reflected in the archaeological sequences at Tarsus and Mersin. A destruction level followed by a rebuilding and continuation of the local ceramic sequence is followed by a level of pits and unstratified fill with Mycenaean Late Helladic IIIC pottery mixed with local wares at both sites (Mee, 1978).

Iron Age (1200–312 BCE). The initial centuries of the Iron Age are documented only in the scanty and disturbed archaeological remains at Mersin and Tarsus. Physical remains of the Late Iron Age exist at Tarsus (Goldman, 1950–1963), Domuztepe, and Karatepe (Bossert and Alkin, 1947). Like their Neo-Hittite counterparts at Carchemish and Malatya, Cilicia was broken into small territorial states with a capital city from which a local dynasty ruled the surrounding villages and towns. [*See* Carchemish.] Karatepe is the best documented example in Cilicia. Located in the eastern mountainous region, where the Amanus and the Taurus Mountains meet, a monumental gate sculpture and inscription dated to the late eighth or early seventh century BCE provide some insight into local dynastic history (Winter, 1979). The inscription is written in hieroglyphic Hittite (Luwian) and Phoenician, and also testifies to the continuity of the Luwian population base in the area. [*See* Luwians.] The agricultural wealth and proximity to mining regions in the Taurus made Cilicia a target for Neo-Assyrian expansion in the seventh century BCE. During this time Cilicia was divided into two kingdoms: Que (classical Cilicia Campestris) on the plain and Hilakku (classical Cilicia Aspera) in the western mountains. Greek colonization of Cilicia is attributed to this period, partly on the basis of the classical legend of Mopsos (Bing, 1968). The Neo-Babylonian Empire took over administration directly from the Assyrians. [*See* Babylonians.] From the sixth century BCE until the conquest of Alexander, Cilicia was ruled from Tarsus by semi-independent rulers with the title *syennesis*.

Hellenistic and Roman Periods (312 BCE–300 CE). For nearly six hundred years, a Greek presence, presumably a merchant class, is documented in Cilicia by the widespread use of imported Greek pottery, the foundation myths of a number of important Cilician cities, and Greek historians (Mutafian, 1988). With Alexander's conquest of the Cilician Gates in 312 BCE, hellenization intensified. Alexander established the first imperial mint at Tarsus, the region's capital. Both Hellenistic and Roman levels are attested in the excavations at Gözlü Kule in Tarsus but appear to be outside the major settlement. The Seleucids acquired Cilicia in the aftermath of Alexander's death and established ports at Aegeae, Alexandretta (Iskanderun), and Seleuia on the Calycadnus (Silifke). [*See* Seleucids.] Royal estates and temple estates formed a major part of the agricultural economy. Sanctuaries included that of Zeus at Olba (Uzuncaburç) and Artemis Perasia at Castabalu (Musti, 1984).

In the first century BCE, pirates based in Cilicia Aspera threatened the Roman sea trade. Pompey defeated the pirates in 67 BCE and took over Cilicia Campestris as well. Recognizing the agricultural potential of the fertile plain, Pompey resettled the area and established new cities, among which was Soli (Pompeiopolis). The presence of citizens who were artisans (linen weavers, dyers, tanners, carpenters) testifies to highly developed trade and craft (Musti, 1984). In 41 BCE, Antony stopped at Tarsus and summoned Cleopatra from Egypt. Her arrival by ship in the lagoon below the town is memorialized by the Roman arch the modern population of Tarsus calls Cleopatra's Gate. In the following centuries the cities of Tarsus, Adana, Mopsuestia, and Anazarbus became wealthy through trade in grain, wine, flax, and linen. Given the region's agricultural basis, it is not surprising that St. Paul pursued the trade of tentmaker in his hometown of Tarsus. The prosperity of Cilicia came to an end when the emperor Valerian was defeated in the third century CE and the Sasanian armies overran Cilician villages and towns on their way through the plain to the Taurus Mountains.

BIBLIOGRAPHY

Beal, Richard H. "The History of Kizzuwatna and the Date of the Šunaššura Treaty." *Orientalia* 55 (1986): 424–445.

Beal, Richard H. "The Location of Cilician Ura." *Anatolian Studies* 42 (1992): 65–73.

Bing, John D. "A History of Cilicia during the Assyrian Period." Ph.D. diss., Indiana University, 1968. The most comprehensive discussion of historical and archaeological sources for Assyrians in Cilicia.

Bossert, Helmuth T., and U. Bahadir Alkim. *Karatepe, Kadirli, and Environments.* Istanbul, 1947.

Desideri, Paolo, and Anna M. Jasink. *Cilicia.* Turin, 1990.

Garstang, John. *Prehistoric Mersin: Yümük Tepe in Southern Turkey.* Oxford, 1953.

Götze, Albrecht. *Kizzuwatna and the Problem of Hittite Geography.* New Haven, 1940.

Goldman, Hetty, ed. *Excavations at Gözlü Kule, Tarsus,* vol. 1, *The Hellenistic and Roman Periods;* vol. 3, *The Iron Age.* Princeton, 1950–1963.

Goldman, Hetty. *Excavations at Gözlü Kule, Tarsus,* vol. 2, *From the Neolithic to the Bronze Age.* Princeton, 1956.

Kümmel, H. M. "Kizzuwatna." In *Reallexikon der Assyriologie,* vol. 5, pp. 627–631. Berlin, 1980. Collection and discussion of all historical references to Kizzuwatna in the Bronze Age.

Mee, Christopher. "Aegean Trade and Settlement in Anatolia in the Second Millennium B.C." *Anatolian Studies* 28 (1978): 121–156. Discusses and tries to account for Mycenaean pottery at Tarsus and Mersin.

Mellink, Machteld J. "The Prehistory of Syro-Cilicia." *Bibliotheca Orientalis* 19 (1962): 219–226.

Mellink, Machteld J. "The Early Bronze Age in West Anatolia." In *The End of the Early Bronze Age in the Aegean,* edited by Gerald Cadogan, pp. 139–152. Leiden, 1986.

Mellink, Machteld J. "Anatolian Chronology." In *Chronologies in Old World Archaeology,* vol. 1, edited by Robert W. Ehrich, pp. 207–220. 3d ed. Chicago, 1992. The most recent discussion of comparative chronology through the end of the Early Bronze Age.

Musti, Domenico. "Syria and the East." In *The Cambridge Ancient History,* vol. 7.1, *The Hellenistic World,* pp. 175–220. 2d ed. Cambridge, 1984.

Mutafian, Claude. *Cilicie au Carrefour des Empires.* Paris, 1988. Collection and translation (in French) of all the primary sources and bibliography referring to Cilicia during the Hellenistic and Roman periods.

Ramsay, William M. "Cilicia, Tarsus, and the Great Tarsus Pass." *Geographical Journal* 22 (1903): 357–413.

Seton-Williams, M. V. "Cilician Survey." *Anatolian Studies* 4 (1954): 121–174.

Winter, Irene J. "On the Problems of Karatepe: The Reliefs and Their Context." *Anatolian Studies* 29 (1979): 115–151.

BONNIE MAGNESS-GARDINER

CIMMERIANS. Since Classical Antiquity it has been believed that the Cimmerians were the early inhabitants of the Pontic steppes, preceding the Scythians there, although an attempt was made recently to use their name only for a small tribe that lived north of Urartu (see esp. A. I. Ivanchik, "K voprosu o etnicheskoj prinadlezhnosti i archeologicleskoj kulture Kimmerijcev," *Vestnik Drevnej Istorii* [1994]: 148–168 and [1995]: 3–22). Archaeologically, their culture stems partly from the previous Belozerka culture of the Pontic area, partly from the Oka-Kama area and Siberia, and partly from the Caucasian tradition of bronzeworking. More distant parallels are also known from other provinces of the eastern koine of the Early Iron Age Geometric styles in Transcaucasia, Iran (Luristan), and the Balkans. Their own archaeological culture in the Pontic area is called Chernogorovka (ninth–early eighth centuries BCE); its late stage—Novocherkassk (late eighth–early seventh centuries BCE)—may have belonged partly to the latest Cimmerians and partly to the earliest Scythians. Cimmerians were among the first mounted nomads to use real cavalry; the objects from their graves include personal ornaments, weapons, and horse harnesses: most importantly horse bits of North Caucasian types (according to H. Potratz, 1966), bimetallic daggers with an iron blade and bronze handle (the latter either in openwork or tanged, with a mushroom-shaped pommel), socketed arrowheads that are a rhomboid in section, and long spearheads. Natural stone whetstones with a hole for suspension were also part of the equipment of the Cimmerians; in addition to openwork bronze belt finials and "birdcage" rattles, cross-shaped ornaments are sometimes found decorated with spirals. Some of the decorated objects have parallels in Assyria. The belt and suspended weapons are depicted on so-called stag stones used as grave stelae, but not the human figure. Stag stones are known across the steppes from central Siberia (Tuva) to eastern Bulgaria (Belogradec, near Varna), while most of the characteristic objects in metalwork come from the Volga-Oka, Kuban, and North Pontic areas. Of more westerly distribution are related Thraco-Cimmerian bronzes from the eastern part of central Europe, evidence of Cimmerian western raids; the Cimmerian and Caucasian influence on the Thracian bronzes from Bulgaria, and Macedonian bronzes from the Axius valley and Chalcidice, may, at the same time, be connected with Strabo's reports of a military alliance between the Cimmerians and Thracian Treres and Edoni (Strabo, C 61, C 627 and C 329 fragment 11). Some Cimmerian decorated bronzes were probably connected with shamanism (there are ethnographic parallels for this usage; see Bouzek, 1983, pp. 219–220), and were adapted as personal ornaments and jewelry even by the European Hallstatt and Villanovan cultures and in Greek Late Geometric art.

There are two groups of written sources on the Cimmerians: Near Eastern and Greek. Most Cimmerians left their country in the Pontic steppes as the Scythians moved westward under pressure from the Massagetes. Herodotus (4.11–13 and 6.20) expressively mentions Tyras (Dniestre) as the place where the Cimmerian kings fought a fratricidal battle and were buried, and from where the common people left their homes along the Black Sea, west of the Caucasus as far as the area of Sinope, followed by the Scythians. The first Assyrian references to Gumurru (the Assyrian equivalent "Cimmerian") date to early in the reign of Sargon II, prior to 713 BCE; the Scythians are also mentioned within the region of Urartu. [*See* Urartu.] Some small groups of Cimmerians, however, remained on the shores of the Azov Sea even later, as recorded by Plutarch (*Life of Marius* xi). The Cimmerian Bosporus, Cimmerian walls (an earthenwork across the East Crimean peninsula, constructed prior to the Greek colonization there), and Cimmerian peninsula are all in this area and the Araxes River (modern Syr Darya), according to Herodotus (4.11), originally formed the Cimmerians' eastern frontier. The battle on the Dniestre apparently marked the last stage of the retreat of the Cimmerians, which lasted for a considerable time, just as happened later in Sarmato-Scythian relations. During the reign of Sennacherib (705–681 BCE), the Cimmerians attacked large areas of Asia Minor and, according to tradition, destroyed the Phrygian Empire (the Phrygian king Midas committed suicide). This probably took place in 696/95 BCE (Eusebius's date)—although a date twenty years later cannot be excluded. Excavations at Gordion revealed destructions, but no characteristic Cimmerian objects. [*See* Gordion.] Only the arrowheads are known from Anatolia, while a few weapons finds and parts of horse harnesses from northeast Anatolia can be ascribed either to Late Cimmerians or Early Scythians. A group of Cimmerians probably settled near

Sinope; Esarhaddon mentions an Assyrian victory over them in 679 BCE: their leader during the 679/78 military campaign is called Tušpa in Assyrian records. Another group of Cimmerians may well have entered Anatolia from Thrace. This is suggested by Strabo, when he speaks about an alliance between the Cimmerians and the Thracian Treres and Edoni (cf. above). The Lydian king Gyges sought an alliance against them with Ashurbanipal. A second attack in 652 BCE was successful: Sardis (with the exception of the citadel) was sacked and Gyges killed. [*See* Sardis.]

The leader of the Cimmerian troops in 652 BCE was called Lygdamis, and there is a parallel name, Tugdammu, in Assyrian records. According to Strabo, Lygdamis was later killed in Cilicia. This happened between 637 and 626 BCE and, according to Herodotus (1.16), the last Cimmerians were driven from Asia Minor by Alyattes in about 600 BCE.

There are no written records on Cimmerian military activities in the eastern part of central Europe, but the numerous destructions and so-called Thraco-Cimmerian bronzes recovered in the area make it probable that the military activities there were Cimmerian because they resembled those of the later Scythians. Because the Thraco-Cimmerian bronzes show some development and appear in contexts from the ninth to seventh centuries BCE, the dominant position of the Cimmerians (or nomads closely related to them) on the Great Hungarian plain must have lasted for more than a century. There were, however, other inhabitants there, who seem finally to have absorbed the nomadic population.

[*See also* Anatolia, *article on* Ancient Anatolia; Cilicia; Persia, *article on* Ancient Persia; *and* Scythians.]

BIBLIOGRAPHY

Bouzek, Jan. *Caucasus and Europe and the Cimmerian Problem.* Sbornik National Museum, 37.4. Prague, 1983. In English with Czech summary.

Diakonoff, Igor M. "The Cimmerians and the Scythians in the Ancient Near East" (in Russian). *Sovetskaya Arkheologiya,* no. 1 (1994): 108–116. Includes an English summary.

Potratz, H. *Pferdetrensen des alten Orients.* Vatican, 1966.

Sulimirski, Tadeusz. "The Cimmerian Problem." *Bulletin of the Institute of Archaeology, University of London* 2 (1959): 45–64.

Terenozhkin, A. I. *Kimmeriity* (in Russian). Kiev, 1976.

JAN BOUZEK

CISTERNS. Designed to collect and store rainwater for drinking, washing, livestock, irrigation, and agricultural installations, a cistern was normally cut out of rock and its interior coated with a thick layer of impermeable plaster. When the rock itself was impermeable, only fissures were coated. Where no solid rock stratum was available, a cistern could be built in an excavated pit in the ground, or partially constructed, incorporating whatever natural rock was available. For built cisterns large stones, sometimes with layers of smaller stones above, were used and then coated with a final layer of plaster.

A cistern's depth would not normally exceed 6 m, so that water could be drawn with relative ease and the cistern could be cleaned by someone upright in it. Neither its width, length, or diameter, would exceed 6–10 m; consequently, a cistern's maximum capacity is a few dozen cubic meters at the most, and no more than 100 cu m. If its dimensions are greater it is properly designated a reservoir. The opening of the cistern was usually narrow in order to prevent falling into it, to prevent evaporation, and to enable convenient pumping.

Canals carved into the earth channeled runoff to a small depression or basin at the side of the cistern, where the soil settled or was filtered. The water was drawn from the cistern by lowering a pail on a rope from the surface through a vertical opening shaped like the neck of a bottle. Sometimes, a pulleylike device made of wood was built above the opening to facilitate drawing water. Pails were also of wood. Al-

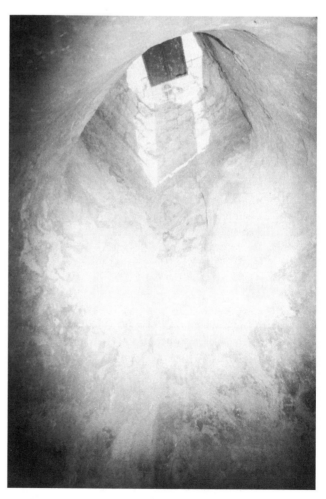

CISTERNS. *View from the bottom of a cistern.* Sepphoris, cistern C-125. (Courtesy E. M. Meyers)

though perishable, some have been found in the excavations of the Agora in Athens.

Bell-shaped cisterns are first evidenced at the end of the Chalcolithic period or the beginning of the Early Bronze Age at Meṣar in Israel. Their form prevents the collapse of the ceiling, which could result if the top of the cistern were too broad. These cisterns are hewn in chalky rock, which allows them to store water without the use of plaster. Cisterns dating from the Middle Bronze Age, such as those discovered at Hazor, are bottle shaped. [See Hazor.] Although they are cut into chalky rock, these cisterns show evidence of plaster used to block up fissures. The Hazor remains, which are the earliest evidence of plaster in water cisterns, invalidate William Foxwell Albright's suggestion (1940, p. 212) that the Israelites invented plastered water cisterns after the Exodus and conquest. Bell-shaped cisterns from the Late Bronze period have been found at Tel Beth-Shemesh. [See Beth-Shemesh.]

During the tenth century BCE, "open" cisterns were in use in the Negev mountains, whose construction also makes them pools by definition. Hewn from the soft rock, they were designed and constructed to store runoff. The region's inhabitants lacked sufficient technical expertise to enable them to create underground cisterns. The depth of the cisterns is not great, and the high rate of evaporation in the region's dry climate suggests that the cisterns were covered with hides to reduce evaporation.

Water cisterns are mentioned often in the Hebrew Bible, and indeed, in the Iron Age II period an increase in the number of cisterns is seen. Excavations at Tell en-Naṣbeh, near Ramallah, have revealed fifty cisterns dating to this period. [See Naṣbeh, Tell en-.] At the Urartian fortress Çavuştepe in eastern Anatolia, square royal water cisterns from the eighth century BCE were discovered hewn into the rock, their fissures filled with plaster.

In the Hellenistic period there appears to have been a great increase in the private use of cisterns, to the extent that each household had one. Many cisterns were found cut into the chalky rock at Mareshah in Israel. They are unplastered, except for the use made of clay to block cracks, and bell shaped, with a volume close to 100 cu m. [See Mareshah.]

The private use of cisterns increased again in the Roman period, reaching its apex during the Byzantine period. Quarried bell cisterns, constructed cisterns with barrel-shaped arches, and cisterns of indeterminate form all existed side by side. Every household had a cistern, with an average volume of 30–50 cu m, that supplied the family with water throughout the year. In the Negev mountain region, underground cisterns (Ar., ḥaraba) were used in the Nabatean-Byzantine period. They are square, with supporting pillars that allow for increased volume. Water cisterns continue to be used throughout the Near East, in areas where a traditional way of life is preserved.

[See also Hydraulics; Hydrology; Pools; and Reservoirs.]

BIBLIOGRAPHY

Albright, William Foxwell. *From Stone Age to Christianity*. Baltimore, 1940.
Brinker, Werner. "Antike Zisternen: Stationen ihrer Entwicklungsgeschichte." *Mitteilungen: Leichtweiss-Institut für Wasserbau der Technischen Universität Braunschweig* 103 (1989): 247–279.
Moran, Uri, and David Palmach. *Cisterns in the Negev Mountains* (in Hebrew). Jerusalem, 1985.
Tsuk, Tsvika. "Survey and Research of Cisterns in the Village of Zikrin (Israel)." *Mitteilungen: Leichtweiss-Institut für Wasserbau der Technischen Universität Braunschweig* 103 (1989): 337–356.

TSVIKA TSUK
Translated from Hebrew by Ilana Goldberg

CIST GRAVES. To construct a cist grave, a rectangular space roughly 2 m long and 1 m wide was lined with stones or mud bricks; occasionally, the floor was paved with cobbles and a superstructure erected. The form remained the same whether constructed within settlements or in extramural cemeteries, for primary interments and secondary burials. The earliest Chalcolithic (4300–3300 BCE) examples were for secondary interments in extramural cemeteries. Early in the Middle Bronze Age (2000–1500 BCE), the intramural cist burial was introduced into Canaan from Syro-Mesopotamia as an exclusive method of primary burial for wealthy or prominent individuals. Late Bronze (1500–1200 BCE) and Iron Age (1200–586 BCE) cist graves for primary interments in extramural cemeteries are attributed to Egyptian influence.

The earliest extramural cemeteries are from the Chalcolithic period. In Palestine, in the cemeteries at Adeimah and Shiqmim, in addition to cist burials, contained secondary burials were found. At Shiqmim bones were also collected in ossuaries.

During the Middle Bronze II, elaborate stone-lined and capped pits were constructed at Ugarit in Syria and at Megiddo and Aphek, in Palestine. In the Aphek cists, the bodies were flexed and oriented east–west, with their heads facing east. Secondary remains were interred in recesses in the side wall of one grave, and a second grave contained a ceramic vessel whose type shows a strong northern connection.

The popularity of extramural cist-grave burial in the Late Bronze and Iron Ages has been attributed to Egyptian influence. Burials at Tell es-Saʿidiyeh provide the clearest Egyptian or egyptianizing features: an east–west orientation, with the heads usually facing west; Egyptian-linen body wrappings; bitumen-covered bodies; an unusually high incidence of metal artifacts; and an absence of bowls and lamps. Cist graves reached the height of their distribution in Palestine in the thirteenth–eleventh centuries BCE, through the lowland regions of the coast, the Besor River valley, and the Jezreel, Beth-Shean, and Jordan River Valleys (Tell Abu Hawam, Afula, Tell el-ʿAjjul, Tell el-Farʿah [South], Tell es-Saʿidiyeh). These were richly provisioned burials for the pri-

CIST GRAVES. *MB I burial in a stone-lined inner chamber.* Cairn 160, from the central Negev highlands. (Courtesy ASOR Archives)

mary interment of one individual and, rarely, two or three. In the case of multiple interments, one of the individuals was frequently an infant or a child. The mortuary provisions were like those in contemporary pit graves, with bowls for serving food predominating along with jugs and accompanying dipper juglets for liquids, plus luxury items such as jewelry, metal objects, and imported pottery. In some cases, pit graves may have sufficed as a simplified version of a cist grave. In the Tell es-Saʿidiyeh cemetery, the cist graves contained aesthetically finer and more precious items than did the interspersed simpler interments.

[*See also* Burial Techniques. *In addition, the sites mentioned are the subject of independent entries.*]

BIBLIOGRAPHY

Avi-Yonah, Michael, and Ephraim Stern, eds. *Encyclopedia of Archaeological Excavations in the Holy Land.* 4 vols. Englewood Cliffs, N.J., 1975–1978. Summary of excavations including results of all earlier expeditions to the sites.
Ben-Tor, Amnon, ed. *The Archaeology of Ancient Israel.* Translated by R. Greenberg. New Haven, 1992. Collection of essays with differing emphases on the Neolithic through the Iron Age II–III periods.

Bloch-Smith, Elizabeth. *Judahite Burial Practices and Beliefs about the Dead.* Journal for the Study of the Old Testament, Supplement 123. Sheffield, 1992. Summary and comprehensive catalog of the Iron Age burials.
Mazar, Amihai. *Archaeology of the Land of the Bible, 10,000–586 B.C.E.* New York, 1990. Comprehensive, detailed, well-illustrated survey of biblical archaeology, limited only by the traditionalist biblical interpretation.
Stern, Ephraim, ed. *The New Encyclopedia of Archaeological Excavations in the Holy Land.* 4 vols. Jerusalem and New York, 1993. Supplements Avi-Yonah and Stern (above), with results of more recent excavations and revised interpretations.

ELIZABETH BLOCH-SMITH

CITIES. [*To survey the city as a form of human settlement in the ancient Near East, this entry comprises five articles:*
An Overview
Cities of the Bronze and Iron Ages
Cities of the Persian Period
Cities of the Hellenistic and Roman Periods
Cities of the Islamic Period
The overview article treats the emergence of cities and the process of ubanization; the remainder treat the development of cities and urban life through time in specific regions.]

An Overview

Cities were the physical focus for the rise of civilization in the ancient Near East. While what constitutes a city in the modern world is fairly clear, there is no uncomplicated definition of a city in the ancient Near East. In the archaeological literature the terms *village, town,* and *city* are usually used interchangeably. A working definition of *city* is that it is a relatively permanent, compact form of human settlement, having a particular kind of relationship to its surroundings, and populated by a fairly large number of diverse individuals who are socially differentiated. Clarity of definition of the city, and the nature of its relationship to other forms of settlement, emerges only in surveys of the relationships of settlement forms to their surroundings.

Center and Periphery. To understand what cities were in the ancient Near East, the ideas of center and periphery need to be examined. Cities, and other forms of permanent settlements, were parts of interdependent systems that included a center and its surroundings. Thus, the modern idea of a rural-urban dichotomy is not helpful in understanding the city in the ancient Near East. Many modern rural-urban differences are typical only of industrial-urban, not of preindustrial societies. Because all ancient Near Eastern cities were part of an agriculturally based economic system, the city and its surroundings were interdependent. People living in the area around a city were dependent on the city, and urbanites depended on the sustaining area of the city's surrounding region. People living in the area around a city were dependent on the city for many things—temples, storage facilities, security, specialists of various kinds, craftspeople who could process goods, and administration or social leadership. Definitive urbanization involved the regulation of the agricultural surplus—that portion of agricultural produce not consumed by the primary producers. The capacity to extract and invest this surplus was a principal function of cities and their administrative officials. As payment for this administrative service, urban officials exacted tribute or taxes from the inhabitants of the surrounding area. Similarly, a city's inhabitants required the agricultural produce of the city's hinterland for their sustenance.

The interdependence between center and periphery becomes recognizable in the archaeological record when the people in the city's hinterland are also organized into settlements, creating a two-level hierarchical system: a city (usually walled) and its villages (usually unwalled), as schematically pictured in figure 1. This interdependence of the city and its surrounding settlements limited the size of such a system. A city and its villages had to be close enough together to make continuous exchange possible. If the system was in a geographic area where there were no physical barriers, it was theoretically possible for it to expand as far as available means of transportation between the center and the most remote village would allow. [*See* Transportation.] The expansion of the system was also a function of the productive capacity of a city's surrounding area.

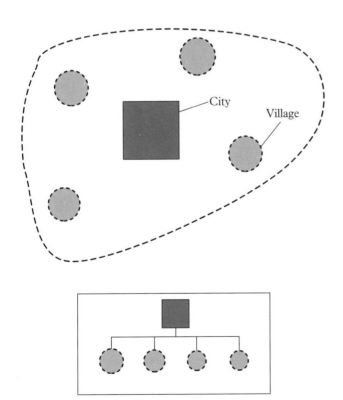

CITIES: An Overview. Figure 1. *A city in relationship to its villages.* (Courtesy F. S. Frick)

As cities that were part of such a simple two-tier system expanded, their sustaining areas would begin to encroach on those of neighboring city-village systems. When this happened, a competitive situation developed between the centers of the two systems. Because of this, a new kind of sociopolitical organization was needed to channel human energy into production rather than destruction. From several systems of two tiers, a new three-tier system was created: a central city that administered an area consisting of several city-village systems (see figure 2). A city that was the center of a two-level system can be thought of as a local center, while the central city in a three-level system is a regional center in a city-state.

Urbanization Process. The process of urbanization is not a unitary, universally homogeneous process; it assumes different forms and meaning, depending on prevailing historic, economic, and cultural conditions. How did urbanization proceed in the ancient Near East and what technologies and forms of social and political organization were involved?

The earliest traces of human existence in the Near East come from the Paleolithic period, where strata indicating short periods of occupation with long intervals between them and skeletal remains have been found in caves (e.g., at Shanidar in present-day Iraq and on Mt. Carmel in present-day Israel). This situation changes with the beginning of the Neolithic period, when the first relatively permanent settlements based on a combination of hunting and gathering and agriculture appear. It is clear, from the fact that archaeological evidence for both phenomena appears at about the same time, that there is a positive correlation between the beginnings of permanent settlements and of food production.

Neolithic settlements were usually some distance from one another and were located in environments where there was ready access to several different ecological niches (food production was still unreliable and had to be supplemented by hunting and food gathering). One of the best-known Neolithic settlements, Beidha, located southeast of the Dead Sea in modern Jordan, is found in such a setting. Another important Neolithic site is Çatal Höyük in modern Turkey. In addition to being located in a differentiated ecological setting, Çatal Höyük is a settlement where a densely built-up area of about 440 sq m has been excavated, in which there were houses of equivalent size and plan, suggesting a socially undifferentiated community. Neolithic Jericho has often been called a city, mostly because of its massive walls and fortification system. While Jericho and other Neolithic settlements anticipate some developments in later cities, they differ from cities, as defined here, because they were not the center of a settlement system. These Neolithic sites should thus be regarded as protourban settlements.

With increasing experience with agriculture came more dependable food production. The necessity of having to settle at sites that offered the safety net of food gathering de-

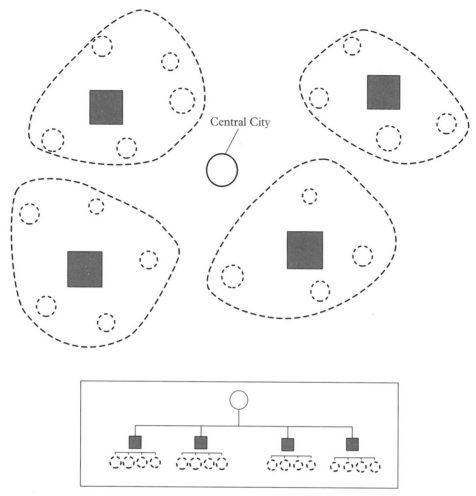

CITIES: An Overview. Figure 2. *A central city in relationship to its associated city-village systems.* (Courtesy F. S. Frick)

creased, and it became feasible to establish settlements in a wider range of environments and nearer one another. With higher agricultural yields, the cultivated area required to feed a person was also reduced. [*See* Demography.] With more intensive agriculture, settlements could be located closer together, a prerequisite for the creation of structured relationships between them in the sense of the formation of settlement systems, which was also a necessary precondition for urbanization. There is, however, no single identifiable cause in the nexus of social, economic, and political transformations that was a sufficient cause for the emergence of cities. Changes in social organization induced by commerce, warfare, or technological advances had to be validated by some instrument of authority if they were to achieve institutional permanence. This instrument of authority, rather than any particular form of activity, was the generating force for urbanization. Gideon Sjoberg (*The Preindustrial City, Past and Present*, Glencoe, 1960, pp. 67–68) equates authority with social power. For him, the preindustrial city was a mecha-

nism by which a society's rulers could consolidate and maintain their power.

Urbanization in Mesopotamia. The first true cities emerged in Mesopotamia in the Early Bronze Age, at the close of the fourth millennium. Habuba Kabira (South), a city on the Upper Euphrates River in present-day Syria, appeared in this period. It had a rectangular layout, a defensive wall, and evidence of social differentiation in the form of a separate block of buildings for the upper class at the southern end of the site. [*See* Habuba Kabira.]

By 3600 BCE the development of urban centers was focused in southern Mesopotamia. Uruk (modern Warka in Iraq) offers an impressive example of urban development in this early period, when isolated settlements gave way to regional centers. Uruk was a substantial ceremonial center and became the largest early city in southern Mesopotamia. Around it lay several small towns and villages. Near the beginning of the third millennium it began to expand rapidly, reaching its greatest size by around 2700 BCE. At that time its population was forty thousand–fifty thousand and its defensive walls enclosed an area of 400 ha (988 acres). [*See* Uruk-Warka.*] Uruk has been excavated (intensively in those areas of the city that were temple sites) and is also known from the Gilgamesh epic, which reflects a much older period, although in the form in which it now exists was written later. Gilgamesh, the hero of the epic, was probably the ruler of Uruk in the Early Dynastic I period (c. 2600 BCE), after the city had reached its largest size. At the beginning of the poem, Gilgamesh has oppressed the people of Uruk in order to build up the massive city wall, which has been identified in excavations as having a circumference of 9.5 km (6 mi.), with about nine hundred semicircular towers. Besides the walls of such early cities, evidence leads to the assumption that the highly developed economic organization of such settlements required not only abstract methods of control, but other forms of social organization.

While some early urban sites on the southern Mesopotamian plains had areas of 400 ha (988 acres) or more, those of Upper Mesopotamia appear to have had a maximum size of only about 100 ha (494 acres). This suggests a ceiling beyond which such sites could not or did not grow. Scholars routinely assume that the size of early cities was limited by the productive capacity of their immediate sustaining area. Fundamental to our understanding of early urban systems is the notion that the extraction of agricultural surpluses enabled early centers to expand and to accommodate specialized economic sectors. While some early centers (e.g., early Uruk) may have been self-sufficient for food, typically it was the outlying settlements that produced the surplus supporting the populations and institutions of urban centers. The latter case is illustrated by the Ugaritic texts that record the contributions of outlying settlements to the centralized economy.

During roughly the first half of the third millennium, wide areas of the Mesopotamian countryside were significantly depopulated, as most of their inhabitants took up residence in politically organized city-states. In the general vicinity of Uruk, for example, the number of villages and towns fell precipitously from 146 at the beginning of the millennium, to only 24 by about 2700 BCE. Meanwhile, the number of cities (i.e., sites exceeding 50 ha, or 123.5 acres, in area) grew from two to eight. Structural changes occurred simultaneously in the newly emergent cities. Accompanying urbanization was increasing militarism, reflected in the construction of massive urban fortifications and in a host of myths, epics, and historical inscriptions recounting the internecine struggles of these city-states. There was also increasing social stratification and the decay of kin-based social units.

The cities of southern Mesopotamia were conquered about 2340 BCE by an invasion of Semites from Babylonia to the north, under Sargon (Sharrukin) of Akkad, who is regarded as the first ruler to create an empire—that is, an expanded state based not solely on cities, but upon territorial control. Administratively, Sargon created a new capital rather than basing his power on an established city. He thus set a pattern of imperial rule in which the capital city became only an administrative center, not an essential political unit. The Akkadian Empire, however, lasted fewer than two centuries. It was overthrown shortly after 2200 BCE by the Guti from the north, who exercised loose administrative control for about a century, allowing the reemergence of independent cities. They were succeeded by the first Babylonian kingdom, whose best-known king was Hammurabi (c. 1792–1750 BCE).

Paralleling these developments in the south was the appearance of a new power in northern Mesopotamia, the Assyrians. The Assyrians marked the realization of a trend in urban development that had begun with Sargon of Akkad—the transition in the city's role from an independent center to the tool of territorial empire builders, a useful administrative unit but no longer an entity that was central to the mentality of ruler or subject. Under Hammurabi, city temples no longer managed land, reducing the city's pivotal role. [*See* Assyrians; Temples, *article on* Mesopotamian Temples.] Thus, "empire" began to be conceived of not as the extension of the control of a city and its ruler, but as the government of a territory by a king and his army. As a consequence, the basis of power shifted from an urban-centered economic organization, with its exploitation of agriculture and trade, to military conquest of and exaction of tribute from subject peoples. The Assyrians thus represent the final shift from control by a city to control on a territorial basis, perhaps exercised through cities but not connected with any specific one. This was the pattern followed by the Persians, by Alexander, and to some extent by the Roman emperors.

Urbanization in Palestine. Urbanization gained momentum in Palestine toward the end of EB I and the beginning of EB II (c. 3000 BCE), as indicated by the sudden appearance of many cities, among them Ai, Beth-Yerah, Bab edh-Dhra', Jericho, Megiddo, Tell el-Far'ah (North), and Tel Yarmut. One feature of these early cities was the appearance of large public buildings, some of which may have been temples.

Toward the end of the Early Bronze Age (EB III, 2650–2350 BCE), urbanization peaked in Palestine and a period of rival city-states emerged in Mesopotamia. In Mesopotamia, urban development was linked to changes in water supply, which not only affected agriculture, but influenced settlement patterns. Because major cities in Mesopotamia were located on watercourses, the receding of water into fewer watercourses must have involved a gradual linkage between the settlements and the remaining watercourses. In addition, it led to the tendency for a few settlements to grow larger at the expense of others. In the area of Uruk, for example, the number of settlements decreased from sixty-two in the Early Dynastic I period to twenty-nine in this period.

While urbanization in Palestine peaked in EB III, by the end of EB IV (2350–2000 BCE), there were no urban settlements left. What caused this disappearance of urban culture? Three explanations have been offered. One is ecological and parallels the Mesopotamian situation of scarce water resources. This explanation maintains that there was a decrease in rainfall and a consequent lowering of the water table, which made concentrated settlements impossible. A second explanation suggests that the urban centers were destroyed or abandoned following incursions from either the north or the south. A third explanation sees the city-state system reaching the point of self-destruction as the result of city-states' raids on one another, as evidenced by the repeated strata of destruction and reconstruction at EB II–III sites.

The second urban period in Palestine, the Middle Bronze Age (2000–1500 BCE), saw the reemergence of urban centers. MB city walls had towers built at intervals of 20–30 m and in MB II (1800–1650 BCE), a glacis at the base of the walls that formed a smooth, steep slope to protect the walls from attackers. While some MB cities were reestablished on EB sites, MB II also saw new, large cities established that were enclosed with earthen ramparts (e.g., Qatna [100 ha, or 247 acres] in Syria and Hazor [60 ha, or 148 acres] in Israel). [See Hazor.] LB cities in Palestine (1500–1200 BCE) showed continuity with MB cities, with few positive developments and a general decline in urban life.

In Late Iron Age I and Iron II Palestine (c. 1000–587 BCE), urbanization flourished with the support of the monarchy, for which cities were an essential part of the administrative system. A hierarchical order of settlements developed, ranging from the capital cities of Jerusalem and Samaria at the top to small fortified sites at the bottom. Between these were major and secondary administrative centers and fortified provincial towns. Most Israelite cities were about 3–7 ha (7–17 acres) in area, with only the central cities of Jerusalem and Samaria being larger, with an area of 30–50 ha (74–123.5 acres). Unlike their Bronze Age predecessors, the Iron II Israelite cities did not accommodate a large number of farmers but were inhabited mostly by families belonging to the political, military, economic, and religious elite.

Significance of the City. Although they are sometimes used interchangeably, there is a distinction between the terms *city* and *urbanism*. Urbanism implies those characteristics that distinguish cities from simpler settlements, but it also refers to the organization of an urbanized society, which includes those settlements associated with cities. A city, on the other hand, is the physical center that manifests many important characteristics of the urban condition. Urbanization refers not exclusively to the processes by which cities are formed and people are incorporated into an urban-centered sociopolitical system. It refers also to the acquisition of characteristics associated with city life and to the changes in the patterns of life that are apparent among city dwellers.

Cities become symbols, as well as things. Humans are not neutral toward cities but surround them with values and beliefs. The city can be seen as the embodiment of good or evil, as representing progress or decline, and as being the site of human alienation or human salvation.

Apart from the usefulness of cities for administration and defense, they appealed to those who felt their individuality was repressed by social organization based on kinship. On the positive side, cities offered these individuals a measure of freedom, anonymity, privilege, the opportunity to develop their skills, and the stimulation of being part of a more heterogeneous sociopolitical unit than a kin-based one. However, the significance of cities in the ancient world was not limited to such opportunities. The status of women, for example, seems to have deteriorated substantially with urbanization. Although archaeologists have only recently begun to examine such issues, inferences can be drawn from ethnographic studies. The advent of permanent settlements initiated changes that led to increased inequality in status between the sexes. The rise of cities also caused more unequal distribution of wealth. Most preurban societies were basically egalitarian with little specialization, except for that determined by age and sex. Urban societies, however, are characterized by specialization of tasks and serious inequalities in the distribution of wealth.

Cities in their physical form are long-lived. At the same time, urban societies change more than any other social grouping. Cities are thus amalgams of physical structures and people. They are settings for daily rituals—the sacred and the secular, the random and the established. Cities are the ultimate memorials of human struggles and achievements: they are where the pride of the past is put on display.

BIBLIOGRAPHY

Eisenstadt, Shmuel N., and Arie Shachar. *Society, Culture, and Urbanization.* Newbury Park, Calif., 1987.

Frick, Frank S. *The City in Ancient Israel.* Society of Biblical Literature, Dissertation Series, no. 36. Missoula, 1977. Survey of urbanization and the significance of the city in ancient Israel.

Nissen, Hans J. *The Early History of the Ancient Near East, 9000–2000 B.C.* Translated by Elizabeth Lutzeier and Kenneth J. Northcott. Chicago, 1988. Revision and expansion of the author's 1983 work. Nissen uses a unique combination of the analysis of material culture and written data to trace the emergence of the earliest isolated settlements, the growth of networks of towns, the emergence of city-states, and finally the appearance of territorial states.

Redman, Charles L. *The Rise of Civilization: From Early Farmers to Urban Society in the Ancient Near East.* San Francisco, 1978. Although a bit dated in parts, Redman's work provides a useful summary mainly for students of archaeology, anthropology, and ancient history. Organized according to developmental stages rather than regionally or chronologically.

Rohrbaugh, Richard L. "The City in the Second Testament." *Biblical Theology Bulletin* 21 (1991): 67–75. Bibliographic essay that includes discussions of works by both ancient historians and modern social scientists.

Trigger, Bruce G., et al. *Ancient Egypt: A Social History.* Cambridge,

1983. Trigger's chapter, "The Rise of Egyptian Civilization," is a valuable piece on urbanization.

Ucko, Peter, et al., eds. *Man, Settlement, and Urbanism.* Cambridge, Mass., 1972. Proceedings of the 1970 meeting of the Research Seminar in Archaeology and Related Subjects. Although somewhat dated, it includes an impressive, wide-ranging, interdisciplinary collection of essays dealing with settlement patterns and urbanization in various parts of the world.

FRANK S. FRICK

Cities of the Bronze and Iron Ages

In the Near East, the type of settlement known as a city, first developed in Mesopotamia during the second half of the fourth millennium and spread to other areas in the region by the beginning of the third millennium. Since that time, the city has embodied a way of life; in the ancient Near East, except in Egypt, "history" has meant the history of cities. A new level of human civilization began with the emergence of urban life, accompanied by other innovations that developed in the fourth millennium and came to fruition in the third: religions with personal gods and mythical tales that expressed people's beliefs and worldviews; mastery of metalworking (the smelting and working of copper and bronze), and the invention of writing as a means of preserving transactions in all areas of society. This transitional period in human civilization was rooted in certain existing technological features: the building of fixed houses out of a variety of materials, the domestication of plants and animals, the use of the wheel, the production of ceramics from clay, and the manufacture of cloth from plant fibers. In spite of the other decisive changes that took place in economic life, in the ancient Near East agriculture remained the basis of the economy. The city did not supplant other forms of settlement, but coexisted with them.

Early Settlements. The founding of settlements begins with the round houses built in the Natufian period (10,000–8,000 BCE). The first round houses at 'Einan ('Ein Mallaha) on Lake Hulah in Israel were constructed of perishable materials on a stone foundation. [*See* 'Einan.] In the Neolithic period, which followed (8000–4000 BCE), air-dried mud bricks became the main building material, combining the advantages of easy manufacture and use with the demands of load-bearing capacity and durability. During this period some settlements already covered a large expanse: Qal'at Jarmo in the region of the Zagros Mountains was about 1 ha (approximately 2.5 acres), Tell Hassuna on the Upper Tigris River was 3 ha (about 7 acres), and Çatal Höyük in Anatolia was approximately 12 ha (30 acres). [*See* Jarmo; Çatal Höyük.] In addition, as the examples of Tell es-Sawwan on the Middle Euphrates River and Tell es-Sultan (Jericho) in the Jordan Valley show, settlements were surrounded by a wall even before it is possible to speak of the city proper. [*See* Jericho; Jordan Valley.] To be sure, fortifications were an important, if not a compellingly nec-

essary criterion in laying out a city; in the Neolithic period, however, all the additional features that legitimate the designation "city" were lacking. In any event, the Neolithic settlements that were fortified were the forerunners of the ensuing urbanization.

Elements of Urbanization. A number of factors inhere in the establishment of the city as a viable community, although not all of them were present to the same degree. Certain natural prerequisites include land that could be cultivated, a sufficient water supply to enable the self-sufficiency of the inhabitants, and a strategic location favorable for commercial traffic. Community life required a stable social order as well as social differentiation. The ruler was at the head of a city and at the top of the social pyramid. The inhabitants in turn formed classes—priests, warriors, merchants, artisans, free workers, peasants, and slaves—in a hierarchy based on the respect accorded to their occupations and their economic strength.

In terms of urbanism's economic foundations, the production of a surplus and the division of labor, which in turn necessitated an exchange of goods and trading activity, is assumed. The invention of writing significantly facilitated the differentiated economic and social systems, as did other organizational mechanisms such as calendars, taxes, and legal systems. In addition to the social, economic, and legal framework, the formal expression of the divine in the form of cult and mythology was a stabilizing element that legitimated the unequal distribution of resources. The combination of characteristics in one place justifies speaking of a settlement as a city. The external appearance of a city devolved from elements of size and planning, fortification, and public buildings that reflect a high level of cultural development.

Earliest Cities. The cities that developed in Mesopotamia in the second half of the fourth millennium had a long history of settlement: the Sumerian settlements at Ur, Uruk, Eridu, and Nippur in southern Mesopotamia and Tepe Gawra on the Upper Tigris. [*See* Ur; Uruk-Warka; Eridu; Nippur; Tepe Gawra.] In these sprawling city complexes the temple precincts, which stood on a raised terrace surrounded by a separate wall, occupied an extraordinarily large area, surpassing the extent of the palace by several fold and reducing the residential quarter to a minimal area of the city. The dominant spatial position of the cult precinct, as well as its social, economic, and political role in urban life, also characterized cities founded later in the third and second millennia (Aššur, Eshnunna; Khafajeh; Hursagkalama, and many others), even when the residential quarters occupied a large area, as at Babylon. [*See* Aššur; Eshnunna; Khafajeh; Babylon.] Only in the Assyrian residence cities like Nineveh, Nimrud, and Khorsabad did the palace of the ruler begin to assume a dominant position, while the space occupied by the temples sharply declined. [*See* Nineveh; Nimrud; Palace.] The division of cities into distinct regions and quarters makes it evident that their layout was planned, a fact also visible in other of its organizational elements, such as the positioning of gates and streets. The city form that was valid for thousands of years came to an end with the decline of the Neo-Assyrian (or Neo-Babylonian) Empire during the middle of the first millennium BCE. [*See* Assyrians; Babylonians.]

City-States. Even before the end of the fourth millennium, elements of urbanization appeared in Syria. The city of Habuba Kabira on the Middle Euphrates River shows all the elements of conscious planning. The temple precinct lies in the southern part of the city, and with the "middle-room house" a well-developed house type was in use (although the city's palace has not yet been discovered). A network of streets divided the residential quarter into individual districts, and the straight city wall displays projecting towers at regular intervals. During the third millennium, the construction of fortified cities spread throughout Syria, with public buildings, a temple, and a palace occupying a dominant position. All the large urban centers—Mari, Alalakh, Ebla, Hama, Ugarit, and Byblos—were founded after 3000 BCE; most of them continued to exist until the invasion of the Sea Peoples at the beginning of the twelfth century BCE. [*See* Habuba Kabira; Mari; Alalakh; Ebla; Hama; Ugarit; Byblos.]

As the area controlled by the city expanded, the palace began proportionally to occupy the largest area. Archives found at sites such as Mari, Ebla, and Ugarit show how the adoption and development of cuneiform script were necessary to facilitate the administrative and diplomatic correspondence this expansion created. [*See* Cuneiform.] Each city was self-sufficient to the extent that its food supply was grown in the surrounding territory and most of its utensils and tools were manufactured within its walls. An extensive trade assured the procurement of necessary raw materials in exchange for certain agricultural products or finished wares. In Syria urbanization led to the establishment of numerouss city-states, whose individual power was reflected in the differing size of the areas under their control. These city-states collapsed during the twelfth century BCE and were not revived until the beginning of the first millennium by immigrant Arameans. [*See* Arameans.] In the center of these new urban centers were extensive palace districts grouped around a building of the *ḫilani* type, as can be seen at Tell Ḥalaf, Tell Taʿyinat, and Zincirli. [*See* Ḥalaf, Tell.]

Bronze Age Palestine. For ancient Palestine there is a lack of the continuity of urban centers found in Syria. Instead, three distinct periods of urbanization are separated from each other by a nonurban interval. The first urban period is identical with Early Bronze II and III (2950–2350 BCE), the second with Middle Bronze II (1950–1550 BCE) and Late Bronze I and II (1550–1200/1150 BCE). At the beginning of the first millennium, during Iron II (1000–587

BCE), a reurbanization, representing a new cultural influx, occurred; this phase may be considered a third urban culture. Each of the three time periods has a distinct character—they do not collectively represent a single culture.

Early Bronze Age. In most places EB I (3150–2950 BCE) open settlements precede the fixed cities of EB II (2950–2650). This continuity of settlement can be firmly established at Kinneret, Khirbet Kerak/Beth-Yeraḥ, Megiddo, Beth-Shean, Tell el-Farʿah (North), Jericho, Tell esh-Sheikh Ahmed el-ʿAreini, and Arad, as well as at other locations. The transition to fortified cities was based on local development and was not the result of foreign influences. [*See* Beth-Yeraḥ; Megiddo; Beth-Shean; Farʿah, Tell el-(North); Arad.] Some cities, such as Hazor and Beth-Shemesh, were founded on previously unsettled territory. [*See* Hazor; Beth-Shemesh.] Others, such as Tell el-Farʿah (North) and Arad, were abandoned again by the end of the period. However, in EB III (2650–2350 BCE) new cities were also founded in some places, such as Ai, Khirbet Yarmuk, Tell el-Khuweilifeh, Tell el-Ḥesi, Tell Beit Mirsim, and Khirbet ez-Zeraqun. [*See* Ai; Ḥesi, Tell el-; Beit Mirsim, Tell; Zeraqun, Khirbet ez-.] None of the EB cities survived the collapse of urban life that took place during the second half of the third millennium.

The large size of some of the EB cities is striking: Khirbet Kerak, Khirbet Yarmuk, and Tell esh-Sheikh Ahmed el-ʿAreini covered an area of 25 ha (62 acres) or more. Somewhat smaller cities include Aphek (12 ha, or 30 acres); Ai (11 ha, or 27 acres); Arad (10 ha, or 25 acres); and Megiddo (6 ha, or 15 acres). [*See* Aphek.] Like the settlements that preceded them, the cities generally lay in the vicinity of water sources on the plains or on hilltops. However, even sloping terrain could be settled, as at Kinneret, Ai, Khirbet ez-Zeraqun, and Arad. The fortifications varied considerably in their means of construction. In some cases, mud-brick walls 2–6 m thick were erected on stone foundations, from which semicircular or quadrangular towers projected. In other cases, the walls were brought to a width of 8–10 m and more when parallel segments were joined; occasionally, the walls were also protected by a glacis. Openings in the city wall were secured by flanking towers, but a separate gate construction had not yet developed. Numerous posterns in the wall and in the towers provided additional entrances. [*See* Fortifications, *article on* Fortifications of the Bronze and Iron Ages.]

In domestic construction the dominant model was the broadroom house, already widely disseminated in the fourth millennium. The single-room basic form could be expanded by extensions and additional rooms, which resulted in farmsteadlike entities that were enclosed by a surrounding wall. The process of subdividing and joining rooms created multiroomed houses and shifted the entrance to the narrow side. Haphazard construction resulted in haphazard streets that occasionally broadened into small squares.

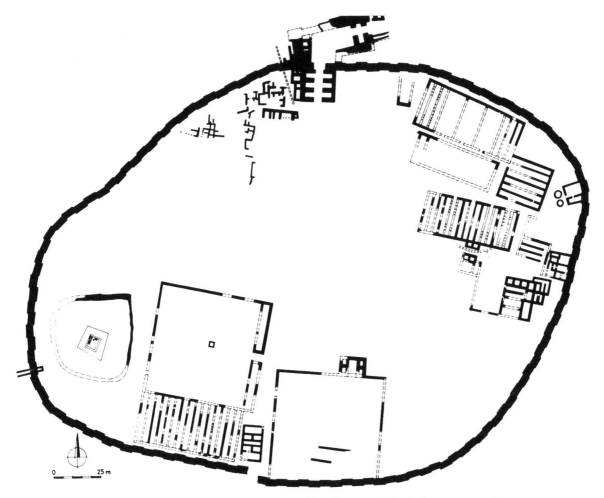

CITIES: Bronze and Iron Ages. *Plan of Megiddo.* City of stratum IVB, ninth century BCE. (Courtesy V. Fritz)

The basic house form was also adopted for public construction; the broadroom temple received an antechamber, however, as the excavated examples show at Megiddo, Ai, Khirbet Yarmuk, and Khirbet ez-Zeraqun. Temples with courtyard altars and subsidiary buildings usually formed a separate cult precinct, which at Ai and Khirbet ez-Zeraqun lay on the highest point of the city. The only EB III palace thus far discovered is at Megiddo, probably depending on foreign influence; like the temple precincts, it was separated from the rest of the city by an enclosure wall. In contrast to domestic construction, the palace was well laid out in groups of rooms accessible from corridors. The ground plan of the palace did not develop from the local types; rather, it is presumed to have been adopted from Mesopotamia. Still, although EB temples and palaces occupied their own districts next to the residential areas, these buildings did not have the spatial dominance characteristic of cities in Mesopotamia.

Overall, during EB II and III urbanization was at a very basic level of development. Only the very beginnings of or-

derly layout and construction are recognizable, and social differentiation is expressed only slightly in architecture, given the limitations of the broadroom house type; large buildings occur rarely. The defense systems show a great concentration of effort, even though gate construction was not developed. The palace at Megiddo implies the existence of centralized rule and political hierarchy, which can be assumed for the other cities as well.

In spite of their predominantly agrarian character, EB cities did not exist in isolation. Agriculture certainly formed their economic foundation; nevertheless, assorted finds point to extensive interregional and intraregional connections. Copper weapons and tools presuppose an intensive trade with the deposit sites in Feinan on the eastern side of the 'Arabah. [*See* Feinan.] The presence of various pottery forms as well as the use of cylinder seals and stamps on vessels indicate connections with Mesopotamia and Egypt. [*See* Seals.] In addition, pieces of imported Palestinian pottery found in Old Kingdom graves prove the existence of trade relations with Egypt. Although writing had not yet been invented in this region, the administration of the cities functioned. It is not known why the cities at the end of EB III were abandoned, but in the period that immediately followed, urban culture was virtually nonexistent.

Middle–Late Bronze Age. The reemergence of urbanization at the beginning of the second millennium bears the stamp of a new culture, with no connection to that of EB II and III. Because this culture seems fully formed at its inception in MB IIA (1950–1750 BCE), it may not have developed locally—it may have been introduced by outsiders, by new immigrants. The majority of the cities, most of which were extraordinarily large, were erected in two waves in the twentieth and the eighteenth centuries BCE. The Old EB hilltop sites of Dan, Hazor, Megiddo, Shechem, Aphek, Gezer, and Jericho were newly fortified, and previously unoccupied sites were settled, as at Akko, Bethel, and Yavneh-Yam. [*See* Dan; Hazor; Shechem; Gezer; Akko; Yavneh-Yam.] Only occasionally did an unfortified settlement precede the fortified city, as at Shechem and Gezer. The MB–LB cities surpassed the EB cities in size. Megiddo reached 10 ha (25 acres), while Dan and Akko covered a surface of about 20 ha (49 acres). The largest cities, such as Ashkelon and Kabri, were built on about 60 ha (148 acres); Hazor was built on 80 ha (198 acres).

The hallmark of the MB–LB cities is their massive fortifications: in addition to the freestanding wall, which had already existed in EB II and III, innovative earthen ramparts were constructed that, including the defensive wall on top of them, could reach heights of up to 12 m. At Hazor and Yavneh-Yam these wall systems are still visible in the landscape; at Dan, Akko, and many other places they were collapsed and eroded into massive mounds of ruins. Parallel to new techniques to strengthen the city's fortifications was the development of the gate structure as an independent component of the wall system. Various gate forms developed from the basic idea of towers flanking an entryway.

Within the city wall, temples and palaces generally occupied a considerable amount of space. In domestic construction a previously unknown form, the courtyard house, appeared (see above). Its hallmark is the arrangement of rooms around a centrally positioned open space that can be bordered on two, three, or four sides by rooms of different sizes. In the process, an attempt was frequently made to establish an approximately square ground plan. With the addition of more rows of rooms, the domestic unit could grow significantly. Because the courtyard provided lighting and ventilation for the rooms, several houses could be contained in individual blocks (the so-called insulae).

In each city there was at least one palace as a residence

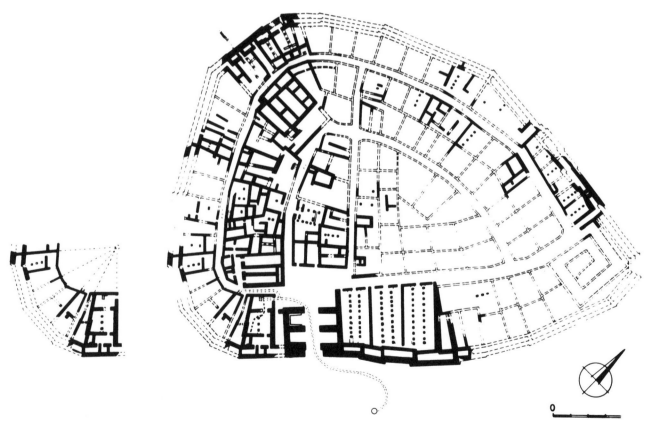

CITIES: Bronze and Iron Ages. *Plan of Tell es-Sebaʿ* (Beersheba). City of stratum II, eighth century BCE. (Courtesy V. Fritz)

CITIES: Bronze and Iron Ages. *City of Lachish.* Reconstruction of the stratum II city, seventh century BCE. (Courtesy V. Fritz)

for the local ruler. A common characteristic of all palaces is the central inner courtyard, around which the rooms were arranged as in the courtyard house. To expand, two rows of rooms could be laid out one behind the other, or the number of inner courtyards could be increased. Although large palace complexes have been uncovered at Hazor, Shechem, Megiddo, Aphek, and Lachish, identifying the functions of their spatial components has so far not been possible. [*See* Lachish.] In temple construction, a new form, the longroom temple, with its entrance on the narrow side, appeared in wide distribution. The type, adopted from a Syrian prototype, was sometimes modified, as at Shechem and Megiddo, by the addition of flanking towers. Other temple forms were also used.

In the course of the millennium, although virtually all the cities were destroyed several times and subsequently rebuilt, their essential elements were maintained. Their complex layout is evidence of a complex social organization: reflections of its defense, domestic life, religious practices, and political features are all visible. Because the city needed commodities from the surrounding countryside, it established control over its hinterland, which presumably consisted of farmsteads and villages. Most of the inhabitants of the city were peasant farmers. Its other inhabitants included

the ruling family and the political elite, artisans, merchants, and sacral personnel. In all respects, the MB II city represents a highly developed culture.

Urban culture entered a decline during the Late Bronze Age: the size of cities as well as their number decreased, and the strength of their fortifications diminished. After 1200 BCE, numerous cities were destroyed and not rebuilt. Even at sites such as Megiddo, which were still inhabited in the twelfth and eleventh centuries BCE, there are signs of a clear break in the material culture, which no longer bears an urban stamp. Explanation for this gradual disappearance of the urban centers in the course of several decades of the twelfth century are still being debated by scholars. Among the possibilities are the invasion of the Sea Peoples, internal conflicts, the end of Egyptian hegemony under the later Ramessides, the collapse of trade with the Mycenaean world, and changes in the natural environment. Some combination of these factors is likely.

Iron Age Palestine. In about 1150 BCE the urban culture that had existed since the beginning of the second millennium disappeared from history. Subsequent occupation preserved isolated elements in some places, but the hallmark of the new nonurbanized period was the founding of numerous small settlements, villagelike in character, outside the territory of the former city-states. It was not until the Israelite kingdom was established in the tenth century BCE, that a reurbanization began within the boundaries of the territorial state. For the royal period the city became the sole settlement form. In that period generally, new cities were founded on the sites of former Bronze Age cities, although occasionally, as at Beersheba, a city could be placed on top of a former settlement from Iron I. [See Beersheba.] The hill-country sites, however, offered the necessary prerequisites for survival with respect to food supply, water sources, and defense. With this reoccupation of the old settlement sites, an urban tradition can be seen, despite differences in the size and layout of the newly founded cities compared to the Bronze Age cities.

The most important element of the Iron Age city was its fortifications. Because all the cities were then under the aegis of a central government, large buildings such as temples and palaces generally declined in significance. Even with some local governance, the Israelite city was subject to the monarchy. The city was thus no longer an independent political entity but was part of a state. The city's agrarian economy meant that its inhabitants were peasants who worked the lands around it. The city's most important function became the protection of its inhabitants.

Iron Age urbanization was the product of a new political situation, not the result of a developmental process. Presumably the establishment of the city was related to the military and administrative demands of the emergent nation-state. Contemporaneous with the spread of the cities, an increase in the population can be seen: on the average, cities were relatively small, with an area of 3–5 ha (7–12 acres), the population varied from a few hundred up to two thousand adult inhabitants. On the basis of their spatial organization, the cities excavated so far can be divided into three groups.

1. *Residential cities.* No form of planning is apparent in residential cities, and as a result their streets form a maze. As in the pre-nation-state villages, the houses are crowded ad hoc within the circuit of the walls. There are no public buildings and a single gate provides access, as, for example at Tell en-Naṣbeh (Miṣpe) and Tell Beit Mirsim. [See Naṣbeh, Tell en-.]

2. *Cities with limited administrative or military functions.* Unlike residential cities, cities with limited administrative or military functions are exemplified by careful planning throughout (e.g., stratum II at Kinneret, stratum II at Beersheba, and stratum VA at Megiddo, even though it lacks an ordered pattern for its streets). A number of pillared houses that served as public buildings appear in the immediate vicinity of the city gate. Residential houses were arranged in rows or in blocks, and the streets either ran parallel to the city wall or were laid out in straight lines and led into an open area in front of the gate. Although the largest portion of the city's total area was taken up by residential buildings,

the city presumably served a broader military or administrative function.

3. *Administrative or military centers.* The development of the city as an administrative or military center appears to have first taken place following the Divided Monarchy, when the demands on and possibilities of the kingdom increased. Buildings with a public function predominated, although a certain number of residential buildings have been excavated (e.g., Lachish strata IV–II, Megiddo stratum IVB). At Lachish a large palace and its subsidiary buildings occupy the center of the site. If this complex was indeed the official residence of a regional governor, Lachish could be described as the earliest provincial capital. At Megiddo several complexes of pillared houses, which may be related to military provisioning, and a palace occupy the largest amount of space. Because troops may have been stationed there, Megiddo may have been a garrison city. Similar arrangements can be assumed for the kingdom's capital cities, Jerusalem and Samaria. In Jerusalem Solomon's royal palace and the Temple and its subsidiary buildings were all in the northern part of the city. [See Jerusalem.] In Samaria the palace formed an independent complex with its own surrounding wall in the center of the city. [See Samaria.]

The early Israelite city was therefore not a uniform entity; its divisions were structured by function—by different economic and political concepts. The three types of city appear in the ninth and eighth centuries BCE. It is not yet known whether they already existed in this form during the United Monarchy in the tenth century BCE. In spite of their differences, the three types of cities share characteristics: a more or less strongly pronounced oval configuration linked to their strategic siting on a tell or a hilltop (cities on a slope, such as Kinneret stratum V, are the exception); a strong circumvallation system, which included massive walls, casemate walls, inset/outset walls, towers projecting from a linear wall; egress and exit through a single gate, which, in the absence of other structures, served civil and defensive functions and could be expanded to a massive building with up to six chambers; and predominating domestic construction (the Israelite pillared house, the three-room house, and the four-room house). [See Four-room House.] A number of cities, such as Jerusalem, Meggido, and Hazor, had their own water systems, which represent not only significant technical achievements but a strong social organization. [See Water Tunnels.]

Many of the cities founded after the beginning of the monarchic period show systematic planning. Only a state with the desire to expand must factor in the need for defense and take corresponding protective measures. Iron II urbanization in Israel, in that it coincided with the formation of the state, was integrally related to political concerns. The settlement was placed within a circumvallation expressly to provide security for its inhabitants in time of war. The technical execution of this arrangement was adapted to the country's construction traditions and topography.

Almost all of these cities were destroyed either during the Assyrian conquest in the second half of the eighth century BCE or in the Neo-Babylonian campaigns at the beginning of the sixth century BCE; they were never rebuilt. The more than two-thousand-year-old continuity of urban construction in the hill country came to an end with the termination of monarchic rule. The few settlements assigned to the end of the Judean monarchy generally lie outside the area of old settlement sites. With the conquest by the Assyrians and the Babylonians, the development of cities in the southern Levant was brought to an abrupt end.

BIBLIOGRAPHY

Adams, Robert McC. *The Evolution of Urban Society: Early Mesopotamia and Prehistoric Mexico.* Chicago, 1971.

Amiran, Ruth. "The Beginning of Urbanization in Canaan." In *Near Eastern Archaeology in the Twentieth Century: Essays in Honor of Nelson Glueck*, edited by James A. Sanders, pp. 83–100. Garden City, N.Y., 1970.

Barghouti, Asem N. "Urbanization of Palestine and Jordan in Hellenistic and Roman Times." In *Studies in the History and Archaeology of Jordan*, vol. 1, edited by Adnan Hadidi, pp. 209–229. Amman, 1982.

Frick, Frank S. *The City in Ancient Israel.* Missoula, 1977.

Fritz, Volkmar. *Die Stadt im alten Israel.* Munich, 1990.

Hammond, Mason. *The City in the Ancient World.* Cambridge, Mass., 1972.

Herzog, Ze'ev. "Israelite City Planning Seen in the Light of the Beer-Sheba and Arad Excavations." *Expedition* 20 (1978): 38–43.

Kempinski, Aharon. *The Rise of an Urban Culture: The Urbanization of Palestine in the Early Bronze Age.* Jerusalem, 1978.

Mellaart, James. *The Neolithic of the Near East.* London, 1975.

Shiloh, Yigal. "Elements in the Development of Town Planning in the Israelite City." *Israel Exploration Journal* 28 (1978): 36–51.

Tcherikover, Avigdor. *Hellenistic Civilization and the Jews.* Philadelphia, 1966.

Ucko, Peter, et al., eds. *Man, Settlement, and Urbanism.* Cambridge, Mass., 1972.

VOLKMAR FRITZ
Translated from German by Susan I. Schiedel

Cities of the Persian Period

Although a large number of sites in Palestine were settled in the Persian period (538–332 BCE), too few remains have been uncovered and insufficient evidence preserved to allow us to reconstruct city plans. The poverty of architectural remains is surprising, for this is a relatively late period, in which, in Persia and Greece, a high standard of building was reached. The scarcity of finds is considered by some scholars to be a result of the widespread destruction in Palestine at the end of the First Temple period. Carl Watzinger maintained that town life in Judah ceased entirely in the Persian period, a view William Foxwell Albright accepted, noting that the results of excavations indicated that the resettlement of Judah was a slow process, and it was not until the third century BCE that the country recovered anything like its old density of population. Kathleen M. Kenyon, in her general discussion of this period, speaks of the decline in town life in Palestine and the concentration of the population in villages. As evidence, she cites both the Persian-period stratum at Tell en-Nasbeh, in which rich finds were discovered without building remains, and the situation at Samaria, where a densely populated urban area was converted into a garden for the Persian governor. However, these theories reflect less the actual situation at that time than the fragmented remains.

Three characteristic features of Persian-period strata have contributed to the archaeological picture and the disappointing results from the excavations at the large mounds: (1) after the Persian period, numerous mounds were abandoned and never resettled (e.g., Megiddo, Tell el-Hesi, and Jericho, among others), and because the stratum from this period was the topmost on the site, it was exposed to the dangers of denudation; (2) at those sites where settlement continued (at Samaria, Shechem, Ashdod, Ashkelon, and Ramat Rahel, for example), the Persian-period level of occupation was severely damaged by intensive building activities in the Hellenistic-Roman period; and (3) at most of the large sites excavated (such as Hazor, Megiddo, Tell Jemmeh, Tel Sera', Lachish, and Tell el-Far'ah [South]), the mound was largely occupied by a palace-fort or other large building.

City Planning. Surveys and excavations of Persian-period settlements throughout Palestine reveal that the coastal plain and perhaps Galilee were very densely populated, while a full account of the cities in the mountain region is yet to be made. The contemporary Greek historian Herodotus describes Gaza as "not inferior to Sardis" (3.5). Indeed, architectural remains in Gaza reveal several examples of well-planned settlements.

Outside Palestine, most cities were built according to the Hippodamic plan (principles of town planning developed by Hippodamus of Miletus in Asia Minor, in the fifth century BCE). The plan divides residential areas into symmetrical blocks, separated by streets that cross each other at right angles. Different functions were assigned to different parts of the town: residential, public, cultic, and recreational (for sport). A fine example of the classic Hippodamic plan is Olynthos, in Macedonia.

There are also examples of well-planned towns along the coast of Palestine, such as at Akko. In the latest city at Tell Abu Hawam, the front of a building was uncovered facing a main road that ran roughly parallel to the city's longitudinal axis. At Shiqmona, a residential quarter consisting of two streets set at right angles to one another contained houses built with considerable symmetry. A similar discovery was made in the excavations at neighboring Tel Megadim, where a quarter was found to be intersected by a broad, straight thoroughfare. The large blocks of buildings flanking the road were separated by lanes that crossed the main road at right angles. The houses themselves were divided into a number of smaller units with a similar plan. Along the southern coast, excavations at Jaffa and Tell el-Ḥesi have revealed a similar well-planned Persian-period stratum.

The recent large-scale excavations at Dor have uncovered another coastal town in which all the strata and remains from the Persian period were strictly laid out according to the Hippodamic plan. Dor's residential quarter is the finest and best-preserved example of Hippodamic planning yet found in Palestine. Its closest parallel is Olynthos. The picture emerging at Dor is that a row of stores and workshops stood along the length of the inner face of the Persian-period city wall. The doors of the shops opened onto a ruler-straight street running parallel to the north–south wall. On the opposite side of the street, whose width is about 2 m, is a fine facade belonging to a long, narrow residential block of buildings. The eastern door of each unit in the row opens onto the street opposite the row of shops. The building is about 20 m wide. Its western side, which faces a street that runs parallel to one on its east, was also uncovered. This elongated block of buildings, preserved to a height of more than 2 m and traced for a length of dozens of meters, was probably crossed by passages leading from one street to the other, but these seem to fall outside the areas excavated so far. Another, identical, building or block of houses existed to the west of this second street. Partition walls divided the block by length and width into small units, or "apartments," whose doors opened, in each case, onto the closest street. In one or two places there are traces of basements. It seems also that the easternmost street, between the residences and the stores, was originally roofed, to provide shelter for pedestrians.

Based on the finds, the latter structures were in use throughout the Persian and Hellenistic periods. There is no indication of violent destruction, but rebuilding took place periodically. With each reconstruction the floor was raised, which resulted in as many as two Persian and three Hellenistic floor levels: the openings were blocked and the walls rebuilt on a higher level. Thus, from one phase to the next, the inner divisions of the building and the function of its rooms varied; for example, in one stage, two small plastered water reservoirs were added. However, none of the alterations affected the external walls. Many coins were found on the different floors, as well as stamped handles from Greek wine amphorae, especially from Rhodes and Knidos, that yielded reliable dates for the building stages. The outer walls of the building were constructed in the style of the period, mostly of well-hewn, hard sandstone ashlars laid in headers. The inner walls and divisions, however, were built in typical Phoenician style: ashlar piers with a rubble fill.

The surprising feature of these plans is that, while the town plan of Olynthos seems to belong to the fourth century BCE—after the time of Hippodamus—Dor was probably laid out in its earliest form in the late sixth century BCE. Dor may thus have served as one of the models from which Hippodamus developed his theories.

Domestic Architecture in Palestine. Remains of houses as well as fortresses and public buildings have been uncovered at Ayyelet ha-Shahar, Hazor, Megiddo, Akko, Gilʿam, Tell Abu Hawam, Shiqmona, Tel Megadim, Dor, Tel Mevorakh, Tel Michal, Tell Qasile, Tell el-Ful, Lachish, Tell el-Ḥesi, Ashdod (fortress north of Ashdod), Tell Jemmeh, Tell el-Farʿah (South), Tel Seraʿ, ʿEin-Gedi, Tell es-Saʿidiyeh, and elsewhere. The plan of these structures indicates that design and construction in the Persian period were surprisingly uniform, whether buildings were private or public. The plan, known as the open-court plan, features an open court surrounded by rooms on several or all sides. The one exception is the Residency at Lachish, which, in addition to an open court, also has two monumental entrances flanked by two columns, typical of the *ḥilani* type. There is no scholarly consensus on the origin of the two building types.

Open-Court Plan. W. F. Petrie sought parallels for the fortress he discovered at Tell Jemmeh and in the two fortresses he had excavated earlier at Daphnae and Naukratis in Egypt. Unfortunately, the data were inadequate for dating. Carl Watzinger accepted Petrie's chronology but rejected his correlation with the Egyptian fortresses, maintaining that fortress A at Tell Jemmeh derived from a Babylonian or an Assyrian source. When similar buildings were subsequently discovered at Megiddo, particularly the fortress and building 736, its excavators, Robert S. Lamon and Geoffrey M. Shipton, recognized the similarity between Building 736 and the earlier open-court buildings at the site, such as buildings 1052 and 1369. They made the comparison with the Residency at Lachish, but their conclusions were too general to be useful. Later assessments usually agree on a Mesopotamian source, either Babylonian or Assyrian (Shmuel Yeivin; Amiran and Dunayevsky, 1958). Ruth Amiran and Immanuel Dunayevsky, after a comprehensive typological analysis of examples from Palestine, Syria, Assyria, and Babylonia, concluded that this type of open-court building was Assyrian and reached Palestine as Assyria's influence spread. Their distinction between an "Assyrian plan," which has rooms flanking the court on all sides, and a "Persian plan," which has rooms only on three sides, may be too fine. The excavators of Megiddo, for example, stated that their fortress may very well have had a fourth row of rooms but that, built so close to the edge, it slid down the slope. This may also have been the case for their building 736, which lacked rooms on the fourth side, perhaps lost to a trench dug by Gottlieb Schumacher that damaged the building on that side.

A survey of the plans of the open-court buildings from the Persian period discussed by Amiran and Dunayevsky and those discovered later reveals that although the basic layout is retained, it is not always uniform. In the Persian period, as in the Iron Age, the arrangement of rooms around a court took on different forms. At Hazor, the rooms of the fortress and the farmhouse enclosed the four sides of the court, a layout also found at Tell el-Ḥesi in F. J. Bliss's city VII and in phase 5d of the recent excavations; at Tell Jemmeh in building B; at Tell Seraʿ in area D, stratum V; in the fortress recently discovered north of Ashdod; and in the fortresses at Tell es-Saʿidiyeh. The courts are surrounded on only three sides in area A at Akko, at Tell Qasile, and in building A at Tell Jemmeh. In some instances, the grouping of rooms varies from place to place (Shiqmona, Tel Mevorakh, Lachish building G/12/13, and ʿEin-Gedi building 234); in others, it is impossible to ascertain (Ayyelet ha-Shahar, the stratum I buildings at Megiddo, Gilʿam, Tell Abu Hawam, Tel Megadim, Ashdod, Tell el-Ḥesi, and Tell el-Farʿah (South), although all the available evidence points to a central court enclosed by rooms. It seems reasonable, nonetheless, to conclude that the open-court plan was introduced into Palestine at the end of the Assyrian period and continued without modification into the Babylonian and Persian periods.

Lachish Residency. Of all the buildings in Palestine attributed by their excavators to the Persian period, only the palace at Lachish deviates in construction from the rest. The main distinction is the two *hilani*-type entrances, not found elsewhere in Palestine. Olga Tufnell (in her final report of Lachish) concurred with Watzinger's earlier interpretation of the building as "Syro-Hittite." Like Watzinger, she encountered difficulties locating appropriate parallels. The closest she found is the palace of the Assyrian governor at Arslan Tash (whose plan it in no way resembles). Finding examples similar to the Lachish Residency led Albright to a strained comparison to early Parthian palaces, such as the small palace at Nippur in Babylon. Yohanan Aharoni's assessment of the plan of the Residency as a combination of a Syrian *hilani* building and an Assyrian open-court house accurately conveys its essence, which is a fusion of two distinct building styles. Moreover, architectural fusion is a characteristic of provincial Persian palaces. The Lachish Residency therefore clearly seems to have been constructed under Achaemenid influence. The reason for its unique appearance among the buildings of the Persian period in Palestine may be that it is the only building that can be interpreted with certainty as a palace; the others may have served different purposes. [*See* Lachish.]

The Fortifications. Defensive walls assigned by their excavators to the Persian period have also been uncovered at Akko, Tell Abu Hawam, Megiddo, Gilʿam, Tel Megadim, Tel Mevorakh, Jaffa, and Tell el-Ḥesi. These towns are on the coast and in the Shephelah, the region between the coast and the Judean hills. Remains of other walls have been cleared at Samaria, Jerusalem, Tell en-Naṣbeh, and Lachish,

as well as at Rabbat Ammon and Heshbon in Transjordan. In the Late Persian period, many city walls were demolished and replaced by smaller fortresses: at Hazor, Megiddo, Dor, Tell Qasile, Tell Jemmeh, Tel Seraʿ, Tell el-Ḥesi, Ashdod, and Tell es-Saʿidiyeh, for example.

At Tell Abu Hawam, a wall was discovered surrounding phase B of stratum II on the south and east. It was built in small sections—each of which stood at a slightly different angle—of fieldstones, with ashlars added for reinforcement at each of its turns. Another small segment of this wall was discovered on the west side of the site. A very similar multiangled wall was also found at Gilʿam belonging to the site's second phase of the Persian-period settlement (fourth century BCE). The wall, which enclosed a rectangular area 100 × 200 m, consisted of two faces of worked or otherwise well-dressed stones taken from the preceding settlement. Between the two faces was a fill of fieldstones. Two segments of this wall, each about 30 m long, were uncovered, one on the east and the other on the north.

The settlement at Tel Megadim was also defended by a wall that enclosed a rectangular area of about 15 dunams (approximately 4 acres). It was built of bricks on a stone foundation. Three sections of the wall have been uncovered so far: about 170 m on the west, about 100 m on the north, and 20 m on the south. This was a typical casemate wall, whose outer and inner walls were divided into rooms that served as dwellings and storerooms. It was apparently erected in stratum III and may have been in use in stratum I. A similar casemate wall was uncovered at Tel Mevorakh in stratum IV (fourth century BCE). The Persian settlement at Tell Abu Zeitun was fortified with a brick wall only in its last phase, according to its excavator, Jacob Kaplan.

Stratum II at Jaffa, which Kaplan assigned to the end of the fifth and beginning of the fourth centuries BCE, was also enclosed by a city wall. One section, about 12 m long and 2.5 m wide, discovered on the east side of the city, was built of well-dressed local sandstone. The stones were shaped like bricks lying on their sides and were set perpendicular to the wall, like headers. At set intervals they were strengthened by piers of stretchers. At Tell el-Ḥesi, the remains of a wall that enclosed both the early and the later phases of the city were found. According to Bliss, its excavator, the north sides of the buildings of city VII (500–400 BCE) leaned against the city wall. This wall continued in use in city VIII (400–332 BCE), during which time it was broadened and strengthened. At Sheikh Zuweid, according to Petrie, city F, which he dated to 497–362 BCE, was enclosed by a thick wall on the west. It was a continuation and repair of the previous wall of city G. It is difficult, however, to establish the true date of the various strata from Bliss's excavation report, leaving the chronology in doubt.

The second group of defense walls from the Persian period in Palestine comes from the cities of Judah. In Jerusalem, Kenyon in her excavations (1961–1967) on the crest of the eastern hill, discovered a fragment of the city wall from the Persian period (which she called Nehemiah's wall) erected on high bedrock. She found settlement levels from the fifth–fourth centuries BCE against it (to which a large tower had been added in the Hasmonean period). Jerusalem in the Persian period had therefore been confined to a narrow strip on the summit of the eastern hill. In Kenyon's opinion, the "Valley Gate," or western gate, uncovered by J. W. Crowfoot, also belonged to the fortifications of that city. The walls were built of large, worked stones whose interstices were filled with smaller stones, a method of construction considered by the excavator to parallel that of the Valley Gate. At Tell en-Naṣbeh, Joseph Wampler assigned a small wall erected outside the large Iron Age city wall to the later phase of stratum I. He interpreted this wall as a modification of the city's defenses which took place after the destruction of the large (previous) wall. Wampler dated this wall to 575–450 BCE.

Clearer remains of Persian-period city fortifications were uncovered at Lachish, where their date parallels that of the Residency (450–350 BCE). Aside from the area of the city gate, which will be discussed subsequently, remains of a wall assigned to stratum I were discovered above the lower wall of the First Temple period. A section of wall investigated was constructed above a 2-m layer of collapsed debris that had piled up after the destruction of the last wall of the First Temple period (stratum II). The upper courses were of worked stones, most of them taken from earlier buildings. The spaces between the stones were filled with clay or small stones. One section of this wall cleared in square E-19 was constructed of fieldstones. The wall was built at a right angle to the road and blocked direct access to the outer gates. The main upper city wall (on the summit of the mound) was built above the course of the stratum II wall. Two sections of this wall were uncovered flanking the gate; in comparison with the previous wall, they were badly constructed. These meager data suggest that the towns in the Judean hills were also fortified, albeit poorly, in the Persian period. [See Judah.]

Towns in Transjordan were also fortified at this time, as is evidenced by recent excavations at Heshbon. A stone wall, 1.10 m thick and preserved to a height of 3–5 m, has been assigned by its excavators to the Persian period. The wall defended the acropolis. Remains of a tower and perhaps also the beginning of a gate were discovered on the eastern side of the excavated area. It recently became clear that the fortresses encircling Rabbat Ammon definitely continue into the Persian period.

Throughout most of the Persian period, Dor's fortifications were the last Iron Age city wall, actually the "Assyrian" wall, with insets and offsets and a two-chambered inner gate. The wall protected the city for the length of time it was a provincial capital: at first of an Assyrian, then of a Babylonian, and finally of a Persian province. It seems that this was also the case at Megiddo. The massive and sophisticated fortification system at Dor was destroyed under Ptolemy II, when the great Phoenician revolt against Persian rule was suppressed in the mid-fourth century BCE. Judging from the archaeological evidence revealed in the excavations, a new fortification system was built at Dor very shortly after, in the late Persian period.

A significant feature of this fortification system is its method of construction: it is clear that the Phoenician building tradition was still alive in Palestine in the mid-fourth century BCE. The outer wall and all of the inner dividing walls were built in its characteristic style: ashlar piers built of headers and stretchers—one stone laid lengthwise and two widthwise across the pier, with a fieldstone fill. As far as we know, all the city walls of coastal Palestine and Phoenicia were built in this way from the tenth to the ninth centuries BCE, as seen at Megiddo and Tyre, down to the third century BCE, at Dor and Jaffa and elsewhere along the coast. The gate of the wall at Dor has not yet been cleaned. Some parts of this Phoenician wall have been preserved to a height of more than 2 m and are among the most impressive examples of their kind yet found in Palestine.

In the third century BCE, when this last "Phoenician" wall from the fourth century, together with its adjacent buildings, was apparently still standing, the city received a new fortification system. This time the wall was built in the Greek style previously encountered only rarely in Palestine (in particular at Samaria, Akko, and Mareshah [Marisa], which had become Greek settlements at the very beginning of the Macedonian conquest).

This new wall was built entirely of large, thick rectangular blocks of sandstone (about 1 m long), most of them laid in headers facing the exterior. The relative flexibility of sandstone and its ability to receive blows without breaking enabled the blocks to withstand the advanced siege machines of the period. It was a massive construction, about 2 m thick, whose foundations cut through all the preceding walls on its eastern side. Square towers, set about 30 m apart and built in the same style, projected beyond the wall. Two of these towers have been uncovered so far, the earliest examples of their type in Palestine. The new wall's distinctive style and towers are unmistakably Greek innovations.

The change at Dor from fortifications built in the Phoenician style to those in the Greek style represents the final stage in the transformation of the Palestinian city from a largely "oriental" city to a Hellenistic one—a process begun much earlier. With this change in the walls, the gates of the eastern tradition, such as those at Megiddo and Dor, were replaced by purely Greek-style gates. These changes were certainly the result of the introduction of the new Greek siege weapons, such as the ballista, as has recently been shown by Ilan Sharon (1991).

The picture that emerges in Ilan Sharon's discussion of Dor's fortifications and their resemblance to those at nearby

Megiddo makes it necessary to reevaluate the latter's fortifications. Scholars have long accepted that the Assyrians established stratum III at Megiddo, rebuilding the offset-inset wall and constructing the two-chambered gate. The findings at Dor will now enable the exact date of the destruction of that advanced system of fortifications at Megiddo to be fixed.

Persian-period remains at Megiddo consisted of three complexes. The third complex, in area D, was interpreted by Ephraim Stern as the entrance gate of the city and dated to stratum I. It includes a building in the north, near the gates from the Israelite period. The building stands somewhat south of these Iron Age gates. Its two parallel rectangular rooms (nos. 603 and 604) are constructed at a distance from each other and are oriented in a line with the Israelite gate. Two other structures near the "gate" are also attributed to the Persian period: a complex of three rooms (nos. 634–635, 576), which is joined by wall 1045 and with it constitutes a separate fortified area; and another complex of rooms (nos. 1346–1348). These two complexes have been interpreted as the barrack of the garrison force.

The wall, gate, and settlement at Megiddo were destroyed in about 350 BCE by the Persian army during the Phoenician revolt. Thus, at both Dor and Megiddo, a two-chambered gate and offset-inset wall existed from the time of the Assyrian conquest to the mid-fourth century BCE. The fortress in area C at Megiddo was built above the offset-inset wall, replacing it, and was the only fortification on the site. Built after the rebellion, this fortification was in place until the city's final destruction by the Greek army and its abandonment in 332 BCE.

The phase at Dor contemporaneous with the fortress at Megiddo contains the "casemate wall," or more precisely, the row of houses that formed a wall around the periphery of the city. These too were built after the destruction of the offset-inset wall in approximately 350 BCE and were later replaced by a solid Hellenistic wall erected by Ptolemy II. It is possible that the Persians—after their bitter experience with the Phoenician rebellion—refused to permit strongly fortified settlements. This may be why so many fifth- and especially fourth-century BCE Palestinian sites have no city walls and small fortresses. For example, at Hazor (strata III–II), the date of fortress III could not be established because it yielded no datable remains. The date of fortress II was fixed by coins to the late fourth century BCE, specifically to the reign of Artaxerxes III (359/8–338/7 BCE). Destroyed during the conquest of Alexander the Great, that fortress also existed only during the last phase of the Persian period, exactly as at Megiddo and Dor.

Fortresses with a similar plan, dating to the same period, have been found at other sites—at Tel Michal, Tell Qasile, Ashdod, Tell Jemmeh, Tell el-Ḥesi, Tel Seraʿ, and Tell es-Saʿidiyeh among them. The poverty of the remains of Palestinian fortifications from the Persian period provides us with only the barest hint of the period's construction practices. What is clear is that the major towns of Palestine in the Persian period were either thoroughly fortified or defended only by fortresses. This can be deduced both from the historical sources and from what is known of the siege techniques of the period, such as those described by the Greek historian Thucydides in the *Peloponnesian War*.

[See also Dor; and Furniture and Furnishings, *article on* Furnishings of the Persian Period. *In addition, many of the other sites mentioned are the subject of independent entries.*]

BIBLIOGRAPHY

Amiran, Ruth, and Immanuel Dunayevsky. "The Assyrian Open-Court Building and Its Derivations." *Bulletin of the American Schools of Oriental Research*, no. 144 (1958): 25–32.

Sharon, Ilan. "Phoenician and Greek Ashlar Construction Techniques at Tel Dor, Israel." *Bulletin of the American Schools of Oriental Research*, no. 267 (August 1987): 21–42.

Sharon, Ilan. "The Fortifications of Dor and the Transition from the Israelite-Syrian Concept of Defense to the Greek Concept" (in Hebrew). *Qadmoniot* 24 (1991): 105–113.

Stern, Ephraim. *Material Culture of the Land of the Bible in the Persian Period, 538–332 B.C.* Warminster, 1982. Covers the architecture of Palestine in the Persian period (pp. 1–67).

Stern, Ephraim. "The Walls of Dor." *Israel Exploration Journal* 38.1 (1988): 6–14.

Stern, Ephraim. *Dor, the Ruler of the Seas: Twelve Years of Excavations at the Israelite-Phoenician Harbor Town on the Carmel Coast.* Jerusalem, 1994. Discussion of the introduction of Hippodamic city planning in the Levant.

EPHRAIM STERN

Cities of the Hellenistic and Roman Periods

Unlike the Mesopotamian temple-cities that emerged in about 2700 BCE whose view of the world was sacral and which were controlled by a priestly caste, the earliest forms of the Greek cities show signs of competing forms of preurban social arrangements—aristocratic warlords, status, property, and kin groups. A radical reorganization in the emerging polis was called for, by which arete, or courage, as the supreme value, was transformed into loyalty to the city and its institutions. Religious commitment played an essential role in terms of devotion to the patron god or goddess, bequeather of the constitution which bound all together.

From its very inception, therefore, the Greek city fostered a more independent character, further developed in the classical period as various forms of government—monarchic, aristocratic, oligarchic, and democratic—established themselves successively between 800 and 400 BCE. The political circumstances of Greece's wars with Persia had led to the formation of various intercity leagues in the fifth and fourth centuries BCE, while leaving intact those institutions that had developed, the hallmark of polis society—the *demos*, or people, *ekklesia,* or "general assembly," and the *boule,* or council. These and other institutions had received theoretical underpining through the writings of Plato and Aristotle and hence became a permanent legacy of the Greek city to Western civilization. In addition, certain architectural features had also emerged, distinct visual expressions symbolic of the city's self-understanding.

Alexander is reputed to have established seventy cities, as his all-conquering campaign took him to the heart of the Persian Empire and beyond. Even if Plutarch's numbers are exaggerated and not all foundations were of equal splendor, the city of Alexandria demonstrates that for Alexander the Greek city had a cultural as well as a defensive or administrative role to play in his grand scheme. Natives were invited to join with Greek settlers to wed east and west into one great cosmopolis. New cities were established and older, Oriental ones were transformed from their hieratic and aristocratic character in accordance with the Greek ideals. The typical institutions of the polis spread the Greek way of life, as can be seen from the many architectural remains, inscriptions, and other signs of the Greek presence in the East. Despite his best intentions, Alexander initiated a subtle change in the role of the city, which was accentuated in succeeding centuries, first under the Hellenistic monarchies and later by Rome (Jones, 1971). The city was to become the instrument of empire and those aspects of its character that impeded this had to be adapted to meet the new agenda. Thus, the Ptolemies and Seleucids continued the policy of establishing new cities, upgrading older ones, or bringing about a synoecism of smaller settlements in their various territories. Some, such as Alexandria, Antioch on the Orontes, and Palmyra were to continue to flourish because of their political and/or strategic locations on the main trade routes between East and West. [See Alexandria, Antioch on Orontes; Palmyra.] Thus the increase in the commercial life of the city in the Hellenistic age, as new trade routes were opened and travel between cities was greatly developed, led to an increase in the ethnic mix within cities and to the establishment of separate quarters in some instances—as, for example, the Jewish quarter in Alexandria. Because cities were no longer fully free and autonomous but subordinate to monarchical rule, the democratic style of government was considerably curtailed. New elites of wealth emerged, favored by central administrations in a patron/client relationship. This in turn meant architectural development, as local wealthy people vied with each other in honoring their patron in the form of public buildings or, as in the case of Herod the Great and his sons, actually founding cities in their honor (Samaria/Sebaste, Caesarea Maritima, Caesarea Philippi, Tiberias). [See Samaria; Caesarea; Tiberias.] Even external appearances were modified as the classical Greek style was blended with more ornate Oriental ones or made to conform to Roman conservative taste, for example, regarding nudity.

These developments continued under the Romans, as they gradually replaced the Hellenistic monarchies from the second century BCE onward (Stambaugh, 1988). The role of the cities then had less to do with the spread of culture than being administrative centers within the provincial system or being rewards for veterans of various campaigns through the founding of colonies. Older cities Rome had destroyed (Carthage, Corinth, Philippi) were reestablished by Julius Caesar. [See Carthage.] These colonies were closely tied to Rome, both politically and culturally, imitating Rome's senatorial form of government and even its architecture: aqueducts, bathhouses, and amphitheaters. [See Aqueducts; Baths.] In some instances their citizens were allowed to vote in Rome itself. Gradually, the right of Roman citizenship was extended to some provincials, thus replacing the privilege of being a citizen of an individual city with the rights of citizenship of the mother of all cities (Acts 21:39, 22:38). Despite these close bonds with Rome, the provincial administration remained intact, acting as a kind of watchdog at the regional level, on behalf of Rome (Sherwin-White, 1963). Cities allowed to mint their own coins, a mark of some independence, had to ensure that the coins bore emblems of Roman imperial rule. Local magistrates were particularly concerned not to prevent anything that could be construed as civil disturbance because this could cause trouble with Rome, as in the case of Paul's visit to Thessalonike (Acts 17:5–9). Yet, they were caught between the task of maintaining law and order and not offending Roman sensibilities when a citizen was involved (Acts 16:37–39).

In the Byzantine period, previous policy with regard to cities continued—namely, to develop them wherever possible, provided there were enough locals willing and able to take on the administrative burdens, particularly the collection of taxes. Throughout the third century CE, there was a serious decline in imperial rule, arrested militarily by Diocletian (r. 284–305). A centralized bureaucracy developed which in time became unwieldy—one reason the Byzantine emperors sought to support local municipalities wherever possible. A network of loyal clients, they allowed local elites to reemerge, curtailing the power of the central civil service. Constantine's declared policy to found new cities and revive others resulted, by the sixth century, in almost all imperial territory being ruled by the cities, with the remnants of the old provincial system carved up among them. In the process, the cities were reduced in importance, their status almost wholly dependent on their performance as outposts of imperial rule. Increasingly, the number of men of substance who might fulfill the role of decurions or magistrates declined, either because they were drawn into the imperial administration or because they decided to withdraw from public life entirely. The architectural trappings of grandeur were maintained, with the development of domed roofs and the free representation of classical motifs, but internally the life had been drained from the towns in supporting a tottering empire. Increasingly, the large villas in the countryside, and of course the Christian monasteries, were the places where the cultural role of the cities of a previous age were maintained and carried forward. [*See* Monasteries.]

Architecture of Ancient Cities. Many handbooks on town planning and architecture are known from Hellenistic and Roman times (e.g., Vitruvius), as well as from the accounts of travelers and geographers, such as Strabo and Pliny, which add to what is known of the visual aspects of ancient cities. The period eclectic styles and conceptions—Etruscan, Greek, Roman, and Semitic—influenced each other at different locations. (Pompeii's state of preservation by the lava from the eruption of Mt. Vesuvius in 79 CE provides a unique example of that eclecticism.) Certain characteristic features emerge with great regularity, however, confirming that it is possible to talk about the ancient city and about architecture playing a role in determining when a settlement was a city.

There is ample evidence to suggest that proximity to a plentiful supply of water was the determining factor in settling most ancient sites, and elaborate measures were taken to ensure one, as can be seen from the arrangements at Hazor, Megiddo, and Jerusalem itself. [*See* Hazor; Megiddo; Jerusalem.] In addition to the supply from a local source, the numbers of cisterns, underground storage pools, channels and conduits which have been unearthed indicate that collection of rainwater was important, for both civic and domestic purposes. [*See* Cisterns; Reservoirs.] The aqueduct, often carrying water from a considerable distance, is associated with Roman hydraulic engineering. It is estimated that in the first century CE Rome itself had as many as nine different ones drawing water from sources 19–80 km (12–50 mi.) away. The remains of aqueducts are scattered throughout the Roman territories, the one at Caesarea Maritima being the most notable in ancient Palestine. The absence of such an amenity was noted and to be remedied at the citizens' expense. Despite the preponderance of Roman remains, however, there is evidence that the Greeks had mastered the technique earlier (Owens, 1991, p. 158). Sometimes water was transported through underground channels, such as at Sepphoris in Galilee, which is fed from two springs, 3 and 5 km (2 and 3 mi.) from the city and with an elaborate system of storage and pressure tanks at various levels along the way. A similar installation has been found at Gadara, Jordan, possibly designed by the same architect (Tsuk, 1995). Population increase meant an extra demand on the water supply, and this was further accentuated in Roman times with the introduction of the public baths, found at almost every significant site from the first century CE onward.

Health needs also demanded sewer and drainage systems. The location of many cities on elevated ground was a natural aid, but the existence of the famous *cloaka maxima,* from the sixth century BCE, still in use in Rome, shows how early this feature had become a part of town planning. At Caesarea there is evidence to suggest that Herod's architects designed the underground sewer chambers so that maximum advantage could be gained from the tides to wash the city's waste out to sea. This feature of Roman towns in particular has been attributed to Etruscan influences on the basis of the evidence from Veii, where rock-cut and stone-built channels have been found. The literary evidence suggests that the sanitary conditions in many cities, especially in the poorer quarters, were virtually nonexistent, however. Thus, the building of public latrines, often ornately decorated on the outside, became a feature of many Roman towns.

The acropolis/*arx* was the city's highest point and also its religious focal point. The temple of the city's chief patron deities (the Parthenon of the goddess Athena in Athens and the temples of Jupiter, Juno, and Minerva in Rome) and their cultic personnel were located on it. It both symbolized the city's freedom and independence and served as a place of refuge, at least for the chief citizens in times of attack. Hence, the notion that walls were essential for the true city was prevalent, even when this was not always the case. Sometimes natural features, such as deep ravines, determined the siting of cities on jagged promontories or inaccessible hills (Pergamon in Asia Minor). [*See* Pergamon.] Josephus's description of Gamla, where Galilean Jews resisted the Romans in 66 CE, also shows a consciousness of the value of natural terrain for defense (*War* 4.4–10). [*See* Gamla.] The Greeks seem to have developed walls as a system of fortification independently of the street plan, so there were interior open spaces which could cause problems if the city came under attack. The Romans, on the other hand, integrated streets and walls to the point that casemate houses formed part of the wall and could function as further support in times of attack or siege.

In the late Roman period walls made a symbolic statement. City walls were poorly constructed in terms of defense, yet functioned as clearly demarcating spatial distinctions between insiders and outsiders: interior walls separated patrician from plebeian quarters and religious from secular ones, and provided toll boundaries and controls for the movement of goods both into and within the city. Walls could also function as status symbols similar to public monuments. In particular, gates took on this feature of public adornment, becoming the focal point for commerce and meeting, sometimes rivaling the agora or forum, which was always located at the center of the settlement. In later times, the streets leading to the gate and from there to the forum were also suitably adorned and were occasionally interrupted with smaller squares which provided for social interaction. Such places also provided welcome for the visitor on the approach to the forum, which otherwise might have appeared forbidding and hostile.

The agora, or forum, was thus the most important central place within the city, not merely for commercial transactions but also for legal, administrative, and religious functions. Their developing location within the overall city plan demonstrates the ways in which the institution of the *polis* was itself transformed over time. As a human community, the polis institution portrayed an ordered way of life in which law was supreme. The idea of a town plan is associated as early as the fifth century BCE, with Hippodamos of Miletus, to whom the notion of the grid system of streets crossing each other in a regular pattern is attributed. [*See* Miletus.] This plan seems to have been almost universally accepted at a relatively early period. In Roman times cities were bissected by a main thoroughfare, running north–south, the *cardo maximus,* which usually led to, and sometimes through the forum. This was intersected by an east–west main street, the *decumanus,* or "tenth street." Shops and other public buildings were located along these two main axes, while the residential areas, the insulae, or blocks of apartments, were on narrower and sometimes unpaved streets.

In some instances, the *cardo* formed a T junction with the *decumanus* and did not carry on beyond the forum, terminating in a basilica, portico, or temple. [*See* Basilicas.] This represented a more conservative approach to spatial organization, suggesting a less open perspective to the visitor. The actual forum area itself seems to have developed from an open area in which everyone intermingled freely to being walled in from the Augustan Age onward, and therefore with controlled entry and egress, as can be seen in the various imperial fora in Rome itself. This development would seem to suggest a concern with policing crowds and the possibility of a more differentiated approach to public social relations between urban elites and ordinary people. Amphitheaters, as enclosed areas for the live animal shows, and bathhouses, both hallmarks of Roman architecture, even when the amphitheaters were not located centrally, indicate similar attitudes: the desire of the imperial administration to offer entertainment and leisure for the masses, while avoiding popular movements of unrest. Despite these developments, architectural evidence for ongoing and varied activity in the forum, essential to the life of the city as a political community—temples, law courts, senate house, rostra, shops—is clear. The theater, which already was very much a feature of the Greek city, continued into Roman times. It was centrally located, which indicates its continued importance to civic life. [*See* Theaters.]

In an honor/shame culture, the endowment of buildings was seen as an act of piety and a demonstration of munificence or generosity, thereby gaining public esteem for the donor. Wealthy people vied with each other in honoring their political master, which from the first century CE onward was the emperor or some member of his family. The Herodian building program in Palestine is an outstanding example, corresponding to the watershed in art and architecture of the Augustan Age generally (Zanker, 1988). The aim was to celebrate Rome's victory in the new age of peace that had dawned. The buildings are larger, more majestic and ornamental; the decorative art was more elaborate, exploit-

ing suitable themes from the classical period to express the new order symbolically—the ultimate political realization on a universal scale of classical ideals. The new artistic expression combined the best traditions of Greek aesthetics and Roman virtue. Statues and busts were not just used for propaganda but to adorn the fora and main thoroughfares; fountains and water houses (nymphaea) were a constant feature, even in private houses. The adornment of buildings with marble facades and the erection of columns, commemorative niches, stairways, and stoas along main thoroughfares all contributed to a splendor which celebrated Rome's glory. Mosaic pavements and frescoed walls were standard decorative elements of both public and private buildings, imposing a uniformity of style and taste throughout the vast territory, often at the expense of local traditions and native habits. [*See* Mosaics; Wall Paintings.]

City as Social System. The Greek polis was first and foremost a community rather than a settlement *(astu)* and this involved political, economic, and cultural organization. These aspects were already well defined in the classical period, and while modifications inevitably occurred under the Hellenistic monarchies, and to an even greater extent under Roman imperial administration, the essential function of its institutions nevertheless continued in place.

Political life. Essential to the very notion of the city was the demos, or people, the body of free citizens who shared in all the rights and privileges associated with such membership and who felt obligated to the maintenance of the polis institutions through services of various kinds as circumstances demanded (Finley, 1983). Not everyone in the settlement was a citizen—slaves, foreigners, and other unpropertied inhabitants were not. In theory, women were equally capable of discharging the duties of the citizen, but in practice their role was restricted to that of the private sphere, except in exceptional circumstances of the wealthy. Thus, despite the evolution from oligarchy to democracy in both Greece and Rome, citizenship was a privilege, not a right. Regular assemblies *(ekklesiai)* of all the citizens were held, but the running of the city's affairs on an on-going basis was delegated to the boule, or council, elected from the citizens with one of its members acting as chief (politarch or archon). There was in addition, a host of other city officials, such as the market manager *(agoranomos),* the chief of police, and tax collectors, among others. As well as the privileges of citizenship there were also responsibilities *(leitourgiai)*—to support a war effort, to sponsor a theatrical performance or religious ceremony, or, in Roman times, to pay for a temple, statue, or other public building. Under the empire the tendency was to revert more and more to the oligarchic style of government as the one which could best be trusted to maintain Roman interests (MacMullan, 1974). Some of the older cities of the east, such as Tyre, were allowed to continue to mint their own coins, as well as Roman imperial ones. [*See* Tyre.] When the right was granted to other, newer foundations, such as Sepphoris (66 CE) and Tiberias (100 CE), Rome was always clearly acknowledged in the emblems and the legend. [*See* Tiberias.]

Rome came to rely more and more on the towns to impose and maintain imperial rule, a policy already well exemplified in the first century through the increased urbanization of Palestine after the First Jewish Revolt (Jones, 1931). [*See* First Jewish Revolt.] Michael Avi-Yonah (1966) has attempted to map the boundaries of the various cities on the basis of such archaeological remains as milestones and such literary sources as Eusebius's *Onomasticon*. More recent archaeological work based on central-place theory and relying on archaeological surveys has developed computer-aided models to understand the role of towns as centers within larger administrative and commercial configurations (Rihll and Wilson, 1991). These studies help to underline the fact that the institution of the city with its own territory was deemed to have on-going relevance in political terms, long after its independence had been drastically curtailed in the interests of empire.

Polis as economic system. The preindustrial city was very dependent on resources available from the immediate hinterland. Scholars agree that the relationship was quite different from that obtaining since the industrial, public health, and transport revolutions. The relationship was symbiotic, but without both benefiting equally from the single most important resource, namely the land (Finley, 1985; Hopkins, 1978, 1980; Wallace-Hadrill, 1991). There is a need to differentiate among the urban elites (a small minority of the total population), the retainer and merchant classes, and the poor, on the one hand, and the large landowners (who often resided in the city and formed an important segment of the urban elite), the small freeholders, the lessees, day laborers, and agricultural slaves, on the other. Thus, access to the basic resource was uneven, and the few at the top of the social pyramid that was the polis stood to gain much more from its successful exploitation than those farther down the social scale. Urban elites needed the peasantry in order to live the life of luxury, and those among the peasantry who had a disposable surplus of grain or other produce needed the cities as places of local demand or as depots and collecting centers for the larger market.

Scientific study of the pottery of Galilee shows that certain villages specialized in supplying the household wares for a wide region, including the urban center of Sepphoris (Adan-Bayewitz, 1993). [*See* Galilee, *article on* Galilee in the Hellenistic through Byzantine Periods.] This is a sign of a developing economy, in which the notion of the village as remote hamlet where peasants lived in total isolation from the larger culture has to be considerably modified, at least beginning in the Hellenistic period. A similar pattern repeated itself in Egypt and Syria as well (Harper, 1928; Bagnall, 1993), so that the prevalent idea of the ancient city as being totally parasitic on the surrounding countryside, following the influential studies of Moses Finley (1977, 1983, 1985), is perhaps overstated (Whittaker, 1990). Nevertheless, it remained true that, as far as peasants were concerned, the countryside was not the city and different norms prevailed. (The peasantry is said to have formed a subculture rather than an independent class.) It was only in the Late Roman and Byzantine periods that the signs of affluence associated with the city flowed into the countryside, as wealthy Romans abandoned crowded cities for their country villas.

Within the confines of the city conceived in narrower terms of the urban center itself, financial considerations loomed large: the costs of building a city and maintaining its public space, even when forced labor and the freely rendered tasks, or *munera*, of the citizens could be relied on to cover a wide range of services. According to a later version of a letter attributed to Hadrian (fl. 130 CE), philosophers, rhetoricians, schoolteachers, and doctors were exempted from the responsibilities of the gymnasium, marketplace, priesthoods, maintaining the supply of corn and oil, jury service, embassies, and obligations to local and provincial offices. However, these exceptions were rare and honor demanded undertaking them with a display of munificence. The competition among the wealthy for popular esteem had its own hazards, as they were expected to make cash handouts to all comers at weddings and other family celebrations. The financial pressures even on the elites were considerable, and the financing of the urban system, which on the whole was not economically productive, was ultimately draining. Little wonder that in some instances, especially at the lower end of the spectrum, people sought to avoid the duties of office. The situation varied enormously from one city to another, especially in the case of older cities in the east that had their own constitutions and other wealth-generating activities, such as their location or a hinterland. By the end of the third century CE, there were signs of increasing state compulsion with regard to the assumption of office, a clear indicator of how the old order had been eroded (Brown, 1971).

Cities as cultural systems. As mediums of culture, cities functioned in many different ways and at several different levels. The spread of Greek as the lingua franca is widely attested from inscriptions, coins, and literary sources. Initially, this was partly the by-product of the cities as administrative and commercial centers, a system in place since Alexander and his immediate successors settled veterans and other Greeks in the new cities. A policy of active hellenization was also part of the underlying philosophy of the new cities within the "one world" vision that inspired the encounter between Greece and the East. Thus, the gymnasium, or Greek school, became one of the essential features of the city, where the *epheboi*, or "elite youth," were given a special education according to Greek ideals comprising both literary and physical aspects. The links between *epheboi* training and citizenship were very strong, but not absolute: these youths could be disqualified from citizen status on other grounds, such as not being freeborn (Tcherikover, 1964; Doran, 1990). The links between the educational system and citizenship remained very close, however.

Religion, as well as education, was intimately bound up with the life of the city and life in the city, from the perspective of a worldview in which there was no separation between the sacred and the secular (Zaidman and Schmitt-Pantel, 1992) The very act of foundation was itself associated with the religious rite of consulting an oracle or the auspices (auguries). Failure to do so might provoke the ire of the gods. The whole subsequent life of the citizens was surrounded by various rituals, private and public, enshrined in laws often inscribed in stone in public places. While certain officials were designated to carry out religious functions on behalf of the citizenry, essentially this was the responsibility of the whole *demos*. The city's charter was a gift from the patron deity, and its due observance meant divine protection for all who dwelt within its walls. The temple in honor of the patron deity; other temples in the fora of the larger cities; shrines, including those in private houses, and sacred groves; and mosaics and frescoes with religious themes all indicate the pervasive role religion played in the life of the average inhabitant of the Greco-Roman city.

It would be a mistake to see the official religious practice of the city as a purely formal affair, devoid of any devotional appeal for the individual. Nevertheless, the Hellenistic period witnessed an amazing increase in the mystery religions, offering the experience of personal intimacy with the divine and mutual support of the members of the various cult groups (*collegia*), in addition to the public religious ceremonies of the city (Cumont, 1956). The various mysteries—Isis, Magna Mater, Dionysus, and Mithras being the most popular and most widely diffused—became a feature of the cosmopolitanism of the age. Originating as local cults in Egypt, Phrygia, and Syria, they traveled widely, even to Rome itself, where they were treated with suspicion, if not downright hostility, at first. Gradually, however, their popularity grew, and the Roman army played a significant role in disseminating them in the West, especially the cult of Mithras. This phenomenon is highly significant to understanding the social situation within the cities and the need for social organizations other than those of the city itself and the extended family or tribe. In addition to the mystery cults, burial associations ensured a decent interment for their members, often consisting of the poor and slaves. [*See* Catacombs.] The insight into urban social relations that can be gleaned from these developments of religion in the city suggest a considerable amount of isolation, even alienation, especially as far as the lower orders were concerned. They also indicate a growing preoccupation with individual identity and uncertainty about life's meaning in an "age of anxiety" (Dodds, 1965). This was fertile soil in which Early Christian groups could sprout. The evidence from the Pauline letters, *Acts of the Apostles,* and the correspondence between Pliny and the emperor Trajan make clear that within less than a century of its inception, the religious movement which had originated in rural Galilee had adapted well to the urban life of the empire (Meeks, 1983; MacMullan, 1984; Stambaugh and Balch, 1986). In this they were merely following patterns already established by Jews in the Diaspora synagogues (Kasher, 1990; Feldman, 1993).

BIBLIOGRAPHY

Adan-Bayewitz, David. *Common Pottery in Roman Galilee: A Study of Local Trade.* Ramat Gan, 1993.

Avi-Yonah, Michael. *The Holy Land from the Persian to the Arab Conquests, 536 B.C.–A.D. 640: A Historical Geography.* Grand Rapids, Mich., 1966.

Bagnall, Roger. *Egypt in Late Antiquity.* Princeton, 1993.

Brown, Peter. *The World of Late Antiquity.* New York, 1971.

Childe, V. Gordon. "The Urban Revolution." *Town and Planning Review* 21 (1950): 3–17.

Cumont, Franz. *The Oriental Religions of Roman Paganism.* New York, 1956.

Dodds, E. R. *Pagan and Christian in an Age of Anxiety.* Cambridge, 1965.

Doran, Robert. "Jason's Gymnasion." In *Of Scribes and Scrolls: Studies on the Hebrew Bible, Intertestamental Judaism, and Christian Origins,* edited by Harold W. Attridge et al., pp. 99–109. New York, 1990.

Feldman, Louis H. *Jew and Gentile in the Ancient World.* Princeton, 1993.

Finley, Moses I. "The Ancient City: From Fustel de Coulanges to Max Weber and Beyond." *Comparative Studies in Society and History* 19 (1977): 305–327.

Finley, Moses I. *Politics in the Ancient World.* Cambridge, 1983.

Finley, Moses I. *The Ancient Economy.* 2d ed. Berkeley, 1985.

Frick, Frank S. *The City in Ancient Israel.* Missoula, 1977.

Harper, George McLean. "Village Administration in the Roman Province of Syria." *Yale Classical Studies* 1 (1928): 105–168.

Hopkins, Keith. "Economic Growth and Towns in Classical Antiquity." In *Towns in Societies: Essays in Economic History and Historical Sociology,* edited by Philip Abrams and E. K. Wrigley, pp. 35–77. Cambridge, 1978.

Hopkins, Keith. "Taxes and Trade in the Roman Empire, 200 BC–400 AD." *Journal of Roman Studies* 70 (1980): 101–125.

Jones, A. H. M. "The Urbanization of Palestine." *Journal of Roman Studies* 21 (1931): 78–85.

Jones, A. H. M. *The Cities of the Eastern Roman Provinces.* 2d ed. Oxford, 1971.

Kasher, Aryeh. *Jews and Hellenistic Cities in Eretz Israel.* Tübingen, 1990.

Lapidus, Ira M. "Cities and Societies: A Comparative Study of the Emergence of Urban Civilization in Mesopotamia and Greece." *Journal of Urban History* 12 (1986): 257–292.

MacMullen, Ramsay. *Roman Social Relations, 50 B.C. to A.D. 284.* New Haven, 1974.

MacMullen, Ramsay. *Christianizing the Roman Empire, A.D. 100–400.* New Haven, 1984.

Meeks, Wayne A. *The First Urban Christians: The Social World of the Apostle Paul.* New Haven, 1983.

Owens, E. J. *The City in the Greek and Roman World.* London, 1991.

Perring, Dominic. "Spatial Organisation and Social Change in Roman Towns." In *City and Country in the Ancient World,* edited by John Rich and Andrew Wallace-Hadrill, pp. 273–295. London, 1991.

Redfield, Robert, and Milton Singer. "The Cultural Role of Cities." *Economic Development and Social Change* 3 (1954): 57–73.

Rich, John, and Andrew Wallace-Hadrill, eds. *City and Country in the Ancient World.* London, 1991.

Rihll, T. E., and A. G. Wilson. "Modelling Settlement Structures in Ancient Greece: New Approaches to the Polis." In *City and Country in the Ancient World,* edited by John Rich and Andrew Wallace-Hadrill, pp. 59–96. London, 1991.

Rohrbaugh, Richard L. "The City in the Second Testament." *Biblical Theology Bulletin* 21 (1991): 67–75.

Safrai, Zeev. *The Economy of Roman Palestine.* London, 1993.

Sherwin-White, A. N. *Roman Society and Roman Law in the New Testament.* Oxford, 1963.

Sjoberg, Gideon. *The Preindustrial City.* Glencoe, Ill., 1960.

Stambaugh, John E., and David Balch. *The Social World of the First Christians.* London, 1986.

Stambaugh, John E. *The Ancient Roman City.* Baltimore, 1988.

Tcherikover, Victor. "Was Jerusalem a Polis?" *Israel Exploration Journal* 14 (1964): 61–78.

Tsuk, Tsvika. "The Aqueducts of Sepphoris." M. A. thesis, Tel Aviv University, 1985.

Wallace-Hadrill, Andrew. "Elites and Trade in the Roman Town." In *City and Country in the Ancient World,* edited by John Rich and Andrew Wallace-Hadrill, pp. 241–272. London, 1991.

Weber, Max. "Die Stadt." *Archiv für Sozialwissenschaft und Sozialpolitik* 47 (1921): 621–772. Translated by Don Martindale and Gertrud Neuwirth in *The City.* Glencoe, Ill., 1958.

Whittaker, C. R. "The Consumer City Revisited: The *vicus* and the City." *Journal of Roman Archaeology* 3 (1990): 110–118.

Zaidman, Louise B., and Pauline Schmitt-Pantel. *Religion in the Ancient Greek City.* Translated by Paul Cartledge. Cambridge, 1992.

Zanker, Paul. *The Power of Images in the Age of Augustus.* Ann Arbor, Mich., 1988.

SEÁN FREYNE

Cities of the Islamic Period

Islamic urbanism maintained and built upon the traditions of the ancient cities and civilizations of the Near East, creating a vibrant urban culture, but one with numerous regional variations in architecture and morphology. Most of what is known about cities in the Islamic period comes from written historical sources and analyses by art and architectural historians of existing monuments published in journals and edited collections. Archaeological excavations of Islamic sites are the exception rather than the rule: many contemporary cities in North Africa and Southwest Asia are built over core Islamic settlements and even earlier ancient sites, inhibiting major excavations.

Islam began in the early seventh century CE and was confined principally to the region of Mecca and Medina until Muhammad's death in 632. Yet, within the next several years most of the Arabian Peninsula was conquered, followed quickly by the Arab conquests to the north in which the weakened Sasanian Empire and the eastern parts of the Byzantine Empire were soon absorbed into the caliphate, the greater Islamic state. [*See* Sasanians; Arabian Peninsula, *article on* The Arabian Peninsula in Islamic Times.] Damascus fell in 636 and northern Syria by 641; Iraqi cities were taken within the first years of the conquests; Hamadan/Ecbatana, Isfahan, and the main cities of western Iran fell by 644; Egypt was conquered by 642 and the rest of North Africa by 711; Spain was absorbed between 711 and 759; and Bukhara and Samarkand were taken in 712 and 713, respectively. [*See* Damascus; Ecbatana; Isfahan.] Within a century after Muhammad's death, the Islamic state reached from Spain and Morocco to Transoxania.

The Muslim conquerors usually established themselves on the outskirts and suburbs of established cities, becoming the ruling and military elites. The local population was subject to taxation but otherwise left to continue its commerce, agriculture, and local customs, including religion. Conversions to Islam for most of the conquered peoples did not, in fact, take place for several centuries (and fully developed Muslim urban societies emerged only by the eleventh and twelfth centuries). Some new garrison towns were initially founded, and these *amsar* (sg., *misr*) housed many of the bedouin warriors from the Arabian Peninsula. Basra and Kufah in Iraq and Fustat in Egypt were the three most important *amsar,* being used as military bases for furthering the Arab conquests. Fustat, founded in 642 just north of the Byzantine fortress of Babylon on the Nile River, is the only early *amsar* that has been excavated. [*See* Fustat.]

Damascus became the capital of the Umayyads (661–750), the first major Islamic empire. The transformation of the Greco-Roman street grid of this city into a more irregular pattern under Islam (Jean Sauvaget, "Esquisse d'une histoire de la ville de Damas," *Revue des Études Islamiques* 8 [1934]: 421–480) became the classic case study that helped promote the erroneous view that all Islamic cities lacked form and order. Baghdad was the newly built capital of the second great Islamic empire, the 'Abbasids (750–1258), a round city possibly based on a Sasanian, Parthian, and/or Median city plan. Located on the southern, or right bank, of the Tigris River, in the center of contemporary Baghdad, there is no trace of the round city today. Continuing an ancient tradition, 'Abbasid caliphs often built new palaces, or even capitals, which sometimes lasted only the lifetime of the ruler. Samarra, located 100 km (62 mi.) north of Baghdad, was such a ninth-century capital. Strung along the Tigris River for many kilometers, the now long-abandoned capital has been the focus of considerable archaeological work, including the German excavations by Ernst Herzfeld in the early twentieth century and the more recent survey operations sponsored by the British School of Archaeology in Iraq. [*See* Baghdad; Samarra, *article on* Islamic Period.]

Islamic cities in Spain often developed on the foundations of Roman towns that had deteriorated for several centuries under the Visigoths. Cordoba, Toledo, Seville, Valencia, and Zaragoza were revived as cities. They contributed to a brilliant Hispano-Arab civilization that, however, began to decline by the eleventh and twelfth centuries and was finally ended by the Christian *reconquista* and the fall of the last Islamic dynasty of Granada in 1492. There were several smaller and newly planned royal cities, including Medina al-Zahira and Medina al-Zahra, the latter on the outskirts of Cordoba and the focus of extensive archaeological excavations by the Spanish.

In Iran many of the Islamic cities were built on Sasanian foundations, which in some instanced represented even earlier settlements. Hamadan, for example, was built on the Median and Achaemenid capital of Ecbatana. Siraf, one of the few excavated Iranian Islamic sites, was built partly over the Sasanian port city of Gur. The Congregation, or Friday, Mosque in many of the first Islamic cities in Iran was often founded on existing Zoroastrian fire temples, providing an additional sacredness to the location and making a symbolic statement: an Islamic building was replacing the principal Zoroastrian place of worship (similar to the Dome of the Rock on the Temple Mount in Jerusalem).

The importance of the religion of Islam in the lives of the inhabitants of the Near East led to the idea by Western Orientalists that there was a unique Islamic city. This model, begun in particular by French scholars working in North Africa, is largely a myth. The cities of the Islamic period resembled their antecedents in morphology and characteristics, except that many Islamic towns became considerably larger and were less likely to be located on a tell. The structure of the towns was often determined by settlements expanding into adjacent agriculture fields; hence, as in many Iranian cities, irrigation systems could also influence morphology. There were palaces, city walls, fortresses, principal places of worship and shrines, residential quarters, and major commercial areas. Major streets were rather straight (only sometimes influenced by the Greco-Roman grid system, as in Herat and Damascus), while residential areas often consisted of numerous dead-end alleyways. Courtyard houses were common in both the ancient and Islamic periods, and where there are tall, multiple-stories buildings, as in Yemen, these types also existed in pre-Islamic times. [See Yemen.] The city continued to be a center for a local agriculture-based hinterland, with long-distance trade being characteristic of certain settlements as well.

By at least the eleventh century, Islamic cities did begin to have some specific characteristics and institutions: religious schools *(madrasah)* for training clergy; mosques, shrines, and mausolea, which proliferated; great bazaar complexes; religiously endowed property *(waqf)*; and merchant guilds *(senf)*. There also developed a rather distinctive separation of public and private space, encouraged by some local interpretations of Islam. How this division differs from the use of space by ancient cities of the Near East is still poorly understood.

Significantly, however, there are considerable similarities in form and function between ancient and Islamic cities within a region, while there are even greater differences in morphology among Islamic cities (and ancient cities) from one region to another. Islamic urbanism, in the guise of a new religion, continued the traditions and patterns of the cities of the ancient Near East.

[*See also* Mosque.]

BIBLIOGRAPHY

Abu-Lughod, Janet L. "The Islamic City: Historic Myth, Islamic Essence, and Contemporary Relevance." *International Journal of Middle East Studies* 19 (1987): 155–176. The historical evolution and problems of the concept of the Islamic City.

Bonine, Michael E. "The Morphogenesis of Iranian Cities." *Annals of the Association of American Geographers* 69 (1979): 208–224. An analysis of the formation and evolution of Iranian settlements; shows how morphology often reflects traditional irrigation and agricultural systems.

Bonine, Michael E., et al. *The Middle Eastern City and Islamic Urbanism: An Annotated Bibliography of Western Literature.* Bonn, 1994. More than seventy-five hundred entries; focuses particularly on the literature on Islamic urbanism in English, French, and German.

Creswell, K.A.C. *A Bibliography of the Architecture, Arts, and Crafts of Islam to 1st January 1960.* Cairo, 1961. Classic and indispensable reference work for studies of architecture and individual monuments, although neither urban nor social studies are included. Supplements appeared in 1973 and 1984.

Creswell, K.A.C. *A Short Account of Early Muslim Architecture.* Revised and supplemented by James W. Allan. Aldershot, 1989. Creswell's 1958 edition of this work was an abbreviated version of his monumental *Early Muslim Architecture*, 2 vols. (Oxford, 1932–1940). His meticulous plans, drawings, and photographs are still largely unrivaled, although many of his dogmatic interpretations have been superseded by subsequent studies and broader viewpoints.

Grabar, Oleg. *The Formation of Islamic Art.* New Haven, 1973. The art and architecture of the Islamic city, including the symbolic significance of the mosque, palace, and other elements.

Hakim, Besim Selim. *Arabic-Islamic Cities: Building and Planning Principles.* London, 1986. Using principally Tunis as an example, this work shows the influence of Maliki Islamic law in many architectural and urban structures, including street widths, use of jointly owned walls, and building heights.

Hourani, Albert, and S. M. Stern, eds. *The Islamic City.* Oxford, 1970. One of the classic collections of papers on the Islamic city, resulting from a symposium at Oxford University in 1965.

Lapidus, Ira M. "The Evolution of Muslim Urban Society." *Comparative Studies in Society and History* 15 (1973): 21–50. Analyzes the components and evolution of Muslim urban society, particularly the role of schools of Islamic law and religious institutions; demonstrates that a true Muslim urban society did not emerge until about the eleventh and twelfth centuries CE.

Von Grunebaum, G. E. "The Structure of the Muslim Town." In Von Grunebaum's *Islam: Essays in the Nature and Growth of a Cultural Tradition*, pp. 141–158. London, 1955. The characteristics of the Islamic city; helped perpetuate and popularize a simplified and mostly erroneous stereotypical model of the Islamic city.

Wirth, Eugen. "Die orientalische Stadt: Ein Überblick aufgrund jüngerer Forschungen zur materiellen Kultur." *Saeculum* 26 (1975): 45–94. The continuities of characteristics of the Islamic city derived from the ancient city of the Near East; emphasizes that many features attributed to the Islamic city are also found in many earlier cities.

MICHAEL E. BONINE

CLERMONT-GANNEAU, CHARLES (1846–1923), French epigrapher, archaeologist, Orientalist, and diplomat and pioneer in the study of ancient Palestinian inscriptions.

Born in Paris, Clermont-Ganneau excelled as a student of Semitic languages and was sent to Jerusalem in 1867 as dragoman-chancellor for the French consulate. In 1869, he was the first to recognize the significance of the Mesha stela discovered at Dibon (Dhiban) in Moab. [*See* Moabite Stone; Dibon.] He subsequently facilitated its purchase and transfer to the Louvre Museum in Paris. Among his later epigraphic discoveries in Jerusalem were the eighth-century BCE Hebrew inscription in the Siloam Tunnel and the Greek inscription from the Herodian period prohibiting the entry of Gentiles into the Temple Court. [*See* Siloam Tunnel Inscription.]

After a transfer to another diplomatic post in Constantinople in 1871, Clermont-Ganneau returned to Palestine in 1873–1874 on special assignment for the British-sponsored Palestine Exploration Fund. His wide-ranging researches included studies of the history of the Dome of the Rock and of ancient Jewish burial customs in Jerusalem and architectural surveys of Gaza, Nablus (Shechem), and Jericho. In his discovery of bilingual Greek-Hebrew boundary inscriptions in the vicinity of Tell Jezer, he was the first scholar to identify the site conclusively with ancient Gezer. [*See* Shechem; Jericho; Gezer.]

Clermont-Ganneau alternated for the next few years between diplomatic and scholarly careers: in 1874, he was appointed to the faculty of the École des Hautes Études in Paris; in 1881, he served as French vice-consul in Jaffa; in 1882, he was chief translator for the foreign ministry in Paris; and in 1883 he was the French consul in London. Following his appointment in 1891 to a professorship in archaeology and epigraphy at the Collège de France, Clermont-Ganneau devoted himself entirely to antiquarian studies. He led an expedition to Crete and Cyrenaica in 1895 and undertook excavations at Elephantine Island in Egypt in 1901. [*See* Crete; Elephantine.]

Clermont-Ganneau was an aggressive and outspoken critic of artifacts he considered forgeries. In 1873, he exposed as modern fakes the so-called Moabite pottery purchased by the Berlin Museum and succeeded in turning scholarly opinion against the *Deuteronomy* manuscript fragments brought to London by a Jerusalem antiquities dealer, Moses Shapira, in 1882.

BIBLIOGRAPHY

Allegro, John M. *The Shapira Affair*. Garden City, N.Y., 1965.
Clermont-Ganneau, Charles. *Archaeological Researches in Palestine during the Years 1873–1874*. 2 vols. London, 1896–1899.
Silberman, Neil Asher. *Digging for God and Country: Exploration, Archaeology, and the Secret Struggle for the Holy Land, 1799–1917*. New York, 1982.

NEIL ASHER SILBERMAN

CLIMATOLOGY.

Paleoenvironmental reconstructions for the ancient Near East rely in part on investigating past weather patterns. These investigations are based on the presumption that a better understanding of ancient climate, should help us know more about the conditions under which a number of civilizations flourished and declined. The region is one in which agriculture and animal husbandry were often marginal even under the best climatic conditions.

Temperature and Precipitation Records. In the Near East, where written records have existed for millennia and significant temperature and precipitation records might be expected to have been kept, there exist, in fact, very few sets of meteorological station records that cover more than one hundred years. The most extended instances of record-keeping available were begun in the nineteenth century: Samsun, Turkey (1819); Haifa, Israel (1842); Beirut, Lebanon (1842); Jerusalem (1846); Athens, Greece (1858); Kom el-Nadura, Egypt (1868); Rome, Italy (1871); Tehran, Iran (1884); Nicosia, Cyprus (1887); Baghdad, Iraq (1888); and Hebron, then Jordan (1896). Other stations have been in existence for only a few decades, so the prospect of developing a long set of gridded records—in which the data from each station are compared with those north, south, east, and west and then analyzed for internal accuracy—is not promising; in addition, the range in time is severely limited for most of the area. The Cyprus Meteorologist's remark about the quality of his own data might well serve as a commentary on that of the rest of the Near East: "Some gauges have been moved so often that they can fairly be described as perambulating. Details are generally, and perhaps mercifully, lacking."

A few nongovernmental records exist such as the diaries of British Residents in Smyrna, Turkey, but at best these cover only the nineteenth century. Some Ottoman archival records were sent to Berlin for analysis at about the time of World War I, but the building in which they were housed burned down. Thus, instrumental data—specifically, temperature and precipitation records—have severe temporal limitations. The data exist for little more than a century and a half at best. Even more limited in time and number of stations reporting are such records as soil moisture, soil temperature, wind speed and direction frequencies, and sunshine, or solar radiation.

Pollen Records. Proxy records, substitutes for thermometric and rain gauge records, such as pollen analyses from stratified cores taken from geological or lake sediments are another step toward developing a climatological record. The most notable work in the Near East has been by Willem van Zeist and his coworkers (1975) in Iran and Turkey; by Aharon Horowitz (1979) in Israel; and by Donald George Sullivan (1994) in Turkey. The spatial coverage is sparse (only two cores for all of Israel, for example); yet, Van Zeist concludes that, although there have been relatively minor fluctuations, there has been no significant change in the climate over the past 7,500 years. Hans J. Nissen (1988) echoes these conclusions for Mesopotamia, Karl W. Butzer for Iran, and Richard Hodges and David Whitehouse for the Late Roman and early medieval world. The potential for pollen records can be measured in millennia, but where hundreds of cores would be desirable in order to get a complete picture of the Near East, only a dozen or two long cores have been taken and properly published. Another problem with pollen cores is dating. Unless multiple radiocarbon determinations are made, which is not always possible with the amount of material available, the time control for each core is severely limited. Recent work by Harvey Weiss and others (1993) at Tell Leilan in Syria is a useful attempt to extract climatic information from a single site, although the method is controversial.

Dendroclimatology. Another proxy technique only now in its initial stages of being exploited in the Near East is dendroclimatology. The work of the Aegean Dendrochronology Project (Peter I. Kuniholm et al.) has produced some six thousand years' worth of tree-ring chronologies, and the tree-ring data are being linked to the observed meteorological record for the last century and a half. The project hopes to extrapolate backward in time to the Early Bronze Age and perhaps even earlier. The potential is for several millennia of information, but limited to the areas where long tree-ring records can be built. This includes all of the Anatolian Plateau, the Taurus Mountains, the Anti-Taurus, and the Lebanon. The method is accurate to the year and sometimes to a specific season.

Historical Climatology. The development of a historical climatology, in which the written record for several millennia is merged with other climatological observations, is the most tantalizing aspect of any consideration of Near Eastern climate. To date, no reliable corpus exists of the entire hieroglyphic, cuneiform, biblical, Greek, Roman, Byzantine, Ottoman, and other records. Once that has been built, the cause-and-effect relationship between a climatic event and a historical event will remain to be demonstrated. The record of Nile floods and their effect on the Egyptian economy is one such example (Lyons, 1905; Bell, 1971, 1975); the time spanned is four to five millennia but with a very uneven distribution of information.

Tentative steps, linking several of the methods noted above, are reported by Kuniholm (1990). For example, a four-decade-long drought in the late 1500s and early 1600s observed in the tree-ring record coincides with a long list of shortages, crop failures, and famines in the same years recorded in the Ottoman Archives in Istanbul. The same kind of linkage among proxies for an instrumental record should some day be possible for the ancient Near East as well. Significant perturbations, still under investigation and not without controversy, include a possible climatic event around 1159 BCE (probably the eruption of Hekla III) associated with the end of the Late Bronze Age; another linked to the eruption of Thera in 1627/28 BCE that pins down the transition from Late Minoan IA to IB; and a possible event in the twenty-third century BCE that interferes with life in the Early Bronze Age in northern Syria.

[*See also* New Archaeology; Paleoenvironmental Reconstruction.]

BIBLIOGRAPHY

Bell, Barbara. "The Dark Ages in Ancient History: I. The First Dark Age in Egypt." *American Journal of Archaeology* 75 (1971): 1–26.

Bell, Barbara. "Climate and the History of Egypt: The Middle Kingdom." *American Journal of Archaeology* 79 (1975): 223–269.

Bryson, R. A., et al. "Drought and the Decline of Mycenae." *Antiquity* 48 (1974): 46–50.

Butzer, Karl W. "Quaternary Stratigraphy and Climate in the Near East." *Bonner Geographische Abhandlungen* 24 (1958): 103–128.

Carpenter, Rhys. *Discontinuity in Greek Civilization.* New York, 1966.

Hodges, Richard, and David Whitehouse. *Mohammed, Charlemagne, and the Origins of Europe: Archaeology and the Pirenne Thesis.* Ithaca, N.Y., 1983.

Horowitz, Aharon. *The Quaternary of Israel.* New York, 1979. See pages 211–230.

Kuniholm, Peter I. "Archaeological Evidence and Non-Evidence for Climatic Change." *Philosophical Transactions of the Royal Society of London, series, A*, 330 (1990): 645–655.

Kuniholm, Peter I. "Overview and Assessment of the Evidence for the Date of the Eruption of Thera." In *Thera and the Aegean World III: Proceedings of the Third International Conference, Santorini, Greece, 3–9 September 1989*, vol. 3, *Chronology*, edited by D. A. Hardy et al., pp. 13–18. Athens, 1990.

Le Roy Ladurie, Emmanuel. *Times of Feast, Times of Famine: A History of Climate since the Year 1000.* Rev. ed. New York, 1988.

Lyons, Henry G. "On the Nile Flood and Its Variation." *Geographical Journal* 26 (1905): 249–272, 395–421.

Neumann, J., and Simo Parpola. "Climatic Change and the Eleventh-Tenth-Century Eclipse of Assyria and Babylonia." *Journal of Near Eastern Studies* 46 (1987): 161–182.

Nissen, Hans J. *The Early History of the Ancient Near East, 9000–2000 B.C.* Chicago, 1988.

Sullivan, Donald George. "Palynological Evidence of Human-Induced Holocene Vegetation in Western Turkey." *Geoarchaeology* (1995).

Weiss, Harvey, et al. "The Genesis and Collapse of Third Millennium North Mesopotamian Civilization." *Science* 261 (1993): 995–1004.

Zeist, Willem van. "Late Quaternary Vegetation History of Western Iran." *Review of Palaeobotany and Palynology* 2 (1967): 301–311.

Zeist, Willem van, and H. E. Wright. "Preliminary Pollen Studies at Lake Zeribar, Zagros Mountains, Southwestern Iran." *Science* 140 (1963): 65–67.

Zeist, Willem van, et al. "Studies on Modern and Holocene Pollen Precipitation in Southeastern Turkey." *Palaeohistoria* 10 (1968): 19–39.

Zeist, Willem van, et al. "Late Quaternary Vegetation and Climate of Southwestern Turkey." *Palaeohistoria* 17 (1975): 53–143.

PETER IAN KUNIHOLM

CLOTHING. Archaeological remains of garments are scarce, with usually only fragments of textiles recovered. What is known about clothing often can be deduced from accessories, which are generally of metal; from the tools used to manufacture cloth—spindle whorls, loom weights, pattern sticks, spools, and needles; and from representations of garments on stone and terra-cotta statuary cut in stone reliefs, engraved on ivory or metal, painted on ceramic, or executed in mosaic. There are text references, but relating them to the archaeological evidence is not reliable. [*See* Textiles.]

In the ancient Near East, the basic garment for men was a simple wraparound skirt—a strip of cloth perhaps 60–75 cm wide wrapped around the waist, descending to just above the knee. In Egypt it was worn to just below the knee and was of plain white linen (*ANEP* 3, 16); in Syria-Palestine it was a brightly patterned linen or wool fabric and often had colored fringes (*ANEP* 3, 6, 35, 36). Early Sumerian carvings show this skirt made of fleece, with hanging locks of wool (*ANEP* 23, 24, 27, 163).

Reliefs and wall paintings show this cloth skirt held in place by a sash of woven cloth, usually in a colored pattern and ending in knotted fringes and tassels (*ANEP* 6, 40, 56). The pin found in burials at the hip of skeletons indicates that it could also be pinned. [*See* Grave Goods.] This was the garment commonly worn by workers (*ANEP* 84, 85, 106) and soldiers (*ANEP* 1, 177) in warm weather; additional upper-body clothing would have been necessary in the cold rainy season (*ANEP* 35).

In Syria the basic garment for women was also wrapped and draped over one shoulder, leaving the arms bare, and reached to mid-calf or slightly below. It was held in place by a pin at the shoulder and was woven in a great variety of bright patterns (*ANEP* 3). In Egypt women wore plain white linen wrapped around the torso and sometimes held in place by a strap over the shoulder. A more elaborate version was gracefully pleated (*ANEP* 407, 408).

Men too wore an over-one-shoulder garment (*ANEP* 3) or sometimes a long garment formed of two separate lengths of cloth woven in elaborate design that were wrapped around the lower body to reach the ankles. The upper ends covered the chest and back and were brought forward over the shoulders to form a cape (*ANEP* 43, 52, 54; *ANEP* II, 3). They may also have worn a separate cape (*ANEP* 5, 62).

In tomb paintings and stone reliefs, in addition to the sash, common clothing fasteners are frequently illustrated: the simple pin, toggle pin (Bronze Age), and fibula (Iron Age and later). The first was of metal or, more commonly, of bone (it can be distinguished from a needle because the needle, whether of metal or bone, has a hole in its upper, thicker end). The bone pins found in many excavations are 5–10 cm (2–4 in.) long, smoothly polished so as not to snag or tear the cloth, and usually have a small head to keep them from slipping through fabric. Many also have decorative bands incised around their circumference. Fashioned out of the bones of domestic animals, they were probably the cheapest clothing fasteners to produce, except perhaps for pins of wood or thorn, which have not knowingly been found in excavations. Small, graceful bone pins were used in all periods to fasten light clothing of linen or wool.

The toggle pin was metal, 15–25 cm long. [*See* Jewelry; Metals.] It had a hole through it halfway down the shaft, through which a fastening cord passed, and decorative bands were worked around it (*ANEP* II, 5). Its size, diameter, and weight indicate that it fastened a coarsely woven heavy woolen cloak rather than a light summer garment, as it would damage a fine fabric.

The fibula (Lat., "safety pin") is a light metal rod fine enough to be bent into a circle and a half in the middle, to form a spring. To use it, both ends are squeezed together and the sharp end is placed into a bend at the other end; when the pressure is released, it fits there firmly. The bent end is sometimes in the form of a tiny metal hand, whose fingers clasp the pointed end; this whimsical form endured for centuries. Both plain and "hand" fibulae are frequently found in excavations.

The number of needles excavated attests to how extensive sewing was in the ancient world. The needles are of metal or bone. [*See* Bone, Ivory, and Shell.] Sewing was essential for tent making, for joining tent panels, and for reinforcing the bands that kept the tent poles from piercing the roof panel. [*See* Tents.] Sewing was also essential in agriculture: folded lengths of heavy cloth were stitched up their sides to make the numerous bags needed for storing the year's harvest of wheat, barley, and lentils; after the bags were filled, they were sewn closed across the top.

Sewing was less essential in the manufacture of clothing because the most common garments had no seams (see above). However, garments did need mending or the decorative colored stitching apparent in carvings and paintings. Those garments that would have needed sewing had an opening at the neck (*ANEP* 3), down the front, or at the arm openings. Garments with sleeves (tubular sleeves, in contrast to a fold of cloth hanging off the shoulder) also would have required sewing. Egyptian tomb paintings show men's robes from Syria with sleeves to the wrist; the seams are covered with decorative embroidery in a contrasting color (*ANEP* 2, 4, 5, 45, 46, 47).

Common headgear for both men and women was a headband tied to hold the hair in place (*ANEP* 3, 4, 5, 6, 27, 43, 54). What may be a hat from the Neolithic period was found in a cave in Naḥal Ḥemar in Israel. To judge from stone reliefs, hats were also commonly worn by men in particular social classes and reflect status or public office (*ANEP* 11, 26, 36, 37, 61; *ANEP* II, 47). Tall, elaborate, and symbolic hats identify deities in monumental stone reliefs and small sculptures, distinguishing them from humans; special hats or crowns commonly appear on reliefs of kings and dignitaries. Ivories from Late Bronze Age Megiddo show women in stiff caps with fabric hanging down behind, like a short veil, but one that does not cover either the face or the ears. (*ANEP* frontispiece, 125) In the Assyrian relief of the conquest of Lachish (*ANEP* 373), women wear hooded cloaks. [*See* Megiddo.]

Sumerian reliefs show men wearing fleece skirts and jackets. Leather was used for shoes and clothing—probably more commonly for military clothing—but it is difficult to identify it in art. Two types of shoes are, however, identifiable in reliefs and paintings: the sandal and the closed shoe. In Egypt, at Beni Hasan, a tomb painting shows women wearing closed shoes with high tops that reach above the ankle; the men are wearing sandals (*ANEP* 3, 39, 40). Both kinds of footwear appear to be of leather, although less costly sandals of woven plant fibers were probably common. Hittite reliefs show men wearing closed shoes that are turned up at the toes, to facilitate walking on rocky terrain (*ANEP* 36). The earliest reference to the different fit of right and left shoes also comes from Hittite culture, from about 1500 BCE.

The Mari tablets and other ancient contracts stipulate that workers are to receive one new garment a year as part of their wages. This rule of thumb indicates that in good times each person would possess more than one garment—perhaps one best dress and several worn ones. The latter would gradually be cut down for children's clothes and the scraps reused for household and pastoral/agricultural purposes. Scraps of cloth could be used to patch other garments, to strain milk, wrap cheese, drain yoghurt, tie small packages of spices, hold seeds, cover the udders of goats when weaning the young, and to wash with; they were also useful as diapers, as parts for donkey and camel harnesses, and as saddle blankets.

BIBLIOGRAPHY

Barber, E. J. W. *Prehistoric Textiles: The Development of Cloth in the Neolithic and Bronze Ages with Special Reference to the Aegean.* Princeton, 1991.

Barber, E. J. W. *Women's Work, the First 20,000 Years: Women, Cloth, and Society in Early Times.* New York, 1994. This and the work above are careful and thorough surveys of textile evidence; because so few garments exist, the study of clothing before the Coptic and Byzantine periods relies on scraps or pictures of textiles.

Houston, Mary G. *Ancient Egyptian, Mesopotamian, and Persian Costume.* 2d ed. London, 1954. Well-illustrated work that considers garments mainly from a technical perspective, analyzing their construction.

Pritchard, James B. *The Ancient Near East in Pictures Relating to the Old Testament (ANEP).* Princeton, 1954.

Pritchard, James B. *The Ancient Near East,* vol. 2, *A New Anthology of Texts and Pictures (ANEP II).* Princeton, 1975.

Schick, Tamar. "Perishable Remains from the Nahal Hemar Cave." *Journal of the Israel Prehistoric Society* 19 (1986): 84–86, 95*–97*.

DOROTHY IRVIN

CODEX. Roman administrators throughout the empire used wooden tablets (Lat., *codices*; sg., *codex*) as registers. Eventually, *codex* became a technical term for an accounting or other financial book or authoritative collection of official or legal writings (cf. *code*). This is how the Romans in the imperial period, the romanized people of the East, and the Byzantines, who succeeded the Romans in the East, understood the word *codex*, regardless of the material out of which it was made.

In modern usage the term refers to ancient or medieval transpositions of an archaic wooden book onto sheets of soft material (papyrus or parchment). These sheets were usually folded down the middle, to form leaves that were then superposed or gathered in various ways. Modern paper books are still codices in form. Historically, this format replaced the papyrus roll (Lat., *volumen*) which, in the Classical East, had been the standard medium for literary, religious, and official writings. The historical problem with the codex is to determine how it came so successfully to rival the scroll in use. This question can be set out in chronological, technical, economic, and cultural terms.

The first archeological examples of ancient codices come from Egypt. Among the literary texts, the codex first appeared in the second century CE. In the third and fourth centuries, it challenged the scroll more and more strongly, eliminating its use by the fifth century. Among administrative texts, the codex appears later (first half of the fourth century); its triumph over the scroll is also late (seventh–eighth century) and not so complete. Although these dates are somewhat precarious, depending in part on paleographic considerations, the Egyptian evidence suggests that the codex appeared during the Roman imperial period, that it was most probably a Roman innovation, and that its diffusion in the East was a correlate of the romanization of the ancient Mediterranean world.

Although it eliminated the scroll (except in Jewish liturgical practice, where it remains in use), the codex borrowed from it a part of its Greek or Latin terminology (e.g., tome, volume, page). Moreover, contrary to the prevalent modern opinion linking codex and parchment, many ancient codices were papyrus books, whose sheets were nearly always cut from rolls. The codex thus appears to be an adaptation of or an improvement on its predecessor: the codex is genuinely technically superior to the scroll (e.g. it gives easier access to a given place in the text and is easier to cross reference).

The material out of which the codex is made, with its attendant physical properties and its economical constraints, determines the shape of the final product and, to some extent, its internal features. Papyrus codices often preserve the height of the roll from which their leaves and sheets were cut (usually about 25–30 cm). The sheets (e.g., in the well-known Nag Hammadi Gnostic manuscripts) were frequently gathered in single quires, sometimes to a considerable thickness. Such an assemblage is not only technically weak, but also unfeasible with parchment sheets, which were always gathered, as paper is today, in superpositions of thin quires, most often of two sheets and four leaves (Lat., *qua-*

terniones, hence, "quire"). Being an inexpensive and ubiquitous material, papyrus had a broader range of use than parchment. Although luxury papyrus codices, with calligraphy and illuminations, do exist, most known codices are of average or low quality and contain mundane texts, such as accounts or private copies of literary works. Expensive parchment was generally preferred for luxury editions or for reference or professional works (e.g., liturgy and law).

Given its Roman background and its coarse wooden archetype, the codex must at first have been perceived by the hellenized Eastern upper classes as a pedestrian format, alien to the liberal Classical culture, whose texts were normally on scrolls. The codex eventually won out, as a consequence of the growing importance in the Roman Empire of religious and intellectual milieux, that had no prejudice for established book standards, namely the Christians and the local academies.

If there is one clear conclusion that the Egyptian evidence permits, it is that the codex was favored by Christians as the exclusive medium for their Holy Scriptures. In addition to the societal generality described in the preceding paragraph, there is no obvious explanation for this fact. Some scholars see the preference as an aspect of the Christian break with the synagogue, where the use of the Torah scroll has survived. It is also possible that the codex appeared to the Christians a better tool than the scroll for teaching purposes.

Thanks to Roman peace and prosperity, many schools flourished in the East, as did other scholarly activities, such as philology and law. This was a time of didactic and practical culture, with bookish tendencies, and that culture was disseminated by a proliferation of handbooks, lexicons, collections of texts, encyclopedias, and codes, for which the practical format of the codex was more suitable than the scroll.

[*See also* Literacy; Nag Hammadi; Papyrus; Parchment; Scribes and Scribal Techniques; Scroll; *and* Writing Materials.]

BIBLIOGRAPHY

Blanchard, Alain, ed. *Les débuts du codex.* Bibliologia, vol. 9. Turnhout, 1989. Original views on the beginnings of the codex.

Robinson, James M., et al. *The Facsimile Edition of the Nag Hammadi Codices: Introduction.* Leiden, 1984. Important for the physical properties and the making of the early papyrus codex.

Turner, Eric G. *The Typology of the Early Codex.* Philadelphia, 1977. Standard work on the subject, based on extensive descriptions of material.

Wouters, Alfons. "From Papyrus Roll to Papyrus Codex: Some Technical Aspects of Ancient Book Fabrication." *Manuscripts of the Middle East* 5 (1990–1991): 9–19. Contains an up-to-date bibliography.

JEAN GASCOU

COELE-SYRIA, the Greek name ("hollow Syria") for the Biqaʿ Valley in southern Syria, between the Lebanon and Anti-Lebanon ranges north of Palestine (i.e., in modern Lebanon)—in the Hellenistic era, considered the southern province of coastal and inland Syria. Under the Ptolemies and Seleucids, all of Phoenicia, and even Palestine, could be designated Coele-Syria. Some modern historical geographies have used the term *Coele-Syria* to distinguish Palestine east of the Jordan River (i.e., Transjordan). This usage derives from Josephus (*Antiq.* 14.ix.5), based on the fact that Herod ruled this territory under the Romans, calling it Coele-Syria in contrast to Judea (Judah), Samaria, and Galilee west of the Jordan River. In the New Testament period, Coele-Syria designated part of the tetrarchy of Philip in northern Transjordan (Josephus, *Antiq.* 12.xiii.3).

[*See also* Phoenicia; Ptolemies; *and* Seleucids.]

WILLIAM G. DEVER

COINS. By interesting coincidence, the initial time range of coinage coincides closely with that of recorded history of the Greek tradition. As strictly defined, its first appearance occurs during the seventh century BCE. By the last quarter of the sixth century it had developed varied and sophisticated forms. Its first currency was in the Lydian kingdom of eastern Anatolia, reflected in the proverbial association of such Lydian rulers as Gyges (c. 679) and Croesus (560–546) with wealth and possession of gold. Simultaneously or soon afterward, coinage began to appear in the Ionian merchant cities of the eastern Aegean, such as Miletus, Ephesus, and Phocaea. Thereafter the spread of coinage continued to parallel that of Greek culture, and its decorative types are noted as fully representative of Greek art. Thus students of Greek and ancient culture and history follow closely the development of coinage and emerging numismatic evidence. In contrast, coin evidence has been of less relevance to prehistorians; and indeed to Assyriologists, though in recent years it has become clear that monetary evidence of a sort was widely present, if formerly unrecognized, in the earlier Mesopotamian archaeological evidence. Though not strictly coinage, this material, broadly categorized as "ingot currency" or "bulk silver," can provide, when studied on numismatic lines, economic and even political data.

The classic definition of coin is that provided by Aristotle in *Politics* 1257a:

> When the community's partners, from whom to import requirements, and to whom to export a surplus, began to extend farther afield, the employment of coinage was devised. For natural commodities are not conveniently transported. Consequently for exchange purposes a medium was agreed to pay and receive, which itself was useful, and had a convenient application in everyday life, such as iron or silver. At first this was measured by size and weight. Eventually an emblem was impressed upon it, so as to free (the users) from the need to measure it. For the emblem (itself) was an indication of the quantity.

Thus, in true coinage the units bear a stamp of authenticity applied by the authority responsible for weight and content. This authority was in most demonstrable cases the state. Suggested ascriptions to merchant guilds, goldsmiths, and other commercial bodies have rarely been substantiated, though these groups may have been responsible for certain punchmarks found on coins. The issue of temple tokens provides a special province of numismatics, going back even to Assyrian times, and later well represented at Palmyra. Thus the *emblems* struck on coins designate the issuing states, often indicating the place and, inferentially, the date of issue. Explicit dates, however, are almost completely confined to the Parthian, Roman, and Islamic series. Because different states maintained specific standards of weight and composition, these—especially the weight—are also characteristic of the issuers. Serious losses could be incurred by a mint issuing precious metal if the weights were inaccurate; therefore, great care was taken to ensure exact standards.

Almost invariably, throughout the history of coinage—normally a prerogative of the state—coins were produced by striking. A blank, which might be cold or hot, depending on size and the practice of the mint in question, was suitably adjusted for dimensions and weight. It was then placed between two dies of bronze or iron, or, by the Islamic period, of steel. The lower die was often fixed in a wooden block, or placed in a fitted recess of an anvil. The upper die, often a punch held freely in the hand or with tongs, was struck once or repeatedly with a sledge-hammer to produce the impression. The decorative subjects of the coins were engraved on the dies in intaglio, commonly freehand, so that every die was distinctly individual. Only in some later periods, and especially in the Islamic era, is there evidence of mass production of the dies by casting or by hubbing, a process of marking out the design on the die by striking this with a punch bearing the subject in relief, before finishing with tools.

The official production of coins by casting has been employed only sporadically, especially in the early Roman, and in the Indian series. Casting from genuine coins is of course the simplest proceedure for producing coin forgeries, detectable by their "soapy" surface, and prevalence of bubbles. In some periods, ancient counterfeits were also produced by casting, and may occasionally even reflect genuine varieties not currently available (Morton, 1975, p. 163).

Since the anvil- or obverse (sometimes also called the "staple") die lasted longer in use, it was customary to engrave here the more difficult or sophisticated subjects. During periods of portrait coinage, especially in Hellenistic times, the royal portrait, the most difficult part of the work, was engraved on the obverse die, whence the present-day terminology of "heads" and "tails" for obverse and reverse. The more ephemeral reverse dies lasted only half, or a third, the life of the obverse. Thus we find coins which are "die duplicates" (i.e., obverse and reverse struck from the same pair of individual dies), and others which share only an obverse (or less frequently a reverse) die, and are said to be "die-linked." It is normally assumed that die-linked coins would be products of the same mint, and close together in time. At the same time, rare instances are known of coindies under the Seleucids, and possibly other Hellenistic kingdoms, being sent to branch mints that are far distant, so that they are linked with issues from totally different series.

From considerable bodies of coinage (coin hoards or museum collections) die-sequences of linked issues can be built up, establishing the chronological series, even when explicit evidence of date is lacking. The rule is now broadly accepted that if in a coin series six examples from each die are present, it may be assumed that every die in the series is known. If however there are some dies represented by fewer than six specimens, allowance must be made for the possibility that several dies are missing, and the sequence consequently incomplete.

The reverse dies (sometimes also called punch dies, or trussels) might for striking, as already noted, be held loose in the hand. The "die-axis," or relation between the orientation of obverse and reverse types upon the resulting coin, would then be haphazard. Sometimes however it appears that guiding lines were marked on the punch die, and upon the anvil, enabling the worker to line up the two dies consistently, though only, of course, with approximate accuracy. Again, in certain series, especially that of Periclean Athens, square-headed dies appear to have been used, which would fit in one of four possible orientations. In other cases, the dies appear to have been hinged, so that a single, mechanically accurate orientation was achieved. This was usually either upright ↑ ↑, or reversed ↑ ↓; and can be expressed more simply with a single arrow as ↑, or ↓. In some periods, variations in die axis help to distinguish the output of different mints or define the chronology of blocks of coinage.

The earliest coinages, in seventh–sixth-century BCE Lydia and Ionia, had a decorative subject engraved only in the obverse die. The reverses were impressions of simple punches, single or double, and designated as "incuse" squares or rectangles. On some thin Greek coinages of southern Italy, the reverses, cut in relief on the dies, closely followed the outlines of the obverse types, producing what are sometimes called "repoussé" coinages. From the late sixth century onward, however, it became customary to engrave both obverse and reverse dies in intaglio, each producing relief impressions on the resulting coins.

The obverse of a coinage is usually distinguished by its convexity, the reverse being concave, a feature resulting from the blow of the die. However, in Islamic coinages, characteristically thin and flat, it is difficult to determine the "technological" obverse. Consequently cataloguers have resorted to the convention that the face bearing the name of Allah and the declaration of faith (*shahādah*) should be considered the obverse. Sometimes the true obverse can be detected as a result of a striking-error known as a brockage, in which a struck flan adheres to the punch die; and the next blank receives, instead of the reverse impression, an intaglio version of the obverse, which thus appears on both faces of the succeeding coin (Bacharach and Awad, 1973, pp. 187–188.)

In this way it will be seen that the technology of coinage, here only briefly outlined, provides special facilities for the analysis of the extensive numismatic evidence surviving from ancient and medieval times (cf. Philip Grierson, *Numismatics*, London and Oxford, 1975, p. 94ff.). The printing of motifs and inscriptions on the metal of coinage preceded by many centuries the introduction of printing on paper. Thus it came to provide perhaps the first historical medium for communication between governments and population. Though full exploitation of this potential for official propaganda was characteristic of the Roman Empire, eastern monarchies such as those of the Parthians and Sasanians used coinage to present an image of the ruler, and to display the ideology and aspirations of the realm.

Coins have several characteristics helpful for conveying historical information. The output of individual mints form *sequences*, from which the chronology of succeeding issues can be deduced. Again, during ancient times, especially in periods of upheaval, a frequent practice was to bury deposits of coins for security. Such coin hoards often come to light, and constitute time capsules, conveying *chronological* information. For study purposes, it is important first to determine which are the latest specimens in each hoard. The sequences contained in overlapping hoards then throw special light on the order of successive issues. "Treasury hoards" consist of stocks of fresh and related coins. "Cumulative" and "savings" hoards may cover long periods of accumulation. "Foundation" deposits (as at Persepolis) have a distinctive character. Sporadic coin *finds*, on the other hand, carefully plotted on the map, throw light on the places of issue when the mints are unknown. "Area finds" recovered in excavation illustrate the economic history of a settlement, and "location finds" contribute to the dating of structures.

Even before the destruction of Assyria in 614–612 BCE by the Babylonians and the Medes, "ingot currencies" of several types circulated in the Near East (see figure 1). It is now realized the "silversmiths' hoards" mentioned in old excavation reports were not mere working stocks, but had a monetary character. The oldest forms in circulation were probably "ring money" of several types, especially the so-called "earrings," also perhaps worn on ringlets of hair. These forms seem characteristic of Babylonia, possibly from the early second millennium. Their weight approximates that of the shekel, but often on standards older and higher than that of the typical Babylonian shekel of 8.40 g. Current later were the rare "slab ingots," monetary "torques," and "cake ingots" (German *Silberkuchen*). These last are known from Zincirli (Luschan, 1943, pp. 119–121) and bear the inscription, incised not impressed, BRRKB BR PNMW, naming

a local ruler who held office around 712 BCE. Although this person is the first ruler named on currency, his ingots do not count as coins since the legend was not mass-produced by stamping; and the weights, though some approach the Babylonian *mina* of 504 g, are very irregular. Cake ingots were also found, with Greek coins among other items, in the Syrian Ras Shamra hoard (Thompson et al., 1973 [hereafter *IGCH*], 1478; Schaeffer, 1939, pp. 464, 466, 486), and in several hoards from Egypt, notably those of Beni Hasan (*IGCH* 1651), Damanhur (*IGCH* 1637), and Mit Rahineh (*IGCH* 1636).

Another form of ingot currency, found at Nush-i Jan in Iran, are the "bar ingots," apparently characteristic of the Median Empire in Iran (seventh–sixth century BCE). The thirteen specimens in this find illustrate a weight range of 12, 18, 24, and 100 g, suggesting a shekel standard around 12g, and representing units of 1, 1½, 2, and 8 shekels. As mentioned, a single piece at 8.40 g represents the Babylonian standard, later revived by the reform of Darius the Great. This last unit, the most influential weight standard of the

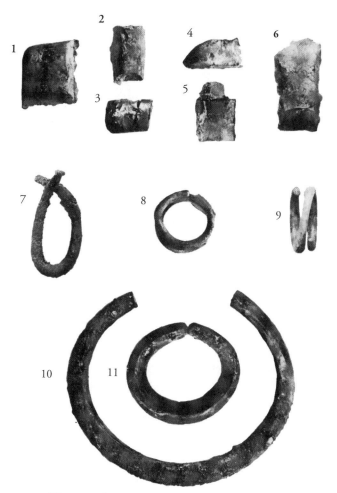

COINS. Figure 1. *Ingot currency.* From Nush-i Jan, Iran, seventh century BCE. Nos. 1-6, "cut-silver" pieces; nos. 7-9, ring-money (shekels); nos. 10-11, large rings ("torques"). (Courtesy David Stronach)

ancient Near East, is hexagesimal, and gives rise to the following correspondences:

60 minas	= 1 talent	= 30,240.00 g
60 shekels	= 1 mina	= 504.00 g
1 shekel	=	8.40 g
1 *zwz* (drachma)	= ½ shekel =	4.20 g

Bar ingots apparently continued in use under the Achaemenids, inspiring the development of the bent bar and punch-marked coinages of ancient India. Finally, "cut-silver" (Ger., *Hacksilber*) makes its appearance as a monetary form, which consists of small chunks of silver cut from larger ingots, bars, or slabs to provide small denominations, usually shekels and their halves. The weights of such fragments are very approximately adjusted, small scraps of silver being used to make up units of weight and bulk payments being weighed out on the balance. Because the shekel standard often fluctuated in the system of ingot currency, payments in silver were simply reckoned on the balance, using the standard weights in force at the time. An increase or reduction of the standard—such as for taxation purposes—could be effected by simply increasing or reducing the weights.

By the end of the sixth century BCE and the beginning of fifth, deposits of bulk silver recorded in Asia east of the Taurus and in Egypt begin to include, together with ingot currency of several kinds, quantities of coined Greek silver, mainly from the areas of silver extraction in Greece (see figure 2). Such regions are the Thraco-Macedonian area; Siphnos, island source of silver used in the Aiginetan "turtle" coinage; and also Athens, a noted producer from the Laurium mines. The mints of Phoenicia, especially Tyre, Sidon, Byblos (Jubayl), and Aradus, probably obtained their bullion by international trade. Hoards of this type are those of Ras Shamra (c. 510–500), the Taranto hoard of 1911 (500–490) with its rare slab ingot, Asyut (c. 475), and the "Jordan 1967" hoard (c. 445). Close dates can be established from the Greek coins present, often heavily chopped or gashed with a chisel—a test for purity of silver probably imposed by the Achaemenid treasuries. The "bulk silver" content probably consisted of pieces retained in circulation from earlier periods. By the second half of the fifth century BCE, the widely distributed hoards of Greek silver in Asia tend to consist entirely of coins. As the study by Daniel Schlumberger (1953) shows, this coinage, received in the Achaemenid Empire by tribute or trade, was widespread in Mesopotamia, Iran, and Afghanistan—a phenomenon illustrated by the hoards of Malayer (discovered 1934), of the Chaman Huzuri at Kabul (discovered 1933), and by C. J. Rich's Tigris Hoard described by G. K. Jenkins (1964).

Although a "silver standard" thus prevailed in the Aegean and in Asia beyond the Taurus, a "gold standard" dominated in the east Anatolian kingdoms of Lydia and Phrygia and the cities of the Aegean coast. The earliest issues were in electrum, a natural alloy of gold and silver. These were "dumps" marked with parallel striations on the obverse, and threefold incuse punch on the reverse. Coins with the legend *Walweš* are ascribed by some to Alyattes, king of Lydia (c. 580), and must come early in the series. Later, respective gold and silver issues of "heavy" standard (about 10.9 g), with types of a confronted lion and bull, are ascribed to Croesus, king of Lydia (560–546). They are followed by issues on a lighter standard with similar emblems, in gold and silver respectively, now increasingly ascribed to Cyrus, king of Persia (550–530), after his conquest of Lydia. These issues, of which the silver denominations reckoned twenty to the gold shekel, weighed respectively 5.4 g and 8 g. Examples were found in the Persepolis foundation deposit toward 511 BCE (Herzfeld, 1938, pp. 413–414; Schmidt, 1957, p. 113). They were quickly followed by the famous "daric-siglos" series, inaugurated no doubt by Darius the Great. The obverse featured a Persian archer, and the reverse had rectangular incuse. It is now known that the sequence of types for both silver and gold was as follows: (1) half-length figure (daric 8 g, siglos 5.4 g); (2) archer shooting with bow (daric 7.87–8.34 g, siglos 5.4 g); (3) archer running with bow and spear, two pellets vertically beneath ear (daric 8.35 g, siglos 5.4 g); (4) archer running with bow and spear, no pellets beneath ear (daric 8.35 g, siglos 5.60 g); and (5) archer running with bow and dagger (daric 8.35 g, siglos 5.60 g). Although the silver coin is known in Greek as the *siglos* (i.e., shekel), it was in fact the gold daric which was to weigh 8.35 g, representing (with a small discount for seigniorage) the standard of the Babylonian shekel (8.40 g) revived by Darius's monetary reforms. The silver denomination of 5.4 g or 5.6 g was adjusted so that it rated twenty to the daric at a silver/gold ratio of 13:1 or 13.3:1. The small fluctuations in the weight standards of silver and gold gave critical clues to the sequence of the daric issues, otherwise differentiated only by details of posture and ornament. Thus, the famous Persian archer series of daric and siglos, effectively the coinage of the Lydian satrapy at Sardis, is recognized by numismatists as typical of the Achaemenids. It is represented in finds far across the empire, although the siglos was treated as bullion in the eastern satrapies (provinces), where there were still no mints for the manufacture of circular coinage until the advent of Alexander the Great. Reports of the minting of sigloi under the Achaemenids elsewhere in the Near East than Sardis (e.g., in Egypt under Aryandes, in Anatolia, or in Babylon) have not yet been confirmed decisively.

If the gold daric was typical of the Lydian satrapy, in some of the Greek cities and islands coinage of the gold-silver alloy electrum persisted. Sometimes it was the natural metal, but increasingly produced as artificial alloy, which was called by numismatists *white gold*. Important centers were Phocaea and Mytilene. Because the Achaemenid satrapy of the Hellespont in northwestern Anatolia produced no coinage of its own, however, the electrum *staters* (units) of Lampsacus

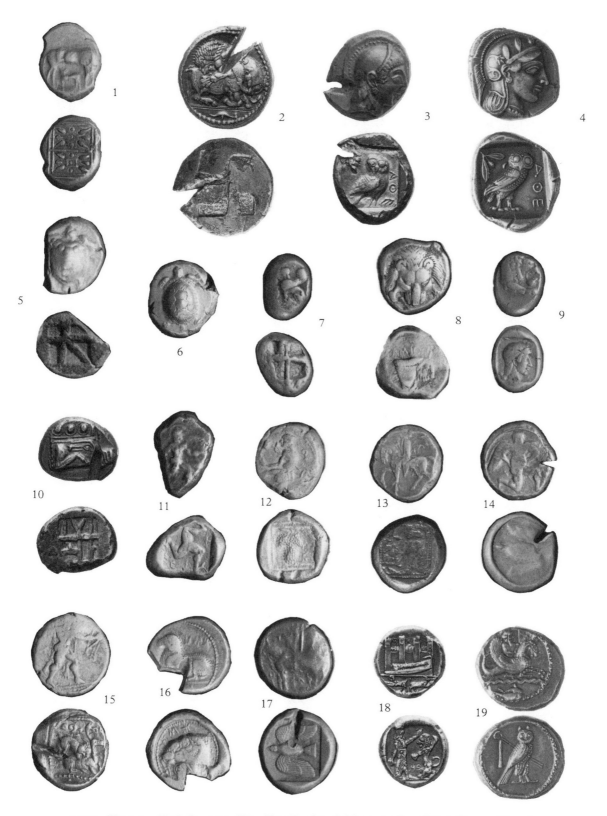

COINS. Figure 2. *Typical contents of Near East silver hoards.* Nos. 1-17, from Kabul, Chaman Huzuri hoard, 1933 (courtesy Kabul Museum, 1962): (1) Kerkyra, (2) Acanthus, (3) Athens (archaic), (4) Athens (c. 430 BCE), (5, 6) Aigina, (7) Chios, (8) Samos, (9) Lesbos, (10) Phaselis, (11) Aspendos, (12) Soloi, (13) Tarsus, (14) Mallus, (15) Kition (King Azbaal), (16) Salamis (Cyprus), (17) Paphos. Nos. 18-19, British Museum (Courtesy of the Trustees): (18) Sidon, (19) Tyre. Note chisel cuts typical of Achaemenid treasury usage. All fifth-fourth century BCE.

and especially of Cyzicus appear to have supplied the need and played an international role in the Black Sea trade. The Cyzicene series, current from the late sixth century until the advent of Alexander, had an extensive repertoire of changing types, always characterized by the accompanying symbol of the tuna fish, the local product. The main *stater* denomination was adjusted to a standard of 16.05 g, and the *hekte* ("sixth") was a common subdivision. The electrum series of Lampsacus bore the winged forepart of a horse and weighed about 15.35 g. Both these coinages bore on the reverse the incuse impression of a plain "mill sail" punch. Toward 400 Lampsacus gave up electrum and produced a distinguished coinage in pure gold with changing obverse types, weighing 8.40 g. This was exactly the standard of the daric and presumably valued against it at par. Important Greek silver coinages of the fifth century BCE circulating in the Near East were the Aiginetan "turtles," the Athenian "owls," the large Thraco-Macedonian pieces and issues of the Phoenician cities of Tyre, Sidon, and Aradus, together with Citium (Kition) in Cyprus.

Hellenistic and Parthian Coinage. Only under Alexander the Great (332–321) was the attempt made to impose a uniform coinage across his territories extending from Macedonia to Iran. The imperial obverse type for gold was a helmeted Athena with her head to right, and the reverse featured a winged Victory holding the *stylis*, a nautical attachment. Athena's helmet was usually ornamented with a coiled serpent, but on some late varieties there was a eagle-griffin, lion-griffin, or sphinx. Remarkably this series seems to have commenced before any victory had actually been won. The silver had the obverse head of Heracles (Herakles) attired in the lion scalp, and on the reverse the Olympian Zeus is enthroned, holding an eagle on his right hand. Separate issues are distinguished in both series by symbols or monograms or both; and the mints, even when not so differentiated, have often been recognized from die links and engravers' styles. Initially the main mints are thought to have been Amphipolis and Pella. Later, as the conquests advanced, coins were issued in many regional centers. The most easterly mint in Alexander's lifetime appears to have been Ecbatana (Hamadan) in Iran. Further east, mixed coinage, "bulk silver," and bars continued to circulate.

The obverse type of Alexander's coinage was not originally a portrait but was quickly taken as such. After the conqueror's death and deification, his portrait in various forms appeared on the coins of the Hellenistic monarchies: on that of Antigonus in Phrygia retaining the Heracles; on that of Ptolemy in Egypt wearing the elephant-scalp commemorative of the Indian conquests; and on that of Lysimachus in Thrace with the ram's horns recalling his sojourn in Egypt. This last was a coinage widely diffused and known throughout the Near East.

Ultimately the diademed portrait of the living ruler be-

came the characteristic obverse of the Hellenistic monarchies, producing some of the finest known Greek portraiture. The Attic standard introduced by Alexander, with a tetradrachm of 17.2 g (.6 oz.), became the most common metrology, but it soon slipped marginally to 16.8 g (.6 oz.), coinciding with the long familiar Babylonian shekel at 8.40 g (.30 oz.), of which it thus represented the double.

The Seleucid kingdom (312–88) in its heyday stretched from the Aegean to Central Asia, and the studies of its mints by Edward T. Newell (1938, 1941) still constitute a model of numismatic method. A characteristic reverse type depicted the god Apollo seated on the Delphic *omphalos* (a rounded stone in his temple regarded as the center of the world) and holding his bow and arrows. Their number, one to three, indicated the mint. Soon the Seleucid eastern territories fell either to the independent Bactrian kingdom or to the advancing Parthians, who pressed forward down the Asian highway from the Caspian to Qumis-Hecatompylos, Rayy (modern Tehran), Hamadan and Seleucia on the Tigris. At first their coinage largely conformed to the Hellenistic pattern, but later the bearded obverse portrait was normally turned to the left. The reverse was soon standardized as the dynastic founder, Arsaces, seated on the *omphalos* or on a throne and holding his bow and arrows. The royal name was inscribed simply as Arsaces, usually accompanied by titles. Thus the absence of the ruler's personal name causes difficulties of identification. Although the drachma denomination was copiously issued at the cities on the Iranian plateau, the large tetradrachms were struck exclusively at Seleucia on the Tigris, where the practice was established of inscribing dates according to the Seleucid era of 312 and frequently also the exact month. Frontal portraits represent pretenders to the Arsacid throne.

The Greek inscriptions on Parthian coins became increasingly conventionalized, and by the reign of Vologeses I (51–78 CE) they are supplemented by initially abbreviated inscriptions in Parthian indicating the royal names, such as WL for Vologeses, later *wlgšy mlk'* ("King Vologeses"). These have the advantage of designating the ruler individually.

COINS. Figure 3. *Early Sasanian coins*. Coins 3, 12, and 15 are ▶ gold; otherwise all are silver. No. 1, Shapur (207 CE), king of Persis. Nos. 2-3, Ardashir I (208-223-241 CE) with successive crowns as king of Persis; no. 4 (223 CE) after defeat of Artabanus V; no. 5 (226 CE) with mural crown after capture of Ctesiphon; no. 6, with definitive crown as Shahanshah, after 228 CE; no. 7, with prince Shapur as heir. No. 8, Shapur I (241-272 CE) with eagle crown as successor in accession year; nos. 9-10, Shapur I with plain crown and crown with cheek-piece. No. 11, Ohrmazd I (272-273 CE). No. 12, Vahram I (273-276 CE). No. 13, Vahram II (276-293 CE). No. 14, Vahram III (293 CE). No. 15, Narseh (293-302 CE). British Museum (Courtesy of the Trustees).

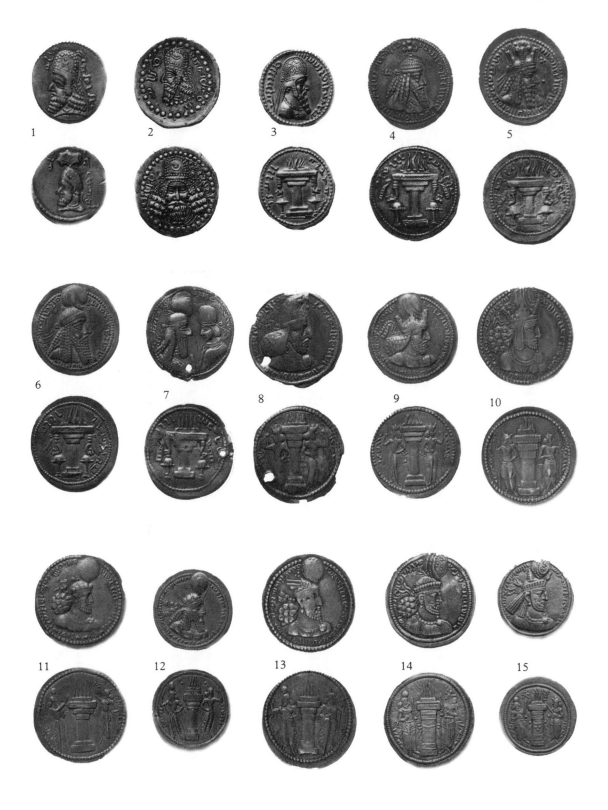

1   2   3   4   5

6   7   8   9   10

11   12   13   14   15

Besides the main series of Parthian coinage, the subordinate kingdoms that were a feature of the Arsacid dispensation—Persis, Elymais, and Characene—intermittently issued their own coinages. Persis indeed produced autonomous tetradrachms and drachms of the Attic standard soon after the death of Seleucus I in 280 BCE. The series is sometimes styled the "Fratadara" coinage from a reading by Ernst Herzfeld (1938) that is now known to be incorrect but nevertheless provides a useful label for the series. These issues bear the Aramaic inscription *frtrk' zy 'lhy'*, apparently "administrator of" (i.e., appointed by) "the gods," in opposition, presumably, to those appointed by the Seleucid kings. Rulers named include Bagadata, Oborzus (*whwbrz*), Artaxerxes ('rthštr), and Autophradates (*wtprdt*), besides others less clearly decipherable. The usual types show the ruler on obverse, wearing the satrapal *tiara*, and a fire temple or fire altar on the reverse. Subsequent coinages on a lighter standard continue until the advent of the Sasanian dynasty (see below).

Elymais, the kingdom in the Zagros foothills east of Susa and Ahvaz, also produced a coinage under its founder, Kamnaskires, a title deriving from that of the Achaemenid treasurers residing at Susa. This quaint designation long remained the throne name of the Elymaean kings. Soon after the start of the Christian era, Greek types and inscriptions gave way to "Oriental" portraits and legends in a local form of Aramaic, naming as kings Phraates, Orodes (*wrwd*), and Chosroes. At the head of the Persian Gulf again lay Characene, a state founded by a chief named Hyspaosines (c. 125), who once more struck large silver coins with Greek legends, beardless portraits, and Heracles on the reverse. His successors Apodakos, Tiraios, and Artabazos continued the tradition until 48–47 BCE. Under later rulers there was progressive debasement of the silver denominations, and here too after about 143 CE, Greek was replaced by a variety of the Aramaic alphabet.

Sasanian Dynasty (223–631 CE). In 223 CE Ardashir I, the local prince of Persis, rebelled against his Parthian overlords, defeated Artabanus V (Ardavan V, sometimes also numbered Artabanus IV), the last Arsacid king, and embarked on the consolidation of Iran. Rigorous reforms were introduced in every theater. Military, administrative, and religious centralization were accompanied by a complete renovation of the coinage. The debased Parthian silver was replaced by a brilliant series in gold and fine silver respectively, the former commemorative, the latter constituting henceforth the principal currency (see figure 3). The weight standard of the silver at 4.1 g, was effectively that of the Attic drachma. The characteristic types showed the royal bust on the obverse now turned toward the right and identified by a specific individual crown. On the reverse was the fire altar symbolic of the dynasty's Zoroastrian faith. This image in the following reigns was flanked by two "guardians." In the

initial period the Pahlavi inscriptions were often blundered because the engravers were not literate. The legends were intended to give on the obverse the name and titles of the ruler with the formula "Mazda-worshiping lord N., king (of kings) of Iran (and non-Iran, whose descent is from the gods)," and on the reverse "fire of N." is written with reference to the royal sacred fires established for every ruler at his accession. With the passage of generations the individual crowns become increasingly complex, occasional mint names appear on the reverses and are eventually standardized in abbreviated form (see figure 4). By the reign of Kavad (488–531 CE), such abbreviations regularly appear to the right of the fire altar, and the regnal date of the issue is indicated in words on the left. The script evolves from the "epigraphic Pahlavi" with its separate characters to the cursive "Book Pahlavi" forms. The volume of coinage was greatly increased under Khusrau I Anushirvan (531–579), revenue thereafter being levied in cash rather than kind. The epic wars against Byzantium waged by Khusrau II Parvez (592–628) demanded vast output of coinage, no doubt often struck from the enormous booty. The Sasanian drachma was by this time a flat and thin module with widely spread flan. It provided the pattern not only for certain Byzantine silver coinages but especially for the dirhams of Islam.

Islamic Coinages. When in 637 the Muslim Arab armies overran Syria and Mesopotamia, they entered a world of two distinct currency systems. That of the Byzantine Empire, based on gold and bronze, functioned farther to the west. That of Sasanian Iran, consisting chiefly of silver, was active to the east. At first the huge quantities of coinage available as tribute or booty sufficed for current needs. Yet already there was being laid the foundation of a coinage system in all three metals. As the Arab armies advanced through Iran, drachmae of the Sasanian pattern continued in issue. Prototypes were naturally coins of the last Sasanian king, Yazdgird III (632–651), dated to regnal year 20, his last, but with slight variations of detail and decoration. For some decades dating continued in Yazdgird's era. The numerous issues of Khusrau II were also imitated and soon began to predominate. Typically, short inscriptions in Arabic appear in the second quarter of the obverse margin, especially *bi-ismi'llāh* ("in the name of Allah") and *jayyid* ("excellent"). The names of the Arab governors, replacing the name of Khusrau, came to be written in Pahlavi in front of the con-

COINS. Figure 4. *Early Sasanian drachmae with mint names.* No. ▶ 1, Vahram I (273-276 CE), mint, rev. above fire altar, Skst'n (for Sistan). No. 2, Vahram II (276-293 CE), with consort, and to right, hier; mint, rev. above fire altar, Ldy for Rayy. No. 3, Ohrmazd II (302-309 CE); mint, rev. on fire altar, Ldy for Rayy. Enlarged about 2x. Note ornate individual crowns of kings. No. 1, Indian National Museum, Parieck Collection. Nos. 2-3, British Museum (Courtesy of the Trustees).

1

2

3

ventionalized portrait. Eventually around AH 60/679–80 CE, the Muslim Hijrah reckoning was introduced for the dates. With the transfer of the caliphal capital to Damascus by the Umayyads, under the caliph ʿAbd al-Malik, the quest began for a definitive Islamic coinage. In gold, the Byzantine "three emperors" type of Heraclius was progressively modified by elimination of the crosses: the "cross on steps" and those on the crowns. Finally, the Arabic declaration of faith appears in the reverse margin. A similar type in silver with the central figure in an attitude of prayer was issued for Bishr ibn Marwan at al-Kufah (Aramaic ʿAqula) and Basra, respectively in 73/692–93 and 75/694–95. Next, the "standing caliph" type appears on the obverse of gold issues for 76/695–96 and on silver from Damascus dated 75/694–95 (cf. Walker, 1956). A remarkable type of 72/691–92 from Sistan has the Muslim Declaration of Faith in Middle Persian written in the Pahlavi script.

The definitive Islamic typology (the "reformed coinage") appears in 77/696–97 for gold and in 79/698–99 for silver. Figural representations are now banned. The types are exclusively inscriptional, obverses bearing simply the Declaration of Faith (*shahādah*) in the central area and the "Prophetic Mission" (Qurʾan 9:33) in the margin. The reverse has the Surat al-Ikhlaṣ (Qurʾan 112:1–3) in the central area. These words—"Allah is one, Allah is eternal, He did not beget, nor was He begotten"—were a formula said to have been inscribed on the banners of armies marching to fight the Byzantines. In the reverse margin is the date-legend with the numeral written in words. On gold, mint names are uncommon. It is assumed that the bulk of coinage was issued at Damascus, although the mint names *Ifriqiyah* (Africa), *al-Andalus* (Spain), and *Maʿdan Amir al-Muʾminin bi al-Hijaz* ("Mine of the Caliph in the Hijaz") are sometimes found. On silver, mint names appear for more than sixty-six provincial and district centers, constituting the main interest of the series. On the Umayyad gold and silver coinage, remarkably no name of any ruler is found. The extensive copper coinage, issued from innumerable local municipalities, at first has only religious formulae. Mint names, names of governors, and ultimately dates progressively make their appearance. Although of humdrum appearance, Islamic copper coinage, which every excavated site introduces in new varieties, has probably the greatest research potential in Near Eastern numismatics. Local knowledge is required to attribute the many "mintless" varieties.

The classically angular Arabic script on these early Islamic coins is designated "Kufic." The diacritical points distinguishing letters of similar form are sparingly found, but they do occur sporadically. Although evolving in detail, forms of the angular script continued until the later twelfth century CE when they were replaced by the joined and flowing "Naskhi" style. Coins of the ʿAbbasid dynasty, who ousted the Umayyads in 132/749–50, are distinguished from earlier issues chiefly by the replacement in the reverse legend of the Surat al-Ikhlaṣ by the words "Muhammad is the Prophet of Allāh." In 146/763–64, the official name of the new ʿAbbasid capital—Baghdad—appeared as Madinat es-Salam ("the city of peace") in the margin. The second city of the ʿAbbasids was Rayy, the ancient predecessor of Tehran, under the designation al-Muhammadiyah. Although the ʿAbbasid gold dinars continued the Umayyad form largely unchanged, the dirhams evolved a slender and elongated Kufic script, which persisted until after the death of Harun al-Rashid in 170–193/786–809. Gradually the brief names of officials begin to appear on the coinage: mint supervisors, princes, ministers, governors, and eventually, the caliph himself with full titles. It was only in the tenth century CE with the increasing fragmentation of caliphal power that local princes bearing the title *amir* became effectively sovereign. They issued coinage, often even gold, in their own names, but still always acknowledging in the legends the ʿAbbasid caliph as overlord. Such rulers were the Ṣaffarids and Ghaznavids in Afghanistan; the Samanids and Qarakhanids in Central Asia; the Buyids, Zaydids, and Musafirids in Iran; and the Hamdanids and Marwanids in Syria and Mesopotamia. Finally, the Turkish dynasty of the Great Seljuqs overshadowed all lesser rivals, and from their capital at Isfahan established perhaps the most stable dispensation, dominating Asian Islam from 429/1038 until 590/1194. During this last phase a "silver famine," variously explained, overtook the treasuries of Islam, coinage seemingly being confined to gold and some copper. This interlude as a whole provides material of striking variety, issued by a galaxy of local mints, and documenting every stage of the complex history. After the brief interlude of the Khwarazmshahs, ʿAla ad-Din Tekish (567–596/1172–1200), and his son ʿAla al-Din Muhammad b. Tekish (596/617–1200–1220), the Mongol avalanche swept away the ʿAbbasid caliphate and its satellites. Their onslaught utterly destroyed the old world of Islam and introduced in due course the late medieval coinage of the Near East with its Naskhi script and innovative designs.

[*See also* Weights and Measures. *In addition many of the ruling dynasties and individual sites mentioned are the subject of independent entries.*]

BIBLIOGRAPHY

Ingot Currency and Archaic Greek Coinage

Balmuth, Miriam S. "The Monetary Forerunners of Coinage in Phoenicia and Palestine." In *International Numismatic Convention, Jerusalem, 17–31 December 1963*, pp. 25–32. Tel Aviv, 1967.

Balmuth, Miriam S. "Origins of Coinage." In *A Survey of Numismatic Research, 1966–1971*, vol. 1, *Ancient Numismatics*, edited by Paul Naster et al., pp. 27–35. New York, 1973.

Balmuth, Miriam S. "Jewellers' Hoards and the Development of Early Coinage." In *Actes du 8ème congrès international de numismatique, New York–Washington, September 1973*, edited by Herbert A. Cahn and Georges Le Rider, pp. 27–30. Paris and Basel, 1976.

Bivar, A. D. H. "A Hoard of Ingot-Currency of the Median Period, from Nūsh-i Jān, near Malayir." *Iran* 9 (1971): 97–111. Illustrates archaeological evidence for the context of bar-ingots.

Bivar, A. D. H. "Bent Bars and Straight Bars: An Appendix to the Mir Zakah Hoard." *Studia Iranica* 11 (1982): 49–60.

Bivar, A. D. H. "Achaemenid Coins, Weights, and Measures." In *The Cambridge History of Iran*, vol. 2, *The Median and Achaemenian Periods*, edited by Ilya Gershevitch, pp. 610–625. Cambridge, 1983.

Carradice, Ian. "The 'Regal' Coinage of the Persian Empire." In *Coinage and Administration in the Athenian and Persian Empires: The Ninth Oxford Symposium on Coinage and Monetary History*, edited by Ian Carradice, pp. 73–95. British Archaeological Reports, International Series, no. 343. Oxford, 1987.

Herzfeld, Ernst. "Notes on the Achaemenid Coinage and Sasanian Mint-Names." In *Transactions of the International Numismatic Congress Organized and Held in London by the Royal Numismatic Society, June 30–July 3, 1936, on the Occasion of Its Centenary*, edited by J. W. Allan et al., pp. 413–426. London, 1938. First publication of the Persepolis foundation deposit, and the pioneer use of Sasanian *bullae* to elucidate the mint signatures on coins.

Jenkins, G. K. "Coins from the Collection of C. J. Rich." *British Museum Quarterly* 28 (1964): 88–95. Literary records of a vast find of Greek coins and ingot currency on the Tigris bank not far from Baghdad.

Kraay, Colin M., and Max Hirmer. *Greek Coins*. London, 1966. Superbly illustrated survey of Greek coinage.

Kraay, Colin M., and P. R. S. Moorey. "Two Fifth-Century Hoards from the Near East." *Revue Numismatique* 10 (1968): 181–235. A "Jordan hoard" and a "Syrian hoard" of mixed Greek coins and scrap silver.

Kraay, Colin M. *Archaic and Classical Greek Coins*. London, 1976.

Kraay, Colin M., and P. R. S. Moorey. "A Black Sea Hoard of the Late Fifth Century B. C." *Numismatic Chronicle* 141 (1981): 1–19.

Luschan, Felix von. *Die Kleinfunde von Sendschirft (Ausgrabungen in Sendschirli V)*. Berlin, 1943, pp. 119–121.

Powell, Marvin A. "A Contribution to the History of Money in Mesopotamia Prior to the Invention of Coinage." In *Festschrift Lubor Matouš*, edited by Blahoslav Hruška and Geza Komoróczy, pp. 211–243. Budapest, 1978. Survey of cuneiform texts illustrating the mechanism of ingot currency and confirming numismatic evidence that weight denominations were only approximately adjusted.

Price, Martin, and Nancy Waggoner. *Archaic Greek Coinage: The Asyut Hoard*. London, 1975. The latest and most complete publication of a large hoard of Greek silver coins from Egypt, buried c. 475 BCE.

Reade, Julian. "A Hoard of Silver Currency from Achaemenid Babylon." *Iran* 24 (1986): 79–87.

Robinson, E. S. G. "A 'Silversmith's Hoard' from Mesopotamia." *Iraq* 12 (1950): 44–51.

Robinson, E. S. G. "The Beginnings of Achaemenid Coinage." *Numismatic Chronicle* 18 (1958): 187–193. Fundamental breakthrough in elucidation of the sequence and weight-standards of the Achaemenid coinage of Sardis.

Schaeffer, Claude F.-A. "Une trouvaille de monnaies archaïques grecques à Ras Shamra." In *Mélanges syriens offerts à M. R. Dussaud*, vol. 1, pp. 461–487. Bibliothèque Archéologique et Historique, vol. 30. Paris, 1939.

Schlumberger, Daniel. "L'argent grec dans l'empire achéménide." In *Trésors monétaires d'Afghanistan*, by Raoul Curiel and Daniel Schlumberger, pp. 3–64. Mémoires de la Délégation Archéologique Française en Afghanistan, 14. Paris, 1953. Publication of the Tchaman-i Hazouri (Kabul) hoard of fifth-fourth century Greek coins and bent bars. Also describes the Malayer hoard of fifth-century Greek coins.

Schmidt, Erich F. *Persepolis* II. Chicago, 1957, pp. 113, pl. 84.

Sellwood, David. "Parthian Coins" and "Minor States in Southern Iran." In *The Cambridge History of Iran*, vol. 3.1, *The Seleucid, Parthian, and Sasanian Periods*, edited by Ehsan Yarshater, pp. 279–314. Cambridge, 1983. Includes excellent illustrations. The second article covers the coinage of Persis, Elymais, and Characene.

Thompson, Margaret, et al. *An Inventory of Greek Coin Hoards. (IGCH)*. New York, 1973.

Hellenistic and Parthian Coinage

Ingholt, Harald, et al. *Recueil des tessères de Palmyre*. Bibliothèque Archéologique et Historique, vol. 58. Paris, 1955. Catalogue of Palmyrene temple tokens (*tesserae*).

Jenkins, G. K. "Coin Hoards from Pasargadae." *Iran* 3 (1965): 41–52. Two hoards of Alexander-coinage and of Seleucus.

Le Rider, Georges. *Suse sous les Séleucides et les Parthes: Les trouvailles monétaires et l'histoire de la ville*. Paris, 1965.

Mørkholm, Otto. *Early Hellenistic Coinage: From the Accession of Alexander to the Peace of Apamea, 336–186 B.C.* Cambridge, 1991.

Newell, Edward T. *Royal Greek Portrait Coins*. New York, 1937. A most useful general survey.

Newell, Edward T. *The Coinage of the Eastern Seleucid Mints, from Seleucus I to Antiochus III*. New York, 1938. Fundamental analysis of the eastern Seleucid coinage and mint-structure, still indispensable today. Covers the mints of Seleucia on the Tigris, Ecbatana, Susa, and Bactria.

Newell, Edward T. *The Coinage of the Western Seleucid Mints, from Seleucus I to Antiochus III*. New York, 1941.

Price, Martin Jessop. *The Coinage in the Name of Alexander the Great and Philip Arrhidaeus*. 2 vols. Zurich and London, 1991.

Sellwood, David. *An Introduction to the Coinage of Parthia*. 2d ed. London, 1980. Very serviceable description of Parthian coinage, with tables for the conversion of Seleucid and Parthian dates (pp. 11–13).

Sasanian and Early Islamic Coinage

Bacharach, Jere L., and H. A. Awad. "The Problem of Obverse and Reverse in Islamic Numismatics." *Numismatic Chronicle* (1973): 183–191.

Broome, Michael. *A Handbook of Islamic Coins*. London, 1985.

Göbl, Robert. *Sasanian Numismatics*. Braunschweig, 1971. Careful description of the coinage.

Göbl, Robert. "Sasanian Coins." In *The Cambridge History of Iran*, vol. 3.1, *The Seleucid, Parthian, and Sasanian Periods*, edited by Ehsan Yarshater, pp. 322–338. Cambridge, 1983.

Gyselen, Rika. "Trésor de monnaies sasanides trouvé à Suse." *Cahiers de la Délégation Archéologique Française en Iran* 7 (1977): 61–74.

Gyselen, Rika. "Un trésor iranien de monnaies sasanides." *Revue Numismatique* 23 (1981): 133–141.

Gyselen, Rika, and Ludvik Kalus. *Deux trésors monétaires des premiers temps de l'Islam*. Paris, 1983. Mixed hoards of Sasanian and early Islamic coins from Syria, with a valuable appendix on the Sasanian mint signatures.

Gyselen, Rika. "Un trésor de monnaies sasanides tardives." *Revue Numismatique* 32 (1990): 212–231.

Herzfeld, Ernst. "Notes on the Achaemenid Coinage and Sasanian Mint-Names." In *Transactions of the International Numismatic Congress Organized and Held in London by the Royal Numismatic Society, June 30–July 3, 1936, on the Occasion of Its Centenary*, edited by J. W. Allan et al., pp. 413–426. London, 1938.

Malek, Hodge Mehdi. "A Seventh-Century Hoard of Sasanian Drachms." *Iran* 31 (1993): 77–93. Up-to-date treatment of a hoard of 296 drachmae of Khusrau II acquired by a collector from Quetta.

Malek, Hodge Mehdi. "A Survey of Research on Sasanian Numismatics." *Numismatic Chronicle* 153 (1993): 227–269. Valuable survey with a comprehensive bibliography of 292 publications in the field (from which the present selection may be supplemented).

Mochiri, Malek Iradj. "A Pahlavi Forerunner of the Umayyad Reformed Coinage." *Journal of the Royal Asiatic Society* (1981): 168–172. Remarkable Arab-Sasanian issue from Sīstān, dated 72/691–692, rendering the Muslim declaration of faith in Middle Persian, written in the Pahlavi script.

Mochiri, Malek Iradj. "A Sasanian-Style Coin of Yazīd b. Muʿāwiya." *Journal of the Royal Asiatic Society* (1982): 137–141. Pseudo-Sasanian drachma, attesting in Pahlavi script "Year 1" of an unspecified ruler Yazīd.

Morton, A. H. "An Islamic Hoard of Forged Dirhams." *Numismatic Chronicle* (1975): 155–168.

Paruck, F. D. J. *Sāsānian Coins*. Bombay, 1924. Comprehensive work for its day, illustrating a wide range of coinage; now increasingly out of date.

Plant, Richard J. *Arabic Coins and How to Read Them*. 2d ed. London, 1980. Useful introduction to the inscriptions on early Islamic coins.

Simon, H. "Die sāsānidischen Münzen des Fundes von Babylon: Ein Teil des bei Koldeweys Ausgrabungen im Jahre 1900 gefunden Münzschatzes." In *Varia 1976*, pp. 149–337. Acta Iranica, vol. 12. Tehran, 1977.

Walker, John. *Catalogue of Muhammadan Coins in the British Museum*, vol. 1, *Arab-Sassanian Coins*. London, 1941. Fundamental study of this series, now somewhat dated. The arrangement by governors' names, rather than by mints, sometimes seems confusing since tenures of office were interrupted. Also the author's transliteration of Pahlavi legends, though logical, was idiosyncratic. Despite such minor shortcomings, this work is essential for serious research.

Walker, John. *Catalogue of Muhammadan Coins in the British Museum*, vol. 2, *A Catalogue of the Arab-Byzantine and Post-Reform Umaiyad Coins*. London, 1956. Indispensable research work for early Islamic coinage, though considerably supplemented in subsequent publications.

Walker, John. "Some New Arab-Sassanian Coins." *Numismatic Chronicle* 12 (1956): 106–110. Four notable additions to the repertoire of Arab-Sasanian coinage, including the astonishing Arab-Hephthalite issue of Yazīd b. al-Muhallab from Guzgān.

A. D. H. BIVAR

COLONIZATION.

The term *colonization* has strong semantic associations with imperialism, especially that of nineteenth-century Europe where colonies were the political, military, and economic possessions of metropolitan powers, held by force and controlled by a bureaucratic machinery. Typical colonial situations involved dominant foreign minority populations that enjoyed juridically privileged access to land, labor, and raw materials, and that retained adherence to metropolitan imperial powers. Ancient empires differed from modern empires in their political structure and in their general emphasis on war loot and tribute payments. Even so, ancient systems minimally involved garrisons and bureaucratic outposts; the Akkadian "palace" at Tell Brak and the Gasur (Nuzi) archive reflect this military and administrative presence in northern Mesopotamia during the twenty-third century BCE. Imperialism could also involve direct control of land, whether by settling soldiers in the margins of empire (e.g., the Ur III state in the twenty-first century BCE and also the Athenian and Roman empires

of later times), or by creating *latifundia*, large plantations worked by bound or slave labor (e.g., Achaemenid Persians in Babylonia). The Assyrian and Babylonian policy of deporting conquered peoples to create pacified labor pools in the first millennium counts as another form of imperial colonization.

New Foundations. Although these imperial situations contain aspects of colonialism, several other kinds of situations in the ancient world created nonimperial colonies. The new Phoenician and Greek foundations around the Mediterranean basin during the Iron Age (eighth–sixth century) exemplifies one of these situations. Here, a population emigrated from an existing city-state to establish another. Unlike imperial colonies, these new communities were politically and economically independent from the founding city-state and displaced the indigenous population. The motives for the colonizing movement were variable, including competition for land and for the wealth that land represents, creation of trading stations with access to new markets, relief from overpopulation and food shortage in the mother city-state, and exile of disaffected political factions.

Trade Colonies. Commercial communities that formed foreign quarters in cities were another, common "colonial" situation in the ancient Near East. In such cases, the foreigners were temporary residents who invested in financial instruments, not land or labor. The activities of these communities were commonly based on agreements between the local ruler and the trading association or foreign state in order to make more predictable (reduce risks) the commercial colony's legal standing, the conditions of trade, and protection costs. These agreements also acted to limit the political, and even economic, power of trading communities. Designated ports-of-trade established analogous legal conduits of trade in which trading privileges and restrictions were established by the local authority. Commercial colonies should be distinguished from trade diasporas in which dispersed members of an ethnic group (e.g., Jews, Greeks, Armenians, and Indians in more recent Asian history) possessed special status as traders across vast regions, but did not enjoy connections to a metropolitan government.

The Akkadian word *karum* refers to the port or commercial quarter of Mesopotamian cities in general where explicit rules of conduct enforced peaceful and profitable trade with neighboring city-states and with more distant regions. The *karum* institution could operate in both nonimperial and imperial settings. For example, the *karum* at Sippar in northern Babylonia provided the institutional setting for traders from other Babylonian kingdoms and from Aššur, early in the second millennium; Sippar also hosted permanent communities from Eshnunna, Isin, and other Mesopotamian cities. Similarly, the Assyrian empire maintained *karum*s for trade with Egypt and with Arwad (and from there with the Mediterranean), in order to regulate and supervise trade with places still outside direct imperial control. Other examples of a similar system, though less well known, include the community of Old Babylonian traders in the Persian Gulf (the *alik Dilmun*), and the Greek emporia (trade centers) at al-Mina (Syria) and Naukratis (Egypt).

The Old Assyrian Cappadocian *karum* system provides the best-known example of ancient commercial colonization. In operation during the early centuries of the second millennium, the *karum* system involved the presence in autonomous (and previously existing) cities of Central Anatolia of Assyrian traders and their families (which often included local wives). The traders represented private family firms or joint investment ventures based in Aššur, under the provisions of treaties between the local Anatolian king and the Assyrian authorities. The traders formed their own institutional structure and offices, to regulate the activities of, and to adjudicate disagreements between, members of the *karum* community, and to represent the *karum* in the local royal court. The best-known Assyrian *karum* in Anatolia is Kaneš (Kültepe) in Cappadocia; the textual evidence indicates that Assyrian trading colonies also existed at Ališar, Boğazköy (the later Hittite capital), and other places. The Kaneš archives record the transactions of Assyrian traders bringing woolen textiles and tin to Kaneš and beyond, where these commodities were exchanged for silver and other commodities to be trafficked in Aššur.

Archaeological Cases. As the review of colonies in the ancient Near East suggests, many of the clearest examples date to the second and first millennia BCE, when the textual sources provide most of the evidence. In earlier periods or in less habitually literate areas of western Asia at any time, archaeological evidence suggests colonialism in certain cases.

The Uruk expansion. The Late Uruk period of southern Mesopotamia presents very strong evidence for a colonial expansion into the surrounding regions. The archaeological evidence falls into several distinct patterns. In the Susiana plain of western Iran, an essentially Uruk assemblage replaced the indigenous culture. The transformation was virtually complete; the previous tradition of painted pottery and stamp seals disappeared, replaced by Uruk pottery and the Uruk administrative technology (cylinder seals, jar sealings, *bullae* [impressed tags of metal or clay that in Uruk times formed hollow balls] and tokens, and eventually numerical notation tablets). This cultural replacement strongly suggests colonization and cultural absorption of the Susiana plain into southern Mesopotamia.

New foundations outside southern Mesopotamia represent a second pattern, best seen at Habuba Kabira, Tell Qannas, and Jebel 'Aruda on the middle Euphrates in Syria. Habuba Kabira South, the town, and Tell Qannas, the acropolis, formed a walled settlement at least 20 hectares (50 acres) in size. The settlement possessed regularly laid-out streets, and gives every indication of being a planned foundation. Just to the north Jebel 'Aruda contained monumental

buildings surrounded by residential structures, and may have been the administrative center for the Uruk communities in the area. The material culture in these sites was almost entirely Uruk in nature, including a wide variety of southern Mesopotamian pottery, administrative devices, and styles of public and private architecture. Habuba Kabira and its sister sites seem to have been occupied 150 years or fewer, toward the end of the Late Uruk period.

Godin, in the Zagros mountains of southwest Iran, presents another distinctive pattern; Uruk materials are associated with a walled compound that contains small rooms arranged around a courtyard (Godin V) within an otherwise local settlement (Godin VI). Inside the Uruk compound, roughly one-third of the pottery is local and the rest Uruk related; in addition to the pottery, Uruk materials include seals and sealings, and numerical notation tablets. Like Habuba Kabira, the Uruk presence at Godin V appears to have been relatively short-lived and dates toward the end of the Late Uruk period. Some scholars have attributed Godin V to the slightly later Proto-Elamite phenomenon.

Other sites combine Uruk and local traits. For example, at Hassek Höyük in southeastern Turkey the architecture is strongly Uruk in character, but the local Late Chalcolithic pottery outnumbers the Uruk-related assemblage and both local and Uruk seals occur. Elsewhere, southern Mesopotamian materials, often only beveled-rim bowls and a few other pottery types, appear as minor elements in otherwise local Late Chalcolithic sites in western Iran, Syro-Mesopotamia, and eastern Anatolia. Southern Mesopotamian materials even appear in the eastern Nile Delta, at Tell Fara'in (Buto).

The Uruk expansion has received several different interpretations. Some have considered it to represent flight from the growing power of state government in southern Mesopotamia. Others have appealed to a Greek analogy, thinking of colonization as relief from overpopulation as well as a search for trading opportunities. The most common explanation is commercial, in which the Uruk settlements and enclaves were optimally situated to direct both riverine and overland traffic into southern Mesopotamia. In its strongest form, this argument considers the Uruk expansion to have been a conscious, state-directed policy of empire, probably the consequence of competition among the emerging city-states. Although sites like Habuba Kabira and Godin V date to the late Late Uruk period, the Uruk expansion actually began in Middle Uruk times. The expansion therefore was not simply a sudden explosive state-administered enterprise, and took several distinct forms (e.g., new foundations, commercial colonies) through time, for which no single explanation can adequately account.

Egypt in Early Bronze Age Palestine. A similar situation appears in southern Palestine and northern Sinai during Early Bronze (EB) Age I times (c. 3400–3000). Surveys and excavations in northern Sinai and southern Palestine have revealed a complex picture of intensifying Egyptian involvement with the southern Levant. Early Gerzean (Naqada II) pottery, both imported and locally made, appeared in sites like Tel 'Erani, Fara H, and Taur Ikhbeineh during the early EBA I period, and the evidence hints that some Egyptians lived in southern Palestine (e.g., the concentration of Egyptian artifacts in a single building at Fara H). In the reciprocal direction, notable amounts of early EB I pottery and some cast copper objects in Palestinian forms appeared at Maadi and Minshat Abu Omar in Lower Egypt. These early EB I manifestations of an Egyptian involvement with southern Palestine culminated during the late EB I, when evidence for colonies becomes widespread.

The two best-known sites are Tel 'Erani and 'Ein-Besor. Egyptian pottery appears virtually throughout the Tel 'Erani sequence, and accounts for nearly half the pottery in stratum V, to which is also assigned a *serekh* (palace-facade design pattern) of dynasty 0 (3200–3100 BCE). Petrographic analysis of the Egyptian pottery indicates that most of it was made in southern Palestine, and only a small proportion was imported from Egypt. The pottery locally made in Egyptian styles significantly has a diversity of functional forms, whereas the imported pottery is mostly containers. At 'Ein-Besor III, roughly 90 percent of the pottery is Egyptian in style, and most of it seems to have been imported; as at Tel 'Erani, the pottery assemblage covers a wide range of functional forms, and other Egyptian objects also occur. A small house built according to Egyptian standards contained a corpus of Egyptian-style clay *bullae* used to track grain and other goods collected as taxes, and their subsequent distribution. Petrographic analysis indicates that the *bullae* were locally made, and the seals impressed on the *bullae* differ in workmanship and sign combinations from those found in Egypt. The *bullae* seem to reflect the internal administrative regulation of an Egyptian community at the site.

Clusters of very small sites of this period are strung out along the northern Sinai coast. The heavy erosion or deflation of these sites may account for the lack of stratigraphy and the apparent absence of architecture. The sites contain cooking and baking installations, domestic pottery (including baking trays and bread molds), and stone tools. Roughly 80 percent of the pottery is Egyptian (dynasties 0–1, c. 3200–2900 BCE); petrographic analysis indicates that it was produced in Egypt. In contrast to the wide functional range of the Egyptian pottery, the local pottery consists mostly of storage jars.

The EB I episode of an Egyptian presence in southern Palestine has been variably interpreted. Most recent assessments of Egyptian colonization indicate that it endured some 150 to 200 years and involved at least several hundred people whose communities performed the full range of activities expected in both domestic and public administrative contexts. Some scholars see these communities as Egypt's first military foray into the area. In this scenario, the Egyptian settlements in northern Sinai and southern Palestine represent way-stations and forts in a crown-sponsored system of administered trade. Other interpretations strip away the aspect of military control, and describe the Egyptian communities as forming a purely peaceful commercial network. State sponsorship of the commercial network is unnecessary to this interpretation, and the local nature of the 'Ein-Besor sealings suggests minimal, direct crown involvement in this community. In both scenarios, the basic incentive for colonies was improved access to Asiatic commodities, which may have included various woods, resins, honey, turquoise, and copper.

Other early cases. The Proto-Elamite period (c. 3100–2900) of southwestern Iran witnessed a phenomenon of expansion similar to that of Uruk Mesopotamia. During this period, an assemblage of beveled-rim bowls, painted pottery, Proto-Elamite seals and sealings, and Proto-Elamite tablets appeared at Susa (immediately after the Late Uruk period) and at Tal-i Malyan in Fars (the Banesh phase). This same complex of items also appeared in local contexts at places like Tepe Sialk on the Kashan plain and Tepe Yahya in Kirman, and elements of the complex have been found as far east as Shahr-i Sokhta in Seistan and Hissar on the Damghan plain. The Proto-Elamite expansion is often seen as an effort to control trade routes and to acquire foreign materials; less thoroughly documented than the Uruk case, however, its use of commercial colonies, new foundations, and/or imperial colonization remains uncertain.

The Indus (Harappan) civilization provides a final example of early colonization, revealed by an enclave of small Harappan settlement in eastern Bactria, and strongly Harappan settlements around the Gulf of Oman. Shortugai in Bactria and approximately 700 km (435 mi.) from the Indus Valley contains a completely Indus assemblage, including painted pottery, inscribed sherds, stamp seals, and construction along Indian standards. On the southeastern Arabian coast, the buildings at Ras al-Junayz belong neither to local nor to Harappan architectural traditions; but the artifacts from these buildings include numerous Indus-style objects (painted pottery, inscribed sherds, seals, beads, and ivory objects) alongside pottery painted in local Arabian styles and locally made stone bowls. The location of Shortugai and Ras al-Junayz at strategic points on trade routes or near raw materials (lapis lazuli, copper, possibly tin) have lead many scholars to interpret them as trading communities. But these settlements represent different situations—Shortugai appears to have been a thoroughly Harappan settlement inhabited by people from the Indus valley, whereas Ras al-Junayz expresses a strong Indian presence in a local context.

Conclusions. In the above examples, a basic distinction is made between nonimperial and imperial varieties of colonization. The clearest examples of nonimperial colonization were commonly associated with trade. In many cases, commercial colonies were permanent communities that operated under formal agreements between local authorities and the metropolitan government or trade association. Greek colonization of the Mediterranean basin aside, these commercial colonies typically were uninterested in agricultural land or labor. Ancient empires focused on extracting tribute payments, rather than direct control over land and labor. This kind of imperialism required that military garrisons and bureaucratic officials be stationed in subject areas, but often did not encourage the presence of wider segments of the dominant society. Accordingly, colonization was a secondary aspect of ancient empires before the Achaemenids. Moreover, empire and trading colony were alternative ways of acquiring foreign goods, and trade often led to empire. An early (literary) example is Sargon's excuse for campaigning in eastern Anatolia to protect Mesopotamian traders there, and the Akkadian habit of referring to places by their desirable products (e.g., the Silver Mountain). The Late Uruk expansion may present an older example, in which new foundations at places like Habuba Kabira may have attempted direct control over trade that previously had been less formally conducted.

[*Most of the sites and civilizations mentioned are the subject of independent entries.*]

BIBLIOGRAPHY

Algaze, Guillermo "The Uruk Expansion: Cross-Cultural Exchange in Early Mesopotamian Civilization." *Current Anthropology* 30 (1989): 571–608. Review of evidence for the Uruk expansion and presentation of the informal empire and control of trade argument. See as well Algaze's *The Uruk World System: The Dynamics of Early Mesopotamian Civilization* (Chicago, 1993), together with critical commentaries from other scholars.

Amiet, Pierre. *L'âge des échanges inter-iraniens.* Paris, 1986. Magisterial overview of interregional connections on the Iranian plateau during the fourth and third millennia BCE, addressing Late Uruk, Proto-Elamite, Indus, and Central Asian materials.

Ben-Tor, Amnon. "New Light on the Relations between Egypt and Southern Palestine during the Early Bronze Age." *Bulletin of the American Schools of Oriental Research,* no. 281 (1991): 3–10. Recent summary of the evidence for the Egyptian presence in southern Palestine during the EBA I, presenting the commercial colonies interpretation.

Boardman, John. *The Greeks Overseas.* Rev. ed. London, 1980. Standard review of Greek colonization in the Mediterranean and Black Sea.

Curtin, Philip D. *Cross-Cultural Trade in World History.* Cambridge, 1984. Reviews "trade diasporas" and commercial colonization in history, with special attention to Asia and Africa, providing a set of useful concepts for understanding these phenomena.

Doyle, Michael. *Empires.* Ithaca, N.Y., 1986. Comparative study of the sociology of ancient and modern empires, with special attention to understanding the conditions of formal versus informal empire and colonization.

Finley, Moses I. "Colonies: An Attempt at a Typology." *Transactions of the Royal Historical Society,* ser. 5, vol. 26 (1976): 167–188. Thoughtful investigation into the varieties of colonialism in the ancient and modern world.

Francfort, H.-P. *Fouilles de Shortugai.* Paris, 1989. Final report on the French excavation at this Indus site in eastern Afghanistan.

Joffe, Alexander. "Early Bronze I and the Evolution of Social Complexity in the Southern Levant." *Journal of Mediterranean Archaeology* 4.1 (1991): 3–58. Interpretive essay on the antecedents to EBA II–III urbanism of the southern Levant that assigns a limited role to EBA I Egyptian colonization.

Kemp, Barry J. "Imperialism and Empire in New Kingdom Egypt, c. 1575–1087. B.C." In *Imperialism in the Ancient World,* edited by P. D. A. Garnsey and C. R. Whittaker, pp. 7–57. Cambridge, 1978. Review of Egyptian imperialism and colonization that distinguishes the situation in Nubia from that in Syro-Palestine during the Late Bronze Age.

Lamberg-Karlovsky, C. C. "The Proto-Elamites on the Iranian Plateau." *Antiquity* 52 (1978): 114–120. Review of evidence for the Proto-Elamite involvement on the Iranian plateau, seen in the context of trade.

Larsen, Mogens T. *The Old Assyrian City-State and Its Colonies.* Copenhagen, 1976. Standard discussion of the political, legal, and economic organization of the Old Assyrian Cappadocian trade.

Larsen, Mogens T., ed. *Power and Propaganda: A Symposium on Ancient Empires.* Copenhagen, 1979. Collection of essays on the motives and representations of imperialism in ancient western Asia, and discussions of the relationship between trade and imperialism.

Oren, Eliezer D. "Early Bronze Age Settlement in Northern Sinai: A Model for Egypto-Canaanite Interconnections." In *L'urbanisation de la Palestine à l'âge du Bronze ancien: Bilan et perspectives des recherches actuelles; Actes du Colloque d'Emmaüs, 20–24 octobre 1986,* edited by Pierre de Miroschedji, pp. 389–405. British Archaeological Reports, International Series, no. 527. Oxford, 1989. Presents the imperial control interpretation of the Egyptian presence in southern Palestine during the EBA I.

Stolper, Matthew W. *Entrepreneurs and Empire: The Murašû Archive, the Murašû Firm, and Persian Rule in Babylonia.* Leiden, 1985. Examines the financial and administrative impact on land-tenure and taxation of the Achaemenids in Babylonia.

CHRISTOPHER EDENS

COLOR. *See* Munsell Chart.

COMPUTER MAPPING. Geographic information systems (GIS), also known as computer mapping technologies, are digital databases that store, manipulate, capture, analyze, create, and display spatially referenced data. The spatial component of these systems make them readily applicable to archaeological research, where archaealogists record location information for everything from individual artifacts to sites in a regional survey. Many projects also record environmental data and such modern features as roads and villages. All of these data are spatially referenced and often best understood when stored as maps, an easy and relatively inexpensive task for a GIS.

Data for building a GIS can come from a number of sources. Remotely sensed data, such as satellite images, aerial photography, and geographic positioning systems, along with more traditional sources, such as paper maps and archaeological databases, can be used to construct a GIS. Unlike paper maps, which store multiple data themes on a single sheet, GIS store data themes in individual layers: a layer for roads, a layer for elevation, a layer for Iron Age sites. Because these map layers are referenced to a common coordinate system, they can be electronically overlaid to create any combination of data themes. The advantage of this type of system is obvious: maps can be quickly and easily revised as new data become available without the expense of traditional cartography.

GIS come in two basic types, vector and raster. Because of the differences in how they manage spatial data, each has its own particular strengths and weaknesses. Vector-based GIS are easily understood because, like paper maps, they store their data as points, lines, and polygons. These entities form the basic data units of a vector GIS, for which spatial information must be explicitly encoded. For example, if a road network is put into a vector GIS as a series of lines, specific X and Y coordinate data must be encoded for each line before the spatial relationships between the various road segments have meaning.

The strengths of vector-based systems lie principally in their familiar format, accuracy, high-quality cartographic output, connectivity to powerful databases, and the relatively small amounts of computer space they require. These strengths make vector-based systems ideal for managing data across large regions and producing detailed and accurate maps. For example, archaeological resource management on a state or national level would be an ideal application for a vector-based system, especially if publication-quality maps are needed. The weaknesses of a vector GIS stem primarily from the necessity to encode spatial data explicitly. This means that continuously changing surfaces, such as elevation and slope, must be generalized as elevation contours or polygons representing slope categories. These are ultimately unsatisfactory for many types of archaeological modeling.

In a raster-based GIS, data are stored in a grid of columns and rows, much like a spreadsheet, that represent X and Y coordinates in the real world. The intersection of each row and column is known as a cell. Each cell represents a specific area in the real world and contains a Z value, or number that can represent anything from elevation values, to sites, to soil types. Unlike vector systems, the basic data unit in a raster GIS is a spatial unit (the cell) for which entity information must be explicitly encoded. For example, if a road network is put into a raster GIS, the X and Y coordinates are implicit because they are determined by their position in the grid; however, Z values corresponding to the various components of the network must be explicitly encoded in each cell for them to have meaning as roads.

The strengths of raster systems are found principally in their ability to manage data that are continuous across a surface, in their simple data structure, and in their ability to use remotely sensed data, such as satellite images, which are stored in a raster format. These strengths make the creation of complex mathematical models possible. For instance, with a raster GIS, it is possible to reconstruct large portions of the paleoenvironment, especially terrain-related data, as continuous surfaces. Rather than representing elevation as a series of contours, each cell in a raster GIS contains a Z value corresponding to the elevation at that location. Because these surfaces are constructed of numbers in cells, they can be subjected to sophisticated mathematical manipulation to create new surfaces. Any equation that can be devised, such as surface 1 + surface 2 = surface 3, can be carried out in a raster GIS. The disadvantages of a raster GIS lie principally in file size and cartographic output. Raster files use large amounts of computer disk space. Even grids representing relatively small areas will contain tens of thousands of cells, and grids with hundreds of thousands of cells are common. Also, because of the raster structure, the traditional cartographic output of points, lines, and polygons is less accurate and of generally poorer quality.

An example of the types of analysis possible with a GIS can be drawn from the Tell el-'Umeiri regional survey in Jordan. The ceramic record from this region indicates a substantial increase in human activity with the change from Iron I to Iron II. To investigate how this increased activity may have modified subsistence strategies, a raster GIS containing several environmental variables was constructed. Eight of the variables were selected and probability models based on a logistic regression were created. This modeling process involved a comparison of the sites from each period with a random sample of 250 nonsite locations. The environmental variables were then weighted, according to their relative importance as revealed by the regression, and summed to create models of the environmental signature for sites from each period. The models illustrated that during the Iron I period the areas considered environmentally suitable for settlement were limited, but that the pressures of increased human activities forced a change in subsistence strategies during the Iron II period, leading to an expansion into areas previously considered unsuitable.

[See also Computer Recording, Analysis, and Interpretation.]

BIBLIOGRAPHY

Allen, Kathleen M. S., et al., eds. *Interpreting Space: GIS and Archaeology*. London, 1990. Collection of articles with the stated purpose to "provide archaeologists with the information to be able to evaluate, purchase, and apply GIS to their work" (p. ix). Practical examples and a theoretical discussion of the relationship between archaeology and GIS, along with discussions of hardware/software considerations.

Burrough, P. A. *Principles of Geographical Information Systems for Land Resources Assessment*. Oxford, 1986. Standard introduction to the fundamentals of GIS.

Kvamme, Kenneth L. "Geographical Information Systems in Regional Archaeological Research and Data Management." In *Archaeological Method and Theory*, vol. 1, edited by Michael B. Schiffer, pp. 139–203. Tucson, 1989. Introduction to using GIS in archaeological research, with a good discussion of the possibilities and practicalities of GIS, including data management and the differences between vector and raster systems.

Kvamme, Kenneth L. "A Predictive Site Location Model on the High Plains: An Example with an Independent Test." *Plains Anthropologist* 37 (1992): 19–40. Accessible example of a probability model based on logistic regression. An understanding of mathematics and statistics is helpful, but not necessary, for understanding the basic principles used to create the model.

Monmonier, Mark. *How to Lie with Maps.* Chicago, 1991. Clever, witty, and informative introduction to basic cartographic techniques; an enjoyable way to gain a basic understanding of maps and map presentations, including some problems specific to GIS. The chapters on maps used for propaganda and disinformation are especially good.

GARY L. CHRISTOPHERSON

COMPUTER RECORDING, ANALYSIS, AND INTERPRETATION.

The introduction of microcomputers in 1976 began to change dramatically and substantively the way in which archaeologists record and analyze data. Suddenly, what had been a scarce resource was nearly universally available. As this technology evolves, researchers will be developing applications not yet envisioned.

Word Processing and Desktop Publishing. Using computer technology, archaeological reports can be prepared quickly and revised conveniently. Archaeologists can now take portable computers into the field to record information at the excavation site. With the advanced capability of software for text manipulation and word-processing software becoming more like desktop publishing software, archaeologists can create reports that include photographs, charts, graphs, diagrams, and drawings in a format ready for publication, substantially decreasing the time between excavation and publication. Powerful new technologies for the dissemination of archaeological information in hypertext format, both on compact disk and on the World Wide Web, are transforming the nature of archaeological publication.

Database Management. Most archaeological projects deal with vast numbers of artifacts. The use of an electronic database to catalog artifacts improves the efficiency of this essential recordkeeping. It is possible to obtain information about excavated material that was once time-consuming or labor intensive: database management programs can quickly sort and reorganize data, making it possible to query, for example, all objects of a particular material or type, from a particular period, and associated with a particular context. Such processes allow a researcher to detect patterns and relationships and to form hypotheses for further investigation that might not have emerged from a simple handwritten or printed catalog. Optimal results are obtained when the software chosen is a fully relational database system, which allows the user to combine information drawn from several different files or catalogs (e.g., an artifact registry, a pottery registry, a file of information about individual loci). The

software should allow the inclusion of graphical information (photographs or drawings) and extensive notation. The ability to export data for use in other computer programs (e.g., for inclusion in reports prepared using a word processor or desktop publishing program or in a spreadsheet or other program for statistical analyses) is very important. Similarly, interactive connections to other computer programs, particularly computer-aided design (CAD) software, are very useful. The context of a particular item recorded in a database can be displayed by a symbol inserted into a drawing to show precisely where the artifact was unearthed. Selecting a particular symbol in a drawing will retrieve the associated information from the database file and display the complete (or selected) material from the catalog. Database management programs easily produce reports that can guide excavation and enhance publication.

Quantitative Analysis and Statistics. Recording and reporting the presence of materials of a particular type (i.e., cooking pots, lamps, nails) or from a particular period (i.e., Early Bronze II, Iron I, Early Roman), is quantitative information that can be very useful in the interpretive process. If the pottery from a particular locus, to take one example, includes a high percentage of vessels used to prepare and consume food, it could support the conclusion that the area in which it was excavated was a kitchen or dining facility; the presence of a very small quantity of such wares, as a percentage of the whole, would weigh against such a conclusion. Similarly, quantitative information about the ceramics from a particular historical/cultural period can be very revealing. When one period is compared with another, relative quantities of material can indicate an increasing or decreasing population, the extent to which an area was used in a given period, or other changes in the demographics or economy that might have occurred over time. The recording, manipulation, and reporting of such numerical information about artifacts constitutes descriptive statistics, which are extremely important for the careful reporting of archaeological excavation and the effective presentation of conclusions drawn by the investigators.

More important, however, are analytical statistics, also referred to as inferential statistics. Archaeology involves the reconstruction of the human past on the basis of the material evidence, and archaeologists' hypotheses about human activity are based on a very small sample of the surviving material. This may be envisioned as follows:

1. *Life assemblage.* In the past there was a complete material culture, including numerous structures and artifacts that were part of a society of living, active human beings.

2. *Deposited assemblage.* When one cultural environment is replaced by another (whether by abandonment, destruction, or natural evolution), there is a residue from the earlier period of those artifacts that come to rest or remain at the site.

3. *Preserved assemblage.* Only a portion of the deposited

assemblage will survive the ravages of time and subsequent activity and be available for excavation and collection.

4. *Sample assemblage.* Only a small portion of the preserved assemblage will actually be recovered and studied by archaeologists.

It is important to note that the several assemblages referred to above become increasingly smaller as the list moves from 1 to 4. This is why analytic, or inferential, statistics are crucial. As the archaeologist theoretically moves from sample data to conclusions about larger populations, there are many computer programs available that will enhance the sophistication and efficiency of statistical analyses.

Computer-Aided Design and Drafting. CAD (or CADD) software offers great potential for recording and interpretating archaeological data. Related tasks, not treated here, are mapping and surface modeling. Drawings are a staple in archaeological recordkeeping, ranging from simple schematic diagrams, to accurate "stone for stone" drawings of individual areas of excavation, to composite drawings of larger fields or sites. They include drawings of individual artifacts (such as the technical rendering of individual potsherds) and projections of buildings and other structures that illustrate their complete form and function. Electronic ("digitized") drawings have many advantages over their paper counterparts: they can be more easily edited, more easily combined into larger wholes, and more easily and precisely compared. If drawing to a different scale or combining elements from several drawings into a new, composite whole is needed, it can be accomplished quickly and easily. Furthermore, with drawings produced accurately to scale, measurements of size or distance and calculations of area become trivial tasks, as "overlays" can be easily and dynamically manipulated. As with numerical data, CAD drawings allow archaeologists to engage in "what if" explorations of hypotheses. That can both guide excavation and assist interpretation.

Archaeologists employ several methods to produce CAD drawings. The following are among the procedures in use:

1. *Tracing.* Conventionally produced drawings can be traced, using a digitizing tablet, to produce an electronic copy of the original.

2. *Scanning.* Conventional drawings, photographs, or slides can be scanned to create copies that can be imported into CAD software. Scanning, however, produces rasterized (bit mapped) images that require raster-to-vector conversion in order to obtain drawings that exploit the full potential of CAD technology. Even with the use of autotrace utilities conversion can be very labor intensive and slow.

3. *Direct entry.* A drawing can be generated electronically from directly entered x–y (or x–y–z) coordinates. These coordinates can be obtained and entered manually or directly through linked electronic surveying equipment.

4. *Photogrammetry.* A number of techniques exist for obtaining digital images from conventional film or digital photography. Photogrammetry can produce highly precise graphic images in either two or three dimensions.

Digital Photography and Scanning. Digital images have become increasingly important for archaeological recording. Whether they are obtained indirectly (e.g. by scanning slides or photographs produced using conventional photography) or directly (i.e, using a digital camera or "frame grabber" and video camera), they offer many advantages over conventional photography. Photographs taken with a digital camera are almost instantly available because they do not require the processing associated with photographic film. Furthermore, digital images, especially those stored on optical disks, are much more stable than images on photographic film. If the electronic data remain intact (multiple backup copies can be maintained to ensure this) the quality of the image will not deteriorate over time. Digital images are also more efficiently kept in archives, where they require far less space and are more easily cataloged and accessed. They can be easily edited (cut, cropped, and enhanced) and quickly imported into documents (from field notes to final publications) or database records. It is quite feasible for a catalog of artifacts, maintained as an electronic database, to include pictures of each object along with text information. Furthermore, digital images can be sent, almost instantly, over computer networks to others throughout the world. Finally, Quick Time™ images, (essentially digital motion pictures) allow an object to be displayed dynamically and seen from all sides and with changing light and shadow, to reveal important detail. Such images can be included with other information as a part of a permanent archeological record or report.

Geographic Information Systems (GIS) and Remote-Sensing and Global-Positioning Systems. Several computer technologies have had an impact on archaeological data collection and interpretation. Geographic information systems (GIS) provide a dynamic link between computer-generated maps or CAD drawings and database files. Thus, the location of any item in a database file can be shown on a map or drawing. Similarly, objects on a map or in a drawing can be linked to related information in a database file. Furthermore, GIS software allows the researcher to explore the spatial relationship of objects to each other as well as to other spatial relationships. Using a survey map and its associated data, relationships can be explored among occupied sites along with their relationship to such ecological and topological features as the availability of water, the proximity of roads, and the nature of the terrain. Similarly, the plan of a building can be used to show the relationship of the artifacts found in it, providing the archaeologist with data to determine the kinds of human activity that took place in it and in its vicinity after it was destroyed or abandoned.

Remote-sensing and global-positioning systems offer the archaeologist means for more rapid and accurate data collection and recording, particularly during surveys, than manual techniques allow.

Advances in computer technology are encouraging archaeologists to adopt standards for data collection and recording and to share information more easily. Computer software programs are facilitating the collection and storage of data and enabling the results from many excavation projects to be drawn together to enhance the understanding of increasingly wider geographic regions and more extended periods of human history.

[*See also* Computer Mapping; Recording Techniques; *and* Statistical Applications.]

BIBLIOGRAPHY

Aldrich, Frank, et al. *Computer Graphics in Archaeology: Statistical Cartographic Applications to Spatial Analysis in Archaeological Contexts.* Arizona State University, Anthropological Research Papers, no. 15. Tempe, 1979.

Archaeological Computing Newsletter. Published quarterly by Oxford University's Institute of Archaeology, this newsletter contains brief articles reporting current work in archaeological computing.

Blakely, Jeffrey A., and William J. Bennett, Jr., eds. *Analysis and Publication of Ceramics: The Computer Data-Base in Archaeology.* British Archaeological Reports, International Series, no. 551. Oxford, 1989.

CSA: Newsletter of the Center for the Study of Architecture. Published quarterly by the Center of Architecture at Bryn Mawr College, this newsletter covers a broad range of computer applications of interest to archaeologists and very often includes information about classical and Near Eastern archaeology.

Gaines, Sylvia W., ed. *Data Bank Applications in Archaeology.* Tucson, 1981.

Gardin, J.-C., with O. Guillaume. *Artificial Intelligence and Expert Systems: Case Studies in the Knowledge Domain of Archaeology.* Translated by Richard Ennals. Chichester and New York, 1988.

Klein, Richard G., and Kathryn Cruz-Uribe. *The Analysis of Animal Bones from Archaeological Sites.* Chicago, 1984. Provides an excellent and easily understandable discussion of statistical theory with an application particularly instructive for archaeologists interested in statistical analyses.

Lock, Gary, and John Wilcock. *Computer Archaeology.* Princes Risborough, 1987. A useful overview of archaeological computing.

Lock, Gary, and Jonathan Moffett, eds. *Computer Applications and Quantitative Methods in Archaeology 1991.* British Archaeological Reports, International Series, no. S577. Oxford, 1992. The most recent in a series of annual volumes of the same title (often with different editors), and the most valuable resource available for those who wish comprehensive and detailed information about applications and advances in archaeological computing.

Richards, J. D., and N. S. Ryan. *Data Processing in Archaeology.* Cambridge, 1985. One of the Cambridge manuals in archaeology, this volume provides a good general treatment of the topic, although one that is rapidly becoming outdated.

Whittlesey, Julian H. *Photogrammetry for the Archaeologist with Calculator Programs for Cartographic Plotting.* Auburn, N.Y., 1979. Although not related to Near Eastern archaeology, this volume provides useful information about photogrammetry.

THOMAS R. W. LONGSTAFF

CONDER, CLAUDE REIGNIER (1848–1910),

principal surveyor for the Survey of Western Palestine (1871–1877). Conder, who as a colonel was to spend much of his career attached to the Ordnance Survey of Great Britain, was commissioned into the Royal Engineers in 1870, having distinguished himself in surveying and drawing. After a two-year professional course at the School of Military Engineering at Chatham, his services were requested by the Palestine Exploration Fund (PEF) for the Survey of Western Palestine, which he joined, as officer in charge, in 1872. Conder also earned honorary Doctor of Civil Law and Doctor of Laws degrees (the latter from Edinburgh, 1891).

The survey's ambitiously wide-ranging undertaking embraced not only the topographical survey itself, but also the recording and investigation of all potential biblical sites, geology, and natural history. To all this, Conder brought his graphical skills and undoubted learning, but these were not matched by his ability to interpret the evidence correctly and many of his identifications were subsequently disproven. Like Charles Warren before him, Conder lacked the technical skills which characterized excavations of the last decade of the nineteenth century and beyond. His outstanding contribution to the archaeology of Palestine lay in his major share of the production of the twenty-six-sheet map of western Palestine which the PEF published at a scale of 1:63,360 in 1880. This project is acknowledged to have contributed more to the understanding of the archaeology and ancient history of Palestine than any other undertaking in the nineteenth century. Conder's popular account of the survey, *Tent Work in Palestine*, first published in London in 1878, had achieved six editions by 1895.

Apart from the maps, the most important publication to result from the survey was The eight-volume *Survey of Western Palestine: Memoirs of the Topography, Orography, Hydrography, and Archaeology* (1881–1885), of which Conder was a principal author and which includes the earliest site-by-site reconnaissance of Palestine. Misinterpretations are substantially compensated for by the richness of meticulous detail Conder recorded. Similarly, his unfinished Survey of Eastern Palestine (1881) is notable for the recording and drawing, in the published maps and *Memoirs*, (London, 1889), of the unusually large number of dolmens in that region. In addition to his prolific contributions over thirty-five years to the PEF *Quarterly Statement*, Conder was the author of fifteen major books on subjects related to the ancient Near East.

[*See also* Palestine Exploration Fund; *and the biography of Warren.*]

BIBLIOGRAPHY

No full biography of Conder has been published, but a brief resume of his life is given in the *Dictionary of National Biography*, supp. vol. 1, pp. 401–403 (Oxford, 1912). Information on Conder's life and work is available in the Archives of the Palestine Exploration Fund, London.

Conder, Claude R. *Tent Work in Palestine*. London, 1878.

Conder, Claude R., and H. H. Kitchener. *The Survey of Western Palestine: Memoirs of the Topography, Orography, Hydrography, and Archaeology*. 8 vols. and set of maps. London, 1881–1885.

Conder, Claude R. *The Survey of Eastern Palestine: Memoirs of the Topography, Orography, Hydrography, and Archaeology*. London, 1889.

Watson, Charles M. "Memoir of Colonel C. R. Conder." *Quarterly Statement of the Palestine Exploration Fund* (April 1910): 93–96.

YOLANDE HODSON

CONSERVATION ARCHAEOLOGY.

In the past, archaeologists treated most sites as mere sources of objects and information, eventually abandoning them to erosion and neglect. Only unusual sites like Jerash (Jordan), Babylon (Iraq), and Qumran (Israel) were treated with conservational care similar to that devoted to the objects taken from them. Today, both regional authorities and archaeologists are becoming more conscious of the archaeological site itself as an object subject to policies and theories of conservation, and rules and strategies for site conservation are being installed everywhere in the Near East. In Jordan, for example, implementation of such strategies has become a cooperative venture involving the local Department of Antiquities, local universities, foreign research institutes and their archaeologists, and cultural and development agencies of foreign governments. International standards for site conservation are overseen by UNESCO and other agencies.

Regional strategies for conservation include setting priorities for exercising damage control on a vast number of known sites, rescuing new sites accidentally exposed, caring for new sites exposed by archaeologists, and developing sites with spectacular cultural remains for touristic and scholarly use. To develop such priorities, ongoing cultural resource management (CRM) programs are essential. CRM involves advance planning, including systematic regional surveys to locate and identify all knowable sites, computer catalogs of those sites with basic archaeological information and significance-priority ranking, archaeological site assessment in advance of commercial site development, rescue archaeology, regulating touristic use of antiquities, setting priorities for sites and site elements for conservation, selecting sites and site features for restoration and antiquities park development, and, tragically, setting criteria under which a site's destruction is to be permitted.

Rescue and maintenance conservation can overwhelm local agency resources. Rescue is frequently built into the planning of major development projects, but a CRM program also must be able to deal with the unexpected, such as the 1993 discovery of a Late Antique mosaic under a modern street in Jerash. The rapid rate of modern development is presently exposing ancient stone surfaces to damage ranging from the tourist's touch to automobile-generated pollution.

New-site conservation follows rescue and maintenance. Primary selection principles are monumentality and extent of preservation. Jerash, for example, has been the focus of numerous Jordanian and international efforts since the 1930s, including the restoration by a French team of the Temple of Zeus and the South Gate, and the restoration by a Polish team of the Hippodrome. Such a site deserves attention not only because its remains are spectacular, but also because it is perceived as an essential component in a widely appreciated human cultural heritage. Other sites may be selected because of specifically focused interests: the mundane architecture at Qumran might not have received such careful attention had it not been associated with the Dead Sea Scrolls. The difficult conservation of the friable granite and sandstone masonry of Islamic Ayla (Aila/Eilat) in 'Aqaba received international funding and local support because of its importance to Jordan's Islamic heritage. Similarly, the extensive reconstruction and development of the antiquities at Sepphoris, in Israel, have received government and private support because of that site's importance for early Judaism and Christianity. Places like Jerusalem, Petra, Giza, Palmyra, and Ur receive conservation attention because of their universal appeal and touristic value. National conservation strategies will tend to count tourism potential in setting priorities.

On-site conservation strategies may range from the complete rebuilding of structures based on archaeologists' theoretical reconstructions, to limited restoration based on components available from collapse debris and to consolidation to prevent still-standing masonry from further collapse and erosion. A classic example of the first is Arthur Evans's restoration of Knossos, Crete, in which the palace superstructure was reconstructed without sufficient archaeological evidence. Although still practiced on occasion, such a procedure is no longer acceptable. Its obvious disadvantages are that the result is more the product of the historical architect's design than a restoration of the ancient structure; the high percentage of new masonry causes the building to lose its aura of antiquity, even if the architectural shape is a faithful reproduction; and such massive reconstruction cannot be reversed to incorporate revisions based on subsequent studies.

In limited restoration, missing fragments may be replaced with newly dressed stones in order to maximize the reuse of existing pieces. A precedent-setting example is the Erechtheion restoration on the Athenian acropolis, which provided the methodological inspiration for the limited restoration of the Temple of Hercules in Amman. Another is the French restoration of the Temple of Zeus temenos wall at Jerash. The most conservative and usually preferable approach is the consolidation only of surviving in situ masonry. This may involve the resetting of dry-laid masonry or the injection of compatible materials into mortar-laid walls.

In all these cases the obvious prerequisite is the careful

study remains by historical architects, including the preparation of preconservation drawings of remains, historical reconstruction drawings of structures, and a detailed method for implementing conservation procedure. Such drawings can be used both for scholarly publications and for site displays to supplement the conserved remains.

Whatever degree of consolidation, conservation, or restoration is adapted, specific technical/structural principles must be followed. The primary one is reversibility, which means that it must be possible to undo all consolidation procedures in case subsequent research indicates contrary procedures. Another is compatibility, which means that new materials introduced into the ancient architectural environment must be in structural balance with it. For example, the structural density of patching mortar has to match that of the masonry being patched, in order to prevent the introduction of stresses destructive to the ancient masonry. For professional results, it may be necessary to engage trained conservation architects and structural engineers to plan and oversee the work.

[*See also* Artifact Conservation; Field Conservation; Tourism and Archaeology. *In addition, many of the sites mentioned are the subject of independent entries.*]

BIBLIOGRAPHY

Cleere, Henry, ed. *Approaches to Archaeological Heritage: A Comparative Study of World Cultural Resource Management Systems.* Cambridge and New York, 1984.

Fagan, Brian. *In the Beginning: An Introduction to Archaeology.* 8th ed. New York, 1994. Chapter 19, "Management of the Past," gives a good overview of the role of conservation in cultural resource management.

Kanellopoulos, Chrysanthos. *The Great Temple of Amman: The Architecture.* Amman, 1995. An excellently illustrated and written example of the right way to conserve a building.

Renfrew, Colin and Paul Bahn. *Archaeology: Theories Methods and Practice.* London, 1991. Chapter 14, "Whose Past? Archaeology and the Public," gives an excellent treatment of the role of ethics in conservation.

BERT DE VRIES

CONSTANTINOPLE, capital of the eastern Roman empire built by Constantine I in 324 CE on the site of the ancient Greek colony Byzantion (41°02′ N, 28°57′ E) and inaugurated in 330. Situated on the Bosporus, Constantinople (modern Istanbul) controlled the entrance to the Black Sea and roads to the East and the West. The development of Constantinople in the early Byzantine centuries was rapid. It extended to the west without disrupting the layout of the ancient city (see figure 1). Constantine I built the Great Palace next to the Roman hippodrome and extended the central colonnaded avenue (known as *Mese*) to the west outside of the ancient walls. There was built the new circular forum of Constantine and the Capitolium at a distance of 1.2 km (.75 mi.). The first line of land fortifications was built by Constantine I and completed by Constantius II in 413. Theodosius II built the second line of walls 1.5 km (.9 mi.) to the west, 6 km (3.7 mi.) long with six gates. Parts of the latter survive. The sea walls along the Propontis and the Golden Horn were built in 439. A third line of fortifications 45 km (28 mi.) long was added by Anastasius at a distance of 65 km (40 mi.) from the city. It was abandoned in the seventh century. Constantine I built the churches of St. Irene (Peace) and the two *martyria* (shrines to martyrs) of St. Acacius and St. Mocius.

In the course of the fourth century, large-scale building construction secured provisions and water supply: to the two ancient harbors on the Golden Horn, the Julian harbor was added in 362 (later renamed Sophia), and the largest Theodosian harbor around 390 with a total length of 4.5 km (2.8 mi.). Several granaries were constructed near the harbors. The long aqueduct of Valens brought water from a distance of 100 km (62 mi.). In the area between the Constantinian and the Theodosian walls three huge open cisterns were built (of Aetius in 421, of Aspar in 459, and of St. Mocius by Anastasius) with a total capacity of 1,000,000 cu cm (59,319 cu. in.). Of the eighty covered cisterns the most impressive is the Basilike cistern (Yerebatan Sarayı) with 336 columns. The forum of Theodosius or Forum Tauri (c. 393) has a spiral-fluted column, two triumphal arches of which one survives, and a basilica copied from Trajan's forum in Rome. In the fifth century were built the forum of Arcadius (c. 403) with arches and a monumental column whose pedestal survives, and the Forum Bovis (after 425).

The next phase of Constantinople's development was marked by a great construction of churches. In the second half of the fifth century and in the early sixth century, large districts of the capital were destroyed by fires and civil riots, the most famous being the Nika revolt in 532. The great building activity of the emperor Justinian (527–565), expressing the spirit of the time focused on Christian structures, churches (thirty-three are mentioned), and philanthropic institutions (Procopius, *Buildings* 1). After the beginning of the seventh century construction in Constantinople ceased. The harbors were reduced to one quarter of their former size; of the five granaries only one survived. The system of water supply was neglected, and the fountains and public baths were closed. The size of the population declined dramatically. This development was a consequence of the unfortunate military circumstances and reduced economic conditions created by the loss of the eastern provinces and Egypt to the Arabs and by the invasion and permanent installation of the Slavs in most of the Balkan territories. In the ninth century Constantinople emerged as a clearly medieval city: there was no longer interest in public buildings other than palaces and churches.

Excavations at the Great Palace started after the fire of 1912–1913 burnt down the district southwest of St. Sophia

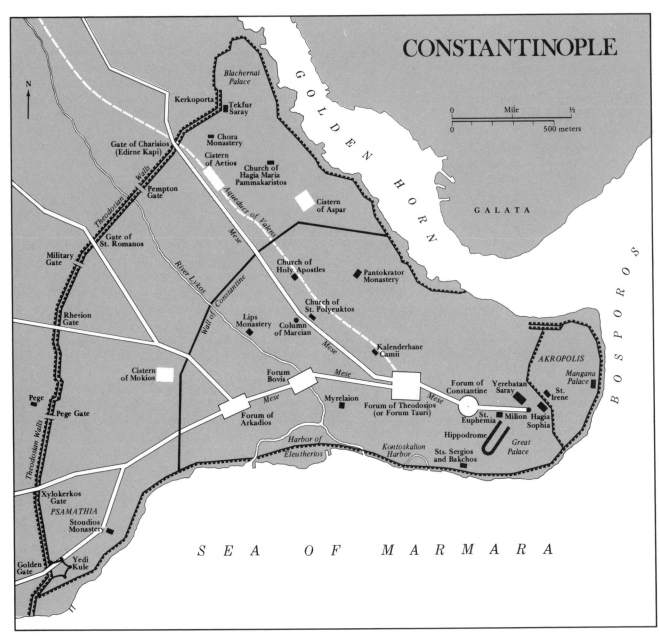

CONSTANTINOPLE.   Figure 1.   *Plan of the city.* (After A. Kazhdan, ed., *The Oxford Dictionary of Byzantium*, New York, 1991)

(1935–1938, 1952–1954). Most important are the remains of an apsed hall, in front of which a peristyle court (66 × 55 m [216.5 × 180 ft.]) is adorned with a magnificent, mosaic probably Justinianic. (Today, contrary to the government's restrictions, most of the area of the Great Palace is covered by new buildings.) The Roman hippodrome, to which Constantine I added an *exedra* (open recess frequently containing seats), was no longer used for athletic competitions but for imperial proclamations, triumphs, and other ceremonies. The *spina* (median) dividing the arena in

two parts was adorned with obelisks, statues, and other ornaments. In 1203 the west wing burned down, and in 1204 the Crusaders, who occupied Constantinople, melted the bronze statues and removed the four gilded horses to decorate the facade of S. Marco in Venice. The east wing of the hippodrome is preserved, and part of the west wing was excavated in 1952. Three of the monuments of the spina survive: the Egyptian obelisk of Thutmosis III (c. 1479–1425 BCE) on a marble basis with reliefs depicting the emperor attending the games (obelisk of Theodosius from 390); the serpent column, the central shaft of the Delphic tripod dedicated to Delphi after the battle of Plataea (479 BCE); the obelisk or colossus with an inscription of Constantine VII.

Two palaces of Byzantine magnates have been excavated. The palace of the *praepositus sacri cubiculi* (grand chamberlain) Antiochus was built around 410–420 CE and confiscated by the emperor about 420. Early in the sixth century its central hexagonal hall was transformed into the church of St. Euphemia. The palace of Lausus was built around 420–430; it included a famous collection of classical statues. After it burned in 476, a hospice was constructed on the same site.

The church of St. Sophia (Holy wisdom) was built near the Great Palace and the hippodrome by Constantius II, (which was inaugurated in 360). Burned by the supporters of the bishop of Constantinople, John Chrysostom, in 404, it was rebuilt by Theodosius II in 415. The colonnade of the facade of the atrium belongs to this period. Destroyed by fire during the Nika riot in 532, it was rebuilt by Justinian and dedicated 27 December 537. The technical problems that the architects Anthemius of Tralles and Isidorus of Miletus encountered in building this domed basilica and their solutions are described in Procopius's *Buildings* 1.1.21–78. The dome collapsed in 558, and it was rebuilt by Isidorus the Younger and rededicated on 24 December 562. The complexity of the architectural plan and the splendor of the mosaic and sculptural decoration are praised in the *ekphrasis* (rhetorical praise) by Paul Silentiarius (P. Friedländer, *Johannes von Gaza und Paulus Silentiarius: Kunstbschreibungen justinianischer Zeit*, Leipzig, 1912, pp. 227–265). The north baptistery survives. To the south was attached the patriarchal palace with offices for the ecclesiastical administration. To the southeast a passage led to the Great Palace.

The second largest church (domed basilica) that survives in Constantinople, the church of St. Irene, was perhaps built on the site of a pagan temple by Constantine I, and it was the cathedral until 360. Forming an architectural complex with St. Sophia, it shared a common administration. The lower part of the church belongs to the Justinianic restoration of 532. The basilica of the Holy Apostles built by Constantius II next to the mausoleum of Constantine I was rebuilt by Justinian in the shape of a cross imitating the plan of the church of St. John at Ephesus with a second mausoleum. The Byzantine emperors were buried there until 1028. The church was demolished and the mosque of Mehmed II Fatiḥ was built on the site. Several imperial sarcophagi are preserved. Of the monastic complex of Sts. Sergius and Bacchus only the church survives. It was built by Justinian and Theodora in the palace of Hormisdas, its octagonal nave inscribed in a rectangle with a dome. Founded before 454, the original three-aisled basilica of St. John Stoudios is partially preserved. The monastery with a renowned library and scriptorium became famous in the fight against the iconoclasts (end of the eight century). The church of St. Polyeuktos, which was built by Anicia Juliana between 524 and 527

on her estate (district of Constantianae, modern Saraçhane), was identified after blocks with the dedicatory epigram (known from the *Anthologia Graeca* 1.10) were discovered in 1960 (Cyril Mango and Ihor Ševčenko, "Remains of the Church of St. Polyeuktos at Constantinople, *Dumbarton Oaks Papers* 15 [1961]: 243–247). Part of the church and a baptistery are excavated. Their sculptural decoration is very elaborate. After it was abandoned in the twelfth century, the architectural ornaments were stolen (e.g., the Pilastri Acritani near the southwest corner of St. Mark's in Venice). Of the church of St. Mary of Chalkoprateia (the copper market), built by the empress Pulcheria or Verina, the apse and parts of the north and south walls survive.

[*See also* Byzantine Empire.]

BIBLIOGRAPHY

Literary sources include the *Notitia urbis Constantinopolitanae,* edited by Otto Seeck in *Notitia dignitatum,* pp. 229–243 (Berlin, 1876), a list of important monuments of Constantinople and account of the features of its urban fabric dating from circa 425. An account of the Justinianic buildings in Constantinople by the sixth-century historian Procopius, *Procopii Caesariensis opera omnia,* has been edited by Jakob Haury and Gerhard Wirth in volume 4 of *De aedificiis* (Leipzig, 1964). Texts on topography and monuments of Constantinople, with related legends, appear in Averil Cameron and Judith Herrin, eds., *Constantinople in the Early Eighth Century: The Parastaseis Syntomoi Chronikai* (Leiden, 1984). For additional research, see the following:

Dagron, Gilbert. *Naissance d'une capitale: Constantinople et ses institutions de 330 à 451.* Paris, 1974. The most authoritative work on the early history of Constantinople, with superb treatment of the literary sources.

Ebersolt, Jean. *Constantinople byzantine et les voyageurs du Levant.* Paris, 1918. Important source for identification of sites and monuments, with information from Western travelers in Constantinople.

Guilland, Rodolphe Joseph. *Études de topographie de Constantinople byzantine.* 2 vols. Berlin, 1969. Collection of studies on districts and particular monuments of Constantinople based primarily on literary evidence.

Harrison, R. Martin. *Excavations at Saraçhane in Istanbul.* 2 vols. Princeton, 1986. Detailed report of the excavations of the church of Saint Polyeuktos, with discussion of the excavated remains and analysis of the literary evidence.

Janin, Raymond. *Constantinople byzantine: Développement urbain et répertoire topographique.* 2d ed. Paris, 1964. Detailed study of Constantinople's topography, focusing primarily on the evidence of written sources, which are treated critically.

Janin, Raymond. *La géographie ecclésiastique de l'empire byzantin I: Le siège de Constantinople et le patriarcat oecuménique,* vol. 3, *Les églises et les monastéres.* 2d ed. Paris, 1969. Study of the churches and monasteries of Constantinople, with identification of the monuments and a detailed account of the sources.

Mamboury, Ernest. "Les fouilles byzantines á Istanbul." *Byzantion* 11 (1936): 229–283; 13 (1938): 301–310; 21 (1951): 425–459. History of the excavations in Istanbul from the nineteenth century to 1951.

Mango, Cyril. *Studies on Constantinople.* Aldershot, 1993. Selection of studies on the development of Constantinople and its monuments.

Mango, Cyril, and Gilbert Dagron, eds. *Constantinople and Its Hinterland. Papers from the Twenty-seventh Spring Symposium of Byzantine Studies, Oxford, April 1993.* Aldershot, 1995.

Müller-Wiener, Wolfgang. *Bildlexikon zur Topographie Istanbuls: Byzantion-Konstantinupolis-Istanbul bis zum Beginn des 17. Jahrhunderts.* Tübingen, 1977. Lavishly illustrated lexicon of the topography of

Constantinople with a description of the monuments, reference to their history, information of travelers, modern excavations, and bibliography.

Stamatopoulos, Kostas, and Akylas Mellas. *Constantinople: Seeking the Ruling City* (in Greek). Athens, 1990. Contains excellent photographs of surviving buildings and monuments.

HELEN SARADI

COPPER SCROLL. The manuscript designated 3Q15, the *Copper Scroll*, was discovered in a cave near Qumran, on the shore of the Dead Sea, on 20 March 1952 by a joint expedition of the École Biblique, the American School of Oriental Research, and Jordan's Department of Antiquities. The scroll contains a list of buried treasure, engraved in Hebrew on thin copper sheets. The sheets were found rolled and so thoroughly oxidized they crumbled to the touch (see figure 1). In 1955–1956, the scroll was opened at the Manchester College of Technology by H. Wright Baker, professor of mechanical engineering, who sawed it into twenty-three segments using an electric circular slitting saw. The nature of the scroll's contents was made public in a press release on 1 June 1956, but the official edition of the Hebrew text, accompanied by a French translation and extensive commentary by J. T. Milik, a Polish member of the international team assembled to edit the Dead Sea Scrolls, was not published until 1962. In the interim, John M. Allegro, a British member of the team, who had supervised the cutting open of the scroll, had published an edition and an English translation of his own in 1960 and had organized unsuccessful attempts to find the buried treasure.

In many ways, the *Copper Scroll* is unique among the Dead Sea Scrolls. It is distinct not only in its subject matter and in the material on which it is written, but also in its script, orthography, language, and literary structure. Moreover, it is the only one of the documents found near Qumran that appears to be an autograph, an original manuscript, rather than a copy.

The text of the *Copper Scroll* breaks down into sixty-four short sections, each typically containing the description of a hiding place and the treasure hidden in it. Enigmatic greek letters appear at the end of sections 1, 4, 6, 7, and 10. The first section establishes the pattern for the text: "In the ruins which are in the Valley of Achor, under the steps which go eastward, forty rod-cubits: a strongbox of silver and its vessels—a weight of seventeen talents." Most of the identifiable hiding places are located in or near Jerusalem, and the treasures usually consist of a specified number of talents of silver and gold, and sometimes other valuable items such as scrolls and cultic vessels or vestments. Section 64 states that a duplicate of the *Copper Scroll*, "and its explanation" (*wprwš*) is included in the last treasure. If the numbers in the treasure descriptions are to be taken at face value, the total weight of the buried treasure is in excess of 200 tons.

Scholarship on the *Copper Scroll* has been sharply divided on two pivotal issues of interpretation: its authenticity and its date. Allegro and others have argued that 3Q15 is an authentic record of buried treasure and is to be dated to around 68 CE, when it was hidden near Qumran together with the other scrolls. Milik and others have claimed that it is a fiction, that it is to be dated well after 68 CE, and that it

COPPER SCROLL.   Figure 1.   *The Copper Scroll, in situ.* (Courtesy ASOR Archives)

has nothing to do with the other scrolls. Still others, like Frank M. Cross, have followed the original press release of 1956 in suggesting that the Copper Scroll, while not describing real treasure, does belong in date with the other scrolls. Finally, we have those, like E. M. Laperrousaz and B. Z. Luria, who accept the authenticity of 3Q15 but date it to the time of the Second Jewish Revolt in 135 CE.

Although there are significant difficulties with each of these positions, it is likely that the majority of scholars are correct in accepting the authenticity of the *Copper Scroll*. (It is possible that the mysterious "explanation" mentioned in the last of the sixty-four sections might be the key to interpreting the improbably high numbers in the treasure descriptions, as well as the puzzling Greek letters.) Furthermore, the archaeological evidence reported by Bargil Pixner suggests that the *Copper Scroll* was hidden at the same time as the manuscript fragments found in the same archaeological context.

If the treasure was real, it almost certainly belonged to the fabled wealth of the Jerusalem Temple and was hidden shortly before the destruction of Jerusalem by the Romans in 70 CE. A connection with the Temple may also be indicated by the high incidence of cultic terms used in the scroll. It is even possible, as Norman Golb has suggested, that 3Q15 had nothing to do with sectarians at Qumran but should be explained simply as a Temple document.

Apart from its possible historical value, the *Copper Scroll* is also significant for the history of the Hebrew language. In morphology, syntax, and vocabulary, the language of the *Copper Scroll* shares with Mishnaic Hebrew linguistic features that distinguish the latter from the Hebrew of the Bible and the other Dead Sea Scrolls. This suggests that a Hebrew dialect similar to Mishnaic Hebrew was spoken in Palestine in the first century CE.

[*See also* Dead Sea Scrolls; Qumran.]

BIBLIOGRAPHY

Allegro, John Marco. *The Treasure of the Copper Scroll*. Garden City, N.Y., 1960. Racy account of the discovery and contents of the *Copper Scroll*, with an imperfect preliminary edition of the Hebrew text and its English translation.

Baker, H. Wright. "Notes on the Opening of the 'Bronze' Scrolls from Qumran." *Bulletin of the John Rylands Library* 39 (1956–1957): 45–56. Contains the text of the 1956 press release.

Golb, Norman. "The Problem of Origin and Identification of the Dead Sea Scrolls." *Proceedings of the American Philosophical Society* 124.1 (1980): 1–24. As an autograph record of real Temple treasures, the *Copper Scroll* provides prime evidence for Golb's theory that the Dead Sea Scrolls come from Jerusalem. See especially pages 5–8.

McCarter, P. Kyle, Jr. "The Copper Scroll Treasure as an Accumulation of Religious Offerings." In *Methods of Investigation of the Dead Sea Scrolls and the Khirbet Qumran Site: Present Realities and Future Prospects*, edited by Michael O. Wise et al., pp. 133–142. Annals of the New York Academy of Sciences, vol. 722. New York, 1994.

Milik, J. T. "Le rouleau de cuivre provenant de la grotte 3Q (3Q15)." In *Les "petites grottes" de Qumrân*, pp. 199–302. Discoveries in the Judaean Desert of Jordan, vol. 3. Oxford, 1962. Standard scholarly edition of the *Copper Scroll*.

Pixner, Bargil. "Unravelling the Copper Scroll Code: A Study of the Topography of 3Q15." *Revue de Qumran* 11.3 (1983): 323–366. An attempt to identify a geographic pattern for the hiding places cited in the *Copper Scroll*, valuable for its archaeological information (pp. 327–329, 334–335), extensive bibliography, and independent English translation.

Wolters, Al. "Apocalyptic and the Copper Scroll." *Journal of Near Eastern Studies* 49.2 (1990): 145–154. Critique of the legendary interpretation of the *Copper Scroll*.

Wolters, Al. "The *Copper Scroll* and the Vocabulary of Mishnaic Hebrew." *Revue de Qumran* 14.3 (1990): 483–495. Identification of fifty lexical items the *Copper Scroll* shares with Mishnaic Hebrew, as distinct from biblical Hebrew.

Wolters, Al. "History and the Copper Scroll." In *Methods of Investigation of the Dead Sea Scrolls and the Khirbet Qumran Site: Present Realities and Future Prospects*, edited by Michael O. Wise et al., pp. 285–295. Annals of the New York Academy of Sciences, vol. 722. New York, 1994.

AL WOLTERS

COPTIC. The latest form of the Egyptian language, Coptic was used from the third century CE onward. The origin of Coptic was concurrent with the rise of Christianity in Egypt and the term *Coptic* is often also applied to the Christian inhabitants of Egypt, their church, and their culture. Coptic remained in use as a language of daily life as late as the twelfth century, although Arabic had already begun to supplant Coptic as early as the ninth century. Coptic as a literary language was moribund by the fifteenth century but was never entirely replaced by Arabic and is still used as a liturgical language.

Coptic and earlier forms of Egyptian constitute a special language group that falls into the Afroasiatic language family. Coptic is very similar to its immediate predecessors, Demotic and Late Egyptian, which favored external marking of forms over the internal changes common in Old and Middle Egyptian. The vocalization of Coptic is more certain than that of its predecessors but is still largely theoretical; the modern pronunciation of liturgical Coptic is heavily influenced by Arabic and is of little use for reconstructing Coptic phonology. Coptic was the only form of Egyptian to indicate vowels and thus the only form in which morphology can be known with certainty. In general, Coptic is characterized by consonantal clusters (especially at the beginnings of words) and doubled vowels in certain contexts; vowelless syllables were marked by a superlinear stroke.

Syntactically Coptic developed many features of Demotic and Late Egyptian. Coptic used nominal, verbal, and adverbial clauses, which were paralleled by nominal, verbal, and adverbial uses of words and phrases. Nouns distinguished number and gender, which were morphologically marked in some cases but usually indicated by articles; case was indicated by sentence position or prepositions. The system of independent, prefix, and suffix pronouns extended and streamlined Demotic and Late Egyptian usage. Adjectives were almost entirely replaced in Coptic by adjective verbs or the attributive use of nouns. The different forms of the verbal infinitive and stative (or qualitative) were often morphologically differentiated; verbs could be conjugated and marked for tense by prefixed conjugation bases or preceded by subject and other markers. As in Demotic, adverbials were usually prepositional phrases placed at the end of a clause. Both verbal and nonverbal clauses could be further marked by converters for preterite, circumstantial, or relative meaning; another converter was the "second tense" marker, which was used to emphasize an adjunct. Negation was accomplished by negative particles, conjugation bases, or infixes (bound morphemes inserted into words), and passive voice was indicated by an impersonal use of the third person plural.

Although Coptic is morphologically and syntactically a direct descendant of Demotic, it marks a radical break in terms of script. Coptic was written with an alphabet of thirty letters (thirty-one in some dialects), twenty-four of which are Greek letters. The remaining letters are derived from Demotic signs. Unlike the Demotic system of ideographic and phonetic characters, the Coptic alphabet included vowels and was much simpler to write and read. It also lacked pagan associations, which made it attractive to the early Christians. Given the importance of Greek in Egypt during the development of Coptic, it is not surprising that Coptic vocabulary derived from both Egyptian and Greek words. Greek terms in Coptic were primarily theological, administrative, or technical; they were treated grammatically as Coptic and were not inflected (except for a few set expressions). A limited number of Latin and Semitic words came into Coptic indirectly through Greek transcription, and later Coptic texts sometimes include transcriptions of Arabic names and words.

Scholars have identified at least ten major dialects of Coptic, with many additional subdialects. Scarcity of evidence makes the earliest dialect history of Coptic uncertain. The main dialect from about the fourth to the eleventh century was Sahidic, in which most early Coptic literary texts were written. Exceptions were mostly regional: the Bohairic dialect prevailed in parts of northern Egypt, and Faiyumic, Akhmimic, and Lycopolitan (among others) are named after their regions of origin in central and southern Egypt. The language of nonliterary texts was highly variable and reflected the dialect geography of Coptic. Most dialects died out by the ninth century, but Bohairic survived and replaced all other dialects. Bohairic remains the dialect of liturgical texts in Coptic to the present.

Although the earliest occurrences of Coptic are in pagan texts, Coptic was ultimately the language of Christianity in Egypt. The earliest Christian writings in Coptic were translations of Greek originals for Egyptians: the New Testament, the Septuagint, apocryphal and patristic works. Early Coptic translations also include important Gnostic and Manichaean texts, including the Nag Hammadi codices, the *Pistis Sophia*, and the Manichaean *Kephalaia*. Original compositions in Coptic are known after the third century. The fifth-century abbot Shenoute, the most important author whose works were originally written in Coptic and not Greek, was one of the earliest writers to treat Coptic as a vehicle for literary expression. Later Coptic authors and translators were highly prolific, resulting in a large body of original compositions, adaptations and translations of a wide range of literature. Saints' lives, homilies, and martyrdoms were popular among monastic audiences, and an extensive body of liturgical texts served the needs of the church. Historiography was limited mostly to church histories, although there are fragments of chronologies and historical "romances." Coptic poetry is attested in a number of forms, culminating in a lengthy poem called the *Triadon*. The decline of Coptic led to the compilation of Coptic-Arabic vocabulary lists known as *scalae*, as well as Arabic grammars of Coptic. Magical texts that combine elements of paganism and Christianity are well attested in Coptic, as are medical, alchemical, astronomical and other scientific writings. Coptic epigraphic texts (mostly stelae and graffiti) and documentary texts (including letters, legal documents, and accounts) are important sources for the economic and social history of Late Antique Egypt. Coptic texts of all genres are essential sources for Christianity and the Christian Community in Egypt.

BIBLIOGRAPHY

Crum, Walter E. *A Coptic Dictionary.* Oxford, 1939. Standard source for Coptic morphology and vocabulary.

Emmel, Stephen. "Nag Hammadi Library." In *The Coptic Encyclopedia*, vol. 6, pp. 1771–1773. New York, 1991.

Frandsen, Paul John and Eva Richte-Ærøe. "Shenoute: A Bibliography." In *Studies Presented to Hans Jakob Polotsky*, edited by Dwight W. Young, pp. 147–176. East Gloucester, Mass., 1981.

Kasser, Rodolphe, ed. "Appendix: Linguistics." In *The Coptic Encyclopedia*, vol. 8, pp. 13–227. New York, 1991. Important, up-to-date survey of Coptic language, especially good for its survey of dialects. Volumes 1–7 of the encyclopedia also contain useful articles on Coptic literature.

Lambdin, Thomas O. *Introduction to Sahidic Coptic.* Macon, Ga., 1983. Standard teaching grammar.

Mallon, Alexis. *Grammaire copte.* 4th ed. Beirut, 1956. Standard grammar for Bohairic dialect of Coptic.

Meyer, Marvin, and Richard Smith. *Ancient Christian Magic: Coptic Texts of Ritual Power.* San Francisco, 1994. Anthology of Coptic magical texts in translation.

Orlandi, Tito. *Coptic Bibliography.* Rome, 1985–. Annually updated bibliography of Coptic studies, especially thorough for language and literature.

Orlandi, Tito. "Literature, Coptic." In *The Coptic Encyclopedia*, vol. 5, pp. 1450–1459. New York, 1991.

Polotsky, Hans Jakob. "Coptic." In *Current Trends in Linguistics*, vol. 6, *Linguistics in South West Asia and North Africa*, edited by Charles A. Ferguson et al., pp. 558–570. The Hague, 1970. Republished in *Afroasiatic: A Survey*, edited by Carleton T. Hodge. The Hague, 1971. General guide to scholarship on the Coptic language.

Robinson, James M., ed. *The Nag Hammadi Library in English.* 3d ed.

New York, 1990. Standard English translation of the Nag Hammadi codices.

Shisha-Halevy, Ariel. *Coptic Grammatical Chrestomathy: A Course for Academic and Private Study.* Orientalia Lovaniensia Analecta, vol. 30. Louvain, 1988. Excellent teaching chrestomathy for Coptic, based on the writings of Shenoute, and a thorough guide to literature on specific aspects of Coptic grammar.

Till, Walter C. "Coptic and Its Value." *Bulletin of the John Rylands Library* 40 (1957): 229–258.

Timbie, Janet. "The State of Research on the Career of Shenoute of Atripe." In *The Roots of Egyptian Christianity*, edited by Birger A. Pearson and James E. Goehring, pp. 258–270. Studies in Antiquity and Christianity, 1. Philadelphia, 1986.

TERRY G. WILFONG

CORBO, VIRGILIO C.

CORBO, VIRGILIO C. (1918–1991), Franciscan priest, teacher, and archaeologist who excavated in the Holy Land: at Jerusalem, Herodium, Magdala, Daburiya, Machaerus, Capernaum, and in the Church of the Holy Sepulcher. After obtaining a degree in Oriental sciences in Rome, Corbo spent his life in the Holy Land. Among his personal discoveries were a number of monasteries in the Judean Desert and St. Peter's house at Capernaum. These monuments were known only through ancient literary sources. It is as a result of his research and archaeological excavations that the location of these sites has been determined. For each site he published a final report; although they are not rich in bibliographic data, they are extremely meticulous. His findings contributed considerably to a better understanding of the structural, historical, and environmental character of the places he excavated.

[*See also* Capernaum; Franciscan Custody of the Holy Land; Herodium; Jerusalem; Machaerus; *and* Magdala.]

BIBLIOGRAPHY

Bottini, Giovanni Claudio, et al., eds. *Christian Archaeology in the Holy Land, New Discoveries: Essays in Honour of Virgilio C. Corbo.* Studium Biblicum Franciscanum (SBF), Collectio Maior, 36. Jerusalem, 1990. Includes a bibliography of Corbo's work.

Bottini, Giovanni Claudio. "In memoriam: Virgilio C. Corbo, ofm, 1918–1991." *Studium Biblicum Franciscanum/Liber Annuus* 41 (1991): 616–625. Includes a bibliography.

Bottini, Giovanni Claudio, ed. *Padre Virgilio C. Corbo: Una vita in Terra Santa.* SBF, Museum, 12. Jerusalem, 1994. Includes a bibliography of Corbo's work.

Corbo, Virgilio. *Gli scavi di Khirbet Siyar el-Ghanam (Campo dei Pastori) e i monasteri dei dintorni.* SBF, Collectio Maior, 11. Jerusalem, 1955.

Corbo, Virgilio. "L'ambiente materiale della vita dei monaci di Palestina nel periodo bizantino." In *Il monachesimo orientale: Atti del convegno di studi orientali, Roma, 9–12 aprile 1958*, pp. 235–257. Orientalia Christiana Analecta, 153. Rome, 1958.

Corbo, Virgilio. *Ricerche archeologiche al Monte degli Ulivi.* SBF, Collectio Maior, 16. Jerusalem, 1965.

Corbo, Virgilio. *The House of St. Peter at Capharnaum: A Preliminary Report of the First Two Campaigns of Excavations, April 16–June 19/ September 12–November 26, 1968.* SBF, Collectio Minor, 5. Jerusalem, 1969.

Corbo, Virgilio, et al. *La sinagoga di Cafarnao dopo gli scavi del 1969.* SBF, Collectio Minor, 9. Jerusalem, 1970.

Corbo, Virgilio. *Cafarnao*, vol. 1, *Gli edifici della città.* SBF, Collectio Minor, 19. Jerusalem, 1975.

Corbo, Virgilio. "La fortezza di Macheronte: Rapporto preliminare della campagna di scavo, 8.09–28.10.1978." *Studium Biblicum Franciscanum/Liber Annuus* 28 (1978): 217–231.

Corbo, Virgilio. "Macheronte, la reggia-fortezza erodiana: Rapporto preliminare alla II campagna di scavo, 3.09–20.10.1979." *Studium Biblicum Franciscanum/Liber Annuus* 29 (1979): 315–326.

Corbo, Virgilio. "La fortezza di Macheronte (al Mishnaqa): Rapporto preliminare alla III campagna di scavo, 8.09–11.10.1980." *Studium Biblicum Franciscanum/Liber Annuus* 30 (1980): 365–376.

Corbo, Virgilio, and Stanislao Loffreda. "Nuove scoperte alla fortezza di Macheronte: Rapporto preliminare alla IV campagna di scavo, 7.09–10.10.1981." *Studium Biblicum Franciscanum/Liber Annuus* 31 (1981): 257–286.

Corbo, Virgilio. *Il Santo Sepolcro di Gerusalemme: Aspetti archeologici dalle origini al periodo crociato.* SBF, Collectio Maior, 29. Jerusalem, 1982. Includes an English summary by Stanislao Loffreda.

Corbo, Virgilio. *Herodion*, vol. 1, *Gli edifici della reggia-fortezza.* SBF, Collectio Maior, 20. Jerusalem, 1989.

Murphy-O'Connor, Jerome. "Review of Christian Archaeology in the Holy Land: New Discoveries." *Revue Biblique* 88 (1993): 615–617. Also appeared in *Biblical Archaeology Review* 19 (1993): 3–4.

GIOVANNI CLAUDIO BOTTINI

COSMETICS

COSMETICS. In the ancient Near East the popular use of cosmetics began with the dawn of civilization and later spread westward, to Greece and then to Rome. Until the advent of Christianity cosmetics were extremely popular, at times even used to excess. Christian thought, which stressed the life of the spirit while rejecting bodily pleasures, led to a decline in the demand for cosmetics and perfumes, although in the East the Arabs continued to enjoy them.

In antiquity, cosmetics first served magicoreligious and healing purposes. To propitiate the gods, cosmetics were applied to their statues and to the faces of their attendants. From this, in the course of time, the custom of personal use developed, to enhance the beauty of the face and to conceal defects.

The most extensive information on personal hygiene and cosmetics in the third and second millennia BCE comes from Egypt. Written and pictorial depictions, as well as rich archaeological finds, all show how important body care and aesthetic appearance were in the lives of the Egyptian aristocracy. For example, bathing for pleasure was a common practice in Egypt, while among other peoples of the ancient Near East it was limited mainly to religious requirements—although it also had hygienic associations. [*See* Baths; Personal Hygiene.] The use of oils and ointments was prevalent in order to protect the face and body from sun, dust, and dryness. These perfumed oils and ointments were not regarded as luxuries and were used by men and women in all strata of the population. It is known that during the reign of Rameses III, the gravediggers of Thebes went on strike to protest a decline in the quality of the food and the quantity of the oils supplied to them.

The Hebrews used ointment in the Temple in Jerusalem and in coronation ceremonies, as recorded in the description of the anointing of David (1 *Sm.* 16:13). The Bible makes no mention of other uses of cosmetics during the First Temple period, but there is evidence of their use for secular purposes in the Second Temple period. Over time, this custom presumably became quite commonplace: in the Talmud it is said that a husband is obliged to give his wife ten dinars for her cosmetic needs (B.T., *Ket.* 66b).

Cosmetic preparations included powders, ointments, perfumes, and fragrant oils, which were produced from various plants and resins mixed with vegetable oil or animal fat. Because of their high price, all these cosmetic substances were marketed in small quantities. This led to the development of an entire industry for the manufacture of tiny containers that became beautifully fashioned luxury articles in their own right. The containers were made of such materials as stone and alabaster, which kept their contents cool. In Egypt, most containers were made of stone, whereas in Greece and Rome they were made of exquisitely painted pottery. When the technique of glassblowing developed in the first century BCE, the perfume industry immediately adopted this lightweight and impermeable material for making perfume containers.

Many perfume containers have been found in tombs, where they were funerary offerings—gifts to the dead or buried with them as cherished personal belongings. The large quantities of perfume bottles found indicate that they were also brought in to freshen the air in the tombs during burial (*Mk.* 16:1; *Jn.* 19:39–40).

Great importance was attached to the care of the hair in antiquity. Long hair has always been considered a mark of beauty, and kings, nobles, and dignitaries grew their hair long and kept it well groomed. Ordinary people and slaves usually wore their hair short, primarily for hygienic reasons: they could not afford to invest in the kind of care that long hair required. The art of hairstyling and hair care reached its apogee during the Roman period, as can be observed from the numerous heads of statues that have survived from that time.

Very early evidence of the use of facial makeup is available from ancient Egypt: cosmetic utensils and materials, numerous written records, and artistic depictions of the subject. The eyes played a central part in facial makeup. Painting the eyes, besides being part of magicoreligious ritual, also served a medical purpose: it protected against eye diseases. Eye paint repelled the little flies that transmitted eye inflammations, prevented the delicate skin around the eyes from drying, and sheltered the eyes from the glare of the desert sun. When Egyptian women realized that the painted frame also emphasized the eyes and made them appear larger, they began using makeup to enhance their beauty. Egyptian women used to paint their upper eyelids and eyebrows black and the lower line of the eye green. They also rouged their lips and cheeks, coloring their face dark red with hematite and red ocher. The Babylonians, too, used red ocher for facial makeup, but the Sumerians preferred yellow (Dayagi-Mendels, 1989, pp. 36–37). The Babylonians painted their faces with vermilion and white lead and their eyes with kohl (*qukhlu;* see R. J. Forbes, *Studies in Ancient Technology,* vol. 3, Leiden, 1965, p. 18).

Whereas the purpose of makeup was to embellish the face and emphasize its features, ointments were used to soften and protect the skin, to preserve its freshness, and rejuvenate its appearance. Ointments were prepared from vegetable oils or animal fat, at times in combination with aromatic resin or perfumed beeswax. An Egyptian papyrus from the sixteenth century BCE contains detailed recipes for ointments to remove blemishes, wrinkles, and other signs of age. Almost nothing is known of the makeup practices among Hebrew women during the Israelite period. However, there is no reason to doubt that making up the face was customary in Israel, mainly because of the many implements and accessories found in excavations, whose shapes attest that they were used for makeup.

The use of kohl for painting the eyes is mentioned three times in the Bible, always with disapprobation (2 *Kgs.* 9:30; *Jer.* 23:40; *Jb.* 42:14). By the Second Temple period, makeup was considered part of a woman's adornment (B.T., *Mo'ed Q.* 9b). Jewish sources distinguish between makeup used for therapeutic purposes and makeup meant merely to embellish the eyes. It was customary to put light-red makeup on the cheeks, and the Mishnah mentions a white cosmetic powder made of flour (*Pes.* 3:1).

In Greece and Rome, facial treatment was very highly developed and women devoted hours to it (Dio Chrysostom, 7.117). They used to spread various creams on the face and apply makeup in vivid and contrasting colors. Greek women would cover their face with a "beauty mask" that consisted mainly of flour, leaving it on all night. The next morning, they would wash it off with milk. This mask was intended to remove blemishes and to endow the skin with a smooth and fresh appearance, ready to receive makeup.

Creating and manufacturing cosmetics and perfumes have always been important and intriguing occupations. People working in this field had to be endowed not only with skill and knowledge, but also with a memory for fragrances and an ability to identify them and to distinguish their combinations. Perfumers in antiquity guarded the secrets of their trade closely, passing on their skills from father to son. The Bible mentions various plants from whose flowers, fruits, leaves, bark, or resin perfumes and ointments were produced (aloe, myrrh, frankincense). Although there is much to be learned in ancient sources about the uses of perfumes, very few describe methods of preparation. Tablets from the second millennium BCE found in Pylos, Greece, list the allocation of raw materials for perfumes but contain no precise recipes. More extensive literary information about perfume production has come down from various classical sources (Theophrastus, Dioscorides, Pliny). The equipment required for perfume manufacture was similar to that in an ordinary kitchen: basins, small pots for steeping and mixing, large jars for storing the oil, and juglets for storing resin.

As perfumes and spices were considered a precious commodity, they were stored with silver and gold. It is recounted in the Bible that when King Hezekiah of Judah received royal guests from Babylon, "he showed them all his treasure house, the silver, and the gold, and the spices, the precious ointment" (*2 Kgs.* 20:13). Classical sources emphasize the widespread use of perfumes in sixth-century BCE Greece, as well as their central place in cultural and social life. Perfumeries functioned as meeting places for all strata of the population (Athenaeus, 12.526A; Xenophon, *Conviv.* 2.3). Philosophers, statesmen, artists, and writers who wished to discuss matters of state would gather in such establishments, and their presence attracted others. Some, however, frowned on such self-indulgence: the renowned fifth-century BCE Athenian statesman Solon prohibited the sale of perfumes and ointments in his state, and the Spartans banished the perfumers from their city. The most lavish consumers of perfumes were the Romans, who perfumed each part of their body with a different scent, sprinkled perfume on their guests at banquets, and even perfumed the walls of their bathrooms. In the houses of the wealthy, beds and banquet couches were filled with fragrant dried flowers. Pliny criticized this excessive and wasteful use of scent, commenting that, despite their costliness—sometimes more than 400 denarii an ounce—perfumes gave pleasure only to others because the user cannot smell them (*Nat. Hist.* 13.20–22).

Perfumes were also commonly used in Palestine during the Second Temple period, and not only among women. The Talmud mentions the priests of the Abtinas family, who maintained a monopoly preparing incense for the Temple. The family refused to let others share in the knowledge of their craft, fearing it might be used for profane purposes. Also, to prevent suspicion that they might be exploiting their skills profanely, their wives were forbidden to use scent, even when they were brides (B.T., *Yoma'* 38a). It is also recorded that perfumers took strict precautions to protect the secrets of their craft and to prevent imitations. Perfumes were sold in shops located in the market, which was often a meeting place for harlots, who used especially large quantities of perfumes (*Shemoth Rabbah* 43:7).

The plants and resins used in producing perfume had to be imported from distant lands, mainly southern Arabia and the Far East. To facilitate their transport, extensive trading networks developed, and the countries the caravan routes traversed enjoyed great economic prosperity as a result. Major land and sea routes led to all the great trading centers in the ancient world. In Palestine the Nabateans functioned as middlemen in the perfume and spice trade. The country played an important role in the overland transportation of those luxury goods to the Mediterranean coast and to the West.

BIBLIOGRAPHY

Abbadie, Jeanne Vandier d'. *Les objets de toilette égyptiens au Musée du Louvre.* Paris, 1972.
Dayagi-Mendels, Michal. *Perfumes and Cosmetics in the Ancient World.* Israel Museum Catalogue, 305. Jerusalem, 1989.
Egypt's Golden Age: The Art of Living in the New Kingdom, 1558–1085 B.C.: Catalogue of the Exhibition. Boston, 1982. See pages 184–227.
Faure, Paul. *Parfums et aromates de l'antiquité.* Paris, 1987.
Paszthory, Emmerich. "Salben, Schminken und Parfüme im Altertum." *Antike Welt* 21 (1990): 1–64.

MICHAL DAYAGI-MENDELS

COUNCIL OF AMERICAN OVERSEAS RESEARCH CENTERS.

Established by the U.S. Congress in 1981, the Council of American Overseas Research Centers (CAORC) is housed in the Smithsonian Institution, with which it is directly affiliated and through which its limited budget for staff is funded. Originally eleven members, and in the mid-1990s fourteen, CAORC's original mandate was to speak with a unified voice in petitioning the government for funds; to act a resource base and clearinghouse for ideas and for other funding; to facilitate and promote overseas research centers; to clarify the role of research centers in enabling cultural exchange, academic programs, and field projects across national boundaries; to promote area studies as a viable discipline; and, where appropriate, to establish new centers. The three centers of the American Schools of Oriental Research (ASOR)—in Jerusalem, Amman, and Nicosia—were among the founding group of eleven.

All of the member centers were formed in response to American interest in fostering primary research in the host country. Their interests are mainly in the humanities and social sciences, though some centers have a keener interest in the natural and technological sciences, which is especially appropriate where archaeology is pursued. CAORC's primary vehicle for promoting scholarly exchange is fellowships for pre- and postdoctoral scholars and senior scholars. Research at the centers is normally devoted to studying either the particular host culture or that of an adjacent region. Most centers were established as consortia of universities in the United States and are governed by the member institutions. Each is independently incorporated as a private, not-for-profit organization. One of CAORC's important roles is to bring together the centers' leadership to exchange scholarly ideas, share management experience, and seek support from government agencies.

In addition to the ASOR group of three centers, CAORC acts as the umbrella for maintaining ties to the following organizations where research pertains to the Near East: the

American Institute for Yemeni Studies, American Institute of Iranian Studies, American Research Center in Egypt, American Research Institute in Turkey, American Academy in Rome, and American School of Classical Studies at Athens. CAORC publishes occasional monographs and papers. It is housed at the Smithsonian Institution in Washington, D.C.

[*See also* American Institute for Yemeni Studies; American Institute of Iranian Studies; American Research Center in Egypt; American Research Institute in Turkey; *and* American Schools of Oriental Research.]

ERIC M. MEYERS

CRESWELL, KEPPEL ARCHIBALD CAMERON (1879–1974), prominent British archaeologist who specialized in Islamic architecture. Creswell was educated at Westminister College in London and began studying Islamic architecture in 1910. He first traveled to the Near East while serving in the Royal Air Corps during World War I. After the war he was assigned to conduct a survey of the monuments in Syria and Palestine. When this was completed, he launched a project to study the history of Muslim architecture in Egypt. In 1931, he was appointed to the faculty of the Egyptian University in Cairo, where he founded and directed the Institute of Muslim Art and Archaeology. In 1956, as a result of the Suez Canal crisis, all British citizens were to be exiled and forced to leave their possessions behind. Creswell, then 75 years old, refused to leave Egypt and his extensive library; he took refuge at the American University in Cairo, where he served as Distinguished Professor and Chair of Muslim Architecture until his death in 1974. His personal library, now known as the Creswell Library of Islamic Art and Architecture, still houses one of the most extensive collections on the subject in the world. His publishing record, which includes several bibliographies of Islamic art and architecture, reflects his passion for the subject and is an invaluable resource for archaeologists. Creswell is best known for his two-volume work *Early Muslim Architecture* (1932–1940), which serves as compendium of the subject. He later condensed and updated his magnum opus as *A Short Account of Early Muslim Architecture* (1989).

BIBLIOGRAPHY

Burns, Kristie. "Cairo's Creswell Collection: A Legacy of Love." *American Libraries* 22 (1990): 940–944. A look at Creswell's life and the establishment of a research library from his personal library.

Creswell, K. A. C. *Early Muslim Architecture.* 2 vols. Oxford, 1932–1940.

Creswell, K. A. C. *A Bibliography of the Architecture, Arts, and Crafts of Islam to 1st Jan. 1960.* Cairo, 1961.

Creswell, K. A. C. *A Bibliography of the Architecture, Arts, and Crafts of Islam: Supplement, Jan. 1960 to Jan. 1972.* Cairo, 1973.

Creswell, K. A. C. *A Short Account of Early Muslim Architecture* (1958). Revised and supplemented by James W. Allan. Aldershot, 1989.

"Creswell, K. A. C." In *Contemporary Authors: Permanent Series,* vol. 1, pp. 147–148. Detroit, 1975. Summary of Creswell's life and work, with a valuable bibliography.

Geddes, Charles L., et al. *Studies in Islamic Art and Architecture in Honour of K. A. C. Creswell.* Cairo, 1965. Festschrift that includes an overview of Creswell's contribution to the field and a valuable bibliography.

Grabar, Oleg, ed. *Muqarnas: An Annual on Islamic Art and Architecture.* Vol. 8, *K. A. C. Creswell and His Legacy.* Leiden, 1991. A collection of papers given at a symposium at Oxford University, which focuses upon Creswell's contribution to the field and includes a short biography.

JOHN D. WINELAND

CRETE. The largest island in the Aegean Sea, Crete is 260 km (about 161 mi.) from east to west. The island is diverse in its geography, with high and rugged mountains, fertile plains, and many low hills that were suitable for flocks and herds as well as agriculture. The climate is Mediterranean, with dry, hot summers and cool winters.

Neolithic Period. The first settlers in Crete arrived in the Early Neolithic period, possibly even before pottery was being used. The earliest pottery on the island, from the second level above sterile soil at Knossos, has affinities with Anatolia. In the subsequent development of the island, this pattern of contacts with the East would never be broken for long: the history of Crete always included a give-and-take with the cultures of West Asia.

The Neolithic period was a time of slow development. Animal husbandry and agriculture were established as the society's economic base, and they would remain such throughout antiquity. By the end of the period, the island was sparsely settled from one end to the other. Contact with the more eastern regions was never close during this time, but it was frequent enough for Crete to benefit from new discoveries, such as better kilns for pottery. A few new settlers seem to have arrived from time to time, especially toward the end of the period.

The earliest phase of the culture known as Minoan is called the Final Neolithic. It must begin well before 4000 BCE, but its dates are far from secure. The phase is first recognized by the beginning of several new cultural traits, probably signaling the immigration of new people into the island. The most important trait for tracing the overseas connections is a dark-burnished pottery in shapes that include jugs with high spouts that look Anatolian. The first beehive-shaped tombs (called tholos tombs) date from this period. The Final Neolithic folk were farmers and herdsmen, and they were probably seafarers as well. They used obsidian from the island of Melos, and their technology for ceramics was on a par with contemporary developments in the Cyclades and Anatolia.

Early Bronze Age. On Crete, the Early Bronze Age is divided into three periods: Early Minoan I, II, and III. In the middle phase of the second period (Early Minoan II), the first real cultural explosion since the advent of the Final Neolithic took place. New objects testify both to an increased technological skill and to a desire for new possessions: sealstones, stone vases, new types of pottery, figurines; and metal objects in a surprising variety of designs. Some writers have seen metallurgy, in its new form as portable wealth, as the main stimulus behind these changes. Certainly, metals played a vital role. Copper was used for jewelry, for tools, and especially for daggers. Silver and gold assumed new roles as symbols of prestige. Because Crete is poor in metallic ores, it is likely that all or almost all of this metal was imported.

Some of the jewelry gives us our best hints about the sources for these new metals. The rich Early Minoan II–III tombs at Mochlos in northeastern Crete have yielded hundreds of pieces of jewelry. They include earrings and pendants with strong stylistic parallels with Troy and nearby parts of the northeast Aegean and with a number of ties to Mesopotamia; quadruple spirals, complex link chains, pierced bands, and flowers and leaves all occur both at Ur in Mesopotamia and at Mochlos on Crete. In addition, the technology of fusing with added fluxes to create filigree and granulation also appears in both areas. Although the lines of transmission are mostly lost, and they were surely distant and indirect, the situation suggests that a general level of technology and a few stylistic details were being transmitted over extremely long distances.

Although invasions and cultural disruptions occurred in Greece and the Cycladic Islands at the end of the Early Bronze Age, Crete does not seem to have been affected. The Middle Minoan period lasted from about 2000 BCE until just after 1700 BCE. The Old Palaces were built during the period, and there is evidence that Crete may have been divided into several kingdoms then, administered from palaces at Knossos, Phaistos, Malia, Zakros, and other centers. The volume of Minoan objects in the East and of Eastern objects on Crete increased appreciably. They suggest economic links in several directions.

Egyptian scarabs and a few other objects occur at several Middle Minoan sites. Minoan pottery, especially the fine Kamares ware of MM II, found its way to Egypt in enough quantity to suggest that it was traded for its own sake rather than as a container. Most of this pottery is palatial (most likely from Knossos), suggesting that the palaces were taking the lead in foreign trade. Objects from Syria, Anatolia, and Cyprus can also be identified on Crete. Among these locations Cyprus is most important, and it may have acted as an intermediary between Crete and ports farther to the east. Eastern products that can be identified from this period include ivory, a few stones, and metals.

Late Bronze Age (Late Minoan I). At the beginning of the Late Bronze Age on Crete (the Middle Bronze IIB in Palestine and Syria), a group of important Minoan wall paintings appears in the East. Examples survive from three sites: Tell ed-Dabʿa in Egypt, Tel Kabri in Palestine, and Alalakh in Syria. At Tell ed-Dabʿa, the Hyksos capital of Avaris, the paintings included bull leapers, Aegean floral motifs, several animals, and abstract designs of Cretan type. Floral ornaments and other designs decorate the palace of Yarimlim at Alalakh. Both a gridded floor and a miniature fresco with buildings, a landscape, and human figures were found at Tel Kabri. In all cases, the technique is true fresco, an Aegean practice previously unknown in Egypt and Western Asia. Apparently, Minoan painters were called in to decorate some of the finer local buildings at this time, using Cretan motifs and techniques. [*See* Dabʿa, Tell ed-; Kabri, Tel; *and* Alalakh.]

Late Minoan I also marks a new height for Cretan trade with the East. Imported commodities are sometimes difficult to trace, but they make a long list. Raw materials include stones like blue lapis lazuli from Afghanistan; white-spotted obsidian from the island of Ghyali; copper; and possibly also tin, ivory, ostrich eggs, gold, silver, and the many products that leave no trace, such as woods, spices, and leathers. If the archaeological record is any indication, finished goods were mostly made at home on Crete. Eastern pottery is rare on Crete. A few pieces came from Knossos, Kommos, Zakros, Pseira, and a few other places, but they were mostly closed containers presumably brought in for their contents. Sealstones from the period are a tiny percentage of the local Minoan seals. Minoan metal objects from this period were almost all manufactured on Crete. It is reasonable to conclude that Crete was an agricultural and a manufacturing center that traded mostly for its raw materials. It must have exported foods, textiles, and especially finished metal goods.

The manufacture of metal objects must have played a large role in this scenario. The final evidence is not in yet, but the best guess is that copper and tin came from somewhere to the east. Large stores of copper ingots must have been needed to supply the bronze-working industry. Hoards of copper ingots have been found at Aghia Triadha and at Zakros, but studies of the ingots by lead isotope analysis have produced a pattern with no known parallel from the eastern Mediterranean. The copper must come from a Precambrian ore body that has not yet been identified. Geographical candidates are Afghanistan or the Caucasus, but little archaeological work has been done in this region. A shipwreck from near Bulgaria, in the Black Sea, with copper ingots on board and with clay weights that are disk-shaped, with holes near the margins (an, Aegean shape), raises the possibility of a seaborne trade in the right direction, but too little research has yet been done to reach any firm conclusions.

At the end of Late Minoan IB, most Cretan sites were destroyed. Many of them were abandoned in LM II, and those that survived have an increased amount of evidence from Mycenaean areas of southern Greece. Most scholars believe that this date marks the arrival of the Mycenaeans on Crete.

Knossos continues to be important in the years of Mycenaean domination, and it must have participated in the international Mycenaean trade in LM III that knit together a great economic network in the eastern Mediterranean. In LM III, the language of Crete was Mycenaean Greek, preserved on tablets written in the script called Linear B. Tablets come from Knossos and Khania on Crete as well as from Mycenae, Pylos, and other sites on the Greek mainland. The tablets, all tallies and other economic documents, describe a thriving economy. Weaving, bronze working, and other crafts were done for the international market as well as for home consumption. Crete's dominant position in the wool trade is demonstrated by the fact that the clay tablets from Knossos list more than 100,000 sheep. By the thirteenth century BCE, iron began to be used in larger quantities than previously, and new customs such as cremation began to appear.

Early Iron Age. Toward the end of the second millennium BCE, all of the Mycenaean world was experiencing disruption. Wars were frequent, and by 1200 BCE most of the great centers had been attacked. A wave of new settlers on Cyprus at about this time coincides with the abandonment of several of the Mycenaean sites. This is the period of the "Sea Peoples," displaced populations who attacked Egypt during the reign of Rameses III. One group of the Sea Peoples, with Aegean population elements, settled in Palestine and became the Philistines. Other groups are more difficult to trace. The coasts of Crete, were so insecure at the time that many harbors were abandoned as people moved inland. Refuge sites on high peaks like Karphi, Vrokastro, and Kavousi-Kastro testify to the new need for defense, rather than access to the coast for trade.

In this period of the Early Iron Age, the Dorians can first be recognized archaeologically on the Greek peninsula and Crete. They spoke a dialect of Greek that was distinct from that of their Mycenaean predecessors, and by the eighth-century BCE they were dominant throughout Crete. The new society was aristocratic, based on land tenure managed by wealthy citizens and worked by slaves and a serf population that was probably the remnant of the island's Bronze Age residents.

Trade revived in the Early Iron Age, and by the ninth century Crete was again a stepping-stone from east to west. In the north, Knossos remained the most important site. In the south, the port of Kommos, on the prosperous plain of the Mesara, was a busy port of call. A temple here, with a shrine of standing stones of Phoenician type and many eastern offsprings, suggests that the Phoenicians used the port on their way east or west. As before, Crete was a link between the eastern and western Mediterranean.

[*See also* Cyprus; *and* Minoans.]

BIBLIOGRAPHY

Evans, Arthur. *The Palace of Minos.* 4 vols. in 6. London, 1921–1935. Publication of the discoveries at Knossos.

Gale, N. H., ed. *Bronze Age Trade in the Mediterranean.* [Göteborg], 1991. Papers on trade delivered at a conference held at Oxford, December 1989.

Lambrou-Phillipson, C. *Hellenorientalia: The Near Eastern Presence in the Bronze Age Aegean, ca.* 3000–1100 B.C. Göteborg, 1990. Summary of the Western Asian–Aegean interrelations, with a list of Eastern objects found in the Aegean and an extensive bibliography.

Muhly, James D. "The Nature of Trade in the LBA Eastern Mediterranean: The Organization of the Metals Trade and the Role of Cyprus." In *Early Metallurgy in Cyprus, 4000–500 BC: Acta of the International Archaeological Symposium,* edited by James D. Muhly et al., pp. 251–266. Larnaca, Cyprus, 1982. Discussion of the trade in metals.

Renfrew, Colin. *The Emergence of Civilisation.* London, 1972. Discussion of the Cyclades and adjacent areas in the third millennium BCE.

Sandars, Nancy K. *The Sea Peoples: Warriors of the Ancient Mediterranean, 1250–1150 B.C.* London, 1978. Discussion of the end of the Bronze Age.

Seager, Richard B. *Explorations in the Island of Mochlos.* Boston, 1912. Publication of the objects from the Early to Middle Bronze Age cemetery at Mochlos, including the gold jewelry.

Smith, William Stevenson. *Interconnections in the Ancient Near-East.* New Haven, 1965. Valuable treatment, especially of art objects.

PHILIP P. BETANCOURT

CROWFOOT, JOHN WINTER

CROWFOOT, JOHN WINTER (1873–1959), director of the British School of Archaeology in Jerusalem (1926–1935). Crowfoot, the son of John Henchman Crowfoot, chancellor of Lincoln Cathedral, was educated at Marlborough College and Brasenose College at Oxford University. His early and lifelong devotion to archaeology led in 1897 to a year of travel in Asia Minor and Greece. He was a lecturer in classics at Birmingham University for two years before going to Egypt as assistant master of education. In 1903 he became deputy principal of Gordon College, Khartoum, in the Sudan. Returning briefly to Egypt as an inspector in the Ministry of Education in 1909, he married Grace Mary Hood, who became a pioneer in the study of ancient and modern textiles and women's crafts. As director of education and principal of Gordon College (1914–1926), he also oversaw the Antiquities Department as well. He was appointed C.B.E. (Companion of the British Empire) for wartime service.

In Palestine from 1926 he directed the British School–Yale University excavation at Jerash (Gerasa) in Transjordan (1928–1930); the joint expeditions to Samaria/Sebaste (1931–1935); and excavations for the Palestine Exploration Fund (PEF) on the Ophel in Jerusalem. On his return to England, he became chairman of the PEF (1945–1950). In

1958 he received the honorary degree of Doctor of Letters from Oxford University.

As recalled by R. W. Hamilton, late keeper of the Ashmolean Museum, Oxford, who first worked with him at Jerash, Crowfoot was known for his tolerance and humor. These qualities proved particularly important in the British School's excavations at Samaria, where his direction facilitated cooperation between his British School, the PEF, the British Academy, Harvard University, and the Hebrew University of Jerusalem. Perhaps his most important achievement was his innovativeness at a time when archaeologists in Palestine were obsessed with the desire to "prove" the truth of the Hebrew Bible. Crowfoot instead turned the activities of the school and its students to Early Christian archaeology, so rich in its architecture, art, and epigraphy, as well as to the classical roots of Western society.

[See also British School of Archaeology in Jerusalem; Jerash; Jerusalem; Palestine Exploration Fund; and Samaria.]

BIBLIOGRAPHY

Crowfoot, John Winter. *Churches at Jerash: A Preliminary Report of the Joint Yale–British School Expeditions to Jerash, 1928–1930.* London, 1931.

Crowfoot, John Winter. *Early Churches in Palestine.* London, 1941.

Crowfoot, John Winter, and Grace Mary Crowfoot. *Early Ivories from Samaria.* Samaria-Sebaste: Report of the work of the Joint Expedition in 1931–1933 and of the Work of the British Expedition in 1935, no. 2. London, 1938.

Crowfoot, John Winter, Kathleen M. Kenyon, and Eleazar L. Sukenik. *The Buildings at Samaria.* Samaria-Sebaste: Report of the Work of the Joint Expedition in 1931–1933 and of the Work of the British Expedition in 1935, no. 1. London, 1942.

Crowfoot, John Winter, Grace Mary Crowfoot, and Katheleen M. Kenyon. *The Objects from Samaria.* Samaria-Sebaste: Report of the Work of the Joint Expedition in 1931–1933 and of the Work of the British Expedition in 1935, no. 3. London, 1957.

ELISABETH CROWFOOT

CRUSADER PERIOD.

On 27 November 1095, Pope Urban II issued a call at Clermont in the Auvergne, France, for European Christians to go to the aid of their Eastern Christian brethren in the Holy Land and to wrest control of the holy sites from the infidels who had desecrated and destroyed them. The four main armies of the First Crusade marched to Constantinople in 1096–1097 and set off across Asia Minor in June 1097.

History. The First Crusade entered Syria-Palestine in 1097, taking Antioch and Edessa in 1098. Continuing south, the Crusaders occupied Bethlehem in June 1099 and conquered Jerusalem on 15 July 1099. Nazareth was taken later in the year by Tancred. Godefroy de Bouillon was elected *Advocatus Sancti Sepulchri* and retained the office until his death on 18 July 1100. Baldwin of Boulogne was crowned king of Jerusalem in the Church of the Nativity in Bethlehem on Christmas day 1100. Gibelin of Arles became the first

uncontested patriarch of Jerusalem in 1108. On 12 July 1109, Tripoli fell to Crusader forces. Thus, during a ten-year period the gains of the First Crusade were slowly consolidated into the establishment of four Crusader states: the Principality of Antioch, ruled by Bohemond of Otranto and his nephew, Tancred; the County of Edessa, ruled by Baldwin of Boulogne and Baldwin of Le Bourg; the Kingdom of Jerusalem, ruled by Baldwin I; and the County of Tripoli, ruled by Bertram, son of Raymond of St. Gilles. By 1110 most of the important port cities on the Mediterranean coast had been taken, with the conspicuous exceptions of Tyre and Ashkelon, which were still in Fatimid hands.

In the newly organized Crusader states, fortifications and churches were needed everywhere. The early kings of Jerusalem, Baldwin I (1100–1118) and Baldwin II (1118–1131) sponsored important castle building in Syria-Palestine near Ashkelon (Israel), at Shaubak (Jordan), and on the Isle de Graye (in the Gulf of 'Aqaba); other patrons built Jubayl (Lebanon) and Saone (Syria). Important commercial arrangements were made by which the Genoese, the Pisans, and the Venetians were given holdings in the port cities, providing the means of trade and a de facto Crusader navy. Coinage generated the earliest Crusader artistic images, in many cases distinctive amalgamations of Byzantine-influenced designs and Western currency types. Metalwork, and especially reliquaries, also proved to be much in demand. A relic of the True Cross became the ensign of the Latin Kingdom and was carried by the patriarch on all important campaigns.

By the time Fulk of Anjou became king, crowned in the Church of the Holy Sepulcher in 1131, the second genera-

CRUSADER PERIOD. *Figural lintel.* A lintel from the south transept facade (west portal) of the Church of the Holy Sepulcher in Jerusalem, c. 1150. Scenes from left to right include Jesus raising Lazarus; Mary Magdalene and Mary, mother of James and John, meeting Jesus; and Jesus directing his disciples to prepare for the Last Supper. (Courtesy École Biblique, Jerusalem)

tion of settlers was in place and social and cultural interpenetration was a feature of life in "outremer" (as the Frankish East was known). As an example of royal intermarriage, the king came from France, but his queen, Melisende, was Greek Orthodox, born of an Armenian mother. Melisende became the most remarkable woman in the Crusader East—daughter, wife, and mother of kings, and patroness of the arts. For her the Melisende psalter was done, the most remarkable illuminated Crusader codex produced in the twelfth century. She, Fulk, and the patriarchs of Jerusalem were responsible for the rebuilding and redecoration of the Church of the Holy Sepulcher: pilgrimage church par excellance, state coronation church, and burial church of the Crusader kings. The aedicule of the Holy Sepulcher had been refurbished immediately after 1099, but an ambitious plan to unify Calvary and the Prison of Christ with the aedicule in a single church was initiated after 1131 with most

of the construction carried out in the 1140s. The church was dedicated on 15 July 1149, after the members of the ill-fated Second Crusade had returned home.

The Holy Sepulcher was the first major holy site to be redone in a distinctive Levantine-Romanesque style of architecture, with complex programs of sculpture and mosaics on the interior and exterior. The Church of the Nativity in Bethlehem was also redecorated in 1167–1169, in a unique joint patronage arrangement between Amaury, king of Jerusalem, the Byzantine emperor, Manuel; and Bishop Ralph of Bethlehem. This church dated to the sixth century CE, but a completely new program of Byzantine- and Crusader-inspired mosaics and frescoes transformed its interior and grotto. By contrast, a third holy site, the Church of the Annunciation in Nazareth, was rebuilt with a very extensive program of figural sculpture making it distinctively different from its predecessors. These holy places strongly shaped the

Crusader artistic agenda in the twelfth century. The Templar and Hospitaller orders, founded in the early part of the century, grew in military power and in their control of castles used to defend these sites and their pilgrims. Otherwise, the Crusaders were less successful on the political and military fronts.

Although the Crusader states proved viable commercially there was the constant threat of Muslim incursions. Edessa had fallen in 1144 and the Second Crusade could do nothing to restore it. It became increasingly evident that the threat from the Turks in the north and the Fatimids in Egypt could successfully be warded off only while the Muslims were divided. When the Crusaders failed to enlist the Byzantines in an efficacious alliance to conquer Egypt in the 1160s and 1170s, Saladin (Salah ad-Din) unified Muslim forces against the Crusaders. Saladin eventually invaded the Latin Kingdom and inflicted a disastrous defeat on the Crusaders at the Horns of Hattin on 4 July 1187. By the end of that year, the Crusaders held only Tyre and Beirut and a few major castles, such as Crac des Chevaliers and Marqab (Syria); all of the major holy places were again in the hands of the infidels.

To regain these sites, the Third Crusade was mounted in 1189. Although it was led by three crowned heads of Europe, including Richard the Lionheart, who delivered Cyprus into Crusader hands, and although it restored the coastline to the Crusaders, symbolized by the retaking of Akko (Acre) in 1191, the Third Crusade failed to regain a single major holy site or to damage a single Muslim center of power. Mindful of this failure, Pope Innocent III organized the Fourth Crusade. It was, however, diverted to Constantinople in 1203–1204. After a terrible sacking of that city in April 1204 a Latin Empire was established for fifty seven years. With Constantinople as its capital, the empire included the territories of Romania, Thessalonike, the Morea, and Crete. Yet, other expeditions were attempted. The Crusade of Pelagius (papal legate and leader of the Crusade to Damietta) attacked Egypt directly in 1218–1221 but was forced to withdraw. Ironically, only Frederick II, twice excommunicated in the process, was able to restore the holy places to Crusader control, by treaty—not by force of arms—with Sultan al-Kamil in 1229.

Crusader jurisdiction over the holy sites after 1229 was tenuous because their military and political power was largely consumed by civil war between 1229 and 1243 and was thus inadequate to reestablish control. In 1244 the Khwarazmian Turks overran Jerusalem, definitively removing the holy city from Crusader access. Yet another Crusade was organized: King Louis IX came east, but his attempt to attack Egypt was repulsed. He then went directly to the Latin Kingdom to aid the Holy Land. Residing in Akko (1250–1254), he set about rebuilding the fortifications at Caesarea, Akko, and Tyre, and he built a new castle at Sidon. He seems to have reinvigorated Crusader painting with his commissions of royal manuscripts, such as the Arsenal Bible. He personally visited the holy site of Nazareth to refocus Crusader goals, but he was unable to restore a single holy site to Crusader control.

CRUSADER PERIOD. *'Atlit castle.* The North Tower wall, looking east with remains of vaulting and three corbels, 1218 CE. (Photograph by J. Folda)

With the Mongol invasion in 1258–1260 and the rise to power of the Mamluk Sultan Baybars, the future of the Crusader states was put in serious jeopardy. Baybars pursued a policy of conquest and destruction, and by 1268 he had taken Nazareth and Antioch. The alarm was sounded and a new Crusade was organized, with Louis IX once again leading the expedition. Louis died in Tunis, en route, in 1270 but Edward I of England continued on to Palestine. Even he could not deter Baybars, however, and in 1271 the Mamluks captured one of the greatest of Crusader castles, Crac des Chevaliers. Only Baybars's death in 1277 foiled his resolve to eradicate the Franks.

In 1280 Baybars's successor, Qalawun, resumed the Mamluk assault on the Crusaders. By 1289 Tripoli had fallen, and Qalawun prepared to attack Akko. Qalawun failed to take Akko only because he died on the march that began the siege; however, his son, Sultan al-Ashraf Khalil, assumed command and the battle was joined. St. Jean d'Acre fell on 28 May 1291. By August, the Mamluks had pushed the Crusaders into the sea, having taken every mainland Frankish fortification. The Latin Kingdom was terminated in Syria-Palestine, and only Cyprus and parts of Greece remained in Frankish hands.

Art and Archaeology. The study of Crusader art was essentially founded and initially carried out by the great French "archéologues" such as Melchior de Vogüé, Emmanuel Rey, Charles Clermont-Ganneau, L.-H. Vincent and F.-M. Abel, and continued by Prosper Viaud, Camille Enlart, and Paul Deschamps, with significant contributions by certain Englishmen such as Claude R. Conder and H. H. Kitchener, William Harvey, and C. N. Johns between 1860 and World War II. In this period the early investigation of the major castles and churches was done with intensive work during the French and British Mandates after 1917, at Crac des Chevaliers and 'Atlit; the site of the Church of the Annunciation, Nazareth, was excavated; archeological studies were done on the Crusader churches of Jerusalem; and specific architectural surveys were carried out on the Church of the Holy Sepulcher, Jerusalem, and the Church of the Nativity, Bethlehem.

Since World War II, archeological investigation has continued with important investigations of the Church of the Holy Sepulcher and specifically the aedicule of the tomb, the castles of Belvoir and Belmont, the Crusader cities of Acre (Akko) and Caesarea, and Crusader settlement in the plain of Sharon. There have been important investigations of the coins and pottery from the Crusader period as well. However, significant art historical research also appeared, starting with the work of T. S. R. Boase, H. Buchthal, and K. Weitzmann. In contrast to the archaeological reports and studies on sites and architecture, the art historical publications have focused more on painting (manuscript illuminations, frescoes, mosaics, and icons), sculpture, and metalwork. These studies have emphasized the figural arts and have made considerable progress in redressing the balance between archaeological and art historical research. For architectural history and archaeology the British School of Archaeology in Jerusalem has recently sponsored important surveys of Mamluk architecture in Jerusalem and a corpus of Crusader churches from the Latin Kingdom of Jerusalem, of which the first volume has appeared (Pringler, 1986). A significant group of Israeli art historians located at Jerusalem, Tel Aviv, and Haifa has also begun making important contributions on painting, sculpture and the minor arts since about 1980.

Of the four Crusader States on mainland Syria-Palestine, the greatest number of Crusader sites and monuments (churches, castles, fortified cities, and towers), including the most important holy places for pilgrimage, is found in the territory of the Latin Kingdom of Jerusalem, which includes today Israel and parts of southern Lebanon, and western Jordan between the Dead Sea and 'Aqaba. In the County of Edessa (Urfa; 1098–1144), which now includes parts of southeastern Turkey and northern Syria, there are some important castle remains, and in the Principality of Antioch (1098–1268), which includes today mainly northwestern Syria and a bit of southern Turkey, there are also important fortifications, but few Crusader churches are extant in either area. The County of Tripoli (1109–1289) was the smallest of these states. running along the coast from Gibelet (Jubayl, Byblos) to the Castle of Marqab (Margat), that is, northern Lebanon and a part of western Syria. Significantly, however, the most impressive extant Crusader castles are located in this region—Crac des Chevaliers. Marqab, and Saone (Sahyun), all in present-day Syria, of which the latter two have never been seriously investigated archaeologically. Indeed, few Crusader castles have been excavated, although several, such as Crac des Chevaliers, have been cleared. Finally, two of the finest extant Crusader churches, at Gibelet and Tortosa (Tartus) are also found in the region of Tripoli.

Jerusalem in the twelfth century and Acre during the thirteenth century were the two primary Crusader artistic centers, along with the important pilgrimage sites such as Bethlehem, Nazareth, and St. Catherine's on Mount Sinai in the Sinai Peninsula. Apart from the decoration of their churches. Jerusalem and Acre were centers for manuscript illumination; in Jerusalem there was also a thriving quarter for goldsmiths and metalwork; and in Acre and at St. Catherine's are found important Crusader panel painting. No Crusader manuscripts from other important centers such as Antioch, Tripoli, or Cyprus have been identified for certain at present, but Antioch may have been important for metalwork, and Lydda, Tripoli, and Nicosia have had Crusader panel paintings attributed to them recently. As with all portable works of art, however, the archaeological evidence for the sources of works such as manuscript painting, icons, and metalwork is difficult to identify in these locations.

[*See also* Akko; Antioch on Orontes; Ayyubid–Mamluk Dynasties; Byblos; Caesarea; Constantinople; Fatimid Dynasty; Jerusalem; Sidon; Tyre; *and the biographies of Abel, Clermont-Ganneau, Conder, Kitchener, Vincent, and Vogüé.*]

BIBLIOGRAPHY

Bagatti, Bellarmino. *Gli antichi edifici sacri di Betlemme.* Jerusalem, 1952.

Bagatti, Bellarmino, and Eugenio Alliata. *Gli scavi di Nazaret*, vol. 2, *Dal secolo XII ad oggi.* Studium Biblicum Franciscanum, Collectio Maior, 17. Jerusalem, 1984.

Benveniste, M. *The Crusaders in the Holy Land.* Jerusalem, 1970.

Biddle, M. "The Tomb of Christ: Sources, Methods and a New Approach." In *Churches Built in Ancient Times: Recent Studies in Early Christian Archaeology,* edited by K. Painter, pp. 73–147. London, 1994.

Boase, T. S. R. "Ecclesiastical Art in the Crusader States in Palestine and Syria" and "Military Architecture in the Crusader States in Palestine and Syria." In *The Art and Architecture of the Crusader States,* edited by Harry W. Hazard, pp. 69–164. A History of the Crusades, vol. 4. Madison, Wis., and London, 1977.

Buschhausen, Helmut. *Die süditalienische Bauplastik im Königreich Jerusalem von König Wilhelm II. bis Kaiser Friedrich II.* Vienna, 1978.

Clermont-Ganneau, Charles S. *Archaeological Researches in Palestine during the Years 1873–1874.* 2 vols. London, 1896–1899.

Conder, Claude R., and H. H. Kitchener. *The Survey of Western Palestine: Memoirs of the Topography, Orography, Hydrography, and Archaeology,* vol. 1, *Galilee;* vol. 2, *Samaria;* vol. 3, *Judaea.* London, 1881–1883.

Corbo, Virgilio. *Il Santo Sepolcro di Gerusalemme.* 3 vols. Studium Biblicum Franciscanum, Collectio Maior, 29. Jerusalem, 1981–1982.

Dean, Bashford. "A Crusaders' Fortress in Palestine." *Palestine Exploration Fund Quarterly Statement* (1928): 91–97.

Deschamps, Paul. *Les Châteaux des Croisés en Terre-Sainte,* vol. 1, *Le Crac des Chevaliers;* vol. 2, *La défense du royaume de Jérusalem;* vol. 3, *La défense du Comté de Tripoli et de la Principauté d'Antioche.* Bibliothèque Archéologique et Historique, vols. 19, 34, and 90. Paris, 1934–1973.

Enlart, Camille. *Les monuments des Croisés dans le royaume de Jérusalem: Architecture religieuse et civile.* 2 vols. Bibliothèque Archéologique et Historique, vols. 7–8. Paris, 1925–1928.

Folda, Jaroslav, et al. "Crusader Frescoes at Crac des Chevaliers and Marqab Castle." *Dumbarton Oaks Papers* 36 (1982): 177–210.

Folda, Jaroslav. *The Art of the Crusaders in the Holy Land, 1098–1187.* New York and Cambridge, 1995. One additional volume is planned.

Johns, C. N. "Excavations at Pilgrim's Castle ('Atlit)." *Quarterly of the Department of Antiquities of Palestine* 1 (1932): 111–129; 2 (1933): 41–104; 3 (1934): 145–164; 4 (1935): 122–137.

Johns, C. N. "The Citadel, Jerusalem: A Summary of Work since 1934." *Quarterly of the Department of Antiquities of Palestine* 14 (1950): 121–190.

Kennedy, H. *Crusader Castles.* Cambridge, 1994.

Kühnel, Bianca. *Crusader Art of the Twelfth Century.* Berlin, 1994.

Kühnel, Gustav. *Wall Painting in the Latin Kingdom of Jerusalem.* Berlin, 1988.

Lane, Arthur. "Medieval Finds from Al-Mina in North Syria." *Archaeologia* 87 (1937): 19–78.

Malloy, A. G., I. F. Preston, and A. J. Seltman. *Coinage of the Crusader States, 1098–1291.* New York, 1994.

Metcalf, David M. *Coinage of the Crusades and the Latin East in the Ashmolean Museum.* London, 1983.

Poree, B. *Un aspect de la culture matérielle des Croisades: Introduction à l'étude de la céramique, XI–XIIIe siècles.* Paris, 1991.

Pringle, Denys. "Medieval Pottery from Caesarea: The Crusader Period." *Levant* 17 (1985): 171–202.

Pringle, Denys, et al. *The Red Tower (al-Burj al-Ahmar): Settlement in the Plain of Sharon at the Time of the Crusaders and Mamluks, A.D. 1099–1516.* British School of Archaeology in Jerusalem, Monograph Series, 1. London, 1986.

Pringle, Denys. *The Churches of the Crusader Kingdom of Jerusalem: A Corpus.* Vol. 1. Cambridge, 1993. Two additional volumes are planned.

Rey, Emmanuel-Guillaume. *Étude sur les monuments de l'architecture militaire des croises en Syrie et dans l'ile de Chypre.* Collection de Documents Inédits sur l'Histoire de France, ser. 1: Histoire Politique. Paris, 1871.

Saller, Sylvester J. *Excavations at Bethany, 1949–1953.* Studium Biblicum Franciscanum, Collectio Maior, 12. Jerusalem, 1957.

Schick, Conrad. "The Muristan, or, The Site of the Hospital of St. John at Jerusalem." *Palestine Exploration Fund Quarterly Statement* (1902): 42–56.

Schultz, Robert W., et al. *The Church of the Nativity at Bethlehem.* London, 1910.

Ulbert, Thilo. *Resafa,* vol. 3, *Der kreuzfahrerzeitliche Silberschatz aus Resafa-Sergiupolis.* Mainz am Rhein, 1990.

Viaud, Prosper. *Nazareth et ses deux églises de l'Annonciation et de Saint-Joseph d'après les fouilles récentes.* Paris, 1910.

Vincent, L.-H., and Félix-Marie Abel. *Jérusalem: Recherches de topographie, d'archéologie et d'histoire,* vol. 2, *Jérusalem nouvelle.* Paris, 1926.

Vogüé, Melchior de. *Les églises de la Terre Sainte* (1860). Toronto, 1973.

The reader should also take note of the archaeological/art historical surveys and excavations in progress (as of 1993). For instance, Israeli and ASOR excavations in Jerusalem and at Caesarea, Belvoir, Acre (Akko), and Ashkelon are regularly reported in the *Revue Biblique* and *Israel Exploration Journal.* The British School of Archaeology is conducting excavations at Belmont castle, west of Jerusalem, reported in *Levant,* and the Lebanese Antiquities Service is currently working at Tyre and Tripoli. Erica Dodd is surveying all the extant Crusader-period frescoes in Lebanon. Martin Biddle's studies of the aedicule of the Holy Sepulcher (with photogrammetry) have appeared in various English archaeological journals as well as the *Illustrated London News.* Other works in progress include surveys of Crusader sculpture in the Latin Kingdom by Zehava Jacoby; mosaics in the Latin Kingdom by Gustav Kühnel; and metalwork by Bianca Kühnel.

JAROSLAV FOLDA

CTESIPHON, city located on the east bank of the Tigris River, 35 km (22 mi.) south of Baghdad in Iraq, and opposite the Seleucid capital of Seleucia on the Tigris and the nearby Sasanian "round city" of Veh Ardashir. Ctesiphon flourished as the Partho-Sasanian capital from the second century BCE until the Arab conquest in 637 CE. The origins and meaning of the Latin name *Ctesiphon* are unknown (Gk., Ktesiphon; Syr., *qtyspwn;* Parthian, Pahlavi, and Sogdian, *tyspwn;* Ar., Taysafun). Contemporaneous classical, Christian, Jewish, and Arab sources refer to several other centers in the vicinity known as "the cities," which has led to considerable confusion as to Ctesiphon's precise location. The most likely site is al-Ma'aridh, where limited German excavations uncovered large Late Sasanian private houses (Kröger, 1982). The origins of Ctesiphon are obscure. It appears to have been founded as a Parthian city following their capture of Mesopotamia from the Seleucids and westward transfer of their capital. It was used as a place of coronation and royal winter residence with treasuries and a garrison; according to one classical author (Ammianus Marcellinus, 23.6.23), the city walls were built by Pacorus I. Owing to its position on the left bank of the Tigris, Ctesiphon was well sited for communicating with the Iranian plateau. (Seleucia, the Parthian foundation of Vologesocerta/Abu Halefija, and the Early Sasanian city of Veh Ardashir controlled access to Babylonia, particularly along canals linking the Euphrates River with the Tigris at this point.) Parthian Ctesiphon was sacked on three occasions by Roman armies, namely by Trajan (116 CE), Avidius Cassius (165) and Septimius Severus (198).

In 224 the Parthians were overthrown by Ardashir, crowned in Ctesiphon in 226 as the first ruler of the Sasanian dynasty. Thereafter, Ctesiphon remained the Sasanian capital, place of coronation, royal mint, and one of the empire's most important administrative and cultural centers. It was strongly fortified with walls of fired brick and a moat. Odenathus of Palmyra unsuccessfully besieged the city in 261, but it was sacked by Carus in 283; Julian attempted to capture it in 363 but failed (Frey, 1967). Ctesiphon was physically connected to Veh Ardashir by a pair of bridges, one of which may have been constructed by Shapur II. Its diverse population included important Christian, Jewish, and Zoroastrian communities. Ctesiphon was the birthplace of the catholicos Elisha, the archdeacon Mar Aba, and Rabbi Hiyya. Mani, the founder of the Manichaean sect, was educated but later crucified at Ctesiphon, and within the city there was a market frequented by local Jews. Heraclius attacked Ctesiphon in 627, and a decade later an Arab army commanded by Sa'd ibn Abi Waqqas captured Ctesiphon and huge quantities of booty after first taking Veh Ardashir and fording the Tigris. Major monuments at this time included a large "White Palace," whose founder was then unknown—suggesting that it was already an old building. Several unidentified mosques were founded after the Arab conquest and Ctesiphon became known as "the ancient city." Despite an unhealthy reputation owing to mosquitoes and malaria, it was occupied by "men of the nobility and distinguished houses of Kufa" (a city on the Euphrates River) with "numerous fighters to watch possible disturbances" (Tabari, I, 2677, 2483; II, 980). With the later foundation of Baghdad, the remaining Sasanian public buildings and fortifications suffered heavily through demolition and removal of bricks for reuse. [See Baghdad.]

Islamic and later European writers have left numerous descriptions of the Ctesiphon area, particularly focusing on a huge vaulted iwan popularly known as the Throne of Khusrau (Taq-i Kisra). Several attempts have been made to reconstruct the historical topography of the site, notably by Claudius Rich (1836), who recognized that eroded mounds on either bank of the present course of the Tigris belonged to a single round city later cut by the river. This he presumed to be Seleucia and the Taq-i Kisra to mark Ctesiphon. Other writers have proposed the existence of a second iwan opposite the first; in 1908, half of the remaining vault and facade of the Taq-i Kisra collapsed, following flooding. Between 1903 and 1911 Ernst Herzfeld conducted architectural surveys in the area. In 1915, there was fierce fighting on the site between Turkish and British armies. Aerial photographs taken during the 1920s confirmed a suggestion that the extensive mounded area immediately west of the round city probably represented Seleucia, as it was laid out on classical principles of urban planning.

Seleucia had been founded by Seleucus Nicator at the junction of a royal canal and the Tigris. [See Seleucia on the Tigris.] A shift in patronage under the Seleucids stimulated its growth at the expense of Babylon. [See Babylon.] Seleucia was fortified; it straddled the canal and was said to have had a population of up to 600,000. It functioned as a mint throughout the Parthian period and was only deserted in the third century when Veh Ardashir was founded. Thereafter, Seleucia was referred to by Syriac and classical authors as "deserted Seleucia" (*Sliq kharawata* or *deserta civitas*) and was used as a place of execution and burial. The city was first excavated by American expeditions initiated by Leroy Waterman in 1927 and concluded by Robert McDowell in 1936–1937. These focused on Tell 'Umar and on an insula near the center of the city (Waterman, 1933; Hopkins, ed., 1972). However, because of the water table, the earliest levels were not reached; much of the published material actually dated to the Parthian period. The round city was assumed to represent Ctesiphon, and excavations were conducted both there and across the present course of the Tigris by German expeditions directed by Oscar Reuther (1928–1929) and Ernst Kühnel (1930–1931). Large quantities of Sasanian decorative stucco were recovered from Tell al-Dhaba'i, Tell Dhahab, al-Ma'aridh, and Umm as-Sa'atir; the church at Qasr bint al-Qadi and a Parthian cemetery were excavated nearby (Kröger, 1982; Hauser, 1993). Further discoveries of stuccoes at other sites in Mesopotamia and Iran stimulated intense interest in the Sasanian period.

Archaeological research in the Ctesiphon area resumed in 1964 with Italian expeditions from the University of Turin directed by Giorgio Gullini (1966) and later by Antonio Invernizzi (1976). At Seleucia, a large Archive Square building, associated with the administration of a salt tax, and a later terra-cotta workshop were excavated. Within the round city, work was concentrated on a stretch of the city walls and an artisans' quarter within (ceramic, glass, and metalworking). Occupation there is dated from the reign of Ardashir I to the fifth–sixth centuries CE, after which low-lying areas of the city were abandoned because of flooding; later occupation was confined to the mound of Tell Baruda (Venco Ricciardi and Negro Ponzi Mancini, 1985). The excavated sequences from the round city, and its location relative to Seleucia and the Taq-i Kisra, demonstrate that this was the site of the city of Ardashir (Veh Ardashir, Bahursir), rather than Ctesiphon. Veh Ardashir was founded by Ardashir on the site of an earlier village known as Kokhé, closer to the Tigris, whose course had shifted slightly. It was intended to replace Seleucia and was, hence, called New Seleucia. Veh Ardashir enjoyed a close relationship with Ctesiphon and was also known as the western city of al-Mada'in or the near city in Arab sources. The fortifications enclosed an estimated area of 700 ha (1,729 acres) of housing separated by cambered asphalted roads and smaller alleys. Public buildings included a major Zoroastrian fire temple, a rabbinic academy, and a citadel or prison called Garondagan or Aqra d'Kokhé; a hay market is also attested in Syriac sources.

Early Islamic descriptions indicate that Ctesiphon lay on the Tigris opposite Veh Ardashir and a mile north of a "great Iwan" that formed part of the separate Late Sasanian royal city of Asbanbur (al-'Ali, 1968–1969). The latter was presumably founded because Ctesiphon had become too cramped to allow the large-scale construction necessary for the administration of the expanded Sasanian Empire. This iwan is the Taq-i Kisra, and possibly the same palace of Khusrau said by the Byzantine historian Theophylact Simocatta to have been constructed using "Greek" marble and with the help of "craftsmen skilled in ceilings" sent by Justinian. In 614 the remains of the "True Cross," captured by the Sasanians in Jerusalem, were taken to a royal treasury, probably at Asbanbur. A church, royal stables, parks, and an aviary were located nearby. There were several other important urban centers in this area, including a city founded by Khusrau I after he sacked Antioch in 542. Known as Khusrau's City of Antioch (Veh-Antiokh-Khusrau, also known as Rumiya); its public buildings included a hippodrome and baths and it was populated with Syrian deportees. Located south of Ctesiphon, that city should be identified with the site of el-Bustan. Finally, although the Sasanian palaces were stripped of their decoration after the Arab conquest, richly decorated private houses continued to be built nearby at Salman Pak as late as the tenth century (excavated by German and later Iraqi expeditions; see Abdul Khaliq, 1985–1986).

[See also Parthians; Sasanians; Seleucids.]

BIBLIOGRAPHY

Abdul Khaliq, 'Hana. "Al-Mada'en." *Sumer* 44 (1985–1986): 111–138. Full preliminary report on more recent Iraqi excavations of Early Islamic housing at Salman Pak.

'Ali, S. A. al-. "Al-Mada'in and Its Surrounding Area in Arabic Literary Sources." *Mesopotamia* 3–4 (1968–1969): 417–439. Detailed study of Arab historical sources, fundamental for the correct identification of cities and monuments in the Ctesiphon area.

Fiey, J. M. "Topography of al-Mada'in (Seleucia-Ctesiphon area)." *Sumer* 23 (1967): 3–38. Reasonably accurate reconstruction of events at Ctesiphon in 363 CE, based primarily on Syriac sources.

Gullini, Giorgio. "Problems of an Excavation in Northern Babylonia." *Mesopotamia* 1 (1966): 7–38. Summary of research prior to the Italian excavations, with the mistaken assumption that the round city is Ctesiphon rather than Veh Ardashir.

Hauser, Stefan R. "Eine arsakidenzeitliche nekropole in Ktesiphon." *Baghdader Mitteilungen* 24 (1993): 325–420, pls. 125–137. Thorough publication and discussion of Parthian tombs excavated at Coche.

Hopkins, Clark ed. *Topography and Architecture of Seleucia on the Tigris.* Ann Arbor, 1972. Detailed historical reconstruction and archaeological report, with summary of excavated finds.

Invernizzi, Antonio. "Ten Years' Research in the al-Mada'in Area, Seleucia and Ctesiphon." *Sumer* 32 (1976): 167–175. Useful account of the early results of Italian fieldwork at Seleucia and Veh Ardashir.

Keall, E. J. "Ayvan-e Kesra." In *Encyclopaedia Iranica*, vol. 3, pp. 155–159. London, 1987. Summary of earlier research on the Taq-i Kisra at Asbanbur near Ctesiphon.

Kröger, Jens. *Sasanidischer Stuckdekor.* Mainz am Rhein, 1982. Detailed and lavishly illustrated final publication of the stratigraphy and stucco from the German excavations in the Ctesiphon area and comparative discussion of Sasanian–Early Islamic art.

Kröger, Jens. "Ctesiphon." In *Encyclopaedia Iranica*, vol. 5, pp. 446–448. London, 1987. The most up-to-date, concise, and accurate description of the site.

Kühnel, Ernst. *Die Ausgrabungen der zweiten Ktesiphon-Expedition (Winter 1931/32).* Berlin. Preliminary report.

Oppenheimer, Aharon. *Babylonian Judaica in the Talmudic Period.* Wiesbaden, 1983. Critical gazetteer of places mentioned in the Babylonian Talmud, with a useful section on the Ctesiphon conurbation under "Mahoza."

Reuther, Oscar. *Die Ausgrabungen der Deutschen Ktesiphon-Expedition im Winter 1928/29.* Wittenberg. Preliminary excavation report.

Rich, Claudius James. *Narrative of a Residence in Koordistan.* London, 1836. A two-volume account of travels in Iraq between 1808 and 1821, with early descriptions of Ctesiphon, Seleucia, and other archaeological sites.

Venco Ricciardi, R., and M. M. Negro Ponzi Mancini. "Coche." In *The Land between Two Rivers: Twenty Years of Italian Archaeology in the Middle East. The Treasures of Mesopotamia*, edited by Ezio Quarantelli, pp. 100–110. Turin, 1985. The most useful summary of the Italian excavations at Veh Ardashir, published in an exhibition catalog.

Waterman, Leroy. *Second Preliminary Report upon the Excavations at Tel Umar, Iraq.* Ann Arbor, 1933. Summary excavation report.

St. John Simpson

CULT. Scholars in religious studies and related disciplines use the term *cult* to refer to the various forms of religious devotion attested for a civilization. This entry will focus on the Northwest Semitic cultural sphere, which in the period before 332 BCE included much of the coastal and inland Levant, from north of present day Syria and Iraq and south to the Sinai Peninsula. In the mid- to late second millennium BCE, the Northwest Semitic cultural sphere also included the Nile Delta in Egypt. During the first half of the first millennium, that cultural sphere moved west with the Phoenician colonization of much of the western Mediterranean. *Northwest Semitic* is a linguistic term used to describe Canaanite and Aramaic, the two primary languages spoken by the inhabitants of the coastal and inland Levant during much of the period before 332 BCE; it is also used by specialists to describe the civilizations of the area and their cults. Canaanite dialects include Phoenician, Punic (Phoenician of the western Mediterranean), Hebrew, Ammonite, Moabite, Edomite, and Ugaritic (though some scholars would dispute this categorization of Ugaritic, viewing it as a separate language). Various Aramaic dialects are also attested in first-millennium BCE texts.

A number of important sources are available for reconstructing religious devotion in the Northwest Semitic cultural sphere. Among these are nonliterary material remains from various excavated sites: altars, temples, cultic utensils, and organic matter (e.g., charred bones from sacrifices); tombs and other burials; figurines, plaques, statues and engraved stelae with representations of deities or their symbols. In addition, literary materials of various stripe are well attested: cycles of myth, "epic" texts, royal inscriptions, treaties, pantheon lists, personal names, dedications to deities, and inscriptions on sarcophagi. The major Northwest Semitic literary corpora from the second millennium of significance for reconstructing cult include the Ugaritic texts (the extant archives of a cosmopolitan center on the northern Levantine coast destroyed in c. 1200 BCE); the Mari documents (letters and other materials from the eighteenth century BCE); and various Egyptian inscriptions from the New Kingdom (c. sixteenth–eleventh century BCE). From the first millennium, the most important sources include the Hebrew Bible (an anthology of Israelite literature spanning 1,000 years); various Phoenician, Punic, and Aramaic inscriptions; and the Canaanite mythic lore attributed to a Phoenician priest, Sakkunyaton, preserved by Philo of Byblos (late first/early second century CE), and transmitted in fragmentary form in Greek by the fourth-century church father Eusebius of Caesarea (in his *Praeparatio evangelica*).

Various aspects of Northwest Semitic cultic devotion have received significant attention from specialists in recent decades. These include general topics that transcend particular cults, such as the relationship of mythic texts to ritual; the functions of sacrifices and offerings; cultic devotion to dead ancestors; gender and the cult; and the relationship of official and popular religion, including attempts to define precisely what constitutes each. In addition, topics pertaining to particular cults, especially that of Israel, have attracted much interest. These include the place of child sacrifice and the role of a goddess or goddesses in the cult of Yahweh, and the broader question of the relationship of Israelite religion to its Northwest Semitic environment. Although all of these topics have attracted sustained attention from the scholarly community and frequently engendered passionate debate, in many cases no broad consensus has been reached.

Deities. Many gods and goddesses appear as actors in mythic and epic texts; they receive dedications from worshipers, support rulers and dynasties according to royal inscriptions, and function as witnesses in treaties; their names are listed in pantheon tabulations and appear as theophoric elements in personal names. Gods receiving cultic devotion are frequently imagined as beneficent parents or kin, providers of progeny and the earth's good bounty to their worshipers. The Ugaritic epic stories "Kirta" and "Aqhat," and *Genesis* 15, each evidence the motif of the heirless patriarch or king provided with a son by his divine benefactor. Various Ugaritic texts state that Baal's rains bring fructification to the earth; in "Kirta," El's command cures Kirta's disease. Names such as Binbaal ("son of Baal"), Bodtannit ("in the hand of Tannit"), Ashtartyaton ("Ashtart gave"), and Yoab ("Yahweh is father") well illustrate the manner in which worshipers imagined their relationship to the divine. Deities such as El, Asherah, Baal/Hadad, and Yahweh are imagined as creators—of the gods, of creatures, of the world. The name *Yahweh* may in fact be a causative form of the verb *to be*, meaning "he creates" with the object ṣĕbāʾôt "(the heavenly) armies" (Cross, 1973, pp. 60–71).

Northwest Semitic gods were typically paired with goddesses, as in other ancient Near Eastern cults: El with Asherah or Ashtart (according to Sakkunyaton); Baal/Hadad with Anat, Ashtart, Pidray or other goddesses; Yarih with Nikkal (*KTU* 1.24). God and goddess pairs are attested among the hundreds of divine figurines discovered throughout the Levant. According to some scholars, Yahweh was probably no exception to this pattern. Inscriptions discovered in the 1970s at Kuntillet ʿAjrud in the Sinai Desert, as well as biblical texts, such as *Deuteronomy* 16:21, suggest the probability of a consort relationship between Yahweh and Asherah, both in popular devotion and in non-Deuteronomistic state religion. However, this view remains controversial (see further, Saul M. Olyan, *Asherah and the Cult of Yahweh in Israel*, Atlanta, 1988; for a different approach, see P. Kyle McCarter, Jr., "Aspects of the Religion of the Israelite Monarchy: Biblical and Epigraphic Data," in *Ancient Israelite Religion*, edited by Patrick D. Miller, Jr., et al., pp. 137–55, Philadelphia, 1987).

It is clear that the idea of a pantheon or divine council was widespread throughout the Northwest Semitic cultural sphere, including in Israel. In the mythic and epic materials from Ugarit, El heads the divine council; in biblical texts such as Psalm 89:6–9 [Eng. 5–8], Yahweh, Israel's national god and likely a manifestation of El, is described similarly (see further, Cross, 1973, on the relationship of El, Baal, and Yahweh). While, the lesser gods in Yahweh's council are nameless and may possess no independent will or authority, this is not the case in the Ugaritic texts, where gods and goddesses are frequently described in conflict, vying for power. In the Baal cycle, Sea claims kingship over the gods, only to be vanquished by Baal; Anat threatens her father El, head of the council; Shapsh, the Sun, threatens Death in the name of El. A number of scholars have argued that El's authority over the pantheon erodes over time, but this remains unproved; in some formulations, El is thought to be displaced by Baal as head of the council (see, for example,

CULT. *Warrior god figure, perhaps Baʿal-Hadad.* Late Bronze Age. (Courtesy ASOR Archives)

Marvin Pope, *El in the Ugaritic Texts*, Leiden, 1955; and, more recently, U. Oldenburg, *The Conflict Between El and Baʿal in Canaanite Religion*, Leiden, 1969). A tendency to elaborate the pantheon through the fusion of divine names to produce new deities is a widely attested phenomenon (e.g., Tannit-Ashtart, Arshaph-Melqart, Eshmun-Ashtart); the divinization of a deity's attributes (e.g., holiness, justice), cultic elements and weapons (e.g., censer, lyre, lance), or the cult place itself (e.g., temple) is also well known in second and first millennium texts.

Israel's religion as attested in biblical sources is better described as monolatry than as monotheism; even biblical texts that insist on the worship of one god acknowledge the ex-

istence of others (e.g., *Dt.* 4:19–20, 29:25) and divine council scenes are not uncommon in biblical narrative. Yahweh's claim to exclusive worship was one component of his covenantal bond with Israel; in a typical ancient Near Eastern suzerain-vassal covenant, after which the Yahweh-Israel bond was modeled, the suzerain demands exclusive rights from the vassal. Israel's monolatry was not altogether different from the national cults of the other kingdoms that emerged in the area at about the same time. What little we know of the cults of Moab, Ammon, and Edom suggest that they too were focused on the worship of a national deity, although devotion to that god was very likely not exclusive.

The preeminent gods of mythic and epic texts, royal dedications, and pantheon lists were sometimes the deities who were most frequently worshipped by elements of the wider populace in a given place at a given time, but not necessarily. A god such as Baal Hadad, a major actor in the mythic cycles from Ugarit and Sakkunyaton's lore, whose name appears near the top of extant pantheon lists from Ugarit, enjoyed widespread popularity in the second and first millennia, among Aramaic as well as Canaanite speakers, given the frequency of his appearance in dedications, treaties, and personal names. A contrasting case is the goddess Astarte, a consort of Baal in some contexts. Though Astarte played a significant role in the official cult of New Kingdom Egypt, appearing in a variety of royal inscriptions, very few personal names compounded with Astarte are attested, suggesting that her role in popular worship might have been limited in that context. More difficult to explain is the evidence attested for the worship of the goddess Tannit (probably an epithet of Asherah) in the Punic colonies of the western Mediterranean. Tannit appears in literally thousands of dedications from the mid- to late first millennium, yet personal names compounded with Tannit are rare. Here we touch on the complex problem of the relationship between official and popular religion on the one hand and of various modes of popular devotion on the other. A deity important in the official cult may not necessarily be important in the quotidian lives of worshipers; a god or goddess important in one class of evidence for popular devotion may hardly appear in another class contemporaneous with it. Such disjunction suggests that there is still much we do not understand about the religious devotion of the ancients.

The study of myth and epic has been the focus of much attention since the initial discovery of ancient Ugarit more than sixty years ago. Three great poetic compositions, the mythic Baal cycle, and the epic stories "Kirta" and "Aqhat," written in a Canaanite dialect in an alphabetic cuneiform script, were unearthed; many lesser mythic texts of interest have appeared as well, some as recently as the last thirty years (see, for example, texts in *Ugaritica*, vol. 5, Jean Nougayrol et al., eds., Paris, 1968). These critical discoveries supplement the largely Phoenician mythological lore of Sakkunyaton from the first millennium; they tend to confirm the basic authenticity of much of Sakkunyaton's lore, even though the latter is frequently shrouded in a hellenized, euhemerized form. Together, these two corpora form the basis for any serious discussion of Canaanite mythology.

The Baal cycle tells of the storm god Baal's battles with two foes: the forces of chaos represented by Sea (Yamm) or sea dragon (Lotan; cf. the cognate biblical word *Leviathan*) and the forces of sterility and death personified in the deity Death (Mot). The battles with Sea and sea dragon are alloforms, both ending in victory for Baal; a third version of this conflict pattern, in which Baal is vanquished by Sea, occurs in Sakkunyaton's lore. This mythic pattern of conflict is widespread, attested elsewhere in the Northwest Semitic cultural sphere, in various Hebrew Bible texts (for example, *Ps.* 29:10, 89:6–13 [Eng. 5–12]; *Is.* 27:1) and in the Mesopotamian myth *Enuma elish*, and has been the subject of much scholarly discussion. The details of each version may differ, but the general pattern is usually the same: Sea or sea dragon, a threatening force, is vanquished by a warrior god (Baal, Yahweh, Marduk) who assumes kingship after victory. The Baal cycle from Ugarit, which is incomplete and sometimes fragmentary, tells of the building of Baal's temple after his victory and his assumption of divine kingship but contains no creation story; in contrast, the *Enuma elish* tells of the creation of the heavens, earth, and humanity by victorious Marduk. *Enuma elish* begins with theogony; in contrast, the Baal cycle contains no theogonic narrative. No consensus has been reached on whether the Baal cycle represents a primitive version of the conflict myth without theogonic and cosmogonic elaboration, or it is incomplete in its present form, lacking a theogonic and/or cosmogonic element that was once present.

The precise relationship between myth and ritual has been widely debated for many decades, and on this no consensus has been reached. Many scholars believe that mythic and epic materials such as the Baal cycle, "the Birth of Dawn and Dusk" (*KTU* 1.23) and "Kirta" had a ritual, or cultic, setting; however, the function of the narrative in such a setting has been difficult to delimit. Some have even argued that ritual drama played a role in the Israelite cult. We know from a colophon that the Baal cycle extant from Ugarit was recited by the chief priest Attanu-Purlianni in the fourteenth century BCE under royal sponsorship (Niqmaddu II, c. 1375–1345), but the purpose of this recitation appears to have been the production of an official written version for the temple archives (*KTU* 1.6 VI 54–58). It has never been demonstrated convincingly that the Baal cycle, "Kirta," or any other mythic or epic narrative was actually acted out in the cult in some kind of ritual drama. (see further I. Engnell, *Studies in Divine Kingship in the Ancient Near East*, Uppsala, 1943, and Helmer Ringgren, *Religions of the Ancient Near East*, Philadelphia, 1973, pp. 162–164, for favorable articulations of the myth and ritual position).

Temples. A deity was worshiped in a holy place that was sometimes located on an elevation, frequently within the confines of a city. A temple, the god's dwelling, or house, often stood within the sanctuary grounds. Divinities were enthroned within their temples; they were served by cultic functionaries—specialists responsible for the upkeep of the sanctuary and its proper functioning. In addition to a cultic image or stelae, the typical temple might also contain incense stands or altars; offering tables, dishes, bowls, or basins; votive items, such as ornaments of precious stone, metal objects, or beads; and burial pits for discarded cultic materials. Where there is evidence for an altar of burnt offerings, it stood outside of the house. A broadhouse structure from Middle and Late Bronze Age Hazor (beginning with stratum III) had a rectangular platform in its courtyard with a drainage channel, evidence of the presence of an altar. An altar of unfinished stones and soil, with plastered channels, was found in the court of the Iron II Israelite temple at Arad (*ANE* 2, picture 105). At Beersheba, a deconstructed horned altar of ashlar blocks was found.

Engraved stelae portray deities receiving offerings from kings (e.g., Yehawmilk of Byblos, *ANE* 1, picture 130, where the goddess, the "Lady of Byblos," raises her right hand in a gesture of blessing). In some cults, royal personages served as hereditary priests or priestesses for their patron deities; Sidon is one example of this, as evidenced in the Tabnit and Eshmunazar inscriptions (*KAI* 13 and 14; English translations in *ANE* 2.227–229). [*See* Eshmunazar Inscription.] Kings frequently boasted of their temple building activities, a pattern ubiquitous in the ancient Near East. When Israel emerged as a significant regional power in the tenth century, a national shrine was constructed under royal patronage for Yahweh in Jerusalem, the imperial capital. A house of cedar, it stood next to the royal palace, a symbol of order, stability, and the eternal rule of both the Davidic dynasty and its patron god. Evidence for the king as a quasi-divine figure, the adopted son of his patron god, is found both in "Kirta" and in Judean royal propaganda (e.g., *Ps.* 2:7–9, 89:20–38 [Eng., 19–37]; *2 Sm.* 7:11b–16).

A number of architectural patterns are attested for temples in the Northwest Semitic cultural sphere. The most common temple design in Canaan proper was the "broad house," with an entry on one long side into a single room; often, a niche was placed in the wall opposite the entrance, within which a divine image or images might rest. This temple design is exceedingly ancient, predating the beginnings of the so-called Bronze Age at Chalcolithic 'Ein-Gedi in Israel (Aharoni, 1982, pp. 43–45); it was utilized at such sites as Hazor, Megiddo, Jericho, and Lachish, as well as at Israelite Arad. Another temple pattern, the "temple tower," is attested at such sites as Shechem, Megiddo, and Hazor in Israel at Alalakh in Syria; it was a broad room with towers flanking the entry area. A third model, the "long house," was used for the Jerusalem temple built by Solomon in the tenth century BCE. It consisted of three rooms, with an entry on one short side. The closest architectural parallel to the Jerusalem temple comes from Neo-Hittite Tell Ta'yinat (ninth century BCE). It has been argued that this version of the long house, along with other Neo-Hittite cultural features, was borrowed during the tenth century BCE, Israel's imperial era.

Many cultic icons have been unearthed, some of which stood on platforms, in cultic niches, or elsewhere within temples. Some of these are clearly representations of deities or divine pairs in a variety of poses; others, such as images of bulls, appear to have served as thrones for deities; in some instances, deity and throne were discovered attached. Icons were often cast in metals such as bronze or copper; some were covered with silver, gold, or electrum. These figurines are generally quite small, especially in comparison to Mesopotamian examples. One example of a divine image is the seated stone figure found in the niche of the Late Bronze Stela Temple excavated at Hazor (*ANE* 2, picture 103). Along with the statue of the deity, there were a number of standing stones (stelae), well-known symbols of divinity found elsewhere. Interesting metal icons from the Levant include a divine couple standing on the back of a bull (Ora Negbi, *Canaanite Gods in Metal*, Tel Aviv, 1976, no. 14) and a consort pair in a chariot (no. 22). Though the cult of Yahweh apparently eschewed images of the deity, the use of stelae to symbolize Yahweh's presence was probably common before the Deuteronomistic reforms of the eighth and seventh centurie BCE, to judge from the archeological finds

CULT. *Bronze figurine of warrior god standing on an oxhide ingot. From Enkomi, height 35 cm. (Archives CFA Schaeffer, Paris)*

at Israelite Arad and the textual evidence (e.g., *Gn.* 28:11–22; 35:14, 20). Besides stelae, some Israelite temples contained icons that functioned as thrones upon which the invisible Yahweh was seated (e.g., the bulls found at Bethel and Dan and, according to biblical texts, cherubs in the Jerusalem Temple). An asherah, likely a stylized wooden tree symbolizing the goddess Asherah, stood in various Yahwistic sanctuaries in Israel and Judah, according to a variety of biblical texts; it is also mentioned in inscriptions from Kuntillet 'Ajrud, Khirbet el-Qom, and Tel Miqne.

Sacrifices. Animal sacrifice and the cultic collection of the products of agriculture and horticulture were activities widely practiced throughout the Northwest Semitic cultural sphere. Sacrifices and offerings had many purposes: they were intended as gifts for deities, from whom worshipers frequently sought blessing; they served as food for the gods; and they were a form of taxation to support the cultic establishment. Other attested purposes include the correction of sin, the fulfillment of vows, and communion with the deity. The system of sacrifices and offerings evidenced in the most detail is Israel's, but there are significant data from Ugarit and the western Phoenician colonies. In many respects, Israelite sacrifice resembled that of other Northwest Semitic peoples. Israelites offered up unblemished sheep, goats, and cattle; birds such as turtledoves and pigeons; oil, wine, and grains in various forms; and incense. From sacrificial lists found at Ugarit there is evidence that cows and sheep were offered to deities of the city's pantheon (*CTA* 34, 35, 36). "Kirta" describes impressionistically a sacrificial ritual in which a lamb and bird are offered, wine is poured out, and prayer is directed toward heaven. Punic sacrifices included goats, sheep, cattle, birds, and grain products. Much Israelite sacrificial terminology is not unlike that found in inscriptional evidence from the Punic west, Ugarit, and elsewhere. Sacrificial tariffs from Marseille (*KAI* 69; English translations in *ANE* 1.221–223) and Carthage (*KAI* 74; translations in *ANE* 1.223–224) list offerings that include such sacrificial terms as *zbḥ*, *kll*, and *mnḥt*, all with biblical cognates [*see* Marseille Tariff]; they bear witness to sacrifices shared by priests and worshipers, as in Israel's cult (cf. Heb., *šělāmîm*, "sacrifices," in *Lv.* 3).

Differences between Israelite sacrifice and that of other Northwest Semitic cults are evident. While the manipulation of blood played a central role in the former, there is little or no indication that it did at Ugarit or in first-millennium Phoenicia or the Punic west (cf. Mesopotamia, where blood played no significant role). Furthermore, purity concerns, so central for Yahweh's cult, are virtually unattested outside of Israelite sources. For example, the Hebrew term *ṭāmē'* ("unclean") and other derivatives from its root, are unattested in the Ugaritic-Phoenician lexicon (however, note the apparent concern for the purity of the sanctuary in Lucian's description of the cult at Hierapolis [*The Syrian Goddess* 52–53] and the evidence for purity concerns in the cult in

Mesopotamia). There are indications that a feeding and pleasing element was present in Israelite sacrifice to Yahweh, but it was at best vestigial (see *Gn.* 8:20–21; *Lv.* 21:22; *Nm.* 28:2; and *Dt.* 33:10, where it occurs).

Textual and archeological evidence indicates that child sacrifice was practiced in much of the Northwest Semitic cultural sphere, including Israel. Sacred precincts (tophets) have been unearthed at a number of sites in the central and western Mediterranean where the Phoenicians had established colonies (e.g., Nora, Sulcis, and Tharros in Sardinia; Motya in Sicily; Carthage and Hadrumetum [Sousse] in North Africa); in the east, the only major site to have been discovered thus far is at the Amman Airport in Jordan. The largest site was found at Carthage. This precinct, which was utilized for nearly six hundred years, contains thousands of burial urns filled with the charred bones of infants, children, or small sacrificial animals and birds, which very likely functioned as substitutes for children; the burials were marked in some phases by stelae, some of which record dedications to Baal Hamon (very likely an epithet of El) and his consort Tannit (very likely an epithet of Asherah). Sakkunyaton records two versions of a myth in which El (called Kronos) sacrifices his "only son" in a threatening situation (war/plague). Various Greek and Latin sources bear witness to Punic child sacrifice and may even allude to the myth of El recorded by Sakkunyaton (e.g., Diodorus of Sicily, *Library of History* 20.14.7; Tertullian, *Apology* 9.4). El and Asherah appear to be the preeminent deities of child sacrifice, at least in the Punic West; for the East only conjecture is possible.

A technical term, *molk*, occurs occasionally in Phoenician and Punic inscriptions, usually compounded with a second term (e.g., *molk 'adam*; *molk ba'l*; *molk 'omor*); in such compounds, *molk* seems to mean a type of sacrifice, either of a child or of an animal substitute for a child (see *Eissfeldt*, 1935). The biblical *molek* is best explained as a sacrificial term cognate to the Punic *molk*, although some scholars argue that *molek* is the name of a god of child sacrifice (e.g., George C. Heider, *The Cult of Molek: A Reassessment*, Sheffield, 1986; John Day, *Molech: A God of Human Sacrifice in the Old Testament*, Cambridge, 1989). Child sacrifice in Israel was more likely directed to Yahweh than a supposed god Molek, as the development of the so-called law of the firstborn (*Ex.* 13:1–2, 11–16, 22:28b–29 [Eng. 29b–30], 34:19–20; *Nm.* 3:11–13, 41), certain prophetic texts (*Ez.* 20:25–26; *Mi.* 6:6–8), and *Genesis* 22 all strongly suggest. The cultic function of child sacrifice is not entirely clear. Evidence suggests that parents sacrificed their children to fulfill a vow; to petition for blessing, health, and happiness; to give thanks for blessings received; or to obey the order of a patron god. Some texts present child sacrifice as a response to crisis and danger (*2 Kgs.* 3:27; Diodorus of Sicily; the El myth recorded by Sakkunyaton); *Micah* 6:6–8 suggests that such sacrifices to Yahweh were presented as sin offerings. Whatever the function of child sacrifice, animal substitution was a widely attested option for parents (see especially the second/third century CE Ngaous inscriptions from Algeria, which contain substitution ritual formulas [Eissfeldt, 1935, pp. 1–7]).

Ancestor Cults. Life after death, the abode of the dead, the archaeology of death, the ritual state of mourning, and cults devoted to dead ancestors have all attracted serious attention from the scholarly community in recent years. Ancestor cults were apparently quite widespread, attested among both Aramaic and Canaanite speakers, to judge from the archaeological and textual evidence. Various sources suggest that members of royal and aristocratic elites, and perhaps others, communed with dead ancestors in the home, in temples, and possibly in the context of a property-owning, feasting society called the *marzēaḥ* (there is, however, much that we still do not understand about this institution, including the extent of its associations with ancestral cults). The Hadad inscription from eighth-century Zincirli (*KAI* 214) mentions the obligation of the heir to invoke the name of the dead king in Hadad's temple in a sacrificial context. This notion of the heir invoking the dead father's name occurs in the Hebrew Bible as well, where the erection of a memorial stela by David's son Absalom is mentioned (*2 Sm.* 18:18; cf. the Ugaritic "Aqhat," where the heir is obliged "to set up a stela for his divine [dead] ancestor," *KTU* 1.17 I 26). The heir may have cared for and fed the dead, as in Mesopotamia, although the exact nature of this activity has been the subject of vigorous debate (see Theodore J. Lewis, *Cults of the Dead in Ancient Israel and Ugarit*, Atlanta, 1989, for a discussion). It seems clear that the dead were deified, even in Israel (*1 Sm.* 28:13 and possibly *Is.* 8:19), but the exact nature of their "divine" status remains unclear. Ugaritic pantheon lists typically begin with or include *'il'ib*, most convincingly explained as "the divine (dead) ancestor." A class of ancestors called Rephaim is mentioned in materials from both the second and first millennia BCE. The meaning of their title ("hale ones"; "healers"; "weak," or "sunken, ones"; and even "great ones"?) and even their status as dead ancestors has been much discussed. No consensus has emerged regarding the meaning of their title, but most scholars now view the Rephaim as dead ancestors rather than living heroes.

Cultic Specialists. Religious practitioners and cultic functionaries such as priests, prophetic figures, mediums, diviners, and professional mourners are all attested in texts from the Northwest Semitic cultural sphere. Each specialization had its own area of influence and control; each probably mediated skills through forms of apprenticeship. The priesthood controlled the sanctuary complex, collecting and processing offerings and sacrifices from worshipers; they oversaw the care of the property, provided for the music and song of cultic rites, blessed worshipers, and practiced divination in some contexts. Evidence suggests that priests also functioned to mediate mythic and epic lore and probably other forms of knowledge (see for instance the role as-cribed by tradition to Sakkunyaton, allegedly a Phoenician priest, or the activity of Attanu-Purlianni in fourteenth cen-tury BCE Ugarit, as witnessed in the Baal cycle colophon [*KTU* 1.6 VI 54–58]). Aside from priests, other specialists and functionaries are attested in various Northwest Semitic cults. A Phoenician inscription from Kition in Cyprus mentions, among others, "servants" (*n'rm*), "sacrificers" (*zbḥm*), "barbers" (*glbm*), "masons" (*ḥršm*), and a chief scribe (*rb sprm*); other lists mention singers, musicians, male and female "holy ones" (some claim these were cult pros-titutes, others deny it. See further, Kavel van der Toorn, "Female Prostitution in Payment of Vows in Ancient Is-rael," *Journal of Biblical Literature* 108 [1989]: 193–205, on the problem of sacred prostitution). Sacrifices and offerings functioned partially to support the cult and its specialists, a form of taxation in kind. There is evidence that at least some temple complexes also had their own flocks and herds: lists of cultic functionaries from Ugarit mention *nqdm*, "herd-ers," along with the priests and other temple officials. In Israel, the priesthood of Yahweh was all male, in contrast to the cults of other Northwest Semitic deities, where women sometimes played a priestly role (e.g., Sidon and Carthage). There is evidence that at least some priesthoods were he-reditary elites. A stela from Carthage lists three generations of high priests from the same family (*KAI* 81); a tomb in-scription lists five generations of priests. In Israel the priest-hood developed over time from a group of specialists (Le-vites) open to the adoption of outsiders as apprentices (e.g., Samuel) into an increasingly exclusive, hereditary elite. Conflict between various priestly clans is well attested in biblical sources.

Prophetic activity associated with the cult is attested in Israel and elsewhere in the Northwest Semitic cultural sphere. Through the oracles of prophets, often delivered in an ecstatic state, a god's message to a king or community was mediated. The twelfth-century narrative of Wenamun, a cultic official from Karnak, reports an incident in which an attendant of Zakarbaal, ruler of Byblos, entered an ec-static state during a sacrifice and delivered a divine oracle (see *ANE* 1.18). The Mari texts attest to the activity of male and female prophetlike figures (e.g., *āpilu* and *āpiltu*, *muḫḫu*). The Aramaic Zakkur inscription from Ḥamath claims that Baal Shamayn (Baal Shamêm) spoke to the king through intermediaries (*KAI* 202). Various anthologies of prophetic oracles survive from Israel, where prophets claimed to mediate Yahweh's word. Intermediation was ac-complished by persons peripheral to the cult, as well as by those who occupied a central position, and positions could change over time (see further, R. R. Wilson, *Prophecy and Society in Ancient Israel*, Philadelphia, 1980, for an interest-ing comparative perspective). Prophetic figures, like priests and others, practiced forms of divination.

Other religious specialists included mediums and necro-

CULT. *Gypsum statuette from Tell Asmar.* (Courtesy Oriental Insti-tute of the University of Chicago)

mancers and professional mourners. Mediums and necro-mancers, many of whom were women, consulted the dead on behalf of the living (*1 Sm.* 28; *Is.* 8:19); some texts suggest that the dead possessed useful information that the living might want to know, as well as the power to bring well-being to those who survived them. Mediums and necromancers apparently communicated with the dead by means of imi-tating their characteristic speech: bird sounds (*Is.* 8:19, 29:4, 38:14; and cf. "Gilgamesh," *ANE* 1.58; "Descent of Ishtar," *ANE* 1.81; and "Nergal and Ereshkigal," *ANE* 2.9, for Me-sopotamian texts in which the dead have the appearance of birds and/or make birdlike sounds). Because they competed with priests and prophets in the arena of divination, medi-ums and necromancers were attacked by their increasingly powerful rivals in Israel during and following the period of the Divided Kingdom (*Dt.* 18:10–12; *Lv.* 19:31; 20:6, 27). Professional mourners, frequently women skilled in weep-ing, wailing, and the composition of lamentations, are at-tested in a number of contexts ("Kirta"; *Jer.* 9:16–18, 19–20 [Eng. 17–19, 20–21]; *2 Sm.* 1:20, 24). It is clear that women played an important role in death-related specializations in at least some Northwest Semitic cults.

[*See also* Arad; Beersheba; Canaanites; Kuntillet ʿAjrud; Mari Texts; Temples, *articles on* Mesopotamian Temples *and* Syro-Palestinian Temples; Ugarit. *In addition, most of the other sites mentioned are the subject of independent entries.*]

BIBLIOGRAPHY

Aharoni, Yohanan. *The Archaeology of the Land of Israel.* Translated by Anson F. Rainey. Philadelphia, 1982.

Albright, William F. *Yahweh and the Gods of Canaan* (1968). Reprint, Winona Lake, Ind., 1990. Classic reconstruction, by one of this century's most talented and influential scholars.

Anderson, Gary A. *Sacrifices and Offerings in Ancient Israel.* Atlanta, 1987. Recent contribution to our understanding of sacrifices and offerings in Israel and the Northwest Semitic cultural sphere.

Anderson, Gary A. *A Time to Mourn, a Time to Dance: The Expression of Grief and Joy in Israelite Religion.* University Park, Pa., 1991. Insightful study of mourning and rejoicing as ritual antitypes.

Attridge, Harold W., and R. A. Oden, Jr., eds. and trans. *Philo of Byblos: The Phoenician History.* Washington, D.C., 1980. Useful text, translation, and introduction to the Sakkunyaton material.

Baumgarten, Albert I., ed. and trans. *The Phoenician History of Philo of Byblos: A Commentary.* Leiden, 1981. Alternative to the edition by Attridge and Oden.

Ben-Tor, Amnon, ed. *The Archaeology of Ancient Israel.* New Haven, 1992. Recent survey, period by period, by one of Israel's leading archaeologists.

Bloch-Smith, Elizabeth. *Judahite Burial Practices and Beliefs about the Dead.* Journal for the Study of the Old Testament, Supplement 123. Sheffield, 1992. Excellent, comprehensive survey of archaeological materials pertaining to death, burial, and ancestor cults in Israel.

Coogan, Michael David, ed. and trans. *Stories from Ancient Canaan.* Philadelphia, 1978. Helpful translation and introduction to the mythological and epic material from Ugarit.

Craigie, Peter C. *Ugarit and the Old Testament.* Philadelphia, 1983.

Cross, Frank Moore. *Canaanite Myth and Hebrew Epic.* Cambridge, Mass., 1973.

Cross, Frank Moore. "The Epic Traditions of Early Israel: Epic Narrative and the Reconstruction of Early Israelite Institutions." In *The Poet and the Historian,* edited by Richard Elliott Friedman, pp. 13–39. Chico, Calif., 1983. The author develops his position on the use of the term *epic* to describe material such as JE in the Pentateuch and "Kirta" and "Aqhat" from Ugarit.

Dietrich, Manfried, Oswald Loretz, and Joaquin Sanmartín. *Die keilalphabetische Texte aus Ugarit,* vol. 1, *Transcription.* Neukirchen-Vluyn, 1976.

Donner, Herbert, and Wolfgang Röllig. *Kanaanäische und aramäische Inschriften.* 3 vols. Wiesbaden, 1962–1964.

Eissfeldt, Otto. *Molk als Opferbegriff im Punischen und Hebräischen und das Ende des Gottes Moloch.* Halle, 1935.

Halpern, Baruch. "'Brisker Pipes Than Poetry': The Development of Israelite Monotheism." In *Judaic Perspectives on Ancient Israel,* edited by Jacob Neusner et al., pp. 77–115. Philadelphia, 1987. Interesting and insightful treatment of a daunting problem.

Herdner, Andrée. *Corpus des tablettes en cunéiformes alphabétiques découvertes à Ras Shamra–Ugarit de 1929 à 1939.* Paris, 1963.

Ottosson, Magnus. *Temples and Cult Places in Palestine.* Uppsala, 1980. Very useful survey of the archaeological data up to the late 1970s.

Pope, Marvin H. "The Cult of the Dead at Ugarit." In *Ugarit in Retrospect: Fifty Years of Ugarit and Ugaritic,* edited by Gordon D. Young, pp. 159–179. Winona Lake, Ind., 1981. One of a number of articles by Pope on this subject. Audacious, controversial, stimulating.

Pritchard, James B., ed. *The Ancient Near East: An Anthology of Texts and Pictures (ANE).* 2 vols. Princeton, 1958–1975. Easily accessible translations of important texts, as well as photographs of sites, inscriptions, and coins. An abridgment of his *Ancient Near Eastern Texts Relating to the Old Testament* (Princeton, 1950), and *The Ancient Near East in Pictures Relating to the Old Testament* (Princeton, 1954).

Stadelmann, Rainer. *Syrisch-Palästinensische Gottheiten in Ägypten.* Leiden, 1967. Interesting study of the data from Egypt on the worship of Northwest Semitic deities there.

Stager, Lawrence E. "The Rite of Child Sacrifice at Carthage." In *New Light on Ancient Carthage,* edited by John G. Pedley, pp. 1–11. Ann Arbor, 1980. Excellent recent overview of the archaeological and epigraphic evidence.

Vaux, Roland de. *Ancient Israel.* 2 vols. New York, 1961. Classic reconstruction of social and religious institutions in Israel, by this century's most accomplished French scholar.

Vrijhof, Pieter Hendrick, and Jacques Waardenburg, eds. *Official and Popular Religion: Analysis of a Theme for Religious Studies.* The Hague, 1979. Useful text on a widely discussed issue.

SAUL M. OLYAN

CUNEIFORM. The first descriptions of cuneiform writing were brought to the West by travellers in the seventeenth century. They used terms such as *pyramid, triangle,* and *delta* to express the configurations of the eye-catching wedge-shaped heads on top or to the side of strokes incised on clay tablets. The use of cuneiform writing covers more than three millennia from the time of its invention (pictographic precursors) at the end of the fourth millennium to the latest datable text attested in 74/75 CE.

G. F. Grotefend's epoch-making thesis, presented in Göttingen in 1802, "Provisional Report on the Reading and Explanation of the So-Called Cuneiform Inscriptions of Persepolis" used *cuneatus,* "wedge shaped," in its Latin title. The term *cuneiformis,* "in the form of a wedge," has given rise to the modern designations cuneiform writing, *écriture cunéiforme* and *Keilschrift.*

The incision made on wet clay with a stylus, usually cut from a reed, automatically leaves a "wedge" at one end of the stroke, where more pressure is exercised. In the period of the Akkadian dynasty (c. twenty-third century BCE) the wedge was already seen as so characteristic of the writing that, although unnecessary, it was used in inscriptions carved in stone or—more rarely—incised in metal as well. Independently of its formal aspects, the term *cuneiform* is used today for a whole system of writing that is distinct from the other early Near Eastern invention, Egyptian hieroglyphic script. The system of the so-called Proto-Elamite script has not yet been fully evaluated because of its still imperfect state of decipherment and scholars' inadequate knowledge of the (Old) Elamite language.

The cuneiform system consists of signs denoting a word (including morphologic affixes or not); signs denoting a syllable, most of these being phonetic abstractions of the sound of a word sign (e.g., *da*, "side"; syllable *da*); and number signs. The system of syllabograms is remarkable (as compared with other syllabographic systems, both ancient and modern) in that it not only denotes v(owels) alone—[a], [i]—or c(onsonant) + v(owel)—[ba], [gu], [ne]—but also v + c—[ab], [id], [ug]—and even c + v + c—[bar], [kal], [tum]. With this system, during the last quarter of the third millennium, scribes handling cuneiform script were already able to yield "visible speech" with a relatively high degree of phonetic exactitude. [*See* Scribes and Scribal Techniques; Writing and Writing Systems.]

Syllabography as described above does not include consonantal clusters—*[tra], *[stra], *[art], *[arst], *[bart]. This means that languages having such clusters had to break them up in writing—ši-pa- for [spa] in Hittite.

In the course of history, cuneiform writing has been applied to far more languages than Sumerian (a language without known linguistic affiliation) and Akkadian (a Semitic language). The number of "cuneiform languages" includes Amorite (Semitic, practically restricted to the notation of proper names); Hurrian and Urartian (of Caucasian descent); Hittite, Luwian, and Palaic (Indo-European); Hattian (in central Anatolia); and Elamite (perhaps a remote cognate of the Dravidian languages). For Ugaritic (Semitic, fourteenth and thirteenth centuries BCE only) and Old Persian (Achaemenid Empire) signs have been invented that are formally cuneiform but are part of a system only loosely related to the one described so far (see below). [*See* Sumerian; Akkadian; Hurrian; Hittite; Ugaritic.]

Writing Cuneiform. From the inception of cuneiform writing, a distinction has been required between the stroke, or line, incised with the sharp end of the stylus and the impression of circles, semicircles, ovals, and triangles administered with its truncated end. The stylus was cut from a reed as a rule, but there were also luxury examples made of precious metal. It is difficult to reconstruct the exact way the stylus was held in the hand, but modern experiments suggest that it was held somehow between outstretched fingers rather than in a closed fist: only in the first manner would it be possible to keep the stylus at a relatively low angle to the tablet.

Whereas in the earliest texts both strokes and curved lines occur, there soon was a tendency toward straightening curves and replacing them with two or more strokes. Because the great majority of signs were composed of two to more than ten strokes or impressions, there most probably were set rules for their sequence, as is the case, for example, with Sino-Japanese signs. To date, almost no research has been devoted to reconstructing stroke and impression sequences.

There has been a long debate on the direction in which ancient scribes of a given period read and how, consequently, cuneiform signs are supposed to read. Pictographic precursors, such as the signs for bird, fish, or the head of a dog only make sense if viewed in their natural position. On stone, the abstract forms descending from the original signs were still written—and certainly were read—in their original sense as late as the eighteenth century BCE, an example being the stela inscription of the code of Hammurabi. On the other hand, everyday writing on clay tablets, as early as the beginning of the second millennium BCE and sometimes even earlier, only makes sense if read at an angle of 90 degrees turned to the left. Therefore, during several centuries two ways must have existed of looking at a cuneiform inscription—one vertical and one horizontal. It is only in about the middle of the second millennium BCE that stone inscriptions begin to be found that are to be read horizontally. Because inscriptions from the first millennium BCE were the first to be known, Assyriologists have become used to reading any cuneiform inscription horizontally, even if it is from the middle of the third millennium, Modern copyists arrange their specimens horizontally. The reason for the change of direction, whenever it definitely took place, can only be surmised and is not of primary concern here.

Ancient Mesopotamians did, in some way, realize that they were practicing "cuneiform." The individual signs had names (like the names of letters of the alphabet), and the name of the vertical wedge, DIŠ with the reading *santag*, in Akkadian *santakku*, became the geometric term for *triangle*. Also, as mentioned above, the wedge-formed heads were deliberately imitated in stone where, theoretically, strokes alone would have been sufficient.

Origin of Signs. It is mainly the research of Denise Schmandt-Besserat that has elucidated the prehistory of cuneiform writing (Schmandt-Besserat, 1992). Until the 1970s, the general opinion was held that writing was an ad hoc invention for administrators in southern Mesopotamia at the end of the fourth millennium. However, the systematic inspection of small, variously shaped clay objects found frequently in prehistoric strata at Near Eastern sites, but also in North Africa and India, has shown that such clay objects, or tokens as they have come to be called, were not haphazard items but part of a system. There is, in fact, a great variety of these objects: spheres (full, three-quarter, half-, or quarter sized), or disks, with or without incision and/or perforation; cylinders, cones, tetra-hedrons, pyramids; and skittles, sometimes with the suggestion of an animal head. At Susa, in Elam, such tokens have been found enclosed in hollow clay balls. The idea therefore arose that these tokens were meant to represent quantities of given things or animate beings. In a few cases, a strong resemblance can be shown to exist between a token and an archaic cuneiform sign. Consequently, it is possible to conclude that certain three-dimensional tokens were transformed into two-dimensional impressions on clay. [*See* Susa.]

Because there are no inventories of tokens for any given site, it is not possible to tell how widespread a consensus there may have been on forms and "meanings." Be that as it may, the fact that there seems to have been, even with local variations, a certain series of one-to-one correspondences between a token and a meaning justifies declaring the tokens to be precursors of writing. This would not belittle the achievement of the real invention of writing, which was the arrangement of signs, in an invariable position, on a two-dimensional surface, with the purpose of communicating an idea or, adversely, with the aim of changing visible speech (writing) back into audible signs (hearing).

The earliest cuneiform texts attested so far are from the southern Babylonian city of Uruk. In their great majority, these texts combine number signs with signs denoting things counted. Thus, the predominantly economical and administrative character of the earliest Mesopotamian writing becomes apparent: it seems in fact to have been the needs of economics—and not of historiography or religion—that prompted citizens of early Sumer to "visualize speech," however rudimentary that may have been. [See Uruk-Warka.]

Sign Types. In general, cuneiform signs can be classified in the following ways:

1. Signs that were, originally at least, the more or less unabbreviated reproduction of the thing they denote—boat, reed, head, hand.
2. Signs where one part stands for the whole (*pars pro toto*)—different heads of animals standing for the respective animal, or a penis for a man.
3. Other kinds of abbreviations—three hills for mountain, mountainous country, foreign country.
4. Signs where the thing reproduced serves as a symbol—a radiating star (or sun) denoting the sky or a divinity and the reed-bundle, symbol of the goddess Inanna standing for the goddess herself.
5. A token impression.
6. Free invention (difficult to prove, but certainly feasible)—signs for which the form had no association whatsoever with its meaning.
7. A rather complicated system of number and measure signs (measurements of length, area, weight, and capacity) in which only the digits 1–9 are multiplications of 1, with 10 corresponding to an invented sign (see above).

Relatively simple signs were soon exhausted when scribes began putting together a system. This is why one of the means of creating new signs was to combine two (or, more rarely, three or even four) individual signs to produce a new meaning. There were three ways of doing this: juxtaposition, incorporation, and ligature or monogram:

1. *Juxtaposition*. Two (or more) signs are grouped and not given their original meaning (and pronunciation)—that is, A.B = a.b, but the combination of the two (or more)

signs yields a new meaning (and pronunciation)—SI.A ≠ * si.a, but *diri(g)*, "exceeding."

2. *Incorporation*. One sign is written within another one, B within A, or, as Assyriologists are used to formulating: A × B ("A times B")—NINDA, "bread" within KA, "mouth," yields gu₇, "to eat."

3. *Ligature and monogram*. In a ligature (joining), signs A and B are put together more closely than would be the case in a simple enumeration of A, then B: for example, MINUS, "woman" + KUR, "foreign country," stands for "slave woman" (*géme*). The border between ligature and juxtaposition is however, a fluid one. A monogram is the ligature of two signs where one element (stroke) is common to both. The sign for *total* (*šunigin*) is very frequently written as a ligature of the signs ŠU and NÍGIN, the final vertical wedge of ŠU and the initial vertical wedge of NÍGIN being identical.

The system of cuneiform signs may have been created in the course of a few generations, but it never ceased evolving.

Signs fell out of use and were completely forgotten; others were newly created, and, most important of all, the forms of the individual signs changed throughout the centuries.

Paleography. The science of studying writing on a given material, with special regard to diachronical change and to different scribal "hands" within a given period, is known as paleography. In the field of cuneiform studies, paleography would ideally imply an ability to determine complete sign inventories for each of a series of narrowly defined periods. Such is not the case, however, in spite of the fact that most publications of cuneiform texts are hand copies of originals that represent individual "hands"—that is, manuscripts in the exact meaning of the word.

The most general tendencies observed in the evolution of cuneiform writing are the elimination of wedges that came to be considered redundant and the reduction of angles at which a stroke or wedge might be written, from the original sixteen to finally only four (horizontal, vertical, oblique upward, and oblique downward). It should be possible, of course, to describe the general aspect of a scribal hand, but next to no preliminary studies have yet been done.

One of the most urgent needs of cuneiform paleography is, as was suggested above, to know the sequence in which the wedges or impressions of an individual sign were made. Close inspection of original cuneiform tablets, but also of first-quality photographs, often shows which of two intersecting wedges or strokes was incised first and which one second: it is frequently possible to see that one incision cuts through or overlaps another. Large-scale work on originals and photos would make significant progress in this area.

Numbers of Signs. Very few cuneiform signs have only a single reading (or value); the great majority have two, three, or, less frequently, even more possible readings. In Sumerian, a single sign may denote only a word or it may also have a syllabic value—*ra* as a verb means "to strike"; as a syllabogram it denotes the dative (*-ra*) in *lugal-ra*, "to the king." In Akkadian, certain Sumerian word signs are used with their Akkadian reading (so-called Sumerograms)—LUGAL is the equivalent of *šarrum*, "king." RI as a syllabic sign may be read *ri* or *dal*, *tal*, depending on the context. In Hittite, there are three levels: syllabic signs, Sumerograms, and Akkadograms—that is, Akkadian words spelled syllabically but read in Hittite.

This polyvalence contributed considerably to reducing the maximal number of signs needed to write literary or highly specialized texts with rare words as well as all sorts of proper names (persons, gods, places). Margaret W. Green's list of the signs found in the corpus of the oldest tablets from Uruk (c. 3000 BCE) contains 771 entries plus 58 number signs (Green and Nissen, 1987). One millennium later, the sign inventory at the time of the Third Dynasty of Ur had about eight hundred signs (no exact count is available). A scribe of the Hammurabi period (eighteenth century BCE) could manage to write Akkadian—entirely excluding Sumerograms—with a minimum syllabary of a little more than eighty signs, and the Old Assyrian merchants in their trading colonies in Asia Minor (nineteenth century BCE) used a syllabary of only sixty-eight signs. Considering these widely differing figures, it is possible to suppose that there were various degrees of literacy. A merchant could handle his correspondence and accounts with five-or six-dozen signs but would have been unable to read (or write) a literary text spelled in a more sophisticated way.

Derived Systems. In the harbor and trade city of Ugarit on the Mediterranean coast, a system of only thirty signs was invented in the fourteenth century BCE to write the local Semitic language. Twenty-seven of these signs denote consonants and the other three stand for *aleph* with inherent a, i, or u—that is, 'a, 'i, and 'u. Formally this writing is cuneiform because the components (one-five) of the individual signs are indeed wedges incised or impressed on wet clay. As a system, however, Ugaritic cuneiform has its closest cognates in the Egyptian one-consonant signs and in various consonantal writing systems of Syria and Palestine. The Ugaritic variety of cuneiform did not survive the invasions of the Sea Peoples in the thirteenth century BCE.

The origin of Old Persian cuneiform is still debated. It was Darius I (521–486 BCE) or one of his predecessors who had writing "invented" for the purpose of representing their tongue. The system comprises three vowel and thirty-three consonant signs with inherent vowels a (twenty-two signs), i (four), and u (six). The sign components similar to Ugaritic cuneiform, but totally independant of it, are wedges, varying between three and five per sign. There were, additionally, eight "logograms" (e.g., for Xerxes, Ahuramazda) that are more complicated. Old Persian cuneiform was exclusively used for monumental inscriptions, whereas the ad-ministration of the empire used either Elamite (on clay tablets) or Imperial Aramaic. The system was in use until Artaxerxes III (358–338 BCE).

BIBLIOGRAPHY

Borger, Rykle. *Assyrische-babylonische Zeichenliste.* 3d ed. Kevelaer, 1986.

Cooper, Jerrold S. "Cuneiform." In *International Encyclopedia of Communications.* vol. 1, pp. 438–443. New York, 1989.

Edzard, Dietz O. "Keilschrift." In *Reallexikon der Assyriologie,* vol. 5, pp. 544–568. Berlin, 1976–.

Englund, Robert K., et al. *Frühe Schrift und Technik der Wirtschaftsverwaltung im Alten Vorderen Orient.* Berlin, 1991.

Gordon, Cyrus H. *Ugaritic Textbook: Grammar, Texts in Transliteration, Cuneiform Selections, Glossary, Indices.* Analecta Orientalia, 38. Rome, 1965.

Green, Margaret Whitney, and Hans J. Nissen. *Zeichenliste der archaischen Texte aus Uruk.* Berlin, 1987.

Kent, Roland G. *Old Persian: Grammar, Texts, Lexicon.* 2d ed. New Haven, 1953.

Labat, René, and Florence Malbran-Labat. *Manuel d'épigraphie akkadienne.* 5th ed. Paris, 1976.

Pallis, Svend Aage. *Early Exploration in Mesopotamia.* Copenhagen, 1954.

Schmandt-Besserat, Denise. *Before Writing.* Vol. 1, *From Counting to Cuneiform;* vol. 2, *A Catalogue of Near Eastern Tokens.* Austin, Tex., 1992.

D. O. EDZARD

CYCLADES. *See* Aegean Islands.

CYPRUS. The third largest island in the Mediterranean Sea (9,251 sq km, or 3,572 sq. mi.), after Sicily and Sardinia, Cyprus has a strategic location in the northeastern corner of the Mediterranean that has proved to be both a blessing and a curse throughout its past twelve thousand years of settlement. Positioned some 70 km (44 mi.) south of Turkey and some 95 km (64 mi.) west of Syria, Cyprus was drawn into the trade and commerce that went east and west between the Aegean and the Levant, as well as north and south between Anatolia and Egypt. Prosperity stimulated plunder and conquest, however. Cyprus caught the eye of the warrior as well as that of the merchant, and there may often have been little difference in motivation between those who came to trade and those out to loot and conquer.

During its long history, Cyprus has been ruled by many groups of people not native to the island: Hittites; Greeks; Phoenicians; Romans (30 BCE–330 CE); Byzantine Greeks (330–1191); Crusaders, including the Knights Templar, Lusignans, and Venetians (1191–1571); Ottoman Turks (1571–1878); and the British (1878–1960). In 1960, Cyprus became an independent republic but was torn asunder only fourteen years later by the Turkish invasion of 1974. Cyprus remains divided, with the northern 37 percent of the island under Turkish military rule.

While this historical pattern of foreign rule has been an obvious force in Cypriot history, it has had a subtle impact on the modern study of Cypriot prehistory and archaeology. Developments on Cyprus came to be seen in terms of foreign invaders and foreign cultural influences, often at the expense of the contribution of native Cypriots to the island's culture. The Greek element in particular, stemming from a colonization of (initially) the western part of the island in the eleventh century BCE (placed by some scholars in the twelfth), had such a profound effect on the island's subsequent history that many modern Greek-speaking Cypriots look on Cyprus as part of the Greek world. The scholarly consequences of that invasion were the cessation of archaeological work in the north, where many of the best-known archaeological sites on Cyprus lie, including Enkomi, Lapithos, Salamis, Soloi, and Vouni. [See Enkomi, Lapithos; Salamis; Soloi; Vouni.] Many Byzantine churches in northern Cyprus have been desecrated. [See Churches.] The international trade in looted icons, mosaics, and wall paintings from these churches has resulted in legal cases that have attracted worldwide interest and resulted in important legislation relating to the shipment and sale of illegally exported antiquities. Prior to 1974, with most archaeological work on Cyprus carried out in the north and northeast, the tourist industry was focused on that general area and especially on the sites of Kyrenia and Ammochostos/Famagusta. Archaeology and tourism are today focused in the south, making Cyprus a tragic example of the ways in which modern politics impacts on the study of the past. [See Nationalism and Archaeology; Ethics and Archaeology; Tourism and Archaeology.]

Cyprus has a geology and an environment that, in many respects, are as unusual and distinctive as its history. Contrary to what was once believed, the island was not originally part of the Anatolian mainland but emerged through volcanic activity from the sea bed. The main mountain range—the igneous rocks of the southern Troodos Mountains—was formed during late Oligocene or Early Miocene times; the sedimentary rocks of the northern Kyrenia range (also known as the Pentadaktylos) emerged during the Late Miocene. Between these two mountain ranges lies the great central plain known as the Mesaoria, access to which is through three main passes from the northern coast. The island has a series of natural harbors, including those at Morphou and Kyrenia on the north coast, Salamis and Ammochostos on the east, Kition and Hala Sultan Tekke and Amathus on the south, and Paphos on the west. [See Kition; Hala Sultan Teke; Paphos.] The special geological history of the Troodos, with their ophiolite copper deposits located in the pillow lavas of the southern part of the range, gave Cyprus its mineral wealth. From the Bronze Age down to modern times, that wealth has been the decisive factor in both the internal and the external affairs of the island.

Even a brief survey of the prehistory and ancient history of Cyprus, seen in light of modern archaeological work on the island, has to include the following periods:

Pre-Neolithic	c. 10,000 BCE
Aceramic Neolithic	c. 7000–5500
Ceramic Neolithic	c. 5000–3700
Chalcolithic	c. 3700–2400
Bronze Age	c. 2400–1125
Iron Age	c. 1125–800
Archaic Period	c. 800–500
Classical Period	499–323
Hellenistic Period	323–30
Roman Period	30 BCE–330 CE

The dating of all periods prior to the Late Bronze Age is based almost entirely upon calibrated radiocarbon dates. The use of such dates is, in some quarters, still regarded as somewhat controversial, but without them it is not possible to study Cypriot prehistory. What gives Cypriot prehistory its special character is that every period prior to the Iron Age has its own group of sites. Long occupation is characteristic of individual sites in the Aegean, Anatolia, the Levant, Iraq, and Iran, but not of Cyprus. For reasons not yet understood, the occupational history of archaeological sites on Cyprus almost never exceeded a single cultural period—nor was a former site ever reoccupied after being abandoned for some period of time. This means that there are no tells in Cypriot archaeology and no long, stratified sequences at major sites, which gives Cypriot prehistory its distinctive episodic character.

The Pre-Neolithic period has only come to light since the mid-1980s and is known only from one site, Akrotiri *Aetokremnos*. This is a rock-shelter at the tip of the Akrotiri peninsula, the southernmost part of Cyprus. It has produced a number of chipped-stone tools plus tens of thousands of fragments of pygmy hippopotamus bones together with a few bones of dwarf elephants (excavated by A. H. Simmons, University of Nevada at Las Vegas). Full-sized elephants and hippos must have made their way to Cyprus during the Last Glacial Maximum, when the distance between the island and the mainland was reduced to about 40 km (25 mi.). These animals, through genetic isolation, eventually evolved into the dwarfed endemic forms (known from Cyprus and from Malta). [See Malta.] The human population at Aetokremnos, presumably of Anatolian origin, seems to represent the initial (apparently unsuccessful) colonization of the island and must also have played some role in the extinction of the island's Pleistocene fauna.

At present it is not possible to make any connection between this pre-Neolithic episode and the following aceramic period, long known as the Khirokitia culture because it was first discovered and is still best documented at the site of Khirokitia *Vouni* (first excavated by Porphyrios Dikaios; current excavations directed by A. LeBrun, CNRS, Paris). The circular, domed houses of Khirokitia, built of river stones and mud brick, were arranged to form a village that is certainly indicative of some degree of town planning and social organization. Ceramics were not in use, but bowls, trays, and figurines of gray-green stone attest to a high degree of technical skill, as well as to a feeling for form and design. One of the houses at the related site of Kalavasos *Tenta* even produced a wall painting, executed in red pigment on an interior plastered wall. It is roughly contemporary with the wall paintings from the site of Umm Dabaghiyah in Iraq (excavated by Diana Kirkbride) and the more elaborate examples from the Anatolian site of Çatal Höyük. [*See* Wall Paintings; Çatal Höyük.]

Following the Aceramic Neolithic of the Khirokitia culture, now known from at least twenty-five sites on Cyprus, there seems to be another break in the archaeological record. There is no evidence relating to the Khirokitia culture later than about 5500 BCE, and nothing from the following Sotira culture (or Ceramic Neolithic) seems to be earlier than about 5000 BCE. Whereas it is conceivable (if unlikely) that the initial human population on Cyprus died out following the abandonment of Akrotiri *Aetokremnos*, (with the Khirokitia culture thus representing a recolonization of the island), it is simply impossible that anything comparable could have happened during the (apparent) hiatus between Khirokitia and Sotira. A deterioration in the climate may have resulted in a change in lifestyle and settlement pattern and the disappearance of major "urban" settlements during the second half of the sixth millennium.

The Sotira culture, named after the site of Sotira *Teppes* (excavated by Dikaios), saw not only the introduction of pottery, but also a significant increase in population. Yet, the period's material culture, as known from such sites as Sotira *Teppes* and Ayios Epiktitos *Vrysi*, has much in common with the earlier aceramic culture. An even greater degree of cultural continuity can be documented for the transition from the Sotira to the Erimi (Chalcolithic) culture, named after the site of Erimi *Pamboula*) (also excavated by Dikaios). Some fifty sites contain traces of both cultures, a very unusual state of affairs in Cypriot prehistory.

As indicated by the use of the term *Chalcolithic*, it is during the period of the Erimi culture that the first evidence exists for the use of metal on Cyprus. It takes the form of a number of small copper artifacts from the sites of Erimi *Pamboula*, Lemba *Lakkous*, Kissonerga *Mosphilia*, and Kissonerga *Mylouthkia* (all excavated by Edgar Peltenburg, University of Edinburgh). It is now claimed (by N. H. Gale, 1991) that these objects were not made of Cypriot native copper and, at least in one case, not even of copper smelted from Cypriot copper ores. Thus, the existence of an otherwise unattested copper trade is implied, presumably between Anatolia and Cyprus.

The Erimi culture represents a great expansion in settlement and population, with more than 125 sites known from across the island. At these sites significant evidence is found for social patterning, emerging social ranking, and control by local elites. A remarkable deposit from Kissonerga *Mosphilia*, including a house (or shrine) model and a number of clay figurines (one of which shows a woman in the act of giving birth), must relate not only to contemporary religious beliefs, but also to some sort of communal ritual activity. [*See* Cult.] The clay figurines from Kissonerga *Mosphilia* must be related to the numerous stone cruciform female figurines made of picrolite, the most distinctive artifact from Chalcolithic Cyprus.

The transition from Chalcolithic to Early Cypriot (marking the beginning of the Bronze Age) is one of the most controversial episodes in Cypriot prehistory. The problem concerns the existence of a distinctive archaeological assemblage known as the Philia culture and the position of that culture in the chronological sequence: is it Late Chalcolithic, Early Bronze, or both? What further complicates the issue is that the Philia culture seems to be associated with major developments in metal technology—including the first use of gold, the use of arsenical copper, and perhaps even the use of bronze—and ceramic links with southern Anatolia, especially the site of Tarsus. All this has suggested to many scholars that the Philia culture (and thus much of the subsequent Early Cypriot period) was brought to Cyprus by invaders (or colonists) from southern Anatolia (cf. Manning and Swiny, 1994; Mellink, 1991).

It seems best presently to discount any strong influence from Anatolia and to regard the Philia culture as a transitional phase, covering a period of about one hundred years (c. 2500–2400 BCE), containing elements of the previous Chalcolithic and the forthcoming Early Cypriot periods. For this reason, A. Bernard Knapp (1990) has proposed that what is represented by Late Chalcolithic, the Philia culture, and Early Cypriot I–III be brought together as Pre-Bronze Age I (with Middle Cypriot I–II being Pre-Bronze Age 2). There is much to be said for this suggestion, save for the fact that changes in terminology almost always create more problems than they solve.

In the Early and Middle Cypriot periods, Cyprus truly became part of the international world of the eastern Mediterranean and the Near East. Prior to the mid-third millennium, imported material was very rare, with the exception of obsidian from Anatolia. Now pottery and metalwork imported from Early Minoan Crete have been found, as well as faience beads and perhaps even the board games Senet and *mehen* from Egypt, and certain metal types from Anatolia. [*See* Glass; Vitreous Materials; Games.] The pair of gold earrings from tomb 6 at Sotira *Kaminoudhia* (excavated by Stuart Swiny; Cyprus American Archaeological Research Institute), the earliest gold objects known from Cyprus, are typologically almost certainly of Anatolian origin.

There are some 270 Early and Middle Cypriot sites, but almost all of them are cemeteries without associated settlements. There are virtually no Bronze Age settlements known on Cyprus that are earlier than about 1700 BCE. With the excavation of an Early Cypriot settlement at Sotira *Kaminoudhia* and Middle Cypriot ones at Alambra *Mouttes* (excavated by J. E. Coleman and J. A. Barlow, Cornell University) and Marki *Alonia* (excavated by D. Frankel and J. Webb, LaTrobe University), this may change. Agricultural practices underwent major changes during the Early Cypriot period with the introduction of cattle and the ox-drawn plow (although there is new, very surprising evidence from the site of Paraklesia *Shillourokampos* (excavated by J. Guilane, CNRS, Paris) that would put cattle on Cyprus as early as the Aceramic Neolithic). [*See* Agriculture; Cattle and Oxen.] The introduction of equids (asses or horses) at this time must have facilitated overland transport on the island. [*See* Transportation.]

During the Middle Cypriot period, the copper industry underwent a great expansion. The first direct evidence for the mining of copper ores has appeared at Ambelikou *Aletri*. This evidence comes from the early second millennium BCE and is contemporary with the first references, in Babylonian cuneiform texts from Mari, to copper from the land of Alashiya. [*See* Cuneiform; Mari.] Although there has been considerable controversy over the identification, it now seems virtually certain that Alashiya was the name used in the Near East (Anatolia, Syria, Palestine, Egypt, Mesopotamia) to designate the island of Cyprus. As Cypriot international relations and copper exports intensified during the Late Cypriot period (c. 1625–1125 BCE), there was a corresponding increase in the number of textual references to Alashiya, especially to copper from Alashiya. With the end of the Bronze Age—on Cyprus and in the eastern Mediterranean—no more is heard of Alashiya. Kypros, the Greek name for the island, appears early—in Mycenaean Greek—and has survived to the present. [*See* Metals, *article on* Artifacts of the Neolithic, Bronze, and Iron Ages.]

The beginning of the Late Bronze (Late Cypriot) period is marked by the establishment of Enkomi (excavated by Dikaios and, in a separate project, by Claude F. A. Schaeffer), on the northeast coast of the island. Enkomi quickly became the most important site on Cyprus and is most prob-

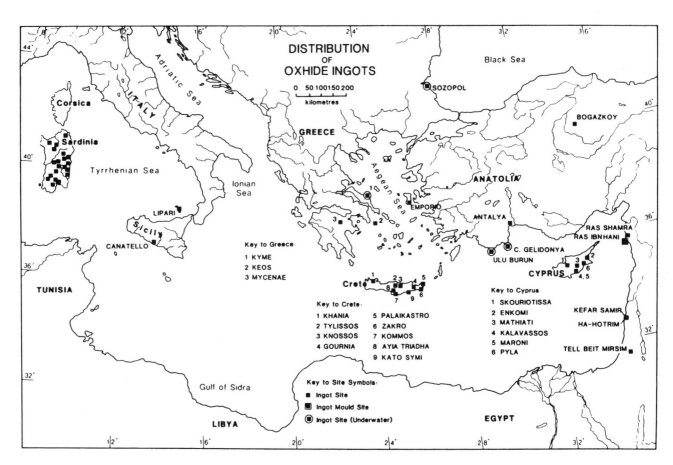

CYPRUS. Figure 1. *Map showing LB distribution of copper oxhide ingots.* (Courtesy J. Muhly)

ably to be identified as the capital of the kingdom of Alashiya. The Late Cypriot period had its own distinctive ceramic repertoire, with Middle Cypriot Red-Polished and White-Painted wares being replaced by Base-Ring, White-Slip, and White-Shaved Late Cypriot wares. These distinctive Late Bronze fabrics seem to have quickly gained popularity outside Cyprus and have been found in considerable quantity at sites in Syria, Palestine, and Egypt. The Uluburun ship that sank off the southern coast of Turkey at the end of the fourteenth century BCE had a cargo that included a large pithos packed with freshly made Late Cypriot pottery, much like a modern "china barrel." [*See* Uluburun.] This pottery must have been destined for western markets. Late Cypriot wares have now been found as far west as the islands of Sicily and Sardinia.

In addition to Enkomi, other important Late Cypriot sites are Kition, Hala Sultan Tekke (also known as Larnaca *Alyki*), Kalavasos *Ayios Dhimitrios,* Maroni *Vournes,* and Alassa *Paleotaverna* (for references, see Knapp et al., 1994). [*See* Kalavasos.] All were connected with copper production and the copper trade and, in some cases, with the production and storage of olive oil. [*See* Olives.] Hala Sultan Tekke seems exceptional in its wealth of foreign imports, especially from Egypt. Tomb 12 at Ayios Dhimitrios, dating to the late thirteenth century BCE, produced a remarkable Hittite silver figurine depicting a male, almost certainly King Tudaliya IV, standing on a stag. [*See* Tombs; Hittites.] This is one of the few known works of Hittite art in precious metal to be found in a controlled excavation (most examples come from the antiquities market). Its presence on Cyprus probably has something to do with Hittite claims of control over Alashiya in the late thirteenth century BCE (during the reigns of Tudaliya IV and Šuppiluliuma II).

It appears that Enkomi dominated the Cypriot copper industry from 1600 to 1300 BCE. Then, in the thirteenth century BCE (Late Cypriot IIC), a decentralization of authority resulted in the establishment of a number of regional centers along the island's south coast. Inland villages, such as Apliki *Karamallos* (excavated by J. DuPlat Taylor), housed the personnel connected with the mining and smelting of the copper ore. [*See* Apliki.] Cypriot copper, in the shape of so-called oxhide ingots (representing one talent, or about 29 kg of copper), were shipped across the Mediterranean, as far west as Sicily and Sardinia (see figure 1). [*See* Sardinia.] The ingots are even found in the Black Sea, at the Hittite capital of Ḫattuša in central Anatolia (modern Boğazköy), and as far east as the Kassite capital of Dur Kurigalzu (modern 'Aqar Quf). [*See* Boğazköy; Kassites; 'Aqar Quf.]

On the basis of present evidence, such ingots represent the form in which raw (or blister) copper was shipped overseas in the Late Bronze Age (see figure 2). Their distinctive oxhide shape is known only from LB contexts. The question is whether all such ingots were cast on Cyprus, of Cypriot copper. The answer is apparently that they were not—the only mold for casting such ingots comes from the Syrian site of Ras Ibn Hani, not otherwise known as a metallurgical site. [*See* Ras Ibn Hani.] Moreover, all the examples known from Minoan Crete—from Ayia Triadha, Gournia, Knossos, Mochlos, and Zakros—seem, on the basis of lead isotope analysis, not to be made of Cypriot copper. All examples from Cyprus itself, on the other hand, as well as those from the Cape Gelidonya and the Uluburun shipwreck, do seem to be made of Cypriot copper. The same origin is claimed for the oxhide ingots from Sardinia—all on the basis of lead isotope analysis. Clearly, Cypriot copper was in wide use across the Mediterranean world, especially in the thirteenth century BCE, but all conclusions based on lead isotope evidence are now under review.

The international character of the Late Bronze Age seems to have come to an end in the early twelfth century BCE, in a sequence of events associated with the invasions and migrations of the Sea Peoples. [*See* Philistines.] Cyprus seems to have suffered less destruction than other areas at this time, perhaps because Bronze Age Cyprus had never developed

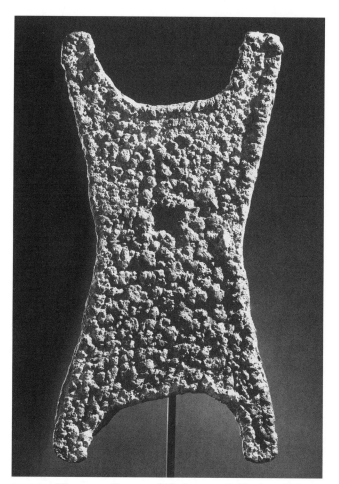

CYPRUS. Figure 2. *Copper oxhide ingot, probably from Enkomi.* (Courtesy Cyprus Mines Company, H. Mudd Collection, Los Angeles; photograph by Tamara Stech)

the highly centralized palace economy so typical of contemporary cultures in the Aegean, Anatolia, and the Levant. [*See* Palace.] Not having been locked into that rigid organization, Cypriots seem to have been better able to respond to the rapidly changing conditions that characterized the Mediterranean world of the twelfth and eleventh centuries BCE. The ability to innovate seems to have been crucial—especially in developing the technology necessary for working in iron, the new metal that achieved such prominence the following centuries come to be known as the Iron Age.

The centuries from about 1100 to 800 BCE were long seen by modern scholars as a dark age—a period of poverty, isolation, and general cultural decline. All knowledge of writing was said to have been lost for several hundred years, along with advanced technological skills in stoneworking, ivory carving, and metal working (precious and base), and that all these skills had to be relearned in the eighth century BCE. [*See* Writing and Writing Systems.] Oriental (especially Phoenician) scribes and craftsmen would have played a key role in this "recivilizing" of the eastern Mediterranean/Aegean world. [*See* Phoenicians; Scribes and Scribal Techniques.] However, this interpretation of the Iron Age is no longer tenable. The evidence now indicates that there was almost unbroken contact between the Aegean (especially Euboea and Crete), Cyprus, and the Levant during those centuries. Three inscribed bronze spits, or *oboleoi*, are known from late eleventh-century Cyprus, from tomb 49 at Palaipaphos *Skales* (excavated by Vassos Karageorghis). One of them is not only inscribed in Greek, but in the Arkadian dialect (in accordance with the later Greek literary tradition that claimed Arkadia as the homeland of the Greeks who colonized Cyprus in the years just after the Trojan War). [*See* Greek.] Fragments of bronze tripods and stands from Iron Age Crete, once seens as heirlooms from a thirteenth–twelfth-century BCE workshop at Enkomi, are now regarded as products of local Iron Age Cretan workshops.

Changes certainly did take place. In the mid-eleventh century BCE Salamis replaced Enkomi as the dominant site in eastern Cyprus, while the Phoenicians moved into Kition. According to the Assyrian king Esarhaddon, in an inscription dated to 673/72 BCE, ten kings of Cyprus ruled over ten separate kingdoms. [*See* Assyrians.] Some of these kings had Greek and some had Semitic names, testifying to the ethnic diversity of Cyprus in the first half of the first millennium BCE. Little is known about the early history of these kingdoms, but they almost certainly go back to at least the eleventh century BCE. The gold scepter from Kourion *Kaloriziki* (early eleventh century BCE), with its pair of Eleonaro's falcons perched on a globe, all decorated with gold and cloisonné work, is quite possibly the standard of authority wielded by one of the early kings of Kourion. [*See* Kourion.]

For Iron Age Greeks, as for their Mycenaean ancestors, Cyprus was called Kypros. For the contemporary Assyrians, however, Cyprus was Yadnana, a land "in the midst of the sea." Esarhaddon (see above) even states that "all kings of the midst of the sea, from Yadnana [Cyprus], the land of Yaman [Ionia], to the land of Tarsisi, bowed down at my feet. I received their heavy tribute." This passage has been the subject of much confused speculation, with Tarsisi even being turned into a reference to Tartessos (in southern Spain). What it really means is that Cyprus, along with the adjacent Anatolian coast (with Tarsus, the principal city, standing for the entire region) was, for the Assyrians, inhabited by eastern Greeks, the Ionians. They are the same Ionians against whom the Assyrian king Sennacherib fought when he sacked the city of Tarsus in 696 BCE.

Relations with Assyria and the Near East were a significant element in the history of Archaic Cyprus. The Assyrian king Sargon II (722–705 BCE) even claimed the conquest of Cyprus in 707 BCE, an event commemorated by the erection of an inscribed stela, apparently in the vicinity of Kition. (The stela was found by chance in the late nineteenth century and is now in the Vorderasiatisches Museum in Berlin.) This so-called conquest seems to have left no more of a trace in the material remains of eighth-century BCE Cyprus than did the earlier conquest claimed by the Hittite king Šuppiluliuma II, at the end of the thirteenth century BCE. Both the Hittite and the Assyrian kings claimed tribute from Cyprus, but these claims probably belong more to the realm of rhetoric than of reality.

Of the ten kingdoms of Archaic Cyprus, the most is known about Salamis as a result of the discovery and excavation of its necropolis by Dikaios and Karageorghis for the Cypriot Department of Antiquities. [*See* Salamis; Necropolis; *and the biography of Dikaios*.] The nine so-called royal tombs in this necropolis, which dates to between about 800 and 600 BCE, produced a rich asemblage of burial goods, including bronze horse trappings and chariot fittings, carved ivories that originally decorated pieces of furniture, and vessels of clay (some even tin-covered) and bronze. [*See* Grave Goods; Bone, Ivory, and Shell, *article on* Artifacts of the Bronze and Iron Ages.] The dromos of tomb 79 at Salamis (end of the eighth century BCE) produced a remarkable bronze cauldron on an iron stand (total height: 1.25 m); the rim of the cauldron is decorated with protomes in the shape of griffins and with bearded sirens. Such cauldrons are known from Delphi, Olympia, and Etruria. All examples date from about 725 to 650 BCE and were most likely manufactured at one or more workshops in Syria (not, as commonly believed, in Urartu).

Similar "royal" tombs are known from the capitals of some of the other Cypriot kingdoms, especially Idalion and Tamassos (excavated by H.-G. Buchholz). [*See* Idalion.] The grave goods from these tombs testify to the wealth and international connections of the rulers of Archaic Cyprus. The latest of the Salamis tombs (no. 3) dates to the early sixth century BCE, shortly before the situation changed dramatically: a short-lived Egyptian rule was followed by the Persian conquest of Cyprus under Cyrus I. Something of the old Archaic lifestyle survived the Persian conquest of about 545 BCE, for Evelthon, king of Salamis in the second half of the sixth century, struck his own silver coins, and the two royal tombs from Tamassos also date to the latter part of the sixth century BCE.

Persian rule over Cyprus seems to have had no more effect on local culture than earlier episodes of foreign rule, although the Persians remained in nominal control down to the conquest of Alexander the Great in 330 BCE. The island seems to have been divided between pro-Greek and pro-Persian camps, a situation that became critical when Cyprus joined the Ionian Revolt in 499 BCE. The intermittent conflicts between Greeks and Persians in the fifth and fourth centuries BCE frequently involved fighting on Cyprus. In 499 the Athenian general Kimon replaced the pro-Persian ruler of Marion with a pro-Greek one—who was then installed in the fortress-palace at Vouni (Nielsen, 1994, pp. 54–61). Kimon, however, was killed shortly thereafter, thus putting an end to this episode of Greek intervention in the affairs of Cyprus.

During the second half of the first millennium BCE, Greek influence was dominated on Cyprus. This can be seen in the numerous terra-cotta figurines from recent excavations (by W. A. P. Childs, Princeton University) at ancient Marion (modern Polis *Chrysochous*), as well as in the Attic pottery and the Attic-inspired grave reliefs from older (informal) excavations at that site, from the magnificent more-than-life-sized bronze head of Apollo from Tamassos (now in the British Museum and known as the Chatsworth head), and the solid cast-bronze cow from the Vouni palace, in the style of the Greek sculptor Myron.

One of the great surprises of recent years was the discovery that there was still a strong Phoenician presence on Cyprus in the fourth century BCE—not only during the first half of the first millennium BCE, the time of the Phoenician temple at Kition. A Phoenician inscription from a fifth-century BCE tomb near Alassa refers to a metalworker named Melekram, and a fourth-century BCE Phoenician inscription from Kition refers to one Eshmounadon, ambassador of the king of Tyre. Recent excavations at Idalion have produced dozens of Phoenician inscriptions, written in black ink on small pieces of local marble. They are administrative texts and, on the basis of an associated coin of Evagoras II, king of Salamis (361–351 BCE), can be dated to the fourth century BCE.

In return for its support, and a gift of one hundred ships, Alexander granted Cyprus its independence. After his death in 323 BCE, however, Cyprus found itself caught up in the power struggle between Ptolemy and Antigonus, two of Alexander's generals. [*See* Ptolemies.] To avoid being captured by Ptolemy, Nicocreon, the last king of Salamis, committed suicide in 311, as did his wife Axiothea and all members of the royal family. In 306 BCE those involved in this mass suicide were given a proper burial in a grand ceremony organized by Demetrios Poliorketes, son of Antigonus and, at that time, ruler of Cyprus. The platform and tumulus erected on that occasion were excavated by Karageorghis in 1964 as Salamis tomb 77. Among the finds, a series of clay portrait heads, in the style of the Greek sculptor Lysippos, are of special interest as they seem to depict members of the royal family.

In 67 BCE, after more than two hundred years of Ptolemaic rule, Cyprus was annexed by Rome and administered, from 58 BCE onward, as part of the province of Cilicia. [*See* Cilicia.] The great orator Cicero was one of the early proconsuls of Cilicia. The Romans bled Cyprus dry, with high taxes and money (to pay those taxes) lent at outrageous rates of interest (as much as 48 percent). Although Salamis continued to be of great importance, the real capital of Roman Cyprus was at Paphos. The harbor town of Nea Paphos (modern Kato Paphos), originally built in the late fourth century BCE, became the center for the Roman administration of the island. Several Roman villas, decorated with wonderful mosaics and dating to the third century CE, have been excavated at Nea Paphos. These include the Villa of Theseus (excavated by W. A. Daszewski on behalf of the Polish Mission to Cyprus) and the House of Dionysus (excavated by Kyriakos Nicolaou on behalf of the Cypriot Department of Antiquities). Similar mosaics are known from Kourion, especially from the House of the Gladiators (end of the third–beginning of the fourth century CE; excavated by D. Christou, Cypriot Department of Antiquities). [*See* Villa; Mosaics; Paphos.]

The monumental (more than 2 m high) bronze statue of Emperor Septimius Severus (193–211 CE), found at ancient Chytroi (modern Kythrea), also attests to the importance of the Roman presence on Cyprus in the third century. The pagan era on Cyprus essentially came to an end with the devastating earthquake of 21 July 365. Following the earthquake, Cyprus was rebuilt as a Christian culture, best seen in the House of Eustolios at Kourion, a public building of the fifth century. A beautiful stone mosaic inscription from this house, written in epic-style verse, proclaims that "In place of big stones and solid iron, gleaming bronze and even hardened steel, this house is girt with the much-venerated signs of Christ" (Soren and James, 1988, pp. 20–23).

BIBLIOGRAPHY

The literature on the archaeology of ancient Cyprus is quite vast. It is impossible to list individual site reports. Recent scholarship on Cypriot archaeology has tended to appear in congress and symposia volumes, most of which have been edited by Vassos Karageorghis on behalf of the Cypriot Department of Antiquities (of which he was director from 1963 to 1988). This bibliography includes only some general works on Cypriot archaeology, followed by a few specialized studies.

General Works

Catling, H. W. *Cypriot Bronzework in the Mycenaean World.* Oxford, 1964. Basic study of Cypriot bronze artifacts, within an Aegeocentric context.

Chypre: Au coeur des civilisations méditerranéennes. Les Dossiers d'Archéologie, no. 205. Paris, 1995. Short articles on recent archaeological work on Cyprus, from Pre-Neolithic to Roman times.

Gjerstad, Einar. *Studies on Prehistoric Cyprus.* Uppsala, 1926. Marks the beginning of the modern study of Cypriot archaeology.

Hill, George F. *A History of Cyprus,* vol. 1, *To the Conquest by Richard Lion Heart.* London, 1940. For many years the standard account of early Cypriot history.

Karageorghis, Vassos. *Cyprus: From the Stone Age to the Romans.* London, 1982. The first general synthesis based on work since 1960.

Karageorghis, Vassos, ed. *Archaeology in Cyprus, 1960–1985.* Nicosia, 1985. Collection of synthetic studies published on the occasion of the twenty-fifth anniversary of the Department of Antiquities.

Karageorghis, Vassos. *Les anciens Chypriotes: Entre Orient et Occident.* Paris, 1991. Contains a valuable list of all archaeological expeditions conducted on Cyprus.

Knapp, A. Bernard, and John F. Cherry. *Provenience Studies and Bronze Age Cyprus: Production, Exchange, and Politico-Economic Change.* Monographs in World Archaeology, no. 21. Madison, Wis., 1994. Comprehensive analysis of the scientific evidence for Bronze Age trade in ceramics and metals.

Peltenburg, Edgar, ed. *Early Society in Cyprus.* Edinburgh, 1989. Important collection of papers on Cypriot prehistory, from Neolithic to Roman times.

Sjöqvist, Erik. *Problems of the Late Cypriote Bronze Age.* Stockholm, 1940. The first important synthesis of the Late Bronze Age on Cyprus.

Specialized Studies

Catling, H. W. "Patterns of Settlement in Bronze Age Cyprus." *Opuscula Atheniensia* 4 (1962): 129–169. The basis for all future survey work on Cyprus.

Gale, N. H. "Metals and Metallurgy in the Chalcolithic Period." *Bulletin of the American Schools of Oriental Research,* no. 282–283 (1991): 37–61. Beginnings of metallurgy on Cyprus.

Knapp, A. Bernard. "Production, Location, and Integration in Bronze Age Cyprus." *Current Anthropology* 31 (1990): 147–176. An important theoretical interpretation of the field that, up to this time, had strongly resisted such interpretation.

Knapp, A. Bernard, et al. "The Prehistory of Cyprus: Problems and Prospects." *Journal of World Prehistory* 8 (1994): 377–453. Interpretive synthesis of current work in Cypriot prehistory, to the end of the Bronze Age, with a rich bibliography on current excavations.

Manning, Sturt, and Stuart Swiny. "Sotira *Kaminoudhia* and the Chronology of the Early Bronze Age in Cyprus." *Oxford Journal of Archaeology* 13 (1994): 149–172. Evanuation of the role of radiocarbon dating in Cypriot prehistory.

Mellink, Machteld J. "Anatolian Contacts with Chalcolithic Cyprus." *Bulletin of the American Schools of Oriental Research,* no. 282–283 (1991): 167–175.

Nielsen, Inge. *Hellenistic Palaces: Tradition and Renewal.* Aarhus, 1994. Excellent discussion of Vouni phase.

Rupp, David W. "The 'Royal Tombs' at Salamis (Cyprus): Ideological Messages of Power and Authority." *Journal of Mediterranean Archaeology* 1.1 (1988): 111–139. Argues for the beginning of Archaic kingdoms in the eighth century BCE.

Soren, David, and J. James. *Kourion: The Search for a Lost Roman City.* New York, 1988. Excavation of Roman Kourion.

J. D. MUHLY

CYPRUS AMERICAN ARCHAEOLOGICAL RESEARCH INSTITUTE. Although archaeological exploration on Cyprus dates back to the mid-nineteenth century when French scholars showed an interest in the distinctly Greek style of sculpture with its perplexing eastern traits, systematic investigation of the island's cultures only began in the 1920s with the arrival of the Swedish Cyprus Expedition. Of considerable importance, however, were the large and rich late nineteenth-century collections made by antiquarians, specifically Luigi Palma di Cesnola, United States consul to Cyprus (1865–1875) and the first American to show an active interest in Cypriot antiquities. Despite the island's proven archaeological wealth, interest in its past was limited and the founding of a foreign school was not contemplated until 1974 when George Ernest Wright, director of the American Schools of Oriental Research (ASOR) Expedition to Ancient Idalion proposed such a move.

In 1978 the president of ASOR, Philip J. King, with the backing of the United States ambassador to Cyprus, approached the Department of Antiquities about establishing a research center to promote dialogue between American and Cypriot scholars and to provide services and facilities for researchers in the fields of archaeology, anthropology, ethnography, history, literature, and related disciplines. The proposal was supported by the far-sighted antiquities director, Vassos Karageorghis. As a result the Cyprus American Archaeological Research Institute (CAARI) came into being and began operating in premises not far from the Cyprus Museum. The board of trustees, which was presided over by Norma Kershaw, appointed Anita Walker as its first director in 1978. Ian A. Todd followed in 1979, and then Stuart Swiny from 1980 to 1995. Initially, the institute's contribution to archaeological research was severely hampered by lack of funds; its impact on Cypriot studies was minimal, being restricted to a one-day symposium on current excavation projects supplemented by the occasional lecture. In 1984, however, the creation of several Fulbright fellowships offered on a yearly basis, the purchase of Claude F.-A. Schaeffer's research library and the reorganization of the board of trustees under the presidency of Charles U. Harris, signaled a change in direction and a period of rapid growth. The combination of library resources, pre- and postdoctoral researchers, as well as increasingly comprehensive reference collections, soon left its mark on American involvement in Cypriot studies.

The emphasis on traditional art historical or archaeological research concurrently began to make way for more problem-oriented, multidisciplinary, and theoretical approaches. A similar evolution occurred in the focus of ASOR-affiliated field projects, both excavations and surveys, which began to be regional and to span several periods.

As CAARI's commitment to Cyprus-based research grew, so too did the number of users, of all nationalities—there is no other foreign archaeological center on the island—and the search for larger, permanent facilities became a priority. In June 1991 the president of the Republic of Cyprus formally inaugurated spacious new premises purchased and renovated through the efforts of CAARI's board of trustees. These fulfilled the requirements of an efficient archaeological research center with a sufficient residence capacity, operating in the 1990s and beyond.

To date the institute's main goals have been to develop its library holdings, to offer more scholarships, to increase its programmatic activities, and to continue sponsoring its own archaeological projects.

Since 1984 the availability of diverse fellowships has significantly expanded the scope and number of researchers in Cypriot studies. In addition to those sponsored by ASOR, there are on average seven grants offered each year by CAARI, lasting from one to ten months. The stipends include travel funds and support for two junior scholars wishing to undertake research projects on ASOR-sponsored excavations. The institute currently offers a full program of lectures and site tours. It also organizes symposia and is now considering a summer teaching program.

In 1981 the first ASOR-sponsored CAARI excavation began work on the Early Bronze site of Sotira *Kaminoudhia*. Other affiliated projects have investigated Akrotiri *Aetokremnos*, ancient Idalion, ancient Kourion, Kalavasos *Ayios Dhimitrios*, *Kopetra*, and *Tenta*, as well as Koletria *Ortos*. Surveys have been undertaken in the Vasilikos Valley, around Kouklia and Mitsero, as well as underwater in the harbor of Paphos.

Since 1986 *CAARI News* has appeared as an annual newsletter. A major publication project in the form of a directory of Cypriot sites is planned as a cooperative project for the future.

The growth of CAARI over a period of fifteen years to a research center offering a fine library, reference collections, fellowships, and excavation programs, has encouraged classicists and Aegean scholars to turn their gaze east, while urging Near Eastern researchers to look west. Once again, Cyprus is assuming its traditional role as stepping stone between the Orient and the Occident.

[*See also* American Schools of Oriental Research; Idalion; Kalavasos; Kourion; Paphos; *and the biographies of di Cesnola, Schaeffer, and Wright.*]

BIBLIOGRAPHY

Davis, Thomas W. "A History of American Archaeology in Cyprus." *Biblical Archaeologist* 52 (1989): 163–169. The most detailed overview to date of American archaeological research on the island.

Harris, Charles U. "The Role of CAARI in Cyprus." *Biblical Archaeologist* 52 (1989): 157–162. Presents the first history of CAARI written by the one person who was instrumental in its creation and development.

King, Philip J. *American Archaeology in the Mideast: A History of the American Schools of Oriental Research.* Winona Lake, Ind., 1983. Reference work for ASOR's role in Near Eastern scholarship. CAARI

would never have been founded without King's belief in the value of a Cyprus center when he was president of ASOR.

STUART SWINY

CYRENE, metropolitan capital of both Cyrenaica and the Libyan Pentapolis during Hellenistic and Roman times (32°48′ N, 21°52′ E). Cyrene is located about 175 km (109 mi.) northeast of Benghazi, 300 km south of Crete and 320 km (198 mi.) west of the Libyan–Egyptian border, and 12 km (7 mi.) inland from the coast on the crest of the Gebel Akhdar or "Green Mountain" at an elevation of 622 m (2,041 ft.). The old village of Shahhat, whose former name Grennah or Gueranna is an obvious corruption of the ancient toponym, has been linked with Cyrene since European travelers first began to seek out its ruins in the early eighteenth century.

The story of Cyrene's foundation around 631 BCE by Therans led by a certain Battus is exhaustively related by Herodotus (4.150 ff.). The founder established a hereditary monarchy that endured foreign attack and internal rebellion until around 440 BCE when Cyrene's last king, Arcesilaus IV, was assassinated. Monarchy was followed by slightly more than a century of erratic republican government, which finally came to an end when Cyrene was brought under Ptolemaic administration in 322.

The Hellenistic period saw the creation of the Pentapolis, or land of the five cities: Cyrene, Apollonia, Ptolemais, Tauchira, and Berenice. Cyrenaica's last Greek ruler, Ptolemy Apion (116–96), willed the region to the Roman Senate, which limited its involvement to collecting the rents from the royal lands previously owned by the Ptolemies. Then, in 74, Cornelius Lentulus Marcellinus was sent out as a quaestor (provincial magistrate) to establish Cyrenaica as a Roman province. The emperor Augustus linked the region administratively with Crete to form a single senatorial province. The unbroken years of prosperity that followed were shattered by a major revolt in 115–116 CE when the province's Jewish inhabitants destroyed much of Cyrene's civic and religious infrastructure. Timely intervention by the emperor Hadrian's government provided a limited recovery, but by the early third century gradual drying up of the climate, extensive earthquake damage, and tribal incursions from the desert renewed the decline. Diocletian (284–305) detached the province from Crete and renamed it Upper Libya or Pentapolis. Its years as a christianized outpost of the Byzantine Empire produced a modest renewal of urban life until the city, along with the rest of the province, fell to the Arabs in 643.

From 1860 to 1861, R. M. Smith and E. A. Porcher led an expedition to collect sculptures for the British Museum. In 1910 R. Norton undertook an investigation, which was aborted, of the acropolis for the American Institute of Archaeology. The subsequent principal excavations at Cyrene fall into two phases. The first was the exclusive domain of Italian archaeologists working between the two world wars to clear the agora-forum area and the sanctuary of Apollo. The second phase, which was initiated shortly after World War II by the British and continues to the present, reflects separate efforts by the Libyan Department of Antiquities (Valley Street and Roman city center, Theater 2, market-theater complex) and by foreign missions: Italian (agora-forum, sanctuary of Apollo, temple of Zeus) and American (sanctuary of Demeter and Persephone).

A rich archaeological record for the city's monarchic period is provided by the physical remains, which consist of civic and religious buildings, locally produced and imported sculpture and pottery and other miscellaneous objects from the city's agora and two principal sanctuaries (Apollo, Demeter and Persephone). Important additional information has also been acquired by the excavation of Cyrene's monumental temple of Zeus, a group of intentionally buried votives (bronze and stone sculptures, columnar sphinx monument) from a unidentified archaic-period precinct, and its various cemeteries lining the major roadways leading from the city. The line of Archaic defenses has yet to be located.

Archaeological data that includes inscriptions recovered from the agora, main religious sanctuaries, and tombs provides a somewhat sketchier account of the republican years that intervened before Cyrene's absorption into the Ptolemaic empire in 322 BCE. Excavation of the same areas have brought to light a full range of Hellenistic remains. Short stretches of the defensive wall system girdling the Ptolemaic city are preserved.

The city's Roman and Byzantine phases have been well documented by the excavation of the Caesareum (monumental complex dedicated to one of the Caesars) and nearby Roman forum area, the Roman city center, the market theater complex, and the city's intramural cathedral, along with the already mentioned santuaries, necropoleis and the agora. On the other hand, the massive acropolis hill and the extramural "caravanserai" and hippodrome all await excavation.

BIBLIOGRAPHY

Chamoux, Franco. *Cyrene sous la Monarchie des Battiades*. Bibliothèque des Écoles Françaises d'Athènes et de Rome, 177. Paris, 1953. Fundamental study of the city from its foundation until the end of the Battiad monarchy, ca. 440 BCE.

Goodchild, Richard G. *Cyrene and Apollonia: An Historical Guide*. 3d ed. [Tripoli], 1970. Written by the former Controller of Antiquities for eastern Libya, this remains the most accessible guide in English but should be supplemented by Goodchild's posthumously published guide in German cited below.

Goodchild, Richard G. *Kyrene and Apollonia*. Ruinenstadte Nordafrikas, 4. Zurich, 1971. The site's definitive archaeological guide.

Goodchild, Richard G. *Libyan Studies: Select Papers of the Late Richard Goodchild*. Edited by Joyce Reynolds. London, 1976. Compilation of articles that includes the author's otherwise unpublished history of Cyrene's exploration and excavation, "A Hole in the Heavens" (pp. 268–341).

Laronde, André, et al. "Cyrene, Apollonia, Ptolemais: Sites prestigieux de la Libye antique." *Les Dossiers d'Archéologie* 167 (January 1992): 1–80. Well-illustrated popular survey of Cyrene and two of its important neighboring towns which includes the most accessible information on work conducted in Cyrenaica during the past decade.

Stucchi, Sandro, et al. *L'Agorà di Cirene*. 4 vols. Monografie di Archeologia Libica, vols. 7, 15–17. Rome, 1965–1984. Final publications of the Italian mission's work in the Agora, fundamental for understanding the city's urban development.

Stucchi, Sandro. *Architettura cirenaica*. Monografie di Archeologia Libica, vol. 9. Rome, 1975. Classic architectural study by Cyrene's premiere excavator that includes an analysis of virtually every monument found at Cyrene.

White, Donald, et al. *The Extramural Sanctuary of Demeter and Persephone at Cyrene, Libya: Final Reports*. 5 vols. University Museum Monographs, 52, 56, 66, 67, 76. Philadelphia, 1984–1993. The most complete publication of the stratigraphical record and various classes of artifacts of a specific complex.

DONALD WHITE

D

DAB'A, TELL ED- (ancient Avaris), site located in the northeastern Nile Delta in the province of el-Sharqiya, 8 km (5 mi.) north of the market town of Faqus (30°47'15" N, 31°49'20" E). The site was the capital of the Hyksos and the southern part of the Delta residence of the Ramessides (nineteenth and twentieth dynasties) under the late name Piramesse (Raamses in the Masoretic Bible text; Ramesse in the Septuagint).

Excavations at Tell ed-Dab'a were begun in 1885 by Édouard Naville. They were resumed in 1941–1942 by Labib Habachi, who suggested the identification with Avaris. Between 1951 and 1954, Shehata Adam discovered a Middle Kingdom temple at 'Ezbet Rushdi. From 1966 to 1969 and from 1975 onward, Manfred Bietak carried out systematic excavations at the site for the Archaeological Institute of Austria, Cairo Department.

Stray finds from the Naqada III period and the beginning of the first dynasty show that the settlement was already inhabited in the fourth millennium. However, the real origin of the settlement at Tell ed-Dab'a was the result of a royal settlement foundation (*ḥwt*) of King Amenemhat I (c. 1963–1934 BCE) to the east of the Pelusiac branch of the Nile River. It probably replaced an older royal foundation of the Herakleopolitan period with the name *Ḥwt R3w3tj Ḥtj* ("royal settlement"), "the two roads" of the Herakleopolitan king Khety.

The center of this settlement during the twelfth dynasty was a royal temple and a palatial building for local officials. An orthogonal, planned workmen's quarter southwest of the town belongs to the construction of this settlement. In the late twelfth dynasty (c. 1800 BCE) Asiatic immigrants were settled to the south of the Middle Kingdom town (stratum H). The type of Middle Bronze weaponry indicates that the settlers were originally soldiers and probably also ship carpenters and sailors in the Egyptian service. Their tombs were found in cemeteries within the settlement, in a layout that is very un-Egyptian. Foreign architectural types also appeared during this period, including a typical Syrian *Mittelsaal* ("middle hall") house and a broadroom house.

During the thirteenth dynasty, the settlement was enlarged to approximately a square kilometer and probably served trading and mining expeditions. A wide palatial building was likely the residence of an Egyptian official, perhaps with the title "overseer of foreign countries" that was found preserved on a magnificent official amethyst and gold seal. While the tombs of the residential officials display Egyptian funerary architectural traditions, the burial customs, such as donkey sacrifices, were Asiatic, as were the Middle Bronze weapons.

During the thirteenth dynasty, one of several kings of Asiatic origin took the throne for a short time. His name was 'Amusa Hornedjherjotef and he was very likely a native of Tell ed-Dab'a. His statue was found in a funerary chapel by Habachi, together with statues of the last queen of the twelfth dynasty, Sobeknofru. The above-mentioned palace dates to approximately this time, as does a smashed colossal limestone statue of a seated Asiatic dignitary with a red mushroom-shaped hairstyle who is holding a throw stick against his shoulder. The destroyed statue and the sudden abandonment of the palace suggest internal political turmoil during the thirteenth dynasty. Soon afterward, the material culture and specific tomb types suggest that new immigrants from Palestine, as well as from Syria and Cyprus, had moved in (stratum G). The percentage of foreign pottery rose from 20 to 40 percent.

In the second half of the eighteenth century BCE there is some evidence that a plague decimated the settlers at Tell ed-Dab'a. Emergency tombs were dug, and bodies were thrown into shallow pits sometimes only 20 cm deep. Changes in the settlement pattern can also be observed between strata G and F, and the eastern part of the town was completely deserted. Soon afterward, an interesting sacred precinct was constructed (stratum F, E/3). In its center was a major Middle Bronze temple of Syro-Palestinian type (approximately 32.7 × 21.4 m). In front of the temple was an altar on which several charred acorns were found. The temple likely belonged to a cult of Asherah, originally the consort of the Canaanite god El, later also considered the consort of Baal. Another broadroom temple in this compound had a separate tower. To judge from inscriptions on door blocks from this area, it seems that this temple precinct, which was surrounded by cemeteries with Egyptian-type mortuary temples, was founded during the reign of King 'Aasehre' Nehesi. (His father, whose name is not known, had split off from the thirteenth dynasty and had founded a small kingdom in the northeastern Delta whose capital was at Tell ed-Dab'a.) From this time onward, the settlement is known as Avaris ("royal foundation of the desert edge"). Nehesi was the first king with the epithet "beloved of the god Seth, the lord of Avaris" (or "lord of Ro-achet," "door of the fertile land").

A cylinder seal found in the earlier palace of the thirteenth dynasty carries a representation of a Syrian storm god. On the basis of this seal, it is assumed that the god Seth of Avaris was syncretized with the northern Syrian storm god Baal, introduced by Asiatic settlers during the late twelfth dynasty. It was only a matter of time before the kingdom of Avaris was replaced by a local Asiatic dynasty that would form the core of the later kingdom of the Hyksos ("rulers of the foreign countries"). Indeed, from the beginning of the Hyksos period (c. 1640 BCE) the town dramatically enlarged to about 2.5 sq km (1.6 sq. mi.)—that is, it was a provincial center that became a metropolis. Very distinct changes appear in the material culture, especially in the pottery. It is tempting to explain the situation as having been created by an influx of new immigrants from Canaan, probably from the southern region around Tell el-'Ajjul (Sharuhen), except that the settlement pattern shows continuity. If there was a population influx, it took place with the consent of the lords of Avaris.

Before the beginning of the Hyksos period there are already very un-Egyptian cemeteries of families arranged around temples and tombs within house precincts. The construction of the tombs shows types of vaulting that were unknown in Egypt but have parallels in ancient Palestine. In domestic architecture the complete adaptation of Egyptian types had taken place during the thirteenth dynasty. Increasing social differentiation can be observed from stratum F onward, with large houses surrounded by smaller houses belonging to the servant class. Typical for the period shortly before the Hyksos, and for the first half of the Hyksos period, are warrior tombs equipped with weapons. Some contain the burial of pairs of donkeys in front of the tomb entrance. Such burials have Palestinian parallels.

In 1991, at the extreme western part of the town, situated directly at the Pelusiac branch of the Nile, remains of a citadel of the Late Hyksos period and of the early eighteenth dynasty were found (strata D2 and C). Along the river there was a fortification wall, 10 Egyptian cubits (5.25 m) strong, with buttresses set in regular intervals of 45 cubits (23.6 m). It is at present unclear if this was the city wall or the enclosure of the citadel. The wall was later enlarged to 16 cubits (8.4 m) and so were the buttresses. Within this wall two layers of garden remains with tree pits and possibly a vineyard were discovered. This scenario—towering fortification walls and gardens—fits perfectly the one referred to in the insulting speech delivered by Kamose against the Hyksos Apophis during his short campaign to Avaris, known to us

from the Kamose stela no. 2. In it he spoke about the wives of the Hyksos peeping through the loopholes in the castle. He also threatens to pull out the trees and to drink the wine from the vineyards of his Asiatic overlord.

At present the structure of the Hyksos citadel is unclear because of the later eighteenth dynasty installations in which older building materials were reused. A part of a monumental doorway of the hitherto unknown Hyksos with the northwestern semitic name *Skr-hr* (= Sikru Haddu, which means "Memories of god Haddu" according to Thomas Schneider, unpublished) was found in the eighteenth-dynasty level (stratum C). It is the first monumental inscription where the title *ḥq3-ḫ3swt* (= Hyksos, ruler of the foreign countries) is used officially. Within this precinct also the stela of the Hyksos Yinassi, who can be identified with the Iannas of the Manethonian list, was found. According to this stela he was the son and probably successor of the great Hyksos Khayan. A house altar dedicated to the Hyksos princess Tany, the sister and possibly consort of the Hyksos Apophis was retrieved by recent channel-dredging within this citadel area.

King Ahmose conquered Avaris about 1530 BCE. From this period there is evidence of an intensive reuse of the citadel after a partial destruction. Near the river was found a palatial construction on a raised platform of 135 × 90 Egyptian cubits (70.5 × 47 m) with a doorway and an access ramp cut through the fortification walls from the riverside. The gardens of the Hyksos period were reestablished. Another much larger palatial compound with huge magazines was constructed south of the platform waiting for future investigation. Both buildings were furnished with Minoan wall paintings, executed by Minoan artists in genuine Minoan style and technique. Motifs such as bull leaping, bull grappling, acrobats, hunting scenes, lions and leopards chasing fallow deer and mountain goats, and representations of griffins display Minoan ideology of hierarchy in nature and are an international scholarly puzzle. Dynastic links with the court of Knossos may explain the wall paintings, which would belong only in a royal palace. It cannot be excluded at present that a part of the Minoan paintings, found in a secondary dump, date from the late Hyksos period, but the only securely dated frescoes came from the early eighteenth dynasty palatial quarter. Perhaps the riddle of the title of the mother of King Ahmose, Queen Ahhotep, as *ḥnwt idbw H3w-nbwt*, "Mistress of the coasts of Haunebut," a country sometimes associated with the Aegean islands, can contribute in future toward an understanding of this puzzling evidence.

The raised platform building must have been in use for a very limited time, as against its weathered eastern face was constructed a very humble settlement of the first half of the eighteenth dynasty, using the platform already as a quarry for building materials. It seems at present that the citadel was used as a royal residence only for a very short time, perhaps during the last years of Ahmose during his campaigns in Canaan. At that time and subsequently the citadel must have been used as an army stronghold. The presence of Nubian mercenaries can be established by remains of Sudanese Kerma-household pottery and by numerous arrowheads of bone and silex.

According to numerous finds of royal name scarabs the settlement of the citadel must have continued at least till the time of Amenhotep II. That it probably continued until the Ramesside period is inferred from the discovery in 1993 of a huge temple complex to the north of the former citadel. Early in the eighteenth dynasty foreign trade flourished again, as in the Hyksos period: amphorae with olive oil and wine were imported in large numbers from Canaan, and Cyprus became a strong trading partner. While most of Avaris, except for the citadel, was abandoned, the quarter of the temple to Seth, in the eastern central part of the site, shows continuity (according to the dating of a lintel its use was renewed). This renovation was carried out during the time of the restoration of the traditional cults in Egypt under the kings Tutankhamun and Horemheb, in the late fourteenth century BCE. New building projects at the temple were carried out under Seti I, the last of which was a large temple to Seth. According to Papyri Anastasi II and IV (1.4–5 and 6.4–5, respectively), it is referred to as the southern topographical fixed point of the Ramesside town. According to the archaeological evidence, the area surrounding this temple was covered with groves of trees.

The continuity of the Seth cult from the Hyksos period to the Ramesside period can be documented by the so-called "Four-hundred-years stela" that probably originally stood in Avaris/Piramesse. This stela was commissioned by Rameses II, whose family most likely originated in Avaris; it can be viewed as a kind of propaganda designed to legitimize the rule of the new dynasty. Seth, in the image of an Asiatic god, with horns and a high crown with a pommel, is presented as the "father of the fathers"—as the ancestor of the new dynasty.

In the Third Intermediate period, Avaris was severely plundered. It had the same fate as the Ramesside town of Qantir and served as a quarry for the new residences of the twenty-first and twenty-second dynasties at Tanis and Bubastis. This explains the secondary use of stone monuments in the last two towns. The plundered monuments are important sources for the history of Avaris and Piramesse. In the fourth century BCE, cults of the gods of Rameses II appeared independently in Tanis and Bubastis. The cults originated from the cult statues that had been transported there. This situation obscured what was known about the original location of the Rameses-town, which had serious consequences for attempts to locate the biblical town of Rameses and its environment (*Ps.* 78:12, 48; *Gn.* 46:28–29 [Septuagint]).

[*See also* Delta; *and* Hyksos.]

BIBLIOGRAPHY

Adam, Shehata. "Report on the Excavations of the Department of Antiquities at Ezbet Rushdi." *Annales du Service des Antiquités de l'Égypte* 56 (1959): 207–226.

Bietak, Manfred. *Tell ed-Dab'a.* Vol. 2. Vienna, 1975.

Bietak, Manfred. "Avaris and Piramesse: Archaeological Exploration in the Eastern Nile Delta." *Proceedings of the British Academy* 65 (1979): 225–290.

Bietak, Manfred. "Canaan and Egypt during the Middle Bronze Age." *Bulletin of the American Schools of Oriental Research,* no. 281 (1991): 27–72.

Bietak, Manfred. *Tell el-Dab'a.* Vol. 5. Vienna, 1991. Includes an up-to-date bibliography (pp. 17ff.).

Bietak, Manfred. "Minoan Wall-Paintings Unearthed at Ancient Avaris." *Egyptian Archaeology* 2 (1992): 26–28.

Bietak, Manfred, et al. "Neue Grabungsergebnisse aus Tell el-Dab'a und 'Ezbet Helmi im östlichen Nildelta, 1989–1991." *Ägypten und Levante* 4 (1993): 9–80.

Bietak, Manfred, and Nannó Marinatos. "Minoan Wall Paintings from Avaris." *Egypt and the Levant* 5 (1995).

Bietak, Manfred, et al. *Pharaonen und Fremde, Dynastien im Dunkel.* Exhibition catalog, Rathaus, City of Vienna, 8 September –12 October 1994. Vienna, 1994.

Bietak, Manfred. *Avaris, The Capital of the Hyksos: New Excavation Results.* The Raymond and Beverly Sackler Distinguished Lectures in Egyptology, no. 1. British Museum Publications. London, 1996.

Habachi, Labib. "Khata'na-Kantir: Importance." *Annales du Service des Antiquités de l'Égypte* 52 (1954): 443–559.

MANFRED BIETAK

DALIYEH, WADI ED-,

DALIYEH, WADI ED-, valley sloping down, sometimes precipitously, from the central ridge of Palestine, northeast of Bethel, all the way to the Jordan Valley, north of Jericho (32°00′ N, 35°25′ E). Its steep, clifflike walls are honeycombed in places with caves, one complex of which was discovered in 1962 by the Ta'amireh bedouin, who had been the first, in 1948, to locate what became known as the Dead Sea Scrolls. The cave that took the name Wadi ed-Daliyeh was excavated on behalf of the American Schools of Oriental Research in 1963–1964 by Paul W. Lapp, after a cache of Aramaic papyrus documents, now known as the Samaria papyri, appeared on the illegal antiquities market. The source of the papyri had proved to be one of the caves in the complex, the Muhgaret Abu Shinjeh, later called Cave I. Another cave, 'Araq en-Na'asaneh, or Cave II, was also excavated.

Cave I produced material that was largely from the Persian period, thus yielding an appropriate date for the papyri in the late fourth century BCE. This included typical Persian–Early Hellenistic horizon pottery, to which must be added the papyri; some 128 clay sealings from the papyri; coins purchased with the papyri from the cave robbers (plus one that was excavated), all of the same period; a scarab; numerous well-preserved textile fragments; pieces of leather sandals and other leather fragments; samples of basketry and wooden implements; glass; and beads and jewelry. The skeletal remains of many individuals were found, all of which had been disturbed by the robbers, who reported finding as many as three hundred skeletons, most of them badly burned.

It appears from the finds that Cave I had been used as a dwelling and no doubt as a hiding place, in this case by Samaritans fleeing the wrath of Alexander and the Macedonians after a revolt in the late fourth century BCE in which the prefect of Syria, Andromachus, had been burned alive. It is likely that Alexander's forces found the Samaritan refugees in the caves in the Wadi ed-Daliyeh and slaughtered them there.

The papyri, which have been extensively treated by Frank M. Cross, support this reconstruction. One mentions "[Yesha]yahû, son of Sanballat, governor of Samaria." Another was "written in Samaria." Other documents bear exact date formulae, reckoned from known Persian administrators in the province of Samaria. The range of these dates is about 375–335 BCE. Many of the papyri are legal or administrative documents, such as refugees would be inclined to take with them. Not only do the personal names, many of them Yahwistic, reveal a great deal about the half-Jewish Samaritan community, they also tell us a good deal about the complex religious and political situation that the returning Jewish exiles met in Palestine in the time of Ezra and Nehemiah. This series of several dozen, closely dated historical documents provides valuable fixed dates for the study of Aramaic and Paleo-Hebrew paleography for the period just preceding the earliest of the Dead Sea Scrolls. Finally, the papyri have increased our knowledge of the Samaritan community, enhanced our understanding of the history of the Samaritan Pentateuch, and contributed to textual studies of the Hebrew Bible and its transmission.

Cave II produced some one hundred pieces of late Early Bronze Age IV pottery (c. 2100–2000 BCE) that has been published by William G. Dever. The corpus belongs to his Family CH (for Central Hills), with some overlap with Family J (for Jericho/Jordan Valley). The group is important partly because it is mostly not from burials but constitutes an assemblage of domestic types, rare in this region of Palestine. It is also evidence for the widely held theory that many EB IV folk were nomadic pastoralists who lived part of the year in caves and other temporary shelters. Also from Cave II was a small collection of Late Roman pottery and objects, indicating a final occupation, probably by refugees during the Second (or Bar-Kokhba) Jewish Revolt in 135 CE.

[*See also* Samaritans.]

BIBLIOGRAPHY

Cross, Frank Moore. "Papyri of the Fourth Century BC from Dâliyeh." In *New Directions in Biblical Archaeology*, edited by David Noel Freedman and Jonas C. Greenfield, pp. 45–69. Garden City, N.Y., 1969.
Lapp, Paul W., and Nancy L. Lapp, eds. *Discoveries in the Wâdī ed-Dâliyeh*. Cambridge, Mass., 1974.

WILLIAM G. DEVER

DALMAN, GUSTAF (1855–1941), theologian and first director of the German Protestant Institute of Archaeology in Jerusalem. Dalman was born in Niesky, in southeastern Prussia, a community dominated by Moravians. After studying Protestant theology he taught at the seminary of the Moravian fraternity in nearby Gnadenfeld (1881–1887). During a stay in Leipzig in 1883, he was promoted to doctor of theology. In 1887 he moved to Leipzig to become an assistant at the Institutum Judaicum, where he earned his Ph.D. He was appointed director of the institute in 1893. Dalman also taught Old Testament at the University of Leipzig, where he became an associate professor in 1896. In 1902 he was elected the first director of the newly founded Deutsches Evangelisches Institut für Altertumswissenschaft des Heiligen Landes in Jerusalem. During World War I he was forced to give up that position because of the political situation. In 1917 he became a full professor in Greifswald, where he founded an institute for research of Palestine. Following his retirement in 1923, Dalman dedicated his life to his magnum opus, *Arbeit und Sitte in Palästina*. He died in Herrnhut, a Moravian village not far from his birthplace.

The Aramaic language was the focus of Dalman's work prior to his directorship at the German institute. He published a grammar and a dictionary of Palestinian Aramaic and a volume on the language of Jesus. In Jerusalem, he collected data on Palestinian customs and manners that is still an important resource for recovering a rapidly vanishing world. His knowledge of the Holy City and its ancient sites, as well as the topography of the land of Israel, appears in his books *Orte und Wege Jesu* and *Jerusalem und sein Gelände*. His exploration of Petra and its vicinity led to his publishing the first description of the now famous site. Dalman published most of the enormous amount of ethnographic material he had gathered before World War I in seven volumes, under the title *Arbeit und Sitte in Palästina* (1928–1942).

[*See also* Deutsches Evangelisches Institut für Altertumswissenschaft des Heiligen Landes; Petra.]

BIBLIOGRAPHY

Dalman, Gustaf. *Palästinischer Diwan*. Leipzig, 1901.
Dalman, Gustaf. *Grammatik des jüdisch-palästinischen Aramäisch*. 2d ed. Leipzig, 1905.
Dalman, Gustaf. *Petra und seine Felsheiligtümer*. Leipzig, 1908.
Dalman, Gustaf. *Neue Petra-Forschungen und Der heilige Felsen von Jerusalem*. Leipzig, 1912.
Dalman, Gustaf. *Jesus—Jeschua; Die drei Sprachen Jesu; Jesus in der Synagoge, auf dem Berge, beim Passahmahl, am Kreuz*. Leipzig, 1922.

Dalman, Gustaf. *Orte und Wege Jesu.* 3d ed. Gütersloh, 1924.

Dalman, Gustaf. *Aramäische Dialektproben.* 2d ed. Leipzig, 1927.

Dalman, Gustaf. *Arbeit und Sitte in Palästina.* 7 vols. in 8. Gütersloh, 1928–1942.

Dalman, Gustaf. *Jerusalem und sein Gelände.* Gütersloh, 1930.

Dalman, Gustaf. *Die Worte Jesu.* 2d ed. Leipzig, 1930.

Dalman, Gustaf. *Aramäisch-neuhebräisches Handwörterbuch zu Targum, Talmud und Midrasch.* 2 vols. 3d ed. Göttingen, 1938.

Männchen, Julia. *Gustaf Dalmans Leben und Wirken in der Brüdergemeinde, für die Judenmission und an der Universität Leipzig, 1855–1902.* Wiesbaden, 1987.

Männchen, Julia. *Gustaf Dalman als Palästinawissenschaftler in Jerusalem und Greifswald, 1902–1941.* Wiesbaden, 1993.

VOLKMAR FRITZ

DAMASCUS, current capital of modern Syria, located in a basin east of the Anti-Lebanon range, at the foot of Mt. Qasiyun (33°30′ N, 36°18′ E). Rainfall in the area is fairly meager (about 250–300 mm/year), but the plain is well watered by the Barada River. The river, augmented with several major irrigation canals, has allowed Damascus to prosper as one of the great oases of Southwest Asia.

Because the city has been occupied since antiquity, often playing an important role in the history of the Levant, very little excavation has been possible in Damascus, and to date, virtually no remains of the city prior to the Roman period are known. However, literary sources from the Late Bronze Age onward refer to Damascus and make it possible to construct its general history from that period through Hellenistic times, in spite of the lack of archaeological data.

History of the City. Although Damascus is popularly called the oldest continuously occupied city in the world, evidence for its existence currently goes back only to the time of the Egyptian pharaoh Thutmosis III, who lists Damascus as one of the cities whose rulers were captured at the siege of Megiddo in the early fifteenth century BCE. In the Amarna letters, Damascus appears as a town in the land of Upu/Upi, an area under Egyptian sovereignty during virtually the entire Late Bronze Age. The Amarna and other Egyptian texts give no indication that Damascus had any major political significance during this period.

During the Iron Age, specifically in the ninth and eighth centuries BCE, however, Damascus became the capital of one of the leading Aramean states of the Levant. It played a significant role in the political life of the kingdoms of Israel and Judah, usually as an antagonist, but sometimes as an ally against the encroachments of Assyria. Portions of the history of this period are known from biblical texts (especially *Kings, Chronicles,* and *Isaiah*), Assyrian records, a few scattered references in Aramaic inscriptions from northern Syria, and the recently discovered Aramaic Stela from Tel Dan in northern Israel (Avraham Biran and Joseph Naveh, "An Aramaic Stele Fragment from Tel Dan." *Israel Exploration Journal* 43 [1993]: 81–98).

In the mid-ninth century BCE, Damascus and the kingdom of which it was the capital (usually called Aram or Aram Damascus) became the preeminent political power in the Levant, and its king, Hadad-idri, led an anti-Assyrian coalition of states in battle against Shalmaneser III in four confrontations between 853 and 845. The reign of Hazael (c. 842–800 BCE) saw Damascus become the head of a substantial empire, dominating most, if not all, of ancient Palestine, including Israel, Judah, and Philistia, and perhaps controlling some parts of northern Syria as well. A decline set in during the reign of Hazael's son, Bir-Hadad, which was not reversed until about 738, when the last independent king of Aram Damascus, Raṣyan (biblical Rezin), came to power and led another anti-Assyrian coalition that included Israel, Philistia, and Tyre against Tiglath-Pileser III. This attempt to secede from Assyrian control was unsuccessful and led to disaster for Damascus, which was captured by the Assyrians in 732 BCE and annexed into the Assyrian provincial system.

Because of its important position on the major trade routes of the Levant, Damascus remained a significant city through the rest of the Assyrian, Babylonian, and Persian periods. The Hellenistic period brought important changes. Following Alexander's conquest of the Levant (333 BCE), the city became the site of a Macedonian colony and was substantially expanded and rebuilt, with new fortifications. In 111 BCE, the city became the capital of Phoenicia and Coelesyria. Following a brief period under the control of the Nabateans, from 85 to 64 BCE, it was incorporated into the Roman Empire. During the Roman period a number of emperors lavished funds on Damascus for public construction: its main temple was spectacularly reconstructed, the city wall was rebuilt, and major colonnaded streets were constructed. The Byzantine period has provided few significant remains, but the city experienced another brief time of glory when it became the Umayyad capital in 661 CE, which climaxed with the building of the Great Mosque. Unfortunately, this period of splendor was short-lived, for in 750 CE the ʿAbbasid caliphs moved the Islamic capital to Baghdad, leaving Damascus without power.

Archaeology of the Site. Archaeological information about the pre-Hellenistic periods of Damascus is scarce in the extreme. Although several limited excavations have been undertaken, none have found those levels. Even the exact location and extent of the ancient site are not yet defined. Scholars generally place the original city within the boundaries of the current "Old City," and propose that the great Umayyad mosque, located on a large, flat plateau in the northwest part of the city, was probably built on the site of the main temple of Iron Age Damascus, which was dedicated to Hadad-Ramman (cf. *2 Kgs.* 5:18). Some scholars argue, however, that the rest of the city was located to the west and south of the temple, while others propose that a group of hills to the east and southeast of the mosque area covers the remains of the settlement. One hill, located some 300 m to the south of the mosque, is generally thought to be the prime candidate for the location of the Iron Age citadel. Only excavation will further illuminate the problem of the location of the original city.

Although no artifacts from Bronze Age Damascus are known, a few items, discovered in secondary contexts, including a carved orthostat, ivories, and bronze ornaments, can be attributed to the Iron Age. The orthostat (about 80 × 70 cm) is basalt and is decorated with a carved relief of a crowned sphinx, stylistically datable to the ninth century BCE. It was found incorporated into the substructure of the wall around the Umayyad mosque and probably belonged to the temple of Hadad-Ramman. Of the two ivories, one was found in the Assyrian fortress town of Til Barsip in northern Syria and the other at the Assyrian capital Kalaḫ, or Kalḫu (Nimrud), in Mesopotamia. They are inscribed with dedications to "our lord Hazael," who may be the Damascene king of that name. Presumably, the ivories were part of the booty taken from Damascus by the Assyrian kings in the eighth century BCE. Each of two bronze horse ornaments, one found on the island of Samos, the other in Eretria in Greece, has an Aramaic inscription mentioning a Hazael, who may be the Damascene king. The ninth-century Bir-Hadad, or Melqart, stela from the North Syrian town of Breij, often attributed to a Damascene king, Bir-Hadad, is now thought by several scholars to belong to the king of a northern Aramean state rather than Damascus (see Wayne T. Pitard, "The Identity of the Bir-Hadad of the Melqart Stela," *Bulletin of the American Schools of Oriental Research* 272 [1988]: 3–21).

Little is preserved from the Hellenistic period as well, although most scholars agree that the general plan of the current Old City is based on the Hellenistic reconstitution of Damascus. Jean Sauvaget (1949) argued that a rectangular city wall was constructed during the Hellenistic period, and this appears likely. However, clear evidence for this wall has yet to be found. The remains of a hippodrome to the north of the Old City probably belong to this era.

Several elements of Roman Damascus are still visible. The most notable examples of Roman architecture are the remains related to the great temple of Damascene Jupiter (Hadad-Ramman) found in the area of the Umayyad mosque. This temple complex, perhaps the largest in Roman Syria, can be reconstructed from the existing remains. Two inscriptions, which can be dated to 15/16 and 37/38 CE, indicate the time of the initial construction of the complex.

The Temple of Jupiter was surrounded by two concentric enclosure walls. The almost-rectangular outer wall encompassed an area of about 380 by 310 meters, creating a large outer court for the temple. The interior side of the wall was covered by a portico, which was occupied by a bazaar. Parts of both the eastern and western gates of this enclosure wall still stand in situ, as do some of the columns from the interior colonnade of the eastern side. Toward the end of the first century, the west and northwest sides of the outer wall were doubled in thickness to create more space for shops. This section was called the gamma, after the Greek letter it resembled.

Within the great courtyard was a second rectangular temenos wall that surrounded the temple proper. It enclosed an area of about 156 by 97 meters and had entrances on all four sides. The exterior was decorated with pilasters, and there were square towers at each of the four corners. A considerable percentage of this enclosure wall is still preserved as the foundation of the current wall surrounding the Umayyad mosque. Much of the principle entrance on the east side, with its impressive propylaeum still exists, as does almost all of the western wall and the lower sections of the south wall.

Within the enclosure, all traces of the Temple of Jupiter have disappeared, and even its location within the enclosure is uncertain.

A study by Klaus S. Freyberger (1989) has shown that the entire complex was substantially refurbished during the reign of Septimus Severus (193–211), including major reconstructions of the south and east gates of the inner temenos wall.

In addition to the temple complex, the main street of Roman Damascus, usually identified with the "Street called Straight" in *Acts* 9:11, can be reconstructed. This street was the city's main artery and was oriented east-west. The eastern city gate that opened onto the street (today called Bab esh-Sharqi) is well preserved and has undergone restoration. The gate has three entries, the largest in the center, which opened onto the street itself. This entry indicates that the street was 13.68 m wide. The other two entries opened onto the sidewalks, which were colonnaded porticoes that flanked the road all the way across the city. The gate has usually been dated to the early third century CE, but Freyberger argues that the decor includes elements that belong to the early first century CE. Thus, the gate and the grand street were probably constructed in the first century and refurbished during the reign of Septimus Severus, as the temple complex was.

About 500 m west of the Bab esh-Sharqi are the remains of an arch that was also related to the street, although its function is not clear. This arch and one about 250 m farther west (no longer in existence) marked spots where the street made a slight shift in direction (thus, Straight Street was not straight). The west gate has not been preserved.

The current wall around the Old City dates largely to the twelfth century CE, and none of it, besides the east gate, to the Roman period, although many Roman stones have been reused in the current wall. Most of the line of the ancient wall remains unknown, although it is commonly believed that it followed the line of the rectilineal Hellenistic wall, rather than that of the current, oval-shaped one. Most reconstructions of the Roman wall show the current wall overlapping the Roman one only near some of the gates.

During the reign of Diocletian (287–305) a fortress was built to the west of the temple complex. It is not clear whether it was outside or inside the city wall because the line of the western wall has not been firmly established. However, its location became the site of the medieval citadel that stands today.

In the reign of Theodosius (379–395), the temple area became the site of a church, dedicated to St. John the Baptist. It is not known whether Theodosius simply converted the old temple into a church or destroyed the temple and constructed a new building within the inner temenos. Very little architectural evidence of this period survives. Virtually nothing is known of the church and the inner court during this period because the entire area within the temenos wall was cleared to build the mosque in the early eighth century. However, the courtyard area between the inner and outer temenos walls was divided up by the erection of colonnades between the entry gates of the outer and inner walls on the north, east, and west. This apparently was done to allow the rest of the outer court to be filled in with new construction while maintaining open ways into the church courtyard. The southern part of the outer court became the site of a new palace at this time. None of the latter has survived, but sections of the western and northern colonnades are still in situ.

The city came under Islamic control in 636 CE, and in 656 the caliph Muʿawiyah made Damascus his capital. This development did not have an immediate impact on the architecture of the city. Muʿawiyah occupied the older Byzantine palace and simply shared part of the inner court of the temple area with the Christians who worshiped in the church. Caliph al-Walid (705–715), however, confiscated the entire complex shortly after coming to power, demolished everything inside the temenos wall, and built the Great Mosque, one of the crown jewels of Muslim architecture.

The inside of the temenos was completely changed. A huge sanctuary (136 m east–west and 37 m north–south) was built along the southern side of the court. Its interior is divided by two rows of columns into three almost-equal aisles. The center is intersected by a transept surmounted by a dome. The interior of the sanctuary was paneled with marble to a height of about 3 m, above which were extensive mosaics.

To the north of the sanctuary was a large open courtyard, paved with white marble and flanked on the north, east, and west by a two-tiered arcade built to match the style of the sanctuary's northern facade. The entire face of the courtyard was decorated, the lower part with marble paneling and the upper part with mosaics depicting landscape motifs. The mosaics in the Great Mosque covered the largest surface ever put to this use. Only a small portion of the marble paneling and mosaics has survived the several disasters that have struck the mosque over the centuries. The most famous surviving section of mosaic is the lovely depiction of trees on the northern face of the transept, although a long section on the back wall of the west portico is equally impressive.

The Umayyad mosque in Damascus had a very strong influence on Muslim architecture and is referred to in Islamic documents as one of the wonders of the world. Al-

DAMASCUS. *Thirteenth-century mausoleum of Rukn ed-Din.* (Courtesy K. Toueir)

DAMASCUS. *Umayyad mosque.* The interior court. (Courtesy W. T. Pitard)

though much of its original splendor has been lost, it remains an imposing complex.

Damascus went into a serious decline with the end of the Umayyad dynasty and the rise of the 'Abbasids, when the capital was moved to Baghdad. In 750, the new rulers sacked Damascus and demolished its city wall. The city lost its important position and went into a long eclipse, marked by little architectural development.

BIBLIOGRAPHY

Creswell, K. A. C. *Early Muslim Architecture.* 2 vols. 2d ed. New York, 1979. Volume 1 includes the best study of the Umayyad mosque available. For an abridged and less technical version of this work, see *A Short Account of Early Muslim Architecture,* revised and supplemented by J. W. Allan (Aldershot, 1989).
Dussaud, René. "Le temple de Jupiter Damascénien et ses transformations aux époques chrétienne et musulmane." *Syria* 3 (1922): 219–250. Significant analysis of the temple complex; still very useful, although it should be read in light of Creswell's (above) analysis.
Freyberger, Klaus S. "Untersuchungen zur Baugeschichte des Jupiter-Heiligtums in Damaskus." *Damaszener Mitteilungen* 4 (1989): 61–86. Important study concerning the date of the Jupiter temple.
Pitard, Wayne T. *Ancient Damascus: A Historical Study of the Syrian City-State from Earliest Times until Its Fall to the Assyrians in 732 B.C.E.* Winona Lake, Ind., 1987. Reconstruction of the historical development of Damascus through the Iron Age.
Sack, Dorothée. *Damaskus: Entwicklung und Struktur einer orientalisch-islamischen Stadt.* Mainz am Rhein, 1989. Important study of the development of the city from the Iron Age to modern times.
Sauvaget, Jean. "Le plan antique de Damas." *Syria* 26 (1949): 314–358. Classic and still useful study of the development of Damascus through the Byzantine period.
Watzinger, Carl, and Karl Wulzinger. *Damaskus: Die Antike Stadt.* Wissenschaftliche Veröffentlichungen des Deutsch-Türkischen Denk-malschutz-Kommandos, 4. Berlin and Leipzig, 1921. Foundational study of the archaeological remains of Damascus, detailed, brilliant, and still very useful.

WAYNE T. PITARD

DAMASCUS DOCUMENT. In 1896, Solomon Schechter of the University of Cambridge, England, discovered two Hebrew manuscripts in the genizah (a storeroom for valued texts) of a Qaraite synagogue in Cairo. He brought them to Cambridge, England, where they were subsequently published, in 1910, as the *Damascus Document.* The first of the two, manuscript A (tenth century CE) contains eight sheets of parchment; manuscript B (eleventh/twelfth century) contains one sheet. Both sides of a sheet were used. Schechter numbered the sheets pages 1–16 and 19–20, respectively; page 19 of manuscript B parallels, with some important differences, pages 7–8 of manuscript A, thus enabling a continuous, but conflated, text to be restored. Page 20 is not paralleled in manuscript A.

The document is comprised of two sections. A paranetic section, the Admonition(s), contains Israel's history, the preservation of a righteous remnant after the Babylonian Exile, and criticism of current religious practice (1–4.12); laws governing a sectarian organization (4.13–7.10); and threats of punishments to outsiders and defectors (7.10–8.19; 19–20). The second section is a collection of laws governing settlements in "camps" and in "cities" (9–16). The name *Zadokite Fragments* derives from a reference in the work to the sons of Zadok; the alternate designation *Damascus Document* derives from a reference to an exile in Damascus.

Fragments of texts that either parallel or are similar to the Cairo manuscripts (designated CD for Cairo Damascus) have been found in three caves at Qumran near the Dead Sea (designated 4Q[umran]D[amascus]a–h, 5QD, 6QD). With the aid of these fragments, some scholars reconstruct an "original" *Damascus Document* in which CD 15 and 16 directly precede CD 9 and other Cave 4 fragments are inserted before CD 1 and after CD 14. However, fewer than half of the QD fragments actually parallel CD.

Schechter and others recognized CD as the product of a Palestinian Jewish sect from the Hellenistic period. Since the Qumran discoveries, CD has played a central role in the dating and identification of the Qumran community. It is acknowledged to contain the most extensive account of the historical and ideological roots of the group that produced it, traced back to the Babylonian Exile, when God revealed to it "the hidden things in which all Israel had gone astray" (3.14)—namely, calendrical and legal observances. These issues surface in other Qumran texts and seem to represent the original cause for the adoption by certain Jews, perhaps in the third or second century BCE, of a segregated life-style governed by a solar year of 364 days (not the standard Jewish lunar year of 354 days) and by their own interpretation of the law of Moses. Their settlements were governed by a *mebaqqer* ("overseer") and a priest, and dealings with the Temple, and with other Jews and Gentiles, were strictly controlled. They regarded themselves as living in an "age of wickedness," in which God's anger with Israel would persist, until "there will arise one who will teach righteousness at the end of days" (6.11).

The relationship between the Damascus communities and the community of the Qumran text known as the *Rule of the Community* (the *yaḥad*) remains unclear. Some scholars identify the two as one because of references in CD to a Teacher of Righteousness as the initiator of a recent penitence movement (CD 1). Many prefer, however, to regard the *yaḥad* as a splinter group because of its clearly different manner of organization and ideology. If so, the *yaḥad* must have written its own creation into the CD's history, perhaps in the light of its belief that the "one who will teach righteousness" had actually arrived. Parts of CD 20 appear to be directed from within the *yaḥad* against those who rejected the "Teacher."

Schechter attributed CD to an otherwise unknown Zadokite sect from which the Dositheans were descended; Israel Lévi (1911) regarded them as Sadducees, but not of the kind depicted in the works of Josephus; Robert H. Charles (1912) saw them as reformed Sadducees. All these scholars identified the Pharisees as the opponents of the sect, although Louis Ginzberg found their laws to be essentially Pharisaic. Since the Qumran discoveries, an Essene identification has been popular; recent studies on CD's legal

traditions (which are congruent with the *Temple Scroll*) again favor the Sadducees, however. The origins of the Damascus community have commonly been ascribed to the Maccabean period, but this conclusion is becoming less certain. Reference to "Damascus" may be taken literally, but Frank M. Cross has proposed that it means Qumran, while Jerome Murphy-O'Connor (followed by Philip R. Davies) has argued that it refers to Babylon.

Recent publication of the 4QD fragments has revived the study of the Damascus communities, with emphasis on the important part legal differences played in creating ancient Jewish sects. The nonlegal material in CD (to which the Qumran texts add little) also maintains a central place in research into the historical and ideological context of the Qumran scrolls, although no theory currently dominates.

[*See also* Dead Sea Scrolls.]

BIBLIOGRAPHY

Baillet, Maurice. "Document de Damas." In *Le "petites grottes" de Qumrân*, pp. 128–131. Discoveries in the Judaean Desert, vol. 3. Oxford, 1962. Publication of the 5QD and 6QD fragments.

Broshi, Magen, ed. *The Damascus Document Reconsidered.* Jerusalem, 1992. Critical text edition, including plates and apparatus, incorporating some Q materials by Elisha Qimron; an essay on the 4QD materials by Joseph Baumgarten; and a bibliography (1970–1989) by Florentino García Martínez.

Cross, Frank M., Jr. *The Ancient Library of Qumran and Modern Biblical Studies.* New York and London, 1958.

Davies, Philip R. *The Damascus Covenant: An Interpretation of the "Damascus Document."* Sheffield, 1982. Analysis of the Admonition, including a discussion of the history of research on CD.

Ginzberg, Louis. *An Unknown Jewish Sect* (1922). New York, 1976. Fullest discussion of the legal material, though the identification of the group concerned is widely challenged.

Murphy-O'Connor, Jerome. "An Essene Missionary Document? CD II, 14–VI, 1." *Revue biblique* 77 (1970): 201–229. Argues that the Damascus Community (identified as the Essenes) immigrated into Palestine from Babylon and formed a sect in the face of opposition to their laws.

Rabin, Chaim, ed. and trans. *The Zadokite Documents.* 2d rev. ed. Oxford, 1958. Includes text, translation, and notes, but no introduction.

Schechter, Solomon. "Fragments of a Zadokite Work." In *Documents of Jewish Sectaries* (1910). Reprint, New York, 1970. Contains a bibliography for 1910–1969, and an updated introduction by Joseph A. Fitzmyer, correcting several misreadings in the original edition's introduction.

Wacholder, Ben Zion, and Martin G. Abegg, comps. and eds. *A Preliminary Edition of the Unpublished Dead Sea Scrolls: The Hebrew and Aramaic Texts from Cave Four.* 2 vols. Washington, D.C., 1991–1992. Contains a computer-generated reconstruction of 4QD^{a-h} based on concordance entries, plus a concordance of CD passages paralleled in the 4Q fragments. See, in particular, pages 1–57, 102.

PHILIP R. DAVIES

DAN (Ar., Tell el-Qadi), site located at the northeast end of the Hula Valley, at the foot of Mt. Hermon and at the headwaters of the Jordan River's most important source (map reference 2112 × 2949). The site is a rectangular, crater-shaped mound that was formed by massive ramparts constructed in the Early and Middle Bronze Ages. It was first identified with biblical Laish/Dan by Edward Robinson in 1838, an identification that has been accepted unanimously since. A bilingual (Greek-Aramaic) stone inscription found at the site also refers to the place name *Dan*. Laish is mentioned in the Egyptian Execration texts, where its king, Horon-Ab is named, and in the Mari texts, in connection with Hazor, in correspondence concerning tin shipments. [*See* Mari Texts.] Later, in the fifteenth century BCE, Laish is again mentioned in the list of cities conquered by the Egyptian king Thutmosis III. Dan is extensively referred to in the Bible, particularly in passages reflecting the Iron Age milieu (e.g., *Jos.* 19:47; *Jgs.* 18; *1 Kgs.* 12:29–31, 15:16 ff.). The latest ancient reference is that in the *Onomasticon* of Eusebius (entry no. 369), who located the place 4 mi. from Panias (Banias).

Trial excavations at the site were carried out in 1963 by Zeev Yeivin, and in 1966 salvage excavations were initiated by the Israel Department of Antiquities under the direction of Avraham Biran. In 1974 the project was transferred to the Nelson Glueck School of Biblical Archaeology of the Hebrew Union College in Jerusalem, still under Biran's directorship. As of 1995 the expedition was still active. Seven excavation areas were opened: A, B, H, K, M, T, and Y. All areas except H and M straddle the perimeter of the tell, exposing the Bronze Age fortifications. The fortifications enclose springs on the west side of the tell, where a high water table and dense vegetation thwart excavation.

Neolithic Period (Stratum XVI). The earliest occupation discerned at Tel Dan dates to the Pottery Neolithic (PN) period, perhaps early in the Wadi Rabah phase (c. 5000 BCE). Occupation remains were encountered in area B, where a deep probe at the base of the MB rampart core reached bedrock. Five stratigraphic phases were distinguished here in 2 m of accumulation. A subsurface infant burial in a jar was uncovered. Significant quantities of PN material were also found in areas M and T, in the fills of the lowest levels, indicating a fairly extensive area of habitation. The material culture features a characteristic flint industry, worked-basalt objects, bone utensils, and pottery—including several complete vessels—of plain, slipped and burnished, and incised wares.

Early Bronze Age (Strata XV–XIV). Surprisingly, Tel Dan seems to be almost devoid of Chalcolithic and EB I occupation. (The exceptions are three or four sherds and a possible "violin figurine," all from fills, objects that may have been transported from elsewhere in a later period.) This implies at least fifteen hundred years of abandonment. EB remains have been found in all the deep exposures (areas A, B, K, M, T, Y)—even those outside the limits of later fortifications—attesting that the EB settlement was the most extensive of all. Massive stone and brick fortifications are in

evidence on the north and east side of the tell and there is a possible gate complex in area K. The pottery sequence makes Dan a type-site for distinguishing earlier (EB II or early EB III) from later (EB III) assemblages. Key finds include animal figurines, models of couches, cylinder-seal impressions (one of the largest groups in the Levant), a bone cylinder, Khirbet Kerak ware, and metal implements. [*See* Seals.]

Middle Bronze Age (Strata XII–IX). Tel Dan was occupied during the Intermediate Bronze Age (EB IV), but without leaving more than some flimsy wall remains and pottery sherds. It is not yet possible to say whether there was a gap in settlement over parts of this period or whether it was partially contemporary with either the previous Early Bronze Age or the subsequent Middle Bronze Age. The MB is represented by four strata (IX–XII) that, in area B, achieved an accumulation of 4–5 m, excluding the interior embankment.

The most prominent features of the MB occupation are its robust fortifications and its uniquely intact mud-brick gate. The initial phases of settlement in stratum XII utilized the remains of the existing EB fortification. Late in this stratum, or perhaps in stratum XI, these fortifications were supplemented by additional embankments and superstructures on the north and east; on the south, a new rampart was constructed by erecting, in stages, a vertical stone core with embankments sloping down to either side. This core was 6.5 m thick and preserved to a height of 10.5 m. The width of the rampart at its base was approximately 50 m. The upper part of the rampart has long since eroded away, and it is not known whether it was crowned with a freestanding wall.

A triple-arched mud-brick gate flanked by two towers may have been built at the same time, possibly on the site of an earlier EB gate. At the time of its discovery, it was preserved almost to its original height. This edifice had been plastered in antiquity. Apparently, however, it was unstable and prone to collapse, as evidence was found of unsuccessful attempts at shoring it up. In the end, it was blocked up and covered by the earthen embankment, resulting in the gate's almost total preservation. A new gate, of stone this time, was apparently built in area AB on the tell's south crest.

The remains inside the MB ramparts (and under them, in the case of stratum XII) seem comprised of rather prosaic courtyard dwellings with baking ovens and cooking and storage facilities. Some of these may have had more than one story. Particularly evocative were the stone-built chamber and cist tombs and infants buried in jars under the floors. No extramural cemetery was found, though a few MB I and II tombs have been found at the nearby sites of Hagoshrim, Gonen, and Kefar Szold. The chamber tombs (of which three were excavated) accommodated the remains of adult and adolescent males and females and included the richest finds: pottery, weapons, bone-inlaid boxes, scarabs, jewelry, and food offerings. Cist tombs held the remains of children above the age of two years and jar burials contained infants or fetuses. The latter two burial types usually included one or two pottery vessels and a scarab or so. These practices appear to be indicative of social status dependent on age. The artifacts from both the tombs (which contain many complete forms) and the floors above them provide a long sequence of material culture from which both typological development and social evolution can be inferred. The MB settlement was destroyed by a great conflagration sometime in the sixteenth or early fifteenth century BCE. [*See* Tombs; Grave Goods.]

Late Bronze Age (Strata VIII–VII). Inside the perimeter of the MB fortifications, LB remains were found in all areas where sufficient depth was attained: stratum VIII represents the LB I and stratum VII the LB II. The occupational remains of stratum VIII were built over the destruction layer of the previous MB stratum and exhibit a similar material culture and a continuation of mortuary practices. At this time the first evidence for metallurgy is found at Tel Dan in the form of melting furnaces, crucibles, slags (especially in area B), and a mold. In area K, a portion of a well-preserved stone-built structure was excavated that contained a terra-cotta mask, a javelin head, and the aforementioned mold (for a scepter?).

Stratum VII was often truncated by the pitting and building activities of the subsequent Iron I strata, VI and V. Its remains testify, however, to public architecture and some degree of wealth. A flagstone pavement or street bordered by structures on either side extended north from the area AB gate. A terra-cotta plaque depicting a dancing figure playing a musical instrument was found under this pavement. During this stage, a metallurgy industry based chiefly on recycling copper and bronze is indicated in areas B and Y by furnaces, slags, blowpipe nozzles, and the like. However, the most impressive assemblage of this period (fourteenth–thirteenth centuries BCE) was found in a large, corbelled, stone-built tomb (T.387) in the MB style, the so-called "Mycenaean tomb." Approximately forty individuals—men, women, and children—were interred over time, with older burials pushed aside to make room for later burials and offerings. Almost five hundred objects were counted among the burial goods, including sheep or goat bones (meat offerings), 108 pottery vessels—28 of which were imported from either the Aegean or Cyprus—alabaster and basalt vessels, bronze tools, weapons and vessels, decorated bone and ivory items, and glass, silver, and gold jewelry.

Iron I (Strata VI–V). Some indications of continuity from the previous period appear in the Iron I strata. In general, pottery forms and metal utensils are clearly descended from LB types. Metallurgy remained an important aspect of the economy, though the Iron I industrial remains are more

extensive than those of the previous period. In Iron I the emphasis is on intensive recycling, and there was a cultic association in area AB in the form of a small appended sanctuary containing such ceremonial objects as a miniature shrine. Nevertheless, important differences and innovations are also present. Myriad deep, often stone-lined, pits are featured in almost all of the excavated areas. Frequently these contained a wide variety and large number of pottery vessels—from large pithoi to small pyxides—animal bones, organic residues, and ash. Particularly suggestive are the many collared-rim pithoi found with pithoi of Galilean and Phoenician types. The collared-rim pithoi are most at home in the central highlands of Samaria and are rare in the north of the country, except at Dan and at a few sites in the eastern, Upper Galilee highlands. Their significant presence at Dan has been attributed to the migration of the tribe of Dan described in *Judges* 18. [*See* Ceramics, *article on* Syro-Palestinian Ceramics of the Neolithic, Bronze, and Iron Ages.]

The floors and architecture of stratum VI (c. twelfth century BCE) were rarely preserved, except for pits. This occupation seems to have been a more ephemeral one, but the lack of preservation is chiefly the result of heavy building and leveling in stratum V (late twelfth–mid-eleventh centuries BCE), one of the most substantial levels at Tel Dan. Stratum V shows a dense array of domestic and industrial architecture in almost every area of the tell. Some of these structures were clearly two stories high. This stratum was destroyed in a great conflagration that apparently enveloped the entire tell, resulting in a rich and varied assemblage of artifacts. Interestingly enough, no burial remains were found from this or the succeeding Iron Age.

Iron Age II (Strata IV–II). Dan's eminence as a cultic center for the Israelite kingdom was responsible for its more or less continuous prosperity and growth in Iron II. The high place in area T and the gate complexes in areas A and AB show a series of major building phases that utilized fine construction and masonry techniques. The excavator discerned three major building phases in the Iron II high place and attributed them to prominent Israelite kings:

1. *Bāmâ A:* Dating to the late tenth century BCE (Jeroboam I), the stratum-IV *bāmâ* is represented by a row of massive rectangular dressed stones laid out under the southern foundations of *bāmâ* B. An ashlar-constructed altar platform, a libation installation (or olive press), and several other richly endowed rooms were associated with this massive substructure.

2. *Bāmâ B:* The ninth-century BCE (stratum III, reign of Ahab) *bāmâ* gave the structure its present form. It is comprised of headers and stretchers dressed with margins in the classic royal Israelite fashion found at Samaria and Megiddo. Cedar beams were integrated at horizontal intervals (cf. *1 Kgs* 7:12). The altar platform was augmented and a

belt of chambers erected around the temple podium and altar precinct, creating an enclosed temenos (or altering the previous one). The in situ work of the stonemasons left a thick yellow travertine floor surrounding this stage's structures.

3. *Bāmâ C:* The eighth century BCE (stratum II, reign of Jeroboam II) *bāmâ* represents a phase of minor alterations and supplements. It was also the phase that revealed a series of cultic objects—altars, incense shovels, a scepter head, and sacrificial remains—in the exterior belt of rooms surrounding the cultic precinct. This was also the stage to which most of the epigraphic material could be attributed.

Like the cultic precinct, the gate complexes also seem to show successive augmentation and aggrandizement. The tenth- and early ninth-century BCE fortification and gate plans have only been recovered in difficult-to-decipher fragments under the well-preserved remains of the assemblage from the ninth–eighth centuries BCE. By the time of *bāmâ* B, the high place and the gates on the southern periphery of the tell were connected by means of a monumental slab-paved avenue found in areas A, M, and T. The excavator has assigned this and its coeval four-chambered gate and buttressed solid fortification wall to Ahab. The last upper gate and some related architecture have been dated to the eighth century BCE and are associated with Jeroboam II. An impressive array of cultic paraphernalia was excavated in and around the gate complex, including an ashlar canopy platform, decorated stone column bases and capitals in the Assyrian style, groups of *maṣṣēbôt* in small "chapels," altars, groups of complete pottery vessels presumed to have a cultic function, and more. Most significant of all is the recent (1993–1994) discovery of fragments of a stela (see figure 1), inscribed in Aramaic, that mentions a king of the House of David and a king of Israel (perhaps Jehoram). Though much controversy surrounds its interpretation, most scholars are now dating its placement to the second half of the ninth century BCE and its shattering to the first half of the eighth century BCE. The last phase was destroyed in

DAN. Figure 1. *Aramaic inscription fragment.* Found in the wall bordering the outer Iron Age gate plaza. The text recounts the exploits of a victorious Aramean king, probably Hazael, and mentions a king of Israel and the house of David. Dated c. 850-800 BCE. (Courtesy Nelson Glueck School of Biblical Archaeology, Jerusalem)

DAN. Figure 2. *Bilingual inscription.* Found in the cultic precinct; Greek above, Aramaic below. The text reads "To the God who is in Dan, Zoilos made a vow" and comprises forceful evidence for the identification of Tell el-Qadi with biblical Dan. Dated c. 200-150 BCE. (Courtesy Nelson Glueck School of Biblical Archaeology, Jerusalem)

the eighth century BCE, in a great conflagration that preserved these finds.

Iron Age III (Stratum I). The period of Assyrian rule over ancient Israel is surprisingly well represented at Tel Dan. While most of the Galilee was devoid of settlement, and even sites of former prominence (Hazor, Tel Kinnerot) were either abandoned or occupied by fortresses alone, Dan experienced a population explosion of sorts. The entire tell was densely occupied by an orthogonal network of domestic structures and streets. Wide-ranging trade relations are evidenced by the presence of Assyrian, Phoenician, Ammonite, Judahite, and Corinthian pottery and other finds. Later Iron Age remains adjacent to the high place were apparently removed by Hellenistic-period modifications, but cultic activity probably continued there because new monumental buildings were erected nearby. Some of these show Assyrian-style pilaster construction. In contrast, the fortifications and gate complexes—perhaps destroyed by the Assyrians—were left in disrepair. The large number of complete vessels and other artifacts found in this stratum indicate sudden abandonment, though no real destruction layer was detected in most parts of the tell.

Persian, Hellenistic, Roman, and Medieval Periods. Tel Dan appears to have lost much of its grandeur and, by inference, part of its original cultic importance, in the Persian through the medieval periods. Occupation was apparently confined to the environs of the high place, where cultic activity did continue. A large cache of Persian-period figurines was recovered in one of the rebuilt temenos chambers. From the Hellenistic period in particular, there is evidence

of the construction of a new cultic precinct based on the same principles that had guided the Iron Age one: a belt of rooms surrounding an open space containing the central platform and altar court. These latter edifices were also supplemented. The most important find from this period came from the area of the cultic precinct: a bilingual (Greek-Aramaic) stone inscription mentioning "the god who is in Dan" (see figure 2). The upper gateway in area AB also continued to function as a passage, if not an actual gate.

The Roman period saw the surfaces in the cultic precinct raised and a new temenos wall constructed. A thick plaster floor was laid over the Iron Age platform. An ashlar-built fountain house was uncovered, fed by terra-cotta pipes drawing water from the nearby spring. All across the southern flank of the tell, above the remains of the Iron Age gates, similar pipes were found in articulation. These carried spring water to irrigate the outlying fields. By this time the cult place at Dan had been largely supplanted by the one at nearby Banias, though the two clearly coexisted over a long period of time. [*See* Banias.] By the end of the Roman period, Tel Dan was abandoned, except for an ephemeral early Ottoman occupation found in area M and its corresponding cemetery found along the margins of the tell, close to the surface.

BIBLIOGRAPHY

Biran, Avraham, and Joseph Naveh. "An Aramaic Stele Fragment from Tel Dan." *Israel Exploration Journal* 43 (1993): 81–98. Detailed account and analysis of the recently discovered stele mentioning the "House of David," including a description of the archaeological context.

Biran, Avraham. *Biblical Dan*. Jerusalem, 1994. Well-illustrated, popular book summarizing twenty-seven seasons of excavation and the excavator-author's interpretations of the finds.

Biran, Avraham, and Joseph Naveh. "The Tel Dan Inscription: A New Fragment." *Israel Exploration Journal* 45 (1995): 1–18.

Biran, Avraham, David Ilan, and A. Greenberg. *Dan I: An Excavation History, the Pottery Neolithic, the Early Bronze Age and the Middle Bronze Age Tombs*. Jerusalem, 1996.

Ilan, David. "Mortuary Practices at Tel Dan in the Middle Bronze Age: A Reflection of Canaanite Society and Ideology." In *The Archaeology of Death in the Ancient Near East*, edited by S. Campbell and A. Green. Oxford, forthcoming. Summary of the MB burial data and an analysis of its cultural significance.

Stager, Lawrence E., and Samuel R. Wolff. "Production and Commerce in Temple Courtyards: An Olive Press in the Sacred Precinct at Tel Dan." *Bulletin of the American Schools of Oriental Research*, no. 243 (1981): 95–102. Alternative explanation (olive press) for the "libation installation" found in the sacred precinct and attributed to stratum IV.

Wapnish, Paula, and Brian Hesse. "Faunal Remains from Tel Dan: Perspectives on Animal Production at a Village, Urban, and Rural Center." *ArchaeoZoologia* 4.2 (1991): 9–86. Revelatory examination of animal husbandry at Tel Dan, showing differing utilization in different parts of the town, exploitation of the site's hinterland, and changing patterns over time.

Yellin, Joseph, and Jan Gunneweg. "Instrumental Neutron Activation Analysis and the Origin of Iron Age I Collared-Rim Jars and Pithoi from Tel Dan." *Annual of the American Schools of Oriental Research* 49 (1989): 133–141. Scientific analysis of a particular pottery type, demonstrating both its local and distant origins.

DAVID ILAN

DARB ZUBAYDAH, pilgrimage road beginning at Kufah in Iraq and ending at Mecca (Makkah) in Saudi Arabia. According to the Qur'an, a "pilgrimage to the Ka'bah (at Mecca) is a solemn duty to God, for all who are able to make this journey." Thus roads from all Islamic countries converged at Mecca. The origin of the Darb Zubaydah may be traced in sections to the early sixth century CE as a trade route linking the Hijaz and central Arabia with al-Hira in Iraq. It was during the 'Abbasid period, however, that its importance grew, and it developed into a full-fleged highway.

The transfer of the 'Abbasid capital from Damascus to Baghdad in AH 132/750 CE necessitated establishment of direct communication between the political and religious centers. The Kufah–Mecca road, existing prior to the 'Abbasid period was linked to Baghdad by extending it farther north. Several earlier 'Abbasid caliphs, especially, Abu'l 'Abbas as-Saffah, Abu Ja'far al-Mansur, al-Maholi, and al-Rashid, took an interest in the establishment of the Kufah–Mecca road and made arrangements for the provisions and facilities essential for travelers.

The 'Abbasid caliph Harun al-Rashid (170–193/786–809) several times visited Mecca accompanied by his wife, Zubaydah. They realized the conditions on the route and lack of facilities available to the pilgrims. Queen Zubaydah took keen interest in the improvement of the Baghdad–Mecca road; she made an outstanding contribution in providing water facilities by digging wells and cisterns along the pilgrim route and by building rest houses and lodgings. Arab geographers such as al-Harbi and Yaqut and the travelers Ibn Jubayr and Ibn Batutah have recorded vivid details of the constructions, facilities, and provisions provided by Zubaydah along the Kufah–Mecca road. She acquired a great reputation for her work. Several places were named after her, that is, Zubaydiyah (known as Umm Ja'far). Later, the road acquired the name Darb Zubaydah.

So far, about one hundred sites on the route have been recorded. Of these thirteen are located within Iraq, and the remaining are situated in Saudi Arabia. According to early geographers, there were twenty-seven main and as many secondary pilgrim stations on the road. There were several other rest places established along the main branches of the road. The most famous of these were al-'Aqabah, Zubalah, Fayd, Samirah, an-Nuqrah, ar-Rabadhah, Ma'din Bani, Sulaym, and Dhat 'Irq. The 'Abbasid caliphs provided milestones, which had Kufic inscriptions giving distances between the stations. Historians such as al-Tabari and Ibn al-Athir furnish details of the erection of milestones and details of the distances along the road starting from Kufah. The road was also provided with road-signs (*a'lam*) and fire signals.

Along the road, Kufic inscriptions are found on rocks at places such as as-Suwargiyah, Hadha, and Samirah. The condition of the road was maintained regularly; it was cleaned and cleared from various obstacles. It was paved in the sandy areas; steep hills and mountains were cut; and smooth tracks were made with steps at some places.

Of archaeological interest are the ruins surviving on the Darb Zubaydah. These are the pilgrim stations, water tanks, wells, forts, rest houses, milestones, and inscriptions (al-Rashid, 1980). Early Islamic pottery, glass, and coins are the main finds along the Darb Zubaydah. The pottery sherds are of a great variety—luster-painted, tin-glazed, splashed, monochrome green-glazed, and unglazed ware with or without decoration. Fragments of soft stone vessels have also been recovered. Minted in different cities, gold dinars, silver dirhams, and bronze coins of the Umayyad and 'Abbasid caliphates have been discovered along the route.

The most remarkable station is ar-Rabadhah about 200 km (124 mi.) southeast of the city of Medina (Madinah al-Munawwrah). At al-Rabadhah excavations under the direction of Sa'ad al-Rashid since 1979 have produced fine architecture and numerous archaeological finds in great variety, such as masonry foundations of houses, mosques, cemeteries, tombstones, and reservoirs and wells. The architecture of the residential houses reveal typical Rabadhah style; independent units are surrounded by strong walls. The structure of the house are defended by towers built along the walls and on the corners. Remains of other buildings, public facilities, small streets between the houses, industrial units, washrooms, and sewage disposal channels have been found. Recent research and archaeological studies on the road has revealed abundant information about the archaeological sites and remains of facilities on the road. From Rabadhah come a variety of metal objects, such as an iron dagger, a spouted receptacle, kohl containers, a dagger sheath, an iron chain, a fragment of an instrument, and animal figures, glass, and jewelry in wood, bone, and ivory.

Two large limestone reservoirs, one circular and the other square at Rabadhah are unique features. The circular structure has a diameter of 64.5 m (211.6 ft.) and its walls rise up to 4.7 m (15.4 ft.) above a gypsum floor. Adjacent to it is filter tank of 55 × 17 × 3.15 m (180.4 × 55.8 × 10.3 ft.) through which the reservoir received flood water after filtering. The reservoir dates to the tenth century, is still in good condition, and had a capacity of 14,250 cu m. The square reservoir, which measures 26 × 26 m (85.3 × 85.3 ft.) has gypsum-plastered walls, strengthened by semicircular buttresses. It has two main inlets, one of them fed by a dam. These reservoirs along with about one hundred tanks of different dimensions and capacity are suggestive of water engineering that existed at Rabadhah and the importance attached to a water supply.

Caliph Harun al-Rashid and his wife Zubaydah not only took keen interest in the establishment of the road but spent large sums for its maintenance and protection. They appointed regular officials for its upkeep and provision of facilities essential for the comfort of travelers. When the road was threatened soldiers were despatched. The traffic on the road was constant and considerable. Caravans by the thousands occasionally traveled at the same time. The road declined from the ninth century CE because of the incursions of various tribes and later by the raids of the Qarmatians. The fall of Baghadad in 1258 to the Mongols was catastrophic for the road. From an archaeological point of view, the Darb Zubayadah is an excellent example of early road systems in Arabia. The excavations along the road, especially at al Rabadhah attest to the flourishing of and advanced civilization and to the mingling of different Islamic countries along the road.

[See also ʿAbbasid Caliphate; Arabian Peninsula, *article on* The Arabian Peninsula in Islamic Times; Mecca; *and* Medina.]

BIBLIOGRAPHY

Atlal: The Journal of Saudi Arabian Archaeology 1–6 (1977–1982).
Ḥarbī, Ibrāhīm al-. *Kitāb al-manāsik wa-amākin ṭuruq al-ḥājj wa-maʿālim al-Jazīrah.* Edited by Ḥamad al-Jāsir. Riyadh, 1969.
Ibn al-Athīr, ʿIzz al-Dīn. *Al-kāmil fī al-tārīkh.* 9 vols. Cairo, 1929–1938.
Ibn Baṭūṭah. *Riḥlat Ibn Baṭūṭah.* 2 vols. Cairo, 1928.
Ibn Jubayr, Muḥammad ibn Aḥmad. *The Travels of Ibn Jubayr.* Edited by M. J. de Goeje. Leiden, 1907.
Ibn Khurdādhbih. *Al-masālik wa-mamālik.* Edited by M. J. de Goeje. Leiden, 1889.
Ibn Rustah, Aḥmad ibn ʿUmar. *Kitâb al-aʿlâk an-Nafîsa.* Edited by M. J. de Goeje. 2d ed. Leiden, 1892.
Jāsir, Ḥamad al-. "Al-Rabadhah fi Kutub al-Mutaqaddimin." *Al-ʿArab* 1 (1967): 5–8.
Muqaddasī, Muḥammad ibn Aḥmad. *Aḥsan al-taqāsīm fī maʿrifat al-aqālīm.* Edited by M. J. de Goeje. Leiden, 1877.
Rashid, Saʿad al-. "Ancient Water-Tanks on the Haj Route from Iraq to Makkah and Their Parallels in Other Arab Countries." *Atlal* 3 (1979): 55–62, pls. 28–43.
Rashid, Saʿad al-. "New Light on the History and Archaeology of Al-Rabadhah (Locally Called Abu Salim)." *Seminar for Arabian Studies* 9 (1979): 88–101.
Rashid, Saʿad al-. "A Brief Report on the First Archaeological Excavation at al-Rabadhah." *Seminar for Arabian Studies* 10 (1980): 81–84.
Rashid, Saʿad al-. *Darb Zubaydah: The Pilgrim Road from Kufa to Makkah.* Riyadh, 1980.
Rashid, Saʿad al-. *Al-Rabadhah: A Portrait of Early Islamic Civilisation in Saudi Arabia.* London, 1986.
Rashid, Saʿad al-. "Nuqud Islamiyya MuktashaFah fi Darb Zubaydah." *Al-Yarmūk Lil-Maskūkāt* 3.1 (1991): 41–56.
Rashid, Saʿad al-. "A New ʿAbbasid Milestone from al-Rabadha in Saudi Arabia." *Arabian Archaeology and Epigraphy* 3 (1992): 138–143.
Samhūdī, ʿAlī ibn ʿAbd Allāh al-. *Wafāʿ al-wafāʿ bi-akhbār Dār al-Muṣṭafā.* 4 vols. Edited by Muḥyi al-Dīn ʿAbd al-Ḥamīd. Cairo, 1955.
Tabarī, al-. *Tārīkh al-rusul wa-al-mulūk.* 15 vols. Edited by M. J. de Goeje et al. Leiden, 1879–1901.
Yāqūt ibn ʿAbd Allāh al-Ḥamawī. *Muʿjam al-buldān.* 5 vols. Beirut, 1955–1957.

SAʿAD ABDUL AZIZ AL-RASHID

DATING TECHNIQUES. Many artifacts and skeletal remains can be dated by reference to an established typological framework. The chronology of such a framework, except within a well-documented historical period, is ultimately based on a chronometric technique such as radiocarbon, thermoluminescence, or dendrochronology. These and other techniques are also used for placement within the framework. The essential characteristic of nearly all these is that they are "absolute," in the sense of giving a date that is based on currently measurable quantities; hence, they are objective, being independent of existing chronologies. The techniques outlined below are: (1) radiocarbon, (2) dendrochronology, (3) luminescence, (4) electron spin resonance, (5) uranium-series, (6) potassium-argon, (7) fission tracks, (8) amino acid racemization, (9) obsidian dating, (10) other chemical techniques, (11) archaeomagnetism, and (12) pollen analysis, climatic change, oxygen-isotope stages, and the Milankovitch timescale. Error limits are quoted at the 68 percent level of confidence (i.e., 1 sigma).

Radiocarbon Dating. The carbon in the carbon dioxide in the atmosphere consists mainly of nonradioactive carbon-12 and carbon-13; there is also a minute amount of weakly radioactive carbon-14 resulting from the interaction of cosmic-ray neutrons with the nitrogen in the upper atmosphere.

Carbon dioxide mixes rapidly throughout the atmosphere, and by photosynthesis enters plant life and hence into animals; atmospheric carbon dioxide also enters the oceans as dissolved carbonate, so that this too contains carbon-14—as do any shells and deposits formed from it. The totality of atmosphere, biosphere, and oceans is known as the carbon-exchange reservoir. The concentration ratio between carbon-14 atoms and nonradioactive carbon atoms is approximately the same (about one in a million million) throughout the reservoir; it also stays approximately constant with time.

In organic matter that is no longer exchanging its carbon with the reservoir, the carbon-14 lost by radioactive decay is not replenished; this is the case, for instance, in the cellulose molecules of wood. From the time of formation, the concentration ratio decreases at a rate determined by the immutable 5,730-year half-life of carbon-14; this means that wood 5,730 years old will have a carbon-14 concentration that is one half of its value at formation; for wood that is 11,460 years old, the concentration will be one quarter of the formation value, and so on—or, the concentration decreases by 1 percent every eighty-three years. Hence, comparing the concentration measured in an ancient organic sample with the assumed value at formation can determine the amount of time that has elapsed.

In practice, the method is useful for the period four hundred to four thousand years ago—although, with special measurement installations, some sample types can reach substantially further back, to about seventy thousand years ago. The error limits on the calendar-year date (i.e., after calibration; see below) are typically in the range ± 50–150 years, being smaller in some millennia than others.

Measurement. The carbon-14 concentration in a sample can be determined by converting the carbon of the sample into a gas or into benzene and measuring the emission rate of beta particles in an appropriate detector system. Since the late 1970s, direct measurement of the concentration by means of accelerator mass spectrometry (AMS) has been increasingly employed. Although such an installation is very expensive, it has the important advantage that the size of the sample required is less by several orders of magnitude—a few thousandths of a gram of carbon instead of a few grams.

Sample types. An essential characteristic of a sample is that over the centuries of burial it should not have acquired any fresh carbon from the atmosphere (e.g., by fungal growth). A minute amount of modern carbon can cause the date that is determined to be substantially too recent, particularly for samples near the forty-thousand-year limit. Conversely, the incorporation of "dead" carbon at formation can cause the opposite effect. Although the sample material itself may have high integrity, intrusive contamination may have been acquired during burial; the humic acids carried in percolating groundwater are an example. It follows that the extent to which a sample is reliable is bound up with the stringency of the laboratory pretreatment that can be applied. The severity that a laboratory can afford to use is dependent both on the size of the initial sample and on the amount of carbon required by the measurement facility; the severity needed depends also on the age.

For wood the use of extracted cellulose avoids lignin and humic acids. For precise dating, a serious problem with wood and charcoal is estimation of the extent to which the wood's formation predated the archaeological event of interest. For bone, use of the extracted protein fraction (collagen, gelatin) is necessary. Unfortunately, the amount remaining decreases with age and in some burial environments, among them the Near East, too little is left in bones from periods earlier than, say, the Neolithic. Charred bone is a good alternative. Grain can be dated reliably, particularly if charred. Single grains can be dated with the AMS technique, but site association is a severe problem. Among other datable sample types are shell, peat, sediment and soils, ivory paper and textiles, straw in mud bricks, and traces of charcoal in iron objects. The golden rule in sample collection is prior discussion with the relevant laboratory.

Calibration. A raw age from a laboratory is given in conventional radiocarbon years BP ("before the present," defined as 1950). This is not the same as the age in calendar years (i.e., sidereal years) because the carbon-14 concentration in the biosphere varies slightly from decade to decade and century to century: thus, wood formed at some time in the past does not necessarily have the same carbon-14 concentration as wood formed today. The variation occurring over the last ten thousand years has now been established by measuring samples of wood for which the age has been determined by dendrochronology. By using this "calibration curve," ages in radiocarbon years can be converted into ages in calendar years or calendar dates—denoted by cal BP, cal BCE, or cal CE. Extension of the calibration curve further back in time is being undertaken by intercomparison with the uranium-series technique using samples of coral.

The terminology just given, BP and so forth, is specific to radiocarbon dating. Most other techniques yield ages directly in calendar years and the use of BP is then confusing (because, it implies radiocarbon years rather than calendar years); exceptions to this are amino-acid dates and obsidian dates calibrated by reference to radiocarbon.

Dendrochronology (Tree-Ring Dating). For some species of trees growing in some climatic conditions, visually recognizable rings form annually with a climatically determined width pattern. This width pattern allows cross dating between trees felled in different periods (the pattern shown by the inner part of a recent tree can be matched with that shown by the outer part of a tree that was felled earlier). In this way a master chronology can be established for a region and building timber of unknown age can be dated by discovering where its pattern fits onto the master chronology. If sapwood is present on the timber, high accuracy is possible; even so, a degree of uncertainty remains as to how many years elapsed between felling and usage on the site concerned. To obtain a reliable fit onto the master chronology, the piece being dated needs to contain a minimum of about fifty rings.

The Californian bristlecone pine chronology and the European oak chronology have made possible the conversion of radiocarbon years to calendar years. The trees concerned are remarkably long-lived and by leapfrogging back from recent trees to successively older fossil trees, as indicated above, it has been possible to cover the last ten millennia.

Luminescence Dating (LD). Thermoluminescence (TL) and optical dating (OD) comprise luminescence dating (LD); OD utilizes optically stimulated luminescence (OSL). These are based on the cumulative effect of nuclear radiation on the crystal structure of certain minerals, mainly quartz and feldspar. The nuclear radiation is provided by trace amounts of potassium-40, rubidium-87, thorium, and uranium that are naturally present in the sample and its surroundings. The dating signal is obtained, in the case of TL, by heating grains extracted from the sample and measuring the light they emit by means of a highly sensitive photomultiplier; in the case of OSL, the measurement is obtained by shining light on the sample; lasers and halogen lamps can be used, as well as infrared-emitting diodes—in which case the luminescence may be termed IRSL.

The TL technique was first applied to pottery, the event dated being the firing by the ancient potter (thereby setting to zero the previously accummulated TL). It was subsequently extended to stalagmitic calcite (which has zero TL at formation) and to burnt flint (heated accidentally by having fallen into fire, or deliberately). The latter application, along with the ESR dating of tooth enamel, has had a particular impact on hypotheses concerning the relationship between anatomically modern humans and Neanderthals. The TL and OSL signals from quartz and feldspar can also be set to zero by exposure to daylight. Thus, windblown sediment (such as loess) is set to zero during its transportation, as is waterborne sediment, though in this case the zeroing process is less effective and the OSL method has a strong advantage over TL.

For either method it is necessary to evaluate the dose rate of nuclear radiation that the sample was receiving during burial. This is done partly by radioactive analysis in the laboratory and partly by on-site measurement (of the penetrating gamma radiation that reaches the sample from surrounding soil and rock, up to a distance of about 0.3 m). It is also necessary to estimate the water content of the sample and soil/rock because any water present attenuates the nuclear radiation. Uncertainty about water content (averaged over the burial period) can limit the accuracy obtained; sites which have always been bone-dry have an advantage.

For pottery and burnt flint, a half-dozen fragments not less than 30 mm across and 10 mm thick are required. For sediment, about half a kilogram is typically needed. Great care must be taken to avoid exposure to daylight, particularly if the OSL method is being used. Hence, the sample collection of sediment should be done by laboratory specialists with appropriate equipment (e.g., a short steel tube which is driven into the section; the material at the exposed ends is discarded in the laboratory); otherwise, the samples should be collected at night and secured in thick, opaque plastic bags. Even slight exposure to light may cause the evaluated age to be too recent.

Age range is highly dependent on sample type and site; several hundred thousand years is a typical upper limit for flint, calcite, and sediment—although with the latter there is a tendency (if some types of feldspar are present in the sample) for the age to be underestimated, particularly beyond fifty thousand years. The lower limit is on the order of one thousand years. With pottery, the lower limit can be on the order of a decade in some cases; the upper limit is usually beyond ten thousand years. The accuracy attainable is usually in the range 5–10 percent of the age (i.e., ±150–300 years at 1000 BCE, ±300–600 years at 4000 BCE). Hence, the main strength of the technique is for sites where there are no samples suitable for radiocarbon and on Paleolithic sites beyond the range of radiocarbon.

Electron Spin Resonance (ESR). Another way of measuring the cumulative effect of nuclear radiation is with electron spin resonance (ESR). Its principal archaeological applications have been to tooth enamel and stalagmite calcite. ESR reaches back several million years; its lower limit is a few thousand years. The above remarks about dose-rate evaluation apply here, but with additional complexity in the case of tooth enamel because of uranium migration. As a result, two ages are quoted, based on the assumptions of early uptake (EU) and linear uptake (LU), respectively (in some cases the EU age is substantially lower than the LU age). Large teeth (elephant, mammoth) are preferred; usually, separate determinations on about a dozen samples are averaged.

Uranium-Series Dating. Stalagmite calcite and other forms of that mineral and also some products from volcanic eruptions lend themselves to uranium-series dating. At formation, only uranium is present in the sample material. With time, radioactive daughter products (thorium-230, protactinium-231) build up slowly; determination of the ratio of daughter product to parent uranium allows the age to be evaluated. Measurement is conventionally by alpha spectrometry, but recently thermal ionization mass spectrometry (TIMS) has been used, which gives much higher precision and needs less of a sample. With TIMS, the age range is approximately 500–500,000 years; with alpha spectrometry, 2,000–350,000 years. In good circumstances, the error limits using TIMS can be as low as ±1 percent of the age; with alpha spectrometry the limits are usually in the range of ±5 percent to ±10 percent.

Potassium-Argon Dating. Of crucial importance in the

study of early hominids, potassium-argon dating is a technique based on the accummulation, in volcanic lava, for example, of argon-40 produced from the slow decay of potassium-40. During a volcanic eruption, previously accumulated argon (a gas) is released, which is the event which is dated. Obviously, to be useful, human occupation must be reliably associated with volcanic products—for example, between two lava beds. Its age range is enormous: from ten thousand years to about four hundred million years.

Fission Track Dating. The main impact of fission track dating has been on the study of early hominids. Its one or two applications to Neolithic obsidian artifacts are to be regarded as exotic rather than useful. The technique is based on the counting of the miniscule tracks left in some minerals by nuclear fragments immediately after the occurrence of spontaneous fission undergone by uranium nuclei present as impurity.

Amino-Acid Racemization. Dating by amino-acid racemization is based on the slow conversion within a protein molecule of an amino acid (such as aspartic) from its **L** form, at formation, to its **D** form, until an equilibrium mixture of the two is reached. Epimerization of isoleucine is another reaction utilized, notably in the dating of ostrich eggshells. These processes are strongly influenced by environmental conditions—by temperature in particular; site-by-site calibration against radiocarbon is usual, along with extrapolation for samples that are beyond the limit of the latter technique.

In its early application the technique acquired a reputation for unreliability, particularly for poorly preserved bone. However, good reliability is now being obtained when sample types are selected carefully (such as ostrich eggshell, well-preserved bone, and tooth enamel), when strict attention is paid to the validity of the radiocarbon dates used for calibration, and when stringent laboratory procedures are followed. Using aspartic acid the last 50,000–100,000 years can be covered; using the epimerization of isoleucine, reaching a half million years is feasible. In addition to the extension of age range, another advantage over radiocarbon is the comparative ease of measurement and, hence, the lower cost. An archaeologist can undertake a much wider sampling of site with amino-acid racemization than could be afforded using radiocarbon only.

Obsidian Dating. Another technique strongly influenced by environmental conditions, particularly temperature, is obsidian dating. It is based on the slow formation of hydration rims on freshly cleaved obsidian. Until the late 1970s, the favored approach was by regional calibration using known-age samples. Since then the emphasis has been on obtaining absolute ages, independent of other techniques or archaeological chronology. This approach requires two major evaluations (in addition to measurement of the hydration rim itself): the effective burial temperature and laboratory

measurement (at elevated temperature and pressure) of the rim growth rate for each type of obsidian that is dated. Dates have been reported in the age range from 200 to 100,000 years ago. Growth rates vary widely between different parts of the world; the comparatively rapid hydration rates in tropical countries allow more recent dating than in Arctic regions.

Other Chemical Processes. The movement of fluorine and uranium into bone and loss of nitrogen are other processes by which some indication of age can be obtained. The bulk contents are strongly dependent on the burial environment; however, this dependence is very much weakened if the depth profile, as measured by a nuclear microprobe, is used instead. Nuclear techniques measuring penetration depth of nitrogen can be used to distinguish between freshly cut surfaces of jade, for example, and those cut in antiquity.

Archaeomagnetic Dating. The direction of the earth's magnetic field (e.g., magnetic north as indicated by a compass) changes very slowly, but it is perceptible over a decade. A fossilized record of past direction is provided by the weak, but permanent, magnetization that is acquired by clay and stones on cooling down after baking and by sediment during deposition (or consolidation). The variation differs from region to region and does not follow a well-defined pattern. Hence, for each region of application it is necessary to establish a calibration curve using kilns, hearths, and silted-up ditches of known age. Consequently, the availability of a reliable archaeological chronology is a necessary prerequisite for applying the method. An alternative possibility is to make measurements on radiocarbon-dated lake sediment, obtained as a long core extracted from the lake bottom.

On a larger time scale, complete reversals of the earth's field provide a worldwide geomagnetic chronology, calibrated by means of the potassium-argon technique. The most recent event (named the Blake event) which is well established and generally accepted occurred at about 110,000 years ago; this was a comparatively brief reversal lasting not much more than ten thousand years. Earlier, at 780,000 years ago, there was the transition from the Matuyama reversed polarity epoch to the present Brunhes epoch.

Pollen Analysis and Other Climatic Indicators. An archaeological site carries a record of past climate notably through preserved tree and plant pollen. Other indicators are faunal assemblage and soil type. This record allows the levels of a Paleolithic site to be described as cold or warm and to be related—often through the intermediate step of a locally defined climatic sequence—to the worldwide climatic chronology, based on oxygen-isotope stages. The successive cold and warm stages of this chronology are defined by the isotope ratio (oxygen-18–oxygen-16) found in marine fossil microfauna. Finest climatic detail is given by the isotope ratio variations measured in long cores drilled into the polar ice cups.

Absolute dating of the marine stages was initially based, via sedimentary remanent magnetization, on potassium-argon dating supplemented by radiocarbon and uranium series. The chronology so obtained has now been refined by reference to the Milankovitch astronomical predictions of the climatic variation resulting from changes in the earth's orbital parameters. The marine stages are now the fundamental time divisions of the Quaternary epoch.

Pollen characteristics (such as the dominant species of tree) can be used to define pollen assemblage zones (PAZ). The succession of such zones can be used as a basis for chronozones, defined in terms of radiocarbon years. For example, at a type-site the boundaries of the major PAZ are dated by radiocarbon and those dates then define the chronozones. Arboreal pollen, expressed as a percentage of total tree and herb pollen, is a useful broad indicator of climate, being high in warm/wet periods and substantially lower otherwise.

BIBLIOGRAPHY

Aitken, Martin J. *Science-Based Dating in Archaeology.* London, 1990. Comprehensive discussion of the techniques outlined in this article.
Aitken, Martin J., et al., eds. *The Origin of Modern Humans and the Impact of Chronometric Dating.* Princeton, 1993. Papers based on a meeting held at the Royal Society, London, February 1992.
Aurenche, Olivier, et al., eds. *Chronologies in the Near East.* British Archaeological Reports, International Series, no. 379. Oxford, 1987. Papers based on an international symposium sponsored by the Centre National de la Recherche Scientifique, Lyon 1986.

MARTIN J. AITKEN

DCP SPECTROMETRY. Direct current plasma (DCP) spectrometry provides an effective means of analyzing the chemical composition of ancient pottery. Similar to inductively coupled plasma spectrometry (ICP), a related spectroscopic method, DCP offers a highly accurate means of determining the presence of a wide range of elements in any given sample, a necessary first step in all provenance studies. By obtaining chemical "fingerprints" of reference materials (e.g., kiln wasters) of known origin and finding compositional "matches" to pottery samples, one is often able to pinpoint the source of manufacture.

The first application of DCP on archaeological artifacts was conducted in 1994: select fired and unfired Jerash bowl fragments recovered from deposits associated with the late Byzantine pottery kilns in the hippodrome at the ancient Decapolis city of Gerasa (Jerash, Jordan) were examined (Lapp, 1994). In combination with petrographic thin-section analyses, DCP subsequently proved invaluable for the chemical characterization of clay oil lamp samples collected from sites once comprising Roman Palestine (Lapp, forthcoming). The team of F. A. Hart and S. J. Adams first used ICP to determine the provenance of select Romano-British pottery from Hampshire (Hart and Adams, 1983). The recent examination of early Bronze Egyptian pottery from Canaan by means of petrography, neutron activation, and ICP analyses successfully combines the analytical strengths of these archaeometric methods for determining provenance (Porat et al., 1991).

DCP centers on the analysis of samples prepared as solutions. The sample itself, whether a ceramic fragment of a Roman oil lamp or of a Persian storage jar, is brought into solution using a lithium metaborate fusion technique. Following the method outlined by E. M. Klein (1991), Lapp mixed 0.1 g of powdered Jerash bowl sample with 0.4 g of ultra-pure lithium metaborate flux and fused the mixture in preignited crucibles at 1040°C for 13 minutes (Lapp, 1994). After fusion, the pebble-shaped melt was dissolved in 0.24 ml of nitric acid; the resulting concentrated solution was then ready to be analysed for trace elements. For the major elements, a dilute solution of each sample consisting of 0.25 ml of the concentrated solution with nitric acid plus lithium was prepared.

Once in solution, the sample was nebulized and its aerosol directed at the plasma. The plasma itself is created by initiating an electrical discharge within a stream of argon flowing between two electrodes (Potts, 1987). After nebulization, the aerosol particles of the sample solution experienced desolation, vaporization, and atomization. This occurred in the "excitation zone" where the sample temperature ranges between 5700 and 6000 K (Potts, 1987). At this temperature, the elements' atoms undergo transitions to lower electronic states and emit their excess energy as a quanta of light. Because these wavelengths of light are specific to the emitting element, the identification of a tested element can be discerned by a proper spectrometer. The intensities of emission are measured by the spectrometer, measurements of which indicate the elemental abundances in any given sample. Potts notes that samples atomized in a direct current plasma experience significantly lower atomization temperatures than those atomized in the inductively coupled argon plasma of ICP analysis (Potts, 1987).

DCP spectrometry has proven to be an effective, accessible, and affordable means of major and trace element analysis of terracotta wares and lamps alike. Undoubtedly, it should also prove useful in future characterization studies with respect to nonceramic objects, as has already been demonstrated by the related archaeometric method of ICP applied to metal artifacts from late Bronze Age hoards in Slovenia (Trampuz-Orel et al., 1991).

[*See also* Neutron Activation Analysis; *and* Petrography.]

BIBLIOGRAPHY

Hart, F. A., and S. J. Jones. "The Chemical Analysis of Romano-British Pottery from the Alice Holt Forest, Hampshire, by Means of Inductively-Coupled Plasma Emission Spectrometry." *Archaeometry* 25.2 (1983): 179–185. The first landmark analysis of ancient pottery using ICP spectrometry.

Klein, Emily M., Charles H. Langmuir, and Hubert Staudigel. "Geochemistry of Basalts From the Southeast Indian Ridge, 115°E–138°E." *Journal of Geophysical Research* 96. B2 (1991): 2089–2107. The methods of sample preparation and procedure for DCP analysis as presented and outlined by Klein were adopted and followed by Lapp in his analysis of Jerash bowl fragments.

Lapp, Eric C. "A Comparative Clay Fabric Analysis of Fired and Unfired Jerash Bowl Fragments by Means of Petrography and Direct Current Plasma (DCP) Spectrometry." In *Proceedings of the 1994 Byzantine and Early Islamic Ceramics Colloquium in Syria-Jordan (Vth–VIIIth Centuries)*, edited by Estelle Villeneuve and Pamela M. Watson. Bibliothèque Archéologique et Historique. Paris, forthcoming. Results of the first application of DCP spectrometry to determine the chemical composition of archaeological artifacts.

Lapp, Eric C. "The Archaeology of Light: The Cultural Significance of the Oil Lamp from Roman Palestine." Ph.D. diss., Duke University, forthcoming. Demonstrates the usefulness of DCP spectrometry in combination with archaeology and epigraphic investigations into the cultural function of oil lamps in ancient daily life.

Plank, Terry A. "Mantle Melting and Crustal Recycling in Subduction Zones." Ph.D. diss., Columbia University, 1993. Highly technical work, written with the geochemist in mind. A model study for understanding the application of DCP spectrometry as it pertains to clay-sediment analysis.

Porat, Naomi, et al. "Correlation between Petrography, NAA, and ICP Analyses: Application to Early Bronze Egyptian Pottery from Canaan." *Geoarchaeology* 6.2 (1991): 133–149. Provenance findings and the value of multiple archaeometric techniques for determining provenance of manufacture.

Potts, P. J. *A Handbook of Silicate Rock Analysis.* Glasgow, 1987. General and succinct introduction to the technique of DCP spectrometry, supplemented with schematic diagrams of the instrumentation involved (see esp. pp. 192–197).

Trampuž-Orel, N., et al. "Inductively Coupled Plasma-Atomic Emission Spectrometry Analysis of Metals from Late Bronze Age Hoards in Slovenia." *Archaeometry* 33.2 (1991): 267–277. Pioneers the application of ICP-AES on metal artifacts, as opposed to pottery.

ERIC C. LAPP

DEAD SEA SCROLLS.

The phrase *Dead Sea Scrolls* is used in two senses, one generic and one particular. In the generic sense the phrase denotes documents and literary texts discovered at various sites along the shore of the Dead Sea and extending up to Jericho. These sites include Masada, Wadi Murabbaʿat, Naḥal Ḥever, Naḥal Ṣeʿelim, Naḥal Mishmar, Khirbet Mird, and Ketef Jericho. In the particular sense the phrase specifies the Hebrew, Aramaic, and Greek literary texts found in eleven caves near the site of Qumran.

Qumran Caves 1–11. The first seven of what have since come to be known as the Dead Sea Scrolls (in the particular sense) appeared in the summer of 1947 in Bethlehem. Coming from the hands of bedouin, their original provenance was unknown. As the significance of these scrolls became apparent, authorities made efforts to determine precisely where they had originated. Qumran Cave 1 was soon identified, and excavations began there in February 1949. These excavations lasted for about one month. The excavators discovered many text fragments, along with pieces of cloth and wood, olive and date stones, leather phylactery cases, and pottery sherds. Some of the text fragments belonged to the seven scrolls the bedouin had offered for sale, thus clinching the identification of the original findspot.

From this time began a competition of sorts between the authorities concerned with preserving manuscripts and recording archaeological details and the bedouin, who were concerned with making a small fortune from the sale of scroll materials. Both groups sought new manuscript-bearing caves. In February 1952, bedouin found Cave 2 and sold some of its fragments. Officials immediately set to investigating the cave systematically, along with all the rock cliffs in the Qumran region. Cave 3 thereupon yielded up its treasures to authorities. Subsequently, two additional rock-cliff caves bearing manuscripts were discovered: Cave 6, found by the Arabs in 1952, and Cave 11, found in 1956. The latter cave contained some of the most important and complete scrolls.

In addition to these natural caves, six caves artificially hollowed out of marl terraces eventually came to light: Caves 4, 5, and 7–10. By far the richest manuscript remains belonged to Cave 4, which was discovered first by the bedouin and then, after it had been badly pilfered, excavated by officials in September 1952. This cave contained portions of hundreds of different manuscripts, many showing evidence of deliberate destruction in antiquity. This same 1952 campaign succeeded in identifying Cave 5. It remained for the campaign of 1955 to discover Caves 7–9. The tenth cave, discovered in the vicinity of Cave 4, contained no manuscripts, only an ostracon inscribed in Hebrew. Altogether, the manuscripts found in Caves 1–11 number approximately 825.

Khirbet Qumran. The presence of eleven manuscript-bearing caves that seemed to radiate north and south from the place known by the Arabic name Khirbet Qumran (its ancient appellation is uncertain) suggested that the site itself ought to be excavated. The Jordanian Department of Antiquities, the Palestine Archaeological Museum (now the Rockefeller Museum), and the École Biblique et Archéologique Française de Jérusalem undertook joint campaigns, beginning in 1951 and continuing for five seasons. The results of those excavations were never published scientifically, although preparations to do so are now underway. Preliminary descriptions written by Roland de Vaux, who headed the project, distinguished four basic occupational levels: one in the seventh century BCE and three others from about 100 BCE to shortly after the fall of Jerusalem in 70 CE.

Recently, questions have been raised about a direct connection between the scrolls and Khirbet Qumran that may lessen the interest of the archaeological data. For example, Pauline Donceel-Voute, one of those responsible for full publication of the de Vaux excavations, has shown that the principal evidence for the "scriptorium"—the plastered "tables" upon which scribes were imagined to have copied out the scrolls—points instead to a triclinium (a dining room). The tables may have been couches on which the diners would have reclined. Furthermore, the identification of hundreds of individual scribal hands for the scrolls and scroll fragments is difficult to square with the notion that Qumran scribes exclusively produced the scrolls at the site. Were that the case, many fewer hands and many more texts traceable to a given scribe could be expected. Recent archaeological investigation has failed to reveal any paths leading from the site to the caves where the texts were cached. This discovery is a formidable obstacle to the popular conception that a community living on the site would have retired to the caves—especially to Cave 4—to study their holy writings.

Finds from Other Sites. Masada, Wadi Murabbaʿat, Naḥal Ḥever, Naḥal Ṣeʿelim, Naḥal Mishmar, Khirbet Mird, and Ketef Jericho have all yielded documentary texts of the late Second Temple period, and in a few cases literary texts were also found. Excavations at Masada from 1963 to 1965, led by Yigael Yadin, discovered seven biblical and nine nonbiblical literary texts. Almost all of the nonbiblical texts seem to have some connection with the Qumran texts, and in at least two cases copies of the same literary work were found at both sites (see below). The Masada excavations also yielded numerous ostraca inscribed in Hebrew, Aramaic, Greek, and Latin, although only the Semitic materials are certainly connected with the Jewish occupation of the years 66–73 (74?) CE. [See Masada.]

Excavations in 1952, combined with bedouin cave combing in the several caves in Wadi Murabbaʿat, resulted in the discovery of nearly one hundred texts, many dating to the time of the Bar Kokhba Revolt (132–135 CE). These finds comprised biblical and nonbiblical literary materials, Hebrew and Aramaic letters and contracts, Greek and Latin documentary materials (mostly from a later date), and five Arabic texts from later centuries. [See Murabbaʿat.]

Naḥal Ḥever, Naḥal Seʿelim and Naḥal Mishmar were explored by a joint expedition from the Hebrew University, the Israel Exploration Society, and the Israel Department of Antiquities in 1960–1961. The finds from Naḥal Ḥever number some sixty-five texts in Hebrew, Aramaic, Nabatean, and Greek. Primary among these finds are the Babatha archive (thirty-seven Greek, six Nabatean, and three Aramaic contracts), the so-called Archive of the En-Gedites (six Hebrew and Aramaic contracts leasing state lands), and a packet of fifteen letters to military leaders in charge of ʿEin-Gedi at the time of the Bar Kokhba Revolt. Indeed, like the Murabbaʿat texts, all of the important Naḥal Ḥever finds date to that approximate period, as do those from Naḥal Seʿelim and Naḥal Mishmar.

The materials originally thought to have come from Naḥal Seʿelim were discovered by bedouin in 1951 or 1952 and sold to authorities. Later, additional fragments belonging to some of these "Naḥal Seʿelim" manuscripts were discovered by archaeologists at Naḥal Ḥever, thereby suggesting that the bedouin finds actually originated there and not at Naḥal Seʿelim. The designation remains as a matter of convenience. These materials include four very fragmentary biblical manuscripts, phylacteries, some fifteen Hebrew and Aramaic documents, five Nabatean deeds, two Greek legal texts, and a scroll of the Minor Prophets written in Greek. Written materials from Naḥal Mishmar are exiguous, comprising papyrus lists of names in Greek.

From Khirbet Mird come portions of a lectionary, an inscription, a letter, and a magical text—all inscribed in Christian Palestinian Aramaic—and one hundred Arabic papyri. [See Palestinian Aramaic.] These texts date a millennium later than the Qumran texts. Excavations by the Israel Antiquities Authority at Ketef Jericho in 1986 and 1994 uncovered portions of at least six economic documents in Aramaic and Greek dating to the period of Bar Kokhba, and two documentary texts dating to the third or fourth centuries BCE.

Biblical Texts from Caves 1–11. Among the manuscripts that have emerged from the Qumran caves scholars have identified about two hundred biblical scrolls and fragments. The number of texts of each book so far identified (the numbers continue to change somewhat as study continues) is as follows: *Genesis* (15), *Exodus* (15), *Leviticus* (8), *Numbers* (6), *Deuteronomy* (25), *Joshua* (2), *Judges* (3), *Ruth* (4), *Samuel* (4), *Kings* (3), *Isaiah* (19), *Jeremiah* (4), *Ezekiel* (6), Minor Prophets (8), *Psalms* (30), *Job* (5), *Proverbs* (2), *Ecclesiastes* (1), *Song of Songs* (4), *Lamentations* (4), *Esther* (0), *Daniel* (19), *Ezra-Nehemiah* (1), and *Chronicles* (1). As the list shows, every book of the Hebrew Bible appears among the Qumran caches, except for *Esther*. It is hard to know whether the absence of this book is purely fortuitous or is meaningful. In the same way, it may or may not be legitimate to draw conclusions from the relative frequency of the various books.

The Dead Sea Scrolls have revolutionized textual criticism of the Hebrew Bible. Previously, scholars had no Hebrew manuscript of any book antedating the medieval period. Now there is access to the Hellenistic and Roman periods, revealing texts in substantial agreement with the Masoretic text as well as widely variant forms. Readings differing from the Masoretic version often agree with known streams of textual tradition, particularly those represented by the Septuagint and the Samaritan Pentateuch. The fact that the major versional types of texts are already present in the Qumran manuscripts has naturally led to attempts to explain the emergence of the later text families. Three basic positions have resulted. The first, known as the theory of local texts, is particularly associated with Frank M. Cross. This theory sees different text forms developing in Babylonia, Palestine, and Egypt—that is, in the three major centers of Jewish civilization in the crucial period 200 BCE–200 CE. Few scholars find this theory convincing; it is simply too artificial and does not account for the complexity of the evidence. A second approach is championed by Shemaryahu Talmon, who hypothesizes that the key to the survival of any particular text type was its acceptance by a definable community. The inference would follow that many text types disappeared in ancient times. The third position is that of Emanuel Tov, for whom the scrolls do not confirm the existence of given text types as such. Rather, because they resist typological differentiation (unlike, e.g., the Byzantine text type of the New Testament), the Masoretic text, the Septuagint, and the Samaritan Pentateuch are representative merely of three texts. One thing is certain: the farther back in time the texts go, the less uniform they are. Pluriformity, not uniformity, was the rule. This realization has heightened appreciation of the versional evidence vis-à-vis the Masoretic text. The Septuagint, in particular, has grown in scholarly estimation.

Of course, the scrolls bear on many other critical matters involved with the Hebrew Bible, of which a few examples must suffice. The absence of verses 42:12–17 from the epilogue of *Job* as represented in *11Q Targum Job* (the designation *11Q* means that the text was discovered in Cave 11 at Qumran) may support the view that the prologue and epilogue (that is to say, the prose portions of the book) are linguistically late and were added recently in the book's history. Text *11QPsalms*[a] raises numerous questions, focusing particularly on the problem of canon in the Second Temple period. The order of the psalms in the 11Q text differs from the Masoretic version, and at least once, the scroll contains a canonical psalm in a different recension (Ps. 145). Certain smaller groupings of psalms, such as the Song of Ascents and the Passover Hallel—viewed by the Masoretic text as units—are scattered throughout the Qumran psalter. Taken together with other "deviant" *Psalms* scrolls, such as 11QPs[b], 4QPs[f], and 4QPs[q], and with the many that appear identical to the Masoretic text, 11QPs[a] indicates that different forms of the biblical book circulated, all apparently equally acceptable to user communities. Various nonbiblical texts described below, which may have had "canonical" status for some groups, support the conclusion arising from the biblical texts: at least the third division of the canon, the *Writings*, was still fluid at the time of the scrolls.

Nonbiblical Writings from Caves 1–11. Important as the biblical materials are, for the student of Second Temple Judaism the real treasures are the nonbiblical scrolls. After all, the books of the Bible have long been known, whereas most of the six hundred-odd nonbiblical texts are new. They increase exponentially what was known of Jewish intellectual life in that period. Most were written in Hebrew, generally in a form of late Biblical Hebrew, but sometimes in a form of the language nearer to the spoken dialects. Slightly more than one hundred texts are inscribed in Aramaic; about twenty are in Greek (mostly from Cave 7). These materials are so rich that the following description pretends to nothing more than a partial and provisional survey.

Legal and regulatory texts. A substantial proportion of the Dead Sea Scrolls are legal and regulatory texts of various kinds. Two of the longest and most common are the *Damascus Document* and the *Rule of the Community*. [*See* Damascus Document; Rule of the Community.]

A third legal work, extant in six copies from Cave 4, is known as *4QMMT* (an anagram for the Hebrew words "Some of the Laws of the Torah"; 4Q394–399). At least one copy of this text begins with a calendrical exposition. Legal rulings on about twenty-three topics follow, all involving temple purity and priestly gifts. The final section of the work is an admonition to right practice. The *MMT* text may have been a letter, although the names of the writer and the addressee have not survived. The work purports to address its urgings to a king. Scholars are still uncertain whether this king was a Hasmonean or a first-century CE figure such as Agrippa I; for adherents of paleographic dating, only the first option seems possible.

Other legal texts include 4Q159, *Ordinances*, extant apparently in two additional copies (4Q513–514). This work interprets biblical laws governing gleaning by the poor, the half-shekel Temple tax, and the prohibition on selling an Israelite into slavery. Text 4Q251 combines portions from the *Rule of the Community* and the *Damascus Document*—with slight differences—with legal materials drawn from other sources. Text 4Q274, *Toharot A*, treats seven-day impurities incurred by touching the dead, skin diseases, and menstruation. Texts 4Q276–277, known as *Toharot B*, deal inter alia with the law of the red heifer (*Nm.* 19). Text 4Q477, known by the title *Decrees of the Sect*, is a record of legal discipline that includes actual proper names—a great rarity among the scrolls. One man, Hananiah Nitos, is reproved for "turn[ing] aside the spirit of the community." A major legal work, one copy of which extends for sixty-six columns, is the *Temple Scroll* (11Q19–20). [*See* Temple Scroll.]

Biblical interpretation. Numerous Dead Sea Scrolls pursue other sorts of biblical interpretation than legal application. Perhaps the most important scrolls here are the so-called *pesharim*. These writings understand prophetic portions of the Hebrew Bible (including *Psalms*, conceived as prophecies) to describe the interpreter's own time. Scholars commonly group these works into two categories: thematic *pesharim* and continuous *pesharim*. Thematic *pesharim* constitute unconnected biblical portions organized around a central theme. Continuous *pesharim* comment seriatim on biblical verses or even whole books. At least fifteen scrolls fit into this latter category.

Continuous *pesharim* ignore what is considered the literal meaning of the biblical text. Their interest is in explaining mysterious truth revealed only to the author and his group. The most complete of these commentaries is the *pesher* Habakkuk. [*See* Habakkuk Commentary.] It preserves thirteen virtually complete columns, covering Habakkuk 1–2. The *pesher Psalms* (4Q171) is also relatively complete, preserved portions commenting on *Psalms* 37:7–40, 45:1–2, and possibly 60:8–9. The writer finds his group's enemies in the biblical text and interprets events in terms of eschatological justification. For the historian, the commentary on *Nahum* (4Q169) is doubtless the cornerstone of the continuous *pesharim*. The author mentions a "Demetrius, King of Greece" and refers cryptically to a Jewish ruler who crucified great numbers of his opponents. These references seem to be to the Seleucid ruler Demetrius III Eucaerus (95–88 BCE) and the Jewish king Alexander Jannaeus, who did indeed—according to the Jewish historian Josephus—put many Jewish insurgents to death in the course of a civil war. Other fragmentary *pesherim* interpreting *Micah, Zephaniah, Isaiah,* and certain psalms have survived.

Of the thematic *pesharim*, none has aroused greater interest than *11QMelchizedek* (11Q13). Thirteen fragments preserve the remains of three columns. The work comments on isolated Hebrew Bible portions, including *Leviticus* 25:9–10, 25:13; *Deuteronomy* 15:2; *Isaiah* 61:1; and *Daniel* 9:26. The events connected with these biblical texts are to take place in "the end of days," which is further identified with the "tenth jubilee." According to the text, Melchizedek will free those who belong to his "inheritance" and (if suggested restorations are correct) "atone for their iniquities." He will further exact divine vengeance upon Belial and those of his "lot." This work presents a conception of Melchizedek approximately contemporary with *Hebrews*, chapter 7, connecting him with heavenly judgment, a day of atonement and a primary role among God's angels. Also of interest is Melchizedek's possible identification with the herald of *Isaiah* 52:7. This identification would represent a combination of scriptural figures and motifs comparable to the New Testament characterization of Jesus.

Two additional thematic *pesharim* are *4QFlorilegium* (4Q174) and *4QTestimonia* (4Q175). The first work combines various biblical portions with interpretive comments relating to the "end of days," when God will have a new "temple of Adam" built. Thus, the author employs an *urzeit/ endzeit* typology, according to which those faithful to God will one day return to an idyllic state of peace. The second writing is a catena of quotations that seem to focus on messianic expectation, including a prophet like Moses (*Dt.* 18:18–19). Though they do not overlap, some scholars believe that these two manuscripts are actually two copies of the same literary work.

The *Genesis Apocryphon* was one of the original seven scrolls found by bedouin and represents a previously unknown example of "rewritten Bible" (a frequent exegetical technique in the Second Temple period that wove comments and expansions into the words of the biblical text itself. [*See* Genesis Apocryphon.] A vaguely similar work, bearing the erroneous preliminary title *Pesher Genesis* (the work is not a *pesher*), survives in three copies (4Q252–254). This writing comments on various problems raised by a close reading of *Genesis*. For example, why did God curse Canaan, the son of Ham, when it was actually Ham who "uncovered his father's nakedness" (*Gn.* 9:26)? The author explains that since God had already blessed Noah's sons, he could not retract that blessing, and, a curse being required, it had to fall on the next generation.

Also in the realm of biblical interpretation are the three Aramaic *targumim* (translations, or paraphrases) so far identified among the scrolls. By far the longest and most complete has already been mentioned, the *targum* to *Job* from Cave 11 (11Q10). The importance of this work is considerable because it represents the only incontestably pre-Christian *targum* of any appreciable length. The surviving portions cover parts of chapters 17–42, with the last six chapters of *Job* the least damaged. The Hebrew *vorlage* of the scroll seems to have been the Masoretic text. The other two *targumim* are extremely fragmentary: 4Q156 renders *Leviticus* 16:12–15 and 18–21 into Aramaic and 4Q157, another targum to *Job*, covers portions of *Job* 3:5–9 and 4:16– 5:4. Both translations are literal rather than expansive.

Pseudoprophetic works (so-called from the modern perspective; it is doubtful they were so regarded by ancient readers) are notable among the Dead Sea Scrolls. According to Josephus, the biblical prophets Jeremiah, Ezekiel, and Daniel each wrote more than one book, so the discovery in Cave 4 of works attributable to those men is intriguing. An apocryphal Jeremianic work is extant in perhaps five copies (4Q383–384, 385[b], 387[b], and 389[a]; their identification is preliminary). Five copies of *Pseudo-Ezekiel* also survive (4Q385, 386, 387, 388, and 391), in which some fragments are of considerable length, allowing the reader to get some feel for the whole. One portion interprets the Vision of the Valley of Dry Bones (*Ez.* 37) in terms of individual resurrection; another declares that in the future "sovereignty will devolve upon the Gentiles for many years . . . in those days a blasphemous king will arise among the Gentiles and do evil things." *Pseudo-Ezekiel* may date from the third century BCE.

A whole series of works is connected with the figure of Daniel. Some of these writings may antedate the biblical book, whereas others are clearly derivative attempts at interpreting some of that book's riddles. In the former category belongs the *Prayer of Nabonidus* (4Q242). This description of a skin disease afflicting Nabonidus (the last of the Neo-Babylonian kings), his healing by an unnamed Jewish exorcist, and his subsequent prayer of thanksgiving may lie behind the story of Nebuchadrezzar in *Daniel* 4. *Pseudo-Daniel* (4Q243–245) falls into the second category, describing what Daniel saw on one or more occasions when he stood before king Belshazzar (cf. *Daniel* 5). The content of the visions given on those occasions goes beyond that of the biblical book, but not much more can be said of it, given the work's extremely fragmentary condition. The *Son of God* text (4Q246) actually quotes *Daniel*, chapter 7, and describes a future figure of some sort. Whether that figure is messianic, angelic, or even a Roman emperor is debatable. Texts 4Q552–553 are two copies of a Danielic work titled the *Four Kingdoms*. They apparently relate to the visions of *Daniel* 2 and 7, wherein four world kingdoms rule in succession until the dawning of a final kingdom of God. This work symbolizes each kingdom not by a bizarre animal or metal, however, as in the biblical book, but by a tree. Finally, two other writings are less certainly related to *Daniel*. Text 4Q558, an extremely fragmentary visionary text inscribed on papyrus, uses important Danielic phraseology. Text 4Q550, *Story Set at the Persian Court*, has been claimed as a precursor to the *Book of Esther*, but it appears rather to be a series of tales about successful Jews in a foreign court, much like Daniel and his friends in the Hebrew Bible.

Also in the category of prophetic works are some dozen pseudo-Mosaic writings of various types. Four copies of a *Pentateuchal Paraphrase* (4Q364–367) admix previously unknown materials—poetry and Temple descriptions—with the books of the Pentateuch. Text 1Q22, the *Words of Moses*, is a type of rewritten Bible. It requires the appointment of priests "to clarify . . . all these words of the Torah." Text 4Q375 relates to the discussion of false prophets in *Deuteronomy* 13 and 18 and raises a point not considered by the biblical portions: What can be done about a false prophet whom one tribe claims is not false? "Then you shall come, with that tribe and your elders and judges . . . into the presence of the anointed priest." A ceremony follows, which would presumably reveal the truth about the disputed prophet. The pseudo-Mosaic *Three Tongues of Fire* (1Q29 and 4Q376) provides guidance on the use of the Urim and Thummim for divination of God's will. A final example of this genre, 4Q390, is particularly concerned with chronology, and also mentions Belial and the angels of Mastemoth. The writing may have been known to the author(s) of the *Damascus Document*, for its view of the apostasy of Israel is similar: "From the end of that generation, corresponding to the seventh Jubilee since the desolation of the land, they will forget law and festival, sabbath and covenant." Only a minority would later know the truth that Israel generally had forgotten.

Calendrical texts. Scrolls concerned at least implicitly with matters of chronology—particularly as measured in jubilee periods of forty-nine years or related to *Daniel's* seventy weeks (*Dn.* 9:25–27)—and the peculiar "Qumran calendar" number in the hundreds. Indeed, concern with calendric and chronological matters is the greatest common denominator among the nonbiblical texts. The calendar is a purely solar, 364-day system that begins on a Wednesday—because that is the day on which the heavenly lights regulating time were created (*Gn.* 1:14–19). The great advantage of this calendar over lunisolar rivals is that it results in fixed dates for the major festivals. This calendar also guarantees that any given day of any month will always fall on the same day of the week forever.

One calendrical text, 4Q321 *Mishmarot B*, tabulates not only the solar year and the holy days thus measured, but also the rotation of the priestly courses into and out of service in the Temple in Jerusalem. The text further deals with the moon, though it is still unclear whether this aspect is an attempt at synchronizing the solar and lunisolar calendars or whether lunar movements are being calculated for other reasons. A second work, 4Q320, *Mishmarot A*, provides three years of such correspondence between the solar calendar and lunar cycles. These two writings list as festivals only those found in the Pentateuch, but some Qumran calendrical works add new, nonbiblical festivals. One such is 4Q325, *Mishmarot D*, which assigns a Festival of New Wine to the third day of the fifth month and a Festival of Wood Offering to the twenty-third day of the sixth month. These festivals and their dates are also known from the *Temple Scroll* and *4QMMT*. What this apparently fundamental disagreement on festivals may imply about the use of the "Qumran calendar" in Second Temple Judaism is a question worth pursuing.

The scroll known as *Otot* (Heb., "signs"; cf. *Gn.* 1:14) evidently calculates those years in which, on the vernal equinox, the sun and moon were aligned as they had been at the creation. The work seeks to align that cycle with both the seven-year cycle of sabbatical years and the jubilees, which measured longer periods of time. Two other Qumran writings concern themselves particularly with lunar movement, one (4Q503) for liturgical purposes and the other (4Q317) to concord the moon's phases with the 364-day calendar. Text 4Q317 is inscribed in a cryptic writing known as cryptic script A; cryptic scripts B and C also existed, and a fourth system of encryption appears in 4Q186 (see below). The full significance of such systems within the context of the Qumran corpus as a whole has yet to be worked out, but it is unsurprising to find one copy of a second calendrical work, *Mishmarot C*, written in cryptic A. Calendrical matters were numinous, inasmuch as these holy patterns were facts not merely observed, but revealed. Not everyone was worthy to read calendrical texts.

Mishmarot C (extant in six copies, 4Q322–324, 324ᵃ, 324ᵇ,

and 324^c) is noteworthy in another respect: along with priestly courses and holy festivals, this calendrical work chronicles historical events important to the work's author(s). This writing would be of surpassing importance to the historian, were it only better preserved. It may still be possible to ferret out certain historical data. For example, one line reads "Hyrcanus rebelled." Although the line breaks after these words, it can be inferred that the context is the civil war between Hyrcanus II and his brother Aristobulus in the years 66–63 BCE. It further appears that the writer favored Aristobulus's faction—otherwise he would not describe Hyrcanus's bid for power as rebellion. Where such points will lead to understanding the historical significance of the Qumran caches remains to be seen.

Wisdom literature. After the period of the biblical writings, wisdom literature continued to develop, and various types are well represented in the Dead Sea Scrolls. One particular sapiential composition is extant in at least six copies (1Q26, 4Q415–418, and 4Q423), but its rationale and perspective are not yet really understood. One clear portion reads: "Honor your father in your poverty and your mother by your behavior, for a man's father is like his arms, and his mother is like his legs. Surely they have guided you like a hand, and just as He has given them authority over you and appointed (them) over (your) spirit, so you should serve them." Text 4Q424 is a collection of proverbs, several quite pithy. For example, one suggests "Do not send the hard-hearted man to discern thoughts because his intuition does not measure up."

The Qumran scrolls are rich in one particular type of wisdom literature important in the Second Temple period, the testament. Thus far, testaments of *Levi*, *Kohath* (4Q542), *Amram*, and *Naphtali* have been identified, and some scholars have seen, in meager fragments, testaments of *Jacob* (4Q537), *Judah* (4Q538), and *Joseph* (4Q539) as well. The *Testament of Levi* is extant in at least two fragmentary copies (4Q213–214) and may be represented by several other manuscripts as well (e.g., 1Q21 and 4Q540–541). Texts 4Q213–214 directly align not with the Greek *Testament of Levi* (part of the *Testaments of the Twelve Patriarchs*), but with the related, yet very different, *Aramaic Testament of Levi*. Scholars have known this work from medieval manuscripts. The *Testament of Naphtali* (4Q215)—unlike the others written in Hebrew, not Aramaic—partially overlaps the long-known Greek *Testament of Naphtali*. It also contains portions unparalleled anywhere in Greek and has an eschatological thrust absent from the Greek version. The *Testament of Amram* (4Q543, 545–548) is notably dualistic in outlook, approaching in this respect the doctrine of the two spirits in the *Rule of the Community.*

Liturgical texts. Whether a given text is liturgical is often debatable—and can be argued for a fair number of writings among the Qumran caches. The *Hodayot* (Hymns of Praise) are perhaps the most notable; these are extant in seven copies (1QHodayot, 4Q427–432). The Cave 1 exemplar comprises eighteen columns and sixty-eight originally unplaced fragments, some of which can now be located with the aid of the Cave 4 texts. The order of the hymns varies from manuscript to manuscript; all begin with either "I thank You, Lord," or "Blessed are You, O Lord." Some of the hymns may be the work of the Teacher of Righteousness mentioned in the *pesharim* and the *Damascus Document*. They seem appropriate to his situation, but such historical identifications are virtually impossible to prove.

A large group of poetic writings is similar to the *Hodayot*. One is the work known after its incipit as *Barki Naphshi* (Bless, O My Soul; 4Q434–438). The poetic quality of all these compositions is uneven, but some passages are striking. In 4Q434, for example, one reads of God: "He opened His eyes to the downtrodden and, inclining His ears, hearkened to the cry of the orphans. In His abundant mercy He comforted the meek, and opened their eyes to behold His ways, and their ears, to hear His teaching. And He circumcised the foreskin of their hearts, and saved them because of His grace. . . ."

The *Songs of the Sabbath Sacrifice* is partially preserved in eight copies from Cave 4 (4Q400–407), as well as in fragments from Cave 11 (11Q17) and, significantly, Masada. It describes heaven as a complicated temple consisting of seven sanctuaries, attended by seven chief prince-priests, their deputies, and seven angelic priesthoods. Simultaneous with earthly sacrifice performed in the Temple in Jerusalem, the truly efficacious equivalents take place in heaven. The work is especially important for the study of angelology and early Jewish Merkavah mysticism.

Other notable liturgical writings include the *Words of the Luminaries* (4Q504–506) and *Berakhot* (4Q286–290). Fragmentary remaining instructions show that the *Words* were intended to be recited on given days of the week. With but one exception—the composition recited on the Sabbath, traditionally a joyous occasion—the mood of the daily texts is penitential. Long passages of the *Berakhot* are similar to the *Angelic Liturgy* and strike the reader as an ecstatic visionary recital. Other portions are equally unrestrained but are directed toward cursing; for example, "They shall answer and say, 'Cursed be Belial in his devilish scheme, and damned be he in his guilty rule. Cursed be all the spirits of his lot in their evil scheme, and may they be damned in the schemes of their unclean pollution.'"

One final liturgical work is most significant for its possible historical implications. This is the *Paean for King Jonathan* (4Q448), apparently celebrating Alexander Jannaeus, whose Hebrew name was Jonathan. The "superscription" describes the work as "A sacred poem for King Jonathan and all the congregation of Your people Israel, who are spread in every direction under heaven." The historical implications concern the work's mere presence among the Dead Sea Scrolls, since from early on in scrolls research, most scholars have thought the scrolls to be anti-Hasmonean. Evidently, the reality was more complicated.

Apocrypha and pseudepigrapha. A fair number of the Qumran writings might easily be designated apocryphal or pseudepigraphic. Copies of some such works known long before the discovery of the scrolls have now turned up in the caves. Most numerous are copies of *Jubilees*, which is represented by fourteen or fifteen manuscripts—more than for any biblical book, except for *Deuteronomy* and *Psalms*. In addition, there are several works designated *Pseudo-Jubilees* (*Pseudo-Jubilees*^{a–c}; 4Q225–227), each apparently a separate composition. These Jubilee works, together with the *Genesis Apocryphon*, *Pesher Genesis*, a *Flood Apocryphon* (4Q370), and *Traditions on Genesis* (4Q422)—to name a few—prove just how lively interest was in interpretating *Genesis*.

First Enoch and other Enochic writings (*Pseudo-Enoch* and the *Book of Giants*) are also numerous among the scrolls. All together, they comprise sixteen manuscripts (4Q201–212, 530–533). At one time, much was made of the absence of the *Book of Parables* (*1 En.* 37–71) from the Qumran *Enoch* texts, but today that lack is no longer considered evidence of a post-Christian origin for the Parables.

Another pseudepigraphic writing, this one not known before the discovery of the scrolls, is the *Psalms of Joshua*, represented by two copies (4Q378–379) and a quotation in the *Testimonia* described above. As for the Apocrypha, there are five or six copies of *Tobit* (4Q196–200; 4Q478 is perhaps another copy): four are in Aramaic and one or two in Hebrew. Which language was original is still uncertain, although there is little question that the most reliable Greek manuscript, *Codex Sinaiticus*, had an Aramaic *vorlage*. *Ecclesiasticus* also appears among the scrolls (2Q18; a second copy was found at Masada).

Miscellaneous. Some of the most interesting Dead Sea Scrolls resist classification into the admittedly arbitrary categories outlined above. One is a manual for the conduct of holy war, designated the *War Scroll* (1QM). Actually, it is inaccurate to refer to it as "the" *War Scroll*, despite scholarly convention, because the Cave 4 copies (4Q471, 4Q491–496) and related writings (4Q471^a and 4Q497) demonstrate that there were various recensions of the work. In this respect, the *War Scroll* is analogous to the *Rule of the Community* and the *Damascus Document*. The weapons and tactics employed in the scroll indicate Roman, rather than Greek, military strategy. For this reason the Cave 1 copy cannot antedate the later decades of the first century BCE. Those reading the final form of the *War Scroll* doubtless conceived of it as a guide to an ultimate revolt against Rome, the foreign power interpreted as the "fourth kingdom" in *Daniel* and related writings. [*See* War Scroll.]

The *Copper Scroll* (3Q15) appears to be a list of treasure removed from the Temple in Jerusalem for safekeeping some time during the First Jewish Revolt. Vastly superior new photographs and renewed scholarly interest in this unique work, inscribed on copper in a "Mishnaic" Hebrew dialect, promise to place it where it belongs: at the heart of discussion about the origins and significance of the Qumran caches. [*See* Copper Scroll.]

Scarcely less intriguing are the several magical and astrological writings found among the scrolls. Magical works include 11QPsAp^a; a ritual for exorcism, 4Q510–511, which contain hymns intended "to scare and alarm" demons; and 4Q560. This last work was once tentatively identified as a collection of proverbs, but it is actually an Aramaic incantation against various types of demons, including male and female "wasting demons"—fever, chilling, and chest-pain spirits. Text 4Q318 is an Aramaic brontologion and lunary, based on the distribution of the signs of the zodiac over the days of the 364-day year. If thunder were heard on a day when the moon stood in a given portion of the sky, this text would enable its reader to divine the future. Text *4QCryptic* (4Q186) is another scroll that presupposes astrological notions. Strictly speaking, it is concerned with physiognomy, but it combines references to astrological signs with that method of divination. Written in Hebrew, it is encrypted by the techniques of transposition and substitution. Text 4Q561 is an Aramaic physiognomic writing that may be related to 4Q186, although it differs in important respects.

Perhaps it is fitting to conclude this overview of the contents of the Qumran texts with a mention of what might be the most important of all the finds, if claims for it are ever proven. A Greek fragment from Cave 7, 7Q5, has been identified as a portion of the *Gospel of Mark*. Very little survives of the text, and if the portion is from *Mark*, it contains a previously unattested textual variant. Virtually all Qumran scholars are sceptical of J. O'Callaghan's identification, preferring to see the portion as the remains of an unknown Old Greek version of the Bible, or even as a line from Homer. The most recent and thorough analysis of the question concludes, however—on the basis of sophisticated statistical techniques—that O'Callaghan's claim cannot be falsified. The question must remain open.

Significance of Written Materials from Other Sites. The manuscripts from Wadi Murabbaʿat, Naḥal Ḥever, Naḥal Seʿelim, Naḥal Mishmar, and Ketef Jericho are particularly important for the light they shed on the period of the Bar Kokhba Revolt. They illumine the course of that revolt, Bar Kokhba's administration, and the prosopography of individuals who took part in those events. [*See* Bar Kokhba Revolt.] In addition, the texts provide information on legal and religious practice, the economics of second-century Palestine, Jewish literacy, and onomastics. The linguistic information they supply is considerable; inter alia they clearly prove the use among the Jews of that period of Hebrew, Aramaic, Greek, and Nabatean. The circumstances of each language's use—that is, the sociolinguistic situation—has yet to be worked out, but the materials have the potential to document such analysis. The texts also provide substantial new information on the development of the Jewish script, especially the cursive varieties, and on the Nabatean cursive and formal scripts.

The Masada discoveries are also important for the linguistic information they supply. In particular, the ostraca are a precious witness to the development of Mishnaic Hebrew dialects. The Masada finds as a whole greatly illumine aspects of the First Jewish Revolt. In this respect, they have the potential to improve understanding of the phenomenon of the Qumran caches because this was when they were hidden. [See First Jewish Revolt.]

Unlike the vast majority of the Qumran scrolls, the finds from the other Dead Sea Scroll sites are, as noted, documentary autographs: contracts, letters, bills of sale, leases, and the like. They are the primary sources for which historians have the greatest use. Extracting history from literary texts such as the Qumran materials is a tricky and tenuous process at best. The discovery of so many documentary materials highlights the anomaly of their virtual absence among the Qumran scrolls. For some scholars this problem is sufficient in itself to raise the question of whether the texts in caves 1–11 really did come from Qumran—because any group resident there presumably also possessed autographic and ephemeral written materials of the sort found at the other sites. Thus, the finds at sites other than Qumran are important both intrinsically and paradigmatically.

Essene Hypothesis for Qumran Text Origins. Shortly after the original seven scrolls from Cave 1 came to be known, Eleazar L. Sukenik queried whether they might not be the writings of an obscure Jewish sect, the Essenes, mentioned by a few classical authors. This view came shortly to be the consensus, maintained to this day, although many advocates concede that a large proportion of the Dead Sea Scrolls are not sectarian and presumably could have been agreeable to most Second Temple Jews. Essentially, the theory rests upon two pillars: the identification of Khirbet Qumran with the Essene dwelling place to the west of the Dead Sea mentioned by Pliny the Elder in *Natural History* 5.73; and a series of correspondences between Josephus's descriptions of the Essenes (mainly *War* 2.119–161) and the contents of the scrolls, the *Rule of the Community* in particular. Many of these parallels are quite general, but the most remarkable—precisely because they are specific and not of general application—are perhaps the rules governing spitting and defecation. A recent monograph by Todd S. Beall compiles and analyzes as many of the parallels as he could identify. [See Essenes.]

Objections to the Essene Hypothesis. The evidence favoring the Essene view has impressed many scholars, but certain thorny problems have yet to be satisfactorily resolved. The question with regard to Pliny is whether he is describing a postbellum or antebellum situation. If he describes a postbellum (post 70 CE) group of Essenes, he can-

not be referring to the site of Qumran because the archaeological research indicates that Romans occupied the site after the war. As for the correspondences between the *Rule of the Community* and Josephus's Essenes, most involve rules for the communal organization of the groups being described. The Essenes are the only Jewish group of the period known to have this communal structure, but they are also one of the few about which we have any substantive information. Many Jewish sects existed: a sample of those named in the sources includes Baptist Pharisees, Boethusians, Galileans, Hemerobaptists, Masbotheans, Samaritans, and Zadokites, in addition to the three groups (Sadducees, Pharisees, Essenes) Josephus mentions. Various other sects are not given names. Together with a proper appreciation of our ignorance, the recent work by Moshe Weinfeld (*The Organizational Pattern and the Penal Code of the Qumran Sect*, Göttingen, 1986) must be factored into the question of Essene identification. He shows that many brotherhood groups of the period—in Egypt, Greece, and elsewhere—shared basic organizational characteristics.

Also problematic are certain fundamental discrepancies between the Essenes of Josephus and the contents of the scrolls. Prominent here are the questions of Essene celibacy and opposition to slavery. None of the scrolls advocates or describes celibacy, and the legal texts regulate slavery just as they do marriage.

To handle such discrepancies scholars choose one of two paths. One way is to argue that, whenever his description conflicts with the contents of the Qumran texts, Josephus was wrong. He was wrong either because he did not know the truth, or because the facts had changed over time. The other way of handling the discrepancies is to say that the Dead Sea Scrolls are not Essene texts. Thus, a sizable number of Qumranologists do not subscribe to the Essene hypothesis, preferring instead to speak of "the sect."

Over the years, several more particular theories have competed with the Essene hypothesis. The most recent challenger is the Jerusalem hypothesis proposed by Norman Golb. This theory holds that the Dead Sea Scrolls represent deposits made by the inhabitants of Jerusalem during the First Jewish Revolt. The texts were not composed at Khirbet Qumran (which Golb believes was actually a fortress), but come from numerous libraries in Jerusalem. In support of this theory, Golb cites the hundreds of scribal hands found in the scrolls—difficult to explain given a thesis that a small group copied texts over several generations. He notes that, with one exception, unlike the other Judean Desert finds, none of the Qumran scrolls is an autograph; all are scribal copies, again problematic if people living at Qumran were responsible for the scrolls. The single exception is the *Copper Scroll*, and for Golb this one autographic text points to Jerusalem as its own place of origin. In his view, the Dead Sea Scrolls are not the work of a single sect, but represent much of the literary heritage of Palestinian Judaism.

While many scholars agree with Golb that a number of the Dead Sea Scrolls probably come from elsewhere, most continue to believe that a sectarian group living at Khirbet Qumran was connected with the texts and was responsible for gathering them into the wilderness caves. Perhaps the most telling objection raised against Golb's position concerns the interrelationship of the texts. In his view, the scrolls should essentially be a random grouping. A few texts might be interrelated, but no intentional principles should link the whole corpus. Yet, most scholars believe such links exist, although they do not always agree on what they are.

Other suggested groups responsible for—or at least connected to—the scrolls include the "Zealots," the Sadducees, and Jamesian Christians. The Zealot connection was argued early on in Qumran scholarship, particularly by C. Roth and G. R. Driver, but was never taken seriously, in part because the editorial team working on the scrolls said that it was wrong. With the recent publication of the materials found at Masada, however, it has become apparent that virtually all of the nonbiblical literary texts found there have connections with the Qumran writings. This new evidence may lead scholars to reconsider some sort of Zealot connection with the scrolls, at least in the final decades before they were hidden.

The Sadducean theory of J. Sussmann and Laurence Schiffman is associated particularly with *4QMMT* because one or two of its laws agree with positions labeled Sadducee in rabbinic literature. This theory has yet to resolve problems of definition (e.g., What does rabbinic literature mean by "Sadducee"? Is that what classical sources mean by the term? How does the term function in each literary context?) and faces the general problem of how—indeed, whether—to use rabbinic literature to write history. Furthermore, many of the scrolls refer to angels and other concepts (e.g., resurrection) that classical sources on Sadducees explicitly say they rejected.

Finally, many scholars have recognized important connections between the Dead Sea Scrolls and early Christianity, especially with John the Baptist. Robert Eisenman, however, has gone much further, arguing for a direct connection between the scrolls and early Christians gathered around James in Jerusalem. For Eisenman, the scrolls *are* Christian—but only because he defines that term much differently than do other scholars. How a collection of texts could be Christian without once mentioning the name of Jesus, Eisenman has yet to explain. His theory has garnered virtually no scholarly support.

Qumran research presently stands only at the end of the beginning. More than half of the texts just recently became available to the generality of scholars, which has had the promising effect of reopening basic issues in the interpretation of the Dead Sea Scrolls.

[*See also* Judean Desert Caves; Murabbaʿat; *and* Qumran.]

BIBLIOGRAPHY

Allegro, John M. *Qumran Cave 4*, vol. 1, *4Q158–4Q186*. Discoveries in the Judaean Desert of Jordan, vol. 5. Oxford, 1968. Includes several important *pesharim*, including the *pesher Nahum*. The volume has been criticized harshly for its many problematic readings and dubious manuscript reconstructions. See the detailed review by John Strugnell, "Notes en marge du volume V des 'Discoveries in the Judaean Desert of Jordan,'" *Revue de Qumran* 7 (1971): 163–276. For bibliography to the individual texts, see the guide by Joseph A. Fitzmyer, "A Bibliographic Aid to the Study of Qumran Cave IV Texts 158–86," *Catholic Biblical Quarterly* 31 (1969): 59–71.

Baillet, Maurice. *Qumrân grotte 4*, vol. 3, *4Q482–4Q520*. Discoveries in the Judaean Desert, vol. 7. Oxford, 1982. Good presentation of extremely fragmentary texts.

Baillet, Maurice, J. T. Milik, and Roland de Vaux. *Le "petites grottes" de Qumrân*. Discoveries in the Judaean Desert of Jordan, vol. 3. Oxford, 1962. Publication of the texts from caves 2, 3, 5–7, and 10, the most important being the *Copper Scroll* (3Q15). The review by Jonas C. Greenfield, "The Small Caves of Qumran," *Journal of the American Oriental Society* 89 (1969): 128–141, offers many important observations and corrections.

Barthélemy, Dominique, and J. T. Milik. *Qumran Cave I*. Discoveries in the Judaean Desert, vol. 1. Oxford, 1955. Publication of 1Q1–72, including 1QSᵃ and 1QSᵇ, originally part of the same manuscript as 1QS, and 1Q33, which flaked off the main scroll of the *War Scroll*.

Beall, Todd S. *Josephus' Description of the Essenes Illustrated by the Dead Sea Scrolls*. Cambridge, 1988. Convenient collection of a substantial amount of material from the Qumran texts that, in spite of grave methodological deficiencies, can serve as a starting point for a more nuanced investigation of the points under discussion.

Beyer, Klaus. *Die aramäischen Texte vom Toten Meer*. Göttingen, 1984. Gathers then-known Aramaic materials from many scattered publications. The adventurous interpretations and reconstructions must be used with caution but are often suggestive. Idiosyncratic on grammatical and linguistic points.

Broshi, Magen, ed. *The Damascus Document Reconsidered*. Jerusalem, 1992. Certain to become the standard edition of the Cairo Genizah texts of the *Damascus Document*, with new photographs and an *apparatus criticus* that collates variant readings from the Cave 4 Qumran copies.

Burrows, Millar, ed., with John C. Trevor and William H. Brownlee. *The Dead Sea Scrolls of St. Mark's Monastery*, vol. 2, fasc. 2, *Plates and Transcription of the Manual of Discipline*. New Haven, 1951. Original and still standard publication of the *Rule of the Community* from Cave 1 (1QS).

Cross, Frank Moore. *The Ancient Library of Qumran and Modern Biblical Studies*. Rev. ed. Garden City, N.Y., 1961. Classic introduction to the scrolls by one of the original editors, arguing unambiguously for the Essene hypothesis. Covers most of the basic questions involved with the texts as seen by the team of editors at about the time they had finished their preliminary reading and transcriptions.

Cross, Frank Moore. "The Development of the Jewish Scripts." In *The Bible and the Ancient Near East: Essays in Honor of William Foxwell Albright*, edited by G. Ernest Wright, pp. 133–202. Garden City, N.Y., 1961. Extremely influential essay detailing the paleographic method of dating the scrolls. The method itself is perhaps dubious because of unproven basic assumptions and the complete lack of dated texts among the scrolls, but a sizable group of Qumranologists continues to rely on Cross's datings.

Cross, Frank M., and Shemaryahu Talmon, eds. *Qumran and the History of the Biblical Text*. Cambridge, Mass., 1975. Useful but dated collection of articles on the scrolls and biblical textual criticism;

should be supplemented with Eugene Ulrich's "Horizons of Old Testament Textual Research at the Thirtieth Anniversary of Qumran Cave 4," *Catholic Biblical Quarterly* 46 (1984): 613–636.

Dimant, Devorah, and Uriel Rappaport, eds. *The Dead Sea Scrolls: Forty Years of Research.* Leiden, 1992.

Eisenman, Robert, and James M. Robinson. *A Facsimile of the Dead Sea Scrolls.* 2 vols. Washington, D.C., 1991. Contains nearly 1,800 photographs of virtually all unpublished materials from caves 4 and 11. See as well, Emanuel Tov et al., eds., *The Dead Sea Scrolls on Microfiche: A Comprehensive Facsimile Edition of the Texts from the Judean Desert* (Leiden, 1993).

Eisenman, Robert, and Michael O. Wise. *The Dead Sea Scrolls Uncovered: The First Complete Translation and Interpretation of Fifty Key Documents Withheld for Over Thirty-Five Years.* Dorset, 1992. Transcription, translation, and analysis of fifty Cave 4 texts, many altogether unpublished, some previously published in part. Eisenman, who wrote the analysis, applies his Jamesian Christian approach to these new materials; readers who are unpersuaded may still find the preliminary transcriptions and translations useful.

Fitzmyer, Joseph A. *The Dead Sea Scrolls: Major Publications and Tools for Study.* Rev. ed. Atlanta, 1990. A very helpful guide to the mass of bibliography generated by the Qumran site and texts, organized both topically and by caves. For the recently released Qumran texts, Fitzmyer's book can be supplemented by the article by Emanuel Tov, "The Unpublished Qumran Texts from Caves 4 and 11," *Journal of Jewish Studies* 43 (1992): 101–136, and Stephen Reed's list (below). Fitzmyer's work also provides bibliography for Masada, Wadi Murabba'at, Nahal Hever, Nahal Se'elim, Nahal Mishmar, and Khirbet Mird.

Golb, Norman. *Who Wrote the Dead Sea Scrolls? The Search for the Secret of Qumran.* New York, 1995. Full statement of the "Jerusalem hypothesis."

Holm-Nielsen, Svend. *Hodayot: Psalms from Qumran.* Aarhus, 1961. Important presentation of the *hodayot* (though it is not the *editio princeps*), including an analysis of how each hymn reuses the biblical text.

Horgan, Maurya P. *Pesharim: Qumran Interpretations of Biblical Books.* Catholic Biblical Quarterly, Monograph Series 8. Washington, D.C., 1979. Full treatment of the *pesharim*, including the Hebrew text, discussion of readings and reconstructions, and interpretive analysis.

Milik, J. T. *The Books of Enoch: Aramaic Fragments of Qumran Cave 4.* Oxford, 1976. Includes virtually all of the Enoch material from Cave 4. The notes and introductions are almost equally valuable for their discussions of various unpublished texts.

Milik, J. T. *Qumrân grotte 4,* vol. 2.2, *Tefillin, muzuzot et Targums (4Q128–4Q157).* Discoveries in the Judaean Desert, vol. 6. Oxford, 1977. Publication of tefillin, mezuzot, and two targums, 4Q156 and 4Q157.

Newsom, Carol. *Songs of the Sabbath Sacrifice: A Critical Edition.* Atlanta, 1985. Includes the materials from Cave 4, Cave 11, and Masada, with an exemplary reconstruction of the original literary work. Weak on historical issues.

Qimron, Elisha. *The Hebrew of the Dead Sea Scrolls.* Atlanta, 1986. The only grammar devoted exclusively to the Hebrew writings among the scrolls. Generally reliable, but questionable at points on phonology and does not include the *Copper Scroll* or, of course, many of the most recently available texts.

Qimron, Elisha, and John Strugnell. *Qumran Cave 4,* vol. 5, *Miqsat Ma'ase ha-Torah.* Discoveries in the Judaean Desert, vol. 10. Oxford, 1994.

Reed, Stephen. *Dead Sea Scroll Inventory Project: List of Documents, Photographs, and Museum Plates.* Claremont, Calif., 1991–1992. The fourteen fascicles of this project provide an invaluable guide to what

there is and where to find it for the Dead Sea Scrolls, in the generic sense. Photograph numbers and other matters of designation are listed for each item. Note as well the author's *Dead Sea Scrolls Catalogue: Documents, Photographs, and Museum Inventory Numbers* (Atlanta, forthcoming).

Sanders, James A. *The Psalms Scroll of Qumrân Cave 11 (11QPs^a).* Oxford, 1965. Original publication of the "deviant" *Psalms Scroll,* with photographs, transcriptions, and translations.

Schuller, Eileen. *Non-Canonical Psalms from Qumran: A Pseudepigraphic Collection.* Atlanta, 1986. Publication of 4Q380 and 4Q381, with a fine discussion of related issues such as Hebrew psalmody in the Persian and Hellenistic periods.

Sukenik, Eleazar L. *The Dead Sea Scrolls of the Hebrew University.* Jerusalem, 1955. Publication with photographs of *1QHodayot* and *1QWar Scroll.*

Vaux, Roland de. *Archaeology and the Dead Sea Scrolls.* London, 1973. Preliminary English publication of the results of five seasons of excavation at Khirbet Qumran. Much of the analysis is debatable, not least because new comparative material has subsequently emerged from Hellenistic-Roman sites at Herodium, Jericho, and Masada, among others. Until the scientific publication of the results becomes available, however, this volume is the place to begin on any point of archaeology. Compare Ernest M. Laperrousaz, *Qoumrân, l'établissement essénien des bords de la Mer Morte: Histoire et archéologie du site* (Paris, 1976).

Vermès, Géza. *The Dead Sea Scrolls in English.* 3d ed. Sheffield, 1987. The most accessible collection of texts in English translation, now badly incomplete (even the 1987 edition was insufficiently revised in relation to the 1975 second edition). See, as well, Florentino García Martínez, *The Dead Sea Scrolls Translated: The Qumran Texts in English* (Leiden, 1994), the largest collection available to date.

Vermès, Géza, and Martin D. Goodman, eds. *The Essenes according to the Classical Sources.* Sheffield, 1989. Helpful collection of the most important Latin and Greek sources on the Essenes, with original text and facing-page translation. For more obscure sources, compare Alfred Adam and Christoph Burchard, *Antike Berichte über die Essener,* 2d ed. (Berlin, 1972).

Wacholder, Ben Zion, and Martin G. Abegg, comps. and eds. *A Preliminary Edition of the Unpublished Dead Sea Scrolls: The Hebrew and Aramaic Texts from Cave Four.* 3 vols. Washington, D.C., 1991–. Based on the readings of the original editors, taken from a concordance and reconstructed into complete texts by computer. For volumes 2 and 3, the authors have compared photographs and other sources, thus offering a critical analysis of the original readings, which they do not always adopt. Volume 1 contains the *4QDamascus Document* materials and calendrical texts; volume 2, a great variety of materials, including many sapiential works; and volume 3, the *4QRule of the Community* materials, *MMT, 4QJubilees* texts, and *Toharot* texts, among others.

Wise, Michael O., et al., eds. *Methods of Investigation of the Dead Sea Scrolls and the Khirbet Qumran Site.* Annals of the New York Academy of Sciences, vol. 722. New York, 1994.

Woude, Adam S. van der, and J. P. M. van der Ploeg. *Le Targum de Job de la grotte XI de Qumran.* Leiden, 1971. Fine original publication of the targum to *Job,* sometimes weak on linguistic analysis. For that aspect of the scroll, see Michael Sokoloff, *The Targum to Job from Qumran Cave XI* (Jerusalem, 1974).

MICHAEL O. WISE

DECAPOLIS (Gk., "ten cities"), an administrative district or region of Greek cities located in northern Transjordan, southern Syria, and northern Palestine. The original cities, ten in number, were attached to the Roman province of Syria in the first century CE. The earliest sources to mention the term date to the first century CE. The Decapolis appears twice in the *Gospel of Mark*: Jesus is said to have passed through "the region of the Decapolis" (7:31), and a healed demoniac proclaimed Jesus' miracle "in the Decapolis" (5:20). The term is also mentioned in the *Gospel of Matthew* (4:25). The most important ancient source is Pliny's *Natural History* (5.74). Pliny states that the Decapolis adjoined the Roman province of Judea (Judah) and names the ten cities: Damascus, Philadelphia, Raphana, Scythopolis, Gadara, Hippos, Dion, Pella, "Galasa" (usually emended as "Gerasa" [Jerash]), and Canatha. Pliny admits, however, that there was some disagreement about specific cities. Josephus, in his account of the first Jewish Revolt against Rome (66–70 CE), notes that "the chief men of the Syrian Decapolis" complained to the Roman emperor Vespasian about attacks on their territory by Jewish insurgents (*Life* 410, cf. 341–342). Josephus also claims that Scythopolis was "the largest city of the Decapolis" (*War* 3.446).

Later sources include Ptolemy, the second-century CE geographer, who provides the only other list of Decapolis cities (*Geography* 5.14–22). His list includes nine of Pliny's original ten cities (Raphana is missing) and adds nine new ones, for a total of eighteen: Heliopolis, Abila, Saana, Hina, Abila Lysanias, Capitolias, Edrei, Gadora, and Samulis. An inscription of 134 CE found in the region of Palmyra in Syria mentions "the good-messenger-Abila of the Decapolis." Somewhat surprisingly, only one other inscription mentioning the Decapolis is known, despite the fact that hundreds of inscriptions have been found in its various cities. Eusebius (*Onomasticon* 1.16), in about 300 CE, refers to the Decapolis as "situated near Peraea around Hippos, Pella, and Gadara." A few more references to the term are found in Byzantine works of the fourth and later centuries. Stephen of Byzantium notes that the Decapolis once included fourteen cities, further evidence that the number of cities varied.

Individual Cities. Most of the Decapolis cities can now be identified with a fair degree of certainty. Scythopolis, the only city of the Decapolis situated west of the Jordan River, is Beth-Shean (Beisan), in Israel's southern Galilee. The southernmost city, Philadelphia, is Amman, in Jordan. Moving north, Gerasa is Jerash in ancient Gilead (modern Jordan); Pella is Ṭabaqat Faḥil, on the eastern side of the Jordan Valley; Gadara is Umm Qeis, just southwest of the Sea of Galilee; and Hippos is Qalʿat el-Ḥusn, at the top of a hill on its eastern shore. Farther east, in northern Jordan, Abila is Qweilbeh, and Capitolias is Beit Ras. Most of the remaining Decapolis cities are located in southern Syria. Raphana is probably to be identified with er-Rafe, and Canatha is probably Qanawat. The location of Dium remains a problem. Some identify it with Tell el-Ḥusn, Kefar Abil, or Edun, all

in northwest Jordan. Others suggest Dium is Tell el-Ashari, in southern Syria.

Nature of the Decapolis. Scholars long regarded the Decapolis as a league or confederation of Greek cities organized by the Roman general Pompey when he brought the region under Roman control in 64–63 BCE. However, no ancient source refers to the Decapolis as a political league or confederation. There is no evidence that there were any special political, military, or commercial arrangements among the member cities, nor was there any sort of federal governmental machinery. Instead, the sources refer to the Decapolis as a region or a district formed by the contiguous territories of the Greek cities. A late first-century CE Greek inscription from the Balkans refers to a Roman prefect of the Decapolis in Syria. This suggests that the Decapolis was then an administrative district attached to the Roman province of Syria under the supervision of a single imperial official. Each city retained local autonomy and administered an extensive rural hinterland. Epigraphic and literary sources provide some evidence as to the territorial boundaries of the individual cities.

Archaeological Evidence. The sites of most Decapolis cities have been surveyed and several have been extensively excavated. Undoubtedly, the best-preserved and most thoroughly excavated city is Gerasa/Jerash. [See Jerash.] The city developed on both banks of a perennial stream, with most public buildings on the west side and most domestic structures on the east. The city was laid out in a typical Roman grid pattern, with a main north–south street (*cardo*) intersected by two major east–west streets (*decumani*). These paved streets were decorated by colonnades lined with shops and other buildings and terminated at monumental gateways. The city was protected by massive walls studded with projecting towers. Other public structures included a "forum" (actually an oval agora, or marketplace), several temples, a theater, an odeon (concert hall), baths, hippodrome (racetrack), triumphal arch, and nymphaeum (fountain house). During the Byzantine period many churches were erected. The other Decapolis cities display similar features typical of Greek cities in the eastern Roman Empire. The most extensively excavated are Philadelphia, Pella, Scythopolis, Gadara, Abila, and Capitolias.

History of the Decapolis Cities. Nearly all the sites of the Decapolis cities were occupied in some fashion in the preclassical period. Yet, most of the cities claimed to have been founded as Macedonian colonies by Alexander the Great or one of his immediate successors in the late fourth century BCE. Philadelphia was founded by Ptolemy II Philadelphus in the early third century BCE. Excavations at Pella, named for the capital of Macedonia, have also produced evidence of this period. The archaeological evidence for early Hellenistic occupation is lacking at some of the excavated cities, however. The cities were generally established on strategic sites, astride major roads, and within fertile agricultural districts. The conquest of Palestine and Transjordan by Antiochus III in 200 BCE brought the entire Decapolis region under the control of the Seleucid Empire. Antiochus and his successors continued to foster the development of the cities, as suggested by their later coins, which reveal Seleucid dynastic toponyms such as Antioch and Seleucia. In fact, it may only have been under Seleucid rule, in the second century BCE, that many of these settlements developed into true urban centers. [*See* Pella; Seleucids.]

The decline of Seleucid power and the consequent rise of the Hasmonean Jewish and Arab Nabatean states in the late second and early first centuries BCE threatened the very existence of these cities. The Hasmoneans conquered Scythopolis, Gadara, Abila, Dium, and Pella, and the Nabateans occupied Philadelphia. When Pompey arrived to establish Roman control in 63 BCE, he posed as a champion of the Greek cities. All the towns were freed from Jewish and Nabatean control, granted ''freedom'' (i.e., municipal autonomy), and placed under the administrative control of the Roman governor of Syria. Many of the cities adopted a new Pompeian era on their coinage, to celebrate their liberation and express gratitude to their liberator.

The Roman emperor Augustus, in 30 BCE, assigned two of the cities (Hippos and Gadara) to the kingdom of his loyal client Herod the Great, despite the objections of their inhabitants. Both cities regained their autonomy and were returned to the province of Syria upon Herod's death in 4 BCE.

The outbreak of the Jewish revolt in 66 CE witnessed attacks by Jewish forces against the territories of several Decapolis cities, including Scythopolis, Pella, Gerasa, Gadara, and Hippos. The people of several of these cities responded by massacring the Jewish minorities in their midst. The people of Gerasa notably did not follow this example, but escorted their Jewish minority safely out of the city. Scythopolis served as an important base for the Roman army of Vespasian during the suppression of the revolt. Eusebius (*History of the Church* 3.5.3) asserts that the Christian community of Jerusalem fled to Pella before Jerusalem fell in 70 CE.

The conversion of the Nabatean kingdom into the new Roman province of Arabia by the Roman emperor Trajan (106 CE) resulted in the effective demise of the Decapolis, for its individual cities were then divided among the Roman provinces of Syria, Arabia, and Palestine. However, the individual cities continued to flourish economically and culturally for many centuries.

Culture of the Decapolis. The uniqueness of the Decapolis was its cultural identity as a group of Greek cities, sharply differentiated from the neighboring Semitic populations. The city plans, individual buildings, tombs, sculpture, and divinities are Greek or Roman, although there are many traces of Near Eastern influences. The vast majority of inscriptions are Greek, with some Latin. Some inscriptions suggest that many of the urban populace were hellenized Semites, although it is entirely possible that some families were descendants of the original Greek or Macedonian colonists. Naturally, much less is known about the population of the rural hinterlands, where Semitic culture may have remained dominant. The high Greek culture of the Decapolis is also clearly reflected by the numerous philosophers, poets, jurists, and other intellectuals from these cities. Among the most famous are the poet Meleager of Gadara (c. 140–70 BCE); the rhetor Theodorus of Gadara (late first century BCE), who was a teacher of the emperor Tiberius; and the mathematician Nichomachus of Gerasa (c. 100 CE).

[*Many of the cities of the Decapolis are the subject of independent entries.*]

BIBLIOGRAPHY

Barghouti, Asem N. "Urbanization of Palestine and Jordan in Hellenistic and Roman Times." In *Studies in the History and Archaeology of Jordan*, vol. 1, edited by Adnan Hadidi, pp. 209–229. Amman, 1982.

Bietenhard, Hans. "Die syrische Dekapolis von Pompeius bis Trajan." In *Aufstieg und Niedergang der römischen Welt*, edited by Hildegard Temporini and Wolfgang Haase, vol. II.8, pp. 220–261. Berlin, 1977. Accepts the traditional view of the Decapolis as a league.

Isaac, Benjamin. "The Decapolis in Syria: A Neglected Inscription." *Zeitschrift für Papyrologie und Epigraphik* 44 (1981): 67–74. Argues convincingly that the Decapolis was an administrative district attached to Syria and under the supervision of a Roman official.

Kraeling, Carl H., ed. *Gerasa, City of the Decapolis*. New Haven, 1938. Indispensable, detailed report of the excavations conducted in the 1920s and 1930s; some of its conclusions have been modified by recent work.

Lenzen, C. J., and Alison M. McQuitty. "The 1984 Survey of the Irbid/Beit Rās Region." *Annual of the Department of Antiquities of Jordan* 32 (1988): 265–274. Suggests continuity of occupation in the territory of Capitolias through the pre- and postclassical periods.

Mare, W. Harold. "Quweilbeh." In *Archaeology of Jordan*, vol. 2, *Field Reports*, edited by Denys Homès-Fredericq and J. Basil Hennessy, pp. 472–486. Louvain, 1989. Summary of what is known about Abila.

McNicoll, Anthony W., et al. *Pella in Jordan 1: An Interim Report on the Joint University of Sydney and the College of Wooster Excavations at Pella, 1979–1981*. Canberra, 1982.

Parker, S. Thomas. "The Decapolis Reviewed." *Journal of Biblical Literature* 94 (1975): 437–441. Rejects the long-held view that the Decapolis ever formed a league or confederation.

Seigne, Jacques. "Jérash romaine et byzantine: Développement urbain d'une ville provinciale orientale." In *Studies in the History and Archaeology of Jordan*, vol. 4, edited by Ghazi Bisheh, pp. 331–341. Amman, 1992.

Smith, Robert Houston. *The 1967 Season of the College of Wooster Expedition to Pella*. Pella of the Decapolis, vol. 1. Wooster, Ohio, 1973.

Smith, Robert Houston, and Leslie P. Day. *Final Report on the College of Wooster Excavations in Area IX, the Civic Complex, 1979–1985*. Pella of the Decapolis, vol. 2. Wooster, Ohio, 1989.

Spijkerman, Augusto. *The Coins of the Decapolis and Provincia Arabia*. Jerusalem, 1978.

Weber, Thomas. "A Survey of Roman Sculpture in the Decapolis:

Preliminary Report." *Annual of the Department of Antiquities of Jordan* 34 (1990): 351–355.

Weber, Thomas. "Gadara of the Decapolis: Preliminary Report on the 1990 Season at Umm Qeis." *Annual of the Department of Antiquities of Jordan* 35 (1991): 223–235. Contains a detailed bibliography on earlier work at the site.

Yeivin, Zeev, et al. "The Bet Shean Project." *Excavations and Surveys in Israel* 6 (1988): 7–45.

Zayadine, Fawzi, ed. *Jerash Archaeological Project, 1981–1983*, vol. 1, *The Hashemite Kingdom of Jordan*. Amman, 1986.

Zayadine, Fawzi, ed. *Jerash Archaeological Project*, vol. 2, *Fouilles de Jérash, 1984–1988*. Paris, 1989.

S. Thomas Parker

DECIPHERMENT. Of the thousands of languages spoken before modern times, a handful developed scripts. The descendants of a few of those are still in use; of a handful of the others, traces have survived the millennia to be discovered by travelers or excavated by archeologists. If the modern descendants diverged considerably from the ancestors, or if there are none, the ancestors need to be deciphered. It is always a script, rather than a language, that is deciphered; if an (ancient) record can be pronounced, but not understood (as with Etruscan), the problem is one of interpretation rather than decipherment.

Decipherment of Scripts. The prerequisite to decipherment is accurate reproduction of the enigmatic inscription. This may seem trivial now that photography has been commonplace for a century and a half, but before 1850 or so—during the quarter millennium when most of the ancient scripts were first found—only the artist's subjective eye served to disseminate an inscription's appearance. The artist's drawings further passed through the engraver's burin and, at the end of the period, the lithographer's crayon. Only with photography, perhaps, does it become apparent how subjective the artist's vision is: witness the depictions of the Sphinx at Giza or the Assyrian bulls that vary with stylistic fashion and the drafting skill of individual artists. The task is especially difficult when the artist is trying to reproduce unfamiliar writing, where apparently trivial details may distinguish two characters (compare the Roman letters C and G), but rather great differences may be completely insignificant (a Roman "t" may be made with or without the lower curve to the right, on the writer's whim). Successive attempts to delineate ancient inscriptions—but not with increasing accuracy—have been published (Daniels, 1988).

Methodology. Given accurate copies of a graphic image, it must first be decided whether the image is in fact writing. The first cuneiform inscriptions, found on doorframes and such at Persepolis, were sometimes considered mere decoration. [*See* Persepolis.] Kufic Arabic inscriptions in mosques are so stylized as to be almost purely decorative rather than linguistic. [*See* Mosque Inscriptions.] The masons' use of South Arabian letters to guide the arrangement of paving stones at Hajar Kohlan provided the first clue to the canonical order of that script. [*See* South Arabian.] The letters' use was functional rather than linguistic, but their function derived entirely from an incidental property of scripts that their characters are learned in a fixed order. It is uncertain whether "potters' marks" dating to the era of the presumed development of Proto-Canaanite writing that might be letters of a script are in fact such or are arbitrary designs with some function or other. [*See* Proto-Canaanite.] Two modes of decipherment ensue when the marks are established as writing. In the exceptional case, the decipherer is very lucky and the new script occurs alongside an inscription in a known language—in a bilingual text. Usually, it is safe to assume that the two texts render the same content—one is a translation of the other (or both are translations of a third).

More often, the unknown script stands alone, and it is up to the ingenuity of the decipherer to discover a virtual bilingual: some stretch of text in a known language that can be presumed to equate to some stretch of text in the unknown one. Most commonly, virtual bilinguals have been at a phonetic level (personal or place names)—although a morphological/semantic level (numbers) figured in at least one case—and sometimes purely graphic (shapes of letters in a known script). This last category comes into play whenever a new text, even in a very familiar language, is unearthed because the ductus of no two scribes is identical. In addition, ancient inscriptions are sufficiently rare that normal variation in script or language will be magnified by the absence of intermediate forms. The history of decipherment is studded with examples of poorly chosen virtual bilinguals, however, and it is difficult to dissuade the proposers from their beliefs.

While the decipherer may formulate a hypothesis about the identity or relationship of the language concealed behind the enigmatic script, this has sometimes proved to be a misstep, misdirecting the investigator. (Most notably, the assumption that Linear B must be some pre-Greek substrate language such as Etruscan delayed success on that script.) It is more useful simply to identify and count the different characters: a small number, about thirty, suggests an abjad (consonantary) or an alphabet; greater variety, about one hundred or more, suggests a syllabary or an abugida, and several hundred or more, a logosyllabary (or a logography—no purely logographic script, if such has ever truly existed, has been deciphered; candidates include Proto-Elamite, Indus Valley script, and Easter Island script). [*See* Writing and Writing Systems.]

Case studies. The surest results have been achieved by those who concentrated on proper names. Such cases include both the first, (Palmyrene, by Jean-Jacques Barthélemy, in 1756), and the two most familiar decipherments (Egyptian, by Jean-François Champollion, in 1823, and Linear B, by Michael Ventris, in 1953), as well as the one that is arguably the most important of all, the Old Persian and

Mesopotamian cuneiform scripts, whose decipherment was begun by Georg Friedrich Grotefend (1802) and climaxed by Edward Hincks (1846–1852). [*See* Cuneiform.] The decipherments of Ugaritic and Himyaritic illustrate different kinds of virtual bilinguals (see Daniels, 1995; Daniels and Bright, 1996, sec. 9). [*See the biography of Champollion.*]

Palmyrene. Palmyra was an independent pagan monarchy on the eastern edge of the Roman Empire. It was fairly well known in the eighteenth century from classical historians. Monuments written in its language, known to be similar to Syriac, had been known in Europe since antiquity and had received the attention of antiquarians since the early 1600s. It was not until 1753 that adventurers traveled to the ruins of the city and brought back accurate copies of some of its inscriptions. Many of the inscriptions in the Palmyrene script and language were accompanied by Greek inscriptions, and it took no great insight to guess that the pairs were equivalent. Barthélemy (1716–1795), in fact, reports that it took him no more than two days to decipher the script. From the thirteen inscriptions that had been accurately published by Robert Wood and James Dawkins (English adventurers who traveled to the ruins of the city in 1753 and brought back accurate copies of some of its inscriptions), Barthélemy chose one in which the Greek parallel began with a proper name, *Septimios.* The seventh letter of the Palmyrene inscription was the same as the first, so (omitting short vowels) there seemed to be a correspondence; the next word, *Ouorōdēn* in the Greek, confirmed the ⟨w⟩ that spelled [o] and gave ⟨r⟩ and ⟨d⟩ as indistinguishable (a characteristic of Aramaic scripts of the period). When the twenty-two letters were identified, their resemblance to the corresponding Hebrew and Syriac forms became clear. A handful of verb forms were nearly identical to Syriac words that could translate the Greek, demonstrating that the language was Aramaic as well (Daniels, 1988). [*See* Palmyra; Palmyrene Inscriptions; Greek; Aramaic; Syriac; Hebrew Language and Literature.]

Mesopotamian cuneiform. Grotefend (see above) used the virtual bilingual of Persian kings' names (known from Herodotus and from formulae in recently deciphered Sasanian inscriptions) to begin the decipherment of the Old Persian version of the trilingual inscriptions from Persepolis. Work on them was greatly advanced by such pioneers of Indo-European and Indo-Iranian studies as Rasmus Rask and Christian Lassen. Henry Creswicke Rawlinson replicated the decipherment of Old Persian, using the huge trilingual inscription at Bisitun that he copied at great personal risk, but he probably knew of Grotefend's insightful virtual bilingual. Rawlinson usually receives credit for deciphering Mesopotamian cuneiform, but his work lagged behind that of Hincks. Although Rawlinson was stationed in Baghdad, he was kept abreast of Hincks's discoveries by a quite efficient postal system. [*See* Sasanians; Persepolis; Bisitun; Cuneiform; *and the biography of Rawlinson.*]

Edward Hincks (1792–1866) was a Church of Ireland country pastor. Unlike the celebrated Champollion and Ventris (see above), he was not a young man when he achieved his decipherment. He was immensely learned in all areas of classical and Oriental (i.e., Near Eastern) studies, and in his first approach to Old Persian he hoped better to understand Egyptian hieroglyphs. In his first lecture on the subject, on 9 June 1846, at the Royal Irish Academy in Dublin (and published in its *Transactions*), he demonstrated that the Old Persian characters denoted consonants plus particular vowels and not a wide variety of consonants. He also showed that the second of the three languages was written with syllabic characters that could be used in the consonant-vowel pattern CV_i-V_iC (*ta-aš*, not *ta-š*). (The second language is what is called Elamite, and it was decades before real progress was made in interpreting it.) [*See* Elamites.] The most important discovery reported in Hincks's second lecture (30 November) was the equivalence between two styles of cuneiform, which he called lapidary and cursive. This made available a great mass of material, which was being brought to the British Museum and the Louvre in Paris by the first excavators in Mesopotamia. In a third lecture (11 January 1847), he refined his readings of many signs and presented the cuneiform system of numerals. The numerals were taken from extensive inscriptions copied in the late 1820s by F. E. Schulz in western Armenia (now eastern Turkey) but not published until 1840 in Paris, and not seen by Hincks until 1846.

It was Schulz's inscriptions, in a language now called Urartian, that proved to be the most important to the decipherment. [*See* Urartu.] The longest one is a royal annal covering thirteen years; each year is introduced by the same formula, but the formula is not always written identically. Hincks discovered certain signs to be optional and identified them as vowel signs. This enabled him to verify the vowel included in preceding CV signs. Moreover, he analyzed the Urartian texts grammatically; his results, including the readings of 110 signs, were published in the prestigious *Journal of the Royal Asiatic Society* (1848). Six months later, Hincks dealt with the inescapable fact that many signs had more than one phonetic value, and semantic values as well. At that point, he suggested the possibility that a different language could underlie the script. Two years later, on 29 July 1850, at the Edinburgh meeting of the British Association for the Advancement of Science, he asserted that the writing system was devised for a non-Semitic language. At that meeting, also, he showed grammatical patterning in the Assyrian language that was fully parallel to that in Hebrew.

Rawlinson's treatment of the Assyrian version of the great Bisutun inscription was published in January 1852. Hincks's last article pertaining to the decipherment per se is dated 24 May 1852: it gives values to 252 characters and identifies elements of Rawlinson's publication that were taken from Hincks's work without acknowledgment. It also includes the first mention of ancient textual material that signaled the close of the decipherment phase of the interpretation of cuneiform. This was a fragment of a lexical list, which Hincks saw comprised a list of signs accompanied by a rendition of their pronunciation. Henceforth, most signs were to be identified from their appearance in such documents, of which thousands of fragments have been recovered from throughout the cuneiform world. Hincks's accomplishment was recognized in his own time; his undeserved eclipse by Rawlinson may be attributable to the personalities of the two men. Hincks was shy and unambitious, with no academic position, rarely leaving the village of Killyleagh, in Ulster. Rawlinson was energetic, well placed in the military and the British Museum, and endowed with dual hagiographers in his brother, a prolific historian, and the immensely powerful E. A. Wallis Budge, who ruled British Oriental studies for decades. Both authors downplay—and distort—Hincks's role. Subsequent chroniclers and historians have not known of the existence of the *Transactions of the Royal Irish Academy* (for details and references, see Cathcart and Donlon, 1983; Daniels, 1994).

Ugaritic. It is Ugaritic that was deciphered by means of numerals, and also by the use of grammatical information. The first texts were excavated at Ugarit in 1929 and published immediately; Charles Virolleaud, the epigrapher, supposed from the location and date of the site and the finds that their language was likely to be Northwest Semitic. He was fortunate enough to discover a tablet that resembled Mesopotamian accounting documents and, in a column that might contain numbers (their names were spelled out), a sequence of symbols like XYX appeared. About the only common word in Semitic with such a consonant pattern is ṯalāṯ, "three." Meanwhile, the eminent scientist Hans Bauer analyzed the letters that appeared at the beginnings or ends of words, or both, and compared them with the limited inventory of affixes in Semitic. Édouard Dhorme noted that a phrase at the beginning of what looked like a letter was identical to a phrase on a sword, with the addition of one letter at the beginning. He surmised that this was the letter *l*, representing the preposition *to*. The work of the three scholars converged, and the Ugaritic script was soon worked out (Corré, 1966). The unique use of three letters for *à*, *ì*, and *ù* was established by Johannes Friedrich. [*See* Ugarit; Ugaritic; Ugarit Inscriptions; *and the biography of Virolleaud*.]

Himyaritic. A Near Eastern script deciphered via the shapes of the characters is the Himyaritic (i.e., Sabaean), as it was called by early researchers. Emil Rödiger discovered two unrelated Arabic manuscripts that contained lists of letters said to be *musnad*, "Himyaritic." The two lists were strikingly similar, suggesting that they might preserve a genuine tradition; indeed, when the first inscriptions from South Arabia were published in 1837 and 1838, Rödiger was able to interpret them fairly successfully, using the manuscript abecedaries. His teacher, the eminent philologist Wilhelm Gesenius, mistrusting that evidence and relying more on comparative philology and limited data from a newly discovered South Arabian language, had an earlier success but went further astray. Unfortunately, the first somewhat extensive text available (ten lines) contained almost nothing but proper names (Daniels, 1986). [*See* Himyar.]

Interpretation of Languages. With the decipherment of ancient scripts came the discovery that they could be used for languages other than those for which they were devised. The recovery of many intermediary forms has enabled the demonstration that all the West Semitic scripts (including Palmyrene, Ugaritic, and Himyaritic, as well as Hebrew and Arabic) belong to a single tree of descent. A productive assumption, as has been seen, was that the languages associated with the unknown scripts were similar to the known Semitic languages: Hebrew, Syriac (Christian Aramaic), Jewish Aramaic, and Arabic. The affinity of the Semitic languages had been recognized since the Middle Ages (previously called Oriental, they did not receive the name "Semitic" until 1781). The four classical Semitic languages are Hebrew, Arabic, Syriac, and Ethiopic, or Geʿez; the language of the Aramaic portions of the Bible was called Chaldee, as were the languages of the rabbinic writings. It is not yet clear when the Aramaic languages were identified as a group (characterized by the phonological change of Semitic interdentals to stops and by a particular selection of the ancestral verb stems); Barthélemy does not use the term of Palmyrene, but it was established by the mid-nineteenth century.

As the decipherment of cuneiform proceeded, several scholars came to believe that cuneiform Assyrian was a Semitic language. This was an assumption rather than a demonstration; however. It was not until Hincks identified the similarity in grammar as well as vocabulary that the identification could be regarded as certain. The other cuneiform languages are more difficult. Those for which the most materials are available are Sumerian, Elamite, Hittite, Hurrian, and Urartian. [*See* Sumerian; Hittite; Hurrian.]

The interpretation of Sumerian was aided somewhat by the discovery, early on, of tablets containing grammatical paradigms. The first interpretations coincided with a vogue for typological classification of language. The German-English philologist Friedrich Max Müller assigned nearly all the non-Indo-European, non-Semitic languages of Eurasia to a phylum he called Turanian (encompassing many more languages than the modern term *Altaic*), largely on the basis of their so-called agglutinative structure. Early Sumerologists, finding similar patterning in Sumerian, believed it, too, belonged in the phylum. They found a worthy opponent in Joseph Halévy (who was actually familiar with a number of Turanian languages). He, however, was of the opinion that Sumerian was not a real language at all, but a code devised by Assyrian priests to maintain the secrecy of the cult (Cooper, 1991). The discovery in the late nineteenth century of archives, notably at Telloh, of the most mundane documents written in Sumerian disproved the notion. Over the following century, attempts have been made to connect Sumerian with virtually every language family on the globe—most recently the Nostratic superphylum encompassing Indo-European and most of its neighbors. So little information is accessible to nonspecialists, however, that no credence can be given to these attempts.

The limited amount of Elamite material and its formulaic nature—even though it crosses several periods in nearly three millennia—make it difficult to analyze. The proposal by David McAlpin to connect it with the well-studied Dravidian family has attracted much notice and entered the handbooks, but it is not accepted by the small corps of Elamitologists. A dispassionate linguist will be immediately suspicious because McAlpin seems to have a Dravidian etymology for *every* Elamite word, an unthinkable occurrence. With cuneiform Hittite, the interpretation is certain. The Czech scholar Bedřich Hrozný (Daniels and Bright, 1996) noted a word that could be transcribed as *watar* in a context that demanded the meaning "water" and successfully interpreted the language as Indo-European. Urartian (so important in the decipherment of cuneiform) resisted interpretation for decades. Extensive studies were published by Archibald H. Sayce in the 1880s, but the ergative type of language was not yet familiar to philologists. Hurrian is known from essentially one document—physically, the largest cuneiform-inscribed clay tablet known—and from many enigmatic ritual bilingual texts with Hittite equivalents. All that can be said is that Hurrian and Urartian are related. It has been suggested they are ancestral to some languages of the Caucasus. Lexical connections with (Indo-European) Armenian have been proposed.

BIBLIOGRAPHY

Cathcart, Kevin J., and Patricia Donlon. "Edward Hincks, 1792–1866: A Bibliography of His Publications." *Orientalia* 52 (1983): 325–356.

Cooper, Jerrold S. "Posing the Sumerian Question: Race and Scholarship in the Early History of Assyriology." *Aula Orientalis* 9 (1991): 47–66.

Corré, Alan D. "Anatomy of a Decipherment." *Proceedings of the Wisconsin Academy of Sciences, Arts, and Letters* 55 (1966): 11–20.

Daniels, Peter T. "'To Prove Him with Hard Questions': The Decipherment of Himyaritic." Appendix 1 of "How to Decipher a Script," in *Writing/Écriture,* edited by Pierre Swiggers and Willy Van Hoecke. Louvain, forthcoming.

Daniels, Peter T. "'Shewing of Hard Sentences and Dissolving of Doubts': The First Decipherment." *Journal of the American Oriental Society* 108 (1988): 419–436.

Daniels, Peter T. "Edward Hincks's Decipherment of Mesopotamian Cuneiform." In *The Edward Hincks Bicentenary Lectures,* edited by Kevin J. Cathcart, pp. 30–57. Dublin, 1994.

Daniels, Peter T. "The Decipherments of Near Eastern Scripts." In *Civilizations of the Ancient Near East,* vol. 1, edited by Jack M. Sasson et al., pp. 81–93. New York, 1995.

Daniels, Peter T., and William Bright, eds. *The World's Writing Systems.* New York, 1996.

Friedrich, Johannes. *Extinct Languages.* Translated by Frank Gaynor. New York, 1957.

Gordon, Cyrus H. *Forgotten Scripts: Their Ongoing Discovery and Decipherment.* 2d ed. New York, 1982.

Pope, Maurice. *The Story of Archaeological Decipherment from Egyptian Hieroglyphs to Linear B.* New York, 1975.

PETER T. DANIELS

DEDAN, site identified with the ruins of al-Khuraybah in the al-ʿUla oasis in Saudi Arabia by Eduard Glaser in 1890, mainly on the basis of geography (26°37′ N, 37°50′ E). This is one of the most fertile valleys in northwest Arabia, where the main route used by the incense trade and pilgrim traffic is restricted by forbidding sandstone mountains, sand desert, and *harra* ("lava flows"). References to Dedan in the Hebrew Bible make it clear that it was one of the most important caravan centers in northern Arabia. The site had been visited by a number of European travelers prior to Glaser, but it was Antonin Jaussen and Raphael Savignac (1914) who were the first (1907–1910) to describe its ruins adequately and to record the many rock inscriptions (in various pre-Islamic Arabian scripts) that amply confirm the identification. Their work remains basic, although it has been supplemented by the more recent, though still very superficial, examination of the site by Fred V. Winnett and William L. Reed (1970), Peter J. Parr and others (1970), and Garth Bawden (1979).

The biblical citations most likely refer to the sixth century BCE, in about the middle of which the site is mentioned (as Dadanu) in an inscription from Harran, in southern Turkey. The inscription records a number of North Arabian centers which the king of Babylon, Nabonidus, attacked at the time of his sojourn in Taymaʾ. Winnett (Winnett and Reed, 1970), whose reconstruction of the history of Dedan based on the epigraphic material is probably the most reliable, postulates the existence of a short-lived, independent "Dedanite" kingdom in about 500 BCE, after the collapse of the Neo-Babylonian Empire and before the Achaemenid rulers had had time to impose their own control over this strategic part of Southwest Asia. Northern Arabia seems to have prospered under Persian rule, and by about 400 BCE an independent—or semi-independent—kingdom, known from the inscriptions as Lihyanite, was centered at Dedan. By about this time also a small trading colony of Minaean merchants from southwest Arabia was established there, leaving inscriptions in their own language and script. Minaean traders were also to be found in Egypt, and Dedan was probably in contact with them, across the Red Sea. Relations with Egypt seem to have been maintained after the fall of the Persian Empire and the establishment of the Greek Ptolemaic dynasty; Ptolemy II is known to have been active in promoting the Red Sea trade and may well have supported the Lihyanite rulers in the face of the rising power of the Nabateans, based farther north at Petra. Nevertheless, Winnett has advanced evidence to suggest that the native Lihyanite dynasty was in fact overthrown by a Nabatean adventurer, Mas'udu, in the second or early first century BCE. Shortly, thereafter, it seems that Dedan was replaced as a trading center by the Nabatean town of Hegra (Meda'in Saleh), a few kilometres farther north. [See Meda'in Saleh.]

In addition to the inscriptions, the archaeological remains at al-Khuraybah comprise a number of simple tomb chambers cut into the cliffs, two of which are flanked by pairs of crudely carved lions, and a low mound of ruins, some 800 × 250 m in extent and just a few meters high. The tomb has been badly disturbed by digging for building material—much of it for the Hejaz Railway, which cuts through it—and only a few traces of ancient walling and much broken pottery can be seen on the surface. Jaussen and Savignac were able to detect part of the plan of a monumental structure, adjacent to which were four statue bases with Lihyanite inscriptions. Winnett (1937) dated them to the late fourth or early third century BCE. Fragments of several nearly life-sized sculptures found close by clearly come from these bases, and presumably represent rulers; their style shows marked egyptianizing characteristics of the late dynastic or Ptolemaic period. All of these remains lay close to the surface of the mound and evidently belong to the last major period of building. Apart from a handful of Nabatean graffiti, there is little evidence for a Nabatean occupation of the site.

[See also Nabateans; and the biography of Winnett.]

BIBLIOGRAPHY

Bawden, Garth. "Khief El-Zahra and the Nature of Dedanite Hegemony in the al-'Ula Oasis." Atlal 3 (1979): 63–72. Most useful for its brief account of recent Saudi Arabian excavations at the site.

Jaussen, Antonin J., and Raphael Savignac. Mission archéologique en Arabie II. Paris, 1914. Long out of print but still the most complete description of the site, and the principal publication of its epigraphic remains.

Nasif, Abdallah A. Al-'Ula: An Historical and Archaeological Survey with Special Reference to Its Irrigation System. Riyadh, 1988. Account of recent work by Saudi Arabian archaeologists, with numerous illustrations (including color plates), but concentrating on the Islamic remains.

Parr, Peter J., et al. "Preliminary Survey in North West Arabia, 1968." Bulletin of the Institute of Archaeology, University of London 8–9 (1970): 193–242. Adds important detail to Jaussen and Savignac's description (see above).

Parr, Peter J. "Aspects of the Archaeology of North-West Arabia in the First Millennium BC." In L'Arabie préislamique et son environnement historique et culturel: Actes du Colloque de Strasbourg, edited by Toufic Fahd, pp. 39–66. Leiden, 1989. Primarily a discussion of controversial issues relating to the archaeology and chronology of another important Arabian oasis center, Tayma', but surveys the history of Dedan as well.

Winnett, Fred V. A Study of the Lihyanite and Thamudic Inscriptions. Toronto, 1937.

Winnett, Fred V., and William L. Reed. Ancient Records from North Arabia. Toronto, 1970.

PETER J. PARR

DEH LURAN ("place of the Lurs," an Indo-European-speaking ethnic group in western Iran), site located in southwestern Iran near the northwestern edge of the Deh Luran plain (32°42' N, 47°14' E). The plain is bounded by the Kuh-i Siah range of the Zagros Mountains to the northeast; Jebel Hamrin, a low anticlinal ridge to the southwest; and the small Dawairij and Mehmeh Rivers on the east and west. The plain lies from 32°30' to 32°42' N and 47°08' to 47° 24' E at an altitude of about 150 m and receives an average of 300–350 mm of precipitation during the winter rainy season. The Deh Luran plain, about 60 km (37 mi.) northwest of Susa, is situated between the base of the Zagros Mountains and the international border with Iraq. It is best known for a series of excavations and surveys of archaeological sites that elucidate the region's history from the oldest agricultural settlements in 9000 BP to the modern era. This small, fertile plain lies about midway between passes that lead into the mountains near modern Dizful and Mandali. Because of the limited availability of fresh water and pasturage, Deh Luran has served as a stopping point for travelers and traders; however, settlement there has generally been sparse and always rural in comparison with Khuzistan, to the southeast.

Most of the natural vegetation has been stripped from this region, leaving it barren and treeless, but pistachio trees once grew along the seasonal streams and there were jujube trees scattered across the steppe. The precipitation is sufficient to grow crops without irrigation during average years, but rainfall is quite variable in intensity and timing so that agricultural success is always uncertain. There is seldom frost in the winter but summer temperatures can rise above 40°C, with high winds, leaving all vegetation scorched by late spring. Because of the heat and summer drought, herders usually take their flocks into the mountains.

The history of Deh Luran reflects that of the surrounding regions: Mesopotamia, Khuzistan, and the Zagros Mountains. As early as the third millennium, and subsequently throughout history, Deh Luran comprised part of one or another larger polity or lay in a boundary zone between those polities. No cuneiform texts have yet been found in the limited excavations at historic sites, but the large walled site of Mussian has been tentatively identified as ancient Urua, an Elamite city. By the second millennium BCE, trade may already have passed through Deh Luran on the route used later by the Achaemenid kings traveling between their capitals at Susa in Khuzistan and Ecbatana at modern Hamadan in the mountains.

The first archaeological investigations were undertaken by Joseph Gautier and Georges Lampre of the French mission to Iran in 1903. They excavated at Tepes Mussian, Khazineh, Aliabad, and Mohammed Jaffar (later known as Ali Kosh) and reported the existence of numerous other tells. Frank Hole and Kent V. Flannery with support from Rice University and the National Science Foundation surveyed the plain in 1961 and began an excavation at Ali Kosh. In 1963, they returned with James Neely, who excavated at Tepe Sabz while Hole and Flannery continued at Ali Kosh and briefly reexamined an old French trench at Tepe Mussian. In 1969 Hole excavated at Chogha Sefid (see figure 1), Neely carried out an intensive survey of the plain, and Michael Kirkby of Bristol University investigated its geomorphic history. Henry Wright of the University of Michigan excavated at Tepe Farukhabad in 1968.

The history of human use of Deh Luran is closely related to changes in the land itself. When people first settled at Ali Kosh and Chogha Sefid, the surface of the land was quite different from what it is today. Flash floods deposited silt washed down from the mountains over the entire plain, regenerating its fertility and creating marshes that abounded with fish, attracted game and migratory fowl, and provided easily tilled, moist soil for agriculture. As the deposition of silt continued, the marshes gradually filled in; by the second millennium, some 4 m of silt had accumulated. The rivers became entrenched, and silt ceased to build up on the plain, leaving much of it unsuited to agriculture except by irrigation. Today, except during winter flooding, both rivers have only meager, brackish flows; the small springs on the piedmont are also brackish.

The American teams focused on prehistoric sites, from the beginnings of human settlement in 7000 BCE to the third millennium. Most of this research was ecologically oriented, with emphasis given to the recovery of seeds, animal bones, and small finds that would inform on environment, agricultural practices, and trade. Ali Kosh and Chogha Sefid document the first settlements by people who combined limited agriculture and stock raising with hunting and collecting. By 6000 BCE, irrigation was introduced during the Chogha Mami period by people who had developed the technology along the Tigris River. Although there were notable changes in the numbers of sites through the various archaeological periods, until the third millennium settlements were small and scattered and populations sparse.

Although the earlier French excavations were not successful in recovering tablets, they did find abundant Jemdet Nasr–Early Dynastic I-style ceramics in proto-Elamite tombs (c. 3200–2600 BCE) at Khazineh and Aliabad, contemporary with substantial settlements at Mussian and Farukhabad. By the early second millennium, populations had declined and the Ur III kings of Mesopotamia were shipping valuable highland commodities such as silver and timber through Deh Luran. Although new towns were established in Deh Luran at Tepes Patak and Goughan during the last half of the second millennium, these had disappeared by the end of the millennium, perhaps victims of the incessant warfare waged between Middle Elamite kings and Babylonia. The Neo-Elamite period (c. 1000–520 BCE) is one of apparent depopulation of the lowlands, perhaps reflecting unsettled conditions in Mesopotamia generally.

DEH LURAN. Figure 1. *Excavation trench in the prehistoric site of Chogha Sefid on the Deh Luran plain.* (Photograph by Frank Hole)

A number of sites were situated on irrigation canals during the Achaemenid, Seleucid and Parthian periods (520 BCE–226 CE). It is probable that the irrigation system was built on Elamite predecessors because several of the towns are in the same locations. The demographic pattern changed dramatically with the Sasanian and Early Islamic periods (c. 226–800 CE), when an entirely new technique of irrigation, based on the *qanat* system of subterranean channels, distributed water to the northern half of the plain. [*See* Irrigation.] This was augmented by a second system that used terraces and check dams to distribute water from the many seasonal streams as a supplement to both irrigation and rainfall. A similar and much more extensive system was also constructed in the previously unsettled piedmont zone. Each of these local systems was designed to serve one or more homesteads. A third Sasanian innovation was a system that took water from springs through canals and drop towers from the upland hills to fields and houses below. One such system, along which there were twenty-two drop towers, has been traced through a course of 6.5 km (4 mi). The drop towers served as penstocks for mills where the force of the falling water turned the blades of a millstone. As a result of these various systems, some 40 percent of the Deh Luran plain was occupied and settlement probably reached its highest total ever.

The later Islamic periods saw a gradual decline in population. From 800 to 950 CE, much of the piedmont system, including the drop towers, was abandoned, as was the *qanat* system that fed the upper plain. Population may have dropped to half that of the previous period. From 950 to 1250, only two functioning irrigation systems remained, one near the modern town of Deh Luran, the other near Tepe Mussian. By 1250, the plain was devoid of settlements, a situation that existed until the twentieth century.

The recent history of the plain has seen seasonal occupation by tribal Luri, Arab pastoralists, and the Wali of Pusht-i Kuh (an Ottoman title), who used Deh Luran as his winter camp and built a fort on top of Chogha Sefid. In the twentieth century, a customs post was established, the British Petroleum Company briefly exporting petroleum products from a natural tar seep by means of a narrow gauge railroad, and the towns of Deh Luran, Mussian, and Bayat were founded. Seismic work established the presence of a major oil deposit beneath the international border, but productions wells were not developed. Until the late 1960s, fresh water was available in Deh Luran only through rainwater or from 'Ain Girzan, the only freshwater spring on the plain. In the 1970s, pumps to deliver fresh groundwater were installed, agriculture was transformed by modern irrigation systems, and bridges were built over the rivers. During the Iraq-Iran war in the 1980s, Deh Luran was invaded and captured by Iraq and subsequently retaken by Iran.

For the prehistoric periods, Deh Luran has one of the best-known sequences in the Near East, and the information on the late historic irrigation and settlement systems is unique. Despite its small size and remote location, Deh Luran continues to hold much potential for elucidating the dynamic history of this region.

[*See also* Ali Kosh; Elamites; Tepe Farukhabad; *and* Tepe Mussian.]

BIBLIOGRAPHY

Excavation and Survey Reports

Gautier, Joseph, and Georges Lampre. "Fouilles de Moussian." *Mémoires de la Délégation en Perse* 8 (1905): 59–149. The first survey and excavations on the plain, including Tepes Mussian, Khazineh, and Mohammad Jaffar, a.k.a. Ali Kosh.

Hole, Frank. "Archeological Survey and Excavation in Iran, 1961." *Science* 137 (1962): 524–526. Discovery and initial excavation of Ali Kosh.

Hole, Frank, and Kent V. Flannery. "The Prehistory of Western Iran: A Preliminary Report." *Proceedings of the Prehistoric Society* 33 (1967): 147–206. General survey of prehistoric sites, including Deh Luran.

Hole, Frank, et al., eds. *Prehistory and Human Ecology of the Deh Luran Plain: An Early Village Sequence from Khuzistan, Iran.* University of Michigan, Memoirs of the Museum of Anthropology, no. 1. Ann Arbor, 1969. Final site report on the excavations at Ali Kosh, Tepe Sabz, and Mussian.

Hole, Frank, ed. *Studies in the Archaeological History of the Deh Luran Plain.* University of Michigan, Memoirs of the Museum of Anthropology, no. 9. Ann Arbor, 1977. Final report on the excavation at Chogha Sefid, with a study of geomorphology and obsidian.

Neely, James A. "The Deh Luran Region." *Iran* 8 (1970): 202–203. First report on the survey of the plain.

Neely, James A. "Sassanian and Early Islamic Water-Control and Irrigation Systems on the Deh Luran Plain, Iran." In *Irrigation's Impact on Society*, edited by Theodore E. Downing and McGuire Gibson, pp. 21–42. University of Arizona, Anthropological Papers, 25. Tucson, 1974. Description of irrigation systems and mills.

Neely, James A., and Henry T. Wright. *Early Settlement Patterns on the Deh Luran Plain: Village and Early State Societies in Southwestern Iran.* University of Michigan, Technical Report of the Museum of Anthropology, no. 26. Ann Arbor, 1994. Description of all prehistoric sites and settlement patterns on the plain as known through survey, from the Bus Mordeh Phase to ED III.

Wright, Henry T., ed. *An Early Town on the Deh Luran Plain: Excavations at Tepe Farukhabad.* University of Michigan, Memoirs of the Museum of Anthropology, no. 13. Ann Arbor, 1981. Final report on the excavation at Tepe Farukhabad.

Environmental Reconstructions

Helbaek, Hans. "Plant Collecting, Dry-Farming, and Irrigation Agriculture in Prehistoric Deh Luran." In *Prehistory and Human Ecology of the Deh Luran Plain: An Early Village Sequence from Khuzistan, Iran*, edited by Frank Hole et al., pp. 383–426. University of Michigan, Memoirs of the Museum of Anthropology, no. 1. Ann Arbor, 1969. Analysis of carbonized seeds from Ali Kosh and Tepe Sabz.

Kirkby, Michael J. "Land and Water Resources of the Deh Luran and Khuzistan Plains." In *Studies in the Archaeological History of the Deh Luran Plain*, edited by Frank Hole, pp. 251–288. University of Michigan, Memoirs of the Museum of Anthropology, no. 9. Ann Arbor, 1977. Geomorphological study of the history of the Deh Luran and Khuzistan plains.

Woosley, Anne, and Frank Hole. "Pollen Evidence of Subsistence and

Environment in Ancient Iran." *Paléorient* 4 (1978): 59–70. Environmental and economic reconstruction based on pollen from the sites.

Trade and Exchange

Renfrew, Colin, et al. "Further Analysis of Near Eastern Obsidians." *Proceedings of the Prehistoric Society* 34 (1969a): 319–331.

Renfrew, Colin. "Sources and Supply of the Deh Luran Obsidian." In *Prehistory and Human Ecology of the Deh Luran Plain: An Early Village Sequence from Khuzistan, Iran,* edited by Frank Hole et al., pp. 429–433. University of Michigan, Memoirs of the Museum of Anthropology, no. 1. Ann Arbor, 1969b.

Renfrew, Colin. "The Later Obsidian of Deh Luran: The Evidence of Chogha Sefid." In *Studies in the Archaeological History of the Deh Luran Plain,* edited by Frank Hole, pp. 289–311. University of Michigan, Memoirs of the Museum of Anthropology, no. 9. Ann Arbor, 1977. Deh Luran in the perspective of the entire Near East.

Wright, Henry T. "A Consideration of Interregional Exchange in Greater Mesopotamia, 4000–3000 B.C." In *Social Exchange and Interaction,* edited by Edwin Wilmsen, pp. 95–105. University of Michigan, Museum of Anthropology, Anthropological Papers, no. 46. Ann Arbor, 1972. Evidence for trade and manufacturing in Deh Luran.

Wright, Henry T., et al. "Early Fourth Millennium Developments in Southwestern Iran." *Iran* 13 (1975): 129–147. Results of survey in Deh Luran and Luristan.

Ancient History and Works of Synthesis

Carter, Elizabeth. "Elam in the Second Millennium B.C.: The Archaeological Evidence." Ph.D. diss., University of Chicago, 1971. Synthesis based on survey and excavations.

Carter, Elizabeth, and Matthew W. Stolper. *Elam: Surveys of Political History and Archaeology.* Berkeley, 1984. Includes Deh Luran in a general review of Elamite history.

Hole, Frank, and Kent V. Flannery. "The Prehistory of Western Iran: A Preliminary Report." *Proceedings of the Prehistoric Society* 33 (1967): 147–206. General survey of prehistoric sites, including Deh Luran.

Hole, Frank. "Chronologies in the Iranian Neolithic." In *Chronologies in the Near East,* edited by Olivier Aurenche et al., pp. 353–379. British Archaeological Reports, International Series, no. 379. Oxford, 1987a. Assessment of carbon-14 dates and chronology of western Iran.

Hole, Frank. "Settlement and Society in the Village Period." In *The Archaeology of Western Iran,* edited by Frank Hole, pp. 79–105. Washington, D.C., 1987b. Deh Luran is compared to other regions of western Iran.

Wright, Henry T., et al. "Early Fourth Millennium Developments in Southwestern Iran." *Iran* 13 (1975): 129–147. Results of survey in Deh Luran and Luristan.

Wright, Henry T., and Gregory A. Johnson. "Population, Exchange, and Early State Formation in Southwestern Iran." *American Anthropologist* 77 (1975): 267–289. Comparison of developments in Deh Luran and Khuzistan.

FRANK HOLE

DEIR ʿALLA, TELL,

DEIR ʿALLA, TELL, site located in the Ghor Abu ʿObeideh in modern Jordan, east of the Jordan River and 4 km (2.5 mi.) north of the bridge over the Zerqa River (map reference 209 × 178). Before considering an identification with a site known from the Bible, the nature of the ruins as Tell Deir ʿAlla and its culture must be identified.

The tell was inhabited from the eighth century BCE until late Persian times and was mentioned by nineteenth-century travelers to the Holy Land (including G. A. Smith and Selah Merrill). Excavation has been underway since 1960, first by the University of Leiden, under the direction of H. J. Franken, and, since 1978, by that university in cooperation with Yarmouk University, Jordan. Excavations have shown that in the Bronze and Iron Ages Deir ʿAlla was a large sanctuary with auxiliary buildings—storerooms, workshops, and dwellings.

Bronze Age. The site's Middle Bronze remains have not as yet been excavated. In the sixteenth century BCE, an artificial hill was constructed that covered the MB ruins. This hill was restricted to the eastern half of the tell and measured more than 90 meters along its northern slope. Its north–south axis was probably the same length. On its north side, which is 7 meters high, a 2-meter-high podium was built of mud bricks, oriented north–south. The podium held a cella (11 m wide and probably 20 m long) built of large river stones. A towerlike structure on this building's north side contained three small rooms. As the mud-brick buildings and mud roofs adjacent to the cella weathered, they caused the surface area to rise, and several times the cella had to be rebuilt on a higher level. In this process, the cella's thick walls served as retaining walls for the platform on which each new cella was erected. The entrance to the latest Late Bronze cella has not been excavated, as it is buried deep within the tell. An earthquake destroyed the building shortly after 1200 BCE.

Storerooms and workshops were built to the west of the cella, against the podium. On the east, rooms were found containing precious objects and clay tablets pertaining to the administration of the temple. Farther east were the living quarters for temple personnel. The nature of these remains creates a question about the function of the complex. It is not part of a village or town; it is a freestanding structure on the plain of Succoth. Petrographic analysis of the pottery revealed that about 20 percent came from areas at a considerable distance from the site, such as basalt areas.

Because there was a strong Egyptian influence, the most likely identification is that the temple served the trade between Egypt and Gilead. This trade is known from biblical sources, in which Midianite and Ishmaelite caravans travel between Gilead and Egypt (*Gn.* 37:28). It was an entrepôt for Gilead's products, collected and harvested by the local population in the hills to the east and north of the site. In the cella, the storerooms, the treasure room, and in one of the houses, fenestrated pots that could be closed were found that had not been used as ossuaries. They may have contained a "document" that testified to special bonds between the sanctuary and certain groups, such as families or tribes. Each pot may have represented a priestly family whose duty it was to serve during a certain period in the temple.

An Egyptian drop vase with the cartouche of queen Tawosert demonstrates that Egyptian trade interests had not yet waned in the early twelfth century BCE. It is not known whether that trade ended with the earthquake that struck shortly thereafter, destroying the sanctuary. While there would have been enough space for the markets in the surrounding fields, the destruction of the administrative center and locations where contracts could be placed under divine authority must have had a disastrous effect on the people's livelihood.

At some point in the early Iron Age, metalworkers leveled part of the surface of the ruined site and, for a short period, settled the tell, where they produced bronze objects. Little is known about this period because the excavation was focused on only a small area. However, there are indications that large buildings had been erected on the east side of the tell—perhaps a new temple complex serving trade, although no longer tied to Egypt. In the following centuries, after the smiths had left the site, there is a rather nondescript collection of small buildings and open spaces at the center of the tell. At one point the area may even have been walled, with a gate between two small watchtowers.

Iron Age. The tradition of Deir ʿAlla as a sacred place was not lost, and in the eighth century BCE a sanctuary existed, designated phase IX, of which a large area was excavated. It is this phase "proto-Aramaic" texts were found in which the prophet Balaam son of Beor plays a role (*Nm.* 22–24). The texts were written on a wall in a room belonging to the large complex of work and storage rooms. East of this complex, of which twenty-two rooms have been excavated, is another complex of ordinary houses with courtyards.

No architectural parallel to this layout has as yet been found in the region. Although this building was also destroyed by an earthquake that shifted walls at ground level, it was still apparent that some rooms could only be entered through a high window or from the roof. This gives the rooms the quality of an artificial cave. It appears that the room in which the Aramaic texts were written belonged to this group. The complex resembles what is described in myths as a labyrinth, although a small one—a place of death and victory over death, a typical theme in religion in the ancient Near East.

According to the Balaam text people believed that there was a pantheon of gods (Heb., *ʾělōhîm*) with a leading goddess, probably Ishtar and Shadday, mythological beings (*Dt.* 32:17). This was a feature of religion in Syria that persisted into the Roman period in Hierapolis (Manbij), where the great Syrian goddess resided. Because the Hebrew prophets describe Canaanite religious practices derogatorily: "under oaks and poplars and terebinths" (cf. *Hos.* 4:13), modern readers may forget that these attributes belonged to a proper religion. Thus, the cult practiced in eighth-century Deir ʿAlla was a primitive "mystery" religion, and not the "state" religion—as was the contemporary cult of Osiris in Egypt and of Attis in Syria itself. The mystery for the living in the latter two cults was the beneficial rising of the Nile water in Egypt and the return of the winter rains in Syria, respectively.

In Israel, the traces of the high places dedicated to Baal disappeared as the hilltops eroded. In Jordan, however, at Tell Deir ʿAlla, later construction buried the remains of a Baal high place and the fertility religion practiced there. A flint inscribed with the name of Sharʿa (the name used by bedouin today for the Jordan River, the "great watering place") was found in a four-room complex with an oversized loom weight and other weaving tools and a libation vessel. Among others, these objects may point to weaving for a water spending deity, a goddess holding power over the water clouds, in the sanctuary.

Tell Deir ʿAlla has often been identified with biblical Succoth (Heb., "huts"), a settlement with "elders" but otherwise unspecified (*Jg.* 8, 16). Succoth may not have been the name used by the local people, but rather was a biblical indication of a place of pagan religion in the Bronze and Iron Ages: the site's sanctuary may have been known as a holy place belonging to certain deities with local names like Beth-Sharʿa (see below). The place name Tarʿalah is Talmudic (J.T. *Sheviʿit* 9.2) and comes from the Hebrew root *rʿl*; the verb is used in connection with drunkenness or to quiver, shake, or reel. It may be that exiles expelled from Jerusalem by the Romans settled in the area and took Psalm 60 to refer to their situation: that is, instead of calling the area Succoth they called it Tarʿalah ("thou hast made us to drink the wine of astonishment", *Ps.* 60–63), from which the corruption Deir ʿAlla followed.

[*See also* Deir ʿAlla Inscriptions.]

BIBLIOGRAPHY

Franken, H. J., with contributions by J. Kalsbeek. *Excavations at Tell Deir ʿAllā*, vol. 1, *A Stratigraphical and Analytical Study of the Early Iron Age Pottery.* Leiden, 1969.

Franken, H. J. *Excavations at Tell Deir ʿAlla, the Late Bronze Age Sanctuary.* Louvain, 1992.

Hoftijzer, Jacob, and Gerrit van der Kooij. *Aramaic Texts from Deir ʿAlla.* Documenta et Monumenta Orientis Antiqui, vol. 19. Leiden, 1976.

Hoftijzer, Jacob, and Gerrit van der Kooij, eds. *The Balaam Text from Deir ʿAlla Reevaluated: Proceedings of the International Symposium Held at Leiden, 21–24 August 1989.* Leiden, 1991.

H. J. FRANKEN

DEIR ʿALLA INSCRIPTIONS. Several groups of inscriptions, now in the Archaeological Museum in Amman, Jordan, were found in the various excavations begun in 1960 at Tell Deir ʿAlla (ancient Penuel or Sukkot?) in the Middle Jordan Valley.

In the site's Late Bronze Age level (c. 1200 BCE), an Egyptian cartouche of queen Tawosert (Yoyotte, 1962) and three small clay tablets inscribed in a linear script were discovered

(Franken, 1964). Although various commentators have proposed interpretations for them, no reading seems satisfactory and they must be classified as undeciphered. It is possible, nonetheless, to hypothesize from the general shape and the vertical stance of the letters that they are Old Arabian script, North and South. Indication for such a reading is to be found in a tablet from Beth-Shemesh in Israel, an abecedary, in the order of the letters in the South Arabian tradition (Sass, 1991). Because the tablets are contemporaneous, this conjecture for the Deir ʿAlla inscriptions appears plausible.

In level M/IX (c. 800 BCE) of H. J. Franken's excavations (1967), several inscriptions attest to the use of Aramaic script. Two incised inscriptions mention "the gate" (šrʿ) and another contains the beginning of an abecedary. Inscriptions on plaster found at the site in 1967 are also written in Aramaic script, in black and red ink. These texts, probably originally written on wall plaster (wall no. 36), were found in many pieces among debris. The details of their language, restoration, script, reading, and interpretation are still under discussion; however, following a preliminary paleographic dating to the Persian period, and then in the *editio princeps* to about 700 BCE (Hoftijzer and Kooij, 1976), most commentators now agree that the paleography fits the dating of the archaeological context: about 800 BCE (Hoftijzer and Kooij, 1991) or the first half of the eighth century BCE. Indeed, the earthquake that destroyed level M/IX at Deir ʿAlla could well be the one mentioned in *Amos* 1:1 (cf. also 4:11, 6:8–11, 8:8, and 9:1; and *Zec.* 14:5), dated to about 760 BCE. Although some scholars prefer to describe this script as Ammonite, and others have attempted to classify it as Hebrew, Midianite, or North Arabic, the texts linguistic features seem to contradict these classifications.

Most specialists agree that the writing is either an unknown Canaanite dialect (Gileadite?) or Old Aramaic. Several linguistic features make the second interpretation more probable: the writing of *q* for *⋆d*; the third-person masculine singular suffix -*wh* in *ʾlwh* (cf. also the plural ending -*n*); the third-person feminine singular -*t* of the perfect tense in the verb in *ḥrpt* and *ḥqrqt*; and the verb *ʾtyḥdw*, among others. This classification fits the archaeological and historical context: during phase M/IX, Deir ʿAlla seems to have been under Aramaic (Damascene) influence.

The restoration of the broken plaster pieces has produced two principal groups of fragments known as combinations I and II. Even if problems with the details remain, it seems possible to restore most of the ten first lines of combination I. Most commentators agree that line 1 contains the title of this combination, written in red ink: *spr (b)lʿm(.br bʿ)r.ʾ š.ḥzh ʾlhn*, "Text of (Ba)laam (son of Be)or, seer of the gods." The text tells the story of the seer Balaam's vision: "The gods came to him at night and *spoke to him according to these words* and told to Balaam son of Beor as follows. . . ." Even though the oracle is difficult to read and interpret, the next lines seem to tell how, on the following morning, Balaam fasts and weeps before telling his vision to his people. The content of this vision is on a plaster fragment and so is incomplete, but it seems to depict a topsy-turvy world overshadowed by an oracle of doom. Combination II is still more difficult to understand because none of the lines can be restored completely (see figure 1). However, from what remains of these two combinations, it is clear enough that they contained literary texts, brief sections of which—probably the most important ones (title, oracle)—were written in red ink.

The original disposition of the text, in one or two columns, also is still debated. Because the inscription on the plaster of wall 36 was in columns, however, it probably resembled a manuscript—a literary text copied from a manuscript by a professional scribe, for the handwriting is both regular and beautiful.

The language of these inscriptions may be an archaic dialect of Aramaic—earlier than the Old Aramaic of the beginning of the eighth century BCE. The redaction of the Balaam text may antedate the Deir ʿAlla copy by one or two centuries, making the Balaam Aramaic text the oldest extant

DEIR ʿALLA INSCRIPTIONS. Figure 1. *Part of Combination II of the Deir ʿAlla Inscriptions.* (Courtesy ASOR Archives)

Aramaic literary text. This example of an Aramaic literary tradition is probably close in time to the origins of the biblical traditions regarding the foreign seer Balaam (especially *Nm.* 22–24).

In addition to an incised "two-shekel" weight (registration number DA 2632) and an Ammonite seal from the seventh century BCE (DA 2550; Kooij and Ibrahim, 1989, p. 106), several Ammonite inscriptions on jars and on ostraca (DA 2555, 2712, 2755; *ibid.*, pp. 103–106) were found in level VI and may date to about 600 BCE. The jar inscriptions have not yet been properly edited but are said to consist principally of personal names, mostly Ammonite. A few Aramaic ostraca (DA 2600, 2768) from the Persian period (fifth century BCE), one of which mentions "stones" (*'bnn*) also awaits a proper *editio princeps*.

[*See also* Aramaic Language and Literature; Deir 'Alla, Tell.]

BIBLIOGRAPHY

Aufrecht, Walter E. *A Bibliography of the Deir 'Alla Plaster Texts.* Newsletter for Targumic and Cognate Studies, Supplement 2. Toronto, 1985.

Eph'al, Israel, and Joseph Naveh. "The Jar of the Gate." *Bulletin of the American Schools of Oriental Research*, no. 289 (1993): 59–65. Study of the Aramaic "gate" inscriptions.

Franken, H. J. "Clay Tablets from Deir 'Alla, Jordan." *Vetus Testamentum* 14 (1964): 377–379.

Hoftijzer, Jacob, and Gerrit van der Kooij. *Aramaic Texts from Deir 'Alla.* Documenta et Monumenta Orientis Antiqui, vol. 19. Leiden, 1976. *Editio princeps* of the Balaam text.

Hoftijzer, Jacob, and Gerrit van der Kooij, eds. *The Balaam Text from Deir 'Alla Reevaluated: Proceedings of the International Symposium Held at Leiden, 21–24 August 1989.* Leiden, 1991. Various linguistic, literary, and archaeological studies dealing with the Balaam text.

Kooij, Gerrit van der, and M. H. Ibrahim. *Picking Up the Threads . . . : A Continuing Review of Excavations at Deir Alla, Jordan.* Leiden, 1989.

Sass, Benjamin. "The Beth Shemesh Tablet." *Ugarit-Forschungen* 23 (1991): 315–326.

Shea, William H. "The Inscribed Tablets from Tell Deir 'Alla." *Andrews University Seminar Studies* 27 (1989): 21–37.

Yoyotte, Jean. "Un souvenir du 'pharaon' Taousert en Jordanie." *Vetus Testamentum* 12 (1962): 464–469.

ANDRÉ LEMAIRE

DEIR EL-BALAḤ (Ar., "house of the dates"), site located in the Gaza Strip, about 13 km (8 mi.) south of the city of Gaza, close to the Mediterranean coast. In antiquity, it was the easternmost point on the ancient road leading across the Sinai desert from Egypt to Canaan. At the site's virgin soil level, a flourishing Late Bronze Age, Egyptian-type outpost, complete with an Amarna-style residence and artificial pool was excavated between 1972 and 1982 on behalf of the Institute of Archaeology of the Hebrew University of Jerusalem and the Israel Exploration Society, under the direction of Trude Dothan. Superimposed on this stratum was a fortress and an artisans' quarter from the time of Rameses II and a contemporary adjacent cemetery. Above these richly documented levels were traces of Philistine, Israelite, and Byzantine settlements, after which the site was abandoned to the encroaching sand dunes.

There were no modern topographic indications of an ancient settlement because of centuries of shifting sand dunes. A bedouin watchman inadvertently discovered the cemetery when an area was cleared for an avocado grove in the late 1960s. Subsequently, the cemetery was emptied by tomb robbers. It was only the sudden appearance of LB burial gifts and anthropoid coffin fragments in the antiquities' market in Jerusalem that alerted the archaeological community to it. [*See* Grave Goods; Ethics and Archaeology.] The site was first examined by archaeologists in 1968, but because of its precarious security situation excavation could not commence until 1972. Every effort was made prior to excavation to locate, register, and photograph all the artifacts that had been purchased by private collectors and museums. Among the artifacts were some fifty anthropoid coffins, the largest and richest group from Canaan so far known; Egyptian scarabs; jewelry; alabaster and bronze vessels; and fine Mycenaean and Cypriot pottery.

The first few seasons were spent excavating the cemetery to the edge of the 132-meter-high sand dunes that bounded the area. Three more anthropoid coffins were found in situ, all containing burials of several individuals. From these burials and those already recorded, it was evident that the coffins had been placed in groups of three or more, with hundreds of simple burials between them, and marked above ground by a Canaanite storage jar. Alongside the coffins were crude, locally made pottery vessels and a diverse assemblage of imported Mycenaean, Cypriot, and New Kingdom Egyptian vessels. Inside the coffins were bronze objects such as mirrors, bowls, a wine set, and knives, apparently once wrapped in linen; alabaster goblets; and jewelry—carnelian and gold beads, gold amulets, gold earrings, scarabs in gold and silver settings, palmette gold pendants, and seal rings. [*See* Jewelry.] Though distinctive Canaanite traits were manifest in the workmanship of some of the jewelry and pottery, the dead were evidently Egyptians or were under Egyptian cultural and religious influence—but losing touch with the cultic significance of the Egyptian symbols. Four local sandstone Egyptian funerary stelae were also found in the cemetery, bearing hieroglyphic inscriptions and depictions of Mut and Osiris, similar to nineteenth-dynasty stelae from Deir el-Medineh in Egypt.

At some distance from the cemetery, mud-brick walls were found that continued under the high dunes. Eventually 175,000 metric tons of sand were removed, revealing an area of 2,000 sq m down to the settlement's earliest occupation level, the mid-fourteenth century BCE. From the architecture, ceramic finds, and other indications, the closest parallels to this stratum are with Tell el-Amarna, the Egyptian capital city of King Akhenaten (1379–1362 BCE). A number of the rooms had well-preserved beaten-earth floors on which were found some locally made Canaanite cooking pots, juglets, bowls, and flasks and a preponderance of Egyptian-type vessels, many painted with "Amarna blue" and some with the additional black and red decoration that was especially popular during the late eighteenth dynasty. Adjacent to the building was a pool or reservoir, also typical of Amarna. [See Amarna, Tell el-.]

Of striking interest were ten cylindrical pieces of carnelian and blue frit, dotted with traces of gold and pierced by a square aperture—parts of a scepter or flail, whose closest parallel comes from the tomb of Tutankhamun. Because flails were a symbol of authority, they can be adduced as evidence that the building complex was either a governor's palace or an administrative residence.

To the west of the residence a pit, possibly a *favissa*, was excavated in which there was a clay bulla, or seal, bearing four hieroglyphs—two *udjat*s and two *nefer*s—another parallel with Amarna.

Superimposed upon the residence was a fortress that appears to have been two stories high, with supporting walls more than 2 m thick. The fortress (20 × 20 m) contained fourteen rooms. It had four corner bastions, which indicated that it had been built in royal Egyptian style, similar to the fortresses shown on the relief of Seti I at Karnak, depicting the ancient route from Egypt to Canaan, "the Way of Horus."

Another area contained an artisans' village, in which traces were found of nearly every craft connected with the production of coffins and burial gifts. There were also fragmentary walls of private buildings, apparently the homes of the artisans, that contained typical such kitchen installations as *tabuns* ("clay ovens") and cooking pots.

Whereas the later archaeological levels were shallow, in the new area layers of ash, rubble, and animal skeletons were packed with enormous amounts of crude pottery fragments, sometimes 6 m deep. Gradually, the semicircular outline of a brick structure built on the fill (of the pool) became evident. Its collapsed domed roof and vitrified walls indicated a pottery kiln, one of several that were found. There was also a large, well-planned building with a water installation in one room, used most likely in the preparation of the clay for the pottery-coffin industry. The installation was built of large slabs of worked sandstone, inlaid with shells and plaster. Also found were large fragments of coffins and a flat, perforated clay disk similar to the coffin bases discovered in the cemetery. Hoards of bronze nails and scraps, a fragment of a divine concubine in carved stone, and spinning bowls used in the production of textiles were also found, as were chunks of ocher for coloring the coffins.

Because of the local topography and the site's unique geopolitical conditions, only a small area was excavated. The site's full size is not known. Nevertheless, the excavations at Deir el-Balaḥ provide an in-depth picture of an Egyptian outpost and cemetery in southern Palestine toward the end of Egyptian influence there.

BIBLIOGRAPHY

Dothan, Trude. "Notes and News." *Israel Exploration Journal* 22 (1972): 65–72; 23 (1973): 129–146; 28 (1978): 266–267; 31 (1981): 126–131.
Dothan, Trude. *Excavations at the Cemetery of Deir el-Balaḥ.* Qedem, vol. 10. Jerusalem, 1979.
Dothan, Trude. "Deir el-Balaḥ." In *The New Encyclopedia of Archaeological Excavations in the Holy Land,* edited by Ephraim Stern, vol. 1, pp. 343–347. Jerusalem and New York, 1993.

TRUDE DOTHAN

DELTA. The Nile Delta extends about 200 km (120 mi.) northward from the area of Cairo to the Mediterranean Sea. In antiquity this flat plain, roughly the shape of an inverted triangle, was traversed by seven branches of the Nile River. Today, only two branches survive: the eastern one emerges near Damietta, while the western one reaches the sea near Rosetta. The Delta's principal topographical features have evolved through the deposition of Nile alluvium and the intrusion of the Mediterranean Sea. Beach ridges, lagoons, and salt marshes are common near the northern coast, while farther south the region is crossed by canals and water channels, and swamps are found frequently in the low-lying areas.

Ancient settlements often developed on the small hills rising above the alluvium, close to the Nilotic branches. The region's economy was based primarily on farming and cattle herding. Other significant economic activities included fishing, commerce, and, in the eastern Delta, viniculture. The local Egyptian population was supplemented by influxes of Asiatics, Libyans, and, especially in the first millennium BCE, people from Cyprus, Anatolia, and the Greek world.

The Delta is much less well known archaeologically than the Nile valley. Many ancient sites are buried beneath either the alluvium or modern occupation. Others have been robbed out by peasants searching for old mud brick for fertilizer or ancient building stone for construction.

Little is known about the Delta in Neolithic times; remains of that period probably lie beneath the high water table and modern alluvium. The earliest excavated village is at Merimde Beni Salame, a large Late Neolithic (early fifth millennium) town on the periphery of the Delta some 59 km (37 mi.) northwest of Cairo.

Evidence of human activity increases somewhat for the Chalcolithic period. Recent excavations at Buto in the western Delta and at Tell Ibrahim Awad and et-Tell el-Iswid (South) in the east have revealed stratigraphic sequences covering the Late Chalcolithic–Early Dynastic periods. The earliest levels at Buto relate archaeologically to finds made years ago at Maadi, which today lies in the southern suburbs of Cairo. In the first half of the fourth millennium, Maadi was a large town that prospered through copper working and trade with Palestine. Buto has also provided evidence for early ties with Mesopotamia, probably via Syria. Finally, a large cemetery from the late fourth–early third millennia at Minshat Abu-Omar in the northeastern Delta has yielded pottery and other imports from Palestine; this site reflects the incursion of Upper Egyptian people into the Delta in the late predynastic period and the expansion of Egyptian trade with the southern Levant.

In pharaonic times the Delta (i.e., Lower Egypt) had a separate series of administrative districts, or nomes, from the Nile valley (i.e., Upper Egypt). Pharaoh ruled over the two halves of the land as "king of Upper and Lower Egypt." The Delta became especially important in the seventeenth–sixteenth and thirteenth–eleventh centuries BCE, and then again during the first millennium BCE. In the fifteenth dynasty (1648–1540 BCE), Asiatic rulers known as the Hyksos dominated northern Egypt from their residence at Avaris (modern Tell ed-Dabʿa), along the former Pelusiac branch of the Nile in the eastern Delta; other Asiatic sites of that period have been found elsewhere in the eastern Delta and in the Wadi Tumilat. In the nineteenth–twentieth dynasties, the Ramessid pharaohs made their home at Piramesse (Per-Rameses), which today encompasses an enormous area extending from Tell ed-Dabʿa north to Qantir.

The Delta reached its cultural and political zenith during the first millennium BCE, when several dynasties came from that area. At Tanis, on the former Tanitic branch of the Nile, a huge capital developed during the twenty-first dynasty. Many earlier monuments removed from other Delta sites have been found there; Tanis also contained a large temple complex dedicated to the god Amun, as well as the tombs of several kings of the twenty-first and twenty-second dynasties. Bubastis, situated farther to the south, was the home of the twenty-second dynasty. This town, founded during the Old Kingdom (c. 2700–2190 BCE), had a temple dedicated to the lioness goddess Bastet, along with large cat cemeteries. [See Cats.]

The twenty-sixth dynasty (664–525 BCE) made its residence at Saïs in the western Delta. In this region, from the sixth century BCE on, there was also a Greek trading colony at Naukratis (modern Kom Ge'if). Located near the old Canopic branch of the Nile, Naukratis was an important commercial center until Ptolemaic times, when the founding of Alexandria on the Delta's northwest coast (in 332–331 BCE) led to the former's decline. The few archaeological remains surviving from Greco-Roman Alexandria include the enormous Column of Diocletian (297 CE) and the theater at Kom el-Dik.

[See also Alexandria; Hyksos; Naukratis.]

BIBLIOGRAPHY

The Archaeology, Geography, and History of the Egyptian Delta in Pharaonic Times: Proceedings of a Colloquium, Wadham College, 29–31 August. 1988. Discussions in Egyptology, no. 1. Oxford, 1989. Proceedings of a conference held at Oxford in 1988 on a variety of subjects and historical periods relating to the Delta. Contains several good papers, but the contributions often lack adequate illustrations.

Baines, John, and Jaromir Málek. Atlas of Ancient Egypt. New York, 1980. Contains a brief, illustrated introduction to the Delta's major archaeological sites (pp. 166–177).

Bietak, Manfred. Tell el-Dabʿa, vol. 2, Der Fundort im Rahmen einer archäologisch-geographischen Untersuchung über das ägyptische Ostdelta. Vienna, 1975. Excellent study of the ancient geography and political organization of the eastern Delta, with special emphasis on the identification of Tell ed-Dabʿa as the Hyksos city of Avaris and the Ramessid residence known as Piramesse.

Brink, Edwin C. M. van den, ed. The Archaeology of the Nile Delta, Egypt: Problems and Priorities. Amsterdam, 1988. Proceedings of a conference held in Cairo in 1986 on the major archaeological problems of the Delta; includes several excellent synthetic contributions.

Brink, Edwin C. M. van den, ed. The Nile Delta in Transition: Fourth–Third Millennium B.C. Tel Aviv, 1992. Well-illustrated, valuable work containing papers from a 1988 conference on the Delta in late predynastic and early dynastic times.

Butzer, Karl W. "Delta." In Lexikon der Ägyptologie, vol. 1, cols. 1043–1052. Wiesbaden, 1975. Solid overview of the geology, geomorphology, and economic basis of the Nile Delta in antiquity.

Fraser, P. M. Ptolemaic Alexandria. 3 vols. Oxford, 1972. Standard reference work on the history and culture of Alexandria in Hellenistic times.

Hoffman, Michael A. Egypt before the Pharaohs. Rev. ed. Austin, 1991. Part 4 (pp. 167–214) provides a survey of the major prehistoric sites in the Delta region.

Kees, Hermann. Ancient Egypt: A Cultural Topography. Translated by Ian F. D. Morrow. London, 1961. Chapter 8 (pp. 83–121) gives a useful political and economic survey of the Delta in antiquity; the archaeological data, especially for the eastern Delta, are largely outdated.

JAMES M. WEINSTEIN

DEMOGRAPHY. For periods in antiquity, where societies are similar and where similar methods of construction and traditions of habitation exist, a fixed coefficient of population density can be determined. More elaborate and advanced techniques, made possible by excavation, surveys, and interpretations of ceramic, faunal, and floral material, will allow future scholars to venture precise estimates for all periods.

Considerable evidence exists to show that in the premodern Near East the average density coefficient was very near 250 inhabitants per hectare (or per 2.5 acres). That figure stems from two systems of calculating population density: by analogy with present-day settlements in traditional societies (the ethnoarchaeological method) and by analysis of the layout of excavated sites.

The first approach shows that the density in villages in various communities in the Near East (Palestinian Arab, Iraqi, and Iranian) averages 250 per hectare. It should be noted though that in ten contemporary "old" cities in the Levant for which data are available, density is 400–500 persons per hectare. Urban settlements in antiquity, as in preindustrial modern cities, must have been considerably denser than in nonurban settlements.

Using the second approach, it can be shown that the mean density of four Iron Age II settlements was fifty-four houses per hectare. If it is assumed that those buildings were occupied by nuclear families, each of five persons on the average, 270 people per hectare can be assumed.

Ancient Sources. Almost invariably, ancient sources supply us with inflated population numbers. The most often-quoted example is the number of Israelites of army age counted during the Exodus—603,550 (*Nm.* 1:45–46 and similar numbers in other places). Because this figure refers to men older than twenty, the total population during the Exodus (the ratio of men of army age to total population is estimated to be 1:3–3.5) would have to have been more than two million—an impossibility. The resources of the Sinai Desert could not have provided enough food or water for such a crowd. The Hebrew Bible contains a wealth of such population figures. Salo W. Baron discusses 345 of them in *Ancient and Medieval Jewish History* (New Brunswick, 1972, pp. 25–38), including the grossly exaggerated results of King David's census: 1,570,000 "sword drawers," which would bring the general population to more than five million (*1 Chr.* 21:5 and elsewhere) and the one million soldiers of Zerah the Ethiopian (*2 Chr.* 14:8).

The figures given by almost all ancient sources are similarly inflated. Flavius Josephus, the first-century Jewish historian who is an otherwise reliable author, supplies mostly fantastic figures when it comes to population estimates. He claims that in 70 CE, during the First Jewish War against Rome, there were 204 villages in the Galilee, the smallest of which numbered 15,000 (*War* 3.43; *Life* 235). This, however, would swell the number of inhabitants in the Galilee in that period to well over three million. It is believed today that at the time the whole country had a population of fewer than one million. Josephus avers that the number of people killed in Jerusalem was 1,100,000 (*War* 5.420)—a figure the city could not possibly have sustained (it must already have been overcrowded, accommodating part of the Roman army).

There are, however, data in Josephus that have the ring of accuracy: the number of the defenders of Jerusalem in 70 CE having been 23,400 (*War* 5.248) and the unrounded numbers and detailed breakdown of troops—how many led by John of Gischala and how many by the Zealots, for example—and their plausible magnitude. Similarly, Josephus's estimate of the number of the inhabitants of Egypt mentioned in the oration of Agrippa II (7,500,000, exclusive of Alexandria) is plausible (*War* 2.385). The reliability of these figures rests on their most probably having been copied from

Roman military records, the *hupomnēmata* (Gk., "commentaries") to which Josephus had access.

The best way to achieve a trustworthy estimate of ancient populations is through a combination of agricultural data, which dictates the carrying capacity of a place, and archaeological data, which helps to estimate population densities.

Estimating Population Size Using Modern Archaeological Data. Western Palestine (modern Israel and the West Bank) is perhaps the most excavated and best-surveyed area in the world. The results of the intensive and extensive surveys and excavations carried out since 1967 enable quite accurate maps of the country to be drawn for certain key chronological periods: 2600 BCE (Broshi and Gophna, 1984); 1800 and 1600 BCE (Broshi and Gophna, 1986); 734 BCE (Broshi and Finkelstein, 1992); and 541 CE (Broshi, 1979). The maximum population ancient Palestine witnessed—about one million inhabitants—was in the year 541, a level not reached again until 1931. That was the heyday of the Byzantine Empire and just one year before the onset of one of the three pandemic plagues recorded in history. It decimated the population of the entire country.

Ancient Palestine. The ability of a given area to support life is its carrying capacity. It is derived from the sum of many factors that limit the amount of food an area can produce. In other words, the carrying capacity of a region is an upper limit. Usually, according to D. J. Greenwood (in W. A. S. Tini, *Nature, Culture, and Human History*, New York, 1977, p. 394), the limiting factors will keep population lower than the theoretical maximum. For ancient Palestine, two ways suggest themselves for estimating carrying capacity: an assessment of its grain-growing capacity and an estimate of its overall food-producing capacity. These methods are based on three assumptions: that annual per capita consumption of food in general and grain products in particular can be calculated; that the country's annual grain-growing capacity can be reckoned; and that Palestine in antiquity was self-sufficient in grain growing and, indeed, in raising all basic commodities but not in refining metals.

Ancient sources, as well as modern parallels, suggest that the annual per capita consumption of ancient Palestine was about 200 kg. Including grain for sowing (20 percent), waste (20 percent), and animal feed (10 percent), the gross consumption reached about 300 kg. It seems that the grain-growing capacity of Palestine is well represented by the harvests of the years 1940–1942. These three years during World War II saw peak harvests, not supplemented with imports. Prices soared and every piece of arable land was cultivated. The 1940–1942 average annual yield of grains (wheat, barley, sorghum, and maize) was 266,411 tons. This amount could feed about 900,000 people.

There is ample evidence to show that ancient Palestine was self-sufficient as far as food production is concerned. Thus, the country was supplying bread to fewer than one million people.

Overall food-production capacity is a quantification method that tries to compute the amount of land needed to feed one person according to the agrotechnical standards of ancient Palestine. Grain was the country's main staple, the source of more than 50 percent of the caloric intake. To produce 300 kg of grain, 0.4 ha (one acre) is needed. With fallow land—a minimum of one-third of the cultivable land—the grain-producing area should reach at least 0.6 ha (1.5 acres).

To supply the other components of the food basket, more area was needed—for vegetables, fruits, legumes, wine, and oil. A certain amount of land also was required for growing fibers for textiles, mostly flax. It is difficult to estimate accurately how much land was needed for these crops, but it seems that 0.4 ha is the bare minimum. Thus, the minimum area necessary to feed one person is one hectare (2.5 acres).

Of the 2,600,000 ha (6,500,000 acres) of Western Palestine, only 937,000 ha are cultivable. For purposes of computation and because a certain amount of arable land has deteriorated in the last thirteen centuries, the number of arable hectares in antiquity can be rounded to one million. Thus, ancient Palestine could have fed some one million people. Although this estimate is lower than most others that are current, it is supported by detailed estimates. Antony Byatt (1973) collected thirteen estimates of the population of ancient Palestine. Only one of them ascribes to Roman Palestine fewer than one million people. The rest run between 1,500,000 and 6,000,000.

Ancient Mesopotamia. The only Near Eastern country other than Israel to benefit from archaeological investigations in assessing demographic history is modern Iraq. A series of reconnaissance projects carried out by Robert McC. Adams and his colleagues between 1956 and 1975, under the auspices of the Oriental Institute of the University of Chicago, covered most of southern Iraq. Adam's work enabled him to draw conclusions about the settlement history of Sumer, Akkad, and later of Babylonia. Ancient Mesopotamia was entirely dependent on vulnerable irrigation systems that can only be maintained by a stable centralized administration. As a result, it suffered more drastic vicissitudes than most Near Eastern countries. Population peaks can be shown for the Late Uruk, Ur III, Neo-Babylonian, and Parthian periods, with marked lows in between, when there was no strong central government. Although Adams refrains from offering absolute population numbers, his data on settlements and their size do enable the development of sound demographic assessments.

[*See also* Agriculture; Ethnoarchaeology; Paleoenvironmental Reconstruction.]

BIBLIOGRAPHY

Adams, Robert McC. *Land behind Baghdad.* Chicago, 1965.
Adams, Robert McC. *Heartland of Cities: Surveys of Ancient Settlement and Land Use on the Central Floodplain of the Euphrates.* Chicago, 1981.
Adams, Robert McC., and Hans J. Nissen. *The Uruk Countryside: The Natural Setting of Urban Societies.* Chicago, 1972.
Broshi, Magen. "The Population of Western Palestine in the Roman-Byzantine Period."*Bulletin of the American Schools of Oriental Research,* no. 236 (Fall 1979): 1–10.
Broshi, Magen. "Methodology of Population Estimates: The Roman Byzantine Period as a Case Study." In *Biblical Archaeology Today, 1990: Proceedings of the Second International Congress on Biblical Archaeology, Jerusalem, June–July 1990,* edited by Avraham Biran and Joseph Aviram. Jerusalem, 1993.
Broshi, Magen, and Israel Finkelstein. "The Population of Palestine in Iron Age II." *Bulletin of the American Schools of Oriental Research,* no. 287 (August 1992): 47–60.
Broshi, Magen, and Ram Gophna. "The Settlements and Population of Palestine during the Early Bronze Age II–III." *Bulletin of the American Schools of Oriental Research,* no. 253 (Winter 1984): 41–53.
Broshi, Magen, and Ram Gophna. "Middle Bronze Age II Palestine: Its Settlements and Population." *Bulletin of the American Schools of Oriental Research,* no. 261 (February 1986): 73–90.
Byatt, Antony. "Josephus and Population Numbers in First Century Palestine." *Palestine Exploration Quarterly* (1973): 51–52.
Stager, Lawrence E. "The Archaeology of the Family in Ancient Israel." *Bulletin of the American Schools of Oriental Research,* no. 260 (November 1985): 1–35.

MAGEN BROSHI

DENON, DOMINIQUE VIVANT (1747–1825), French diplomat, artist, colleague of Napoleon Bonaparte, and founder of the Louvre in Paris. This truly universal man may be considered the first Egyptologist for the detailed and profusely illustrated observations that he published following his participation in the Napoleonic expedition to Egypt (1798–1801). In his fifties and distinguished as a diplomat, art connoisseur, and artist, Denon was one of the more senior and brilliant members of the commission of science and arts attached to the general staff of Napoleon's army of Egypt.

Denon proved to be an energetic explorer and tireless recorder, often working under the most difficult and dangerous conditions as he followed General Desaix's army through Egypt, sketching monuments and recording his impressions in writing. He discovered the zodiac on a ceiling in the temple of Dendera, which the French were the first Europeans to view. Because some of the temples that Denon documented with precision no longer survive, the *Description d'Égypte* and his additional works preserve the only records.

When Bonaparte abandoned his troops in Egypt in August of 1799, he took Denon back to Paris with him. From his large collection of drawings, Denon published his *Voyage dans la Basse et la Haute Égypte* (1802), in two volumes with 141 plates, which appeared twenty years before the Commission of Science and Arts' *Description,* and thus gave to the West the first professional portrayal of the wonders of

Egypt. The book was enormously popular, and went through forty editions, was translated into English and German, and provided the inspiration for the Egyptian revival in architecture and the decorative arts that marked the early nineteenth century.

Denon was appointed director general of museums by Napoleon and went on to be the founder of what is now the Louvre. He played a major role in forming its collections when he accompanied Napoleon on subsequent campaigns in Europe giving advice on the choice of artistic spoils from vanquished cities.

BIBLIOGRAPHY

Dawson, Warren R., and Eric P. Uphill. *Who Was Who in Egyptology.* 2d rev. ed. London, 1972.
Denon, Dominique Vivant. *Voyage dans la basse et la haute Égypte* (1802). Paris, 1990.
Nowinski, Judith. *Baron Dominique Vivant Denon, 1747–1825.* Rutherford, N.J., 1970.

BARBARA SWITALSKI LESKO

DER, TELL ED-, site located in northern Babylonia, halfway between the Tigris and Euphrates Rivers, 25 km (15.5 mi.) south of Baghdad (33°6′ N, 44°18′ E). Tell ed-Der covers an area of about 50 ha (123.5 acres). The site was probably founded slightly before the Ur III period (2112–2004 BCE), but its name at that early stage in its history is not known. However, the information yielded from the archives found in the area its excavators call operation E ascertain its identification with the Old Babylonian town of Sippar-Amnānum that appears in written sources during the reign of Sinmuballit (1812–1793 BCE); on the other hand, Dominique Charpin (1992) has shown that the names of Sippar-Amnānum, Sippar-Annunītum, Sippar-rabûm and Sippar-dūrum probably designate the same town. Later on, only Sippar-Anunītu is cited by the Assyrian king Tiglath-Pileser I (1114–1076 BCE) among his conquests—the name that remained until the Persian period (539–333 BCE). The meaning of *Der* as "cloister" or "enclosure" has not yet been established with certainty.

DER, TELL ED-. Figure 1. *Operation E.* View of the house of Ur-Utu, chief dirge singer of the goddess Annunitum. (Courtesy H. Gasche)

In 1891, E. A. W. Budge drew many thousands of clay tablets out of the mounds at ed-Der. Three years later, Victor Scheil made a more modest find but presumed that ancient Sippar-Amnānum lay hidden underneath the ruins. Walter Andrae and Julius Jordan visited the site in 1927 and drew the first precise plans; it was not until 1941 that excavations were organized, by Taha Baqir and Mohammad Ali Mustafa under Iraqi government auspices. Since 1970 a Belgian team directed by Léon De Meyer and Hermann Gasche has systematically investigated the site. In the area the excavators call operation A an area with private houses was selected for stratigraphic analysis: seventeen successive building stages are represented by some 6 m of cultural debris, from the twenty-first to the end of the eighteenth centuries BCE. The considerable information gathered is featured in various synthetic studies (e.g., urbanization, domestic architecture, graves, pottery, terra-cotta figurines, texts).

The results of the work undertaken on the imposing peripheral levee (operation B) were unexpected. This impressive mass does not hide a traditional city wall, as had been anticipated, but an earthen dike (with a width of a least 45 m; see De Meyer, Gasche, and Paepe, 1971, plan 1), whose function was to protect the town from flooding. It is known, however, that Sippar-Amnānum was encircled by a real fortification wall because King Samsuiluna (1749–1712 BCE) mentions it in a letter. This wall can now be identified with a structure 6 m wide that appeared under the slightly later earthen dike mentioned above. Archaeological evidence has ascertained that the wall was destroyed by floods and then replaced by the earthen dike that, prior to the Kassite period (1595–1155 BCE), was raised several times.

The most important discoveries were made in operation E and came from the house of Ur-Utu (see figure 1), chief dirge singer *(gala.mah)* of Annunitum, the main goddess of Sippar-Amnānum. More than two thousand tablets give invaluable information not only concerning social, economic, and religious life but also about the mutable commercial activities of Ur-Utu, a highly placed religious dignitary at that time. Ur-Utu's house was burned in 1629 BCE, that being the date of the latest text found in the archives. The ruins were totally covered with a sandy sediment, which indicates a period of abandonment of the area until it was reoccupied in about 1400 BCE. Installations from that reoccupation were cleared in operation E3, where the most recent remains are probably from the time of Šagarakti-Šuriaš (1245–1233 BCE).

The excavations at Tell ed-Der have not yet revealed material from the Neo-Babylonian period. The question, then, is where the Temple of Annunitu, commemorated in an inscription of Nabonidus (555–539 BCE) as the work of that king, is to be found.

[*See also* Babylonians; Cuneiform; Mesopotamia, *article on* Ancient Mesopotamia; Sippar; *and* Tablet.]

BIBLIOGRAPHY

Charpin, Dominique. "Sippar: Deux villes jumelles." *Revue d'Assyriologie et d'Archéologie Orientale* 82 (1988): 13–32. Essential study of the toponyms in the area of Sippar in the Old Babylonian period.

Charpin, Dominique. "Le point sur les deux Sippar." *Nouvelles Assyriologiques Brèves et Utilitaires*, no. 114 (1992): 84–85. Supplement to the aforementioned study.

De Meyer, Léon, Hermann Gasche, and Roland Paepe. *Tell ed-Dēr I*. Louvain, 1971. Preliminary reports on the first excavation season at Tell ed-Der (Old Babylonian period).

De Meyer, Léon, ed. *Tell ed-Dēr*. Vols. 2 and 4. Louvain, 1978–1984. Progress reports including reports of excavations, publication of texts, cylinder seals, metal vessels and metal analysis, studies on regional geomorphology, fauna and botanical remains (Ur III, Isin-Larsa, and Old Babylonian periods).

Gasche, Hermann. *La Babylonie au 17e siècle avant notre ère: Approche archéologique, problèmes et perspectives*. Ghent, 1989. The house of Ur-Utu, gala.mah of Annunītum, followed by a study of the declining Old Babylonian period.

Gasche, Hermann, et al. "Tell ed-Dēr, 1985–1987: Les vestiges méso-babyloniens." *Northern Akkad Project Reports* 6 (1991): 9–94. Reports on the Kassite remains found at Tell ed-Der, including the pottery, epigraphic finds, and the fauna.

Lerberghe, Karel van, and Gabriela Voet. *Sippar-Amnānum: The Ur-Utu Archive*. Vol. 1. Ghent, 1991. Publication of 106 texts found in the Ur-Utu archives, with a study of the seal impressions and sealing practices.

LÉON DE MEYER

DEUTSCHE ORIENT-GESELLSCHAFT.

Founded in 1898 and charged with conducting excavations in the ancient Near East, the Deutsche Orient-Gesellschaft (DOG) carried out numerous projects under their direction of such noted archaeologists as Robert Koldewey, Walter Andrae, and Rudolf Borchardt. These include Babylon (1899–1917), Aššur (1902–1913), Jericho (1908/09), Abu Sir (1902–1907), Amarna (1911–1914), Boğazköy (since 1906), Uruk-Warka (beginning in 1912/13), and at many other sites. This period of active fieldwork came to end with World War I, but some of the research was later continued in cooperation with the Deutsches Archäologisches Institut (German Archaeological Institute). The necessary funds were contributed by the more than one thousand members of the DOG, the German emperor, and the government of Prussia.

The DOG's most important sponsor was James Simon, a Jewish merchant from Berlin, who donated the finds from Amarna to the Egyptian Museum in Berlin. Publication of the excavation results began in 1900 with a new series, Wissenschaftliche Veröffentlichungen der Deutschen Orient-Gesellschaft, edited by the secretary of the society. More than fifty volumes appeared between 1901 and 1936, when Bruno Güterbock held the office. After 1933, the society lost most of its members; in 1949, it was restituted and Andrae was elected president. Publication of the rich harvest from DOG's early excavations continued with thirty volumes of the Wissenschaftliche Veröffentlichungen and a new series, Abhandlungen, was established.

Independent fieldwork began again in 1968, with excavations at Habuba Kabira and Munbaqa in Syria, under the presidency of Ernst Heinrich. This work continues, as does publication of the results and the finds from earlier projects. Of special significance is the rich material from Aššur housed in the Vorderasiatisches Museum in Berlin, which is in an advanced stage of preparation for publication. Recent papers appear in the periodical *Mitteilungen der Deutschen Orient-Gesellschaft*. Today the society has about eight hundred members and is actively engaged in scholarly work concerning the ancient Near East, with an emphasis on Mesopotamia and northern Syria.

[*See also the biographies of Andrae and Koldewey.*]

BIBLIOGRAPHY

Nagel, Wolfram. "Die Deutsche Orientgesellschaft: Rückblick 1976." *Mitteilungen der Deutschen Orientgesellschaft* 108 (1976): 53–71.
Schuler, Einar von. "Siebzig Jahre Deutsche Orientgesellschaft." *Mitteilungen der Deutschen Orientgesellschaft* 100 (1968): 6–21.

VOLKMAR FRITZ

DEUTSCHER PALÄSTINA-VEREIN.

By 1876 the need for a scientific society to coordinate and support the efforts of German scholars exploring Palestine—Arabists, archaeologists, geographers, historians, Orientalists, theologians—became urgent. In addition the religious and scientific interests of scholars and scientific societies in Palestine were in competition. The initiative to establish the Deutscher Palästina-Verein (German Palestine Society) finally came from the Basel rector Carl Ferdinand Zimmermann (d. 1889). He met at Bâle with the biblical scholar Emil Kautzsch and the Arabist Albert Socin, who was at Tübingen in summer 1876 to discuss founding a Palestine society. Their recommendation was then sent to fifteen distinguished scholars who might serve as its governing committee. The three men presented their plans to the members of the Deutsche Morgenländische Gesellschaft (German Oriental Society) that same year. The conceptualization of the future society was refined and a new proposal was sent to about seventy scholars in Germany, Austria, Switzerland, and Russia requesting support. In 1877 Kautzsch, Socin, and Zimmermann distributed a proposal to the general public bearing the signatures of fifty-two respected individuals. Within a short time about fifty members enrolled in the new society. The three initiators held a meeting of the constituents at Wiesbaden, on 28 September 1877, the Deutscher Verein zur Erforschung Palästinas (German Society for the Exploration of Palestine) was formally founded; rules for the society were adopted and a committee of nineteen and an executive committee of five established.

The society's goals are to advance all aspects of the scientific exploration of Palestine and to make those activities accessible to a wide audience. Their aims were to be achieved through the publication of a journal and by scientific research in Palestine, be carried out by a German field expedition. To that end, a portion of the membership fees and other monies would contribute to an expedition fund. The legal seat of the society was to be at Leipzig. From 1877 to 1903 the society's affairs were managed by the first members of the executive committee: Hermann Guthe, Kautzsch, Otto Kersten, Socin, and Zimmermann. Beginning in 1903, one member of the committee served as chair: Kautzsch (1903–1910); Guthe, (1911–1925); Albrecht Alt (1925–1950); Martin Noth (1952–1964); Otto Plöger (1964–1974); Herbert Donner (1975–1992); and Helga Weippert (since 1993). Membership remains relatively constant: in 1879 it was 268; from 1911 onward it was more than 400; in 1920 it dwindled to 273 but reached a new peak in 1929 of 391; it fell again to 255 in 1942 and to 114 in 1964. Since then membership has climbed to 360 (1995).

The founders of the society planned a journal, the *Zeitschrift des Deutschen Palästina Vereins* (*ZDPV*), to report on topographic, ethnographic, historical, numismatic, epigraphic, and archaeological problems as well as on subjects in the natural sciences (e.g., geology, climatology) relevant to the study of Palestine and its neighboring countries—articles that would advance knowledge of the Bible. It was also to contain critical summaries of relevant foreign scholarly literature and statistical and political news about the conditions of life in modern Palestine. The first issue appeared in April 1878; volume 110 appeared in 1994. The editors were Guthe (1878–1896); Immanuel Benzinger (1897–1902); Carl Steuernagel (1903–1928); Noth (1929–1964); and Arnulf Kuschke (1965–1974). Since 1974 Siegfried Mittmann and Manfred Weippert have been co-editors; Weippert was succeeded by Dieter Vieweger in 1994.

News about the society and reports on different general subjects were published separately from 1895 to 1912 as *Mitteilungen und Nachrichten des Deutschen Vereins zur Erforschung Palästinas* (edited by Guthe until 1901 and then by Gustav Hölscher). In addition, from 1914 to 1927 the society published *Das Land der Bibel: gemeinverständliche Hefte zur Palästinakunde*, a more popular series (edited by Hölscher and then by Peter Thomsen). To supplement the *ZDPV*, a new series, *Abhandlungen des deutschen Palästina-Vereins*, was established in 1969 to publish longer monographs.

Another prominent institution, the German Protestant Institute of Archaeology of the Holy Land, directed from 1902 to 1917 by Gustav Dalman, is organized and financed by the German Protestant Churches; it is completely independent of the German Palestine Society, but a close cooperation exists between them and they share a roster of prominent members, mostly biblical scholars and theologians. [*See*

Deutches Evangelisches Institut für Altertumswissenschaft des Heiligen Landes.]

The history of the German Palestine Society can be divided into four periods, with the activities of major figures often belonging to more than one of them.

1877–1918. As documented in the *ZDPV* and other publications, the society shaped the various aspects of the new discipline of *Palästinakunde* (the historical geography and archaeology of Palestine). Research on the architecture and topography of Jerusalem and its surroundings was carried out by such pioneers at Conrad Schick (1822–1902) who, in 1880, discovered the Siloam Tunnel inscription (*ZDPV* 3, 1880): Schick published about fifty articles in the *ZDPV*. [See Siloam Tunnel Inscription; *and the biography of Schick*.] In 1881 Guthe conducted the first excavations on behalf of the society. His work on Jerusalem's southeastern hill (the Ophel) was carried out on a small scale, before systematic excavation methods had been developed (*ZDPV* 5, 1882). [*See* Jerusalem.] Gottlieb Schumacher (1857–1925), the architect and cartographer, began surveying parts of Transjordan in 1884 on behalf of the society; between 1906 and 1924 he published the maps the work produced. From 1903 to 1905 Schumacher directed the society's first (and last) large-scale excavation at Megiddo, except the fall season of 1903, which was led by Benzinger (Silberman, 1982, p. 169). [*See* Megiddo; *and the biographies of Schumacher and Benzinger*.] Max Blanckenhorn, a geologist, investigated the geology of Palestine; beginning in 1894 he installed a series of weather bureaus for the society and published the results of his observations (e.g., temperature, rainfall, wind) in the *ZDPV* annually. In 1901 the society underwrote the drawing of the mosaic map of Madaba discovered in 1884. [*See* Madaba.] This was completed by the Jerusalem architect Paul Palmer and was subsequently published in 1906 by him and Guthe. The excavations of Ernst Sellin (1902–1904) at Taʿanach, with Schumacher's temporary assistance, and at Jericho (1907–1909) with Carl Watzinger, as well as his preliminary work at Shechem (1913–1914), belong to this pioneering period. In particular, the exactness of the descriptions in the report on Jericho (1913) makes it still useful. [*See* Taʿanach; Jericho; Shechem; *and the biography of Sellin*.] The research of Heinrich Kohl and Watzinger on synagogues in Galilee (published in 1916) represent another aspect of the discipline, now also covering the New Testament period. Gustaf Dalman's research on topography and ethnology was intensive during this period as well. Already in 1908, 1913, and 1915–1917 Albrecht Alt worked in Jerusalem. [*See the biographies of Watzinger, Dalman, and Alt*.]

1919–1932. In spite of Germany's political and economic difficulties after World War I, the interdisciplinary, interreligious, and international cooperation of the society and its foreign members grew constantly. A new generation came into office: Alt was elected to the society's executive committee in 1923 and became chairman in 1925; Noth became editor of the *ZDPV* in 1929 (see above). Whereas the society's only project in Palestine was its series of weather bureaus, the Deutsches Evangelisches Institut in Jerusalem (see above), directed by Alt from 1921 to 1923, gained new importance: German scholars assembled there to continue their research. From 1924 to 1931, Alt conducted an annual *lehrkurs* (seminar) for a period of three or four months. He placed more emphasis on the history of Palestine than on ethnology, as Dalman had done. During field trips, reconnaissance of small areas was carried out by thorough surveys and ceramic sherds at settlement sites were collected and read as basic sources for the history and patterns of those settlements. The stress Alt placed on the close connection between research on the land (archaeology through survey and excavation) and critical readings of the biblical text (exegesis) in reconstructing a history of Palestine was the main contribution he (and his generation) made to the discipline of biblical archaeology.

Other major figures working in Palestine during this period include Sellin at Shechem (1926–1927, 1932 and 1934); Kurt Galling at Shechem with Sellin (1926) and at Tell Beit Mirsim with William Foxwell Albright (1930). Joachim Jeremias a New Testament scholar did research in Jerusalem (1931, 1932); and Noth, scholarship student at the institute in 1925, was a guest there of the *lehrkurs* (1931, 1933). This group of distinguished scholars subsequently published important books or articles based on the research they developed during their respective stays in Palestine.

1933–1964. Hitler's rise to power in 1933 was very soon felt by Alt and others as a danger to the work of the society (and the institute) at home and in Palestine. Because the Nazi authorities did not make sufficient foreign exchange available to the institute and because of the political disturbances in Palestine, Alt was no longer able to offer the *lehrkurs*. In addition, he and a few other scholars could travel to Palestine only sporadically and work there for only some months respectively doing their research: Alt was there in 1933 and 1935, also taking some field trips. From July to September 1935 Galling continued Dalman's research on the necropolis in Jerusalem and finished it (*Palästina Jahrbuch* 32 [1936]: 73–101); he took some short field trips in 1937 and 1938. His *Biblisches Reallexikon* was published 1937. In it, for the first time, mainly archaeological findings were used to describe the subjects of the entries, a first attempt to develop within the discipline of biblical archaeology the topic of "systematic archaeology." [*See the biography of Galling*.] The beginning of World War II put a stop to research in Palestine, only the *ZDPV* was still published, from volume 62 (1939) to volume 67 (1944). In 1943 the society lost its entire archive in Leipzig: all its files and stock of publications from 1877 onward, its library, and its ethnological and archaeological collections. From 1945 to 1952 the society's activities were—out of political and even legal reasons—completely suspended and therefore the *ZDPV* could not be published. Instead from 1946 onward Noth edited three issues of *Beiträge zur biblischen Landes- und Alterumskunde*, 1951, which was counted as volume 68 of the *ZDPV*. By 1950 the society, whose legal seat was still at Leipzig, was liquidated by the East German authorities, but on 31 July 1952, it was reestablished in West Germany, in Bonn. Noth, still editor of the *ZDPV*, also became its chairman. [*See the biography of Noth.*] After that the *ZDPV* has been published again continuously from volume 69 (1953) onward. Slowly, studies in *Palästinakunde*, mainly by the above-named scholars, began again. The *lehrkurs* at the institute, then located in the Old City of Jerusalem (Jordan), was resumed in 1953, the first conducted by Galling.

Since 1965. The *ZDPV*, again a journal of international repute, is publishing more articles by foreign scholars. In 1964 Noth was nominated director of the institute in Jerusalem. However, expectations for furthering *Palästinakunde* were destroyed by his early death in 1968. Since 1970 young German scholars have begun taking part in excavations: Kuschke, Mittmann, Martin Metzger, Ute Lux, and August Strobel in Lebanon and Jordan; and Volkman Fritz and Diethelm Conrad in Israel. The society now organizes symposia, the first two of which took place in 1977 and 1982. Since 1988 they have been held every two years. It is through these activities that the German Palestine Society and its members hope to make a special contribution to *Palästinakunde*, or biblical archaeology, further developing the best traditions of Alt and Noth.

[*See also* Biblical Archaeology.]

BIBLIOGRAPHY

To date, no comprehensive history of the society has been published. Because the archive of the society was destroyed in 1943, all facts had to be extracted from the society's publications: *Zeitschrift des Deutschen Palästina-Vereins*, vols. 1–67 (Leipzig, 1878–1944/45), and vols. 69/110 (Wiesbaden, 1953–1994); *Mitteilungen und Nachrichten* (Leipzig, 1895–1912); and from *Palästinajahrbuch des Deutschen Evangelischen Instituts für Altertumswissenschaft des Heiligen Landes zu Jerusalem* (Leipzig, 1905–1941). The latter is the organ of the institute, with news on its activities and important articles on results of research. The reader may also consult the following:

Alt, Albrecht. "Protokoll der 24. Generalversammlung des Deutschen Vereins zur Erforschung Palästinas (23. August 1928 in Bonn)." *Zeitschrift des Deutschen Palästina-Vereins* 51 (1928): 302. Remarks on the fifty-year-old society.

Kautzsch, E. "Vorwort." *Zeitschrift des Deutschen Palästina-Vereins* 1 (1878): 1–9. Preface to the first volume of *ZDPV*, containing details about the founding of the society.

Silberman, Neil Asher. *Digging for God and Country: Exploration, Archaeology, and the Secret Struggle for the Holy Land, 1799–1917.* New York, 1982. Explores the connections between religiously motivated scientific exploration of Palestine in the nineteenth century and the political struggles among rival European powers for dominance in the region.

Steuernagel, Carl. "Ein Rückblick auf 50 Jahre der ZDPV." *Zeitschrift des Deutschen Palästina-Vereins* 51 (1928): 1–4. Review of the main stages of the then fifty-year-old journal.

Zobel, H.-J. "Geschichte des Deutschen Evangelischen Instituts für Altertumswissenschaft des Heiligen Landes von den Anfängen bis zum Zweiten Weltkrieg." *Zeitschrift des Deutschen Palästina-Vereins* 97 (1981): 1–11. The first short history of the German Protestant Institute of Archaeology, from its founding to World War II, with comparative assessments of Dalman and Alt.

DIETHELM CONRAD

DEUTSCHES ARCHÄOLOGISCHES INSTITUT, ABTEILUNG DAMASKUS.

The founding of the Deutsches Archäologisches Institut (DAI; German Archaeological Institute) in Damascus in 1980 came out of the long-standing tradition of German archaeological research in Syria. The institute, which opened in 1981, works in close cooperation with the Syrian Directorate General of Antiquities and Museums. The institute supports the investigation of all archaeologically relevant periods in Syria and its neighboring regions. At present, the emphasis of its research is on the Late Bronze Age, Roman, Byzantine, and Islamic periods. In addition to numerous small survey and conservation projects, work is underway at the following sites: at Late Bronze Age Tell Bazi at Tishrin (rescue excavations directed by Berthold Einwag); Roman (first–third centuries CE) temple complexes in the Hauran (at Atil, Brekeh, Mushennef, Qanawat, as-Sanamain, directed by Stefan Freyberger); a Roman (second–third centuries CE) temple complex in Middle Syria, (Temple of Esriye, with a survey of the adjoining settlement, directed by Rüdiger Gogräfe); a third-century temple grave at Palmyra (no. 36, a joint project of the DAI and the Antiquities Administration of Palmyra, directed by Andreas Schmidt-Colinet and Khaled al-As'ad); the first–sixth-century limes on the Middle Euphrates River (Qseir es-Seile/Tetrapyrgium and Sura, directed by Tilo Ulbert and Michaela Konrad); Rusafa/Sergiopolis (first–thirteenth-century martyr's city of St. Sergius, directed by Ulbert); ar-Raqqa, the eighth-century palace city of the 'Abbasid caliph Harun al-Rashid (rescue excavations directed by Michael Meinecke until his death); and the fourteenth-century Hammam Mangak at Bosra (restoration and construction of a small Islamic museum, a joint project of the DAI and the Antiquities Administration of Bosra, directed by Meinecke and Riad al-Muqdad).

The institute houses a specialized library, which is open to the public and currently contains about eight thousand volumes, as well as a photo library with about twenty-five thousand negatives and a slide library. Its publications are *Damaszener Mitteilungen* (*DaM*) a periodical with essays by international researchers covering the institute's entire field of activity—so far volumes 1 (1983) through 6 (1993) have appeared; and *Damaszener Forschungen (DaF)* a monograph series, of which five volumes have appeared.

[*See also* Bosra; Palmyra; Raqqa, ar-; *and* Rusafa.]

TILO ULBERT
Translated from German by Susan I. Schiedel

BIBLIOGRAPHY

Bittel, Kurt. *Beiträge zur Geschichte des Deutschen Archäologischen Instituts 1929 bis 1979.* Das Deutsche Archäologische Institut, Geschichte und Dokumente, 3. Mainz, 1979. See pages 65–91.
"Jahresbericht des Deutsches Archäologisches Instituts 1989." *Archäologischer Anzeiger* (1990): 590–600.

WOLF KOENIGS

DEUTSCHES ARCHÄOLOGISCHES INSTITUT, ABTEILUNG ISTANBUL.

One of the nine branches of the German Archaeological Institute (DAI) in Berlin in countries in the Mediterranean basin and the Near East, the institute in Istanbul was founded in 1929 to organize German archaeological research in Turkey. That research had begun with surveys and excavations in Anatolia in 1828 by F. E. Schulz, A. D. Mordtmann, Heinrich Schliemann, Karl Humann, Theodor Wiegand, Wilhelm Dörpfeld, and many others. As a result of the interest the newly established Republic of Turkey took in the country's history, the goals of the DAI in Istanbul were defined in a much wider sense than just archaeology. They comprise research and publications on all the cultures of Anatolia from prehistoric times until the end of the Ottoman Empire. The DAI's staff of thirty in Istanbul includes eight German scholars in prehistorical and classical archaeology, Byzantine studies, the history of architecture, and turcology. The institute cooperates with Turkish universities in research and teaching and provides a library of about 55,000 volumes, including 245 scholarly periodicals.

An archive of about 150,000 photographs of archaeological objects and sites in Anatolia also includes a collection of negatives and prints from 1860 to 1920. Under the auspices of the institute, prominent scholars have made considerable contributions to what is known of Anatolia's history and culture: Kurt Bittel in prehistory and the Hittites; Rudolf Naumann in Hittite and classical architecture; Martin Schede in classical archaeology and architecture; Alfons Maria Schneider in the history of Byzantium; Wolfgang Müller-Wiener in the topography of Istanbul; Paul Wittek in Ottoman history; and Kurt Erdmann in Islamic art.

Currently, the institute is involved in archaeological excavations and to some extent in restoration at the Hittite capital city of Boğzköy/Hattuša, the ancient city of Miletus, the classical cities of Aizanoi, Miletus, Pergamon, and Priene, and the classical sanctuary at Didyma. In Istanbul, topographic surveys and research on single monuments have always been part of the institute's program.

The institute publishes the yearbook *Istanbuler Mitteilungen* (Tübingen, 1966–) with occasional monographs and the series of *Istanbuler Forschungen* (Berlin, 1932–). Some of its reports appear in the *Archäologischer Anzeiger*, Berlin.

[*See also* Boğazköy; Didyma; Miletus; Pergamon; Priene; *and the biography of Schliemann.*]

DEUTSCHES EVANGELISCHES INSTITUT FÜR ALTERTUMSWISSENSCHAFT DES HEILIGEN LANDES.

The German Protestant Institute for Archaeology of the Holy Land, located in Jerusalem, was founded in 1900 by Germany's Protestant churches and has been sponsored by them ever since. The first director, Gustaf Dalman (1902–1917), initiated a wide range of activities—his own major fields having been the ethnography of Palestine, tombs in the vicinity of Jerusalem, and Petra. During the British Mandate, Albrecht Alt was appointed director; Alt did not actually reside in Jerusalem but, conducted the famous summer courses about aspects of his research in historical geography in the country. The institute was closed during World War II but was reopened by Martin Noth in 1964. After Noth's untimely death in 1968, Ute Lux served as director until 1982. Lux excavated at Gadara (Umm Qeis). A branch of the institute was founded in Amman in 1973. The institute in Jerusalem was directed, from 1982 until 1992, by August Strobel, who undertook several excavation projects in Jordan. Volkmar Fritz, appointed director in 1994, is continuing the tradition of geographic research and archaeological projects.

From the beginning, the work of the institute was handicapped by the lack of its own building. Then, in 1982, a house in the compound of the German Augusta Victoria Compound on Mt. Scopus was made available as the institute's center. A board of trustees representing German churches and theological faculties is responsible for its budget and staffing.

Between 1905 and 1941, the institute published a yearbook, *Palästina Jahrbuch*, founded by Dalman and later edited by Alt. In 1989, Strobel revived it as the *Jahrbuch des Deutschen Evangelischen Instituts für Altertumswissenschaft des Heilingen Landes.* Articles on the activities of the institute also appear in the *Zeitschrift des Deutschen Palästina-Vereins (ZDPV).*

[*See also* Historical Geography; Jerusalem; Petra; Umm Qeis; *and the biographies of Alt, Dalman, and Noth.*]

VOLKMAR FRITZ

DE VAUX, ROLAND. *See* Vaux, Roland de.

DEVELOPMENT AND ARCHAEOLOGY.

Nowhere has the dialogue between the past and the present had a greater impact on current economic, political, and religious realities than in the modern nation-states of the ancient Near East. There, the past is visible in nearly every field, village, town, and city, often creating a sense of identity and continuity, or in some cases alienation, for its modern inhabitants. Throughout all periods of time, the past was visible as ruins above the surface, inspiring curiosity and speculation from travelers and pilgrims, who saw in them their own religious and political heritage, and from local inhabitants, who saw the ruins as landmarks and as part of the natural landscape, often connected with local legend or holding traditional significance.

Since the nineteenth century, archaeological excavation, or the systematic recovery and recording of ancient ruins, has revealed the concealed past. During the period of domination of the Near East by foreign powers and until World War II, most archaeological investigations were directed and sponsored by individuals or private institutions from the industrialized Western world who had religious or academic research goals; they, in turn, were often encouraged by national or government institutions having an imperialistic agenda in the Near East. The excavations were almost exclusively financed by private or foreign government funds and were initiated because of a site's historic or biblical significance—Jerusalem, Megiddo, Beth-Shean, Samaria, and Jericho in Palestine. [See Jerusalem; Megiddo; Beth-Shean; Samaria; Jericho.] However, during the last half of the twentieth century, with the creation of independent nation-states and their increasing economic prosperity, locally directed and locally funded excavations often outnumber foreign expeditions. [See Nationalism and Archaeology.]

Today, archaeology is financially accountable to economic forces. Private and government agencies concerned with conservation and the presentation of public sites employ large numbers of trained archaeologists and are keen to promote contract archaeology connected with land development. Fewer and fewer sites are being excavated purely for research purposes: they are being excavated because of their impending destruction or their commercial, national, or touristic value.

A recent phenomenon is the growing influx of foreign tourism to the region of the ancient Near East as a result not only of the romantic appeal of its great cultures and their religious significance, but to the open borders resulting from peace treaties between Arab nations and Israel. The massive rise in revenues from foreign tourism has added incentive to preserving and presenting ancient ruins: the past is now understood to be a valuable natural resource. The use of archaeology to encourage tourism and economic development in an underdeveloped town or region has made it a tool for solving social and economic problems, as well.

Thus, archaeological excavation for the sake of tourism is an impetus to development, and development creates a need for more archaeological work in the form of salvage excavation. Conflicting needs exist however: excavation, preservation, and publication costs compete for funds with construction and development and the desires of local populations. This competition often forces difficult compromises between economic profit and the ideal of preserving the past.

Impact of the Past. Although development affects archaeological remains and historic buildings throughout the world, in the Near East the situation is especially complex because multilayered, or stratified, tells characterize many sites. The overlay of periods, cultures, and peoples requires choosing which part of the past is to be preserved: whether the Hittites, Canaanites, Egyptians, Philistines, Israelites, Assyrians, Phoenicians, Babylonians, Persians, Greeks, Romans, Arabs, Crusaders, Mamluks, Ottoman Turks, or Palestinians (both Jewish and Arab) are to be highlighted on the personal, political, or economic criteria of the body within the society that chooses to initiate a project. In short, the "victor" writes and interprets the past.

Economic development and archaeology have been especially intertwined in modern Egypt. Under colonial rule, Egypt experienced massive looting of its ancient treasures, particularly by European explorers, conquerors, and scholars. Following independence from British colonial rule, many Egyptians closely identified with the glories of pharaonic Egypt—most notably during the governments of Gamal Abdel Nasser and Anwar Sadat. Today, however, Islamic fundamentalists view the pharaohs as the evil oppressors they have been portrayed as in Islamic literature and Muslim tradition. It is the ancient monuments of the pharaohs, visited by millions of tourists each year, that provide one of Egypt's most important sources of foreign currency. The significance of tourism generated by the archaeological treasures of Egypt and the vulnerability of this source of income are illustrated by the attacks on tourists by Islamic fundamentalist groups attempting to influence political developments.

Ancient Nubia, located in modern southern Egypt, is the site of perhaps the best-known international archaeological rescue operation of the twentieth century. [See Nubia.] In the 1960s, the Aswan High Dam and Lake Nasser were created in this region of Upper Egypt, where the New Kingdom pharaoh Rameses II constructed numerous rock-cut temples. As a result of the construction, a number of those monuments were removed and reconstructed at different sites, following an appeal by the United Nations Educational, Scientific, and Cultural Organization (UNESCO) to its member states to assist in a rescue operation. At Abu Simbel, the site of the most spectacular temples, the temple facades and walls were dismantled and re-sited next to Lake Nasser. Today, these temples are one of Egypt's most popular tourist spots. [*See* Abu Simbel.]

Ironically, the very source for much of Egypt's economic development also is the greatest threat to its future: Egyptian authorities have become increasingly concerned with conserving the country's treasures—its pyramids, sphinx, and several of the decorated New Kingdom tombs at ancient Thebes. The tomb of Nefertari has been the subject of an extensive renovation and conservation project by the Egyptian Antiquities Organization and the Getty Conservation Institute in California. Now reopened, only a limited number of tourists are allowed to view the tomb, under carefully controlled conditions.

During the 1970s, Carthage, an important Phoenician and Roman port located near Tunis, the modern capital of Tunisia, was the focus of a second international campaign commissioned by UNESCO. Rapid urban and tourist development along the Tunisian coast was threatening the ancient remains of Carthage. With the cooperation of the Institut National d'Archéologie et d'Art, the Tunisian authority responsible for antiquities, and under the aegis of UNESCO, international teams were invited to assist in the excavation and presentation of the city's archaeology. Ten foreign missions participated in the Save Carthage Project in the 1970s and early 1980s. They were required, in addition to funding the excavations and their publication, to finance its touristic presentation. Today, Carthage appears on the World Heritage List and is a national park. [*See* Carthage.]

In the Republic of Turkey, considerable funding has been allotted to excavating Neolithic and Bronze Age sites in Asia Minor, especially ancient Hittite sites, with an eye toward highlighting Turkey's glorious non-Islamic past. [*See* Hittites.] More recently, with the massive growth of tourism, especially along Turkey's western coast, the focus has shifted to the splendors of classical Turkey in the Hellenistic and Roman periods: Ephesus, Pamukale, Aphrodisias, Sardis, and Pergamon have been extensively excavated and restored for tourism, completely transforming the economic base and development of many villages and towns, such as Kusadasi, Bodrum/Halikarnassos, Marmaris, and Antalia. [*See* Ephesus; Aphrodisias; Sardis; Pergamon; Halikarnassos.]

Since achieving independence in 1960, Cyprus has also had to contend with the pressures of local development, especially following the 1974 partition that divided the island into two sections, a Turkish enclave in the north and a Greek Cypriot one in the south. [*See* Cyprus.] This resulted in a migration of Greek refugees to the south and compounded pressures on the island's infrastructure. During the 1970s and 1980s, Cyprus's rapidly developing economy encouraged private, commercial, and government construction. In addition to the needs generated by an increased population, tourism to the south (especially in Limassol and Paphos)

demanded rapid development of the coastal cities. [*See* Paphos.] During the course of construction activities, a number of significant sites requiring salvage excavation were revealed. Kalavasos-*Ayios Dhimitrios* (an important Late Bronze Age settlement located between Nicosia and Limassol), Skales (an Iron Age cemetery near Palaipaphos), and Amathus (a Phoenician settlement east of Limassol) have undergone emergency salvage excavations by both the Cypriot Department of Antiquities and foreign expeditions. [*See* Kalavasos; Amathus.]

The premiere site and major tourist attraction on Cyprus, Nea-Paphos, was the capital of ancient Cyprus during the Hellenistic and Roman periods and played an important role in the spread of Christianity. The archaeological site, the only open space in an otherwise overdeveloped area, is known for its richly decorated mosaic pavements dating to the Roman period. [*See* Mosaics.] The site, which since 1980 has appeared on UNESCO's World Heritage List, has become a symbol of Greek Cypriot cultural heritage for its modern inhabitants, especially since the division of the island. Today, Nea-Paphos is a major source of revenue and economic development for modern Paphos.

Jordan, a region largely undeveloped and unexcavated until the 1970s, is now a focus of increasing archaeological exploration and economic development. In 1987, the Jordanian government adopted an organized approach to the problem of archaeological heritage and economic activities, combining governmental, private, and academic agencies and organizations into a cooperative program referred to as the Jordan Cultural Resource Management (CRM) Project. It is supported by the Department of Antiquities of Jordan, the American Center of Oriental Research (ACOR), and the United States Agency for International Development (USAID). [*See* American Center of Oriental Research.] Its goals include encouraging communication and coordination among the departments, organizations, and agencies involved in preserving Jordan's cultural heritage and developing its economy; assisting in salvage excavations at endangered sites; and training and educating professional staff—local and international members of the archaeological community. CRM contributed to the development of a computerized database for ancient sites in Jordan: the Jordan Antiquities Database and Information System (JADIS), designed to assist in planning the future development and protection of cultural resources. Initially, the CRM project focused on salvage excavations—especially in the rapidly growing metropolis of Amman, but in areas outside the capital city as well—and on cultural resource management. [*See* Amman.] In the 1990s, USAID funding of archaeological activities in Jordan shifted from rescue excavations and cultural resource management to tourist-oriented projects, such as those at Aila (the ancient Islamic port of ʿAqaba), restoration of the Amman Citadel, the Madaba Urban Development Project, the Umm Qeis/Gadara Museum, the Pella rest stop, and the Petra Church Project. [*See* 'Aqaba; Madaba; Umm Qeis; Pella; Petra.*]

Antiquities in Lebanon, a country devastated by civil war from 1975 to 1990, were not only damaged during hostilities but were victims of large-scale looting. During the chaos that reigned following the mid-1970s, the country's heritage was plundered for profit on the antiquities market. Although an illicit antiquities market exists throughout the region, Lebanon has been the most severely affected by illegal excavations, to supply the demands of primarily foreign private collectors. [*See* Ethics and Archaeology.]

Lebanon's economic recovery from civil war, beginning in the early 1990s, included the massive development and reconstruction of many of its cities. Its population's urgent needs and the desire for rapid economic recovery clashed with preserving an archaeological heritage that spans the Canaanite, Phoenician, Roman, Byzantine, Crusader, and Islamic periods. An international team of archaeologists from Europe and Lebanon began conducting salvage excavations in 1993 over an area of about 48,000 sq m in downtown Beirut, currently being rebuilt by SOLIDERE, Lebanon's largest commercial enterprise. [*See* Beirut.] While the fate of many of these ancient structures remains in question, on 6 November 1995, Reuter Information Service in Beirut reported increasing public interest and personal identification with the antiquities being uncovered in salvage excavations in the city's center.

Archaeology played a key role in the modern State of Israel's political, cultural, and economic development even before the establishment of the state in 1948. With the increasing Jewish immigration to Palestine following World War I, Palestinian Jewish scholars became involved in the archaeology of ancient synagogues, finding personal identification and political justification in discovering Israelite and early Jewish remains. The focus of Israel's newly established Department of Antiquities was on the excavation, preservation, and restoration of sites exhibiting clear evidence of a Jewish presence in antiquity. In the 1950s, the Government Committee for the Preservation of Landscape and Antiquities (today the Israel National Parks Authority) was created to administer archaeological sites considered to be of national interest. Attention during the 1950s and 1960s was directed toward the excavation and reconstruction of monumental Crusader castles, such as those at Caesarea and Belvoir, and of Christian Byzantine churches, in order to attract Christian pilgrims. [*See* Crusader Period; Caesarea; Churches.] The only two biblical sites open to the public were Megiddo, excavated between the two world wars by the Oriental Institute at the University of Chicago, and Hazor, excavated with support from James A. de Rothschild, the Anglo-Israel Exploration Society, and the Government of Israel, in the late 1950s and early 1960s. [*See* Hazor.]

In the 1960s, Masada was excavated and soon became the most visited site in Israel. [*See* Masada.] Located in the Judean Desert on a cliff overlooking the Dead Sea, the visual impact of the site and evocation of the events that took place there during the First Jewish Revolt against Rome inspired an entire generation of Israelis who saw in Masada a romantic symbol of the besieged modern state. [*See* First Jewish Revolt.] The 1960s also witnessed heightened archaeological activity in the Negev desert, a by-product of Prime Minister David Ben Gurion's vision of developing the Negev for Jewish immigration. [*See* Negev.] Large-scale excavations and reconstruction were conducted at a number of Nabatean sites there—at Avdat, Kurnub, and Shivtah/Subeita—and were opened to the public by the National Parks Authority. [*See* Nabateans; Avdat; Kurnub; Subeita.]

Following the Six-Day War in 1967 and the resulting Israeli sovereignty over the eastern part of Jerusalem, historical and biblical Jerusalem became accessible to Israelis for the first time since 1948. The impact of a unified Jerusalem on the city's economic and archaeological development is reflected in the three large-scale excavations begun in its eastern part shortly after the Six-Day War: along the southern and western walls of the Temple Mount, in the historic Jewish Quarter within the walls of Old City, and later in the City of David, located at the edge of the Kidron Valley in the Arab village of Silwan. [*See* Jerusalem.]

The renewed excavations (1978–1984) in the City of David were sponsored by the City of David Society, the Institute of Archaeology of the Hebrew University, the Israel Exploration Society, and the Jerusalem Foundation. [*See* Israel Exploration Society.] The goals were to excavate, preserve, and restore the archaeological remains on government lands in Jerusalem's historic core. Since the conclusion of those excavations, the site has at times become a focal point of debate regarding land ownership and residential development in Jerusalem. Today the site is an archaeological park. It was there that the opening ceremonies took place in 1995 to mark the three-thousand-year anniversary of the establishment of Jerusalem as King David's capital.

The renovation of the Jewish Quarter by the Company for the Reconstruction and Development of the Jewish Quarter, established by the Israeli government and the Institute of Archaeology of the Hebrew University of Jerusalem, entailed extensive excavations of and below pre-1948 (medieval- and Ottoman-period) buildings. Significant Roman- and Byzantine-period remains are incorporated or preserved as part of or below the restored and reconstructed houses in the Jewish Quarter, and several underground archaeological sites are now open to the public. Jewish families who inhabited the quarter before 1948 were encouraged to return to live in its renovated houses as a means of engendering a strong identification and sense of continuity with the past. Because many Arab families were relocated to accommodate the demographic change, the Israeli excavations in the Jewish Quarter and near the Western Wall of the Temple Mount met with considerable criticism on a political level.

A similar renovation project underway in the Old City of Akko in Israel is the combined restoration of currently inhabited houses and structures of historic interest with the excavation of the well-preserved Crusader city beneath the modern dwellings. [See Akko.] This endeavor, under the auspices of the Israel Government Tourist Corporation, the Old Acre Development Company, the Israel Antiquities Authority, and the Ministry of Tourism, involving one of the best-preserved towns of the Ottoman period in the region, is proceeding without displacing the inhabitants. [See Israel Antiquities Authority.]

Archaeological sites in Israel are occasionally excavated and developed because of local interest and national identification. The modern Jewish city of Qazrin, located in the Golan Heights, was established in the mid-1970s because of its proximity to the ancient site of Qaṣrin, a Jewish village and synagogue dating to the Byzantine period (fourth–eighth centuries CE). Excavations and subsequent reconstruction of the village, under the auspices of the Qazrin Local Council and the Israel Government Tourist Corporation, have created a popular tourist site that provides employment opportunities for residents. Ancient Qasrin has also become, for many Golan residents, a symbol of modern Jewish settlement in the Golan and is the setting for community celebrations and political rallies. [See Qaṣrin; Golan.]

A different, and largely ignored, past is significant to the Palestinian population. The Palestinian link with the past is mainly through the traditional village—the settlement type that predominated for the last thirteen centuries of Palestine's history. From 1948 to 1950, during and following the establishment of the State of Israel, many of those villages were obliterated, severing the connection many Palestinians had with the land. As a result, there has been limited interest by, and even the alienation of, the Arab population in the archaeology of Israel. Today, there is renewed interest among Palestinian scholars in documenting and preserving traditional houses in towns such as Ramallah and in excavating Ottoman villages such Jenin and Ta'anach on the west bank of the Jordan River. [See Ta'anach.]

The 1990s ushered in a new era of archaeological investigation in Israel closely tied to national economic interests. This coincided with the establishment in 1990 of an independent authority, the Israel Antiquities Authority, with expanded jurisdiction over archaeological sites in Israel, replacing the Israel Department of Antiquities. The decade has been characterized by the excavation of major archaeological sites of national significance undertaken to encourage tourism and development. The year-round excavations at the classical (Hellenistic–Byzantine periods) sites of Beth-

Shean, Caesarea, and Mareshah/Beth-Guvrin were initiated primarily to solve local social and economic (employment) problems. [See Mareshah.] In addition, large-scale construction (the response, in part, to massive immigration from countries belonging to the former Soviet Union), has required unprecedented salvage excavations at hundreds of sites yearly. The large residential communities currently under construction in the northern suburbs of Jerusalem, in Modi'in (north of Jerusalem), and in Beth-Shemesh; the construction of Highway 6 transversing the country from north to south; and a series of bypass routes on the west bank of the Jordan have not only resulted in an unprecedented number of excavations, but have transformed the local topography. [See Beth-Shemesh.] A landscape has been created that never existed. Although a number of sites will be preserved or not excavated, the new residential communities will create artificial "islands" of cultural heritage cut off from their natural setting. Thus, in the 1990s in Israel archaeology became inseparable from tourism, economic development, and growth.

This rapid development and the resulting increase in salvage excavations and attempts to preserve Israel's cultural heritage have been challenged by several sectors of the Israeli populace. At a number of construction sites, Jewish tombs have been inadvertently uncovered, requiring salvage excavations. The removal of human bones from their final resting place, forbidden by Jewish religous law, and their disturbance by bulldozers or archaeologists have provoked violent demonstrations and political upheaval. Compromise solutions have included the rerouting of major roads or the cessation of excavations and the sealing of tombs thought to be Jewish. Development has also been prevented on the Haram esh-Sharif (the Temple Mount), the region's most significant site for Jews, Christians, and Muslims. Today, it is under Muslim jurisdiction, with Israel honoring an arrangement made when the eastern part of Jerusalem was under Jordanian rule before 1967. Because of Muslim concerns over the character and future of the site and of fears enforced by several attempts in recent decades to destroy Islamic structures on the Haram, all archaeological activity there is forbidden. The battle over whose past is presented in Jerusalem has extended to the south of the Temple Mount, where excavations uncovered not only the glories of Herod's Jerusalem but also public structures dating to the Umayyad period. [See Umayyad Caliphate.] Municipal plans to reconstruct and preserve the Umayyad monuments were met with demonstrations by nationalistic groups in Israel who oppose presenting Islamic Jerusalem to the public.

Future of the Past. The threat to the past presented by development in the majority of modern nation-states in the ancient Near East is unprecedented in history as a result of population growth, economic prosperity, and the earth-moving machines used in today's building projects. The ideal is a balanced approach to preserving cultural heritage without unnecessarily impeding economic growth and development. Several measures need to be taken in advance of planned development, including surveys and inventories of sites and historic buildings. This policy has been implemented, with varying degrees of success in Israel and Jordan, and on a smaller scale in surrounding countries. Close coordination needs to be encouraged and enforced by government agencies, municipalities, and private contractors on the one hand, and by departments of antiquities on the other, to minimize damage to archaeological sites and to avoid unnecessary delays or expense to contractors and investors. Cooperation during initial planning stages can often benefit all parties. Local and foreign tourism are encouraged through well-conserved sites accessible to the public and by public buildings and residential neighborhoods in which archaeological remains are preserved or incorporated into modern structures.

To effectively manage historical and archaeological resources, clear legal, planning, policy, and academic frameworks are necessary. Such well-defined guidelines can assist greatly in resolving the conflicts of interest that are unavoidable when development affects archaeological remains. Relevant information must be accessible to decision makers involved in planning and development as well as to those protecting archaeological resources. The management of archaeological sites, particularly in an urban environment, requires a well-trained, professional staff as well as funding and other resources to collect and record archaeological remains and to implement policy.

Tourism requires infrastructure and facilities for visitors to sites in order to avoid adverse effects on the environment of a region and on ancient remains. [See Tourism and Archaeology.] In addition to the legal, administrative, and economic factors of archaeological resource management, perhaps the most important aspect of cultural heritage is the relationship between the archaeological site and the public. Public awareness and education are crucial to the conservation of cultural heritage and planned development and can be encouraged through local associations and societies, in schools, and in the media. This communication is essential to raising awareness of the value of archaeological heritage as an endangered finite natural resource.

The past is perceived through the eyes of the living, and as contemporary values and beliefs change, so will interpretations of the past. Historic remains are not static, and each site may have a diversity of meanings for different publics. As interpreters of cultural heritage, it is the task of archaeologists to convey the relevancy of the past, to promote dialogue between professionals and lay persons, and to encourage constructive cooperation between those desiring to preserve archaeological resources and developers responding to the needs of a modern society.

BIBLIOGRAPHY

Broshi, Magen. "Religion, Ideology, and Politics and Their Impact on Palestinian Archaeology." *Israel Museum Journal* 6 (1987): 17–32. Survey of the development of Palestinian archaeology and its significance for Jews, Christians, and Muslims.

Economic Development and Archaeology in the Middle East. Amman, 1983. Booklet published by the Department of Antiquities of Jordan, American Schools of Oriental Research and the American Center of Oriental Research, outlining current Jordanian policy regarding development and archaeology.

Glock, Albert E. "Archaeology as Cultural Survival: The Future of the Palestinian Past." *Journal of Palestine Studies* 23 (1994): 70–84. Article presenting the largely ignored Palestinian past.

Greene, Joseph A. "Preserving Which Past for Whose Future? The Dilemma of Cultural Resource Management in the Mediterranean Region." In *Interpreting the Past: Presenting Archaeological Sites to the Public,* edited by Ann Killebrew and G. Lehmann. Forthcoming. Detailed account of government policy regarding cultural resource management in Tunisia, Cyprus, and Jordan.

Kempinski, Aharon. "Synagogues, Crusader Castles, and Nabatean Cities: Restoration in Israel during the 1950s and 1960s." In *Interpreting the Past: Presenting Archaeological Sites to the Public, May 30th–June 4, 1993 (Abstracts),* edited by Ann Killebrew, p. 39. Haifa, 1993. Summary of lectures delivered at an international symposium.

Knoop, Riemer. "Public Awareness and Archaeology: A Task for the Voluntary Sector." *Antiquity* 67 (1993): 439–445. Article on the importance of local community involvement in the preservation and protection of historic and archaeological sites.

Leone, Mark P. "Archaeology's Relationship to the Present and the Past." In *Modern Material Culture: The Archaeology of Us,* edited by Richard A. Gould and Michael B. Schiffer, pp. 5–13. New York, 1981. Essay on the interaction between the public and the archaeological site, stressing the importance of changing interpretations and its relevance to modern society.

Lowenthal, David. *The Past Is a Foreign Country.* Cambridge, 1985. Fascinating, well-written account of modern society's interest in the past.

McManamon, Francis P. "The Many Publics of Archaeology." *American Antiquity* 56 (1991): 121–130. Essay on the importance of public education and involvement in archaeology.

Miller, Daniel. "Archaeology and Development." *Current Anthropology* 21 (1980): 709–715. Important article on archaeology and development outlining various approaches to archaeology and its relationship to local communities. Miller draws on his experiences in the Solomon Islands as a case study of archaeology and development in non-Western countries.

Rabinovich, Abraham. "Inside the Israel Antiquities Authority." *Biblical Archaeology Review* 20.2 (1994): 40–45. Brief account of the recent reorganization of the Israel Antiquities Authority, including its new mandate and goals for the future of archaeology in Israel.

Reich, Ronny. "The Archaeologist's Dilemma." In *ICOMOS International Symposium, "Old Culture in New Worlds,"* vol. 2, pp. 1009–1015. Washington, D.C., 1987. Problems relating to the preservation and presentation of archaeological remains on multilayered tells.

Reid, Donald M. "Indigenous Egyptology: The Decolonization of a Profession?" *Journal of the American Oriental Society* 105 (1985): 233–246. Development of an Egyptian approach to Egyptology.

Seeden, Helga. "Lebanon's Past Today." *Berytus* 35 (1987): 5–12. Summary of the disastrous affects of Lebanon's civil war on its archaeological sites and antiquities.

Silberman, Neil Asher. *Between Past and Present: Archaeology, Ideology, and Nationalism in the Modern Middle East.* New York, 1990. Series of essays on different countries in the Middle East that demonstrates how the past and present are linked as modern nation-states using archaeology to reinforce their international prestige.

Tilly, Christopher. "Archaeology as Socio-Political Action in the Present." In *Critical Traditions in Contemporary Archaeology: Essays in the Philosophy, History, and Socio-Politics of Archaeology*, edited by Valerie Pinsky and Alison Wylie, pp. 104–116. Cambridge, 1989. Discusses the importance of relating archaeology and the past to contemporary culture and society.

Uzzell, David L., ed. *Heritage Interpretation*. Vol. 1, *The Natural and Built Environment*; vol. 2, *The Vistor Experience*. London, 1989. A two-volume collection of papers dealing with all aspects of world heritage management and interpretation and its interaction with the public.

Wainwright, G. J. "The Management of Change: Archaeology and Planning." *Antiquity* 67 (1993): 416–421. Charts recent developments in archaeological site and landscape management in England.

Wensinck, A. J., and Georges Vajda. "Fir'awn." In *The Encyclopaedia of Islam*, new ed., vol. 2, pp. 917–918. Leiden, 1960–. Muslim attitudes toward pre-Islamic pharaonic history in Egypt.

ANN KILLEBREW

DE VOGÜÉ, MELCHIOR. *See* Vogüé, Melchior de.

DHRA', site located about 5 km (3 mi.) east of the famous Early Bronze Age city Bab edh-Dhra', which is in the Lisan area of the Dead Sea in modern Jordan (31°14'30" N, 35°35' E; map reference 204 × 073 [Bennett, 1980, p. 30; Raikes, 1980, p. 56]). The name *Dhra'* is identified with the Arabic word for "arm."

Dhra' was first discovered and investigated in 1976 under auspices of the Department of Antiquities of Jordan by Thomas D. Raikes, who emphasized that its flint industry, which included Khiamian points, could be compared with that of other late ninth- and early eighth-millennium BCE sites in Jordan, Israel, and Syria. Queisa and Sabra I in southern Jordan are similar to and contemporaneous with Dhra' in the very early stages of the Neolithic period.

Wadi Dhra', a perennial stream that runs to the northeast of the site, supplies it with water. Dhra' has been described as a flint-tool factory because of the large number of unfinished tools and wasters found there (Raikes, 1980, p. 56). Blade cores, long thin blades, scrapers, chisels, arrowheads, polished basalt axes, chipped and limestone objects of horn or phallus shape were collected. Raikes also noted the presence of Roman buildings, graves, and a well.

Crystal-M. Bennett made soundings at the site briefly in 1979, excavating six areas. In area I, the largest (27 m north–south × 5 m east–west), she laid out four one-meter-square probe trenches on the east. Bennett (1980) published the flints from these test trenches. She reached bedrock in this and other areas, encountering very well-defined floors as well as a destruction level above floors 5 and 6 (Bennett, 1980, p. 33). In area I, she found pit dwellings with floors

ending at thin walls of pisé and stone. Mud brick was also used.

The published pottery from Dhra' all comes from area IV, immediately under the topsoil. Bennett reached bedrock in this area at a depth of 85 cm in the northeast corner and at 40 cm in the northwest corner. The pottery corpus is comparable to Jericho stratum IX, Pottery Neolithic A (PNA), although the Dhra' ware is not crumbly and had been fired at a higher temperature. Bennett argued that some of this pottery assemblage, particularly the thinner ware, seems closer to Jericho VIII/Pottery Neolithic B (PNB) than to Jericho IX/PNA (1980, p. 36). However, other PNA and PNB sites in Jordan, such as Wadi Shu'eib, 'Ain Ghazal, and Dharih, have also recently been sounded or excavated. [See 'Ain Ghazal; Shu'eib, Wadi.]

Although Bennett did not find the Khiamian points in good stratigraphic contexts, this does not necessarily mean that the site was not occupied in the Early Neolithic period. Dhra' may have been a base camp during the earliest phase of the Neolithic and a farming village in the sixth and fifth millennium.

[See also the biography of Bennett.]

BIBLIOGRAPHY

Bennett, Crystal-M. "Sounding at Dhra', Jordan." *Levant* 12 (1980): 30–39.

Raikes, Thomas D. "Notes on Some Neolithic and Later Sites in Wadi Araba and the Dead Sea Valley." *Levant* 12 (1980): 40–60.

ZEIDAN A. KAFAFI

DIBON, village in modern Jordan (31°30' N, 35°42' E) on the ancient, but still used, main north–south road (the "King's Highway" of *Nm.* 20–22), located about 64 km (40 mi.) south of Amman and 3 km (2 mi.) north of Wadi el-Mujib (the Arnon River of *Nm.* 21:13, 14, 24, 26; 22:36; *Dt.* 2:24; *Jgs.* 11:26; *Is.* 16:2; *Jer.* 48:20). An adjacent hill, northwest of this village, is the site of the ancient Moabite city of Dibon, pronounced Dībôn in Hebrew and possibly Daibôn in Moabite (Septuagint of *Jos.* 13:17) and transliterated as Dhībân in modern Arabic.

Its natural defenses are deep valleys on the southwest, west, and north; on the east, erosion from the tell has made the contour less steep. The southeast corner, however, slopes down more gently and is joined by a saddle to the next hill, on which the modern village lies. When excavation was begun, this area was marked by two knolls: the eastern one supported a ruined building surmounted by a sheikh's tomb; the western knoll remained unexcavated until recently, when illegal digging revealed a small square stone tower, possibly Roman. Between them, the slope is slightly concave; this came to be known as the gateway area.

The site has no natural water supply except from the winter rains that are still conserved in scores of cisterns. The site's economic importance was guaranteed by its key position at the crossroads of the main north–south road already mentioned and a less obvious east–west track that passes immediately south of the site and joins grain-raising and sheep-goat-rearing lands to the east and west. It was also a major center politically for any power wishing to control territory north of the Arnon River gorge. Evidence for the site's long occupation was the presence, until fifty years ago, of ruins on its surface dating from Byzantine and Arab times.

There seems never to have been doubt that this was the site of the ancient city of Dibon, but the discovery there, in 1868, of a stela bearing an inscription memorializing the deeds of King Mesha (hereafter MI) focused attention on the site. [See Moabite Stone.] The inscription refers to events and persons until then known only from the Bible (e.g., *1 Kgs.* 16:23–24; *2 Kgs.* 3:4–27).

History. Such references make it possible to reconstruct, in part, the history of Moab and Dibon. [See Moab.] The earliest references occur in the biblical accounts of Israel's traditional movement from Egypt to Canaan via Transjordan. In them (*Nm.* 21:21–31) Sihon, king of the Amorites, whose capital was at Heshbon, had seized the land of the king of Moab as far south as the Arnon River, including Dibon. The Israelites, having apparently bypassed that part of Moab south of the Arnon (*Nm.* 21:11–13), defeated Sihon's forces and took possession of the land north of the Arnon. The tribe of Reuben was assigned this territory (*Jos.* 13:15–23), but it seems to have been partly occupied by Gad (*Jos.* 13:24–28; *Nm.* 32:34; MI 10). Israelite control of the Transjordanian kingdoms was not assured, however (*Jgs.* 3:12–14, 11:1–40; *1 Sm.* 12:9, 14:47), until David conquered Moab north of the Arnon (*2 Sm.* 8:2) and even included it in his general census (*2 Sm.* 24:5). Israel's control, while it probably continued under Solomon, no doubt ceased with the breakup of David's empire under Rehoboam.

Two events—the attack by Moab and its allies against Judah (*2 Chr.* 20:1–30) and the counterattack (?) by Israel and Judah (*2 Kgs.* 3:4–27) against Mesha's (?) rebellion—should probably be attributed to the time of Mesha's father, Kemosh[yat], for both are routed south of the Dead Sea; the latter is directed against Kir-Ḥareset, Moab's southern capital (usually identified with modern Kerak).

It was Omri of Israel who subdued Moab (MI 4–9), and his heirs held it until Mesha, king of Moab and residing at Dibon, revolted and extended his kingdom some 35 km (22 mi.) northward, as far as Nebo (modern Khirbet el-Mukhayyat). To give thanks to his god Kemosh and to celebrate his victories, Mesha built a new royal quarter adjacent to the earlier city, which he called Qarḥoh "the prominent" or "the eminent" (MI 21–26). It contained a high place for Kemosh, a palace, an acropolis with gates and towers, and houses for the growing population (each of which was to be provided to have a cistern). Finally, he set up his stela, recounting his achievements, quite possibly in Kemosh's high place near where it was found.

There is little information about the history of Dibon and Moab immediately after Mesha. The statement in *2 Kings* 10:32–34) that Hazael of Damascus had seized from Israel the lands as far south as the Arnon River suggests that those lands had reverted to Israelite control. It is, however, difficult to see how, in the face of Syrian threats, Israel could have accomplished this. It is to be noted that *Amos* (1:3) seems to restrict Hazael's conquests to Gilead (in central Transjordan), while the reported raids (*2 Kgs.* 13:20) by Moabites suggest that Moab was by no means powerless. There is no evidence that Jeroboam II was able to restore Israelite control. Furthermore, there is no sign of violent destruction at Iron Age Dibon.

The Moabite kingdom and Dibon came under Assyrian domination by 731 BCE, when a king of Moab paid tribute to Tiglath-Pileser III and continued to do so under three subsequent Moabite kings. The capital appears to have remained at Dibon (*Is.* 15:2 RSV; *Jer.* 48:18). Such pussilanimity (or so it was interpreted by Judah) was infuriating and led to dire oracles against Moab (*Is.* 15, 16:6–13, 25:10–12; *Jer.* 48; *Ez.* 25:8–11; *Zep* 2:8–11), but it was the key to survival. Finally, however, Moab, too, joined a general revolt against Nebuchadnezzar that led to the state's destruction in 582 BCE.

Archaeological Research. Excavation at Dibon did not begin until 1950, when Fred V. Winnett, director of the American School of Oriental Research in Jerusalem, initiated a series of campaigns in the site's southeast quadrant, where the Moabite stone had been found. Expeditions under a succession of directors were in place in 1951–1953, 1955–1956, and 1965. The most recent archaeological results were achieved by William H. Morton on the summit and northern part of the site. Here, for the first time, Dibon's complete archaeological history was defined: from its beginning in the Early Bronze Age it continued directly—without any trace of Middle or Late Bronze Age occupations—into Iron Age II (Moabite), Nabatean, Roman (?), Byzantine, Umayyad, and later deposits.

The Moabite levels included a north gateway (much modified in the Nabatean period), silos for grain, and, nearby, carbonized grain similar to that found by William L. Reed in the southeast quadrant (Winnett and Reed, 1964, pp. 48–50). Most significant were the remains of a major rectangular stone building (42.9 m × 21.10) that Morton called the Moabite Palace Complex (Morton, 1989; pp. 244–246). This palace apparently had an adjoining sanctuary, for cultic objects, including a proposed Iron I incense stand and fertility figurines were found in the vicinity. Perhaps this was the sanctuary of Ashtar-Memosh (MI 17).

Winnett's work in 1950–1951 in the southeast quarter (Winnett and Reed, 1964) identified vertical retaining walls and a great battered stone wall supporting a 10-meter-deep artificial fill extending to bedrock. He traced the outer sloping wall for about 12 m, including two sharp right-angled turns in its course to enclose a square stone tower (about 6 × 6 m). The wall rests on bedrock and still reaches a height of 10 m in places (section E-E in Tushingham, 1972). The tower was excavated internally for about 11 m without reaching bedrock; its original entrance, approached from inside the city, stands at least 12 m above bedrock. The heavy battered wall has also been found at the south side of the quadrant (Tushingham, 1972, pl. V. 1, 2 and Section G-G [wall]). It was in this area that Reed discovered, on bedrock, the remains of domestic occupation. Its contemporary pottery and quantities of charred grain could be Carbon-14 dated to about 850 BCE. Resting on this deposit or on bedrock were heavy stone walls Reed thought could be defensive. This area was engulfed by a great artificial fill whose depth probably averages about 3 m, as compared with the 10 m of the fill above bedrock Winnett had traced. As all of this fill must postdate about 850 BCE and required both stabilizing walls and the great stone retaining wall revealed on both the east and south sides of the area (see above), it is logical to consider it the podium of Mesha's royal quarter. Its original surface is not preserved anywhere in the area excavated, but the entrance to the stone tower is. It and other clues establish the level on which Mesha's buildings were founded. Few of these can, at present, be identified, but it seems probable that Kemosh's high place lay beneath the later Nabatean temple. It was near here that the Mesha inscription was found.

Several Moabite tombs were excavated, one containing a clay sarcophagus, with quantities of jewelry and pottery that were, however, so mixed they could not provide a datable sequence. These were probably family tombs.

For about five and a half centuries the site was deserted. Then, with the renaissance in Transjordan under the Nabateans, Dibon again became important. The walls on the summit were rebuilt, as was a north gate overlying the Moabite gate. In the southeast quarter, a major temple, reminiscent of the main temple at Petra, was erected; it was surrounded by an unwalled sacred precinct approached by a grand staircase leading up from the south. It is to be dated to the first century CE. [See Petra.] Two inscriptions and the remains of a bath indicate that there was a Roman garrison here in the 3rd century CE.

After another break, Dibon shared in the general prosperity of the Byzantine period. Architectural features include a large church dated to the sixth century. There were also many burials in the general area, with some sarcophagi inserted into the ruins of the Nabatean temple.

The Umayyad period was brief but left evidence of construction, including two small, but virtually complete, domed buildings on the summit Morton, 1989, p. 245). The Ayyubid/Mamluk occupation is evidenced by the reuse of Byzantine and Umayyad remains—in many cases scrappily preserved because of a later cemetery. Coins and pottery, however, are sufficient to indicate the presence and date of this occupation. The ancient site of Dibon was abandoned (except as a cemetery) when the village moved to its present location, probably in the 14th century CE.

[See also the biography of Winnett.]

BIBLIOGRAPHY

Bienkowski, Piotr, ed. *Early Edom and Moab: The Beginning of the Iron Age in Southern Jordan.* Sheffield Archaeological Monographs, 7. Sheffield, 1992.

Dearman, Andrew, ed. *Studies in the Mesha Inscription and Moab.* Atlanta, 1989.

Dornemann, Rudolph Henry. *The Archaeology of the Transjordan in the Bronze and Iron Ages.* Milwaukee, 1983.

Freedman, David Noel. "A Second Mesha Inscription." *Bulletin of the American Schools of Oriental Research,* no. 175 (1964): 50–51.

Morton, William H. "Report of the Director of the School in Jerusalem." *Bulletin of the American Schools of Oriental Research,* no. 140 (1955): 4–7.

Morton, William H. "Dhiban." *Revue Biblique* 64 (1957): 221–223.

Morton, William H. "A Summary of the 1955, 1956, and 1965 Excavations at Dhiban." In Studies in the Mesha Inscription and Moab, edited by Andrew Dearman, pp. 239–246. Atlanta, 1989.

Murphy, Roland E. "A Fragment of an Early Moabite Inscription from Dibon." *Bulletin of the American Schools of Oriental Research,* no. 125 (1952): 20–23.

Mussell, Mary-Louise. "The Seal Impression from Dhiban." In *Studies in the Mesha Inscriptions and Moab,* edited by Andrew Dearman, pp. 247–251. Atlanta, 1989.

Reed, William L., and Fred V. Winnett. "A Fragment of an Early Moabite Inscription from Kerak." *Bulletin of the American Schools of Oriental Research,* no. 172 (1963): 1–9.

Tushingham, A. D. "An Inscription of the Roman Imperial Period from Dhiban." *Bulletin of the American Schools of Oriental Research,* no. 138 (1955): 29–34.

Tushingham, A. D. *The Excavations at Dibon (Dhîbân) in Moab: The Third Campaign, 1952–53.* Annual of the American Schools of Oriental Research, 40. Cambridge, Mass., 1972.

Tushingham, A. D. "Three Byzantine Tombstones from Dhîbân, Jordan." In *Studies in the Ancient Palestinian World,* edited by John W. Wevers and Donald B. Redford, pp. 29–33. Toronto, 1972.

Tushingham, A. D. "Dhîbân Reconsidered: King Mesha and His Works." *Annual of the Department of Antiquities of Jordan* 34 (1990): 183–191.

Tushingham, A. D., and Peter H. Pedrette. "Mesha's Citadel Complex (Qarhoh) at Dhîbân." *Studies in the History and Archaeology of Jordan,* vol. 5, pp. 151–159. Amman, 1995.

Winnett, Fred V., and William L. Reed. *The Excavations at Dibon (Dhîbân) in Moab: The First Campaign, 1950–51, and the Second Campaign, 1952.* Annual of the American Schools of Oriental Research, 36/37. New Haven, 1964.

A. D. TUSHINGHAM

DI CESNOLA, LUIGI PALMA

DI CESNOLA, LUIGI PALMA (1832–1904), soldier, diplomat, antiquarian and ultimately museum director. Throughout his long life Emmanuele Pietro Paolo Maria Luigi Palma di Cesnola was always a colorful and controversial figure. After seeing military action in Italy and the Crimea, he traveled extensively throughout the Ottoman

Empire and then emigrated to the United States. During the American Civil War, Cesnola distinguished himself as a colonel in the Union cavalry; he was wounded, captured, and exchanged in a release of prisoners. Without private means, he was fortunate later to be offered a consulship in Cyprus, then a backwater of the Ottoman Empire. Shortly after arriving there, Cesnola emulated his French and British consular colleagues by collecting ancient Cypriot art, a pursuit that became a major preoccupation and lucrative source of income. Ultimately, it also brought him fame. With determination the consul toured the island from 1865 to 1875 with his gangs of laborers, opening thousands of tombs and cursorily "exploring" numerous ancient city and temple sites.

The resulting collection of antiquities, ranging from over life-size statues to fine jewelry, numbering in the tens of thousands, was offered to various great museums around the world. Some works went to London and Paris; but after much negotiating the Metropolitan Museum of Art in New York City purchased more than four thousand items, the nucleus of its antiquities collection. They also received Cesnola, who, for better or for worse, became the first director. His tenure was beset by allegations of unethical practices concerning the restoration of statues and the provenance of the so-called Treasure of Curium. The latter, much like Priam's Treasure excavated by Heinrich Schliemann (who Cesnola attempted to upstage) was not a single deposit but a heterogeneous collection of gold jewelry and other valuables from local tombs. Although much criticized today for his lack of scientific method, Cesnola must be given credit for propelling Cypriot art onto the world stage for the edification of future generations.

BIBLIOGRAPHY

Di Cesnola, Luigi P. *Cyprus: Its Ancient Cities, Tombs, and Temples*. 2d ed. New York, 1878. Reprint, with a forward by Stuart Swiny. Limassol, 1991. Cesnola's embellished and often inaccurate account of his activities on Cyprus over a decade. Nonetheless, an important work, the first detailed publication of a large and representative sample of Cypriot antiquities, and an entertaining introduction to contemporary life on the island.

Di Cesnola, Luigi P. *A Descriptive Atlas of the Cesnola Collection of Cypriote Antiquities in the Metropolitan Museum of Art, New York*. 3 vols. Boston and New York, 1885–1903. Fine quarto publication, reproducing the best pieces in the collection. Available in major libraries, these massive volumes are now collector's items.

McFadden, Elizabeth. *The Glitter and the Gold: A Spirited Account of the Metropolitan Museum of Art's First Director, the Audacious and High-Handed Luigi Palma di Cesnola*. New York, 1971. Very well researched. The subtitle is no overstatement!

Myres, John. *Handbook of the Cesnola Collection of Antiquities from Cyprus* (1914). New York, 1974. Standard reference work to the collection by the leading expert of the day.

Wright, G. R. H. "Louis Palma di Cesnola and Cyprus." *Archiv für Orientforschung* 38–39 (1991–1992): 161–167. The only work to question the psychology of this nineteenth-century adventurer, with in-

teresting comparisons to Henry Austen Layard and Heinrich Schliemann.

STUART SWINY

DIDYMA (formerly Branchidai; modern Yenihisar, formerly Yoran), site in Vilayet Aydın, a regional sanctuary in the area of the Carian-Ionian border (Strabo 14.1.2) situated on a limestone plateau 75 m above sea level on the Gulf of Akbük.

Didyma became famous as a spring/oracle of Apollo (Herodotus 1.92, 2.159; Pausanias 7.2.6) and for the size of the Temple of Apollo (Strabo 14.1.5), one of the best-preserved large-scale buildings from antiquity. From 1765 to 1856 investigations were carried out at Didyma by English scholars, and between 1873 and 1896 a French mission researched the Temple of Apollo. From 1906 to 1925, excavations and the conservation of the temple were conducted by the Berlin Museum; those activities have been continued, since 1962, by the German Archaeological Institute. [*See* Deutsches Archäologisches Institut, Abteilung Istanbul.] In addition to the Temple of Apollo, a sanctuary in the northwest, which was built over in modern times, has been investigated. The oldest archaeological remains date to about 700 BCE, although obsidian artifacts from the Neolithic period were found 4 km (2 mi.) to the south at Didim plaji. Written traditions concerning the site's pre-Greek foundation first appear in the Hellenistic-Roman periods. More than six hundred inscriptions are related to cult, donations, building activities, the "sacred grove," and the settlement. [*See* Cult.] From the seventh century BCE until the seventh century CE, Didyma was the best-known oracle shrine of Apollo in Asia Minor.

The core of the cult place was the freshwater springs on which the shrines of the main god, Apollo, and of Artemis developed. According to cult legend, the union of Zeus and Leto took place in Didyma (*SIG* 590). In the pre-Greek period (Herodotus 1.157; Pausanias 7.2.6) a female nature divinity was probably worshiped there. In the pre-Hellenistic period, the *Branchidae*, likely an association of members of the local oligarchy, were the cult's prophets and priests and gave their name to the place. Royal donations were given by Pharaoh Necho at the end of the seventh century BCE) and by the Lydian King Croesus in the mid-sixth century BCE (Herodotus 2.159, 1.92). The Persian king Darius is said to have confirmed in writing the shrine's right of asylum (Tacitus, *Annals* 3.63). No archaeological evidence exists for the "looting and firing" by the Persians recorded by Herodotus (6.19); its dating to the time of Darius in 494 BCE or to Xerxes in 479 BCE, "during the second defection of Ionia" from the Persians (Herodotus 9.104; Pausanias 8.46.3), is controversial.

Processions from Miletus to the shrine were reestablished in 479/78 BCE. [*See* Miletus.] The purported surrender of the sanctuary to the Persians by the *Branchidae* (Strabo 14.1.5, 11.11.4) is explained as a Milesian invention. Beginning in the last third of the fourth century BCE, at the instigation of Miletus, the organization and activity of the oracle (Strabo 17.1.43) were fundamentally changed, based on the model of Delphi. An annual official of the polis functioned as the *prophetēs* and sacrificing priest of Apollo. A *hydrophoros*, or the female water-bearer, performed the office of the priestess of Artemis. In this period new building activities took place (Temple of Apollo III), while the older structures were maintained.

The Seleucids supported the sanctuary and returned the city's votive statue of Apollo, the work of the sculptor Kanachos, to Miletus, which the Persians had stolen (Pausanias 1.16.3, 8.46.3). [*See* Seleucids; Persians.] The *Didymeia* were celebrated as a five-year festival, beginning in about 200 BCE. The sanctuary was looted in 277/76 BCE by pirates. In 44 BCE Caesar enlarged the site's area of asylum as a sanctuary. Otherwise, only occasional evidence exists for a Roman presence in the first century BCE. Under Emperor Trajan, the Sacred Way (see below) and the pavement within the sanctuary were rebuilt. "Emperor worship" began under the name of *Kommodeia* in 177 CE. In the fourth and seventh centuries CE the sanctuary was destroyed by earthquakes. Cult practices came to an end with the advent of the fourth century.

The first evidence of the presence of Christians in the sanctuary also dates to the beginning of the fourth century. In the fifth–sixth and tenth–twelfth centuries, new building activities took place at the site, and the seat of a bishop was installed. At the end of the fifteenth century, the site was again destroyed by an earthquake; it was only reoccupied at the end of the eighteenth century.

Architectural Remains. For the most part, local limestone was used as the building material at the site. The spring precincts of Apollo, located in a hollow, and of Artemis, to the northwest on a rocky ledge, have existed since about 700 BCE.

Sanctuary of Apollo. In the western part of the adytum, foundation remains of the mud-brick walls of a courtyard (10 × 30 m, reconstructed) have been excavated. The cult monument of the spring had been located in the courtyard (*Sekos* I). About 100 m east of the spring precinct was a slope marked by five steps. South of it a supporting wall for a terrace was found that had held two hall-type buildings. The slope formed a bow-shaped boundary for an area with an unroofed, round construction. The latter has been called the sanctuary's main altar, but that designation is questionable. In the first half of the sixth century BCE, the spring precinct was enlarged when the Temple of Apollo (II) was constructed, along with a two-winged surrounding colonnade. The building materials used were limestone, poros, and marble. In the western part of the cult courtyard lime-

stone foundations with five pilasters have been preserved. Also preserved are the remains of walls in the so-called *naiskos*, whose function was presumably that of a springhouse to protect the cult monument and the seat of the oracle *(manteion)*. The sanctuary's most recent construction phase, according to the entablature reliefs, which show gorgons, belongs to about 500 BCE.

Sometime after the mid-fourth century BCE, the buildings were systematically demolished and construction of the Hellenistic-Roman marble temple (III) begun. This temple was erected upon a seven-stepped foundation that, with the retention of the enlarged cult courtyard and the surrounding colonnades (see above), covers 2.5 times the surface area of its predecessor (the stylobate was 51.13 × 109.34 m). Inscriptions (third–second centuries BCE) and sketches of the construction on the inner courtyard walls document the building process. Marble quarries have been discovered near Heraklea sub Latmus. In about 170 BCE, the sanctuary's central building, with a cult courtyard and *prodomos*, was erected. A pedestal in the courtyard was 5 m high and the courtyard's upper walls, with pilasters, were 20 m high. The *prodomos* (a columned hall) was a dodecastyle with two tunnel passages leading to the cult courtyard and to a Great Gate whose unpassable threshold was 1.5 m high. Still standing are a hall with two columns and staircases, a wall with three doors in it, and an open stairway to the cult courtyard. The construction of the surrounding colonnades (interior 8 × 19 columns; exterior 10 × 21 columns) and its roof was never completed. Literary sources testify that a grove (*alsos*, Strabo 14.1.5) was planted inside and outside the temple precinct.

After 250 CE, the spaces between the columns on the east side were walled up, and steps were built in front of the Great Gate. In the fifth–sixth centuries, a gallery basilica was erected in the cult courtyard. [*See* Basilicas.] After the earthquakes in the seventh century, the temple was fortified; the fortifications were destroyed by fire in the tenth century. The temple itself was finally destroyed in an earthquake in 1493; its stones were looted in the nineteenth century.

Sanctuary of Artemis. The worship of Artemis is attested from the sixth century BCE. Evidence exists for a hieron and a cult statue in the third century BCE. Structures on a rocky ledge in the spring precinct have been identified with the Artemis cult *(hydrophoria)*. In about 700 BCE, the southern spring basin was enclosed by a wall; the precinct was enlarged in the sixth century BCE, and in the third–first centuries BCE the spring basins, which had dried out, were replaced with wells. Leveling and the construction of a complex of individual buildings reached the sanctuary's northern boundary. Walls separated the sanctuary from the Sacred Way; colonnades of limestone columns with wooden entablatures were erected in front of the walls. In the second century CE, the sanctuary was remodeled. It was destroyed in the fourth century, probably by an earthquake, and was then abandoned.

Sacred Way. The construction of a 5–6-meter-wide road more than 20 km (12 mi.) long overland from Miletus to Didyma is attested stratigraphically for the second half of the sixth century BCE and also by the cult regulations of the *Molpoi* pertaining to processions with stations for local divinities. From about 530 to the fourth century BCE, at the top of the pass, there was a cult precinct with a group of seated statues in the middle and sculptured sphinxes. It is assumed that in the last section of the processional road the course veered to the west and south of the Apollo temple (called the "stadium" by Theodor Wiegand).

Hellenistic-Roman constructions. At Didyma, near the Sacred Way and beyond it, burial sites have been identified, mostly dating to the Roman period. The settlement and some secular buildings have also been excavated from the period.

Byzantine constructions. During the fifth–sixth centuries, the Sacred Way was furnished with an arcaded hall, and a basilica was built within the Temple of Apollo. There is archaeological evidence of a village settlement, including churches and interments, from the ninth-tenth centuries. [*See* Churches.]

Finds. Didyma is the site of the richest source of Early Greek sculpture in Anatolia. Starting in the early sixth century BCE, all the important types are represented: *kouroi* and *korai,* male and female seated statues, standing and reclining clothed male statues, lion and sphinx statues, or architectural sculpture. In about 500 BCE Kanachos of Sikyon made a bronze statue of Apollo commissioned by the city of Miletus (Pliny, *Nat. Hist.* 34.75; Pausanias 2.10.4, 9.10.2). Honorific bronze statues from the Hellenistic-Roman periods can only be inferred from their bases. In addition to these, only fragments from a few marble statues and reliefs and terra cottas have been preserved from the period. The ceramic ware is local, and imports are rare. The metal finds consist mostly of vessels but do include weapons and statuettes, however rarely. [*See* Weapons and Warfare.] Only a few pre-Hellenistic coins have been found—the others date to the fourth century BCE–seventh century CE. In addition to animal bones from burnt offerings, there are deposits of unburned bones, which would be in accordance with a "Carian" ritual (*Suidas* s.v. *karikon thyma*).

Divinities. Cult places for Apollo and Artemis have been identified through inscriptional evidence (Callimachus Lyr. 229 v. 11 ed. Pfeiffer; Schol. Clem. Alex. Protr. 45.2). Such evidence also exists for precincts of Aphrodite, Zeus Soter, Zeus Kataibates (?), Angelos, and Phosphorion (Hecate? Artemis?). Most of the dedications are to Apollo and Artemis Pytheie; in addition, there are dedications to Hecate, Zeus and Leto, Dionysus, Kurotrophos, Aphrodite Urania and Katallakteria, Soteria, Pan and the Nymphs, the Muses, Cybele, Telesphorion, Zeus Hyetios and Telesiurgos, Poseidon Seisichthon, Agathe Tyche, Osiris, Serapis-Isis-Anubis, and the Sebastoi. Except for nameless altars from the archaic period, there are altars for Artemis Lykeie, the Curetes, Zeus Phaneios and Hypsistos, Asphaleios Poseidon, Asclepius Soter, Demeter Karpophoros, Sotira Kore, and Tyche. [*See* Altars.]

BIBLIOGRAPHY

Didyma Wegweiser. Vols. 1–31. Berlin, 1984–1993. Series of brief current reports.

Drerup, Heinrich, et al. "Bericht über die Ausgrabungen in Didyma 1962." *Archäologischer Anzeiger* (1964): 333–383.

Fontenrose, Joseph. *Didyma: Apollo's Oracle, Cult and Companions.* Berkeley, 1988.

Günther, Wolfgang. *Das Orakel von Didyma in hellenistischer Zeit: Eine Interpretation der Stein-Urkunden.* Istanbuler Mitteilungen, 4. Tübingen, 1971.

Haselberger, Lothar. "Bericht über die Arbeit am Jüngeren Apollontempel von Didyma." *Istanbuler Mitteilungen* 33 (1983): 90–123.

Haselberger, Lothar. "The Construction Plans for the Temple of Apollo at Didyma." *Scientific American* 253 (1985): 126–132.

Knackfuss, Hubert. *Didyma I: Die Baubeschreibung.* 3 vols. Berlin, 1941.

Rehm, Albert. *Didyma II: Die Inschriften.* Berlin, 1958.

Schneider, Peter. "Zur Topographie der Heiligen Strasse von Milet nach Didyma." *Archäologischer Anzeiger* (1987): 101–129.

Schneider, Peter, et al. "Ein Temenos an der Heiligen Strasse von Milet nach Didyma." *Archäologischer Anzeiger* (1989): 147–217.

Tuchelt, Klaus. *Die archaischen Skulpturen von Didyma: Beiträge zur frühgriechischen Plastik in Kleinasien.* Istanbuler Forschungen, 27. Berlin, 1970.

Tuchelt, Klaus. *Vorarbeiten zu einer Topographie von Didyma: Eine Untersuchung der inschriftlichen und archäologischen Zeugnisse.* Istanbuler Mitteilungen, 9. Tübingen, 1973.

Tuchelt, Klaus. "Didyma or Branchidai." In *The Princeton Encyclopedia of Classical Sites,* pp. 272–273. Princeton, 1976. Includes the scholarly literature up to 1975.

Tuchelt, Klaus. *Branchidai-Didyma: Geschichte und Ausgrabung eines antiken Heiligtums.* Zaberns Bildbände zur Archäologie, vol. 3. Main, 1992. Includes additional scholarly literature up to 1990.

KLAUS TUCHELT

DIKAIOS, PORPHYRIOS (1904–1971), one of the most infuential Cypriot archaeologists. Dikaios studied at the universities of Athens, Liverpool, Lyons, and the Sorbonne. In 1929 he was appointed assistant curator of the Cyprus Museum, and two years later he became curator. In 1961, after Cyprus became an independent republic, Dikaios became the first Cypriot director of the Department of Antiquities. In 1963 he left Cyprus for the United States, where he taught at Princeton and Brandeis for the following three years. He then became professor of archaeology at the University of Heidelberg, a post he held until his death in 1971.

While in the Department of Antiquities, Dikaios played a leading role in the reorganization of its administrative system. He was also responsible in 1935 for introducing a new, scientifically based system for cataloging finds and presenting exhibits in the Cyprus Museum. This accomplishment was followed by the publication of the first modern *Guide to the Cyprus Museum* (Nicosia, 1947; 2d ed., 1953; 3d ed., 1961; Greek ed., 1951).

One of the founders of modern Cypriot archaeology, Dikaios excavated and published widely on a variety of subjects, concentrating mainly on Cypriot prehistory. With his publications of his excavations at Khirokoitia, Troulli, Kalavasos, and Sotira, Dikaios defined the character and lay the foundations for all subsequent studies on Neolithic Cyprus. He also investigated the Chalcolithic Period at Erimi, Ambelikou, and Kalavasos and the Early Bronze Age at Vounous and Philia. Of great importance is his work on the Late Bronze Age sites of Pyla-*Kokkinokremos*, Maa-*Palaeokastro*, and, above all, Enkomi which was the subject of one of his major publications (*Enkomi Excavations, 1948–1958,* 4 vols, Mainz, 1969–1971). Dikaios also excavated the Iron Age necropolis of Salamis, and located a large number of sites, several of which were later excavated by other archaeologists. He lectured widely in the United States and Europe and was honored by many institutions.

BIBLIOGRAPHY

Dikaios, Porphyrios. *Khirokitia.* London, 1953. The starting point for any study of this important site and Neolithic Cyprus in general.

Dikaios, Porphyrios. *Sotira.* Philadelphia, 1961. A touchstone in Cypriot prehistory.

Dikaios, Porphyrios, and James R. Stewart. *Swedish Corpus Expedition,* vol. 4.1A, *The Stone Age and the Early Bronze Age in Cyprus.* Lund, 1962. Still the basic work on the subject.

Ieromonachou, Lyghia. "Bibliography of Porphyrios Dikaios." In *Studies Presented in Memory of Porphyrios Dikaios,* pp. 216–217. Nicosia, 1979. Contains a full bibliography of Dikaios's work.

The Large Cypriot Encyclopaedia (in Greek). Nicosia, 1986. See volume 4, pages 267–268.

Nicolaou, Kyriakos. "Porphyrios Dikaios: Necrology" (in Greek). *Report of the Department of Antiquities of Cyprus* (1973): 226–229.

DEMETRIOS MICHAELIDES

DILMUN, the Sumerian name (cf. Akk., Tilmun; Gk., Tylos/Tyros; Lat., Tyrus) given to a country bordering the body of water known in cuneiform sources as the Lower Sea (Persian/Arabian Gulf). Culturally and territorially outside the bounds of Mesopotamia proper, Dilmun is attested as early as the late fourth millennium in the Archaic texts from Uruk-Warka. During the late Early Dynastic period (c. 2500–2350 BCE), Dilmun emerged as an important source of raw materials for the kings of the city-state of Lagash. Ur-Nanshe (c. 2550 BCE) "had ships of Dilmun transport timber from foreign lands" to his city, while Lugalanda (c. 2400) and Urukagina (c. 2380) purchased copper in exchange for milk and cereal products, fat, silver, and wool. Sargon of Agade (c. 2334–2279 BCE) boasted that ships from Dilmun, Magan (Oman peninsula), and Meluḫḫa (Indus Valley?)

docked at the quay of his capitol, Agade (Cooper, 1986, p. 22ff.). During the Isin-Larsa and Old Babylonian periods, Dilmun was most famous as a retailer of copper (probably of Omani origin) to the seafaring merchants of Ur, such as one Ea-nasir, some of whose letters were found by Leonard Woolley during his excavations there (Leemans, 1960). At the same time, diplomatic ties linked Dilmun with the Old Assyrian king Shamshi-Adad and his son Yasmakh-Adad, and caravans are known to have traveled up the Euphrates River between Dilmun and Mari. In the Middle Babylonian period, as two letters found at Nippur show, Dilmun was under the control of a Kassite governor with close family ties to the elite of Nippur. By the Neo-Assyrian period Dilmun, though perhaps independent, was nevertheless tributary to Assyria. The Dilmunite kings Uperi and Aḫundara, who lived, "like a fish, thirty double-hours away in the midst of the sea of the rising sun" (e.g. *Annals of Khorsabad,* Sargon II, section 41), both brought gifts to Sargon II, and a later king called Ḫundaru sent tribute to Ashurbanipal's court at Nineveh. A Babylonian "administrator of Dilmun" (Akk., *lúbēl pīḫāti Dilmunki*) is mentioned in 544 BCE during the reign of Nabonidus.

In addition to these historical and economic references, literary sources attest to the special regard in which Dilmun was held in Mesopotamia. In the Sumerian myth Enki and the World Order, for example, Enki is said to have "cleaned and purified the land of Dilmun," while in Enki and Ninhursag, Dilmun is described as a pure, bright and clean land flowing with the "water of abundance."

Given the relatively abundant written references to Dilmun, it is hardly surprising that many scholars, from the mid-nineteenth century CE onward, have tried to fix the precise location of this land. The French Assyriologist Jules Oppert was the first scholar to link the Akkadian toponym *Tilmun* with the Greek name *Tylos,* the descriptions of which (e.g., by Theophrastus, Strabo, Pliny, and Arrian) leave no doubt of its identity with the largest of the Bahrain islands. The only problem with this identification for the earliest phases of Dilmun's existence (i.e., pre-Old Akkadian) is the complete lack of archaeological evidence for settlement on Bahrain during the late fourth and early third millennia. By contrast, the northeast Arabian mainland contains many sites, such as Tarut Island just opposite the Qatif oasis, Abqayq, Umm an-Nussi, and Umm ar-Ramad, that were inhabited then and show evidence (pottery, carved soft-stone vessels, and statuary) of contact with Jemdet Nasr through Early Dynastic Mesopotamia. It has therefore been suggested that the original center of Dilmun lay on the mainland, and that only toward the end of the third millennium did it shift to Bahrain.

Archaeological investigations on Bahrain since 1879 have documented the existence there of more than one hundred thousand burial mounds dating to the Bronze and Iron Ages, as well as large cemeteries (e.g. at Karranah and Abu Saybi) of Hellenistic and Parthian date. Danish archaeological excavations led by Peter Vilhelm Glob and T. Geoffrey Bibby from the University of Aarhus during the 1950s and early 1960s revealed for the first time the existence of several settlements (e.g., Qal'at al-Bahrain, Saar) and a number of sanctuaries (e.g., Barbar, Diraz, 'Ain Umm es-Sejour) on the island as well. The British archaeologist T. Geoffrey Bibby proposed a comprehensive periodization for Bahrain, based on the Danish work at Qal'at al-Bahrain, using the terms city I–VI to denote individual periods. A distinctive type of circular stamp seal with a high, perforated boss was developed on Bahrain at the very end of the third millennium and was further elaborated during the first centuries of the second millennium BCE (see figure 1). By contrast, cylinder seals were rarely used except during the Middle Babylonian and Neo-Assyrian periods. A local ceramic industry grew up during the city I (so-called chain-ridged ware) and city II (red-ridged ware) periods (i.e., c. 2300–1600 BCE). In addition, Bahrain has always been in contact with neighboring parts of Mesopotamia, Iran, Oman, and the Indus Valley, and the ceramic repertoire found there is accordingly varied. Shortly after 2000 BCE, a satellite settlement was founded on the island of Failaka off the coast of Kuwait. The material culture of the earliest settlement there is so identical to that found on Bahrain at the same time that it is certain the foundation must have been a Dilmunite colony, probably of merchants and their families.

The rich system of aquifers underlying eastern Arabia en-

sured a plentiful supply of water on Bahrain in antiquity, permitting the cultivation of dates, cereals, and other fruits. Freshwater springs emerge both on land and in the shallow waters offshore. It was its role as a commercial center in international trade, however, that made Dilmun famous—although the goods it sold to Mesopotamian merchants were not local products but originated farther east. Copper from the Oman peninsula, tin from Afghanistan (?), exotic woods and ivory from India were purchased by Dilmunite merchants and then reexported to cities like Ur, Lagash, and Mari. Throughout most of the third, second and first millennia BCE, Dilmun was Babylonia's most important southern source of copper, timber, and exotic goods; and at Ur, "Dilmun merchants" (Akk., *alik Tilmun*) formed a particular subgroup of merchants engaged in trade with the Lower Sea.

[*See also* Bahrain; Failaka; Girsu and Lagash; *and* Qal'at al-Bahrain.]

BIBLIOGRAPHY

Bibby, Geoffrey. *Looking for Dilmun*. New York, 1969. Popular account of the Danish Gulf expedition, with primary reference to the work carried out on Bahrain and the search for Dilmun.

Cooper, Jerrold S. *Sumerian and Akkadian Royal Inscriptions*. New Haven, 1986. Reliable, up-to-date translations of third millennium royal texts concerning Dilmun.

Khalifa, Shaikha Haya A. al-, and Michael Rice, eds. *Bahrain through the Ages: The Archaeology*. London, 1986. Wide-ranging proceedings of a conference held in 1983; touches on many aspects of Dilmun's history.

Larsen, Curtis E. *Life and Land Use on the Bahrain Islands: The Geoarcheology of an Ancient Society*. Chicago, 1983. Geoarchaeological approach to ancient Bahrain which must be read critically.

Leemans, Wilhelmus F. *Foreign Trade in the Old Babylonian Period*. Leiden, 1960. Basic study of Ea-nasir's activities.

Potts, Daniel T., ed. *Dilmun: New Studies in the Archaeology and Early History of Bahrain*. Berlin, 1983. Collection of essays on Dilmun, primarily by Assyriologists, on the cuneiform sources of various periods, as well as a number of archaeological studies.

Potts, Daniel T. "Reflections on the History and Archaeology of Bahrain." *Journal of the American Oriental Society* 105 (1985): 675–710. Critical review of a number of studies in Bahraini archaeology which appeared in the early 1980s; contains a great deal of environmental and demographic information on Bahrain and extensive discussions of questions connected with Dilmun.

Potts, Daniel T. *The Arabian Gulf in Antiquity*. 2 vols. Oxford, 1990. General survey of the archaeology of the Gulf region, with a discussion of Dilmun in all periods.

D. T. POTTS

DILMUN. Figure 1. *Circular stamp seal.* A typical stamp seal of early second millennium BCE, showing human and animal figures. (Courtesy D. T. Potts)

DIYALA, a tributary of the Tigris River that catches its water from the Zagros Mountains northeast of Baghdad. After it escapes from the mountains, the Diyala crosses two plains: a triangular basin northeast of a low row of promontories, Jebel Hamrin, and the alluvium surrounding the river south of the Hamrin before it joins the Tigris at Baghdad. The Diyala region is traditionally divided into three zones: the Upper Diyala, referring to the course of the river through the mountainous Zagros; the Middle Diyala, which includes the Hamrin basin and immediate catchment areas; and the Lower Diyala, the areas southwest of the Hamrin range.

The Diyala River traverses the central western Zagros Mountains and the northeastern part of the Mesopotamian alluvium. One of the oldest known trade routes, the Silk Road, is located in this region. Connecting the Mediterranean with China, the route is also called the Great Khorasan Road between Baghdad and Kermanshah. The route follows the Diyala River up from Baghdad through the Hamrin, where it crosses to the Iranian plateau through passes in the Zagros Mountains. These geographic details are important in reconstructing ancient human exploitation of the region.

In archaeological terms, the Diyala traditionally refers to the Lower Diyala region and includes the countryside receiving water from the Diyala River by irrigation canals. Recent archaeological results from the Hamrin make it plausible to include this region as well. The Lower Diyala region has been identified at the province of Eshnunna, an important city-state during the Isin-Larsa period. Eshnunna is modern Tell Asmar. Other important sites have also been identified, such as Khafajeh as the ancient town of Tutub.

The first systematic archaeological investigation of the Lower Diyala plain took place from 1930 to 1938 with the Iraq Expedition, directed by Henri Frankfort. It was the first large-scale expedition from the Oriental Institute of the University of Chicago to Iraq. Among others, the staff also included Thorkild Jacobsen as epigrapher, Seton Lloyd, Gordon Loud, and Pinhas Delougaz. One reason for choosing the Diyala region was the increasing number of clay tablets and art objects being brought to the antiquities market in Baghdad from illicit digging into the mounds in the area. It was also assumed that the region was historically important and that Tell Asmar was indeed the ancient city of Eshnunna. The Oriental Institute expedition concentrated on the excavations of four sites: Khafajeh, Tell Asmar, Tell Agrab, and Ishchali. It built its expedition house at Tell Asmar. [See the biographies of Frankfort, Jacobsen, and Lloyd.]

Extensive surveys of the Lower Diyala plain combined with excavations were carried out in 1957–1958 by Thorkild Jacobsen, Robert McCormick Adams, and Fuad Safar under the Diyala Basin Archaeological Project. [See the biography of Safar.] The project, aimed at investigating agricultural history and irrigation—the salinity of irrigated fields and its impact on social and economic subsystems—mapped the cultural landscape through more than six thousand years. It was the first comprehensive archaeological regional analysis of the Mesopotamian alluvium.

During the 1970s, intensive archaeological rescue operations took place in the Hamrin Basin as a result of construc-

tion for a new dam at the point where the Diyala River cuts through the Hamrin Mountains. The aggregated archaeological investigations of the Diyala region have made it one of the best-documented provinces of Mesopotamia.

The excavations at Tell Asmar, Khafajeh, Tell Agrab, and Ishchali resulted in the development of a long-range chronology for the Lower Diyala region. These sites cover a period from the Late Uruk into the Old Babylonian Period (c. 3500–1800 BCE). Their stratigraphic sequences partly overlap and provide the basis for a diachronic study of architecture and artifacts. In 1952, Delougaz (1952) published a comprehensive pottery corpus, still one of the most useful references for studying the third- and early second-millennium BCE pottery of Mesopotamia. The repertoire of seals also has contributed essentially to establishing a sequence for glyptic styles in Mesopotamia (Frankfort, 1955). The architectural remains from the beginning of the third millennium, in particular temple buildings, have resulted in the subdivision of the ED period into three phases: I–III (Delougaz and Lloyd, 1942). The terminology Frankfort and others introduced does differ at some points from that traditionally used (e.g., the Protoliterate period equals the Uruk and Jemdet Nasr periods; late ED III is labeled the Protoimperial period).

Robert McC. Adams's 1957–1958 surveys added details about settlement patterns and canal systems from the Ubaid period through the nineteenth century CE. The intensive investigation of the Hamrin basin by many international archaeological teams extended the chronology for the entire Diyala region and widened its geographic range.

Except for a single aceramic site, the earliest settlements in the Hamrin date to the Samarra period (c. 6000–5500 BCE). This could be expected, as the region is in the middle of traditional Samarran territory, the marginal zones for dry farming. The first substantial human activities can be attributed to the Ubaid period (5500–4000 BCE). At Tell Abada, located south of the Diyala River in the Hamrin, almost an entire Ubaid village was excavated by an Iraqi expedition under the direction of Sabah Abboud Jasim (1985). The village consists of several building compounds in which a central building differs both in size and finds from the rest and suggests an advanced state of social stratification in the order of chiefdoms. Houses show a typical tripartite ground plan, with a T-shaped central room. These are prototypes for the following Uruk and ED temple and house plans. At Tell Madhhur, in the northern part of the Hamrin, a particularly well-preserved house with almost a complete household inventory was excavated by a British-Canadian team (e.g., Roaf, 1989). In the Lower Diyala Region, sparse Ubaid remains were observed, but the location of sites shows the basic outline of the irrigation canal system. There, as at several other Mesopotamian sites, the fact that Ubaid remains were found under the major urban sites shows that the principle urban settlement pattern took shape during the Ubaid with the establishment of villages at natural or artificial watercourses. [See Ubaid.]

Few finds are available from the Uruk period (4000–3100 BCE). In the Hamrin, villages founded during the Ubaid disappear, while in the Lower Diyala region there is an increasing area of land under exploitation. This development can be tied to the urbanization process for the entire region, in which centers experiencing strong population growth became large towns.

During the Jemdet Nasr and Early Dynastic periods (3100–2400 BCE), the Diyala region experienced steady population growth, to judge from the increase in the number of sites and in settlement size. In the Lower Diyala region, urban centers surrounded by a pattern of sites in hierarchical clusters developed at Khafajeh, Tell Asmar, and Tell Agrab. Of ninety-six surveyed sites, ten can be classified as large towns (greater than 10 ha, or 25 acres), nineteen as small towns (4–10 ha, or 9–25 acres), and sixty-seven as villages (fewer than 4 ha, or 9 acres). The ED period is one of the best documented in the region. Extensive excavations at sites in the Lower Diyala and the Hamrin give a comprehensive impression of the architecture, burial traditions, art, and material culture in the early third millennium. At Khafajeh and Tell Asmar, sequences of temples were found, some of them identified by historical sources. In Khafajeh a sequence of temples dedicated to Sin dates back to the Jemdet Nasr period. The temple type is initially tripartite but evolves into a closed compound with internal courtyards. In contrast to contemporary and earlier temples, these temples were originally built on the ground floor. In the ED II period, a large temple complex was constructed at Khafajeh, characterized by two large oval enclosure walls. Between the two walls was a house interpreted as the house of the priest. Inside the oval enclosure walls the temple rose on a platform. It was surrounded by workshops, perhaps a production center administrated by the priest of the temple (Delougaz, 1940). At Tell Agrab a monumental temple was dedicated to Shara. The ground plan shows a traditional Mesopotamian building pattern, in which the cella is located within a large square complex of rooms and courtyards and the entire building is enclosed with a heavy outer wall. At Tell Asmar, the temple sequence produced several spectacular finds. Best known is the hoard of sculptures from the ED II period found in a pit under the floor of the so-called Square Temple. The sculptures are carved in stone and are typically Sumerian in style and dress. ED domestic architecture is less well known. In the Hamrin remains of round structures were found that are dated to the beginning of the ED period. Both at Tell Gubba and Tell Razuk, complete round buildings were preserved to a degree that had left part of the corbelled vaulted ceilings intact. These round structures are assumed to have served as fortifications along the northeastern frontier, constructed and maintained by the large town centers in the Lower Diyala region. One reason for setting up such strongholds was to protect the vulnerable outlets for the vital irrigation canals at the point where the Diyala River cuts through the Hamrin Mountains.

The excavation of ED sites gives detailed insight into the technological and artistic level of the population. In particular many cylinder seals, bronze tools, sculptures, and carved relief plaques were recovered. The pottery tradition during the ED I–II periods shows regionalization at the southeastern fringe of Mesopotamia: polychrome painted Jemdet Nasr pottery develops into local styles; and in the Lower Diyala and the Hamrin, so-called Scarlet Ware, a jar painted in red and black with geometric and naturalistic motifs, appears. This distribution of ceramic styles makes it possible to recognize the Diyala region as one cultural entity during ED I–II.

In the Akkadian period (2400–2200 BCE), the region continues to develop along the lines laid out during the ED period. At Tell Asmar, private houses and monumental buildings have been exposed. The Northern Palace, a large building complex with several domestic sectors, may have already been built at the end of ED III. While the palace was apparently ruined with the Guti invasion at the end of the Akkadian period, the private houses and dwellings continued in use. The town lost its administrative function, but it remained inhabited. In the Hamrin, Akkadian cuneiform tablets have been found, probably within an administrative context (Whiting, 1987).

The archaeological record remains poor through the Ur III dynasty, during which period Eshnunna/Tell Asmar was controlled by governors appointed by the kings of Ur. During the following era, the Isin-Larsa period (c. 2000–1800 BCE), the region reached a political peak, beginning with the move toward independence by the governor of Eshnunna, Ituriya. Although the settlement pattern continued, there was a tendency for a few centers to grow, perhaps as a result of the centralization of administrative institutions and power in Eshnunna. The importance of the region and its history during the Larsa period is well documented because of the finds of archives and inscriptions. Large temple complexes were constructed, and, in the case of the Shu-Sin temple at Eshnunna, the temple was combined with a palace. At Ishchali, the monumental temple of Ishtar-Kititum comprises interior courtyards and broadroom antecella and cella temple plans. From this era, several sites in the Hamrin that most likely profited from the interest of Eshnunna have produced remains, particularly towns that dominated the main routes.

The flourishing of the Diyala during the hegemony of Eshnunna ended with the reign of Hammurabi of Babylon. According to survey results (Adams, 1965), the larger towns entered a period of decline that lasted for several hundreds of years. Data from the Hamrin speak of a population settled primarily in villages scattered over the plains. A regeneration of the settlement pattern and population growth first occurs in the Seleucid-Parthian period. Despite poor archaeological documentation, survey data suggest extensive urbanization. Development culminated in the Sasanian period, during which the region, in ecological terms was brought to its limits. As the agricultural hinterland for the Sasanian capital at Ctesiphon, large canal systems were laid out and the agricultural potential exploited to a maximum. During the Islamic period, the Diyala region again experienced a decline in organization and population size, despite the rise of Baghdad.

[*See also* Eshnunna; Hamrin Dam Salvage Project; *and* Khafajeh.]

BIBLIOGRAPHY

Adams, Robert McC. *Land behind Baghdad.* Chicago, 1965. The most comprehensive study of ancient settlement patterns in the Diyala.

Delougaz, Pinhas. *The Temple Oval At Khafajah.* University of Chicago, Oriental Institute Publications (OIP), 53. Chicago, 1940. Excavation report.

Delougaz, Pinhas, and Seton Lloyd. *Pre-Sargonid Temples in the Diyala Region.* OIP, 58. Chicago, 1942. Excavation report with a description of the Sumerian temples found at Tell Asmar, Khafajeh, and Tell Agrab (except the Oval Temple).

Delougaz, Pinhas. *Pottery from the Diyala Region.* OIP, 63. Chicago, 1952. The basic reference book for Mesopotamian pottery.

Delougaz, Pinhas, et al. *Private Houses and Graves in the Diyala Region.* OIP, 88. Chicago, 1967.

Frankfort, Henri. *Sculpture of the Third Millennium B.C. from Tell Asmar and Khafājah.* OIP, 44. Chicago, 1939. Detailed presentation of Sumerian sculptures from the Diyala.

Frankfort, Henri, Seton Lloyd, and Thorkild Jacobsen. *The Gimilsin Temple and the Palace of the Rulers at Tell Asmar.* OIP, 43. Chicago, 1940. Excavation report.

Frankfort, Henri. *More Sculpture from the Diyala Region.* OIP, 60. Chicago, 1943. Detailed presentation of Sumerian sculptures from the Diyala. See as well Frankfort (1939).

Frankfort, Henri. *Stratified Cylinder Seals from the Diyala Region.* OIP, 72. Chicago, 1955

Gibson, McGuire, ed. *Uch Tepe I.* The Chicago-Copenhagen Expedition to the Hamrin, Hamrin Report 10. Chicago and Copenhagen, 1981. A broad review of the settlement history and archaeological results from the Hamrin basin, together with a detailed report on the excavation of the ED round fortification at Tell Razuk.

Hill, Harold D., et al. *Old Babylonian Public Buildings in the Diyala Region.* OIP, 98. Chicago, 1990. Conclusive report on the excavations of the Kititum Temple at Ishchali.

Jacobsen, Thorkild. *Salinity and Irrigation: Agriculture in Antiquity.* Bibliotheca Mesopotamica, 14. Malibu, 1982. Based on manuscripts twenty years older than the year of publication.

Jasim, Sabah A. *The 'Ubaid Period in Iraq: Recent Excavations in the Hamrin Region.* British Archaeological Reports, International Series, no. 267. Oxford, 1985. Report on the important finds of an Ubaid village, with a summary of the Ubaid period in Mesopotamia based on the new finds.

Roaf, Michael. "Social Organization and Social Activities at Tell Madhhur." In *Upon This Foundation—the Ubaid Reconsidered,* edited by E. F. Henrickson and Ingolf Thuesen, pp. 91–145. Copenhagen, 1989. Comprehensive analysis of an Ubaid period household.

Whiting, Robert M., Jr. *Old Babylonian Letters from Tell Asmar.* University of Chicago, Oriental Institute, Assyriological Studies, 22. Chicago, 1987. The most recent and detailed scholarly work on letters from the archives at Tell Asmar.

INGOLF THUESEN

DODECANESE. *See* Aegean Islands.

DOGS. The dog (*Canis familiaris*) evolved from the wolf (*Canis lupus*) in a number of parallel and independent episodes of domestication. Domestication is inferred in the archaeological record from skeletal changes in the teeth and skull—in particular, crowding of the tooth row. Additional changes include an overall diminution in size and increased variability in domesticates. The earliest claim of domestic dog in the Near East comes from the Palegawra cave in Iraq, in a deposit dated to about 10,000 BCE. However, both the date and the morphological identification of this canid is contested. In Natufian levels (c. 9600 BCE) at 'Ein Mallaḥa in northern Israel, a woman was buried with a wolf or dog puppy. Although, the wild or domestic status of the puppy cannot be determined, it documents the first ceremonial relationship between humans and canids in the region.

The ceremonial treatment of dogs took several forms. Interment, with or without accompanying human burial, is known throughout the ancient eastern Mediterranean, but only in Egypt and Israel was it practiced on a large scale. Dogs were used in sacrificial and exorcistic rites in Anatolia. Among the western Semites, puppies were specified for sacrifice to conclude a covenant. In Mesopotamia and Anatolia, dogs and puppies played a role in cultic healing and rites to eliminate impurity. Dogs were used in healing rituals in Greece, but they were also sacrificed and apparently eaten in conjunction with human burials.

In Egypt, in a few cases, dogs have been found accompanying human burials in deposits as early as the Neolithic and Badarian periods. Large-scale burial of mummified remains are known from the Hellenistic and especially Roman periods. At the Chalcolithic cemetery at Gilat in the Negev, two dogs with grave goods were recovered. Also in southern Israel, more than 1200 dog interments were excavated from Persian and Early Hellenistic levels at the site of Ashkelon. In Mesopotamia, the dog was associated with the goddess Gula in her function as healer, and a number of puppies and adults were found in a ramp of her temple at Isin (c. 1000 BCE). Dog burial was widespread but does not seem to have been similarly motivated in each region. At Ashkelon, for example, the dogs were carefully interred in separate pits, but no grave goods accompanied them, and the burials were not associated with architecture of any notable scale. The reason for their burial remains a mystery.[*See* Gilat; Ashkelon; Isin.]

Egyptian and Mesopotamian art contains numerous images of dogs that have been identified as representing ancient breeds, often greyhounds and salukis or mastiffs. These are not confirmed by the osteological evidence from Egypt and the Near East, however. Reconstructions of the size, weight, limb proportions, and head shape of ancient dogs shows that prior to the Roman period selective dog breeding was not practiced in a way that produced distinctive populations. Rather, the osteological evidence reveals that the dogs of the region can be referred to the "pariah"—medium-sized animals varying in body and head from a sheep dog to a greyhound type.

[*See also* Animal Husbandry; Cult; Ethnozoology; *and* Paleozoology.]

BIBLIOGRAPHY

Churcher, C. S. "Dogs from Ein Tirghi Cemetery, Balat, Dalkhleh Oasis, Western Desert of Egypt." In *Skeletons in Her Cupboard,* edited by Anneke Clason et al., pp. 39–59. Oxbow Monograph, 34. Oxford, 1993. Critical survey of appearance of dog types in ancient Egypt.
Day, Leslie P. "Dog Burials in the Greek World." *American Journal of Archaeology* 88 (1984): 21–32. Reviews the evidence for Greek dog sacrifice and its underlying motivations.
Haddon, Kathleen. "Report on a Small Collection of Mummy Dogs." In *The Cemeteries of Abydos,* part 1, *1909–1910: The Mixed Cemetery and Umm el-Ga'ab,* by Edouard Naville, et al., pp. 40–48. Memoir of the Egyptian Exploration Society, 33. London, 1913. Despite its age, the best zoological evaluation of the dog "types" in Egyptian mummified remains.
Olsen, Stanley J. *Origins of the Domestic Dog: The Fossil Record.* Tucson, 1985. Global review of the osteological evidence for dog domestication.
Wapnish, Paula, and Brian Hesse. "Pampered Pooches or Plain Pariahs? The Ashkelon Dog Burials." *Biblical Archaeologist* 56.2 (1993): 55–80. Although focused on the burials at Ashkelon, the article provides a regionwide review of dogs in the historic period.

PAULA WAPNISH and BRIAN HESSE

DOLMEN. A megalithic burial structure shaped like a table (from whence its Breton name) a dolmen is usually comprised of a capstone resting on upright stones. It most often occurs in groups and is frequently associated with enigmatic stone circles, one-course stone rows, and tumuli.

Dolmens can take on a number of forms. Though their typologies do not completely coincide, both Claire Epstein (1985) and Mattanyah Zohar (1992) have discerned six general types, based on shape, size, depth, and association with

DOLMEN. *Dolmen with a carved stone aperture from ed-Damiyeh, Jordan.* (Courtesy D. Ilan)

other features such as stone tumuli, rings, and walls. The simplest type, the trilithon, is the most common form. Different forms often occur together, but specific fields and certain regions generally show a preponderance of a particular type—perhaps an expression of tribal traditions. Many dolmens show signs of originally having been enclosed by tumuli, and it is possible that all were. [See Tumulus.]

In the Levant, dolmen fields are concentrated along the Syro-African Rift, as far north as southern Turkey and as far south as Ma'in in Jordan. They do not occur in the southern deserts of Sinai, Arabia, and the Negev, nor are they found in southern Mesopotamia or northern Anatolia. Dolmens most commonly occupy lands best suited for pasture and that are less amenable to field-crop agriculture, leading most researchers to associate them with nomadic pastoralist populations. However, Lipaz Vinitzky (1992) has shown a clear nexus between Early Bronze Age settlements and dolmen fields in Israel's Golan Heights and Galilee region. Topographically, dolmens tend to be concentrated on escarpment piedmonts (e.g., Shamir in Israel or Adeimah in Jordan) and along wadi slopes (e.g., the Golan Heights), where large slabs can be transported downslope, or in places of prominence on extensive plateaus. It is now recognized that dolmens were erected at least as early as the late fourth millennium (EB I) and at least as late as the second or early third millennium BCE (Intermediate Bronze Age). Disagreement exists as to whether the floruit of the phenomenon came about in the Early Bronze (e.g., Vinitzky) or the Intermediate Bronze Age (Zohar, Epstein). Finds indicate that some monuments continued to be utilized throughout the second millennium BCE and even later.

Dolmens are most often found empty or containing only fragmentary and exiguous artifacts. Nevertheless, the fact that a few dolmens have been found to contain human skeletal material has lead virtually all researchers to conclude that they functioned as tombs. The scarcity of bones suggests to some that dolmens were intended for primary burial, after which the bones were moved elsewhere for final, secondary burial; this is unlikely, however, because few, if any, necropoli containing secondary burials can clearly be related to dolmens. They may represent a netherworld abode or locus of transition between the realms of life and death. For the living, they may have served as local territory markers—particularly in times of scarce pasture—or as symbols of power and ideological affiliation.

[See also Burial Sites; Cave Tombs.]

BIBLIOGRAPHY

Epstein, Claire. "Dolmens Excavated in the Golan." 'Atiqot (English Series) 17 (1985): 20–58. Contains a good sample of dolmen forms and recovered artifacts that illustrate reuse from the Intermediate Bronze Age through the Late Bronze Age.

Prag, Kay. "The Dead Sea Dolmens: Death and the Landscape." In The Archaeology of Death in the Ancient Near East, edited by Stuart Campbell and Anthony Green. Oxford, 1995. Regional study utilizing ethnographic and ecological data to interpret the dolmen phenomenon and their appearance in EB I.

Vinitzky, Lipaz. "The Date of the Dolmens in the Golan and the Galilee: A Reassessment." Tel Aviv 19.1 (1992): 100–112. Regional study incorporating recent data to show that the floruit of dolmen building occurred during the Early Bronze Age in association with settlements.

Zohar, Mattanyah. "Megalithic Cemeteries in the Levant." In Pastoralism in the Levant: Archaeological Materials in Anthropological Perspectives, edited by Ofer Bar-Yosef and Anatoly Khazanov, pp. 43–63. Prehistory Press Monographs in World Archaeology, no. 10. Madison, Wis., 1992. The most up-to-date synthesis of dolmens in the Levant and one of two studies that attempt serious socioecological explanation (the other is Prag, above).

DAVID ILAN

DOR, eastern Mediterranean seaport mentioned in biblical accounts in connection with the Israelite conquest of Canaan. The site is located on the Carmel coast, about 21 km (13 mi.) south of Haifa, at the site of modern-day Khirbet el-Burj.

History. An Egyptian inscription found in Nubia that dates to the reign of Rameses II (thirteenth century BCE) contains the earliest known reference to Dor in a list of Syro-Phoenician coastal cities. Dor is cited also in the account of the Egyptian emissary Wenamun's journey to Byblos (c. 1100 BCE), as is Dor's ruler, Beder, king of the Tjeker (Sikels), one of the marauding Sea Peoples who invaded the Levant in the twelfth century BCE.

In the Bible, the king of Dor is listed among the many defeated Canaanite rulers whose lands were distributed to the Israelites (Jos. 12:23). Material remains suggest, however, as does Joshua 17:12–13, that the site, allotted to the tribe of Manasseh, was populated by Canaanites until the reign of King David in the tenth century BCE, when Dor was finally conquered by the Israelites. Later, when King Solomon reorganized Israel into administrative districts, he made Dor the capital of the fourth administrative district, with his son-in-law Ben-Abinadab as governor (1 Kgs. 4:11).

After the entire coastal region of the northern kingdom was conquered by Tiglath-Pileser III in 732 BCE, Dor became the capital of an Assyrian province extending from the Carmel range to Jaffa. Sidon apparently ruled Dor in the Persian period (sixth–fourth centuries BCE), but in the Hellenistic period the city became a powerful fortress that two Seleucid kings were unable to take, either by land or sea. Dor and its fortified neighbor, Straton's Tower (later Caesarea), were ruled by the despot Zoilus until the two cities were conquered by Alexander Jannaeus in the late second century BCE. [See Caesarea.] The Hasmoneans then ruled Dor until 63 BCE, when the Roman general Pompey conquered the city but granted it independence. Coins minted at Dor during the Roman period indicate that the inhabitants worshiped Zeus and Astarte, but there are literary references to a Jewish community and synagogue during the reign of Agrippa I (41–44 CE). At the beginning of the third century Dor was abandoned.

In the late fourth century CE, St. Jerome described Dor as lying in ruin, but excavators have uncovered two distinct periods of Byzantine church constructions, beginning in the fourth century and ending in the seventh century CE, outside and at the front of the mound. The area lay uninhabited until the eleventh century, when the Crusader fortress of Merle was built on the mound; it was destroyed shortly thereafter.

Excavations. The first excavations at Dor were conducted in 1923 and 1924 by the British School of Archaeology in Jerusalem under the direction of John Garstang. J. Leibowitz, on behalf of the Israel Department of Antiquities, excavated north of the mound in 1950 and 1952. Leibowitz discovered sections of a Roman theater as well as the Byzantine church mentioned above. Located east of the mound, the church complex, comprising about 1,000 sq m, was fully excavated between 1979 and 1983 by an Israel Department of Antiquities and Museums team led by C. Dauphin.

Beginning in 1980, large-scale excavations were resumed at the site by Ephraim Stern under the auspices of the Institute of Archaeology at the Hebrew University of Jerusalem and the Israel Exploration Society. Findings from seven main areas of the mound indicate that Dor was first inhabited at the beginning of the Middle Bronze Age IIA (c. 2000 BCE) and was occupied virtually without a gap until the third century BCE. After Herod the Great built the harbor at Caesarea in the first century BCE, Dor began to decline and eventually was abandoned.

Archaeological Remains. A few MB IIA buildings were uncovered along the western edge of the site, which the sea has eroded to bedrock. No Late Bronze buildings were uncovered, but scarabs and pottery from the period were found.

A massive mud-brick wall running north–south along the eastern fringe of the mound is the characteristic feature of Early Iron Age Dor. This wall (about 3 m high and 2.5 m deep) was reinforced along its exterior by a sand rampart. Two rooms were partially excavated along the wall's interior and several vessels, similar to ones uncovered at other sites

DOR. *View of excavated areas from the east.* (Courtesy E. Stern)

along the Syro-Phoenician coast, were found in situ. These rooms were destroyed by a conflagration, after which the wall went out of use. These Early Iron remains at Dor probably date from 1150 to 1050 BCE and likely are evidence of an impressive fortified Sikil settlement.

Several new settlement phases dating from the second half of the eleventh century BCE were uncovered in various areas of the mound. Among the important material finds from these Iron Age strata were Early Cypriot vessels, some Phoenician bichrome ware and black-on-red vessels, and local pottery. Dor was destroyed at the end of the tenth century BCE, probably at the hands of the Egyptian pharoah Sheshonq (biblical Shishak). The town was refortified during the ninth century BCE with the addition of a solid offset-inset wall and a four-chambered gate. Not long after the destruction of this fortification by Tiglath-Pileser III, at the end of the eighth century BCE, the Assyrians rebuilt the wall and added a two-chambered gate; this fortification system lasted until the mid-fourth century BCE, when it was probably destroyed in the Sidonian revolt against the Persians (348 BCE).

Dor's cosmopolitan character during the Persian period is indicated both by abundant and varied material remains and by evidence of imported city planning. The eastern part of the mound was a residential district laid out according to the orthogonal Hippodamian plan, in which living units were divided into long, narrow blocks (about 15 m wide) separated by streets intersecting at right angles. Lengthwise streets ran parallel to the city wall. Unusually large quantities of local and imported pottery, especially Attic ware, were uncovered in two Persian period strata; some types were rare—such as large wine amphoras, the first found in coastal Israel. Many figurines, statuettes, and seals also were uncovered, as were several ostraca—among them the first Greek inscriptions from the Persian period discovered in Israel—and many Phoenician cult objects, primarily pottery figurines, stone statuettes, and faience amulets, some recovered in situ.

The orthogonal layout remained virtually unchanged during the Hellenistic period, when urban planning was evident in the southern as well as eastern areas of the mound. Houses at least two stories high were built on the same narrow blocks as in the Persian period, but with different partitions between them, and in the same Phoenician style, with outer walls of alternating ashlar piers and a rubble fill. Some residences had cellars.

The remains of some of the largest temples yet uncovered in Israel were exposed on the western slope of the mound. These temples—all located near the seashore—probably were built in the Hellenistic period but continued in use into the Roman period. A virtual ceramic typology of Hellenistic Palestine was uncovered in these strata. By this period Dor had become a thoroughly Greek city, as indicated by such pagan finds as a marble head of Hermes, the head of a pot-tery figurine (probably of Aphrodite), and a "temple-boy" pottery figurine.

Late Roman remains were uncovered in two main strata. In the earlier stratum a spacious piazza was discovered at the intersection of the city's main street, which extended out from the eastern gate, and a long north–south street. A well had been dug in the center of the piazza, which was paved with large, dressed stones. A drainage system, with its main drain running east–west and auxiliary channels joining it from the north and south, was uncovered under the pavement of the street and the piazza. Public buildings surrounded the piazza in this period. One of them—a storehouse, khan, or barrack—had an internal courtyard surrounded by rows of rooms. One row abutted and ran parallel to the long north–south street; each of its rooms opened onto the courtyard, but only the entrance hall also opened onto the street. Other building remains from the earlier Roman stratum included a spacious and well-planned residential quarter with intersecting streets and a large ashlar structure; the latter was uncovered at the foot of the mound, indicating that construction in this period extended beyond the boundaries of the mound.

Four large square piers were exposed outside and east of the city gate. These piers mark the western terminus of the Roman aqueduct through which water was brought to Dor from springs in the Carmel range. A paved path ran between the piers, at least one of which apparently had an arch. A sacred enclosure on the western slope of the mound seems to relate to a massive retaining wall whose orientation follows that of an earlier north–south street just east of it that was the main access road to the Hellenistic temples (see above). In the later Roman period the street was blocked by the retaining wall. Sherds were uncovered along the wall of the enclosure that seem to belong to the foundation trench of the retaining wall—further evidence that these remains belong to the later Roman stratum. Also part of that stratum was a large piazza at the center of the mound. Two massive foundations north of the piazza extend east and west of it and may have carried a portico that surrounded the city's forum. Two more structures dating to the later stratum were uncovered on the mound's western slope. One was a bath, in which two rooms, perhaps the caldarium and tepidarium, were excavated. The other structure, which had a barrel-vault roof, was only partially excavated.

BIBLIOGRAPHY

Dahl, George. "The Materials for the History of Dor." *Transactions of the Connecticut Academy of Arts and Sciences* 20 (1915): 1–131. General study of all written sources related to the city of Dor.

Stern, Ephraim. *Dor, the Ruler of the Seas: Ten Years of Excavations in the Israeli-Phoenician Harbor Town on the Carmel Coast.* Jerusalem, 1994. Summary of the recent excavations at Tel Dor.

EPHRAIM STERN

DOTHAN (Ar., Tell Dothan), site located in the northern Samaria Hills on the east side of the Dothan Valley, some 22 km (about 14 mi.) north of Shechem. Dothan is a prominent mound, composed of nearly 15 m of stratified remains superimposed on a natural hill nearly 45 m high. The summit comprises approximately 10 acres, and the occupied area of the slopes includes another 15 acres. The plain has always been of strategic importance as the most easterly of the three main passes of the coastal plain from the Sharon to the Jezreel Valley through the mountainous ridge created by the northern Ephraimite hill country and the Carmel ridge.

Dothan has been identified with the biblical city of the same name, mentioned in *Genesis* 37 as the place where Joseph found his brothers in the course of their wanderings with their father's flocks. The narrative describes the intrigue that led to Joseph's being taken to Egypt by a caravan of Ishmaelites (or Midianites) traveling via Dothan from Gilead. During the period of the monarchy, Dothan is described as a well-fortified city to which the Aramean king sent emmisaries in search of the prophet Elisha (2 Kgs. 6:13–14). Other literary references include three notations in the *Book of Judith* and one in the *Onomasticon* of Eusebius.

The site was excavated by Joseph P. Free of Wheaton College, Illinois, in nine seasons between 1953 and 1964. According to the excavator, Dothan yielded a nearly continuous occupational sequence from the Chalcolithic (3200 BCE) through the Byzantine period with later occupation as late as the fourteenth century CE. The site was investigated in six major areas of excavation (T, B, A, D, L, and K, moving from east to west.) The western cemetery is located in area K.

From 1960 to 1964, Robert E. Cooley excavated three tombs in area K. Tomb 1 is the western cemetery's largest, richest (more than 3,400 objects), and best-preserved of the burial chambers. In addition to an abundant collection of human bones, a variety of small finds was recovered from it: pyxides (most with painted decoration), lamps, bowls, biconical jars, kraters, chalices, flasks, juglets, stirrup jars, jewelry, bronze weaponry, beads, bone-carved objects, an important group of scarabs, and several unique artifacts, such as a figurine lamp.

The tomb's architectural plan is tripartite: a basically rectangular tomb chamber with rounded corners, a stepped entryway on the west, and entry through a vertical shaft. The shaft gave access to the stepped entryway that, in turn, led into the tomb chamber. Eight loculi, or crypts, were located along the walls of the chamber, whose orientation is west–east.

Tomb 1 is a successive multiple-burial tomb. Five distinct levels of stratification were discerned, dating from the Late Bronze 11 period into the Early Iron Age. The total number of burials has been calculated to be between three hundred

and five hundred. Although tombs 2 and 3 appear to share the chronology of tomb 1, they were not stratified.

Area D, on the south side of the summit of the tell, yielded a massive city fortification that was dated to the earliest phases of the Early Bronze Age. Area T, located on the highest part of the mound, was designated by Free as the acropolis area. Notable among the discoveries there was a medieval fortress-palace from the fourteenth century CE. Published data for area B are exceptionally lean and consist only of the observation that the area embraced remains from the Roman and Hellenistic periods. The central section of the top of the mound (area A) was occupied by a Hellenistic settlement, embracing the third and second centuries BCE. Substantial remains of an Iron Age settlement were uncovered beneath the Hellenistic occupation. Notable among the architectural features of the Iron Age was a substantial section of a wide street (33.5 m long and 1.20 m wide) bordered by well-preserved structures. The largest of the areas of excavation was area L, on the western summit of the mound. The sloped section of this area yielded substantial fortifications from the Early Bronze Age. The area also produced sections of the city's Middle and Late Bronze Age fortifications. Substantial remains of an Iron Age administrative building were also discovered in this area. Several structures were uncovered in area L that were reminiscent in architectural plan of the so-called open-court building regarded as a hallmark of Assyrian influence. The associated pottery was clearly in the Assyrian tradition of the eighth–seventh centuries BCE.

BIBLIOGRAPHY

Cooley, Robert E. "Gathered to His People: A Study of a Dothan Family Tomb." In *The Living and Active Word of God: Studies in Honor of Sameul J. Schultz,* edited by M. Inch and R. Youngblood, pp. 47–58. Winona Lake, Ill., 1983.

Free, Joseph P. "The First Season of Excavation at Dothan." *Bulletin of the American Schools of Oriental Research,* no. 131 (1953): 16–20.

Free, Joseph P. "The Second Season at Dothan." *Bulletin of the American Schools of Oriental Research,* no. 135 (1954): 14–20.

Free, Joseph P. "The Third Season at Dothan." *Bulletin of the American Schools of Oriental Research,* no. 139 (1955): 3–9.

Free, Joseph P. "The Fourth Season at Dothan." *Bulletin of the American Schools of Oriental Research,* no. 143 (1956): 11–17.

Free, Joseph P. "The Fifth Season at Dothan." *Bulletin of the American Schools of Oriental Research,* no. 152 (1958): 10–18.

Free, Joseph P. "The Sixth Season at Dothan." *Bulletin of the American Schools of Oriental Research,* no. 156 (1959): 22–29.

Free, Joseph P. "The Seventh Season at Dothan." *Bulletin of the American Schools of Oriental Research,* no. 160 (1960): 6–15.

ROBERT E. COOLEY and GARY D. PRATICO

DOUARA, cave located about 18 km (11 mi.) northeast of Palmyra in central Syria (34°38′42″ N, 38°25′58″ E). Excavation has shown that the site was inhabited during the

Middle Paleolithic and Epipaleolithic periods. Douara is unusual because it is one of the few Paleolithic sites that have been excavated in Syria's semiarid interior. The sequence of occupation at Douara is unusually long, although the episodes of use were separated by long intervals of abandonment. The material recovered has provided extensive information about the history and nature of its human occupation.

The cave is set in the south face of a steep rock scarp on the southern edge of the Jebel Abu Rujmein, a range of hills that extends northeastward across central Syria. The cave is more than 10 m wide at the entrance and extends 14 m back into the hillside. The site was identified in 1967 by a Japanese team from the University of Tokyo and was excavated by them in 1970 (under the direction of Hisashi Suzuki), 1974 (Kazuro Hanihara), and again in 1984 (Takeru Akazawa).

The archaeological sequence consisted of two upper deposits, horizons I and II, and two lower ones, horizons III and IV (Endo et al., 1978, pp. 88–93). Horizon I contained mainly modern and Neolithic material. The deposits of horizon II filled a pit 1.5 m in diameter near the cave's entrance. The artifacts in this horizon were characteristic of the Geometric Kebaran phase of the Epipaleolithic period. The two lower horizons were much older: both contained Middle Paleolithic artifacts that were presumably made by Neanderthal people. The flint tools from horizon III were typical of the Levantine Levalloiso-Mousterian culture, whereas the assemblage from horizon IV, although still with Middle Paleolithic affinities, was significantly earlier (Akazawa, 1987, pp. 155–156)—it was principally composed of flint blades that had been struck from prismatic cores. The lower part of horizon IV, level IVB, consisted of a large hearth full of ashes.

The excavators experienced some difficulty in determining the ages of these deposits, in part because horizons III and IV were too old to be dated satisfactorily by the radiocarbon method. They obtained a fission-track date of about 75,000 BP for a burnt pebble from the IVB hearth. The date was confirmed by the thermoluminescence dating of other burnt pebbles from the same deposit. This date is probably of the right order of magnitude for the horizon IV deposits, although horizon III could be twenty thousand years younger. A weathered layer at the junction of horizons III and IV suggested that the site was little used by humans between these two episodes of occupation. The horizon II Epipaleolithic deposits would date to about 13,000–14,000 years BP, based on analogy with other sites.

The main animals hunted by the inhabitants of the cave in all periods were wild sheep, goats, camels, and a small equid. These species are typical of a semiarid steppe like that around Douara today, suggesting that conditions were quite similar to the present during each period of occupation (Payne, 1983). The inhabitants also collected seeds of perennial steppe plants and the fruits of hackberry trees that grew in the hills behind the site. People probably occupied the cave seasonally, perhaps during the winter and spring.

BIBLIOGRAPHY

Akazawa, Takeru. "The Ecology of the Middle Paleolithic Occupation at Douara Cave, Syria." In *Paleolithic Site of the Douara Cave and Paleogeography of Palmyra Basin in Syria*, part 4, *1984 Excavations*, edited by Takeru Akazawa and Yutaka Sakaguchi, pp. 155–166. University of Tokyo, University Museum, Bulletin no. 29. Tokyo, 1987. Summary of the results of the excavations and studies of Douara's environment.

Akazawa, Takeru, et al. "1984 Excavations at Douara Cave: Methods and Techniques." In *Paleolithic Site of the Douara Cave and Paleogeography of Palmyra Basin in Syria*, part 4, *1984 Excavations*, edited by Takeru Akazawa and Yutaka Sakaguchi, pp. 41–48. University of Tokyo, University Museum, Bulletin no. 29. Tokyo, 1987. Description of the final excavation season.

Endo, B., T. Fujimoto, T. Akazawa, and K. Endo. "Excavation at the Douara Cave." In *Paleolithic Site of Douara Cave and Paleography of Palmyra Basin in Syria*, part 1, *Stratigraphy and Paleography of Palmyra Basin in Syria*, edited by Kazuro Hanihara and Yutaka Sakaguchi, pp. 83–98. University of Tokyo, University Museum. Tokyo, 1978.

Payne, S. "The Animal Bones from the 1974 Excavations at Douara Cave." In *Paleolithic Site of the Douara Cave and Paleogeography of Palmyra Basin in Syria*, part 3, *Animal Bones and Further Analysis of Archeological Materials*, edited by Kazuro Hanihara and Yutaka Sakaguchi, pp. 1–108. University of Tokyo, University Museum, Bulletin no. 21. Tokyo, 1983. Definitive analysis of the faunal remains from the second season of excavations and their interpretation for human use of the site and its environment.

Suzuki, H., and I. Kobori. "Report of the Reconnaissance Survey on Palaeolithic Sites in Lebanon and Syria." In *Bulletin of the University Museum* (University of Tokyo), no. 1 (1970): 41–48. Account of the discovery of Douara cave.

A. M. T. MOORE

DUNAND, MAURICE (1898–1987), French archaeologist best-known as the director, for more than fifty years, of the excavations at Byblos in Lebanon. Dunand was born and died in Haute-Savoie. His interest in Levantine archaeology began when he participated in the 1919–1920 French military campaign in Syria. After graduating from the École du Louvre, he continued his education at the École Biblique et Archéologique Française in Jerusalem (1924–1925). While working at the 1924 Palmyra and Byblos excavations, he initiated excavations at Eshmun, near Sidon. In 1925, he undertook epigraphic expeditions to Safa, the Hauran, and on Jebel al-Druze and reorganized the Museum of Suweida. In the following year he excavated in Syria in the Ledja and the Jezireh and farther east, at Arslan Tash, Til Barsip, and Luristan.

From 1940 to 1945, Dunand served as director of the French high commission for Syria-Lebanon and excavated Hellenistic Umm el-'Amad (1943–1945). In 1948, with the end of the French Mandate, the Lebanese Department of Antiquities authorized him to continue the Byblos excavations. With his wife Mireille, he developed a ceramic typology, plus field techniques using the 10-m × 10-m site grid and the excavation of 20-cm levels. Byblos architecture and forty-five thousand artifacts were analyzed by level, as opposed to natural stratigraphy. This now-outmoded system was Dunand's attempt to objectify excavation. From 1954 to 1974, Dunand excavated the Greco-Persian temple of Amrit (Syria) and Tell Kazel on the Syrian coast. From 1961 to 1976 he continued his work at the Eshmun temple.

The French government awarded Dunand the Legion of Honor and made him an honorary conservator of the national museums. He left Lebanon during the civil strife of the 1970s. His prolific publications include five Byblos volumes, *Fouilles de Byblos* (1937–1958), *Oumm el-'Amed* (1962), and *Le Temple d'Amrith* (1985), and his bibliography appears in fasicle I of *Mélanges de l'Université Saint-Joseph de Beyrouth* (1970).

[See also 'Amrit; Byblos; Kazel, Tell al-; Suweida; *and* Til Barsip.]

BIBLIOGRAPHY

Dunand, Maurice. *Fouilles de Byblos.* 5 vols. Paris, 1937–1958.
Dunand, Maurice. "Rapport préliminaire sur les fouilles de Byblos." *Bulletin du Musée de Beyrouth* 9 (1949–1950): 53–74; 12 (1955): 7–23; 13 (1956): 73–86; 16 (1964): 69–85.
Dunand, Maurice. *Oumm el-'Amed, une ville de l'époque hellénistique aux échelles de Tyr.* Paris, 1962.
Dunand, Maurice. *Byblos: Its History, Ruins, and Legends.* 2d ed. Beirut, 1968.
Dunand, Maurice. "La Piscine du Trône d'Astarté dans le Temple d'Echmoun à Sidon." *Bulletin du Musée de Beyrouth* 24 (1971): 19–25.
Dunand, Maurice. "Le Temple d'Echmoun à Sidon: Essai de chronologie." *Bulletin du Musée de Beyrouth* 26 (1973): 7–25.
Dunand, Maurice. Article in *Mélanges de l'Université Saint-Joseph de Beyrouth* 48 (1974–1975): 3–8.
Dunand, Maurice. *Le temple d'Amrith dans la pérée d'Aradus.* Bibliothèque Archéologique et Historique, vol. 122. Paris, 1985.
Mélanges de l'Université Saint-Joseph de Beyrouth 46.1 (1970): 3–8. Bibliography of Dunand's work to 1970.

MARTHA SHARP JOUKOWSKY

DUNAYEVSKY, IMMANUEL (1906–1968), consulting architect for many important early excavations in Israel. Born in Odessa (Ukraine) and educated as a structural engineer, Dunayevsky emigrated to Palestine in 1934. He worked first as an engineer, but after participating part-time at Benjamin Mazar's excavations at Beth-She'arim, Beth-Yeraḥ, and Tell Qasile (1949–1951), he abandoned engineering and joined Yigael Yadin's excavation at Tel Hazor as staff architect (1955). Dunayevsky joined the Department of Archaeology at the Hebrew University of Jerusalem and, until his death, served either as the architect or consulting architect for the excavations at 'Ein-Gedi, Hammath Tiberias, Masada, and Megiddo, among many others.

In addition to surveying and preparing and drawing final plans, Dunayevsky applied himself to architectural and

stratigraphic analysis, in which he was gifted and insightful. Through on-site checking of walls, floors, and their interrelationships, he established the true sequence of strata and the architectural history of a site. It was, perhaps, because he was not trained as an archaeologist that he was free of the burden of preconceived theories. Dunayevsky was a master at reading a site's relative chronology, as preserved in its architectural history. His contribution to the Hazor expedition (1954–1956, 1968), was the final and perhaps the best example of his work.

[See also the biographies of Mazar and Yadin. In addition, the sites mentioned are the subject of independent entries.]

BIBLIOGRAPHY

Netzer, Ehud. "A List of Selected Plans Drawn by I. Dunayevsky." *Eretz-Israel* 11 (1973): 13*–24*. (I. Dunayevsky Memorial Volume).
Netzer, Ehud, and Aharon Kempinski. "Immanuel (Munya) Dunayevsky, 1906–1968: The Man and His Work." In *The Architecture of Ancient Israel from the Prehistoric to the Persian Periods: In Memory of Immanuel (Munya) Dunayevsky,* edited by Aharon Kempinski and Ronny Reich, pp. vii–ix. Jerusalem, 1992.

RONNY REICH

DURA-EUROPOS, site located near the modern village of as-Salihiyeh, 92 km (57 mi.) southeast of Deir ez-Zor (Dayr az-Zawr), Syria, on a promontory along the southern bank of the Euphrates River (34°46′ N, 40°46′ E); the escarpment down to the river formed a natural rampart on the east with deep wadis on the north and south. The ancient city covered approximately 180 acres, with its main gate facing west, toward Palmyra. The ruins were first noted in the late nineteenth century by travelers and archaeologists but were generally assumed to be Arab because Greek, and, especially Roman, sites were not thought to extend this far east. A city with the double name "Dura, called Europos by the Greeks" was known from the first-century geographer Isidore of Charax/Bosra, but the name had been erroneously attached to the unexcavated tell at Abu'l Hassan. The ruins at as-Salihiyeh yielded some ancient materials in a 1912 survey by Friedrich Sarre and Ernest Herzfeld, but the advent of World War I precluded further investigation. [See the biography of Sarre.]

The site was rediscovered in 1920 by a company of British soldiers in the aftermath of World War I. While digging emplacements for bivouac among the visible ruins, they uncovered "some ancient wall paintings in a wonderful state of preservation . . . in the west corner of the fort." After reporting to the garrison commander at Abou Kemal (now in Iraq), a request was made to James Henry Breasted, who had been surveying potential excavation sites in the region, to confirm the find. He viewed the finds (located in what is now known as the Temple of the Palmyrene Gods) and identified the scene from the depiction and *dipinto* as the Roman tribune Julius Terentius in the act of sacrifice. It was to date the easternmost find of any Roman remains. Another *dipinto* from the same painting referred to the *Tyche* ("Fortune") of Dura, thus providing clear identification with the double-named city of Isidore. [*See the biography of Breasted.*]

In the following years, the area came under the French Mandate. In November 1922 and October–November 1923, the first brief seasons of archaeological work were conducted by Franz Cumont under the auspices of the French Academy of Inscriptions and Letters in Damascus. While some initial discoveries were made, largely in the northwest corner of the city, the excavations had to be abandoned because of political unrest. When relative peace was restored in 1926, the site's remoteness hindered resuming work until a joint expedition between the French Academy and Yale University was arranged. Mikhail I. Rostovtzeff, who had just joined the Yale faculty, was eager to involve the university in the burgeoning archaeology of the region. The first joint expedition was conducted in 1928, and ten campaigns were completed through 1937. Cumont and Rostovtzeff initially served as the project directors, with Maurice Pillet of the French Academy as field director. The field directorship continued under Clark Hopkins (1931–1935) and Frank E. Brown (1935–1937), both of Yale. The field seasons were published serially under the title *Excavations at Dura-Europos: Preliminary Reports* (New Haven, 1929–1952). Subsequent research and analysis of the finds removed to the Damascus Museum and the Yale University Art Gallery resulted in a series of *Final Reports* (New Haven, 1943–1977), as yet incomplete.

The site may have been settled in earlier periods, but no significant levels of occupation are known prior to the establishment of the Hellenistic city by Seleucus I Nicator in about 300 BCE. In 114 BCE it was ceded to the Parthians, who remained in control until the Roman expansion under Trajan (116). Following the Roman withdrawal (118), it returned to Parthian control. [*See Parthians.*] Eventually, the campaign of Lucius Verus (168) brought the entire region firmly under Roman control. The city was a fortified station along the ancient trade routes between Seleucia/Ctesiphon and Charax/Bosra to the east, and to the west either Antioch (by way of Ciresium and Aleppo) or Damascus (by way of Palmyra). In 209–211 it was garrisoned by the Romans and in the 220s–230s was further reinforced against the rising Sasanian kingdom. After withstanding an initial attack under Ardashir in 239, it was besieged in 253/54 by his son Shapur I (240–264). Despite substantial defense efforts, including sacrificing the area along the interior of the western city wall as fill for an embankment, it fell and was razed in 256. While much of Dura is now known through excavation of the foundation plans and debris from the destruction, it is the embankment that has yielded the most remarkable finds left intact from the time they were buried (see below).

Excavation of this single-stratum site revealed a complex and intersecting pattern of habitation that included influences from periods of Hellenistic, Parthian, and Roman control as well as local cultures including Persian, Palmyrene, Aramaic, Safaitic, and other Semitic linguistic groups. The Hellenistic and Early Parthian city was grouped around the central area. The western defense wall and the main gate (called the Palmyra Gate) were added by the Parthians, probably sometime in the late first century BCE. Under the Romans (or later the Parthians), a regular grid plan was imposed on the city; it provides the basic plan from which the excavators developed their reference notation (see figure 1). Epigraphic, papyrological, and documentary remains have been found in Greek, Latin, Aramaic, Palmyrene, Safaitic, and Middle Iranian (Pahlavi). At least by the later Parthian and Roman periods, Dura seems to have had strong cultural, commercial, and administrative ties to Palmyra. In addition to the Temple of the Palmyrene Gods (J3–5; a triad of military deities associated with Bel and Iarhibol), the *Tyche* of Palmyra was publicly displayed. There is also a Temple of Palmyrene Gad(de) (H1). Other regional cults include two temples for the Parthian deities Aphlad (N8) and Artemis-Azzanathkona (E7). The latter is a compound of Anat; the name and iconography suggest affinities to Atargatis (also called Dea Syria), where Aphlad would be the expected consort. In addition, there is a separate temple to the Syrian/Phoenician Atargatis (H2) with her regular consort, Hadad. Traditional Hellenistic and Roman cults are represented by temples to Adonis (L5), Greek Artemis (H4), Zeus Kyrios (N7), Zeus Theos (B3), Zeus Megistos (C4), and Jupiter Dolichenus (X7). In several of these cases the central cult figures, either in frescoes or reliefs, were also found. These religious monuments clearly show the mixture of regional Syro-Phoenician, Palmyrene, and Parthian traditions with both Hellenistic and Roman elements. [*See Phoenicians; Palmyra.*] Zeus Kyrios is identified with Ba'al Shamin (Ba'al Shamêm), and Zeus Theos is depicted in Parthian-style dress. The art also shows a mixture of Hellenistic and so-called orientalizing influences and has sometimes been labeled proto-Byzantine, especially in its use of frontality.

The temples span several phases in the occupation of the city and continued in use to the end, with some reflecting continued expansion. Some peculiarities in their plan and architecture are collectively known as "the Durene temple type." This type of planning seems to have stretched from the Late Hellenistic occupation of the city down through end of the Roman period. Typically, these Durene temples employed a spacious walled temenos (sacred precinct), often with multiple small chapels or dining rooms around the outer walls. The main sanctuary of the god(s) was a smaller enclosure (the naos proper), usually set off at one end and sometimes with flanking chambers. The archaeological evidence further indicates that considerable renovation and enlargement occurred in these temples (especially of the Palmyrene Gods) over time; some of the temples were built

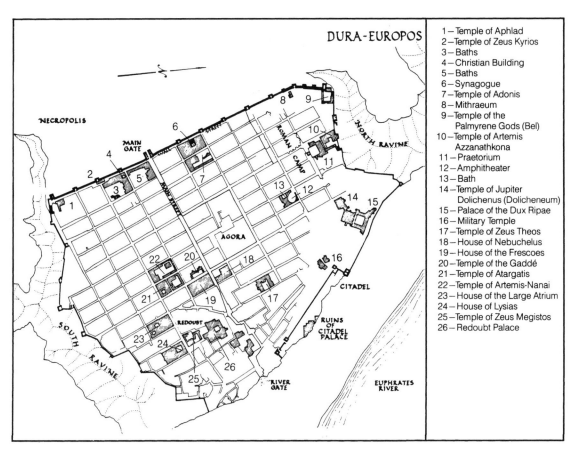

DURA-EUROPOS. Figure 1. *Plan of the city.* (Drawing by David O. Kiphuth, Courtesy ASOR Archives)

on or from existing residential areas (especially those of Atargatis and Gadde).

The Hellenistic city was clustered in the center of the walled area around an open central agora (G1–8) that had, in earlier stages, functioned like a bazaar. By the Roman period, the agora had been developed architecturally into a market center, with less open space. A proliferation of domestic blocks and other, larger buildings during the late second and early third centuries CE filled the walled areas, especially along the city's western and southern sections. This phase of civic building corresponds to the consolidation of Roman control and the period of reinforcement of the garrison under the Severan emperors. At this time, the northern section of the city was partitioned off for the military garrison, and a new palace (X3–5) of the river commander and a bath (E3) were begun in upper part of the city. [*See* Palace; Baths.] The garrison incorporated the areas around the temples of Azzanathkona and the Palmyrene Gods; added to the same area was a sanctuary of Jupiter Dolichenus, a favorite among the legions. Under Caracalla, the city was reinforced by troops from the Fourth Scythian and Sixteenth Flavia Firma Legions, under the commander Antonius Valentinus. Later detachments of the Third and Fourth Cyrenaica (from Bosra) are also recorded. In its final days, the city was the headquarters of the Twentieth Palmyrene Cohort, under the military tribune Julius Terentius. A graffito records that the Persians first attacked the city in 239 CE, at which time Julius Terentius was killed. The city was further reinforced by elements of the Second Paphlagonian (Galliena Volusiana) Cohort. In addition to numerous inscriptions, contracts, and literary documents, the excavations yielded a number of military records, including pay rosters and census records. A number of the records referring to Roman cleruchs indicate that Dura was considered a colony for veterans of these eastern legions. Military accouterments were well preserved in the fill. One such find was a Roman wooden shield with decorated leather covering; among the painted decorations was a ship and a list (partially damaged) of the posts of the legionnaires from the Black Sea to Dura. Individual studies of parchments and papyri, coins, textiles, glassware, and several ceramic classifications appear in the *Final Reports.*

The excavations along the city's western wall produced the most interesting finds because of their level of preservation (they had been buried during the final siege of the city). One such edifice was a suite of rooms renovated from two neighboring houses that had served as the offices of a scribal guild. Most of the areas along the western wall had earlier been domestic blocks (insulae) of contiguous private homes. Three of the most significant discoveries for the city's religious history were found in such houses along the western wall. In each case, the existing domestic edifice had been renovated in one or more stages for use as a religious center. These include a sanctuary of Mithras (or mithraeum; see figure 2), a synagogue, and a Christian building. The mithraeum (block J7) went through three distinct phases of renovation and enlargement from its original form as a private house; the first occurred shortly after the Roman takeover in 168 CE, and abundant graffiti and inscriptions make it clear that the membership was largely from the military. In the middle phase (c. 209–211), when a major structural renovation project transformed the building into a more formal religious hall, the main donor was the garrison commander Antonius Valentinus. The final renovation (c. 240s) included an elaborate decorative program. While the mithraeum should not be overlooked as a contribution to the study of the Roman cult of Mithras, it is really the other two that have attracted the most attention. The Christian building at Dura is the earliest clearly identifiable church building from the Roman world. The Jewish edifice is one of the earliest known synagogue sites from the Diaspora and is especially important for its development of synagogue planning and decoration. [*See* Churches; Synagogues.]

The synagogue (block L7) was originally installed in a house facing the western wall in the middle of an insula of ten houses. The house was typical of Durene private architecture: several rooms were grouped around a central open court, from which a corridor gave access to the street. The function of some of the rooms in the house continued to be domestic, but one room was adapted for use as a Hall of Assembly. There is some evidence of minimal decoration and seating in this early hall. The first synagogue installation

DURA-EUROPOS. Figure 2. *The late sanctuary of the Mithraeum.* Dated to the last half of the fifth century CE. (Courtesy ASOR Archives)

dates to the last quarter of the second century CE. Numismatic evidence indicates that there might have been Jews present in the city from the earlier Hellenistic and Parthian periods, especially during the Hasmonean dynasty (late second–first centuries BCE). No other direct evidence exists for a permanent synagogue community prior to the adaptation of the house, however.

It would appear that the early Hall of Assembly had a Torah niche or ark (*'aron ha-qōdeš*) installed along the western wall, although it may have been a secondary installation. Nonetheless, it would be one of the earliest known Torah niches from all ancient synagogues. In approximately 244–246 CE this edifice was extensively remodeled to form an even larger and more formal synagogue. The renovation involved gutting the interior of the earlier house (including the hall) and tearing down two exterior walls. New, heavier walls were built, and the area of the earlier house was divided into two main areas: a large, rectangular Hall of Assembly and an entry court with *tristoa* colonnade. In addition, the adjacent house to the east was annexed to the synagogue building and used as a suite of entry chambers and for the quarters of a resident caretaker. Thus, the total area of the new complex was more than double that of the earlier one. Within a few years of the renovation, the Hall of Assembly was further decorated with an elaborate series of figural paintings depicting biblical scenes. [*See* Wall Paintings.] These paintings seem to be a professional commission, perhaps by Jewish artists from Lower Mesopotamia using an established pattern of artistic renderings of biblical stories. Many of the paintings are signed with Pahlavi *dipinti*, while the other signatures on the paintings and inscriptions in the hall are in Greek and Aramaic. The paintings are grouped in patterns around the center of the hall's long, western wall, in which an integral single-block Torah niche had been installed opposite the room's main door. Stepped benches also lined the walls. The plan of the hall and the paintings clearly reflect a focal orientation toward the Torah niche. There is no indication of other areas for assembly in the later synagogue hall.

The Christian building was installed by a single stage of renovation of a private home (block M8) just a little farther to the south. [*See* House Churches.] A graffito in the undercoating of the wall plaster indicates that the house was built (or rebuilt) in 231 CE; therefore, the renovation for Christian usage likely occurred in about 241. No other direct archaeological evidence of a Christian presence in the city is known prior to the renovation. The basic domestic plan was retained, but regular household activities ceased. The renovations were concentrated in two main areas. On the south side, the partition wall between two adjoining rooms was removed in order to create a long, rectangular hall oriented toward a low dais on the eastern end. No other decoration or accouterments are known from this room, except for some damaged graffiti that seem to refer to some of the

Christian leaders. On the other side of the courtyard, a small room in the northwest corner of the house was converted into a baptistery. [*See* Baptisteries.] It is, to date, the earliest known from archaeological sources. The square baptismal font (approximately one meter deep) was set into the floor; above, an arched canopy was carried by two columns. The room was fitted with a low ceiling just above the canopy. The baptistery was finished with a program of figural paintings depicting a combination of biblical scenes (Adam and Eve, David and Goliath) and scenes from the life of Jesus (the Samaritan Woman at the Well, the Healing of a Lame Man, and Jesus and Peter Walking on Water). The central scene in the arch lunette of the canopy above the font is that of a Good Shepherd. Unfortunately, the rear portions of the room were more heavily damaged and the upper register of the artistic program is lost. In the lower register, the main scene stretched as a single narrative composition from the rear (east) wall around the side (north wall) and up toward the font itself. It seems to depict five women bearing torches in procession toward a sarcophagus. The scene is usually read as the Women at the Tomb of Jesus. The fact that there are five women likely comes from a blending of the different Gospel stories, such as in Tatian's *Diatessaron*, a second-century harmonized version of the four Gospels known to have been used in some Syrian churches. A fragment of a Greek version of the *Diatessaron* on parchment, the earliest manuscript evidence for the document, was also found in the fill along the western wall, although not in the immediate context of the Christian building.

BIBLIOGRAPHY

Cumont, Franz. "The Dura Mithraeum." In *Mithraic Studies*, vol. 1, edited by John R. Hinnels, pp. 151–214. Manchester, 1975. Published posthumously from notes and edited by E. D. Francis.

Francis, E. D. "Mithraic Graffiti from Dura-Europos." In *Mithraic Studies*, vol. 2, edited by John R. Hinnels, pp. 424–445. Manchester, 1975.

Gilliam, James F. *Roman Army Papers*. Amsterdam, 1986.

Gutmann, Joseph. *The Dura-Europos Synagogue: A Re-Evaluation, 1932–1972*. Chambersburg, Pa., 1973.

Hopkins, Clark. *The Discovery of Dura-Europos*. New Haven, 1979. Includes a complete list of the preliminary and final reports published to date.

Kraeling, Carl H. *The Synagogue*. The Excavations at Dura-Europos, Final Report 8, part 1. New Haven, 1956.

Kraeling, Carl H. *The Christian Building*. The Excavations at Dura-Europos, Final Report 8, part 2. New Haven, 1967.

Millar, Fergus. *The Roman Near East, 31 BC–AD 337*. Cambridge, Mass., 1993.

Perkins, Ann. *The Art of Dura-Europos*. Oxford, 1973.

Rostovtzeff, Michael. *Dura-Europos and Its Art*. Oxford, 1938.

Welles, Charles Bradford. "The Epitaph of Julius Terentius." *Harvard Theological Review* 34 (1941): 79–102.

Welles, Charles Bradford. "The Population of Roman Dura." In *Studies in Roman Economic and Social History in Honor of Allan Chester Johnson*, edited by Paul R. Coleman-Norton, pp. 251–274. Princeton, 1951.

White, L. Michael. *Building God's House in the Roman World: Architectural Adaptation among Pagans, Jews, and Christians.* Baltimore, 1990.
White, L. Michael. *The Social Origins of Christian Architecture.* 2 vols. Minneapolis, 1995.

L. MICHAEL WHITE

DUSSAUD, RENÉ (1868–1958), French Orientalist and archaeologist who organized the Syrian Antiquities Department and, over a period of twenty years, various French expeditions to Syria. Dussaud graduated from the École Centrale des Arts et Manufactures in Paris, with an assured career in engineering. He chose to investigate the Near Eastern world of his father, who had worked on the Suez Canal. Trained in the classics, Dussaud embarked on learning Arabic and Classical Hebrew. He was encouraged in his work by Charles S. Clermont-Ganneau, whom he accompanied on several archaeological missions to Syria and Lebanon. Dussaud was an energetic scholar who published Nabatean, Greek, and Latin inscriptions. Submitting his thesis to the École des Hautes Études in 1899, he thereafter published *Introduction à l'histoire des religions* (1914) and *Les Arabes en Syrie avant l'Islam* (1907).

Dussaud theorized about Near Eastern cultural exchanges. Enthusiastic about Arthur Evans's discoveries on Crete, he visited the island and in 1910 produced *Les civilisations préhelléniques dans le bassin de la mer Égée* (1914). Following World War I, Dussaud returned to Syria, which was then under French mandate. There he presided over the opening of the Byblos excavations and ensured French expeditions to Ras Shamra/Ugarit and Mari.

Dussaud was codirector of the *Revue de l'histoire des religions,* and in 1920 founded the periodical *Syria.* In 1923 he was appointed to the *Académie des inscriptions,* replacing his mentor, Clermont-Ganneau. He continued to research Canaanite cults and their interconnections with the Hebrew Bible in a two-volume work, *L'art phénicien du IIe millénaire* (1949).

[*See also* Mari; Ugarit; *and the biography of Clermont-Ganneau.*]

BIBLIOGRAPHY

Dussaud was a prolific writer, interested in many fields, including philology, epigraphy, numismatics, and archaeology. He published articles on Safaitic, Nabatean, Greek, Arabic, Aramean, Phoenician, and Neo-Punic. His early bibliography, listing almost three hundred articles and volumes, appears in *Mélanges Syriens* 30 (1939). Other works by Dussaud include the following:
Les Arabes en Syrie avant l'Islam. Paris, 1907.
Les civilisations préhelléniques dans le bassin de la mer Égée. Paris, 1914.
Introduction à l'histoire des religions. Paris, 1914.
Les origines cananéennes du sacrifice israélite. Paris, 1921.
Topographie historique de la Syrie antique et médiévale. Paris, 1927.
Les découvertes de Ras Shamra (Ugarit) et l'Ancien Testament. Paris, 1937.
Les religions des Hittites et les Hourrites. Paris, 1945.
L'art phénicien du IIe millénaire. 2 vols. Paris, 1949.
La pénéntration des Arabes en Syrie avant l'Islam. Paris, 1955.

MARTHA SHARP JOUKOWSKY

E

EAST AFRICA. *See* Ethiopia; Nubia.

EBAL, MOUNT, located some 50 km (30 mi.) north of Jerusalem, one of the highest peaks in Israel, rising to about 940 m above sea level. It is located in the Manasseh tribal allotment in the heart of the hill country of Samaria. Opposite, to the south, is the slightly lower Mt. Gerizim, with several excavated ruins. Between the two mountains, in a well-defined pass, lies Shechem (Tell Balaṭah), once the capital of ancient Israel, on the main road leading north from Jerusalem to the Esdraelon Valley.

No archaeological sites on Mt. Ebal were known before 1980, when a survey team, led by Adam Zertal, discovered what appeared to be an Early Israelite mountaintop high place on a rocky ridge high on the eastern slopes, 800 m above sea level (map reference 1773 × 1829). The survey covered 2,000 sq km (or 1,240 sq. mi.) of the Manasseh hill country. The site overlooks the eastern Samaria hill country, the Wadi Farʿah region, and parts of Transjordan. It was excavated by Zertal in the course of eight seasons (1982–1989), on behalf of Tel Aviv and Haifa Universities and the Israel Exploration Society.

The site was founded during the Late Bronze Age IIB/Iron Age IA transitional period (late thirteenth century BCE). The dating is based on pottery, including a few Mycenaean IIIC sherds, a dated stone seal, and two egyptianized scarabs from the latter part of the reign of Rameses II (c. 1240–1215 BCE).

Both of its levels were excavated. In level 2 (c. 1240–1200 BCE), a small stone circle 2 m in diameter was found filled with ash and animal bones; near it were two walls and an area covered with large potsherds. The circle had been arranged directly on the bedrock. Sections under later courtyards (level 1B) revealed intensive use of fire on the rock and many animal bones. On a lower terrace west of the circle, between a low rock cliff and an enclosure wall built with large boulders, a structure resembling an Iron Age four-room house was excavated and attributed to level 2. [*See* Four-room House.] Southeast of it, along the same wall, a portion of a storehouse was unearthed, with eleven large pithoi of the collared-rim type lying in stone "cells."

Sometime in the early twelfth century BCE, the site underwent major changes (level 1B), without evidence of destruction or abandonment. At the center of the site was a structure measuring about 9 × 14 m; built of large, undressed stones, it is preserved to a height of 3.25 m. Two walls led from the structure's outer section to its inner section, which was filled with stones, ash, burnt animal bones, sherds, and other debris. The excavators distinguished four fill levels in the debris, which seemed to have been sealed over by a stone pavement. Surrounding the central level 1B structure on three sides, and about 0.8 m lower than it and connected to it, was a stone wall about 1 m wide. A double stone ramp led up from the outside to the central structure: the main ramp, leading to the top, was 1.2 m wide; the secondary ramp, joined to it and leading to the surrounding wall, was 0.8 m wide. The structure was built as part of a stone enclosure (26 × 26 m) whose southwestern side consisted of two adjoining, stone-paved open-air courtyards. Built into these courtyards were eleven pitlike installations, containing ash, animal bones, and pottery vessels. Some ninety similar installations were found outside the central structure on all sides. These contained metal objects, seals and scarabs, and vessels of different types.

Other changes in level 1B included the closing and covering over of the level 2 four-room house, converting it into an open square in front of the central structure, and the building of a double temenoslike enclosure with a central complex inside it. The two enclosures were connected by a flight of three stone steps 7.5 m wide. Level 1B was occupied for fifty-seventy years (c. 1200–1130 BCE); pottery finds indicate that it did not survive into the eleventh century. The site was systematically abandoned: there was no sign of destruction or fire, and it had been deliberately sealed with a stone cover (level 1A).

The excavators suggest a connection between the twelfth-century BCE level 1B complex and the traditions in *Deuteronomy* 27:1–9 and *Joshua* 8:30–35. These describe a large, stone-built sacrificial altar erected by Joshua on Mt. Ebal, under the command of Moses, where the people of Israel gathered and an important ceremony took place. Evidence for this identification—one of the few instances in Syro-Palestinian and biblical archaeology where a structure mentioned in biblical texts can be correlated with a specific archaeological discovery—is seen in the level 1B complex as a whole. It is interpreted as a raised altar surrounded by a temenos wall. The stone installations, intended for offerings; the absence of living quarters in level 1B; some special types of pottery; and, particularly, the nearly three thousand animal bones, 96 percent of which are from cattle, sheep, goats, and fallow deer (17 percent of the total sample of burnt material) attest to the area's cultic use. All but fallow deer are considered sacrificial animals in biblical and later rabbinic traditions. The installation itself can be compared with similar altars mentioned not only in *Deuteronomy* and *Joshua*, but also in *Ezekiel*, in the writings of Josephus, in the Temple Scroll, and in the Mishnah. Moreover, the site conforms with the biblical account in date, in the character of the place, and in geographic setting.

The cultic and biblical interpretation of the site, while strongly maintained by the excavator, has not gone unchallenged. Some archaeologists (Aharon Kempinski, 1986; Anson F. Rainey; and William G. Dever) deny the cultic connection altogether and suggest that this be seen as an isolated house or watchtower. Other specialists, however, concur as to its cultic nature, but interpret it differently: Michael David Coogan suggests a non-Israelite cult; Israel Finkelstein (1986) accepts that it is an early Israelite cultic high place, but not an altar; and Amihai Mazar (1990) concurs with its possible biblical connection. Such biblical scholars as Moshe Anbar (1985) and André Lemaire (1990) accept the site's cultic character but go no further. Finally, some historians (Nadav Na'aman and Gösta W. Ahlström) suggest that the Mt. Ebal installation may be the biblical "Tower of Shechem," the cultic center of Israelite Shechem mentioned in *Judges* 9. Nevertheless, there is wide agreement over the dating of the site to the late thirteenth/early twelfth centuries BCE.

The vigor of the debate concerning the Mt. Ebal site is related to its importance regarding the problem of the date of the Israelite settlement in Canaan, the origins of Israel, and, above all, the historicity and dating of the pentateuchal traditions, thought by many to be late and ahistorical.

[*See also* Altars; Samaria; Samaritans; *and* Shechem.]

BIBLIOGRAPHY

Anbar, Moshe. "The Story about the Building of an Altar on Mount Ebal." *Das Deuteronomium* 68 (1985): 304–309.

Brandl, Baruch. "Two Scarabs and a Trapezoidal Seal from Mount Ebal." *Tel Aviv* 13–14 (1986–1987): 166–173.

Finkelstein, Israel. *The Archaeology of the Period of Settlement and Judges* (in Hebrew). Tel Aviv, 1986. See pages 82–85.

Harper, Henry A. "Ebal and Gerizim." *Palestine Exploration Fund Quarterly Statement* (1896): 85–86.

Horwitz, Liora K. "Faunal Remains from the Early Iron Age Site on Mount Ebal." *Tel Aviv* 13–14 (1986–1987): 173–189.

Kempinski, Aharon. "'Joshua's Altar': An Iron Age I Watchtower." *Biblical Archaeology Review* 12.1 (1986): 42–53.

Lemaire, André. *La protohistoire d'Israël*. Paris, 1990. See pages 199–201.

Mazar, Amihai. *Archaeology of the Land of the Bible, 10,000–586 B.C.E.* New York, 1990. See pages 348–351.

Tonneau, Raphael. "Le sacrifice de Josué sur le Mont Ébal." *Revue Biblique* 35 (1926): 98–109.

Zertal, Adam. "Has Joshua's Altar Been Found on Mount Ebal?" *Biblical Archaeology Review* 11.1 (1985): 26–43.

Zertal, Adam. "How Can Kempinski Be So Wrong!" *Biblical Archaeology Review* 12.1 (1986): 42–53.

Zertal, Adam. "An Early Iron Age Cultic Site on Mount Ebal: Excavation Seasons 1982–1987." *Tel Aviv* 13–14 (1986–1987): 105–165.

ADAM ZERTAL

EBLA (mod. Tell Mardikh), large Bronze Age site in northern Syria, located 60 km (37 mi.) south of Aleppo. The tell, a slightly irregular oval, has a surface area of nearly 60 ha (148 acres). The large lower town surrounds the acropolis, which reaches a height of 431 m and is located almost at the center of the settlement. At the tell's extreme periphery, the outline of the town's ancient outer fortification, 22 m higher than the level of the surrounding fields, is relatively visible. The Italian Archaeological Expedition of the University "La Sapienza" of Rome has worked at the site every year since 1964, under the direction of Paolo Matthiae.

Before the excavations at Tell Mardikh, Ebla was known from two copies of Old Akkadian royal inscriptions by Sargon and Naram-Sin of Akkad, who both boasted of conquering the town; from the Sumerian statue B of Gudea of Lagash as the region of provenance of precious wooden objects; and from economic texts of the Third Dynasty of Ur. [*See* Akkadian; Akkade; Lagash; Ur.] During the seventeenth and fifteenth centuries BCE, Ebla appears in rare quotations in the texts of Alalakh VII and IV; after its final destruction, at the beginning of the fifteenth century BCE, Ebla is mentioned in a Hurrian fragment dealing with ritual from the archives of Ḫattuša and on the hieroglyphic list at Karnak of Pharaoh Thutmose III's Syro-Palestinian conquests. [*See* Alalakh.] The identification of Tell Mardikh with Ebla was made in 1968 after the discovery, in the western part of the acropolis, of a basalt torso with an inscription of Ibbit-Lim, son of Igriš-Khep, king of Ebla, dedicated to the goddess Ishtar (c. twentieth century BCE). The formative period of Mardikh I (c. 3500–3000 BCE) is known from fragmentary levels of its central and final phases on the acropolis.

Stratum IIB. The city's development peaked in Mardikh IIB1 (c. 2400–2300 BCE), the period of Royal Palace G and of the cuneiform tablets in the state archives (see below). [*See* Cuneiform; Tablet.] The extent of the urban center probably reached nearly 50 ha (124 acres) before the end of Mardikh IIB1, whose destruction is attributed to Sargon II of Assyria. [*See* Assyria.] That destruction brought to an end a phase of great economic and political expansion. The settlement was then reduced in size and may have been limited to only its northern region in Mardikh IIB2 (c. 2300–2000 BCE).

The Mardikh IIB2 period corresponds to the chronological horizon of 'Amuq J. [*See* 'Amuq.] It is thus far represented in the lower town on the northwest only by an imposing building, called the Archaic Palace, nearly 500 sq m of whose trapezoidal plan have been exposed. The still poorly known intermediate palace of Mardikh IIIA was erected over part of this building, and, later, the large and quite well-preserved northern palace of Mardikh IIIB (see below). The Archaic Palace was quite probably the royal residence contemporary with the Third Dynasty of Ur. [*See* Palace.]

Stratum III. Following a presumed second destruction, a renaissance took place in the urban center in the Mardikh IIIA phase (c. 2000–1800 BCE), whose ceramic horizon largely corresponds to Hama H (twentieth century BCE). [*See* Hama.] The settlement at Ebla was rebuilt according to a precise urban pattern: the town had a double fortification wall composed of an inner wall surrounding the citadel, and an outer circumference wall with four imposing gates that enclosed a belt of large secular and religious buildings in the lower town and public buildings on the citadel. The outer wall, nearly 3 km long, was a typical earthen rampart that enclosed nearly all of the site's 60 ha. It was limited at the bottom by a revetment of large stone blocks; a relatively shallow wall was constructed at the top, lost almost everywhere except east of the southwest gate. The inner wall also had a high sloping revetment rising out of stone blocks at its base; a high slope in the middle was dug from the side of the ancient tell on the acropolis; and, at the top, a mud-brick wall had a deep scarp at its base, also constructed of mud brick. The stratum IIIA buildings underwent reconstruction in the following phase, Mardikh IIIB (c. 1800–1600 BCE). After the total destruction of Mardikh IIIB (c. 1600 BCE), provoked by the invasion of the Old Hittite king Ḫattušili I (or, more probably, of his successor, Muršili I), a large part of the town was finally abandoned. [*See* Hittites.]

Palace G. Large sectors are known of the extensive Royal Palace G, from the first great period at Mardikh (IIB1), which corresponds to Early Bronze IVA. Nearly 2,400 sq m of the palace have been excavated, mostly on the western and southern slopes of the acropolis; the complex probably extended across the top of the acropolis. The peripheral quarters of its western wing specialized in food production, and the southern wing was devoted to storage; both are quite badly preserved. The well-preserved area on the southwest slope was the most important: it included a large exterior space with a porch, called the Court of Audience; the royal dais was on its north. On the east, a monumental stairway (22 m long) overcame the nearly 6-meter difference in the level between the lower town and the acropolis. South of the gateway, which was really the main entrance to the palace, the administrative quarter was divided into a limited outer

sector below the porch and an inner sector with a court (also with a porch) that opened, to the south, to the throne room (L. 2866); the throne room was nearly 16 × 11 m in size.

Archives. The cuneiform tablets of the state archives, which include more than seventeen thousand inventory numbers of complete and fragmentary documents, were placed in the major archive room (L. 2769) in the outer sector of the administrative quarter; a smaller number were found in a lesser archive (L. 2712) below the eastern porch of the Court of Audience, but north of the gateway, in a trapezoidal storeroom (L. 2764). [*See* Libraries and Archives.] The archives, which include economic, administrative, juridical, and lexical accounts and literary texts and letters, offer exceptional documentation of the city's social and economic structure, as well as information about administrative organization, religion, and literature. Particularly important is the contribution they make to linguistics: the language of the archives is a very archaic Semitic language that some scholars consider to be a dialect of Old Akkadian; others believe to be an older, independent Semitic language called Eblaic; and still others consider an antecedent of later Northwestern Semitic languages. The texts cover a period of not more than forty or fifty years and are contemporary with Kings Igriš-Halam, Irkab-Damu, and Išar-Damu, who ruled with the help of some very high officials—Ibrium, Ibbi-Zikir, and Dubukhu-Adda, who also succeeded from father to son, like the kings.

Small finds. The discovery, in the inner court of the administrative quarter, of several fragments of Egyptian bowls of diorite and alabaster from the pharaonic period and a lid with the name of Pharaoh Pepi I of the sixth dynasty, offers a basic synchronism between Sargon of Akkad, Pepi I of Egypt, and Išar-Damu of Ebla, at about 2300 BCE. In the royal palace of Mardikh IIB1 (see above), whose ceramic horizon corresponds to phases J8–6 at Hama, and perhaps to the final phase of 'Amuq I, several fragmentary masterpieces have been found of ancient palatial furniture. Among these, of primary importance are two steatite plaques of headdresses, originally belonging to two royal figures, a male and a female; wooden carvings with mother-of-pearl inlays, primarily of animal figures, decorating a chair and a table; several fragments of composite panels of a series of figures of officials, carved in high relief in wood, covered with gold leaf, and completed with limestone, steatite, and lapis-lazuli detailing for the clothing and headdresses; and cylinder seals known from impressions on clay sealings with friezes of athletic contests typical of the late Early Dynastic tradition in Mesopotamia, but with several typically Syrian figures (e.g., the great goddess dominating wild animals and the cow woman, inspired by the figure of the bull man). The noteworthy Standard of Ebla that was discovered belongs to an early phase of Mardikh IIB1 (c. 2400 BCE). Several of its figural marble inlays are preserved, with scenes of triumph and divine figures representing the lion-headed eagle over two human-headed bulls, a symbol of an early Syrian deity of war—of the Sumerian Ningirsu or Ninurta type. [*See* Sumerians.]

Sacred and royal architecture. The citadel also contained temple D, dedicated to the goddess Ishtar, with a longitudinally tripartite typology. The temple may be considered a very old antecedent of Solomon's Temple in Jerusalem, built in the tenth century BCE. [*See* Jerusalem.] In the lower town, a belt of sacred buildings surrounded a large part of the acropolis. In the northeast sector was the temple of the god Shamash. To the northwest were the northern palace and the sacred area of Ishtar, with the great temple P2 and monument P3, an imposing cult terrace with a court that hosted the sacred lions of the goddess. In the west and southwest sectors were the large western palace (more than 7,500 sq m); temple B of the god of the netherworld, Resheph; and sanctuary B2, dedicated to the cult of the royal deified ancestors.

The northern palace was a ceremonial building related to kingship, and the western palace was the residence of the crown prince.

Necropolis. It is meaningful that the area of the royal necropolis was situated among the western palace, temple B, and sanctuary B2. [*See* Necropolis.] Three important tombs, dating from between 1825 and 1650 BCE, were excavated: the Tomb of the Princess (c. 1800 BCE), the only intact one, from which a group of jewelry (including six bracelets, an earring decorated with granulation, a pin with a star-shaped head, and a necklace) and more than sixty clay pots were recovered; the Tomb of the Lord of the Goats, found with gold jewelry, bronze weapons, stone vases, ivory talismans, more than seventy clay pots, and an Egyptian ceremonial mace belonging to Pharaoh Hetepibre Harnejheryotef (r. 1770–1760 BCE); and the Tomb of the Cisterns, closed in about 1650 BCE, but sacked at the time of the conquest of the town in about 1600 BCE. [*See* Tombs; Jewelry; Weapons.]

Art and iconography. Several fragments of very important sculptures were found in the Old Syrian town of the end of Mardikh IIIA, and of the first and central phases of Mardikh IIIB: carved double basins with ritual and mythical reliefs from temples B, D, and N (c. 1850–1750 BCE) and large fragments of important royal statues, particularly from temple P2, of a seated king and of a standing queen (c. 1700 BCE). These were the first evidence of the great statuary of inner Syria, contemporary with the classical style of the Old Syrian culture. Although at Ebla remains of Old Syrian glyptics are rare, several impressions on jars from the western palace produced a dynastic seal belonging to a crown prince, king Indilimgur's son (reigned c. 1650 BCE), with the figures of Hadad, Khebat, and of the owner, who receives life from the two great gods. Another significant example of art produced in Mardikh IIIB is the ivory carvings, in an egyptianizing style, discovered in the northern palace: elegant fig-ures, carved in the ajouré technique, represent the gods in the Egyptian pantheon, from Horus to Sobekh and Hathor to Montu; heads wearing Osiris's atef crown presumably are representations of deified Old Syrian kings. These ivories probably date to about 1700–1650 BCE; they likely decorated the back of a throne or of a ceremonial bed. Other ivory pieces, probably slightly older, include a miniature figure in the round of an offering bearer carrying a gazelle and an ajouré figure of a king wearing the typical ovoid tiara. These pieces are evidence of the activity at Ebla of workshops whose output was in the Old Syrian style.

Strata IV–VI. The remains of Mardikh IVA–B (c. 1600–1200 BCE) are scattered and limited to sectors on the acropolis. Traces of rural settlement mark the Mardikh VA phase (c. 1200–900 BCE); the settlement was enlarged in Mardikh VB–C (c. 900–535 BCE). In a central phase of Mardikh VIA–B (c. 535–60 BCE), a small rural palace was built on the northern part of the acropolis. During the second century BCE, or slightly afterward, the tell was totally abandoned. The last evidence of a human presence at Tell Mardikh is scant: traces of scattered houses belonging to a third-century CE agricultural settlement; some remains, as yet unexcavated, of a poor monastic settlement that may date to the fourth–fifth centuries; and, in a peripheral region, some reused stone blocks with short Arabic inscriptions in Kufic script that may date to the ninth century—the period in which the First Crusade passed through the region and in which the name *Mardikh* appears in written sources for the first time.

[*See also* Eblaites; Ebla Texts; Furniture and Furnishings, *article on* Furnishings of the Bronze and Iron Ages; *and* Syria, *article on* Syria in the Bronze Age.]

BIBLIOGRAPHY

Ebla retrouvée. Histoire et Archéologie, Dossier 83. Dijon, 1984.

Lebrun, René. *Ebla et les civilisations du Proche-Orient ancien.* Louvain-la-Neuve, 1984.

Matthiae, Paolo. "Empreintes d'un cylindre paléosyrien de Tell Mardikh." *Syria* 46 (1969): 1–43.

Matthiae, Paolo. "Princely Cemetery and Ancestors Cult at Ebla during Middle Bronze II: A Proposal of Interpretation." *Ugarit-Forschungen* 11 (1979): 563–569.

Matthiae, Paolo. "Scavi a Tell Mardikh–Ebla, 1978: Rapporto sommario." *Studi Eblaiti* 1 (1979): 129–184.

Matthiae, Paolo. "Campagne de fouilles à Ebla en 1979: Les tombes princières et le palais de la ville basse à l'époque amorrhéene." *Comptes Rendus de l'Académie des Inscriptions et Belles-Lettres* (1980): 94–118.

Matthiae, Paolo. *Ebla: An Empire Rediscovered.* Translated by Christopher Holme. Garden City; N.Y., 1980.

Matthiae, Paolo. "Fouilles à Tell Mardikh–Ebla, 1978: Le Bâtiment Q et la nécropole princière du Bronze Moyen II." *Akkadica* 17 (1980): 1–51.

Matthiae, Paolo. "The Princely Tombs of Middle Bronze II at Ebla and the Contemporary Syro-Palestinian Cemeteries." *Studi Eblaiti* 2 (1980): 195–204.

Matthiae, Paolo. "Sulle asce fenestrate del 'Signore dei Capridi.'" *Studi Eblaiti* 3 (1980): 53–62.

Matthiae, Paolo. "Two Princely Tombs at Tell Mardikh–Ebla." *Archaeology* 33 (1980): 8–17.

Matthiae, Paolo. "A Hypothesis on the Princely Burial Area of Middle Bronze II at Ebla." *Archiv Orientální* 49 (1981): 55–65.

Matthiae, Paolo. "Osservazioni sui gioielli delle tombe principesche di Mardikh IIIB." *Studi Eblaiti* 4 (1981): 205–225.

Matthiae, Paolo. "Fouilles à Tell Mardikh–Ebla, 1980: Le Palais Occidental de l'époque amorrhéene." *Akkadica* 28 (1982): 41–87.

Matthiae, Paolo. "Fouilles de 1982 à Tell Mardikh–Ebla et à Tell Touqan: Nouvelles lumières sur l'architecture paléosyrienne du Bronze Moyen I–II." *Comptes Rendus de l'Académie des Inscriptions et Belles-Lettres* (1982): 299–331.

Matthiae, Paolo. "Die Fürstengräber des Palastes Q in Ebla." *Antike Welt* 13 (1982): 3–14.

Matthiae, Paolo. "The Western Palace of the Lower City of Ebla: A New Administrative Building of Middle Bronze I–II." *Archiv für Orientforschung* 19 (1982): 121–129.

Matthiae, Paolo. "Ebla Discovered." In *Ebla to Damascus, Art and Archaeology of Ancient Syria: An Exhibition from the Directorate-General of Antiquities and Museums of the Syrian Arab Republic,* edited by Harvey Weiss, pp. 134–139. Washington, D.C., 1985.

Matthiae, Paolo. *I tesore di Ebla.* 2d ed. Rome, 1985.

Matthiae, Paolo. "Le palais royal d'Ebla." *Archéologia* 238 (1988): 34–43.

Matthiae, Paolo. *Ebla, alle origini della civiltà urbana: Trent'anni di scavi in Siria dell'Università di Roma "La Sapienza."* Milan, 1995. Catalog of an exhibition held in Rome in 1995.

Mazzoni, Stefania. *Le Impronte su Giara Eblaite e Siriane nel Bronzo Antico.* Materiali e Studi Archeologici di Ebla, 1. Rome, 1992.

Pinnock, Frances. "Nota sui 'sonagli' della 'Tomba del Signore dei Capridi.'" *Studi Eblaiti* 1 (1979): 185–190.

Pinnock, Frances. *Le perle del Palazzo Reale G.* Materiali e Studi Archeologici di Ebla, 2. Rome, 1993.

Scandone Matthiae, G. "Un oggetto faraonico della XIII dinastia dalla 'Tomba del Signore dei Capridi.'" *Studi Eblaiti* 1 (1979): 119–128.

Scandone Matthiae, G. "Ebla und Aegypten im Alten und Mittleren Reich." *Antike Welt* 13 (1982): 14–17.

PAOLO MATTHIAE

EBLAITES. Scholars utilize the ethnonym *Eblaites* to refer to the people of Ebla, a major Bronze Age city-state in northern Syria. Discussions about the identity of peoples, especially in the Near East, typically rely on factors such as the identification of the language utilized and the gods worshiped. Thus, because the eblaite language is Semitic and many of the gods worshiped at Ebla occur elsewhere in the pantheons of other Semitic peoples, it is generally accepted that the Eblaites were a Semitic people. However, a host of problems specific to refining this statement continues to be debated.

The classification of the Eblaite language within the Semitic family of languages is the center of a sharp debate. Some scholars view Eblaite as a dialect of Old Akkadian, in which case it would be proper to speak of the Eblaites as a branch of the East Semites (Akkadians, Assyrians, and Babylonians). Other scholars view Eblaite as a branch of West Semitic, with an especially close relationship to other West Semitic languages utilized in Syria (in particular, the roughly contemporary Amorite and the later-attested Aramaic). The majority of the evidence favors the latter opinion. To cite one example, the Eblaite first-person independent pronoun *I* is *'ana,* exactly as in Amorite and Aramaic. It is thus preferable to speak of the Eblaites as West Semites. [*See* Semitic Languages.]

The deities attested at Ebla likewise share greater similarities with the West Semitic world than with the East Semitic world. Important gods are Dagan, Hadd/Baal, Rashap, Ashtar, Kamish, Malik, and Qura (as well as the sun and moon deities whose Eblaite names are unknown because Sumerograms always are used). To illustrate connections with the West Semitic world, the god Kamish may be highlighted. This deity appears in the city name Kar-Kamish (Carchemish) in northern Syria; is attested in the pantheon of Ugarit on the Syrian coast; and appears much later as the national god of the Moabites (written almost always as Kamosh [Chemosh], but in one biblical passage as Kamish).

Although the Eblaites can be seen to have been West Semites, it is important to note that they had intimate connections with Mesopotamia. Because the Eblaites were based in a major urban center (unlike other West Semites, who may have been more rural or pastoral), the links with the large cities of Mesopotamia were strong. This will explain the fact that about fifty different Ebla texts (especially lexical texts) are duplicates of texts known from sites such as Fara and Abu Salabikh. Especially close cultural contacts appear to have existed with Kish; for example, it is known from one text that a mathematics professor from Kish worked or taught at Ebla. The city of Mari presumably served as the conduit through which much of Mesopotamian culture reached Ebla. [*See* Fara; Abu Salabikh; Kish; Mari.]

In conclusion, the Eblaites were a West Semitic people, similar to other peoples of Syria (e.g., the Amorites). However, because their culture was urban based, there were strong influences from Mesopotamia.

[*See also* Ebla; Ebla Texts.]

BIBLIOGRAPHY

Buccellati, Giorgio. "Ebla and the Amorites." In *Eblaitica: Essays on the Ebla Archives and Eblaite Language,* edited by Cyrus H. Gordon and Gary A. Rendsburg, vol. 3, pp. 83–104. Winona Lake, Ind., 1992. Addresses the problem of the relationship between the Eblaites and the Amorites.

Gelb, I. J. "The Language of Ebla in the Light of the Sources from Ebla, Mari, and Babylonia." In *Ebla, 1975–1985,* edited by Luigi Cagni, pp. 49–74. Naples, 1987. Final article written by the leading scholar of Akkadian, Amorite, and Eblaite languages.

Gelb, I. J. "Mari and the Kish Civilization." In *Mari in Retrospect: Fifty Years of Mari and Mari Studies,* edited by Gordon D. Young, pp. 121–202. Winona Lake, Ind., 1992. Article prepared for publication by the editor, following Gelb's death.

Matthiae, Paolo. *Ebla: An Empire Rediscovered.* Translated by Christopher Holme. Garden City, N.Y., 1980. Written by the chief archaeologist of Tell Mardikh, with particular attention to Ebla's archaeological and historical significance.

Pettinato, Giovanni. *Ebla: A New Look at History.* Translated by C. Faith Richardson. Baltimore, 1991. Synthesis of the epigraphic finds from Tell Mardikh by the excavation team's former chief epigrapher.

Rendsburg, Gary A. "Monophthongization of *aw/ay* > *ā* in Eblaite and in Northwest Semitic." In *Eblaitica: Essays on the Ebla Archives and Eblaite Language,* edited by Cyrus H. Gordon and Gary A. Rendsburg, vol. 2, pp. 91–126. Winona Lake, Ind., 1990. Argues for a Syrian Semitic *Sprachbund* consisting of Eblaite, Amorite, and Aramaic.

Stieglitz, Robert R. "Ebla and the Gods of Canaan." In *Eblaitica: Essays on the Ebla Archives and Eblaite Language,* edited by Cyrus H. Gordon and Gary A. Rendsburg, vol. 2, pp. 79–89. Winona Lake, Ind., 1990. Discusses the West Semitic identification of the major and minor deities in the Eblaite pantheon.

GARY A. RENDSBURG

EBLA TEXTS. The tablets discovered in Royal Palace G at Ebla in Syria by Paolo Matthiae of the University of Rome are written in cuneiform script and dated to about the first half of the twenty-fourth century BCE. The texts were excavated between 1974 and 1976; since that time there have been only sporadic discoveries. The tablets recount activity during the reigns of three generations of sovereigns: Igriš-Ḫalab, Irkab-Damu, and Išar-Damu, for a period estimated to cover forty to fifty years. The only synchronism with other previously known dynasties is with Iblul-Il, king of Mari, who is mentioned in two documents that refer to the first contacts between the two Syrian cities. The lid of a vase with the cartouche of Pepi I, found in the same level as the tablets, constitutes a *terminus post quem* for the destruction of the palace.

All the texts come from Palace G. The central archive was preserved in one room (locus 2769), on the east side of the internal portico of the Audience Hall (see figure 1). The tablets (1,727 of them) that are either complete or preserved in large part come from there, along with 9,483 fragments and numerous chips. The original number can be estimated at 2,500 documents. Except for the large tablets, which were placed directly on the ground, the tablets were stored on wooden shelving, which was completely burned. From the adjacent vestibule (locus 2875) come, in addition to 276 texts, fragments of bone that could belong to styluses and a stone for smoothing the surface of a tablet, an indication that this was one of the places where the tablets were written. Records concerning foodstuffs consumed at the court (242 texts) were found in a small room in the northeast corner of the Audience Hall. An additional twenty-two texts were found on a wooden table about 10 m west of there. A small archive of predominately agricultural texts, consisting of seventeen lenticular tablets and more than one thousand fragments, was found in the vicinity of an internal courtyard. Another room contained a group of thirty-two lenticular tablets.

Most of the texts are administrative in character and relate to palace activity. Also preserved in the central archive were guides for the correct use of the cuneiform script, which, in addition to syllabic signs for the Eblaite language, made use of numerous Sumerian logograms. Some forty lists contain Sumerian words arranged by subject: names of professions, of cities, of animals, and of objects. These are of Mesopotamian origin and present a canonical arrangement already fixed in the examples known from the archives at Shuruppak

EBLA TEXTS. Figure 1. *Ebla tablets in situ.* (Courtesy A. Archi)

EBLA TEXTS.   Figure 2.   *The Sumerian-Eblaite vocabulary.* (Courtesy A. Archi)

and Abu Salabikh. Another eight lists, with words or expressions arranged according to acrophonic principles (the longest has 1,204 terms), were composed at Ebla. One of these served as the basis for bilingual Sumerian-Eblaite lists, which are the most ancient dictionaries known (see figure 2). Manuscripts A and C contain approximately 1,200 Sumerian words, the greater number of which are given an Eblaite translation. The list continues in A₂, which has about 350 additional words. Manuscript D, consisting of five smaller tablets, stops at number 880. A more recent recension is B, a large tablet that includes the entire list. Another eighteen smaller texts give various sections.

Literary texts are represented by one Sumerian hymn and two Semitic hymns (one of these and the Sumerian one are also known in versions from Abu Salabikh) as well as by eighteen incantations, the majority of which are in Sumerian. A long ritual for the enthronement of the royal couple, in two parallel versions written on the occasion of the marriage of the last two kings, describes cult rites for the gods and the deceased sovereigns. The chancery texts include political agreements (with Mari, Ibal, and Abarsal; this last one is made up of a long series of symmetrical clauses following a pattern that will reappear a millennium later in Syrian-Anatolian treaties), diplomatic reports, letters, and royal decrees. One letter from Enna-Dagan, king of Mari, in which he describes the conquests of his own ancestors, comes from the chancery of that city. [*See* Mari.] Compared to the economic documents, these texts show a less frequent use of Sumerograms.

The most consistent group of economic documents is made up of 543 monthly statements concerning the distribution of clothing to foreign kings and their officials and to dependents of the Eblaite administration; altogether it covers at least forty years. Twenty-seven annual registers (large tablets with up to thirty columns per side) concern consignments of gold and silver articles on the part of the administration. Sixty tablets are devoted to the palace revenues (mu-DU) remitted by the more important officials. Thirty of these date back to the most ancient phase (the reign of Igriš-Ḥalab); the others are dated to the vizier Ibrium and to his son and successor Ibbi-Zikir (seventeen and thirteen documents, respectively) and show an annual pattern. Other groups of texts are concerned with the assignment of fields, with accounts regarding agricultural production (primarily barley but also olive oil and wine) and the raising of animals, and with consignments of sheep for sacrifices to the gods and for meat consumption at the palace. In addition, there are hundreds of small- and medium-sized tablets with individual administrative records.

Eblaite is the oldest documented Semitic language and was spoken in all of northern Syria, although there may have been dialectic variants. It belongs to the archaic Semitic type, which continued in Mesopotamia with Akkadian, and of which some elements were preserved in the second millennium BCE in Ugaritic and surface later in the most ancient dialects of the southern Arabian Peninsula. However, Eblaite presents its own innovations (such as verbal nouns with the prefix t- and the infix -t-), and does not share some of those to be found in Akkadian (such as the declension of pronominal suffixes in the dual). [*See* Akkadian; Ugaritic.]

The archives reveal the history of central Syria in the third millennium. The entire area was organized into city-states that had their center in a palace, where the king and the queen, *mal(i)kum maliktum,* resided. [*See* Palace.] One offering list (*ARET* [=*Archivi Reali di Ebla. Testi*] 7.150) gives the names of ten kings of Ebla in chronological order: Abur-Lim, Agur-Lim, Ibbi-Damu, Baga-Damu, Enar-Damu, Išar-Malik, (I)kun-Damu, Adub-Damu, Igriš-Ḥalab, Irkab-Damu. This list appears again (*TM* [= *Tell Mardikh*] 74.G.120) giving twenty-six royal names, from Kulbanu, the most ancient, to Išar-Damu, the successor of Irkab-Damu and the last king of Ebla. The dynasty therefore goes back to about the twenty-seventh century BCE, proving that Semitic populations had settled in northern Syria by at least the beginning of the third millennium and that they are responsible for the process of "secondary urbanization" that took place in that epoch.

Ebla became a regional state under Irkab-Damu, when its territory included the plain of Antioch, Carchemish to the north, and Hama to the south. It finally succeeded in setting itself up in opposition to Mari, to which it had to pay a tribute for a period of fifteen years (from Ibul-Il to Enna-Dagan) that in its entirety amounted to 1,028 kg of silver and 63 kg of gold. Under Irkab-Damu, Ibrium was placed at the head of the administration, a post he held for at least fifteen years, during which time there was an annual flow into the palace of 200–300 kg of silver, 200–500 kg of copper, 3–5 kg of gold, and about 2,000 pieces of clothing. With Ibbi-Zikir, Ibrium's son, who became vizier during the reign of Išar-Damu, there was a notable increase: 420–730 kg of silver, the same amount of copper, 2–20 kg of gold, and at least five thousand garments. The structure of the state was strongly centralized: about five thousand lower officials, artisans, and workers, and eight hundred women—practically the entire active population of the city—depended directly on the palace. The production of woolen cloth was well developed, as was metallurgy, which employed as many as five hundred workmen. It is not possible to deduce from the texts which enemy brought an end to this period of splendor.

The pantheon included Semitic divinities and local ones. Among the latter is Kura, the principal god of the city, along with his wife Barama, the goddess Išḫara (more important than Ishtar), and possibly Idabal. Semitic gods are the weather god Hadda of Ḫalab (Aleppo), the sun goddess (written with the Sumerogram *Utu*), Dagan, Rashap, and Kamish. *Il* is a frequent element in the theophorous personal names, but it does not appear in the lists of gods; it expresses the visible manifestation of the divine (originally of the divinity of the group), but found no place in Ebla's polytheistic system. Il/El, the lord and father of gods and men described in the Ugaritic myths, is the product of later theological speculation.

The series *Archivi Reali di Ebla. Testi* (Rome, 1981–) is dedicated to the publication of the texts; other documents have been published in the series *Materiali epigrafici di Ebla* (Naples, 1979–).

[See also Cuneiform; Ebla; Eblaites.]

BIBLIOGRAPHY

Archi, Alfonso. "The Archives of Ebla." In *Cuneiform Archives and Libraries,* edited by Klaas R. Veenhof, pp. 72–86. Leiden, 1986. Description of the archives and general classification of the texts.

Archi, Alfonso. "How a Pantheon Forms: The Cases of Hattian-Hittite Anatolia and Ebla of Third Millennium BC." In *Religionsgeschichtliche Beziehungen zwischen Kleinasien, Nordsyrien und dem Alten Testament im 2. und 1. Jahrtausend,* edited by Bernd Janowski et al., pp. 1–18. Orbis Biblicus et Orientalis, vol. 129. Göttingen, 1993. The first classification of the Eblaite pantheon.

Archi, Alfonso. "Trade and Administrative Practices: The Case of Ebla." *Altorientalische Forschungen* 20 (1993): 43–58.

Conti, Giovanni. *Il sillabario della quarta fonte della lista lessicale bilingue eblaita.* Quaderni di Semitistica, vol. 17. Florence, 1990. Results of study of a section of the lexical lists.

Fronzaroli, Pelio. "Per una valutazione della morfologia eblaita." *Studi Eblaiti* 5 (1982): 93–120. Short grammar of the Eblaite language.

Fronzaroli, Pelio, ed. *Literature and Literary Language at Ebla.* Quaderni di Semitistica, vol. 18. Florence, 1992. Up-to-date presentation of the literary and lexical texts.

Matthiae, Paolo. "The Archives of the Royal Palace G of Ebla: Distribution and Arrangement of the Tablets According to the Archaeo-

logical Evidence." In *Cuneiform Archives and Libraries,* edited by Klaas R. Veenhof, pp. 53–71. Leiden, 1986.

Milano, Lucio. "Food Rations at Ebla." *Mari: Annales de Recherches Interdisciplinaires* 5 (1987): 519–550. Study of the alimentary supply for the Eblaite court.

Pettinato, Giovanni. *The Archives of Ebla: An Empire Inscribed in Clay.* New York, 1981. The first evaluation of the archives, which needs extensive revision.

ALFONSO ARCHI
Translated from Italian by Susan I. Schiedel

ECBATANA (modern Hamadan, at 34°48′ N, 48°31′ E and 1,800 m above sea level), site located at the base of the eastern slope of the 3,571-meter-high Kuh-e Alvand range in the Zagros mountains of west-central Iran. The city is bisected from south to north by the Alusjerd River. The identification of the site with Hamadan is solidly based on both historical and archaeological evidence. The ancient name of the city appears in the Bisitun inscription of Darius II in Old Persian ha ^{m}gmatana, Elamite ag-ma-da-na, and Akkadian a-ga-ma-ta-nu and is usually interpreted as *hang-mata* "(place of) gathering." In classical, biblical, and other sources, the name variously occurs as Agbatana, Ecbatana(s), Ecbatanis Partiorum, Ekbatan, Achmetha, Ahmatan, Hamatan, and Ahmadan. Founded as the capital of the state of Media (Herodotus, Hist. 1.97), the city subsequently served as the satrapal seat of the province of Media from the Achaemenid to the Sasanian period. In addition, it served as a royal treasury and summer residence. It was in Ecbatana that Cyrus's order for the rebuilding of the Jerusalem Temple was found (*Ez.* 6:2). The city fell to Cyrus II in 550/49 BCE, to Alexander the Great in 330 BCE, to Seleucus I in 305 BCE, to Mithridates I in 147 BCE, to Ardashir I in 226 CE, and to the Muslims in 642 (AH 23), after which it became a provincial capital, which it has remained.

Ecbatana's location provides strategic control over the major east-west route, the so-called High Road, through the central Zagros mountains. An extensive fertile plain lies to the east and, in antiquity, the area was famed for its horse rearing and wheat production (Polybius, *History,* 544.1). The city's major topographical features are al-Musalla, an 80-meter-high natural rock outcrop in the southeastern quarter, topped by the ruins of a rectangular citadel, probably of the Parthian period (238 BCE–224 CE). The barren hill of Sang-i Shir lies on the city's southeastern perimeter and features a colossal stone lion, possibly from the Hellenistic period. Nearby is Tell Hagmataneh, a 30-meter-high mound in the city's northeastern quarter, which has been identified by chance finds and archaeological investigation as the site of the Median citadel and of subsequent Achaemenid royal construction. The so-called Tomb of Esther and Mordechai, associated by long tradition with Esther, the Jewish bride of Ahasuerus (Xerxes I or Artaxerxes I), and her uncle, Mordechai, is more likely the sepulcher of Shu-shan-Dukht, the Jewish consort of Yazdigird I (399–420 CE). The most detailed and probably the most reliable ancient description of the city, renowned in antiquity for its vast wealth and splendid royal architecture, is provided by Polybius, *History,* (10.27.1–13), who describes the palace area as having a circumference of nearly seven stades (1.4 km), a measurement that corresponds closely to the circumference of Tell Hagmataneh. Various early travelers recorded observations of Persepolis-style column bases and other ancient masonry reutilized in later structures or lying in heaps in the river. They identify the city as a source of an extensive trade in antiquities and forgeries. French archaeologist Jacques de Morgan collected numerous antiquities in Hamadan in the late nineteenth century. Charles Fossey directed the earliest archaeological excavations in 1913, under the auspices of the French archaeological mission in Iran (see Chevalier, 1989). In 1920 and 1923, two large treasure troves, both probably from the reign of Artaxerxes II (404–359 BCE) or later, surfaced in the city, but their precise provienience is unknown. In 1956, road construction cut through the western slope of Tell Hagmataneh to a depth of 7 m and revealed a massive zigzagging outer defensive wall constructed in mud brick that is probably Median (seventh century BCE; see Dyson, 1957). In 1971, Stuart Swiny conducted an archaeological survey of the area around Hamadan for the British Institute of Persian Studies, and Massoud Azarnoush of the Iranian Archaeological Service partially excavated a Parthian cemetery from the first century BCE to the first century CE partially excavated in the city's southeast quadrant, near Sang-i Shir (see Swiny, 1975; Azarnoush, 1975). Two trilingual (Old Persian, Neo-Babylonian, and Elamite) rock-cut inscriptions are located at Ganj Nameh, 12 km (7 mi.) southwest of Hamadan, in a 2,000-meter-high pass over the Kuh-e Alvand. The texts praise Ahura Mazda and record the royal lineages and conquests of Darius I (521–485 BCE) and Xerxes I (485–465 BCE).

[*See also* Medes; Persia, *article on* Ancient Persia; *and* Sasanians.]

BIBLIOGRAPHY

Azarnoush, Massoud. "Hamadan: Excavation Report." *Iran* 13 (1975): 181–182.

Brown, Stuart C. "Ecbatana." In *Encyclopaedia Iranica*. New York, in press. Detailed discussion of pre-Islamic Hamadan, with extensive bibliography.

Chevalier, N. "Hamadan 1913: Une mission oubliée." *Iranica Antiqua* 24 (1989): 245–253.

Dyson, Robert H. "Iran, 1956." *University Museum Bulletin* (Philadelphia) 21.1 (1957): 27–39.

Frye, Richard N. "Hamadhān." In *Encyclopaedia of Islam*, new ed., vol. 3, pp. 105–106. Leiden, 1960–. Brief history of Hamadan in the Islamic period.

Swiny, Stuart. "Survey in North-West Iran, 1971." *East and West* 25 (1975): 77–96.

STUART C. BROWN

ÉCOLE BIBLIQUE ET ARCHÉOLOGIQUE FRANÇAISE. The oldest graduate school for biblical and archaeological studies in the Holy Land was opened in Jerusalem by Father Marie-Joseph Lagrange, O.P., on 15 November 1890, on the premises of the Dominican Monastery of St. Stephen, which had been established in 1882. He named it the École Pratique d'Études Bibliques (The Practical School of Biblical Studies) in order to underline its distinctive methodology—combining text and monument; the Bible would be studied in the physical and cultural context in which it had been written. The name was modified in 1920 when the Académie des Inscriptions et Belles-Lettres in Paris, rather than create a sister in Jerusalem to the celebrated École Française de Rome and the renowned École Française d'Athenes, decided to recognize the achievements of the École Biblique by designating it the École Archéologique Française. The honor, as will become apparent, was well merited. Alone of the national archaeological schools in Jerusalem, it has a developed teaching program and offers a doctorate (but no lower degrees) in biblical studies. Its extensive library holdings are made accessible by a uniquely detailed subject index.

None of the original staff, apart from Lagrange himself, had any professional qualifications. Very quickly, however, he selected and trained a faculty envied by all, drawing from among the Dominican novices forced to study in Jerusalem by anticlerical laws in France. Marius Antonin Jaussen (1871–1962) became a pioneering Arabic ethnographer. Louis-Hugues Vincent (1872–1960) developed into the preeminent Palestinian archaeologist of his generation. Antoine Raphael Savignac (1874–1951) made his mark as a semitic epigrapher, particularly for his work during three dangerous expeditions to northern Arabia with Jaussen in 1907, 1909, and 1910–1912. The acute critical judgment of Félix-Marie Abel (1878–1953) focused his vast erudition into unrivaled mastery of the Greek sources for the history and geography of Palestine. Edouard Paul Dhorme (1881–1966) became a noted Assyriologist and was the first to decipher Ugaritic and produce a continuous translation of the original tablets discovered in 1929.

In the fifty years of their intense interdisciplinary cooperation (1890–1940), the members of this small group produced 42 major books, 682 scientific articles, and more than 6,200 book reviews. The two latter categories appeared in the *Revue Biblique* (founded in 1892) and the former in the series *Études Bibliques* (begun in 1900).

They also trained their own successors, who began to appear in the 1930s. Bernard Couroyer (1900–) published extensively in Egyptology but also taught Coptic and Arabic. Roland de Vaux (1903–1971) was noted for both biblical scholarship and field archaeology. Raymond Tournay (1912–) is renowned for producing the best translation of the Psalms in any language. Pierre Benoît (1906–1987) and Marie-Emile Boismard (1916–) produced highly significant work in New Testament. It was they who, with the survivors of the first generation, gave Lagrange's ideal its ultimate expression with the publication of *La Bible de Jérusalem* (1956). The quality of the introductions, translations, and notes reflected the best of contemporary ecumenical scholarship, and the layout both delighted the eye and facilitated comprehension—for example, by printing poetry as poetry. A radical break with traditional presentation, it set the standard for all subsequent modern bibles and has been translated into most major languages (*The Jerusalem Bible* 1966; 2d ed., 1985). This Bible highlights the central place of biblical studies at the École Biblique.

Digging the foundations for the monastic church in 1889 became an archaeological excavation when elements began to come to light of the fifth-century basilica erected by the empress Eudocia to receive the relics of St. Stephen. It was to be a long time before the École Biblique could afford another excavation. Instead, it focused on a critical reevaluation of all topographical references, combined with intense and systematic surface exploration that involved all its professors and students. Particular attention was paid to the recovery of inscriptions. A simple listing of the reports in the *Revue Biblique* must suffice to indicate the scope of these expeditions: Masada, Transjordan, and southern Lebanon (1894); the Jordan Valley (1895, 1910–1913, 1931–1932); Sinai (1896); Petra (1897); the Hauran (1898); Gezer (1899); Philistia (1900); Avdat (1904–1905); the Dead Sea (1909–1910); the coastal plain (1914); Palmyra (1920); Qadesh Barnea (1921, 1938); central Samaria (1922–1923); southern Transjordan (1935); and Ephraim (1946).

For the same financial reasons, the École Biblique was attracted to the study of monumental complexes that did not need excavation. The Church of the Nativity in Bethlehem (1914) and the Ḥaram el-Khalil in Hebron (1923) were studied in exhaustive detail by Vincent with the assistance of Abel for the former and of E. J. H. Mackey and Abel for the latter. From the first article in the first fascicle of the *Revue Biblique* (by Lagrange in 1892), which destroyed the then current consensus by correctly locating the biblical Mount Zion on the Ophel ridge, Jerusalem provided an inexhaustible subject. A systematic research program was established in 1912 under Vincent's direction. Over and above his listed collaborators, he mobilized the resources of the École for the publication of the massive volumes *Jérusalem Antique: Topographie* (Paris, 1912); *Jérusalem Nouvelle* (Paris, 1914, 1922, 1926), with Abel; and *Jérusalem de l'Ancien Testament* (1954–1955), with A.-M. Stève. A member of the École Biblique, Charles Coüasnon (1904–1976), served as architect for the Latin community in the restoration of the Holy Sepulcher from 1959 to his death. His 1972 Schweich Lectures of the British Academy on the architectural evolution of the monument were published as *The Church of the Holy Sepulchre, Jerusalem* (London, 1974).

Inevitably, the British mandatory authorities drew on the accumulated expertise of the École Biblique for salvage operations. In 1919 the École Biblique both cleared the synagogue at Naʿaran, near Jericho, and mapped the monumental tomb at Khirbet Askar in Nablus, to which it returned for a more in-depth study in August 1921. In December 1921 the École Biblique cleared the magnificent mosaic floor at Beth-Guvrin, and excavated the entire Roman villa there in 1924 to establish its context. In 1937 the discovery of a "cities" mosaic floor at Maʿan in Jordan led to the excavation of a Byzantine church.

The first full-scale dig undertaken by the École Biblique was in 1924–1925, when Vincent excavated the churches at Imwas. Abel contributed the textual evidence to the final report, *Emmaüs: Sa basilique et son histoire* (Paris, 1932). This quickly led to others. In 1926, A. G. Barrois began a two-season excavation at Nerab, near Aleppo in Syria; his conclusions were published in *Syria* and the *Revue Biblique*. Mobilized into the French consular service during World War II, de Vaux was directed, in 1944, to research the history of the French government property at Abu Ghosh. His conclusions appeared as *Fouilles à Qaryet el-Enab, Abu Gosh, Palestine* (Paris, 1950). In 1945–1946 he and Stève excavated and published the baptistery, monastery, and fortress at ʿAin el-Maʿamudiyeh, west of Hebron.

Such small excavations prepared the École Biblique to attempt a major site. With the financial support of the French government de Vaux, who had become director of the École in 1945, selected Tell el-Farʿah (North), 11 km (7 mi.) northeast of Nablus. Between 1946 and 1962 he excavated there for nine seasons, each year publishing preliminary reports in the *Revue Biblique*. Unfortunately, he died before writing a final report, largely because of his involvement in the purchase of the Dead Sea Scrolls and the excavation at Qumran and the nearby caves.

In 1951 the École Biblique participated in the excavation of Cave 1 at Qumran, together with the Palestine Archaeological Museum (now the Rochefeller Museum) in Jerusalem, over whose trustees de Vaux presided, and with the Jordanian Department of Antiquities, headed by Gerald Lankester Harding. The latter's preoccupations in Amman, however, meant that daily responsibility devolved on the École Biblique and, to a lesser extent, the museum, both represented by de Vaux. Thus, the École Biblique excavated at Qumran in four seasons (1953–1956), and spent one season each in the caves of Wadi Murabbaʿat (1952) and at ʿAin Feshkha (1958). In 1952, with the aid of the American Schools of Oriental Research in Jerusalem, it conducted a systematic search of 270 caves in the vicinity of Qumran. Preliminary reports appeared annually in the *Revue Biblique*; the closest to a final report is the English version of de Vaux's 1959 Schweich Lectures, *Archaeology and the Dead Sea Scrolls* (London, 1973).

Dominique Barthélemy, O.P. (b. 1921), was the only member of the École Biblique to belong to the original group of three entrusted with publishing the scrolls in 1952; the other two were Josef Tadeuz Milik and Maurice Baillet. Recognizing that the material was too abundant and potentially too sensitive to be dealt with by this small group of Roman Catholic priests, de Vaux called on scientific organizations and eminent scholars for nominations to an interdenominational and interconfessional team of eight that would publish the scrolls. Once these had been selected and the documents divided among them (described in the *Revue Biblique* 63 [1956]: 49–67), neither de Vaux nor the École Biblique had any control over the fragments. Pierre Benoît, O.P. (1906–1987), also a professor at the École Biblique, was coopted to edit the few Greek and Latin fragments and, because he had published his assignment, he was named to succeed de Vaux as general editor of *Discoveries in the Judaean Desert* when the latter died in 1971. Émile Puech of the French National Center for Scientific Research, who resides and teaches at the École Biblique, is still working on unpublished texts from Qumran. [*See* Qumran; Dead Sea Scrolls.]

The cooperation of the École Biblique in Kathleen M. Kenyon's excavation on the Ophel ridge (1961–1963) was cut short by political objections to the proximity of the squares to the Ḥaram esh-Sharif. Just before his death in 1971, de Vaux selected Tell Keisan, between Haifa and Akko, as the next major excavation of the École Biblique. Between 1971 and 1980 a series of directors—Jean Prignaud, Jacques Briend, and Jean-Baptiste Humbert—conducted eight campaigns there. The first part of the final report appeared as *Tell Keisan (1971–1976), une cité phénicienne en Galilée* (Fribourg, 1980). In order to provide a context for the inscribed Syro-Palestinian tombstones discovered by Savignac in 1924, the École Biblique dug for six seasons at Khirbet es-Samra (1978–1986), some 50 km (36 mi.) north of Amman, under the direction of Humbert. The latter, however, was less interested in churches of the seven–eighth centuries than in the Aramean migrations in the Iron Age; in 1986 he moved his team to el-Fedein, close to the Jordanian border with Syria. There he had the misfortune to find extensive Umayyad ruins, which the Jordanian government decided to preserve. In exchange, the École Biblique was invited, in 1988, to excavate the third terrace of the lower city of the citadel in Amman, in cooperation with the Department of Antiquities. A preliminary report of the first three seasons (1988–1991) appeared in the centenary issue of the *Revue Biblique* (1992).

[*See also the biographies of Abel, Barrois, Lagrange, Vaux, and Vincent.*]

BIBLIOGRAPHY

Benoît, Pierre. "French Archaeologists." In *Benchmarks in Time and Culture: An Introduction to Palestinian Archaeology Dedicated to Joseph A. Callaway*, edited by Joel F. Drinkard et al., pp. 63–86. Atlanta,

1988. Full bibliographical references for all the archaeological work of the École Biblique to 1986.
Murphy-O'Connor, Jerome, with a contribution by Justin Taylor. *The Ecole Biblique and the New Testament: A Century of Scholarship, 1890–1990*. Novum Testamentum et Orbis Antiquus, vol. 13. Fribourg, 1990. Profiles of the École's seven New Testament professors, with full bibliographies.
Vesco, Jean-Luc, ed. *L'Ancien Testament: Cent ans d'exégèse à l'École Biblique*. Cahiers de la Revue Biblique, vol. 28. Paris, 1990. Surveys and evaluates the contribution of the École Biblique to biblical, intertestamental, and Oriental studies.
Viviano, Benedict T. "École Biblique et Archéologique Française de Jérusalem." *Biblical Archaeologist* 54 (1991): 160–167. Current faculty and work of the École Biblique.

JEROME MURPHY-O'CONNOR, O.P.

EDOM. The early history of Edom, a small Iron Age Kingdom southeast of Judah, is obscure. It flourished under the Assyrians (eighth–seventh centuries BCE) and was destroyed by the Babylonians in about 550 BCE. The Hebrew name *Edom* ("red") primarily referred to the mountains south of the Dead Sea and east of the Wadi 'Arabah, but Edomites also settled in the region west of the Wadi 'Arabah, their western boundary abutting Judah's between Qadesh and the southern end of the Dead Sea (cf. *Nm.* 34:3ff.; *Jos.* 15:1–4; *Dt.* 2:8). This western region was called Seir (cf. *Jos.* 11:17; 1 *Chr.* 4:42ff.), a name in some biblical texts virtually synonymous with Edom (cf. *Gn.* 32:3, 36:8ff.; *Jg.* 5:4).

Scholarly exploration of Edom began in the nineteenth century with Ulrich J. Seetzen (1806–1807); Jean Louis Burkhardt (1812), who rediscovered Petra; Charles Leonard Irby and James Mangles (1818); Léon de Laborde (1828); Edward Robinson (1838); and others. Louis Lartet and Edward Hull published geological studies (1876, 1883). Alois Musil (1896–1898, 1900–1902), and Rudolf Ernst Brunnow and Albert von Domaszewski (1897–1898) recorded visible ruins. In 1933–1935 Nelson Glueck explored Edom; in 1937–1938 he excavated the Nabatean site of Khirbet et-Tannur and in 1938–1940 the Iron Age Tell el-Kheleifeh. In the 1950s and 1960s Diana Kirkbride excavated at Beidha, Peter Parr at Petra, and Crystal-M. Bennett at Umm el-Biyara, Tawilan, and Buṣeirah. In the 1980s Stephen Hart excavated in south-central Edom, Manfred Lindner explored west-central hilltop sites, and Andreas Hauptmann and others studied mining sites in the 'Arabah. The 1970s and 1980s saw important surveys in the Wadi el-Hasa region (Burton MacDonald, Manfred Weippert), at Ras en-Naqb (Hart), in the Ḥisma region (William Jobling), and in the Ghor and northern Wadi 'Arabah (Walter Rast and Thomas R. Schaub, and MacDonald).

Edom's prehistoric sites have been researched by Donald Henry, Mary O. Rollefson, and others. Human activity is evidenced through the Lower, Middle, and Upper Paleolithic, Epipaleolithic, Neolithic, and Chalcolithic periods (c. 100,000–3,000 BCE), especially in more moist periods when settlement could spread from the terraces of the scarp to the central plateau, where grazing animals might be hunted. A number of Epipaleolithic-Natufian sites are known from the eleventh–tenth millennia in the Wadi el-Hasa, near Petra, and in the Wadi Judaiyid. The Pre-Pottery Neolithic period is well evidenced at Beidha. There is little Pottery Neolithic, but Chalcolithic sites appear south of Ras en-Naqb and in the Wadi 'Arabah, where copper was mined and smelted.

Early Bronze Age sherd scatters on the plateau evidence temporary settlements and pastoral activity. Surveys show an absence of MB pottery, but a handful of sites with late Bronze pottery suggests the start of renewed population growth. In the Wadi 'Arabah, however, carbon-14 datings from charcoal suggest smelting activities at Khirbet en-Nahas in MB II and at Feinan in LB II. Smelting took place at Timna' under the Egyptian nineteenth and twentieth dynasties. The Egyptians knew Edom and Seir's inhabitants as *shosu* ("wanderers"), bellicose pastoralists who migrated to Egypt in times of hardship. LB Transjordan was subject to Egyptian control and lay on the very fringe of the wealthier Aegean world, whose trade reached the Jordan Valley.

In Iron Age I, the population and number of settlements increased. Terraces, houses, small farms, a cemetery, a possible village, and a possible fortress suggest an agricultural community, mainly in the west-central region. In Iron II the population grew significantly. Surveys reveal buildings, hamlets, unwalled villages, a significant number of fortresses on the plateau, and a number of mountaintop settlements in the west (cf. *Ob*.3). Defense seems to have been important, with the fortresses perhaps defending official interests in trade and agriculture and the minor clifftop settlements defending the local population against intruders. Crystal-M. Bennett excavated a short-lived seventh-century BCE domestic settlement on the top of Umm el-Biyara, an eighth–fifth century BCE unfortified agricultural town at Tawilan, and an eighth–fifth (?) century BCE major city at Buṣeirah (biblical Bozrah), with a casemate town wall, domestic buildings, and an enclosed acropolis with an Iron II palace or temple, succeeded by a smaller "winged" building possibly built for the Persian administration. Glueck excavated Tell el-Kheleifeh, assigning it five occupation levels from Solomon to the Persian period; however, recent study has demonstrated two levels, a casemate-walled fortress and a larger, solid-walled fortress, dated by the Iron II pottery to the eighth–fifth centuries BCE. The site is now identified with Uzziah's Eilat (*2 Kgs*. 14:22), rather than with Solomon's Ezion-Geber (*1 Kgs*. 9:26). Evidence of an Iron II copper industry, active from the eighth to the fifth centuries BCE, perhaps encouraged by the Assyrian administration, appears at Feinan and elsewhere in the 'Arabah (cf *Jb*. 28:1–4); it produced enough copper to leave 100,000 tons of slag.

Thus, early Edom was primarily a rural society of subsistence farmers and pastoralists, presumably tribal in structure. Central administration was probably first imposed by Judah (*2 Sm*. 8:14). The "Edomite king list" of *Genesis* 36:31–39, an Israelite compilation of monarchic date or later, offers uncertain evidence for the early period but may suggest some regionalism in Edom, Bozrah, and the land of the Temanites (the southern region?) being clearly well known. Political development could begin only when Judah's rule ended; monarchy was established in about 850 BCE (*2 Kgs*. 8:20). Population expansion, the appearance of villages, hilltop settlements, fortresses, towns, a major city, the copper industry, and evidence of foreign trade belong, together with vassaldom to the Assyrians, to the eighth–seventh centuries BCE; Edomite tribute is mentioned in the records of Adad-Nirari I, Tiglath-Pileser III, Sargon II, Sennacherib, Esarhaddon, and Ashurbanipal; the last two kings required military service also. Assyrian rule may help explain Edom's relative prosperity and security.

Edom's material culture was similar to that of its Transjordanian neighbors. Standard pottery shapes include platters, bowls, cups, cooking pots, jugs and juglets, storage jars, and lamps. Plain coarse ware is found everywhere, but fine painted ware, presumably for the wealthier classes, is found especially at Buṣeirah (and also at some Iron II sites in the Negev). Assyrian bowls and cups are also found. More decorative objects include cosmetic palettes, carved tridacna shells, seals, beads, and jewelry. Major inscriptions are lacking, but the seventh–sixth-century BCE seals, seal impressions, and ostraca, with some fifth–fourth-century BCE evidence from Tell el-Kheleifeh, suggest that the script was of Phoenician origin, increasingly influenced by the Aramaic script used by the Assyrian administration. The language was a variant of Northwest Semitic, close to Hebrew, Ammonite, and Moabite.

Archaeological evidence for religious practice is limited. Buṣeirah's building B, with its courtyard, cisterns, and steps flanked by pillar bases leading to an inner room, was probably a palace rather than a temple (cf. *Am*. 1:12). Censers witness a common cultic practice, female figurines perhaps indicate devotion to Astarte, and a scarab from Tawilan picturing a crescent on a pole may symbolize the moon god Sin of Harran in Syria. The evidence of seals, ostraca, and biblical Edomite names suggests that the deities Baal, Hadad, and El were known. The element *qws* in theophoric names from later seals, ostraca, and inscriptions suggests that Qos (personifying the bow?) was worshiped in Edom. Qos was a war or weather god of North Arabian origin, but when this cult was introduced into Edom is not clear. The Israelites knew Edom as the home of Yahweh (*Jgs*. 5:4) and recognized the Edomites as their brothers and fellow Yahweh-worshipers (*Dt*. 23:8; *1 Sm*. 21:7).

[*See also* Beidha; Buṣeirah; Feinan; Kheleifeh, Tell el-; Tawilan; *and* Umm el-Biyara.]

BIBLIOGRAPHY

This entry is based mainly on archaeological reports and research published in archaeological journals. Full bibliographies will be found in the works of Bartlett and MacDonald cited below.

Bartlett, John R. *Edom and the Edomites.* Sheffield, 1989. First major scholarly synthesis of the evidence for the history of Edom since Frantz Buhl's *Geschichte der Edomiter* (Leipzig, 1893), with detailed bibliography of the scholarly literature.

Bienkowski, Piotr, ed. *The Art of Jordan.* Stroud, England, 1991. Series of scholarly articles accompanying an exhibition of artifacts from Jordan, including ancient Edom. Note especially the chapters on sculpture, pottery, art and technology, and writing.

Bennett, Crystal-M. "Excavations at Buseirah." *Levant* 5 (1973): 1–11; 6 (1974): 1–24; 7 (1975): 1–15; 9 (1977): 1–10. Reports of excavation at Edom's major city.

Burckhardt, Jean L. *Travels in Syria and the Holy Land.* London, 1822. Classic of early exploration, full of well-observed detail.

Glueck, Nelson. *Explorations in Eastern Palestine.* Vols. 1–3. Annual of the American Schools of Oriental Research, 14, 15, 18/19. New Haven, 1934–1939. Glueck's surveys in Edom, Moab, and Ammon. Glueck based his results on a pottery classification that has since been considerably refined. His work must now be interpreted in the light of subsequent field research by Burton MacDonald, Stephen Hart, Manfred Lindner, Manfred Weippert, William Jobling, and others.

Glueck, Nelson. *The Other Side of the Jordan* (1940). Rev. ed. Cambridge, Mass., 1970. Popular account of Glueck's surveys and excavations in modern Jordan in which he revises some of his original conclusions.

Hadidi, Adnan, ed. *Studies in the History and Archaeology of Jordan.* Vols. 1–3. Amman, 1982–1987. Presentations delivered at three international conferences by leading scholars of the history of Jordan. Note especially papers by Peter J. Parr, Manfred Weippert, and Crystal-M. Bennett in volume 1; and E. Axel Knauf and C. J. Lenzen, Manfred Weippert, and Gerrit van der Kooij in volume 3.

MacDonald, Burton. *The Wadi el Ḥasā Archaeological Survey, 1979–1983, West-Central Jordan.* Waterloo, Ontario, 1988. Results of a detailed survey of the region immediately south of the Wadi el-Ḥasa in northern Edom.

MacDonald, Burton. "Archaeology of Edom." In *The Anchor Bible Dictionary,* vol. 2, pp. 295–301. New York, 1992. Survey, with a detailed bibliography of literature in archaeological journals.

Sawyer, John F. A., and David J. A., Clines, eds. *Midian, Moab, and Edom: The History and Archaeology of Late Bronze and Iron Age Jordan and North-West Arabia.* Sheffield, 1983. Includes important studies on Edomite pottery (Marion F. Oakeshott) and "Midianite" pottery (Benno Rothenberg and Jonathan Glass).

JOHN R. BARTLETT

EGYPT.

[*This entry provides a broad survey of the history of Egypt as known primarily from archaeological discoveries. It is chronologically divided into five articles:*

Prehistoric Egypt
Predynastic Egypt
Dynastic Egypt
Postdynastic Egypt
Islamic Egypt

In addition to the related articles on specific subregions and sites referred to in this entry, see also History of the Field, *article on* Archaeology in Egypt.]

Prehistoric Egypt

Although Egypt has been inhabited for at least 500,000 years, unfortunately, we know almost nothing about the way of life in Egypt for at least the first half of this period, largely because intensive erosion has destroyed most of the deposits in which settlements might have been preserved. Our information is a little more complete for the next 200,000 years (the Middle and Upper Paleolithic), but it is not until almost 20,000 BP, in the Late Paleolithic, that we really begin to be able to reconstruct the functioning of prehistoric Egyptian societies, the character of their food economies, and the distribution of their settlements across the landscape.

Lower Paleolithic. The earliest evidence of human presence consists of crude handaxes, classified as Middle Acheulean, found in older stream gravels at a few localities along the Nile and in the Sahara. None of these sites is dated or has associated fauna. Several more localities in Egypt have yielded the more evolved handaxes of the Late and Final Acheulean, probably dating between 250,000 and 400,000 BP, but again none seems to occur in a primary context, and only one locality (Bir Sahara East in the Western Desert) has any associated fauna. There is good sedimentary evidence, however, for Lower Paleolithic occupation of the Sahara during intervals of greatly increased rainfall, when large permanent lakes and at least ephemeral streams existed.

Middle Paleolithic. The data on the Middle Paleolithic in Egypt are considerably more numerous than those for the earlier period. Most Middle Paleolithic tools are made from large stone flakes, often produced by a prepared-core technique known as Levallois. Almost all of the assemblages include high frequencies of unretouched Levallois flakes (most of which are rejected tool blanks), sidescrapers, denticulates, and retouched pieces. Some assemblages also include high proportions of burins and endscrapers, and others have a few bifacial foliates and stemmed tools. Most of the assemblages are generally similar to the Mousterian of Southwest Asia and western Europe.

The best information on the Middle Paleolithic in Egypt comes from the two neighboring depressions of Bir Tarfawi and Bir Sahara East, some 350 km (about 220 mi.) west of Abu Simbel. Both basins have a sequence of five Middle Paleolithic wet intervals with permanent lakes, dating between about 175,000 and 70,000 BP. The numerous Middle Paleolithic sites associated with the lakes occur in a variety of settings, which seem to have been used for different purposes. Several sites were in fossil soils that developed in swamps adjacent to the lakes; others were in beaches formed with considerable wave action. Both of these settings were used as secondary workshops and for processing marshland plants. The paucity of bones suggests that meat was not an important food during the season when these sites were occupied.

Most of our information on the late Middle Paleolithic comes from a series of quarries on the west bank near Qena in Upper Egypt. Thermoluminescence dates for the Late Middle Paleolithic aggradation indicate that it occurred between 62,000 and 45,000 BP; the quarries probably date somewhere in that interval. Irregular trenches and pits testify to the ability of the people to quarry for stone, although their efforts were neither as systematic or efficient as those seen at the Upper Paleolithic quarries in the same area.

Near the end of the Middle Paleolithic, the river began a cycle of downcutting, incising a deep channel to a level near that of the river today. There are no sites in Egypt that can be correlated with this period, although some are known north of the Second Cataract in Sudan.

Upper Paleolithic. Around 33,000 BP, the Upper Paleolithic appeared in Upper Egypt. It is characterized by a new technology based on the production of long, narrow blades, rather than the short, wide flakes of the Middle Paleolithic. Our only information comes from quarries north of Nag Hammadi, which consist of a systematic series of deep pits, galleries, and chambers excavated to extract flint cobbles. The oldest human skeleton from Egypt is associated with one of these quarries. It is a *Homo sapiens sapiens*, slightly more primitive than, but of the same type as, the skeletons found at several Late Paleolithic sites in this area.

The late Upper Paleolithic is known from three settlements dating to about 25,000–22,000 BP. The tools are made on large blades and include denticulates, retouched pieces, burins, and endscrapers; backed blades are rare. The associated fauna are mostly wild cattle, hartebeest, gazelle, and a few fish. At this time, the Nile was probably very similar to that of the late Middle Paleolithic, and once again the valley began to fill with silt.

Late Paleolithic. Around 21,000 BP, stone technology shifted from large to small blades or bladelets. This change marks the beginning of the Late Paleolithic, which lasted for more than ten millennia in the Nile Valley. A complex series of Late Paleolithic industries has been defined for both Lower Nubia and Upper Egypt, each with a distinctive tool kit. Similar modifications in artifacts occurred at about the same time throughout the Valley, with intervals of cultural turmoil and rapid change. A few of these changes are so numerous and abrupt that they must represent new populations. The beginning the Late Paleolithic saw more use of Nilotic resources: fish, shellfish, migratory water fowl, and marshland plants. Large animals were still hunted, but they were now a relatively minor part of a rich and highly diverse subsistence.

From Wadi Kubbaniya, north of Aswan, came the best data on subsistence. The onset of the Nile flood in summer was an important time for food collection. At this time catfish moved to the edge of the floodplain to spawn and were easily taken in great numbers. The Kubbaniya sites contain thousands of their bones. Some of the fish may have been dried or smoked for later consumption, as suggested by several suitable pits with burned areas on their floors. The inhabitants also began to collect seeds of marshland plants, such as chamomile and club rush. In winter, they harvested the tubers of nut grass and club rush, both of which contain complex carbohydrates and volatile toxins and excess fibers. They can be made edible by grinding and roasting, and the

Kubbaniya sites contain heavily worn grinding stones and charred fragments of several varieties of the wetland plants. As with the catfish, surplus tubers may have been processed for later use. In the late winter and spring, when the river was at its lowest level, the inhabitants moved to the mouth of the wadi and other localities where bedrock outcrops and shoals facilitated the gathering of the Nile oyster and other shellfish.

Late Paleolithic human remains are all of the same physical type: the robust but fully modern Mechta el-Arbi type found throughout North Africa between 20,000 and 10,000 BP. They resemble the contemporaneous Cro-Magnons of southwestern Europe. Many of the Late Paleolithic skeletons show signs of violence. A skeleton of a male found at Kubbaniya, for example, had several healed wounds and two bladelets in the abdominal cavity that were presumably the cause of death. More dramatic is the Late Paleolithic graveyard at Jebel Sahaba, where 40 percent of the fifty-nine men, women, and children had artifacts embedded in their bones or showed other signs of trauma. This graveyard has a radiocarbon date of 13,740 BP, and may contain the earliest evidence of warfare. It certainly suggests that the Late Paleolithic was a period of intense competition in the Nile Valley.

Around 13,000 BP, temperatures increased in East Africa, and there was more rainfall in the headwaters of the Nile. The river became a massive stream more like that of today. After a series of large floods about 12,500 BP, the river began to cut a deep channel into the silts. From the onset of this downcutting until shortly before 8000 BP, the only site known in the valley is a small camp, occupied about 11,500 BP; it differs little from the sites occupied a thousand years earlier.

Several eighth-millennium sites have been excavated in the Faiyum, where they are associated with sediments that accumulated when Nile floodwaters entered the Faiyum depression and formed a large lake. Other sites include a group at el-Kab in Upper Egypt, and a small cave in Egyptian Nubia. All of these localities have yielded numerous fish bones, together with a few presumably wild cattle, hartebeest, and gazelle; fishing, hunting, and probably plant-gathering continued as major economic activities. There are no traces of pottery or domesticated species.

Neolithic on the Nile. As recently as 7000 BP, the Egyptian Nile was still occupied by small groups of people whose subsistence patterns were similar to those of the Late Paleolithic—fishing, collecting, and hunting. About 6000 BP (5200 BCE), there was a dramatic change in cultural developments. In Lower Egypt, in the Faiyum depression and farther north on the edge of the Delta, a complex Neolithic economy appeared suddenly and without local antecedents. It was based on domesticated species from southwestern Asia, used in combination with the already known wild foods.

The earliest attested of these Neolithic sites are in the Faiyum and date to 5230–4450 BCE. The sites are much larger than before and were probably occupied for several months after the summer floods, when fish could be easily harvested in the cut-off pools and swales and also when cereals were planted for harvest in winter. There are no traces of permanent houses, only a few post holes suggesting temporary huts made of poles covered with brush, reeds or mats. Deep accumulations of cultural debris, however, exist. The sites contain numerous bones of fish, domestic cattle, sheep or goat, pig, and a variety of wild fauna, including hartebeest, gazelle, hare, hippopotamus, crocodile, turtle, and waterfowl. Plants include emmer wheat and barley.

Pottery is abundant and very different from that in contemporaneous sites in the southern Western Desert. There are many large storage jars, which are fiber tempered, rough, and undecorated, and a few small, open bowls, which are sand tempered, frequently smudged, and either smoothed or burnished. None of the pottery is painted.

The Faiyum Early Neolithic villages may each have contained two hundred people. Because all of the known sites were inundated by the summer floods (except the granary pits, which were above the inundation level on an adjacent hill), they cannot have been occupied year round. We do not know where the Faiyum Neolithic people went during the rest of the year. There are several sites in the Sand Sea, near the Libyan border, with similar fiber-tempered pottery, a comparable range of lithic artifacts, including concave-based arrowheads, and of about the same age. Some of the Faiyum groups may have included the Sand Sea in their seasonal movements, or the similarities may indicate only that the two groups were closely related.

Although the sudden appearance of the Faiyum Neolithic just as the drying desert was becoming uninhabitable suggests a Saharan origin, there is little evidence to support such a hypothesis. Indeed, the origin of the Neolithic anywhere in the valley is obscure and controversial, and there is no firm evidence that Saharan groups played a significant role in these developments in Lower Egypt. The importance of Levantine domesticates, the distinctive fiber-tempered pottery, and the presence of several lithic elements not known in the desert (such as maceheads) may indicate that derivation or influence from southwest Asia. However, the apparent absence of similar complexes in the Sinai, southern Israel, and southern Jordan argues against migration.

Merimde Beni Salame, at the western edge of the Delta, was first occupied only slightly later than the Faiyum Neolithic and was partially contemporaneous with it. Merimde is one of the largest prehistoric sites in Egypt, and at its maximum, there may have been more than a thousand people living there. The houses in the lowest levels were oval huts with walls of upright poles covered with mats or brush, similar to those suggested for the Faiyum. They had firepits equipped with burned clay firedogs to support a cooking pot, and some had pots sunk into their floors. Near each house was a large storage pit. Burials were placed in simple oval pits within the village and without grave offerings.

In the upper levels of Merimde, dating to around 4,300 BCE, the houses were more substantial, partly dug into the ground with the above-surface walls made of mud bricks. The entries to the houses, all on the same side, had thresholds of hippopotamus tibiae. The interiors were sometimes partitioned into activity areas by posts set into the floor. The houses were separated by reed fences and arranged in irregular rows on either side of a street or alley. Large storage jars, baskets, and pits were placed near the houses. The size of the community, the alignment of the houses, and the abundance of the storage features suggest that around 4,300 BCE, Merimde witnessed a new level of village organization, which provides the basis for the early Predynastic period of Lower Egypt, which is documented at such sites as el-Omari and Maadi, near Cairo. [See Merimde.]

In Upper Egypt, the earliest-known Neolithic phase is the Badarian, recorded at forty habitation sites and a similar number of cemeteries, south of Asyut. These are clustered into three large communities, each consisting of several dispersed villages and homesteads. The Badarian represents a sharp break from the fishing, hunting, and gathering groups of less than a millennium earlier, and, like the early Neolithic period in Lower Egypt, appears suddenly and without local precedent. The possible role of the Desert Neolithic in this is difficult to evaluate. Cultural complexity is evident earlier in the desert, and there are similarities in the pottery and some of the stone tools, particularly with the Saharan Late Neolithic, which suggest that the desert people did contribute. Unfortunately, our lack of data from the Nile between 6,000 and 5,000 BCE prevents further evaluation.

The Badarian phase is not well dated. Several thermoluminescence dates on pottery range from 5,580 to 4,510 BCE, but all have large standard deviations, and the higher dates seem to be too old when compared to the dates for the fishing and hunting sites at el-Kab and the small cave in Egyptian Nubia. The best indication of the age of the Badarian phase is that it is older than the Amratian, a Predynastic complex that has several calibrated radiocarbon dates of around 4,200 BCE, and is thus of about the same age as the upper level at Merimde. The earliest Badarian phase was probably contemporaneous with the oldest Faiyum Neolithic.

Badarian villages have simple brush- or mat-covered huts, with large storage pits and pens for sheep or goats. Their economy was based on the cultivation of wheat, barley, and chickpeas. They also gathered nut-grass tubers, fished in the Nile, and did some hunting. Their economy and houses were thus not very different from those in the Faiyum, and they also had comparable concave-based projectile points. However, their other crafts were more developed. They had well-made pottery, almost all of it polished, red or black in color, or red with a black rim. Some had comb-impressed designs on the exterior, often partially obliterated by polishing. A few pots were decorated with incised geometric designs. There were carefully shaped stone palettes and quantities of red and green pigments. Animal and human clay figurines, and carved ivory tools also indicate the Badarian emphasis upon ornamentation.

It is in burials, however, that the Badarians differ most from their contempories in Lower Egypt. Most burials were not in the villages, but in separate graveyards. Most of them also have offerings, including pottery, beads and other ornaments. Some graves were much richer than others, indicating that there were differences in wealth and status. These Badarian traits were further emphasized in the Predynastic cultures of Upper Egypt, and reached their apogee in pharaonic civilization.

[*See also* Delta; Faiyum; Lower Egypt; Nag Hammadi; Nile River; *and* Upper Egypt.]

BIBLIOGRAPHY

Caton-Thompson, Gertrude, and E. W. Gardner. *The Desert Fayum.* London, 1934. The best available study of the early Neolithic in the Fayum. Subsequent studies show that the Fayum A to Fayum B sequence is reversed.

Caton-Thompson, Gertrude. *Kharga Oasis in Prehistory.* London, 1952. Classic study of Lower and Middle Paleolithic remains in the Egyptian Sahara. Recent research, however, suggests that the proposed cultural and climatic sequences should be used with caution.

Close, Angela E. "Living on the Edge: Neolithic Herders in the Eastern Sahara." *Antiquity* 64 (1990): 79–96. Describes the use of the hyperarid Safsaf sandsheet by Holocene herding groups.

Hoffman, Michael A. *Egypt before the Pharaohs.* Rev. ed. Austin, 1991. Excellent popular summary of Egyptian prehistory, with several interesting stories about early personalities.

Klees, Frank, and Rudolph Kuper, eds. *New Light on the Northeast African Past.* Cologne, 1992. Contains several excellent summaries of the prehistory of Egypt, ranging from the Lower Paleolithic to the Neolithic.

Paulissen, Etienne, and Pierre M. Vermeersch. "Earth, Man, and Climate in the Egyptian Nile Valley during the Pleistocene." In *Prehistory of Arid North Africa: Essays in Honor of Fred Wendorf,* edited by Angela E. Close, pp. 29–67. Dallas, 1987. Excellent survey of Pleistocene prehistory in the Nile Valley, particularly good for Upper Egypt.

Vermeersch, Pierre M., et al. "33,000 Year Old Chert Mining Site and Related *Homo* in the Egyptian Nile Valley." *Nature* 309 (1984): 342–344. Describes the excavation of an early Upper Paleolithic flint mine and associated human remains.

Wendorf, Fred, ed. *The Prehistory of Nubia.* 2 vols. Dallas, 1968. Volume 2 contains technical reports on several prehistoric sites in Egyptian Nubia. This was the first "modern" study of Nubian prehistory and has now been largely replaced by Wendorf et al. (1989).

Wendorf, Fred, and Romuald Schild. *Prehistory of the Nile Valley.* New York, 1976. Describes and dates several Late Paleolithic industries, particularly useful for the Fayum.

Wendorf, Fred, and Romuald Schild. *Prehistory of the Eastern Sahara.* New York, 1980. Technical study of the prehistory of the Western Desert of Egypt; for more recent information see Wendorf et al. (1984).

Wendorf, Fred, et al. *Cattle Keepers of the Eastern Sahara: The Neolithic of Bir Kiseiba.* Dallas, 1984. Contains the most recent information on Holocene archaeological remains in the Western Desert of Egypt. Following A. Gautier in the same volume, the authors propose that the cattle found in early Holocene sites are domestic; however, for a contrary view see A. B. Smith, "The Origins of Food Production in Northeast Africa," in *Palaeoecology of Africa and the Surrounding Islands,* edited by J. A. Coetzee and E. M. Van Zinderen Bakker, pp. 327–324 (Rotterdam, 1982).

Wendorf, Fred, et al. *The Prehistory of Wadi Kubbaniya.* Vols. 2–3. Dallas, 1989. Technical report describing the Late Paleolithic occupation near Aswan, with important new data on the food economy. The conclusions in volume 3 will be useful to the general reader.

FRED WENDORF and ANGELA E. CLOSE

Predynastic Egypt

The later Neolithic in Egypt, known as the predynastic period, represents the transition to a single unified state in about 3100 BCE. Two separate ceramic and lithic traditions are evidenced during this era—one in northern, or Lower, Egypt and the other in Southern, or Upper, Egypt (which extended into Lower Nubia). Both the ceramics and lithics can be equated with finds from the Sudan and belong to a characteristic African technology. The type-site for the Upper Egyptian culture was excavated by William Matthew Flinders Petrie at Naqada; through his development of sequence dating, or seriation, he was able to order his material chronologically through stylistic development. [*See Naqada.*]

Petrie divided his finds into various phases. The first is known as the Amratian period, named for the site of el-Amra, near Abydos. This period, which dates to between 4200 and 3700 BCE, is characterized by red-fired Nile-silt ceramics and vessels that often have a black top and that occasionally are decorated with yellowish or white pigment. The second period, the Gerzean, shows a change in ceramic technology that is represented by the use of higher-fired, white-to-buff marl clays, sometimes ornamented with patterns in red ocher. This period dates from 3700 BCE to the beginning of the first dynasty, although it is sometimes subdivided into a later phase known as Late Gerzean. Petrie termed this last period the Semainean and equated it with a dynastic race that migrated into the Nile Valley and brought about a unified state (Petrie, 1921). Helene Kantor (1952) however, clearly disproved the theory of such a massive population influx and demonstrated that, aside from a few imports, the material culture of the Upper Egyptian predynastic sequence and that of dynastic Egypt belonged to the same tradition.

The sequence dates Petrie assigned to these periods began with the number 30, to leave room for earlier cultures, should they be discovered. This turned out to be the case with the Badarian culture of the prehistoric period. The evolutionary framework for this period, set by Petrie a century ago, now has largely proven correct. Further refinements were added by Werner Kaiser (1957), however. Kaiser sub-

EGYPT: Predynastic. Figure 1. *Painting from the "Decorated Tomb" at Hierakonpolis.* The painting depicts some Mesopotamian motifs, including the "divine hero" holding off two lions at the lower left. Dated to the Naqada II period, c. 3500 BCE. (Courtesy P. Lacovara)

divided the Amratian into Naqada I A, B, and C; the Gerzean into Naqada II A, B, C, D1, and D2; and the Late Gerzean into Naqada III A1, A2, and B.

The Lower Egyptian sequence is less well documented, but it appears to be related to ceramic and tool types found in Syria-Palestine. There is a greater amount of material from settlements rather than graves, which may exaggerate the difference between the north and south. The principal sites here are in the area of the Faiyum and at Maadi near Cairo. [*See* Faiyum.] Lower Egyptian ceramics appear far more utilitarian than Upper Egyptian examples. They are usually of simple, baggy shapes with thick walls and abundant chaff temper.

The only large settlement site to be extensively explored from this period in Upper Egypt is that of Hierakonpolis. Excavations there by Michael Hoffman revealed a temple and settlements dating to the Naqada I and II periods (Hoffman, 1982). In addition, a series of kilns found along the desert margins of the site may have been employed to produce ceramics for mortuary use. Often, the ceramics found in Upper Egyptian graves show no sign of use and may have been especially made for burial. [*See* Grave Goods.] Such pottery is characterized by fine wares with simple, elegant shapes and decoration in red or white pigment. Some examples have applied decoration in the form of animal figures or symbols. Other types imitate the appearance of stone vessels, which were made of a number of hard and soft stones such as basalt, granite, breccia, and alabaster (calcite or travertine).

Elizabeth Finkenstaedt (1980) has shown that several schools, or local styles, of painted pottery are to be found in predynastic ceramics that may point to the development of regional centers or small states. Eventually, the tradition of

painted pottery died out, perhaps replaced by the growing production of stone vases to equip the tombs of the elites. [*See* Tombs.] For this era, the cemeteries excavated demonstrate an increasing social stratification, with more and more elaborate tombs provided for the wealthy. One particular tomb at Hierakonpolis had a painted mural decoration (see figure 1) that contained motifs related to the art of Mesopotamia. [*See* Wall Paintings.] Foreign influence, as evidenced by both imported materials and adaptations of stylistic motifs (animal phyle, "divine hero," composite monster), suggest that the exchange of ideas with the Near East at this juncture played a pivotal role in the development of art, writing, and the formation of the pharaonic state.

[*See also the biography of Petrie.*]

BIBLIOGRAPHY

Arkell, Anthony J., and Peter Ucko. "Review of Predynastic Development in the Nile Valley." *Current Anthropology* 6 (1965): 145–166.

Baumgartel, Elise J. *The Cultures of Prehistoric Egypt.* 2 vols. Oxford, 1947–1960.

Finkenstaedt, Elizabeth. "Regional Painting Style in Prehistoric Egypt." *Zeitschrift für Ägyptische Sprache und Altertumskunde* 107 (1980): 116–120.

Hoffman, Michael. *The Predynastic of Hierakonpolis.* Cairo, 1982.

Holmes, Diane L. *The Predynastic Lithic Industries of Upper Egypt.* 2 vols. British Archaeological Reports, International Series, no. 469. Cambridge, 1989.

Kaiser, Werner. "Zur Inneren Chronologie der Naqadakultur." *Archaeologia Geographica* 6 (1957): 69–77.

Kantor, Helene J. "Further Evidence for Early Mesopotamian Relations with Egypt." *Journal of Near Eastern Studies* 11 (1952): 239–250.

Petrie, W. M. Flinders. *Corpus of Prehistoric Pottery and Palettes.* British School of Archaeology, Publications, no. 32. London, 1921.

PETER LACOVARA

Dynastic Egypt

In his *History of Egypt* (Gk., *Aegyptiaka*), the early third-century BCE Egyptian priest Manetho organized the kings of Egypt from Menes to Alexander of Macedon (c. 3100–332 BCE) into thirty consecutive "dynasties," or families. A thirty-first dynasty was later added to Manetho's treatise, which is preserved only in corrupted and fragmentary form in the epitomes of later authors. Some of his dynasties probably have no historical basis, while others were overlapping rather than successive.

The relative chronology of the dynastic period is based on a number of sources in addition to Manetho. These include king lists, genealogical data, historical and biographical texts, dated monuments and papyri, and archaeological remains. Conversion of Egypt's relative chronology into an absolute chronology has been achieved through the use of astronomical data; historical synchronisms between Egyptian kings and several Hittite, Babylonian, and Assyrian rulers; classical sources; and radiocarbon dating.

The archaeology of dynastic Egypt can be divided into two major categories of material remains: one relating to the elite, the other to ordinary people. Most books and articles focus on the kings and members of the royal family, the bureaucrats and provincial officials, the military, and the temple priesthood. These groups together constituted only a small percentage of the country's inhabitants, but their wealth and material achievements vastly exceeded those of the illiterate peasants, whose existence probably changed little over several thousand years of dynastic rule. Hence, the "archaeology of ancient Egypt" largely reflects the material culture of the country's political, religious, and military institutions.

Early Dynastic Period (First and Second Dynasties: c. 3100–2700 BCE). Egyptologists sometimes group the rulers of Upper Egypt just prior to the beginning of the early dynastic period (such as Ka and Scorpion) as dynasty 0. Later tradition records that a king Meni (Gk., Menes), from This in Upper Egypt, united the two halves of the country and founded a new capital at Memphis, situated just south of Cairo. Menes is probably to be equated with Narmer, a king whose large commemorative palette found at Hierakonpolis in Upper Egypt shows him wearing the White Crown of Upper Egypt on one side and the Red Crown of Lower Egypt on the other. The reign of Narmer (c. 3100 BCE) inaugurated the first dynasty and the beginning of the early dynastic period (see figure 1).

The early dynastic period was a formative era in the evo-

EGYPT: Dynastic. Figure 1. *Palette of King Narmer.* To the left, King Narmer is seen holding a captive by the hair, and he wears the crown of Upper Egypt. On the reverse side, to the right, King Narmer appears as the largest human figure in the upper scene, wearing the crown of Lower Egypt. Dated c. 3100 BCE. (Courtesy ASOR Archives)

lution of Egypt's political and religious institutions. An important element in the development of these institutions was writing, which first appeared (possibly as the result of cultural influence from Mesopotamia) at the end of the predynastic era. Other significant achievements of the early dynastic period included the development of major elements of the Egyptian artistic canon and the first use of stone in construction (though most buildings of the period were made entirely of mud brick).

In foreign affairs, the kings of the first dynasty campaigned against Nubian and Libyan tribes. Trade with Palestine, which had been extremely active in late predynastic times and dynasty 0, declined during the course of the first dynasty. Domestically, the country was politically stable during the first dynasty, but conflict between Upper and Lower Egypt appears to have broken out in the early second dynasty.

The history and material culture of this period are known principally from Abydos and Saqqara. Both sites have yielded rectangular mastaba tombs containing the names of early dynastic kings. The kings of the first dynasty and of the end of the second were probably buried at Abydos, whereas the rulers of the early second dynasty may have been interred in subterranean galleries at Saqqara. The rich contents of the Abydos and Saqqara tombs included inscribed sealings, labels, and stelae; copper and stone tools and weapons; stone vessels; ivory and stone statuary; wood and ivory furniture; and jewelry.

Old Kingdom (Third–Sixth Dynasties: c. 2700–2190 BCE). The Old Kingdom is frequently labeled the Pyramid Age. The country was administered by a strong, highly centralized government headed by a monarch whose absolute authority and divinity were reinforced during the fifth dynasty by his formal claim to be the son of the sun god Re. On a day-to-day basis, the government was run by a large bureaucracy managed by high officials who often were members of the royal family.

The Old Kingdom was a period of economic prosperity and political unity. Commercial and military expeditions traveled south to Nubia, which in pharaonic times provided Egypt with such items as ivory, ebony, gold, and animal skins. The turquoise mines of western Sinai were opened up for exploitation at least as early as the third dynasty. The coastal cities of the northern Levant, especially Byblos, were visited by Egyptian diplomatic and commercial missions, and several military campaigns were conducted in Palestine as well as against the Libyans. Large state building projects were undertaken, especially for pyramid complexes and, in the fifth dynasty, temples for the solar cult. Most of the laborers on these projects were peasants, whose work in the fields came to a halt during the Nile's annual inundation.

Memphis was the capital and royal residence throughout the period. Stretching many kilometers north and south of Memphis were the great royal and private cemeteries. The first pyramid was erected at Saqqara during the early third dynasty. Designed by Imhotep for King Netjerikhet (later called Djoser), this step pyramid is the oldest major building constructed entirely of stone. The first true pyramid was built at Dahshur at the beginning of the fourth dynasty. To that dynasty also belong the pyramids of Khufu, Khafre, and Menkaure (Gk., Cheops, Chephren, and Mycerinus) at Giza. Later Old Kingdom pyramids were smaller and not as well constructed. Around each Old Kingdom pyramid complex were large mastaba tombs for the king's relatives and other officials who wished to share in their ruler's eternal life. The mastabas of the fifth and sixth dynasties were larger than their predecessors, and the interior rooms of their superstructures were decorated with scenes of daily life.

The absolute power of the monarchy began to deteriorate during the fifth dynasty. The decline is attributable to the growing importance of the solar cult at Heliopolis (which increased the power of that cult's priesthood) and the increasing wealth of the nobility, who now often were provincial governors (nomarchs) rather than royal relatives and who could pass their offices on to their sons. Exemption from taxation for temples and the great royal mortuary cults also took its toll on the treasury. In about 2200 BCE, shortly after the extended reign of the sixth dynasty king Pepi II, the country's central government collapsed.

First Intermediate Period (Seventh–mid-Eleventh Dynasties: c. 2190–2033 BCE). For about half a century after the demise of the Old Kingdom, the kings of the seventh and eighth dynasties attempted to maintain order from the capital at Memphis. Eventually, the country broke up into several independent political units, famine and anarchy were rampant in the land, and Asiatic nomads wandered into the Delta. The literature of the period speaks of economic and social hardship. The closing of the royal ateliers in the old capital led to the development of crude provincial art styles.

Contemporary with the eighth dynasty, a line of Herakleopolitan princes (Manetho's ninth and tenth dynasties) united the middle reaches of the Nile valley under their rule. Civil war later broke out between Herakleopolis and the newly emerging town of Thebes in Upper Egypt. Eventually, the eleventh-dynasty Theban ruler Nebhepetre Mentuhotep (2033–1982 BCE) defeated the Herakleopolitans, bringing about a new era of national unity and prosperity.

Middle Kingdom and Early Second Intermediate Period (Mid-Eleventh–Thirteenth Dynasties: 2033–1648 BCE). The late eleventh dynasty saw mining expeditions once again going to Sinai and trade missions setting out for the Levant. Nebhepetre Mentuhotep's principal building achievement was his funerary complex at Deir el-Bahari in western Thebes; the early eighteenth-dynasty pharaoh Hatshepsut used Mentuhotep's complex as a model for her own magnificent funerary complex immediately to the north. Following a brief period of disorder at the end of the eleventh dynasty, the throne of Egypt was secured by Amenemhet I, whose reign begins the twelfth dynasty (1963–1786 BCE).

Amenemhet I moved the royal residence from Thebes to Itjtawy, located in the vicinity of Lisht in the Faiyum region. In the Faiyum itself, the kings of the twelfth dynasty undertook major irrigation projects to reclaim a large amount of land for farming. Throughout the twelfth dynasty, the kings were buried in pyramids. Following the reign of Amenemhet I, the pyramids were built of mud brick supported by interior stone crosswalls; later on, they were constructed of mud brick with a limestone casing. Around the pyramid complexes stood the mastabas of their officials.

The provincial authorities continued to wield substantial authority until Senwosret III (1862–1843 BCE) put an end to their power (see figure 2). The institution of coregency, whereby the king took his son as coruler to ensure a smooth transition of power, became a regular feature of the monarchy in the twelfth dynasty, and a middle class began to develop. Scarabs inscribed with royal names and the names and titles of officials first appear in the Middle Kingdom.

EGYPT: Dynastic. Figure 2. *Head of Senwosret III*. Red granite; nineteenth century BCE. (Courtesy ASOR Archives)

The foreign policy of the twelfth dynasty included several campaigns into Nubia, where a line of fortresses was erected in the second cataract region to protect Egypt's southern frontier. Egyptian armies also campaigned northeast of the Nile valley, possibly even reaching the northern Levant during the reign of Amenemhet II (1901–1866 BCE). Expeditions went out to the mines of Sinai on a regular basis, and trade and political contacts with Syria were on a larger scale than ever before. At Byblos, along the southern Syrian coast, the local rulers employed Egyptian hieroglyphs for writing their names and used Egyptian titles. Egyptian hieratic inscriptions on clay figurines and pottery bowls contain curses (the so-called Execration Texts) directed against rulers and places in Syria-Palestine, Libya, and Nubia; these documents reflect Egypt's extensive knowledge of foreign lands and, perhaps, the extent of her power and influence.

The Middle Kingdom was a golden age for Egyptian literature and art. This was the time of Middle Egyptian, the classical phase of the Egyptian language. Famous works of the era, such as the Story of Sinuhe and the Instruction of Amenemhet I, were copied as schoolboy exercises for hundreds of years thereafter. The art is notable for its royal portrait sculpture: the serious, often somber look on the faces of the kings is unique in the history of pharaonic art. The jewelry is exquisite, yet simple, and includes some extraordinary inlaid pieces.

The kings of the thirteenth dynasty (1786–1648 BCE) continued to reside at Itjtawy, and the art, pottery, and seals of the period reflect a continuation of Middle Kingdom traditions. Nonetheless, a rapid turnover in occupants of the throne, the end of pyramid construction, and, toward the end of the eighteenth century BCE, the decline or abandonment of a number of sites in the Faiyum region herald a weakening of the central government. At the same time, an influx of Asiatics into the eastern Delta led to a deterioration in royal control over that part of Lower Egypt. Eventually, in 1648 BCE, the ruler of Avaris (modern Tell ed-Dabʿa), the center of Asiatic activity in the Delta, captured the old Egyptian capital at Memphis and took over northern Egypt.

Late Second Intermediate Period (Fifteenth–Seventeenth Dynasties: 1648–1540 BCE). A nineteenth-dynasty king list preserved in Turin reports that six "rulers of foreign countries" (i.e., Manetho's fifteenth, Hyksos Dynasty) controlled Egypt for 108 years. During the late seventeenth and the first half of the sixteenth centuries BCE, Asiatics came to dominate the Delta, Memphis, and part of the Nile Valley, while a line of Theban princes (the seventeenth dynasty) controlled southern Egypt. The Asiatics adopted many aspects of Egyptian culture, including the use of the hieroglyphic script for writing their documents and transcribing their personal names. Recent excavations at Tell ed-Dabʿa have revealed extensive contact with the Levant, Cyprus, and the Aegean world. In the mid-sixteenth century BCE, the

Theban ruler Kamose recaptured Memphis and drove the Hyksos back to Avaris. His brother and successor, Ahmose, the first king of the New Kingdom, captured Avaris and drove the Hyksos out of Egypt.

New Kingdom (Eighteenth–Twentieth Dynasties: 1550–1069 BCE). Several kings of the early eighteenth dynasty—most notably Ahmose (1550–1525 BCE), Amenhotep I (1525–1504 BCE), and Thutmose I (1504–1492 BCE) and III (1479–1425 BCE; see figure 3)—campaigned widely in the Levant and Nubia, establishing an empire that, at its height, extended from Napata in the northern Sudan to the Euphrates River in western Syria. The inhabitants of this empire provided Egypt with a wide variety of tribute and trade goods. Commercial relations, which throughout pharaonic times were conducted under royal authority, were active with the Aegean world, Anatolia, Syria-Palestine, Mesopotamia, and Nubia. For the next several hundred years, Egypt was the wealthiest country in the ancient world, a phenom-

EGYPT: Dynastic. Figure 3. *Statue of Thutmose III.* Fifteenth century BCE. (Courtesy ASOR Archives)

enon reflected in the enormous temples and magnificent royal and private tombs at Thebes.

During most of the eighteenth dynasty (1550–1295 BCE) the royal residence was at Thebes, whereas in the nineteenth and twentieth dynasties (1295–1069 BCE) the kings lived at Per-Rameses in the eastern Delta. The pharaohs were buried in large rock-cut tombs in the Valley of the Kings in the Theban necropolis, while the nobility were buried in tombs cut in the nearby hills. Memphis continued to function as a major administrative center during the New Kingdom.

In the mid-fourteenth century BCE, Pharaoh Amenhotep IV abandoned the worship of the god Amun, changed his name to Akhenaten, and with his family and a small coterie of followers moved north from Thebes to Amarna, where he could worship the sun in its manifestation as the sun disk (the Aten). A hoard of several hundred cuneiform tablets found at Amarna and written mostly in Babylonian, the lingua franca of the Near East in the Late Bronze Age, contains letters addressed to the Egyptian royal court from the major rulers of western Asia and the vassal princes of Syria-Palestine, as well as archival copies of a smaller number of letters sent from Egypt in the opposite direction.

Following Akhenaten's death, his second successor, Tutankhamun, departed from Amarna. Not long after, a new dynasty arose in Egypt, under the leadership of a military officer named Rameses (who was the first of eleven kings to use that nomen). For more than two centuries, the Rameside kings ruled Egypt as Manetho's nineteenth and twentieth dynasties.

The greatest challenge to Egypt in the early nineteenth dynasty came from the Hittites in Anatolia. Rameses II (1279–1213 BCE) fought the Hittites to a standstill at Qadesh on the Orontes River in western Syria, but much of the Egyptian Empire in Syria was subsequently lost. Egypt continued to prosper during the nineteenth dynasty, despite internal political problems in the early twelfth century BCE. The art and jewelry of the period are gaudy and inferior to that of the eighteenth dynasty; the scenes in the tombs of the nobles focus more on the afterworld than daily life; and the temple architecture and royal sculpture are more notable for their monumental scale than their artistic quality (the temple of Rameses II at Abu Simbel being a fine example).

In the eighth year of Rameses III's reign (1184–1153 BCE), in the early twentieth dynasty, much of the eastern Mediterranean world was overwhelmed by tribal groups from the northern Mediterranean known collectively as the Sea Peoples. After devastating Asia Minor and the Levantine coast, they were defeated by the Egyptians and forced back into Palestine. Egypt managed to sustain its empire in parts of Palestine for another generation or two, but what was left of the empire collapsed in about the third quarter of the twelfth century BCE. From then on, Egypt began a long period of political, economic, and social decline. The Nubian portion of the empire was lost in the early eleventh century BCE, and shortly thereafter the country once again split apart.

Third Intermediate Period (Twenty-first–Twenty-fifth Dynasties: 1069–664 BCE). The Third Intermediate period opened with the kings of the twenty-first dynasty residing at Tanis in the northeastern Delta and a line of high priests of Amun dominating Upper Egypt from Thebes. For the next four hundred years, the country lurched from one political and military crisis to another. During the twenty-first dynasty (1069–945 BCE) there were competing rulers at Tanis and Thebes. The twenty-second dynasty (945–715 BCE) saw a line of rulers of Libyan origin dominating Egypt from Bubastis in the eastern Delta. The first of these kings, Sheshonq I (945–924 BCE), campaigned in Palestine and pillaged the temple in Jerusalem. Later in the dynasty the country again fragmented, leading to competing kingdoms at Saïs in the western Delta, Thebes, and Herakleopolis (the period of the twenty-third dynasty). In the mid-eighth century BCE, a Sudanese king, Kashta, gained control of Thebes. Soon thereafter, another Napatan king, Piye (otherwise known as Piankhi), swept north into Egypt and established Kushite domination of the country as far downstream as Memphis; his successor, Shabako, finished the conquest of northern Egypt. The twenty-fifth (Napatan) dynasty (747–656 BCE) rebuilt and enlarged Egypt's temples, especially those favoring the god Amun, and reasserted the country's old traditions. In 664 BCE, however, the Assyrians marched into the Nile valley and captured Thebes.

Because most of the capitals of the Third Intermediate period are in the Delta, relatively little is known about the archaeology of this period. Many of the sites are buried beneath the alluvium or modern occupation, or have had their stone monuments completely robbed out. At Tanis, an enormous temple complex associated with the god Amun has been excavated. Within the temple enclosure was a royal necropolis for several kings of the twenty-first and twenty-second dynasties.

Late Period (Twenty-sixth–Thirty-first Dynasties: 664–332 BCE). Threats against their empire from the east soon forced the Assyrians to leave Egypt. They entrusted control of the country to a number of local princes, one of whom, Psammetichus, soon became king, founding the twenty-sixth dynasty (664–525 BCE) at Saïs. During the Saïte dynasty, the country regained its independence; rebuilt its military forces (which now included large numbers of foreign mercenaries, many of whom settled in Egypt); and expanded its commercial activities throughout the eastern Mediterranean. An attempt by Pharaoh Necho II (610–595 BCE) to reestablish Egyptian hegemony in the Levant led to a disastrous defeat at the hands of the Babylonians at Carchemish in 605 BCE. The strongly nationalistic views of the period are reflected in the archaizing features of the art, which hearken back to the Old Kingdom.

In 525 BCE, a Persian army under Cambyses defeated the last Saïte king, Psammetichus III, at Pelusium, bringing Egypt into the Achaemenid Empire. During the twenty-seventh (Persian) dynasty (525–404 BCE), the bureaucratic language was Aramaic rather than Egyptian. Egypt regained its independence during the twenty-eighth–thirtieth dynasties (404–343 BCE). The thirtieth dynasty is notable for the extensive temple-building activity undertaken by Nectanebo I and II. In 343 BCE, the Persians recaptured Egypt, but they held it for only a short time. In 332 BCE, Alexander of Macedon led his army into Egypt and made the country part of his burgeoning empire.

[*See also* Abydos; Dab'a, Tell ed-; Delta; Heliopolis; Hyksos; Lower Egypt; Memphis; Pyramids; Saqqara; *and* Upper Egypt.]

BIBLIOGRAPHY

Baines, John, and Jaromir Màlek. *Atlas of Ancient Egypt.* New York, 1980. Well-illustrated, semipopular introduction to ancient Egypt.

Gardiner, Alan H. *Egypt of the Pharaohs.* Oxford, 1961. History of ancient Egypt, based almost entirely on textual sources, by the leading British Egyptologist of the twentieth century.

Gardiner, Alan H., T. Eric Peet, and Jaroslav Černý. *The Inscriptions of Sinai.* 2 vols. Egyptian Exploration Society, Memoir 45. 2d ed. London, 1952–1955. Basic publication of Egyptian inscriptions from the mining areas of western Sinai.

Grimal, Nicolas-Christophe. *A History of Ancient Egypt.* Translated by Ian Shaw. Cambridge, Mass., 1992. Good history of ancient Egypt, much more balanced in its use of source material than Gardiner's book; contains a lengthy bibliography.

Hayes, William C. *The Scepter of Egypt: A Background for the Study of the Egyptian Antiquities in the Metropolitan Museum of Art.* 2 vols. New York, 1953–1959. Examination of Egypt to the end of the New Kingdom, illustrated by objects in the museum's collection. Chapters on the Middle and New Kingdom are especially valuable because of the richness of the museum's collections for these periods.

Helck, H. Wolfgang. *Die Beziehungen Ägyptens zu Vorderasien im 3. und 2. Jahrtausend v. Chr.* 2d ed. Wiesbaden, 1971. The only comprehensive study of Egyptian relations with the Near East during the Bronze Age. The text is out of date for some periods and must be used with caution.

Helck, Wolfgang, and Eberhard Otto. *Lexikon der Ägyptologie.* 7 vols. Wiesbaden, 1972–1991. Massive reference work containing articles in English, French, and German on virtually every topic relating to ancient Egypt; includes extensive notes and bibliography.

Kemp, Barry J. *Ancient Egypt: Anatomy of a Civilization.* London, 1989. Original and interesting socioeconomic interpretation of the development of the Egyptian state, administration, and economy.

Kitchen, K. A. *The Third Intermediate Period in Egypt, 1100–650 B.C.* 2d ed. Warminster, 1986. Dry but authoritative history of Egypt during a long period of decline.

Kitchen, K. A. "Egypt, History of (Chronology)." In *The Anchor Bible Dictionary,* vol. 2, pp. 322–331. New York, 1992. Up-to-date overview of the current status and major problems of Egyptian dynastic chronology.

Lichtheim, Miriam, comp. *Ancient Egyptian Literature.* 3 vols. Berkeley, 1973–1980. Excellent translations of many important Egyptian texts.

Lucas, Alfred. *Ancient Egyptian Materials and Industries.* 4th ed., rev. and enl. by J. R. Harris. London, 1962. Classic work in the field, now outdated in such areas as metals and faience but still extremely useful.

Quirke, Stephen, and A. Jeffrey Spencer, eds. *The British Museum Book of Ancient Egypt*. London, 1992. Excellent introduction to the history and material culture of ancient Egypt, illustrated by objects in the British Museum.

Redford, Donald B. *Egypt, Canaan, and Israel in Ancient Times*. Princeton, 1992. Stimulating, somewhat idiosyncratic history of Egyptian relations with Palestine.

Strouhal, Eugen. *Life of the Ancient Egyptians*. Norman, Okla., 1992. Beautifully illustrated survey of the daily life of the ancient Egyptians, providing a perspective on ancient Egypt different from other books cited here.

Trigger, Bruce G., et al. *Ancient Egypt: A Social History*. Cambridge, 1983. The social, economic, and political history of dynastic Egypt. Each chapter contains its own bibliography. The first three chapters were originally published in volume 1 of *The Cambridge History of Africa* (New York, 1975).

Waddell, W. G., ed. and trans. *Manetho*. Cambridge, Mass., 1940. Greek text and English translation of the epitomes of Manetho's *Aegyptiaka*.

JAMES M. WEINSTEIN

Postdynastic Egypt

Research into the history and culture of Egypt from the arrival of Alexander the Great in November of 332 BCE to the conquest by the Islamic forces of Amr ibn al-ʿAs in 640 CE are currently in a state of flux because of an intensive interdisciplinary approach to this very complex era. Much of what has been written in the past is no longer valid, and some of what is to be stated herein is only provisional. The brunt of these assertions are immediately evident on examination of the brief stay of Alexander the Great in Egypt.

It is now generally acknowledged that Egyptian Alexandria was already inhabited at Alexander's arrival and that, far from founding a new city, the conqueror merely replanned the existing one. Growing evidence also suggests that there was a flourishing, contemporary cult of Osiris-Apis in the city, which Alexander (of Macedonian-Greek birth) embraced under the name of Serapis. The contours of the city, compared to that of a *chlamys* (Macedonian riding cape) emphasized its Greek, not Egyptian, sociopolitical orientation, which was reinforced by its name, Alexandria ad Aegyptum ("Alexandria by the side of [but not within] Egypt").

Ever the pragmatist, Alexander did little to interfere with the existing administrative bureaucracy of the land. In fact, many former officials who had served with distinction under the Persians, who had occupied Egypt before Alexander, were permitted to remain in their same offices. When Ptolemy I Soter declared himself pharaoh in 305/304 BCE, he did little to change this system. The administration of Ptolemaic Egypt is currently regarded as self-generated, addressing issues on an ad hoc basis as the need arose; it was not a consciously developed administration.

The ethnicity of Ptolemaic Egypt has been much discussed, in particular the relationship between the native Egyptians and the Macedonians and other Greeks who were encouraged to immigrate to Egypt early on to serve in the

EGYPT: Postdynastic. *Statue of an official.* The figure is wearing a traditional Egyptian tripartite costume. Black granite; height 1.165 m. Provenance unknown (perhaps Dendera). Metropolitan Museum of Art. (Rogers Fund, 1965)

armies of the Ptolemies or in other capacities in exchange for prime arable lands. The consensus is that the culture of Ptolemaic Egypt can be characterized as one of two societies, the immigrant Greek and the native Egyptian; both were separate and mutually unequal in their spheres of activity. This opinion masks the existence of numerous other nationalities and languages in the cultural record of the Ptolemaic Period, from Aramaic to Carian and Phoenician. Despite the continuity of these diverse peoples and their native tongues, there is a certain uniformity in the material culture, at least on the pharaonic side, to suggest that the native Egyptians were themselves highly resistant to foreign influences. Indeed, the attraction of Egypt was so great that all immigrants were soon acculturated to Egyptian norms.

With the passing of time, the indigenous Egyptians became more assertive. There are at least ten documented revolts by the Egyptians during the Ptolemaic Period, the most famous of which saw the Thebaid (that region of Upper Egypt, extending roughly from Coptos in the north to Edfu in the south, that was under the administrative authority of Thebes) effectively gain a modicum of independence and local autonomy from the crown during the reigns of Ptolemy IV Philopator and Ptolemy V Epiphanes when two Egyptians, Horwenenefer and Anhkwenenefer (perhaps father and son) established themselves as counter-kings in succession. The revolt of the Delta city of Lycopolis was particularly long-lived and bloodily quelled only in 186 BCE. Whereas some may ascribe the causes of these armed insurrections to economic or social inequities, the xenophobia of the Egyptians toward their Greek overlords cannot be overlooked as a prime contributing factor. The frequency with which asylum decrees are promulgated, granting Egyptian felons immunity from persecution, are indicative of just how far the Ptolemies would go in order to pacify a generally hostile population. It is within this broader cultural context that one can understand why, perhaps, Cleopatra VII was the only member of her dynasty to speak Egyptian.

The precipitous return to Egypt from Syria by Ptolemy III Euergetes I, which effectively enabled the Seleucids to regroup and eventually to invade Egypt, was probably due to his need to address such a rebellion at home. The overseas empire of Ptolemaic Egypt, which was won by Ptolemy II Philadelphus and his sister-consort, Arsinoe II, was now threatened by the Seleucids. The successful invasion of Egypt by the Seleucid monarch Antiochus III Epiphanes was reversed by Roman intervention in the form of the ultimatum that Popilius Laenas personally issued to Antiochus. Certain important details to this episode, recorded by Polybius and Livy, have now been recovered from an Egyptian archive unearthed at Saqqara, from which one learns the name (Nounenios) of the envoy dispatched by Ptolemy IV Philopator to thank the Roman Senate for Laenas's intervention. From that moment on, Egypt was to be drawn into the affairs of Rome. Those interactions accelerated during the course of the first century BCE, but here again a revisionist approach to many of the events is currently gaining favor.

So, for example, the alleged will of Ptolemy X Alexander I (r. 110–109; again 107–88 BCE) in which he is said to bequeath his kingdom to Rome is based on a misinterpretation of the evidence. A careful reading of the relevant passages in Cicero in conjunction with Egyptian sources reveal that Ptolemy X borrowed money from Rome, which was deposited at the city of Tyre. Upon his demise, the Romans attempted to recover the principal. The agreement, as it can now be reconstructed, merely grants the Romans the right to repayment; it does not name them heirs to his kingdom.

It was for similar financial considerations that Ptolemy XII Auletes (r. 80–58; again in 55–51 BCE) fled to Rome in 58 following his ouster by the Alexandrians. He was reinstated in 55, having returned with Roman legions commanded by Gabinius. The financial affairs of Ptolemy XII were managed by Gaius Rabirius Posthumus in an attempt to recover the debt of 10,000 talents of silver, which Auletes had borrowed earlier.

Before his death, Ptolemy XII Auletes elevated his daughter Cleopatra VII, aged seventeen, to the throne as coregent together with his son Ptolemy XIII, aged six. The queen, far from being illegitimate (as implied by Strabo) asserted her right to the throne and issued at least three documents in which she is named as Egypt's sole monarch. Julius Caesar, pursuing Pompey to Alexandria in the wake of Rome's civil wars, arrived in Alexandria to find a city divided by internecine strife. In short order, Caesar sided with Cleopatra, and the two embarked on a conscious campaign of political domination. Cleopatra aspired to restore Egypt to her former glory and thus decorated Egyptian temples, such as Dendera, where she is depicted as the legitimate successor of the pharaohs of old. The untimely assassination of Caesar in 44 BCE left the queen without an ally, but she soon associated herself with Marc Antony, the politically weaker of the two. Together Cleopatra and Antony challenged the might of Rome. In the waters off Actium, a promontory of southwestern Greece, the combined naval forces of Cleopatra and Antony confronted those of Octavian, thereafter called Augustus, Julius Caesar's heir and future first emperor of Rome. Contrary to popular opinion, Cleopatra herself planned the strategy for the battle and was in command of part of the fleet, which consisted of some of the largest men-of-war ever constructed in the ancient world. The battle lost, Cleopatra and Antony withdrew to Egypt and there elected suicide rather than capture and disgrace. The death of Cleopatra VII ended the Ptolemaic period, one of Egypt's most brilliant cultural epochs.

In general, native pharaonic art forms were continued during the Ptolemaic period. There is virtually no evidence whatsoever of foreign intrusions into the form or functions of such a major temple at Edfu, which was built and constructed entirely during the Ptolemaic period. There the Ptolemies are depicted in several scenes as the dutiful officiants, solemnly offering a variety of items to the various deities of the temple. Their appearance masks the fact that the most important theological aspect of this temple revolves around the falcon-deity Horus in his role as the universal monarch. As a result, the image of this aspect of Horus at Edfu enabled the native priesthood to conduct their rituals in the name of this falcon-pharaoh rather than in the name of one of the Ptolemies, with whom the priesthood was often at odds.

Likewise, the funerary stelae (commemorative tablets) and statues of officials eschew Hellenistic forms and remain loyal to pharaonic sculptural tenets. On occasion one sees what appears to be Hellenistic-looking hair on the heads of some of these officials, who may also be holding foreign attributes. In the final analysis, however, those coiffures and emblems are rendered in accordance with the mimetic principles of ancient Egyptian art and cannot be cited as examples of foreign influence on native traditions.

On the other hand, the Macedonian-Greek overlords of the land did attempt to incorporate into their art aspects of Egypt's long cultural heritage. This process could be accomplished in several ways. On a basic level, the Hellenistic artists could simply sculpt, for example, an image of the goddess Isis in classical style. Several such examples are known. On the other hand, Egyptian concepts were often clothed in Greek garb. So, for instance, the Macedonian appropriation of the native Alexandrian deity Osiris-Apis, who represented the deified and resurrected Apis bull, was given Hellenistic form as Serapis, represented in art as a full bearded, long haired male deity, resembling Zeus or Hades but bearing as his attribute a modius (corn measure) on his head. The completely Hellenistic idiom in which these images are sculpted belies the fact that these images can only be fully understood with reference to the cult of the Egyptian god Osiris. In other cases, the Macedonians felt compelled to inscribe an epitome, usually in Greek, on a pharaonic-styled object, which served as a gloss explaining the nature of the statue to an audience not familiar with Egyptian art. There is no corresponding example of a Hellenistic work of art inscribed in Egyptian for the benefit of the Egyptians.

These artistic differences are graphically understood by a comparison of the architecture and decoration of the three extant Hellenistic tombs at Mustafa Kamal in Alexandria with the temple of Horus at Edfu. In the former, Egyptian elements, such as the sphinx, are used decoratively to suggest an Egyptian ambience, whereas there are no analogous quotations from the Hellenistic record at Edfu.

Furthermore, borrowing of visual motifs and other art forms is not the only manifestation of Macedonian appropriations of pharaonic culture. Recent studies suggest that the idea behind the creation of the great library at Alexandria as a repository for books was a Macedonian response to the "Houses-of-Life," the scriptoria (writing centers) that were attached to the temples of ancient Egypt (Bianchi, 1989–1990, p. 3). Manetho, for example, writing during the reign of Ptolemy II (285–246), had access to such scriptoria when he wrote a history of pharaonic Egypt in Greek for the benefit of the Macedonians. No Greek penned a similar history in Egyptian. This appropriation of things Egyptian by the Greeks of Egypt is nowhere more graphically illustrated than in the so-called *Romance of Alexander the Great,* in which the Macedonian conqueror is depicted as the son of the Egyptian god Amun and the legitimate successor of Nectanebo II, the last native pharaoh of the thirtieth dynasty (360–342).

The defeat of Cleopatra and Antony at Actium, the last naval battle of antiquity, and their suicide the following year in 30, left Octavian master of the known Mediterranean world. Fearing that another Egyptian may again rise up to challenge his authority, Augustus, the former Octavian, decreed Egypt the private domain of the Roman imperial household and forbade Romans from visiting the land without first having obtained his authorized visa. As part of this conscious policy, Augustus named Gallus to be the first prefect (governor) of the land. Shortly thereafter, Gallus became inebriated with Egyptian culture and soon erected monuments in his own name near the great pyramids at Giza and at other sites throughout the land. Augustus recalled him, and Gallus, disgraced, committed suicide. When a revolt in southern Arabia forced Augustus to dispatch his Egyptian legions under the direction of his second prefect to the troubled area across the Red Sea, the southern frontier of Egypt revolted, led this time by another woman, the Candace (queen), of the Nubians. Her forces succeeded where Cleopatra's had failed by successfully defeating the Roman legions sent against her in combat. In time, the third prefect, Petronius, reached an accommodation with this Nubian Candace, whereby Roman taxes were remitted and a common border between the Kingdom of Meroë, the Candace's realm, and Roman Egypt was established. [*See* Meroë.] This frontier would be respected until the time of the Roman emperor Diocletian, when the marauding tribes of the Blemmyes brought instability to the region.

The cultures that developed during the course of the early Roman Empire in Egypt are difficult to define with any precision because ideology is not often made manifest in art. To be sure, classical art forms continued, as revealed by the marble images of Roman emperors Augustus, Hadrian, and others found in Egypt and now on view in the Greco-Roman Museum in Alexandria. The cults of the gods and goddesses of Greece and Rome as well as cult of Serapis in his Macedonian form were popular, but worship of these deities was not permitted within Egyptian temples proper.

In time the Romans attempted to discourage the pagan Egyptian practices in Egypt. The most graphic expression of this curtailment of religious rights is seen within the temple of Luxor. The central doorway, giving access to the inner sanctum or barque station, was intentionally blocked up and converted into a niche in which the image of the reigning emperor was duly erected. The entire room was then covered with plaster and adorned with frescoes depicting the emperor and his entourage. This remodeling of the Luxor temple effectively prevented the Egyptian priests from carrying the sacred barques of the gods in procession during the annual festivals, thereby depriving the Egyptians of the most popular means of worshiping their deities.

During the course of the first and second centuries CE Egypt prospered, and the city of Alexandria flourished, propelled doubtless by the pharaonic canal that the Roman emperor Trajan reopened to link the Nile and the Red Sea, along which many trading centers were established. As a result, the luxury goods of the Orient—spices and silk—began to appear in quantity in Mediterranean markets. It was doubtless such mercantile interests that caused the Palmyrenes, in the person of Queen Zenobia, to occupy Egypt in the late third century CE. The armed struggles between the forces of Zenobia and those of the Roman emperor Aurelian in the decade between 270 and 280 CE effectively reduced the city of Alexandria to rubble. It has been suggested that these disturbances were the major factors contributing to the damage to the Great Library and the tomb of Alexander the Great in Alexandria herself (see P. M. Frazer, *Ptolemaic Alexandria* I, Text, Oxford, 1972, p. 16).

At the same time, Christianity, traditionally arriving in Egypt with St. Mark in the first century CE, began to make inroads. By the third century Christians formed thriving communities in Egypt as elsewhere in the Mediterranean world. Soon, for reasons that are too complex to outline here, Christians were subjected to persecutions by the pagans. The pogroms against the Christians in Egypt initiated under Emperor Decius (r. 249–251) were so destructive that the Copts, the present Egyptian Orthodox Christians, mark the beginning of their liturgical calendar with the age of the martyrs who fell during that time. The persecutions escalated in time and culminated during the reign of Diocletian (284–305), who vented his anger not only against the Christians in Egypt but also against the pagans in Alexandria, whose massacre he ordered in 295 CE. To commemorate this triumph, Diocletian erected a single column in Alexandria, which is known locally but erroneously as Pompey's Pillar.

The Edict of Milan, issued in 312 and reaffirmed in 323, granted all the freedom to practice the religion of one's choice. Christians were not favored by the Edict, they were simply no longer persecuted for their beliefs. In 324 Constantine the Great transferred the capital of the Roman Empire from Rome to Byzantium, changing the name of that city to Constantinople; the Byzantine period was thereby inaugurated, and Christianity was openly encouraged. Christian theologians soon began heated theological debates among themselves regarding such matters of doctrine as the nature of Christ. Alexandrian clergymen, doubtless because of the long intellectual tradition enjoyed by the city because of its Great Library and numerous institutions of higher learning, played major roles in these lively dialogues. In 325 the views of Arius, an Alexandrian prelate, on the less-than-divine nature of Christ were condemned by the Council of Nicaea. Between the years 379 and 395, the Roman emperor Theodosius formally declared Christianity the religion of the empire and systematically closed down all pagan institutions, a process that led to the physical destruction by zealous Christians of the great temple of Serapis in Alexandria.

Nevertheless, some pagans continued to practice their older religion. As late as 415, Hypatia, a fascinating woman who is traditionally regarded as the last pagan intellectual in Alexandria, was savagely stoned to death by Christian monks goaded on by the patriarch, Theophilos. Despite these attacks, pagan Egyptians remained loyal to their traditional beliefs. The very last pagan Egyptian inscription ever carved in Egypt is a demotic graffito on the island of Philae dated to 452, one year after the fateful meeting of the Council of Chalcedon in 451.

During the proceedings of this, the fourth ecumenical council, the assembled clerics debated the nature of Christ. The council condemned as heretical the position of the Egyptian Christians and their coreligionists wherein the nature of Christ was monophysite, meaning that Christ's divine and human nature were commingled simultaneously. Insulted by the decision, the Egyptian Christians returned home and steadfastly refused to abide by the decision of the Council, thereby causing an early schism within the Church. Their tenacious embrace of the monophysite ("one nature") doctrine led to an awkward situation among the Christian community in Egypt because the recognized clerical authority in Alexandria, the Christian patriarch, appointed by the council, was at theological odds with the majority of his fellow Christians throughout the land. The rift was never healed. To this day the Copts of Egypt, descended from those pagan Egyptians who converted to Christianity, remain monophysites. Their liturgical language, Coptic, is itself an alphabetic script based on hieroglyphs and employs letters based on the Greek alphabet to which have been added seven signs modified from demotic, the most cursive form of the ancient Egyptian language. [*See* Coptic.]

The struggles between the monophysitic Copts and their nominal rulers, the administrators and prelates dispatched to Egypt from Constantinople, created friction within the Christian community. The Sasanians, or Persians, led by Chosroes II, invaded Egypt in 619, having defeated the armies of the Byzantine emperor Heraclius. Three years later in 622, the Prophet Muhammad embarked on the Hijrah, his "flight" from Mecca to Medina, thereby firmly establishing Islam in the Arabian Peninsula. In 626 Heraclius expelled the Sasanians and regained Egypt for Byzantium. For the next fourteen years, Heraclius was engaged in a series of military confrontations with the leaders of Islam, whose defeat of the Persians in 637 at al-Qadisiya signaled the end of the Sasanian Empire. The Byzantines and Muslims now engaged in a struggle to control the lands of the Middle East. In 640, Amr ibn al-'As, the general of the Islamic caliph 'Umar, overran the Egyptian outpost at Pelusium and defeated the Byzantine garrison at Babylon, today Old Cairo. The Copts perhaps acquiesced to this takeover, preferring to pay taxes to the caliph in exchange for their religious freedom, rather than to be subjects of their adversarial coreligionists. Amr ibn al-'As he proceeded to Alexandria, and captured it in 642. The city was freed by the Byzantine fleet in 645, only to be retaken by Amr ibn al-'As the following year. Egypt had fallen, and the path to Spain across North Africa lay open to the Muslims.

During their formative period, Christians and their pagan counterparts were not clearly distinguished. In some instances, the blurring of distinctions among disparate sects existed in antiquity, as the gnostic archive from Nag Hammadi and the religious books recently uncovered at Ismant in the oasis of Dakhleh reveal, in which there appears to be an unmistakable mixture of Christian and decidedly pagan elements. [*See* Nag Hammadi.]

As difficult as it is to separate Christians from pagans, it is often more problematic to distinguish monophysitic Copts from Byzantine Christians on the basis of the monuments without recourse to textual information. That data enables identification of the clerics within the monastery of Abu Jeremiah at Saqqara as monophysitic Copts. Nevertheless, more progressive academics are beginning to regard Christian art produced in Egypt as a branch of Byzantine art. There is a growing tendency as well to dismiss as Christian many of the monuments, often sculpted in the soft, local limestones, the motifs of which are taken over directly from the repertoire of classical, not pharaonic, Egyptian mythology (Johnson, ed., 1992). Although these monuments are often called "Coptic," they are better regarded as examples of pagan art, created for those living in Egypt during the Roman Empire, whose roots and traditions can be traced back to the Macedonian-Greek immigrants.

[*See also* Alexandria; Alexandrian Empire; Byzantine Empire; Ptolemies; Roman Empire; Saqqara; *and* Seleucids.]

BIBLIOGRAPHY

Alexandria and Alexandrianisms: Proceedings of a Symposium Held at the J. Paul Getty Museum in May, 1993. Malibu, forthcoming.
Bianchi, Robert Steven. *Cleopatra's Egypt: Age of the Ptolemies.* Brooklyn, 1988.
Bianchi, Robert Steven. "The New Alexandriana: A Personal View of the History of the Great Library of Alexandria and the Current Plans for its Revival." *Newsletter of the American Research Center in Egypt,* no. 148 (Winter 1989–1990): 1–5.
Bowman, Alan K. *Egypt after the Pharaohs: 332 BC–AD 32.* Berkeley, 1986.
Dack, E. van 't, et al. *The Judean-Syrian-Egyptian Conflict of 103–101 B.C.: A Multilingual Dossier Concerning a "War of Sceptres."* Collectanea Hellenistica, 1. Brussels, 1989.
Johnson, Janet H., ed. *Life in a Multi-Cultural Society: Egypt from Cambyses to Constantine and Beyond.* University of Chicago, Oriental Institute, Studies in Ancient Oriental Civilization, no. 51 Chicago, 1992.
Pearson, Birger A. "Earliest Christianity in Egypt: Some Observations." In *The Roots of Egyptian Christianity,* edited by Birger A. Pearson and James E. Goehring, pp. 132–160. Studies in Antiquity and Christianity, 1. Philadelphia, 1986.
Ray, J. D. *The Archive of Hor.* Egypt Exploration Society, Texts from Excavations, Memoir 2. London, 1976.
Samuel, Alan E. *The Shifting Sands of History: Interpretations of Ptolemaic Egypt.* Publications of the Associations of Ancient Historians, 2. Lanham, Md., 1989.

ROBERT STEVEN BIANCHI

Islamic Egypt

Following the death of the prophet Muhammad in Medina in AH 10/632 CE his community of believers quickly consolidated their control of Muslims, particularly among those tribes people who believed that their submission to the prophet was personal, hence temporary. The way became clear for carrying the message of Islam to the northern and northeastern areas of the Arabian Peninsula, which were in thrall either to the Sasanian padishah or the Byzantine emperor. Within five years Jerusalem, Damascus, and Ctesiphon were in fealty to the caliph in Medina and very soon thereafter Muslim armies had entered Anatolia and crossed the Oxus River.

Amr ibn al-'As convinced the caliph, 'Umar, that with Greater Syria and Iraq under Muslim control, the logical step would be an invasion of Egypt. Commanding an army of about four thousand horsemen, Amr entered Egypt at al-Arish in AH 18/639 CE, took the port city of Pelusium, and arrived at the Byzantine fortress of Babylon early in 640. With reinforcements sent from the Hijaz, Amr proceeded to invest the fortress since it proved impossible to take by storm. Amr positioned his army slightly north of the fortress in a very large encampment surrounded by a ditch where the troops were assigned living areas on the basis of tribal affiliation. In April 641 Babylon fell. Amr continued his campaign toward Alexandria without fear of rear attack. Parts of the original army invaded the Faiyum and eventually conquered Middle and Upper Egypt up to the First Cataract at Aswan. By the end of the year Alexandria was in Muslim hands.

By 'Umar's orders Amr returned to Fustat and made it his headquarters and capital (*'asimah*) from which to plan the further conquest of the contingent portions of the southern littoral of the Mediterranean and the assimilation of Egypt into the ever-expanding *dar al-Islam* (Muslim territory). Although this action triggered a certain eclipse of Alexandrian prominence, it laid the foundation for the modern city of Cairo.

It is difficult to understand fully the reasons that facilitated the seemingly easy conquest of so rich and vitally important a part of the Byzantine Empire. Egypt had been rent by the Sasanian invasion of 619 and the subsequent decade of occupation, a ravaged pawn in the larger unresolved power struggle of the Sasanian and Byzantine polities. The religious doctrinal strife that accompanied the advent of Christianity was fully echoed in Egypt where the Melkites (those loyal to the Orthodox church) proved unequal to the task of converting the very strongly monastic-oriented Coptic-speaking masses (the Monothelites). Whereas the Melkites might be seen as dominating the cities and fortresses along the Nile, the Copts won the allegiance of the peasantry. Their apparent neutrality during the Arab conquest facilitated Amr's progress and thus guaranteed sympathetic treatment at his hands. Culturally, the countryside had been but lightly hellenized, insuring the longer life of Coptic as compared with Greek in the slow arabization of Egypt.

Immediately following the conquest, three parallel and intermingling processes can be identified. First, Arabic replaced Greek as the linguistic medium of government, and the Umayyad caliph 'Abd al-Malik ordered Hellenic and Sasanian effigies to be removed from the coinage. All the inscriptions were in Arabic. Bilingual documents were gradually replaced by entirely Arabic texts written by a new scribal class, most of whom were recruited from among the large number of early converts to Islam or the swell of immigrants arriving from the Arabic-speaking provinces of the Arabian Peninsula. So great was the prominence of Arabic as the mode of contact with the authorities that even the religious teaching texts of the Coptic church became bilingual toward the end of the tenth century.

Second, as the scanty sources imply, there was very little pressure on the Egyptian population to convert. However, advancement and full admission to governing status entailed conversion to Islam. Early in the eight century local Coptic dignitaries were replaced by Arabic-speaking Muslims as tax collectors and adjudicators, and the scene for accelerated conversion was set. Exact figures are rare, but the greater part of the population seems to have been Muslim at the time of the Fatimid conquest in AH 358/969 CE.

Third, a process of acculturation began with soldiers from the conquering army who settled down in Egypt and immigrants in ever-increasing numbers from Greater Syria, the Arabian Peninsula, Iraq, and even Iran. The long history of the Nile Valley dictated an adaptation to the mores and regulations (particularly agricultural) so delicate that to impose others too harshly would disturb the rich ebb and flow of daily life. Very soon the settlers found themselves celebrating national feasts of pharaonic origin, utilizing the millennial norms of planting and harvesting to schedules that followed Ptolemaic and Coptic formulas and finding themselves accommodating rather than dictating.

Politically, Egypt mirrored the shifts of power within the dar al-Islam without substantial injury. The seizure of the caliphate by the 'Abbasids in AH 132/750 CE signaled little to the population except at Fustat when a new government precinct called al-Askar appeared slightly to the north. When Ahmad ibn Tulun became governor in 254/868, the calm was somewhat broken as he assumed autonomous authority. He reduced the revenues paid to Baghdad and used this extra income to raise his own army with which he arrogated the role of protector of Syria. These new moneys also permitted an ambitious building program centered on Ibn Tulun's new ruling quarter of al-Qata'i ("the fiefs," which were parceled to his most loyal officers) to the northeast of Fustat-Askar. Ibn Tulun's crowning works were his palace at the foot of the Muqattam Hills; his Friday mosque, one of the pearls of Islamic architecture, on Jabal Yashkur; and an aqueduct to carry water to al-Qata'i. [See Mosque.]

Nevertheless, the Tulunids remained loyal to the 'Abbasid caliphate. Egypt was prosperous and generally at peace. However, a new and powerful threat attended from the west where the heterodox Isma'ili Fatimid dynasty had established its own caliphate. Baghdad reacted quickly, sending in 292/905 an army under Muhammad ibn Tughj, who ruled under the title of al-Ikhshid. The 'Abbasids repelled the early Fatimid attacks and concentrated their efforts on maintaining the prosperity of the country. A large number of Iraqi Arabs and Turks came to Egypt as soldiers and bureaucrats. Eventually, Baghdad was too strapped to send yet another army when the Fatimid forces under Gawhar appeared in 358/969. Egypt was taken and loyalty was sworn to a Shi'i caliphate for the next two centuries.

The Fatimid dynasty (AH 358–567/969–1171 CE) represents a watershed in Egyptian Islamic history. Because the Fatimids could not destroy the Sunni 'Abbasid caliphate and were unable to maintain their ascendancy in the Maghrib, they concentrated on Egypt. They gave to the country an independence that capped the autonomy achieved by the Tulunids. Egypt enjoyed an unparalleled prosperity based on improved agriculture; on control of the trade with China and southwestern Asia; and on discovery of large gold deposits in the Wadi Allaqi in Nubia. The Fatimids regularized trade between Egypt and inner Africa, which offered slaves and ivory, and welcomed European and Byzantine merchants with whom they expanded their commercial and industrial endeavours, particularly in textiles.

The Fatimids had a high sense of their mission to win the allegiance of the entire dar al-Islam and particularly to propagandize of their family descent from the Prophet's daughter. It would seem that they were imbued with an almost Byzantine sense of ritual and ceremonial. All of these aspirations were bodied forth in their splendid new walled capital of Cairo (Ar., al-Qahira, "the Victorious"), laid out as a formally divided rectangle with eight gates to the northeast of the amalgamated Fustat-Askar-Qata'i. Within were two palaces divided by a plaza and al-Azhar Mosque, originally an institution for training Fatimid propagandists. Later the mosque of al-Hakim was built immediately adjacent to the two principal northern gates and dedicated in 400/1010.

Fatimid piety echoed the ancient Egyptian veneration of the dead and the importance of the tomb structure. Domed mausolea appeared in the Southern Cemetery honoring ancestors and immediate family. The purported head of the Prophet's grandson Husayn was interred in a splendid mausoleum-cum-mosque within the royal quarter. All of these shrines were visited and venerated by Sunni and Shi'i alike.

This glamour and prosperity were threatened. The Seljuk Turks who took over the 'Abbasid hegemony declared an aim of destroying the heretical Fatimid dynasty. Despite the conquest of Anatolia and the incursion of the Crusaders against the Seljuks, the Fatimids did not take advantage of their reprieve, except to rebuild the walls of Cairo in stone and to enclose the mosque of al-Hakim. They could not govern either their armies or their bureaucracy. Succession was attended by family friction, deceit, and the mishandling of policy by successive viziers, some of whom were Christians and Jews, who were proof of Fatimid tolerance. Low Nile floodings caused famine. The new Seljuk principates of Syria were pressing upon the Crusader states; both hungered for the riches of Fatimid Egypt and by 564/1169 both were marching on it. The vizier Shawar set fire to the older parts of the city, particularly Fustat, and then invited the Syrian army to enter Cairo to protect it from the forays of the Crusader army. The commander, Shirkuh, had himself proclaimed vizier, and after his death his nephew, Salah ad-Din (Saladin) assumed command and deposed the Fatimid caliph in 567/1171.

The peaceful transition of religious allegiance to the 'Abbasid Sunni caliphate was proof of just how little the Fatimid ideology had penetrated the Egyptian community. Salah ad-Din introduced strict Sunnism on Egypt inspired by the thrust of what can be termed the "Seljuk dispensation." With the introduction of the *madrasah* (theological school), he insured an orthodox legal system and a cadre of specifically trained bureaucrats. He imposed the *iqta* system whereby the productive land of Egypt was tied to the maintenance of the army with a consequent diminution of private property. When his nominal ruler, Nur ad-Din of Damascus, died, Salah ad-Din assumed the title of sultan and took charge of the counter-Crusade that eventually restored Jerusalem to the *dar al-Islam* and secured Greater Syria to the rule of his dynasty, the Ayyubids. The final portion of the dispensation, the *khanqah* (a convent for the training of Sufis to eliminate the possibility of any Shi'i strain taking root), was firmly established in Egypt through the patronage of the sultan and his family.

In all other respects the Ayyubids built on the heritage of the Fatimids. They destroyed none of the mausolea, which through visitation and invocation had become part of Cairene life; indeed they went further by turning the idea toward Sunni ends with the erection of the large domed structure in the Southern Cemetery, which housed the remains of Imam Shafi'i (d. 204/820), the founder of the *madhhab* (legal school) now professed by the majority of Egyptians.

Where taste was concerned, the earlier Fatimid tendencies toward revived classical and Maghribi models were replaced by those emanating from Greater Syria. This was particularly noticeable in the great Citadel (initiated by Salah ad-Din) built on the middle peaks of the Muqattam hills with walls spreading to take in al-Qahira to the north and much of Fustat to the south. By the end of the twelfth century CE Egypt was orthodox in belief, prosperous, well protected, and connected to the markets of the Mediterranean, the Far East, and southeast Asia. In the following century, this strong entity eliminated the Crusader states and protected itself from the Mongols.

[*See also* 'Abbasid Caliphate; Ayyubid-Mamluk Dynasties; Cairo; Fatimid Dynasty; *and* Fustat.]

BIBLIOGRAPHY

For the only synoptic surveys of Islamic Egypt, see Stanley Lane-Poole, *A History of Egypt in the Middle Ages* (London, 1901,) and Gaston Wiet, *L'Égypte arabe* (Paris, 1937.) A deeper, more idiosyncratic study of the evolution of Egypt's history in the Islamic period is available in Jean-Claude Garcin, *Espaces, pouvoirs et idéologies de l'Égypte médiévale* (London, 1987.)

The classic study of the Conquest remains Alfred J. Butler, *The Arab Conquest of Egypt,* edited by P. M. Fraser (Oxford, 1978.) A far more mettlesome argument is conveyed in Vassilios Christides' article on the period 602–750, "Miṣr," in *Encyclopaedia of Islam,* new ed., vol. 7, pp. 152–160 (Leiden, 1960–).

For the development of the capital through the Fatimid period, see the article on Fustat. For more particular aspects of the Fatimid period, see Leila Al-Imad, *The Fatimid Vizierate, 969–1172* (Berlin, 1990), and Paula Sanders, *The Court Ceremonial of the Fatimid Caliphate in Egypt* (Syracuse, 1994). Important economic data is provided in Claude Cahen, *Makhzumiyyat* (Leiden, 1977). Wheeler M. Thackston's fully annotated translation, *Nasir-i Khusraw's "Book of Travels"* (Albany, N.Y., 1986), adds depth to the received view of Cairo's apogee of prosperity in the first half of the eleventh century CE. The architecture of the period is surveyed in K. A. C. Creswell, *Early Muslim Architecture,* vol. 2 (Oxford, 1940,) and *The Muslim Architecture of Egypt,* 2 vols. (Oxford, 1952–1959.)

Short though it was, the Ayyubid period was of vast importance in that it set the scene for the Mamluks. See the crucial bibliography in Heinz Halm, "Miṣr," *Encyclopaedia of Islam,* new ed., vol. 7, pp. 164–165 (Leiden, 1960–), covering the period 1171–1250 CE. For the urban growth of Cairo, see Neil D. Mackenzie, *Ayyubid Cairo: A Topographical Study* (Cairo, 1992).

GEORGE T. SCANLON

EGYPT EXPLORATION SOCIETY. Founded in 1882 by Amelia Edwards, an English writer who had visited Egypt in 1873 and had seen the need for organized excavation, the Egypt Exploration Society of London aims to undertake surveys and excavations at ancient sites in Egypt and to publish the results of this work. The earliest excavations concentrated on trying to establish links between archaeological remains in the Nile Delta and the stories of the Hebrew Bible, but activities soon expanded to cover all areas of the country and all periods of ancient Egyptian history. Many excavators have worked for the society including one of the most influential figures in Egyptian archaeology, Sir W. M. F. Petrie.

The society is currently working at a number of sites. The Survey of Memphis aims to illuminate the topography of the ancient capital. At Saqqara a joint expedition with the National Museum of Antiquities, Leiden, The Netherlands, concentrates on the New Kingdom cemetery in which the tombs of important officials are being recorded. At Amarna, the city of Akhenaten and Nefertiti, the society has resumed excavation and survey in a place of major importance. Qasr Ibrim, the last surviving site available for excavation in Egyptian Nubia, is a fortress-town and religious center that has yielded vast quantities of material remains and written documents.

In addition to reports of excavations and publications of texts, the society publishes an annual periodical, *The Journal of Egyptian Archaeology.* Since 1991 the *JEA* has been joined by a color magazine, *Egyptian Archaeology,* which presents excavation reports and other articles in a more popular form.

The Egypt Exploration Society remains one of the major excavating bodies in Egypt and has an international membership now amounting to nearly three thousand individuals and libraries. Membership is open to all with an interest in the civilization of ancient Egypt.

[*See also* Amarna, Tell el-; Saqqara; *and the biography of Petrie.*]

BIBLIOGRAPHY

Dawson, Warren R., and Eric P. Uphill. *Who Was Who in Egyptology.* 2d rev. ed. London, 1972. Brief biographies of major figures in the history of exploration and excavation in Egypt. A third edition is in press.

Drower, Margaret S. *Flinders Petrie: A Life in Archaeology.* London, 1985. The period of Petrie's work for the Egypt Exploration Society is covered in early chapters.

Edwards, Amelia B. *A Thousand Miles Up the Nile* (1877). London, 1982. Edwards's account of her visit to Egypt in the winter of 1873–1874.

James, T. G. H., ed. *Excavating in Egypt: The Egypt Exploration Society, 1882–1982.* London, 1982. Illustrated history of the Society's work, published to coincide with its centenary.

PATRICIA SPENCER

EGYPTIAN. The language of ancient Egypt represents an autonomous branch of one of the most widespread language families in the world, variously called Afroasiatic, Hamito-Semitic, or Semito-Hamitic and comprising, from antiquity to the present time, the entire area of the eastern Mediterranean, northern Africa, and western Asia. The six individual branches of the Afroasiatic family are Ancient Egyptian, Semitic, Berber, Cushitic, Chadic, Omotic. Ancient Egyptian shows the closest relations to Semitic and Berber, more distant ones to Cushitic (except Beja, a Northern Cushitic language possibly derived from the language of the people called *mdꜣw* in Egyptian texts) and Chadic. Afroasiatic languages are generally characterized by the following linguistic features not all of which are shared by Egyptian: the presence of bi- or triconsonantal lexical roots; a consonantal system displaying a series of ejective, emphatic, or glottalized phonemes (sound units) alongside the voiced and the voiceless series; a vocalic system originally limited to the three phonemes /a/ /i/ /u/; a nominal feminine suffix ⋆*-at;* a rather rudimentary and often lexicalized case system; a nominal prefix *m-;* an adjectival suffix *-ī,* called *nisba;* a basic opposition between prefix (dynamic) and suffix conjugation (stative) in the verbal system; a conjugation pattern 1st sg. ⋆*'a-,* 2d ⋆*t-,* 3d masc. ⋆*y-,* fem. ⋆*t-,* 1st pl. ⋆*n-,* with supplementary suffixes in the 2d and 3d fem. pl.

The history of the Egyptian language, which remained in use over more than four millennia (c. 3000 BCE–1300 CE), can be divided into two main stages, characterized by a major typological change from synthetic to analytic patterns in the nominal syntax and in the verbal system. Each of these two stages of the language can be further subdivided into three different phases, affecting primarily the sphere of graphemics.

Older Egyptian. The forms of Older Egyptian consisted of the language of all written texts from 3000 to 1300 BCE, surviving in formal religious texts until the second century CE. It has three main phases: Old Egyptian, Middle Egyptian, and Late Middle Egyptian.

Old Egyptian. The language of the Old Kingdom and the First Intermediate Period (3000–2000) is known as Old Egyptian. The main documents of this stage of the language are represented by the religious corpus of the Pyramid Texts and by a sizable number of so-called autobiographies on the external walls of the rock tombs of the administrative elite.

Middle Egyptian. Also termed *Classical Egyptian,* Middle Egyptian lasted from the Middle Kingdom to the end of the eighteenth dynasty (2000–1300). Middle Egyptian is the classical language of Egyptian literature, expressed in a variety of texts that can be classified according to two main genres. The first, the "Instructions," are wisdom texts normally addressed from a father to a son, which conveyed the educational and professional expectations of Egyptian society. The most renowned examples are the *Instructions of the Vizier Ptahhotep* and the *Instructions for Merikare.* Some of these moral texts, such as the *Admonitions of Ipu-Wer,* are in fact philosophical discussions *ex eventu* on the state of the country taking as a point of departure the political evolution from the Old to the Middle Kingdom, a period generally refered to as the First Intermediate Period. The second, the *Tales,* are narratives relating the adventures of a specific hero and representing the vehicle of individual, as opposed to societal, concerns. The most famous specimens of this genre are the *Tale of Sinuhe* and the *Shipwrecked Sailor.* Some texts, such as the *Eloquent Peasant,* combine features and contents of both main genres.

Late Middle Egyptian. In use from the late New Kingdom to the end of Egyptian civilization, Late Middle Egyptian is the language of mainly religious texts (rituals, mythological inscriptions, hymns). It maintains the linguistic structures of the classical language, but especially in the Greco-Roman period (Ptolemaic Egyptian: third century BCE–second century CE), it shows an enormous extension in its set of hieroglyphic signs.

Older Egyptian is characterized by its preference for synthetic grammatical structures. It displays a full set of morphological suffixes indicating gender and number; it exhibits no definite article: *rmt* "the man," "a man"; it maintains the verb-subject-object order in verbal formations (*sḏm=k n=f* "may you listen to him").

Later Egyptian. The forms of Later Egyptian are documented from the nineteenth dynasty to the Middle Ages (1300 BCE–1300 CE) and consisted of Late Egyptian, Coptic, and Demotic.

Late Egyptian. In use from 1300 to 700 BCE, Late Egyptian was the language of written records from the second part of the New Kingdom. It primarily conveys the rich entertainment literature of the nineteenth dynasty, consisting of both traditional forms, for example, the *Tale of the Two Brothers,* the *Tale of Wenamun,* or the *Instructions of Ani* and the *Instructions of Amenemope,* and of new literary genres, such as the mythological tale or love poetry. Late Egyptian was also the idiom of the Ramesside bureaucracy: for example, archival documents from the Theban necropolis or school texts such as the *Miscellanies.*

Demotic. In use from the seventh century BCE to the fifth century CE, Demotic was the language of administration and literature during the Late Period (seventh–fourth century BCE). Although grammatically it closely continues Late Egyptian, Demotic differs radically from it in its graphic system. Important texts in Demotic are the narrative cycles of Setne-Khaemwase and of Petubastis and the instructions of Papyrus Insinger and Onkhsheshonqi.

Coptic. In use from the fourth through fourteenth centuries CE, Coptic was the language of Christian Egypt, written in a variety of the Greek alphabet completed by six or seven Demotic signs to indicate Egyptian phonemes absent in Greek. As a spoken language Coptic was superseded by Arabic from the ninth century, but it survives to the present in the liturgy of the Coptic Orthodox Church of Egypt.

As opposed to Older Egyptian, Later Egyptian developed analytic features. Suffixal markers of morphological oppositions are dropped and functionally replaced by prefixal morphemes, the demonstrative "this" and the numeral "one" evolving into the definite and the indefinite article respectively. Periphrastic patterns in the order subject-verb-object supersede older verb-subject-object verbal formations.

Unless otherwise specified, the following grammatical sketch refers to Older Egyptian, more specifically to the language of classical Middle Egyptian literature.

Writing System. The language of Ancient Egypt was written in a monumental script and its cursive varieties. The monumental script is known as hieroglyphs. These are pictographic signs that represent living beings and objects, such as gods or people, animals, parts of the human or animal body, plants, stars, buildings, furniture, containers, and so forth. The number of hieroglyphic signs varied from approximately one thousand in the Old Kingdom down to about 750 in the classical language, but—following the decline of a centralized school system—increased dramatically to many thousands during the Ptolemaic and Roman rule in the country.

In this writing system, phonological and ideographic prin-

ciples appear combined: a written word consists of a sequence of signs, called *phonograms,* which convey a substantial portion of its phonological structure: normally all the consonants, occasionally also the semivocalic phonemes. Each phonogram can express one, two, or three consonants of the language. The sequence of phonograms is usually followed by a "determinative," which indicates iconically the semantic sphere of the word: for example, a sitting god expresses the lexical sphere of "god, divine," a scribe's outfit indicates the semantic realm of "writing," a stylized desert landscape denotes the word as a foreign toponym. Although some words in common use may be written only with phonograms, many items of the basic vocabulary are expressed by hieroglyphic signs that represent, evoke, or symbolize their own meaning: these are called *logograms* or *ideograms:* for example, the hieroglyphic sign representing a human head is used to signify the lexeme "head." The use of a hieroglyphic sign as logogram or ideogram is made visually explicit through a vertical stroke following the sign.

As part of its inventory of phonograms, hieroglyphic writing displayed a set of twenty-four "alphabetic" signs that expressed one consonantal phoneme. Each of these signs corresponded to one consonantal or semiconsonantal phoneme of Egyptian; in this way, we can obtain an insight into the complete phonological system of the language, the only exception being the consonant /l/, for which a distinct grapheme appears only in Demotic. In spite of the presence of this exact correspondence between monoconsonantal signs and the phoneme inventory, hieroglyphs never developed a genuine alphabetic system. This was due to the culturally significant connection between the hieroglyphic sign and its pictographic content, a connection that in the later periods of the history of the hieroglyphic system, especially in Ptolemaic Egyptian, led to the emergence of hitherto unknown signs, of new phonological values for known signs, and of cryptographic solutions.

The hieroglyphic system was mostly used for monumental purposes, and only rarely in a cursive form adopted in religious texts of the Middle and the New Kingdom. During the three millennia of their productive use, hieroglyphs developed two manual forms: while Hieratic (2600 BCE–third century CE) represents a direct cursive rendering, with ligatures and diacritic signs, of individual hieroglyphs, Demotic (seventh century BCE–fifth century CE) modifies completely the writing conventions by introducing a simplification of hieratic sign-groups. In Coptic, the hieroglyphic-based system is replaced by an alphabet derived from the Greek one, with the addition of six or seven Demotic signs for the indication of phonemes absent from Greek.

The basic orientation of the Egyptian writing system, and the only one used in the cursive varieties, is from right to left; in epigraphic, that is, monumental texts, this order is

TABLE I. *Consonants of Older Egyptian*

Consonants	Labial	Apical	Alveo-palatal	Palatal	Velar	Uvular	Pharyngeal	Glottal
Stops								
Voiceless	p /p/	t /t/		ṯ /c/	k /k/	ḳ, q /q/		ì /ʔ/
Voiced	b /b/	d /d/		ḏ /ɟ/	g /g/			
Fricatives								
Voiceless	f /f/	s /s/	š /š/	ẖ /ç/	ḫ /x/		ḥ /ħ/	h /h/
Voiced		z /z/					ʿ /ʕ/	
Nasals	m /m/	n /n/						
Lateral		ꜣ, n, r /l/						
Vibrant		r /ʀ/				ꜣ /ʀ/		
Glides	w /w/			y, jj /j/				

often inverted for reasons of symmetry or artistic composition.

Phonology. The exact phonological value of many Egyptian consonants is obscured by difficulties in establishing reliable Afroasiatic correspondences: Vocalism and prosody can only be reconstructed by combining the contemporary Akkadian transcriptions of the second millennium with the later Greek transcriptions of the Late Period (corresponding roughly to spoken Demotic) and the Coptic evidence of the first millennium CE.

For Older Egyptian, we can posit the phonological inventory shown in table 1 (the conventional Egyptological transcriptions are indicated in italics). The Egyptian phonological system does not display the "emphatic" phonemes common to many Afroasiatic languages. Voiced stops, however, were often articulated as "glottalized" consonants; thus, /d/ = [t'], /j/ = [c'], /g/ = [k']. The phoneme conventionally transcribed ꜣ (aleph), originally a uvular vibrant probably articulated like *r (grasseyé)* in French, corresponds to Afroasiatic *r or *l. The existence of a phoneme /l/ in Egyptian is well established on the basis of Afroasiatic correspondences and of its presence in Coptic; yet, unlike all other consonantal phonemes, /l/ shows no unequivocal graphic rendering, being expressed in different lexemes by ⟨ꜣ⟩, ⟨n⟩, ⟨r⟩ or ⟨nr⟩.

The opposition between voiced and voiceless consonants tends to be progressively neutralized into the voiceless variant. During the second millennium, the following sound changes took place: (a) the uvulat vibrant /ʀ/ acquired the articulation /ʔ/ (glottal stop); (b) the point of articulation was progressively moved to the front—velar to palatal, palatal to apical; (c) oppositions between fricatives in the palatal region (/š/, /ç/, /x/) tended to be neutralized into /š/; and (d) final /r/ and /t/ tended to become /'/, then to disappear. During the first millennium, the opposition between ʿayin /ʕ/ and ʾaleph /ʔ/ was also neutralized.

The original set of vowels (see table 2) underwent a certain number of historical changes. Already during the second millennium, short stressed /i/ and /u/ merged into /e/, and long /u:/ turned into /e:/. Around 1000, long /a:/ became /o:/, a phonetic evolution similar to the contemporaneous "Canaanite shift" in Northwest Semitic. There was also a change in the short tonic from /a/ to /o/, but Coptic shows that this affected only a portion of the Egyptian linguistic domain. Egyptian unstressed vowels progressively lost phonological status and became realized as *schwa* (ə).

In the classical language, the stress could lie only on the ultimate or penultimate syllable. Although both closed and open syllables are found in pretonic position, the only possible structure in syllables following the stress is the closed syllable with short vowel. The stressed vowel of a penultimate open syllable is long; some scholars posit the existence of extralong syllables under oxytone stress. In addition to final /j/, /w/, /t/ and /r/, unstressed vowels were dropped between 2000 and 1600.

Morphology. The basic Egyptian morphological unit of nouns is a biliteral or triliteral root, which is modified by flectional suffixes (see table 3). Although some scholars detect remnants of the Afroasiatic case system in the Egyptian verbal paradigm, the syntactic structure of classical Egyptian was so rigid that cases could not have played a productive role in the language in historical times. Short unstressed vowels in final position are not posited for classical Egyptian.

Adjectives are morphologically and syntactically treated like substantives. Very common is the derivational pattern called *nisbation,* in which a morpheme -*j* is added to a noun to form its corresponding adjective: *nṯr,* "god," *nṯrj* "divine."

The three types of pronouns are listed in table 4. Inde-

TABLE 2. *Vowels of Older Egyptian*

Vowels	Short	Long
Front	/i/	/i:/
Middle	/a/	/a:/
Back	/u/	/u:/

TABLE 3. *Nominal Morphology in Older Egyptian*

	Masculine	Feminine
Singular	.ɸ, .w	.t
Dual	.wj	.tj
Plural	.ɸ, .w, .ww	.t, .jjt, .wt

pendent pronouns are used for the topicalized subject of sentences with nominal or adjectival predicate in the first person (*jnk jtj=k* "I am your father") and for the focalized subject of nominal or verbal cleft sentences: *ntf z3 Wsjr* "*he is Osiris' son*"; *jnk jnj=j sw* "it is I who shall bring it." Dependent pronouns are used as the object of a transitive verb (*sḏm=f wj* "he will hear me"), as the subject of a qualifying nominal sentence (*nfr ṯw ḥnʿ=j* "you are happy with me") and of an adverbial sentence in the first and second persons only after an initial particle (*mk wj m-b3ḥ=k* "Look, I am in front of you"). Suffix pronouns are used as the subject of verbal forms, as possessive pronoun, and as object of prepositions: *ḏj=k r=k n=j ḥ.t=j* "you shall truly (lit., to-you) give me (= to-me) my possessions."

Demonstratives are characterized by a deictic (specifying) element preceded by the indicator of gender and number (masc., *pn, pf, pw*; fem., *tn, tf, tw*; *rmṯ pf* "that man"; *ḥjm.t tn* "this woman"). They normally follow the noun to which they refer. The plurals *nn, nf, nn* are also used with following genitive as pronouns in partitive constructions: *nn nj srjw.w* "these officials." Later Egyptian developed a set of definite articles from the proclitic demonstrative series *p3, t3*, pl. *n3*; *p3-rm(t)* "the man"; *t3-ḥm(.t)* "the woman"; *n3-srj.w* "the officials," as well as an indefinite article from the numeral *wʿj* "one": *wʿ-rmt* "a man."

The relative pronoun is masc. *ntj*; fem. *nt.t*; pl. *ntj.w* "who/

TABLE 4. *Personal Pronouns in Older Egyptian*

	Independent	Dependent	Suffix
Singular			
1 c.	*jnk*	*wj*	*=j*
2 m.	*ntk, ṯwt*[1]	*ṯw*	*=k*
2 f.	*ntṯ, ṯmt*[1]	*ṯn*	*=ṯ*
3 m.	*ntf*, swt[1]	*sw*	*=f*
3 f.	*nts, stt*[1]	*sj, st*	*=s*
Dual			
1 c.		*nj*	*=nj*
2 c.	*ntṯnj*	*ṯnj*	*=ṯnj*
3 c.	*ntsnj*	*snj*	*=snj*
Plural			
1 c.	*jnn*	*n*	*=n*
2 c.	*ntṯn*	*ṯn*	*=ṯn*
3 c.	*ntsn*	*sn, st*	*=sn*

[1]*ṯwt, ṯmt, swt,* and *stt* are archaic forms found mainly in Old Kingdom religious texts.

which/that." It only refers to specific (i.e., semantically determined) antecedents because in Egyptian indefinite antecedents are not resumed by a relative, but by a circumstantial, clause: *rmṯ ntj rḥ.n=j sw* "the man whom I know" (lit., "man that I know him," as opposed to *rmṯ rḥ.n=j sw* "a man that I know," lit., "man—I know him"). Peculiar to Egyptian is the presence of a relative pronoun, which semantically incorporates negation: masc. *jwtj*, fem. *jwt.t*, pl. *jwtj.w* "who/which/that not."

Basic interrogative pronouns are *m* "who?", "what?", *jḫ* "what?", *jšst* "what?". They can be combined with prepositions or particles to form complex pronouns: *jn-m* "who?", literally, "FOCUS-who"; *ḥr-m* "why?", literally, "on-what?".

The most common numerals show etymological connections with other languages of the Afroasiatic family: *wʿj* "one," *sn.wj* "two," *ḥmt.w* "three," *jfd.w* "four," *dj.w* "five," *srs.w* "six," *sfḫ.w* "seven," *ḥmn.w* "eight," *psḏ.w* "nine," *mḏw* "ten," *ḏw.tj* "twenty," *mʿb3* "thirty," *ḥm* "forty," *ty.w* "fifty," *sjsy.w* "sixty," *sfḫy.w* "seventy," *ḥmny.w* "eighty," *psḏy.w* "ninety," *šn.t* "one hundred," *ḫ3* "one thousand," *ḏbʿ* "ten thousand," *ḥfn* "one hundred thousand," *ḥḥ* "one million." It is noteworthy that *five* is etymologically a *nisba* of Afroasiatic *⋆yad* "hand," which is no longer a productive word in historical Egyptian, that "twenty" is an old dual of "ten," that "thirty" and "forty" are independent lexemes but cardinals from "fifty" to "ninety" represent the plural forms of the respective units "five" through "nine." Numbers are seldom written out; they are mostly rendered graphically, strokes indicating the units, and special hieroglyphs being used for the powers of "ten." Ordinals are derived from cardinals through the addition of a suffix .*nw* (from 2 to 9, e.g., *ḥmt.nw* "third"), or the prefixation of the participle *mḥ* "filling" to the cardinal number (from 10 onward, e.g., *mḥ-20* "twentieth").

Finite verbal forms are built by annexing a suffix pronoun to the root, either directly or after a morpheme indicating tense, aspect, or voice features. The most important verbal indicators are .*n* (past tense; *sḏm.n=j* "I heard"), .*t* (perfective, sometimes prospective aspect, *n sḏm.t=f* "he had not heard," *jw.t=f* "he shall come"), .*w* (prospective aspect and passive voice, *jrj.w=f* "it has been/shall be done"), .*tw* (passive voice, *sḏm.tw=k* "you are heard"). Classes of so-called "weak" verbal roots, whose third radical is a semiconsonantal *j* or *w*, show the reduplication of the second radical and the presence of a stressed vowel between the two consonants in a form indicating in Semitic languages the imperfective aspect or the factitive stem, such as the imperfective in Akkadian and the D-stem throughout Semitic: In Egyptian this form, which is conventionally called *emphatic*, fulfills the function of pragmatic "theme" of the sentence in which it appears: *mrr=s wj* "(the-fact-that-)she loves me." In such sentences, the attentional stress normally lies on an adverbial modifier. The nonreduplicated verbal form is further subdivided into temporally unmarked or future functions, depending on the temporal setting of the context. The imperative has no suffix element in the singular, but sometimes, especially with weak verbs, a suffix .*w* or .*y* in the plural.

Egyptian also exhibits a verbal form, variously called *old perfective, stative,* or *pseudoparticiple,* which indicates the wide semantic range of verbal "perfectivity," from perfective aspect with intransitive verbs to passive voice with transitive verbs. This form displays a set of suffix pronouns that are etymologically linked to the forms of the Semitic suffix conjugation. Examples are *prj.kw* "I have come forth," *ḫpr.tj* "you have become," and *rdj.w* "it has been given."

Nonfinite forms of the Egyptian verb are (1) the participle *(nomen agentis),* which exhibits nominal morphology and is derived from the verbal stem (2) the infinitive *(nomen actionis),* which shows a suffix .*ø* in the regular verbs and a suffix .*t* in some classes of weak verbs (*mrj.t* "to love," "love"). A special type of infinitive characterized by a suffix .*w* is used after verbs of negative predication, such as *tm* "not to do." It is a matter of scholarly dispute whether the radical element in finite forms was originally a *nomen agentis* (*mrj=f* "*a-loving-one-is-he*" > "he loves") or a *nomen actionis* (*mrj=f* "loving-of-him" > "he loves"). Verbal predications could also be expressed by prepositional constructions (*sw ḥr sḏm* "he is on hearing" > "he is hearing"; *jw=f r mrj.t* "he is toward loving" > "he is going to love," "he will love"); constructions such as these characterize the evolution of the verbal system in Later Egyptian.

The most frequent prepositions are *m* "in," "with"; *n* "to," "for"; *r* "toward"; *mj* "as," "like"; *ḥr* "on"; *ẖr* "under"; *ḥnˁ* "with"; *ḫft* "according to"; and *ḫntj* "before." Prepositional phrases follow the noun or the verb they modify. Particularly noteworthy is the presence of the preposition *ẖr* "near", whose original semantic value (*A ẖr B* "A is near B") was applied to any situation in which the two participants A and B find themselves at different hierarchical levels, A being socioculturally higher than B (*sḏd=f ẖr msj.w* "he will speak to the children") or vice versa B higher than A (*jmꜣḫy ẖr nṯr ˁꜣ* "honored by the great god").

The basic negative particle is *n* (cf. Semitic *laʾ): *n rḫ.n=f* "he does not know": A variant of this, conventionally transcribed *nn,* is used as predicative negation: *nn mꜣˁ.tjw* "there are no trustworthy people."

Syntax. Egyptian exhibits three sentence types, nominal, adverbial, and verbal, which are classified on the basis of the syntactic nature of their predicate—the subject being always a nominal phrase.

1. *Nominal sentences,* in which the predicate is either a substantive or an adjective. In categorical statements or qualifying adjectival sentences, the normal order of constituents is predicate-subject: *Rˁw pw* "this is Ra"; *nfr mtn=j* "my path is good." This sequence is modified into subject-predicate in identifying sentences when both the subject and the predicate are semantically determined or specific (*sn.t=f spd.t* "his sister is Sirius"), or in cleft sentences, when the subject is focalized (*jn sn.t=f sˁnḫ rn=f* "it is his sister who causes his name to live"). Topicalization is achieved by means of extraposition, the topicalized syntagm being resumed by a coreferential pronoun in the main clause.

2. *Adverbial sentences,* in which the predicate is an adverbial or prepositional phrase; the order is always subject-predicate: *jw NN jr p.t* "NN is towards heaven"; *ẖr.t=k m prw=k* "your rations are in your house."

3. *Verbal sentences,* with verbal phrase; in which the order is predicate-subject (-object): *ḫˁ.y=k* "you shall appear"; *ḫˁm.n=f wj* "he charged me."

In Egyptian sentences, verbal forms often appear embedded as theme or rheme of the utterance. In the Egyptological literature, this phenomenon is known as "transposition." The theme-rheme sequence is labeled "complex adverbial sentence": *wgg ꜣs.n=f wj* "(as for) weakness, it has seized me" > "weakness has seized me". Thus, Egyptian syntax displays a comparatively high degree of topicalization and focalization phenomena. The bare verbal sentence with the sequence predicate-subject appears less frequently than in related languages, being limited to modal (including prospective) functions.

[*See also* Hieroglyphs.]

BIBLIOGRAPHY

Allen, James P. *The Inflection of the Verb in the Pyramid Texts.* Bibliotheca Aegyptia, vol. 2. Malibu, 1984.

Černý, Jaroslav, and Sarah I. Groll. *A Late Egyptian Grammar.* 3d ed. Studia Pohl, Series Maior, vol. 4. Rome, 1984.

Doret, Éric. *The Narrative Verbal System of Old and Middle Egyptian.* Cahiers d'Orientalisme, vol. 12. Geneva, 1986.

Edel, Elmar. *Altägyptische Grammatik.* 2 vols. Analecta Orientalia, vols. 34–35. Rome, 1955–1964.

Englund, Gertie, and Paul J. Frandsen, eds. *Crossroad: Chaos or the Beginning of a New Paradigm; Papers from the Conference on Egyptian Grammar, Helsingør, 28–30 May 1986.* Carsten Niebuhr Institut Publications, 1. Copenhagen, 1986.

Erman, Adolf, and Hermann Grapow. *Wörterbuch der ägyptischen Sprache.* 7 vols. Leipzig and Berlin, 1926–1963.

Faulkner, Raymond O. *A Concise Dictionary of Middle Egyptian.* Oxford, 1962.

Frandsen, Paul J. *An Outline of the Late Egyptian Verbal System.* Copenhagen, 1974.

Gardiner, Alan H. *Egyptian Grammar: Being an Introduction to the Study of Hieroglyphs.* 3d ed. Oxford, 1957.

Johnson, Janet H. *The Demotic Verbal System.* University of Chicago, Oriental Institute, Studies in Ancient Oriental Civilization, no. 38. Chicago, 1976.

Junge, Friedrich. *Syntax der mittelägyptischen Literatursprache.* Mainz, 1978.

Loprieno, Antonio. *Das Verbalsystem im Ägyptischen und im Semitischen: Zur Grundlegung einer Aspekttheorie.* Göttinger Orientforschungen, vol. IV.17. Wiesbaden, 1986.

Loprieno, Antonio, ed. *Crossroads II: Proceedings of the Second International Conference on Egyptian Grammar, Los Angeles, October 17–20, 1990.* Lingua Aegyptia, vol. 1. Göttingen, 1991.

Ossing, Jürgen. *Die Nominalbildung des Ägyptischen.* 2 vols. Mainz, 1976.

Polotsky, Hans Jakob. *Collected Papers.* Jerusalem, 1971.

Polotsky, Hans Jakob. "Les transpositions du verbe en égyptien classique." *Israel Oriental Studies* 6 (1976): 1–50.

Polotsky, Hans Jakob. *Grandlagen des koptischen Satzbaus.* 2 vols. American Studies in Papyrology, vols. 28–29. Decatur, Ill., 1988–1990.

Schenkel, Wolfgang. *Einführung in die altägyptische Sprachwissenschaft.* Darmstadt, 1990.

Shisha-Halevy, Ariel. *Coptic Grammatical Categories.* Analecta Orientalia, vol. 53. Rome, 1986.

Vernus, Pascal. *Future at Issue: Tense, Mood, and Aspect in Middle Egyptian; Studies in Syntax and Semantics.* Yale Egyptological Studies, vol. 4. New Haven, 1990.

ANTONIO LOPRIENO

EGYPTIAN ARAMAIC TEXTS.

[*The tables referred to throughout this entry appear as an appendix in volume 5.*] Aramaic texts from the twenty-sixth dynasty through the Ptolemaic period were written (or found) in Egypt on papyrus, parchment, wood, ostraca, stone out croppings, sarcophagi, funerary stelae, altars, jars, bowls, coins, statuettes, seals, and bullae. Major centers of discovery were Memphis-Saqqara and Elephantine from the Persian period and Edfu from the Ptolemaic period, but graffiti have turned up all along the Nile from northern Giza to Nubian Tumas. The particulars of discovery and publication of papyri, ostraca, and jar inscriptions are listed chronologically in tabular form according to category of text (tables 1, 14–15). Other texts, including ostraca and jar inscriptions, are arranged typologically and listed alphabetically according to museum or library (tables 2–13).

Papyri and Parchments. These documents fall into six categories: (1) thirty-six letters on papyrus and fourteen on parchment, plus numerous fragments. Twenty-eight papyri belong to Elephantine (*TAD* [= Porten and Yardeni, 1986–1993] A3.1–10; 4.1–10; 5.2, 5; 6.1–2) or Syene (Aswan; *TAD* A2.1–4) and seven elsewhere—el-Hibeh (*TAD* A3.11), Luxor (*TAD* A2.5–7), Saqqara (*TAD* A1.1; 5.1), and an unknown locality (*TAD* A5.3, 4). A unique letter is from Adon, king of Ekron (c. 604–603 BCE), seeking aid from the pharaoh against the Babylonian onslaught. (2) forty-three contracts from Elephantine Island, mostly intact (495–400); one from el-Hibeh (515 [*TAD* B1.1]) and fragmentary court protocols from Saqqara (*TAD* B8.1–12). (3) two or three literary texts—*The Words of Aḥiqar* (*TAD* C1.1) and one or two fragmentary reworked Egyptian tales (*TAD* C1.2). (4) one historical text—a fragmentary version of Darius' Bisitun inscription (*TAD* C2.1). (5) thirty accounts from Elephantine and Saqqara in the Persian period and Edfu in the Ptolemaic period (*TAD* C3.1–29). (6) nine lists, likewise from Elephantine and Saqqara (*TAD* C4.1–9).

There was a distinctive mode of writing for each type of document. Letters and contracts were written in a single column on a roll held vertically, perpendicular to the fibers and parallel to the joins. Although a letter frequently continued on the verso, contracts rarely did (exceptions are *TAD* B1.1; 2.3; 3.3; 4.4). All other texts were written in columns on a roll held horizontally, parallel to the fibers and perpendicular to the joins. At the end of the fifth century a few contracts were also written this way (*TAD* B4.6; 7.1–3).

Letters. Letters may be classified according to four categories—private, communal, official, and satrapal. At least eighteen letters may be assigned to the first category (*TAD* A2.1–7; 3.1–11). They are dispatched by peripatetic correspondents, Jewish and Aramean soldiers receiving government allotments (*prs* [*TAD* A2.3:8, 3.3:3; B4.2:6]). Their letters send and seek greetings, communicate matters of concern, issue instructions, enter requests, and occasionally contain such a significant piece of historical information as the succession to the throne of Nepherites in Epiph (= 27 September–26 October 399 BCE [*TAD* A 3.9]).

The ten papyri in the communal archive of leader and perhaps chief priest Jedaniah, son of Gemariah, are historically the most significant of the Elephantine texts (*TAD* A4.1–10). The fragmentary Passover letter sent to him in 419/18 by one Hananiah instructs the Jewish garrison in the proper observance of the two festivals (*TAD* A4.1). Three other letters attest to the tension between the devotees of YHW and of Khnum (*TAD* A4.2–4) that ultimately led to the destruction of the Jewish temple on the island by the Khnum priests in connivance with the Persian governor Vidranga (*TAD* A4.5–10). The most informative pieces are two drafts of a petition addressed to Bagohi, governor of Judah, on 25 November 407 BCE by Jedaniah and his colleagues, with a copy to the sons of Sanballat, governor of Samaria (*TAD* A7–8). In an oral memorandum, Bagohi and Delaiah, son of Sanballat, agreed to a limited reconstruction of the temple "on its site as it was formerly" but omitted permission to offer animal sacrifices (*TAD* A4.9). Blood on the altar was to be the exclusive prerogative of Jerusalem. The Jews at Elephantine accepted the limitation and in a further petition to "our lord," perhaps Arsames, offered him a rich reward if he would allow reconstruction of the temple (*TAD* A4.10). The last contract of the Anani(ah) archive (13 December 402 BCE) records the continued presence of the temple of YHW (*TAD* B3.12:18–19), indicating that if it had not yet been rebuilt, its place had not been taken by another structure.

Five fragmentary letters may be classified as official, two from Elephantine concerning an hereditary land lease (*TAD* A5.2, 5), one from Saqqara dated 436/35 BCE (*TAD* A5.1), and two of unknown provenance (*TAD* A5.3–4). The persons involved in these letters are either Persians or Egyptians. The letters associated with the satrapal house of Arsames (*TAD* A6) illustrate well the bureaucratic procedures pursued in handling complaints and issuing instructions and orders.

Legal Documents. The most intact of all the papyri are those acquired by purchase on the antiquities market. These constitute two family archives. The other legal documents (loosely referred to as "contracts") may be divided into five categories—deeds of obligation (*TAD* B4.1–6), conveyances (*TAD* B5.1–5), documents of wifehood (*TAD* B6.1–4), judicial oaths (*TAD* B7.1–4), and court records (*TAD* B8.1–12). Representative documents from the first three categories appear also in the family archives. The parties regularly (except for Egyptians), and witnesses and neighbors occasionally, were identified by ethnicity (Aramean, Babylonian, Bactrian, Caspian, Jew, Khwarezmian), occupation ([member] of a [military] detachment, builder, boatman, [temple] servitor), and usually by residence (Elephantine, Syene) as well. The numerous witness signatures attest a high degree of literacy among the colonists.

The Mibtahiah archive contains eleven documents and spans three generations (471–410 BCE) of one of Elephantine's leading Jewish families. Mahseiah ("YH is refuge"), son of Jedaniah, may have named his daughter Mibtahiah ("YH is trust") with the biblical verses *Psalms* 91:2, 118:8–9 (*ḥsh* > *bṭḥ*) in mind, and she gave her two sons the patronyms Jedaniah and Mahseiah. Mibtahiah was twice married, the second time to an Egyptian, Eshor, later known as Nathan. She accumulated three houses and four slaves; the houses passed on to her eldest son and the slaves were divided between her two sons (*TAD* B2.1–11).

The Anani(ah) archive contains thirteen documents and spans two generations (456–402 BCE) of two interrelated families. The first family consists of the minor temple official Anani(ah), son of Azariah; his Egyptian slave-wife, Ta(pa)met; their two children, Pelatiah/Pilti and Jehoishma; and their son-in-law, Anani(ah), son of Haggai. The second family consists of the creditor and slave owner Meshullam, son of Zaccur, and his son, also named Zaccur. The elder Anani(ah) had but one house, acquired as a piece of abandoned property from a Caspian couple (*TAD* B3.4 [437 BCE]) and disposed of in parts and stages by bequest and sale, first to his wife (*TAD* B3.5), then to his daughter (*TAD* B3.7, 10, 11), and finally to his namesake son-in-law (*TAD* B3.12). When the elder Anani(ah) married the handmaiden Ta(pa)met, her master Meshullam barely provided her with a dowry (*TAD* B3.3), but Anani(ah)'s emancipated daughter was handsomely endowed by her adoptive brother, Zaccur (*TAD* B3.8).

Literary and Historical Text. Eleven sheets containing fourteen columns of the Ahiqar text from Elephantine are preserved (*TAD* C1.1). The first five columns are narrative, relating the story of the "wise and skillful scribe . . . counselor of all Assyria and [be]arer of the seal" for King Sennacherib and his son, Esarhaddon. Decipherment of the erased customs account (*TAD* C3.7) underlying the Ahiqar text corroborates the present order of the narrative, mandates a rearrangement of the plates with the proverbs, and suggests that the conclusion of the narrative followed the end of the proverbs. Being on the outside of the scroll, it was lost (introduction to *TAD* C1.1–2). The two fragments of *The Prophecy of Hor* and *The Demise of Righteousness* (*TAD* C1.2) are joined together by a thin strip in the middle (as proposed by Bezalel Porten and Ada Yardeni). The upper half of a fragmentary column is preserved on each side. On the recto the Egyptian magician Hor, known also from demotic texts, elusively tells the pharaoh "your bones shall not go down to Sheol." The verso details the breakdown of social order followed by a divinely proclaimed redeemer.

The one historical text is a fragmentary copy of the original Bisitun inscription dispatched by Darius I to centers throughout the empire recording his victory over nineteen rebels in one year (*TAD* C2.1). The original Aramaic text must have consisted of eleven columns of seventeen to eighteen lines each, yielding a total of approximately 190 lines, of which seventy-nine have been recovered. A date in the Record of Memoranda on the verso (year 7 = 417 BCE [*TAD* C3.13:34]) suggests that the present copy may have been written to commemorate the hundredth anniversary of the great victories of Darius I, which fell shortly after the accession of his later namesake.

Accounts and Lists. There are significant accounts from the three major sites, dealing with the disbursement or receipt of such commodities as silver (*TAD* C3.2, 4–5, 7, 11, 15, 25), grain (*TAD* C3.13–14, 16–18, 25–28), wine and oil (*TAD* C31, 7, 11–12, 18, 28–29). Only a few are intact. The most significant religiously and onomastically is the eight-column Collection Account from Elephantine, probably of 400 (*TAD* C3.15), listing 128 Jewish contributors of two shekels each, initially designated for YHW the God but at the end divided up between him and the deities Eshembethel and Anathbethel. Economically, the most significant text is the newly deciphered (Yardeni and Porten) Customs Account (*TAD* C3.7). Written on both sides of a fifty-sheet scroll in 475 BCE at one of Egypt's custom's stations, either Migdol (*Jer.* 44:1, 46:14; *Ez.* 29:10, 30:6; *TAD* A3.3:4), Daphne-Tahpanhes (*Jer.* 43:9), or Memphis (*TAD* C3.8IIIA:11, IIIB:16), it was subsequently erased to make way for the *Words of Ahiqar*. It attests to forty-two sailings in ten months of four different kinds of ships (thirty-six Ionian and six "Phoenician") and the duty (*mndt*) in kind paid on entry and the dues (*tšy* = *t3 šy.t*) paid on exported natron. The import duty on the Greek ships includes gold staters, silver, Ionian wine, oil, a wooden support(?), coated and uncoated jars.

The "Phoenician" ships bring a variety of items—Sidonian wine of year 10 and of year 11; two kinds of iron (*pkrn* and *sny*), bronze, and tin; wood by weight and by number, including four different cuts of cedar (*sy* ["beam"?], *mlwt* ["board"?], *pq* ["plank"?], and *p'my* [translation unknown]); two kinds of wool, designated by their village of origin; and clay. The turnaround time is one to three weeks, and a certain Glaphyros is known to have sailed twice (*TAD* C3.7Kv2:22f; Gr2:15f). Some Babylonian-Egyptian double dates allow the reconstruction of several sheets from the

Memphis Shipyard Journal for the years 473–471 (*TAD* C3.8). North Saqqara has yielded several very fragmentary land registries (*TAD* C3.20–24), using Persian words to describe the type of property (*rstkh*, *'wpsth*) and measuring the area in arouras (*'šln*). Third-century BCE accounts, probably from Edfu, display Greek names (e.g., Apollonios, Bacchios, Herakleides, Hermias, and Jason) alongside a few northwest Semitic ones (e.g., Abdi, Abieti [*'byty*], Judah, Nathan, and Shabbethai).

Ethnically, the nine lists (*TAD* C4.1–9) display the cosmopolitan nature of society in the Persian period. A single onomastic group usually dominates each list. Lacking or missing title, they conceal their intent. Perhaps they constituted military units, collection lists (*TAD* C3.15), or ration lists (*TAD* C3.14, 27).

Ostraca and Jar Inscriptions. Ostraca are texts written on pot shards and limestone flakes, while jar inscriptions were written, incised, or inked on the jar, usually at the top, at the time of its manufacture, transport, or storage. Some 330 Aramaic ostraca have been discovered, almost all from excavations at Elephantine (table 2). Unlike the papyri, which appeared in major collections, the ostraca were never assembled into one publication and there is no standard method of citation. There are twenty-six jar inscriptions, mostly fragmentary, from Elephantine, Saqqara, and Edfu (table 3).

The ostraca may be divided into four groups—letters, lists, accounts, and two abecedaries. The largest category is letters. Almost all of the Elephantine ostraca were written by a single scribe in the first quarter of the fifth century BCE taking dictation at Syene from soldiers needing to communicate with their family and friends in Elephantine. The letters were written on randomly shaped ostraca that measured roughly 7 × 10 cm, beginning regularly on the concave side and continuing on the convex and averaging a dozen lines. A ferry service plied the waters of the Nile between Syene (Aswan) and Elephantine (Gazirat al-Aswan) in Persian times as today, and these notes were sent with the boatman of these ships. Communication was meant to be immediate, and often a sense of urgency pervades the letters. They are full of reports and requests for objects and information. One ostracon reports an unsettling experience—"Now, lo a dream I saw and from that time I am very hot. May Jhamoliah see my wellbeing" (table 2.1). In the realm of religion, they are a valuable source of information on divine epithets, divine intervention in personal affairs, the Jewish temple, oaths, Sabbath, Passover, and purity. The divine name spelled *YHW* in the later papyri is written in the early papyri and in all these ostraca *YHH*. Orthographic evidence indicates that it was pronounced something like "Yaho" and not "Yahu." One of the strangest instructions, backed by an oath-supported threat, is contained in a letter to the woman Islah, "Now, behold, legumes I shall send tomorrow. Meet the boat tomorrow on the Sabbath. Lest, if they get lost, by

the life of YHH, if not (= surely) yo[ur] life I shall take. Do not rely on Meshullemeth and on Shemaiah" (table 2.63). Almost as cryptic is the query of Hoshaiah, "Send me (word) when you will do (observe/perform) the Passover" (table 2.40). Is it a matter of calendar or purity? One ostracon may be reconstructed to read, "Do not dispatch to me bread without it being sealed *(htm)*. Lo, all the jars are impure *(tm'n)*. Behold, the bread which [yo]u disp[atched] to me yesterday is im[pure]" (table 2.62)." The *marzeah*, barely alluded to in the Bible (*Jer.* 16:5; *Am.* 6:7), appears prominently in one of the ostraca (table 2.46).

Fifteen ostraca may be classified as lists (table 2a), twelve as accounts (table 2b), and they bear the same features as their papyrus counterparts. Some are onomastically homogeneous (all Jewish [tables 2.8 = 2b.3] or all Egyptian [tables 2.6 = 2b.2]), and others are mixed (tables 2.79 = 2a.14). One exclusively Egyptian list, uniquely written on both sides, includes a couple names that are popular in demotic documents but otherwise absent from the Aramaic texts—Es(p)metsheps (*'smtšbs* ["He of the glorious staff"]) and Espetensene (*'sptnsny* ["He of him who is in Bigeh"]) (tables 2.80 = 2a.15). The ostraca accounts are all Ptolemaic and probably all, with but one exception, from Edfu. The names are followed by monetary or other notations. The names in one account are distinctly mixed—Greek (Theodore [*twdrs*], Egyptian (Taba), Hebrew (Shabbethit and Abram), and Aramaic (Abieti) (tables 2.3 = 2b.1). Several of the Jewish names are characteristic of the Ptolemaic period and do not appear in Achaemenid Elephantine—Abieti ("[my] father will come"), Abram, Dallui, Jidleh, Jotakum ("YW, may you arise"), Judith, and Simeon. The abecedaries come from Elephantine (table 2.78) and North Saqqara (table 2.81).

Eight of the Elephantine jar inscriptions were written by the same scribe (table 3.3, 7–8, 10, 13–14, 16, 18). Two reconstructed Elephantine jars show three names each, one written in Aramaic by this scribe at the top of the jar near the handle and two in a different hand in Phoenician farther down, one below the other (table 3.13–14) A large percentage of the Phoenician theophorous names are compounded with Ptah or Apis, the deities of Memphis, and so the jars must have subsequently passed into the hands of Phoenicians there and only later made their way down to Elephantine. Numerous sherds bear the Phoenician inscription *lmlk* followed by the *tet*-like sign (believed by some to mean "royal measure" [Orli Goldwasser and Joseph Naveh, "The Origin of the Ṭet Symbol," *Israel Exploration Journal* 26 (1976): 15–19]), and two sherds carry this formula in Aramaic (table 3.5). Two jars from Abu Sir contain an unexplained fragmentary text—*lslk 'm lbwš h /// /// ///* (table 3.1–2). One fragmentary inscription reads "To Psamshek . . . cohort commander (*rb ksr*'; table 3.15). The Saqqara jars contain an incised potter's mark (*bb* [table 3.19a]), an inked notation of contents (*mglt* or simply *mg* [table 3.22,

26], "scroll," that is, papyrus rolls), or a dedication "To Nabu" (table 3.23), known to have a temple at Syene (*TAD* A2.3:1; table 10.8).

Sundry Inscriptions with Names. The inscriptions on other small objects (stone plaques [table 4], wood [table 5], seals and bullae [table 6], statuettes [table 7], silver bowls [table 8], mummy labels [table 9], and coins), as well as on sarcophagi (table 10), and tombstones (table 11) are mostly names. The seals, bullae, and coins, some of the wooden inscriptions, a bowl, a statuette, two mummy labels, three sarcophagi, and a tomb inscription all have but a single name each. Once more, the outstanding feature about these fifteen names is their onomastic and presumably ethnic diversity— Aramean (Aḥinuri, Hadadezer, and Ezer [seals (tables 5.6, 6.1, 4)]; Ammishezib [wooden palette (table 5.3)]; Sharah [mummy label (table 9.7)], Assyrian (Belsaruṣur [statuette (table 7.1)]), Egyptian (Harkhebe [seal (table 6.6)], Hor [sarcophagus (table 10.2)]), and *Teehur* [mummy label (table 9.8)]), Hebrew (Shabbethai [sarcophagus (table 10.1)] and Uri [tombstone (table 11.6)]), and Persian (Bagamarazdiya [seal (table 6.2)] and Bukhsha [sarcophagus (table 10.15)]). As recently read by Naveh, one seal bears the Arabian name Ubaid son of Siniyad (table 6.5).

Most of the names recorded on mummy labels (table 9), sarcophagi (table 10), and tombstones (table 11) give both prenomen and patronym. As expected, Elephantine shows Jews (Shabah, son of Hosea [mummy label (table 9.1)]; see also table 4.2) and Syene, Arameans (Abutai, daughter of Shamashnuri [sarcophagus (table 10.3)]). The material from South Saqqara displays a mixed Aramean-Egyptian ambience with a touch of Persian. Burial proximity and prosopographical considerations on six sarcophagi permit the reconstruction of three family groups—(1) †Agri(ya), son of †Bethelzabad, son of Eshemram (tables 9.3, 6; 10.10); (2) Heremnathan, son of Besa, son of Zabdi (table 9.5; 10.12); (3) Heremnathan, son of Peṭ(e)esi, son of Sharah, son of Pasi (table, 10.7, 16–17, 20). At least three of the dead were temple officials, one far from home—the priest Heremshezib, son of Ashah (table 10.5); "Sharah the servitor" (table 9.7), who may be the same as the above Sharah; and Sheil, a priest of Nabu at Syene (table 10.8). The names of two brothers appear on either side of a ceramic mummy label (table 9.4)—Pahe, son of Bagadata, and Bagafarna, son of Bagadata. Perhaps they died young and belong to the twin heads from a fragmentary unpublished coffin lid (Egyptian Museum, Cairo, JE 55246). Four of the buried parties are women. The mummy labels were usually placed on the chest of the deceased. The coffin inscriptions were written twice or three times, either inscribed and painted or just painted above the head or on the chest of the lid and on the side, usually at the shoulders on the outside, but twice on the inside (table 10.9, 13), allowing the deceased to "look" at his name. Twelve Jewish tombstones of the Ptolemaic period have been uncovered—three at the necropolis at el-Ibrahimiya in Alexandria and nine in Edfu. Only one of the

Alexandrian inscriptions is fully intelligible (table 11.2) and it bears the unique Hebrew names Akabiah, son of Elioenai ("to YW are my eyes [directed]"). Is he related to one of the last biblical Davidic descendants, Akkub, son of Elioenai (1 *Chr.* 3:24)? Like the Arameans of Saqqara, the Jews of Edfu were buried with their families. Obadiah, son of Simeon, written on a reused offering table (table 11.5), and Nathn(a)i, son of Simeon, (table 11.7) were probably brothers. A third Edfu stone (table 11.4) bears four names, apparently father and children—Azgad, son of *Mdy/Mry* and the three persons related to Azgad, namely the woman Shelomzi(o)n, Zebadiah, and Meshullam. Azgad appears as the name of a family head among the Judean repatriates (*Ezr.* 2:12, 8:12; *Neh.* 7:17, 10:16), and the name Shelomzion ("welfare of Zion") is well known in Second Temple times, as are Nathn(a)i, Obadiah, and Simeon.

A unique memorial inscription of uncertain provenience (table 11.14) reads "To Anan (*'nn*), son of Elish (*'lyš*), the priest of Baal, husband (*b'l*) of Anoth (*'nwt*)." Neither of the personal names is attested elsewhere, and the form of the divine name is strange. Some scholars doubt the inscription's authenticity. Other items inscribed on these small objects include accounts on both sides of a wooden palette (table 5.5), a duplicate date formula ("On the 24th of Ab, year 2 Artaxerx[es]") incised and inked on a triangular limestone plaque from the Apries palace in Memphis (table 4.1), and the words *'wy ly*, ("woe unto me"?) incised on a small figurine (table 7.3).

Funerary, Votive, and Dedicatory Inscriptions. The Aramaic-speaking peoples in Egypt were not only buried in Egyptian style but they also produced Egyptianizing funerary stelae and offering tables (table 12). The stelae depict familiar funerary scenes in two or three upper registers with a one- or four-line Aramaic inscription at the bottom (table 12.1–3) or between two registers (table 12.5–6). One stela (table 12.1) also has a hieroglyphic inscription. The embalmed deceased is lying on a (lion) couch above four canopic jars (table 12.2–3), flanked by the goddesses Nephthys and Isis (table 12.3) and anointed by the god Anubis (table 12.1, 3–4). A second register depicts mourners in Semitic garb and coiffure (table 12.1, 4–5). The third register, usually the upper one, shows offerings being made by the deceased to Osiris (table 12.1, 3), with Isis (and Nephthys) standing behind him. Most of the names and patronyms or matronyms of these defunct Arameans are Egyptian and they are to be blessed by Osiris—Taba, daughter of the woman Taḥapi (table 12.3); Ankhoḥapi, son of the woman Taḥabes (table 12.5); Tumma (*tm'* [Aramaic]), daughter of Bocchoris (*bkrnp*) (table 12.2); and Peṭeesi, son of *Yḥ'* . . . (table 12.4). The mixed onomastic situation is best illustrated by a dated stela (Mehir, year 4 of Xerxes = 21 May–19 June 482 BCE [table 12.1]) prepared by the Aramean Absali for his Aramean father, Abah, son of Egyptian Ḥor and Aramean mother, Aḥatabu, daughter of the Jew Adaiah. A new reading (Yardeni) shows that the couple came from the city *ḥstmḥ* = *Ḥꜣs.t Ṯmḥy*, near Marea on the Lybian border (Herodotus, 2.30; Henri Gauthier, *Dictionnaire des noms géographiques contenus dans les textes hiéroglyphiques*, vol. 4, Cairo, 1927, p. 159). One stela with three Egyptian loanwords (table 12.3) is a quatrain of three four-beat bicola with an occasional hint of internal rhyme and a concluding three-beat bicolon—"Nothing of evil has she done/Nor slander of anyone has she spoken at all." The four-line inscription on the offering table (table 12.6) begins "the offering table (*ḥtpy*) for the offering (*lqrbt*) of Banit to Osiris-Ḥapi (= Serapis) made Abitab, son of Banit, for her" (*lh* [sic, according to Yardeni]).

The milieu of these stelae may be Egyptian, but the inscription genre background is West Semitic. Comparison may be made with the four inscribed libation bowls from Tell el-Maskhuta in the eastern Delta (table 8.1–4). These votive offerings are inscribed "to Han-Ilat" (*lhn'lt*); "which Seha, son of Abdamru (*'bd'mrw*), offered to Han-Ilat"; "which Qainu, son of Geshem, king of Qedar offered to Han-Ilat"; "Harbek ["Horus (the) falcon"], son of Pasiri, offered to Han-Ilat the goddess." A generation after Geshem the Arabian opposed Nehemiah's fortification of Jerusalem (*Neh.* 2:19, 6:1–2, 6), his son and others bearing Egyptian names were worshiping at the shrine of an Arabian goddess in the Nile Delta. A similar bowl, also presumably from Egypt and dated a century later, is inscribed with a single Persian name Tirifarna (*tryprn* [table 8.5]).

The presence of Persians in Aramaic dedicatory inscriptions is evidenced from a sandstone building inscription from Aswan (table 12.7). An upper panel is possibly missing; what is visible reads "this shrine (*brzmdn*), garrison commander of Syene, made in the month of Sivan, that is Meḥir, year seven of Artaxerxes the king (= 6–14 June 458 BCE). . . ." The inscription follows a pattern known in early Phoenician dedicatory inscriptions (*KAI* 7) and continued into contemporary Aramaic inscriptions from Cilicia (*KAI* 258 = Gibson, no. 33). In both the Cilician and Elephantine inscriptions the object described is indicated by a Persian word—*patikara-* and **brazmādāna-* respectively. Another Old Persian loanword, *drwt* ("welfare"), must have introduced the concluding blessing to be bestowed upon the garrison commander (the reading Vidranga is excluded) who built the shrine and set up the inscription.

Graffiti. Almost fifty Aramaic graffiti have been located at eleven locations in Egypt from Giza, Maʿsarah, and Dahshur near Memphis, through Wadi Sheikh Sheikhun, Abydos, Wadi Hammamat, and Wadi Abu Qwei north of Thebes, Gebel Abu Gurob, Wadi el-Shatt er-Rigal, Aswan, and Wadi el-Hudi, and as far south as Tomas in Lower Nubia (table 13). Almost all of these sites have yielded numerous inscriptions, small and large, and the Aramean-writing travelers followed in the path of their predecessors and contemporaries. Most inscriptions remain in situ and require collation. One was a royal dedicatory inscription of unknown provenance with an incised prenomen (table

13.51). The Egyptian-Aramean ambience is again prominent here—for example, Abitab son of Shumtab, Zur son of Kamam, Belhabeh ("Bel, give him"), Heremnathan, Heremshezib, Jinamiom (*yn'mywm*, "may day be pleasant" [unlocated]), Nabunathan, and Shumieti (table 13.3–4, 9, 19, 22, 27, 33–34, 51) are Aramean, and Eshor, Hori, Patou, Petemun, Peteesi, and Peteneesi son of Petosiri are Egyptian (table 12.7–8, 13–14, 20, 23–24, 26–27). One name is Babylonian ([Mar]dukshumukin [table 13.1]), another possibly Arabian (Ḥaggag son of Ablat [table 13.12]), and a couple may be Anatolian (table 13.17–18). Not one is distinctly Jewish. At some sites the traveler simply wrote his name (Maʿsarah, Dahshur, Gebel Abu-Gurob, and Tomas). Often he incised a proskynema, that is, an obeisance—"blessed be PN (son of PN) to/before DN." At the temple of Seti I in Abydos (table 13.7–18), the visitor came, along with so many others, as a pilgrim to Osiris. Elsewhere other deities were invoked—Horus, Isis, and Khnum at Wadi el-Shatt er-Rigal (table 13.37–41); the god of the eastern desert, Min, at Wadi Abu Qwei and probably at Wadi Sheikh Sheikhun (table 13.6, 26–29); and Shamash (or Sun), "the great god," the god of the rock and the god of Egypt in Wadi el-Hudi above Aswan (table 13.43–45, 47). The Giza graffito records the arrival of a caravan (table 13.1); that in Wadi Hammamat is an abecedary (table 13.25); and A. H. Sayce imagined the word *by*, "house," written three times at the Aswan sandstone quarry (table 13.42). The longest graffito is dated, runs nine lines (table 13.47), and contains a blessing formula whose first part is unique and whose second half is reminiscent of an epistolary praescriptio—"blessed be he who wrote this inscription before the god of the mountain and the god of Egypt that they grant me welfare and favor . . . and blessed be he who will read this inscri[ption]" (cf. *TAD* A4.3:2–3, 4.7:1–2]).

A Romance? Last but not least and perhaps the most fascinating of all the Aramaic texts is an extremely fragmentary seventeen-panel inscription in a cave some 8 km (5 mi.) northeast of Sheikh Fadl. It was discovered by Flinders Petrie while excavating at Bahnasa (Oxyrynchus) and reported by Noel Aimé-Giron (*Ancient Egypt* 2 [1923]: 38–43). The text mentions King Taharqa, Pharaoh Necho, and a Psamtik/Psammetichus (but not the king of that name). A tantalizing line reads *l' 'kl 'šbqnh 'škb 'mh rḥm 'nh lhy* [according to Ada Yardeni, not *lhy/sgy*, "I cannot leave her. I shall lie with her. I love her abundantly." A cryptic colophon mentions "year 5."

[*See also* Aramaic language and Literature; Elephantine; Giza; Oxyrhynchus; *and* Saqqara.]

BIBLIOGRAPHY

Aimé-Giron, Noël. *Textes araméens d'Égypte.* Cairo, 1931. Publication of 112 items (papyri, sarcophagi, graffiti, mummy labels) discovered by French expeditions, mostly at Saqqara. Contains a valuable introduction and topical treatments, although readings must be checked against later publications.

Aimé-Giron, Noël. "Adversaria semitica." *Bulletin de l'Institut Français d'Archéologie Orientale* 38 (1939): 1–63. Corrigenda and continuation of *Textes* (1931), from nos. 113 to 121 (new material from Saqqara and Edfu).

Aimé-Giron, Noël. "Adversaria semitica." *Annales du Service des Antiquités de l'Égypte* 39 (1939): 339–363. Continuation of "Adversaria semitica" from numbers 122 to 124 (unique graffiti from Wadi el-Hudi).

Bresciani, Edda. *Missione di scavo a Medinet Madi (Fayum-Egitto).* Milan, 1968.

Bresciani, Edda. "Una statuina fittile con inscrizione aramaica dell'Egitto." In *Hommages à André Dupont-Sommer,* pp. 5–8. Paris, 1971.

Corpus inscriptionum semiticarum. Part 2.1. Paris, 1888–1893. Publication of all known Aramaic texts to date (funerary stelae, graffiti, ostraca, papyri, seals), with valuable plates and a commentary in Latin.

Cowley, Arthur E. *Aramaic Papyri of the Fifth Century B.C.* Oxford, 1923. The most convenient collection of all papyri published to that date. Readings must be checked against later publications.

Driver, Godfrey R. *Aramaic Documents of the Fifth Century B.C.* Oxford, 1954. Superb publication of parchment letters sent from outside Egypt to satrapal officials, with excellent full-size plates. Abridged and revised (without plates) in 1957 and 1965.

Dupont-Sommer, André. "Un ostracon araméen inédit d'Éléphantine (Collection Clermont-Ganneau no. 44)." In *Hebrew and Semitic Studies Presented to G. R. Driver,* edited by D. Winton Thomas and W. D. McHardy, pp. 53–58. Oxford, 1963.

Ebers, Georg. *The Hellenic Portraits from the Fayum.* New York, 1893.

Fitzmyer, Joseph A., and Stephen A. Kaufman. *An Aramaic Bibliography,* part 1, *Old, Official, and Biblical Aramaic.* Baltimore and London, 1992. Complete listing of all texts and extensive bibliography for each. Classification according to *TAD* sigla where available; otherwise classification is cumbersome.

Greenfield, Jonas C., and Bezalel Porten. *The Bisitun Inscription of Darius the Great: Aramaic Version.* Corpus Inscriptionum Iranicarum, part 1, vol. 5: Texts 1. London, 1982. New edition with restored text, with a comparison to the Akkadian version and papyrological treatment. Minor revisions in *TAD* C2.1.

Grelot, Pierre. *Documents araméens d'Égypte.* Paris, 1972. French annotated translation of 109 texts, including papyri, ostraca, and other small inscriptions, plus an elaborate onomastic treatise.

Hinz, Walther. *Altiranisches Sprachgut der Nebenüberlieferungen.* Wiesbaden, 1975.

Kraeling, Emil G. *Brooklyn Museum Aramaic Papyri: New Documents of the Fifth Century B.C. from the Jewish Colony in Elephantine.* New Haven, 1953. Publication of the Anani(ah) family archive discovered in 1893 by Charles Edwin Wilbour, with a comprehensive introduction. Readings must be checked against later publications.

Naveh, Joseph. "The Development of the Aramaic Script." *Proceedings of the Israel Academy of Sciences and Humanities* 5 (1970): 21–43. Basic work for palaeographical dating of all Aramaic texts.

Parlasca, Klaus. *Mumienporträts und verwandte Denkmäler.* Wiesbaden, 1966.

Petrie, W. M. Flinders. *The Palace of Apries (Memphis II).* London, 1909.

Porten, Bezalel. *Archives from Elephantine: The Life of an Ancient Jewish Military Colony.* Berkeley, 1968. The most comprehensive synthesis of the material. A thoroughly revised edition (Brill) is planned for 1998. The treatment of legal topics is updated in joint studies by Porten and Szubin.

Porten, Bezalel, and H. Z. Szubin. "'Abandoned Property' in Elephantine: A New Interpretation of Kraeling 3." *Journal of Near Eastern Studies* 41 (1982): 123–131.

Porten, Bezalel, and H. Z. Szubin. "Exchange of Inherited Property at Elephantine (Cowley 1)." *Journal of the American Oriental Society* 102 (1982): 651–654.

Porten, Bezalel, and H. Z. Szubin. "Litigation Concerning Abandoned Property at Elephantine (Kraeling 1)." *Journal of Near Eastern Studies* 42 (1983): 279–284.

Porten, Bezalel. "The Jews in Egypt." In *The Cambridge History of Judaism,* vol. 1, edited by W. D. Davies and Louis Finkelstein, pp. 372–400. Cambridge, 1984. Update of Porten (1968), with basic bibliography.

Porten, Bezalel, and H. Z. Szubin. "Hereditary Leases in Aramaic Letters." *Bibliotheca Orientalis* 42 (1985): 283–288.

Porten, Bezalel, and Ada Yardeni. *Textbook of Ancient Aramaic Documents from Ancient Egypt (TAD A, B, C).* 3 vols. Jerusalem, 1986–1993. The most up-to-date collection of Egyptian Aramaic papyri and parchments, including letters (*TAD* A), contracts (*TAD* B), literature, accounts, and lists (*TAD* C), with detailed excurses. Each text is newly collated at the source and reproduced in hand-copy. *TAD* D is in preparation and will include papyrus and parchment fragments and inscriptions on material other than papyrus.

Porten, Bezalel, and H. Z. Szubin. "A Dowry Addendum (Kraeling 10)." *Journal of the American Oriental Society* 107 (1987): 231–238.

Porten, Bezalel, and H. Z. Szubin. "Litigants in the Elephantine Contracts: The Development of Legal Terminology." *Maarav* 4 (1987): 45–67.

Porten, Bezalel, and H. Z. Szubin. "Royal Grants in Egypt: A New Interpretation of Driver 2." *Journal of Near Eastern Studies* 46 (1987): 39–48.

Porten, Bezalel, and H. Z. Szubin. "An Aramaic Deed of Bequest (Kraeling 9)." In *Community and Culture,* edited by Nahum M. Waldman, pp. 179–192. Philadelphia, 1987.

Porten, Bezalel. "The Calendar of Aramaic Texts from Achaemenid and Ptolemaic Egypt." In *Irano-Judaica,* vol. 2, *Studies Relating to Jewish Contacts with Persian Culture throughout the Ages,* edited by Shaul Shaked and Amnon Netzer, pp. 13–32. Jerusalem, 1990. Detailed examination of every date, with discussion of dating patterns in contracts, letters, and accounts, and synchronous Babylonian-Egyptian dates.

Porten, Bezalel. "Elephantine Papyri." In *The Anchor Bible Dictionary,* vol. 2, pp. 445–455. New York, 1992. Detailed survey of discovery and contents of all Elephantine papyri, with an elaborate bibliography.

Répertoire d'épigraphie sémitique. Paris, 1901–1917. Most convenient single collection of nonpapyrological epigraphic material for those years.

Sachau, Eduard. *Aramäische Papyrus und Ostraka aus einer jüdischen Militärkolonie zu Elephantine.* Leipzig, 1911. Publication of seventy-five papyrus items and numerous inscriptions on shards, jars, wood, stone, and leather, mostly from the 1906–1908 Elephantine excavations by Rubensohn and Zucker. Indispensable plates.

Sayce, A. H., and Arthur E. Cowley. *Aramaic Papyri Discovered at Assuan.* London, 1906. Mibtahiah archive plus several ostraca. Contains full-size plates and an excellent bibliography of all Aramaic texts to date by Seymour de Ricci. Readings must be checked against later publications.

Segal, Judah B. *Aramaic Texts from North Saqqâra.* London, 1983. Publication of 202 papyrus items and 26 Aramaic and Phoenician ostraca found by Walter Emery (1966–1967) and Geoffrey Martin (1971–1973). Elaborate apparatus but disappointing plates. Readings must be checked against reviews and later publications. New collation essential.

Szubin, H. Z., and Bezalel Porten. "'Ancestral Estates' in Aramaic Contracts: The Legal Significance of the Term *mḥḥsn.*" *Journal of the Royal Asiatic Society of Great Britain and Ireland* (1982): 3–9.

Szubin, H. Z., and Bezalel Porten. "Testamentary Succession at Elephantine." *Bulletin of the American Schools of Oriental Research,* no. 252 (1983): 35–46.

Szubin, H. Z., and Bezalel Porten. "A Life Estate of Usufruct: A New Interpretation of Kraeling 6." *Bulletin of the American Schools of Oriental Research*, no. 269 (1988): 29–45.

Szubin, H. Z., and Bezalel Porten. "An Aramaic Joint Venture Agreement: A New Interpretation of the Bauer-Meissner Papyrus." *Bulletin of the American Schools of Oriental Research*, no. 288 (1992): 67–84.

Weigall, Arthur E. P. *A Report on the Antiquities of Lower Nubia.* Oxford, 1907.

Weigall, Arthur E. P. *Travels in the Upper Egyptian Deserts.* London, 1909.

BEZALEL PORTEN

'EINAN (Ar., 'Ain Mallaḥa), an important Natufian site located 72 m above sea level near a freshwater spring in Israel's Hulah Valley. The site was excavated by Jean Perrot (1955–1971), who was joined in 1971 by François R. Valla, who later continued excavation in the uppermost layer. Excavation exposed four major building strata, all constructed within the slope of colluvial deposits. The lowest strata (IV–III) were assigned to the Early Natufian and strata II and I to the Middle and Late Natufian, respectively (c. 10,000–8,000 BCE).

The earliest building, which was found in stratum IV, is a large subterranean house, 9 m in diameter. Its rear walls were constructed as terraces and still stand to a height of one meter. Six well-preserved postholes indicate that wood supports probably held the structure's roof. Two fireplaces were found in the floor, as well as more than twenty multicolored pebbles and three whetstones. A large number of stone and bone tools were found, along with broken mortars and pestles. The round houses of strata III and II are 3–6 m in diameter, all with semisubterranean stone foundations. While little is known about their superstructure, the interiors of several of these houses reveal squarish fireplaces. The houses of stratum I are smaller in diameter but always have a central fireplace. In this layer, numerous bell-shaped subterranean pits were found, some one meter deep and with sides coated with a thick layer of clay. Other, shallower pits were covered with a thin lime plaster and may have been storage facilities, although they were often used secondarily for burials.

Both single and communal burials were found in strata III and IV, mostly in a semiflexed to flexed position. Several of the skeletal remains exhibit decorated headpieces of dentalium beads, as well as necklaces or bracelets made of these or other shells. The burials, even when found under floors, had originally been dug outside the structures. It has been suggested that some were dug in family burial grounds. One distinctive grave was of an older woman interred with a puppy, illustrating the special relationship between humans and domesticated animals. The stratum II burials often lack decoration and are less flexed than the earlier ones. The burials in stratum I were commonly pits in secondary use

and generally contained more than one individual. One special grave is covered by a rock pile and contains the remains of four–eight individuals. Based on cranial morphologies from these burials, the population from 'Einan is believed to be descended from local Levantine Upper Paleolithic groups.

'Einan's lithic industry led Valla to propose the subdivision of the Natufian into four stages of lithic development. The dominant types are microliths, especially Helwan lunates in the lower part of the sequence, and increasingly dominant backed lunates. Burins from another important group, with fewer endscrapers, sickle blades, and a few elongated picks considered the forerunners of Neolithic axes. The ground-stone industry is rich in mortars and pestles, and a very large goblet-shaped basalt mortar should be noted in particular. Numerous whetstones and shaft straighteners were recovered. Artistic activity was expressed in a series of schematic figurines, mainly carved or incised in stone.

Although plant remains were not preserved, the presence of sickle blades probably indicates the harvesting of wild cereals. Animal bones are numerous and consist mainly of gazelle and deer, with a noticeable presence of wild boar. Other important food sources were tortoises, fish from Lake Hulah, and waterfowl, especially migratory species present in winter. Animal bones and marine shells provided raw material for jewelry; shells were brought mainly from the Mediterranean Sea, with a few specimens from the Red Sea and the Nile Valley.

The site of 'Einan was probably one of the major villages of the Natufian culture in the Levant. Although the site was abandoned several times, the presence of domesticated animals and the evidence for a seasonal distribution of food indicate that when the settlement was occupied, habitation was nearly year-round.

BIBLIOGRAPHY

Bouchud, Jean. *La faune du gisement Natoufien de Mallaha (Eynan) Israel.* Mémoires et Travaux du Centre de Recherche Française de Jérusalem, 4. Paris, 1987.

Perrot, Jean, and Daniel Ladiray. *Les hommes de Mallaha, Eynan, Israel.* Mémoires et Travaux du Centre de Recherche Française de Jérusalem, 7. Paris, 1988.

Valla, François R. "Aspects du sol de l'Abri 131 de Mallaha (Eynan)." *Paléorient* 14.2 (1988): 283–296.

Valla, François R. "Les Natoufiens de Mallaha et l'espace." In *The Natufian Culture in the Levant,* edited by Ofer Bar-Yosef and François R. Valla, pp. 111–122. Ann Arbor, 1991.

OFER BAR-YOSEF

'EIN-BESOR (or 'En Besor), site located in Israel's northwest Negev desert, on a small loess hill of about one-half acre in area, approximately 350 m south of the Besor springs ('Ain Shellala; map reference 1013 × 0795). During excavations carried out from 1970 to 1983 by an expedition on behalf of the Israel Department of Antiquities and the Institute of Archaeology of Tel Aviv University headed by Ram Gophna and Dan Gazit, about 400 sq m were exposed at the site. Three Early Bronze Age strata and one Hellenistic stratum were uncovered.

In stratum IV (EB IB) the slope of the eastern hill was sparsely settled. A round silo base was excavated as well as the solitary remains (partial floors) of structures. Also recovered were sherds of the period, flint tools, bones of sheep and goats, and a variety of carbonized agricultural products (wheat, barley, peas, grapes). This settlement was abandoned, but the material culture of the following new stratum (III) is also dated to EB IB. Part of a brick building, A (approximately 85 sq m), was excavated at the top of the tell that had been constructed directly above remains of stratum IV. The finds it and its surroundings produced, the dimensions of the mud bricks used (8 × 12 cm), and the bricklaying and bonding techniques indicate that the builders were Egyptian. To the east of the building's west wing, which was used as a residence, was an open courtyard. Several industrial installations (probably a bakery and a brewery) were uncovered in building A's south wing. Most of the finds from building A and its refuse pits were characteristically Egyptian in style or design: ceramics, flint knives and sickle blades, a copper pin and harpoon, a marble bull's-head pendant, the bottom half of a faience statuette of a baboon, a cylinder seal, a sherd incised with a *serekh* (a rectangular frame, with the name of an Egyptian king in hieroglyphs), and quantities of unfired clay bullae bearing impressions from Egyptian cylinder seals that had been used in Egypt to seal receptacles in which dry food products were stored. [*See* Seals.] Stratum III "Egyptian" sherds were subjected to petrographic and chemical analyses that showed most to be of pots of local origin. [*See* Petrography.]

Building A was first dated to the first dynasty—that is, to the EB II—based on A. R. Schulman's deciphering of the impressions on the unfired bullae (see figure 1) and the *serekh*. He identified the names of three first-dynasty kings, high-ranking Egyptian officials (Schulman, 1983). However, subsequent dating of these materials (first suggested by Siegfried Mittmann) to the beginning of the first dynasty, or even earlier—to the end of dynasty 0—shifts the date of stratum III back to the conclusion of EB IB, a date further comparative analysis of the Egyptian pottery corroborated. The petrographic tests demonstrating that the clay is local indicate that the seals on the storage receptacles (see above) were applied in Canaan. The building's construction was likely the work of a royal Egyptian expedition to establish a way station on the route from northern Sinai to Canaan. The route traversed the area midway between the wells in North Sinai and the springs on the central coastal plain. From 'Ein-Besor, the Egyptians exercised control over the largest perennial water sources between the desert and the sown land.

The stratum II remains (dated to the end of EB II/begin-

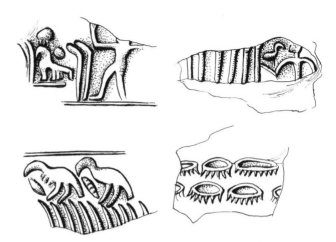

'EIN-BESOR. Figure 1. *Egyptian cylinder seal impressions.* (Courtesy R. Gophna)

ning of EB III) include part of a broadhouse (building B). It and the local pottery were uncovered on the mound's southeastern slope. The stratum's ceramics included fragments of storages jars, jugs, and ledge handles. Graves dug by bedouin on the summit of the hill destroyed almost all of the stratum I remains, which are from the Hellenistic period. Dated to the second–mid-first century BCE, sections of a wall and a floor, sherds, and a coin (surface find) represent the stratum I occupation.

BIBLIOGRAPHY

Gophna, Ram. "Excavations at 'En Besor." *Atiqot* 11 (1976): 1–9.
Gophna, Ram. "Excavations at 'En Besor, 1976." *Atiqot* 14 (1980): 9–16.
Gophna, Ram. "The Egyptian Pottery of En Besor." *Tel Aviv* 17 (1990): 144–162.
Gophna, Ram. "The Early Bronze I Settlement at 'En Besor Oasis." *Israel Exploration Journal* 40 (1990): 1–11.
Gophna, Ram, and Dan Gazit. "The First Dynasty Egyptian Residency at En Besor." *Tel Aviv* 12 (1985): 9–16.
Gophna, Ram, and Erich Friedmann. "The Flint Implements from Tel 'En Besor." *Tel Aviv* 20 (1993): 147–163.
Quack, Joachim F. von. "Die Datierung der Siegelabdrucke von Tel 'En Besor." *Zeitschrift des Deutschen Palästina-Vereins* 105 (1989): 18–26.
Schulman, A. R. "On the Dating of the Egyptian Seal Impressions from 'En Besor." *Journal of the Society for the Study of Egyptian Antiquities* 13 (1983): 249–251.

RAM GOPHNA

'EIN-BOQEQ, oasis in Israel on the southwest shore of the Dead Sea (31°10′ N, 35°20′ E; map reference 1854 × 0676). Its ancient name is unknown. After a Late Roman *castellum* was constructed here, it may have been known as Tetrapyrgia (cf. Anastasius Sinait., Interrog, in J. P. Migne, *Patrologia Graeca*, Paris, 1857–1886, 89, col. 744).

The site's ideal growing conditions for pharmaceutical

plants, such as balsam, and choice fruits such as the Nicolaus date, caused the Hasmoneans (perhaps under Alexander Jannaeus) to extend their most lucrative plantations, maintained in neighboring 'Ein-Gedi, to 'Ein-Boqeq. A tower of typical Hasmonean chisel-smoothed whitish ashlar, pottery, and two coins connect the initial terracing and field enclosures with them. Because aqueducts—one 1.2 km long and the other 300 m long—and reservoirs (which served the oasis in later periods) were a precondition for settlement here, their construction must also be attributed to the Hasmoneans (in the site's phase I). At its greatest expanse, perhaps in the Byzantine period, the cultivated area covered 180,000 sq. m.

The Officina. Under King Herod the products of the plantations, supplemented by asphalt from the Dead Sea and ingredients provided by the Arabian caravans passing to the south of it, were used to operate a factory *(officina)* for producing pharmaceutical and cosmetic products. The *officina* was a nearly rectangular building (20 × 20 m). Its walls, preserved to a height of 1.5 m, are 80 cm thick, have two faces of roughly dressed stones set in mud mortar, and have a rubble core. The rooms are arranged around a central courtyard that runs from the northern to the southern (main) entrance.

The evidence suggests that the main entrance chamber gave access on the left into a storeroom for precious raw materials and on the right to a workroom furnished with two low, plastered basins. One basin has a posthole and may have been a bag press operated by a single worker. The relatively small site of these basins and most of the other installations at the site attests to how delicate the raw materials—petals, buds, and leaves—were, as well as to the small quantities of liquids, resins, and powders extracted.

The main production line was in the southeastern part of the courtyard. This industrial compound included, in its most elaborate phase (phase II), a stone chest for raw materials, a fireplace for preheating (esp. boiling); a grinding platter; a stone vat, or mortar; and an upper and lower beehive-shaped oven that created regulated temperature to heat vessels set upon the opening in their apex. These installations served processes such as crushing, pounding, mixing of ingredients, their maceration (dipping in hot fats and oils), decoction (boiling down to essence), evaporation, or sublimation (non-liquid condensation). (The same techniques of production existed already in Old Testament times, as proven by Egyptian wall paintings.) Two additional ovens, in work areas created by walls that jut into the courtyard, served or were served by the production line. Room 4 (10 × 3.75 m), west of the courtyard, was heavily plastered. The floor in its northern part, also plastered, sloped slightly toward a sunken pit (55 × 35 × 50 cm) that collected the substances squeezed out of plants by treading or crushing. In the opposite room (no. 6), a handmill or similar device seems to have been operated in phases I–II

on a round table surrounded by a round flagstone floor. The Hasmonean tower, incorporated into the structure's southwest corner, provided security. The plantation's four phases of occupation of the factory are allocated to Herod, the first procurators, Agrippa I and the second procurators, and to a haphazard refurbishing by Bar Kokhba following the destruction that took place during Vespasian's war against the Jews.

The Castellum. The subsequent history of 'Ein-Boqeq is obscure until a courtyard-type *castellum*, or fortress, was built by Constantine or, more probably, his sons. The fort is a typical *quadriburgus* (16.5 × 16.5 m). Its walls, built with two roughly dressed faces and a rubble core, are 1.80–2 m thick and are 6 m high. The four corner towers (each is 6 × 6 m) provided complete protection for a garrison of forty-five to sixty-five men (based on a reconstruction of the barrack blocks), with either one or two stories. The barracks were leaning onto the curtains and used their inner face as a back wall. Considerable skill was exercised in setting this structure firmly into a mound of loose gravel and making it almost completely resistant to the shock of earthquakes or attempts at separate capture. Yet, such attempts have left their imprint: destruction layers separate the four phases during which it functioned as a stronghold at the Dead Sea of the *limes Palestinae* (the fortified borders of Roman Palestine).

Phase I extended to Valentianus, phase II to the mid-fifth century (?), phase III to the Persian invasion (614 CE), and phase IV to Heraklius (c. 624 to the Arab conquest, c. 634 CE). Although the plantations ceased to operate at about the time of the Arab conquest, life went on for two or three more generations in the *castellum*. It became a collection center for nitrates gathered from the Dead Sea, which were used for fertilizer and in the manufacture of glass.

BIBLIOGRAPHY

Fischer, Moshe. "En Boqeq: An Industrial Compound from Herodian Times" (in Hebrew). *Nophim* 11–12 (1979): 21–38. Discusses the functioning of the *officina*.

Fischer, Moshe, and Tzvi Shacham. "The Water System of the En Boqeq Oasis" (in Hebrew). In *Aqueducts of Ancient Palestine*, edited by David 'Amit et al., pp. 289–298. Jerusalem, 1989.

Gichon, Mordechai. "Das Kastell En Boqeq." *Bonner Jahrbücher* 171 (1971): 386–406.

Gichon, Mordechai. "Excavations at En-Boqeq: The First Season." In *Roman Frontier Studies 1969*, edited by Eric Birley et al., pp. 256–262. Cardiff, 1974.

Gichon, Mordechai. *En Boqeq: Ausgrabungen in einer Oase am Toten Meer.* Mainz, 1993. Final excavation report of the *castellum*, including historical background and a detailed comparative discussion of the small finds.

Sheffer, Avigail, and Amalia Tidhar. "The Textiles from the En Boqeq Excavation in Israel." *Textile History* 22.1 (1991): 3–46. Technical treatise on the production and composition of the textiles produced at 'Ein-Boqeq, of special importance for research into the textiles of Byzantine Palestine.

MORDECHAI GICHON

'EIN-GEDI, oasis located on the western shore of the Dead Sea and named for the perennial spring that flows from a height of 200 m above it (map reference 1870 × 0965).

Biblical and Historical References. 'Ein-Gedi was part of the wilderness territory assigned to Judah after the Israelite conquest of Canaan (*Jos.* 15:62). It was also where David took refuge from Saul (*1 Sm.* 23:29). The fruitful vineyards of 'Ein-Gedi are mentioned in the *Song of Songs* (1:14), and it is included in a prophetic image of prosperity related by Ezekiel (47:10).

According to Josephus, 'Ein-Gedi was a Roman headquarters in the first century CE (*War* 2.55), and Pliny mentions its destruction during the First Jewish Revolt against the Romans in 66–70 CE (*Nat. Hist.* 5.73). [*See* First Jewish Revolt.] During the Second Jewish Revolt, the town was one of Bar Kokhba's military and administrative centers. [*See* Bar Kokhba Revolt.] By the early second century it was the site of a Roman garrison. In his *Onomasticon* (fourth century CE), Eusebius refers to 'Ein-Gedi as a large Jewish village (86.18), which apparently was celebrated for its dates and for balsam, which was used in the manufacture of perfume. The Jewish settlement was destroyed by fire in the sixth century CE (see below).

Excavation History. The initial survey of the oasis was carried out in 1949 by Benjamin Mazar for the Hebrew University of Jerusalem. Two additional surveys, both on behalf of the Hebrew University, were conducted in 1956 and 1957, the first directed by Yohanan Aharoni, the second by Joseph Naveh. Yigael Yadin, Nahman Avigad (in the 1960s), and Gideon Hadas (1980s) surveyed Jewish tombs in the oasis. [*See the biographies of Mazar, Aharoni, Yadin, and Avigad.*] Mazar excavated at 'Ein-Gedi from 1961 to 1965 and Dan Barag and Yosef Porath from 1970 to 1972, both projects on behalf of the Hebrew University. The excavations were focused on Tel Goren, the most prominent area of the oasis; structures were also uncovered to the east and northeast of the mound. The earliest remains date to the Chalcolithic period, but most finds are much later, dating to the Late Iron Age and beyond.

Chalcolithic Period. The only Chalcolithic (fourth millennium BCE) structure uncovered was a sacred enclosure situated on a terrace, about 150 m north of the spring. Within the enclosure were two buildings linked by a stone wall. A circular structure about 3 m in diameter stood at the center of the enclosed courtyard. Excavators found no evidence of multiple construction stages or repairs, and they determined that the enclosure, which probably served as a cultic site, had not been destroyed but abandoned.

Iron Age. A Late Iron Age settlement (630–582 BCE) was uncovered at Tel Goren. Among the numerous finds from this stratum were large barrel-shaped pithoi and numerous pottery vessels characteristic of the period. Based on a group of similar buildings cleared on the mound's northern slope,

excavators conjectured that 'Ein-Gedi had been a center of perfume production in this period, perhaps in the royal service. The settlement was destroyed by fire, perhaps in 582–581 BCE, during Nebuchadrezzar's conquest of Judah. [*See* Judah.]

Persian Period. The most impressive remains from the Persian period stratum (fifth–fourth centuries BCE) were those of a large building on the mound's northern slope. This structure (about 550 sq m in area) was probably a dwelling of one of the town's officials; it had twenty-three rooms, enclosed courtyards, and various storerooms. Most of the pottery was characteristic of the period and included Attic ware. Among the seal impressions was a jar handle stamped *Yhwd*. [*See* Seals.]

Hellenistic Period. A few coins and potsherds dating from the late fourth to the early second centuries BCE were found, but most of the relatively few Hellenistic remains dated to the Hasmonean period, especially between the reigns of Alexander Jannaeus and Herod the Great (103–37 BCE). A Late Hellenistic citadel built in two separate sections was uncovered on the top of the mound. This defensive system was destroyed in 40 BCE, during the Parthian invasion and in the last war of Hasmoneans against Herod (Josephus, *War* 3.55, 4.402).

Roman Period. An impressive citadel and a large, rectangular tower, both destroyed during the First Jewish Revolt, were uncovered on top of the mound. The pottery from the tower, which resembles the ceramic material from nearby Qumran and Masada, was used to date this stratum to the period of the Herodian dynasty (4 BCE–68 CE). However, the level may be earlier than 4 BCE. [*See* Qumran; Masada.]

Late Roman–Byzantine Period. Tel Goren was not a permanent settlement in the Late Roman–Byzantine period, but on the nearby plain, between Nahal David and Nahal 'Arugot, excavators uncovered several structures dating from the second to the sixth centuries CE. One of these structures was a Roman bathhouse (40 × 50 m) that dates to between 70 CE and 132 CE.

Several synagogues were excavated east of the summit. The earliest, which was probably built at the end of the second century or at the beginning of the third century CE, was a trapezoidal (13.5 m long on the east, 15.5 m long on the west, and 9–10.5 m wide). The orientation of its northern wall, which had two entrances, was toward Jerusalem. A mosaic pavement with a nonfigural design was executed in coarse white stones and black and colored tesserae. It is unclear whether the entire pattern was laid at the same time. [*See* Mosaics.] When this synagogue was renovated, the central entrance in the northern wall was turned into a niche where the Torah ark apparently was placed. A stepped seat was added to this wall, and three stepped benches were built along the southern wall. Pillars divided the interior—formerly one large hall—into a nave and two aisles, and three entrances were added on the west. The mosaic pavement continued in use. A new synagogue was built in the late fifth century. It featured a rectangular wooden structure that housed the Torah ark and a new mosaic pavement executed with colored tesserae that contained numerous inscriptions in Hebrew and Aramaic, one of them biblical. This synagogue, along with the rest of the settlement, was destroyed in the sixth century.

BIBLIOGRAPHY

Barag, Dan, et al. "The Synagogue at En-Gedi." In *Ancient Synagogues Revealed*, edited by Lee I. Levine, pp. 116–119. Jerusalem, 1981. Story of the discovery of the ancient synagogue at 'Ein-Gedi.

Hadas, Gideon. "Nine Tombs of the Second Temple Period at 'Ein Gedi." *'Atiqot* 24 (1994).

Mazar, Benjamin, et al. "En-Gedi: The First and Second Seasons of Excavations, 1961–1962." *'Atiqot* 5 (1966). The final excavation report on the Tel Goren dig.

Ussishkin, David. "The Ghassulian Shrine at En-Gedi." *Tel Aviv* 7 (1980): 1–44. Study of the Chalcolithic shrine found at 'Ein-Gedi.

EPHRAIM STERN

'EIN-GEV (Ar., Khirbet el-'Asheq), site located at the estuary of the 'Ein-Gev River on the eastern coast of the Sea of Galilee (32°48′ N, 35°22′ E; map reference 210 × 243). The houses of Kibbutz 'Ein-Gev are built over most of the ancient site (250 m long × 120 m wide). The suggested identification with Aramean Aphek of *1 Kings* 20:26–30 and *2 Kings* 13:14–17 is supported by the results of the regional archaeological exploration conducted by the Land of Geshur Project (see below). The ancient place name is preserved at the site located by the springs of the 'Ein-Gev River, 6 km (4 mi.) uphill, known in Arabic as Fiq, and in the name of the Second Temple period village of 'Afiqa, modern Kibbutz Afiq. No Iron Age remains have been attested there. Iron Age Tel Soreg, at the foot of Kibbutz Afiq, proved, after excavation, to have been just a small hill fort, which does not comply with the biblical description of the war with the Arameans that took place on the plain and of Aphek being a major base for the Aramean army. 'Ein-Gev is, however, located on the plain and excavation has shown that it was an important fortified Aramean town in the ninth century BCE. [*See* Aphek.]

In 1961 Benjamin Mazar and others undertook rescue excavations at the southern and northern tips of the site on behalf of the Israel Department of Antiquities. In 1990–1992, in the framework of Tel Aviv University's Land of Geshur Project, three seasons of excavations were conducted by the Japanese Expedition to 'Ein-Gev headed by Hiroshi Kanaseki and Hideo Ogawa. As most of the lower tell is built up, the expedition concentrated its efforts on the northern tip of the tell, the acropolis. The rescue excavation discerned five Iron Age strata on the lower tell and four on the acropolis. The Japanese expedition distinguished three

Iron Age strata, one from the Persian period and one from the Hellenistic period. Final correlations for the stratigraphy of the various excavated areas is not yet possible, but the conclusions reached by the recent excavation are presented here.

In stratum V two thick, parallel walls were found at the foot of the acropolis. The inner wall (1.7 m wide) was built of large basalt boulders and its foundations were sunk more than 4 m in the ground. This wall supported the fill for the acropolis and served as a defense wall as well. A more shallow counterpart of this wall ran parallel to it, and the space between the two was left open as a ditch. A 1.5-meter-thick layer of black decomposed organic material mixed with sherds was found in the ditch. The lowest layers of pottery dated to the tenth century BCE and the uppermost to the eighth. This fortification system resembles the one found by the rescue excavation's stratum IV on the lower tell.

In stratum IV fragmentary remains of a public building at least 18 m long were uncovered. It was probably a storehouse. The stratum III tripartite pillar buildings were built on top of it, following the same orientation. The pillars are square-section monoliths without holes in them or troughs between them. The function of these buildings was probably connected with the trade of goods that took place on the main road from the Bashan to Akko and to the Via Maris. In the Iron Age II, well-fortified and with important public buildings, 'Ein-Gev assumed the economically central role previously played by Iron I Tel Hadar, 7 km (4 mi.) to the north. [*See* Hadar, Tel.]

The rescue excavation exposed a room rich in finds at the southern end of the site. There, a complete storage jar with the word LŠQY (Aram. *le-shaqya*, "belonging to the cup bearer") inscribed on its shoulder was found. "Cup bearer" was a title carried by very high officials in the courts of kings in the ancient Near East. The importance of 'Ein-Gev in the Aramean Kingdom of Damascus is thus attested by these finds. [*See* Arameans.]

In stratum II pits from the Persian period were cut into the debris of the last Iron Age town, which was probably destroyed during Tiglath-Pileser III's onslaught on Damascus and northern Israel in 732 BCE. The site was resettled in the Hellenistic period (stratum I, third–second centuries BCE). Private houses, but no fortifications, were found on the acropolis. Hellenistic 'Ein-Gev was the harbor town of the newly established city of Hippos/Susita, 2 km to the east.

BIBLIOGRAPHY

Aharoni, Yohanan. *The Land of the Bible.* 2d ed. Philadelphia, 1979. Identifies 'Ein-Gev with Aramean Aphek (p. 335).

Dothan, Moshe. "Aphek on the Israel-Aram Border and Aphek on the Amorite Border" (in Hebrew). *Eretz-Israel* 12 (1975): 63–65. Identifies 'Ein-Gev with Aramean Aphek.

Kochavi, Moshe. "Israelites, Arameans and Geshurites East of the Sea of Galilee" (in Hebrew). *Ariel* 102–103 (1994): 98–109. Latest treatment of the subject.

Mazar, Benjamin, et al. "Ein-Gev: Excavations in 1961." *Israel Exploration Journal* 14 (1964): 1–49. Report on the rescue excavation.

MOSHE KOCHAVI

'EIN-SHADUD, site located about 200 m east of Tel Shadud (map reference 1724 × 2294), on the northwest edge of Israel's Jezreel (Esdraelon) plain. The site, unknown to archaeologists until 1979, was almost completely destroyed by modern construction. Its ancient name is obscure; its present identification is derived from the name of an adjacent spring.

Salvage excavations were carried out under the direction of Eliot Braun and Shimon Gibson of the Israel Department of Antiquities and Museums in two areas, A and B. Separated by an unexcavated strip 20 m wide, the areas yielded evidence of two successive occupational strata.

Stratum II, the earlier stratum, was established on virgin soil and was represented by a number of disjointed, fragmentary stone wall foundations and one partially sunken rectangular broadroom. Its pebble-paved floor, bench-lined interior, and large flat stone pillar bases are in keeping with Early Bronze I architectural traditions. One corner was occupied by a basalt-paved grinding installation on which several basalt querns were found.

The stratum I houses, constructed directly on top of the remains of the earlier buildings, were similarly oriented. Although somewhat better preserved, the structures in this level suffered from changes in elevations that produced a warping effect: originally horizontal layers were pushed up in places and were undulating rather than level.

A sausage-shaped house with parallel walls ending in two opposing, curvilinear apses—otherwise typically a broadroom with internal benches and stone pillar bases—was associated with this stratum. Its affinities with early northern EB I curvilinear constructions, such as those found at Yiftahel II (Braun, 1985–1986), Tel Teo V–IV (Eisenberg, 1989), and Palmahim Quarry 3, are somewhat modified by its broadroom. Similar contemporary structures have been uncovered at Qiryat Ata II (Eliot Braun and A. Golani, "Kiryat Ata," *Hadashot Archeologiot*, in press [Hebrew]), Tel Kabri (Scheftelowitz, 1992), and Megiddo, stage IV (Engberg and Shipton, 1934, fig. 2).

Completely rectilinear buildings, some with deliberately rounded corners, are also associated with the stratum I occupation at 'Ein-Shadud. They exhibit two building phases, in the latter of which there is a marked tendency toward thickening walls.

Additional structures—including a double broadroom with a flagstone floor, several curvilinear walls, and fragmentary pebbled surfaces—were also encountered in the excavations. However, because of the site's poor state of preservation, they could not be attributed to either stratum.

In agreement with the architectural evidence for continuity is a collection of well-stratified diagnostic pottery types that show strata II and I to be roughly contemporary and of relatively brief duration.

A quantity of late-style bowls of Gray-Burnished (Esdraelon) Ware emphasizes a somewhat early date on the EB I horizon for the overall occupation. Ceramics typical of this assemblage, indicating a somewhat advanced (post-Yiftahel II) and northern facies of the EB I, include red-slipped and burnished vessels, rail-rim and bow-rim pithoi, hemispherical bowls with conical projections, and grain-wash decoration.

The flint tool kit (Rosen, 1985), based on analysis of all artifacts, including cores and debitage, is significant for its sizable collection of locally produced "ad hoc" tools and an imported Canaanean blade component, including sickles.

Evidence that grains were harvested and flour produced is found in sickle blades with gloss and numerous grinding stones. An osteological study (Horwitz, 1985) suggests that animal husbandry must also have played a significant part in the economy of the 'Ein-Shadud villages. Sheep, goat, cattle, pig, and ass appear in quantities sufficient to suggest their utilization for primary and secondary products, as well as possibly being employed as beasts of burden.

Trade and outside contacts seem to have been limited and probably extended only over short distances. Shared architectural and ceramic styles; lithic imports, including flint and some ground stone objects; and occasional instances of the use of cylinder seals, probably by itinerant potters, brought this village into contact with contemporary settlements, especially within the Jezreel plain. Presumably, small surpluses would have been used to barter for imported goods.

[*See also* Yiftahel.]

BIBLIOGRAPHY

Braun, Eliot. *En Shadud: Salvage Excavations at a Farming Community in the Jezreel Valley, Israel.* British Archaeological Reports, International Series, no. 249. Oxford, 1985.

Braun, Eliot. "Of Megarons and Ovals: New Aspects of Late Prehistory in Israel." *Bulletin of the Anglo-Israel Archaeological Society* 6 (1985–1986): 17–26.

Eisenberg, Emmanuel. "Chalcolithic and Early Bronze I Occupations at Tel Teo." In *L'urbanisation de la Palestine à l'âge du Bronze ancien: Bilan et perspectives des recherches actuelles; Actes du Colloque d'Emmaüs, 20–24 octobre 1986,* edited by Pierre de Miroschedji, vol. 1, pp. 29–40. British Archaeological Reports, International Series, no. 527. Oxford, 1989.

Engberg, Robert, and Geoffrey Shipton. *Notes on the Chalcolithic and Early Bronze Age Pottery of Megiddo.* University of Chicago, Oriental Institute, Studies in Ancient Oriental Civilizations, no. 10. Chicago, 1934.

Horwitz, Liora K. "Appendix C: The En Shadud Faunal Remains." In *En Shadud: Salvage Excavations at a Farming Community in the Jezreel Valley, Israel,* edited by Eliot Braun, pp. 168–177. British Archaeological Reports, International Series, no. 249. Oxford, 1985.

Rosen, Steven A. "Appendix B: The En Shadud Lithics." In *En Shadud: Salvage Excavations at a Farming Community in the Jezreel*

Valley, Israel, edited by Eliot Braun, pp. 153–167. British Archaeological Reports, International Series, no. 249. Oxford, 1985.

Scheftelowitz, Na'ama. "Area B: Architecture, Stratigraphy, and Pottery." In *Excavations at Kabri 6: Preliminary Report of 1991 Season,* edited by Aharon Kempinski and Wolf-Dietrich Niemeier, p. 1. Tel Aviv, 1992.

ELIOT BRAUN

'EIN-YA'EL (map reference 16687 × 12777), terraced farm at a hand-dug spring in the Rephaim Valley, 3 km (5 mi.) southwest of Jerusalem. The ancient name of the site is unknown, but in Arabic it is called 'Ain Yalu. Based on archaeological survey, the site has been inhabited from the Canaanite period (2000–1600 BCE) until modern times, although not continuously. Excavation has revealed structural remains from the First Temple (800–700 BCE), Roman (100–300 CE), Byzantine (400–640 CE), Early Arab (700–800 CE), and Ottoman (1516–1917) periods.

The remains of agricultural terraces surrounded by stone fences can still be seen in aerial photographs and topographical maps of the Judean hills. As far as is known, such terraces were first built in this region at the beginning of the Iron Age (twelfth–eleventh centuries BCE) and continued to be used until modern times.

The farm at 'Ein-Ya'el was built near the foot of the hill and consisted of eight terraces constructed along its contours. The terraces were surrounded by a stone fence with access on both its west and east sides. In all periods of settlement at 'Ein-Ya'el, the buildings were constructed at the uppermost part of the farm.

The terraces were irrigated by a water system consisting of a tunnel hewn horizontally into the hill. At one end of the tunnel, rainwater filtering through the rock was collected in a cave. The tunnel opens into a series of plastered channels leading to several pools that regulated the amount of water used for irrigation. Two levels of channels beneath the modern channels attest to the similarity of the modern and ancient water systems. The imprints of metal tools are still visible on the rock walls of the tunnel and the cave.

The terrace walls were laid on bedrock and the empty space created between the wall and the slope was filled with soil and stone. The earliest structure excavated is a corner of a building dated to the First Temple period. Pottery and stone tools were found scattered on its floor. Among the inscriptional finds are two seal impressions, the first with an undeciphered personal name in the Hebrew script common to the period and the second with a *lmlk (lamelekh)* seal imprint on a jar handle.

On the three highest terraces, the remains of a Roman villa (approximate area, 4,500 sq m) were discovered and partially excavated. On the uppermost terrace, the frescoed, stone walls of a corridor, a room, and a triclinium (formal dining room) were uncovered, all with mosaic floors (see figure 1). Scattered on the floor of the triclinium were hundreds of fragments of fresco decorated with flowers and human faces and chunks of plaster with a painted diamond pattern that had probably fallen from the ceiling. A stuccoed frieze decorated with stylized flowers, geometric patterns, and human faces adorned the room's edges. One panel of the mosaic floor features the sea goddess Tethys surrounded by fish and sea creatures; depictions of Medusa flank the scene. The second panel of this mosaic bears scantily clad

'EIN-YA'EL.   Figure 1.   *Overall view of the villa's mosaic flooring.* (Courtesy Lucille Roussin)

'EIN-YA'EL. Figure 2. *Part of the mosaic floor.* From the triclinium, showing nereids and icthyo-centaurs offering platters with gifts. (Courtesy Israel Antiquities Authority)

nereids seated on the tails of ichthyocentaurs (creatures with the head, arms, and bust of a man; the forelegs of a horse; and the tail of a fish) (see figure 2); this scene is bordered by depictions of fish and ducks flanking two cupids riding on dolphins. In the center of this second panel, a marble slab forming part of a fountain was found together with a bronze nozzle; lead pipes through which the water circulated were found under the mosaic.

The mosaic in the corridor consists of four panels, each containing a personification of one of the four seasons, with birds in each corner. An additional rectangular panel contains a scene of a satyr weaving garlands, while a figure carrying a basket approaches from behind. Only the last word, *kalē* ("good"), of the Greek inscription below the satyr has been read.

The triclinium opened onto a small room with a mosaic floor displaying a medallion with a badly preserved face. A bird is depicted in each corner of the floor and an animal is depicted on each edge. Two theatrical masks on this floor allude to the cult of the wine god Bacchus.

On the second terrace of the villa, the remains of a Roman bathhouse were uncovered. Sections of two of its rooms still stand from floor to ceiling, one with a domed roof. The roof of the second room was barrel vaulted, and beneath the floor brick arches were found that supported the hypocaust. Pottery pipes—part of the heating system—were found attached to the walls of both rooms. A cross painted on one wall of the domed room confirms the ceramic evidence of occupation during the Byzantine period, whereas an oven was dated to the Early Arab period.

On the villa's third terrace, the remains of a pool were found; its position indicates that it formed part of the Roman irrigation system. Well-preserved rooms from a second Roman bath were excavated on this terrace. In the two rectangular rooms, the mosaic floor above the hypocaust was supported by columns. The floor had mostly collapsed in these rooms, but a mosaic depiction in a third (circular) room resembles a *magen David* (Heb., "shield of David"). The wall of the circular room had frescoes painted with geometric lines and swirls and representations of fruit. A layer of plaster painted with colored lines was applied on top of this fresco; this layer is not clearly dated. The mosaic floors and the ceramic as well as the numismatic finds in the villa date to the Late Roman period (late second to third century CE); additional pottery sherds were dated to the Early Arab period. On top of this material lay roof tiles, some bearing seals of the Roman Tenth Legion, and boulders that had slid from the hill.

The Roman villa at 'Ein-Ya'el was built after the Bar Kokhba Revolt (132–135 CE) and the expulsion of the Jews from all of Judea [*see* Judah]. The villa forms part of the romanization of Judea, which included the construction of Aelia Capitolina on the ruins of the city of Jerusalem. The earlier farms surrounding Jerusalem were probably replaced by Roman-style farms and villas similar to those at 'Ein-Ya'el. Some of the villa's buildings were in use more than four hundred years later, until the earthquake that shook Jerusalem in 732.

All the remains of the villa were deliberately covered with soil, probably during the Ottoman period, and the site was used as a farm. Today the site houses the 'Ein-Ya'el Living Museum.

BIBLIOGRAPHY

Applebaum, Shimon. *Judaea in Hellenistic and Roman Times.* Leiden, 1989.
Edelstein, Gershon. "What's a Roman Villa Doing Outside Jerusalem?" *Biblical Archaeology Review* 16.6 (1990): 32–42.
Edelstein, Gershon, and Ianir Milevsky. "The Rural Settlement of Jerusalem Re-valuated: Surveys and Excavations in the Rephaim Valley and Mevasseret Yerushalaim." *Palestine Exploration Quarterly* 126 (1994): 2–23.
Gibson, Shimon, and Gershon Edelstein. "Investigating Jerusalem's Rural Landscape." *Levant* 17 (1985): 139–155.
Hopkins, David C. *The Highlands of Canaan: Agricultural Life in the Early Iron Age.* Sheffield, 1985.

GERSHON EDELSTEIN

'EIN-ZIPPORI, TEL, site located in Israel in the Lower Galilee, along the Naḥal Zippori, 5 km (3 mi.) from the modern city of Nazareth (32°45′ N, 35°15′ E; map reference 1761 × 2374). It is adjacent to one of the only currently active springs and spring-fed streams in the Galilee. The site is well positioned to take advantage of neighboring arable land and a perennial water supply. 'Ein-Zippori was initially surveyed by Zvi Gal (*Lower Galilee during the Iron Age,* Winona Lake, Ind., 1992), and two seasons of excavation were carried out (1993, 1994) by the Sepphoris Regional Project, sponsored by Duke University, Wake Forest University, and the University of Connecticut at Storrs, under the direction of Eric Meyers, Carol Meyers, Ken Hoglund, and J. P. Dessel.

Tel 'Ein-Zippori is approximately 1.5 ha (4 acres) in size. Its northern and western sides were cut, probably during the last two hundred years, to increase the area of the valley under cultivation. Other recent modifications of the tell include the construction of a well on the eastern slope. Based on its construction style and on ethnohistorical data, the well was also built within the last two hundred years. Closer to the center of the tell there are indications of another well.

The depth of the archaeological deposits reaches at least 4 m. Excavation exposed a sequence of occupation from the Late Bronze Age I (1550 BCE) through the Iron Age II (ninth century BCE). The highest and most pronounced part of the tell has two terraces: an upper terrace (field I) and a lower terrace (field II). A 2-meter vertical face separates them. Field III is located along the western edge of the tell.

Stratum I (ninth century BCE) is most clearly seen in field III. The remains of a stratum I pillared building were found along the western slope of the tell. Excavation on these slopes also clearly demonstrated that the site was unfortified in Iron II. Stratum II (tenth century BCE) contained a large, well-constructed, multiroomed building in field I that has been partially excavated (see figure 1). The complex (at

least 11 × 15 m) is oriented northeast–southwest, with two primary interior dividing walls perpendicular to each other. One interior wall carries a stone bench along its northern face. Both walls have well-hewn stones as door jambs. The complex has two building phases. The destruction debris found within the complex included a great deal of burned mud brick.

In field II a series of terraced, well-integrated domestic buildings and alleys was uncovered. The southernmost terrace wall is more than 11 m long and more than 1 m wide, suggesting a large, well-planned residential area. Rectangular rooms with domestic ceramic assemblages, including three cup-and-saucer vessels, were found along both sides of this east-west wall. Another large rectangular building was found in field II that was partially cobbled and contained several large column bases. A drainage system on the upper terrace channeled runoff away from the structure's southwestern corner.

The strata III–IV remains of a large building complex in field II are dated to the thirteenth–twelfth centuries BCE. The complex is oriented east–west and opened onto a large unroofed courtyard area to the north. Several large storejars were set in the courtyard and used as small *tabuns* or jar stands. Along with local pottery, imported Cypriot wares

'EIN-ZIPPORI, TEL. Figure 1. *Eastern portion of a large tenth-century BCE building complex in field I.* (Courtesy Sepphoris Regional Project)

were found, including Base Ring II and White Slip II. The building was constructed in LB II and reused, with some modification, in Iron I.

Stratum V is represented by a narrow exposure that revealed a rich assemblage of LB I pottery smashed on a surface. The remains of at least thirteen restorable vessels included several large pithoi; the Bichrome Ware and imported Cypriot White Slip I pottery suggest an LB IA date.

In summary, Tel 'Ein-Zippori has five main occupational strata. Little is known about the LB I village, but it appears to end abruptly. In LB II the site was rebuilt along a different orientation, and there is complete continuity from LB I into Iron I. In the tenth century BCE the site was rebuilt for the third time, again with a different architectural plan. There is good evidence for large monumental buildings. This occupation ends in a partial destruction. The orientation of a ninth-century BCE pillared building differs significantly from the tenth-century architecture. It appears that the site was temporarily abandoned sometime in the late tenth century BCE. Although Tel 'Ein-Zippori was undoubtedly a village, the size and construction of the buildings suggest a degree of rural complexity for the tenth century BCE.

J. P. DESSEL

EKRON. *See* Miqne, Tel.

ELAMITES. From the early third through mid-first millennia BCE, Elam was one of the major powers in the ancient Near East. Its territory encompassed parts of southern and western Iran, and comprised both lowland (modern Khuzistan) and highland Zagros Mountain components (Fars, and parts of Kerman, Luristan, and Kurdistan). Susa, in central Khuzistan, and nearby sites in the Khuzistan lowlands have been the primary focus of research. [*See* Susa.] Anshan (modern Tall-i Malyan) was the major highland site, 500 km (310 mi.) to the southeast, in western Fars. [*See* Malyan.] Carter and Stolper (1984) provide the essential synthesis of Elamite history and material culture, and the following discussion draws on the framework that they have established and the evidence that they present. The modern name *Elam* derives from the biblical Hebrew *'elām*, Akkadian *elamtu*, Sumerian *elam(a)*, and ultimately native Elamite *hatami* and *haltamti*. Elamite was not closely related to any known ancient language, and no direct derivative survives.

Throughout Elamite history, the balance between the highland and lowland regions shifted back and forth. While the geographic distributions of archaeological assemblages (material culture) can be defined through fieldwork, linking the ancient political and cultural geographies referred to in texts to the topography and assemblage distributions remains difficult. Historical sources document political ties of varied strengths among the regions as changing with time, as did the material culture. Because of its ease of access, lowland Elam was periodically involved in Mesopotamian political developments and even incorporated into Mesopotamian states. Elamite polities in the Zagros highlands from the north to the southeast, however, were better able to sustain some autonomy, protected by the rugged topography. At times, the highland polities developed sufficient cohesion to be able to dominate the lowlands.

Native Elamite textual sources are sparse and episodic, leaving long periods of history obscure. Most of the texts come from Susa, where Mesopotamian influence often was strong. Almost no highland sites have yielded texts. Much of Elamite history must thus be extracted from tendentious, often hostile Mesopotamian texts. Their links between Elamite and Mesopotamian history provide the basic chronology for Elam.

Archaeological data are the major indigenous source for Elamite cultural history. Although excavation and survey had concentrated on Khuzistan, especially the area around Susa, the research ended by political events in 1978–1979 had begun to illuminate basic highland developments. Throughout Elamite history material culture, such as ceramics, was strongly regional. Thus, the absence of a single distinctive "Elamite" style exacerbates the problem of defining even the geographic scope of Elam. Elam's historical geography remains problematic, especially in the highlands, as a result of a dearth of native textual sources and the essential Mesopotamian ignorance of the highlands. The location of toponyms, cities, regions, and even important polities often remains uncertain. Texts and rock reliefs document an Elamite presence throughout lowland Khuzistan, southward along the Persian Gulf to at least Bushire (ancient Liyan), and eastward in the highlands into Fars (ancient Anshan in the Marv Dasht). The Elamite sphere in the highlands to the north of Khuzistan remains ill defined.

Physical Geography. Differences in gross topography, climate, ecology, and natural resources yielded a regionally diverse mosaic of subsistence and economic potentials that were ultimately reflected in cultural regions. Khuzistan is an extension of the Mesopotamian lowlands east of the Tigris River. [*See* Tigris.] Although dry farming is possible, irrigation provides a more dependable agricultural base. [*See* Irrigation; Agriculture.] Resource poor, Khuzistan depended on the surrounding highlands for many basic materials, such as metals, hard and semiprecious stones, and wood. [*See* Wood.] River valleys, particularly those of the main rivers, provide the primary routes into the highlands through the rugged parallel ridges of the Zagros Mountains.

East of Khuzistan, in Fars, almost half of the Kur River basin (2,200 sq km, or about 1,350 sq. mi.), at an elevation of 1,600 m in the Zagros Mountains, is arable. There lay

Anshan, the ancient name of both the regional polity and the largest known Elamite site (mod. Tall-i Malyan) in the highlands. North of Khuzistan, the intermontane valleys of Luristan and southern Kurdistan tend to be relatively small, with a mixed agricultural-pastoral economy. Limited routes lead northward to the Great Khorasan Road, the primary east–west route linking the Iranian plateau and areas farther east to central Mesopotamia, where it entered the lowlands along the Diyala River. [*See* Diyala.] Sociopolitical organization has tended to be tribal throughout history, with marked cultural and ethnic regionalism. Farther to the east, the Kerman range provides a link between the eastern valleys of the central Zagros and the great salt deserts (Dasht-i Kavir and Dasht-i Lut) of the central Iran.

Research on Elam. Susa, always an important center, underpins the archaeology and history of Elam. The early excavations there, directed by Jacques de Morgan (1897–1908) and Roland de Mecquenem (1908–1946), who had both trained as mining engineers, were massive in scale. Mud-brick architecture, characteristic of southwest Asia, was not recognized, so that the excavations essentially yielded artifacts, monuments, graves, and occasional baked-brick structures without contexts. Roman Ghirshman (director from 1946 to 1967) concentrated on the second millennium BCE, excavating a residential area of almost 10,000 sq m on the Ville Royale mound at Susa, as well as temples and the city wall at the nearby monumental site of Chogha Zanbil. [*See* Chogha Zanbil.] Under Jean Perrot (director from 1967 to 1990), stratigraphic excavations at Susa and at smaller sites on the surrounding plain yielded a detailed sequence for the region.

Between the late 1950s and the revolution in 1978–1979, the scope of excavation and survey expanded greatly. In Khuzistan, Pinhas Delougaz and Helene Kantor excavated at Chogha Mish, concentrating on the prehistoric phases, and Etat O. Neghaban worked at Haft Tepe. [*See* Haft Tepe.] Numerous surveys and smaller-scale excavations throughout Khuzistan and the Zagros piedmont clarified the history of Elamite settlement. In Fars, Louis Vanden Berghe and later William M. Sumner constructed the Kur River basin sequence. Sumner's excavations at Tall-i Malyan/Anshan dramatically increased the geographic scale of Elam and highlighted the role of the highlands. Excavations at sites in the Kerman range, such at Tepe Yahya, Tall-i Iblis, Tepe Sialk, and Shahdad, yielded evidence of the exploitation of natural resources and contacts with the Elamite west. [*See* Tepe Yahya.] Growing numbers of surveys and excavations began to clarify developments in highland Luristan and southern Kurdistan and their relationships to lowland Khuzistan. T. C. Young's excavations at Godin Tepe provided a dependable archaeological sequence for the late fourth through late second millennia BCE. [*See* Godin Tepe.]

Although changes in archaeological assemblages do not often proceed in lockstep with political events, the following historical periodization corresponds workably (dates are approximate).

Proto-Elamite Era (c. 3400–2600 BCE). Elamites are first identified historically in the Proto-Elamite era; ethnic affinities in prehistory are problematic.

Early stages of writing. The Acropole I excavation by Alain Le Brun at Susa have distinguished several stages in the development of writing, although it is not certain that the innovation itself first took place there (Le Brun and Vallat, 1978). [*See* Writing and Writing Systems.] Small, variously shaped clay tokens were used as counters or, as Denise Schmandt-Besserat suggests represent set amounts of specific commodities. By level 18 (3200 BCE), tokens were placed inside a hollow clay ball (bulla) whose surface was impressed with one or more seals to provide a sealed record. [*See* Seals.] Sometimes, signs corresponding to the shape and number of the enclosed tokens were impressed on the exterior. In level 17 (3200–3100 BCE) numerical tablets replaced bullae, counters, and tallies. [*See* Tablet.] A more complex system of numerical signs, in which various shapes and sizes of marks had specific values, was impressed on pillow-shaped lumps of clay. The limited information recorded suggests short-term administrative records for local use. In levels 16–14B (and Ville Royale I, levels 18–13), pictographic signs were added to identify the item counted. This developed into the Proto-Elamite A script, consisting of perhaps four hundred to eight hundred distinct characters, one hundred of them common, and suggesting a predominantly logographic writing system. The Proto-Elamite B script dates to the late third millennium BCE and is found on statues, vessels, and large clay tablets at Susa and Shahdad; fewer than one hundred characters are known.

The basic script on Proto-Elamite tablets is similar to scripts of southern Mesopotamia, but it is distinct in all details, suggesting a different language and perhaps parallel but independent development. Proto-Elamite script was probably used to write an early form of Elamite and may thus define the minimal geographic extent of early Elam. In the later third millennium BCE, the Mesopotamian cuneiform writing system displaced Proto-Elamite script for writing Elamite. [*See* Cuneiform.]

Material culture

Khuzistan. During the later Susa II period (3500–3100 BCE), which corresponds to the Late Uruk in Mesopotamia, the population of Susiana had declined and was concentrated into two enclaves focused on the towns of Susa and Chogha Mish, separated by an empty zone 14 km (9 mi.) wide. Scenes of organized warfare in seals and sealings illustrate conflict. Numerical tablets, found at Susa in Le-Brun's Acropole I excavation levels 18–17 (see above), provide evidence for deep penetration into the highlands at Godin (V), Sialk (IV1), and Tall-i Ghazir.

In about 3000 BCE, Susiana separated culturally from the Mesopotamian world, and a polity began to emerge at Malyan 500 km (310 mi.) to the southeast, in Fars. During the Susa III period (3100–2700 BCE), Susa expanded, while the overall settlement density in Susiana remained low. The ceramic assemblage was basic: common types include coarse-ware goblets and trays, beveled-rim bowls, red-slipped basins, and jars. A new glyptic style emerged, using deep linear engraving to depict animals in human stances. Glazed steatite seals (the surface vitrified by heating) have geometric or sometimes plant or animal motifs; this "piedmont" style extended into the highlands. Proto-Elamite A tablets and associated pottery and glyptic, found at Malyan (Banesh period, 3400–2600 BCE), Sialk (IV2), Yahya (IVC), and even Shahr-i Sokhta/Sistan provide evidence for an even more extensive outreach into the highlands. On the Deh Luran plain, 60 km (37 mi.) to the northwest, the population peaked. [See Deh Luran.] The ceramic assemblage was much more Mesopotamian in character, with parallels to the Jemdet Nasr–Early Dynastic I Diyala region; red- and black-painted ware was related to Early Dynastic I–II Scarlet ware.

Fars. The Banesh period (see above) corresponds to late Susa II–III. Malyan reached 50 ha (124 acres) in size in the early third millennium BCE. In area ABC, large public buildings had painted wall decoration, while area TUV yielded a more "industrial area," with Proto-Elamite A tablets and Susa III ceramics. [See Wall Paintings.] By the late Middle Banesh period (c. 3000 BCE), a massive city wall was built.

Kerman. Proto-Elamite A tablets, Susa III pottery, and glazed steatite seals in a single large building on top of the mound at Tepe Yahya mark an extended reach to the east into Kerman. Numerical tablets and Susa III pottery also are found at Tepe Sialk (IV1), near the crossing of north–south routes with the Great Khorasan Road. Tall-i Iblis, a copper metallurgical site, yielded Susa III pottery.

Luristan. At another junction of north–south routes and the Great Khorasan Road, an oval enclosure on top of Godin Tepe (period V) yielded Susa III ceramics and numerical tablets. The surrounding settlement, however, continued to use the local traditional pottery. Other sites along important routes through Luristan have also yielded late fourth–early third millennia lowland types of pottery, suggesting a network of lowland-connected sites in the highlands.

Proto-Elamite phenomenon. The distribution of numerical and Proto-Elamite A tablets deep into the highlands suggests an outreach toward resource areas and routes. At sites like Godin V and Yahya IVC, late Susa II or Susa III pottery and tablets were essentially confined to a single building complex within a settlement where the preexisting local material culture continued with only slight changes. The presence of blank tablets at highland sites (Godin and Yahya) implies local use. Impacts on the highlands were highly variable. In many regions the lowland emplacements were short-lived. Banesh Malyan, however, developed into a sizable city. During Susa III, Elamite culture was becom-ing less Mesopotamian. It was then, at the very beginning of Elamite history proper, that the pattern of highland-lowland interrelationship, which was to characterize Elam throughout its history, first appeared.

Late Third Millennium (c. 2600–2100 BCE). References to Elam appear in Sumerian historical and literary texts of the mid-third millennium BCE from southern Mesopotamia. [See Sumerians.] For example, the Enmerkar and the Lord of Aratta epic recounts an expedition to Anshan and beyond for metals, lapis lazuli, and craftsmen; inscriptions from Early Dynastic Lagash already record conflicts with Elam, especially Susa (c. 2450–2375 BCE). The Sumerian King List includes a dynasty of Awan, an Elamite center.

In the Old Akkadian period (c. 2350–2200 BCE), Mesopotamian texts record Akkadian kings waging war and diplomacy against both lowland and highland Elam, although the historical geography, and thus the scope, remains problematic. [See Akkadians.] Susa and the Khuzistan plains were vassals or may have been incorporated into the Akkadian state; Susa has yielded Old Akkadian texts, school tablets, and other evidence of typical Mesopotamian administrative activity. Highland regions experienced both military and diplomatic pressure (Akkadian royal inscriptions record campaigns to Anshan). Texts document commercial ties among Umma in southern Mesopotamia, Susa, and areas farther east.

Material culture

Khuzistan. At Susiana, the population gradually returned to levels reached in the fourth millennium. Susa itself grew from 10 to 46 ha (25 to 106 acres) in area. Small settlements were scattered across the plain, with two weak clusters, one of them centered on Susa. In Deh Luran, Tepe Mussian remained a large town (14 ha, or 35 acres). Eastern Khuzistan, however, seems to have lacked permanent settlement. [See Tepe Mussian.]

Evidence for the later third millennium at Susa is fragmentary. Banded plain-ware pottery typical of Susa III disappeared. Susa IV monochrome painted buff ware had decoration arranged in registers on the upper body; focal motifs included naturalistic, geometric, and abstract designs. This ceramic tradition is closely related to the early phases of the Godin III tradition in Luristan. Painted wares decreased in frequency through Susa IV, as Mesopotamian types of Akkadian date, such as jars with ribbed shoulders, became more common. Increasing Mesopotamian cultural impact is evident in the styles of cylinder seals, wall plaques, and votive sculpture. The Proto-Elamite A script went out of use, and the increasing use of Akkadian-style glyptic and ceramics reflected Akkadian domination of Khuzistan.

Fars and Kerman. In Fars, a gap separated the Proto-Elamite Banesh (3200–2600 BCE) and Kaftari (2200–1600 BCE) periods (see below). Kerman was culturally distinct from the Elamite regions but long-distance trade contacts continued. "Intercultural style" chlorite bowls link Tepe Ya-hya IVB (2800–2300 BCE), lowland Elam, and Early Dynastic II–III (2700–2400 BCE) Mesopotamia. Made at Yahya and other (still unknown) sites, such vessels had their surface covered with incised decoration; characteristic motifs include intertwined snakes, humpback bulls, date palms, eagles with lion heads, and architectural facades whose geometric patterns seem to portray reed-mat, bundled-reed, and brick construction. All other aspects of material culture, such as glyptic and ceramics, show that Yahya's ties were to the Indo-Iranian traditions to the south and east. North of Yahya, Shahdad lies between the Kerman range and the Dasht-i Lut desert, astride major trade routes. Its material culture seems to have derived from the Proto-Elamite tradition, but it developed as part of the northeastern Iranian and south-central Asian world.

Luristan. In Luristan, the Godin Tepe III monochrome-painted buff-ware ceramic tradition, related to and perhaps derived from that of Susa IV, spread northward through the eastern valleys. Godin Tepe itself overlooks the junction of north–south routes from Khuzistan and the Great Khorasan Road. The expansion of the monochrome-pottery distribution may reflect an early Elamite attempt to tap, or perhaps even control, the flow of materials from the Iranian plateau to the Mesopotamian lowlands. In the western valleys (the Pusht-i Kuh), the economy seems to have been predominantly pastoral. Megalithic stone-built communal tombs (*lihaqs*, 6–13 m long) yielded bronze artifacts and monochrome-painted buff ware associated with the early Godin III tradition. [*See* Tombs.]

Dynasty of Shimashki and the Sukkalmah (c. 2100–1600 BCE). A century after the collapse of the Old Akkadian state, Ur under the Ur III dynasty reunified southern Mesopotamia and again moved against Elam (2100–2000 BCE). [*See* Ur.] Susa and the Khuzistan lowlands were incorporated into the Ur III provincial system. Although the polities in the highland Zagros maintained their basic autonomy, they experienced military and diplomatic activity. This intensive Ur III pressure on highland polities stimulated defensive alliances. From this emerged the Shimashki dynasty (c. 2100–1900 BCE), which regained the lowlands and led the destruction of the Ur III state. Shimashki probably lay to the north of Khuzistan in the highlands. The decentralized government structure characteristic of the following *sukkalmah* period may have emerged at this time. Conflict with Mesopotamia continued after the fall of the Ur III dynasty.

The Sukkalmah era (c. 1900–1600 BCE) is the best-documented period of Elamite history, based on building and cylinder-seal inscriptions and royal texts. The transition from the dynasty of Shimashki to the Sukkalmah remains unclear. As seen in texts from Susa, power was held by the *sukkalmah* ("grand regent"), the *sukkal* of Elam and Shimashki ("senior co-regent"), and the *sukkal* of Susa ("junior co-regent"), all drawn from a dynastic family. If more were

known from other regions, such as Anshan, the picture might well become more complex. Although Elam was a major independent power, private legal documents from Susa, and the names of many individuals in them, were written in Akkadian or Sumerian rather than Elamite, although some legal terms and usages were non-Mesopotamian.

By the early eighteenth century BCE, Elam was one of the largest states in the area. It extended southward along the Persian Gulf and eastward into Fars (Anshan), although its ultimate eastern and northern limits remain uncertain. Elam exerted influence, if not actual control, over the city-states along the eastern edge of Mesopotamia, north to the Diyala River and beyond to the Lower Zab River; its diplomatic and economic contacts stretched across Mesopotamia and northern Syria to the Mediterranean coast. Susa's role in the tin trade is clear in texts from Mari on the Middle Euphrates River. [*See* Mari; Euphrates.] In the mid-eighteenth century BCE, Elam and Mesopotamian allies campaigned into northern Mesopotamia and Syria, before finally being pushed back by Hammurabi of Babylon. [*See* Babylon.] Elam then seems to have spent several centuries in decline.

Material culture

Khuzistan. In Khuzistan during the Shimashki period, Susa was the only city (85 ha, or 210 acres); most of the population lived in towns (4–10 ha, or 10–25 acres) rather than villages. [*See* Villages.] Under the *sukkalmah*, three additional settlements grew to cities (of greater than 10 ha, or 25 acres) and the number of villages increased. Susa and its hinterland grew. (Political disarray in southern Mesopotamia and Elamite independence would have encouraged such growth.) The population in Deh Luran declined, and the plains in eastern Khuzistan seem not to have had permanent occupations.

At Susa, elaborate administrative and religious buildings stood on the Acropole, and perhaps the Apadana mound, but they were badly damaged by later building activity. A temple with terra-cotta lions may have stood on the Ville Royale. A dense urban residential neighborhood on the Ville Royale had streets that intersected obliquely and alleys between houses. The typical house plan consisted of mud-brick rooms around a courtyard. Burials were placed below house floors or courtyards. [*See* Burial Techniques.] Shimashki-era burials tended to be placed in an inverted, tub-like terra-cotta sarcophagus. [*See* Sarcophagus.] During the Sukkalmah period, vaulted tombs built of baked brick were used for repeated (family?) burials, a practice that continued into the first millennium BCE.

Pottery from the early second millennium BCE bears a close resemblance to that from contemporary Mesopotamia, despite political independence. During the Sukkalmah period, new forms related to the Kaftari assemblage at Fars appeared. Shimashki glyptic was very similar to Ur III Mesopotamian types; with presentation scenes the typical motif. Sukkalmah glyptic includes both Mesopotamian types, such as Old Babylonian-style worship scenes, and local types made of bitumen or soft stones with scenes of banquets, files of animals, or dancing. Vessels made of bitumen have handles, feet, and spouts in animal forms, for which there are parallels from Larsa-period Mesopotamia (2000–1800 BCE). Chlorite bowls, flasks, and compartmented containers are associated with Persian Gulf seals and suggest trade among southern Mesopotamia, Susa, the Gulf, and southern Iran. Popular art includes molded naked female figurines with headdresses, jewelry, and belts. [See Jewelry.]

Fars. Following an apparent occupational hiatus after the Banesh period, population grew during the Kaftari period in Fars (2200–1600 BCE). Malyan was a large regional center (150 ha, or 371 acres) dominating a four-level hierarchy of site sizes. The regional distribution of sites suggests a complex irrigation network. Excavations at Malyan uncovered substantial buildings and portions of the city wall. Ceramic parallels between the *sukkalmah* phase and the Kaftari assemblage reflect the close lowland-highland political connections. The black-painted buff ware of the Kaftari ceramic assemblage tended to have overall decoration. Plain and painted red wares provide parallels to Susa. Kaftari glyptic has both Susian-style scenes (a worshiper facing a table with food) and Mesopotamian types. Cuneiform texts from Malyan reflect Mesopotamian scribal traditions but are not written in Elamite, despite Elamite autonomy. [See Scribes and Scribal Techniques.]

Along routes from Susiana to Malyan (Kurangun) and from Malyan to the Iranian plateau (Naqsh-i Rustam), are rock carvings that may have been shrines. [See Naqsh-i Rustam.] In each, the central scene shows worshipers approaching a divine couple seated on serpent thrones beneath flowing streams.

Luristan. The later phase of the Godin III monochrome painted tradition is found throughout the region. The ceramic assemblage is quite standardized, although red-slip or bichrome-painted decoration marks regional variants. Settlement density reached a peak, and valleys had central towns surrounded by villages. The western, outer Zagros valleys seem to have been essentially deserted, except by pastoralists, as a buffer against lowland Mesopotamian states. [See Pastoral Nomadism.] By the middle of the second millennium, BCE the density of settlement and complexity of the economy seem to have declined markedly.

Transitional and Middle Elamite Periods (1600–1100 BCE). Elam regained strength throughout the fourteenth century BCE, and the titulary of the king at Susa claimed control of Anshan. By the thirteenth century BCE, Elam had reemerged as a major power, with a geographic scope comparable to that under the *sukkalmah*. Kings undertook extensive building programs. Untash-Napirisha carried out large construction projects at a number of centers in Khuzistan—the largest was the building of a new center, Al Untash Napirisha (modern Chogha Zanbil), 40 km (25 mi.) southeast of Susa. [See Chogha Zanbil.] In the twelfth cen-

tury BCE, Elam had major military and political impacts on Mesopotamia, ousting the Kassite dynasty in Babylonia and effecting dynastic changes in other cities as well. [See Kassites.] At the zenith, under Shilhak-Inshushinak, Elamite forces again pushed deep into Mesopotamia, as far north as the Lower Zab and as far west as the Euphrates.

Material culture

Khuzistan. The Middle Elamite state reached its zenith in the thirteenth–twelfth centuries BCE and represents something of a break with the past. The much broader use of Elamite for inscriptions and the development of a distinctive style of art and architecture all served to illustrate and emphasize Elamite power and independence.

Although the area west of Susa seems to have been abandoned as a buffer zone against southern Mesopotamian states, settlement across Khuzistan grew. Susa itself seems to have declined in size and importance, while a series of large new settlements, which may have been funerary cult centers, were founded outside central Khuzistan. [See Cult.] Susa's role as a religious center must have suffered. At first, the number and size of villages and small towns remained unchanged; later, however, population seems to have concentrated in large towns along major routes. The depopulation of Deh Luran continued.

Stamped baked bricks attest to repeated royal renovations of the Temple of Inshushinak at Susa, for which molded glazed frit bricks may have been used as a facing. The techniques used to make the molded-brick facade of another temple to Inshushinak were similar to those used by the Kassites in Mesopotamia. Large houses on the Ville Royale had a standard plan, distinct from the ones in contemporary Mesopotamia, with courtyard(s) surrounded by rooms; a large rectangular room with pilasters probably served as a reception room.

Haft Tepe (ancient Kabnak[?]) 20 km (12 mi.) south of Susa was built by Tepti-ahar (c. 1375 BCE). No houses have been excavated there. A funerary temple complex consisted of a walled compound with a baked-brick pavement. Two halls opened off of a portico; beneath each was a large vaulted tomb chamber. Some bodies had been carefully laid out and covered with ocher; others had been interred much more haphazardly. Two mud-brick terraces were found nearby, one of which was 14 m high and surrounded by halls with polychrome painted decoration. Crafts at the site included elephant-bone working, tablet firing, potting (ceramic kiln), and metalworking.

Untash-Napirisha (1260–1235 BCE) founded Chogha Zanbil (ancient Al Untash-Napirisha) on a ridge overlooking the Diz River after Haft Tepe was abandoned. Within an area of 100 ha (247 acres) enclosed by a city wall were a ziggurat complex and several monumental buildings. [See Ziggurat.] Courts, shrines, and temples to various gods inside a double wall surrounded the ziggurat with its temple to Inshushinak and Naparisha (the complex had undergone several major changes of plan). Decorated pegs attached glazed tiles to doorjambs, wooden doors had glass-bead decoration, and glazed frit griffins and bulls guarded the zigurrat's staircases. [See Glass.] In the eastern corner of the city, three monumental complexes consisted of large courtyards surrounded with rooms and storerooms; one contained five underground vaulted tomb chambers.

Through the second millennium BCE, the Elamite pottery assemblage became more uniform and simpler, which suggests more centralized production. The Middle Elamite assemblage included wide varieties of jars and goblets. Pottery at Deh Luran had more Mesopotamian Kassite parallels, while eastern Khuzistan had parallels to the Qaleh pottery tradition of Fars.

Royal Elamite seals from the seventeen to fourteenth centuries BCE display a deity seated on a serpent throne. Middle Elamite glyptic includes scenes of banqueting and hunting, mythical beasts, and geometric patterns; other seals have Old Babylonian or Kassite Mesopotamian parallels. Middle Elamite craftsmen were skilled in metalwork, glass, faience, and glazing. A fragmentary monumental stone stele shows Untash-Napirisha and his family in a religious procession. A massive solid bronze statue of Napirisha (although incomplete it weighs 1,750 kg), a serpent offering table, and a religious-offering tableau demonstrate bronze-casting skill.

Fars. In Fars, the regional population declined. On a high point at Malyan, a building whose plan consisted of a rectangular courtyard surrounded by corridors off of which rooms opened, yielded Middle Elamite pottery and accounting tablets dealing with precious metals, food, and animal products. Only Malyan itself has pottery with clear lowland connections. Distinct local ceramic assemblages seem to be at least contemporary with one another, suggesting a fragmentation of local (material) culture. The Qaleh assemblage is related to the earlier Kaftari in forms and decoration. The handmade Shogha assemblage has black-painted decoration on an orange ground, with animal, plant, and geometric motifs. Teimurran pottery is wheelmade, with extremely regular decoration that was probably painted on a turntable.

Luristan. Ceramic distributions suggest a complex cultural situation in Luristan. Elamite goblets and some related forms are found throughout the southern and western valleys. Eastern Luristan was either abandoned or had perhaps shifted to a heavily pastoral economy. Elements of the Iron I–II western gray-ware assemblage characteristic of northwestern Iran (e.g., Hasanlu V–IV), such as button-base goblets, appear in graves in the northern and eastern valleys of Luristan. [See Hasanlu; Grave Goods.] Local traditions, if any, are difficult to identify. The beginnings of the elaborate "Luristan bronze" tradition also appear, probably drawing on the lowland Elamite bronzeworking tradition.

Neo-Elamite Period (1100–500 BCE). Nebuchadrezzar I (1125–1104 BCE) defeated Elam but seems not to have gained long-term control. After a period of historical obscurity, Elam again reemerged as a political refuge for Babylonian opponents of Assyria; at the same time, the Assyrians

were moving into the central western highlands and establishing control along the valleys along the Great Khorasan Road. [See Babylonians; Assyrians.] By the second quarter of the first millennium BCE, Elam was under ever-increasing pressure from all sides: the Assyrians and Babylonians from the west, the Medes and Assyrians in the northern highlands, and the Persians in the southeast. [See Medes; Persians.] From about 750 to 650 BCE, Elam experienced a slow decline during nearly constant political and military conflict with Mesopotamian powers. Finally, in 646 BCE, the Assyrian king Ashurbanipal conquered Khuzistan and sacked Susa. Assyrian palace reliefs provide detailed information on dress, architectural facades, and other aspects of Elamite material culture.

Fragments of Elam, mostly in the highlands, maintained a political identity, but by the mid-sixth century BCE, former Elamite areas had fallen under Achaemenid control. Elam ceased to exist as a power. Under the Achaemenids, the Elamite language continued in use for display inscriptions, such as at Bisitun, and in administrative documents. [See Bisitun.] Although references to Elamites persist into the Hellenistic era, Elam's importance and independent identity had come to an end.

Lowland Elam had been in decline by the beginning of the first millennium BCE. The number of villages decreased, and many Middle Elamite towns were abandoned by about 1000 BCE (cultural developments in the highlands may have played a major role in this). During the second half of the second millennium BCE, many indigenous traditions disappeared as new groups appeared. The changes in the highlands accelerated through the first millennium BCE, sweeping away the past. Susa revived as a regional center by the end of the eighth century BCE. Neo-Elamite architecture shows a strong continuity with the past in location and ornamentation: a small temple on the Acropole had green-glazed bricks, and the pegs attaching glazed frit tiles to the walls bear knobs in the form of animal forequarters, humans, or bull men. Burial practices continued second-millennium BCE practices, including the use of painted clay funerary heads.

Neo-Elamite I pottery (1000–700 BCE) is little known; Neo-Elamite II pottery (700–500 BCE) is simple and demonstrates continuity. This is noteworthy because the Assyrian conquest of Elam and the sack of Susa in 646 BCE had little effect on the ceramic assemblage and other types of artifacts. The second half of the first millennium BCE is poorly known archaeologically.

[See also Mesopotamia, *article on* Ancient Mesopotamia; *and* Persia, *article on* Ancient Persia.]

BIBLIOGRAPHY

Amiet, Pierre. *Glyptique susienne: Des origines à l'époque de Perses-Achéménides.* Mémoires de la Délégation Archéologique en Iran, 43. Paris, 1972. Comprehensive study of Susiana glyptic.
Amiet, Pierre. "Archaeological Discontinuity and Ethnic Duality in

Elam." *Antiquity* 53 (1979): 195–204. Important essay on the low-land-highland dynamic of Elamite history.

Amiet, Pierre. *L'âge des échanges inter-iraniens.* Paris, 1986. Synthesis of interregional connections.

Berghe, Louis Vanden. *Bibliographie analytique de l'archéologie de l'Iran ancien.* Leiden, 1979. This and the two supplements below are an exhaustive bibliographic resource, site by site.

Berghe, Louis Vanden, and E. Haerinck. *Bibliographie analytique de l'archéologie de l'Iran ancien: Supplément 1, 1978–1980.* Leiden, 1981.

Berghe, Louis Vanden, and E. Haerinck. *Bibliographie analytique de l'archéologie de l'Iran ancien: Supplément 2, 1981–1985.* Leiden, 1987.

Cahiers de la Délégation Archéologique Française en Iran. Paris, 1971–. Reports on the French excavations at Susa and other prehistoric Khuzistan sites since 1967.

Carter, Elizabeth, and Matthew W. Stolper. *Elam: Surveys of Political History and Archaeology.* Berkeley, 1984. Essential synthesis of Elamite history and archaeology.

Gasche, Hermann. *La poterie élamite du deuxième millénaire A.C.* Mémoires de la Délégation Archéologique en Iran, 47. Paris, 1973. Second-millennium BCE Elamite pottery corpus from Ghirshman's Ville Royale excavations at Susa.

Harper, Prudence, Oliver, et al., eds. *The Royal City of Susa: Ancient Near Eastern Treasures in the Louvre.* New York, 1992. Catalog from an exhibition at the Metropolitan Museum of Art, New York City, with numerous illustrations, extensive essays on many aspects of Elamite art and culture from Susa, and recent bibliography.

Hinz, Walther, and Heidemarie Koch. *Elamisches Wörterbuch.* Archäologische Mitteilungen aus Iran, vol. 17. Berlin, 1987.

Hole, Frank, ed. *The Archaeology of Western Iran: Settlement and Society from Prehistory to the Islamic Conquest.* Washington, D.C., 1987. Comprehensive survey of development in western Iran, providing the Iranian context of Elam.

LeBrun, Alain, and François Vallat. "L'origine de l'écriture à Suse." *Cahiers de la Délégation Archéologique Française en Iran* 8 (1978): 11–60. Stratigraphic evidence from Susa for the development of writing.

Mémoires de la Délégation en Perse, Mémoires de la Mission Archéologique en Iran, Mémoires de la Délégation Archéologique en Iran (series name changes over time). Paris, 1900–. Reports of the French excavations, primarily at Susa, by Jacques de Morgan, Roland de Mecquenem, and Roman Ghirshman.

Mésopotamie et Elam: Actes de la XXXVème rencontre assyriologique internationale, Gand, 10–14 juillet 1989. Ghent, 1991.

Miroschedji, Pierre de. "Fouilles du chantier Ville Royale II à Suse, 1975–1977, I: Les niveaux Élamites." *Cahiers de la Délégation Archéologique Française en Iran* 12 (1981): 9–136. The first millennium BCE sequence at Susa.

Nicholas, Ilene M. *The Proto-Elamite Settlement at TUV.* Malyan Excavation Reports, vol. 1. Philadelphia, 1990. Report on the area TUV excavation at Malyan.

Pittman, Holly. *The Glazed Steatite Style: The Structure and Function of an Image System in the Administration of Protoliterate Mesopotamia.* Berlin, 1994.

Sumner, William M. "Proto-Elamite Civilization in Fars." In *Gamdat Nasr: Period or Regional Style?*, edited by Uwe Finkbeiner and Wolfgang Röllig, pp. 199–211. Beihefte zum Tübinger Atlas des Vorderen Orients, Reihe B, vol. 62. Wiesbaden, 1986.

Sumner, William M. "Anshan in the Kaftari Phase: Patterns of Settlement and Land Use." In *Archaeologia Iranica et Orientalis: Miscellanea in honorem Louis Vanden Berghe*, edited by Léon De Meyer and E. Haerinck, pp. 135–161. Ghent, 1989.

Vallat, Françoise. *Suse et l'Élam.* Paris, 1980.

Voigt, Mary M., and Robert H. Dyson, Jr. "The Chronology of Iran, ca. 8000–2000 B.C." In *Chronologies in Old World Archaeology,* edited by Robert W. Ehrich, pp. 122–178. 3d ed. Chicago, 1992. Provides

the most detailed synthesis of the archaeological evidence for the fourth and third millennia BCE.

ROBERT C. HENRICKSON

ELEMENTAL ANALYSIS. *See* Neutron Activation Analysis.

ELEPHANTINE (Egyp., 3bw; Aram., Jeb [or Yeb]; Gk., Elephantine; Ar., Geziret-Aswan), the southern frontier town of pharaonic Egypt, situated on an island in the Nile River opposite modern Aswan, whose ancient predecessor it is (24°6′ N, 32°54′ E). The modern remains consist of a tell up to 15 m high about 350 m in diameter.

The first excavations, by missions of the Berlin Museums and the Paris Académie des Inscriptions et Belles Lettres, took place at the beginning of the twentieth century and were primarily aimed at recovering papyri. A comprehensive examination of the city by the German Institute of Archaeology together with the Swiss Institute for Architectural Research, has been underway since 1969; it is allowing the most important features of its history to be determined with increasing accuracy.

The earliest traces of settlement so far determined date to the Middle Naqada period (c. 3500 BCE) and are concentrated on the eastern part of the island, which was at that time still divided into two flood-free granite ridges. The sacred precinct of the antelope goddess Satet, the historical "mistress of the city," which at first consisted of nothing more than a modest brick hut between three towering granite rocks, can be traced at least as far back as the Late Naqada period (c. 3200 BCE). It is, however, unclear whether the inhabitants of the early settlement consisted largely of egyptianized Nubians, whose settlement area then extended to the north, beyond the first cataract, or whether the oldest Elephantine was already an extended outpost of Egypt proper. Its function, at the northern end of the hard-to-navigate cataract region, must have been related primarily to trade with the south.

With the final development of the Egyptian state, the function of state border post was added to that of exchange place; during the course of the first dynasty (c. 3000/2950–2800 BCE), a fortress protected by towers was erected on the highest point of the east island, close to the bank; it was, so far as can be determined, staffed with nonlocal—but certainly Egyptian—forces. A little later, the entire settlement area was also surrounded with a strong brick fortification. From the third/fourth dynasty onward (c. 2600 BCE), the city gained in significance because of increased quarrying of its valuable hard stone, of which the so-called Aswan granite, in particular, remained one of Egypt's most beloved materials for monumental buildings, statues, and stelae throughout the pharaonic period.

With the conquest of Lower Nubia by Sesostris I (c. 1950 BCE) in the early twelfth dynasty, Elephantine, for the first time, lost its function as a frontier town; however, as compensation, it became an even more important administrative and trading center for traffic to the south, beyond the first cataract. The western island, which had served primarily as a cemetery, was increasingly included in the settlement area of the city. Sesostris I had the first stone temple erected to the city goddess Satet; next to it he built a festival court for the celebration of the Nile flood, which, according to Egyptian belief, had its point of origin in Elephantine. At about this time, the ram-headed god of the cataracts, Khnum, also received his own temple in the city. A third sacred precinct that had already developed in the course of the eleventh Dynasty (c. 2050 BCE) was refurbished for the worship of a former governor of Elephantine by the name of Heqaib. In the difficult period during which the Old Kingdom declined, Heqaib apparently distinguished himself, so that he was made the protective saint of the city after his death. Even his successors in the twelfth and thirteenth dynasties (c. 2000–1650 BCE) all erected their own commemorative chapels in his precinct, in addition to their rock-cut tombs on the east side of the Nile; other officials, even from outside Elephantine, dedicated statues and stelae there.

The disintegration of the Egyptian state in the second interregnum (c. 1650–1550 BCE) returned the southern boundary of Egypt to Elephantine for a while. When the kings of the early eighteenth dynasty (c. 1550–1300 BCE) renewed their conquest of Nubia, this time extending beyond the fourth cataract, a new period of prosperity began for the city. Its boundaries expanded once more (they can no longer

be precisely determined under the modern village toward the north). Hatshepsut and Thutmosis III (c. 1490–1440 BCE) had new and larger temples erected to Satet and Khnum; especially the one to Khnum was considerably enlarged during the later eighteenth and the nineteenth/twentieth dynasties (c. 1300–1020 BCE). The two temples, together with their administrative and commercial buildings, occupied almost a third of the city's preserved surface area. It is, therefore, probably no coincidence that at this same time Syene (modern Aswan) made its first appearance in Egyptian texts.

With the beginning of the third interregnum (1080–710 BCE), Nubia's independence, and Egypt's continually erupting internal conflicts, Elephantine's significance must have again been predominantly military. During the Persian occupation of Egypt (525–404 BCE), Elephantine's renewed character as a fortress was most probably not directed solely against possible threats from outside Egypt. The garrison stationed by the Persians, which consisted at least in part of members of the Aramaic/Jewish colony (which had its own temple to Yahweh in Elephantine before the Persian period) points in this direction. Nothing of the Yahweh temple remains, probably as a result of the enlargement of the Khnum temple during the thirtieth dynasty (380–342 BCE); there are, however, probably remains of a number of houses of a non-Egyptian type, from which important papyrus finds relating to early Judaism have been recovered. [See Papyrus.]

With the last native kings of the thirtieth dynasty, another extended period of prosperity began for Elephantine, even though it was soon under Greek and then (from 30 BCE onward) Roman rule. Nectanebo II (360–342 BCE) began a

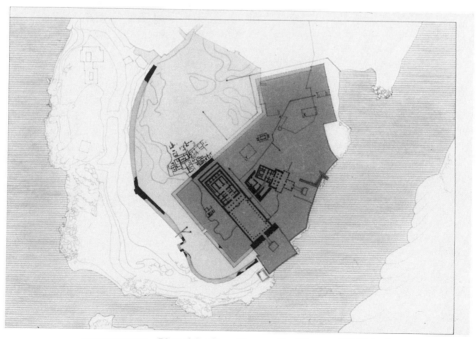

ELEPHANTINE. *Plan of the Greco-Roman city.* (Courtesy W. Kaiser)

large restoration of the Khnum temple. The Ptolemies (305–330 BCE), especially Ptolemy VI and VIII, continued the work, which was finally completed under Augustus with a large riverside terrace. The restoration of the considerably smaller Temple of Satet was begun by Ptolemy VI and was also outfitted with a riverside terrace and a Nilometer. During the Roman period there was additional construction along the bank between the two temple terraces; to the north, at some distance to the Nilometer of the Satet temple, a monumental staircase with a sacred precinct to the Nile was erected at the city's port. Two more temple buildings, whose exact location has not yet been determined, were built inside the sacred area; with its administrative and commercial buildings, this area ultimately occupied almost half of the old area of the city. At the same time, the everyday life of trade and probably also administration shifted more and more to Syene; this helps to explain why, with the triumph of Christianity in the early fourth century CE, Elephantine fell decisively behind modern Aswan. Arabic sources from the early Middle Ages still report a cloister and two churches in Elephantine. Remains of a small church from the early sixth century and the scattered remains of a somewhat later large basilica are preserved. [*See* Churches; Basilica.] However, with the increasing islamization of Egypt, even this last Christian phase in the history of the city did not last long. In the absence of the tell's upper layer, the definitive end of the settlement cannot be determined precisely. It can, however, hardly be later than the tenth or twelfth century.

BIBLIOGRAPHY

Dreyer, Günter. *Der Tempel der Satet*. Elephantine, vol. 8. Mainz, 1986.

Franke, Detlef. *Das Heiligtum des Heqaib auf Elephantine*. Heidelberg, 1994.

Gempeler, Robert D. *Die Keramik römischer bis frühharabischer Zeit*. Elephantine, vol. 10. Mainz, 1992.

Grossmann, Peter. *Kirche und spätantike Hausanlagen im Chnumtempelhof*. Elephantine, vol. 2 Mainz, 1980.

Habachi, Labib. *The Sanctuary of Heqaib*. Elephantine, vol. 4. Mainz, 1985.

Jaritz, Horst. *Die Terrassen vor den Tempeln des Chnum und Satet*. Elephantine, vol. 3. Mainz, 1980.

Jenni, Hanna. *Die Dekoration des Chnumtempels durch Nektanebos II.* Elephantine, vol. 15. Mainz, forthcoming.

Junge, Friedrich. *Funde und Bauteile*. Elephantine, vol. 11. Mainz, 1987.

Kaiser, Werner, et al. "Stadt und Tempel von Elephantine, 21st/22nd Grabungsbericht." *Mitteilungen des Deutschen Archäologischen Instituts Kairo* 51 (1995): 99–187. Includes references to the first twenty excavation reports for the site.

Kraeling, Emil G. *The Brooklyn Museum Aramaic Papyri*. New York, 1953. See especially pages 7–18 for the earlier excavations.

Laskowska-Kusztal, Ewa. *Die Dekorfragmente der späten Tempel*. Elephantine, vol. 14. Mainz, forthcoming.

Pilgrim, C. V. *Grabungen in der Stadt des Mittleren Reiches*. Elephantine, vol. 18. Mainz, forthcoming.

Porten, Bezalel. *Archives from Elephantine: The Life of an Ancient Jewish Military Colony*. Berkeley, 1986.

Ricke, Herbert, and Serge Sauneron. *Die Tempel Nektanebos' II. in El-
ephantine und ihre Erweiterungen*. Cairo, 1960. See especially pages 2–3 for the earlier excavations.

Valbelle, Dominique. *Satis et Anoukis*. Mainz, 1981.

Ziermann, Martin. *Befestigungsanlagen und Stadtentwicklung in der Frühzeit und im frühen Alten Reich*. Elephantine, vol. 16. Mainz, 1993.

WERNER KAISER
Translated from German by Susan I. Schiedel

EMAR (mod. Meskene), site located on the right bank of the Euphrates River in Syria. Today it is submerged under the Tabqa dam, el-Assad lake. Emar/Meskene is situated at the juncture of the region's land and water routes (east–west) and its two main topological features—the steppe, on which the site leans, and a fluvial plain, rich and fertile as a result of irrigation. Farther southeast on the Euphrates are the cities of Tuttul and Mari; to the north is Carchemish and Anatolia; to the west, where transportation to Cyprus and the Mediterranean Sea would have been available, are the cities of Aleppo (Yamḫad), Qatna, and, on the coast, Ugarit; Damascus is to the south; and to reach Canaan it was necessary to go through Hazor. In short, Emar was a vital crossroads for trade, east–west relations, and travel by water to Babylon, Mari, and the lands of the Hittites.

Until 1972, Emar was known only through the archives of Mari, Nuzi, and Ugarit, as their political or commercial partner. The construction of the Tabqa dam where the Euphrates, after leaving the mountains of Anatolia, turns toward Mesopotamia and the Persian Gulf, led to the exploration of Emar/Meskene, directed by Jean-Claude Margueron, under the auspices of the French Commission of Excavations of the Ministry of Foreign Affairs. In six campaigns (1972–1978), archaeological and epigraphic documentation was recovered that opened a new chapter in the history of Late Bronze Age Syria. The city uncovered was not, however, the one mentioned in the Middle Bronze Ebla or Mari texts but a city erected entirely in the Late Bronze Age on a site prepared especially for that purpose. None of the soundings showed any trace of a city earlier than the LB city, which existed only until the beginning of the fourteenth century BCE, when it was violently destroyed—a little after 1187 BCE (Arnaud, 1975).

The contradiction between the texts and the archaeological reality has led investigators to believe that the city of the third and second millennia BCE was actually located several hundred meters away from the excavated city, at the foot of the mound, in the valley itself. Doubtless eroded away by a meander of the Euphrates and close to disappearing in the Late Bronze Age, it would have been reconstructed on the edge of the plateau in order to avoid erosion by the river. The work would have been sponsored by the Hittite king Šuppiluliuma I (1380–1340 BCE), who dominated North Syria at the time, or by his son Muršili II (1339–1306 BCE), to safeguard a vital commercial link. Abandoned after its destruction in 1187, in the first millennium BCE, the site was partly reoccupied in the Roman period by a modest city named Barbalissos. Within the walls of the Byzantine period lay the medieval city of Balis that continued to exist until the end of the Ayyubid period.

The Ebla archives provide evidence that Emar existed in the mid-third millennium—a dynastic alliance facilitated commercial relations between the two cities. At the beginning of the eighteenth century BCE, the archives of Mari show Emar to be a true economic hub, connecting the great Syrian centers (see above). [*See* Ebla Texts; Mari Texts.] The discovery of several hundred texts (a priest's library of private and royal archives) that cover the period of nearly a century and a half from the end of the fourteenth century to 1187 BCE, has permitted the history of the LB city to be written. Emar, then the capital of a Hittite province named Astata, was accountable directly to the kingdom of Carchemish, itself dependent upon Ḥattuša (Boğazköy), the center of the Hittite Empire; a ranking general called the Head of the Chariots represented the central power. The texts are concerned, for the most part, with judicial, legal, and economic matters—the society and its system of relationships based on economics and trade.

It is always risky to link LB tablets to the Bible, even though they shared a cultural domain. The most obvious parallels among LB texts and some of the biblical narratives involve the institution of the family and societal customs—for example, the customs of inheritance and the sale of family property owned by the eldest in the texts from Emar are reminiscent of customs in other patriarchal societies, such as Nuzi and Ugarit. The importance of soothsayers from Babylon and prophets are documented in the Emar texts as is the ordination of priests and priestesses and other rituals that took place during important celebrations.

The LB builders chose an arm of the rocky, rectangular plateau that borders the valley on its southern edge—a mountainous location, not one in the plain or valley, as was the Syrian tradition. They completely altered the topography by creating staggered terraces and cutting an artificial channel or ravine (about 500 m long, 50 m wide, and more than 20 m deep), to create a site whose commanding view of the surrounding area made it easy to defend and convenient for commerce. The residential quarters were built upon that infrastructure. Two were excavated extensively (trenches A and D). The buildings were constructed gradually, as a need evolved. Elsewhere, the plan of the city and its natural and hewn topography suggest that the main gates were located in the middle of the sides of the quadrilateral, about a kilometer to a side. One portion of its rampart was located on the western side of the site, along the artificial ravine. The ruins of a fortress responsible for the defense of Emar, at Tell Faq'us, a site about 10 km (6 mi.) downstream, was excavated by the French team in its last campaign in 1978.

The plans of the thirty or so private houses that were excavated are quite uniform: at ground level a large, rectangular room opens directly onto the street; opposite the entrance are two small rooms of equal size, with separate entrances. The method of construction, the frequent appearance of interior steps, and the traces of charred wood in the debris suggest that this group of rooms was roofed and that another story extended over some, if not all, of them, while a terrace provided an open-air space. This particular architectural plan seems to have been popular on this bank of the Euphrates, in North Syria in general, and sometimes in neighboring regions in the second millennium BCE. Terra-cotta models of houses or temples were found among the ceramic remains during excavation.

The palace belonging to the governor or local "king" who deferred to the overlordship of the Hittite king was uncovered. Installed on the northwest promontory, it dominated both the valley and the port. It takes the form of a *hilani*, the distinctive residence of Iron Age North Syria. The *hilani* is characterized by a facade (see figure 1) with a columned portico leading to a pair of oblong rooms, the second of which here certainly served as a throne room, and upper floor. This is the earliest known example of a *hilani* in Syria. It was provided with additional rooms installed at various levels more than a meter apart on the southern slope of the promontory, which make its plan difficult to understand because of the differences of level of each part of the dependancies of the building (see figure 2). A Hittite origin for this architectural formula seems probable.

Four temples have been excavated. They all belong to the northern long style of temple formed by an elongated room that served as a holy space, with an offering table, a podium for the god, and some furnishings used in carrying out rituals; this room was fronted by a vestibule that opened to the exterior via a porch with columns. Associated with the temple, a large esplanade or raised terrace was equipped with an altar where sacrifices and possibly other rites were practiced.

The principal sanctuary was formed by two temples dedicated to Baal and to Astarte, both situated at the highest point of the site on both sides of a street that led to the sacrificial terrace. A third temple, dedicated to all the gods, was attended by a priest whose reputation had reached the court of the Hittite king; his library and archives constitute one of the most important discoveries at Emar because they explain the progress of divination by observation of animal livers from Mesopotamia toward Anatolia and the classical Mediterranean world. A fourth temple, whose dedicant remains unknown, preserved especially rich furnishings.

The city of Emar never played a particularly important political role, but from the third millennium, as a point of exchange in the relations between Syria and Mesopotamia, it was one of the principal elements in the system that dominated the economic life of the Near East during the Bronze

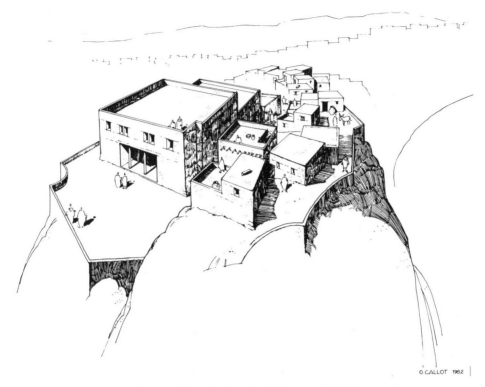

EMAR. Figure 1. *Facade of the ḫilani.* (Courtesy J.-C. Margueron)

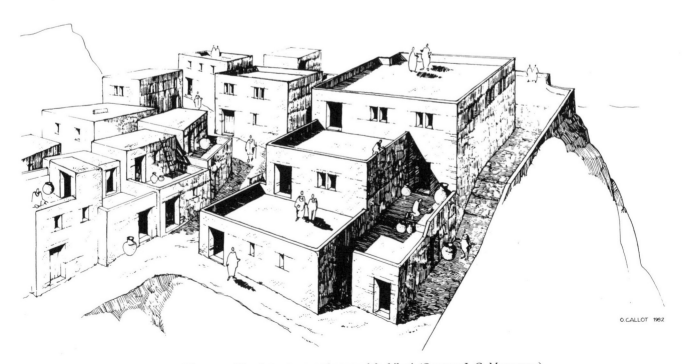

EMAR. Figure 2. *Tiered structures at the rear of the ḫilani.* (Courtesy J.-C. Margueron)

Age. Emar provides a clear idea of the life of a Hittite province at the time of the greatest expansion of the empire, of the organization of the territory, and of the role that this crossroads played in international life.

[*See also* Babylon; Boğazköy; Carchemish; Ebla; Emar Texts; Hittites; Mari; Nuzi; *and* Ugarit.]

BIBLIOGRAPHY

Arnaud, Daniel. "Les textes d'Emar et la chronologie de la fin du Bronze Récent." *Syria* 52 (1975): 87–92.

Arnaud, Daniel. *Emar VI: Textes sumériens et accadiens.* 4 vols. Paris, 1985–1987.

Badre, Leila. *Les figurines anthropomorphes en terre cuite à l'Âge du Bronze en Syrie.* Paris, 1980. Includes some unpublished material on Emar.

Beyer, Dominique, ed. *Meskéné-Emar: Dix ans de travaux, 1972–1982.* Paris, 1982. Succinct presentation of aspects of the city and the finds, with a bibliography of all articles appearing before 1982.

Bunnens, Guy. "Emar on the Euphrates in the Thirteenth Century B.C.: Some Thoughts about Newly Published Cuneiform Texts." *Abr-Nahrain* 27 (1989): 23–36.

Margueron, Jean-Claude. "Les fouilles françaises de Meskéné-Emar (Syrie)." *Comptes Rendus de l'Académie des Inscriptions et Belles-Lettres* (1975): 201–211.

Margueron, Jean-Claude. "Quatres campagnes de fouilles à Emar, 1972–1974." *Syria* 52 (1975): 53–85.

Margueron, Jean-Claude. "Rapport préliminaire sur les deux premières campagnes de fouille à Meskéné-Emar, 1972–1973." *Annales Archéologiques Arabes Syriennes* 25 (1975): 73–86.

Margueron, Jean-Claude. "La campagne de sauvegarde des antiquités de l'Euphrate." *Ktèma* 1 (1976): 63–80.

Margueron, Jean-Claude. "'Maquettes' architecturales de Meskéné-Emar." *Syria* 53 (1976): 193–232.

Margueron, Jean-Claude. "Un exemple d'urbanisme volontaire à l'époque du Bronze Récent en Syrie." *Ktèma* 2 (1977): 33–48.

Margueron, Jean-Claude. "Un 'Hilāni' à Emar." *Annual of the American Schools of Oriental Research* 44 (1979): 153–176.

Margueron, Jean-Claude, ed. *Le Moyen Euphrate, zone de contacts et d'échanges: Acts du colloque de Strasbourg, 10–12 Mars 1977.* Leiden, 1980. Includes articles by Margueron, Daniel Arnaud, Dominique Beyer, and Emmanuel Laroche.

Margueron, Jean-Claude. "Aux marches de l'Empire hittite: Une campagne de fouille à tell Faq'ous (Syrie), citadelle du pays d'Astata." In *La Syrie au Bronze Récent: Recueil publié à l'occasion du cinquantenaire de la découverte d'Ugarit–Ras Shamra,* pp. 47–66. Paris, 1982.

Margueron, Jean-Claude. "Rapport préliminaire sur les 3e, 4e, 5e et 6e campagnes de fouilles à Meskéné-Emar, 1974–1976." *Annales Archéologiques Arabes Syriennes* 32 (1982): 233–249.

Mari: Annales de Recherches Interdisciplinaires 6 (1990). Special issue of the journal entitled "Imâr avant le Bronze Récent," edited by Jean-Marie Durand and Jean-Claude Margueron, including articles by Alfonso Archi, Dominique Beyer, Bernard Geyer, Joannes F. Geyer, Durand, and Margueron.

Tsukimoto, Akio. "Emar and the Old Testament: Preliminary Remarks." *Annual of the Japanese Biblical Institute* 15 (1989): 3–24.

JEAN-CLAUDE MARGUERON and MARCEL SIGRIST
Translated from French by Nancy Leinwand and Monique Fecteau

EMAR TEXTS. Excavations in the mid-1970s at the Syrian site of Meskene (ancient Emar), located at the great bend of the Euphrates River, yielded some eight hundred cuneiform tablets and fragments. Internal evidence shows that the texts date from the end of the fourteenth to the beginning of the twelfth century BCE.

Four languages are represented in the cuneiform script at Meskene. A few texts are Hittite, including a royal letter (there are also seals with hieroglyphic Luwian legends). Several Hurrian texts were also found. Neither the Hittite nor the Hurrian texts have as yet received full publication. Most of the texts are Akkadian and Sumerian and have been published in copy, transliteration, and translation in four large volumes (Arnaud, 1985–1987).

A wide range of genres is represented in the Sumero-Akkadian tablets. There are roughly 150 economic texts (records of deliveries, inventories, lists of sacrifices, lists of personnel, memoranda); 200 contracts (adoptions; antichretic contracts; debt payments; guarantees; inheritance divisions; lawsuits; loans; property exchanges; purchases of fields, houses, orchards, and slaves; ransoms; sales of children, houses, orchards, and slaves; verdicts; wills); and about twenty letters (between nonroyal persons). These texts reveal many details about everyday life in Late Bronze Emar. Texts recording purchases and sales of real estate are normally provided with specific references to the location of the property in question, including mention of the property on all sides; tabulation of this information might well yield a detailed layout of at least some parts of the town.

Many Mesopotamian canonical texts were also discovered at Emar. There are, for example, more than sixty lexical texts and more than one hundred omen texts, in both cases reflecting many of the canonical series; also represented are incantations and rituals. Literary texts are few in number, but include fragments of Gilgamesh (tablets 4 and 6) and of The Tamarisk and the Date Palm. A significant discovery was a wisdom text also known from Ugarit and from Ḫattuša but not yet found in Mesopotamia.

Certainly the most unexpected texts unearthed at Meskene are the roughly two hundred tablets and fragments that describe otherwise unknown festivals and rituals, shedding much new light on Late Bronze Syrian religious practices. The festival texts include lengthy descriptions of the installation ceremonies of the priestess of the storm god and a priestess called a *maš'artu,* and of festivals called *kissu* ("throne"?) and *zukru* ("commemoration"?); the level of detail presented in these documents is quite unprecedented. Other types of local religious texts are annual and monthly liturgies, offering lists, and rituals for Anatolian deities (Fleming, 1992).

Besides the texts edited in Arnaud (1985–1987), several hundred tablets from the immediate vicinity of Emar have also been published in the last decade (see, e.g., Arnaud, 1987, 1991; Beckman, 1988; Dalley and Teissier, 1992; Huehnergard, 1983; Tsukimoto, 1988, 1990, 1991, 1992). The majority of these are economic and legal texts.

The Akkadian texts that were not copied from Mesopotamian originals betray in their grammar the fact that they were written by scribes whose native language was not Akkadian. Like contemporary Akkadian texts from Ugarit, Alalakh, and el-Amarna, these texts frequently betray elements of the scribes' own tongues. The most obvious of these elements are the large number of unusual words found in the Emar texts, some of which, at least, appear to derive from a Northwest Semitic language. In the legal and economic texts and in the letters, too, most of the names of the local Emarites are Northwest Semitic.

[*See also* Akkadian; *and* Emar.]

BIBLIOGRAPHY

Arnaud, Daniel. "Les textes d'Emar et la chronologie de la fin du Bronze récent." *Syria* 52 (1975): 87–92. On dating the Meskene text finds.

Arnaud, Daniel. *Emar VI.* 4 vols. Paris, 1985–1987. Official publication of the tablets found during the French excavations in the 1970s.

Arnaud, Daniel. "La Syrie du moyen-Euphrate sous le protectoral hittite: Contrats de droit privé." *Aula Orientalis* 5 (1987): 211–241. An edition of seventeen texts.

Arnaud, Daniel. *Textes syriens de l'âge du Bronze récent.* Aula Orientalis Supplementa, 1. Barcelona, 1991. An edition of 197 texts.

Beckman, Gary. "Three Tablets from the Vicinity of Emar." *Journal of Cuneiform Studies* 40 (1988): 61–68.

Dalley, Stephanie, and Beatrice Teissier. "Tablets from the Vicinity of Emar and Elsewhere." *Iraq* 54 (1992): 83–111.

Fleming, Daniel. *The Installation of Baal's High Priestess at Emar: A Window on Ancient Syrian Religion.* Harvard Semitic Studies, 42. Atlanta, 1992. In-depth study of one of the longest local festival texts and a discussion of its cultural context.

Huehnergard, John. "Five Tablets from the Vicinity of Emar." *Revue d'Assyriologie* 77 (1983): 11–43. Five texts and a summary of the grammatical features of Emar Akkadian.

Tsukimoto, Akio. "Sieben spätbronzezeitliche Urkunden aus Syrien." *Acta Sumerologica Japan* 10 (1988): 153–189. Publication of texts from Emar and vicinity.

Tsukimoto, Akio. "Akkadian Tablets in the Hirayama Collection." *Acta Sumerologica Japan* 12 (1990): 177–259; 13 (1991): 275–333; 14 (1992): 289–310. Publication of texts from Emar and vicinity.

Wilcke, Claus. "Die Emar-Version von 'Dattelpalme und Tamariske': Ein Rekonstruktionsversuch." *Zeitschrift für Assyriologie* 79 (1989): 161–190. Detailed consideration of one of the Mesopotamian literary texts found at Meskene.

JOHN HUEHNERGARD

EMMAUS, important market town and spa in the Judean piedmont, halfway between Jaffa and Jerusalem (31°50′ N, 34°57′ E; map reference 1494 × 1388). Its Greek name derives from Hamath or Hamta ("hot springs"; *Ecclesiastes Rabbah* 106b). Granted a town charter by Elagabalus in about 230 CE, it took the name *Nicopolis-Antoninopolis.*

Emmaus's strategic location made it the site of many battles, from Joshua's Ayalon valley campaign to the British general Allenby's campaign in 1917 CE and beyond. The site is first mentioned in *1 Maccabees* 3:40 as the site of Judas's great victory in 166 BCE over the Seleucids, and it was sub-

sequently the capital of a Herodian toparchy. As an outpost opposite the mainly pagan plains, during the Second Temple period it acquired its character as a center of religious fervor and, at times, of armed militancy. Gaius Cassius sold Emmaus's inhabitants into slavery. Following Herod's death, Athronges led his rebellion against Rome from Emmaus and was crushed there by Varus, then governor of Syria. During the Jewish War of Vespasian and Titus, the Fifth Legion was based at Emmaus, and in Bar Kokhba's time, the Twelfth Legion may have been annihilated nearby (*Ekhah Rabbah* 2.4.22a). The literary and archaeological evidence points to Judean-Samaritan and later also to Christian coexistence in Emmaus. The site's epigraphic material consists of tombstones of soldiers of the Fifth Macedonian Legion (first–second centuries CE) and inscriptions on lintels from a Samaritan synagogue and from the mosaic floors in a fifth-century church (see below).

Emmaus has been identified, but not later than by Eusebius (*Onomasticon* 90.16), with the locality of Christ's revelation to his disciples in the aftermath of the crucifixion (*Lk.* 24). One of the major Byzantine basilicas in the Holy Land was erected there and refurbished by the Crusaders in the twelfth century. The identification with the Emmaus in *Luke* rests on the preference of the fourth-century Codex Sinaiticus, Palestinian Syriac (based on sundry Greek translations and the Peshitta), and other fifth–sixth-century texts, which quote 160 stadia as its distance from Jerusalem, against the 60 stadia given by various Latin, Greek, and other sources commencing with the fourth-century Codex Vaticanus. These encouraged rival identifications, up until the Crusader period: al-Qubaibah (map reference 1631 × 1386), Qaloniye (map reference 1656 × 1338), or Abu Ghosh (map reference 1604 × 1349).

Villa and Churches. The oldest remains recovered beneath the site's two Byzantine churches were of a fourth–fifth-century CE building, possibly a *villa rustica.* The older (?), fifth-century church was an elongated basilica (18 × 10 m), divided by two rows of six columns each into a nave and two aisles, with a triple entrance. Its mosaic floors were decorated with guilloches and floral, bird, and animal designs. It was probably joined with the large sixth-century basilica to its right (but cf. Avi-Yonah, 1976). The basilica (46.4 × 24.4 m) was constructed of very large, smooth ashlar blocks. Two rows of thirteen columns formed its broad nave and narrow aisles. On its exterior, the central apse was trapezoidal. The side apses are preserved up to and including their exquisite hemispherical ashlar vaulting. A smaller Romanesque Crusader church incorporated the nave and central apse of the destroyed Byzantine basilica, adding to the size of its hall (23 × 10.25 m) with a vault carried on four pointed arches that rested on a solid buttressed wall.

Bathhouse. The third-century thermae belong to monoaxial bathhouses, all of whose installations are arranged adjacent to each other on a straight line. Parts of the building collapsed during one of the earthquakes recorded for the fourth–fifth centuries. The surviving structure was partly buried to its roof by a subsequent landslide, which explains its state of preservation. The thermae were built of smooth and well-fitting ashlars. The walls measured between 1 and 1.5 m. The extent of the refurbished part is 14 × 7.5 m. After the refurbishing, the entrance was through the former tepidarium, which had been converted into a frigidarium. Passage was then available into a former caldarium, then the tepidarium; the second adjoining caldarium retained its function. The sweat chamber was built over the boiler room on the west. Another room preserved an entire original stone cupola, constructed of four hemispherical segments that leaned against each other, leaving an air-regulation aperture in its apex (cf. Vitruvius 5.10.5).

Two other rooms contained two apses each in opposing walls. Each has a barrel-vaulted roof constructed of tiles and rubble cement, respectively. The former is of Byzantine and the latter of Ottoman date. The original ashlar vaults caved in at the same time the rest of the building collapsed. Some of the pottery pipes are preserved that heated the wall of the *suspensura*. The latter was composed of an upper floor constructed of marble slabs on cement that, in turn, had been spread on large tiles resting on rows of brick arches (cf. Vitruvius 5.10.2). These combined resilience, so important in this earthquake-prone region, with good air circulation. Three interconnected tanks provided, one each, cold, tepid, and hot water (cf. Vitruvius 5.10.1).

Yizhar Hirschfeld (1989) traced two parallel aqueducts for 1.5 km from ʿEin Eqed to the town. Their method of construction changed from subterranean tunnels to rock-cut or stone-built channels. The tunnel has an inspection chamber with a pointed Byzantine-period (?) arch.

[*See also* Aqueducts.]

BIBLIOGRAPHY

For the identification of Emmaus, see the bibliography collected in Yoram Tsafrir et al., *Tabula Imperii Romani: Iudaea-Palaestina*, p. 105 (Jerusalem, 1994).

Churches

Vincent, L.-H., and Félix-Marie Abel. *Emmaüs, sa basilique et son histoire*. Paris, 1932. Comprehensive excavation report and historical discussion, although it lacks clear stratigraphic data and the chronological conclusions are suspect.
Vincent, L.-H. "Chronique: Autour du groupe monumental d'ʿAmwas." *Revue Biblique* 45 (1936): 403–415.
Vincent, L.-H. "La chronologie du groupe monumental d'ʿAmwas." *Revue Biblique* 55 (1948): 348–375.

The following items are critical discussions of the findings and dating of Vincent and Abel.
Avi-Yonah, Michael. "Emmaus." In *Encyclopedia of Archaeological Excavations in the Holy Land*, vol. 2, pp. 362–364. Jerusalem and Englewood Cliffs, N.J., 1976. In this critical evaluation of the relative dating of the two basilicas (repeated in the 1993 Hebrew edition), Avi-Yonah proposes to predate the larger basilica to the smaller one.

The typological reasons are unclear as well as the proposed relationship of the supposedly coexisting edifices.
Bagatti, Bellarmino. *I monumenti di Emmaus et Qubeibeh e dei dintorni*. 2 vols. Jerusalem, 1947.
Chen, Doron. "On the Golden Gate in Jerusalem and the Baptistry at Emmaus-Nicopolis." *Zeitschrift des Deutschen Palästina-Vereins* 97 (1981): 171–177. Examination of the baptistry and its dating to the fourth century CE as terminus a quo.
Crowfoot, J. W. "Emmaüs: Sa basilique et son histoire. Reviews." *Palestine Exploration Fund Quarterly* 70 (1935): 40–47.
Crowfoot, J. W. *Early Churches in Palestine*. London, 1941. See pages 71, 125, and 145.
Finegan, Jack. *The Archeology of the New Testament: The Life of Jesus and the Beginning of the Early Church*. Princeton, 1969.
Ovadiah, Asher. *Corpus of the Byzantine Churches in the Holy Land*. Bonn, 1970. Proposes the most logical reconstruction of the eastern basilica, including the baptistery (see pp. 63–65, fig. 54).

Thermae and Aqueducts

Gichon, Mordechai. "Roman Bath-Houses in Eretz Israel" (in Hebrew). *Qadmoniot* 11 (1978): 22–35. The ʿEin-Boqeq thermae and their typology within the framework of bathhouses discovered in Israel.
Gichon, Mordechai. "The Roman Bath at Emmaus: Excavations 1977." *Israel Exploration Journal* 29 (1979): 101–110.
Gichon, Mordechai, and Robert Linden. "Muslim Oil Lamps from Emmaus." *Israel Exploration Journal* 34 (1984): 156–169. Examination of the conch-shaped, open oil lamp, a continuing Iron Age tradition.
Gichon, Mordechai. "The Bath-House at Emmaus." *Bulletin of the Anglo-Israel Archaeological Society* 6 (1986–1987): 54–57.
Hirschfeld, Yizhar. "The Aqueducts of Emmaus-Nicopolis." In *The Aqueducts of Ancient Palestine* (in Hebrew), edited by David ʿAmit et al., pp. 197–204. Jerusalem, 1989. Includes a discussion of the early pointed arch of the inspection chamber in one of the aqueduct's tunnels.

MORDECHAI GICHON

EN _____. *For toponyms beginning with this element, see under* ʿEin-.

ENKOMI, site in Cyprus (35°10′ N, 33°53′ E), named after the village located 1 km (.6 mi.) to the east. It extends some 46 km (29 mi.) east of Nicosia, 8 km (5 mi.) northwest of Famagusta, and 3 km (2 mi.) southwest of Salamis on ground that slopes gently from east to west, from the foot of a low cliff down to the bed of the river Pediaios. In antiquity, the estuary of the river probably reached inland as far as Enkomi and sheltered its harbor.

Official excavations started in 1896 with the British Museum Expedition, which was led by A. S. Murray. Numerous campaigns followed: Sir John Myres and Menelaos Markides in 1913, on behalf of the Cyprus Museum Committee; Rupert Gunnis in 1927; the Swedish Cyprus Expedition (SCE) under Einar Gjerstad and Erik Sjöqvist in 1930; Claude F.-A. Schaeffer in 1934; and a French expedition, led by Schaeffer from 1946 to 1970, later by

Olivier Pelon from 1971 to 1973. From 1948 to 1958, a Cypriot team directed by Porphyrios Dikaios joined the French expedition. The Cypriots worked on their own and in separate areas. The 1974 war put an end to field research. [*See the biographies of Myres, Gjerstad, Schaeffer, and Dikaios.*]

The first excavators considered Enkomi as a Bronze Age necropolis of an unknown settlement. They dug through the upper archaeological layers, taking no notice of them or regarding them as medieval. The British Museum pioneer excavations yielded some of the most impressive objects ever found in Enkomi, such as an ivory game box with relief decoration, a bronze cultic stand, ivory mirror handles, and a large Egyptian necklace of gold with paste inlay. The publication (Murray, 1900) made Enkomi a major site for the Cypriot Late Bronze Age. The Swedish expedition published twenty-two tombs (Sjöqvist, 1934, 1940). Careful study of the stratification in each tomb provided new firm ground for the relative and absolute chronology of the Late Bronze Age. In 1934, Schaeffer soon realized that the walls he had encountered while digging for tombs belonged to the Bronze Age. He laid bare a building made of ashlar (dressed) masonry with a hoard of bronze objects (the so-called Maison des Bronzes).

The way was open for the exploration of the ancient town of Enkomi. Its equation with Alashiya, the capital of the kingdom of Alashiya, was proposed by Dussaud and by Schaeffer. It is generally rejected, but final decision must await new textual evidence. Some significant points in the chronology of Enkomi have not yet been settled. Schaeffer's and Dikaios's stratigraphies cannot be precisely correlated. For simplicity's sake, a division into three phases is used here, corresponding roughly to the traditional partition of the Late Cypriot Bronze Age: I (c. 1600–1450/1400 BCE), II (1450/1400–c. 1200), III (c. 1200–1050).

Phase I (c. 1600–1450/1400) has been studied extensively only by Dikaios. In his Area III (and grid area 1W, see below), at the northern limit of the town, Dikaios uncovered a long rectangular building that he understood to be a fortress, in which he identified a metallurgical workshop. In Area I (4W), near the center of the settlement, were small houses. The destruction of this phase is ascribed to an earthquake. Two exceptional built tombs, irregular *tholoi* (beehive-shaped tombs), can be dated to phase I (SCE tomb 21, probably in 6W) and to early phase II (French tomb at point 1336, in 5E).

Phase II (1450/1400–c. 1200) eventually saw a radical development in the urban organization of Enkomi from an open, loosely occupied town to a fortified, dense, and strictly planned city, and a boom in metallurgical activity. According to Dikaios, this boom was caused by Mycenaean settlers during phase II, but the geometrical town plan, the final construction of the rampart, and the introduction of ashlar masonry all belong to the beginning of phase III, after a destruction and the arrival of newcomers related to the so-

called Sea Peoples, with a strong Mycenaean element among them. For Schaeffer, the changes date back to a time well before the end of the thirteenth century and belong to phase II. Recent discoveries (ashlar masonry of the thirteenth century at Kition and Kalavasos, for example) have in the main confirmed Schaffer's reconstruction. [*See Kition; Kalavasos.*]

The city wall encloses a roughly semicircular area, some 406 m (1,332 ft.) north–south and 350 m (1,148 ft.) east–west. Basically, it consists of an inner wall with an upper part of mud bricks and of an outer strengthening of very large, minimally hewn rocks. It is in places protected by small bastions. A northern and a western gate have been found.

The town is divided by one north–south street and ten east–west streets into large rectangular blocks, which measure approximately 33 × 170 m (108 × 558 ft.) numbered 1W to 12W and 1E to 12E, starting from the north. This geometrical grid was in use until the final destruction. A paved square (from the beginning of phase III in its present state) marks the center of the city.

In grid area 6E is a rectangular tripartite construction of large ashlar masonry, probably a temple. A square base supports a pillar with a stepped capital, a type also known from Kition, Palaipaphos, and other Cypriot sites. Along street 5, in grid area 5W, extends Building 18, named after Swedish Tomb 18 discovered by the Swedish Cyprus Expedition (see figure 1). It was erected around the middle of the thirteenth century BCE, apparently as a residence for a wealthy leader, the earliest indication of a political authority in the city. The facade, nearly 40 m (131 ft.) long with four wide doors, is partly made of blocks of ashlar masonry, one of them no less than 3 m (10 ft.) long. This technique, although reminiscent of Ugarit, is used here in a way peculiar to Cyprus. The central part of the building recalls Building X at Kalavasos, near Limassol. Four chamber tombs of ashlar masonry of the fourteenth and thirteenth centuries in areas 3E and 4E may indicate that some aristocratic families from Ugarit had settled in Enkomi.

During phase II there is a great increase in industrial production, exchanges, and prosperity. The funerary furniture becomes very rich with a wealth of imported Mycenaean pottery. Many copper smelting and working places are attested, especially in area 1W. At the beginning of phase III (c. 1200–1050) although Building 18 had lost its aristocratic character, a large residence of ashlar masonry was built in area 4W. It comprised a series of three communicating spaces, one of them with a central hearth, a feature equated by Dikaios (1969–1971, p. 187) with the Mycenaean "megaron." The whole settlement was destroyed by a violent fire, ascribed to the Sea Peoples around 1190 BCE.

Activity and wealth, again based on metallurgy, were rapidly restored. Nevertheless the dwellings are usually smaller than in phase II. Profound cultural changes are noticeable in the funerary customs. Shaft graves supersede rock-cut chamber tombs. Judging by the small number of *intra muros* inhumations, most of the dead were buried outside the settlement. The bulk of the local painted pottery now reflects Mycenaean tradition.

The sanctuaries of the "horned god" and the "ingot god" are of particular interest. The rituals for both deities show great similarities—libations and offerings of bucrania (oxen skulls)—that reflect Aegean, Near Eastern, and local tradition.

The sanctuary of the horned god occupied the profoundly remodeled residence in area 4W. Oxen skulls and other offerings lay on the floors. The cult statue was set in the southernmost part of the former megaron where 276 one-handled libation bowls have been found. The bronze figure, 55 cm high, shows a young athletic god wearing a short kilt and a curly cap from which two ox horns emerge. The attitude is static, the right hand extended with its palm facing downwards. The god has been tentatively described as an archaic Apollo, a protector of the cattle. A space was also dedicated to a female deity, represented by a tiny bronze figurine with a headdress resembling that of the Egyptian goddess Hathor.

The sanctuary of the ingot god, in area 5E, is quite different in its layout. Its main feature is a large rectangular, partly covered hall. West of it, nearly 250 fragments of clay figurines have been collected. They were originally standing in circles on disk-shaped bases, clearly an Aegean tradition.

In the hall are a hearth and a sacrificial altar. Benches run along the walls; on or near them have been found most of the offerings, such as oxen and fallow-deer skulls, possibly used as ceremonial masks, notched animal shoulder-blades, libation bowls, and two large painted clay figurines of double-headed sphinxes (see figure 2). The 35-centimeter-high bronze cult statue found in a small room arranged in the northeast corner of the hall is that of an oriental smiting god standing on an ingot in the shape of an oxhide. It is a base added to characterize the deity as a protector of metallurgy. A figurine of a goddess standing on an ingot, probably from Enkomi, is now in the Ashmolean Museum, Oxford.

At the end of the twelfth century, Enkomi suffered new destruction, possibly by an earthquake. A vivid revival ended with a final destruction before 1050. Part of the population probably moved to Salamis. [*See* Salamis.]

This description of the excavation can convey but a faint idea of Enkomi's contribution to the study of Cyprus in the Late Bronze Age, on matters such as the presence and role of the Aegeans, the transition to the Iron Age, the problem of the Sea Peoples, and the religion. The material (pottery, jewelry, ivories, faience, stone vases, and cylinder and stamp seals) illustrates how Cyprus, in close contact with Egypt, the Aegean, and the Asiatic Near East, took part in the elaboration of the aristocratic international culture of the Eastern Mediterranean Late Bronze Age. Worthy of mention are the funerary gold "mouthpieces" with stamped decoration, the silver bowl with gold and niello bull heads, faience goblets

ENKOMI. Figure 1. *The southern facade of building 18, along east-west street no.* 5. Looking east-northeast, during 1950 excavation. (Archives CFA Schaeffer, Paris)

ENKOMI. Figure 2. *Front view of a painted terra-cotta double-headed "sphinx" or "centaur."* Found in the sanctuary of the ingot god. Height, 31 cm. (Archives CFA Schaeffer, Paris)

in the shape of a woman's or an animal's head. Metallurgy is illustrated by a great variety of bronze tools, weapons (swords of the Nenzingen type), armor (bronze greaves of SCE Tomb 18), figurines (seated drinking deities, cult-chariot), molds, and copper oxhide ingots (the main export of Cyprus, a symbol of richness and power). Iron appears in phase III. Cuneiform archives are missing as yet, but a wealth of information may be hidden in the undeciphered Cypro-Minoan texts.

BIBLIOGRAPHY

Courtois, Jacques-Claude. *Alasia*, vol. 2, *Les tombes d'Enkomi: Le mobilier funéraire (fouilles C. F. A. Schaeffer, 1947–1965)*; vol. 3, *Les objets des niveaux stratifiés d'Enkomi (fouilles C. F. A. Schaeffer, 1947–1970)*. Paris, 1981–1984.
Courtois, Jacques-Claude, Jacques Lagarce, and Elisabeth Lagarce. *Enkomi et le Bronze récent à Chypre*. Nicosia, 1986.
Courtois, Jacques-Claude, and J. M. Webb. *Mission archéologique française d'Alasia: Les cylindres-sceaux d'Enkomi (fouilles françaises, 1957–1970)*. Nicosia, 1987.
Dikaios, Porphyrios. *Enkomi: Excavations, 1948–1958*. 3 vols. Mainz, 1969–1971.
Dussaud, René. In *Comptes rendus de l'Académie des inscriptions et belles-lettres*, January–March, 1949, p. 20.
Lagarce, Jacques, and Elisabeth Lagarce. *Alasia*, vol. 4, *Deux tombes du Chypriote récent d'Enkomi (Chypre): Tombes 1851 et 1907*. Paris, 1985.
Murray, A. S. In "Excavations at Enkomi, 1896." In *Excavations in Cyprus*, by A. S. Murray et al., pp. 1–54. London, 1900.
Schaeffer, Claude F.-A. *Missions en Chypre, 1932–1935*. Paris, 1936.
Schaeffer, Claude F.-A. "Note sur l'enceinte mycénienne d'Enkomi (Chypre)." In *Mélanges d'archéologie et d'histoire offerts á Charles Picard á l'occasion de son 65e anniversaire*. Vol. 2, pp. 926–935. Paris, 1949.
Schaeffer, Claude F.-A. *Enkomi-Alasia: Nouvelles missions en Chypre, 1946–1950*. Paris, 1952.
Schaeffer, Claude F.-A., et al. *Alasia*. Vol. 1. Paris and Leiden, 1971.
Schaeffer, Claude F.-A. *Corpus des cylindres-sceaux de Ras Shamra-Ugarit et d'Enkomi-Alasia*. Vol. 1. Paris, 1983.
Sjöqvist, Erik. "Enkomi, the Necropolis." In *The Swedish Cyprus Expedition: Finds and Results of the Excavations in Cyprus, 1927–1931*, vol. 1, by Einar Gjerstad et al., pp. 467–575. Stockholm, 1934.
Sjöqvist, Erik. *Reports on Excavations in Cyprus*. Stockholm, 1940.

JACQUES LAGARCE

ENTERTAINMENT. *See* Games; Stadiums; Theaters.

ENVIRONMENTAL ARCHAEOLOGY. Interest in what is now called environmental archaeology was probably stimulated by the long-discredited views of Ellsworth Huntington, who, in the first decade of the century, proposed that climatic change had played a major role in the rise and fall of civilizations in the Near East. For example, he claimed that purported desiccation in early postglacial times had forced people to congregate in river valleys, where they began to domesticate plants and animals. Similarly, he believed that the abandonment and desertification of Palestine in the Late Byzantine period were a result of desiccation, just as he claimed periodic nomadic eruptions from Central Asia could be explained by climate. Climate became the engine of history and with it, "environmental determinism" took root.

The Huntington legacy was insidious. Despite repeated and effective refutation, some scholars continue to explain archaeological displacements or sociopolitical discontinuities by "climatic change." Recently, climatic change was linked to the Aegean dark age and the "Peoples of the Sea" (after 1225 BCE), as well as to the fall of the Akkadian Empire and synchronous political collapse in adjacent regions (c. 2200 BCE). On the other hand, there has also been to exploring flexible environmental constraints on particular economic activities and the possible complementary role of adverse environmental trends in more complex, systemic crises.

In 1925, the British archaeologist Gertrude Caton-Thompson invited a geologist, Elinor Gardner, to assist her with prehistoric projects in the Faiyum and Khargah oases in Egypt. [*See* Faiyum; *and the biography of Caton-Thompson*.] Gardner helped to tie various archaeological sites into specific landscapes, both temporal and spatial, by establishing a succession of environmental changes. Thus, a site was contemporary with a particular lakeshore or spring deposit, which provided a relative date as well as a unique environmental setting (Caton-Thompson and Gardner, 1934). This was achieved by interpreting the conditions of geological formation, relating them to other features in stratigraphic terms, and using associated molluscan collections to amplify or confirm ecological inferences. This prototype of multidisciplinary fieldwork was also pioneered elsewhere. It did not become an instant success in the Near East but received significant impetus in the 1950s through the efforts of Robert J. Braidwood. Frustrated by the difficulty of analyzing agricultural origins, Braidwood collaborated with a geologist and brought in a zoologist to study animal bones (to determine whether potential livestock were domesticated), a paleobotanist to study seed grains, and eventually a palynologist to identify the pollens in cores drilled into nearby lake or marsh beds (to provide a detailed and often continuous record of vegetation change). He also worked with a ceramicist (to examine pottery-making techniques and identify clay sources) and an ethnographer (to observe village life in remote areas and provide analog information on a broader range of material culture and its social replication) (Braidwood and Howe, 1960).

The numbers and specializations of collaborating environmental scientists and their opportunities to influence excavation strategies and publications continues to vary. Increasingly, environmental archaeologists seek independent funding: much of the information now available for the Near East, mainly for the Paleolithic and Neolithic periods, was generated independently. Environmental archaeology is still all too rarely applied to historical time periods, such as at Bronze and Iron Age settlements.

Environmental archaeology can be categorized at different operational and conceptual levels. Paleoenvironmental studies are the most common, and have direct and indirect applications to archaeology—primarily as background information for local or regional settlement histories (Brice, 1978; Bintliff and van Zeist, 1982). Such macroscale research is complemented by site-specific studies that document local geographies and settings (with reference to patterns of topography, soils, and vegetation) or directly address site-formation processes (geoarchaeology) or site economies (zooarchaeology and archaeobotany) (Butzer, 1982, 1960, 1959). Finally, a number of regional or local studies also explicitly address such broad issues as subsistence and settlement patterns and resource opportunities, utilization, and management (Butzer, 1981, 1976; Larsen, 1983). At whatever scale, the work emphasizes the complex interdependence of multiple variables, the role of feedback—positive (change enhancing) or negative (change buffering)—shifting equilibrium levels, and the impact of human land use on environment.

Agricultural Origins in Western Asia (c. 10,000 BP). One old and tenacious explanation of agricultural origins is known as the oasis-propinquity theory. It holds that the initial domestication of plants and animals was the result of

climatic stress. It is based on the incorrect assumption that glacial-age climate in the Near East was wetter than today and became markedly drier at the beginning of the Holocene or Recent period, in about 10,000 BP. Hunter-gatherers would have been faced with declining game resources and plant foods, as forests were reduced to dry scrub and grasslands to sparse steppe. Confronted with ever-scarcer surface water, people and game would have gravitated to reliable sources of water along more richly vegetated riverine lowlands or scattered oases. There, the enforced proximity of hunter-gatherers with game and residual plant foods should have favored a symbiosis that brought the domestication of plants and animals.

Numerous pollen and geological studies provide a very different picture: glacial-age climates were harsh in the Near East and Mediterranean basin; forests were very rare (widely spaced trees were found mainly at intermediate elevations), with steppic grasslands in what are now subhumid environments, particularly on south-facing slopes in hill country; rivers were more seasonal; and oases were few. Archaeological investigations in northeast Africa show human settlement limited to the Nile Valley (c. 20,000–10,000 BP), with no traces of habitation in the Saharan oases. At the beginning of the Holocene, Saharan climate became moister for several millennia; however, in the highland belt, from Greece and Anatolia to Syria-Palestine and the Zagros ranges, forest recolonization was slow, taking up to fifteen hundred years in the west and more than four thousand years in the east (Bintliff and van Zeist, 1982; van Zeist and Bottema, 1991).

Thus, the hill country of Southwest Asia, where the critical steps to early domestication were taken between perhaps 12,000 and 8000 BP, was overwhelmingly open and grassy. This matches the habitat preferences of the earliest plant domesticates—barley and wheat—which cannot compete in closed woodlands, as well as the first animals to be domesticated—goat and sheep—both adapted to open environments. [See Cereals; Sheep and Goats.] If anything, initial domestication of these key plants and animals was facilitated by their wider distribution and greater abundance. This allowed intensive collecting or hunting of the wild forms, and presumably also initial manipulation and experimentation, over a vast area of open, hilly environments (Butzer, 1990, 1982).

Agricultural expansion into the riverine floodplains of western Asia was in fact delayed by several millennia, until agricultural communities first settled the woodlands of the western Mediterranean and central Europe. While forests gradually recolonized the hill country of western Asia, marginalizing that environment, it is more probable that demographic expansion led to agricultural colonization farther afield. After all, woodlands along the Mediterranean coastlines and deep inside Europe were being occupied, implying that people had acquired skills for clearing forests by fire or by stripping leaves from tree branches to reduce the canopy.

Settlement of riverine floodplains demanded similar skills because the areas were partly wooded and required accommodation to periodic flooding.

Between 7900 and 7300 BP (end of the Pre-Pottery Neolithic B) a crisis occurred in the agricultural development of much of the Fertile Crescent. For a time there is very little archaeological visibility, suggesting settlement retraction. When sites reappeared in quantity, there seems to have been an adaptive change between a previously flexible mix of hunting-gathering and herding-farming to a more standardized form of primarily agricultural settlement. Mobility also seems to have been reduced. A climatic crisis is commonly assumed during the intervening centuries, but a fundamental social transformation can be posited: increasing population may have led to greater competition for and pressures on limited resources. On the desert margins of Transjordan, for example, excessive exploitation of trees had previously destroyed the open oak woodlands.

The question of agricultural origins in Southwest Asia illustrates the importance of investigating the changing environment as a context for socioeconomic transformation. Synthesis of a wide range of paloenvironmental information provides insights in systemic terms. The global perspective of independent agricultural origins in other parts of the world, in a broadly similar time range but with distinctive domesticates and in radically different environments, suggests that the evolutionary trajectory of that larger system was related to the dynamism of human culture, not to environmental change.

Desert Adaptations in the Eastern Sahara (c. 9000–4500 BP). In about 9000 BP there is evidence of increasing rainfall, rising water tables, and the formation of numerous ephemeral or semipermanent lakes in the lowlands of the Sahara. There also is higher archaeological visibility after more than twenty millennia. The greater moisture persisted, with fluctuations, and, during the next forty-five hundred years or so, several peoples left a discontinuous settlement record across much of that great desert.

There is a good possibility that the southern margins of the Sahara were an independent center of agricultural innovation; pottery making is verified there by 9000 BP, some fifteen hundred years earlier than in Syria-Palestine. African sorghum and millet were grown in a small, south Egyptian oasis in 8000 BP, with a clear morphological indication that the sorghum was in the process of domestication (Wasylikowa et al., 1993). By then, cattle bones are sufficiently common to suggest domestication, a millennium or more before the appearance of domesticated sheep/goat of western Asian origin: sheep or goats suitable for domestication were not found in Africa, but the wild progenitors of cattle were long indigenous to the Egyptian Nile Valley. [See Cattle and Oxen.] Yet, throughout this period, until 6500 BP in Egypt and 4700 BP in central Sudan, archaeology shows that occupation was limited to hunters, fishers, and gatherers. [See Hunting; Fishing.]

Climatic amelioration in the Sahara toward 9000 BP created new but modest opportunities for a mobile and precarious subsistence by hunters and fishers, following a number of different trails between waterholes, marshes, and small lakes. The geoarchaeology at several such oases indicates that there was little lag between improving ecological conditions and initial colonization efforts; furthermore, maximum archaeological visibility matches optimal water availability. Final abandonment of a deteriorating location appears to have been delayed, perhaps as people tried to find solutions to growing resource scarcity.

Groups occupying the rich riverine environments along the Nile remained "conservative" in their subsistence pursuits, despite their adoption of pottery and their inevitable awareness of alternative subsistence strategies, such as herding and cultivation (Butzer, 1982). Presumably, fishing, hunting, and plant gathering provided an ample and reliable food supply, with less labor investment. Nonetheless, when agriculturalists did finally appear on the Nile floodplain, their subsistence activities were able to support much larger populations, in greatly expanded and more clearly nested settlements.

By contrast, those groups that moved from one desert oasis to another appear to have been unusually innovative. Their mainstays were hunting, trapping, or fishing, but they also carried seed grains from the Nile margins or the Sahel to new marginal or ephemeral habitats, deliberately or inadvertently propagating such plants. They also somehow controlled and drove cattle from the thickets of the Egyptian Nile into the Sahara to sparse seasonal pastures (transhumance). Ecologically, this is the only way cattle can have survived in the Sahara, given their fodder and water requirements. Such a process will have selected for small and lean stock, quite possibly used for blood-letting rather than milk, in analogy to the practice of Nilo-Saharan-speaking cattle pastoralists in East Africa (verified archaeologically since 4000 BP). Eventually goat/sheep were acquired from southwestern Asia, while leaving no imprint along the Nile; such small stock were much less difficult to adapt to desert transhumance. These pioneers in desert colonization were not the victims of increasing aridity, but, rather, adventurous and innovative groups developing a versatile, adaptive repertoire that has persisted (or was reinvented), in various forms, in Arabia and other arid environments under the guise of nomadic pastoralism. [See Pastoral Nomadism.]

There are also some commonalities in lithic technology between the Nilotic hunter-fishers of Egypt and the desert pastoralists and between the pottery traditions of the latter and of hunter-fishers in the central Sudan. More significant is that the lithic assemblage found with the Faiyum Neolithic (the earliest known agricultural group in Egypt—6500–5500 BP) is close to that of hunter-gatherers near the Khargah oasis (7200 BP or earlier) and near the Dakhla oasis (6200–5100 BP). Yet, the Faiyum Neolithic combined fishing (a Nilotic adaptation), wheat and barley planting (Near Eastern domesticates), and stock raising (a desert adaptation of African and Near Eastern origins). In about 5800 BP at Merimde, next to the Nile Delta, and after 5500 BP at Khargah, similar lithic assemblages incorporated sickle blades, a Near Eastern tradition of long standing. [See Merimde.]

To what extent the agricultural traditions in Lower and Upper Egypt that subsequently evolved autochthonously into the predynastic cultures of the Nile floodplain and Delta initially involved information exchange or small-scale population movements is obscure, but Egypt at that time should be seen as an open system with diverging adaptations and increasing interchange. When most of the desert populations (always very small) disappeared from the record (c. 4500 BP), some of those small groups may have trickled into the Nile Valley.

Environmental Crisis (c. 2200 BCE?). Between about 2300 and 2100 BCE, the Aegean world and much of the Near East was engulfed in turmoil commonly attributed to invaders from the Balkans, the Zagros Mountains, the Syrian desert, and elsewhere. From the Balkans to Mesopotamia and Palestine, most urban sites were abandoned, destroyed, or reduced in size. Even where settlement was not abandoned, the archaeological components or the dynasties changed—the end of the Akkadian Empire in Mesopotamia and the Old Kingdom in Egypt (both perhaps c. 2230 BCE). Equated with the end of the Early Bronze II in Anatolia or the Early Bronze III in Palestine, this sociopolitical discontinuity could have transpired within less than a century or been more complex and prolonged. Subsequently, reduced archaeological visibility (e.g., the EB IV in Palestine) may have spanned some three centuries, to about 1900 BCE.

Such apparently synchronous events have led some scholars to invoke a super-regional causal mechanism such as climatic change. Weiss and others (1993), base their suggestion on studies of northeastern Syria (Khabur plains), where wind-borne deposits, arid conditions of soil alteration, and long-distance volcanic ash mark the onset of perhaps three centuries of drier climate—fixed at 2200 BCE, the date of the abrupt abandonment of Tell Leilan. [See Leilan, Tell.] It is even speculated that a cataclysmic eruption by an unknown volcano may have caused a "volcanic winter," destabilizing global climate (Courty, 1994).

The evidence for a period of drier climate comes from widely separated locations, but is by no means universal:

1. *Lake Van.* Enrichment of the isotope ^{18}O was experienced by Lake Van near the Anatolian headwaters of the Tigris and Euphrates Rivers (c. 2300–2100 BCE), based on varve correlation and dating from the lake bed (Degens and Kurtmann, 1978). The implication is reduced precipitation in the catchment, and if the dating can be trusted, would argue for a diminution of river discharge in Mesopotamia (Kay and Johnson, 1981), and might help explain increasing salinization and declining crop productivity (2350–1850 BCE), although land-use problems appear to have played a key part in this (Adams, 1981).

2. *Lake Zeribar.* A single pollen profile, from Lake Zeribar in the Zagros Mountains (van Zeist and Bottema, 1991), shows an abrupt decline of oak pollen (by 40 percent), disappearance of maple and willow, and a corresponding increase of grass and composite pollen (c. 2200 BCE). Recovery of the high-elevation woodlands was delayed by perhaps six hundred years. However, Holocene forest recolonization of the mountain ranges around Lake Van (see above) was only briefly interrupted at this time, judging by a core from that lake.

3. *Lake Beysehir.* The pollen profile from Lake Beysehir in southcentral Anatolia offers dubious support for greater aridity in about 2200 BCE (300-cm level, interpolated from carbon-14 dates)—namely, a strong decline of pine and cedar and an increase of grasses; however, oak and ash began to increase steadily at the same time. Equally problematic is the oxidation of pollen in a core from Lake Koycegiz in southwestern Anatolia, perhaps by a temporary drying out of the lake at roughly this time.

Examination of some two dozen other pollen profiles from Lake Urmia (northeastern Iran), Syria, northwestern Anatolia, southern and northern Greece, Dalmatia, and North Africa fails to reveal evidence of a woodland decline or drier ground conditions from about 2300 to 1800 BCE; in general, the period from about 2700 to 1500 BCE was climatically uneventful in these areas, except for scattered episodes of anthropogenic disturbance (Bottema et al., 1990). In Palestine, Lake Kinneret (Sea of Galilee) shows a submaximum of deciduous oak pollen (c. 1900 BCE), as does Lake Hulah (c. 2250 BCE), while ^{18}O readings on dated land snails in the Negev suggest a wetter climate phase (2450–2050 BCE) prior to a rapid shift to essentially modern conditions. Stream behavior in western Asia is ambiguous. The Khabur River indicates a shift to a semiarid, periodic flow regime (braiding, then channel incision) in about 4000–2000 BCE, before resuming a more equitable, meandering flow, by perhaps 1800 BCE (Courty, 1994). In Palestine, Nahal Lachish, near the tell of that name, had a broad, "wet" floodplain from the EB into the MB II period, when slope soils were eroded; only thereafter did the stream cut down its channel and strip away its agriculturally attractive floodplain (Goldberg, 1986; Rosen, 1986).

The only other environmental "event" in about 2200 BCE was in the Nile Valley, where the Old Kingdom state dissolved amid dynastic anarchy and disastrous famines (e.g., c. 2200, c. 2100, and 2002 BCE). Various textual elaborations of failing Nile floods, famine, abandoned farmland, dislocated people roaming the countryside, and even cannibalism illustrate the scope of this disaster (Butzer, 1984). The texts are complemented by information from the Upper Nile region, where Lake Rudolf abruptly switched to a shallower and more alkaline lake (c. 2300 BCE), while the discharge of the Omo River, draining western Ethiopia, reached a minimum shortly after 2200 BCE, before recovering somewhat in about 2150–1950 BCE. That rapid recovery was evident in the Faiyum Depression in Egypt, where a flood surge filled most of the basin with water in about 2000 BCE. The data, however, support only one interval of Nile failure, during the rule of the Upper Egyptian governor Ankhtifi (c. 2210–2185 BCE).

The available evidence, although scant, suggests that Nile failures did not unleash decentralizing forces and chaos that took almost two centuries to tame. Central authority declined markedly during the sixth dynasty (c. 2380–2230 BCE); during its second half there was progressive economic decline and impoverishment in the capital and some of the provinces, while the aristocracy began to create local power bases (Butzer, 1984). In an even broader perspective, two centuries of political fragmentation preceded any Nile-related disasters, although these may have triggered the social unrest that ultimately led to a reassessment of traditional values.

Because periodic Nile failures could have begun as much as a century earlier, and the destruction of Byblos by invaders had already taken place within the reign of Pepi II of Egypt (died c. 2250 BCE), it is helpful to look at another agricultural crisis (c. 1170–1000 BCE) that may have brought down the New Kingdom (Butzer, 1984). [See Byblos.] Spiraling and wildly fluctuating food prices are documented, peaking in 1130 BCE. There were food riots; the temple granaries were empty, in part through embezzlement; and the countryside was increasingly abandoned because of overtaxation and banditry. However, corruption had already been rampant before the subsistence crisis began; two foreign invasions (1207 and 1177–1171 BCE) took place prior to the rise in food prices; and two bouts of civil war were not reflected in food-price fluctuations. This suggests that although environmental stress and the resulting economic crisis were implicated in the disempowerment of the last New Kingdom pharaohs, the sociopolitical processes of devolution were far more complex. Indeed, this crisis period with its foreign invaders and widespread political discontinuity in the Near East (the fall of the Hittite Empire) had been underway some thirty years before Egypt plunged into ecological crisis.

A synoptic overview of the environmental evidence for the crisis of 2000 BCE suggests a trend to aridity only within the area between the Euphrates River and the Zagros Mountains. [See Euphrates.] Syria-Palestine, Greece, and northwestern Anatolia, as well as northwest Africa, did not experience greater aridity; any anomalies favored a moister climate and forest expansion or recovery. Even within the region possibly affected by drought, the Khabur River had documented an increasingly semiarid stream regime since 4000 BCE, and in the Zagros forests expanded steadily until about 2200 BCE. Climatic trends were not in phase, and whatever environmental crisis there may have been, or however severe it may have been locally, was limited to a circumscribed area.

As the relevant archaeological record becomes more tangible, it suggests great circumspection in interpretating episodes of urban decline and political simplification. Thus, in Palestine (Miroschedji, 1989), EB III urban sites were largely destroyed or abandoned between 2250 and 2200 BCE. However, ruralization rather than depopulation followed, and during the next three or four centuries, the Negev and Sinai were the focus of countless small settlements. Only at the end of EB IV (c. 1850 BCE) were these desert areas abandoned—until the Roman-Nabatean period. [See Nabateans.] Even on the Syrian Euphrates renewed urbanism appears as Tell Leilan declines. The inherent complexity of crisis periods may, thus, stem from the systemic interdependence of larger political entities; the latent, sociopolitical instability of some; and the advantages of technological, military, or adaptive innovations within the larger region (which also applies to hypotheses invoking climate to explain the end of Mycenaean and Minoan civilization after 1200 BCE and the political devolution of Mesopotamia in the eleventh century BCE).

Cultural Transformation of the Landscape. More productive than climate and migration as explanatory models is the human use of and impact on environmental resources. While Near Eastern hunters and gatherers (20,000–10,000 BP) utilized natural resources in increasingly complex ways, their environmental impact probably was both localized and ephemeral. Agricultural land use is another matter, involving vegetation clearance, soil manipulation, irrigation works, and potentially heavy grazing. [See Irrigation.] With the emergence of the high civilizations, tied to dense rural populations and growing urban centers, resource pressures and ecological impacts take on yet another dimension, including an insatiable demand for timber and fuel wood. This is fundamental to understanding the geographic stage on which socioeconomic and political history was played out in the Near East.

The single most important tools currently available to identify and gage human impact on the environment are palynology and the identification of botanical and animal remains from archaeological sites. Pollen cores can provide a continuous trace of composite ecological change, commonly from lakes or swamps at some distance from settlement centers—primarily a macroscale approach. Paleobotanical remains from sites provide more discontinuous records, from close proximity to settled areas. They emphasize plants and animals of economic importance and tend to offer a more finely textured picture, complementing that of the pollen profiles that document change through time (Van Zeist and Bottema, 1991). Equally important is evidence for human impact on the soil mantle. Erosion leaves thinned soil profiles or exposed rock; eroded soil material accumulates downslope as hill wash or is swept away by stream floods, to be deposited on floodplains farther downstream.

Dry-Farming and Pastoralism. The impact of Neolithic agricultural or pastoral land use was localized and mainly ephemeral, exerted primarily through the use of fire to clear woodland for cultivation and perhaps also as pasture. Subsistence was still heavily dependent on hunting, and even on wild plant foods. This does not preclude almost complete clearance of woodland in proximity of occupation sites—whether for cultivation, construction timbers, or fuel. Neolithic dispersal was also directed toward more arid environments and rudimentary irrigation was practiced in some places. Noteworthy is the first settlement of the deltaic wetlands of southern Mesopotamia a little after 7000 BP, where people probably practiced simple floodwater farming.

There is no correlation between cultural designations such as Neolithic and permanent or prominent settlements. Some of the latter, with rectangular houses with stone foundations, predate the Neolithic, while in parts of the Mediterranean basin some agricultural peoples moved between caves and clusters of seasonal huts as late as 2000 BCE. It also is not self-evident that mobile hunter-pastoralists with supplementary seasonal farming had less ecological impact than clusters of farming villages. Sedentary farmers could not persist indefinitely in a particular area without developing conservationist strategies based on cumulative experience. Long-term success is predicated on minimizing both long-term environmental damage and short-term subsistence risk (Butzer, 1996). That may be easy enough on level land with productive soils, but when expanding populations required the cultivation of fragile soils on steeper hill country (e.g., olive groves or vinyards on terraced hillsides), long-term productivity could only be assured with considerable and sustained labor input. [See Viticulture.]

The archaeological record appears to approximate such a model. Agricultural landscapes with prominent villages are found scattered across stretches of fertile, level land from Mesopotamia to central Europe by 5000 BCE. Permanent hillside cultivation seems to have been associated with the expansion of olive and grape orchards beginning as early as 3500 BCE in Syria-Palestine and a millennium or so later in Greece. This Mediterranean-style pattern of land use, emphasizing arboriculture, emerged in a subhumid environment with mild winters and sustained large populations during later parts of the Bronze Age and again in Hellenistic-Roman times. It did not lend itself well to irrigated desert in arid settings—despite their best efforts, the Egyptian elite had to import considerable olive oil and wine from Syria. A similar form of land use did not develop in the hill country east of the Euphrates, at least not until Hellenistic times and on a local scale. There, agriculture tended to remain on the valley floors, except in eastern Anatolia and the Caucasus, where orchards of fruit trees substituted for olive groves and vinyards.

Pollen records suggest that deforestation or other vegetation disturbance became increasingly common in the hill country of the Near East and Greece after about 5000 BCE, before the establishment of Mediterranean-style farming (Butzer, 1996). This can best be attributed to early pastoral activity, which subsequently became more directly linked to agricultural pursuits—the same villages farmed, planted orchards, and moved herds of livestock up into the hills and back in a seasonal round. This promoted a more judicious form of pastoral land use, favoring greater ecological stability. Slowly, the initially small patches of planted fields, pastures, and secondary woodland expanded until, by the Late Bronze Age, about 1500 BCE (Bottema et al., 1990), the warm-temperate hill country west of the Euphrates exhibited large tracts of well-tended agricultural landscape.

The ecological record is by no means one of harmony between land use and the environment. Episodes of destructive impact were commonly limited to land abandonment, either in the course of political devolution, or in the wake of intrusive populations with a greater emphasis on pastoral herding (Butzer, 1996). New pastoral colonists from humid, northerly woodlands probably lacked experience with the more fragile ecology of an unfamiliar Mediterranean environment. One such period was the Early Iron dark age, but impact on vegetation was not synchronous: 1500–400 BCE in Epirus; 1100–1000 BCE in Macedonia; and 1000–900 BCE in southwestern Anatolia. Much the same happened in medieval times: in about 400–1100 CE in Palestine; 1200–1350 CE in southwestern Anatolia; and 1000–1500 CE in Epirus and North Africa—involving Vlach and Slavic pastoralists or Arab bedouin. Local land-use histories have varied, and broad generalizations are prone to be simplistic. Overall, the marginal agricultural lands of Syria-Palestine were abandoned at different times, in part as a result of Byzantine-era insecurity, in part because of economic decline, following the shift of power from Umayyad Damascus to 'Abbasid Baghdad after 750 CE. [See Umayyad Caliphate; 'Abbasid Caliphate.] It was this abandonment, which persisted into the 1920s, that gave Huntington the impression of climatic deterioration.

The location of major pollen cores at some distance from major urban sites limits information on whether large and expanding towns may have so depleted their environmental resources as to contribute to local population decline or even abandonment. A record of discontinuous but repeated soil erosion from Hellenistic to late Byzantine times in the Aegean region suggests that this is at least a possible scenario. The irrigated floodplains of the arid Near East present a distinctive land-use trajectory, with different environmental repercussions.

Nile Valley Irrigation. Agricultural settlements began to proliferate in the Nile Valley in about 4000 BCE. Preferred site locations gradually shifted from the desert edge to the naturally raised levees running along the margins of the Nile and its secondary channels. The Nile floodplain was subdivided into shallow basins, as a result of the intersection of various active and older levees (Butzer, 1976). These basins flooded naturally at the time of annual inundation (August or September), the excess water draining back out into the channel six to ten weeks later, as the flood waned. The clayey soils retained sufficient moisture to bring a crop seeded in October or November to harvest in February or March. This natural pulse of irrigation was adequate to cultivate extensive floodplain tracts without artificial irrigation. Technological intervention was incremental, first by means of controlled breaches in the levees that regulated the influx as well as outflow of water from the basins. Short canals were eventually built to distribute water within basins that were subdivided into more manageable units by transverse earthen dikes. The bucket-and-lever device, known in Arabic as *shaduf*, was introduced about 1500 BCE to allow the small-scale, mechanical lifting of water for vegetable and pleasure gardens. [*See* Gardens, *article on* Gardens in Preclassical Times.] Large-scale water lifting was only possible with the animal-drawn waterwheel, or *saqiya*, however, first verified in Ptolemaic times.

Human modification of the Nile Valley, thus, took place gradually, beginning in predynastic times. During the Old Kingdom, fruit orchards were widely planted on new estates in the southern delta, with vineyards placed along the delta margins (Butzer, 1976). Middle Kingdom development apparently focused on controlling the quantity of water entering the Faiyum Depression, where settlement was probably expanded. The New Kingdom and late periods saw land reclamation in the delta marsh fringe and greater irrigation control in the less manageable, larger basins of Middle Egypt. There never was a tall, dense riparian forest, and from the earliest times, acacia represented the key local timber; productive groves of date palms probably soon dominated the riparian fringe. Finally, salinization was not a problem in flood basins flushed on a regular basis. Thus, the Nile Valley and Delta were not degraded, but progressively converted into a carefully tended, cultural landscape that was indefinitely sustainable.

Mesopotamian Irrigation. The alluvial and deltaic plains of Lower Mesopotamia were different from those of Egypt (Adams, 1981). The narrow Tigris floodplain is entrenched well below the alluvial land created by the Euphrates, and the Tigris was therefore quite difficult to harness for more extensive irrigation. Whereas the Nile floods were modulated, to allow winter cultivation (as elsewhere along the Mediterranean coastlands), the Euphrates was erratic and often violent. Its floods reflected the snow cover in eastern Anatolia, and when and how quickly it melted. Sweeping down a much shorter trajectory, floods arrived between late April and early June, breaking out from the shifting channels to drain into a vast marshland, instead of filling shallow basins before emptying back into the main river. Simple floodwater farming had only limited scope, and the floods were hazardous to settlements. Accumulating across broad, marshy zones in the lower delta, dissolved salts were retained and built up in the soil and groundwater. In addition, the Euphrates silts included less fertile clay than did the Nile muds.

Mesopotamia, therefore, required substantial modifica-

tion and costly maintenance to achieve productive, irrigated landscapes. The main channels had to be tapped by long feeder canals that fanned out across the plain and replaced former flood breaches and temporary overflow channels. These required massive reconstruction and cleaning out after most flood seasons, before labor would be available for planting crops downstream; by then, however, water volume had sharply diminished. This may explain why traditional irrigation farming could not take advantage of a possible postflood crop season, delaying planting until river discharge slowly increased again in October or November. One advantage of an almost flat plain was that canals could tap river water even at an intermediate stage of flow. The disadvantage was that regular incremental tapping of canal water implied evaporation of slightly saline water in the fields, creating salinization over time.

Effective water control in Mesopotamia consequently meant a quantum change in potential agricultural productivity; it also required an elaborate canal network and costly labor input (Adams, 1981). Such a system was probably inaugurated by Early Uruk times (c. 4000–3500 BCE), and the transformation of natural Euphrates tributaries into a great network of artificial canals completed by 2000 BCE. Maintenance could not be guaranteed during periods of political devolution, however, resulting in periodic abandonment of much of the arable land. Overirrigation further led to salinization of the lower ends of the irrigation system, possibly favoring an upstream shift of the prime agricultural lands and, with them, the clusters of population. Equally so, this upstream shift may have enabled protection of towns from destructive floods by the new technology of massive rings of dikes.

The conversion of Lower Mesopotamia into an agricultural landscape was a less harmonious affair than in Egypt. The system was more fragile, its operation discontinuous, and its ecological impact negative. Unlike Egypt, which remained a breadbasket without interruption, most of Lower Mesopotamia lay waste from about 1000 CE until after World War I. Furthermore, the creation and management of this system required either centralized control or unusual levels of cooperation among the various polities embedded within it. That assigned a major role to mediating "bureaucracies" and enhanced the dependency of individual cultivators—unlike in Egypt, where irrigation was managed locally, well into the last century.

Tells. The potential to produce a detailed site history exists at excavations where archaeologists and environmental archaeologists collaborate on-site. In the Near East, a tell, or artificial hill, typically formed by the residues of mud (adobe) bricks used across successive occupations to build houses, public buildings, and fortifications, is an anthropogenic landform that can be in excess of 50 m deep (Rosen, 1986). It usually incorporates between 1 million and 10 million cu m of sediment. Many of the larger abandoned tells on the plains of northern Syria are sufficiently prominent to be visible on conventional satellite imagery. Similar town sites on the Nile floodplain are equally large, but their forms are low and less conspicuous, as a result of protracted alluviation of the surrounding floodplain.

Such mounds record millennia of settlement history, documented not only by architectural structures and archaeological inventories, but also by a detailed sedimentary record that reflects the use and disposal of a perishable building material (Butzer, 1982). Individual houses are built, eventually collapse, and must be rebuilt with new mud bricks, as older debris is reworked into a prepared "floor." New quarters of a town grow, while old ones decay. Middens of highly organic, ashy or sandy refuse accumulate in disused rooms, abandoned houses, or decaying quarters. A whole town is destroyed or abandoned and a new one is raised on its ruins. As sediment continues to accumulate, with little net loss of material, the mound progressively increases in elevation. Each occupation phase included multiple levels of house floors, each structure partially filled by several thin strata. These levels not only record the progression of local construction and collapse, or site growth and decay, but also provide details about each room's original function, as well as the physical processes of microaccumulation.

Until very recently, archaeologists limited their attention to the three-dimensional architectural matrix of mounds and the artifacts therein. As a result, no tell has yet been comprehensively studied by a geoarchaeologist, despite a number of exploratory efforts, to identify the changing nature of domestic occupation, microenvironmental dynamics, and demographic trends. [See Demography.] The processes of chemical alternation or enrichment within a site, or the agencies of contemporary or subsequent deposition of erosion, might highlight a climatic signal.

A particularly useful link between the tell and its environmental context is provided by mud bricks (Rosen, 1986). Their texture, color, and calcium-carbonate content are diagnostic markers that vary remarkably from site to site. Even within a single site, mud bricks can identify the different materials used for monumental structures and simple houses, or clay sources quarried at different times—including some sources exposed, buried, or exhausted during specific periods. Tell-derived hill wash from different ages also tends to be distinctive and traceable to specific microstratigraphic units exposed in an adjacent alluvial profile. That, in turn, may allow correlation between settlement and landscape histories, in regard to changing human use of, and impact on, the environment.

The point of this example is that Bronze Age and historical settlement sites remain the most neglected arena of potential research in Near Eastern environmental archaeology. The tons and tons of sediment excavated from such sites every year could be used to richly complement standard archaeological interpretation. But in the past it has simply been thrown out, without the excavators drawing in the requisite geo-archaeological expertise.

Perspectives. Ideally, the scope of environmental archaeology goes well beyond data gathering to explore fresh vistas for major issues. In terms of the rise and fall of empires, for example, the most tangible variables are political centralization/decentralization, economic expansion/dissipation, and demographic growth/decline. Two of the questions to be answered are which was dependent and which independent and whether change was externally or internally stimulated. A systemic analog, instead of a causality model, allows for external inputs and breaking away from biological systems centered on energy flows (e.g., economic and geopolitical priorities). Systemic thinking is primarily heuristic, designed to enhance sophistication in analyzing change, rather than to predict or retrodict outcomes (Butzer, 1990). If indeed a climatic anomaly is demonstrated, the questions should be who was affected, where, and how; what risk-minimizing strategies were in place; what experience was available to cope with subsistence shortfalls or to adapt to a recurrence of such a crisis; and which institutions could be mobilized to mitigate social stress? Questions might next shift to the resilience of the economic and political structures of a particular state under external or internal "siege." Answers are usually difficult to provide, but the questions ideally upgrade the sophistication of research designs and the categories of empirical investigation.

Human populations have always interacted with their environment in multiple ways, using it, shaping it, and devising alternative ways to bend its constraints—but also abusing and sometimes degrading it. At the core of human history is a long tradition of persistence in the face of adversity and resilience in the throes of crisis. Especially in an era with increasing interest in the impact of long-term land use on sustainability or ecological equilibrium, environmental archaeology has a unique capability to examine such issues empirically (Butzer, 1996). Five millennia of intensive agriculture and town life in the Near East provide an unusual opportunity to monitor human impact on the environment.

[See also Computer Mapping; Ethnoarchaeology; Ethnobotany; Geology; Historical Geography; New Archaeology; Paleobotany; Paleoenvironmental Reconstruction; and Paleozoology.]

BIBLIOGRAPHY

Adams, Robert McC. *Heartland of Cities: Surveys of Ancient Settlement and Land Use on the Central Floodplain of the Euphrates.* Chicago, 1981.

Bintliff, J. L., and Willem van Zeist, eds. *Palaeoclimates, Palaeoenvironments, and Human Communities in the Eastern Mediterranean Region in Later Prehistory.* Oxford, 1982.

Bottema, Sytze, et al., eds. *Man's Role in the Shaping of the Eastern Mediterranean Landscape.* Rotterdam, 1990.

Braidwood, Robert J., and Bruce Howe, eds. *Prehistoric Investigations in Iraqi Kurdistan.* University of Chicago, Oriental Institute, Studies in Ancient Civilization, no. 31. Chicago, 1960.

Brice, William C., ed. *The Environmental History of the Near and Middle East since the Last Ice Age.* London, 1978.

Butzer, Karl W. "Environmental and Human Ecology in Egypt during Predynastic and Early Dynastic Times." *Bulletin de la Société de Géographie d'Égypte* 32 (1959): 43–87.

Butzer, Karl W. "Archeology and Geology in Ancient Egypt." *Science* 132 (1960): 1617–1624.

Butzer, Karl W. *Early Hydraulic Civilization in Egypt: A Study in Cultural Ecology.* Chicago, 1976.

Butzer, Karl W. "Rise and Fall of Axum, Ethiopia: A Geo-Archaeological Interpretation." *American Antiquity* 46 (1981): 471–495.

Butzer, Karl W. *Archaeology as Human Ecology: Method and Theory for a Contextual Approach.* Cambridge, 1982.

Butzer, Karl W. "Long-Term Nile Flood Variation and Political Discontinuities in Pharaonic Egypt." In *From Hunters to Farmers*, edited by J. Desmond Clark and Steven A. Brandt, pp. 102–112. Berkeley, 1984.

Butzer, Karl W. "A Human Ecosystem Framework for Archaeology." In *The Ecosystem Approach in Anthropology*, edited by Emilio F. Moran, pp. 91–130. Rev. ed. Ann Arbor, Mich., 1990.

Butzer, Karl W. "Ecology in the Long View: Settlement Histories, Agrosystemic Strategies, and Ecological Performance." *Journal of Field Archaeology* 23 (1996).

Caton-Thompson, Gertrude, and E. W. Gardner. *The Desert Fayum.* 2 vols. London, 1934.

Courty, M.-A. "Le cadre paléogéographique des occupations humaines dans le bassin du Haut-Khabour, Syrie du Nord-Est." *Paléorient* 20 (1994): 21–60.

Degens, Egon T., and Fikret Kurtmann, eds. *The Geology of Lake Van.* Ankara, 1978.

Goldberg, Paul. "Late Quaternary Environmental History of the Southern Levant." *Geoarchaeology* 1 (1986): 224–244.

Kay, P. A., and Douglas L. Johnson. "Estimation of Tigris-Euphrates Streamflow from Regional Paleoenvironmental Proxy Data." *Climate Change* 3 (1981): 251–263.

Larsen, Curtis E. *Life and Land Use on the Bahrain Islands: The Geoarchaeology of an Ancient Society.* Chicago, 1983.

Miroschedji, Pierre de, ed. *L'urbanisation de la Palestine à l'âge du Bronze ancien: Bilan et perspectives des recherches actuelles; Actes du Colloque d'Emmaüs, 20–24 octobre 1986.* British Archaeological Reports, International Series, no. 527. Oxford, 1989.

Rosen, Arlene Miller. *Cities of Clay: The Geoarchaeology of Tells.* Chicago, 1986.

Wasylikowa, Krystyna, et al. "Examination of Botanical Remains from Early Neolithic Houses at Nabta Playa, Western Desert, Egypt." In *The Archaeology of Africa*, edited by Thurstan Shaw et al., pp. 154–164. London, 1993.

Weiss, Harvey, et al. "The Genesis and Collapse of Third Millennium North Mesopotamian Civilization." *Science* 261 (1993): 995–1004.

Zeist, Willem van, and Sytze Bottema. *Late Quaternary Vegetation of the Near East.* Wiesbaden, 1991.

KARL W. BUTZER

EPHESUS, major ancient Greek city now in western Turkey, situated on the western coast of Asia Minor (37°50′ N, 27°15′ E). There has never been any question about the site's identification. In the Late Bronze Age the name of the site was perhaps Apasa, the capital of the empire of Arzawa. Under the first Hellenistic king, Lysimachos, the town was called Arsinoeia, but after his death the traditional name was maintained. During the Byzantine period, after the main town was abandoned, the site around the hill, east of the Artemision (temple sacred to the goddess Artemis), was called Ayasoluk, which nowadays is the Turkish town of Selçuk.

Ephesus and the surrounding area have been settled since the Bronze Age. During Mycenaean times the hill of Ayasoluk and the Artemision showed remains of occupation. Until now little was known about the earlier Ionian migration period, but since the eighth century BCE, Ephesus has played an important role within the Ionian civilization. Remains below the lower agora of the Roman town and a peripteros in the central base of the Artemision underline the specific significance of the site (see figure 1). Other than the Artemision, little is known about the remains of the site in the sixth and fifth centuries BCE. In the fourth century the temple of Artemis remained the center of activities, but after a new town was founded by the *diadoch* (follower of Alexander the Great) Lysimachos, Ephesus began to flourish. The new urbanization was the basis for the development of Ephesus into a metropolis in the Roman empire.

Although Ephesus has been visited by many people since the time of Cyriacus of Ancona, one of the first scholarly travelers (1446 CE), archaeological investigations did not begin until the second half of the nineteenth century. John Turtle Wood began excavating there in 1864 and continued his archaeological work until he discovered the Artemision in January, 1870. Some of the marbles that he excavated can now be seen in the British Museum. In 1904 and 1905 the British Museum undertook another excavation in the Artemision and David G. Hogarth discovered the earlier strata of the sanctuary. The Austrians started their work at Ephesus in 1895, an ongoing undertaking that has been interrupted only by the two world wars. The emphasis of the Austrian research was on the Roman town; however, since 1965 the Artemision has also been included in the activities.

The Artemision. The temple of Artemis is situated outside the Roman town in the plain, east of the hill of Ayasoluk, and its remains lie partly in the groundwater. In the center of the temple a *peripteros* (colonnaded rectangle) 9.5 m (31 ft.) wide and 13.3 m (43.5 ft.) long with columns arranged four by eight, was excavated (see figure 2). Within the cella (inner part) is a rectangular base surrounded by six column bases of green schist. Beneath it a hoard of jewelry was found, perhaps the necklace for the *xoanon* (statue in wood of the goddess). The whole construction is to be dated in the eighth century. The eastern part of the cella was reused in the middle of the sixth century as a foundation for a shrine in marble, perhaps the shelter for a new cult statue. Therefore the coins of electrum (alloy of gold and silver) found below its floor give a terminus ante quem of around 560, the year in which Croesus gained political power.

Two other large constructions, Temple C, as designated by Hogarth, in the center of the temple, and orthogonal to it the so-called *hekatompedos* in the west, existed before the first big marble temple was erected. Designated after an early temple to Athena on the Acropolis in Athens, the *hekatompedos* (meaning "one hundred feet long" in Greek) was the first construction at the site made with marble and measured 100 Ionian feet long. Temple C had *antae* (pilasters) on the west side. This arrangement implies that around 600 BCE two main cults existed at the site. Numerous votive offerings in gold and ivory, some of them female figurines, as well as the animal bones of the sacrifices, emphasize the special character of the early cults at the site. Pigs were especially common as a sacrifice, more in the central base than at the other locations; however, donkeys, dogs, bears, and lions were also used as a sacrifice to the goddess. Even human sacrifices, called *pharmakos* by the Lydian poet Hipponax, are archaeologically evident.

The great marble temple, also called the temple of Croesus, was 59.9 m (194.5 ft.) wide including the *krepidoma* (solid base of the building); however, its length is not yet known. Eight of the thirty-six Ionian sculptured columns, which stood at the entrance, and the *sima* (gutter) in marble, which was covered by a sculptural frieze, were some of the remainders from the temple, which was burnt down in 356 BCE. This temple was rebuilt with the same dimensions but on a higher level. Once again some of the column pedestals and drums were sculptured. Pliny tells us that 127 columns existed and of them thirty-six were sculptured. Some of the remains of both these columns and the archaic columns are now in the British Museum. With the erection of the marble temple of Croesus all earlier cults were suppressed, and the worship of Artemis alone was established. An archaic sacrificial area, consisting of a ramp and two bases with a water pipe made of lead, was surrounded by a courtyard, axial to the temple of Croesus. Their foundations were reused in the fourth century, and a new altar with a screen wall was built on them. This screen wall was composed of a frieze on a socle and was topped with an Ionian colonnade. The cella of the temple was reused as a church in early Byzantine times.

Hellenistic and Roman Town. Lysimachos of Thrace (322–281) founded a new city between the two hills Panayirdağ and Bülbüldağ. It was designed in a rectangular grid system that was oriented to the axis of the Artemision. The Embolos (Gk., "wedge," in general also late antique streets) was not adapted to this hippodamic (rectilinear) system, but instead, it used the archaic processional road in the valley between the two hills. The new urbanization included an archaic settlement, which was probably the ancient town Smyrna, at the valley's entrance. The town walls enclosed a big area that went along the ridges of the two hills.

During the Roman times the Hellenistic urbanization was completed. Some of the main constructions included a sheltered harbor north of the Bülbüldağ and the water supply from the surrounding mountains to the town. A procession road partly covered by the sophist and philosopher Damianos led around the Panayirdağ to the Artemision.

Temples. Many shrines for the cult of the emperors existed in the Roman towns, such as a twin shrine perhaps one

EPHESUS. Figure 1. *The Roman town.* View from above the embolos with the monument of Memmius in front. The harbor gymnasium can be seen toward the rear. (Courtesy A. Bammer)

EPHESUS. Figure 2. *Peripteros in the Artemesion.* Eighth century BCE. (Courtesy A. Bammer)

west of the Monument of Memmius. Along the Embolos stood the *hydrekdocheion* ("water castle") of Trajan (*IvE*, nos. 415–416, 419, 424, 435–436, 4249), and near the street to the Magnesian gate another fountain for the same emperor was erected. South of the upper agora a semicircular water container was built, and at the southwest corner of the upper agora stood the *hydrekdocheion* of Laecanius Bassus (*IvE*, nos. 232–421).

Public Squares and Administrative Buildings. The upper agora had a political connotation. Its northern front was covered by the basilica with three naves, sponsored by C. Sextilius Pollio and his wife, Ofilia Bassa (*IvE*, no. 404). It was decorated with bull-head capitals on the inner colonnade. Behind it stood the *prytaneion* (headquarters of the city administrative body) with the sanctuary for Hestia, which in late antiquity was decorated with heart-leaf columns.

The lower agora seems to have served more for commerce, but a Doric stoa on a higher level at its eastern edge had perhaps also an administrative purpose. The agoras and main streets were divided by arches and gates. In late antiquity the public squares, like the agoras, were built over by private buildings. Their function was taken over by larger streets with colonnades like the Arkadiane from the theater to the harbor or the stoa of Servilius to the stadium.

Private Buildings. Private buildings were on the slopes of the Panayırdağ and the Bülbüldağ, but only two *insulae* (squares surrounded by streets) south of the Embolos have been completely excavated. They are composed of flats lying on several terraces. The dwellings themselves were mostly composed around a courtyard, often a peristyle. The walls of the rooms were decorated with paintings and marble revetments. Among the paintings scenes of dramas and comedies of Euripides and Menander should be mentioned. The floors were worked in mosaics. Remains of the furniture in bronze and ivory have also been found. The decorations as a whole belong to the most outstanding in Asia Minor.

Heroa and Tombs. Among the tombs outside the city wall, only one along the street to Magnesia, which today is beside the street to Aydın, has been excavated, and it has the form of a *tholos* (beehive-shaped structure). Within the city wall the monument of Pollio, the sponsor of the aqueduct over the River Marnas and the basilica is known. At the courtyard of Domitian, the monument for C. Memmius, a grandson of Sulla (*IvE*, no. 403) in the form of a tetrapylon with niches at the same place, was erected around 51 BCE. The octagon, a grave for a maiden, perhaps Arsinoe IV, killed by Cleopatra VII, stands at the Embolos. Next to it another *heroon* (shrine for a deified deceased person) is situated, which may have been built by Androklos. At the end of the Embolos the library of Celsus Polemaeanus (*IvE*, no. 5101) erected around 117 CE was built over the sarcophagus of its sponsor.

for the Divus Iulius and the other for Dea Roma (Dio Cassius, 5120.6) near the Prytaneion at the upper agora, a temple for Domitian and Titus (*Die Inschriften von Ephesos* [*IvE*], nos. 232–242, 1498, 2048) south of the courtyard of Domitian, a small temple for Hadrian at the Embolos, built by C. Quintilius (*IvE*, no. 429), and a huge temple in Hadrianic times, maybe the Olympieion (Pausanias, *Periegesis* 7.2.6) at the harbor. Sanctuaries for non-Greek gods are still more difficult to identify, but at the upper agora stood a temple, possibly for Isis (or Dionysos?) and a sanctuary, perhaps for Serapis, was discovered west of the lower agora.

Gymnasia and Baths. Because gymnasia needed much space, two of them were built near the northern and eastern city wall, two in the plain between the theater and the harbor, one east of the upper agora and only one, the baths of Varius, later restored by Scholastikia, at the Embolos in the center of the town (*IvE*, nos. 431, 453, 500, 1313–1315, 3008). Most of the gymnasia were constructed in the second and third century CE, and all of them were restored up to the fourth and fifth century.

Fountains. Most of the fountains stood in the upper part of the town, near the upper agora, the courtyard of Domitian, and the Embolos. A fountain with a big niche was constructed by the proconsul Calvisius Ruso in honor of the emperor Domitian (92 CE), and then another one was built

Churches in Late Antiquity. Smaller churches and chapels were built all over the town, one in the northern wall at the stadium, another one into the gymnasium close to the eastern city wall. The biggest church was the church of Holy Mary in the harbor area perhaps used for the council of Ephesus 431 CE. The basilica of St. John at the hill of Ayasoluk was first built in the fifth century, then rebuilt under Theodosius in the sixth century. Two churches were built into the Cemetery of the Seven Sleepers at the east side of the Panayirdağ. Finally, the church in the courtyard of the Artemision must be mentioned, also one of the largest and earliest churches.

Sculpture. Although Ephesus did not have a sculptural school like the one at Aphrodisias, sculptures played a great role in decorating buildings. The richly decorated Artemision has certainly been a model. Also of great importance are the Statues of Amazons dedicated in the fifth century to the Artemesion but only conserved as copies from Roman times. Androklos, the mythical founder of Ephesus, is often represented. For instance, he is represented in a frieze at the *heroon* near the octagon, in the frieze of the temple of Hadrian, and in the sculptures of the fountain for Trajan. At the end of the Roman republic the monument of Memmius was highly decorated with caryatids at the pillars and officials and soldiers on the surrounding frieze on top of the arches. The facade of the substructure of the temple of Domitian was decorated in the second floor with male and female barbarians. In the *prytaneion* three statues of Artemis Ephesia have been found. The library of Celsus was decorated with the allegories of the virtues of Celsus. However, the most important frieze is that of the so-called monument of the Parthians with battle scenes and the adoption of Lucius Verus. The foundation of this important altar still has to be identified.

BIBLIOGRAPHY

Bammer, Anton. *Ephesos: Stadt an Fluss und Meer.* Graz, 1988.
Bammer, Anton. "A *peripteros* of the Geometric Period in the Artemision of Ephesus." *Anatolian Studies* 40 (1990): 137–156.
Engelmann, Helmut. "Zum Kaiserkult in Ephesos." *Zeitschrift für Papyrologie und Epigraphik* 97 (1993): 279–289.
Foss, Clive. *Ephesus after Antiquity.* Cambridge, 1978.
Friesen, Steven J. *Twice Neokoros, Ephesus, Asia and the Cult of the Flavian Imperial Family.* Religions in the Graeco-Roman World, 116. Leiden, 1993.
Die Inschriften von Ephesos (IvE). 8 vols. Bonn, 1979–1984.
Knibbe, Dieter. *Via sacra Ephesiaca I.* Berichte und Materialen, 3. Vienna, 1993.
Le Monde de la Bible, no. 64 (1990). Special issue entitled "Éphèse, la cité d'Artémis."
Muss, Ulrike. *Die Bauplastik des archaischen Artemesions, Sonderschriften,* vol. 25. Vienna, 1994.
Oster, Richard E. *A Bibliography of Ancient Ephesus.* Metuchen, N.J., 1987.
Rogers, Guy M. *The Sacred Identity of Ephesos: Foundation Myths of a Roman City.* London, 1991.
Strocka, Volker M. "Zeus, Marnas und Klaseas, Ephesische Brunnenfiguren von 93 n. Chr." In *Festschrift für Jale Inan,* pp. 79–92. Istanbul, 1989.
Thür, Hilke. "Arsinoe IV: Eine Schwester Kleopatras VII, Grabinhaberin des Oktogons von Ephesos?" *Jahreshefte des Österreichisches Archäologisches Institut* 60 (1990): 43–56.
Torelli, Mario. "Il monumento efesino di Memmius." *Scienze dell'Antichità* 2 (1988): 403–426.

ANTON BAMMER

EPHRAIM, SURVEY OF. *See* Southern Samaria, Survey of.

EPIGRAPHY. *See* Inscriptions.

EQUIDS. The horse, ass, and onager, all members of the genus *Equus*, family *Equidae*, order *Perissodactyla* (odd-toed ungulates), are found in the ancient Near East both as wild and domestic stock. The equids were secondary domesticates—chronologically later additions to husbanded sheep, goat, cattle, and pig—apparently more valued for their labor than for meat, milk, fiber, or hides. The wild ass, *Equus africanus*, is known from Nubia and the eastern desert of Egypt; it recently was identified in southwest Asia. Previously thought to have been domesticated only in Egypt, it now appears that this could have occurred in the Syro-Arabian region as well. Remains of the domestic ass, *E. asinus*, appear in fourth-millennium deposits in both areas. Among the earliest remains from Israel are those in Early Bronze I–II levels at Arad. In all periods after the beginning of the second millennium BCE, the ass was the most common equid, used for plowing and as the primary beast of burden.

Remains of caballine wild horse, *E. ferus*, are known from Pleistocene sites in the Levant. Once thought to have disappeared from there at the end of the Ice Age, recently identified remains from a Chalcolithic deposit in the northern Negev have provisionally been identified as *E. ferus*. This would mean that the species persisted later into the Holocene and farther south than previously thought. Current opinion on the domestication of the horse, *E. caballus*, places it on the Eurasian steppe in the late Neolithic. From there it spread to various regions, reaching the ancient Near East in the first half of the third millennium. The earliest archaeological evidence places the domestic horse in Mesopotamia in about 2300 BCE. The domestic horse in Israel is noted from a slightly earlier context, again from Early Bronze I–II levels at Arad. [*See* Arad, *article on* Bronze Age Period.]

In greater Mesopotamia the onager, or half ass, *E. hemionus*, ranged from the Mediterranean to the Caspian Seas.

During the Neolithic, according to evidence from such sites as Umm Dabaghiyeh in Iraq, the animal was hunted for its meat and skin. It was once thought that the onager had been domesticated in Mesopotamia, but recent summaries of the philological, osteological, and behavioral evidence make clear that onagers were and are intractable. Onagers were used as studs to produce hybrids with donkeys during the early dynastic period in Mesopotamia. However, this practice seems to have died out with the arrival of the horse. Mules (hybrids produced by crossing a horse with an ass) have been attested on the basis of bone finds; the earliest are from Iran at the end of the third millennium BCE.

Equids figured in ritual activity. In Mesopotamia, equids were interred with humans and even wheeled vehicles, beginning in the late fourth and continuing until the first half of the second millennium BCE. Among the western Semites, as documented at Mari, asses were sacrificed to conclude a covenant. During the Middle Bronze Age both asses and horses were buried by western Asiatics in southern Canaan and the Egyptian Delta in ritual contexts. At Tell el-'Ajjul, near ancient Gaza, horses and asses were interred with human remains. At the Hyksos capital of Avaris in the Delta, asses accompanied some human burials. This was repeated at other sites in the southern tier of Canaan and the Delta as well. The Canaanite material also may have been sacrificial meals, for many of the equid skeletons are missing limbs or pelvic parts. At Tell el-'Ajjul and nearby Tell Jemmeh in southern Canaan, equids were also used as foundation deposits. In Egypt, outside the time and sphere of Asiatic influence, equids were occasionally interred with humans as part of the great Egyptian preoccupation with providing familiar and necessary items for the deceased's afterlife. [See 'Ajjul, Tell el-; Jemmeh, Tell.]

Throughout the ancient Near East, horses were always associated with elite classes, most often in their capacity to draw light chariots and, later, in the development of mounted cavalry. The equipment used to handle equids seems to have derived from that used for cattle. The earliest true bits appear in the sixteenth century BCE, but earlier evidence of mouth gear is known from marks left on teeth. Because they conferred considerable prestige on their owners, horses were highly prized. The horse is one of the few animals for which there is a demonstrated ancient interest in selective breeding. Horse texts from second-millennium Nuzi record genealogies, a parallel component of modern breed maintenance. [See Nuzi.] Mid-second-millennium Ugaritic texts include a discussion of veterinary issues in horse husbandry.

[See also Animal Husbandry; Cult; Ethnozoology; Leather; and Paleozoology.]

BIBLIOGRAPHY

Azzaroli, Augusto. *An Early History of Horsemanship.* Leiden, 1985. Includes extensive discussion of Near Eastern traditions of horsemanship.

Boessneck, Joachim. *Die Tierwelt des Alten Ägypten: Untersucht anhand Kulturgeschichtlicher und Zoologischer.* Munich, 1988. Presents summaries of the Egyptian evidence by a zoologist who studied the faunal remains from hundreds of sites throughout the ancient world.

Clutton-Brock, Juliet. *Domesticated Animals from Early Times.* Austin, 1981. Global summary of the equids, with a useful review of their biology and behavior.

Meadow, Richard H., and Hans-Peter Uerpmann, eds. *Equids in the Ancient World.* 2 vols. Wiesbaden, 1986–1991. Important studies of the philology and osteology of the Old World equids by J. N. Postgate, Uerpmann, Pierre Ducos, Juris Zarins, Juliet Clutton-Brock, and Meadow.

PAULA WAPNISH and BRIAN HESSE

'ERANI, TEL (also 'Areini; Tel Gath), site located on Israel's southeastern coastal plain, on Naḥal Lachish (Wadi Qubeiba), at the twenty-fourth kilometer of the historical Ashkelon-Hebron road, north of the modern town of Qiryat Gat. The tel contains an acropolis and a high and low terrace. It is 60–90 acres in size and 120–152 m above sea level. Although the site has been identified as Libnah by Claude R. Conder and H. H. Kitchener, as Gath of the Philistines by Hermann Guthe, as *mmšt* of the *lmlk* impressions and as Eglon by Shmuel (1958, p. 276; Yeivin 1961 p. 10), and as Makedah (Kallai, 1986, p. 381) it still lacks a solid identification. Its Hebrew name derives from the tomb (Ar. *weli*) of Sheikh Aḥmed el-'Areini that stood on the acropolis (area E).

Victor Guérin visited the site in 1863, Conder in 1875, and William Foxwell Albright in the 1920s. Yeivin and Shalom Levy carried out six seasons of excavations from 1956 to 1961, on behalf of the Israel Department of Antiquities and Museums, with the participation of Antonia Ciasca and Gherardo Gnoli of the Istituto Italiano per il Medio ed Estremo Oriente in Rome in the last three seasons. In 1985, 1987, and 1988 Aharon Kempinski and Isaac Gilead excavated in area D-II on behalf of Tel Aviv and Ben-Gurion Universities (Kempinski and Gilead, 1991; Kempinski, 1992; 1993). Smaller excavations and inspection work at the southern part of the site were undertaken in 1960 by Ephrat Yeivin (area Y), in 1966 by David Ussishkin (area U), in 1983 by Arieh Rochman-Halperin (area R), and in 1994–1995 by Eliot Brown and Edwin C. M. van den Brink (area O), on behalf of the Israel Antiquities Authority (reports are in the Antiquities Authority archive).

The excavation results are mainly Yeivin's. More than thirty-two strata were observed, but only preliminary reports have been published. Yeivin's independent sequences (areas A/G, D) are reported here out of necessity; Yeivin's and Kempinski's interpretations differ on several points. The analysis of the Early Bronze and Iron Age finds is not yet complete, so that the following stratigraphic and chronological picture is provisional, especially regarding Iron II.

Chalcolithic Period. No architectural remains were exposed for the earliest settlement (stratum pre-XII [Brandl, 1989, p. 365, n. 4], areas D and D-II). Its finds were recovered in later contexts and include basalt fenestrated bowls and pottery cornets.

Early Bronze Age I. Strata XII–IV in area D and strata D to early B in area D-II reflect the most important period at the site, when it was the center of the Egyptian colonization of the coastal plain and lowlands of Canaan and reached its greatest size (Brandl, 1992). [*See* Canaan.] According to the Canaanite pottery, the lower four strata belong to the earlier part of the period and the upper five to its later part. The exposed area of the former is limited, but it is clear that the strata, except for stratum XII, which included only pits, reflect the same Egyptian architectural tradition as the later EB I strata: no stone foundations, brick bonding techniques, and matting on the floors. Parts of several buildings were uncovered. More than two thousand of the finds are Egyptian in character—most are locally made, as is indicated by their clay and the flint and other stones.

Early Bronze Age II. The site may have been smaller in EB II than in EB I but was larger than in EB III, as the city wall of the latter was built on EB II wall stumps. It is not clear if the Egyptians stayed on during this period (strata III–II, area D; late stratum B, area D-II). The pottery finds include Abydos jars and other forms that are parallelled at Arad. [*See* Arad, *article on* Early Bronze Age Period.] The seven skeletons found in a room destruction are among the few human remains of EB II date uncovered in Palestine.

Early Bronze Age III. The settlement (stratum I, areas D, F, K–O; stratum A, area D-II), with its massive city wall, glacis, and possible indirect-entry gate in area N (attributed by Yeivin to stratum VI; Brandl, 1989, pp. 379–383), seems to extend across the high terrace. The material culture was purely Canaanite, its pottery including Metallic ware and some Khirbet Kerak vessels. [*See* Canaanites.] The nature of the architecture may be similar to area G at Tel Yarmut. [*See* Yarmut, Tel.]

Late Bronze Age II B. During the thirteenth century BCE, after a long gap, a new settlement (areas A, B, F, G; stratum A, area D-II [Kempinski and Gilead 1991]) covered the entire acropolis and perhaps a little beyond. Traces of a massive structure (palace?), originally identified as a gate, were found in area G under the Iron II fortifications. Two tombs were discovered in area D-II. The pottery reflects the international contacts of the period as well as the Egyptian colonization under Rameses II: Cypriot Base Ring II, White-Slipped and White-Shaved Wares, and locally made Egyptian vessels.

Iron Age I. The settlement (areas B, F, G), in Iron I was most probably Philistine and covered the same area as the previous one. It contained Philistine Bichrome pottery, including mourners and Ashdoda figurines. [*See* Philistines, *article on* Early Philistines.]

Iron Age II. The site (strata XIII–IV, areas A, E–H, K, R, U) seems to have been a border town of Judah in Iron II. [*See* Judah.] The settlement was concentrated on the fortified acropolis, while potters' kilns and other polluting man-

ufacturing were located on the high terrace. The proximity to Philistia may account for the few Ashdod Ware vessels recovered. The excavators had assigned thirteen Iron II strata to the Hellenistic period in areas A and G. The lowermost four were identified only in the fortifications in a trench west of area G. Their relationship to stratum IX is still an open question, and they may have to be "moved" upward.

Of stratum IX, only a large plastered surface (a piazza inside a now eroded gate?) was exposed. In stratum VIII two ninth-century BCE buildings with inner courtyards were constructed over the piazza, possibly reflecting population growth. Stratum VII was originally dated to the late eighth–early seventh centuries BCE, but should be redated to the mid-eighth century, following the redating of stratum VI. Remains of two buildings with inner courtyards and a street, which continued the previous outline of this area, were uncovered, together with smashed pottery vessels, one with the Hebrew inscription *lyhz'*.

Stratum VI is dated to the late eighth century BCE, on the basis of a complete stamped *lmlk* jar found in situ. Altogether twenty *lmlk* impressions and one official impression (*ltnḥm mgn*), most from later or mixed contexts, can be attributed to this stratum. Two four-room houses were also uncovered. [*See* Four-room House.] This stratum was destroyed by the Assyrians in 701 BCE, as is attested by numerous slingstones, mainly from Area A.

Stratum V represents the Judean, post-Assyrian rebuilding of the seventh century BCE. The acropolis was refortified: an upper wall and its glacis were found in area G and its lower supporting wall in area F. A structure that Yeivin believed to be a great square inner tower seems to be another Israelite house. Among the finds are a jar handle with a rosette impression, East Greek pottery (including wine jars from Chios and Lesbos), oenochoes, and Ionic cups. Another find attributable to this stratum is a fragment of a bearded human terra-cotta head (Yeivin, 1961, pl. III:3), probably from an anthropomorphic vessel similar to finds from Horvat Qitmit and Haseva. [*See* Qitmit, Horvat.] Stratum IV (beginning of the sixth century BCE) was heavily disturbed by Persian-period silos. It seems that this last Judean stratum was destroyed by the Babylonians.

Persian Period and Later. In strata III and II (fifth–fourth centuries BCE), as at many sites in Palestine, the acropolis was partially abandoned and its summit pitted by numerous silos. Only one undisturbed room was found in stratum III, while the main settlement moved to the high terrace. The excavators identified almost no architecture; the settlement is deduced from the wide distribution of Persian-period pottery, such as high-footed mortaria and Attic Ware from areas A, B, D–G, and K–M. A *favissa* in area D contained fragments of stone statuettes and terra-cotta figurines, pointing to the existence of a temple on the high terrace.

Stratum I (Hellenistic period) was a smaller settlement. It

yielded much-disturbed remains in area A and pottery in areas B, C, and F. During the Byzantine and Mamluk periods, graves were dug into several areas. The settlement, a village, moved to the south (this may have already occurred in the Roman period), where the later village of 'Iraq el-Manshiyyeh was located. A Mamluk inscription of AH 717 (1317 CE) mentioning the construction of a khan, presumably nearby, was found in secondary use in the *weli*.

BIBLIOGRAPHY

Albright, William Foxwell. "Notes and Comments: One Aphek or Four?" *Journal of the Palestine Oriental Society* 2 (1922): 184–189.

Brandl, Baruch. "Observations on the Early Bronze Age Strata of Tel Erani." In *L'urbanisation de la Palestine à l'âge du Bronze ancien: Bilan et perspectives des recherches actuelles; Actes du Colloque d'Emmaüs, 20–24 octobre 1986*, edited by Pierre de Miroschedji, pp. 357–387. British Archaeological Reports, International Series, no. 527. Oxford, 1989.

Brandl, Baruch. "Evidence for Egyptian Colonization in the Southern Coastal Plain and Lowlands of Canaan during the EB I Period." In *The Nile Delta in Transition: Fourth–Third Millennium B.C.*, edited by Edwin C. M. van den Brink, pp. 441–477. Tel Aviv, 1992.

Ciasca, Antonia. "Tel Gat." *Oriens Antiquus* 1 (1962): 23–39.

Ciasca, Antonia. "Un deposito di statuette da Tell Gat." *Oriens Antiquus* 2 (1963): 45–63.

Ferembach, Denise. "Les restes humains de Gat." In *Preliminary Report on the Excavations at Tel Gat (Tell Sheykh Ahmed et 'Areyny)*, by Shmuel Yeivin et al., pp. 12–20, pls. 11–12. Jerusalem, 1961.

Horwitz, Liora K., and Eitan Tchernov. "Animal Exploitation in the Early Bronze Age of the Southern Levant: An Overview." In *L'urbanisation de la Palestine à l'âge du Bronze ancien: Bilan et perspectives des recherches actuelles; Actes du Colloque d'Emmaüs, 20–24 octobre 1986*, edited by Pierre de Miroschedji, pp. 279–296. British Archaeological Reports, International Series, no. 527. Oxford, 1989.

Ilan, Ornit, and Michael Sebbane. "Metallurgy, Trade, and the Urbanization of Southern Canaan in the Chalcolithic and Early Bronze Age." In *L'urbanisation de la Palestine à l'âge du Bronze ancien: Bilan et perspectives des recherches actuelles; Actes du Colloque d'Emmaüs, 20–24 octobre 1986*, edited by Pierre de Miroschedji, pp. 139–162. British Archaeological Reports, International Series, no. 527. Oxford, 1989.

Kallai, Zecharia. *Historical Geography of the Bible: The Tribal Territories of Israel.* Leiden, 1986.

Kempinski, Aharon. *The Rise of an Urban Culture: The Urbanization of Palestine in the Early Bronze Age.* Jerusalem, 1978.

Kempinski, Aharon, and Isaac Gilead. "New Excavations at Tel Erani: A Preliminary Report of the 1985–1988 Seasons." *Tel Aviv* 18 (1991): 164–191.

Kempinski, Aharon. "Reflections on the Role of the Egyptians in the Shefalah of Palestine in the Light of Recent Soundings at Tel Erani." In *The Nile Delta in Transition: Fourth–Third Millennium B.C.*, edited by Edwin C. M. van den Brink, pp. 419–425. Tel Aviv, 1992.

Kempinski, Aharon. "'Erani, Tel: Area D." In *The New Encyclopedia of Archaeological Excavations in the Holy Land*, vol. 2, pp. 419–421. Jerusalem and New York, 1993.

Mayer, Leo A. "Satura Epigraphica Arabica I." *Quarterly of the Department of Antiquities in Palestine* 1 (1932): 37–43.

Moscati, Sabatino. "L'archeologia italiana nel Vicino Oriente." *Oriens Antiquus* 3 (1964): 1–14.

Porat, Naomi. "Local Industry of Egyptian Pottery in Southern Palestine during the Early Bronze I Period." *Bulletin of the Egyptological Seminar* 7 (1986–1987): 109–129.

Porat, Naomi. "An Egyptian Colony in Southern Palestine during the Late Predynastic–Early Dynastic Period." In *The Nile Delta in Transition: Fourth–Third Millennium B.C.*, edited by Edwin C. M. van den Brink, pp. 433–440. Tel Aviv, 1992.

Rosen, Arlene Miller. "Early Bronze Age Tel Erani: An Environmental Perspective." *Tel Aviv* 18 (1991): 192–204.

Rosen, Steven A. "A Preliminary Note on the Egyptian Component of the Chipped Stone Assemblage from Tel 'Erani." *Israel Exploration Journal* 38 (1988): 105–116.

Slatkine, A. "Comparative Petrographic Study of Ancient Pottery Sherds from Israel." *Museum Haaretz Yearbook* 15–16 (1972–1973): 101–111.

Smith, Patricia M. "The Skeletal Biology and Paleopathology of Early Bronze Age Populations in the Levant." In *L'urbanisation de la Palestine à l'âge du Bronze ancien: Bilan et perspectives des recherches actuelles; Actes du Colloque d'Emmaüs, 20–24 octobre 1986*, edited by Pierre de Miroschedji, pp. 297–313. British Archaeological Reports, International Series, no. 527. Oxford, 1989.

Smith, Patricia M. "People of the Holy Land from Prehistory to the Recent Past." In *The Archaeology of Society in the Holy Land*, edited by Thomas E. Levy, pp. 58–74. New York, 1994.

Weinstein, James M. "The Significance of Tel Areini for Egyptian-Palestinian Relations at the Beginning of the Bronze Age." *Bulletin of the American Schools of Oriental Research*, no. 256 (1984): 61–69.

Yeivin, Shmuel. "Notes and News: Tell Gath." *Israel Exploration Journal* 8 (1958): 274–276.

Yeivin, Shmuel. "Chronique archéologique: Tell Gath." *Revue Biblique* 67 (1960a): 391–394.

Yeivin, Shmuel. "Notes and News: Tell Gath." *Israel Exploration Journal* 10 (1960b): 122–123.

Yeivin, Shmuel. "Early Contacts between Canaan and Egypt." *Israel Exploration Journal* 10 (1960c): 193–203.

Yeivin, Shmuel, et al. *Preliminary Report on the Excavations at Tel Gat (Tell Sheykh Ahmed el 'Areyny): Seasons 1956–1958.* Jerusalem, 1961.

Yeivin, Shmuel. "Further Evidence of Narmer at 'Gat.'" *Oriens Antiquus* 2 (1963): 205–213.

Yeivin, Shmuel. "The Chalcolithic Cultures of Canaan." In *VI Congreso Internazionale delle Scienze Preistoriche e Protostoriche*, vol. 2, *Communicazioni, sezioni I–IV*, pp. 355–357. Rome, 1965.

Yeivin, Shmuel. "A New Chalcolithic Culture at Tel 'Erani and Its Implications for Early Egypto-Canaanite Relations." In *Fourth World Congress of Jewish Studies*, pp. 45–48. Jerusalem, 1967.

Yeivin, Shmuel. "Additional Notes on the Early Relations between Canaan and Egypt." *Journal of Near Eastern Studies* 27 (1968): 37–50.

Yeivin, Shmuel. "El-'Areini, Tell Esh Sheikh Ahmed (Tel 'Erani)." In *Encyclopedia of Archaeological Excavations in the Holy Land*, vol. 1, pp. 89–97. Jerusalem, 1975.

Yeivin, Shmuel. "'Erani, Tel." In *The New Encyclopedia of Archaeological Excavations in the Holy Land*, vol. 2, pp. 417–419, 421–422. Jerusalem and New York, 1993.

BARUCH BRANDL

ERIDU, Sumerian city and cult center located on the southwestern periphery of the southern Mesopotamian floodplain (30°52' N, 46°3' E). It is the site of é-abzu, temple of Enki (Akkadian Ea), god of the subterranean freshwater ocean, and consists of seven mounds, whose occupations range in date from the Ubaid to the Persian period. The main mound (mound no. 1) is called Abu Shahrain or Abu Shuhur but is also reported to have been called Nowawis in the late nineteenth century. Either French Assyriologists Charles François Lenormant or Joachim Ménant first identified Abu Shahrain as ancient Eridu (Zehnpfund, 1909, pp. 291–298), apparently on the basis of inscribed bricks from the site.

The first archaeological work at Abu Shahrain was carried out in 1854, when J. E. Taylor undertook excavations there on behalf of the British Museum. In a paper read before the Royal Asiatic Society on 5 May 1855, Taylor described his work at the site as "unproductive of any very important results" (Taylor, 1855, p. 404). In 1918, R. Campbell Thompson carried out a season of excavation at the site, also on behalf of the British Museum. In the following year, Harry R. Hall continued the museum's work with a single season of work. From 1946 to 1949, Fuad Safar, Mohammad Ali Mustafa, and Seton Lloyd undertook extensive excavations at Eridu on behalf of the Iraqi Directorate General of Antiquities. [*See the biographies of Safar and Lloyd.*]

Eridu is best known for its sequence of temples excavated by the directorate general. Eighteen building levels above a 30-centimeter-thick layer of occupational debris (level XIX), spanning a period from the Early Ubaid period into the Late Uruk period, were uncovered. The earliest temple identified in this sequence belongs to level XVI. It consisted of a small rectangular mud-brick building with a deep recess in its northwest wall. The building had a podium, perhaps an offering table, in the center of its main room and a second one—in all likelihood the pedestal on which the cult statue would have stood—in a niche in the northwestern wall. A circular oven was found outside the temple's south wall. As the level XVI temple was rebuilt time and again, the building grew larger and more elaborate. The later temples, whose ground plans consisted of a long rectangular central room flanked by rows of rooms on its northwestern and southeastern sides, were set elevated on platforms and had elaborate niched and buttressed facades. Inside the central room was a high podium or offering table; against the southwestern wall was a second podium or pedestal on which the cult statue would have stood. Large quantities of fish bones were found on the floors of the level VII temple and mixed with ashes on and around the podium in the central room of the level VI temple. The bones are likely the remains of offerings to Enki. Of the Uruk-period temple levels (V–I), only portions of the temple platforms remained. [*See* Ubaid; Uruk-Warka.]

Joan Oates (1960) used the Eridu sequence of temples and painted pottery recovered from them to divide the Ubaid period into four phases: Ubaid 1, or Eridu (levels XIX–XV); Ubaid 2, or Hajji Muhammad (levels XIV–XII); Ubaid 3, or Ubaid (levels XII–VIII); and Ubaid 4, or Late Ubaid (levels VII–VI). A phase (Ubaid 0, or 'Oueili) that antedates the Ubaid 1, or Eridu, phase was subsequently recovered at Tell el-'Oueili (Huot, 1987, pp. 11–120). [*See* 'Oueili, Tell el-.] The Eridu temple sequence provides archaeological support for a lengthy, in-place cultural development in southern Mesopotamia from the earliest-known prehistoric period to the point when the written language can be identified as Sumerian; it has been used to argue that the Sumerians were the original inhabitants of the southern floodplain (Oates, 1960, pp. 44–50). [*See* Sumerian; Sumerians; Ur.]

The topography of the main mound at Eridu is dominated by a large ziggurat dated to the Ur III period. This ziggurat, constructed of a mud-brick core and an outer facing of baked bricks set in bitumen, is 61.8 m long × 46.5 m wide. Its eroded ruins stand 9.5 m high. Construction of the ziggurat was initiated by Ur-Nammu (2112–2095 BCE) and completed by his grandson Amar-Suen (2046–2038 BCE). Stamped bricks also provide evidence that a king of Larsa, Nur-Adad (1865–1850 BCE), carried out work on the ziggurat. [*See* Larsa.] A single inscribed brick bearing the name of Nebuchadrezzer II (604–562 BCE) was found lying to the west of the ziggurat, probably in a secondary context. Althought there is a gap in the temple sequence between the Uruk levels and the Ur III ziggurat, the ziggurat can be viewed as the culmination of a long developmental sequence of Mesopotamian temple architecture stretching back to the Ubaid period.

One of the largest Ubaid cemeteries known was excavated at Eridu by the Iraqi Directorate General of Antiquities. The burials date to the end of the Ubaid period. Of an estimated 800 to 1,000 burials in the cemetery, 193 were excavated. The burials, cut through a layer of rubbish containing Ubaid 2 or Hajji Muhammad pottery, consisted of a square shaft lined with mud-brick walls. One or more individuals were placed in this shaft along with burial goods; the chamber was then filled with earth and sealed with mud brick.

Other areas excavated at Eridu include the Hut Sounding, a small excavated unit located 80 m southeast of the ziggurat. The Hut Sounding included fourteen levels of Ubaid-period occupation and the Early Dynastic palaces excavated on the North Mound (mound no. 2). Considered to be among the oldest cities in Mesopotamia, antedating the Flood, and the first city to hold kingship, Eridu figures prominently in Sumerian literature (Green, 1975, 1978).

[*See also* Ziggurat.]

BIBLIOGRAPHY

Coon, Carleton S. "The Eridu Crania." *Sumer* 5 (1949): 103–106.

Flannery, Kent V., and Henry T. Wright. "Faunal Remains from the 'Hut Sounding' at Eridu, Iraq." *Sumer* 22 (1966): 61–64.

Green, Margaret Whitney. "Eridu in Sumerian Literature." Ph.D. diss., University of Chicago, 1975.

Green, Margaret Whitney. "The Eridu Lament." *Journal of Cuneiform Studies* 30 (1978): 127–167.

Hall, Harry R. *A Season's Work at Ur.* London, 1930.

Huot, Jean-Louis. *Larsa(10e campagne, 1983) et Oueili (4e campagne, 1983): Rapport préliminaire.* Paris, 1987.

Lloyd, Seton, and Fuad Safar. "Eridu: Preliminary Communication on the First Season's Excavations, January–March 1947." *Sumer* 3 (1947): 84–111.

Lloyd, Seton, and Fuad Safar. "Eridu: Preliminary Communication on the Second Season's Excavations, 1947–1948." *Sumer* 4 (1948): 115–127, 276–283.

Oates, Joan. "Ur and Eridu: The Prehistory." *Iraq* 22 (1960): 32–50. Seminal division of the Ubaid period into phases.

Safar, Fuad. "Excavations at Eridu." *Sumer* 3 (1947): 219–235; 5 (1949): 116–117, 159–173; 6 (1950): 27–38.

Safar, Fuad, et al. *Eridu*. Baghdad, 1981.

Taylor, J. E. "Notes on Abu Shahrein and Tel el Lahm." *Journal of the Royal Asiatic Society* 15 (1855): 404–415.

Thompson, R. Campbell. "The British Museum Excavations at Abu Shahrein in Mesopotamia in 1918." *Archaeologia* 70 (1920): 101–145.

Zehnpfund, Rudolf. "Die Lage der Stadt Eridu." *Hilprecht Anniversary Volume*, pp. 291–298. Leipzig, 1909.

MICHAEL D. DANTI and RICHARD L. ZETTLER

ERMAN, ADOLF (1854–1937), eminent German Egyptologist. Born in Berlin of Swiss descent, Jean Pierre Adolphe (Johann Peter Adolf) Erman became one of the best-known and most influential Egyptologists in the world. He was trained in Leipzig and Berlin by Georg Ebers and Richard Lepsius. By 1884, he was the director of the Egyptian and Assyrian Department of the Egyptian Museum in Berlin and professor of Egyptology.

Erman was one of the "founding fathers" of modern Egyptology, for it was he who first organized ancient Egyptian into three separate phases: Old, Middle, and Late. He followed this groundbreaking theoretical division with the publication of grammars of the stages. Erman also wrote about the relationship between ancient Egyptian and Semitic languages. His talents, however, were not limited to philological theory, for he was a gifted translator and an avid scholar of all aspects of Egyptology. His many volumes of translated texts were invaluable to scholars and represented the means by which the public could understand and appreciate the wealth of Egyptian literature.

Erman wrote a monograph on the hieroglyphic inscriptions accompanying the figures decorating the walls of Old Kingdom tombs. He recognized that these texts represented the figures' actual conversations. They are, therefore, much like the speech balloons that appear near the characters in our modern cartoons. Erman's extensive knowledge of every aspect of ancient Egypt civilization was the source for his book *Life in Ancient Egypt* (1894), which is still in use today. His works on art, archaeology, history, and religion are equally valuable sources of information.

Erman's most ambitious project, for which he is best known, was his dictionary of the ancient Egyptian language. The *Wörterbuch der ägyptischen Sprache*, produced jointly with Grapow, was in progress when Erman died in Berlin. It stands today as a fitting monument to this enormously talented individual whose innumerable contributions were instrumental in unraveling the many mysteries of ancient Egypt.

BIBLIOGRAPHY

Erman, Adolf. *Life in Ancient Egypt*. London, 1894.

Erman, Adolf, and Hermann Grapow. *Wörterbuch der ägyptischen Sprache* (1926). 7 vols. 4th ed. Berlin, 1982.

DAVID P. SILVERMAN

ESDAR, TEL, a 2-ha (5 acre) loess hill located 3 km (2 mi.) north of Tel 'Aro'er in the Negev desert (31°09′ N, 34°59′ E; map reference 1475 × 0645). The site was discovered by Nelson Glueck in 1956 (his site 308; Glueck, 1957) and excavated by Moshe Kochavi on behalf of the Israel Department of Antiquities in 1963–1964. Five periods of occupation were discerned in three areas of excavations. Avraham Biran proposed identifying Tel Esdar with 'Aro'er in the Davidic cycles (*1 Sm.* 30:28) because no Iron Age I remains were found in his excavation at nearby Tel 'Aro'er (Biran, 1993). [*See* 'Aro'er.]

Stratum IVB, found in all the excavated areas, belongs to the Beersheba culture (Chalcolithic period). It consisted of several beaten-earth living surfaces with fireplaces and ash-pits. The small finds were typical of the culture: churns, decorated bowls, flint axes, and an agate pendant. Stratum IVA, also found in all the excavated areas, belongs to the Early Bronze Age II. Several living floors constructed of pebbles and some stone-lined silos were among its remains. Besides the pottery, known from Arad and EB II Sinai and Negev sites, a cache of giant fan scrapers was found on one of the floors. The scrapers were made of tabular flint and incised with different patterns on their backs; some of the motifs resemble those from Megiddo stratum XIX.

Tel Esdar was the first of the Iron I sites excavated in the Negev. In stratum III several buildings were found arranged in a defensive circle on the spur of the tell (area C). A test pit was dug in the area they surrounded but no remains were found, indicating that the area had been used as an open space. Of the eight buildings excavated, the plan of only one was preserved in its entirety; however, sufficient evidence was left to show that all had followed approximately the same plan. These were three-room houses, with dividing walls formed by rows of pillars and a main entrance in the long wall, facing an interior open space. Dozens of smashed vessels were found on the floors, indicating a violent destruction. The crude, undecorated pottery dates the destruction to the late eleventh century BCE. Many comparisons could be found between it and the pottery of Tel Masos III–II. [*See* Masos, Tel.] Of special importance are the thirty-six complete storage jars, all of the same distinctive transitional type, and the use of chalices as stands for oil lamps.

In stratum II, three structures, dated to the tenth century BCE, had been constructed close to one another on the slope of the tell. They were situated beyond the stratum III enclosure and built on a different plan and consisted of a farmhouse and its related buildings. They suffered no sudden destruction and only a few red-slipped sherds and many stone agricultural implements were found on their floors.

Stratum I consisted of agricultural terrace walls. Pottery sherds of the Roman-Byzantine period define the stratum.

In summary, the earliest levels of occupation at Tel Esdar fit well with the pattern of settlement in the Chalcolithic Beersheba culture and EB II in the Negev. These two periods of occupation are well represented in the Beersheba–Arad valley and the long gap of occupation between them and the Iron Age finds a good comparison at Tel Arad. [*See* Arad, *article on* Early Bronze Age Period.] Tel Esdar stratum III is to be interpreted either as a satellite of Tel Masos or as its small rival, destroyed by the inhabitants of the larger, much stronger community. Stratum II was part of the revival of the valley in the tenth century BCE, when Tel Malhata was resettled and strongly fortified.

BIBLIOGRAPHY

Biran, Avraham. "Aroer (in Judah)." In *The New Encyclopedia of Archaeological Excavations in the Holy Land*, vol. 4, p. 1272. Jerusalem and New York, 1993. Proposes an identification with ʿAroʿer.

Cohen, Rudolph. "Tel Esdar, Stratum IV." *Israel Exploration Journal* 28 (1978): 185–189. Corrects the dating of stratum IV and divides it into IVA and IVB.

Glueck, Nelson. "The Fifth Season of Exploration in the Negeb." *Bulletin of the American Schools of Oriental Research*, no. 145 (1957): 14. First description of the site, but the dating is incorrect.

Kochavi, Moshe. "Excavations at Tel Esdar." *ʿAtiqot* 5 (1969): 2*–5*, 14–48. Publication of the excavation.

Kochavi, Moshe. "Esdar, Tell." In *The New Encyclopedia of Archaeological Excavations in the Holy Land*, vol. 2, p. 423. Jerusalem and New York, 1993. Short description of the excavation with corrected stratigraphy.

MOSHE KOCHAVI

ESHMUNAZAR INSCRIPTION. The discovery in 1855 of an anthropoid sarcophagus near the Phoenician port city of Sidon brought to light an important Phoenician text. The stone coffin belonged to a Sidonian king, Eshmunazar II, who most likely reigned in the first half of the fifth century BCE; on the lid of the sarcophagus was inscribed the twenty-two-line text now known as the Eshmunazar Inscription.

On 19 January 1855, workmen hired to hunt for treasure on behalf of the chancellor of the French consulate general in Beirut discovered the basalt sarcophagus within an ancient necropolis, a rocky knoll and grotto known as Mugharat Ablun, about a kilometer southeast of Sidon's port. The large sarcophagus (110 × 225 cm) had been buried 2 m deep in an open rock-cut grave and, in antiquity, apparently had a small stone-built entrance chamber to protect it. Disinterred, the sarcophagus was shipped to France, where it resides in the Louvre Museum.

The style of the features carved on the lid of the stone coffin—an almond-eyed face, chest-length striated wig, chin beard, and falcon-headed *usech,* or broad collar—is typically Egyptian. Most likely fashioned in Egypt, the coffin may have been brought to Sidon as booty or as a purchased order, where it was inscribed following Eshmunazar's death.

The text is inscribed below the funerary mask. In the first four lines we read that King Eshmunazar, son of King Tabnit, reigned for fourteen years and lived a short life. Eshmunazar describes himself as an "orphan, the son of a widow"; Tabnit apparently died before or shortly after his son's birth, making Eshmunazar a child-king and his mother, the regent. After imprecations directed toward would-be grave plunderers (ll. 4–13), the text recounts the cultic shrines Eshmunazar and the queen-mother (re)built (ll. 13–18), a notable one being the Temple of Eshmun. It further declares that the "lord of kings," most probably the king of Persia, ceded Levantine territory, particularly the cities of Dor and Jaffa, to Sidon in return for services rendered (ll. 18–20). The nature and date of these rendered services remain unknown: perhaps Persia ceded the territory to Sidon for assisting Cambyses' invasion of Egypt in 525 BCE or for naval support during the battle of Salamis in 480 BCE or because of changes in Persian satrapy boundaries in the generation after 480 BCE. Additional imprecations complete the inscription (ll. 20–22).

The first thirteen and a half lines also appear in seven lines on the head end of the base. The reason for the duplication may be that the inscriber could not fit the full text there or wanted to start anew after committing several writing errors.

The text, because of its length and degree of preservation, provides significant insight into the characteristics of the Phoenician language in general and the Tyro-Sidonian dialect in particular. The inscription also reveals meaningful affinities with other Semitic languages, seen, for example, in its idioms, word pairs, and use of repetition.

[*See also* Phoenician-Punic; *and* Sidon.]

BIBLIOGRAPHY

Gibson, John C. L. *Textbook of Syrian Semitic Inscriptions*, vol. 3, *Phoenician Inscriptions Including Inscriptions in the Mixed Dialect of Arslan Tash*. Oxford, 1982. Discusses historical circumstances and dating (pp. 101–102), and includes Hebrew transliteration, English translation, philological analysis of the text, and bibliography (pp. 105–114, Text 28).

Jidejian, Nina. *Sidon through the Ages*. Beirut, 1971. Discussion of the discovery of the sarcophagus and the excavations at the Temple of Eshmun, with bibliography in the side margins. See figures 5–9 for photos and drawings of the sarcophagus.

Peckham, J. Brian. "Tyre, Sidon, and Vicinity." Chapter 3 of *The Development of the Late Phoenician Scripts*. Harvard Semitic Studies, no. 20. Cambridge, Mass., 1968. Discussion and bibliography about the issues involved in dating Eshmunazar's reign (pp. 77–87).

GARY ALAN LONG

ESHNUNNA (modern Tell Asmar), site located in the Diyala River basin, about 81 km (50 mi.) northeast of Baghdad, Iraq, in a very arid region in which the productivity of the land was exhausted through overirrigation in antiquity (33°32′ N, 44°58′ E). Eshnunna was also the name for the entire region of which Tell Asmar/Eshnunna was the main town and often the administrative center. Excavations conducted at Tell Asmar by the Iraq Expedition of the Oriental Institute of the University of Chicago in the 1930s uncovered important and monumental remains from the early third through the early second millennia BCE. The results of the excavations there provide the basis for the Mesopotamian chronology used today.

The name of the town may have been pronounced "Eshnun" in the Akkadian through Ur III periods; the long form, Eshnunna, appeared first in the Ur III period. Although the name *Eshnunna* was known from historical texts to the first scholars of the ancient Near East, the site was not located until 1930. Bricks inscribed with the name *Eshnunna* were already turning up on the antiquities market in the late nineteenth century. Some of those inscriptions were published in 1892 by French antiquarian and Assyriologist Henri Pognon, who, for obscure reasons, refused to divulge the location of the site from which the inscriptions came. Edward Chiera of the Oriental Institute had collected some bricks inscribed with the names of rulers of Eshnunna from Tell Asmar; the site was chosen for archaeological exploration partially on the basis of his observations. In addition to the Oriental Institute's excavations under the direction of Henri Frankfort, the Diyala Basin Archaeological Project was carried out between 1957 and 1958 under the direction of Thorkild Jacobsen. The project was conceived as both a textual and field investigation of settlement and irrigation in the whole Diyala region. [*See* Diyala; *and the biographies of Frankfort and Jacobsen.*]

Although regional surveys have indicated that the earliest settlements in the Diyala River basin date to the Ubaid period (fifth–early fourth millennia), at Tell Asmar, virgin soil underlay remains of the late fourth millennium. Ubaid sherds were found at Tell Asmar, but they were in secondary association with later materials; there was no primary Ubaid deposit. The Early Dynastic period was a period of substantial growth in the Diyala, in which Tell Asmar was at the high end of a hierarchy of towns and villages. During the Ur III and Isin-Larsa periods, although there was continuity of settlement in the Diyala, there was a trend toward more dispersed rural settlement with a decline in the total amount of built-up areas occupied by towns as opposed to villages. The northwest area of the mound of Tell Asmar seemed to have been the site of the Early Dynastic–early Ur III period town. The town greatly expanded during the later Ur III and Isin-Larsa periods. The main loci of habitation shifted, so that the previously sparsely occupied southern two-thirds of the mound became the site of the most important monumental public buildings of the city of the Late Ur III through the Isin-Larsa periods. Tell Asmar was abandoned in the Old Babylonian period, presumably at or about the time of the conquest of Eshnunna by Hammurabi of Babylon in 1763 BCE or of the final Babylonian conquest of Eshnunna by Samsuiluna. [*See* Ur; Ubaid; Isin; Larsa.]

The most important early remains from Tell Asmar are a long series of temples built one on top of another, perhaps indicating continuity in religious tradition. The latest of the temples was apparently dedicated to the local god, Abu (the earlier ones may also have been devoted to the cult of this deity). The stratigraphy of the temples and the associated objects provided the basis for determining the chronology of the Early Dynastic period. The excavators divided it into three distinct phases based on the identification of three main phases in the Abu Temple above an early Protoliterate period (late fourth millennium) shrine: the Archaic Shrine dating to Early Dynastic I, the Square Temple dating to Early Dynastic II, and the Single Shrine dating to Early Dynastic III and the so-called Protoimperial periods. This schema has since been modified.

The Square Temple (Early Dynastic II period) consisted of three separate shrines around a square central room. Each shrine had a rectangular altar at one end. In one of the shrines, the excavators found a hoard of sculpted figures, both males and females, buried beneath the floor in a recess north of the altar. The findspot of the hoard may actually predate the temple. It is not possible to determine whether the statues were made as a group and dedicated at the same time or were accumulated by the temple over a period of time. They are characterized by rather naive, abstract geometric forms the excavators thought were typical of the ED II style throughout Mesopotamia. However, it is now believed that because Eshnunna was a provincial town, the unsophisticated style of the statues cannot be considered typical of Mesopotamian art in general. In addition, the so-called Early Dynastic II pottery from the Square Temple consists of types that continue from ED I to ED III or that can be found either in ED I or ED III. According to the current trend of thought, ED II as a distinct period may only have validity in the Diyala, where it was contemporary with the late ED I period in southern Mesopotamia.

The most important structure of the Akkadian period was the so-called Northern Palace. Abutting that building to the south was a house adjacent to the Abu Temple. The earliest version of the Northern Palace, dating to the very Early Akkadian period seemed to have served as a residential compound, perhaps somehow associated with the nearby Abu Temple. There is also evidence that some industrial activity may have taken place within the complex. This evidence consists of a rather elaborate system of drains, several rooms identified as toilets or bathrooms by the excavators, and a large cistern. Whatever the function of this early version of the Northern Palace, the succeeding phase, called the main level, was not a palace at all but rather a large building devoted to manufacturing. It consisted of a central block of

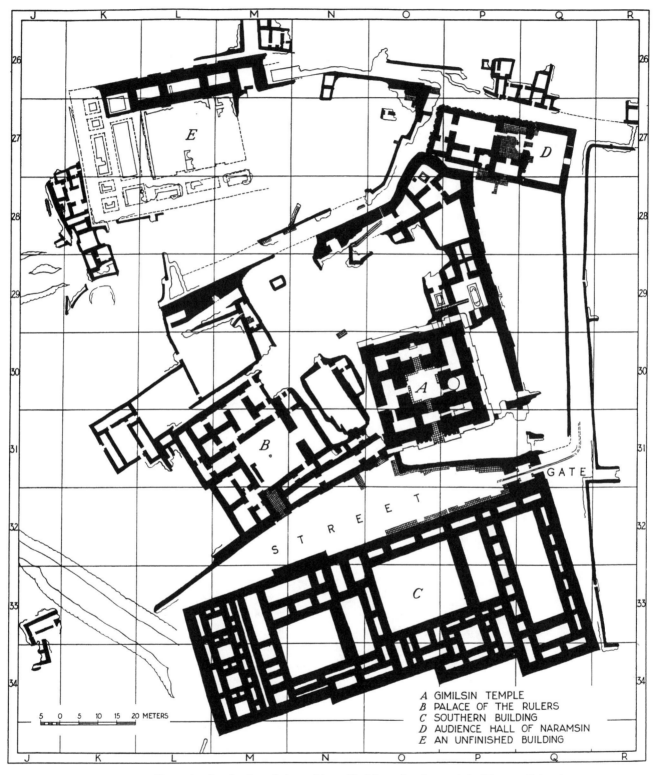

ESHNUNNA.   *Composite plan showing relative positions of buildings of various periods.* (Courtesy Oriental Institute of the University of Chicago)

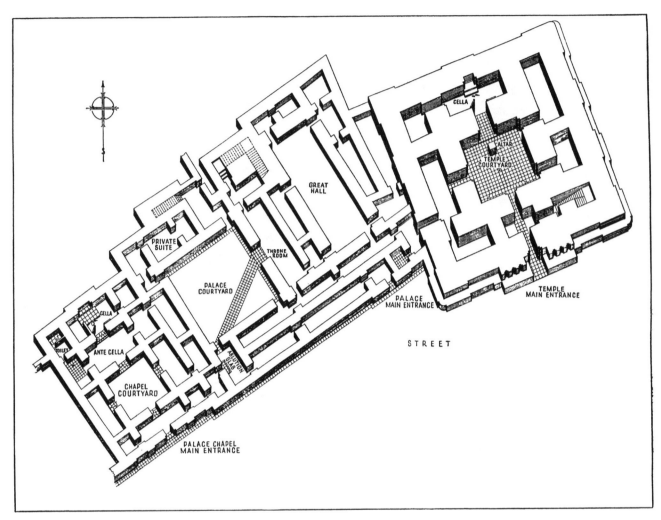

ESHNUNNA. *Projected plan of the Gimilsin Temple and the Palace of the Rulers in the reign of Ilushuila.*
(Courtesy Oriental Institute of the University of Chicago)

rooms with a large courtyard, a northern group separated from the main suite by a long vestibule, and a southern wing identified by the excavators as a women's residential quarters. This level also contained an elaborate drainage system with many drains, some with large vats at their heads, and floors paved with bitumen. Several of the rooms containing water installations had drains that emptied into a sewer in the street.

Although the excavators speculated that the large number of water installations in the building suggested a leather workshop, it now seems more likely that textiles dyeing took place there and that the establishment was devoted to textile production, probably employing numbers of female workers. Weaving and dyeing were not the only industries there. [*See* Textiles, *article on* Textiles of the Neolithic through Iron Ages.] There were also workshops for stone and shell inlay and ornamental stoneworking, as well as a food-processing and storage area, probably to feed the workers in the

various operations, and perhaps a potter's workshop. Above the palace were some fragmentary remains of what appears to have been flimsy rebuildings of the Northern Palace of the Ur III and perhaps the very early Isin-Larsa period. Some Akkadian tablets found in robber holes cut into the palace walls refer to a "women's house" in which women worked in a textile industry.

Excavations in the northwest section of the mound revealed a large residential area that was occupied continuously from the late ED III through the Early Isin-Larsa periods. Some of the houses of the Akkadian period included what could have been shops fronting the street; some others appeared to have altars, perhaps for private or family devotions. The Late Akkadian period occupation in this area may have been the most extensive; by the Late Ur III period, the main focus of occupation had already shifted south.

Late in the Ur III period, the *išakku,* or city ruler, of Eshnunna, Ituriya, had a temple built to his overlord, the deified king of Ur Shu-Sin, in the southern area of the site, where there had been no monumental buildings before. This building is unique among Mesopotamian temples in that the deity worshiped in it was a ruler actually living at the time it was built and dedicated. The temple was very regular in plan, with exceptionally wide walls. It was square, with a square, central courtyard with regular rooms arranged around it. The state temple was a testimony to the suzerainty of Ur over Eshnunna, an important administrative center near the border of the limits of the area controlled directly by the central government at Ur.

Somewhat later, at the time Eshnunna was breaking away or had just broken away from the authority of Ur, the Palace of the Rulers was built abutting the Shu-Sin Temple. As the palace underwent alterations, the temple, which had ceased being used for divine service, was eventually fully incorporated into the palace. The palace, an administrative building rather than a residence for the ruler, was altered many times by rulers throughout the twentieth century BCE, or the Early Isin-Larsa period. In that period Eshnunna was often independent but was sometimes subordinate to the rule or influence of Elam to the east. [See Elamites.] Many administrative texts dating to the twentieth–nineteenth centuries BCE were found in this building.

The mound of Tell Asmar was seriously eroded so that, although there is historical evidence that Eshnunna was very powerful until Hammurabi conquered it in 1763 BCE, the expedition was able to find only the foundations of massive buildings of the late nineteenth and early eighteenth centuries BCE but no stratified deposits. The remains of those monumental public buildings in the southern sector of the mound only hint at the power and prestige of Eshnunna in the late nineteenth and early eighteenth centuries BCE, when it was one of the important players on the international political scene.

BIBLIOGRAPHY

Adams, Robert McC. *Land behind Baghdad: A History of Settlement on the Diyala Plains.* Chicago, 1965. Excellent source for information on the topography, hydrology, land use, and settlement history of the entire Diyala region.

Delougaz, Pinhas, and Seton Lloyd. *Pre-Sargonid Temples in the Diyala Region.* Oriental Institute Publications (OIP), 58. Chicago, 1942. Detailed description of the series of ED temples said to be dedicated to the god Abu.

Delougaz, Pinhas. *Pottery from the Diyala Region.* OIP, 63. Chicago, 1952.

Delougaz, Pinhas, et al. *Private Houses and Graves in the Diyala Region.* OIP, 88. Chicago, 1967. Includes a detailed description of the Northern Palace and the residential areas at Tell Asmar.

Frankfort, Henri. *Sculpture of the Third Millennium B.C. from Tell Asmar and Khafājah.* OIP, 44. Chicago, 1939. Detailed description of the hoard of stone statues from the Abu Temple.

Frankfort, Henri, et al. *The Gimilsin Temple and the Palace of the Rulers at Tell Asmar.* OIP, 43. Chicago, 1940. Publication of the Isin-Larsa period public buildings at Tell Asmar; see the introduction for a good though outdated discussion of the site's history.

Frankfort, Henri. *Stratified Cylinder Seals from the Diyala Region.* OIP, 72. Chicago, 1955.

Henrickson, Elizabeth F. "Non-Religious Residential Settlement Patterning in the Late Early Dynastic of the Diyala Region." *Mesopotamia* 16 (1981): 43–133.

Henrickson, Elizabeth F. "Functional Analysis of the Elite Residences in the Late Early Dynastic of the Diyala Region: House D and the Walled Quarter at Khafajah and the 'Palaces' at Tell Asmar." *Mesopotamia* 17 (1982): 5–33. This and Henrickson's article above represent an interesting attempt at a functional analysis of the use of space in the residential quarters at Tell Asmar and nearby Khafajeh.

Jacobsen, Thorkild. *Salinity and Irrigation: Agriculture in Antiquity.* Bibliotheca Mesopotamica, 14. Malibu, 1982. Report on the results of the Diyala Basin Archaeological Project's regional survey.

Whiting, Robert M., Jr. *Old Babylonian Letters from Tell Asmar.* University of Chicago, Oriental Institute, Assyriological Studies, 22. Chicago, 1987. Good, up-to-date source for the chronology of the rulers of Eshnunna.

ELISE AUERBACH

ESKI MOSUL DAM SALVAGE PROJECT. A

long-planned dam on the Tigris River, just upstream from Eski Mosul (Balad) in Iraq was built between 1981 and 1985. As with the Hamrin and Haditha Dam Salvage Projects, Iraqi and foreign expeditions cooperated in investigating the sites to be flooded in the Eski Mosul Dam Salvage Project (later called the Saddam Dam Basin Salvage Project).

The major crossings of the Tigris River are outside the area of the project at Nineveh, Balad (Eski Mosul), and Cizre, but the Tigris can be readily crossed when it is not in flood and routes cross the region at Abu Dhahir and at Zummar. In general, however, the main routes avoid the broken terrain beside the river and follow courses outside the area. The main road north from Nineveh skirted the southeastern part of the area of the project, however.

The geomorphology of the region has not been adequately investigated, but excavations at sites such as Tell Kutan and Kharabeh Shattani showed that there has been considerable erosion and deposition. After rainstorms, the wadis were very active. It would be unwise to infer that the present topography closely resembles the ancient, but it is likely that in general the environment has not changed greatly since prehistoric times. Beside the river was a narrow floodpain bordered by rolling hills, often with the bedrock emerging: indeed, the area had been used as a quarry. The region is cut by a series of wadis draining into the Tigris. Most of these are dry for most of the year, but the Baqaq stream is perennial. The annual rainfall is about 450 mm and, where the soils were suitable, it was possible to practice dry farming. There is evidence for small canals, particularly along the Baqaq stream, that seem to be associated with a series of water mills of fairly recent date rather than with irrigation.

The top of the dam is 317.5 m above mean sea level and about 435 sq km (270 sq. mi.) is to be flooded. The lake extends about 70 km (43 mi.) upstream, as far as the Syrian border, and covers a ribbon of land which at its widest point is fewer than 8 km (5 mi.) from the old river course. In the original survey of the area by the Iraqi State Organization for Antiquities and Heritage, 149 sites were identified. There were only a few large sites: the most impressive (550 × 300 m) was Tell Jikan (Jigan), where Victor Place had excavated briefly in the nineteenth century; also impressive were Tell Selal and Tell Abu Dhahir, which also covered several hectares. These major sites were situated where wadis and relatively easy routes reached the Tigris and where the immediate terrain was quite flat and suitable for agriculture. Most of the sites in the region were small and occupied for limited periods. Some sixty-three sites were excavated in the course of the project, including twenty-one not located in the original survey. Most of the excavated sites were situated in the southeastern part of the area and along the south side of the river. For security reasons, only a few sites were investigated farther upstream on the north side of the river.

The Iraqi State Organization for Antiquities and Heritage excavated some twenty-three sites. The University of Mosul excavated four important sites on the south side of the river, Abu Dhahir, Mseifneh, Tell Dhuwaij, and Tell Selal. British teams from the British School of Archaeology in Iraq, the British Museum, the University of Edinburgh, and the University of Manchester worked on some fifteen sites, mostly in the southeastern part of the area and in the region near Abu Dhahir. Japanese archaeologists from Kokushikan University worked on seven sites near Jikan and near Zummar. A Polish team excavated sites near Rifan Ulya and at the Aceramic Neolithic site of Nemrik. In addition, Austrian, French, German, German/Italian, Italian, and Russian teams worked on a smaller number of sites.

A Polish survey in the region of Rifan identified some twenty-two locations where Lower Paleolithic tools were found; sixty Middle Paleolithic and twenty-three Upper Paleolithic tools also were recovered. Hand axes were occasionally found elsewhere in the project area. Two Pre-Pottery Neolithic sites were excavated. At Nemrik, which lies just above the area to be flooded, semisunken round houses with tauf (Ar., similar to *terre pisé*) and mud-brick walls were found. At Der Hall, an aceramic level was found, but the artifacts were not in situ.

Five Hassuna sites were excavated. The Hassuna remains at Tell Abu Dhahir could be traced over an area of about 2 ha (5 acres). At Kharabeh Shattani, the Hassuna level was covered by a compacted silty layer 1.2 m thick, on which a Halaf settlement was built. Only one site was excavated for which Samarra pottery has been published, but as many as nine sites were excavated with Halaf pottery. At Kharabeh Shattani several round houses (tholoi) were uncovered. At Khirbet Derak a series of bullae with stamp-seal impressions on them were found. At Derak and at Khirbeh Hatareh there was evidence for a gradual transition from the Halaf to the Ubaid pottery style, with intermediate types being recognized. Some eight sites with Ubaid pottery were excavated.

No substantial architecture of the period has been published.

Early Uruk or Gawra period occupations were identified on four sites. At Tell Mishrifeh houses with possibly tripartite plans and at Tell Karraneh 1 and 2 megaron-type buildings like those from Tepe Gawra levels IX–XI were found. The impression given by the results of the investigations in the Eski Mosul Dam Salvage Project strongly supports the view that the Gawra period precedes the Late Uruk period. It has been suggested that two rival cultures coexisted in northern Mesopotamia; a local one typified by Gawra and a second heavily influenced by the southern Uruk civilization represented by level IV at Nineveh. This southern-influenced culture was thought to have formed an elite dominating the local culture. The idea, however, receives no support from the excavations in the Eski Mosul region.

Local Late Uruk occupations characterized by beveled-rim bowls, incised jars, and spouted vessels, for example, were found on some eight sites. Excavations at a number of sites, particularly at Tell Mohammed Arab, have elucidated the sequence from the Late Uruk to the Ninevite 5 period and have resolved some of the long-standing problems of ceramic development in this period. A gradual transformation from the painted Uruk pottery to the painted Ninevite 5 and from the fineware Uruk vessels to the Ninevite 5 could be shown. The gradual introduction and development of incised gray ware and excised gray ware were demonstrated by the stratigraphic excavation at Tell Mohammed Arab and by a comparison with assemblages from shorter-lived sites. Also for the first time, an exposure of architecture revealed that small two-room rectangular dwellings were the norm in the Ninevite 5 period. Some nineteen sites with Ninevite 5 levels were excavated. Most of these occupations were small and were not long-lived. Thus, although the number of sites was large, the population in any one period could have been quite small. It should be noted that Painted Ninevite 5 pottery was found in widely separated soundings on Tell Jikan, suggesting that an extensive area, perhaps as much as 15 ha (37 acres), was occupied in this period.

The fine decorated gray ware of the Ninevite 5 period appears to have been the forerunner of the distinctive hard fineware of the Taya period. The transition from one to the other has not been found in excavations to date, and there seem to be important changes that occurred with the introduction of this new style. In particular, at Tell Jikan the construction of the city wall was associated with this new style. Similar indications of urbanization have been found elsewhere in northern Iraq and in the Khabur region in this period. At Tell Karraneh 1 an interesting group of six terracotta objects was recovered, five shaped like phalli and the sixth with a molded stylized human head. In the Eski Mosul Dam Salvage Project, nine sites of this period were excavated, which corresponds roughly to the Akkadian and Ur III periods in the south.

The largest number of sites excavated (twenty-two) belonged to the Khabur period. On many of these, areas of housing consisting of large buildings with many rectangular rooms were excavated. Nuzi ware was recovered at about a dozen sites, but for the most part these were occasional sherds and did not form a large proportion of the pottery assemblage.

A similar number of sites belonging to the Middle Assyrian period was excavated. Tell Mohammed Arab provided a good sequence of pottery and associated buildings. At this site a characteristic plan of a rectangular building with one large rectangular room and three or four smaller squarish rooms was identified.

Expectations that important Late Assyrian remains would be found were high, as inscribed bricks of Sargon II had been published as coming from Jikan; it was also speculated that Jikan might have been ancient Kurbail. Further research showed that the bricks in question came from Khorsabad, and excavations at Jikan failed to reveal substantial buildings of the Late Assyrian period. At Tell Baqaq 2, beside the main road leading north, however, the remains of a small palace were found. It included several courtyards, a throne room with stone tramlines, (parallel lines of stone paving, commonly found in the throne rooms of Assyrian palaces, perhaps used for a brazier on wheels), a bathroom, and a few cuneiform tablets dated to about 800 BCE. At Khatuni-yeh, the vivid remains of the site's destruction, presumably at or near the time of the destruction of Nineveh, were revealed. About a dozen other sites with less substantial remains of the period were excavated, but it does not seem to have been a time of particular prosperity in the region. It seems probable that in the Late Assyrian period arable farming was concentrated on the more fertile plains of northern Mesopotamia, and that areas such as that of the Eski Mosul region were used for animal husbandry, perhaps including horse rearing.

Following the destruction of Nineveh it is uncertain whether northern Iraq was under the control of the Medes, the Babylonians, or neither. In the second half of the sixth century BCE it became part of the extensive empire of the Persian king Cyrus, but details of the history of northern Iraq under the Achaemenids are not known. It was, therefore, surprising to find an extensive (but shallow) site at Khirbet Qasrij of the sixth or fifth centuries BCE with evidence for industrial activities, though Xenophon (Anabasis) mentioned extensive settlements when the ten thousand (the Greek mercenaries) retreated through this area at the end of the fifth century BCE.

In the Hellenistic period, perhaps with the revival of political stability, there were numerous relatively rich agricultural villages in the area. Apart from the pottery, which included fish plates with stamped palmettes, the most characteristic feature of these settlements was the number of deep bell-shaped grain silos dug into the ground. A small building (18 × 5.5 m) at Tell Deir Situn has been interpreted as a police post or waystation close to the main route from Nineveh leading north.

Parthian remains were identified at a few sites, but it was not clear how Parthian sites were distinguished from Hellenistic—and indeed the reports on many sites combined the two periods. In the early centuries of the first millennium CE, this region at times lay on the borders between the empires of Rome and Iran. The site of Seh Qubba may have been an outpost of Roman rule on the west bank of the Tigris, and traces of a mosaic floor were found. The site stayed in use in the Sasanian period; the walls of the city, which encircle an area of more than 100 hectares (247 acres), may have been built then.

The Sasanian period was recognized at about ten sites. The only site with substantial architectural remains was at Mseifneh, where a monastery with a fine basilican church constructed from worked stone was uncovered. This building may have been constructed in the fifth century CE; it remained in use (though perhaps not as a Christian religious building) until the Il-Khanid period. A cemetery at Tell Mohammed Arab provided evidence for the burial customs of the period. Most of the inhumations lacked funeral offerings, but a few were plentifully supplied with jewelry (e.g., beads, seals, earrings, rings, bracelets) and with glass bottles that may have held perfume.

As might be expected, almost half the sites excavated had remains from the Islamic period. Sometimes these were a few burials, but some sites had substantial buildings. At Tell Khirbet Saleh a stone and mortar structure with columns was interpreted as a heathen temple built in the 'Abbasid period. At Deir Situn a church was dated to the thirteenth century, but fragmentary architectural remains may belong to an earlier church, perhaps originally constructed in the Sasanian period. At Mishrifeh village, a khan built in the 'Abbasid period remained in use until the Il-Khanid period. At Tell Baqaq 3, another khan in use in the Il-Khanid period was found. At Kharabok a large courtyard building constructed in the 'Abbasid period was rebuilt in the Il-Khanid period, when an elaborate water system was installed. Tell Selal had substantial fortifications from the Middle Islamic period.

The project area has no natural boundaries and is divided by the Tigris River and the wadis flowing into it. The majority of sites in the project were small and occupied for short periods. One consequence of this is that only very few cuneiform tablets were recovered: two Middle Assyrian tablets from Tell Madhhur, two Late Assyrian tablets from Tell Baqaq 2, and a curious hemerological tablet (tablets that list activities to be done on different days of the month) from a Hellenistic pit at Tell Fisna. These do not contribute greatly to a deeper understanding of the history of the region. The archaeological results, however, were extremely interesting: in particular, the elucidation of the chronology of the Late

Uruk and Ninevite 5 periods is of importance for the whole of northern Mesopotamia.

BIBLIOGRAPHY

For preliminary reports on the sites excavated in the Eski Mosul Dam Salvage Project, see the following: Robert Killick and Michael Roaf, comps., "Excavations in Iraq, 1981–82," *Iraq* 45 (1983): 207–220; Robert Killick and James Black, comps., "Excavations in Iraq, 1983–84," *Iraq* 47 (1985): 227–239; W. Ball and James Black, comps., "Excavations in Iraq, 1985–86," *Iraq* 49 (1987): 234–250. The State Organization of Antiquities and Heritage has published *Researches on the Antiquities of Saddam Dam Basin Salvage and Other Researches* (Baghdad, 1987), a special volume containing reports on many of the excavated sites. New information about the Ninevite 5 period is summarized by Michael Roaf and Robert Killick in "A Mysterious Affair of Styles: The Ninevite 5 Pottery of Northern Mesopotamia," *Iraq* 49 (1987): 199–230. The same period is given comprehensive treatment in *The Origins of North Mesopotamian Civilization: Ninevite 5 Chronology, Economy, Society*, edited by Harvey Weiss (in press), based on proceedings of a conference held at Yale University, New Haven, Connecticut, 15–19 December 1988. Evidence for settlement in the Zummar region is discussed in W. Ball, ed., *Ancient Settlement in the Zummar Region: Excavations by the British Archaeological Expedition to Iraq in the Saddam Dam Salvage Project, 1985–86* (in press).

MICHAEL ROAF

ESSENES. Known primarily in the late Second Temple period, especially from about 146 BCE to about 70 CE, the Essenes were a movement within Judaism, a communal association, entered by initiation. They considered themselves to be the predestined remnant of those who truly observed God's will and pursued their own interpretation of Torah and prophecy. Although Essenes influenced the development of rabbinic Judaism and of Christianity, neither of those groups affirmed the Essene's self-description, and the history of the Essenes has often been considered enigmatic.

The Name *Essenes*. The name *Essene* has two forms in Greek, *Essaioi* and *Essēnoi;* the English pronunciation comes from the latter form, but the *Essaioi* spelling appears to be the earlier and more Semitic form. Because the solution is crucial, more than fifty different etymologies have been proposed, but no scholarly consensus has yet been achieved. Some have proposed another Greek word to explain the origin of the name, for example—a similar, though not identical, name for certain priests of Artemis in Ephesus, *Essēnas*. Most scholars have concluded, however, that the Greek forms of the name *Essene* derive from a Semitic (Hebrew or Aramaic) root. The two most often-repeated guesses involve two Aramaic words, *ḥasayyâ* ("pious") and *'āsayyâ* ("healers"), but neither appears in any known ancient text in a reference to the Essenes. A Hebrew proposal is the root *'aśah* in the participle form *'ôśin* and the construct form *'ôśê hatorah* ("doers of torah"); this appears as a self-description in several Dead Sea Scrolls. It parallels some other relevant group self-understandings (e.g., Samaritans as "keepers" of torah), and it corresponds with Philo's et-ymological guess of *hosios*, Josephus's transliteration of the Hebrew *hôšen* as *essēn*, and Epiphanius's spelling of this Jewish sect as *Ossaioi* and *Ossēnoi*. This Hebrew solution was proposed long before the Qumran discoveries (see, e.g., Jost, 1839); while it accords well with the evidence, no consensus yet exists.

Sources on Essenes. Several ancient descriptions of the Essenes have survived in Greek and Latin texts. Among the most important are those by the three earliest authors, Philo, Josephus, and Pliny. Later accounts by Hippolytus and Epiphanius, among others, also preserve important additional observations (see Adam and Burchard, 1972; Stern, 1976–1984; and Vermès and Goodman, 1989). Most of these ancient accounts were addressed to non-Jewish audiences, which influenced the selection of Essene characteristics and the manner in which they were described. These texts show philosophical (especially Stoic) and ethnographic interests typically found in Hellenistic history and geography texts. Several of these descriptions relied on earlier, now-lost texts, including at least one Greek source earlier than Philo, whose account is the earliest extant. Posidonius, Strabo, and Marcus Vipsanius Agrippa are among the likely authors of now-lost descriptions of Essenes (see Goranson, 1994).

The Qumran Evidence. Pliny located an Essene settlement near the Dead Sea. In the analysis of most scholars, the ruins at Qumran and the scrolls from surrounding caves belonged to a group of Essenes. While a few argue that Khirbet Qumran might have been a fort or a winter villa, the majority of historians and archaeologists regard Qumran as one of the Essene settlements. Other settlements or community centers were located in Jerusalem and in the "land of Damascus" (beyond the Jordan River) and elsewhere. According to Philo, the Therapentae, who lived in Egypt, were related to the Essenes.

Several of the Qumran manuscripts include parallels to the teaching, practices, and self-description of the Essenes (see, e.g., Beall, 1988). Surely some of the texts found at Qumran are Essene, including the *Serek ha-Yaḥad* (Rule of the Community or Manual of Discipline), several Bible commentaries *(pesharim)*, and the text designated 4QMMT, *Miqṣat Maʿaśê ha-Torah* (Certain Enactments of the Torah). Such texts as *Jubilees* and portions of *Enoch* and *Testaments of the Twelve Patriarchs* likely are pre-Qumran texts written within the Essene (or pre-Essene) movement. Many new publications concerning the texts and the archaeology of Qumran will continue to appear whose conclusions may modify some currently held views.

Beliefs and Practices. Essene teachings shared much with those accepted by other Jews, such as the Torah and the writings of the Prophets, but they claimed a special, sometimes esoteric interpretation of Scripture. Essenes regarded the Jerusalem Temple high priests (sometimes associated with Sadducees) as misled, following wrongful practices and the wrong calender. Although Essenes were careful in their legal deliberations, they never referred to this exercise as "*halakhah,* instead alluding to that term only in a repeated and negative pun against Pharisees as the "seekers of smooth things" *(dōrĕšē ha-hălāqôt).* Essenes observed Torah strictly but according to their own interpretation and described themselves as doers of torah. Essene beliefs included predestination, important roles for angels, and resurrection, but not necessarily including bodily resurrection (Josephus and Hippolytus differ on this; see Puech, 1993). They expected a messiah, or, in some descriptions, priestly and royal messiahs. The Essene apocalyptic and dualistic worldview is more similar to the *Book of Daniel* than to *1* and *2 Maccabees.* (The latter are not found among the eight hundred or so texts from Qumran; God and the angels—not men—will destroy the community's enemies.)

The Essene communal organization had rules for initiation and punishments, including expulsion. Some Essenes were celibate and some observed periods of celibacy limited to certain times or places. Essenes kept no slaves, and at least the full members held property in common. Agriculture was their main occupation; they made no weapons. They avoided the courts of outsiders. Their rules for ritual purity were strict. The extent to which they participated in the Jerusalem temple cult is an issue still debated.

History of the Essenes. Josephus wrote that Essenes existed in 146 BCE (*Antiquities* 13.171), probably because his source, Strabo, began his *History* then. No year of origin can be pinpointed with the evidence available, perhaps because the Essene movement developed gradually or because the movement preceded the Greek form of its eventual name. Three of the four Essene individuals mentioned in Josephus are known for prophecy and were present in Jerusalem. Josephus also located an Essene gate in southwest Jerusalem (*War* 5.145). The fourth, John the Essene, who joined the Zealots, is less typical; John—a common name—was given the additional descriptive, Essene, because it was not usual to find an Essene relying on human weapons.

Qumran texts describe certain individuals, especially an Essene Teacher of Righteousness and his opponent, the Wicked Priest—some scholars suggest there was more than one of each. Jonathan (161–143/2 BCE) is considered by many to be the best candidate for the Wicked Priest, but Alexander Jannaeus (103–76 BCE) is another possible contender. Although most scholars believe that the Teacher of Righteousness cannot be identified with any known historical personality, a potential candidate is Judah the Essene. Josephus (*War* 1.78–80; *Antiquities* 13.311) places him teaching in about 104 BCE, soon before Alexander's rule. He may be the same Judah recorded in the Babylonian Talmud (*Qid.* 66a), in which he asks Alexander to give up the priesthood, and perhaps also in the Habbakuk Commentary from Qumran (1QpHab 12.4). The Essenes' negative view of the latter Hasmoneans was shared by Strabo, who wrote (*Geography* 16.2.35–40) that Alexander was among the tyran-

nical and superstitious leaders who departed from the honorable teachings of Moses.

The Essenes disappeared from history sometime after the First Jewish War against Rome (66–70). While considerable debate continues concerning the many aspects of the movement's history, research has succeeded in revealing much diversity within late Second Temple Period Judaism.

[*See also* Dead Sea Scrolls; *and* Qumran.]

BIBLIOGRAPHY

Adam, Alfred, and Christoph Burchard. *Antike Berichte über die Essener.* 2d ed. Berlin, 1972. The most comprehensive available collection of ancient texts on Essenes, with useful notes and bibliography. Includes selected texts from seventeen authors and extensive references to other writers who, with more or less small variations, repeated the earlier accounts of Essenes.

Beall, Todd S. *Josephus' Description of the Essenes Illustrated by the Dead Sea Scrolls.* Cambridge, 1988. A worthwhile comparison of selected passages from Josephus with some Qumran texts; not the last word on the subject because additional observations have been made, some using recently published texts.

Goranson, Stephen. "Posidonius, Strabo, and Marcus Vipsanius Agrippa as Sources on Essenes." *Journal of Jewish Studies* 45 (1994): 295–298. According to proposals here, Posidonius and Strabo were among the sources for Philo and Josephus, and M. Agrippa was a source for Pliny.

Jost, Isak M. "Die Essäer." *Israelitische Annalen* 19 (1839): 145–147. On the etymology of the name.

Puech, Émile. *La croyance des Ésséniens en la vie future.* 2 vols. Paris, 1993. Discusses the issue of resurrection as it appears in ancient descriptions of Essenes and in some texts from Qumran.

Stern, Menachem, ed. and trans. *Greek and Latin Authors on Jews and Judaism.* 3 vols. Jerusalem, 1976–1984. Fine collection in which the reader may compare ancient descriptions of Essenes, including those by or addressed to non-Jews, with the broader category of descriptions of Jews.

Vermès, Géza, and Martin D. Goodman, eds. *The Essenes according to the Classical Sources.* Sheffield, 1989. Selection of texts from six ancient authors, with English translations, an introduction, brief notes, and a bibliography; a handy volume but considerably less comprehensive than Adam and Burchard.

Wagner, Siegfried. *Die Essener in der wissenschaftlichen Diskussion.* Berlin, 1960. Extensive survey and bibliography of the vast pre-Qumran scholarship and speculation on Essenes, with special attention to nineteenth-century German writers.

STEPHEN GORANSON

ETHICS AND ARCHAEOLOGY.

Ethics are standards of moral judgment and conduct to which individuals or groups subscribe. Ethics flow from the ongoing life of a community as it questions whether its practices are appropriate or valid. Each community discusses these questions in order to define standards for its members. Smaller groups or individuals then translate the standards to fit their particular situations. In effect, ethics represent values and ideals that are continually negotiated by those who subscribe to them, based on factors within and outside the group. Ethics constantly evolve, but they are fundamentally conservative in that they are meant to protect the group and its members from internal discord and from external attack by those who might have an interest in the community's activities.

Archaeological ethics exemplify these principles. The community primarily defines itself as having an interest in exploring and understanding the past. Subgroups form around these interests, and each then defines its ethics. For example, formal or informal groups may form around the study of archaeology from a certain region, such as the Near East or North America. Others may form around study of a particular time period, such as the Upper Paleolithic or the Ottoman Empire. Still others may form around specialities, such as museum studies or heritage management. An overlapping of interests and standards is common among subgroups, but to assume that there is or ever can be a single set of ethics would be erroneous. At the same time, groups do deal with similar issues as they define their ethics.

Among the first and most important questions addressed by each group is: Who is or is not an archaeologist? As cultural resources management specialist Leslie Wildesen has pointed out (in Greene, ed., 1984), this usually means who is or is not a "real" archaeologist. The distinction is drawn between archaeologists as members of a peer group and outsiders who lay claim to membership but are not accepted by the group. These outsiders may range from amateurs to journalists to dealers in antiquities. The integrity of the group is assessed on the basis of the integrity of its members. Groups therefore may demand that its members have well-defined credentials—formal education, often at least a graduate degree, and other sorts of training, such as internships or attendance at field schools, where proper excavation techniques are learned and practiced.

Membership standards have changed dramatically since archaeology began. People such as Heinrich Schliemann and Jean-Baptiste Belzoni, who in their own time were accepted as archaeologists, might now be labeled as little more than looters, grave robbers, or publicity seekers—at best, "historical figures" or sophisticated amateurs. These standards are obviously subject to changes in the group's intellectual climate. To some degree, members may reflect the views of outsiders, who may, for example, be concerned with matters of cultural patrimony. As segments of the archaeological community professionalized and established formal organizations, these associations took it upon themselves to establish minimal standards for membership. Some, as in the cultural resources management community in the United States, lobbied outside entities to codify these standards into government regulation. The membership standards have sometimes been hotly debated, but the issue has been relatively simple because the group involved is relatively small and controllable. Vastly more complex is the question of the accountability of group members.

To whom should archaeologists be accountable? From the early days of archaeology into the present, some archae-ologists have believed they should be held accountable only to their profession (i.e., subgroup). Their primary responsibility, some believe, is to their "science" or to "the past" or to another abstract entity. Most archaeologists recognize, however, that from the outset, archaeology has almost always been conducted for a client—whether a patron, a museum, or a government agency. Clients have vested interests, and thus a say in how every aspect of archaeology is done, from excavation to the interpretation and use of information. At the same time, archaeologists have recognized that they are themselves members of other groups, whose views influence archaeological practice. In other words, archaeology is done within a framework of the larger society. Questions of accountability result in a profoundly more difficult matter: Who sets the agenda for archaeology?

Another way of phrasing this might be: For whom do archaeologists do archaeology? Certainly one answer is that they do it for themselves. Archaeology can both provide a livelihood and satisfy curiosity about the past. Some would maintain that this is enough. Professional archaeologists, at the very least, question their role in relation to the sciences and humanities. They understand that their theoretical approaches and excavation techniques have an impact on the sites and materials they study. Most also recognize that their discipline plays a role in the larger society. Therefore, most realize that they are accountable to outsiders as well as to their profession.

Awareness of these other constituencies to archaeology has only come in recent decades. Initially, as archaeology became professionalized, the group's definition took precedence, as did clarifying appropriate methods and techniques of archaeology. As archaeology began to look outward, it noted the concerns of outside groups and the issues became both complex and intertwined.

Among the most important of these issues is the preservation of archaeological sites from destruction by forces such as those accompanying economic development. Archaeologists have been extremely vocal in demanding that outside groups pay attention to the loss of sites that many maintain are part of the world's heritage. They have called for site protection on national and international levels and have succeeded to some degree. For example, the League of Nations Mandate for Palestine, ratified in 1923, outlined the excavation and preservation of archaeological remains. All league nations were given equal rights to excavation, overseen by a Department of Antiquities whose director could requisition land for excavations, deny permits to unqualified archaeologists, and punish looters of antiquities. In the United States, antiquities received some protection under the Antiquities Act of 1906, but vastly more under the Historic Preservation Acts of 1966 and 1974 and the Archaeological Resources Protection Act of 1979. Under these laws and their accompanying regulations, any federal government action involved in disturbing the landscape must provide for the location, protection, or mitigation of the loss of sites (usually by excavation) that are potentially eligible for inclusion on the National Register of Historic Places. While, however, preservation of sites may seem a noble goal, it raises difficult problems.

By working toward implementing preservation policy and law, archaeologists recognize their dependency on governments, thereby legitimizing nonarchaeological interests and giving them a voice in archaeological practice. Among the most knotty problems is preservation for what and for whom? The dilemma is a simple one: How is potential economic benefit from a development project to be weighed against potential scientific and humanistic benefit from an archaeological site? The interests behind economic development are vast and often very powerful. A government, for example, may promote an open-pit mine that will allow it to compete more powerfully in the import-export market. Increased revenues may bring jobs and a higher quality of life to citizens. At the same time, construction of the mine may destroy important sites from which everyone can learn important lessons about their heritage (which also may be said to improve quality of life).

While some archaeologists would urge protection of the pit-mine site, others would urge excavation if it could not be preserved. Excavation benefits archaeologists scientifically; it can also benefit financially, if a developer pays for the excavation and analysis of the artifacts. Archaeologists can find themselves in an ethical dilemma: wanting to preserve sites, while wanting access to the information and funds for excavation. In fact, developers, the public, and government agencies have accused archaeologists of stopping progress or of seeking personal gain through laws the archaeologists sought to implement. Additional questions relate to how a site's significance is determined: Who is most capable of making such a determination? Archaeologists maintain that they are. Again, the question of self-interest can be raised.

Once the economics of excavating is settled, other issues come into play. If a site is preserved as a part of peoples' heritage, how it is to be treated raises additional internal ethical problems: Should the site even be excavated? Excavation is, after all, a destructive process. Some archaeologists urge no excavation, preferring preservation. As David Lowenthal (1985) cautions, however, preservation reveals that permanence is an illusion. Even untouched, a site and its significance are continually altered and reinterpreted. Other archaeologists suggest conservation, by which, subsequently, one part of a site might be excavated while the rest is left undisturbed, in expectation of renewed study at some point in the future when advanced theories and techniques may be available.

Whether the decision is preservation or conservation, nonarchaeologists still have a say. If sites are in fact a public heritage, they should be accessible. What then is archaeo-logy's responsibility in interpreting sites for the public? At a minimum, archaeologists recognize that they must complete the analysis of their work and publish their findings. How sensitive, then, do archaeologists need to be to the accusation that they often use jargon incomprehensible to nonspecialists. Many archaeologists believe that they have an obligation beyond publication to educate the public about what they do. In many countries they have developed public education programs: ninety-seven countries are linked in the Associated Schools Project (ASP) affiliated with UNESCO. One ASP project, the Fifth Lyceum School on Cyprus, decided to explore four rescue archaeology operations: Nubia and Philae, Borobudur, the Acropolis, and Paphos on Cyprus. Such projects raise a question already asked: Whose agenda is paramount in educational projects, those of teachers, archaeologists, government entities, or other interested parties?

Closely tied to projects like these are entities linked to the protection and presentation of the past of which museums are the most visible. Although archaeologists are frequently associated with museums, the objectives of the two are not always compatible. Museums have their own ethical concerns, which sometimes involve purchasing or trading antiquities. Many archaeologists believe that assigning a monetary value to antiquities promotes the looting of sites. As a result, some professionals have recently debated whether, ethically, the discipline of archaeology can include the study objects in a museum that were purchased or otherwise obtained under ethically questionable circumstances. Governmental entities have sometimes determined that the past can be used for financial gain through tourism. This may involve support for museums, but it may also encompass developing certain important monuments or archaeological sites as tourist attractions.

During the mid-1960s, concerns about how such sites should be treated led to the development of a set of principles to guide the conservation and restoration of sites and monuments. The International Council on Monuments and Sites and associated committees were formed to promote these principles. Crucial ethical concerns about the protection and development of archaeological sites involve the expenditure of funds and who decides what will be developed. Developing sites whose significance is questionable depletes funds available for locating, exploring, and interpreting sites of equal or greater potential scientific merit.

A case in point is the (High Dam) Nubian rescue campaign in Egypt in the 1960s. Might the $63 million spent on moving and restoring Abu Simbel (whose inscriptions had long been recorded and that some argue is aesthetically mediocre) been better applied to locating and excavating unrecorded sites that would have given a more complete picture of Nubian archaeology before the dam also covered them with water? Might a fraction of that money have been usefully dedicated to upgrading the Cairo Museum, which houses Egypt's most significant national treasures? Some Egyptologists argued the case, contending that the overall scientific goals at Abu Simbel were more important. In the end, the decision to save Abu Simbel was made by Egyptian politicians acting on behalf of the Egyptian public. Archaeologists who questioned whether the scholarly community was capable of judging Abu Simbel's worth supported the politicians. Was the decision vindicated by the more than a thousand tourists per day who paid to visit the site, more than the number who formerly saw it in a month?

Archaeologists face other challenging problems relating to site protection: What should be the role of archaeologists in instances of international, regional, or civil conflict, when important archaeological sites are endangered? During the Gulf War, Allied bombing jeopardized numerous sites in Iraq (ancient Mesopotamia). Nine of the seventy-seven nations ratifying the 1954 UNESCO Convention for the Protection of Cultural Property in the Event of Armed Conflict were directly involved in the conflict (the United States never ratified the agreement). The Department of Defense of the United States, a major participant in the war, reportedly did not give these matters much thought, for which it was strongly criticized. Civil conflict produces similar situations. During Lebanon's civil war in the 1970s and 1980s, the National Museum was looted, vandalized, and hit by shelling. Museum staff attempted to protect its well-known Roman and Phoenician sarcophagi by encasing them in concrete. Roman and Iron Age Phoenician cemetery sites in Tyre were looted and their gold, jewelry, and pottery sold to antiquities dealers. A 1988 decree passed by the Lebanese Ministry of Tourism, which oversees the Department of Antiquities, makes dealing in antiquities illegal. The Lebanese army has stopped most site looting, and transportation authorities have been on the lookout for antiquities smuggling. Archaeologists who involved themselves directly in saving sites and seeking solutions to the postwar return of antiquities did so at some personal risk. Even when political situations stabilize, matters of funding are primary. How is limited money best spent: in repairing sites, monuments, and museums or in returning and caring for Lebanese antiquities?

Governments recognize that the past is a very powerful tool and they have used it as such, sometimes with the complicity of archaeologists. The history of archaeology is intimately linked with colonialism. Some of the field's first knowledge of the past was directly related to conquest. Neil A. Silberman (1982) recounts the international struggle for control of the archaeological resources of the Holy Land, where Western (largely Christian) nations, Jews, and Muslims have contested control of the region's antiquities for generations. Governments have also used the results of archaeological investigation for nation building. During the Gulf War, Iraqi leader Saddam Hussein, hoping to build internal support for his regime's activities, compared his empire with that of ancient Mesopotamia. Modern Israel is a powerful example of archaeology effectively used to provide direct historical links to a land. Its archaeological and political agendas have often been fundamentally the same, as in the excavation in the 1960s of Masada, whose historical reconstruction has only recently undergone critical reexamination. The siege of Masada became a national symbol for a besieged Israel and a connection to a heroic past. For a time national defense forces used Masada as a place for swearing in new tank corps recruits who vowed that "Masada shall not fall again." New analyses suggest that archaeological evidence may not support the first interpretations of events at the site. At the same time, Israeli archaeologists and the government remain at odds about antiquities traffic. The government allows some traffic in Holy Land relics as a means of promoting the centrality of the nation: it enables Jews and Christians in other countries to possess something of ancient Palestine in the hope that they will support Israel politically. Some of that country's most important archaeological finds were looted and turned up in dealers' shops, the best-known example being the Dead Sea Scrolls. Archaeologists' own perception of their role varies. Most recognize the ethical dilemmas posed by the traffic in antiquities.

Archaeology in a postcolonial world poses other ethical quandaries. Among the most delicate are matters of cultural patrimony, indigenous rights, and representations of the past; the three are usually integrally linked. Some nations, recognizing the power of the past as a nation-building tool, have demanded the return of antiquities taken from their territory. These demands have especially been aimed at museums in North America and Europe and pose major problems. Notable examples include the so-called Elgin Marbles, which reside in the British Museum but were taken between 1803 and 1812 by Lord Elgin (Thomas Bruce) from the Parthenon in Athens. The legal complexities of Priam's Treasure, now in Russia at the Pushkin Museum, supposedly taken from Hissarlik/Troy by Schliemann in 1873, are tangled. No fewer than five nations have some claim to it. These claims range from rights of possession and war claims (United States and Russia), to rights of the excavator (Germany), to rights of location (Turkey), to rights of cultural patrimony (Greece). Indigenous peoples or religious groups in some regions have demanded the return of sacred objects and the skeletal remains of their ancestors. Groups now protest the excavation of any archaeological sites by outsiders, or at least place limits on their work. In Israel, archaeologists and rabbis often struggle over excavations, especially those involving burials. Sarcophagi recently recovered in rescue excavations in Jerusalem's French Hill neighborhood and just outside the Old City walls near the Jaffa Gate were turned over by the director of the Antiquities Authority to a burial society for immediate reinterrment under Jewish religious law. Archaeologists have filed legal action so that they can study the caskets. Across the Middle East, Muslim laborers have had to be assured that they were not excavating the remains of Muslims. In part out of cultural patrimony and in part of Muslim sensibilities, the Egyptian government requested return of mummies and their display in museums has been curtailed.

Many peoples have also claimed that because the archaeology done in the past on their lands was done by outsiders, the past created was a colonial tool used to dominate them. They protest that their oral histories are neglected in impersonal archaeological models and chronologies. As a consequence, some groups employ only archaeologists sympathetic to their concerns, train their own citizens to do archaeology, or in some cases outlaw archaeology altogether, stirring international debate among archaeologists.

There is concern among some archaeologists that returning artifacts and remains destroys the archaeological data base. They ask whether artifacts will be properly cared for if repatriated or, as has been documented, they will end up on the antiquities market. Those who believe that archaeological sites and artifacts are a universal heritage have been outraged when objects fall under the control of a nation or an ethnic group that keeps them forever out of reach of others to see or study. There is also concern about the limits set on academic freedom by religious and political groups by dictating research agendas.

Archaeologists who recognize the colonial nature of their enterprise have attempted to reach compromises. In the United States, for example, the Native American Graves Protection and Repatriation Act of 1990, passed over the objection of many archaeologists, was supported by others, who helped to write it and lobbied for its passage. It requires the U.S. government to fund museums and laboratories to inventory sacred objects and skeletons and make a good-faith effort to return them. The law also demands consultation with tribal groups over how archaeological research is carried out on tribal lands.

Some organizations have come to recognize that archaeology is fundamentally a political exercise that places archaeologists in tenuous ethical positions. For example, the explicit goals of the World Archaeological Congress (WAC), formed in 1986, are to incorporate archaeologists from underdeveloped countries and indigenous peoples and to examine the political and ethical ramifications of archaeology. These issues are central themes at their meetings and in the numerous WAC publications in the One World Archaeology series. At the 1990 WAC 2 meeting in Venezuela, the WAC Executive passed a code of ethics for dealing with the primacy of indigenous peoples to control any archaeology that studies their pasts. Significantly, the code was generated by indigenous peoples.

At no time in the history of archaeology have archaeological ethics been under greater scrutiny than since the early 1980s. At no time in the past was there greater disagreement about what is or is not ethical practice. The issues are complicated and there are few easy solutions. For each subgroup formed and for each ethical question posed, a continuum of opinion exists about how to behave ethically. What is undeniable is that by continually reassessing ethics in archaeology, the discipline undergoes continual change.

[*See also* Nationalism and Archaeology; Tourism and Archaeology.]

BIBLIOGRAPHY

Adams, William Y. "Science and Ethics in Rescue Archaeology." *Boreas: Uppsala Studies in Ancient Mediterranean and Near Eastern Civilizations* 13 (1984): 9–15. Discussion of the interaction of science, public interest, and rescue archaeology during the Nubian rescue campaign of the 1960s.

Cleere, Henry F., ed. *Archaeological Heritage Management in the Modern World.* One World Archaeology, 9. London, 1989. Thorough examination of issues surrounding heritage management, with case studies from all continents.

Fleming, Arlene Krimgold. "Securing Sites in Time of War." *Archaeology* 44.3 (1991): 43. Deals with the UNESCO Convention for the Protection of Cultural Property in the Event of Armed Conflict during the Gulf War.

Greene, Ernestene L., ed. *Ethics and Values in Archaeology.* New York, 1984. Twenty-six chapters explore issues relating to an archaeologist's responsibilities to the profession and the public, giving the ethical codes of several American organizations.

Lowenthal, David. *The Past Is a Foreign Country.* Cambridge, 1985. Examines complex process by which views of the past become subject to the needs of the present.

Maisels, Charles K. *The Near East: Archaeology in the Cradle of Civilization.* London, 1993. Current research agendas in the Near East and several factors influencing them are examined in the final chapter.

Raschka, Marilyn. "Salvaging a Scarred Land." *Archaeology* 47.1 (1994): 64–67. Case study of archaeological responses to the destruction of antiquities during the civil war in Lebanon.

Silberman, Neil A. *Digging for God and Country: Exploration, Archeology, and the Secret Struggle for the Holy Land, 1799–1917.* New York, 1982. Explores the connection between religion and archaeology in the Holy Land.

Silberman, Neil A. *Between Past and Present: Archaeology, Ideology, and Nationalism in the Modern Middle East.* New York, 1990. Essential reading about Middle East governmental uses of archaeology for national political agendas, with case studies from the Balkans, Turkey, Cyprus, Israel, Egypt, and South Arabia.

Stone, Peter, and Robert MacKenzie, eds. *The Excluded Past: Archaeology in Education.* London, 1990. Case studies detail concerns of both archaeologists and indigenous people over how the past is presented in archaeological education programs.

Watzman, Herbert M. "Religious Dispute over Excavations of Burial Sites Pits Israel's Archaeologists against Rabbis." *Chronicle of Higher Education,* 24 March 1993: A31. Describes debates over research agendas, in which questions have been raised similar to those in disputes over the treatment of indigenous remains.

LARRY J. ZIMMERMAN

ETHIOPIA. The name Ethiopia was adopted into the Geʿez dialect in early Christian times by the Axumites in the northern part of the land from the Septuagint equivalent of

Hebrew Kush. The name *Eritrea/Ertera*, or more commonly *Bahra Ertera* in Geʿez, referred to the Red Sea until modern times when it came to designate the northern plateau of the Horn of Africa after it was colonized by the Italians at the end of the nineteenth century. There are many ancient names that refer to one or another part of Ethiopia. The Egyptian Punt or biblical Put referred to one or another part of the Horn of Africa. Three identifiable biblical names also designate Ethiopia and those parts of modern Sudan and Yemen that were once controlled by the Axumite Empire. Kush is known from about fifty references to individuals, peoples, and lands, their merchandise, and political influence. It is also associated with the Garden of Eden river Gihon, the name Ethiopians give the Blue Nile, Sheba recalls the famous queen, who was visitor of King Solomon. Hawilah, like Kush, was one of the lands of the Garden of Eden; its river, Pishon, was once identified with the rivers of Ethiopia, those tributaries of the Nile called Gihon in Geʿez literature.

Habashat, from which the modern name *Abyssinia* is derived, is one of the toponyms found in the Proto-Ethiopic/Sabean inscriptions. It was once thought to be the name of a major tribe that entered Ethiopia from Yemen. The epigraphist A. J. Drewes first noted in 1962 that the name appears in Yemeni inscriptions but not until about 350 CE in Ethiopian inscriptions. Others have subsequently argued that the name is topographical and the territory most reasonably covers the Ethiopian regions.

Origin. The origin of ancient Ethiopia as a political state goes back to the first millennium BCE, a centralized kingdom with Axum as its capital came into being in the north. There exist extensive archaeological and epigraphic evidence about this kingdom gathered from the surroundings of Axum and from such sites as Matara, Qasqase, Taconda, Qohaito, and others in the neighboring state now known as Eritrea. According to these archaeological sources, ancient Ethiopia, from about the fifth century BCE until the early Christian period, was an area comprising the wedge-shaped, northernmost Ethiopian plateau, including the Eritrean seacoast where the ancient international port of Adulis was located. With the conquest of many of the surrounding peoples and states, the original kingdom expanded far into the interior highlands and eventually gave rise to a large kingdom, which came to call itself Ethiopia in early Christian times.

Archaeological evidence, internal inscriptions, and external information show that the large kingdom grew into an empire at the dawn of the period we call the Middle Ages in Europe. Comprising a territory almost the size of western Europe, Ethiopia's borders extended from beyond the island of Meroë to Marib in the heart of the Arabian Peninsula. Only Rome and Persia could compare to it in size and power until the about the eighth century CE.

Prehistoric Archaeology. Some of the earliest human remains have been found in the Awash River valley, the Omo River valley, Malka Qunture, and other regions throughout the Ethiopian Rift valley. These regions link the Paleolithic Rift valley with historic Nile civilizations. Among the most recent discoveries is one of the most complete (nearly 60 percent) skeleton of a hominid named *Australopithecus afarensis*, popularly known as Lucy, and believed to be over three million years old. Discovered in 1974 by a joint Ethiopian-American expedition, it is now thought to be an important link between humans and apes. This skeleton and other recent discoveries, which are coming to light even now, point to the Ethiopian Rift valley as an important area of early human evolution, if not indeed the place of our origin (Johanson and Edey, 1981). [See Hadar.]

Evidence from the Neolithic period (c. 10,000) also points to the existence of African peoples who developed in Ethiopia various agricultural techniques such as terrace farming and crops such as millet, sorghum, and cotton. Cotton is thought have developed in southwestern Ethiopia from a primitive herbaceous plant. According to some botanists, all prehistoric survey evidences point to Ethiopia as a major center of ancient agricultural evolution and the birthplace of most African crop plants.

Connection with Ancient Egyptian Archaeology. About 2200 a group of people described as the C-group by Egyptologists, entered the Meroitic region and eventually western Eritrea. This group left its impression through its rippled pottery found at Agordat.

Not much earlier, in the time of the Egyptian pharaoh Sahure (c. 2458–2446), the earliest expedition to the land of Punt (which had the epithet "god's land" in Egyptian) took place. The identity of Punt is still a matter of debate, but the goods brought from there—resins, frankincense, ointment, myrrh, electrum (gold with silver alloy), and ebony—point to the Horn. Although myrrh grown in the Horn of Africa was already known in the time of the first and second dynasties (c. 2920–2649), and a slave from Punt was present in Cheop's court (fourth dynasty, c. 2575–2465), this is the first time specific mention of an expedition to the land of Punt is mentioned. Likewise, the Egyptian reference to an island prince who claims to be a serpent and controls spice and animal trade, may also point to the same region.

Other pharaohs, up to at least the time of Rameses III (c. 1198–1167), sent expeditions to Punt. It was in the time of Queen Hatshepsut (c. 1473–1458) of the eighteenth dynasty, however, that the most extended expedition took place to the land of Punt. It took beads, daggers, bracelets, to Punt and brought back fragrant woods, ebony, fresh myrrh trees, myrrh resin, incense, gold, ivory, panther skins, and live animals (panthers, monkeys, baboon, and cattle) and people. Carlo Conti Rossini as early as 1928 argued that Ethiopia is best identified with this combination of merchandise in antiquity (for a more recent confirmation of this view, see Kitchen, 1993). This expedition was truly a glorious one, recorded on the impressive temple reliefs of Hatshepsut's mortuary temple at Deir el-Baḥari on the western bank of Thebes at modern Luxor.

Although no doubt contact between Ethiopia and Egypt persisted throughout history, we do not find enough archaeological evidence about it on Ethiopian soil until the time of the Ptolemies. Ptolemy II Philadelphus (c. 285–246) fought against the Seleucids with elephants possibly brought from Ethiopia. One of his successors, Ptolemy III Euergetes (c. 246–221) left an inscribed tablet at the ancient port of Adulis.

Axumite Archaeology. Excavations at Axum and the surrounding regions have uncovered many objects, including altars, incense burners, decorated pottery, buildings, dams, stelae, coins, and many more objects, which throw light on the artistic trends current in Axum at the time. The art of stonecutting and engineering was perfected at Axum as evidenced by the still-standing stelae, the ruins of the palace of Enda Mika'el, the 66.8-meter-long dam at Qohaito, and the temple at Yeha, among other works.

The later Christian kings continued this skill to build churches, such as the church at Abba Garima by Emperor Gabra Masqal (c. 550–575), the monastery of Dabra Damo,

ETHIOPIA. *Early Ethiopian altar dedicated to the moon god Almaqah.* From Malazo, near Axum; dated to the fifth century BCE. Archaeological Museum, Addis Ababa, Ethiopia. (Werner Forman/Art Resource, NY)

or even the famous church of gold and marble at San'a in Yemen built by the Ethiopian viceroy Abraha. The foundations of the famous church of Axum, where Ethiopians believe the original Tablets of the Law given to Moses or the Ark of the Covenant are found, go back to this period.

Both the type of earth and the artistic style of Axumite architecture and pottery have been influential in Marib and pre-Christian Yemen (Van Beek, 1967). The northern sluice of the great dam at Marib constructed between the fourth and sixth centuries with headers protruding beyond the face of the wall was an Axumite technique with no real construction antecedent in South Arabian architecture or evidenced in the Marib region (Van Beek, 1967).

One of the most important archaeological sites in Ethiopia is the commercial port of Adulis, not far away from the modern port of Asab in Eritrea. Probably going back to the late Hellenistic times or the early period of the Roman Empire, Adulis came to international prominence. In later times, especially the reign of Emperor Kaleb (513–547), it was a base of an important military fleet. It controlled international maritime trade moving through the Red Sea and the Indian Ocean, connecting Asia with the Near East and the Mediterranean world. Adulis traded in ivory, tortoise shell, apes, hippopotamus hides, and obsidian (used for jewelry and mirrors). Trade enhanced the ancient Ethiopian Empire to establish cultural interchange not only with Asia but also with Rome. Archaeological remains point to Adulis as the area where the early Christian missionaries, who were Red Sea traders and travelers, began their evangelizing activities. Adulis was sacked in 640 CE by an Arab force.

In the nineteenth century, the first almost simultaneous discovery of Sabaean or Proto-Ethiopic inscriptions in Yemen and Ethiopia by David Heinrich Müller (1894) and Theodore Bent (1893) respectively, and by J. Halevy subsequently in both countries opened a new era of archaeological and epigraphic research in the region. Eduard Glaser (1891, 1895) in Yemen and Enno Littmann in Ethiopia (1913) advanced the research for these inscriptions which continue to be discovered up to today but which still require a more extensive survey. Many of the inscriptions found in and around Axum help us outline and understand not only the history of Ethiopian wars and expeditions and political state but also the character of ancient Ethiopian society and religion. Even in pre-Christian times, the author of the *Periplus of the Erythraean Sea,* who visited Axum around the second century BCE and wrote of its important commercial relations with the Greco-Roman world, observed that the Ethiopian king "Zoskales" was well acquainted with Greek literature. Numerous Greek inscriptions, including the important trilingual inscription of Ezana, have also been found in northern Ethiopia.

Among the numerous stone stelae with detailed inscriptions are three inscriptions of Emperor Ezana (c. 320–360). The first of these is a trilingual inscription about the war

ETHIOPIA. *Altar with Sabaean inscription in the service of the moon god Almaqah.* From Melazo, near Axum, dated to the fifth century BCE. Archaeological Museum, Addis Ababa, Ethiopia. (Werner Forman/Art Resource, NY)

with Tsarane in nonvocalized Ge'ez, Sabaean (Proto-Ge'ez), and Greek. The second written in Ge'ez and Greek deals with the conquest of the Beja, a nomadic and warlike tribe. The third, perhaps the most important, deals with the conquest of the Noba, who occupied much of Nubia. The first two inscriptions call Ezana the son of the god Mahrem, son of Ares, whereas the third is dedicated in the name of the Lord of Heaven. From this evidence, historians have deduced that Ezana was the first Ethiopian king to be converted to Christianity. Others, however, hold that inscriptions of the later centuries including those of Emperor Kaleb (c. 514–546) that call upon the Trinity are evidence not only of Ethiopia's conversion to Christianity but of Christianity's triumph in Africa.

After about the middle of the seventh century Ethiopia lost control over the Red Sea trade, which had been a major source of economic and international strength, and entered a period of isolation. The decline of its maritime trade became one of the main reasons for an interest in Ethiopia's hinterland for other areas of economic wealth and stability. Probably in the tenth century the capital was moved to Agaw in the middle highlands, where Christianity was translated into indigenous African cultural terms. The north remained the spiritual center of the nation and Axum the national holy city.

The techniques of stonecutting and building continued. There have been discovered all over northern and central Ethiopia more than two hundred churches hewn out of rock. Beginning in the tenth century there was a cultural reawakening. A city of rock-hewn churches was built at new site called Lalibela, supposedly named for the king who founded the city. Although general and artistic descriptions of these churches abound in modern writings on Ethiopia, and Lalibela itself is a major tourist attraction, very little archaeological work has been done in and around its churches.

One of the most important archaeological finds in Ethiopia is a diverse and large amount of ancient coins dating from the third to the seventh century CE. In many of the ruins of the great structures of Axum and the surrounding regions, large finds of coins have been made. These coins not only reflect upon the wealth of ancient Ethiopia, but they also bear an important record of history and help us directly with reconstructing Axumite chronology and ancient Ethiopian history. Ethiopia was the only ancient kingdom in all of Africa to issue its own coinage.

The use of foreign money by international merchants in Adulis, which is reported first in the *Periplus of the Erythraean Sea* about two thousand years ago, has been confirmed by the discovery of foreign coins in recent excavations, which have also brought to light diverse indigenous Ethiopian Axumite coinage. Originating from at least early Christian times, it was struck of gold, silver, bronze, and other metals overlaid with gold. The coinage exhibits the royal head, the crown, and, in later times, the cross. Other coin finds feature half-length profile busts of kings wearing fringed robes and necklaces, bracelets, and armlets or holding a sword, a spear, or a hand cross and framed by two stalks of wheat. Some coins have a double representation of the royal image thought to be unique in ancient coinage.

The most common reverse motif on silver and bronze coins after the conversion of Ezana in 330 CE is the cross (Latin and Greek, diamond-shaped, and other variants). According to Bent Juel-Jensen (1991) and Stuart Munro-Hay (1984), the Axumite kings were the first Christian rulers to display the cross on their coins. Less common motifs depict an architectural reverse. One type shows an arch supported on double columns. The second (of Armah) depicts the columns supporting a central gold-inlaid cross flanked by two others with a key-shaped object under the arch. According to the numismatist Munro-Hay (1989a, 1993), these pieces may refer to both the conquest of Jerusalem by the Persians in 614 and either to Calvary or to the Holy Sepulcher.

Greek was used primarily on gold coins, but Ge'ez came to predominate later on coins of other metals. King Wazeba used Ge'ez on his gold and silver coins. On earlier coins the inscriptions call the kings "Son of Mahrem." Some of the earliest Christian coins depict the cross framed by the words "May this please the people." Other phrases and statements "by the grace of God," "MHDYS, by this cross he will conquer," "joy and peace to the people," "Christ is with us," or "mercy and peace."

The inscriptions also reveal the names of a dozen well-known and about two dozen lesser-known kings of Axum. They span approximately the late third and the seventh centuries, representing the period of the rise and decline of the Axumite Empire. Among the finds are thin gold coins of kings Allamidas, Ella Gabaz, Ioel, Hataz/Iathlia, Israel, and Gersem. Emperor Kaleb, whose famous campaign against Dhu-Nawwas in Yemen took place about 525, is one of the last Axumite kings who issued a large number of gold coins.

Axumite coinage fluctuated in weight. According to Munro-Hay (1984, 1993), the fluctuations parallel those of Roman coinage. The heaviest gold coins equal the Roman half-aureus standardized at about 1.6g, like the Roman *tremissis* of the monetary reforms of Constantine the Great. The gold content also varies, the earlier coins being up to 90 percent. In the mid-fourth century King Ezana's issues were 80 percent. Fifth- and sixth-century coinage was 60–70 percent; Kaleb's coins had 64.2 percent; and Ella Gabaz' and Yoel's coins possessed only 50 percent. Numismatists think that the decline in the gold content of the coinage must have caused the collapse of the monetary system in the seventh century.

The oldest extant coins date to the fourth quarter of the third century and depict King Endubis, king of Axum, and his divine symbol. The king wears a helmet, depicted on both the obverse and reverse of his gold coins. Aphilas, Endubis's successor, issued coins made of gold, silver, and bronze with different sizes and designs. These exhibit variously the disk and the crescent, which were religious symbols, above an elaborate high tiara situated on a colonnade or a tiered bust. Although the reverse was inscribed, the obverse had no text.

The Axumite Empire is distinguished among many ancient states not only for its production of coinage but also for the minting of gold coins, as in Rome and Persia. The coins witness the great economic and political influence of the empire and its international trade connections with the Roman and Persian empires and the Indian continent. Unfortunately, with the decline and disintegration of the Red Sea trade in the seventh century, the Ethiopian capital moved further inland, and the international monetary system was no longer of use. With the demise of Axum, the production of coins dwindled and thereafter ceased probably around 630.

Archaeological Potential of Ethiopia. Ethiopia is still a largely unexplored archaeological paradise. Even many structures that stand above ground have not been fully recorded and studied.

According to Ethiopian Church tradition, the Ethiopian eunuch of the *Book of Acts* (8:27–39), was the first Christian missionary to Ethiopia. Christian missionary activities must have indeed begun all along the Red Sea regions beginning in the first century. Scholars believe that Ethiopia did not adopt Christianity as the state religion until the fourth century, when Ethiopia was at the height of its political, military, and economic power. The claim that Christianity did not gain eminence until the sixth century that occasionally is aired is speculation based on the tradition that the first Ethiopian Christian kings were Abraha and Asbaha, who ruled in that later period. In a highly africanized form, Christianity gave rise to the dominant culture of Ethiopia—its literature, art, music, law, and architecture. During the fourth and fifth centuries the entire Ethiopian plateau in the north was so thoroughly christianized that Cosmas, the famous Egyptian monk who visited Ethiopia about 525, returned impressed that there were "everywhere churches of the Christians, bishops, martyrs, monks, and hermits, by whom the gospel . . . is proclaimed." The sites of many ancient churches still remain unexcavated.

During the fifth through fifteenth centuries, there arose in the east several Muslim states such as Ifat, Dawaro, Hadya, Saho, Bali, and Afar that were assimilated into the Ethiopian empire. Little archaeological work has taken place in these regions. Likewise, many Christian sites of the twelfth through the fifteenth centuries await excavation. This era, which was a period of ecclesiastical revival, consists of the Zagwe dynasty (1137–1270) and the so-called Solomonid dynasty (1270–1527).

[*See also* Adulis; Axum; Hadar; Maṭara; *and* Meroë.]

BIBLIOGRAPHY

Alvares, Francisco. *Prester John of the Indies.* Translated by Lord Stanley of Alderley. Edited by C. F. Beckingham and G. W. B. Huntingford. Cambridge, 1961.

Anfray, Francis. "Chronique archéologique, 1960–64." *Annales d'Éthiopie* 6 (1965): 3–48.

Anfray, Francis. "Le Musée Archéologique d'Asmara." *Rassegna di Studi Etiopici* 21 (1965): 5–15.

Anfray, Francis. "Enselale, avec d'autres sites du Choa, de l'Arssi et un ilot du lac Tana." *Annales d'Éthiopie* 11 (1978): 153–180.

Athanasius. *Historical Tracts.* Translated by John Henry Newman. Oxford, 1843. See pages 182–183.

Athanasius. *Apologia ad imperatorum Constantium.* In *Patrologia graeca.* Vol. 25. Paris, 1857. See page 636.

Azaïs, François, and Roger Chambard. *Cinq années de recherches archéologiques en Éthiopie.* 2 vols. Paris, 1931.

Bent, J. Theodore. *The Sacred City of the Ethiopians.* London, 1893.

Bianchi Barriviera, Lino. *Le chiese in roccia di Lalibelà e di altri luoghi del Lasta.* Rome, 1963.

Bureau, Jacques. "Note sur les églises du Gamo." *Annales d'Éthiopie* 10 (1976): 295–303.

Caquot, André. "Note sur Berber Māryām." *Annales d'Éthiopie* 1 (1955): 109–116.

Caquot, André, and Pierre Nautin. "Une nouvelle inscription grecque d'Ézana, roi d'Axoum." *Journal des Savants* 72 (1970): 260–274.

Casson, Lionel, ed. and trans. *The "Periplus Maris Erythraei": Text with Introduction, Translation, and Commentary.* Princeton, 1989.

Cecchi, Antonio. *Da Zeila alle frontiere del Caffa.* Rome, 1886.

Cerulli, Enrico. "Documenti arabi per la storia dell'Etiopia." In *Memorie della Reale Accademia dei Lincei,* 6th ser., vol. 4. Rome, 1931.

Cerulli, Enrico. *Etiopi in Palestina: Storia della comunita etiopica di Gerusalemme.* 2 vols. Rome, 1953–1957.

Cerulli, Enrico. *Storia della letteratura etiopica.* Milan, 1956.

Christliche Kunst aus Äthiopien und Nubien. Vienna, 1964. Exhibition catalogue, Museum für Völkerkunde.

Conti Rossini, Carlo. *Storia d'Etiopia.* Bergamo, 1928.

Cosmas Indicopleustes. *The Christian Topography of Cosmas, an Egyptian Monk.* Translated and edited by John W. McCrindle. London, 1897.

Drewes, Abraham J. *Inscriptions de l'Éthiopie antique.* Leiden, 1962.

Gerster, Georg. *Churches in Rock: Early Christian Art in Ethiopia.* London, 1970.

Gigar, Tesfaye. "Inscriptions sur bois de trois églises de Lalibala." *Journal of Ethiopian Studies* 17 (1984): 107–126.

Glaser, Eduard. *Nochmals die Adulitanische Inschrift.* Das Ausland, 1891.

Glaser, Eduard. *Die Abessier in Arabien und Afrika.* Munich, 1895.

Groom, Nigel. *Frankincense and Myrrh: A Study of the Arabian Incense Trade.* London, 1981.

Heldman, Marilyn E. "Early Byzantine Sculptural Fragments from Adulis." Paper presented at the Tenth International Conference of Ethiopian Studies, Paris, 1988.

Heldman, Marilyn, et al. *African Zion: The Sacred Art of Ethiopia,* edited by Roderick Grierson. New Haven, 1993.

Huntingford, G. W. B., ed. and trans. *The Periplus of the Erythraen Sea.* London, 1980.

Ibn Hishām, 'Abd al-Malik. *Kitāb sīrat Rasūl Allāh.* 2 vols. Edited by Ferdinand Wüstenfeld. Göttingen, 1858–1860.

Isaac, Ephraim, and C. Felder. "Reflections on the Origins of the Ethiopian Civilization." In *Proceedings of the Eighth International Conference of Ethiopian Studies,* vol. 1, pp. 71–83. Addis Ababa, 1984.

Johanson, Donald, and Maitland Edey. *Lucy: The Beginnings of HumanKind.* New York, 1981.

Juel-Jensen, Bent. "Was the Design of One of Offa's Coins Inspired by the Silver of King Abana of Aksum?" *Spinks Numismatic Circular* 97 (1989): 296.

Juel-Jensen, Bent. "A New Aksumite Coin from the Early Christian Period." *Spinks Numismatic Circular* 99 (1991): 39.

Kitchen, Kenneth A. "The hand of Punt." In *The Archaeology of Africa: Food, Metals, and Towns,* edited by Thurstan Shaw et al., pp. 587–608. London and New York, 1993.

Kobischanov, Yuri M. *Axum.* Translated by Lorraine T. Kapitanoff. State College, Pa., 1979.

Lepage, Claude. "Les monuments chrétiens rupestres de Degum, en Éthiopie (rapport préliminaire)." *Cahiers Archéologiques* 22 (1972): 167–200.

Littmann, Enno. *The Legend of the Queen of Sheba in the Legend of Aksum.* Leiden, 1904.

Littmann, Enno. *Publications of the Princeton Expedition to Abyssinia.* 4 vols. Leiden, 1910–1915.

Littmann, Enno, et al. *Deutsche Aksum-Expedition.* 4 vols. Berlin, 1913.

Maqrīzī, Ahmad ibn 'Alī. *Historia regum Islamiticorum in Abyssinia.* Translated and edited by Friedrich Theodor Rink. N.p., 1790.

Moberg, Axel, ed. and trans. *The Book of the Himyarites.* Lund, 1924.

Moore, E. "Ethiopian Crosses from the Twelfth to the Sixteenth Century." In *Proceedings of the First International Conference on the History of Ethiopian Art, London, 1986,* pp. 110–114, figs. 148–182. London, 1989.

Müller, David Heinrich. *Epigraphische Denkmäler aus Abessinien.* Berlin, 1894.

Munro-Hay, Stuart C. *The Coinage of Aksum.* New Delhi, 1984.

Munro-Hay, Stuart C. "The al-Madhāriba Hoard of Gold Aksumite and Late Roman Coins." *Numismatic Chronicle* 149 (1989a): 83–100.

Munro-Hay, Stuart C., et al. *Excavations at Aksum: An Account of Research at the Ancient Ethiopian Capital Directed in 1972–4 by the Late Dr. Neville Chittick.* Memoirs of the British Institute in Eastern Africa, no. 10. London, 1989b.

Munro-Hay, Stuart C. "A New Silver Coin of King Aphilas of Aksum." *Numismatic Chronicle* 150 (1990): 238.

Munro-Hay, Stuart C. "Aksumite Coinage." In *African Zion: The Sacred Art of Ethiopia,* edited by R. Grierson. New Haven, 1993.

Oddy, W. A., and Stuart C. Munro-Hay. "The Specific Gravity Analysis of the Gold Coins of Aksum." *Metallurgy and Numismatics* 1 (1980): 73–82, pls. 2–4.

Procopius. *De bello Persico.* Translated by H. B. Dewing. Cambridge, Mass., 1914.

Schneider, Madeleine. "Stèles funéraires arabes de Quiha." *Annales d'Éthiopie* 7 (1967): 107–122.

Schneider, Madeleine. "Documents épigraphiques de l'Éthiopie." *Annales d'Éthiopie* 9 (1972): 103–113; 10 (1973): 81–93; 11 (1974): 128–133.

Schneider, Madeleine. "Trois nouvelles inscriptions royales d'Axoum." In *IV congresso internazionale di studi etiopici,* vol. 1, pp. 767–786. Accademia Nazionale dei Lincei, Quaderno 191. Rome, 1974.

Schneider, Madeleine. "Deux inscriptions éthiopiennes." *Journal of Ethiopian Studies* 15 (1982): 125–130.

Schoff, Wilfred H., ed. and trans. *The Periplus of the Erythraean Sea.* New York, 1912.

Strelcyn, Stefan. "Quelques inscriptions éthiopiennes." *Bibliotheca Orientalis* 36 (1979): 137–156.

Uhlig, Siegbert. *Äthiopische Paläographie.* Äthiopistische Forschungen, 22. Stuttgart, 1988.

Van Beek, Gus W. "Monuments of Axum in the Light of South Arabian Archaeology." *Journal of the American Oriental Society* 87.2 (1967): 113–122.

EPHRAIM ISAAC

ETHIOPIC. A language belonging to the Ethiopic Semitic subcategory of the southern group of Semitic, Ethiopic is more specifically known as classical Ethiopic or Ge'ez (Eth., *gə'əz,* perhaps derived from a root *g'z* "become free"; less probably, "depart," "change camp"). Ethiopic Semitic, a highly differentiated family of some fifteen languages, probably developed out of a lingua franca based on one or more varieties of South Semitic imported into the Horn of Africa from Southern Arabia (modern Yemen), perhaps in connection with Southern Arabian migration or trading activity at some time during the first millennium BCE. Ge'ez belongs to the Northern group of Ethiopic Semitic languages, as does its close relative Tigrinya, the language of modern Eritrea. It is attested in its full classical form by the fourth century CE but probably had disappeared as a spoken language by the tenth century. Ge'ez has survived as an ecclesiastical and liturgical language. Until the nineteenth century, it was, for all practical purposes, the sole written language of Ethiopia. The official language of modern Ethiopia is Amharic, one of a dozen or more languages making up the Southern group of Ethiopic Semitic languages.

TABLE 1. *Ethiopic writing systems.* Columns 1–8 show the Ethiopic syllabary (each sign represents the row/column consonant-vowel combination); columns 9-10 show the Old South Arabian alphabet (OSA signs for s³, theta, delta, ẓ, and gamma not used in Ethiopic).

1	2 Ca	3 Cu	4 Ci	5 Cā	6 Ce	7 Cə	8 Co	9 OSA	10
h									h
l									l
ḥ									ḥ
m									m
š									s²
r									r
s									s¹
q									q
b									b
t									t
ḫ									ḫ
n									n
ʾ									ʾ
k									k
w									w
ʿ									ʿ
z									z
y									y
d									d
g									g
ṭ									ṭ
ṗ								–	
ṣ									ṣ
ḍ									ḍ
f									f
p								–	
qʷ									
ḫʷ									
kʷ									
gʷ									

The writing system used for all Ethiopic Semitic languages (see table 1) clearly developed from a South Semitic consonantal script of the type attested in Epigraphic South Arabic. A unique feature distinguishing this from all other West Semitic scripts is its evolution in the direction of a syllabary by the introduction of a distinct modification of the basic consonantal character for each of the seven vowels (/i e a ā ə o u/) of the language. There is, however, no special sign for a consonant not followed by a vowel (the Cə sign is used), or for consonant gemination (doubling), an important feature of Geʿez morphology. The consonantal inventory of Geʿez contains most of the "emphatic" and laryngeal consonants expected in a Semitic language. It is important to note, however, that the set of consonants is unique in having both an "emphatic" (glottalized) /p'/ and a class of "labio-velar" consonants (velars with a *w*-offglide) /kʷ gʷ qʷ hʷ/.

In verbal morphology Geʿez shares with other Western Semitic languages (Arabic, Hebrew, and Aramaic) the de-velopment of a perfective (past) tense based on suffixed subject elements; its imperfective (present-future), how-ever, preserves an archaic construction found elsewhere only in Akkadian. In the paradigm of the base form of the perfective and imperfective of the verb qtl ("kill") shown in table 2, note also the /k/ in the first person singular and sec-ond person perfective subject suffixes, instead of the /t/ found in the other languages.

Of the three Common Semitic nominal case suffixes, nominative /-u/, genitive /-i/, accusative /-a/, only the accu-sative survives in Geʿez. Like Arabic and South Arabian, Geʿez forms the plural of a large portion of its nouns by replacing the vowel pattern of the singular: *kalb/aklāb* "dog/dogs," *wald/wəlud* "son/sons," *kanfar/kanāfər* "lip/lips." Syntactically, Geʿez tends to follow the verb-subject-object clause word-order pattern favored in West Semitic lan-guages but less rigorously than some of the other languages.

The written attestation of Geʿez starts with a limited num-ber of monumental inscriptions in an archaic nonvocalized form of the script. By the time of the fourth-century CE king Ezana, we find a number of long, vocalized, and monumen-tal texts on stelae (essentially campaign narratives) from the capital, Axum, monotheistic (presumably Christian) in con-tent, which show both the language and script in their es-sentially classic form. There are earlier polytheistic texts in nonvocalized Ethiopic script from the same ruler. Some of these texts are accompanied by Greek translations and tran-scriptions into South Arabian script. Properly speaking, the earliest period of Geʿez literature seems to date from the evangelization of Ethiopia, perhaps from the sixth century. (Few, if any, of the preserved Geʿez manuscripts can be dated confidently before the twelfth century.) This literature consists largely of translations and adaptations from Greek and possibly Syriac: the Bible and Apocrypha, liturgical texts, rules of Pachomius, collections of extracts from the Church Fathers, and hagiographical accounts. After a "dark period," which began in the eighth century and lasted for several hundred years, the literary tradition picks up again in connection with new monastic foundations and reesta-blishment of a link with the Alexandria patriarchate in the eleventh century. There is still a strong translation compo-nent, now largely from Arabic (itself in turn frequently a translation from Greek, Coptic, or Syriac), but there are also

TABLE 2. *Perfective and Imperfective of the Verb* Qtl *("Kill")*

	PERFECTIVE		IMPERFECTIVE	
	Sg.	Pl.	Sg.	Pl.
1	qatal-ku	qatal-na	ə-qattəl	nə-qattəl
2 m	qatal-ka	qatal-kəmmu	tə-qattəl	tə-qattəl-u
2 f	qatal-ki	qatal-kən	tə-qattəl-i	tə-qattəl-ā
3 m	qatal-a	qatal-u	yə-qattəl	yə-qattəl-u
3 f	qatal-at	qatal-ā	tə-qattəl	yə-qattəl-ā

new, original, and indigenous works in an ecclesiastical vein. These works include hagiography, local chronicles, and liturgical, devotional, and apocalyptic literature. Furthermore, court literature includes royal chronicles, a "national epic" (*Kəbra Nagast*—"The Glory of Kings"—recounting the origins of the ruling dynasty from a union of Solomon and Sheba, here, an Ethiopian queen), and legal documents. A tradition of magical texts continues into the twentieth century, its most visible manifestation being the ubiquitous "magic scrolls" composed in Ge'ez for individual clients by learned clerics and worn as an amulet, rolled up in a leather case.

[*See also* Semitic Languages.]

BIBLIOGRAPHY

Dillmann, August. *Lexicon linguae aethiopicae.* Leipzig, 1865. The basic lexicographic work, with Ethiopic script, textual citations, headwords ordered according to script order, and translations into Latin. The etymologies are unreliable and should be consulted with Leslau (1987).

Dillmann, August. *Ethiopic Grammar.* 2d ed. London, 1907. The basic grammar.

Hetzron, Robert. *Ethiopian Semitic: Studies in Classification.* Journal of Semitic Studies, Monograph no. 2. Manchester, 1972. Consult for the relations of Ethiopic Semitic languages to one another, and to Semitic generally.

Lambdin, Thomas O. *Introduction to Classical Ethiopic (Ge'ez).* Harvard Semitic Studies, no. 24. Missoula, Mont., 1978. Good for self-instruction; exercises and grammar given in Roman transcription only.

Leslau, Wolf. *An Annotated Bibliography of the Semitic Languages of Ethiopia.* La Haye, 1965.

Leslau, Wolf. *Comparative Dictionary of Ge'ez (Classical Ethiopic).* Wiesbaden, 1987. Entries and subentries in Roman transcription, ordered by transcription alphabet, with up-to-date and reliable etymologies.

Leslau, Wolf. *Concise Dictionary of Ge'ez (Classical Ethiopic).* Wiesbaden, 1989. Same basic vocabulary coverage as above, excluding etymologies. Entries are given in Ethiopic script, according to Ethiopic script order.

Ricci, Lanfranco. "Ethiopian Christian Literature." In *The Coptic Encyclopedia,* vol. 3, pp. 975–979. New York, 1991. Contains extensive bibliography.

GENE GRAGG

ETHNOARCHAEOLOGY.

The wide variety of approaches, methodologies, and questions designed to enhance archaeological interpretation through the application of ethnographic data to material remains recovered through excavation is collectively known as ethnoarchaeology. More technically, ethnoarchaeology refers to ethnographic study conducted for the purpose of applying it to a particular archaeological problem, such as tool construction and use, population density, use of domestic space, or pottery production. Archaeologists observe a living culture that is similar in both environmental setting and cultural character to the ancient culture they are attempting to reconstruct. The data from the living culture are then applied to the ancient setting in order to allow a more informed interpretation of the material culture. Some scholars therefore restrict the term *ethnoarchaeology* to describe and define problem-oriented fieldwork. Others prefer a broader definition and refer to problem-oriented field archaeology as either action archaeology (Kleindienst and Watson, 1956) or living archaeology (Gould, 1977).

Archaeologists and anthropologists have used ethnographic data to aid in interpretation and reconstruction since at least the mid-eighteenth century. Initially those data were used to study hunting-and-gathering societies. They were usually collected to study modern examples of those societies and were only secondarily applied to archaeological interpretation. In 1900, J. W. Fewkes used the term *ethnoarchaeology* to describe this type of research, but for much of the twentieth century the term has been only loosely defined (Gould and Watson, 1982). In the last forty years, advances in methodology have allowed ethnoarchaeology to emerge as a distinct discipline within the fields of anthropology and archaeology. Two important changes have taken place: there has been a linkage between archaeological and ethnographic fieldwork, so that the primary purpose of collecting ethnographic data is to assist in reconstructions; and scholars have consciously expanded the boundaries of ethnoarchaeology to include virtually all preindustrial societies—horticultural, agrarian, herding, nomadic, and maritime.

Methodology. Ethnoarchaeologists generally agree that the primary purpose of ethnoarchaeology is to aid archaeologists and anthropologists in the difficult task of interpretation. This occurs primarily in two ways: hypotheses concerning the use and origin of particular artifacts or architectural remains in ancient cultures are generated, and theories explaining the relationship between material remains and the human culture that produced them are developed and tested (Gould and Watson, 1982, pp. 356–357). However, debate continues over the role of "analogy" or "analogical reasoning" in the interpretative process. Specifically, questions remain about the appropriate limits and controls for the use of analogy. Some suggest loose controls (Robert Ascher, "Analogy in Archaeological Study," *Southwestern Journal of Anthropology* 17 [1961]: 317–325; Yellin, 1977); others propose that the scientific method be imposed rigidly on the interpretive process (Binford, 1967, 1982). While most recognize the need for caution in applying analogy, a minority of scholars suggest that analogical reasoning should be abandoned altogether on the grounds that it is circular and overly subjective (Freeman, 1968; Gould, in Gould and Watson, 1982).

In analogical reasoning, archaeologists seek analogs, or points of comparison, between a source society (contemporary, but premodern) and a subject society (ancient, often prehistoric). Those who favor the use of analogy generally agree that for analogical reasoning to be valid, several levels of similarity must exist—in cultural organization, environmental setting, subsistence strategy, and technology—between the ethnographically documented culture and the archaeologically documented culture (Kramer, 1979).

In his programmatic article, Ascher (1961) drew attention to the need for a more sophisticated methodology to govern analogical reasoning. He points out that anthropologists frequently applied data directly from one cultural context to another (in what he called the direct-historical approach) with little sensitivity to the levels of continuity or discontinuity between the analog and the culture to which it was applied. He suggests that ethnoarchaeologists adopt a more nuanced approach to the data to include the use of multiple analogs in interpretation; ranking the usefulness of those analogs; incorporating more ethnographic data in interpretation; and showing greater sensitivity to the differences between living and dead cultures under study. Lewis Binford (1967) argues that Ascher's suggestions are inadequate and that if analogy is to be used in archaeological reconstructions it must be governed by scientific method. He called for archaeologists to state clearly the assumptions underlying their research and to frame and test hypotheses concerning the cultures being studied.

Patty Jo Watson (Gould and Watson, 1982) and Alison Wylie (1985) claim that analogical reasoning is indispensable to the interpretative process. Wylie maintains that a major reason for the resistance to analogical reasoning is its early naiveté, its evolutionary determinism, and its lack of adequate controls. She further argues that because ethnoarchaeologists have advanced more sophisticated methodologies, the distrust of analogy is no longer valid—that, at its core, all archaeological interpretation is analogical. According to Watson, the purpose of ethnoarchaeology is twofold: to collect analogs from as many contexts as possible and to develop theories and methodologies to govern the application of these analogs to the archaeological record. She readily admits the tentative nature of analogical inference but seeks to offset any subjectivity through evaluating each proposed analog for its degree of similarity between source and subject culture. In addition, Watson emphasizes the need of further scientific testing that would demonstrate both similarities and differences among the cultures under question.

According to Richard Gould, analogy is fundamentally flawed. He objects to its use on three points: analogical reasoning tends to be circular, it assumes a high degree of continuity (when it observes real or apparent parallels it claims to prove the uniformity that it has assumed); and apparent similarity among cultures does not prove that specific relationships actually exist between present and past practices or cultural patterns. Gould insists that analogical reasoning, and the apparent continuity it claims to prove, cannot adequately explain the variables inherent in human culture. Thus, he suggests that ethnoarchaeologists should concentrate on levels of cultural dissonance and anomaly rather than seek to demonstrate cultural similarities through analogy. Gould and others who oppose analogical inference frequently cite "cautionary tales" to demonstrate the weaknesses of analogy and to call either for better methodology or for the abandonment of analogical reasoning. These tales generally demonstrate that the proposed relationship between an ancient artifact and its contemporary analog does not exist, based either on problem-oriented research or newly gathered ethnographic information.

The concerns regarding the use of analogy are particularly important when prehistoric, hunter-gatherer societies are the focus of the study. In such cases, the time gap between the society from which the ethnographic data are gathered and the culture to which they are applied often approaches thirty thousand–forty thousand years. In the case of the earliest hominid remains, in which tool production or even subsistence patterns may be studied, the gap may increase substantially into the hundreds of thousands or even millions of years. Generally, the greater the time gap between the two cultures being studied, the more difficult it is to show that analogies truly exist and the more speculative the conclusions. As noted, most early ethnoarchaeological research focused on prehistoric cultures. However, recent ethnographic studies have been applied to historical societies for which scholars may possess both written and archaeological remains; in these cases, levels of continuity or discontinuity may be more easily discerned and analogy applied with greater accuracy.

Despite the concerns expressed by Gould and other scholars, analogy will probably continue to play an important role in ethnoarchaeological studies. Gould's criticisms have prompted scholars to be more sensitive to similarity and dissonance (or anomaly) between source and subject cultures; ethnoarchaeologists continue to be self-critical and more objective in the ways in which they apply analogical reasoning to the archaeological record.

Ethnoarchaeology and the Biblical World. As ethnoarchaeology has emerged as a separate discipline, it has increasingly been applied to the archaeology of the ancient Near East. Several important studies have been conducted throughout the region, from Cyprus to the Zagros Mountains, and have contributed to a greater understanding of numerous cultural patterns, including use of domestic space, pottery manufacture, population, pastoral nomadism, architecture, technology, and production. Among these issues three stand out as most significant in dealing with ancient Israel: pastoral nomadism, population, and production.

Pastoral nomadism. One of the major theories about the origins and emergence of Israel claims that the earliest Israelites were pastoral nomads who, for various socioeconomic reasons, chose a sedentary lifestyle over nomadism. This theory initially applied analogical parallels from late nineteenth- and early twentieth-century models of bedouin culture and camel nomadism to the biblical texts (see, for example, Johannes Pederson, *Israel: Its Life and Culture*, London, 1926; W. Robertson Smith, *Lectures on the Religions of the Semites: The Fundamental Institutions*, Edinburgh, 1889). Albrecht Alt (1925) and Martin Noth (*The History of Israel*, New York, 1958) then used this model in their "peaceful infiltration" theory to explain Israel's emergence in Canaan. George Mendenhall (1962) subsequently showed the weaknesses of this theory, particularly because it relied on relatively late and highly idealized pictures of nomadism, and proposed an alternative model for Israel's origins. [*See* Israelites; *and the biographies of Alt and Noth.*] Recent scholarship has refined the model of pastoral nomadism through ethnoarchaeological and anthropological studies of various types of nomadic societies; rather than use one rigid model of nomadism, scholars are now able to differentiate among transhumant pastoralism, camel nomadism, and traditional pastoral nomadism (see, in particular, *Biblical Archaeologist* 56.4 [1993]).

One of the difficulties in reconstructing nomadic societies and testing their applicability to earliest Israel has been the paucity of material remains such societies leave. However, new techniques of investigation (some developed from intensive studies of living nomadic societies) allow archaeologists to retrieve data even from scant archaeological remains of ancient nomadic groups (Rosen and Avni, and Banning, in *Biblical Archaeologist*, 1993). Other studies concentrate on the complex social forces involved in the process of sedentarization, the origins of the four-room or broadroom house, the way in which traditional and nomadic societies maintain ethnicity, subsistence strategies, and settlement design. While these studies cannot prove or disprove the peaceful infiltration theory proposed by Alt, they have allowed for its refinement and for a more nuanced understanding of a societal type that was present in Syria-Palestine in antiquity.

Population. Perhaps the least controversial use of ethnoarchaeology is its application to population density in antiquity. Ethnoarchaeologists have examined various aspects of population density in rural villages in Iran and Syria-Palestine (including areal density and spatial patterning). Archaeologists most commonly use areal analysis to estimate the population of ancient Syria-Palestine. The density of population in a contemporary village is studied, and a population-to-area coefficient is applied to ancient settlements. Early studies suggested that as many as 450 to 500 persons lived on one hectare (2.5 acres) of settled space, which led to somewhat inflated estimates of population of cities and villages in antiquity.

As a result of several recent and more accurate studies of population density, the most widely accepted population-to-area coefficient is now 250 persons per hectare (25 persons per metric dunam [0.25 acre]). To compute population, archaeologists estimate a site's total settled area and then multiply the figure by the population coefficient. For example, a series of articles on the population of Syria-Palestine for the Early Bronze, Middle Bronze, Iron II, and Roman-Byzantine periods indicates that there were three population peaks for Syria-Palestine: the Middle Bronze Age II, Iron Age II, and Roman-Byzantine periods (Broshi and others: 1979, 1984, 1986, 1992). Such studies allow for a better understanding of the settlement and population patterns in particular periods and throughout the history of an entire region and thus for more accurate reconstructions of the larger socioeconomic and cultural patterns in antiquity. (Broshi, one of the pioneers in population studies, initially used the higher 450 persons per hectare coefficient; some of his early results should be recalculated using 250 persons, which will reduce estimates by about 45 percent.) [*See* Demography.]

Production. Cultural reconstruction also involves the mode and types of production. Scholars examine such features as crop types and yields, the relative importance of particular crops in production; technological innovations that affect crop types or yields, economic interrelationship among villages, and the degree to which villages were exploited by larger cities and their social elites.

With the assistance of the allied fields of ethnobotany and paleobotany, it is relatively easy to assess the types of crops that were most significant in the overall agrarian regimen. [*See* Ethnobotany, Paleobotany.] Similarly, technological shifts tend to be well represented in the archaeological record. However, additional sources of information are needed to answer questions about agricultural production and socioeconomic interrelationships. Israel Finkelstein (*The Archaeology of the Israelite Settlement*, Jerusalem, 1988) and Baruch Rosen ("Subsistence Economy of Stratum II," in *Izbet Sarta. An Early Iron Age Site near Rosh Ha'ayin, Israel.* Oxford, 1986), for example, have turned to two sources to supplement the archaeological data: sixteenth-century CE taxation and census documents from the Early Ottoman period in Syria-Palestine and documents and statistics from the early British Mandate of Palestine (1917–1948). Although these materials were not compiled to assist archaeological interpretation, their use would be allowed under a definition of ethnoarchaeology that views archival data as legitimate for analogical inference.

Using the data from these two sources, Finkelstein and Rosen attempt to reconstruct the levels of crop yields possible for a particular region of Syria-Palestine. These reconstructions form the basis of their detailed analysis of village and regional economies, which shows how patterns of surplus or deficit affect the production of certain crops and how patterns of trade among villages offset environmentally influenced patterns. However, the data from the sixteenth- and early twentieth-century studies have been applied directly to the past without enough sensitivity to the sources of data or to the possible differences between the source and subject cultures (Carter, 1992). Although the approach may hold promise for future economic reconstructions of ancient Syria-Palestine, testable hypotheses need to be devised to determine whether the apparent continuity between these traditional cultures and those of antiquity is genuine. Only when adequate similarity between source culture and subject culture is demonstrated can the data be applied to ancient Israel.

Ethnoarchaeology shows significant potential for helping archaeologists interpret and understand the remains they excavate. It sheds light on the problematic archaeological issues of cultural patterns, socioeconomic setting, means of production, population, ethnicity of ancient societies, and the relationship between ideological and material aspects of culture.

BIBLIOGRAPHY

Alt, Albrecht. "Die landnahme der Israeliten in Palastina: Territorialgeschichtliche studien." Leipzig, 1925. See also the English translation in *Essays in Old Testament History and Religion.* Oxford, 1968, pp. 135–169.

Bar-Yosef, Ofer, and Anatoly Khazanov, eds. *Pastoralism in the Levant: Archaeological Materials in Anthropological Perspectives.* Prehistory Press Monographs in World Archaeology, no. 10. Madison, Wis., 1992. Important contribution to the discussion of pastoralism, including reports of ethnographic research, discussions of anthropological and ethnoarchaeological method, and examinations of pastoralism in specific archaeological periods, regions, or sites in antiquity.

Biblical Archaeologist 56.4 (1993): "Nomadic Pastoralism: Past and Present." Includes five articles on ethnoarchaeology as it relates to pastoral nomadism and as recorded in archaeological remains and Near Eastern texts (see the articles by Augustin F. C. Holl and Thomas E. Levy, Ilse Köhler-Rollefson, Stephen Rosen and Gideon Avni, David C. Hopkins, and E. B. Banning).

Binford, Lewis R. "Smudge Pits and Hide Smoking: The Use of Analogy in Archaeological Reasoning." *American Anthropology* 32 (1967): 1–12. In this and the article below, Binford discusses the uncritical use of analogy and advocates the application of scientific method and the development of testable hypothesis as a means of bringing greater control to analogical reasoning.

Binford, Lewis R. "Meaning, Inference, and the Material Record." In *Ranking, Resource, and Exchange,* edited by Colin Renfrew and Stephen Shennan, pp. 160–163. Cambridge, 1982.

Broshi, Magen. "The Population of Western Palestine in the Roman-Byzantine Period." *Bulletin of the American Schools of Oriental Research,* no. 236 (Fall 1979): 1–10. This and the following articles by Broshi, Gophna, and Finkelstein represent studies of population and demography based on ethnoarchaeological assessments of population density. They show the methodological advances in such studies, demonstrating the use of population studies in the reconstruction of wider social and economic patterns.

Broshi, Magen, and Ram Gophna. "The Settlements and Population of Palestine during the Early Bronze Age II–III." *Bulletin of the American Schools of Oriental Research,* no. 253 (Winter 1984): 41–53.

Broshi, Magen, and Ram Gophna. "Middle Bronze Age II Palestine: Its Settlements and Population." *Bulletin of the American Schools of Oriental Research,* no. 261 (February 1986): 73–90.

Broshi, Magen, and Israel Finkelstein. "The Population of Palestine in Iron Age II." *Bulletin of the American Schools of Oriental Research,* no. 287 (August 1992): 47–60.

Carter, Charles E. "A Social and Demographic Study of Post-Exilic Judah." Ph.D. diss., Duke University, 1992. Includes a discussion of ethnoarchaeological method and devises testable hypotheses to evaluate the assumption of continuity that underlies recent attempts to use premodern data from Palestine to reconstruct economic patterns of that region in antiquity.

David, Nicholas. "Integrating Ethnoarchaeology: A Subtle Realist Perspective." *Journal of Anthropological Archaeology* 11 (1982): 330–359. Study of methodological issues confronting ethnoarchaeologists, distinguishing between two basic models: the "Binfordian" model, which concentrates on material remains, and the "Hodderian" model, which focuses on ideational aspects of culture.

Freeman, Leslie G., Jr. "A Theoretical Framework for Interpreting Archeological Materials." In *Man the Hunter,* edited by Richard B. Lee and Irven DeVore, pp. 262–267. Chicago, 1968. Calls for the abandonment of analogical reasoning, suggesting that the similarities between ancient and modern societies and/or behavior are only apparent and that analogical inference impedes the interpretive process.

Gould, Richard A. "Some Current Problems in Ethnoarchaeology." In *Experimental Archaeology,* edited by Daniel Ingersoll et al., pp. 359–377. New York, 1977. Presents a broadly based definition of the term *ethnoarchaeology* and suggests that problem-oriented ethnographic research should be called living archaeology.

Gould, Richard A., and Patty Jo Watson. "A Dialogue on the Meaning and Use of Analogy in Ethnoarchaeological Reasoning." *Journal of Anthropological Archaeology* 1 (1982): 355–381. Opposing viewpoints on the use of analogy present and a discussion of the appropriate methods of ethnoarchaeological interpretation.

Heider, Karl G. "Archaeological Assumptions and Ethnographical Facts: A Cautionary Tale from New Guinea." *Southwestern Journal of Anthropology* 23 (1967): 52–64. Uses ethnographic research to show that certain assumptions concerning tool use in prehistoric hunter-gatherer societies, arrived at through analogical reasoning, are incorrect; advocates greater caution in applying analogy to the archaeological record.

Kleindienst, Maxine, and Patty Jo Watson. "'Action Archaeology': The Archaeological Inventory of a Living Community." *Anthropology Tomorrow* 5 (1956): 75–78. Pioneering article on the nature of ethnoarchaeology.

Kramer, Carol, ed. *Ethnoarchaeology: The Implications of Ethnography for Archaeology.* New York, 1979. Essential introduction to the recent use of ethnoarchaeology and ethnography in the archaeology of the ancient Near East, including a critical introduction to ethnoarchaeology and several studies in which ethnographic information from the Near East is applied to the archaeological record of that region in antiquity.

Mendenhall, George. "The Hebrew Conquest of Palestine." *Biblical Archaeologist* 25 (1962): 66–87.

Wylie, Alison. "The Reaction against Analogy." In *Advances in Archaeological Method and Theory,* vol. 8, edited by Michael B. Schiffer, pp. 63–111. New York, 1985. Perhaps the best synopsis of the recent discussion of the use and abuse of analogy, suggesting that all ethnoarchaeological inference is analogical. Wylie attempts to show that recent developments in methodology make the objections to analogy groundless.

Yellin, John E. *Archaeological Approaches to the Present: Models for Reconstructing the Past.* New York, 1977. Pragmatic treatment of the problems involved in archaeological reconstructions that identifies past problems and recent advances in ethnoarchaeological methodology.

CHARLES E. CARTER

ETHNOBOTANY. By examining modern plant use and the interrelationship between humans and their environment, archaeologists and paleoethnobotanists can gain insight into ancient uses of plants and the processes responsible for the deposition of the variety of botanical remains found at archaeological sites. Among the many uses of plants, that of food is perhaps the most critical. Past subsistence practices, diet, and nutrition can be reconstructed by observing traditional methods and tools used in food preparation and processing. To understand how plants have been used for food, how they were deposited, and how they were collected, it is helpful to turn to the practices of comparable modern societies.

Studies have been carried out in Turkey and Greece to identify the by-products of crop processing activities, with a view to determining which plants and plant parts are likely to be preserved in various contexts at a Neolithic or Bronze Age site. One such study (Hillman, 1984) identified nearly thirty different steps necessary to process emmer wheat. From threshing, winnowing, and sieving, to final sorting before grinding, each step in the process produced various weed seeds, chaff fragments, or other plant parts that were ultimately deposited elsewhere on the site as fodder, mudbrick temper, or refuse. The disposal of certain by-products in hearths or middens that are subsequently burned, or the accidental destruction of a storage or processing facility by fire, will result in at least some of the specific by-products being carbonized and thus potentially preserved. It may then be possible to correlate similar types of deposits on archaeological sites with the processing step(s) used.

The ethnobotanist observes seasonal plant use, often for several years within a given community or region, in order to observe how some plants are stored while others are eaten immediately upon collection or harvest. In the course of several years it may also be possible to examine plant reactions to stresses such as crop failure from drought or other climatic disasters, depletion of wild resources as a result of the expansion of agricultural lands, or loss of wood for fuel as a result of deforestation. Most or all of these stresses were probably also felt by societies and communities in the ancient Near East at one time or another. It is, thus, possible to formulate hypotheses about the reactions of ancient populations based on a modern society's methods of coping with the stress on flora.

There is some uncertainty attendant in this type of ethnographic analogy: the by-products of different processing steps may not have been mixed in the same deposit, particular tool types found on sites may not always have been used for the same purposes, and people may not, in fact, always

react in the same ways to similar stresses. Still, ethnobotany provides a framework for speculation. It also allows an examination of the archaeological data from a different perspective, in order to reach the most reasonable explanation of the ancient record.

[See also Agriculture; Cereals; Ethnozoology; Paleobotany; and Paleoenvironmental Reconstruction.]

BIBLIOGRAPHY

Forbes, Mary. "Gathering in the Argolid: A Subsistence Subsystem in a Greek Agricultural Community." In *Regional Variation in Modern Greece and Cyprus: Toward a Perspective on the Ethnography of Greece*, edited by Muriel Dimen and Ernestine Friedl, pp. 251–264. Annals of the New York Academy of Sciences, vol. 268. New York, 1976. A look at some wild plant foods that would not be preserved archaeologically and might, therefore, be overlooked as part of the ancient diet.

Hillman, Gordon. "Interpretation of Archaeological Plant Remains: The Application of Ethnographic Models from Turkey." In *Plants and Ancient Man: Studies in Palaeoethnobotany*, edited by Willem van Zeist and W. A. Casparie, pp. 1–41. Rotterdam, 1984. Discusses crop-processing activities observed in Turkey over a number of years, the various by-products from each step, and analytical methods useful for grouping archaeological samples for comparison with an ethnobotanical counterpart.

Jones, Glynis E. M. "Interpretation of Archaeological Plant Remains: Ethnographic Models from Greece." In *Plants and Ancient Man: Studies in Palaeoethnobotany*, edited by Willem van Zeist and W. A. Casparie, pp. 43–61. Rotterdam, 1984. Statistical analysis of weed seeds to identify the most likely steps in the processing sequence by which archaeological samples were produced.

JULIE HANSEN

ETHNOZOOLOGY. The study of the way people and animals interact in a particular zoocultural system, ethnozoology seeks appropriate cultural definitions for animals as economic, symbolic, and ritual markers in a society. To study communities and their animals in the past, ethnozoology follows ethnoarchaeology in observing how modern societies use animals to discern patterns of behavior. From this, appropriate models are constructed against which the archaeological record can be tested. Because much ethnozoology has been directed to revealing how in the past people produced animals and animal products, it has focused its research on modern pastoral societies. The limitations of ethnoarchaeology in general have applied here: extinct cultural processes cannot be found through ethnographic analogy. Its potential to inform, however, is great, if appropriate examples are chosen. In the ancient Near East, the range of animals (sheep, goat, cattle, pig, donkey, camel) exploited for food and labor was small and has not changed appreciably for much of the region—with the possible exception of the increased use of domestic chicken and the decrease, since late antiquity, in the use of pig. The great difference between ancient and modern stock is the introduction of improved breeds since World War II. However, because such animals are found only in the most sophisticated centers, sophisticated breeding techniques do not confer a substantial increase in product potential.

To study animal production systems, ethnoarchaeologists have lived with modern pastoral societies and learned much about how their management choices are influenced by environmental, social, political, and economic factors. These field studies have contributed enormously to models of the domestication process. Ethnozoological research also concerns the mechanisms for the distribution of animal products. Both ethnographic and ethnohistoric records have been evaluated to produce models of the kinds of animals—by age, sex, and class—that are manipulated by central political authorities and markets. Together these studies have produced a sophisticated understanding of the relationship between the "desert and the sown" and the significance of pastoral resources in the construction of political and economic power. They have been significant in the evaluation of the extensive cuneiform record of centralized animal management. Another aspect is the study of cuisine, an ethnographic understanding of cooking and meal presentation in different social settings. This has proved beneficial in interpreting archaeological data at the household level. A final ethnoarchaeological aspect is actualistic studies of taphonomy (the study of processes that affect remains between their deposition and recovery). Bones are subject to numerous biases—that is, to processes associated with burial that differentially destroy them. Experimental research has provided techniques for minimizing the distortion these biases might bring to the historical interpretation of archaeological materials.

Ethnozoology also refers to the way people conceptualize animals. The study of folk taxonomy, a subdiscipline of cognitive anthropology, has revealed universal patterns in the way folk categorize and group animals. Because the basic level in studying animal production systems is predicated on animals as scientific categories that may have little or no intersection with the folk category, any complete understanding of how such a system functioned must comprehend both. The underlying psychology of folk taxa and their arrangements explicates the similarities and differences between folk and scientific systems. In studying the past, folk taxonomic principles can usefully be applied to ancient texts to facilitate a more accurate identification of animal terms. For example, philologists translating ancient animal terms would try to use contextual clues about morphology and behavior to match with a modern animal identified as a Linnaean category in a scientific classification. While this is a proper route to identification on one level, few philologists have understood modern zoological classification well enough to use it effectively: many times a term is equated with a modern species when there is insufficient evidence to make such a judgment, or when the folk category is, in fact, closer to a higher-level scientific grouping. In most instances, there has been little recognition that the ancients had no concept of Linnaean categories, and so only one side of the equation was revealed. The starting point of all "ethno-" study is to discover culturally conditioned units for investigation. Textual evidence can provide important ethnozoological data when critically evaluated.

[See also Animal Husbandry; Camels; Cattle and Oxen; Equids; Ethnoarchaeology; Ethnobotany; Paleobotany; Paleozoology; Pigs; and Sheep and Goats.]

BIBLIOGRAPHY

Atran, Scott. Cognitive Foundations of Natural History: Towards an Anthropology of Science. Cambridge, 1990. Penetrating study of the universal patterns underlying the cognition and arrangement of animate, as opposed to inanimate, objects and their influence on modern studies of natural science.

Aurenche, Olivier, ed. Nomads and sédentaires: Perspectives ethnoarchéologiques. Centre Jean Palerne, Mémoires, 4. Paris, 1984. Important detailed studies of communities in Syria and Iraq.

Berlin, Brent, et al. "General Principles of Classification and Nomenclature in Folk Biology." American Anthropologist 75 (1973): 214–242. Major initial statement of the principles of folk classification.

Berlin, Brent. Ethnobiological Classification: Principles of Categorization of Plants and Animals in Traditional Societies. Princeton, 1992. Incorporates Berlin's many studies of ethnobiological classification and presents fresh insights into his pioneering theories. It will stand for many years as the seminal work in the field of folk classification.

Cribb, Roger. Nomads in Archaeology. Cambridge, 1991. Important ethnoarchaeological study of nomads in Turkey and Iran with broad utility in the construction of models for the ancient Near East.

Kramer, Carol. Village Ethnoarchaeology: Rural Iran in Archaeological Perspective. New York, 1982. Pioneering study of the implications of the characteristics of a village in Iran for archaeological reconstructions.

Watson, Patty Jo. Archaeological Ethnography in Western Iran. Tucson, 1979. Important details about animal management in a sedentary society.

PAULA WAPNISH

EUGENICS MOVEMENT. The term eugenics, defining a theory of human evolutionary genetics and "racial improvement" that exerted a profound influence on archaeological interpretation in the Mediterranean basin and Near East, was coined in 1883 by Francis Galton. A widely respected Victorian statistician and social critic, Galton sought to apply the principles of Darwinian "natural selection" to the improvement of the human race. According to the genetic theory first detailed in Galton's most famous work, Hereditary Genius: An Inquiry into its Laws and Consequences (New York, 1870), human races possess varying levels of intelligence and physical capabilities. Indeed, the ability of each race—so the theory went—could be measured, to provide a clear hierarchy of racial groups.

The movement of history, Galton contended, was propelled by the effects of this hereditary inequality, with "superior" races naturally conquering and subsequently dominating "inferior" ones. Galton and his followers further believed that uncontrolled interbreeding between superior and inferior races led inevitably to the degeneration of the former, and to their inevitable conquest by yet purer and superior racial groups. The early supporters of the eugenics movement in England were primarily concerned with modern racial issues: the social effects of massive immigration into the country in the late nineteenth and early twentieth centuries and the often problematic relationship between British imperial administrators and the millions of Asians, Africans, and Middle Easterners they presumed to rule. Yet, one of the most important intellectual tasks undertaken by the supporters of eugenics was to demonstrate that racial inequality had been an operative factor throughout history—and that uncontrolled "race mixing" had uniformly disastrous results in all societies in which it occurred.

William M. Flinders Petrie was among the first archaeologists to be deeply affected by Galtonian eugenics in the reconstruction of past societies. In 1885, Petrie accepted employment by Galton to travel up the Nile River and photograph ancient Egyptian reliefs. The expectation was that the standard complement of human races, identifiable by their standard facial and bodily characteristics, could be traced back to pharaonic times. The result of this expedition was Petrie's book *Racial Photographs from the Egyptian Monuments* (1887), which was among the first archaeological works to describe the various ethnic groups of the ancient Near East with modern racial terminology. Petrie further elaborated the idea of racial hierarchy in the ancient Near East in his later excavations both in Egypt and Palestine. His recognition of successive strata of occupation at every site was linked to a sequence of historical conquests. Indeed, Petrie and the generation of Near Eastern archaeologists he trained and influenced grew accustomed to associating the appearance of new classes of artifacts at stratified sites such as Gurob in Egypt and Tell el-Ḥesi in Palestine with the arrival (and conquest) of aggressive and technologically superior ethnic groups.

The legacy of Petrie's eugenical thinking continued to exert an effect on the implicit racial thinking of Near Eastern archaeology until long after his death in 1940. The statistical assumptions underlying the seriation techniques used to construct a chronological typology of ceramic types (pioneered by Petrie at Naqada, Hu, and Abadiya in Egypt) were based on the acceptance of the inevitability of a rise-floruit-fall cycle in every aspect of human cultural production—implicitly paralleling the supposed genetic rise-floruit-fall of every interbreeding racial or ethnic group. Moreover, the identification of external invasion as the primary motivation for the major cultural breaks in every major archaeological period, from the Chalcolithic to the end of the Crusader period, served to transform modern archaeological research, at least partially, into an ideological justification for the aggressive expansion into the Near East of the profess-

edly superior European imperial powers. The assumptions of Petrie and his followers about the cultural superiority of the supposedly northern Hyksos or Aegean-based Philistines are two cases that illustrate his eugenical belief about the effect exerted by superior, or more innovative, races on the basically uncreative culture of Palestine.

Racial terminology and eugenical thinking remained prominent in archaeological thinking through the 1930s. Considerable attention was paid by scholars to the racial origins of excavated skeletal remains and the racial connections of cultural forms and artifact types. Through the continuing use of Petrie's basic methodology of distinguishing discrete strata often uncritically linked to invasions of historically mentioned ethnic groups, race remained a prominent (though scientifically unverified) element in reconstructions of ancient Near Eastern history. In the continuing, uncritical acceptance of rise-floruit-fall cycles in pottery types, and in the undefined attribution of social or cultural change to outside "influence" or internal "disintegration," some scholars may still implicitly promulgate the basic concepts of eugenical history. When, or if, they do, those concepts are promulgated as inherited ideology rather than empirically verified fact.

In the wake of World War II, however, the scientific bases for eugenical theories were largely undermined. Revulsion at the Nazis' final solution to the problem of "racial degeneration" ultimately paved the way for the final fall of eugenics, both as a modern social program and a scientific theory. In the 1950s and the 1960s, with the discovery of DNA and the beginning of research into population biology and the complexity of genetic inheritance, it became clear that the concept of "races" as distinct or even measurable entities was a dangerous oversimplification. New approaches—economic adaptation, innovation, cultural borrowing and exchange—in addition to invasion, came to be examined as the cause for changes in patterns of material culture.

[*See also the biography of Petrie.*]

BIBLIOGRAPHY

Cowan, Ruth S. "Francis Galton's Statistical Ideas: The Influence of Eugenics." *Isis* 63 (1972): 509–528.

Galton, Francis. *Hereditary Genius: An Inquiry into Its Laws and Consequences.* New York, 1870.

Kendall, David G. "A Statistical Approach to Flinders Petrie's Sequence Dating." *Bulletin of the International Statistical Institute* 40 (1963): 657–681.

Kevles, Daniel J. *In the Name of Eugenics: Genetics and the Uses of Human Heredity.* New York, 1985.

Lorimer, Douglas. "Theoretical Racism in Late-Victorian Anthropology, 1870–1900." *Victorian Studies* 31 (1988): 405–430.

Petrie, W. M. Flinders. *Racial Photographs from the Egyptian Monuments.* London, 1887.

Petrie, W. M. Flinders. "The Earliest Racial Portraits." *Nature* 39 (1888): 128–130.

Silberman, Neil Asher. "Petrie and the Founding Fathers." In *Biblical*

Archaeology Today, 1990: Proceedings of the Second International Congress on Biblical Archaeology, Jerusalem, June–July 1990, edited by Avraham Biran and Joseph Aviram, pp. 545–554. Jerusalem, 1993.

NEIL ASHER SILBERMAN

EUPHRATES.

In Sumerian the name of the Euphrates River is *BURANUN;* in Akkadian, *ÍD.KIB.NUN.KI* (lit., "Sippar River"); in Assyro-Babylonian, *Purattu;* in Old Persian, *Ufratu;* and in Greek, *Eufrates.* The river originates in eastern Turkey and flows into the Arab-Persian Gulf, a distance of almost 2,700 km (1,674 mi.), making it the longest river in western Asia. It currently traverses three modern Near Eastern states and a tiny part of a fourth. The total area of the Euphrates basin is 444,000 sq km (275,280 sq. mi.), of which 27 percent (125,000) is found in Turkey, 18 percent (76,000 sq km) in Syria, 40 percent (177,000 sq km) in Iraq, and 15 percent (66,000 sq km) in Saudi Arabia (Wakil, 1993, p. 67); 84 percent of its waters originates in Turkey, 13 percent in Syria, and 3 percent in Iraq. South of the Balikh and Khabur Rivers, rainfall ceases to be an important contributing factor to the Euphrates flow. The annual rate of flow fluctuates, depending on the climatic conditions affecting runoff and recharge. During the flood stage (March–June), when meltwater from eastern Anatolia Taurus ranges and spring rains are at their peak, 70 percent of the annual flow is generated. The summer low (July–October) generates only 10 percent of the annual flow, and the rainy season (November–February) creates the remainder: 20 percent of annual flow. The rate of flow fluctuates correspondingly. Within the Middle Euphrates area, reports of rate flow vary from 840 to more than 1,000 cu m per second) (Hardan, 1993, pp. 75–78; Tomanbay, 1993, p. 60; Akkermans, 1990a, p. 123; Sanlaville, 1985, p. 24). The annual rate also varies from year to year, with a typical average for several years reported at 2,600 million cu m per year (Sanlaville, 1985, p. 24).

The river can be divided into a number of distinct geographic units, depending on geomorphological conditions. First, the Upper Euphrates is found in eastern Anatolia, Turkey (from the Turkish perspective, the Lower Euphrates). There, two separate branches can be considered the source of the river. The western branch, the Kara Su, begins in a small lake north of Erzurum and flows west. The eastern branch, the Murat Su, also begins as a small lake east of Erzurum and flows west, paralleling the Kara Su. The two branches join north of Malatya to form the Euphrates (Tk., Firat) proper. Crossing the Taurus and the front range, the river then flows several hundred kilometers in a southerly direction, until it enters the Syrian plain at ancient Carchemish. There, the Middle Euphrates (sometimes called the Upper Jezireh) receives its Syrian tributaries; first, the Sadjur (100 million cu m per year), then the Balikh (190 million

cu m per year), just below ar-Raqqa, draining a large area to the north, and finally the Khabur at Bouqras (1,575 cu m per year). The river crosses into Iraq at Abu Kemal, near the site of ancient Mari. [*See* Carchemish; Raqqa, ar-; Bouqras; Mari.]

From the Khabur south, until Ramadi, the Middle Euphrates area is often called the Lower Jezireh (steppe), and the river is entrenched between this landform to the east and the Arabian plateau to the west. It does not enter the Mesopotamian floodplain until well south of Hit, 160 km (99 mi.) from the Iraqi-Syrian border (Sanlaville, 1985, p. 19). The current 250-millimeter isohyet in this region of the Jezireh determines the difference between dry farming, irrigation, and the development of pastoral nomadism (Zarins, 1990, fig. 3; Sanlaville, 1985, p. 20). [*See* Agriculture; Irrigation; Pastoral Nomadism.] The Lower Euphrates consists of a series of subgeomorphological units:

Alluvial plain. A typical alluvial plain of braiding streams creates natural levees, or river embankments, characterized by seasonal inundation and alluvial flats. Siltation and salt become problems as transported silts in the water (from repeated evaporation in alluvial basins or irrigated flats) cause channel closing and salinization. The river reaches its closest point to the Tigris River near ancient Sippar and modern Baghdad. [*See* Sippar; Baghdad.] There, it enters the delta plain and divides into two branches.

Delta plain. The main branch in the delta plain, the Hindiyah, flows to Samawa; the minor branch, the Hilla, continues past ancient Babylon and Kish to Diwaniya, joining the Hindiyah past Samawa. [*See* Babylon; Kish.]

Marsh/lake. The river creates a marsh/lake environment as it flows past Nasiriyyah, skirting north of Lake Hammar, then joining the Tigris at Qurmat Ali. The combined streams form the Shatt al-Arab in the estuarine zone.

Estuarine zone. The single stream of the Shatt al-Arab flows past Basra, where it is joined by the Karun and Karkheh Rivers from Iran. All four flow past Abadan and create a delta near Fao as they empty into the Arab-Persian Gulf. In this area, the pinching Batin and Karun and Karkheh River deltas constrict the modern Shatt al-Arab (Buringh, 1957; Sanlaville, 1989).

Ten existing dams are currently operating on the river system. The Hindiyah barrage is the oldest, having been built in 1911–1914. (The others are the Keban, Karakaya, Atatürk, Tabqa, Haditha, Baghdadi, Ramadi, Falluja, and Hilla.) The latest dams, such as the Ataturk in Turkey, were completed in 1990. On-line (i.e., functioning) dams such as the Keban in Turkey, the Tabqa in Syria, and Haditha in Iraq have created unique archaeological opportunities in areas otherwise poorly known (see below). Additional dams are in various stages of construction or planning on the river or its tributaries—particularly in Turkey and Syria (Khata, Bireçik, Carchemish, Saab, Shouher, Taaf). As a result of modernization plans, annual usage will be increased dramatically both for agricultural and industrial use. Because the river flows through three countries, future regulation of the Euphrates's waters is essential—a situation exacerbated by increasing competition for its waters and an incomplete understanding of the amount of water available annually.

Geological examination of the river's history has been spotty. Little is known from the source areas and the upper region; the Lower Euphrates has been more intensively examined. Initial work in the Middle Euphrates area suggests that the entire system originated in the Miocene graben, or depression, with subsequent Pliocene-Pleistocene depressions leading to the creation of a modern Euphrates. Tectonic movement during those two periods largely determined the course of fossil and present-day streams (Akkermans, 1990a, p. 122; 1990b, pp. 15–17). In Syria, terrace remains are attributed to multiple periods, from the Lower through the Upper Pleistocene. At Mari, Paul Sanlaville suggests that a four-terrace system (T4–T1) can be recognized, with the highest at +40 m. The middle terrace (+20–30 m) belongs to the Lower Paleolithic (c. 250,000 BP), and the +5–8-meter terrace has been identified as belonging to the Würm (Sanlaville, 1985, p. 22, fig. 4).

In Iraq, researchers have suggested that three or more terrace systems may belong to the Middle Pleistocene (Paepe, 1971). Perhaps as far back as 500,000 years ago, and as recently as 10,000 years ago, the Euphrates on the central Iraqi alluvial plain was part of a single river system emanating from Wadi Tharthar. Alluviation and tectonic activity not only created terraces but the current Euphrates River valley. (Paepe, 1971). Bifaces found on several of the highest terraces suggest a clear-cut Lower–Middle Paleolithic affiliation.

The Wadi Rimah/Wadi al-Batin complex, draining some 70,000 sq km (43,400 sq. mi.) in Kuwait and Saudi Arabia, also follows a graben system and was a tributary system to an ancient Euphrates basin in the Late Pliocene and Pleistocene. [See Kuwait.] While ephemeral flow has been noted only for the last five thousand years, the latest water data suggest that 32 million cu m per year flow past stations in the Wadi Rimah basin (Sowayan and Allayla, 1989, p. 482). At least two or three terraces of fluvial/eolian origin are noted of Quaternary date (Sanlaville, 1989, fig. 3, p. 10). Aquifer water studies confirm the Pleistocene nature of the stream flow.

By Early Holocene times, the Middle Euphrates river was in its present form. Western tributaries in Iraq and Syria traversing the desert are almost always associated with Early Holocene industries, suggesting active river systems. These flowed into either the current Euphrates or playa lakes west of the modern river (Khor Habbaniya, Abu Dibbis/Bahr al-Milh; Zarins, 1990, p. 50). One of the main Early Holocene channels then passed Ramadi to Kerbala-Najaf. According

to J. Boerma, the Upper Euphrates channelization has been entrenched since 8000 BCE (Boerma, 1983, p. 362). Archaeologists have also suggested that the Tigris-Euphrates emanated south of Baghdad as one stream, out of which numerous branches emerged (Crawford, 1991, p. 8; Adams, 1972, maps 2–3; Adams 1981, figs. 9, 27). By the sixth millennium, only the main channel remained in the middle of the alluvium. Even as late as the third and second millennia BCE, branches of the Euphrates continued to dominate the Sippar area (Gasche, 1985, p. 581). Subsequently, in the late first millennium BCE, the river began its migration westward, to its present position. In the marsh/lake region, prior to 5000 BCE, the Euphrates ran across what is today the southern Khor al-Hammar to Zubair and then to Umm Qasr, forming two channels past Bubiyan Island (Zarins, 1992, fig. 1). The Wadi Batin river and delta near Zubair may have been reactivated in this period as well. The effects of the Flandrian Transgression affected the Euphrates Delta, and the marine shoreline was considerably inland in historical times (c. 5000–2500 BCE). By 2000 BCE, the more modern conditions were reached (Sanlaville, 1989; Zarins, 1992, fig. 1).

Archaeological associations with the river are numerous (for a recent summary, see Wright, 1992). The most recent detailed work has taken place in the Upper Euphrates region. Sites threatened by flooding brought archaeologists to examine the Altinova plain associated with the Keban dam—and more recently sites associated with the Atatürk dam. A rich association of tell sites stretching from the Pre-Pottery Neolithic (Çafer Höyük, Hayaz Höyük) through the Ceramic Neolithic/Chalcolithic (Tepeçik, Norsuntepe, Koruçutepe) to the late third millennium BCE (Hassek Höyük, Kurban Höyük, Lidar Höyük) suggests that the archaeology of the region has close ties to the Middle Syrian Euphrates region to the south (Mellink, 1992, pp. 208–214). These and other sites (e.g., Samosata, Zeugma-Apamea, Tille) also cast light on later historical groups—Hittites and Neo-Hittites, Assyrians/Urartians, Arameans, and Partho-Romans—and on the Islamic period (Ward, 1990). [See Hittites; Assyrians; Urartu; Arameans.]

In the Middle Euphrates region, archaeological sites are to be found associated directly with the river, with the Balikh tributary, the Khabur triangle, and areas to the west, such as Jebel Bishri and the el-Kowm region. Archaeological work in the region has increased considerably as a result of now-completed or ongoing dam construction. Sites in the Taqba dam reservoir have, in particular, changed the perception of the region. Especially important are the sequences from Mureybet and Abu Hureyra, which shed light on the agricultural revolution from the tenth to sixth millennia (Sanlaville, 1985, p. 18). [See Mureybet.] From the Late Uruk period, sites such as Habuba Kabira, Jebel 'Aruda, and other have shown direct connections with the Late Uruk of southern Mesopotamia, suggesting the establishment of Late Uruk "colonies" from the south. [*See* Habuba Kabira; Colonization.] In addition to well-known tributary sites such as Tell Ḥalaf and Chaghar Bazar, recent work has considerably advanced what is known of the prehistoric to historical periods. Tell Leilan, identified with Shubat-Enlil, in the Khabur triangle, may be the most important recent discovery. [*See* Ḥalaf, Tell; Leilan, Tell.] The site of Mari, known from the French excavations begun in the 1930s, has yielded not only tremendous second-millennium BCE textual and artifactual data, but recently data stretching back to the Early Dynastic I period (Schwartz and Weiss, 1992, pp. 221–243). North of Mari, ongoing work at Dura-Europos will also elucidate the problems of the classical period both within the Euphrates valley and in such desert centers as Palmyra. [*See* Dura-Europos; Palmyra.]

From the Middle Euphrates Haditha dam reservoir in Iraq the sites of the Early Dynastic–Ur III periods are particularly important, painting a picture of Sumerian civilization on the Middle Euphrates hitherto only vaguely known (Roaf and Postgate, 1981, pp. 192–198; Killick and Roaf, 1983; Abdul-Amir, 1988; Porada et al., 1992). [*See* Sumerians.] The Euphrates entered the Mesopotamian alluvial plain south of Ramadi; survey work in the region, principally by Adams (1972), has shown that few sites are to be found there. Rather, civilization got its start on the delta plain beginning at ancient Sippar. This area is divided archaeologically and historically into two parts: Akkad, covering the northern portion, and Sumer, to the south. The main channel(s) of the Euphrates in Akkad in the fifth–third millennia lay well to the east of the present Euphrates course and, upon reaching Sumer, it (they) became extremely diffuse, or braided (Adams, 1981, fig. 9). Hans J. Nissen has suggested that with the lowering sea level in the fourth millennium, Sumer required less natural irrigation, population became consolidated in towns, and social stratification became more extreme (Nissen, 1988, pp. 65–71, 74, 129–132). City states were created, which led to buffer zones and more constant warfare. Lack of raw materials heightened long-distance trade and the subsequent empire building became characteristic (Wright, 1992, p. 723). Akkad relied less on such changes and became a distinct entity, based in part on the Euphrates channelization and the active tributaries to the western plateau (Steinkeller, 1992; Zarins, 1990). The Euphrates's principal channels and offtake canals had been creating silt and salt for the region at least since the third millennium (Jacobsen and Adams, 1958). These factors, plus the shifting of the Euphrates westward, eventually brought about the dissolution of Mesopotamian civilization.

The Euphrates as the dominant source of water for Akkad and Sumer, and later for Babylonia, played an integral role in agriculture, communications, and the creation of political structures in the region. The occupation of Eridu and later of the other Sumerian towns of the delta alluvium as the primary centers of Sumerian political and religious focus left its imprint on biblical studies as well (especially *Gn.* 1–11)— in the Flood stories, Creation accounts, and the explanation for the origin of cities (Kramer, 1963, pp. 269–299).

BIBLIOGRAPHY

Abdul-Amir, Sabah J. "Archaeological Survey of Ancient Settlements and Irrigation Systems in the Middle Euphrates Region of Mesopotamia." Ph.D. diss., University of Chicago, 1988.

Adams, Robert McC. "Settlement and Irrigation Patterns in Ancient Akkad." Appendix 5 in McGuire Gibson's *The City and Area of Kish*, pp. 182–208. Miami, 1972.

Adams, Robert McC. *Heartland of Cities: Surveys of Ancient Settlement and Land Use on the Central Floodplain of the Euphrates.* Chicago, 1981.

Akkermans, P.M.M.G. "The Neolithic of the Balikh Valley, Northern Syria: A First Assessment." In *Préhistoire du Levant: Processus du changements culturels*, vol. 2, edited by Olivier Aurenche et al., pp. 122–134. Paris, 1990.

Akkermans, P.M.M.G. *Villages in the Steppe.* Amsterdam, 1990.

Boerma, J. "Bouqras Revisited: Preliminary Report on a Project in Eastern Syria." *Proceedings of the Prehistoric Society* 49 (1983): 362–365. See the section "Environmental Conditions."

Buringh, P. "Living Conditions in the Lower Mesopotamian Plain in Ancient Times." *Sumer* 13 (1957): 30–46.

Crawford, Harriet. *Sumer and the Sumerians.* Cambridge, 1991.

Gasche, Hermann. "Tell ed-Dēr et Abu Ḥabbah: Deux villes situées à la Croisée des Chemins nord-sud, est-ouest." *Mari* 4 (1985): 579–583.

Gibson, McGuire. *City and Area of Kish.* Miami, 1972.

Hardan, Adai. "Sharing the Euphrates: Iraq." *National Geographic: Research and Exploration* 9 (1993): 73–79.

Jacobsen, Thorkild, and Robert McC. Adams. "Salt and Silt in Ancient Mesopotamian Agriculture." *Science* 128 (1958): 1251–1258.

Killick, R. G., and Michael Roaf. "Excavations in Iraq, 1981–1982." *Iraq* 45 (1983): 199–224.

Kramer, Samuel Noah. *The Sumerians: Their History, Culture, and Character.* Chicago, 1963.

Lloyd, Seton. *The Archaeology of Mesopotamia: From the Old Stone Age to the Persian Conquest.* London, 1978.

Mellink, Machteld J. "Anatolian Chronology." In *Chronologies in Old World Archaeology,* edited by Robert W. Ehrich, vol. 1, pp. 207–220, vol. 2, 171–184. 3d ed. Chicago, 1992.

Nissen, Hans J. *The Early History of the Ancient Near East, 9000–2000 B.C.* Chicago, 1988.

Paepe, Roland. "Geological Approach of the Tell ed-Dēr Area." In *Tell ed-Dēr I,* edited by Leon De Meyer et al., pp. 9–27. Louvain, 1971.

Porada, Edith, et al. "The Chronology of Mesopotamia, ca. 7000–1600 B.C." In *Chronologies in Old World Archaeology,* edited by Robert W. Ehrich, vol. 1, pp. 77–121, vol. 2, 90–124. 3d ed. Chicago, 1992.

Roaf, Michael, and J. N. Postgate. "Excavations in Iraq, 1979–80." *Iraq* 43 (1981): 167–198.

Sanlaville, Paul. "L'espace géographique de Mari." *Mari* 4 (1985): 15–26.

Sanlaville, Paul. "Considérations sur l'évolution de la Basse Mésopotamie au cours des derniers millénaires." *Paléorient* 15 (1989): 5–27.

Schwartz, Glenn M., and Harvey Weiss. "Syria, ca. 10,000–2000 B.C." In *Chronologies in Old World Archaeology,* vols. 1–2, edited by Robert W. Ehrich, pp. 221–243, 185–202. 3d ed. Chicago, 1992.

Sowayan, A. M., and R. Allayla. "Origin of the Saline Ground Water in Wadi ar-Rumah, Saudi Arabia." *Ground Water* 27 (1989): 481–490.

Steinkeller, Piotr. "Mesopotamia in the Third Millennium B.C." In *The Anchor Bible Dictionary*, vol. 4, pp. 724–732. New York, 1992.

Tomanbay, Mehmet. "Sharing the Euphrates: Turkey." *National Geographic: Research and Exploration* 9 (1993): 53–61.

Wakil, Mikhail. "Sharing the Euphrates: Syria." *National Geographic: Research and Exploration* 9 (1993): 63–71.

Ward, Diane R. "In Anatolia, A Massive Dam Project Drowns Traces of the Past." *Smithsonian Magazine* 21 (1990): 28–41.

Wright, Henry T. "Prehistory of Mesopotamia." In *The Anchor Bible Dictionary*, vol. 4, pp. 720–724. New York, 1992.

Zarins, Juris. "Early Pastoral Nomadism and the Settlement of Lower Mesopotamia." *Bulletin of the American Schools of Oriental Research*, no. 280 (1990): 31–65.

Zarins, Juris. "The Early Settlement of Southern Mesopotamia: A Review of the Recent Historical, Geological, and Archaeological Research." *Journal of the American Oriental Society* 112 (1992): 55–77.

JURIS ZARINS

EUPHRATES DAMS, SURVEY OF. During the second half of the twentieth century CE, nine dams were built or were under construction on the Euphrates River. The enormous number of antiquities lost from those projects was offset in part by intensive archaeological salvage efforts. The largest dam in Syria, the al-Thawra (Ar., "revolution"), whose reservoir (625 sq km, or 387 sq. mi.) is called Lake Assad, was constructed at the village of Tabqa in the late 1960s and early 1970s. Just above it construction of a second, the Tishreen (Ar., "October") dam, begun in the late 1980s, will be completed by the twenty-first century; its reservoir (70 sq km, or 43 sq. mi.) will extend about 60 km (37 mi.) north, almost to Jerablus (Carchemish) and the Turkish border. During the 1970s in the Lake Assad flood zone, excavations were conducted at more than twenty-five sites; in the early 1990s fifteen sites were excavated in the Tishreen innundation area. The results of those excavations enable the charting of the early trend to sedentarism, the emergence of agriculture, the formation of states, and the incorporation of the Middle Euphrates into empires and world systems.

In the Epipaleolithic (Mesolithic; 12000–8000 BCE) period the cultural sequence is Kebaran, Natufian, and Late Natufian, although there is some question whether the term *Natufian* can properly be used for Euphrates sites so distant from its core area. The site of Nahr al-Homr, which produced a Kebaran lithics assemblage, is succeeded in the Natufian period at the sites of Tell Abu Hureyra (excavated by A. M. T. Moore) and Tell Mureybet. During period I at Abu Hureyra, in which deposits span 11500–10000 BCE, there were semisubterranean round houses 2 m in diameter. Subsistence was based on hunting, predominantly gazelle, and collecting plants, of which 150 species have been identified. Phases I and II at Mureybet are assigned to the late Natufian and transitional Khiamian, respectively. Subsistence there was diversified: hunting (mainly gazelle) fishing, and gathering.

In the early aceramic Neolithic, the Mureybetian period (8000–7600 BCE)—represented at Mureybet (phase III), Tell Sheikh Hassan (excavated by Jacques Cauvin), and Tell Jerf al-Ahmar (excavated by Thomas McClellan and M. Mottra)—is part of the Pre-Pottery Neolithic A (PPNA) culture that is better known in the southern Levant. Although round houses continue to be used, internal divisions made with straight walls begin to be found in some. Rectilinear buildings appear for the first time in history at Jerf el-Ahmar, in phase III at Mureybet, and at Sheikh Hassan. Female figurines are found in stone and clay from Mureybet, and at Jerf el-Ahmar geometrically decorated shaft straighteners and a limestone human head with carefully modeled hair reveal a complex symbolic repertoire.

The degree to which cereals were gathered or cultivated is debatable, depending on how modern specialists define this important transition. Another problematic issue is the extent of sedentarism. In fact, this was the time for the transition to full village life, a process some call neolithicization. Jacques Cauvin, the excavator of Mureybet and Sheikh Hassan, stresses the mental transformation of the society reflected in the new cult of the female deity (represented by the figurines at Mureybet), the new cult of the bull (first observed in Mureybet phase II), and new burial practices. The emergence of agriculture is yet another result of changes in societal organization, according to Cauvin, rather than its underlying economic or technological cause, as postulated by some cultural evolutionists such as Marvin Harris, Elman Service, and Julian Steward.

The Pre-Pottery Neolithic B (PPNB) period is known at Mureybet (phase IV), Abu Hureyra II, Tell Halula (excavated by Miguel Molist), and Tell Dja'de el-Mughara (excavated by Eve Coqueugniot). Byblos points and large "naviform" blades distinguish the lithics, and rectangular houses become common. At Halula a PPNB "city gate" and portions of a "city wall" have been discovered. Cereal cultivation and animal husbandry combined to form the full agricultural system that became common to the Near East.

In the Chalcolithic period (5500–3400 BCE), the Halaf and Ubaid cultures, both of which are thought to have had their origins farther east, successively extended across northern Syria. The Halafian is best known from the site of Tell Shams ed-Din Tannira (excavated by Selina al-Radi and Helga Seeden) and is well represented at Halula, whereas Tell 'Abr (excavated by Hamidu Hammade and Yayoi Koike) provides important evidence for the western Ubaid tradition.

The Uruk period (3400–3100 BCE) in the Thawra and Tishreen dam areas marked what historians refer to as the beginning of civilization and anthropologists call the emergence of complex society and the process of state formation. It was not an indigenous development in northern Syria but was introduced from southern Mesopotamia. Excavations at the sites of Habuba Kabira South and Jebel 'Aruda in the Lake Assad region revealed the expansion of Uruk culture far from its core region. These sites have not merely borrowed southern Mesopotamian cultural traits, they are in fact Uruk colonies. Habuba Kabira South was a large fortified city in which residential dwellings are grouped into city blocks. Within Habuba Kabira South, a complex called Tell Qannas (excavated by André Finet) was found to contain back-to-back temples with decorative mud-brick buttressing, one of which has a tripartite layout—both are features of Uruk temples in southern Mesopotamia.

Several kilometers away and 60 m above the river plain, on a spur of the mountain Jebel Aruda (excavated by G. van Driel), was a second, smaller Uruk settlement. It was dominated by two Uruk-style temples (although some scholars question their having been temples), with a tripartite layout, mud-brick construction, and decorative buttressing. Associated with the temples are a number of large domestic structures, tripartite in plan, that are similar to those at Habuba Kabira South. Both sites exhibit typical Uruk, southern Mesopotamian traits, including beveled-rim bowls, jars with nose lugs and drooping spouts, Protoliterate seals and sealings, tokens, counters, and tablets for numeration. Uruk assemblages have also been encountered at Tell Sheikh Hassan, Tell Jerablus Taḥtani, Tell 'Abr, and Tell Banat.

The discovery of two major and numerous minor Uruk settlements on the Middle Euphrates in northern Syria raised several issues regarding the transmission of cultural ideas and traits to the less developed area (periphery) of northern Syria. Using the core-periphery model popularized by Immanuel Wallerstein, Guillermo Algaze has seen these sites as colonies that were part of a large trading network in which the resource-poor Uruk homeland of lower Mesopotamia exploited peripheral zones for such raw materials as timber and metals. The relationship to local populations is unclear, but a hierarchy of Uruk settlements is thought to have included colonies (Habuba Kabira South and Jebel 'Aruda), stations, and outposts. Both Habuba Kabira South and Jebel 'Aruda were occupied for short time spans of no more than 150 years; they were built on virgin sites and after their destruction were never reoccupied. Uruk occupation at Sheikh Hassan lasted for a considerably longer period.

Northern Syria, including the region of the two dams, is thought by some to have undergone a gap in occupation after the destruction of the Uruk colonies and the collapse of Uruk cultures in southern Mesopotamia. Consequently, the introduction of complex societies into Syria in about 3300–3100 BCE was abortive and had no lasting effect on the cultures of the region. Following this scenario, the first indigeneous Syrian states may not have emerged until later, in about 2600 BCE—not along river courses but in dry-farming areas—with the emergence of Ebla and large settlements in the Khabur Triangle, such as Tell Chuera and Tell Leilan. An alternative reconstruction of the period sees a reduced, but unbroken, cultural continuity at sites along the Euphrates in the first half of the third millennium (Early Bronze Age). Tell Hadidi has produced "EB I" and "EB II" material (see below), and some of the strata at Tell Halawa date to the first half of the third millennium. There are indications that a continuous sequence exists at a cluster of four EB sites centered at Banat.

No consensus exists for the terminology of the Early Bronze Age (c. 3100–2000 BCE); the first half (3100–2500 BCE) is often called EB I and II, or sometimes Mesopotamian terms are applied: Jemdet Nasr, Early Dynastic I–III. The second half of the period (2500–2000 BCE) is generally referred to as EB IV; none of these terms are fully satisfactory. The third millennium is well represented by sites in the Thawra and Tishreen dam regions: Tell Hadidi, Tell Habuba Kabira North, Tell Halawa, Tell Tawi, Tell Sweyhat, Tell Selenkahiyeh, Tell Munbaqa, Tell Ahmar, and Tell Banat, including Tell Kabir and Tell Banat North, and Tell Qara Qusaq. At Halawa (excavated by Winfried Orthmann) there was an EB occupation on tells A and B. On tell B, dating to the first half of the third millennium, three phases of a temple, entered from the structure's broad south side, were constructed on a large platform. The orientation changed in a final phase to the structure's broad east side. Three strata of tell A date to the second half of the third millennium; in the earliest, stratum 3, portions of the settlement excavated contained a defensive wall, city gate, domestic dwellings, and a stone, long-room temple in antis (with columns set between two piers) that opened toward the east. A similar structure was found at Tell Kabir (excavated by Anne Porter) in the Tishreen dam flood zone. At Tell Banat (excavated by Thomas McClellan) there are fragments of a public building, possibly a palace, with large limestone column bases. Cemeteries of the period were recovered at Tawi and Halawa; the Hypogeum Tomb at Ahmar (excavated in the 1930s by François Thureau-Dangin and Maurice Dunand) was an elite burial that contained more than a thousand vessels and a rich collection of bronzes. Another high-ranking burial at Banat dates to about 2600 BCE and contained Plain Simple Ware, Euphrates Banded Ware, Metallic Ware, and Red-Black Burnished Ware.

In the Middle Bronze Age (2000–1600 BCE), Old Babylonian texts indicate that Carchemish (which lies at the northern end of the Tishreen flood zone) and Emar (old Meskene) were important centers, but occupation from this period has never been located archaeologically at Emar. Excavations at Tell Qara Qusaq (excavated by Emilio Olávarri and Gregorio del Olmo Lete for the University of Barcelona) show that it was a storage depot in which circular stone-lined silos were found to contain barley, perhaps for shipment to Mari. At el-Qitar part of a structure with orthostat dados was excavated, and there are also occupation layers at Kabir, Halawa, Habuba Kabira North, and Hadidi, with ceramic repertoires produced at the latter.

Large portions of settlement plans for the Late Bronze Age (1600–1200 BCE) have been recovered at Munbaqa/Ekalte (excavated by Dittmar Machule) and el-Qitar/Til-Abnu and a major archive at old Meskene/Emar. Some of these sites may have been destroyed in the Euphrates campaign of Thutmosis III. There were three long-room temples at Munbaqa and three at Emar. Regarding fortifications, at Munbaqa an offset-inset mud-brick city wall was found encased in massive ramparts of river pebbles. Several city gates were excavated, including the northwest gate, in which a mud-brick arch across the passageway was preserved. At el-Qitar two city gates had limestone orthostat piers. Cuneiform tablets have also been found at Hadidi, Munbaqa, Tell Fray, and el-Qitar.

The Iron Age is best represented by occupations at Carchemish and Tell Ahmar (Til Barsip), as well as Tell Jurn Kabir (excavated by Jesper Eidem and Karin Pütt). At Tell Ahmar Aramean stelae were noted by travelers in the late nineteenth century, and in the early 1930s, a major Neo-Assyrian palace with extensive wall paintings was found. Recently, Guy Bunnens has found more Neo-Assyrian buildings, one with a black-and-white checkerboard pebble mosaic, along with a constructed burial vault, cuneiform texts, ivory objects, and Assyrian Palace Ware.

The mountain Jebel Khalid (excavated by Graeme Clarke and Peter Connor) was the site of a major Hellenistic fortress in the third century BCE. During the Roman period, the Middle Euphrates sometimes became the frontier in a long-running conflict between the Roman/Byzantine empires in the west and the Persians (Parthians/Sasanians) who, on occasion, reached Balis (Meskene). Small tumuli from this period may reflect the burial customs of European troops stationed in the region during the Roman Empire. Occupation on this part of the Euphrates was not dense in the Islamic period, although there are surface indications of small villages and farmsteads; the main settlement was Balis, the site adjacent to LB Emar and on the outskirts of the modern town of Meskene. The fortress at Qal'at Nejim guarded a crossing point in late medieval times.

[See also Carchemish; Chuera, Tell; Colonization; Ebla; Emar; Euphrates River; Habuba Kabira; Hadidi, Tell; Leilan, Tell; Mureybet; Qitar, El-; Ubaid; and Uruk-Warka.]

BIBLIOGRAPHY

Algaze, Guillermo, *The Uruk World System.* Chicago, 1993.

Beyer, Dominique, ed. *Meskéné-Emar: Dix ans de travaux, 1972–1982.* Paris, 1982.

Bunnens, Guy, ed. *Tell Ahmar: 1988 Season.* Supplement to Abr-Nahrain, 2. Louvain, 1990.

Freedman, David Noel, ed. *Archaeological Reports from the Tabqa Dam Project—Euphrates Valley, Syria.* Annual of the American Schools of Oriental Research, 44. Ann Arbor, Mich., 1979.

Hammade, Hamido, and Yayoi Koike. "Syrian Archaeological Expedition in the Tishreen Dam Basin: Excavations at Tell al-'Abr 1990 and 1991." *Damaszener Mitteilungen* 6 (1992): 109–175.

Kampschulte, Ingrid, and Winfried Orthmann. *Gräber des 3. Jahrtausends v. Chr. im syrischen Euphrattal,* vol. 1, *Ausgrabungen bei Tawi*

1975 und 1978. Saarbrücker Beiträge zur Altertumskunde, 38. Bonn, 1984.

Machule, D., et al. "Ausgrabungen in Tall Munbāqa/Ekalte 1990." *Mitteilungen der Deutschen Orient-Gesellschaft* 124 (1992): 11–40. See other preliminary reports in volumes 117–123.

Margueron, Jean-Claude, ed. *Le Moyen Euphrate, zone de contacts et d'échanges: Acts du colloque de Strasbourg, 10–12 Mars 1977.* Strasbourg, 1980. Essential collection of preliminary reports.

Moore, A. M. T. "A Pre-Neolithic Farmers' Village on the Euphrates." *Scientific American* 241.2 (1979): 62–70.

Olmo Lete, Gregorio del, ed. *Tell Qara Qūzāq I: Campañas I–III (1989–1991)* Barcelona, 1993

Orthmann, Winfried. *Halawa 1977 bis 1979.* Saarbrücker Beiträge zur Altertumskunde, 31. Bonn, 1981.

Orthmann, Winfried. *Halawa, 1980–1986.* Saarbrücker Beiträge zur Alterumskunde, 52. Bonn, 1989.

Radi, S. al-, and Helga Seeden. "A Stone Age Village on the Euphrates: I. The AUB Rescue Excavations at Shams ed-Din Tannira." *Berytus* 28 (1980): 87–126. See *Berytus* 28–30 for parts II–V.

Strommenger, Eva. *Habuba Kabira: Eine Stadt vor 5000 Jahren.* Mainz am Rhein, 1980.

Sürenhagen, Dietrich. "The Dry Farming Belt: The Uruk Period and Subsequent Developments." In *The Origins of Cities in Dry-Farming Syria and Mesopotamia in the Third Millennium B.C.,* edited by Harvey Weiss, pp. 7–43. Guilford, Ct., 1986.

Sürenhagen, Dietrich. *Keramikproduktion in Habuba Kabira-Süd.* Acta Praehistorica et Archaeologica 5/6. (1994–1995), pp. 43ff.

Thureau-Dangin, François and Maurice Dunand. *Til-Barsib.* Paris, 1936.

Van Driel, Govert, and Carol Van Driel–Murray. "Jebel Aruda, 1977–78." *Akkadica* 12 (1979): 2–28.

Van Driel, Govert, and Carol Van Driel–Murray. "Jebel Aruda: The 1982 Season of Excavation." *Akkadica* 33 (1983): 1–26.

Wallerstein, Immanuel. *The Modern World System.* Vol. 1. New York, 1974.

THOMAS L. McCLELLAN

EVANS, ARTHUR (1851–1941), principal excavator of Knossos, Crete, and preeminent scholar of the Cretan Bronze Age. The son of antiquarian-industrialist Sir John Evans, Arthur was educated at Harrow and Brasenose College, Oxford, where he read history and graduated in 1874. He became involved in Balkan politics as a correspondent for the *Manchester Guardian*. As a champion of the Slavic independence movement, Evans carried out archaeological researches, later published in his "Antiquarian Researches in Illyricum" in 1885–1886. He became keeper of the Ashmolean Museum, Oxford, in 1884.

Evans's involvement with Crete began in 1894 when he traveled the island in search of seal stones bearing "pre-Phoenician" script, which he published in the *Journal of Hellenic Studies* (1894, 1897); the journeys are recorded in letters to *The Academy*. During this time he identified remains of the "Minoan" civilization suspected to be earlier than the Mycenaeans of Greece and bought the tell called Tou Tseleve he Kephala (the headland or bluff of the local Turkish landowner) near the classical Greek and Roman remains of Knossos, where others had found traces of pre-Hellenic antiquities. He excavated at a number of sites in the Knossos valley during large-scale intensive campaigns from 1900 to 1905. Evans concentrated his efforts, however, on the tell that had covered the successive phases of the complex architectural remains called the "Palace of Minos" after the legendary ruler of Crete. Detailed preliminary reports on the palace appeared in the *Annual of the British School at Athens* (7–11 [1901–1905]), and final reports on late cemetery sites in the region were published in *Archaeologia* in 1905.

The stratigraphy at Knossos formed the basis for Evans's proposed tripartite relative chronological sequence for the Cretan Bronze Age, which he called Early, Middle, and Late Minoan with further tripartite subdivisions. His Minoan scheme was adapted for the neighboring Cycladic islands and Greek mainland and remains the most useful relative chronology for the Aegean Bronze in the absence of absolute dates.

Evans's re-creation of the Bronze Age Cretans, whom he called "Minoans," is set out in the rambling chapters of *The Palace of Minos*, published in four volumes between 1921 and 1935. Initially conceived as the final report on his work at Knossos, it became a widely ranging synthesis of archaeological research in the Aegean and the leading role Evans felt the Minoans to have played. There can be little doubt that Evans was very intuitive, but his preoccupation with associating the early Cretans with the later Greeks and thus modern Europeans led to the frequent use of Greek myths as possible explanations for the early Cretan iconography without full consideration of Near Eastern and Anatolian possibilities. Nonetheless, *The Palace of Minos* remains the most influential and basic source for students of the Aegean Bronze Age.

The first biography of Evans, *Time and Chance: The Story of Arthur Evans and his Forebears*, was published by his half-sister, Joan Evans, in 1943; a second, *The Find of a Lifetime: Sir Arthur Evans and the Discovery of Knossos*, by Sylvia Horwitz appeared in 1981. Neither was critical of Evans's work.

[*See also* Aegean Islands; Minoans.]

BIBLIOGRAPHY

Evans, Arthur. "Antiquarian Researches in Illyricum, I–II and III–IV." *Archaeologia* 48 (1885): 1–105, 49 (1886): 1–167.
Evans, Arthur. *Cretan Pictographs and Prae-Phoenician Script*. London, 1895.
Evans, Arthur. *The Prehistoric Tombs of Knossos*. London, 1906.
Evans, Arthur. *The Palace of Minos*. 4 vols. in 6. London, 1921–1935.
Evans, Joan. *Time and Chance: The Story of Arthur Evans and His Forebears*. London, 1943.
Horwitz, Sylvia. *The Find of a Lifetime: Sir Arthur Evans and the Discovery of Knossos*. London, 1981.

J. ALEXANDER MACGILLIVRAY

EXCAVATION STRATEGY. There is no one universal excavation strategy because developing one depends in part on the type of site being excavated and the purpose of an excavation. Therefore, an important characteristic of any strategy is flexibility in meeting the new problems, questions, and goals that will emerge during excavation.

With the advent of processual archaeology (also referred as the New Archaeology) in the 1960s, archaeologists began to ask questions of intention prior to going into the field. This process of developing a hypothesis and then testing it has reshaped the way archaeological excavation is undertaken today. Prior to processual archaeology, much of Near Eastern archaeology was more site oriented, with archaeologists interested primarily in cultural history. That approach stressed the excavation of large, multiperiod sites, especially prominent tells, to discover unusual art objects or "museum pieces," to uncover monumental remains, and to establish the political history of a site. [*See* New Archaeology.]

Since the early 1960s the theoretical component of archaeology has become a driving force in determining how, why, and where excavation will be initiated. Most archaeologists now begin with a problem orientation and from it derive a theoretical model they will test with empirical data. Problem orientation is more formally developed as a research design, which articulates how specific archaeological methodologies employed at a specific site or in a specific region will address theoretical goals. Thus, a site must be selected that best meets the needs of the research design. Although there is no guarantee that the questions archaeologists ask will ultimately be answered by the material they excavate, there is almost always an attempt to link a problem orientation to an excavation strategy.

A good excavation strategy is the means by which to connect theory to data and must be predicated on the purpose or function of the proposed excavation. A strategy employed in salvage archaeology, where time is a critical factor, will greatly differ from the strategy used in a research excavation. The type of site will also directly affect the excavation strategy employed. Single-period sites are excavated much differently than multiperiod, or tell, sites. Prehistoric sites, classical sites, and underwater sites all have distinct archaeological configurations and attendant methodological approaches. However, almost all archaeologists are interested in the interpretation of archaeological data, rather than mere collection and/or description. To that end, most archaeological investigations in the Near East now include a multidisciplinary orientation and some degree of interest in environmental data. Archaeologists are increasingly turning to computers to assist in statistical analyses, data storage, artifact and architectural reconstruction, and systems modeling. [*See* Statistical Applications.]

The first step in almost any archaeological excavation is preexcavation research. Any previous excavation or survey of the site is studied, along with relevant maps, historical documents, drawings, and photographs. Geological and other types of areal research or survey are reviewed. This phase of research should also include historical and ethnographic assessments of the area under investigation, including visits to local museums and conversations with local professional and amateur archaeologists and any local residents familiar with the site or its environs. [*See* Site Survey.]

Following this phase of research, the site itself is surveyed and mapped. Artifacts from the site are collected systematically and then analyzed. The site is mapped and examined for signs of human or natural modifications. Areal photographs are also useful in discerning anomalies or other noteworthy characteristics. The site's environment is also surveyed in order to understand its ecological context.

A thorough preexcavation investigation is crucial because it will help refine the problem orientation and define specific research goals. However, as the excavation progresses, new hypotheses will be generated and new problems and questions will arise that should be systematically integrated into the research design and then field tested. Specific research problems lead to the collection of specific types of data. The method of collection, analysis, and publication is shaped by the research design. The research design should also help the archaeologist better define and determine appropriate methodological approaches.

The preexcavation phase can be the most important part of an archaeological project. In this formative period sites, regions, research hypotheses, and excavation methodologies are linked. In effect, the actual excavation should be putting a well-conceived and detailed research design into operation: the actual process of gathering empirical data with which to assess a theoretical model. The better crafted the research design, and the more thorough the preexcavation research, the more likely the research goals are to be met.

Once the formulation of the problem orientation and preinvestigation research is complete, the excavation, or acquisition of data, can begin by utilizing one of two standard approaches. A research design involving diachronic issues—such as culture change and continuity over time—will usually utilize a penetration methodology, probing subsurface deposits with deep trenches. This method stresses stratigraphic relationships (the vertical layering of artifacts and architecture). For synchronic issues a horizontal, or clearing, methodology stressing the spatial arrangements of artifacts and architecture at one point in time is more useful. Most excavation strategies employ both approaches in order to achieve the best possible context for all the archaeological data. With either method, the types of data collected and how they are collected should be systematically articulated in the research design.

Once the data are collected, they must be analyzed. Data analysis is as important as fieldwork. This phase of an excavation project generates the inferences on which archaeological interpretations and reconstructions are based. The analysis phase is often mediated by specialists who should be familiar with the field methodology in order to avoid inherent biases, which could affect interpretation.

The final stage of an excavation project is publication. Deciding which data will be published and how they will be presented are part of the excavation strategy. How the publication is organized is predetermined by the research design, excavation methodologies, and types of analyses.

BIBLIOGRAPHY

Dever, William G. "Two Approaches to Archaeological Method: The Architectural and the Stratigraphic." *Eretz-Israel* 11 (1973): 1*–8*. Clear and concise description of the horizontal and stratigraphic methods of excavation used in Syria-Palestine.

Dever, William G. "The Impact of the 'New Archaeology' on Syro-Palestinian Archaeology." *Bulletin of the American Schools of Oriental Research,* no. 242 (1981): 15–29. Useful overview of the history of the discipline in terms of field methodology for Syria-Palestine.

Drinkard, Joel F., et al., eds. *Benchmarks in Time and Culture: An Introduction to Palestinian Archaeology Dedicated to Joseph A. Callaway.* Atlanta, 1988. Very useful volume that includes articles addressing the history of the discipline of archaeology, techniques and methods of excavation practiced in the Near East, and theoretical overviews of different approaches to archaeology.

Joukowsky, Martha Sharp. *A Complete Manual of Field Archaeology: Tools and Techniques of Field Work for Archaeologists.* Englewood Cliffs, N.J., 1980. Excellent how-to guide for fieldwork; useful for anyone involved in the field, from the inexperienced volunteer to the excavation director. Details fieldwork techniques used internationally.

Renfrew, Colin, and Paul Bahn. *Archaeology: Theories, Methods, and Practice.* New York, 1991. Valuable, up-to-date sourcebook on all aspects of archaeology.

Sharer, Robert J., and Wendy Ashmore. *Archaeology: Discovering Our Past.* Palo Alto, Calif., 1987. Comprehensive introductory textbook for archaeology.

J. P. DESSEL

EXCAVATION TOOLS. A fundamental development took place in the range of tools used in Near Eastern archaeology once field operations were resumed following World War II. During the first century or so of archaeological fieldwork, the two primary tools of exploration had been borrowed from road construction: a large pickax for breaking up soil and a broad-bladed hoe for scooping loosened soil into baskets to be carried away. As long as the basic strategy of digging was to locate buried wall segments and expose them down to their founding surfaces, those tools were adequate.

Beginning in the 1950s, an important development in digging strategy led to a dramatic increase in the use of small hand tools, nearly rendering the large pick and hoe obsolete. The initial primary interest in architecture moved to a concomitant concern for the careful separation of soil layers to gain better stratigraphic control, more complete retrieval of data, and a clearer interpretation of the evidence. In Palestine, Kathleen M. Kenyon's excavations at Tell es-Sultan (Jericho) in 1952–1957 and her use of the so-called Wheeler-Kenyon grid technique demonstrated the need for small tools to provide closer control of the digging process. [*See* Excavation Strategy.]

Most of the newer small tools have also been borrowed

from other endeavors—from geology and mountain climbing (hand pick) to dentistry (dental pick). Three tools have come to dominate: the handpick, the trowel, and the soft-bristled hand brush. Light vertical downstrokes using the handpick's flat chisel-headed blade can dislodge small clumps of soil, thus exposing potsherds and small artifacts in situ. Used in this way, the handpick also allows the excavator to notice changes in the color and consistency of soil that can signal the transition to a different layer. A mason's trowel is commonly used in conjunction with the handpick. Alternating vertical strokes of the pick with horizontal scraping motions of the trowel brings newly loosened soil toward the kneeling digger. This process turns over the loosened earth to reveal still-hidden objects and clears it away to allow the digger to see soil changes more clearly. A soft-bristled hand brush is then used to clear away the smaller particles of loosened soil, further revealing the character of the newly exposed earth below. The brush is later used to prepare the area for photography.

A variety of even smaller implements has been employed to clear soil from delicate objects (such as skeletal remains, mosaic tiles [tesserae], or necklace beads) or multielement complexes. Some of the tools found useful in such delicate work are teaspoons, dental picks, and soft-bristled artists' brushes.

The process of removing dirt from the excavation area has also undergone refinement. Reed baskets gave way by midcentury to buckets, known as *gufas* (or *goufas*, from Arabic), made from discarded automobile or truck tire tube casings. Those are now increasingly being replaced with plastic pails. The long-handled hoe, used to scoop up soil, has given way at most excavations to the trowel, hand brush, and dustpan. Between the digging area and the dump, a fine-mesh sieve is frequently used to sift excavated soil in order to reveal small objects (such as beads, coins, bone fragments, and stone-tool flakes) that might otherwise have eluded workers. Where there is a concern for retrieving ancient seed and pollen data, fine sieves or flotation devices are also used to recover material from the soil being discarded.

An increasing array of utensils and supplies now finds its way into the archaeologist's field kit. Laying out an area for excavation requires stakes and string, a measuring tape, and a line level to set balk lines; taking elevations of excavated features requires a transit and range rod; collecting and transporting potsherds, bones, flints, and other artifacts require buckets, paper bags and boxes, and cotton padding; and the all-important recording and registering of finds utilize a variety of tags, gummed labels, and waterproof marking pens. [See Recording Techniques.]

In the excavation camp, a complementary assortment of tools completes the recording and conservation process: toothbrushes and cotton swabs for cleaning finds and rulers, calipers, and circumference gauges for measuring potsherds and other objects that are to be drawn. [See Conservation Archaeology.]

BIBLIOGRAPHY

Cole, Dan P. "Archaeological Tools and Their Use." In *A Manual of Field Excavation: Handbook for Field Archaeologists*, edited by William G. Dever and H. Darrell Lance, pp. 123–145. Cincinnati, 1978. Proper use of tools.

Heizer, Robert F., and John A. Graham. *A Guide to Field Methods in Archaeology: Approaches to the Anthropology of the Dead*. Palo Alto, Calif., 1967. Brief discussion of excavation tools (see chap. 5.A); of comparative value because it reflects New World conditions and methods.

DAN P. COLE

EXPERIMENTAL ARCHAEOLOGY. Archaeologists design experiments to re-create or reproduce ancient artifacts, technologies, and behaviors to help interpret ancient material culture and events. The experiments reconstruct the human and natural causes of the manipulation, damage, wear, breakage, deposition, and disintegration of artifacts prior to, during, and subsequent to their deposition. Researchers ask questions about the relationship between the person and the product; how manufacture influences the appearance of artifacts; and the sources of diversity and variation in the artifacts.

Experimental archaeology began in Europe in the eighteenth century when bronze horns were found in Scandinavian and British peat bags. A certain Dr. Robert Ball from Dublin died as a result of blowing an Irish horn too hard. In recent decades there has been a resurgence in such studies with an emphasis on the rigorous control of well-documented, recorded, and repeatable experiments. Experimental settings vary, depending on the questions under investigation. For example, pottery firing techniques can be studied by using a gas kiln in a laboratory or by firing wood in a pit dug in the ground. The purpose of each test would be to create and control the causes of firing time and temperatures. What would be learned would be the effect of each variable on the finished product.

Archaeologists begin by explicitly stating an experiment's theoretical basis, its variables, selected materials, and methods; finally, they state its results. Controlled experiments involve the use of pertinent materials, ideally those that would have been available to a society in antiquity, such as local clays or stones. Experiments should include as many variables as possible. To learn the impact of dung added to clay as a tempering material ideally means varying the clays, the size of the dung fragments, the proportions of clay to dung, and the firing temperatures. As the clay is worked its pliability, workability, elasticity, and the ease with which pots can be made from it are assessed. The effects are observed, recorded, and interpreted as inferences for archaeology.

Experimental archaeology involves the reproduction of human behaviors associated with the use of artifacts: butchering studies reveal the physical appearance and deposition of bones after the flesh has been removed with a stone implement. Observing the collapse of walls leads to the ability to identify the archaeological remains of such an event and so to understand the difference between a deposit that is the direct result of the collapse and one that is evidence of scavenging, reuse, or other disturbances.

In addition to studies replicating or imitating ancient artifacts and behaviors, experimental archaeology includes testing the usefulness of methodological assumptions. For example, one can test the validity of population estimates based on animal bone counts by studying what happens to bones when animals are killed. Retrieval techniques can be assessed to learn if plant remains collected by dry sieving provide valid samples of ancient flora and/or diet. Finally, some consider ethnoarchaeology to be a type of experimental archaeology.

[*See also* Ethnoarchaeology.]

BIBLIOGRAPHY

Coles, John M. *Experimental Archaeology*. London, 1979. Overview of the topics and results.
Ingersoll, Daniel, John E. Yellen, and Wm. Macdonald. *Experimental Archaeology*. New York, 1977. Individual experiments concerning ancient technologies; quantitative methods; and site formation.
London, Gloria Anne. "Dung-Tempered Clay." *Journal of Field Archaeology* 8 (1981): 189–195. A series of experiments adding dung to clay.

GLORIA ANNE LONDON

F

FAILAKA, an island (approximately 14 × 5 km, or 9 × 3 mi.) in the State of Kuwait, located at the mouth of Kuwait Bay, at the northern end of the Arab-Iranian Gulf (29°26′ N, 48°20′ E). Excavations by Danish teams (1958–1962) revealed what continue to be the earliest (c. 2000 BCE) traces of habitation on Failaka Island. That Bronze Age settlement, at the island's southwest corner, consists of clusters of small domestic structures executed in a casual stone-mortar construction. The principal feature of the tallest tell (designated F-3, 6 m above sea level) is an open-air platform temple. Associated with the three architectural levels of the temple and surrounding buildings are hundreds of fragments of decorated soft-stone vessels. A number of the fragments with representational designs have parallels with complete dated bowls excavated at sites in Mesopotamia; other comparable, but not securely stratified, material is found at Tarut (eastern Arabia), Susa, and Tepe Yahya (Iran). [*See* Susa; Tepe Yahya.] The Failaka fragments, some dated as early as 2500 BCE, must have been retrieved from temple destructions in southern Mesopotamia and brought as votives by sailors coming from Sumer—their first sheltered port would have been the harbor at Failaka. One of the most historically interesting of the vessel fragments carries the inscription "Temple of Inzak." According to Mesopotamian texts, Inzak is the titular deity associated with the land of Dilmun," one of several reasons for the suggestion that Kuwait together with Bahrain, and the eastern coast of Arabia were regarded as Dilmun by the Mesopotamians in the late third and early second millennia BCE. [*See* Dilmun.]

Equally significant among the Bronze Age finds are hundreds of circular stamp seals, also of soft stone. The iconography and style of Gulf seals (including those from Bahrain) constitute a unique group featuring elements of Gulf culture (e.g. date palm, gazelle, reed stool, water bird, bullman). Yet, the evidence for foreign contacts is far ranging, extending north to Babylonia, Assyria, Syria, and Turkey; south to Oman and Egypt; and east to Margiana, Bampur, Dasht-i-Lut, and the Indus Valley.

A substantial amount of the excavated material relates to the bronzeworking industry: metal slag, copper ingots, metal objects, and tools. This indicates that ingots were imported from Iran even in the early settlements, and a reasonable number of objects were manufactured for export or exchange. Many of the bronze tools identified would have been used in seal cutting, shellworking, and woodworking.

Some 200 m north of the harbor settlement mound, on a lower, sprawling tell, the Danes located the Ruler's Villa, a modest building containing reception and administrative rooms in the front, a central court marked with four square corner pillars (presumably to support a loggia), and residential quarters to the rear. Other finds throughout the site included imported pottery, square stamp seals, cylinder seals, and metal materials, attesting to foreign contacts with Mesopotamia, Abu Dhabi, and Oman and, in the second millennium BCE, the Indus Valley. [*See* Oman.]

Major architecture from the Hellenistic period consisted of a square enclosure with quadrangular corner bastions. Two entrance doors permitted access to this "fortified" area, which contained the site's earliest Greek settlement (300–250 BCE); the central portion consisted of a religious precinct that may have included two sanctuaries. One was a small Greek cella constructed in well-dressed stone masonry with two columns *in antis*. The capitals betray an Ionic influence, and the bases are inspired by Achaemenian prototypes. In the latest Hellenistic phase the entire enclosure was surrounded by a dry moat.

A large inscribed stela that had fallen from its original position was found in front of the temple. This public letter to the people of Ikaros (the Greek name for Failaka Island) gives instructions for moving the Artemis Temple and establishing a gymnasium. The inscription is dated to a Greek satrap at Susa in the late third century BCE. Another stone inscription from Tell Khazneh, a kilometer to the north, also mentions Artemis, together with Zeus Savior and Poseidon Savior. It has been suggested that the Greek goddess Artemis may have been assimilated with Ninsikilla, the original goddess of Bronze Age Dilmun, noted in Sumerian mythology as the place where all animals live in peace.

Another rectangular building with many rooms located on the seashore and referred to as the Terracotta Workshop contained a number of figurines, as well as ancient molds for terra cottas of types familiar in the Hellenistic world.

Other figurines found throughout the sites illuminate the variety of cults and diverse artistic influences: Mesopotamian, orientalizing Greek, and Hellenistic Tanagra styles.

American excavations by Theresa Howard-Carter for the Johns Hopkins University under auspices of the Kuwait Ministry of Information (1973, 1974) exposed an industrial and crafts area adjacent to the Ruler's Villa, identified by at least six large circular kilns. Raw materials were stored in vats constructed of stone slabs. The contents of the vats were used in the manufacture of a gypsum organic building material, hunks of which appeared in the fill. The kilns were commonly used for firing pottery and baking bread. A trench along the outer wall of the Villa revealed a sophisticated stone-built sewage system with a covered drain running under the wall to a large, covered cesspool outside.

Finds in the crafts workshops next to the Villa included fragments of soft-stone bowls with figural decoration; stamp seals in steatite, ivory, mother-of-pearl, and jasper; imported cylinder seals and inscribed Indus seals; jewelry of bronze, silver, gold, agate, carnelian, and lapis; and bronze tools and implements, shields, greaves, and other armor.

The French excavations under the direction of Yves Calvet, Jean-François Salles, and Jacqueline Gachet of La Maison de l'Orient of the Université de Lyon (1983–1989) in the same area revealed a large, important, and badly denuded stone building whose internal features (water basins and drains) suggest a religious use. The thick walls and prominent staircase indicate some sort of temple tower, which would have been visible to passing ships. The building's meager contents—tripods, seals, decorated soft-stone vessel fragments, bronze tools, and ceramics comparable to those found at Bahrain—indicate that it was constructed at the turn of the second millennium BCE. [See Bahrain.]

It is not possible to identify distinct architectural remains on Failaka between the Late Kassite and Hellenistic periods. A number of Neo-Assyrian inscriptions from Mesopotamia mention Dilmun as located on the mainland, but it is not ascertainable whether the border was in the southern Iraqi marshes or Kuwait, or on the eastern Arabian shore. Some small finds, including a cylinder seal, attest to limited Assyrian contact.

The Neo-Babylonian period is more tangibly represented by a stone architectural member bearing an inscription of Nebuchadrezzar. Other Neo-Babylonian epigraphic materials refer to a temple now presumed to have been situated on Failaka; a scarcely definable building at the inland sanctuary site of Tell Khazneh is a possible candidate. Terracotta figurines from this period date to the Neo-Babylonian and Seleucid periods. The Achaemenid period is further represented in pottery types and characteristic bronze arrowheads.

The French added two new Hellenistic sanctuaries to the architectural corpus, one of them on the beach to the east of the fortress. Dedicated to Artemis, it dates to the first half of the second century BCE. The other sanctuary, at Tell Khazneh, is constructed over the earlier Neo-Babylonian/Achaemenid building.

Much additional work has been done to clarify the architecture and stratification of buildings within the Hellenistic fortress. Two hoards of coins found in the complex date to Antiochus III; others imitate the "Alexander style." Numismatic evidence from the Artemis sanctuary on the beach point to the mint at Gerrha; the numerous Seleucid coins were minted either at Susa or Seleucia on the Tigris.

A location called al-Quṣur ("the castles") in the center of the island has traditionally been identified as an archaeological site because it is marked by stone walls and ceramic debris. Initial exploration by the French team led to the discovery of three steps of a staircase and fragments of a stucco frieze bearing an unmistakable Christian cross. Excavation revealed a church (36 × 19 m) constructed basically of mud brick/terre pisé with some courses of small-stone facing; a thick white plaster overlaid all its walls and floors. The building's bipartite structure consisted of the "public" nave (narthex and aisles) and the "restricted" area (two aisles with chapels, the choir, and dependencies utilized for priestly functions). The stucco crosses presumably date to the fifth–sixth centuries CE; however, the pottery associated with the church's establishment is Sasanian/Early Islamic (first half of seventh century). The building was abandoned in the second half of the eighth century and reused for domestic quarters in the late eighth/ early ninth centuries.

[See also Kuwait.]

BIBLIOGRAPHY

Bernard, Vincent, et al. "L'église d'al-Qousour Failaka, État de Koweit." *Arabian Archaeology and Epigraphy* 2 (1991): 145–181.

Calvet, Yves. "Failaka and the Northern Part of Dilmun." *Proceedings of the Seminar for Arabian Studies* 19 (1989): 5–11.

Connelly, Joan Breton. "Votive Offerings from Hellenistic Failaka: Evidence for a Herakles Cult." In *L'Arabie préislamique et son environnement historique et culturel: Actes du Colloque de Strasbourg*, edited by Toufic Fahd, pp. 145–158. Leiden, 1989.

Højlund, Flemming. *Failaka/Dilmun: The Second Millennium Settlements*, vol. 2, *The Bronze Age Pottery*. Jutland Archaeological Society Publications, 17.2. Aarhus, 1987.

Howard-Carter, Theresa. "Modern Excavations on Failaka Island." *Arts of the Islamic World: Kuwait Supplement* 3.1 (1985): 70–73, 96.

Howard-Carter, Theresa. "Voyages of Votive Vessels in the Gulf." In *DUMU-E₂-DUB-BA-A: Studies in Honor of Åke W. Sjöberg*, edited by Hermann Behrens et al., pp. 253–266. Occasional Publications of the Samuel Noah Kramer Fund, 11. Philadelphia, 1989.

Kjærum, Poul. *Failaka/Dilmun: The Second Millennium Settlements*, vol. 1.1, *The Stamp and Cylinder Seals*. Jutland Archaeological Society Publications, 17.1. Aarhus, 1983.

Potts, Daniel T., ed. *Dilmun: New Studies in the Archaeology and Early History of Bahrain*. Berliner Beitrage zum Vorderen Orient, vol. 2. Berlin, 1983.

Potts, Daniel T. *The Arabian Gulf in Antiquity*. 2 vols. Oxford, 1990.

Salles, Jean-François, et al. *Failaka: Fouilles français*. 3 vols. Travaux de la Maison de l'Orient, nos. 9, 12, 18. Lyon, 1984–1990.

Salles, Jean-François. "The Arab-Persian Gulf under the Seleucids."

In *Hellenism in the East,* edited by Amélie Kuhrt and Susan Sherwin-White, pp. 75–184. London, 1987.

THERESA HOWARD-CARTER

FAIYUM. To the ancient Egyptians, the lake at the center of the Faiyum Depression was a holy place, sacred to Sobek, the crocodile god, whose material manifestations swarmed the lake's beaches. The high religious significance of the lake was paralleled in several periods with considerable economic importance, based on the fecundity of the Faiyum's well-watered farmlands and fish, fowl, and other resources from the lake itself. In modern Arabic, the lake is known as Birket Qarun. In ancient Egyptian it was originally She-resy ("southern lake") and later divided into She-resy and Mer-wer ("The Great Lake").

In early antiquity the Faiyum lake was fed by a branch of the Nile; therefore the lake rose and fell annually with the river, and in the flood season it covered a large area. Beginning probably in the twelfth dynasty (c. 1991–1783 BCE) the water flow into the lake was artificially restricted, probably in order to reclaim land for farming. Land reclamation over the centuries eventually reduced the lake to less than 20 percent of its original extent. In the early 1990s water runoff from agricultural fields has increased the size of the lake slightly and made it so saline that most aquatic animal species disappeared.

Traces of human activity in the areas around the Faiyum Depression region go back hundreds of thousands of years, but the earliest substantial and well-preserved occupations date to about ten thousand years ago when hunters and gatherers began intensive exploitation of the rich terrestrial and lake resources along the shore. Remains of these early occupations are marked by many small chert blades and other tools (known as the Qarunian Industry) and include numerous remains of fish, gazelle, hartebeest, hippo, and other animals. These early Faiyum groups appear not to have been in the process of domesticating plants or animals, or using these domesticates in any form of agriculture.

About 7,500 years ago, the Faiyum hunter-fisher-foragers were replaced, displaced, or "converted" (the evidence is still uncertain) to "Neolithic" cultures, which were based in part on domesticated wheat, barley, sheep, goats, and cattle. Artifacts and sites of this period are found in heavy concentrations on most of the perimeter of the lake. There is no question that these people cultivated wheat and barley. In the 1920s archaeologist Gertrude Caton-Thompson (Caton-Thompson and Gardner, 1934) found silos full of well-preserved wheat and barley that also contained sickles and other tools of these early cultivators. Except for a few possible traces of poles for huts, no dwellings of the Faiyum Neolithic have been found, and it seems likely that these people lived in reed huts.

The Faiyum seems to have been nearly abandoned soon after 4,000 BCE, but only a few sites that date to 4000–3000 have been found, perhaps because the main Nile Valley offered better conditions for agriculture than the Faiyum.

Only a few sites dating to 3000–1550 have been found in the Faiyum. Stone quarries on the northern side of the lake were worked during this period, and a small temple (known as Qaṣr el-Sagha) was built there in the Middle Kingdom (2040–1640).

King Amenemhet I of the twelfth dynasty (c. 1991–1962) moved the administrative capital of Egypt and his royal residence from Thebes to Itjtawy—now known as Lisht—which was located on the west bank of the Nile between the Faiyum and Memphis. Little remains of the town except two small pyramids and some tombs and cemeteries, but the emergence of Lisht as an important settlement probably resulted in attempts to develop the Faiyum. Amenemhet III (c. 1844–1797) built a temple in the southern Faiyum at Medinet Madi, as well as a pyramid at Hawara, at the eastern entrance to the Faiyum. Underground burial chambers near the Hawara pyramid were probably the "Labyrinth" described by the Greek historian Strabo. Amenemhet III is also associated with two large stone constructions at Biahmu, which apparently were the bases of two colossal statues of him. Once on the shore or actually in the lake, they were described by Herodotus and perhaps were still partially preserved in the seventeenth century CE, according to travelers' reports, but no longer exist.

Between about 300 BCE and 300 CE, the Greco-Roman era, the Faiyum became one of the richest and most important provinces of Egypt. During this time the agricultural produce of the Faiyum was exported to many towns and cities, some of them outside of Egypt, and several Faiyum towns grew into major metropolises. Some of these cities, such as Dimai on the northern shore of the lake and Karanis at the eastern entrance to the Faiyum, are remarkably well preserved even today. We know much of this period because thousands of documents have been found, almost all of them written on papyrus in demotic Egyptian or Greek and documenting the social and economic life of these communities. The Faiyum prospered during the medieval and modern periods as well, and today it is one of the most densely settled and agriculturally productive regions in Egypt.

BIBLIOGRAPHY

Caton-Thompson, Gertrude, and Eleanor Gardner. *The Desert Fayum.* London, 1934.

Ginter, Bronislaw, and J. K. Kozlowski. "Investigations on Neolithic Settlement." In *Qasr el-Sagha 1980,* edited by J. K. Kozlowski, pp. 37–67. Warsaw, 1983.

Wendorf, Fred, and Romuald Schild. *Prehistory of the Nile Valley.* New York, 1976.

Wenke, Robert, Janet Long, and Paul Buck. "The Epipaleolithic and Neolithic Subsistence and Settlement in the Fayyum Oasis of Egypt." *Journal of Field Archaeology* 15.1 (1988): 29–51.

ROBERT J. WENKE

FAKHARIYAH, TELL, site, whose modern Arabic name means "mound of sherds," located immediately south of the modern town of Ras al-'Ain ("fountainhead") in Syria (40°01′ N, 36°09′ E), 65 km (38 mi.) northwest of the modern city al-Hasakah (Hasseke) and about 100 km (62 mi.) west of the modern town of Qamishli (Nisibin). Hundreds of springs in the environs form the headwaters of the Khabur River. This part of Syria is called Jezireh ("island") and is equivalent to Upper Mesopotamia.

Tell Fakhariyah was first observed by Baron Max von Oppenheim in 1899, during his visit to the source of the Khabur. Von Oppenheim worked at Tell Ḥalaf from 1911 to 1913, in 1927, and in 1929, searching for the Mitanni capital, Waššukanni. However, his work indicated that Ḥalaf was the ancient city of Guzana (Aram., *gwzn*). He moved to Tell Fakhariyah in 1929, to supervise a survey of the tell, which produced a contour map but no excavation.

Later, in 1940, the Oriental Institute of Chicago decided to change the focus of its research from the 'Amuq region in Syria to Mesopotamia. Its goal was to clarify the cultural relationship between the 'Amuq basin and Upper Mesopotamia in the second millennium BCE, in the belief that Waššukanni, the capital of Mitanni, was located at Tell Fakhariyah.

In 1940, the institute received permission to excavate from the French High Commission of Syria. The expedition consisted of Calvin W. McEwan and his wife, the former as director; Harold D. Hill as architect; and Abdullah Said Osman al-Sudain as superintendent. The American expedition came to an unexpected halt when von Oppenheim protested to the Vichy French government about its presence. Although the Americans withdrew from the field, the baron did not excavate the site himself. In 1955, Anton Moortgat received a license to excavate Tell Fakhariyah in the name of the Oppenheim Foundation. [*See the biography of Moortgat.*]

In the short time they were in the field, the Americans were able to make nine separate soundings, distinguishing eight levels: the upper four yielded Arab/Islamic, Byzantine, Roman, and Hellenistic remains. The fifth level belongs to the Aramaic period (or Iron Age, 900–600 BCE), the sixth to the Middle Assyrian period (thirteenth century BCE); and the seventh to the Mitannian period (fifteenth–fourteenth centuries BCE). So-called Khabur ware was found in level eight (first half of the second millennium BCE). Moortgat made similar observations. The results from both excavations are described here.

The tell was settled in the Umayyad period. In the preceding Byzantine and Roman levels, the settlement was fortified. Sections of a double city wall were unearthed: two limestone walls running roughly parallel to each other. The inner wall was clearly the more important, as it contained a series of curtains with projecting towers and buttresses.

In level five, in sounding IX, the American expedition partially exposed a palace dated to the Aramaic period (Iron Age II, sixth–seventh centuries BCE). It is essentially a *ḥilani* (or pillared) type of structure. In 1979, at the southwestern edge of the tell, a tractor turned up a basalt statue (1.65 m high) of the Aramean king Hdys'y, King of *gwzn*, *skn*, and *'zrn*. It was consecrated to the god Hadad of Sikani (Aram., *Hadd zy skn*).

The most important level at Tell Fakhariyah is level six, the Middle Assyrian period. Many small objects, among them ivory pieces and seal impressions, were found in this level. The ivories were recovered in sounding IX, from floor 6, below the Iron Age palace. They are very fragmentary and appear to have been ornamental inlays for furniture or boxes. Only five pieces are undecorated; the majority are decorated with geometric designs, flower patterns, animal and human figures, Hathor heads, winged sun disks, and a griffon/demon. In a building dated to the thirteenth century BCE, twelve cuneiform tablets, ten with 116 seal impressions on them, were found. The style of most of the seal designs is exactly that of the Middle Assyrian seal impressions on tablets from Aššur dated to the thirteenth century. The repertoire of designs is relatively small: recurring elements are ritual scenes, heroes and animals, monsters and animals in conflict, and animals in tranquil settings. In addition to these seal impressions, there were an old Babylonian cylinder seal, thirteenth-century BCE stamp seals, and typical Late Assyrian (Iron Age) scaraboids and bulla bearing the impression of a scarab. Of the twelve tablets and tablet fragments found at Fakhariyah in sounding VI, four are letters and eight are legal/economic documents. Four of the legal documents bear names of Limmu: of these four eponyms, one belongs to the reign of Shalmaneser I (1272–1243 BCE) and one to the reign of his son, Tukulti-Ninurta (1242–1206 BCE).

In level seven, there were traces of the Mitanni at Tell Fakhariyah, as well as of earlier periods. These remains, represented mainly by pottery sherds, were not as well attested as the quantity of Assyrian remains from the following period.

The American and German expeditions expected to find Waššukanni at Tell Fakhariyah. Instead, they found Sikani, an identification confirmed by the inscription of King Hadys'y, who placed his statue in the Temple of Hadad at Sikani, the statue found at Tell Fakhariyah.

[*See also* Mitanni.]

BIBLIOGRAPHY

Assaf, Ali Abou, et al. *La statue de Tell Fekheryé et son inscription bilingue assyro-araméenne.* Paris, 1982.

McEwan, Calvin, et al. *Soundings at Tell Fakhariyah.* Oriental Institute Publications, 79. Chicago, 1958.

Moortgat, Anton. *Archäologische Forschungen der Max Freiherr von Oppenheim-Stiftung im nördlichen Mesopotamien 1955.* Cologne, 1957.

Moortgat, Anton. *Archäologische Forschungen der Max Freiherr von Oppenheim-Stiftung in nördlichen Mesopotamien 1956.* Arbeitsgemeinschaft für Forschung des Lands Nordrhein-Westfalen, Wissenschaftliche Abhandlungen, vol. 7. Cologne, 1957.

ALI ABOU ASSAF

FAKHARIYAH ARAMAIC INSCRIPTION.

The inscribed statue of a bearded male, Hadad-Yis'i, with hands crossed on the stomach, was discovered accidently in 1979 at Tell Fakhariyah in northeast Syria. The statue stands 1.65 m high. The subject is clothed in a shawl and a long tunic with a fringed border and his feet are clad in sandals.

The statue's bilingual inscriptions, in Akkadian and Aramaic, are divided into two parts. The Akkadian text, thirty-eight lines long, is engraved on the front of the tunic; the Aramaic, twenty-three lines long, is on the back. In the Aramaic text words are separated by two dots, occasionally three, vertically oriented. This text contains new paleographic elements, and the iconography of the statue has proven useful for dating.

The inscriptions are similar in structure: they are dedications to the storm god Hadad; the identity of the dedicator is Hadad-yis'i, son of Shamash-nuri king of Gozan; they wish for a long, prosperous life; and they offer threats to anyone who would try to erase his name. A second inscription follows in both languages: the dedicator has increased his territory; restored or reengraved his dedications; and threatens whomever would erase his name from the property of the Temple of Hadad (the threatened punishment would be accomplished by Hadad and his consort, Shala/Sawl, supported by Nergal). Many of the phrases in the Aramaic version are more adaptation than translation, but it does contain elements that are not common to both versions.

In the version intended for their Assyrian masters, Hadad-yis'i and his father Shamash-nuri are called governor of Guzana (šakin), but in the Aramaic version, intended for their underlings, they are called king of Gozan (mlk). In the Akkadian, the god resides at Guzana, in the Aramaic at Sikan. Perhaps at first two statues were erected, one at Guzana and one at Sikan, each inscribed with the Akkadian (ll. 1–18) and the Aramaic (ll. 1–12) texts. The second text (Akkadian, ll. 19–38; Aramaic, ll. 12b–23) may have been written later, after the annexation of Sikan and 'Azran, no doubt with Assyrian help.

The threats, brief in the first part, are more detailed in the second. Were these copied from a vassal treaty linking the dynasty of Guzana to the king of Assyria? Some Aramaic words are borrowed from the Akkadian, and sometimes the word order copies the Akkadian with the verb at the end of the sentence. The inflection of nouns in the nominative plural (nšwn, "women") and in the oblique case (l'lhyn, "for the gods") recall the case system of classical Arabic. The last part of the Aramaic texts contains images present in the Bible: l. 22, Aramaic, l. 35ff., Assyrian (cf. Lv. 26:26).

The Aramaic writing does not preclude a date of about 1100 BCE (Naveh, 1987, pp. 214ff., 221), but the statue and the costume suggest a date within the ninth century BCE (Spycket, 1985, p. 67f.; Sader, 1987, pp. 26ff.). The latter date is supported by the following historical data: the Assyrian eponym for the year 866 BCE is Shamash-nuri, and in the eighth century BCE the succession of eponymous governors in Tushan and Guzana is frequent, as in 794–793, for example. If this custom existed in the ninth century, the eponym of 867 being governor of Tushan, that of 866 called Shamash-nuri could have been the governor of Guzana. Furthermore, some details of the Assyrian are characteristic of the period of Ashurbanipal (c. 850 BCE).

Some of the Aramaic letters are archaic (e.g., /D/ and /'ayin/); others are known in the tenth century BCE, or even in the ninth (e.g., /B/, /Z/, and /H/), while others anticipate the writing of the eighth century BCE. The /W/ with a foot, the /L/ in the form of a question mark, the upright /M/, the /N/ with a right angle, and the /S/ are all unusual forms.

A new argument may be adduced dating the inscription to about 800 BCE: word dividers are identical to those of more ancient Greek inscriptions from about 750 BCE (Jeffery, 1982, fig. 104, pp. 820ff., 823). That fact also reinforces the traditional idea that the Greeks borrowed the Phoenician alphabet in the eighth century, probably by still-undiscovered northern channels. The Aramaic inscription from Tell Fakhariyah remains for the time being a unique example of this northern graphic tradition.

[See also Fakhariyah, Tell.]

BIBLIOGRAPHY

Assaf, Ali Abou, et al. La statue de Tell Fekheryé et son inscription bilingue assyro-araméenne. Paris, 1982.

Fitzmyer, Joseph A., and Stephen A. Kaufman. An Aramaic Bibliography, part 1, Old, Official, and Biblical Aramaic. Baltimore and London, 1992. See pages 36ff.

Jeffery, Lilian H. "Greek Alphabetic Writing." In The Cambridge Ancient History, vol. 3.1, edited by John Boardman et al., pp. 819–833. 2d ed. Cambridge, 1982.

Naveh, Joseph. An Early History of the Alphabet. 2d ed. Jerusalem and Leiden, 1987.

Sader, Hélène. Les états araméens de Syrie depuis leur fondation jusqu'à leur transformation en provinces assyriennes. Beiruter Texte und Studien, vol. 36. Beirut, 1987.

Spycket, Agnès. "La statue bilingue de Tell Fekheriyé." Revue d'Assyriologie et d'Archéologie Orientale 79 (1985): 67–68.

"The Tell Fakhariyah Bilingual Inscription." Newsletter for Aramaic and Targumic Studies, Supplement 4 (1988): 1–7.

PIERRE BORDREUIL

Translated from French by Melissa Kaprelian

FARA, city mound in Iraq, located about halfway between Baghdad and the Persian Gulf, on the dry bed of the ancient Euphrates River (31°42' N, 45°32' E). The mound is large (220 ha, or 524 acres) and low (10 m at its maximum height). It was visited by three Europeans before serious excavation was begun: by William Kennett Loftus in 1850, William Hayes Ward in 1885, and Hermann V. Hilprecht in 1900.

A pottery cone with an inscription of Halada, *ensi* (governor) of Shuruppak, son of Dada, *ensi* of Shuruppak, found by the Deutsche Orient-Gesellschaft expedition on the surface of the mound, identified Fara as Shuruppak in 1902. In Near Eastern literature, Shuruppak is the home of Utnapishtim, the hero of the Babylonian Flood story. It appears as one of the five antediluvian cities on the Sumerian king list. [*See* Sumerians.]

Excavations and surveys indicate that the first settlement at Fara took place shortly before 3000 BCE. There is a Jemdet Nasr, or Late Uruk, level about 2 m thick at the base of the mound. [*See* Jemdet Nasr.] The site was then continuously occupied until shortly after 2000 BCE. Although a large city in Early Dynastic (ED) I, it does not appear among the ED III dynasties on the Sumerian king list. Shuruppak was one of eighteen *ensi*ships under the control of Ur in the Ur III period (2112–2004 BCE). [*See* Ur.] There are few traces of later habitation; presumably, the site was abandoned as the Euphrates changed course. [*See* Euphrates.] Archaeologically, Fara is remarkable for having ED IIIA and II remains at surface level in most areas, later deposits having eroded away.

The Deutsche Orient-Gesellschaft (DOG) excavated at Fara for nine months beginning in June 1902 (Heinrich, 1931). [*See* Deutsche Orient-Gesellschaft.] In that time, approximately two hundred men under two supervisors excavated twenty-one trenches consisting of about 855 3- ×-8-meter "squares." In the last few months of the excavation, the archaeologists began recognizing and tracing mud-brick architecture, and a few house plans were recovered.

From this massive earth-moving effort, about twenty-five hundred objects were recovered and registered. Of these, about eight hundred were early cuneiform tablets, about thirteen hundred were seal impressions, and 171 were complete pots or decorated sherds. [*See* Cuneiform; Tablet; Seals.] The tablets, found at twenty-four sites across the mound, were ED IIIA in date. They attest the organization of large numbers of workers by a number of large administrative units within the city.

Most of the seal impressions were found either in a large dump area (trench Id–e, ED I–II) or in houses with ED IIIA tablets. These huge collections of seal designs have been vital to the study of Early Dynastic glyptic (see figure 1), although the exact dating of the mixed I–II group is still debated.

In 1931 Erich Schmidt excavated at the site for three months for the University of Pennsylvania (Schmidt, 1931). His deep sounding in DE 38/39 established the presence of a thick Jemdet Nasr stratum followed by a "Flood stratum"

FARA. Figure 1. *Seal impression.* Early Dynastic IIIa period. (Courtesy H. P. Martin)

and then more than 6 m of ED I–II deposits. ED IIIA tablets were found in drainpipes penetrating the debris from later, now eroded, levels. Schmidt excavated Early Dynastic II house remains in FG 42/43 and ED IIIA remains in HI 47/48/58. In addition, he cleared two of the massive Early Dynastic "silos" that dot the site. [*See* Granaries and Silos.] These had filled with rubbish, dating from the ED III through Old Babylonian periods.

Between 1968 and 1982, Harriet P. Martin, while doing doctoral research at the University of Chicago, reexamined all of the finds and records from both excavations and conducted a surface survey of the site (Martin, 1983, 1988). This enabled her to establish findspots for many of the objects from the DOG excavations and to put them in context by fully publishing Schmidt's excavations.

Using Schmidt's records, Martin defined a corpus of ED II pottery for central and southern Babylonia (Martin, 1982). She also suggested a stylistic and chronological classification of the ED I–II seal impressions; it has been widely debated, however, largely because the total cultural assemblages of these periods have not been defined through published excavation: Schmidt's excavations were too small in scale to do this and the DOG's were too crudely executed. The DOG trenches can still be discerned on Fara's surface, broken in places by more recent illegal excavations.

[*See also* Mesopotamia, *article on* Ancient Mesopotamia; *and the biography of* Hilprecht.]

BIBLIOGRAPHY

Primary Sources for Archaeological and Philological Material

Deimel, Anton. *Die Inschriften von Fara*, vol. 1, *Liste der archaischen Keilschriftzeichen;* vol. 2, *Schultexte aus Fara;* vol. 3, *Wirtschaftstexte aus Fara.* Wissenschaftliche Veröffentliche Deutsch Orient-Gesellschaft, 40, 43, 45. Leipzig, 1922–1925.

Heinrich, Ernst, and Walter Andrae, eds. *Fara: Ergebnisse der Ausgrabungen der Deutschen Orient-Gesellschaft in Fara und Abu Hatab 1902/3.* Berlin, 1931.

Jestin, Raymond R. *Tablettes sumériennes de Šuruppak conservées au Mu-*

sée d'Istanbul. Mémoires de l'Institut Français d'Archéologie d'Istanbul, 3. Paris, 1937.

Jestin, Raymond R. *Nouvelles tablettes sumériennes de Šuruppak au Musée d'Istanbul*. Bibliothèque Archéologique et Historique de l'Institut Français d'Archéologie d'Istanbul, 2. Paris, 1957.

Kramer, Samuel Noah. "New Tablets from Fara." *Journal of the American Oriental Society* 52 (1932): 110–132.

Martin, Harriet P. "The Early Dynastic Cemetery at al-'Ubaid: A Re-evaluation." *Iraq* 44 (1982): 145–185.

Martin, Harriet P. "Settlement Patterns at Shuruppak." *Iraq* 45 (1983): 24–31.

Martin, Harriet P. *Fara: A Reconstruction of the Ancient City of Shuruppak*. Birmingham, 1988.

Schmidt, Erich F. "Excavations at Fara, 1931." *University of Pennsylvania Museum Journal* 22 (1931): 193–235.

Biblical and Literary References

Although Shuruppak has indirect biblical connections as the home of the Babylonian "Noah" (Utnapishtim), it is not explicitly mentioned in the Bible. Shuruppak appears in ancient literature because there was an antediluvian dynasty there mentioned in three king lists; the Instructions of Shuruppak were a type of ancient wisdom text in which "Shuruppak," a man, is passing on advice to his son; and the hero of the Babylonian Flood story (known variously as Ziusudra, Utnapishtim, or Atrahasis) is king of and/or comes from the city of Shuruppak. Some principal works related to this literature are:

Civil, Miguel, and Robert D. Biggs. "Notes sur des textes sumériennes archaïques." *Revue d'Assyrologie et Archéologie Orientale* 60 (1966): 1–5.

Finkelstein, Jacob J. "The Antediluvian Kings: A University of California Text." *Journal of Cuneiform Studies* 17 (1963): 39–51.

Jacobsen, Thorkild. *The Sumerian King List*. Oriental Institute, Assyriological Studies, 11. Chicago, 1939.

Jacoby, Felix. *Die Fragmente der griechischen Historiker*, part 3, *Geschichte von Städten und Völkern (Horographie und Ethnographie)*. Leiden, 1955.

Lambert, W. G. *Babylonian Wisdom Literature*. Oxford, 1960.

Langdon, Stephen H. *Sumerian Epic of Paradise: The Flood and the Fall of Man*. University of Pennsylvania, the University Museum Publications of the Babylonian Section, vol. 10.1. Philadelphia, 1915..

Langdon, Stephen H. *The Weld Blundell Collection in the Ashmolean Museum*, vol. 2, *Historical Inscriptions, Containing Principally the Chronological Prism, W–B 444*. Oxford, 1923.

Poebel, Arno. *Historical and Grammatical Texts*. University of Pennsylvania, the University Museum Publications of the Babylonian Section, vol. 5. Philadelphia, 1914.

Thompson, R. Campbell. *The Epic of Gilgamesh*. Oxford, 1930.

HARRIET P. MARTIN

FAR'AH, TELL EL- (North), site located in the Samaria hills, 10 km (6 mi.) northeast of Nablus (map reference 1823 × 1882). Situated on a high bluff at the western end of Wadi Far'ah, a major east–west avenue from the hill country to the Jordan Valley, the site overlooks the valley and perennial springs of 'Ain el-Far'ah and 'Ain el-Duleib. The mound's area is approximately 10 ha (25 acres). The site is called Tell el-Far'ah (North), to distinguish it from Tell el-Far'ah (South) in Nahal Besor.

Tell el-Far'ah (North) is identified with biblical Tirzah, briefly the royal residence and capital of the northern kingdom of Israel until Omri's founding of Samaria (*1 Kgs.* 16:23–24). The identification was made by William Foxwell Albright (1931). Gustaf Dalman and Albrecht Alt suggested that the site was Ophrah, home of Gideon; and Félix-Marie Abel suggested that it was Beth-Barah. The name *Tell el-Far'ah* (Ar., "mound of the elevated ridge") offers no clue as to the site's ancient identity. The site's excavator, Roland de Vaux, agreed with the identification of Tell el-Far'ah with Tirzah (see Vaux, 1956). However, while the identification remains persuasive, the archaeological evidence is ambiguous. [*See the biographies of Albright, Dalman, Alt, Abel, and Vaux.*]

De Vaux excavated at Tell el-Far'ah for the École Biblique et Archéologique Française in Jerusalem for nine seasons, from 1946 to 1960. De Vaux died before writing final reports. To date, reports have been produced for the Middle Bronze IIA and IIB–C by Joel Mallet (1973, 1988) and the Iron Age by Alain Chambon (1984). De Vaux's field methods emphasized large architectural exposures, giving little attention to stratigraphy. The architectural stratigraphy and poor recording do not allow a detailed picture of the site's internal development. Nevertheless, Tell el-Far'ah stands with Megiddo and Hazor as foundations for understanding the hill country and northern Canaan. [*See* Megiddo; Hazor.]

The site's first significant material comes from the Chalcolithic period. An important Chalcolithic tomb, "grotto U," was excavated in a cave on the southern edge of the tell and was the first discovery of the Beersheba-Ghassul horizon in the north. The material de Vaux called Late Chalcolithic is now understood as early Early Bronze I, represented by pottery and circular pit dwellings. The primary evidence from EB I comes from the extensive cemeteries to the south, north, and recently along Wadi Far'ah northeast of the tell. The majority of the tomb material is EB I, with only 10 percent belonging to EB II, and none to EB III. There are at least five EB phases on the tell, which are comprised of rectilinear buildings with common walls around streets or lanes. Remains of the earliest known updraft kilns and pottery workshops were found there.

The site was partially surrounded by a fortification wall of mud-brick on stone. The wall defended it on its open flank to the west. Steep slopes to the east and south made walls unnecessary. Other features included rectangular towers and a gateway. The gate was a narrow passageway set between projecting mud-brick towers. The gate was rebuilt in a later phase, then blocked, and then rebuilt entirely. In a later, EB II phase, part of the wall was reconstructed in stone on the remains of the earlier wall; at the same time, another section of mud-brick wall was strengthened with a stone wall and rampart. Still later a glacis was added to the rampart.

There is disagreement about the dating of Tell el-Far'ah in the Early Bronze Age, with de Vaux arguing that the first two phases date to the EB IB and the rest to EB II. Refinements in ceramic chronology suggest that all the phases could be placed in EB II. There is no material from the tell or tombs from EB III or IV.

The site was resettled in the MB IIA. A large village was built above the ruins of the EB II town. Excavated remains are limited, consisting of fragmentary walls and sherd material. A dozen tombs were found containing MB IIA or IIB burials. The MB IIC remains are more substantial and include a mud-brick-on-stone fortification wall and a layered stone and earth glacis built on top of the ruins of the EB wall. A large two-entryway gate with offset entry was incorporated into the wall. Two cult installations are attributed to MB IIC. One, temple 1–2, may have been a dome-shaped granary. The gate shrine near the city gate may have been a cultic installation. Continuity is suggested by an overlying sanctuary and Iron Age maṣṣēbâ and olive oil press. Domestic remains of the MB IIC show continuity and accumulation from the previous phase. Houses, courtyards, and installations were found, as well as infant jar burials beneath floors.

The Late Bronze Age strata are poorly preserved and reported. The only significant structure, the sanctuary, was erected above the gate shrine. It is a long room with a two rows of pillars, in which a small bronze statue of Hathor covered in silver was found. This structure has been reassigned to the Iron Age and reinterpreted as a four-room pillared house. [See Four-room House.] Few stratified remains can be assigned to the Late Bronze Age. The cemeteries continued to be used, and there were infant jar burials beneath floors. The date and circumstances of the site's abandonment remain unclear.

The Iron Age strata are better preserved than those of the Late Bronze Age. Chambon's final report provides a fuller picture of the site in that period (Chambon, 1984). Four basic strata are evident. The site was reoccupied in the twelfth century BCE. The first Iron Age stratum, VIIa (de Vaux's 4), is fragmentary and contains partial remains of four-room houses. The next stratum, VIIb (de Vaux's 3), is more substantial, with four-room houses oriented on a rectangular plan. This stratum is dated to the tenth century.

A problem arises with stratum VIIC (de Vaux's Intermediate). De Vaux deemed one structure, building 411, an "incomplete building," regarding it as an unfinished palace abandoned by Omri's shift of the Israelite capital from Tirzah to Samaria. This is not, however, supported by the evidence. Virtually no material or other structures can be assigned to this stratum, and Thomas L. McClellan's reanalysis of the stratigraphy (1987) indicates that the incomplete building should be reassigned to stratum VIId (de Vaux's 2). Similar problems appear with stratum VIId (de Vaux's 2), in which de Vaux saw a socioeconomic gap between rich and poor during the eighth century BCE. McClellan shows that "poorer" buildings should be reassigned to the earlier stratum VIIb (de Vaux's 3). The four-room houses and courtyards remaining in stratum VIId (de Vaux's 2) are highly standardized, with little evidence of socioeconomic differentiation.

Tell el-Far'ah was destroyed by the Assyrians in 723 BCE. Its final Iron Age stratum, VIIe (de Vaux's 1), shows evidence of a rebuilding of the administrative building of the previous stratum and of Assyrian pottery. At the end of the seventh century BCE, Tell el-Far'ah was abandoned and was never reoccupied.

BIBLIOGRAPHY

Albright, William Foxwell. "The Site of Tirzah and the Topography of Western Manasseh." *Journal of the Palestine Oriental Society* 11 (1931): 241–251. The first identification of Tell el-Far'ah (North) with Tirzah and an extensive discussion of classical sources.

Chambon, Alain. *Tell el-Fâr'ah I: L'âge du fer.* Paris, 1984. Final report of the Iron Age strata.

Dever, William G. "Review of J. Mallet, *Tell el-Fâr'ah (Région de Naplouse)." Journal of Biblical Literature* 94 (1975): 607–608.

Dever, William G. "Review of *Tell el-Fâr'ah II, 1; 2. Le Bronze moyen." Paléorient* 15.2 (1990): 154–158. This and the review above help place the MB materials from Tell el-Far'ah (North) in their larger Canaanite context, something not attempted by the authors of the final reports.

Huot, Jean-Louis. "Typologie et chronologie relative de la céramique du Bronze ancien à Tell el-Fâr'ah." *Revue Biblique* 74 (1967): 517–554. Fairly comprehensive publication of the EB pottery typology; marred by poor drawings and now outdated comparative materials.

Mallet, Joel. *Tell el-Fâr'ah (Région de Naplouse): L'installation du moyen Bronze antérieure au rempart.* Paris, 1973.

Mallet, Joel. *Tell el-Fâr'ah II, 1; 2. Le Bronze moyen stratigraphie des vestiges du Bronze moyen II.* Paris, 1988.

McClellan, Thomas L. "Review of A. Chambon, *Tell el-Fâr'ah I." Bulletin of the American Schools of Oriental Research,* no. 267 (1987): 84–86. Review of the final report on the Iron Age strata and an important reanalysis of some of the stratigraphy.

Vaux, Roland de. Excavation reports. *Revue Biblique* 54 (1947): 394–433, 573–589; 55 (1948): 544–580; 58 (1951): 393–430; 59 (1952): 551–583; 62 (1955): 541–589; 64 (1957): 552–580; 68 (1961): 557–592; 69 (1962): 212–253.

Vaux, Roland de. "The Excavations at Tell el-Fâr'ah and the Site of Ancient Tirzah." *Palestine Exploration Quarterly* 88 (1956): 125–140. Elegant summary statement of the work at Tell el-Far'ah by the excavator; identification of the site with Tirzah.

Vaux, Roland de. "Tell el-Far'a North." In *Encyclopedia of Archaeological Excavations in the Holy Land,* vol. 2, pp. 395–404. Englewood Cliffs, N.J., 1976. Final summary of the work at Tell el-Far'ah by the excavator; too general to be useful.

ALEXANDER H. JOFFE

FAR'AH, TELL EL- (South), site located on the west bank of the Wadi Gaza, about 29 km (18 mi.) southeast of Gaza, at 31°17' N and 34°29' E (map reference 100 × 076). The tell, covering approximately 15 acres and protected on three sides by natural slopes, is one of the largest in the northwestern Negev. The site sits along a route linking the coast to Beersheba in the north-central Negev. The site is designated "south" to distinguish it from the northern Palestinian site of the same name.

Tell el-Far'ah (South) was excavated in 1928–1929 by W. M. Flinders Petrie, who misidentified the site as biblical Beth-Pelet. William Foxwell Albright subsequently connected the site with Sharuhen, an Asiatic stronghold captured by the Egyptian king Ahmose at the beginning of the eighteenth dynasty (c. 1540 BCE). Albright's view was widely accepted until the mid-1970s, when Aharon Kempinski suggested that Sharuhen should be placed at Tell el-'Ajjul in the Gaza district. Kempinski's proposal has gained support from an increasing number of archaeologists (although recently Anson Rainey has proposed that Tell Abu Hureirah [Tel Haror] should be identified with Sharuhen); it leaves Tell el-Far'ah (South) without a known ancient name.

Occupation on the mound is attested starting in the Middle Bronze II–III period. At that time the town had a defense wall, glacis, and fosse and counterscarp on the west and a triple-entryway gate with a pair of flanking towers on the south. A cemetery (designated cemetery 500 by Petrie) was in use northwest of the tell; a scarab from tomb 550 contained the name of the Hyksos (i.e., fifteenth dynasty) ruler Maaibre. The site was abandoned in the second half of the sixteenth century BCE, possibly as the consequence of an early eighteenth-dynasty Egyptian military campaign; it was not reoccupied until the fourteenth century BCE.

In the thirteenth century BCE, a large brick building was constructed on top of the MB II rampart at the north end of the mound. Fronted by a paved courtyard and containing an entrance and external stairway at one corner and a central courtyard with rooms on all four sides, this Egyptian-style structure (designated the Residency by its excavator) was probably erected in connection with Egyptian administrative and military control of Palestine during the Ramessid period. A jar fragment found in the building's central courtyard contains the cartouches of the nineteenth-dynasty Egyptian king Seti II (1200–1194 BCE). A smaller building on the west side of the Residency probably was used for offices. Cemetery 900, which belongs to the thirteenth–early twelfth century BCE, contained numerous Egyptian objects.

There was an important Philistine component at the site in the mid-twelfth and eleventh centuries BCE. To this period belong several large rock-cut chamber tombs in cemetery 500 that contained pottery and other goods associated with the Philistines; tombs in several other cemeteries around the mound yielded similar remains. Two of the cemetery 500 tombs (nos. 552 and 562) contained anthropoid coffins, a burial custom adopted by the Philistines from the Egyptians. The Philistines apparently settled at Tell el-Far'ah while the town was still under Egyptian control and remained there after the Egyptians withdrew from southern Palestine in about the third quarter of the twelfth century BCE.

The evidence for human activity at the site during the first millennium BCE is scattered. There appears to have been limited occupation during the tenth–early ninth centuries BCE (most of the tombs in cemetery 200 belong to this period) and then again during the seventh–sixth centuries BCE. Occupation in the Persian period is attested by burials in several cemeteries. A rich tomb of that period, number 650, contained a silver dipper and fluted bowl. Another decline in activity followed that lasted until the Early Roman period, when a small fort was constructed at the north end of the mound. Several coin hoards helped to date the structure to the first century CE.

BIBLIOGRAPHY

Cohen, Rudolph. "Tell el-Far'ah (South)." *Israel Exploration Journal* 27.2–3 (1977): 170. Brief report on the discovery of Iron Age remains at the site in 1976.

Dothan, Trude. *The Philistines and Their Material Culture.* New Haven, 1982. Comprehensive study of Philistine archaeological materials, including those at Tell el-Far'ah (South).

Kempinski, Aharon. "Tell el-'Ajjul—Beth-Aglayim or Sharuhen?" *Israel Exploration Journal* 24.3–4 (1974): 145–152. Questions the identification of Tell el-Far'ah (South) with ancient Sharuhen, suggesting that Tell el-'Ajjul is a more likely candidate.

Macdonald, Eann, J. L. Starkey, and Lankester Harding. *Beth-Pelet,* vol. 2, *Prehistoric Fara; Beth-Pelet Cemetery.* British School of Archaeology in Egypt, Publications of the Egyptian Research Account, no. 52. London, 1932. Final report on Petrie's 1929 season at Tell el-Far'ah (South), written by members of his staff.

Maxwell-Hyslop, K. R. "A Silver Earring from Tell el-Farah (South)." In *Archaeology in the Levant,* edited by Roger Moorey and Peter Parr, pp. 180–182. Warminster, 1978. Publication of a Persian-period earring from Tomb 725 at Tell el-Far'ah (South).

Oren, Eliezer D. " 'Governor's Residencies' in Canaan under the New Kingdom: A Case Study of Egyptian Administration." *Journal of the Society for the Study of Egyptian Antiquities* 14 (1984): 37–56. Analysis of a group of Egyptian-style buildings in Canaan during the thirteenth and twelfth centuries BCE, including the Residency at Tell el-Far'ah (South).

Petrie, W. M. Flinders. *Beth-Pelet.* Vol. 1. British School of Archaeology in Egypt, Publications of the Egyptian Research Account, no. 48. London, 1930. Petrie's final report on his 1928 season at this site.

Price-Williams, David. *The Tombs of the Middle Bronze Age II Period from the "500" Cemetery at Tell Fara (South).* University of London, Institute of Archaeology, Occasional Publication, no. 1. London, 1977. Detailed reexamination of the principal Middle Bronze Age cemetery at the site.

Rainey, Anson F. "Sharhân/Sharuhen—The Problem of Identification." *Eretz-Israel* 24 (1993): 178*–187*. Disputes the identification of Tell el-'Ajjul with Sharuhen; proposes Tell Abu Hureirah (Tel Haror) as a better alternative.

Waldbaum, Jane C. "Philistine Tombs at Tell Fara and Their Aegean Prototypes." *American Journal of Archaeology* 70.4 (1966): 331–340. Attributes the tombs in Cemetery 900 to a pre-Philistine group of Aegean Sea Peoples and the tombs in Cemetery 500 to the Philistines. The latter claim is now generally accepted; the former is not.

Weinstein, James M. "Egypt and the Middle Bronze IIC/Late Bronze IA Transition in Palestine." *Levant* 23 (1991): 105–115. Compares the evidence for Tell el-'Ajjul and Tell el-Far'ah (South) as Hyksos-period Sharuhen, favoring the former site.

JAMES M. WEINSTEIN

FARIS, KHIRBET, ruined agricultural village, located 3 km (2 mi.) northeast of al-Qaṣr in Jordan (31°24′ N, 35°44′ E). From the eighteenth to early twentieth centuries, Khirbet Faris was known as Khirbat Tadun; it derives its present name from Faris al-Majali, its owner, who was buried there in about 1930. There is evidence of occupation at the site since the Bronze/Iron Age.

Khirbet Faris was visited by several nineteenth-century European travelers including Ulrich J. Seetzen, Félicien de Saulcy, and Alois Musil, and surveyed by J. Maxwell Miller (1991) and Udo Worschech (1985). It was excavated between 1988 and 1993 by the British Institute at Amman for Archaeology and History and the University of Oxford, under the direction of Jeremy Johns and Alison McQuitty. The excavation set out to investigate a specific set of problems. Regional surveys in Jordan had indicated dramatic fluctuations in the pattern of Islamic settlement, generally attributed to the varying ability of the state to keep the bedouin from invading the settled region. The excavations at Khirbet Faris sought to test this model by studying a rural community from the seventh century to the present, reconstructing its material culture and socioeconomic structure through a combination of excavation and postexcavation analysis of finds, architectural survey, paleoenvironmentology, field survey, historical studies, and ethnoarchaeology.

Preliminary results suggest that human occupation at Khirbet Faris is best understood not in terms of settlement or abandonment, but rather as a continuum of differing intensities of occupation, ranging from permanent, year-round settlement in structures built de novo, to seasonal occupation involving the reuse and slight modification of existing structures. Khirbet Faris was always occupied at some level on this scale, and there was extensive de novo building or major architectural modification of domestic and agricultural structures in the first–second centuries CE, fifth–mid-eighth centuries CE, twelfth–sixteenth centuries CE, and late nineteenth–early twentieth centuries. The postexcavation analysis of finds, especially of the organic remains, is providing evidence for the socioeconomic trends behind the variations in the scale of occupation.

BIBLIOGRAPHY

Johns, Jeremy, and Alison M. McQuitty. "The Fāris Project: Preliminary Report upon the 1986 and 1988 Seasons." *Levant* 21 (1989): 63–95.

Johns, Jeremy. "Islamic Settlement in Ard al-Karak." In *Studies in the History and Archaeology of Jordan*, vol. 4, edited by Ghazi Bisheh, pp. 363–368. Amman, 1992.

Johns, Jeremy. "The *Longue Durée*: State and Settlement Strategies in Southern Transjordan across the Islamic Centuries." In *Village, State, and Steppe: The Social Origins of Modern Jordan*, edited by Eugene L. Rogan and Tariq Tell, pp. 1–31. London and New York, 1994.

McQuitty, Alison M., and Robin Falkner. "The Fāris Project: Preliminary Report on the 1989, 1990, and 1991 Seasons." *Levant* 25 (1993): 37–61.

Miller, J. Maxwell, ed. *Archaeological Survey of the Kerak Plateau.* Atlanta, 1991.

Worschech, Udo F. Ch. *Northwest Arḍ el-Kerak, 1983 and 1984: A Preliminary Report.* Munich, 1985.

JEREMY JOHNS

FARMSTEADS. Research into the rural zone has burgeoned in the past two decades. Archaeologists of the Greek and Italian countryside offer studies ranging from luxurious wine-producing villas like Settefinestre to small-holdings of Roman colonists (Potter, 1987). In the Near East, surveys have produced a great body of data identifying and documenting the hinterland's farmstead—the buildings, fields, and activity loci of a farm—as a conspicuous feature of the ancient landscape and a telling indicator of the ebb and flow of settlement. Surface dating has demonstrated the association of farmsteads with periods of high-intensity land use, a barometer of the growth of the urban sphere and its sway over the surrounding territory. Thus, the appearance of farmsteads is related to heightened security conditions and the burgeoning demand for specialized economic goods—that is, marketable commodities. Nevertheless, there remains precious little published archaeological data regarding the hinterland's farmstead.

A host of difficulties hinder the detailed investigation of the farmstead: chief among these is the normally limited accumulation and eroded condition of artifact-bearing sediments that hamper the dating of the structures. Nevertheless, probes alongside the walls of rural buildings in the vicinity of Tell el-ʿUmeiri (Jordan), for example, often have been successful in pinpointing the buildings' period of construction. [*See* ʿUmeiri, Tell el-.] Architectural typologies—building size and materials—help to date those farmstead structures that themselves lack significant stratified remains. Still, the installations and features that surround a rural building almost always lack a stratigraphic context. However, certain features regularly appear in association with farmstead buildings. Rock-cut wine presses, cupholes, reservoirs, cisterns, and caves, along with terrace and perimeter walls, comprise a constellation of activity loci that was probably constructed contemporaneously with the farmstead building.

The advantages of farmstead residence include a decrease in time lost to commuting back and forth to the fields from town and a greater ability to devote constant attention and surveillance to the farm and its holdings. Both of these advantages permit a farming family to make more use of its labor force or a commercial enterprise to supervise its hired or enslaved labor force. The farmstead also offers greater efficiency in developing a holding of contiguous land units (as opposed to the fragmented holdings that characteristically surround villages). The disadvantages of rural residence include social isolation and vulnerability—greater risk through the inability to call upon neighbors for defense and reciprocal labor exchanges.

Khirbet er-Ras, just south of Jerusalem is a well-published farmstead (Edelstein et al., 1983). A fieldstone perimeter wall surrounded the site, enclosing an area of about 1.8 ha (4.5 acres) located on a slope just above a wadi floor. Terraces ran laterally across the farmstead, which also included two buildings, cisterns, a cave, a beam-type wine press, and other walled enclosures. The central house (about 12.8 × 9.7 m) is a courtyard ("four-room") house with remnants of paved flooring. Among the Late Iron II pottery (mostly holemouth jars and bowls), its excavators recovered two jar handles with *lmlk* ("the king's") seal impressions. These finds link the farmstead and its winery directly to the royal Judean economic program and suggest that the occupants of the farmstead were related socially and politically to the elite leadership. Though the term *farmstead* connotes the rural residence of a hardscrabble farming family, Iron Age farmsteads may well represent the penetration of the countryside by the managerial arm of the city-based administration.

[*See also* Agriculture.]

BIBLIOGRAPHY

Dar, Shim'on. *Landscape and Pattern: An Archaeological Survey of Samaria, 800 B.C.E.–636 C.E.* 2 vols. British Archaeological Reports, International Series, no. 308. Oxford, 1986. Decade-long survey with some excavation of sites. The rich rural life of this hill country region—lime kilns to threshing floors—is amply documented in word, line drawing, and photograph.

Edelstein, Gershon, et al. "Food Production and Water Storage in the Jerusalem Region" (in Hebrew). *Qadmoniot* 16.1 (1983): 16–23. Reports the authors' study of 'Ein-Yalu, Khirbet er-Ras, and el-Tauvil. See also Gershon Edelstein and Shimon Gibson, "Ancient Jerusalem's Rural Food Basket," *Biblical Archaeology Review* 8.4 (1982): 46–54.

Hopkins, David C. *The Highlands of Canaan: Agricultural Life in the Early Iron Age.* Sheffield, 1985. Contains a systematic, anthropologically oriented presentation of the nature of agriculture and its particular manifestations in Early Iron Age Palestine.

Potter, Timothy W. *Roman Italy.* Berkeley, 1987. Contains a succinct review of archaeology in the Italian countryside.

Younker, Randy W. "Architectural Remains from the Hinterland Survey." In *Madaba Plains Project 2: The 1987 Season at Tell el-'Umeiri and Vicinity and Subsequent Studies,* edited by Larry G. Herr et al. Berrien Springs, Mich., 1992.

DAVID C. HOPKINS

FATIMID DYNASTY. Shi'i in origin, the Fatimid dynasty takes as its eponym Fatimah, the daughter of the prophet Muhammad and the wife of 'Ali, the fourth of the earliest "rightly guided" caliphs. But for its real individuality, one must look to the schism within the Shi'i movement, which divided on politically strategical lines when Isma'il, the oldest son of the sixth Imam (in direct line from the sons of 'Ali and Fatimah), was superseded by his younger brother. Part of the Shi'i community remained loyal to the senior line and espoused a policy of political intervention and subterfuge toward achieving legitimacy. This group was known as the Isma'ili branch, and those who followed the younger Imam down to the twelfth and last Imam are termed Ithna 'Ashari, or "Twelver," a group regnant in Iran and espoused by a significant percentage of the present population in Iraq and Lebanon.

It has been difficult to forge direct lineage between the family of the Imam Isma'il and the founder of the Fatimid branch, Ubaydallah. Believers hold that the Imamate was vouchsafed to the father of Ubaydallah, Maymun al-Qaddah, by one of the heirs of Isma'il. This claim was so difficult to prove that the 'Abbasid caliphate refused to consider Fatimid legitimacy, denouncing them as impostors both to the Prophetic family and to the religious legitimacy, which it unwillingly acknowledged of the sons of 'Ali and Fatimah and their heirs. (Such acknowledgement motivated the 'Abbasid caliph al-Ma'mun to surrender his power temporarily to the Twelver Imam, 'Ali ibn Musa al-Kadhim, in AH 201/817 CE.) Nevertheless, Ubaydallah operated out of Salamiyah in Syria, setting up a network of undercover agents whose objective was to secure him a base of power from which to begin his vaunted quest to unseat the 'Abbasid caliphate. By shrewd and secret propaganda, these agents secured such a base among the Kutama Berbers, long disgruntled with the 'Abbasid/Aghlabid hold on the eastern half of the Maghrib. By 297/909, Ubaydallah was in the Maghrib and declared himself the rightful imam and caliph, taking the almost prophetic regnal title of al-Mahdi. He constructed a new capital, al-Mahdiyah south of the old seat of power in Ifriqiyah, Qayrawan. (Soon after the Umayyad ruler of Spain, 'Abd al-Rahman III, also assumed caliphal rank; thus by the mid-tenth century there were three caliphs in the *dar al-Islam* [Islamic world].)

Ubaydallah's success brought large sections of the Berber population to his side with whom he and his son, al-Qa'im, were able to subdue all of the Maghrib and, for a time, Sicily. Inevitably forays were made against Egypt, most signally in 913–915, 919–921, and 925. Eventually, the Fatimid general Jawhar (a slave of Sicilian origin) entered Fustat in Cairo in July 358/969 and welcomed his master, the caliph al-Mu'izz in 362/973. Very soon thereafter, the regents left in charge of the Fatimid dominions in the west returned to the Sunni allegiance, recognizing the suzerainty of the 'Abbasid caliph in Baghdad. (In the next century, the Fatimids of Egypt wrought their revenge by allowing free passage of the marauding tribes of Sulaym and Hilal through Egypt and into the Maghrib, which they proceeded to devastate.)

Until 567/1171 Egypt was the center, indeed the linchpin of Fatimid power. The Fatimids paid lip service to the quest toward the east and Baghdad, a quest that necessitated the conquest of most (but never all) of Greater Syria. (Yet for one year, 451/1059, the Fatimid caliph replaced the 'Abbasid caliph in the *khutbah* in Baghdad.) In time the Fatimids were thwarted by two successive phenomena, the rise of the Seljuk (Saljuq) dynasty, which was adamantly Sunni, and the appearance of the Crusaders toward the end of the eleventh century CE. Indeed, it was to the crusaders that the Fatimids lost their last holding in Syria, Ashkelon, in 548/1153. [See Crusader Period.]

With a few hard years following low Nile floods and subsequent dysynchronous famine (i.e., intermittent but related to the flooding pattern), the Fatimid period represents the apogee of wealth of medieval Egypt. On the economic side, one may cite three strokes of fortune: a superb, even reformed, agricultural system, which permitted three harvests in one year and found rich return in exporting the surplus of cereals, sugar, and linen; the presence of a supply of gold in the Wadi Allaqi in Nubia, so bounteous that there was very little silver coinage in the eleventh century and so well controlled that Egypt essentially set the prices for its imports, thereby freeing itself from the medieval vagaries of the barter system; and control of the Indian and Far Eastern trade, which shifted to the Red Sea sometime after the beginning of the eleventh century as a measure of how tremulous the Persian Gulf route had become. Although it is true that the effects of the famines in 446/1054–55 and 457–464/1065–1072 were almost catastrophic (all sources agree on the suffering), so much so that the caliph al-Mustansir was forced to disgorge the treasures of his palace to allay the disaster, it is equally true that the recovery was quick and the prosperity renewed. This process held true to the very end of the dynasty. In pursuit of wealth, a protean economic endeavor, the Crusader states at the behest of Venetian and Genoese merchants attacked Egypt in 563/1168 without cause. To counter such trespass Egypt was forced to call on its sworn Sunni enemy, Nur ad-Din of Damascus, to assist the dynasty already in the throes of its political dessication.

From the beginning, the Fatimid dynasty sought to call attention to its legitimacy and its ambitions. A whole new "city" was laid out to house the caliph and his entourage, the military and the governmental bureaus to the northeast of the conglomerate capital of Fustat/al-Askar/al-Qata'i. This royal quarter was dubbed *al-Qahira* (Mars, "the conquering star," was in the ascendant when the urban lines were laid out), which was transliterated *Cairo* by Italian merchants. Al-Azhar was founded a year after the conquest as a training school for the propagandists (sg., *al-da'i*) of the creed. Eventually, the caliph al-Hakim (386–411/996–1021) built a Friday mosque directly adjacent to the earlier brick north wall, which had a beautiful facade with an imposing monumental entrance (a copy of the one at the mosque of al-Mahdiyah) and superb stone minarets at either end. Toward the end of the long reign of al-Mustansir (427–487/1036–1094) and under the stress of Seljuk incursions into Greater Syria, a second set of stone walls was erected, which enclosed the mosque of al-Hakim on the north side. Through its three superb gates, Bab al-Nasir and Bab al-Futuh on the north and Bab al-Zuwaylah on the south, passed not only the population of the expanded capital (for the old one had simply crept up and glued itself unto al-Qahira), but men from all over the Mediterranean and the *dar al-Islam*, particularly those of the Isma'ili persuasion.

One other quite surprising aspect of the Fatimid rulers of Egypt, which contributed to their phenomenal success within Egypt, was the constant display of tolerance. It is true that some unusual forms of practice were introduced, particularly in the *adhan* (the call to prayer) and the Qur'anic verses used in inscriptions and recited during public ceremonies; nevertheless, Sunni allegiance was hardly touched during their two centuries of dynastic rule. Craftsmen and scholars were welcomed and lavishly patronized. Men of all religious persuasions assumed the wazirate (vizierate) or headed the various governmental *diwans* (administrative offices), and, in some cases, held military command. Though some converted, there was no policy of enforced conversion. Perhaps only the leadership of the *duwwat*, the system of training and directing the Fatimid propagandists, was allocated specifically to a Fatimid Isma'ili Shi'ite. The Shi'ite worship of the 'Alid and Imamate families, which accorded with Egyptian traditions concerning the dead and their monuments, in taking the form of rather splendid mausolea and their visitation, struck a sympathetic chord throughout Egypt. (It is interesting to note that not a single Fatimid public inscription was destroyed or defaced by Salah ad-Din and his successors.) In their public rituals, public ceremonies, and court etiquette the Fatimids raised the tone of society to a level that had only been touched during the Ptolemaic period.

Quite another aspect of the Fatimids' effect upon Egypt was in the realm of art and architecture. They freed artists from their implicit dependence on 'Abbasid models, as is quite obvious from the two sets of stucco decoration at al-Azhar. On the one hand, the pre-Islamic classical style, which is preserved in Coptic monasteries, reemerged particularly in the variations on the vine and *rinceau* (circle or spiral) themes; on the other hand, a whole cycle of courtly motifs came to dominate the arts. These decorations were available to the bourgeois as well as the royal patrons. Insinuating all was the apogee of floriated Kufic calligraphy, which is easily traced on the buildings of the period. In architecture the patrons of the Fatimid period respected innovation above all; there was no low point, no tapering off of form or decoration, from al-Azhar to the mosque of as-Salih Tala'i built in 555/1160. Unlike the Mamluks style, the Fatimids had an aesthetic of decorous verve subsuming the undercurrents of millennial Egyptian motifs and influences from countries as diverse as Tunisia, China, Byzantium. In the Fatimid epoch, marriage contracts were woven in silk; chess was played with rock crystal figures; family tombs were replete with mosque and bath; luster ware and imported porcelain were readily available; and the textiles of the world could be had for a bride's trousseau.

Yet for all the public prestige and prosperity, the continuity was internally challenged from the beginning. Legitimacy may have been the constricting problem. Although European merchants and Byzantine diplomats beat a path to Cairo, Sunni Islam was as determined to destroy the Fatimid dynasty as to retrieve the lands usurped by the Crusaders. The overwhelming majority of Egyptians did not convert to Isma'ilism; hence the need for external military personnel. The Berbers were undependable and melted back to the Maghrib; the black troops (Nubians and Ethiopians) were obstreperous and a civil menace; Daylami Persians never came in sufficient numbers; and itinerant Turks made manifest their quixotic loyalties. A strong caliph such as al-Hakim went to extremes in ordering a decent 'Alid society, including burning the Church of the Holy Sepulcher in Jerusalem in 400/1009–10. Others came to depend on military strong men, such as Badr al-Jamali, a converted Armenian, who restored order in Cairo and built the second set of walls. He was succeeded by his son al-Afdal who interfered in the succession process following the death of al-Mustansir in 487/1094 and had a more pliable second son, al-Musta'li (487–495/1094–1101) put on the throne rather than al-Nidhar the eldest, thus repeating the pattern of the imam Isma'il's rejection. Once broken, it was almost impossible to resurrect caliphal influence and direction; one caliph, al-Hafidh (525–544/1130–1149) was only a cousin of his predecessor. The weak and the young succeeded one another; they were pawns of unstable wazirs and/or powerful generals, who had to be eliminated at great cost to the dynasty's prestige. All such fissiparous tendencies did not impinge on the public prosperity of Fatimid Egypt, but they weakened whatever direction the dynasty signaled to the populace. When the Crusaders attacked, help had to be sought from the Sunni constituencies, making the return to orthodoxy inevitable.

In September 567/1171 Salah ad-Din al-Ayyubi (Saladin) had the *khutbah* (the Friday sermon) read in the name of the 'Abbasid caliph in Baghdad. As sultan of Egypt, he used its resources to commence his conquest of Greater Syria and his counter-Crusade, which culminated in the retaking of Jerusalem in 583/1187. He treated the Fatimid family with great kindness, simply making sure there was very little procreation.

The dynasty was remembered outside Egypt through two movements: the Druze in Greater Syria, who maintained a sacral reverence for the caliph al-Hakim; and the Nizari Isma'ilis known more familiarly as the Assassins, from which today the Iranian, Indian, and African branches give allegiance to the family of the Aga Khan. Within Egypt, the memory faltered after the advent of the Ayyubids and the dominance of the Mamluks who moved the center of government from al-Qahira to the new Citadel. The two paradisiacal palaces of the Fatimids along the great north–south artery were reduced and then removed to make way for imposing religious structures. Only in the very beginning of the fourteenth century does a glimmer of interest reappear in the quest of the historian al-Maqrizi to understand the Fatimid effect in Egypt's history. The people of Cairo have continued to visit and venerate the Fatimid tombs to the present time. Perhaps in the pomp and prestige they evinced, however, the historian senses the move from the puissant autonomy of the Tulunids to an achieved independence of Egypt within the fuller medieval Islamic polity. This Fatimid legacy has proven more important than their chimerical origins.

[*See also* Ayyubid–Mamluk Dynasties; Cairo; Egypt, *article on* Islamic Egypt; *and* Fustat.]

BIBLIOGRAPHY

For the best digest of the primary sources and analysis of the research up to c. 1970 on the subject, see the incomparable article by Marius Canard, "Fāṭimids," in *Encyclopaedia of Islam*, new ed., vol. 2, pp. 850–862 (Leiden, 1960–). (The accompanying article on Fatimid art by Georges Marçais needs serious updating.)

A number of new editions of older sources have appeared which throw considerably more penetrating light on the history of the Fatimids. See, for example, al-Musabbihi, *Al-juz' al-arba'in min akhbar misr*, edited by Thierry Bianquis and Ayman Fu'ad Sayyid (Cairo, 1978); Ibn al-Ma'mun al-Bata'ihi, *Nusus min akhbar misr*, edited by Ayman Fu'ad Sayyid (Cairo, 1983); and, though later, Claude Cahen's various studies on the known fragments of the bureaucrat al-Makhzumi, which can be extrapolated to take in the final part of the Fatimid dynasty, collected in *Makhzumiyat* (Leiden, 1977). For the death and veneration of al-Hakim, see Joseph van Ess, *Chiliastische Erwartungen und die Versuchung der Göttlichkeit der Kalif al-Hakim (386–411 H.)* (Heidelberg, 1977).

All the new subgroup Fatimists are hugely in debt to the extraordinary work of S. D. Goitein based on the examination and rescension of the Geniza documents. Canard surveyed all the printed preparations toward Goitein's five-volume study, *A Mediterranean Society* (Berkeley, 1967–1988), but would have been very slightly dismayed to find that the materials were more pertinent to the twelfth than the eleventh century. A sixth volume of referential indices has been published jointly by Goitein and Paula Sanders (Berkeley, 1993). For the analysis of the Fatimid financial/commercial system, in a sense the first "spin-off" of Goitein's survey, see Abraham Udovitch, *Partnership and Profit in Medieval Islam* (Princeton, 1970).

Two very important monographs have recently appeared which flesh out Canard's rather acute analysis of the subjects: Paula Sanders, *Ritual, Politics, and the City in Fatimid Cairo* (Sarasota Springs, N.Y., 1994), and Leila Al-Imad, *The Fatimid Vizierate, 969–1172* (Berlin, 1990). Yaacov Lev's *State and Society in Fatimid Egypt* (Leiden, 1991) is much less convincing as a commentary on Canard's precis. For the most insightful analysis of the propaganda bureau *(duwwat)*, see Paul Walker, "The Ismaili Da'wa in the Reign of the Fatimid Caliph al-Ḥākim," *Journal of the American Research Center in Egypt* 30 (1993): 161–182.

For the marriage contract on linen, see Y. Ragib, "Un contrat de marriage sur soie d'Égypte fatimide," *Annales Islamologiques* 16 (1980): 31–37. Two important articles by Oleg Grabar discuss the artistic wealth of the Fatimids and its meaning: "Imperial and Urban Art in Islam: The Subject Matter of Fatimid Art," in *Colloque international sur l'histoire du Caire*, pp. 173–191 (Cairo, 1969), and "Fatimid Art: Precursor or Culmination," in *Isma'ili Contributions to Islamic Culture*, edited by Seyyed Hossein Nasr, pp. 207–224 (Tehran, 1977). Two important studies on the architecture of Fustat during the Fatimid period are Antoni A. Ostrasz, "The Architectural Material for the Study of the Domestic Architecture at Fustat," *Africana Bulletin* 26 (1977): 57–

86, and Wladyslaw B. Kubiak and George T. Scanlon, *Fustat Expedition: Final Report*, vol. 2, *Fustat-C* (Winona Lake, Ind., 1986). The recent work of Roland Gayraud on the Fatimid Funerary Complex at Stabl Antar in Fustat has not been fully published, but see his reports in *Annales Islamologiques* 23 (1987): 55–72; 25 (1991): 57–88; and 27 (1993): 225–232. Nothing specifically Fatimid has been published from the Polish excavations at Kom el-Dikka in Alexandria; however these results should form a governor to the excavations at Fustat and elsewhere in Egypt. A newer light on the question of Chinese imports and their influence can be found in George T. Scanlon, "Egypt and China: Trade and Imitation," in *Islam and the Trade of Asia*, edited by D. S. Richards, pp. 265–274 (Oxford, 1970); and B. Gyllensvard, "Recent Finds of Chinese Ceramics at Fustat," *Bulletin of Far Eastern Antiquities* (Stockholm), no. 45 (1973): 99–119, and no. 47 (1975): 99–119.

For a more searching survey of the post-Canardian bibliography, the reader should consult the *Index Islamicus* for the work of scholars such as Ayman Fu'ad Sayyid, Thierry Bianquis, Abbas Hamdani, Oleg Grabar, Y. Ragib, and George T. Scanlon, as well as the article "Fustat," *infra*.

GEORGE T. SCANLON

FEINAN, site located at the eastern margin of the Wadi 'Arabah, halfway between the Dead Sea and the Red Sea (30°37′36″ N, 35°29′ E). The Byzantine ruins of Feinan (Fenan, Phinon, Punon) are but one prominent archaeological site in a copper ore district that covers about 500 sq km (310 sq. mi.). It is part of the original sedimentary copper deposit of Timna'-Feinan-Eilat-Abu Kusheiba, which is divided by the tectonic activities of the Wadi 'Arabah rift valley. [*See* Timna' (Negev).] In the Feinan area, more than 250 ancient mines and 150,000–200,000 tons of slag were discovered. The history and development of metallurgy in the area has been studied by archaeologists and scientists from the Deutsches Bergbau-Museum, Bochum, Germany, and the Jordanian Department of Antiquities since 1984. The area has been intensively surveyed and settlements from different periods and mines have been excavated (Wadi Ghwair 1, Tell Wadi Feinan, Wadi Fidan 4, Khirbet Hamra Ifdan, Barqa el-Hetiye, Wadi Khalid, Qalb Ratiye). Analytical work for provenience studies and reconstructions of smelting processes is done in the laboratory on ore, slag, and metal.

Archaeological excavation and the radiocarbon dating of fifty-two samples have made it possible to trace the exploitation of the ore deposit over a period of nine thousand years. The earliest settlements belonged to the Pre-Pottery Neolithic period, when copper ores ("greenstones") were utilized for making beads and for cosmetic purposes. The ores were traded as far as 'Ain Ghazal in Transjordan and Jericho in ancient Palestine. Samples of pure copper ores have also been found at Tell Wadi Feinan (sixth/fifth millennium), some 2 km (1 mi.) west of the ruins of Feinan. Pyrometallurgy developed in the middle of the fourth millennium. Metal was smelted on a small scale inside of settlements ("household metallurgy"). High-grade secondary ores were used that left only very small amounts of slag.

Copper ore was also traded to Abu Matar, Shiqmim, Wadi Ghazzeh, and Tell Maqass/'Aqaba, where it was smelted inside the Chalcolithic settlements. [*See* Shiqmim.]

At Feinan, mining and smelting peaked in the Early Bronze Age II–III (first half of the third millennium). New technologies, such as the use of manganese oxide for fluxing, increased the exploitation of ores considerably. Twelve slag heaps in the area of Feinan point to a large-scale copper production that was the basis for the export of metal to cities in the Levant. The survey produced only sparse evidence for metal production there in the Middle Bronze Age. As at Timna', production increased again in the Late Bronze Age. Excavations at Barqa el-Hetiye/Feinan revealed Midianite pottery from the thirteenth/twelfth centuries BCE.

Innovations in mining and smelting developed during the Iron Age IIB and IIC, and copper was produced on an industrial scale. The industry was organized by the Edomite towns on the Jordanian plateau, such as Buseirah and Umm el-Biyara. [*See* Buseirah and Umm el-Biyara.] Remote parts of the ore deposit were made accessible by sinking shafts as deep as 70 m. Smelting was concentrated at two major centers—at Khirbet en-Nahas ("ruins of copper") and at Feinan—and led to the formation of the largest slag heaps in the southern Levant. This copper boom, which is paralleled in other copper districts in the Old World, arose in a period when the popularity of iron and steel increased.

Major mining activity resumed centuries later, in the Roman period (first century BCE—fifth century CE). By then the richest minerals appear to have been so completely exhausted that the Romans had to resort to low-grade copper ore. The church fathers Eusebius and Hieronymus (see Geerlings, 1985) describe the cruelty of the work in the mines of Feinan ("*damnatio ad metallam*"). One of the most impressive technological monuments is the mine at Umm el-Amad (6,600 sq m), some 15 km (9 mi.) south of Feinan. It is the only complete mine known from the Roman period. The Romans transported the ore over a distance of 12 km (7 mi.) to a central site located very close to the ruins of Byzantine Feinan. The large amount of metal produced here is demonstrated by the 50,000–70,000 tons of slag left behind.

After 500 CE, Feinan's role as a major copper supplier in the southern Levant ended; however, textual evidence and the remains of churches and a monastery indicate that the town maintained a certain importance as the bishop's see in the Early Byzantine period. In the Mamluk period, some minor mining and smelting activities took place there.

The copper produced at Feinan throughout history is characterized by a low trace-element content—except for lead, which sometimes ranges up to the percent level. This indicates that high-purity copper must not necessarily derive from native copper, clearly distinguishing Feinan copper from the copper-arsenic-antimony alloys found at Chalcolithic sites such as Nahal Mishmar, Shiqmim, and Tell Abu

Matar. The lead isotope ratios are clearly different from ore deposits in Cyprus, Anatolia, and the Aegean Sea, but it is difficult to distinguish between Timnaʿ and Feinan.

[*See also* Mines and Mining.]

BIBLIOGRAPHY

Adams, Russel, and Hermann Genz. "Excavations at Wadi Fidan 4: A Chalcolithic Village Complex in the Copper Ore District of Feinan, Southern Jordan." *Palestine Exploration Quarterly* 127 (1995).

Fritz, Volkmar. "Ergebnisse der Grabungen in Barqa el-Hetiya im Gebiet von Fenan, Wadi el-Araba (Jordanien)." *Zeitschrift des Deutschen Palästina-Vereins* (in press).

Geerlings, Willem. "Zum biblischen und historischen Hintergrund der Bergwerke von Fenan in Jordanien." *Der Anschnitt* 5–6 (1985): 158–162.

Hauptmann, Andreas, et al. "Archäometallurgische und bergbauarchäologische Untersuchungen im Gebiet von Fenan, Wadi Arabah." *Der Anschnitt* 5–6 (1985): 163–195.

Hauptmann, Andreas. "The Earliest Periods of Copper Metallurgy in Feinan." In *Old World Archaeometallurgy*, edited by Andreas Hauptmann et al., pp. 119–135. Der Anschnitt, Beiheft 7. Bochum, 1989.

Hauptmann, Andreas, et al. "Early Copper Produced at Feinan, Wadi Araba, Jordan: The Composition of Ores and Copper." *Archeomaterials* 6.1 (1992): 1–33.

Hauptmann, Andreas, et al. "Chalcolithic Copper Smelting: New Evidence from Excavations at Feinan/Jordan." *Proceedings of the 29th International Conference on Archeometry.* Ankara, 1995.

Knauf, E. Axel, and C. J. Lenzen. "Edomite Copper Industry." In *Studies in the History and Archaeology of Jordan,* vol. 3, edited by Adnan Hadidi, pp. 83–88. Amman, 1987.

Najjar, Mohammed, et al. "Tell Wadi Feinan: The First Pottery Neolithic Tell in Southern Jordan." *Annual of the Department of Antiquities of Jordan* 34 (1990): 27–56.

ANDREAS HAUPTMANN

FIELD, HENRY (1902–1986), physical anthropologist, active in Iraq, Iran, Jordan, Saudi Arabia, India, Pakistan, Europe, and Northeast Africa and prolific writer and editor. Field was born in Chicago and received his B.A. (1925) and D.Sc. (1937) from Oxford University. His appointments in anthropology include the Field Museum, Chicago (1926–1941); United States Navy, Washington, D.C. (1941–1945); Peabody Museum, Cambridge, Massachusetts (1950–1986); and the University of Miami, Florida (1966–1986). He directed the Field Research Projects, Coconut Grove, Florida (1963–1986), issuing an eclectic series of reports begun in 1953 at the University of Miami Press. The series focused on the anthropology, archaeology, and natural history of Southwest Asia.

Under his curatorship at the Field Museum, the influential Halls of Prehistoric Mankind and of the Races of Mankind were created in 1933. The cooperative efforts involved were described in Field's *The Track of Man: Adventures of an Anthropologist* (New York, 1953). The great range of modern humans throughout the world was represented in the exhibition by bronze figures sculpted from life by Malvina Hoffman.

Expeditions to Iraq and Iran provided material for Field's memoir on the Arabs of central Iraq (Field, 1935), volumes on these peoples (Field, 1939; 1952), and many short articles. An expedition to Northeast Africa yielded anthropological contributions on the Sudan and Egypt (Field, 1949; 1952). Field reviewed and interpreted anthropological research reported from eleven countries in Southwest Asia (Field, 1956; 1961). His 1925–1950 survey work in Jordan, Arabia, and Iraq was published in 1960 (Field, 1960). Expeditions to India and Pakistan widened his views on this link in human history (Field, 1970). Field is altogether credited with more than six hundred publications.

As a naval officer and anthropological adviser to U.S. presidents Roosevelt and Truman (1941–1945), Field and his coworkers reviewed world literature on patterns of migration and settlement (Field, 1969). His bibliographies of Southwest Asia (Field, 1953–1961) remain central for students and advanced researchers studying the region.

BIBLIOGRAPHY

Field, Henry. *Arabs of Central Iraq: Their History, Ethnology, and Physical Characteristics with Introduction by Sir Arthur Keith; Field Museum–Oxford University Joint Expedition to Mesopotamia.* Field Museum of Natural History, Anthropology Memoirs, vol. 4. Chicago, 1935. Pioneering presentation containing more than a thousand photographs and anthropometric data on modern Arabs of the Kish area. The text is expanded in the 1939 report (below) and supplemented by Field with articles in 1937, 1940, 1943, 1950–1952, and 1955.

Field, Henry. *Contributions to the Anthropology of Iraq.* 2 vols. Field Museum of Natural History, Anthropological Series, vol. 29.1–2. Chicago, 1939. Extends early work at Kish, with discussions of land, people, and physical anthropology of racial groups.

Field, Henry. *The Northern Sudan.* University of California, African Expedition Scientific Paper, no. 1. Berkeley, 1949. Basic early anthropological data.

Field, Henry. *The Anthropology of Iraq.* 3 vols. Papers of the Peabody Museum of Archaeology and Ethnology, vol. 46.1–3. Cambridge, Mass., 1951–1952. Kurds and other groups.

Field, Henry. *Contributions to the Anthropology of the Faiyum, Sinai, Sudan, and Kenya.* Berkeley, 1952. Early observations and interpretations, some of seldom-studied groups.

Field, Henry. *Bibliography of Southwestern Asia.* 7 vols. Coral Gables, Fla., 1953–1961. Indispensable source of selected titles in anthropology, anthropogeography, and natural history from Anatolia to the Arabian Sea, from the Nile River to the Indus Valley. Access is facilitated by subject indices released by Field and others. See as well the eight supplements compiled by Field and E. M. Laird (Coconut Grove, Fla., 1968–1973).

Field, Henry. *Ancient and Modern Man in Southwestern Asia.* 2 vols. Coral Gables, Fla., 1956–1961. Original observations and sources from the literature, with extensive anthropometric data, maps, and graphs. Twenty-nine plates show Paleolithic and Neolithic implements from Saudi Arabia.

Field, Henry, et al. *North Arabian Desert Archaeological Survey, 1925–50.* Papers of the Peabody Museum of Archaeology and Ethnology, vol. 45.2. Cambridge, Mass., 1960.

Field, Henry. *"M" Project for F.D.R.: Studies on Migration and Settlement.* Coconut Grove, Fla., 1969. Definitive summary of 665 reports, compiled in 1943–1945 at the Library of Congress, Washington,

D.C., on world population, refugees, migration, and settlement, that are essential for understanding these historic problems.

Field, Henry. *Contributions to the Physical Anthropology of the Peoples of India*. Coconut Grove, Fla., 1970. Physical observations interpreted in support of the author's late views on the subcontinent's role in the historical distributions of human populations.

WILLIAM C. OVERSTREET

FIELD CONSERVATION. Each archaeological discovery, from the merest fragment of an object to a very complex structure, should be maintained with care, ensuring that it can be admired and studied by future generations. This is a generally accepted premise, but of the considerable amount of material buried in antiquity, only a fraction survives. What does survive can be said to have achieved an equilibrium between itself and its environment: when excavated material is exposed to atmospheric conditions different from those to which it was accustomed, its equilibrium is upset and, if no care is taken, the material will eventually disintegrate. Some archaeological discoveries are portable and can be lifted and transferred to a safer location for conservation and study. Others (i.e., remains of built structures) cannot be moved and must be treated and protected in situ.

Portable Artifacts. Classified into organic and inorganic, recovered portable objects are crafted or otherwise produced in a variety of materials.

Organic material. Leather, bone, ivory, wood, and textiles are among the organic materials that rarely survive. When they do, their condition is usually fragmentary and very fragile. Organic material buried under favorable conditions—in permanently dry, wet (as a bog), or freezing circumstances—has the best chance of survival. For example, if an ivory object excavated from damp soil dries quickly, it will crack or warp. [*See* Bone, Ivory, and Shell; Textiles.]

Inorganic material. Objects out of stone, terra cotta, metal, and glass are more resistant to decay than those out of organic materials, but, for example, if a stable, dry bronze object gets wet, it will begin to corrode. [*See* Metals; Vitreous Materials.]

When an object of any kind is found in the field, it must first be protected so that the equilibrium that existed between it and the environment will not be radically disturbed. Before it is removed from the ground, however, photographs must be taken of it in situ, so that its exact position, condition, and relationship to its surroundings are recorded. This information will be useful to the laboratory conservator and restorer. How carefully an object is removed from the ground increases or diminishes the success of the available preservation techniques that can be used on it in the laboratory. [*See* Recording Techniques; Restoration and Conservation.]

An artifact, whether it is recovered from an archaeological excavation, survey, or rescue operation, or it is a chance find

(see below), must be lifted and transferred for treatment and protection. When it is not possible to lift an object in one piece—as with a very fragile artifact or one that is not flat (e.g., a skeleton or a rhyton)—the block-lifting method is recommended: the object is lifted together with the soil that surrounds it (in a "block") and is then transferred to the laboratory for treatment. If an object needs consolidation before it is lifted, it must be cleaned well, in situ, using the least possible quantity of consolidant, which subsequently often will have to be removed in the laboratory. An emulsion will be needed, for example, when the object is damp and needs consolidation. In any case, when used, the consolidant must be allowed to dry before the object can be lifted.

The packaging, transfer, and storage of objects found in the field are also components of field conservation. Their objective is to keep the artifact in a stable condition until it undergoes conservation treatment in a conservation laboratory.

Structural Remains. Built structures, usually out of stone, brick, mud brick, wood, or some combination of these materials, are stationary artifacts. Because wood is an organic material that survives only under very favorable conditions, "building material" usually refers to stone, brick, and mud brick. Secondary materials used in construction are mortar, fresco, and mosaic. [*See* Wall Paintings; Mosaics.] All of these materials must be protected immediately upon discovery, and on a long-term basis must be protected against weathering (Price, 1984).

Systematic Excavation. Conservation complications begin in the field, when important late remains are built on top of earlier ones that also need excavating (Sease, 1992). Ideally, the latest structure can be transferred as intact as possible to a nearby location. However, an excavation's budget and intentions toward protecting the site, structures, and artifacts may be incompatible. Thus, moving a structure is rarely practical because of lack of funds, space, or personnel or because its building material is in reuse (belongs to an earlier period) or the existing structures were used in more than one period. When, however, a built structure is to be dismantled or transferred, photographs, drawings, measurements, and other documentation must be made before it is disassembled, and its individual stones must be numbered for re-placement.

When the last layer to be excavated is exposed, it must be protected immediately, as must its portable discoveries (see above). It is best to build a shelter for it. Some opposition to this method exists, based on the argument that a shelter will disturb the environment. If, however, the shelter or roofing is compatible in material, shape, and color, it has a better chance of being accepted (Getty Conservation Institute, 1991).

Features associated with structures, such as mosaics or frescoes, should be sheltered within the structure. If there is no danger of theft, all should remain in situ. Otherwise, they must be lifted and transferred to an otherwise protected location.

When a site is of archaeological, historical, ethnic, religious, or touristic interest and will likely draw many visitors, paths should be built to protect both the visitors and the site. When a site is discovered accidentally and excavation is either postponed or initiated but then halted, or if a site is isolated and protection against theft or weathering may not be possible, full recording procedures should be followed, including photographs and drawings. The site should then be backfilled, including using geotextiles, a patented synthetic substance, separating the finds from the fill. In a rescue excavation the only option is usually to remove structures, after documenting them as completely as possible. Only rarely will it be possible to transfer them to another location.

[See also Artifact Conservation; and Photography, article on Photography of Fieldwork and Artifacts.]

BIBLIOGRAPHY

Dowman, Elizabeth A. *Conservation in Field Archaeology.* London, 1970. Deals with newly excavated finds.

Getty Conservation Institute. *The Conservation of the Orpheus Mosaic at Paphos, Cyprus.* Marina del Rey, Calif., 1991. Describes the process of rolling, treating, reinstalling, and protecting a mosaic with a specially designed shelter.

Hodges, Henry, and Miguel Angel Corzo, eds. *In Situ Archaeological Conservation: Proceedings of the Meetings, April 6–13, 1986, Mexico.* Marina del Rey, 1987. Deals with the in situ conservation of different materials.

Price, N. P. Stanley, ed. *Conservation on Archaeological Excavations with Particular Reference to the Mediterranean Area.* Rome, 1984. Collection of essays on the treatment and protection of excavated finds: mosaics, stucco, mud-brick structures.

Sease, Catherine. *A Conservation Manual for the Field Archaeologist.* 2d ed. Los Angeles, 1992. Excellent manual for field conservation.

ANDREAS GEORGIADES

FIRST JEWISH REVOLT. The main source for the First Jewish Revolt, also called the Great War, is Josephus' *Jewish War* (books 2–7) as well as his autobiography, the *Vita.* The events of the first century leading up to the war can be found in his *Antiquities* (books 18–20, with parallels in his *War* books 1–2). Except for Tacitus's *Histories* 5, very little is known about the revolt from gentile Greek and Latin sources. The revolt, which started in 66 CE had several causes. It ended with the total defeat of the Jews and the destruction of their Temple in Jerusalem. Scholars have pointed to socioeconomic causes—that is, to the growing rift between the rich and the poor in Palestine. They have emphasized the polarity between Jews and non-Jews there, religious conflicts with the Romans, and Rome's alienation from the ruling class (see below). The circumstances that brought about the war were primarily the cruel and foolish behavior of some of the later Roman procurators and the hostile activity of the extreme Jewish groups usually identified with the Zealots and the Sicarii. In the years that led to the outbreak of the revolt the latter two became factions in the so-called Fourth Philosophy group, which claimed that no ruler except God could rule the Jews, and therefore the Jews must free themselves from the yoke of Roman rule in Palestine.

The first Jewish Revolt was preceeded by intensive fighting between the gentiles and the Jews in the mixed cities of Palestine. In April/May 66 CE, both the emperor and the Roman governor of Palestine, Florus, sided with the non-Jews of Caesarea in a conflict there. Florus irritated the Jews even more by his confiscation of seventeen talents from the Temple's treasury. As a result there was a disturbance in Jerusalem that led to the seizure of the Temple by the crowds and to clashes between the Jews and the two Roman cohorts brought up to Jerusalem from Caesarea. When Agrippa II, king of the former tetrarchy of Philip, heard of these stormy events, he hurried to Jerusalem and attempted to stop the insurrection. His speech is given at length by Josephus (*War* 2.345–401).

Agrippa's attempts turned out to be futile, and the situation in Jerusalem worsened when Eleazar, the son of Ananias the high priest, who was a clerk in the Temple, persuaded his colleagues to stop the daily sacrifice offered on behalf of the emperor. Most of the more moderate circles in Jerusalem were against this decision, but they could not oppose the militant majority. This led to civil strife within Jerusalem in summer 66 CE. The Jewish leaders of Jerusalem and the high priests called in an army, provided by both Florus and Agrippa II, and fought the rebels who were holding the lower city and the Temple Mount. Within a short time the rebels, together with the Sicarii, managed to gain the upper hand against Agrippa's soldiers, the Romans, and the moderates, who were concentrated in the upper city. While doing so the rebels caused a great deal of damage: they set fire to the public archives in order to gain sympathy from the debtors in the city. In addition, the high priest Ananias was murdered; Agrippa's troops were driven out; and the Roman soldiers were killed, in spite of an agreement they had reached beforehand with the rebels. The Sicarii left Jerusalem after one of their leaders, who had gone to sacrifice in the Temple arrayed in royal robes, was murdered. They retreated to Masada and did not thereafter participate in the war in Jerusalem. [See Masada.]

While these events were taking place in Jerusalem, a terrible war broke out all over the country between non-Jews and Jews, in places such as Caesarea, Philadelphia (Amman), Gerasa (Jerash), Scythopolis (Beth-Shean), and Ashkelon. As a result of these events, Cestius Gallus, the governor of Syria, attempted to quell the fighting. He advanced with the Twelfth Legion and forces he had collected from various towns and then made his way toward Jerusalem (September/October 66 CE). The Jews managed to crush the

Twelfth Legion, an event that, tragically, encouraged them to read the military and political map falsely. They began to prepare for their own political independence as early as 66 CE, as can be seen clearly from the first series of coins they struck at the time (Meshorer, 1982). The nature of the Jewish central government created at this juncture, as well as of the generals chosen to command the different regions of Palestine is revealing. All were selected from among the moderate section of the aristocracy and from the priestly order; no Zealots were included. At this point many still thought that God had led them into the war, and that they would succeed.

The central government in Jerusalem was active during the winter of 66 and in the first months of 67 CE, but it had difficulty imposing its influence on the different regions in the country. Some local leaders, such as Shim'on bar Giora acted independently. He, with a private army, terrorized and robbed the rich in the region of Akraba in Samaria and later terrorized the Jews in the region of Idumea. There was also tension between the central government and Josephus (Yoseph ben Mattithias), who was the general in the Galilee. The support the central government gave to Josephus's fierce opponent, John of Gischala (Gush Halav), at the beginning of 67 CE shows that it did not control the country very decisively (Josephus, *War* 2.583–594; *Life*).

By the time the Roman general Vespasian landed in Palestine in spring 67 CE, there was no united Jewish front against Rome. It does seem, however, that the majority did support the first stages of the war, which had been presented as a defensive war against Rome and the gentiles living in the land of Israel. Opposition to the war was symbolized by cities such as Sepphoris, which minted coins in 68 CE with the inscription "the city of peace" (Meshorer, 1982). [*See* Sepphoris.] The Galilee fell quickly to the Romans after the immediate collapse of Josephus's army. He himself was besieged by the Romans in Jotapata (Yodefat). The fortress there fell to the Romans in June or July 67 CE. [*See* Jotapata.] Josephus surrendered to the Romans, and when he appeared before Vespasian prophesied to him that the general would become the future emperor of Rome. By the end of 67 the Romans had managed to regain control of the whole of the Galilee and part of the Golan (*War* 4.1–83). Thousands of Jews were killed or deported to be sold as slaves. During this time the Roman forces also demolished Jaffa and killed 11,600 Samaritans (*War* 3.414–431; 3.307–315). The campaign of 67 CE ended with the conquest of Jamnia and Ashdod. After a winter break, Vespasian resumed operations, and by the end of spring 68, the whole of Transjordan, Judea (Judah), and Idumea were subdued. Only Jerusalem and Masada were left unconquered. Thus started the last stage of the war.

Meanwhile, civil strife had begun in Jerusalem, caused in part by the defeat of the Jews of Palestine. Vespasian's operations in Palestine in late spring 68 resulted in a terrible refugee problem in the capital. Many Jews had escaped from the Romans to Jerusalem, which was still firmly in Jewish hands. One group that reached there safely in autumn 67 was led by John of Gischala. In June 68, Nero committed suicide, and a great turmoil ensued in the empire. In summer 69, the legions declared Vespasian emperor. Titus, his son, was left to continue the war in Judea, but he did not manage to continue the operation against Jerusalem until spring of 70. Thus, for about two years the citizens inside the city, instead of preparing for an imminent war, carried out dreadful attrocities against each other. The Zealots fought both each other and the moderate groups and, among many others, murdered two of the most distinguished moderate leaders, Hanan the high priest and Joseph ben Gurion. It was because of, and during, these fights that the moderate Rabban Johanan ben Zakkai left Jerusalem for Javneh. According to a rabbinic tradition, it was ben Zakkai who allegedly greeted the emperor with the words "Vive domine imperator" when he met him (B.T., *Git.* 50 a–b).

In spring of 70 Titus besieged Jerusalem. John of Gischala managed to penetrate the courts of the Temple compound and brought the Zealots under his control. Simeon bar Giora became the high commander of most of the city, while John of Gischala was responsible for the Antonia fortress and the Temple Mount. Nevertheless, a great deal of fighting continued within the city during the siege, described by Josephus, who was with the Roman forces outside the city (*War* 5–6). Josephus made continuous attempts to encourage the besieged Jews to surrender, but his attempts were in vain. The city fell to the Romans on the tenth of Tammuz (summer 70 CE), and the Temple was destroyed. The so-called Burnt House and other archaeological remains excavated in the upper city of Jerusalem are mute evidence of the city's last hours (Avigad, 1983). Masada fell in spring of 73, after a three-year siege. The Jewish Revolt was over, and the whole of Palestine was again subdued. Reactions to the destruction of Jerusalem and the Temple can be found in certain of the Gospels, *Luke–Acts*, in *2 Baruch*, *4 Ezra*, as well as in rabbinic sources.

[*See also* Biblical Temple; Jerusalem.]

BIBLIOGRAPHY

Avigad, Nahman. *Discovery Jerusalem*. Nashville, 1983.
Cohen, S. J. D. *Josephus in Galilee and Rome: His Vita and Development as a Historian*. Leiden, 1979.
Goodman, Martin D. *The Ruling Class of Judaea: The Origins of the Jewish Revolt against Rome, A.D. 66–70*. Cambridge, 1987.
Hachlili, Rachel. *Ancient Jewish Art and Archaeology in the Land of Israel*. Leiden, 1988.
Hengel, Martin. *The "Hellenization" of Judaea in the First Century after Christ*. London, 1989.
Hengel, Martin. *The Zealots: Investigations into the Jewish Freedom Movement in the Period from Herod I until 708 AD*. Edinburgh, 1989.
Kasher, Aryeh. *Jews and Hellenistic Cities in Eretz Israel*. Tübingen, 1990.

Kuhnen, Hans-Peter. *Palästina in griechisch-römischer Zeit.* Munich, 1990.

Mendels, Doron. *The Rise and Fall of Jewish Nationalism.* New York, 1992.

Meshorer, Ya'acov. *Ancient Jewish Coinage.* 2 vols. Dix Hills, N.Y., 1982.

Rajak, Tessa. *Josephus: The Historian and His Society.* London, 1983.

Schürer, Emil. *The History of the Jewish People in the Age of Jesus Christ, 175 B.C.–A.D. 135.* 4 vols. Revised and edited by Géza Vermès et al. Edinburgh, 1973–1987.

Smallwood, E. Mary. *The Jews under Roman Rule from Pompey to Diocletian.* Leiden, 1976.

Stern, Menachem, ed. and trans. *Greek and Latin Authors on Jews and Judaism.* 3 vols. Jerusalem, 1976–1984.

DORON MENDELS

FISHER, CLARENCE STANLEY (1876–1941),

American archaeologist and architect; innovator in the techniques of stratigraphic analysis at excavations in Egypt and Palestine. Born in Philadelphia, Fisher was trained as an architect at the University of Pennsylvania. In 1898, after a brief period of professional employment in St. Louis, he joined the university's expedition to Nippur. He spent the next few years as a research fellow in Babylonian architecture at the University Museum. In 1909, Fisher was recruited for the Harvard University Expedition to Samaria and began a close partnership with Egyptologist George Andrew Reisner. At Samaria, the two men paid close attention to patterns of debris deposits and fills. Indeed, Fisher's carefully drawn stratigraphic sections from Samaria became prototypes for subsequent generations of archaeological architects.

Fisher remained in the Near East throughout World War I, working as a volunteer on various humanitarian relief missions; later in life he would devote considerable time, energy, and personal funds for charitable works in Jerusalem. During his extended wartime stay in Egypt, Fisher expanded his research interests and was named chief archaeologist and Egyptologist in Cairo for the University of Pennsylvania Museum. In the early 1920s, Fisher alternated his time between Egypt and Palestine. From 1921 to 1925, he served as director of the University of Pennsylvania excavations at Tell Beth-Shean, where he and his team uncovered a sequence of New Kingdom temples and directed limited soundings down to Neolithic levels. He also devoted part of every year to his work with Reisner, serving as chief architect at Reisner's important excavations at Girga, Giza, Memphis, and Luxor. Fisher was also later called on to direct the University of Chicago Oriental Institute's excavations at Megiddo (1925–1927) and Haverford College's expedition to Beth-Shemesh (1928–1929).

Fisher was named professor of archaeology at the American School of Oriental Research (ASOR) in Jerusalem in 1925 and participated in many of the school's field projects. The last major project of his career, an ambitious "Corpus of Palestinian Pottery," remained unfinished at the time of his death.

[*See also* American Schools of Oriental Research; Beth-Shean; Beth-Shemesh; Giza; Megiddo; Memphis; Samaria; *and the biography of Reisner.*]

BIBLIOGRAPHY

Fisher, Clarence S. *Excavations at Nippur.* Philadelphia, 1905.

Glueck, Nelson. "Clarence Stanley Fisher in Memoriam." *Bulletin of the American Schools of Oriental Research,* no. 83 (1941): 2–4.

King, Philip J. *American Archaeology in the Mideast: A History of the American Schools of Oriental Research.* Winona Lake, Ind., 1983.

Reisner, George A., Clarence S. Fisher, and David G. Lyon. *Harvard Excavations at Samaria, 1908–1910,* vol. 1, *The Text;* vol. 2, *Plans and Plates.* Cambridge, Mass., 1924.

NEIL ASHER SILBERMAN

FISHING. Long considered a humble occupation, fishing has been part of human activity in the Near East since the beginnings of settled habitation, either temporary or permanent, near bodies of water. Although fishing and hunting may have evolved at about the same time and may share origins, the mythology of hunting involves the braver "royal huntsman," whereas fishing involves those of more humble social standing.

In an Egyptian papyrus from 2000 BCE, the Satire of the Artisans, a pupil is warned by his teacher, a scribe, about the hardships and dangers of fishing—that is, about the attendant high taxes on the fish caught and about the crocodiles in the Nile River. In the Hellenistic period, taxes on a catch came to 25 percent of its value. Herodotus (2.164) classifies those who fish at the lowest of all social levels—the seventh—together with sailors.

Those for whom fishing was an occupation sometimes also held political office, however. The mayor of Tiberias at the time of the first Jewish Revolt against Rome in Galilee was the head of the "marine union," which undoubtedly included both fishermen and sailors (Josephus, *Vita,* 12). Together with the fishermen of Magdala, they represented the uncompromising forces of Jewish nationalism, as against the Peace party of the rich (Josephus, *War,* 2.21.3). Two hundred years later, the Talmud describes the powerful fishermen's unions of Tiberias and Akko as differing in their readiness to work during the intermediate days of Passover and the Feast of Tabernacles (J.T., *Mo'ed Q.* 2.5; B.T., *Mo'ed Q.* 13.2).

Ancient fishing techniques and technologies can be reconstructed based on existing documentation: Egyptian reliefs and tomb paintings beginning in the third millennium, texts from Mesopotamia, references in the Bible and the Talmud, and excavated fishing implements. The similar climate found throughout the Levant and the cultural exchanges made among ancient societies resulted in a uniformity of fishing techniques. Many Near Eastern sources

FISHING. *Ancient fishermen catching barbels with hook and line.* Top: Egyptian; bottom: Assyrian. (After Nun, 1989)

record catching and preserving fish as a well-developed and important industry. Fish were transported, alive or preserved (by drying, salting, or pickling), across considerable distances and constituted both an article of trade and of tax payment. Competition regarding fishing waters and concession rights created conflicts as early as the third millennium in Sumer and, in the biblical period, in the Sea of Galilee.

For large industrial catches, however, fishermen in Egypt, as elsewhere, used nets. All industrial fishing in the world today is based on methods that originated in the ancient Near East. The oldest and most important type of net is the dragnet, or seine (Gk., *sagēnē*; Ar., *jarf*; Heb., *ḥērem*). Mentioned nine times in the Hebrew Bible (more than any other method) and once in the Parable of the Seine in the Gospels, the dragnet is a kind of wall of netting spread from a boat parallel to the shore and then dragged to land with the catch. It is 250–300 meters long, 2 meters high at its "wings," and 4–5 meters high at its center. A foot rope, weighted with stone or lead sinkers, is used with the dragnet, as are papyrus or wood floats to keep the wall upright. The first ancient nets were made of plant fibers; later examples are of linen or cotton. As a result of the region's dry climate, nets from

the second millennium BCE have been found in Egyptian tombs as at Gebelin, and a piece of a net from the second century CE was discovered in the Cave of the Letters near the Dead Sea.

The cast net (Gk., *amphiblēstron*; Ar., *shabakeh*; Heb., *qelaʿ*) was popular in antiquity and is still used. It is circular, 6–8 meters in diameter, with stone or lead sinkers attached to its edge. It is tossed by a lone individual who stands on the shore, in shallow water, or in a boat; the net lands like a parachute and sinks into the water. Complete cast nets from the second millennium BCE have been found in Egyptian tombs as at Deir el-Baḥari. The Talmud (B.T., *B.Q.* 81b) and the Gospels (*Mk.* 1:16; *Mt.* 4:18) contain references to them.

Netting needles, the tool used to weave and repair nets, have been found in Egyptian tombs and at sites on the Mediterranean coast of Israel near Gaza and Jaffa. On the Sea of Galilee, these needles have been found at Beth-Yerah, and at Magdala, in first-century contexts. Made of bone, bronze, iron, or wood (and today, plastic), the netting needle is from 10 to 30 centimeters long. It differs from the sewing needle in that the thread used is wound right on the needle.

In Sumer, fishing rights belonged to temples and local rulers, who leased them to fishermen. The right to fish in canals belonged to owners of the adjacent lands, who received these rights as compensation for maintaining the canals. As elsewhere, line and cast-net fishermen worked alone; those using larger nets worked in groups.

At Khafajeh, near Baghdad (2700 BCE), fifty ring-shaped ceramic sinkers (5–6 cm in diameter) were discovered, a few of which still had small pieces of netting attached. Bronze fishhooks have been recovered at Ur (third dynasty), in Egyptian tombs, at Capernaum, and elsewhere. Stone and lead net sinkers, stone net anchors, and stone boat anchors are the most commonly found of all fishing accessories.

Sumerian and Akkadian mythologies contain many references to fishing in parables and analogies, a tradition also found in the Hebrew Bible and New Testament. Gilgamesh, the hero of a Mesopotamian flood myth, is depicted carrying a catch of fish, and the major Sumerian deity, Ea, the all-wise earth and water god, is described as owning a fishnet.

FISHING. *Egyptian fishermen with a dragging net.* Sixteenth century BCE. (After Nun, 1989)

His son Adapa is the hero of a remarkable adventure involving providing fish for the gods.

The first maritime empire was ruled by the Minoan civilization on Crete. At its height (c. 1600 BCE) it controlled the islands in the Mediterranean and Aegean Seas. Depictions of fish and fishing are prominent in Minoan wall paintings and on their ceramics, and the figure of a fish was typically placed on the prow of a ship. The Philistine "Sea Peoples," who probably originated in the Aegean, brought their knowledge of techniques for catching and preserving fish to ancient Palestine. [See Minoans; Philistines.]

None of the several references to fishing in the Hebrew Bible includes a single personality occupied with fishing or the name of a single fish. Only the prophets, notably Ezekiel (26:5, 14) and Isaiah (19:5), mention fishing in their parables. The coastal tribes of Zebulon and Asher, along with the Phoenicians, probably fished on the shore of the Mediterranean (*Gn.* 49:13). According to a tradition preserved in the Talmud (Tosefta, *B.Q.* 8), the tribe of Naphtali was given exclusive fishing rights by Joshua, entitling them to "set seines and spread cast nets" around the entire shoreline of the Sea of Galilee.

The New Testament Gospels include fishing vignettes on the Sea of Galilee, the scene of most of Jesus' ministry and where his earliest disciples fished. However, the descriptions of the Miraculous Drought (*Lk.* 5:1–7; *Jn.* 21:1–9) are not technically accurate, perhaps because the authors were already distant in time and place from the experience of fishing in the Galilee. Problems of translation (especially of "dragnet" and "cast net") add to the lack of accuracy. Nevertheless, it is safe to say that fishing methods on the lake have not changed greatly since Second Temple times.

In February 1986, a sensational discovery was made on the muddy beach near Migdal (Magdala), on the Sea of Galilee: an ancient wooden boat, dating to the first century CE, miraculously preserved by the mud into which it had sunk. The boat is 8.8 meters long, 2.5 meters wide, and 1.25 meters deep, almost exactly the measurements of the boats used by seine net fishermen in the Sea of Galilee until the mid-twentieth century. The planks were made of cedars of Lebanon and the ribs of unworked oak branches. The boat was likely used for both transportation and fishing. [See Galilee Boat.]

Other important finds were made at the same location between 1989 and 1991, when drought drastically reduced the water level in the Sea of Galilee. Hundreds of stone net sinkers, net anchors, and boat anchors of varying sizes and shapes were recovered, objects that will contribute greatly to what is known about early fishing technology.

[See also Anchors; Hunting; Ships and Boats.]

BIBLIOGRAPHY

Brandt, Andres von. *Fish Catching Methods of the World.* 3d ed., rev. and enl. Farnham, England, 1984.

Dalman, Gustaf. *Arbeit und Sitte in Palästina.* 7 vols. in 8. Gütersloh, 1928–1942.

Frost, Honor. "From Rope to Chain: On the Development of Anchors in the Mediterranean." *The Mariners Mirror* 49.1 (1963): 1–20.

Hooke, S. H. *Middle Eastern Mythology.* Middlesex, 1963.

Hornell, James. *Fishing in Many Waters.* Cambridge, 1950.

Nun, Mendel. *Ancient Jewish Fishery* (in Hebrew). Tel Aviv, 1963.

Nun, Mendel. "Fishing" (in Hebrew). In *Encyclopaedia Mikrait* (Biblical Encyclopaedia), vol. 6, pp. 720–726. Jerusalem, 1971.

Nun, Mendel. *The Sea of Galilee and Its Fisherman in the New Testament.* Kibbutz Ein Gev, 1989.

Radcliffe, William. *Fishing from the Earliest Times.* 2d ed. London, 1926.

MENDEL NUN

FOOD STORAGE. The need to store food arose early in human history. Food had to be saved in times of plenty for times of need, especially when human resourcefulness created a surplus either by hunting and gathering or by production through domestication. With the evolution of social structures, surplus could be traded, a notion that made storage attractive. To carry out food storage successfully, two issues needed to be addressed: food processing and containers.

In some environments food tends to spoil, hence, it has to be processed so that it can be stored for long periods. Processed foods were not only consumed locally, but also sold or bartered. Food processing took the form of drying, salting, smoking, or producing by-products, such as wine. Because most vegetables were not processed, they were used as seasonal foods. Certain fruits, such as grapes, figs, dates, and apricots, could be hung on string for drying and storage, pressed into cakes, or kept in containers. In addition, grapes, and other fruit were crushed and their juice processed into wine, syrup, and vinegar and stored in containers. Olives were crushed and pressed, producing an oil that was also stored in containers. Treating raw olives with salt or other additives for consumption was introduced in the Hellenistic or Roman period (Borowski, 1987, p. 123). [See Olives; Viticulture.]

Other raw foods could also be processed for long storage and transport. Both meat and fish were preserved by being dried, salted, or smoked in thin strips. Fish bones discovered at sites distant from any body of water suggests that they had been transported there after being processed. Milk was churned, turned into cheese, and dried in blocks that could be reconstituted with water, a practice still prevalent among nomadic bedouin.

Grain for consumption could be preserved for a long period by heating to kill the germ, after setting aside seed for future seasons. This practice was not a common one, however. Grain was stored in bulk or in containers. To protect the seed from spoilage and rodents, it was fumigated (Borowski, 1987, p. 156). Because it was not processed before it was used, it was ground daily for baking and cooking. Storing flour was neither customary nor efficient, although a case is known of wheat flour stored in a Roman amphora (Renfrew and Bahn, 1991, p. 241).

In most instances, pottery vessels were used for food storage. Prior to the invention of pottery, in its absence, or for special purposes, however, containers were made out of animal skins, tree bark, wood, rush mats and baskets, and stone. Some of the earliest stone vessels found in villages in Mesopotamia, as at Maghzaliyeh, date to 6500–6000 BCE and were made of gypsum, in the tradition of Zagros Mountain societies (Huot, 1992, p. 189).

Whether storage was in private or public hands, special areas and facilities were set aside in the community, with an eye toward ease of use and efficient collection and distribution (Borowski, 1987, p. 82). Studies of space utilization at archaeological sites demonstrate that the majority of private dwellings contained areas designated for food preparation and storage (Daviau, 1990). This is corroborated by ethnoarchaeological studies that show well-defined space for food storage in dwellings (Kramer, 1979, pp. 144–145). In the Chalcolithic period, food-storage installations were built in the courtyard, which was surrounded by rooms (Porath, 1992, p. 45). In the Early Bronze Age, food was stored in large pithoi, and the jars were placed on the floors of rooms and courtyards or sometimes sunk into the floor (Ben-Tor, 1992, p. 67). In the Middle Bronze Age, with the development of the courtyard house, space for food storage was set aside in the courtyard and in some of the rooms, a practice continued into the Late Bronze Age (Ben-Dov 1992, pp. 100–104). With the development of the two-story residence, foodstuffs were mostly stored on the ground floor, in small rooms surrounding a central space, possibly a courtyard. Whether the ground-floor space was covered is still being debated. Iron Age houses in ancient Palestine are often found with storage rooms (Borowski, 1987, p. 82). Although cellars were not as common as storage rooms in dwellings or in public buildings, examples have been uncovered at Tell Beit Mirsim, Beersheba, and Tell Jemmeh (Borowski, 1987, pp. 75–76).

In dwellings, foodstuffs were stored mostly in jars, whose shape and size changed based on new influences in a period and needs. While storage jars in EB Palestine had a characteristic flat bottom, MB storage jars featured a pointed bottom that allowed the sediments in such liquids as oil and wine to settle. Such jars were also used to store grain; when used in large numbers, they were placed close to each other for support and cushioned with chaff and straw against breakage, as at Gezer (Borowski, 1987, p. 69). Individual jars were placed in corners, along walls, inside depressions in the floor, and in round clay stands.

The soft limestone bedrock of the Shephelah was hewn to create underground work and storage spaces, as at Mareshah (Marisa) as early as the Hellenistic period. During the Roman period, in part for reasons of security, the soft rock was hewn to create underground storage facilities for agricultural produce. Of interest are four rooms found at the Ahuzat Hazan hiding complex, where the floors were hewn with rows of depressions for storage jars, each connected to the other by a narrow channel in which spilled oil could be directed into a collection basin (Kloner and Teper, 1987, pp. 115–127). The size of this installation and the quantity of oil that could have been stored (10,500 liters) suggest that it did not belong to an individual, but may have played a role in the community's preparation for the impending turmoil that culminated in the Bar Kokhba Revolt (132–135).

Certain food-processing activities, such as wine making, required particular storage facilities, such as those evident in the winery at Gibeon. [See Gibeon.] The excavator found a series of caves, used as fermentation cellars, in which the wine was kept undisturbed at a constant temperature until it was drinkable (Pritchard, 1964, pp. 1–27).

Public storehouses, under the control of the civic or religious authorities, were placed in a city's administrative section, near the main gate, near the governor's or the king's palace, or inside the cult compound. Most public storage installations were repositories for grain, oil, and wine—commodities that could be distributed to functionaries. For their daily needs, palaces and temples stored foodstuffs in facilities similar to those in private dwellings. These practices were common throughout the Near East: at the palaces at Ebla and Mari, in Syria, documents related to food supplies and agricultural production were found in the former, and related to food storage and disbursement in the latter. At Amarna, in Egypt, granaries and storage areas were uncovered, and at Kuntillet ʿAjrud, a way station and cult center in the Sinai Desert, large pithoi found in long, narrow rooms demonstrate how foodstuffs were stored. Long and narrow rooms were popular for storage of foodstuffs, as evident from the tripartite buildings in Beersheba, Tel Hadar, and other sites.

Although their function is still being debated, the Samaria ostraca deal with the collection of oil and wine in ancient Israel, either as taxes in kind, provisions for the palace, or produce from royal estates shipped for certain functionaries (Smelik, 1991, pp. 56–57). [See Samaria Ostraca.] Distribution of food by the central government in ancient Israel is illustrated by the Arad ostraca, which contain instructions for rationing certain measures of bread or flour, wine, and oil to functionaries, possibly Greek mercenaries. From the ostraca it appears that the ration was one loaf of bread per person per day, and the bread remained edible for four days. [See Arad Inscriptions.] Beyond this period, flour was given in the amount of one liter per loaf. Wine was rationed at a quarter to a third of a liter per person per day (Smelik, 1991, p. 106). Additional information about the collection and distribution of foodstuffs by the central government in ancient Israel are the lmlk stamped jar handles, dated to the time of Hezekiah's revolt against Sennacherib in 701 BCE. The present consensus among scholars is that these stamped jar handles designated containers used for supplying Judean cities with provisions to withstand the Assyrian siege.

Foodstuffs were transported from one location to another on land by wagons and pack animals, mostly donkeys, and on sea by boats. On land, liquids were transported in jars as well as in skins. Other foodstuffs were probably transported in jars or sacks. Transport by boat involved the use of amphoras, tall jars designed to fit in the hold and stabilized by tying their large handles to beams in the body of the boat.

There are very few references to food storage in the Hebrew Bible. From *1 Kings* 17:12, 14, and 16 it appears that household flour was kept in a jar (*kad*) and oil was stored in a flat jar (*sappaḥat*), possibly the Iron Age type known as a pilgrim's flask. Two terms are clearly associated with public food storage facilities: *'ôṣārôt* (*Jl.* 1:17; *Neh.* 12:44; 13:12; *1 Chr.* 27:25, 27–28; *2 Chr.* 11:11) and *miskĕnôt* (*2 Chr.* 32:28). However, their literary context implies that these facilities were not used exclusively for foodstuffs.

What is known about food storage in antiquity will increase as the technology of archaeology advances. That is, chemical analyses of storage jars and other vessels will give more accurate assessments of the commodities they held. More sophisticated studies of space utilization will help to identify the configurations of storage space and the nature and quantities of the goods stored in them.

[*See also* Granaries and Silos.]

BIBLIOGRAPHY

Ben-Dov, Meir. "Middle and Late Bronze Age Dwellings." In *The Architecture of Ancient Israel: From the Prehistoric to the Persian Periods*, edited by Aharon Kempinski and Ronny Reich, pp. 99–104. Jerusalem, 1992.

Ben-Tor, Amnon. "Early Bronze Age Dwellings and Installations." In *The Architecture of Ancient Israel: From the Prehistoric to the Persian Periods*, edited by Aharon Kempinski and Ronny Reich, pp. 60–67. Jerusalem, 1992.

Borowski, Oded. *Agriculture in Iron Age Israel.* Winona Lake, Ind., 1987. The most recent work on the topic; combines biblical and archaeological information.

Daviau, Paulette M. Michele. "Artifact Distribution and Functional Analysis in Palestinian Domestic Architecture of the Second Millennium B.C. (Bronze Age)." Ph.D. diss., University of Toronto, 1990. Study of space utilization.

Huot, Jean-Louis. "The First Farmers at Oueili." *Biblical Archaeologist* 55 (1992): 188–195. Early Mesopotamian settlement; issue devoted to the region.

Kloner, Amos, and Yigal Tepper. *The Hiding Complexes in the Judean Shephelah* (in Hebrew). Tel Aviv, 1987. The only treatment of the topic.

Kramer, Carol. "An Archaeological View of a Contemporary Kurdish Village: Domestic Architecture, Household Size, and Wealth." In *Ethnoarchaeology: Implications of Ethnography for Archaeology*, edited by Carol Kramer, pp. 139–163. New York, 1979. Comparison of space utilization in a modern village with archaeological finds.

Netzer, Ehud. "Domestic Architecture in the Iron Age." In *The Architecture of Ancient Israel: From the Prehistoric to the Persian Periods*, edited by Aharon Kempinski and Ronny Reich, pp. 193–201. Jerusalem, 1992.

Porath, Yosef. "Domestic Architecture of the Chalcolithic Period." In *The Architecture of Ancient Israel: From the Prehistoric to the Persian Periods*, edited by Aharon Kempinski and Ronny Reich, pp. 40–48. Jerusalem, 1992.

Pritchard, James B. *Winery, Defenses, and Soundings at Gibeon.* Philadelphia, 1964.

Renfrew, Colin, and Paul Bahn. *Archaeology: Theories, Methods, and Practice.* New York, 1991. Excellent work on the topic.

Smelik, K. A. D. *Writings from Ancient Israel: A Handbook of Historical and Religious Documents.* Translated by Graham I. Davies. Louisville, 1991. Excellent treatment of written records from ancient Israel.

ODED BOROWSKI

FORTIFICATIONS. [*To survey the historical development, forms, and functions of fortifications, this entry comprises five articles:*

An Overview

Fortifications of the Bronze and Iron Ages

Fortifications of the Persian Period

Fortifications of the Hellenistic, Roman, and Byzantine Periods

Fortifications of the Islamic Period

The first provides a general typology and morphology of fortifications, particularly in Syria-Palestine; the remainder treat remains of specific periods.]

An Overview

Fortifications are an important component of the ancient urban settlement, aimed at preventing access of hostile elements as well as demarcating the limits of the city. Their construction necessitated the mobilization of many members of the community. As part of the urban matrix, fortifications share both military and civic functions; their structure usually reflects a compromise between those conflicting roles. Attempts to associate the shape of fortification systems directly with the invention of new weapons (Yadin, 1963) are not supported by the accumulating factual data. [*See* Weapons and Warfare.] Rather, the nature of the fortifications appears to have been dictated by a variety of combinations of military, political, economic, demographic, and ideological factors. The history of alterations in shape, structure, and building materials of fortification systems demonstrates the shifting priorities made by the community within the scope of the military-civic continuum.

Fortification systems consist of several different elements: the circumferencial unit that provides the physical barrier or the demarcation line of the settlement; a gate or gates; posterns; towers and bastions; and glacis and water systems.

Circumferencial Defense Systems. The use of the term *circumferencial defense systems* instead of the popular designation *city walls* denotes the wide range of functions that should be attributed to the structure of the settlements' boundaries, beyond an exclusive military role. The following typology reviews the various ways in which communities shaped the edges of their cities and towns in order to meet their military and socio-economic needs.

Solid city walls. A solid wall appears to be the earliest type of fortification, the concept stemming, perhaps, from the fences built around animal pens in sedentary farming communities. Solid walls were the simplest structure that could provide a physical barrier against intruders or attackers. In the Early Bronze Age the walls were made of fieldstones, sometimes constructed in segments, with narrow intervals to diminish damage from earthquake, such as at Megiddo XVIII. At many sites additional lines of solid walls were added outside the first one (totaling more than 15 m in width) to gain better protection (e.g., Ai, Tel Yarmut). The walls of Middle Bronze Age cities were commonly constructed of clay bricks and were of modest width (2–3 m) but reinforced by a well-constructed glacis.

In Iron Age II, ashlar blocks were used sparsely in the outer faces of solid walls. At Megiddo and Tell en-Nasbeh a type of offset-inset wall was in place. [*See* Megiddo; Naṣbeh, Tell en-.] The wall was made of sections about 6-meter-long that alternately projected and receded and was constructed of fieldstones faced with ashlars. This method provided more stability to the wall with minimal cost for material and labor. Balconies used to protect the "dead area" at the foot of the wall could be constructed over the insets on their outer side. At Beersheba and Arad, such solid walls were built in a sawtooth fashion, in which sections deviate at intervals in the same direction (some 0.3–0.5 m)—like teeth on the blade of a saw. [*See* Beersheba; Arad, *article on* Iron Age Period.] This technique may have been meant to create vertical shadow, which would have made the wall appear higher and more formidable.

Casemate wall. A unique type of fortification, common in Iron Age II, was composed of two parallel walls with a space between them: the casemate wall. This method was evidently applied as a way to economize on construction costs by decreasing the amount of material and labor; it was also a means to gain additional storage space within the city. Casemate walls were often integrated into dwellings inside the city, as at Beersheba and Tell Beit Mirsim. [*See* Beit Mirsim, Tell.] The casemate rooms served in these cases as the rear broadroom of a house. At Hazor, the casemate wall was built as an independent structure: a street separated the wall from neighboring houses. [*See* Hazor.] In a few instances, such as at Samaria, the casemates were filled with soil and served as structural foundations. [*See* Samaria.] In Anatolia and Northern Syria, underground "boxes" completely filled with soil and debris, termed *Kastenmauer,* were used as structural foundations from the Middle Bronze Age (Naumann, 1971, pp. 249–256). At Hazor and in the fortress of Arad, casemate walls were converted into stronger solid walls by the intentional filling of the casemates with soil and stones.

Earthen rampart. Several MB cities were surrounded by magnificent earthen ramparts. The most prominent example is the Lower City of Hazor, where the rampart rises to 90 m. These structures were considered by many scholars (Albright, 1960; Yadin, 1963; Mazar, 1968) to be a new type of defense introduced by the Hyksos. [*See* Hyksos.] Investigations by Peter J. Parr (1968) and Jacob Kaplan (1975), as well as new data from the sites of Dan, Akko, and Tel Yavneh-Yam, indicate that earthen ramparts already existed in the MB IIA period. [*See* Dan; Akko; Yavneh-Yam.] Furthermore, it has been clarified that nowhere was a city wall incorporated into an earthen rampart; thus, their function must be considered to have been a means for demarcating the city's limits (Herzog, 1992) or providing a psychological deterrent (Finkelstein, 1992).

Belt of houses. Communities that could not afford the cost of constructing an elaborate fortification system chose to protect their settlement by arranging an outer belt of houses. The rear wall of these structures provided the necessary barrier, at least against thieves or robbers. This concept is commonly found at Late Bronze Age and Iron I settlements.

Glacis. Consolidated layers of soil, bricks, or stone to protect the slopes of a mound are known as a glacis. To assure drainage, layers of different types of soil were alternated. The foot of the glacis was retained by brick or stone walls. Occasionally, the outer face of the glacis was covered with stone paving. Earthen or stone-built glacis were also considered a Hyksos invention. However, Parr (1968) convincingly demonstrates that the phenomenon has a wider chronological range and already existed at EB cities. For practical reasons, every fortification system had to include some kind of glacis to prevent damage to the wall's foundations by erosion. A glacis also provided smooth slopes around the walls that obstructed attackers from climbing them. Indeed, glacis were applied in every period in which cities were fortified by walls. The common use of mud bricks for MB city walls may have necessitated the development of more elaborate glacis in that period.

Moat. A deep ditch was cut at the foot of some mounds in order to increase their height. This method was especially important in places were the natural hill was not sufficiently prominent to invest and attack. In many cases, the moat can be considered to be a by-product of removing much needed soil and stone for earthen fills and construction. Digging the soil in the area around the mound created a ditch that impeded the enemy's attack. A moat was exposed on the western side of the MB II Lower City at Hazor and around the newly exposed fortified Iron II city at Tel Jezreel. [*See* Jezreel, Tel.] In addition, because these moats were cut deep into the bedrock, they probably served as a quarry for construction stone. Moats were also observed at the Hittite capital of Ḫattuša (Boğazköy) in central Anatolia, in northern

Syria at Carchemish, and at Tell Halaf in northern Mesopotamia (Naumann, 1971, pp. 305–308). [*See* Boğazköy; Carchemish; Halaf, Tell.]

Gates. City gates dramatically represent the architectural dilemma created by a settlement's military and civil needs. As an entrance to the city, the gate needed a wide opening and a location at the easiest approachable point, however, defensive considerations demanded a narrow and hard-to-enter location. The planners of city gates throughout the ages had to find an adequate compromise between these two conflicting demands. The following typology of city gates portrays different solutions developed to cope with the dilemma.

Gates with projecting towers. The simplest way to protect a gate was to flank the approachway between two towers. The top of the city wall above the gate and the roof of the projecting towers provided the defenders with strategic firing platforms that controlled the area in front of the gate from three sides. This arrangement also minimized the size of the dead area next to the foot of the wall. Wooden doors were reinforced with strips of metal to prevent their burning. A well-preserved example of this type are the EB II gates at Tell el-Farʿah (North). [*See* Farʿah, Tell el- (North).] When the main gate was erected inside the fortification line, the protection of the area was achieved by constructing an outer gate. Such installations were popular at such Iron Age cities as Tel Beersheba, Dan, and Megiddo.

Fort gates. A unique type of gate was developed in the MB II period, apparently initiated at cities demarcated by earthen ramparts. In these unfortified cities, the ruling class needed strongholds to protect them both from outside enemies and inside rebels. Such double protection was accomplished by erecting city gates as separate forts. These forts consisted of two huge towers with internal rooms and a gateway narrowed by three pairs of pilasters. The location of door sockets indicates that the gates were shut off by two pairs of doors, facing the outer and inner sides of the city. When the doors of these gates were closed, the structures were transformed into independent strongholds in which members of the ruling class could find shelter in an emergency.

Gates with two, four, or six rooms. During the Iron Age, city gates often consisted of two large towers flanking the gateway. However, unlike the shallow recesses between the piers of MB II gates, the long rooms of the towers opened fully into the gateway. Another essential difference is the location of the doors. Instead of two sets of doors, as in MB II, the Iron Age gates were closed only by a single pair of doors located behind the first set of piers. This arrangement indicates that the function of the gate rooms at the floor level was civil and not military.

Iron Age gates differ in the number of their rooms. The most common are gates with four or six rooms; a few were equipped with only two rooms. Yigael Yadin (1963) assumed that the number of rooms changed during the period and affected the protective strength of the gates. Detailed analysis (Herzog, 1986) indicates that these gate types were used simultaneously throughout the period, with the number of rooms reflecting the intensity and diversity of a gate's uses. In addition, the gate rooms could be used by guards, as well as by political, judicial, religious, and commercial institutions. The military role of some gates was reinforced by adding an outer gate in front of the main gate.

Ceremonial gates. At least one gate, in stratum XV at Megiddo, seems to reflect a ceremonial function. The gate was furnished with two wide, straight, parallel gateways with stairs that led up to the cultic compound.

Secondary gates and posterns. Multiple narrow, secondary gates were used as civilian passageways through the city walls, mainly during the EB II–III period. These gateways were 0.80–1 m wide and allowed the farmers a shortcut to their fields. In the Iron Age, narrow posterns were utilized for escaping from a besieged city or for a surprise attack on the enemy.

Bastions and Fortresses. The rise of a military establishment demanded appropriate structures for its use. These needs were best met by bastions or forts, erected in connection with a fortification system. A large bastion was built next to the water system at Arad in EB II, and several huge bastions were erected at Tel Yarmut in EB III. [*See* Arad, *article on* Bronze Age Period; Yarmut, Tel.] The gate forts of the MB IIA, described above, are another type of independent stronghold. Isolated Iron I forts have also been observed in the hill country of Judah. [*See* Judah.]

BIBLIOGRAPHY

Albright, William Foxwell. *The Archaeology of Palestine.* Rev. ed. Harmondsworth, 1960.

Finkelstein, Israel. "Middle Brone Age 'Fortifications': A Reflection of Social Organizations and Political Formations." *Tel Aviv* 19 (1992): 201–220.

Herzog, Ze'ev. *Das Stadttor in Israel und in den Nachbarländern.* Mainz am Rhein, 1986.

Herzog, Ze'ev. "Settlement and Fortification Planning in the Iron Age." In *The Architecture of Ancient Israel: From the Prehistoric to the Persian Periods,* edited by Aharon Kempinski and Ronny Reich, pp. 231–274. Jerusalem, 1992.

Kaplan, Jacob. "Further Aspects of the Middle Bronze Age II Fortifications in Palestine." *Zeitschrift des Deutschen Palästina-Vereins* 91 (1975): 1–17.

Mazar, Benjamin. "The Middle Bronze Age in Palestine." *Israel Exploration Journal* 18 (1968): 65–97.

Naumann, Rudolf. *Architektur Kleinasiens: Von ihren Anfängen bis zum Ende der hethitischen Zeit.* 2d ed. Tübingen, 1971.

Parr, Peter J. "The Origin of the Rampart Fortifications of Middle Bronze Age Palestine and Syria." *Zeitschrift des Deutschen Palästina-Vereins* 84 (1968): 18–45.

Yadin, Yigael. *The Art of Warfare in Biblical Lands in the Light of Archaeological Study.* 2 vols. New York, 1963.

ZE'EV HERZOG

Fortifications of the Bronze and Iron Ages

Fortifications were a fundamental aspect of urbanization in antiquity. While the need to protect a settlement arose with the development of social institutions, the very existence of fortifications generated the evolution of the military establishment. The size and the nature of fortifications were determined by the community's level of social complexity, which was affected by the role of the site within larger geopolitical units.

Neolithic and Chalcolithic Periods. The appearance of what seemed to be a fortified city in Pre-Pottery Neolithic Jericho has puzzled scholars since its discovery. [*See* Jericho.*] A satisfying solution suggests interpreting the structures not as fortifications but as a retaining wall against floods and a tower for ceremonial purposes (Bar-Yosef, 1986). Enclosure walls of temenoi at Chalcolithic sites such as 'Ein-Gedi and Teleilat el-Ghassul in Israel may have been the conceptual inspiration for the first defensive walls. [*See* 'Ein-Gedi; Teleilat el-Ghassul.]

Early Bronze Age. The earliest fortifications so far uncovered in modern Israel belong to the Early Bronze Age IA (Kempinski, 1992a). At Tel 'Erani/Tel Gath, on the southern coastal plain, excavation exposed a 3-meter-wide city wall, an outer glacis, and two towers in a limited area, contemporary with a public building inside the settlement. [*See* 'Erani, Tel.] From about the same time (late fourth millennium), an elaborate fortification system was found at Habuba Kabira in Syria. [*See* Habuba Kabira.] It consisted of a 3.40-meter-wide city wall constructed on the western side of the city in a straight line, for about 600 m. Rectangular towers were spaced at regular intervals of 14 m and in front of them a thin (.70 m) outer wall was added. There were two identical city gates in the main wall, each with two towers and two doorways, and an additional outer gate through the outer wall (Strommenger, 1980).

Evidently, toward the end of EB I, more sites were fortified: Jericho, with a city wall 1.10 m wide and semicircular towers; Tell Shalem, protected by two parallel walls (inner wall, 4.5 m wide; outer wall, 2.80 m wide); and Aphek, with a city wall 2.90 m wide. [*See* Aphek.] The first phase of the fortification systems at Tell el-Far'ah (North) and Ai is attributed by some scholars to late EB I and by others to EB II. [*See* Far'ah, Tell el- (North); Ai.] At Tell el-Far'ah (North), a city wall 2.20 m wide is joined to a remarkable city gate. The gate consists of two huge towers that project 7 m outward from the wall; each tower is about 8 m wide. The towers commanded a 4-meter-wide approach that narrowed to a 2-meter-wide entrance. The gate was closed by double doors, as is evident from the two door sockets found in situ. At Ai, the first city wall (C), 5–5.50 m thick, was built of large stones and strengthened by semicircular towers. Two narrow (only 1 m wide) passages were uncovered, but no main gate has so far been found.

In EB II, fortified cities became common all over the Levant (Richard, 1987). In addition to the above-mentioned sites, fortified cities have been found at Beth-Yerah, Megiddo, Ta'anach, Khirbet Makhruk, Dothan, Tel 'Erani, Tel Yarmut, Arad, and Bab edh-Dhra'. [*See* Beth-Yerah; Megiddo; Ta'anach; Dothan; 'Erani; Tel; Yarmut, Tel; Arad, *article on* Bronze Age Period; Bab edh Dhra'.] A typical feature at most of these sites was the attempt to increase the strength of the city walls by making them very thick and by erecting additional parallel walls with fills between them. These accumulative fortification systems of walls and fills reached unusual widths (and apparently considerable heights)—up to 15 m wide at Tell el-Far'ah (North) and more than 10 m wide at Ai (walls C and B). The wall at Arad is only 2–2.50 m thick, indicating the site's lessened role as a fortified urban center. In some cases, such as at Megiddo and Jericho, the city wall was constructed in sections approximately 20 m long, with narrow gaps of about 0.20 m between them—presumably to prevent the collapse of the wall in the event of an earthquake.

The EB II cities are also characterized by the existence of more then one gate (Herzog, 1986a, pp. 12–23). Each city had at least one large gate (more than 2 m wide), such as the main gates at Tell el-Far'ah (North) and Arad, through which fully laden beasts of burden could pass. In addition, many cities had several narrow passages (only .80–1 m wide), often called posterns. This duality reflects attempts to counterbalance the conflicting military and civilian requirements of very large cities inhabited mostly by agriculturalists: multiple passages saved the farmers from traveling a distance of several kilometers in order to reach their fields. Vulnerability was minimized by making the secondary gates as narrow as feasible. Such gates could be blocked quickly in case of an emergency or effectively defended from the top of the ramparts.

An additional defensive aspect of the system was provided by towers projecting outward from the wall, thus enabling flanking fire. Most common are semicircular towers attached to the wall and incorporating a narrow doorway, like the ones at Arad, where the towers were built at intervals of 25–40 m. In some cases the towers were rectangular; such towers are depicted on Egyptian pallets (Yadin, 1963, pp. 122–125). An interesting innovation is the massive (25 m long and 13 m wide) bastion attached to the city wall at Tel Yarmut. A similar structure (18 × 8 m) at Arad dominated the reservoir inside the city.

At several sites, such as at Tell el- Far'ah (North), Khirbet Makhruk, and Jericho, the slopes around the city walls were reinforced by a glacis—a structure consisting of alternating layers of different kinds of soils and/or stones. The glacis served to prevent erosion, to force an attacking enemy to climb a slippery ascent, and to make any attempt to undermine the city wall more difficult. The bastion at Tel Yarmut is surrounded by an imposing stone glacis at least 6 m wide.

EB III settlers exploited the fortifications of the preceding period with few alterations. Basically, the technique was to increase the width of the earlier city walls. The addition of wall A at Ai created a complex of fortifications 17 m wide, and wall 4045A at Megiddo doubled the width to 8.50 m. At Tel Yarmut, the fortifications in EB III reached a total width of 36 m. Rectangular towers were a typical feature in this phase.

The bastions incorporated into the circumference of the city wall became more popular in EB III. They were constructed of heavy walls with inner divisions into rooms, some of which were narrow stairwells that led to upper stories. Such bastions are found at Jericho (16 × 7 m), Tell el-Hesi (18 × 9 m), and Taʿanach (10 × 10 m). [See Hesi, Tell el-.] In the absence of fortified palaces or acropola, these bastions served as a power base for the city's military elite.

The city gate in stratum XV at Megiddo had a ceremonial rather than a military function. Two wide parallel gateways with stairs led up to the temple area, between three rectangular units. At Beth-Yerah, stairs between two solid towers led down into the city.

Middle Bronze Age. During the Middle Bronze Age I, there was no urban settlements in Israel—the population being rural or nomadic. However, there are fortifications attributable to this period in Transjordan, specifically at Khirbet Iskander, where a 2.50-meter-wide perimeter wall with reinforced corners and a two-chambered gate was excavated. [See Iskander, Khirbet.] Fortified cities reappeared in Israel in MB IIA, at first along the coastal plain and the interior valleys (Kochavi et al., 1979). Fortification systems included city walls, mighty city gates, towers, glacis, and earthen ramparts. The walls were made of sun-dried bricks above stone foundations with a moderate width of about 2 m. In some cases, such as at Megiddo and Aphek, the wall was reinforced by pilasters on the exterior. [See Megiddo; Aphek.]

The common use of bricks as the main constructional material stimulated the wide introduction of the glacis, which protected the bottom of the city wall on its outer side and the slope immediately below it. The elaborate MB IIA glacis at Tel Gerisa is composed of several courses of bricks (up to thirteen in one spot) laid on the slope of the mound and covered by a layer of crushed sandstone. [See Gerisa, Tel.] This was a great improvement over the earthen glacis of the Early Bronze Age. [See Building Materials and Techniques, article on Materials and Techniques of the Bronze and Iron Ages.]

In addition to fortified cities built on hills or tells, large settlements surrounded by earthen ramparts were erected outside the tells in the lowlands. These ramparts were built by a variety of techniques: with or without a stone core; with internal, boxlike brick constructions; or, most commonly, with sloping layers of alternating soil types. There is not a single case where a city wall was found to be incorporated

within the rampart. This absence of a defensive wall means that these earthen ramparts cannot be interpreted as fortifications against military attack: they were neither designed to prevent the access of chariots nor could they provide a response to the battering ram, allegedly introduced at that time (Yadin, 1955). It is more likely that the earthen ramparts were a quick and easy means to demarcate the city limits of unusually large communities during peaceful times (Herzog, 1986b, 1992a; Bunimovitz, 1992; Finkelstein, 1992). These communities could erect an earthen rampart within a few months, with their own hands, without investing in professional builders and expensive materials. Such enclosures are known at the huge sites of Qatna and Tell Mardikh/Ebla in Syria and at Hazor, Yavneh-Yam, Tel Kabri, Tel Dan, and Akko, in Israel. [See Ebla; Hazor; Yavneh-Yam; Dan; Akko.] They were erected over areas of 20–100 ha (49–247 acres) during MB IIA–B. The incorporation of city gates within earthen ramparts does not contradict the demarcation function but rather supports it. The gates were not attached to any city wall; they were merely anchored to the rampart by short walls (as for their function, see below).

City gates in MB IIA present several competing conceptional approaches (Herzog, 1986a). A gate with an approach constructed at right angles to the gateway has been found at Megiddo, stratum XIII, forming a bent entrance, which was easier to defend then a straight entrance. The stepped approach to the gate indicates that only pedestrians or pack animals, but not wheeled vehicles, could enter the city. A second gate type was found at Tel Akko. It consisted of a gate chamber (8.25 × 7 m) with a 10-meter-long corridor, almost on the same axis. However, there also the narrow (1.75 m) entrance and two steps in front of the corridor prevented use by wagons or chariots.

The long stepped approach leading to the gate at Tel Dan points to similar constraints, but the plan of the gatehouse is different. It is a roughly square building (15.45 × 13.50 m) divided into four large rooms, two on each side of the gateway. The gate, including the front arches and half-barrel roof (all made of mud brick), is exceptionally well preserved because it was intentionally and totally buried by the builders of the slightly later earthen rampart. The MB IIA gate at Dan bears a strong resemblance to the Iron Age II four-room gate type.

The fourth type of gate, which developed in Syria at Tell Mardikh/Ebla and was introduced into Israel at Yavneh-Yam in MB IIA, has six piers. The type became dominant in MB IIB. City gates in this group are composed of formidable pairs of towers flanking straight gateways that are narrowed by three piers on each side. The towers' thick walls (2 m and more) point to their considerable height, with rooms on several floors. Some of these rooms served as stairwells; others were probably used as barracks for the city guards as well as to store their equipment and food. The gates of this type had wide, straight entrances (2.80–4.00 m)

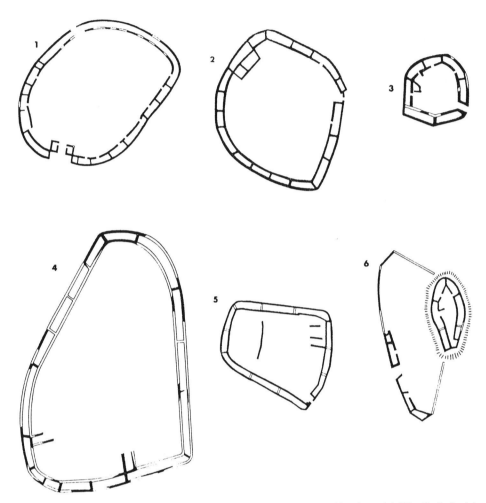

FORTIFICATIONS: Bronze and Iron Ages. *Examples of Iron Age Fortifications.* (1) 'Ein-Qadesh; (2) Atar ha-Ro'a; (3) Ḥorvat Ḥaluqim; (4) Ḥorvat Raḥba; (5) Ḥorvat Ketef Shivta; (6) Ramat Matred. (After A. Mazar, *Archaeology of the Land of the Bible*)

and no stairs in either the approach or in the gateway. This clearly indicates daily use by wheeled vehicles.

The interpretation of the function of the six-pier gate type is based on the location of the door sockets at both the front and rear ends of the gatehouse (Herzog, 1986a, pp. 62–66). This proves that the gate passage was closed off by two sets of doors, one set toward the exterior of the passage and the other on the city side. The dual closure system converted the gate into an independent defensive unit, a kind of fort; it was vital in cities enclosed by earthen ramparts and lacking proper city walls. This fort controlled the wheeled transportation in and out of the city and could serve as the only defensible structure for the local elite. In fortified cities, a gate with a dual closure system may indicate internal social tension and an attempt by the ruling class to protect itself against attack from within the city, as well as from without.

Six-pier city gates are known in Syria at Tell Mardikh/ Ebla (14.70 × 22 m), Qatna (36 × 29 m), Carchemish (25 × 18 m), and Alalakh (23 × 17 m); all of these cities were enclosed by earthen ramparts. [*See* Carchemish; Alalakh.] In Israel such gates have been found attached to the earthen enclosures at Yavneh-Yam (25 × 18 m) and Hazor (20.60 × 16.20 m). They were also adapted for use in walled cities at Megiddo (18 × 10 m), Shechem (17 × 19 m), Gezer (22 × 14 m), Beth-Shemesh (16.50 × 12.40 m), and Tell el-Far'ah (South; 21.60 × 18 m). [*See* Shechem; Gezer; Beth-Shemesh; Far'ah, Tell el- (South).]

Bastions incorporated into city walls, which, like the glacis, seem to revive an EB III tradition, are another typical component of MB II fortifications. Moderately sized bastions (10 × 5 m) have been found at Tel Zeror, Tel Poleg, and Megiddo, while large bastions were uncovered at Gezer (26 × 16 m) and Tell Mardikh/Ebla (65 × 30 m). [*See* Zeror, Tel.]

Late Bronze Age. The people of the Late Bronze Age for the most part reused the fortification systems of the previous period and seldom erected new elements. One of the exceptions was in the newly built city at Tell Abu Hawam, which had a city wall 2 m wide. [*See* Abu Hawam, Tell.] Usually, when the earlier walls were destroyed, cities (e.g., Megiddo) were surrounded solely by a belt of houses and not by an independent city wall. Egyptian accounts and reliefs referring to captured LB cities in Canaan relate in many cases to the king's palace rather than to a fortified city (Herzog, 1986a, p. 73).

On Israel's southern coastal plain, a series of forts or "governors' palaces" evidently served the Egyptian administration in Canaan (Oren, 1984). These solid square structures (about 20 × 20 m) are found from Tel Mor to Deir el-Balah, in addition to the one at the Egyptian center at Beth-Shean. [*See* Mor, Tel; Deir el-Balah; Beth-Shean.] These forts or palaces are usually isolated structures and are not incorporated into a fortification system. This indicates that not only the Canaanites, but also their Egyptian overlords, refrained from constructing fortified cities, perhaps to prevent their potential use as bases for revolt against Egypt.

Iron Age. Real fortification systems are also absent in Iron Age I. The new settlements of the twelfth–eleventh centuries BCE adapted the principle of a peripheral belt of houses, creating either an enclosed settlement (with an empty central courtyard) like the one at 'Izbet Sartah, stratum II, and Beersheba, stratum VII, or as a settlement village (with dwellings filling the inner space), as at Ai and Beth-Shemesh. [*See* 'Izbet Sartah; Beersheba.]

The earliest Iron Age city wall seems to be at Ashdod, stratum 10, belonging to a Philistine city of the late eleventh century. [*See* Ashdod; Philistines, *article on* Early Philistines.] The city has a brick wall 4.50 m wide adjoining a four-room gate protected by two solid towers. At Megiddo, stratum VIA, a simple two-room gate was incorporated in the belt of dwellings that encircled the city then. Yigael Yadin developed a theory of chronological-typological attribution regarding Iron II fortifications: he assumed that only casemate walls and six-room gates were used in the tenth century BCE, during the reign of Solomon, and that they were without exception replaced by solid walls and four-room gates in the ninth century BCE, during the reign of Ahab (Yadin, 1963, pp. 322–325). However, the wide variety of fortification systems now observed in every century of Iron II disproves Yadin's schematic approach (Herzog, 1992b).

Tenth century BCE. All three types of city gates were used in the tenth century BCE. A peripheral belt of houses was still in use at Megiddo, stratum VA; Gezer, stratum 6; and Lachish, level V. [*See* Lachish.] A casemate city wall unconnected to dwellings has been found at Hazor, stratum X, and apparently at 'Ein-Gev, stratum IV. [*See* 'Ein-Gev.] Casemates integrated with dwellings are attributed to this phase at Tell Beit Mirsim, stratum B3. [*See* Beit Mirsim, Tell.] Simple solid walls encircled the cities at Ashdod, stratum 9; Beersheba, stratum V; and, eventually, at Tel Dan. An offset-inset city wall was built at Megiddo, stratum IVB, while a solid wall with towers protected Lachish, level IV,

and Gezer. Six-room gates were used at Ashdod, stratum 9; Hazor, stratum X; Gezer, stratum 6; Megiddo, stratum IVB; and Lachish, level IV. Four-room gates were used at Beersheba, stratum V; Megiddo, stratum IVA; and, eventually, at Dan. Two-room gates were found at Megiddo, stratum VA, and at Tell Beit Mirsim, stratum B3. Four-room gates were also popular in North Syria from the tenth century onward at sites such as Carchemish and Tell Halaf. [*See* Halaf, Tell.]

Ninth century BCE. A casemate city wall integrated with dwellings was built at Beersheba, stratum III, and casemates filled with earth were built at Samaria, stratum II, and at Hazor, stratum VII. A solid wall with towers has been found at Tell en-Nasbeh attached to a four-room city gate at an early stage and to a two-room gate in the final stage. [*See* Nasbeh, Tell en-.] A four-room gate was also erected at Beersheba, stratum III.

Eighth–seventh centuries BCE. During the eighth–seventh centuries BCE only solid city walls were constructed. Simple solid walls have been found in Jerusalem; at Tel Batash, stratum III; and at Lachish, level II; a solid wall with towers was built at Hazor, stratum VA. [*See* Jerusalem.] The six-room city gate reappeared in the eighth century BCE at Tel 'Ira; a two-room gate was erected at Tell Beit Mirsim, stratum A2, and in the Assyrian city of Megiddo, stratum III. [*See* 'Ira, Tel.] A gate complex in the form of an elaborate fort is represented at Lachish, stratum II.

Fortresses and Their Functions. Iron II military units were mainly fortresses erected along borders and trade routes. Whereas architects in Judah preferred rectilinear forms at the southern end of their kingdom, the round type of fort seems to have been chosen at the eastern front of the

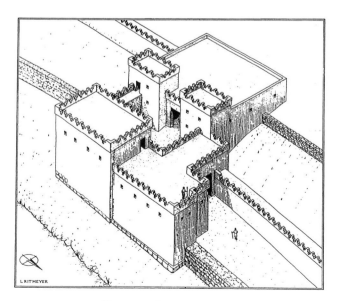

FORTIFICATIONS: Bronze and Iron Ages. *The Iron Age Gate at Timna'*. (Drawing by L. Ritmeyer; copyright G. Kelm)

kingdom of Israel. [See Judah.] A sequence of six square forts (about 50 × 50 m) dating from the tenth through the sixth centuries BCE has been uncovered at Arad. [See Arad, article on Iron Age Period.] Periods of shorter use (eighth–sixth centuries BCE) are ascribed to the rectangular fortresses at Qadesh-Barnea (60 × 40 m) and Ḥorvat ʿUza (51 × 42 m). [See Qadesh-Barnea.] All these units had elaborate fortified walls with towers and gates, systems for water supply and storage, and at Arad even a royal temple. Unlike their southern counterparts, the circular forts of the northern kingdom (late tenth or ninth century BCE), like the one at Khirbet Makhruk, were small—only 19.50 m in diameter (about 300 sq m). The small space was filled by three concentric walls, leaving room for only a few soldiers and their equipment.

The diversity of Iron II fortifications as described above establishes that no single factor was responsible for all of them. Rather, it seems plausible that the decision as to which type of defensive system was suitable for a certain city was dictated by the state's general economic conditions, by the role of the city within the hierarchy of the royal administration, and by the location of the city in terms of the state's overall defense lines. These considerations affected the choices: economical enclosure by a belt of houses, a casemate wall with its savings in space and construction costs, or the more costly—but much stronger—solid city wall. Similarly those considerations influenced the decision between two-, four-, or six-room gates and whether to use inexpensive mud bricks, fieldstones, or ashlar masonry as the construction material.

The complexity of the roles city gates played is very clear in their construction when they served daily as civilian entrances into the city. Along with the variety of forms, Iron II city gates also display uniformity in one basic feature: deep rooms open to their full width to the passageway. This characteristic is particularly striking when compared to MB II gates, whose rooms were enclosed in the towers and where only short piers projected into the passageway. Another important difference in the Iron Age was the presence of a single pair of doors closing off the entrance into the city from the outside only; they allowed free access into the gatehouse from the city side. These characteristics indicate that, in contrast to MB II gates, Iron Age gates had civilian functions above and beyond their purely military/defensive role. This conclusion is further supported by several installations in or next to the gates. Large plazas adjoining the gate inside the city, which could accommodate large audiences or serve as a marketplace, were found at every site. Reservoirs outside the gate (such as at Megiddo and Beersheba) mainly served caravans and bypassers. [See Reservoirs.] Ceremonial installations (e.g., at Megiddo and Dan) testify to cultic activities conducted near the gate. [See Cult.] Benches found built into some of the side rooms (e.g., at Dan, Gezer, and Beersheba) were outfitted for use by merchants, judges, and prophets.

BIBLIOGRAPHY

Bar-Yosef, Ofer. "The Walls of Jericho: An Alternative Interpretation." *Current Anthropology* 27 (1986): 157–162.

Bunimovitz, Shlomo. "The Middle Bronze Age Fortifications in Palestine as a Social Phenomenon." *Tel Aviv* 19.2 (1992): 221–234.

Finkelstein, Israel. "Middle Bronze Age 'Fortifications': A Reflection of Social Organization and Political Formations." *Tel Aviv* 19 (1992): 201–220.

Herzog, Ze'ev. *Das Stadttor in Israel und in den Nachbarländern.* Mainz am Rhein, 1986a.

Herzog, Ze'ev. "Social Organization as Reflected by the Bronze and Iron Age Cities of Israel." In *Comparative Studies in the Development of Complex Societies,* vol. 2, edited by T. C. Champion and M. J. Rowlands. Southampton, Eng., 1986b.

Herzog, Ze'ev. "Administrative Structures in the Iron Age." In *The Architecture of Ancient Israel: From the Prehistoric to the Persian Periods,* edited by Aharon Kempinski and Ronny Reich, pp. 223–230. Jerusalem, 1992a.

Herzog, Ze'ev. "Settlement and Fortification Planning in the Iron Age." In *The Architecture of Ancient Israel: From the Prehistoric to the Persian Periods,* edited by Aharon Kempinski and Ronny Reich, pp. 231–274. Jerusalem, 1992b.

Kempinski, Aharon. "Chalcolithic and Early Bronze Age Temples." In *The Architecture of Ancient Israel: From the Prehistoric to the Persian Periods,* edited by Aharon Kempinski and Ronny Reich, pp. 53–59. Jerusalem, 1992a.

Kempinski, Aharon. "Middle and Late Bronze Age Fortifications." In *The Architecture of Ancient Israel: From the Prehistoric to the Persian Periods,* edited by Aharon Kempinski and Ronny Reich, pp. 127–142. Jerusalem, 1992b.

Kochavi, Moshe, et al. "Aphek-Antipatris, Tēl Pōlēg, Tēl Zerōr, and Tēl Burgā: Four Fortified Sites of the Middle Bronze Age IIA in the Sharon Plain." *Zeitschrift des Deutschen Palästina-Vereins* 95 (1979): 121–165.

Oren, Eliezer D. "'Governors' Residencies' in Canaan under the New Kingdom: A Case Study of Egyptian Administration." *Journal of the Society for the Study of Egyptian Antiquities* 14 (1984): 37–56.

Richard, Suzanne. "The Early Bronze Age: The Rise and Collapse of Urbanism." *Biblical Archaeologist* 50 (1987): 22–43.

Strommenger, Eva. *Habuba Kabira, eine Stadt vor 5000 Jahren: Ausgrabungen der Deutschen Orient-Gesellschaft am Euphrat in Habuba Kabira, Syrien.* Sendschrift der Deutschen Orient-Gesellschaft, 12. Mainz, 1980.

Yadin, Yigael. "Hyksos Fortifications and the Battering Ram." *Bulletin of the American Schools of Oriental Research,* no. 137 (1955): 23–32.

Yadin, Yigael. *The Art of Warfare in Biblical Lands in the Light of Archaeological Study.* 2 vols. New York, 1963.

ZE'EV HERZOG

Fortifications of the Persian Period

A primary means of defense in the Near East was the wall systems surrounding cities. In the case of the Persian Empire, a distinction must be made between urban fortification systems within the traditional Persian heartland and the fortifications in those areas acquired by conquest and consequently under imperial control. The varying Persian approach to urban fortifications is best seen by comparing the

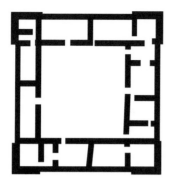

North of Ashdod

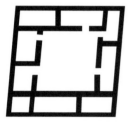

Ḥorvat Mesora

Tell es-Saʻidiyeh

FORTIFICATIONS: Persian Period. *Plans of excavated mid-fifth century fortresses.* (Courtesy K. G. Hoglund)

fortifications of the traditional capitals of the empire with urban areas outside the Iranian plateau.

Cyrus the Great (560–530 BCE), founder of the Persian Empire, established the imposing site of Pasargadae as his capital. No remains of major fortifications have been found relating to Cyrus's rule, although under his successors a significant complex of mud-brick and stone structures was built at the site. Within the complex was a structure the excavators identified as a citadel. It consisted of a large, nearly square courtyard (31 × 32 m) with rooms along its eastern and western sides. Its overall form was rectangular. The citadel and its surrounding structures were enclosed by a mud-brick double wall 8 m thick. There is evidence that large towers projected from the walls at regular intervals. [See Pasargadae.]

Darius I at his accession in 522 BCE selected another city, Susa, to be the capital of the Persian Empire. Although Susa had been largely ruined, the king had it completely rebuilt. A large citadel was built on the acropolis, and the combined palace and residential district was contained within a rectangular enclosure wall of unbaked mud brick more than 20 m thick at its base and tapering upward. Entering the palace of Darius, the Apadana, required passing through a second mud-brick enclosure some 17 m wide at its base. [See Susa.]

Persepolis, a Persian capital also established by Darius, was built on an expansive terrace. There is scattered evidence of a massive mud-brick wall surrounding the whole terrace, and certain areas were protected behind bulky mud-brick defenses. A wall 10 m thick and an estimated 11 m high, sheltered an important administrative building the excavators identified as the Treasury. [See Persepolis.]

In general, these imposing defensive works seem to have functioned less as effective protection from external enemies than as intimidating symbols. Ancient Persia's fortification systems were part of a larger design based on the spatial impact of the royal cities. They could not fail to impress on visitors the awesome power of the empire.

In contrast to those territories securely within the heartland of the Persian Empire, urban centers lying in conquered territories could present a threat if fortified. There was no priority for fortifying cities outside of the Iranian plateau.

Babylon under Persian domain is a clear example of the threat a fortified urban center could pose. Though apparently receptive to Cyrus's conquest of the city in 539 BCE, Babylon attempted to revolt when Darius I came on the throne. Once the city was pacified, Darius ordered the inner walls of its citadel to be destroyed. Babylon attempted to revolt again in 484, when Xerxes came to the throne; following the reassertion of Persian control, Xerxes had the outer city walls destroyed. Deprived of its defenses, in the future Babylon would have faced the unchecked military force of the empire should it have sought independence. [See Babylon.]

A similar concern over the danger presented by urban fortifications can be seen in the biblical narratives surrounding the rebuilding of the walls of Jerusalem during the Persian period. Apparently, imperial officials rapidly stopped an early attempt to erect city walls without authorization, ostensibly because of Jerusalem's history of revolt against imperial rulers (*Ezr.* 4:7–23). When the Persian monarch Artaxerxes formally authorized a refortification effort to launch the career of Nehemiah, neighboring rulers raised the specter of revolt against the empire in an effort to derail the work (*Neh.* 6:5–9). The archaeological remains of a city wall around Jerusalem that best correlate with these biblical notices suggest that the wall was quite rough but was some 2.75 m thick (Kathleen M. Kenyon, *Jerusalem: Excavating 3000 Years of History,* London, 1967, pp. 110–112). It would appear that this rapidly constructed fieldstone wall enclosed only the eastern hill of the city, the area known as the City of David. [See Jerusalem.]

Without fortified urban centers, the Persian Empire directed its strategic planning toward establishing an intricate network of small and medium-sized forts. Staffed by imperial troops, these forts were positioned along the essential routes that tied the vast areas of the empire together. The importance of these forts is evidenced both in written sources and in the archaeological record.

Several ancient Greek writers make specific reference to the essential function of forts in the context of Persian im-

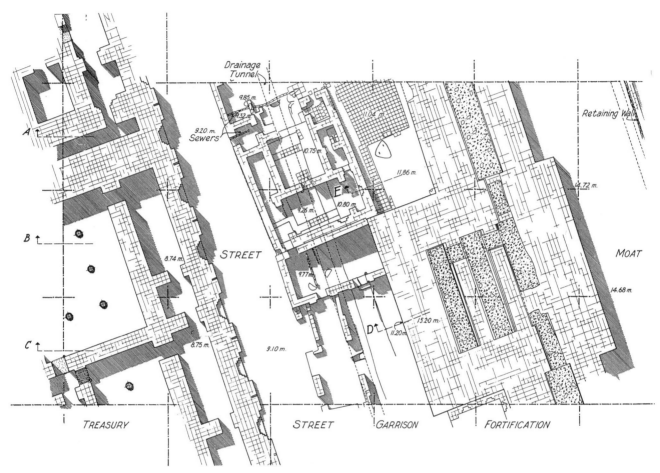

FORTIFICATIONS: Persian Period. *Plan detail of a fortification wall outside of Persepolis.* (After Schmidt, 1953)

perial administration. Xenophon, in his *Cyropaedia* and *Oeconomicus,* emphasizes the necessity both of garrisoned forces for maintaining Persian imperial security and of taxing local populations to support those installations. Xenophon's comments have led some scholars to suggest that these garrisons served the empire as the primary collecting stations for imperial taxes, even though the evidence is ambiguous on this point (see C. Tuplin, "Persian Garrisons on Xenophon and Other Sources," *Achaemenid History* 3 [1988]:67–70).

An analysis of inscriptions, historical references, and a few contemporary documents yields a total of approximately 139 forts constructed throughout the empire. This number is undoubtedly only a fraction of the number of forts actually established, however, because many in addition to those named in literary sources have been uncovered in archaeological excavations.

In Palestine, a number of forts have been recovered. As a result of increased imperial concern over this region following a serious revolt in Egypt, many forts were constructed in the mid-fifth century BCE. In general, they are located on

elevated sites overlooking trade routes, often removed from settled areas. They are square, with a central courtyard and rooms arranged along all four sides. The exterior wall is usually about one meter thick and made of fieldstones. These forts range from 20 to 40 m on a side, their overall size being determined by that of the garrison to be stationed there. The following examples demonstrate the typical forms of these forts.

In 1969, a Persian fort was excavated north of the ancient site of Ashdod along Israel's Mediterranean coast. The fort occupied a hilltop, although there was no sign of a Persian settlement nearby. The structure was nearly 30 m square with an exterior fieldstone wall approximately 1.5 m thick. The central courtyard was 16 m square and surrounded by sixteen rooms. Imported Greek pottery found within the structure placed the use of the fort in the mid-fifth century BCE. [*See* Ashdod.]

In Jordan, the excavations at Tell es-Sa'idiyeh encountered a building exactly 22 m square on the upper part of the site. Its exterior fieldstone wall was 1.25 m thick, and the central courtyard, surrounded by ten rooms; was 9.5 × 8 m.

The few excavated remains in the structure suggest that its first phase dates to the mid-fifth century BCE, although there was no evidence of any occupation of the tell in the Persian period as a whole. [*See* Saʿidiyeh, Tell es-.]

At Tel Michal, on Israel's Sharon plain, excavators encountered a series of small forts. In the first Persian phase at the site a fort, 15 m square was constructed, with rooms on at least one side (the preservation of this phase was poor) and walls approximately 1.2 m wide. A number of grain silos were associated with this structure. The presence of imported pottery dated the phase to the late sixth century BCE. By the end of the fifth century BCE, a new fort was constructed, with fieldstone walls 1 m thick and a central courtyard some 11 m square. It is not preserved well enough to recover the entire plan, but there is evidence for rooms arrayed around the courtyard on some sides. An impressive stairway led up to the fort. This same fort saw use with little alteration until the end of the Persian period. [*See* Michal, Tel.]

Although it is not certain how widely distributed these Persian forts were, it appears that, in some areas of Palestine small forts were placed at 5–8 km (3–5 mi.) intervals overseeing major routes. This pattern suggests that one of the most pervasive archaeological indications of a Persian imperial presence would be the remains of such forts. It also suggests that the local populations under imperial control were faced with a constant reminder of the military power the Persian monarchs could direct.

[*See also* Cities, *article on* Cities of the Persian Period; *and* Building Materials and Techniques, *article on* Materials and Techniques of the Persian through Roman Periods.]

BIBLIOGRAPHY

Herzog, Zeʿev, George Rapp, and Ora Negbi, eds. *Excavations at Tel Michal, Israel.* Publications of the Institute of Archaeology, no. 8. Minneapolis, 1989.

Hoglund, Kenneth G. *Achaemenid Imperial Administration in Syria-Palestine and the Missions of Ezra and Nehemiah.* Society of Biblical Literature, Dissertation Series, no. 125. Atlanta, 1992. Study linking the historical and archaeological evidence, including remains of forts, for an increased Persian military presence in Palestine in the mid-fifth century BCE, with the biblical narratives recalling this period.

Parrot, Jean. "L'architecture militaire et palatiale des Achéménides à Suse." In *150 Jahre Deutsches Archäologisches Institut, 1829–1979,* pp. 79–94. Mainz, 1981. Concise overview of several decades of the work of French excavators at Susa.

Pritchard, James B. *Tell es-Saʿidiyeh: Excavations on the Tell, 1964–1966.* University Museum, Monograph 60. Philadelphia, 1985.

Schmidt, Erich F. *Persepolis,* vol. 1, *Structures, Reliefs, Inscriptions.* University of Chicago Oriental Institute Publications, vol. 68. Chicago, 1953.

Stronach, David. *Pasargadae.* Oxford, 1978.

Tuplin, Christopher. "Xenophon and the Garrisons of the Achaemenid Empire." *Archaeologische Mitteilungen aus Iran* 20 (1987): 167–245. Exhaustive discussion of the literary sources for Persian forts, including a comprehensive catalogue of garrisons.

Williamson, H.G.M. "Nehemiah's Walls Revisited." *Palestine Exploration Quarterly* 116 (July–December 1984): 81–88. Up-to-date sur-

vey of the archaeological and literary evidence for Nehemiah's re-fortification of Jerusalem in the mid-fifth century BCE.

KENNETH G. HOGLUND

Fortifications of the Hellenistic, Roman, and Byzantine Periods

The historical development, forms, and functions of fortifications from Alexander the Great (336–323 BCE) to the rise of Islam in the seventh century present a complex picture. Primary sources are mostly archaeological, although literary sources provide useful details and especially aid in understanding the function of various fortifications. Also helpful are depictions of fortifications in mosaics and other contemporary art. [*See* Mosaics.] The following survey will proceed chronologically, from the beginning of the Hellenistic period to the Muslim conquest.

Hellenistic Period. Fortifications in the Hellenistic period witnessed some assimilation between intrusive Greco-Macedonian and indigenous Near Eastern cultures. Near Eastern peoples had a long tradition of sophisticated fortifications, prompted by the efficiency in siege warfare among many Near Eastern peoples, such as the Assyrians. In the Greek Aegean, in contrast, relative backwardness in siege warfare meant that fortifications were rarely taken by assault before the fourth century BCE. Fortified Greek cities normally fell only to starvation or through internal treachery. Improvements in siege warfare and artillery in the fourth century BCE changed the balance in favor of the besiegers: assault causeways, mounds, wheeled towers, battering rams, mines, and catapults were employed effectively by Alexander during his conquest of the Near East. Even seemingly impregnable fortress cities, such as the island of Tyre, fell victim to Macedonian siege warfare. [*See* Tyre.]

The challenge improved siegecraft posed was met by designers of fortifications in the Hellenistic period. Stone was the preferred building material, although mud brick remained common in regions lacking suitable stone, such as Mesopotamia. Ditches or other obstacles in front of curtain walls were designed to obstruct the approach of siege engines. Curtain walls, often of ashlar construction, became thicker and stronger, both to resist siege engines and to support artillery. In some cases crenellated parapets, which would have been vulnerable to artillery bombardment, were replaced by solid screen walls pierced by windows. Interval towers were erected closer to each other and at higher elevations. These towers projected from the curtain in order to direct enfilading fire at attackers. Towers above all functioned as platforms for defensive artillery, and thus required stronger foundations and internal walls. Gates, which were naturally the weakest point of the defensive perimeter, were flanked by projecting towers and further strengthened by gate courts with both inner and outer entrances. Attackers who penetrated the outer entrance merely broke into a gate court, a small area open to missile fire from all sides. Posterns or sally ports, sometimes hidden behind towers, gave the defenders the opportunity to launch surprise assaults to disrupt attackers and destroy siege equipment. Finally, a heavily fortified citadel was often built within the curtain wall to enable the defenders to continue resistance even after the curtain had been breached.

Virtually all these elements, with the exception of artillery, were well known in the Near East long before Alexander, however. Hellenistic military architects seem merely to have made marginal improvements in Near Eastern fortifications. On the other hand, there is some evidence for a Near Eastern influence on Greek fortifications in this period. The use of mortar as binding material, for example, long known in the Near East, was introduced into the Greek Aegean in the Hellenistic era (Winter, 1971, pp. 93, 95).

Hellenistic city fortifications in the Near East may be best appreciated by examining the new foundations laid by Alexander and his successors. [*See* Cities, *article on* Cities of the Hellenistic and Roman Periods.] Unfortunately, little is known about some of the most important, such as Alexandria in Egypt or Seleucia on the Tigris. [*See* Alexandria; Seleucia on the Tigris.] Better-preserved examples of Hellenistic urban fortifications include the Seleucid foundations of Antioch on the Orontes and Dura-Europos. The defended area of Antioch, founded in 300 BCE, eventually measured 3.2 × 1.2–1.5 km. This huge expanse was apparently deemed necessary by the inherent tactical weakness of the site on the east bank of the Orontes River, which was dominated by Mt. Silpius. The city walls were thus extended far up the mountain slopes, even though this resulted in extensive uninhabited areas within the fortifications; the walls terminated in a citadel on top of the mountain to prevent its use by attackers. In stark contrast, Dura-Europos, also founded in about 300 BCE, exploited a tactically strong position on the Middle Euphrates River. Its curtain wall on three of its four sides zigzagged to exploit defensible ground. The east wall directly overlooked the Euphrates; the north and south walls were erected on top of the banks of steep ravines, leaving the western wall to bar the only approach over relatively flat ground. Rectangular interval towers projected from the curtain and flanked the main gateway in the west wall. Within the fortifications a citadel was built against the east wall, overlooking the river plain. [*See* Antioch on Orontes; Dura-Europos.]

Even towns of more modest size were protected by substantial fortifications in the Hellenistic period. The city of Dor on the Palestinian coast has yielded important evidence suggesting change in fortifications that may reflect cultural distinctions. A rebuild of the city's walls in the fourth century BCE remained in the Phoenician tradition of ashlar pillars surrounding a rubble fill. In the third century BCE, however, the walls were rebuilt "in the entirely different Greek style" of header-stretcher masonry with projecting rectan-

gular towers (Stern, 1993, p. 366). [*See* Dor.] Tel Beth-Yeraḥ (Khirbet Kerak), on the southwest shore of the Sea of Galilee, was defended by a brick wall erected on top of a massive basalt rubble foundation 4.8–7 m wide and 3.5 m high. The wall was defended by alternating rectangular and circular interval towers (Hestrin, 1993, pp. 255, 258). [*See* Beth-Yeraḥ.] Round towers were in fact common in the Hellenistic period, attested at such sites as Caesarea, Ptolemais (Akko), and Sebaste (Samaria). [*See* Caesarea; Akko; Samaria.]

The Hellenistic cities and their hinterlands were often defended by outlying fortifications. A relatively well-preserved and closely dated example is the fort on top of Jebel Ṣarṭaba, 2 km (1 mi.) southeast of Pella in the Jordan Valley and surmounting the highest elevation in the region, with views up to 25 km (16 mi.) away. The fort measures about 55–70 m on each side. It was defended by a curtain wall approximately 2 m thick and by eight towers projecting from the curtain, all of local cherty limestone. The towers were located at each corner and in the middle of each side of the curtain wall. Access was provided by four posterns one on each side and each directly adjacent to a projecting tower. Within the fort, two rock-cut cisterns sealed with cement held the water supply (McNicoll et al., 1982, pp. 64–67).

In addition to fortified cities and forts, fortified palaces constitute an important strand in the Hellenistic tradition in the Near East. Especially notable are the Herodian fortified palaces of the late first century BCE, such as Masada, Herodium, and Machaerus. The palace on top of Masada, for example, occupied a flat-topped mountain rising 100–400 m above the surrounding terrain. The curtain wall was of casemate construction with thirty rectangular towers spaced at irregular intervals of 35–90 m, as dictated by tactical considerations. The four original gates were all of the courtyard type, with inner and outer entrances. Machaerus similarly occupied a mountaintop. Herodium was built on top of a hill about 60 m above the surrounding terrain but formed a double circular enclosure about 62 m in diameter. A corridor about 3.5 m wide ran between the two walls and provided access to four semicircular towers spaced equidistant from one other at the cardinal points. Both the towers and outer wall were founded on a series of vaults. [*See* Masada; Herodium; Machaerus.]

Roman Period. The advent of Roman rule in the first century BCE did not significantly affect city fortifications in the Near East: Rome's many client rulers in the region continued Hellenistic traditions. When Rome annexed most of its clients, by the late first century CE, Roman forces were deployed along a military frontier stretching from the Black Sea to the Red Sea. There was a sporadic threat in the north from Parthia, and low-intensity raids by Arab nomads recurred in the south, but neither possessed significant siege capability. [*See* Limes Arabicus.]

The Romans introduced their own distinctive military architectural tradition into the Near East. Roman armies on campaign usually constructed a temporary camp at the end of each day's march. These so-called "marching camps" were simply constructed of earth and timber. The soldiers dug a ditch enclosing a rectangular area sufficient for the entire army. They piled the excavated earth from the trench into a rampart, often topped by wooden stakes carried by each soldier. The army then camped that night within the defended enclosure. These rectangular marching camps typically had rounded corners, giving rise to the term "playing-card forts" by modern scholars. Such forts are attested in the Near East in the early Roman period. These include both temporary siege camps, such as those in the circum-

vallation at Masada, and permanent forts, such as the late first-century CE playing-card fort on the summit of Tell el-Hajj on the Syrian Euphrates. The fort (about 120 × 160 m) shared key characteristics with contemporary forts in the Western empire: rounded corners, nonprojecting internal towers, and a relatively thin (about 1.2 m wide) curtain wall fronted by a ditch (Bridel, 1972). Aerial photography suggests that other early Roman playing-card forts probably await excavation in the region (Kennedy and Riley, 1990, pp. 95–110).

Otherwise, the Romans were content to base a significant portion of their Near Eastern units in towns and cities, which were usually fortified. It is likely that the situation at Dura-

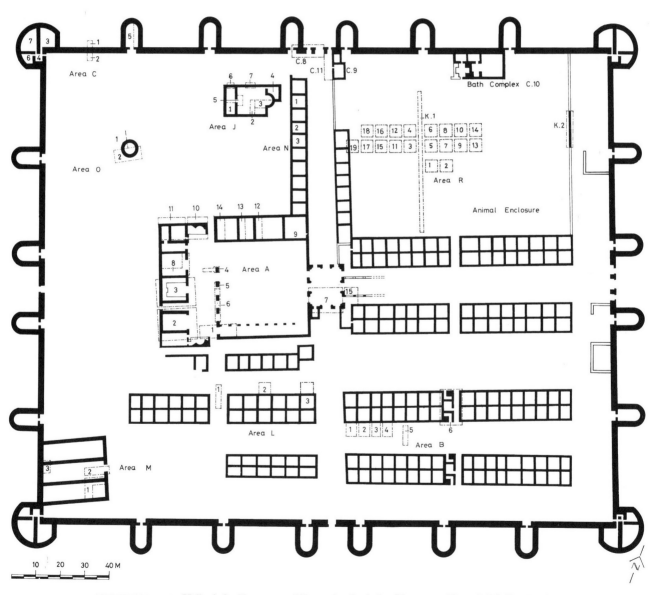

FORTIFICATIONS: Hellenistic, Roman, and Byzantine Periods. Figure 1. *Plan of el-Lejjun (ancient Betthorus).* A later Roman legionary fortress east of the Dead Sea. Built around 300 CE for *legio IV Martia.* (Courtesy S. T. Parker)

Europos, garrisoned by the Romans beginning in about 165 CE, was typical. There the garrison simply walled off a quarter of the city for its exclusive use. At Bosra, capital of provincial Arabia, the legionary base was attached as an annex to the city's northern curtain wall. [See Bosra.] At Satala in Cappadocia, the late first-century CE legionary fortress compares closely in size and plan with contemporary examples from the Western empire. [See Cappadocia.] Forts with projecting rectangular towers appear no later than the late second century, as revealed by new evidence from Humeima (ancient Avara) in southern Jordan. [See Humeima.]

Noticeable changes occur in fortifications in the late third century. These are no doubt connected with the increased threats posed by the Sasanians, with their sophisticated siege capability, and the nomadic Arabs, with their fine light cavalry (but still lacking siege technology). Warfare between Rome and Persia from the third century onward usually centered on sieges of well-fortified strongpoints. Many fortified cities fell to determined assaults, such as Dura-Europos to the Sasanians and Palmyra to the Romans. The late third-century defenses of Palmyra in Syria graphically illustrate hurried attempts at refortification by many cities in this period. The so-called Zenobia's wall at Palmyra incorporates much *spolia* (reused architectural fragments) and several preexisting monuments along its line. The curtain is defended by projecting towers of varied sizes and plans (Gawlikowski, 1974). [See Palmyra.] In contrast, the fortifications at Gerasa (Jerash) in Transjordan present a fairly regular program. The curtain wall (3.5 m wide) was defended by a series of 101 rectangular towers spaced at intervals of 16–22 m and projecting from the curtain. Although the fortifications at Gerasa were long dated to the end of the first century CE, recent excavations around the south gate suggest that at least this portion of the fortifications, and perhaps the entire circuit, actually date to the turn of the fourth century (Seigne, 1992). [See Jerash.]

Late Roman military architecture reflects a marked change from the previous period. The playing-card plan was completely abandoned in favor of rectangular forts defended by projecting towers. There was also a marked reduction in areal size, presumably corresponding to the reduced strength of individual garrison units. The tetrarchic legionary fortress at el-Lejjun, for example, was only 20 percent the size of legionary fortresses of the principate (see figure 1). Similar reductions are observable in Late Roman auxiliary forts, which usually ranged from about 35 to 60 sq m (0.12–0.36 ha). Although smaller in size, the Late Roman forts were more heavily fortified, with thicker walls, larger and higher projecting towers, and strongly defended gates. One notable change was the shift in the construction of curtain walls from solid ashlar masonry to a rubble core surrounded by two faces of coursed mortared masonry.

The towers were intended partly as platforms for defensive artillery. In smaller forts most interior rooms were built as casemates against the curtain wall, surrounding a central courtyard. An especially well-preserved example of a Late Roman fort is Qasr Bshir (castra praetorii Mobeni), erected in 293–305 CE of roughly cut, dry-laid masonry (see figure 2). Four large angle towers, each of three stories with a central staircase, dominate the plan and two smaller interval towers flank the main gate. A sally port in one wall and slit windows in the tower walls illustrate key elements of the defenses. The internal rooms against the curtain wall were built in two stories: the lower story apparently served as stables, the upper story as a barrack.

Diverse types of towers were employed in the Late Roman period, at times even in the same structure. U-shaped towers, which may have been imported from the lower Danubian frontier by Roman military architects in the late third century, project from both Near Eastern city walls, such as Singara in northern Mesopotamia, and legionary fortresses (el-Lejjun and Udruh in Transjordan). These two latter fortresses also were protected by large (about 20 m in diameter) semicircular towers at each corner. These corner towers contained several internal rooms on each floor, connected by an interior staircase that wound around a central pier. Rectangular towers, usually projecting from the curtain wall, are attested at numerous sites. Rectangular towers were presumably easier to construct than U-shaped or semicircular towers, but the right-angled corners of rectangular towers were more vulnerable to battering rams and other siege en-

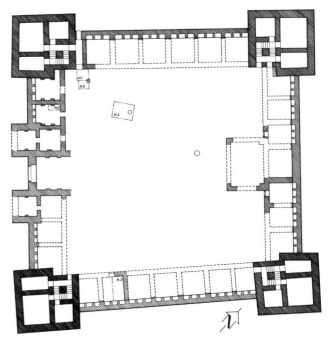

FORTIFICATIONS: Hellenistic, Roman, and Byzantine Periods. Figure 2. *Plan of Qasr Bshir (castra praetorii Mobeni).* A late Roman *castellum* erected in Moab between 293 and 305 CE, probably designed for a cavalry unit. (Courtesy S. T. Parker)

gines. Towers also stood as independent structures, often on high elevations with extensive views. Epigraphic evidence reveals that these were constructed both by the Roman soldiers and by civilians, presumably for a multiplicity of purposes.

Byzantine Period. The basic type of fortifications with rectangular towers projecting from the curtain wall continued through the Byzantine period in the Near East, as evidenced by such examples as Sergiopolis (Rusafa) in northern Syria and Zenobia (Halabiyya) on the Syrian Euphrates. [*See* Rusafa.] The preeminent example, of course, dating to the mid-fifth century, is the Theodosian wall of Constantinople (Foss and Winfield, 1986; pp. 41–77). [*See* Constantinople.] Interestingly, however, some Byzantine *castella*, such as the early fifth-century forts at Qaṣr el-Baʿiq and the contemporary barracks at Umm el-Jimal, lack projecting towers (Parker, 1986; pp. 24–29). [*See* Umm el-Jimal.] All this suggests considerable variation in the types of fortifications in the Byzantine period.

An interesting feature of Byzantine fortifications is the revival of a fortified citadel within the walled enclosure, an element found in Hellenistic and earlier Greek fortifications but generally lacking in the Roman tradition. Zenobia on the Euphrates provides a good example, where the surviving remains can be compared to a detailed description by Procopius (*De Aedificiis* 2.8–25). The walls form a triangle whose base rests on the right bank of the Euphrates. The two remaining sides of the curtain extend up the slope to meet at a citadel on top of a hill that dominates the site. The citadel itself was further strengthened by a glacis at the base of its walls. The curtain walls were punctuated by closely spaced rectangular towers that projected quite far beyond the line of the wall (Lauffray, 1983).

Representations of various urban fortifications depicted in Byzantine mosaics, such as the Madaba map and the city vignettes from the Church of St. Stephen at Umm er-Rasas/Kastron Mefaa in Transjordan offer important evidence for the superstructure of curtain walls and towers. [*See* Umm er-Rasas.] The mid-sixth-century Madaba map, for example, depicts Jerusalem as defended by interval towers that rise above the curtain wall; windows are visible in the upper story of some of the towers. Each gate is flanked by twin interval towers. Further details of Jerusalem's defenses are depicted in the mosaic of the Church of St. Stephen. That vignette also shows interval towers of three stories rising above the curtain wall. The towers have flat roofs, presumably to facilitate their use as fighting platforms. Windows are visible in both the towers and curtain wall and the entire circuit of walls and towers is topped by a crenellated parapet. [*See* Jerusalem.] The vignettes of other cities in Palestine, Egypt, and Transjordan depicted in the mosaic, including that of Kastron Mefaa itself, display similar features (Piccirillo, 1993). It is useful to compare these elements with the detailed descriptions of fortifications in Procopius. These

basic principles of Byzantine fortifications continued well into the medieval period, as seen for example in the Byzantine fortifications of Armenian Cilicia (Edwards, 1987).

[*See also* Alexandrian Empire; Byzantine Empire; *and* Roman Empire.]

BIBLIOGRAPHY

Bridel, Philippe. *Tell el Hajj in Syrien.* Bern, 1972.

Edwards, Robert W. *The Fortifications of Armenian Cilicia.* Dumbarton Oaks Studies, 23. Washington, D.C., 1987.

Foss, Clive, and David Winfield. *Byzantine Fortifications: An Introduction.* Praetoria, 1986. Focuses almost exclusively on Anatolia and the Balkans.

Gawlikowski, Michal. "Le défences de Palmyre." *Syria* 51 (1974): 231–242.

Hestrin, Ruth, "Beth Yerah." In *The New Encyclopedia of Archaeological Excavations in the Holy Land,* vol. 1, pp. 255–259. Jerusalem and New York, 1993.

Karnapp, Walter. *Die Stadtmauer von Resafa in Syrien.* Berlin, 1976.

Kennedy, David L., and Derrick N. Riley. *Rome's Desert Frontier from the Air.* Austin, 1990. Essential for its rare aerial photographs and accompanying line drawings of many key Roman fortifications.

Lander, James. *Roman Stone Fortifications: Variation and Change from the First Century A.D. to the Fourth.* British Archaeological Reports, International Series, no. 206. Oxford, 1984. Valuable synthesis of Roman fortifications throughout the empire, although the material on the Roman Near East is now somewhat dated in light of recent excavations.

Lauffray, Jean. *Halabiyya-Zenobia: Place forte du limes oriental et la Haute-Mésopotamie au VIe siècle,* vol. 1, *Les duchés frontaliers de Mésopotamie et les fortifications de Zenobia;* vol. 2, *L'architecture publique, religieuse, privée et funéraire.* Paris, 1983.

McNicoll, Anthony W., et al. *Pella in Jordan 1: An Interim Report on the Joint University of Sydney and the College of Wooster Excavations at Pella, 1979–1981.* Canberra, 1982.

Netzer, Ehud. *Greater Herodium.* Qedem, vol. 13. Jerusalem, 1981.

Netzer, Ehud. *Masada 3: The Buildings, Stratigraphy, and Architecture.* Jerusalem, 1991.

Parker, S. Thomas. *Romans and Saracens: A History of the Arabian Frontier.* American Schools of Oriental Research, Dissertation Series, 6. Winona Lake, Ind., 1986. Contains plans of most Roman and Byzantine fortifications in Jordan.

Parker, S. Thomas, ed. *The Roman Frontier in Central Jordan: Interim Report on the Limes Arabicus Project, 1980–1985.* 2 vols. British Archaeological Reports, International Series, no. 340. Oxford, 1987. Includes detailed architectural and stratigraphic analysis of several Late Roman fortifications east of the Dead Sea, including el-Lejjun and Qasr Bshir.

Parker, S. Thomas. "The Typology of Roman and Byzantine Forts and Fortresses in Jordan." In *Studies in the History and Archaeology of Jordan,* vol. 5, edited by Safwan Tell. Amman, forthcoming.

Parker, Safwan Thomas. "Roman Legionary Fortresses in the East." In *Roman Legions and Their Fortresses.* London, forthcoming.

Piccirillo, Michele. *The Mosaics of Jordan.* Edited by Patricia M. Bikai and Thomas A. Dailey. American Center of Oriental Research, Publications, 1. Amman, 1993. Lavishly illustrated with detailed photographs.

Seigne, Jacques. "Jérash romaine et byzantine: Développement urbain d'une ville provinciale orientale." In *Studies in the History and Archaeology of Jordan,* vol. 4, edited by Ghazi Bisheh, pp. 331–341. Amman, 1992. Major reinterpretation of the history of this Decapolis city.

Stern, Ephraim. "Dor." In *The New Encyclopedia of Archaeological Ex-*

cavations in the Holy Land, vol. 1, pp. 357–368. Jerusalem and New York, 1993.

Winter, Frederick E.. *Greek Fortifications.* London, 1971. Still the standard survey of the topic.

S. Thomas Parker

Fortifications of the Islamic Period

A fortified castle or urban citadel served both for defense and to forestall an attack by its mere presence. Fortresses protected against incursions of a nearby foe; they were even more necessary when the vulnerable area was sparsely populated, as was often the case in Islam's frontier zones. Fortifications also served for the surveillance and control of the domestic landscape, particularly in areas where a minority of Muslims ruled over a larger non-Muslim majority. However, there was always the danger of a fortress becoming the seat of internal revolt, as in the case of Ibn Hafsun, who held out against the Umayyad emirs of Cordoba at Bobastro in the mountains above Malaga. Situated at important points in the landscape, such as mountaintops, seaports, fords and bridges, fortresses regulate the passage of traffic from one critical point to another and prevent an enemy from gaining access. A fortress is often part of a large network, such as the littoral *ribat*s stretching along the coast of Tunisia in the Aghlabid period. The Tunisian *ribat*s, furthermore, were linked by the ability to communicate via signals emitted from their lighthouse towers. Such communication was hardly unusual: Islamic Spain had a similar system of towers, which could relay a smoke signal from Soria to Cordoba in half a day.

Islam's earliest fortifications were the late classical, Byzantine, Sasanian, and Soghdian fortresses taken over by Islamic armies and the newly founded garrison cities *(amsar)*, such as Kufah, Basra, Wasit, Fustat, and Kairouan (Qayrawan), which secured the territory held by Islam and provided stations from which to launch campaigns farther afield. There is very little information on the early state of these centers; utilitarian at first, the construction of a congregational mosque and governor's residence *(dar al-imarah)* soon followed.

In addition to wholly defensive fortresses guarding critical points in the landscape, there was a variety of other fortified buildings where defense was secondary. One was the isolated agricultural estates, such those built by the Umayyads in Syria and Transjordan in the late seventh and early eighth centuries. In the course of conquering the Levant, Islam had encountered Roman fortifications from the Gulf of 'Aqaba to Damascus and from Damascus to Palmyra. Moreover a great many of these fortresses, such as Qasr al-Hallabat (213–217, 529 CE) in Transjordan, served as temporary residences to Umayyad princes. Thus, when the Umayyad patrons began to build large residences in their so-called desert estates—Jabal Says and Khirbet al-Minyeh *(705–715)*, Qasr al-Hayr West (c. 727), Qasr al-Hayr East (729), Khirbat al-Mafjar (c. 725–750), and Qasr al-Meshatta and Qasr al-Tuba (c. 744)—they adopted the *appearance* of the defensive architecture inherited from the Romans, although their mil-

FORTIFICATIONS: Islamic Period. Figure 1. *Qasr al-Hayr East.* Small enclosure with facade entrance gate with machicolation. (Courtesy D. F. Ruggles)

itary service was minimal. Buildings such as the large and small enclosures at Qaṣr al-Ḥayr East had tall, windowless stone walls with corner towers from which the surrounding area could be watched. Access was limited to a few closely guarded portals flanked by half-round towers and overlooked by a machicolation on three brackets with two openings. [See Qaṣr al-Ḥallabat; Qaṣr al-Ḥayr ash-Sharqi; Qaṣr al-Ḥayr al-Gharbi; Mafjar, Khirbat al-; and Qaṣr al-Meshatta.]

Machicolation consists of a high balcony projecting on brackets with gaps in the floor for dropping heavy objects or hot liquids. Although western Europe did not learn the device until the late twelfth century, K. A. C. Creswell (1952) states that it was known in pre-Islamic Syria. The first construction of machicolation in Islamic architecture occurred at Qaṣr al-Ḥayr East (see figure 1). An older and more rudimentary machicolation with only one opening may be found at Qaṣr al-Ḥayr West; it was part of an existing monastery tower incorporated into one side of the Qaṣr's enclosure walls.

A second semifortified type was the caravanserai, which offered overnight lodgings to merchants traveling along key commercial arteries. Inns, such as the Ribat-i Malik (c. 1068–1080), which proliferated in the eleventh and twelfth centuries in Iran and Central Asia, were built not to withstand the direct attack of armies but rather to offer safe haven against bandits. Thus caravanserai portals are more decorative than formidable, yet their outer walls are tall, windowless, marked by corner towers, and pierced usually by a single well-guarded entrance. [See Caravanserais.]

A third type was the well-fortified *ribat*, a frontier outpost inhabited by warrior monks (*murabiṭin* and *ghazi*). The Sousse Ribat (771–788, tower 821) consisted of an impenetrable square enclosure with stone walls that now rise 8.5 m (28 ft.) above ground level and are supported by eight towers (see figure 2). The walls were topped by a crenelated battlement consisting of raised merlons (the solid parts of the wall between the openings) alternating with open crenels; Sousse's crenelations are somewhat unusual in that the merlons were pierced by narrow windows for shooting arrows. Inside are two stories of small unadorned living cells intended for individuals rather than families. One of the towers soars above the rest: 15.38 m (50.45 ft.) high, it offers a magnificent view of the coast and could communicate with

FORTIFICATIONS: Islamic Period. Figure 2. *The ribat at Sousse, Tunisia.* (After Georges Marçais, *L'Architecture Musulmane d'occident*, Paris, 1954)

the Monastir Ribat (796) to the south as well as other *ribats*, if pirate ships were sighted off the Tunisian coast.

Fortifications exploit natural topographic features such as height, sheerness of rock face, or the isolation of a peninsula as at Mahdiyah (912). Additional measures for security were implemented by architectural design. The Merida Alcazaba (835), for example, had an ample interior for the storage of food and an internal cistern with which to withstand long sieges. More direct implements and methods of attack such as ladders for scaling the walls, catapults (*manjaniq* and '*arrada*), battering rams *(kabsh)* for breaching the walls, siege towers on wheels *(burj),* or digging under the foundations could be withstood by a portcullis, the doubling of thick stone walls, and steeply sloping glacis foundations *(zallaqa)* that exposed would-be scalers and made undermining impossible. Calatrava la Vieja in Spain and Raqqa in Iraq (both ninth century) had moats. The portcullis, an iron grate that could be raised or lowered along grooves to block an entrance, was an ancient Near Eastern device that was employed at Ukhaidir (764–778). Rather than preventing ingress, the portcullis was used to trap enemy soldiers between the outer and inner walls of the portal where they could be assailed by archers above. Additionally, running all the way around Ukhaidir's outer walls at a height of five m (16.5 ft.) was a gallery with openings in its floors through which arrows and projectiles could be fired at attackers.

Fortification had a psychological as well as military purpose, giving the impression of invincibility and formidable strength to allies and enemies alike. In situations in which full-scale military attack was not expected, architecture could be embellished with a fortified exterior that was unnecessary or even nonfunctional but served a symbolic role. The city of Baghdad (begun 762) was located at the center of the 'Abbasid realm where attack was unlikely, yet the round city was surrounded by double walls, 35–40 m (114.8–131.2 ft.) apart. The walls were tall (outer 14 m [46 ft.], inner 17 m [55.8 ft.]) and thick (outer 4 m [13.1 ft.], inner 5 m [16.4 ft.]), and the inner wall was crenelated. The walls were flanked by 112 towers and pierced by four gates, one of which was described by a medieval historian as having a bent entrance. According to Creswell (1952), the bent entrance was known to neither the Romans (who employed only oblique entrances) nor the early Byzantines. Its origins are to be found in Central Asia, and the appearance of the device in Islamic architecture at this time is the result of the 'Abbasids' orientation toward Iran rather than the Hellenistic Mediterranean. A bent entrance prevented direct access into an enclosure and instead forced the intruder through a short maze of two turns. The strategic advantage was that the enemy encountered his opponent at a right angle, with his right side exposed (the left hand holding the shield, the right clenching the sword). Bent entrances existed in a variety of configurations and were used both for defense and visual privacy. [*See* Baghdad.]

The improved fortification of Cairo's city walls in 1087 by Badr al-Jamali included many defensive features, including slippery stone glacis foundations. Today a portion of the original walls and three stone gates survive: the Bab al-Nasir, Bab al-Futuh, and Bab Zawayla. The Bab al-Nasir's portal had a rampart walk with a crenelated parapet. Its square towers were three storied and solid in their lower two stories. They flanked a vaulted passageway (20.89 m high × 24.22 m wide × 20.47 m long [68.5 × 79.5 × 67.2 ft.]). Above was another passage in the floor out of which were five openings, similar to those at Ukhaidir, for throwing projectiles at the enemy beneath. Halfway up the first story there were stone columns laid horizontally as a bond between the inner rubble core and the outer ashlar (dressed masonry) facing. More importantly, the columns also supported the walls in the event that a battering ram was applied to the base, a tunnel was dug under the walls and set on fire, or the stones were pried loose by miners. Such elaborate and expensive precautions were deemed strategically necessary at the time they were built. Almost impossible to destroy by fire, undermining, and battering, Cairo's monumental gates have withstood the ravages of time equally well. [*See* Cairo.]

BIBLIOGRAPHY

Bosworth, Edmund. "Armies of the Prophet: Strategy, Tactics, and Weapons in Islamic Warfare." In *The World of Islam*, edited by Bernard Lewis, pp. 201–212. London, 1976. More useful on the subject of objects and practice than architecture.

Creswell, K. A. C. "Fortification in Islam before A.D. 1250." *Proceedings of the British Academy* 38 (1952): 89–125. Excellent though conservative discussion of Islamic fortification techniques and their origins, focusing on center lands and largely ignoring the Maghrib and Central Asia.

Creswell, K. A. C. *Early Muslim Architecture.* 2 vols. 2d ed. Oxford, 1969. Archaeologically reliable survey of Islamic architecture from the beginning through the ninth century CE. The reader may consult an abridged version, which has the advantage of including recent discoveries and theories: *A Short Account of Early Muslim Architecture* (Aldershot, 1989).

Grabar, Oleg. "Palaces, Citadels, and Fortifications." In *Architecture of the Islamic World*, edited by George Michell, pp. 65–79. London, 1978. Nicely complements Creswell's 1952 article because it is thematic rather than chronological, stresses the history of conquest rather than architectural typology, and examines the means as well as psychology of fortification.

Hogg, Ian. *The History of Fortification.* New York, 1981. Discusses fortifications in all places and periods, and thus skims lightly over Islam, but includes a description of medieval techniques of attack, siege, and defense.

Zozaya, Juan. "The Fortifications of al-Andalus." In *Al-Andalus: The Art of Islamic Spain*, edited by Jerrilynn D. Dodds, pp. 62–73. New York, 1992. Short but useful discussion of fortification systems in Spain.

D. FAIRCHILD RUGGLES

FOUNDATION TRENCH. In order to support the base of a wall or other construction element, ancient builders dug foundation trenches. A trench for a wall generally ran for the length of the wall. The depth and width of the trench depended on both the stability of the matrix on which the wall was founded and the weight of the structure being supported. If bedrock, an earlier wall, or firm soil formed a stable foundation for supporting a wall, the foundation trench did not need to be wider than the wall laid in it. Builders frequently bedded walls in an unstable tell matrix, which necessitated a wider trench to spread the weight of the wall and its foundation over a greater surface and thus prevent the wall from sinking. Occasionally, sand was spread in the bottom of the trench to facilitate drainage away from the base of the wall.

Two methods were commonly employed in constructing the foundation. In the first, a foundation trench with vertical sides was prepared. Then stones were laid against the sides and the core was filled with stones and perhaps mortar. In many cases, the stones of the superstructure or wall formed a smoother vertical edge than those of the foundation trench, so even at sites where floor surfaces have not been preserved, it is possible to tell, when excavating, when the bottom of the foundation trench is reached. In the second type, the foundation trench was cut wider than the foundation wall, usually in a V-shaped configuration, to minimize soil cave-ins and to simplify digging. After the wall was constructed in the center of the trench, the space between it and the trench's sloping sides was filled with small stones and earth. This second type is more easily detected in excavation.

On sites that are tells—that is, at sites where there is a buildup of material from earlier occupation and construction—builders often simplified their work by reusing stones from earlier walls. Thus, all that may remain of a wall and its foundation is a "robber's trench," an empty trench that follows the course of the original foundation trench.

[*See also* Stratigraphy.]

BIBLIOGRAPHY

Kempinski, Aharon, and Ronny Reich, eds. *The Architecture of Ancient Israel: From the Prehistoric to the Persian Periods.* Jerusalem, 1992. Concise and well-illustrated introduction to building materials and construction methods, followed by essays on each period.

ELIZABETH M. BLOCH-SMITH

FOUR-ROOM HOUSE.

Together with the three-roomed variation, the four-room house was the dominant house form in ancient Israel (see figures 1a and 1b respectively). A shed was sometimes added along one side (see figure 1c). An uncommon two-roomed variant lacked the characteristic transverse rear room. For functional and structural reasons the form was highly standardized. As a result, unusual or extensively elaborated plans should be closely examined to ensure that they do not represent architectural reconstructions of more than one building or stratigraphic phase. This distinctive house is found through-

out Israel and Judah, from the earliest hill settlements (Marquet-Krause, 1949; Callaway, 1983; Stager, 1985) to the latest Iron II towns. [*See* Judah.] While not the only house form seen in Israelite cities, it is found nearly universally in lightly fortified desert farms (Cohen, 1979), farming hamlets and villages, towns, and military outposts.

Door placement and other details apart, the form was highly stylized almost from the start (e.g., at Khirbet Radannah and Ai), although it could be fitted into an existing space by tapering its overall shape (or by repositioning the rear room or even eliminating it) if alternative storage space were available nearby. [*See* Radannah; Ai.] Ethnographic parallels and architectural analysis support the conclusion that this house was highly adapted to normative Israelite family structure, modes of production (mixed peasant dry-farming and/or horticulture and animal husbandry: Hopkins, 1985) and socioeconomic organization (Holladay, 1995, pp. 391–393). The sporadic earlier appearance of similar houses in Late Bronze Age Syria is of interest and may have something to say about the emergence of early Israel.

Palestinian House Forms and Ethnicity. In Palestine, with the exception of a few examples at tenth-century BCE Philistine sites (e.g., see Maisler [Mazar], 1951), all occurrences of the four-room house known to date seem to be limited to Israelite or Judean sites. Typical Philistine houses were quite different (Dothan, 1971; Gitin, 1989). [*See* Philistines.] The form also appears in Transjordan, with other styles of pillared house construction, but not enough is known of its dating or archaeological contexts there to allow for a clear interpretation. In general, however, even when the form appears at a non-Israelite site, it does so during such periods of overwhelming Israelite hegemony as the United Monarchy. In those cases, the buildings may well have housed ethnic Israelites. Though data are sparse, the form does not seem to have survived the Babylonian Exile. For all these reasons, it seems legitimate to call this the Israelite house.

Architectural Reconstruction and Functional Interpretation. Extremely few four-room houses are preserved to the second story, most being known only from their stone foundations and floor surfaces. Thus, details of the upper story or stories, roof, and so forth must either be extrapolated from a few known details or inferred from constructional features (see below). Similarly, functional interpretations must proceed on the basis of inference from architectural details in the light of ancient and ethnographic parallels, along with a smattering of meaningful artifact distributions. As a negative case in point, rows of storejars in the stabling areas of houses destroyed by enemy action may reasonably be construed as exceptional, reflecting preparations for siege and not normal storage patterns (cf. Holladay, 1986, p. 160). As is often the case in archaeology, even the name *four-room house* is misleading, describing only the main structural divisions of the ground floor—one or two side aisles, a misnamed "courtyard," and a rear room in the

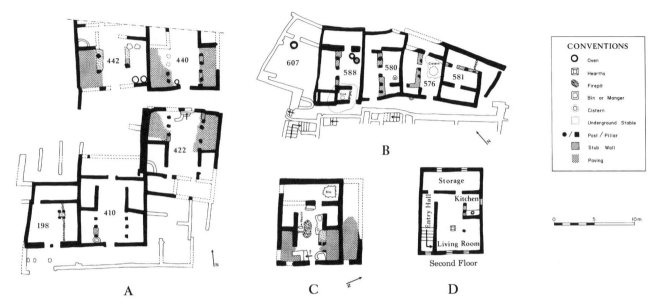

FOUR-ROOM HOUSE: Figure 1. *House plans.* (a) Four typical four-room houses, and one slightly atypical three-room house, from Tell el-Farʿah (North) (Chambon, 1984); (b) three typical and one "squeezed in" three-room house from Tell en-Nasbeh (McCown, 1947, survey map); (c) four-room house with added side-hall or shed from Shechem (Wright, 1965, fig. 76); (d) a proposed second-floor plan of the house figured in (c) above. (Courtesy J. S. Holladay)

usual terminology—and ignoring both the characteristic second story (the structural reason for the massively pillared construction) and the frequent divisions in the side and back "rooms." In fact, apart from their very unitary character (each household clearly is an independent social unit), the pillars and cobbled side aisles are the chief distinguishing characteristics of these houses. The pillars are of a variety of locally available materials—from well-shaped caprock (Ar., *nari*) monoliths to stacked, roughly dressed stone drums or slabs to heavy wooden or mud-brick pillars. Occasionally, the beams borne by the pillars were also stone monoliths or were complexly built up of cantilevered stone slabs. Only high loading factors would ensure the integrity of the stacked stone-boulder or stone-slab construction; the massiveness of all the other forms similarly attests to the tremendous load-carrying capacity of the line or lines of pillars.

Floor surfaces range from hardened surfaces composed of cobbles or flagstones bedded in ashy soil for the pillared side aisle/s to relatively clean packed earth, often multilaminated, with a few flat-lying sherds and occasional slivers of bone, for the rear room, small side rooms, and the center room or courtyard. Rarely, the center room was whitewashed or surfaced with a thin white marly "plaster." Some small side rooms lack clear surfaces and may be interpreted as mirey, uncleaned stalls for the penned-up "fatted calf" (*1 Sm.* 28:24; *Am.* 6:4; see below). Ethnographically, the first five floor surfaces noted here are associated with such different functions such as stabling (Holladay, 1986), store-rooms and kitchens (the latter having an ashy floor), living rooms, and nonhardened (lacking cobbles or flagstones) domestic stables (Kramer, 1979, pp. 147–149; Watson, 1979, p. 121). That the so-called center room or "courtyard" is an interior surface is easily tested by an objective (e.g., granulometric) comparison of its surfaces with other surfaces known to be exterior (e.g., streets and other open areas: Kramer, 1979, pp. 148–149; Watson, 1979, pp. 157–159, pls. 5.3–5), as well as by the fact that, although the "courtyard" surfaces are often lower than exterior street levels, with high thresholds to keep water out, no provision was made for the internal drainage required if they were open to the sky.

Stairways are commonly noted and can be reconstructed in other instances. From everything presently known, the first story was low, averaging under 2 m, with considerably less clearance under the beams. It was, thus, unsuited to human habitation.

Interior Features. Most houses had stub walls between the supporting pillars with, where preserved, mud-and-stone mangers on top. The mangers are similar to those found in stables at Hazor and Beersheba and would have been used for donkeys and, probably, cattle (the standings are too short for horses). [*See* Hazor, Beersheba, Stables; Cattle and Oxen.] Semicircular ground-level mangers ("bins") are common and may have been used for sheep and goats, but possibly also for cattle. [*See* Sheep and Goats.] Fire pits or hearths in the courtyard are characteristic at Radannah and at Tel Masos, but in general they are rarely found. [*See* Masos, Tel.] Other types of hearths are found occasionally, mostly in the central space, or "courtyard" (e.g., the "pi"-shaped hearths in the Drainpipe House at Taʿanach and in house 1727 at Shechem, and in the hearths contained in the overturned upper portions of storejars sunk into the ground in buildings at Shechem, Hazor, and Meṣad Ḥashavyahu). A large industrial hearth, which replaces an earlier wine press at Shechem in house 1727 seems to be unique. [*See* Taʿanach; Shechem; Meṣad Ḥashavyahu.]

Hearths are by no means commonly found. However, it is clear that every household must not only have had cooking facilities (cooking pots are one of the most common vessel types), but, in most parts of the land, also hearths for heat in winter. (Ovens served for bread making, not cooking.) Ethnographically, hearths are one of the chief markers of living rooms (Watson, 1979, p. 122, fig. 5.2; Kramer, 1979, pp. 147–148). These are rooms within which the entire nuclear family cooks, entertains, eats, sleeps, and performs daily indoor activities. Families having two living rooms use the second one for entertaining or rent it. At Patty Jo Watson's "Hasanabad" and "Ain Ali" bread ovens were not used: one hearth served for winter warmth, cooking, and—through the use of the *saj*, the modern descendent of the baking tray—baking (Watson, 1979, pp. 205, 283). During the summer, cooking fires were relocated into exterior courtyard spaces. Carol Kramer (1979, pp. 147–148, emphasis added) presents illuminating data: "Hearths are peculiar to living rooms. . . . In contrast to ovens, such hearths, found throughout the Zagros . . . and elsewhere in Southwest Asia, *are often situated in second-story rooms*, and as such have been found at an archaeological site near Shāhābād." Ovens, on the other hand, are generally placed out of the wind at points of easy access from outside (e.g., Tell el-Farʿah [North]; Chambon, 1984); they are not normally found in or adjacent to every house. This implies communal use, as in present-day traditional villages. [*See* Farʿah, Tell el- (North).]

Silos or grain pits have been found in the rear room and elsewhere (Watson, 1979, pp. 125–126, fig. 5.4). Multiple exterior grain pits were common before and during the United Monarchy but are not characteristic of later periods (Holladay, 1995, pp. 377–379, table 3). Vermin-resistant above-grade grain and flour bins or chests constructed of mud and chaff are common in ethnographically witnessed villages in Iran (Kramer, 1979, pp. 144, 147; Watson, 1979, pp. 67, 162, figs. 5.42–43), suggesting that they might have been used for domestic storage in Israel; none have yet been identified, however. Where cisterns were used, they would have been located either beneath the house or outside. [*See* Cisterns.] In some cases, houses may have been built over preexisting cisterns.

Functional Aspects of the Ground-Floor Plan. The ground floor in the four-room house falls entirely within the family's economic domain. Stalls for donkeys and large cattle are readily identified by their similarity to standings in chariotry stables (cobbled or flagstoned surfaces, bench-style mangers, pillared construction). Floor-level mangers may attest to the feeding of sheep and goats. By analogy with modern European modes of veal production, small rooms with blocked doorways and miry surfaces may have housed the "fatted calf." Small storerooms with packed-earth or mud-plaster surfaces probably served for specialized storage, while the back room seems to have been the main locus for heavy storage: ethnographically, the items stored in such rooms change with the season. In ancient Israel they would have included young animals, bulk quantities of wine and oil, fodder, grains and legumes, reserved seed grain, straw, dung, twigs and dung cakes (the primary fuel source), pottery vessels not in use, timbers, raw materials for craft production, and a plow, yoke, and other farm implements (DeBoer and Lathrup, 1979, pp. 110–121; Hall, McBride, and Riddell, 1973; Jacobs, 1979, p. 179; Kramer, 1979, pp. 144, 147, 154; Watson, 1979, pp. 160, 294–296). Light items—dried fruits and dairy products, spices, textiles, and other domestic goods—would have been stored on the second floor (Kramer, 1982, p. 105). The large central space seems to have functioned by day as a work area and is where large limestone mortars (used with long wooden pounders for pearling barley?) were typically located. At night and during winter storms this area would have served as a secure folding area for the family's small sheep and goat herd (Hopkins, 1985, pp. 245–250).

It has often been suggested that the rear room served as the family's living room, and that the Israelite house evolved from this original nucleus, perhaps originally imitating a nomad's tent (Fritz and Kempinski, 1983, pp. 31–34; Herzog, 1984, pp. 75–77). However, there is absolutely no evidence for this type's existence in the second millennium BCE. Against this, the mean width of ninety-five identifiable rear rooms in Frank Braemer's catalog (1982, pp. 160–269) is 1.98 m, while the mean widths of ethnographically described living rooms range from 2.78 m at "Hasanabad" to 2.9 m at Aşvan to 3.02 m at "Aliabad" (Watson, 1979; Hall, McBride, and Riddell, 1973; Kramer, 1982)—their width being determined by the length of the available roofing timbers. In short, a family of four to five persons cannot live, work, cook, eat, entertain, and sleep in a 2-meter-wide hallway with 1.52 m of head room.

Second Story. A second story must be inferred for the four-room house on the basis of its constructional characteristics: its massive load-bearing pillars in a roofed-over courtyard and lack of provision on the ground floor for living quarters or, in most cases, for cooking or heating facilities. Given the lack of these facilities on the ground floor, the second floor should constitute the family's "living domain": the living rooms should have widths and overall floor areas similar to those in the ethnographic literature—or an average living room size of between 15 and 20 sq m (Kramer, 1979; Watson, 1979), although larger and smaller ones do occur. Living rooms should have other dimensions (e.g., headroom), facilities (e.g., hearths), and functionality not available on the ground floor (cf. Hopkins, 1985, pp. 144–148). An entry hall at the head of the stairs, used to store outer clothes and men's portable tools, is suggested by the ethnographic data. Kitchen facilities and one or two light storage rooms would round out the second floor plan (see figures 2b, 3). The second story's walls may have been thinner because of their reduced load-carrying requirement. This would have increased its area slightly. A third-floor 'ălîyyâ, "upper room, or roof chamber," preferably accessed by an external staircase, might also be present, whether for rent or use as a guest room (see figure 3). Balustraded windows, unsuitable for ground-floor use, would be perfectly in place in the higher stories, providing good light and ventilation. Domestic versions would have been more rustic than the palatial one featured in the "woman at the window" ivories from Nimrud. [See Nimrud.]

Roofs were flat, of packed mud and chaff ("straw"), with new layers applied annually. Following a rainstorm they were rolled with limestone rollers or carefully compacted by foot (Wright, 1965, p. 161, fig. 80; Watson, 1979, pp. 119–120). Sprouted grain on the rooftops was a proverbial sign of spring (Ps. 129:6; Is. 37:27). Parapets, stipulated by Deuteronomic legislation (Dt. 22:8), were necessary to enable the use of the roof as an outdoor workspace (i.e., it would have functioned analogously to enclosed courtyard space) and as a safe place for women and their small children to socialize. With no roof overhang, rainwater runoff would

have eroded the mud-brick (adobe) fabric of the house. Thus, jutting wooden (or ceramic) "gargoyles" (Watson, 1979, p. 159) or internal drainpipes leading to an in-house cistern (Lapp, 1967, pp. 2–39, fig. 14), would have been needed to drain the roof. The gargoyles' individual splash areas or runoff channels (Watson, 1979, p. 159) would have been visible on exterior, street, or lane surfaces. Ethnographic parallels show that brush shelters (biblical sûkkôt, Neh. 8:16) are set up to soften the summer sun and that during the hottest months, families often sleep on the roof. Ethnographically, this is the woman's domain—house tops being the common pathways between closely packed neighboring households in some modern walled villages (Jacobs, 1979, p. 179). There, and by parallel in ancient Near Eastern cities and villages, cultic ceremonies are conducted on rooftops (Jer. 19:13; Zep. 1:5), as were corporate mourning and rejoicing (Is. 15:3, 22:1), sleeping (1 Sm. 9:25), bathing (2 Sm. 11:2), washing, and clothes drying, basket making, baking, and drying food and fodder for storage, dung and brush for fuel, and flax and other agricultural products for processing (Jos. 2:6). They probably were also used for storing beams and large household and farming implements during the rainless months (Jacobs, 1979; Kramer, 1982, p. 111; cf. Hall, McBride, and Riddell, 1973, p. 248).

Economic Significance. Except for the large numbers of grain silos (averaging a storage capacity of about a ton each) occasionally found near certain houses prior to and

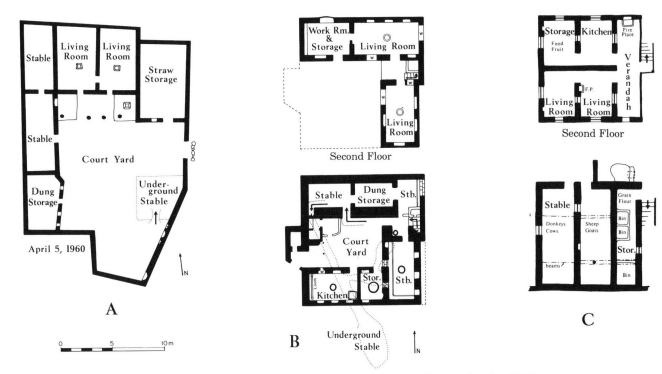

FOUR-ROOM HOUSE: Figure 2. *Selected ethnographically documented peasant housing.* (a) One-story house from Hasanabad, Iran (Watson, 1979); (b) two-story house from Aliabad, Iran (Kramer, 1982, fig. 4.7); (c) two-story house from Aşvan, Turkey (Hall et al., 1973, fig. 4). (Courtesy J. S. Holladay)

FOUR-ROOM HOUSE: Figure 3. *Reconstruction of the house in figure 1: c-d, featuring a hypothetical* '*ăliyya, or upper room.* (Drawing by Megan Williams; courtesy J. S. Holladay)

during the Solomonic era (Greenberg, 1987; Finkelstein, 1986, pp. 1–20, fig. 4), but not met with later, large-scale facilities for accumulated agricultural surpluses are not known from the period of the Israelite monarchy. This stands in marked contrast to the military and economic policies of the Persian period, as witnessed by the large number of great store pits at such sites as Tell el-Hesi (Bennet and Blakely, 1989, p. 67) and Beersheba (Naveh, 1973). [*See* Hesi, Tell el-.] Nor are redistributive mechanisms, such as the large-scale bakeries found in conjunction with granaries in Saite through Ptolemaic Egypt (at Tell el-Maskhuta) known from either Israel or Judah. Even the three hundred-odd jars filled with oil, wine, and grain in the Phoenician "fort" excavated by Zvi Gal (1992) at Horvat Rosh Zayit fall into different focus when it is realized that it would have taken at least ninety-one jars to store the subsistence and seed-grain requirements of one typical Israelite household and its flocks and herd, to say nothing of their olive oil and wine. In terms of scale, the storage capacity of the back rooms of only thirty-one typical Israelite houses more than equaled the capacity of silo 1414 at Megiddo, the largest storage facility presently known for either Israel or Judah (Holladay, 1995, p. 393).

Except for chariotry, frontier forts such as Tell Arad, palaces, and—perhaps—the cultus, neither ancient Israel nor Judah seems to have operated on a redistributive basis: there could have been no widespread issuing of grain and other rations to large numbers of the civilian population. Simply put, Israelite peasant farmers operated with a house (and agricultural regime) specifically designed to accumulate surpluses. The specific mechanisms by which those surpluses entered either domestic or international commerce are matters for future research, although it should be noted that a whole series of small ports, conveniently spaced about a half-day's journey apart, existed along the Palestinian coast during the Iron II period, providing a cost-effective mechanism for the long-range movement of such low-value, high-bulk goods.

[*See also* Building Materials and Techniques, *article on* Materials and Techniques of the Bronze and Iron Ages; Ethnoarchaeology; *and* House, *article on* Syro-Palestinian Houses.]

BIBLIOGRAPHY

Aharoni, Yohanan, ed. *Beer-sheba I: Excavations at Tel Beer-sheba, 1969–1971 Seasons.* Tel Aviv, 1973.

Bennett, W. J., Jr., and Jeffrey A. Blakely. *Tell el-Hesi: The Persian Period (Stratum V). The Joint Archaeological Expedition to Tell el-Hesi.* Vol. 3. Winona Lake, Ind., 1989.

Braemer, Frank. *L'architecture domestique du Levant à l'Âge du Fer.* Paris, 1982.

Callaway, Joseph A. "A Visit with Ahilud." *Biblical Archaeology Review* 9 (1983): 42–53.

Chambon, Alain. *Tell el-Farah I: L'âge du Fer.* Paris, 1984.

Cohen, Rudolph. "The Iron Age Fortresses in the Central Negev." *Bulletin of the American Schools of Oriental Research,* no. 236 (1979): 61–78.

DeBoer, Warren R., and Donald W. Lathrup. "The Making and Breaking of Shipibo-Conibo Ceramics." In *Ethnoarchaeology: Implications of Ethnography for Archaeology,* edited by Carol Kramer, pp. 102–138. New York, 1979

Dothan, Moshe. *Ashdod II–III: The Second and Third Seasons of Excavations 1963, 1965: Text and Plates.* 'Atiqot, English series, 9–10. Jerusalem, 1971.

Finkelstein, Israel. *'Izbet Sartah: An Early Iron Age Site near Rosh Ha'ayin, Israel.* British Archaeological Reports, International Series, 299. Oxford, 1986.

Fritz, Volkmar, and Aharon Kempinski. *Ergebnisse der Ausgrabungen auf der Hirbet el-Mšāš (Tel Māśōś) 1972–1975.* Weisbaden, 1983.

Gal, Zvi. "Hurbat Rosh Zayit and the Early Phoenician Pottery." *Levant* 24 (1992): 173–186.

Gitin, Seymour. "Tel Miqne-Ekron: A Type-Site for the Inner Coastal Plain in the Iron Age II Period." In *Recent Excavations in Israel: Studies in Iron Age Archaeology*, edited by Seymour Gitin and William G. Dever, pp. 23–58. Annual of the American Schools of Oriental Research, 49. Winona Lake, Ind., 1989.

Greenberg, Raphael. "New Light on the Early Iron Age at Tell Beit Mirsim." *Bulletin of the American Schools of Oriental Research*, no. 265 (1987): 55–80.

Hall, G., S. McBride, and A. Riddell. "Architectural Analysis." In *Aşvan 1968–1972: An Interim Report*, edited by David French et al., pp. 245–269. *Anatolian Studies* (1973): 71–309.

Hamlin, Carol Kramer. "Seh Gabi, 1973" *Archaeology* 27 (1974): 274–277.

Herzog, Ze'ev. *Beer-sheba II: The Early Iron Age Settlements*. Tel Aviv, 1984.

Herzog, Ze'ev. "Administrative Structures in the Iron Age." In *The Architecture of Ancient Israel from the Prehistoric to the Persian Periods*, edited by Aharon Kempinski and Ronny Reich, pp. 223–230. Jerusalem, 1992.

Holladay, John S., Jr. "The Stables of Ancient Israel: Functional Determinants of Stable Construction and the Interpretation of Pillared Building Remains of the Palestinian Iron Age." In *The Archaeology of Jordan and Other Studies, Presented to Siegfried H. Horn*, edited by Lawrence T. Geraty and Larry G. Herr, pp. 103–165. Berrien Springs, Mich., 1986.

Holladay, John S., Jr. "The Kingdoms of Israel and Judah: Political and Economic Centralization in the Iron IIA-B (ca. 1000–750 BCE)." In *The Archaeology of Society in the Holy Land*, edited by Thomas E. Levy, pp. 368–398. London, 1995.

Hopkins, David C. *The Highlands of Canaan: Agricultural Life in the Early Iron Age*. Sheffield, 1985.

Jacobs, Linda K. "Tell-i Nun: Archaeological Implications of a Village in Transition." In *Ethnoarchaeology: Implications of Ethnography for Archaeology*, edited by Carol Kramer, pp. 175–191. New York, 1979.

Kempinski, Aharon, and Ronny Reich, eds. *The Architecture of Ancient Israel from the Prehistoric to the Persian Periods*. Jerusalem, 1992.

Kramer, Carol. "An Archaeological View of a Contemporary Kurdish Village: Domestic Architecture, Household Size, and Wealth." In *Ethnoarchaeology: Implications of Ethnography for Archeology*, edited by Carol Kramer, pp. 139–163. New York, 1979.

Kramer, Carol. *Village Ethnoarchaeology: Rural Iran in Archaeological Perspective*. New York 1982.

Lapp, Paul W. "The 1966 Excavations at Tell Ta'annek." *Bulletin of the American Schools of Oriental Research*, no. 185 (1967): 2–39.

Maisler (Mazar), Benjamin. "The Excavations at Tell Qasile, Preliminary Report." *Israel Exploration Journal* 1 (1951): 61–76, 125–140, 194–218.

Marquet-Krause, Judith. *Les fouilles de 'Ay (et-Tell), 1933–1935: Entreprises par le Baron Edmond de Rothschild . . . La risurrection d'une grande cité biblique*. Bibliothèque archéologique et historique, 45. Paris, 1949.

McCown, Chester C. *Tell en-Nasbeh I*. Berkeley, 1947.

Naveh, Joseph. "The Aramaic Ostraca." In *Beer-sheba I: Excavations at Tel Beer-sheba, 1969–1971 Season*, edited by Yohanan Aharoni, pp. 79–82. Tel Aviv, 1973.

Stager, Lawrence E. "The Archaeology of the Family in Ancient Israel." *Bulletin of the American Schools of Oriental Research*, no. 260 (1985): 1–35.

Watson, Patty Jo. *Archaeological Ethnography in Western Iran*. Tucson, 1979.

Wright, G. Ernest. *Shechem: The Biography of a Biblical City*. New York, 1965.

JOHN S. HOLLADAY, JR.

FRANCISCAN CUSTODY OF THE HOLY LAND.

The order of the Franciscan Friars, founded by Francis of Assisi (Italy), became a presence in the Near East in 1221, the same year it was officially approved by the Pope. The founder himself visited the region in order to preach the Gospel to the Muslims, whom he saw as brothers. The mission resulted in a meeting with the sultan of Egypt. The Franciscan Province of the East extended to Cyprus, Syria, Lebanon, and the Holy Land (ancient Palestine). Before the Muslims took Akko in 1291, there were Franciscan friaries there and in Sidon, Antioch, Tripoli, Jaffa, and Jerusalem.

At the end of the Latin Kingdom, the Franciscans took refuge on Cyprus, where they began planning their return to Jerusalem, given the goodwill between Christian governments and the Mamluk sultans in Egypt. In about 1333, a friar, Ruggero Garini, succeeded in buying the Cenacle on Mount Zion and some nearby land on which to build a monastery for the friars, using funds provided by the king and queen of Naples. In 1342, Pope Clement IV, in two papal bulls (Gratias Agimus and Nuper Carissimae) approved and created the new entity, which became known as the Franciscan Custody of the Holy Land (Custodia Terrae Sanctae). The friars came from the order's provinces and were placed under the jurisdiction of the father-guardian (superior) of the monastery on Mt. Zion. They were instated in the Cenacle and in the Church of the Holy Sepulcher in Jerusalem and in the Basilica of the Nativity in Bethlehem. Their principal activity was to ensure liturgical life in those Christian sanctuaries, to give spiritual assistance to pilgrims and merchants coming from the West, and to have a direct and authorized relationship with the Christian oriental communities.

In 1551 the Turkish Authority expelled the friars from the Cenacle and the adjoining monastery. However, they were granted permission to purchase a Georgian monastery for nuns in the city's northwest quarter, which became the new center of the Custody in Jerusalem, and they developed the Latin Convent of St. Savior (Ar., Dayr al-Latin). In 1620 the Franciscans received Mt. Tabor in Galilee and the venerated Grotto of the Annunciation in Nazareth from Fakhr ed-Din, the Druze amir of Sidon. In the following year they were permitted to rebuild part of the church of St. John the Baptist at 'Ein-Kerem near Jerusalem, and open a new friary. In the nineteenth century, new churches and monasteries were built at other, already venerated sites, above the ruins of older churches: the Chapel of the Flagellation along the Via Dolorosa in Jerusalem (1838); a chapel at Emmaus/Qubeibeh (1872); the church at Cana (Ar., Kafr Kana; 1880); and a chapel each in the village of Naim (1885), at Bethpage (1883), and at Dominus Flevit (1891)—the latter two on the Mt. of Olives. New basilicas were built at Emmaus/Qubeibeh (1901); at Nazareth (the so-called Church of Nutrition; 1911–1914); at Gethsemane (Basilica of the Agony; 1919–1924); and on Mt. Tabor (Basilica of the Transfiguration; 1921–1924). New chapels followed:

the Chapel of the Good Shepherd in Jericho (1924); the chapel on the west bank of the Jordan River (1934); and the Chapel of Primacy at Tabgha, on the shore of the Sea of Galilee. Church buildings and additions included the Church of the Visitation at 'Ein-Kerem (1938–1940); a church in Bethany (1952–1954); a chapel at Shepherds' Field, outside the village of Beit Sahur/Bethlehem; and a new chapel at Dominus Flevit (1955). The new great Basilica of the Annunciation in Nazareth, begun in 1955, was consecrated in 1969, and the Memorial of St. Peter at Capernaum was completed in 1990.

The Franciscan presence in the Holy Land has provided continuity in the recording of local tradition since the Crusader period. Since 1342 they have functioned as custodians of the Christian shrines on behalf of the Catholic church, as guides for Christian pilgrims to the Holy Land, and as authors of many publications intended to increase the knowledge of the Holy Land among the Christians of Europe.

The restoration and rebuilding during the nineteenth century of sanctuaries owned by the Custody of the Holy Land resulted in the archaeological exploration of those sites. Such projects are entrusted to the archaeologists of the Studium Biblicum Franciscanum (SBF), an institute founded in 1923 to continue the work done by the Franciscan fathers in previous centuries. As a scientific institution, the SBF is closely related to the Franciscan presence in the Holy Land. A Roman Catholic faculty teaches biblical and archaeological studies, sponsored by the Franciscan Custody of Terra Sancta. The SBF is located in the Old City of Jerusalem, in the Monastery of the Flagellation, at the Second Station of the cross, on the Via Dolorosa. As a research center, the SBF fosters work on New Testament sites, as well as the study of the early Christian church in the Holy Land, by means of literary sources and excavations. It publishes reports on excavations annually in the review *Liber Annuus*, begun in 1950, and in the series *Collectio Maior* and *Collectio Minor*. Exegetical studies are published in the series *Analecta*, and the archaeological collections of the SBF are illustrated in the series *Museum*. As a learning center, the SBF is presently authorized to confer pontifical academic degrees of baccalaureate, licentiate, and doctorate in biblical theology.

The SBF opened an archaeological museum in 1902 in the Monastery of St. Savior, whose collection was transferred to the Monastery of the Flagellation in 1931. Findings from SBF excavations, along with liturgical Latin codices from the fourteenth and fifteenth centuries, a treasure of liturgical medieval objects from the Basilica of the Nativity in Bethlehem, and eighteenth-century pots from the pharmacy in the Monastery of St. Savior, are displayed there. The collection also includes a numismatic section specializing in the city coins of Palestine, the Decapolis, and the Provincia Arabia.

SBF-sponsored archaeological fieldwork includes the following sites. The excavations in Nazareth were begun by Prosper Viaud at the beginning of the twentieth century and were resumed by Bellarmino Bagatti in 1954. Along with the discovery of the ancient village, he found the first signs of a Christian presence there in graffiti scratched on plaster found under the Crusader and Byzantine Basilica of the Annunciation. [*See* Nazareth; *and the biography of Bagatti.*] At Capernaum, the excavations in the synagogue initiated by Gaudenzio Orfali in 1921 were resumed in 1968 by Virgilio Corbo and Stanislao Loffreda and are still underway. The excavators have discovered the *insula sacra* (the area of sacred buildings) among the ruins of the houses in the ancient village, with the *domus ecclesia* (house-church) of St. Peter under the Byzantine octagonal basilica. They have also unearthed structures under the synagogue that date to the Late Roman period. [*See* Capernaum.] The excavation of the palace at Herodium, near Bethlehem, was carried out by Corbo, between 1962 and 1967. He also directed the excavations of the Herodian fortress of Machaerus in Jordan, in which, according to Josephus Flavius, John the Baptist was jailed and murdered. [*See* Machaerus.] One of the institute's main excavation and restoration projects is on Mt. Nebo in Jordan. The project was begun in 1933, under the direction of Sylvester Saller. The work was focused mainly on the Memorial Church of Moses Prophet and Man of God. This memorial was built by Christians in the region in the fourth century, on the western peak of Siyagha. A monastery developed around it in the Byzantine period. Excavations were expanded to the nearby ruins of Khirbet el-Mukhayyat on the southern peak of Mt. Nebo, where an Iron Age fortress and Roman-Byzantine village identified with Nebo are located. [*See* Nebo, Mount.] Since 1984, the SBF has been excavating two Byzantine churches in the valley of 'Ain Musa and a monastery in the valley of 'Ayn al-Kanisah, simultaneously cooperating with the Jordanian Department of Antiquities in excavating several monuments in the city of Madaba, such as the Church of the Virgin, the Hippolythus Hall, the Cathedral, and the Burnt Palace. [*See* Madaba.]

In summer 1986, work started at Umm er-Rasas, in the steppe 30 km (19 mi.) southeast of Madaba, where the ancient name of the ruins, Kastron Mefaa, was rediscovered in the inscriptions in the rich mosaic floor of the church of St. Stephen, built in the Umayyad period. [*See* Umm er-Rasas.] Moreover, a city plan of Kastron Mefaa was found along with the inscriptions. In summer 1989, a second plan of the city of Kastron Mefaa, depicted in the mosaic floor of the Church of the Lions, was unearthed. It is now possible to accept the identification of Umm er-Rasas/Kastron Mefaa with biblical Mepha'at proposed by Eusebius (*Onomasticon* 128.21; *Jos.* 13:21, 21:27; *Jer.* 48:21).

BIBLIOGRAPHY

Amico, Bernardino. *Trattato delle piante et imagini de i sacri edificii di Terra Santa/Plans of the Sacred Edifices of the Holy Land* (1620). Studium Biblicum Francescanum, Publications, no. 10. Jerusalem, 1953.

Bagatti, Bellarmino. *Il Museo della Flagellazione in Gerusalemme*. Jerusalem, 1939.

Bagatti, Bellarmino, ed. *Studium Biblicum Franciscanum nel 50° della fondazione, 1923–1973*. Jerusalem, 1973.

Golubovich, Girolamo. *Biblioteca bio-bibliografica della Terra Santa e dell'Oriente Francescano*. Vols. 1–14. Florence, 1906–1933.

Niccolò da Poggibonsi. *A Voyage beyond the Seas, 1346–1350*. Translation of *Il libro d'oltramare* by T. Bellorini and E. Hoade. Studium Biblicum Franciscanum, Publications, no. 2. Jerusalem, 1945.

Piccirillo, Michele, ed. *La custodia di Terra Santa e l'Europa*. Rome, 1983.

Piccirillo, Michele. *Studium Biblicum Franciscanum Museum*. Jerusalem, 1983.

Quaresmo, Francesco. *Historica theologica et moralis Terrae Sanctae* (The Illustration of the Holy Land). 2 vols. Antwerp, 1639.

Rossi, Berardo. *The Custody of the Holy Land*. Jerusalem, 1981.

Suriano, Francesco. *Il trattato di Terra Santa e dell'Oriente* (Treatise on the Holy Land; 1485). Milan, 1900.

MICHELE PICCIRILLO

FRANKFORT, HENRI (1897–1952), eminent scholar of the ancient Near East. Born in the Netherlands, Frankfort began his studies in history at the University of Amsterdam but subsequently transferred to London to work with Flinders Petrie at University College. He obtained his M.A. there in 1924 and his Ph.D. at the University of Leiden in 1927.

From 1925 to 1929 Frankfort served as director of excavations for the Egypt Exploration Society, chiefly at Tell el-Amarna, Abydos, and Armant. In 1929, he was invited to take charge of the University of Chicago's recently organized Oriental Institute Iraq Expedition and served as its field director until 1937. In 1932, Frankfort was appointed Research Professor of Oriental Archaeology at the Oriental Institute of the University of Chicago and concurrently held the position of Extraordinary Professor in the History and Archaeology of the Ancient Near East at the University of Amsterdam. When World War II ended the field activities of the Iraq Expedition, Frankfort took up residence in Chicago to concentrate on research, publication, and teaching. During the war years, he served as acting chairman of the Department of Oriental Languages and Literatures. In 1949 he accepted the directorship of the Warburg Institute and a professorship of the history of preclassical antiquity at the University of London.

The various archaeological expeditions that Henri Frankfort directed rank among the most carefully conducted, most fruitful, and best published of any of his time. Frankfort's numerous seminal published works range over many fields of ancient Near Eastern studies. They include excavation reports of work in both Egypt and Iraq, major synthetic monographs that sought to organize large quantities of data into meaningful frameworks for the relatively new field of ancient Near Eastern studies, and sensitive and penetrating essays. Frankfort traveled to the Near East for the last time in the fall of 1952 as a Guggenheim fellow to research and write *The Art and Architecture of the Ancient Orient*, which was published in 1954.

BIBLIOGRAPHY

Delougaz, Pinhas, and Thorkild Jacobsen. "Henri Frankfort." *Journal of Near Eastern Studies* 14 (1955): 1–13.

Frankfort, Henri. *Studies in the Early Pottery of the Near East*. 2 vols. London, 1924.

Frankfort, Henri, ed. *The Mural Painting of El-ʿAmarneh*. London, 1929.

Frankfort, Henri. *The Cenotaph of Seti I at Abydos*. 2 vols. Egypt Exploration Society, Memoir 39. London, 1933.

Frankfort, Henri. *Preliminary Report of the Iraq Expedition, 1st–5th, 1930/31–1934/35*. 5 vols. University of Chicago, Oriental Institute Communications, nos. 13, 16, 17, 19, 20. Chicago, 1931–1936.

Frankfort, Henri. *Cylinder Seals: A Documentary Essay on Art and Religion of the Ancient Near East*. London, 1939.

Frankfort, Henri. *Sculpture of the Third Millennium B.C. from Tell Asmar and Khafājah*. University of Chicago, Oriental Institute Publications, vol. 44. Chicago, 1939.

Frankfort, Henri, et al. *The Gimilsin Temple and the Palace of the Rulers at Tell Asmar*. University of Chicago, Oriental Institute Publications, vol. 48. Chicago, 1940.

Frankfort, Henri. *More Sculpture from the Diyala Region*. University of Chicago, Oriental Institute Publications, vol. 60. Chicago, 1943.

Frankfort, Henri, et al. *The Intellectual Adventure of Ancient Man*. University of Chicago, Oriental Institute Essays. Chicago, 1946. Expanded and later published as *Before Philosophy: The Intellectual Adventure of Ancient Man*. Baltimore, 1967.

Frankfort, Henri. *The Art and Architecture of the Ancient Orient*. Harmondsworth, 1954.

Frankfort, Henri, with a chapter by Thorkild Jacobsen. *Stratified Cylinder Seals from the Diyala Region*. University of Chicago, Oriental Institute Publications, vol. 72. Chicago, 1955.

Frankfort, Henri. *Kingship and the Gods*. University of Chicago, Oriental Institute Essays. Chicago, 1978.

KAREN L. WILSON

FRENCH ARCHAEOLOGICAL MISSIONS. In France, the archaeology of the Near East has long been a concern of the state. Since the nineteenth century, French political authorities have concerned themselves with archaeological exploration, often on the heels of military expeditions. The best example of this kind occurred at the beginning of the nineteenth century in the company of the expedition of Napoleon Bonaparte in Egypt. The artistic, archaeological, and scientific observations (from botany to zoology and ethnography) of the enterprise produced the monumental work *Description de l'Égypte*. France, like other European countries, were later attracted to other parts of the Near East, such as Mesopotamia, the Levant, and Iran. French teams sought to discover the history of civilizations in which the common past of humanity could be seen (and in which the Bible played an important role). The quest for inscriptions was a prime motivation. Furthermore, archaeological research aimed to enrich museums. The formation of the great Near Eastern collections of the Louvre in Paris dates from this period, as also the British Museum in London, and the Vorderasiatische Museum in Berlin, as well as in numerous other museums of Europe and America, not to mention private collections.

A first phase, begun in the 1840s, could be considered the "period of the diplomats." First, in Mesopotamia, the French consul Paul-Émile Botta discovered the palace of Sargon at Khorsabad in 1843–1844. Interest in the Bible also explains the innumerable expeditions undertaken under diverse sponsorship (public and private) in Syria and Palestine (then under Ottoman rule), notably by Félicien de Saulcy in Jerusalem in 1850. In 1860, accompanying the French army of the Levant, the Mission de Phénicie (Phoenician Expedition) was officially sent by the government of Napoleon III under the direction of Ernest Renan, in the name of the Académie des Inscriptions et Belles-Lettres. The campaign led by Melchior de Vogüé to Cyprus complemented the work in Phoenicia.

A coherent policy of archaeological research developed in France and England at the end of the nineteenth century. This was the "period of the engineers." France wished to undertake large, long-term excavations in the Near East at prestigious sites, as had been done earlier by French expeditions in Delphi in Greece. In 1884 Marcel Dieulafoy initiated archaeological study of Iran with the exploration of Susa, which entailed the creation of a permanent organization in 1897, the French Delegation in Persia, under the direction of Jacques de Morgan. In Mesopotamia, Ernest de Sarzec opened the way to the discovery of the Sumerians with the excavation of Tello beginning in 1877.

In the twentieth century, the "scientific phase" of Near Eastern archaeology with the creation of archaeological services, museums, and the foundation of archaeological institutes and schools. France participated actively in these places of research in foreign countries.

Beginning in 1912, Roland de Mecquenem resumed excavations at Susa. After World War I, Abbé Henri du Verdier de Genouillac continued the excavations in southern Mesopotamia at Tello. He was replaced by André Parrot, who subsequently excavated at the neighboring site of Larsa.

In the Levant, after the fall of the Ottoman Empire, the creation of a French Antiquities Service of the Mandate in Lebanon and Syria made the excavations of large sites possible: Byblos on the Mediterranean coast, previously dug by Pierre Montet in 1921–1924 and then by Maurice Dunand beginning in 1926; Ras Shamra/Ugarit beginning in 1929 by Claude Schaeffer; and Mari on the Euphrates, excavated by André Parrot beginning in 1933.

Currently official archaeological activity outside French territory is state-run under the Ministry of Foreign Affairs. Modern French archaeological policy began with the creation of a special commission of this ministry in 1947, the "Commission Consultative des Fouilles," since 1970 "Commission Consultative des Recherches Archéologiques à l'Étranger" (Consulting Commission for Foreign Archaeo-

logical Research), under the authority of the General Directorate of Cultural, Scientific, and Technical Relations. This commission, which meets annually, submits proposals to the Foreign Ministry about the allocation of subventions to the French archaeological missions in different countries.

A great diversity exists among the "missions." Some large projects include multidisciplinary programs extending over many years. The oldest in progress is the excavation at Ras Shamra/Ugarit in Syria. Other projects, however, involve surveys that are limited in time and area, such as emergency exploration required in some countries (for example, building projects such as dams that will permanently inundate archaeological sites).

The state provides financing of the projects through the recommendation of the Ministry of Foreign Affairs, but also through other public institutions which occasionally provide their own contributions. In fact, government's scientific programs that support the missions in the Near East also rely on various research institutes, such as those at the universities of Paris, Lyon, and Strasbourg, the teams of researchers of the CNRS (Centre National de la Recherche Scientifique), the Départment des Antiquités Orientales au Musée du Louvre (Department of Eastern Antiquities, Louvre Museum), which in turn come under the jurisdiction of various ministries: the Ministry of National Education, the Ministry of Research, the Ministry of Culture, and of course, the Académie des Inscriptions et Belles Lettres.

The French archaeological missions around the world are divided into five subcommittees of the Committee of Excavations of the Ministry of Foreign Affairs. The Near East currently represents about a third of the activities. Thus, for 1994, of 205 applications for 46 countries, 68 requesting subventions were designed to conduct research in the countries of the Near East subcommission: Syria (22), Jordan (10), Lebanon (3), Israel (8), Turkey (13), Cyprus (5), Greece (4), and intercountry programs (3). In other Near Eastern countries political turmoil has interrupted several missions of long duration (e.g., Susa in Iran or Larsa in southern Mesopotamia/Iraq).

The Ministry of Foreign Affairs also maintains several institutions that represent French archaeology of the Near East within the host countries. Financed by public money, these institutes support a large number of archaeological projects carried out under the auspices of the French government. The Institut Français d'Archéologie de Beyrouth (IFAB), founded after World War II with Henri Seyrig as its first director to accommodate fellows and a specialized library, has become today the Institut Français d'Archéologie du Proche-Orient (IFAPO), with offices in Beirut, Damascus, and Amman. Other institutions ensure the official presence of French archaeology in the Near East: the Institut Français d'Études Anatoliennes (IFEA) in Istanbul (Turkey), the Institut Français de Recherches en Iran (IFRI) in Teheran, the Délégation Archéologique Française en Iraq

(DAFIQ) in Baghdad, the Institut Français d'Archéologie Orientale (IFAO) in Cairo, as well as a section of the Institut Français d'Études Arabes de Damas (IFEAD) in Syria for the medieval period.

Among private scientific undertakings, the Jesuit-run Université Saint-Joseph (USJ) in Beirut has received subventions from the French government for archaeological and museographical projects. The École Biblique et Archéologique Française (EBAF) in Jerusalem, a Dominican monastery, has also received subsidies from the Ministry of Foreign Affairs for excavation projects as well as stipends contributed by the Académie des Inscriptions et Belles Lettres.

[See also École Biblique et Archéologique Française; Institut Français d'Archéologie du Proche Orient; Institut Français d'Archéologie Orientale; Institut Français d'Études Anatoliennes d'Istanbul; Institut Français d'Études Arabes; *and the biographies of Botta, Dunand, Montet, Parrot, Renan, Saulcy, Schaeffer, Seyrig, and Vogüé. In addition, many of the sites mentioned are the subject of independent entries.*]

BIBLIOGRAPHY

Caubet, Annie. "Donateurs du Louvre: Archéologiques et fouilleurs." In *Les donateurs du Louvre*, pp. 55–67. Paris, 1989.
Chevalier, Nicole. "L'administration de la recherche archéologique française dans le Moyen Orient du milieu du XIXe siècle à la seconde guerre mondiale." Ph.D. diss., University of Paris I, 1993.

MARGUERITE YON
Translated from French by Nancy Leinwand

FRENCH SCHOOL (Jerusalem). *See* École Biblique et Archéologique Française.

FRESCOES. *See* Wall Paintings.

FUL, TELL EL- (Ar., "mound of beans") site situated on the crest of the watershed about 5 km (3 mi.) north of the Old City of Jerusalem, rising 862 m above sea level (map reference 172 × 137). Tell el-Ful is not strictly a tell; it rises about 30 m above the surrounding plain with occupational debris usually less than 2 m deep in an area approximately 150 × 90 m, north–south and east-west, respectively.

Tell el-Ful's identification with Gibeah of Saul (*1 Sm.* 10:26, 14:2, 15:34) was confirmed by William Foxwell Albright's excavations for the American Schools of Oriental Research (ASOR) in 1922, after a lively debate of more than eighty years. Albright's identification was widely accepted until the 1960s when the debate resurfaced. Although Paul Lapp's excavations under the auspices of ASOR and the Pittsburgh Theological Seminary (1964) largely confirmed Albright's conclusions, the site's identification with Gibeah

is still not accepted by all scholars. However, no other excavated site in the area indicates occupation in the periods necessary to correlate with the biblical traditions.

The American explorer Edward Robinson describes Tell el-Ful in his *Biblical Researches in Palestine* (vol. 1, 1874, p. 577), and Charles Warren carried out the first excavations there, of two weeks' duration, in 1868. Warren for the Palestine Excavation Fund published a brief description of his work (*PEF Quarterly*, 1869–1870, p. 66), and his plans were published by Claude R. Conder and H. H. Kitchener in 1883 (*The Survey of Western Palestine*, vol. 3). Albright (1924) excavated the site for seventeen months (1922–1923) and promptly published his results. He returned to the site for about a month in 1933 (Sinclair, 1960). The most recent excavations were Lapp's 1964 six-week salvage operation prior to modern building operations there. The expedition's final report (Lapp, 1981) reexamines the evidence from the earlier excavations and the new (1964) data, distinguishing five periods of occupation. The first, Iron IA (c. 1200–1150 BCE), is brief and without extensive finds. It is usually associated with the Benjaminites as recorded in *Judges* 19–20. The second period, Iron IC (c. 1025–950 BCE), is the period of Saul's fortress, which was the principle standing ruin at the site. It was largely excavated by Albright, but Lapp generally confirmed his conclusions in 1964 and refined his plans. It is the assignment of the date of construction of this fortress to the time of Saul that is the principle reason for Tell el-Ful's identification with Gibeah.

By the time of Lapp's excavations, pottery dating had been sufficiently refined to date period III to Late Iron II and the period of the Exile (c. 700–538 BCE). The fortress was probably rebuilt during Josiah's reign (640–609 BCE) with a casemate wall. That fortress was most likely destroyed in Nebuchadrezzar's campaign (588–587 BCE), but some occupation continued at the site until 538 BCE. During the pe-

FUL, TELL EL-. *Revetment against the southwest tower.* (Courtesy N. L. Lapp)

riod-IV Hellenistic occupation (175–63 BCE), which flourished toward the end of the second century BCE, the tower was rebuilt, elaborate bath installations were added, and the casemate rooms were reused. In addition to the pottery, coins, and stamped jar handles (*yršlm* and *yrd* + symbol), as well as an ostracon (Aramaic, c. 100 BCE), provide chronological pegs. Period V was a brief Roman occupation in about 70 CE.

[*See also the biographies of Albright, Conder, Kitchener, Lapp, Robinson, and Warren.*]

BIBLIOGRAPHY

Albright, William Foxwell. *Excavations and Results at Tell el-Fûl (Gibeah of Saul)*. Annual of the American Schools of Oriental Research, 4. New Haven, 1924. Final report of the first campaign, including the original publication of the fortress and important finds.

Lapp, Nancy L., ed. *The Third Campaign at Tell el-Fûl: The Excavations of 1964*. Annual of the American Schools of Oriental Research, 45. Cambridge, Mass., 1981. Takes into consideration earlier campaigns and presents the finds and various archaeological problems of the site.

Lapp, Paul W. "Tell el-Fûl." *Biblical Archaeologist* 28 (1965): 2–10. Summarizes the results of the third campaign.

Sinclair, Lawrence A. *An Archaeological Study of Gibeah (Tell el-Fûl)*. Vol. 1. Annual of the American Schools of Oriental Research, 34. New Haven, 1960. Report of the 1933 campaign, generally less reliable than earlier or later publications.

NANCY L. LAPP

FUNERARY MONUMENTS.

FUNERARY MONUMENTS. [*To provide a morphology and typology of funerary monuments and a survey of their development, forms, and functions in the ancient Near East, this entry is chronologically divided into two articles:* Monuments of the Hellenistic and Roman Periods *and* Monuments of the Late Roman through Islamic Periods.]

Monuments of the Hellenistic and Roman Periods

The funerary architecture of the Near East is eclectic and resists easy categorization, having offered scope for the public display of status, wealth, and, to a much lesser extent, personal beliefs. In Anatolia, monumental funerary architecture is attested as early as the Archaic period, where the rich variety of tomb types is represented by such monuments as the prominent tumuli and rock-cut tombs of Phrygia in central Anatolia, tombs on podia with pyramidal roofs found in the western coastlands, and the elevated sarcophagi and pillar tombs of Lycia in southwest Asia Minor. By the fourth century BCE, a fusion of Greek religious architecture and indigenous, elevated tomb types had taken place, the first example of such a structure being the Nereid monument at Xanthos in Lycia. The construction of tombs that resembled religious monuments (with, for example, peripteral columns) was to have a profound impact on the development of funerary architecture in the Near East. An outstanding Anatolian tomb of the Hellenistic period is the Mausoleum at Halikarnassos, no longer extant but tentatively restored on the basis of ancient testimonia and surviving fragments. The Mausoleum, one of the Seven Wonders of the ancient world, was the tomb of Mausolos, a satrap of Caria, and was completed in about 350 BCE. The tomb was the location for lavish sculptural displays depicting mythological battles. Above a tall podium was a peripteral cella of Ionic columns, surmounted by a pyramidal roof; its form influenced tomb design not only in Anatolia, but throughout the eastern Mediterranean. At Belevi, near Ephesus, a tomb of uncertain patronage mimics the Mausoleum in form, with its tall lower story, central cella of freestanding columns, and probable pyramidal roof. [*See* Mausoleum.]

Throughout the Hellenistic period the notion of the hero cult played a role in the funerary architecture of Anatolia. Such burial locations, known as *heroa* (sg., *heroon*), are found at Termessos in Pisidia and Gölbaşi-Trysa in Lycia, both dating to the Early Hellenistic period. These *heroa* suggest the apotheosis or divinization of the deceased with some provision for ritual or cultic activity—for example, a tomb in the form of a temple or the presence of an altar or a sacred temenos enclosure in which the tomb structure itself is not necessarily the dominant feature. Farther east in Anatolia, the influence of Syrian (and North African) tombs becomes apparent in such monuments as the early first-century BCE tower tomb at Olba-Diocaesarea in Cilicia (see figure 1). In addition to these freestanding tombs, rock-cut facade tombs were common in mountainous regions in Anatolia, for example in Lycia and Caria in the southwest and in Phrygia.

The tomb monuments of Roman Anatolia continued the Hellenistic traditions of visibility in the landscape and reliance on cut-stone construction, combined with the new possibilities provided by the western Roman podium temple. Monumental temple tombs, often enclosed within a temenos and elevated on a tall podium approached by a frontal staircase, are preserved throughout Anatolia (e.g., at Pergamon, Iasos, and Side). Such tombs preserve the idea of the Hellenistic *heroon*, yet their ostentation and lavish use of marble reflect the new economic conditions of the Roman Empire.

As in Anatolia, in Syria-Palestine evidence for monumental tomb architecture predates the Hellenistic period; mausolea of considerable size, dating to the fifth century BCE, are also preserved in the Arabian Peninsula. It is to the Hellenistic period, however, that many outstanding tombs of Syria-Palestine belong. In the Kidron Valley north and east of Jerusalem, a number of monumental tomb complexes are extant, all unique in form but often combining familiar architectural elements; the so-called Tomb of Zachariah (late first century BCE; see figure 2), with its half-columns engaged to a cubic central story surmounted by a pyramidal roof, and the nearby Tomb of Absalom, another freestanding

FUNERARY MONUMENTS: Hellenistic and Roman Periods.   Figure 1.   *Temple-tombs.* Located near the ancient site of Olba-Diocaesarea, near the modern Turkish village of Demicirli, in southeastern Asia Minor. Second century CE. (Courtesy S. H. Cormack)

tomb with engaged Ionic columns, Doric entablature, and concave conical roof, exemplify the eclecticism and imposing scale of the Late Hellenistic Kidron Valley tombs. Other tombs near Jerusalem are rock-cut, with substantial exterior courtyards and Doric architectural facades screening an interior burial chamber(s) (e.g., the Cave of Umm el-Ammed, the Deir ed-Derb tomb, and the Sanhedrin tombs north of Jerusalem). Outside Jerusalem there is little evidence for monumental tomb architecture, although ancient authors such as Josephus do refer to the existence of such monuments (*Antiquities* 13.211–213, 20.95).

In Syria and Lebanon, freestanding monuments such as the Tomb of Hamrath at Suweida and the tomb at Hermel are further representatives of the Hellenistic monumental stone tomb with one or more cubic stories, engaged columns, and an imposing pyramidal roof. In the former tomb the burial took place below ground level, with the architectural superstructure serving as a symbolic marker. The imposing tomb at Kalat Fakra (central Lebanon), more than 37 m in height, with a staircase, central cubic element, and pyramidal roof, dates to the Claudian period (41–54 CE) and

reveals the lingering influence of monumental Hellenistic tombs into the Roman period.

The rock-cut temple tomb tradition is well represented at Petra (Jordan), where more than five hundred tombs are preserved. Although the most common tomb type at Petra is the pylon tomb, a simple rock-cut facade tomb with a central doorway and, in the attic zone, crenellated relief carving of non-Greek inspiration, there are a number of ostentatious, two-storied rock-cut tombs, among them the el-Khazneh ("treasury"), the Deir ("convent"), and the Palace Tombs. In the first two, a central doorway in the lower story is flanked by engaged columns and recessed niches; the central feature of the upper story is a partially freestanding tholos, or circular structure, flanked by broken pediments. These tombs are without local precedent in Nabatean architecture, and the intrusion of the Hellenistic Greek architectural vocabulary, perhaps via Alexandria, is clear. The elaborate Petra tombs are controversial in date and patronage, with suggested dates ranging from the early first century BCE to the second century CE; it is likely that they were commissioned by local rulers. [*See* Petra.]

The city of Palmyra (Syria) preserves a vast necropolis with more than 150 tombs of the Hellenistic and Roman periods. The tombs belong to three basic types: hypogea (underground tombs with loculi for cremation burials), funerary towers of up to five stories, and funerary temples. The hypogea are the earliest burials at Palmyra and continue a tradition of Syrian hypogeum burials; they are categorized typologically according to the interior layout of their rooms. Funerary towers, the latest example of which dates to 128 CE, were originally provided with loculi at their lowest level; gradually, the entire interior of the tower was exploited and was often lavishly decorated with busts of the deceased. Funerary temples first appear at Palmyra in the second century CE; their interior arrangement allowed for either cremation burial in loculi or inhumation burial in sarcophagi. [See Palmyra; Sarcophagus.]

In North Africa, there are well-preserved tombs of the Hellenistic period at Cyrene and Alexandria in the east, and tower tombs of the Greco-Punic type farther west, at Sabratha (Libya), Dougga (Tunisia), and El-Khroub (Algeria). At Cyrene, elevated sarcophagi, mausolea, stone-revetted tumuli, and courtyard tombs are found. At the many necropoli in Alexandria, the courtyard tomb, with sunken peristyle, vestibule, and burial chamber(s), predominates. In many of the Alexandrian tombs (e.g., the Mustafa Pasha cemetery), the decorative details (painted scenes of garlands, horsemen, and the like) betray a Macedonian influence. In Libya, Tunisia, Algeria, and Morocco, the Hellenistic tower tombs combine elements of the multistoried tombs of Anatolia, with indigenous Punic features such as relief sculpture in native designs, Phoenicio-Cypriot capitals, and concave-sided pyramids as crowning elements. Mausoleum B at Sabratha (also known as the tomb of Bes, or Bisu) is a unique creation in the realm of funerary architecture, having a triangular base with concave sides, a middle story with a false door of Egyptian design, an upper story decorated with colossal statues above seated lions, and a crowning pyramid. The monument, which attained a total height of about 24 m, dates to the early third century BCE. Similar monuments with varying degrees of architectural elaboration were constructed at Dougga, El-Khroub, and Siga (Algeria). The North African tower tomb with a pyramidal or an obelisk-shaped roof had a long history, as a number of tombs in Algeria dating to the first–third centuries CE indicate.

In addition to these North African tower tombs, there are circular North African tombs with applied architectural elements; these represent the transformation of an earlier, indigenous circular tomb type with rings of stones (known as a *bazina*) into an architecturally developed monument. The Medracen and the tomb at Kbour er-Roumia (also known as the Tomb of the Christian Woman), both in Algeria, are two examples of monumental tumulus burials, with a cylinder of engaged columns surmounted by a conical stepped pyramid. The Medracen is an early example of Numidian tumulus architecture, perhaps dating to the early third century BCE (although a second century BCE date has also been proposed), whereas the Kbour er-Roumia tomb is later, perhaps suggesting links with tumulus burials from Republican Italy in the first century BCE. That the cylindrical type sur-

FUNERARY MONUMENTS: Hellenistic and Roman Periods. Figure 2. *Tomb of Zechariah near Jerusalem.* (Courtesy Pictorial Archive)

vived well into the Roman period is attested by the tomb of Q. Lollius Urbicus, prefect of the City of Rome, built in the second century CE in Algeria.

[*See also* Burial Sites. *In addition, many of the sites mentioned are the subject of independent entries.*]

BIBLIOGRAPHY

Browning, Iain. *Palmyra*. Park Ridge, N.J., 1979. See especially pages 192–214 for an accessible, well-illustrated account of the tombs.
Burns, Ross. *The Monuments of Syria: An Historical Guide*. New York, 1992. Historical guidebook for the Western traveler, with clear maps and plans; useful entry on tombs at Palmyra (pp. 167–170).
Cassels, J. "The Cemeteries of Cyrene." *Papers of the British School at Rome* 23 (1955): 1–44. Still the primary publication in English.
Colvin, Howard. "The Romans and Their Monuments." In Colvin's *Architecture and the After-Life*, pp. 55–100. New Haven and London, 1991. Clear, concise, and well-illustrated account of funerary architecture of the Roman period, incorporating Italian and Western monuments in addition to those of the Near East. Extensive bibliography.
Dent, J. "Burial Practices in Cyrenaica." In *Cyrenaica in Antiquity*, edited by Graeme Barker et al., pp. 327–336. British Archaeological Reports, vol. 14. Oxford, 1985. Overview of Cyrenaican tombs, including a discussion of tomb morphology (with a debt to Cassels's work in the area duly noted), chronology, and the relationship between tomb type and social structure.
Fedak, Janos. *Monumental Tombs of the Hellenistic Age: A Study of Selected Tombs from the Pre-Classical to the Early Imperial Era*. Toronto, 1990. Fundamental and concise survey of Hellenistic tombs throughout the ancient world, lavishly illustrated, with full bibliographic references.
Gawlikowski, Michal. *Monuments funéraires de Palmyre*. Warsaw, 1970. As there is no monographic treatment of the tombs at Palmyra in English, this remains the fundamental publication of this vast Syrian necropolis.
McKenzie, Judith. *The Architecture of Petra*. London, 1990. Complete and up-to-date treatment of the rock-cut tombs at Petra, including an immensely useful discussion of the Hellenistic tombs at Alexandria and their relationship to the tombs at Petra. The author bases her chronology on a stylistic analysis (where secure dating evidence is lacking). Extensive bibliography; richly illustrated.
Ridgway, Brunilde Sismondo. *Hellenistic Sculpture*, vol. 1, *The Styles of ca. 331–200 B.C.* Madison, Wis., 1990. Thorough, English-language treatment of the controversial tomb at Belevi near Ephesus in Turkey (pp. 187–196), reviewing arguments for its chronology and discussing the placement of the sculpture.
Roos, Paavo. *The Rock-Cut Tombs of Caunos*. 2 vols. Studies in Mediterranean Archaeology, vol. 34. Göteborg, 1972.
Roos, Paavo. *South-Eastern Caria and the Lyco-Carian Borderland*. Studies in Mediterranean Archaeology, vol. 72. Göteborg, 1985. This and the volume above provide thorough publication of the impressive rock-cut tombs of Caria in southwest Turkey, with detailed analysis of the small finds and pottery.
Sartre, A. "L'architecture funéraire de Syrie du sud." In *Archéologie et histoire de la Syrie*, vol. 2, *La Syrie de l'époque achéménide à l'avènement de l'Islam*, edited by Jean-Marie Dentzer and Winfried Orthmann, pp. 423–446. Saarbrücken, 1989. Discusses the major typological groups of Syrian funerary architecture and their possible derivation from outside Syria; extensive bibliography, mainly in French.
Toynbee, Jocelyn M. C. *Death and Burial in the Roman World*. Ithaca, N.Y., 1971. Although now out of print, this useful handbook of funerary monuments throughout the Roman Empire includes a summary of tombs in the eastern Mediterranean, arranged by type.
Waelkens, Marc. "Hausähnliche Gräber in Anatolia vom 3. Jht. v. Chr. bis in die Römerzeit." In *Palast und Hütte: Beiträge zum Bauen und Wohnen im Altertum von Archäologen. Vor- und Frühgeschichtlern*, edited by Dietrich Papenfuss and Volker M. Strocka, pp. 433–445. Mainz am Rhein, 1982. In the absence of an English-language study of Anatolian tombs of the Hellenistic and Roman periods, this article provides a useful summary of the major types. The role of domestic architecture in the formation of Anatolian funerary architecture is stressed, at the expense of religious architecture.

SARAH H. CORMACK

Monuments of the Late Roman through Islamic Periods

Funerary monuments of the Near East in late antiquity varied in their morphology, based upon local environmental situations, the economic or social status of the deceased, and religious convictions. As a result, no unilinear typological evolution encompasses the variety of monuments in the Near East from the fourth through the eleventh centuries CE. The morphology of funerary monuments from late antiquity, when separated from associated epigraphic and material evidence, can thus provide only a meager indication of a burial's chronological and socioreligious context. Funerary monument and sepulchral typology falters because of the continuous and contemporaneous use of types by divergent religious groups.

Pagan Funerary Monuments. From the Late Roman period onward, pagan funerary monuments preserved the variety of forms, such as inscribed stelae and supraterranean structures, of the Greco-Roman period because pagans were generally free from religious restrictions. These monuments are identified by inscriptions indicating devotion to the gods of the pagan pantheon, the presence of pagan grave goods, and the absence of formulaic expressions and symbols of monotheistic piety. In pagan monuments, inscriptions typically identify the owner of a tomb and the owner's greatest accomplishments, such as service in the imperial armies. These monuments attempted to preserve an eternal memory among the living. The ostentatious style of the pagan funerary monuments of the Greco-Roman periods, such as the mausoleum at Quweismeh in Jordan, continued to be followed, but new constructions declined in the fourth century and disappeared in the fifth, as a result of economic constraints, philosophical changes, and eventually the pressure of the antipagan legislation of the Christian emperors.

Jewish Funerary Monuments. In late antiquity the Jewish community of the Near East built upon ancient Hebrew traditions in erecting funerary monuments and grave markers. Hebrew traditions and teachers such as Rabban Simeon ben Gamaliel minimized the utilization of portraiture and the construction of ostentatious monuments. The most common Jewish funerary monument was a simple, uninscribed, annually whitewashed stela that served to protect passersby from ritual defilement or to warn against the pursuit of activities prohibited in cemeteries, such as grazing animals. Because these grave markers were of ritual significance, they were highly regarded and were maintained by family members. The practice of adorning funerary monuments with Jewish religious symbols such as the shofar and *měnôrôt* ("lamps") increased over time; they often adorned the lintel of the entrance to polyandria or multiperson burial grounds, as well as the interior walls of hypogea, or catacombs.

Jewish religious convictions regarding ritual defilement through contact with the dead made funerary monuments necessary; at the same time, such monuments were not ostentatious because there was no belief that spiritual benefits might be obtained or that one's afterlife depended on the retention of one's memory. Thus, while Talmudic literature mentions the use of graves, family sepulchers, and mausolea, they were not places of worship, and graves were not located in synagogues.

Christian Funerary Monuments. The Byzantines utilized a variety of funerary monuments because Christian scriptures have no specific restrictions about them. Christian attitudes toward worldliness did provide some restraint, but some tombs, such as those at el-Kahf, near Amman, Jordan, were quite elaborate. Most Christians were buried in cemeteries in single graves or in hypogea, where the bedrock permitted the excavation of polyandria. These polyandria served as family tombs that were enlarged at times, over generations, and could also be developed into catacombs, which, used as communal burial places, were of more extended public usage. Beyond these subterranean burial places, for which there was access, supraterranean sepulchral monuments included mausolea, ciboria, and martyria.

Headstones stood over Byzantine graves, displaying the name of the deceased and religious symbols, such as the cross. The decoration and quality of these monuments varied with the deceased's status. Examples of such gravestones can be seen at the village of Nebo in Jordan. Christians who retained Jewish traditions combined crosses and Jewish symbols. Undergound, the walls of hypogea provided space for funerary monuments. Arcosolia provided a tympanum, or recessed space, beneath the arch for paintings incorporating Christian symbolism. Christians buried in loculi within polyandria also had their tombs decorated with painted plaster. Epitaphs in these areas were typically brief, with the name of the deceased, such expressions of piety as crosses or doctrinal statements, and the date of death. Many Byzantine burials utilized polyandria from earlier periods and even closed shaft graves with *pellaicon* (especially shaped stones with notches on the sides or holes in them that allowed a tool to be inserted or provided a handhold), which facilitated the removal of sealing stones and the grave's reuse. The Christians who reused graves generally left no independent funerary monument.

Funerary monuments intended for public display in churches and martyria were typically those of wealthy patrons of the church or of pious persons the community venerated. Such sepulchral monuments proliferated with the evolution of the belief that spiritual benefits could be acquired through venerated Christians.

Islamic Funerary Monuments. Religious restrictions played a key role in the minimization of Islamic funerary monuments among the faithful in the early centuries. Muhammad considered elaborate funerals and monuments to be a retention of paganism and subsequently prohibited the plastering of the surface above graves and the construction of memorial structures on graves. Islamic burials of the faithful thus were typically very simple shaft graves surmounted by a vertical stela at the head and foot. These gravestones were occasionally inscribed with an epitaph, but iconography was not utilized. Less rigorous and proud individuals, such as the 'Abbasid caliph Harun al-Rashid, ordered mausolea to be built for themselves, however.

In spite of Muhammad's proscriptions against funerary monuments and his condemnation of those who made graves of prophets and venerated places of worship and prayer, mosques and canopy tombs appeared over burials in the Umayyad and 'Abbasid periods, such as at the Cave of the Seven Sleepers near Amman. The proliferation of complex funerary monuments greatly increased after the eleventh century, with the belief that benefit might be gained from prayers in such places.

[*See also* Burial Sites; Burial Techniques; Catacombs; Cave Tombs; Martyrion; *and* Mausoleum.]

BIBLIOGRAPHY

Bagatti, Bellarmino. *The Church from the Circumcision: History and Archaeology of Judaeo-Christians.* Translated by Eugene Hoade. Jerusalem, 1971. Contains examples of Jewish-Christian funerary monuments.

Bagatti, Bellarmino. *The Church from the Gentiles in Palestine: History and Archaeology.* Translated by Eugene Hoade. Jerusalem, 1971. Contains examples of non–Jewish-Christian funerary monuments.

Canaan, Taufik. "Mohammedan Saints and Sanctuaries in Palestine." *Journal of the Palestine Oriental Society* 4 (1924): 1–84; 5 (1925): 163–203; 7 (1927): 1–88. An account of nineteenth-century practices, with reference to real monuments.

Creswell, K. A. C. *A Short Account of Early Muslim Architecture.* Rev. ed. Aldershot, 1989.

Goldziher, Ignácz. "On the Veneration of the Dead in Paganism and Islam." In *Muslim Studies,* vol. 1, edited by S. M. Stern, pp. 229–238. London, 1967.

Kurtz, Donna C., and John Boardman. *Greek Burial Customs.* Ithaca, N.Y., 1971.

Kyriakakis, James. "Byzantine Burial Customs: Care of the Deceased from Death to the Prothesis." *Greek Orthodox Theological Review* 19 (1974): 37–72.

Rahmani, L. Y. "Ancient Jerusalem's Funerary Customs and Tombs." *Biblical Archaeologist* 44 (1981): 171–177, 229–235; 45 (1982): 43–53, 109–119.

Rush, Alfred C. *Death and Burial in Christian Antiquity.* Edited by Johannes Quasten. Studies in Christian Antiquity, vol. 1. Washington, D.C., 1941.

Saller, Sylvester J., and Bellarmino Bagatti. *The Town of Nebo (Khirbet el-Mekhayyat) with a Brief Survey of Other Ancient Christian Monuments in Transjordan (1949).* Jerusalem, 1982. Examples of Christian funerary monuments and information regarding the veneration of martyrs.

Toynbee, Jocelyn M. C. *Death and Burial in the Roman World.* Ithaca, N.Y., 1971.

Zlotnick, Dov. *The Tractate "Mourning."* Yale Judaica Series, vol. 17. New Haven, 1966.

ROBERT WAYNE SMITH

FURNITURE AND FURNISHINGS. [*This entry surveys the history of domestic furniture and furnishings as preserved in the archaeological record. It comprises five articles:*

An Overview

Furnishings of the Bronze and Iron Ages

Furnishings of the Persian Period

Furnishings of the Hellenistic, Roman, and Byzantine Periods

Furnishings of the Islamic Period

Following the overview, which provides a general introduction to the subject, the remaining articles treat the artifacts of specific periods and regions.]

An Overview

Permanent settlement was a precondition for the emergence of furniture: nomads would have had little use for it. This discussion of furniture consists of primarily utilitarian, movable household pieces such as low- and high-back chairs, stools, tables, stands, beds, and couches. Ancillary furnishings consist of secondary movable pieces such as boxes and chests, pottery and metal vessels, gameboards, rush mats, and built-in items such as shelves and benches. The existing data suggest that several millennia passed between permanent settlement and the introduction of furniture. There is no evidence for the existence of furniture in Egypt or Mesopotamia before the beginning of the third millennium. Nevertheless, since the earliest Egyptian furniture already displays a remarkable virtuosity there was, in all likelihood, a period of gestation of unknown duration.

The introduction of furniture for general use represented a significant degree of sophistication and refinement originally reserved for royalty and those in the highest ranks of society. No longer content with sleeping on reed mats, or sitting on the floor to eat food spread on platters on the ground, or leaving clothing in a bundle up against a wall, ordinary people of Egypt and elsewhere in the Near East began to fashion beds, chairs, stools, tables both for eating and to support gaming boards, chests, and boxes to contain jewelry, cosmetics, and other sundries. Nevertheless, as can

readily be observed in scanning the evidence from Egypt, the furniture recovered from the royal tombs is far more elegant and sophisticated than the furniture found even in the tombs of the nobles. Yet, ancient dwellings were sparsely furnished. The Shunemite couple's construction of bed, table, chair, and lampstand for the prophet Elisha (*2 Kgs.* 4:10) would have represented a fully furnished room and a considerable investment. However, in addition to the utilitarian function of furniture, such archaeological and pictorial evidence as exists suggests designs intended to create not only functional, but also beautiful objects to decorate the home.

Sources. Because almost all ancient furniture was made from wood, which for the most part deteriorated in the wet climate zones, any reconstruction of furniture in the ancient Near East remains incomplete. The examples of ancient furniture preserved in the dry climate of Egypt and the desert of western Palestine, as well as artistic representations and models of furniture, do provide invaluable information. The Egyptian repertoire is based on furniture from Egyptian Old Kingdom to Late Period tombs (Queen Hetepheres at Giza, Yuya and Thuya and Tutankhamun at the Valley of the Kings) wall paintings and reliefs, statuary, and models of furniture. The picture of Mesopotamian furniture is more difficult to reconstruct because in contrast with Egypt, few furniture remains are preserved as a result of that area's heavy annual rains. With exception of the Mari palace, which yielded schematized pictures of stools, no significant wall decorations depicting furniture are known until the Neo-Assyrian period. Nevertheless, a general picture of Mesopotamian furniture is reconstructed on the basis of such Early Dynastic finds as the furniture depicted on the Royal Standard at Ur (Strommenger and Hirmer, 1964, fig. 72), cylinder seals and stone sculpture, and seals and sculpture of the Akkadian to Kassite periods where both stools and high backed chairs are in evidence (Frankfort, 1963, pls. 54A, 57; Strommenger and Hirmer, 1964, figs. 73, 128 above, 129 right, 157, 159). Though a harpist on a terracotta relief sits on a folding stool, folding stools are rare in Mesopotamian art (Frankfort, 1963, pl. 59B). Likewise, the enthroned god depicted on the top of the stele of the Code of Hammurabi rests his feet on a footstool (Strommenger and Hirmer, 1964, fig. 159), footstools are relatively rare in Mesopotamian art. The most detailed views of Mesopotamian furniture are preserved in Neo-Assyrian wall reliefs that depict palace furniture (Strommenger and Hirmer, 1964, figs. 195, 241 below, and 260 below). Archaeological remains of ivory plaques (the largest assemblage coming from Nimrud [Mallowan, 1966, figs. 381–583]) and bronze furniture parts help to complete the picture. [*See* Mari; Ur; Nimrud.]

The Palestinian repertoire is based on the generally warped, fragmentary, yet informative furniture remains from Middle Bronze Age tombs at Jericho, sculpture from Late Bronze Age Hazor and Tel Sippor in the Philistine plain; LB ivories from Megiddo and Tell el-Far'ah (South) and Iron Age ivories from Samaria, terra-cotta models and wall reliefs from Sennacherib's throne room that depict Assyrians carrying off furniture from Lachish. Though Ugarit has provided an important assemblage of LB ivories that originally come from wood furniture, the furniture has deteriorated. The ivories thus provide little information about the furniture they decorated. However, the Iron Age ivories from Nimrud, Arslan Tash, and Samaria enable the reconstruction of a more vivid picture of Syrian style furniture in the Iron Age. [See Hazor; Megiddo; Far'ah, Tell el- (South); Samaria; Lachish.]

Style and Repertoire. Furniture from Egypt and the Near East shared a repertoire, materials, and technology. It also shared in the conceptual transference of the idea of four-legged animals as the model for four-legged furniture. Nevertheless, in furniture as in art chronological and regional differences exist. For example, while bovine legs characterized Egyptian Archaic period furniture, Old Kingdom furniture is characterized by lions' legs. Furniture proceeds generally from simple forms and unostentatious decoration as in the furniture from the fourth-dynasty tomb of Queen Hetepheres, to more complex and ornate forms seen particularly in the New Kingdom examples from the tomb of Pharaoh Tutankhamun and in wall paintings and reliefs. Furniture represented in Mesopotamian third millennium statuary and cylinder seals is simpler and less ornate, and has softer, rounder forms that accord with Mesopotamian art in general. Thus, extrapolation can only be taken so far for example, to Early Bronze Age Palestinian and Syrian furniture (for which there are no data) from Egyptian Old Kingdom furniture, where third-millennium furniture is best represented. Indeed, comparing Egyptian Middle Kingdom furniture with the known examples of MB furniture from Jericho illustrates the problem. While the furniture from both regions generally shares techniques, the remarkable similarity among the Jericho examples demonstrates that this assemblage, which differs from the characteristic Egyptian furniture, was made at a location other than Egypt. Indeed, it may have been made locally or at least at some location in Syria-Palestine.

Some of the earliest-known furniture, consisting of the ivory bovine legs of couches and gameboards, comes from a first-dynasty cenotaph at Abydos, Egypt. [See Abydos.] Furniture items, consisting of two low-backed chairs with side rails, a curtain box, a bed and neck rest, and a litter entirely covered with gold foil, are among the reburied finds belonging to Queen Hetepheres (fourth dynasty) and are restored masterpieces of Egyptian furniture. By the Old Kingdom period, all the furniture types that characterize the furniture of the ancient world, and for that matter modern furniture, and all of the basic Egyptian woodworking techniques were already known. Like Egyptian art in general, Egyptian furniture is shaped at right angles and consummately crafted.

Evidence of high-backed chairs, a major contribution by Egypt to the evolution of furniture design, comes from Egyptian furniture (Manuelian, 1982, figs. 37, 38), from LB stone sculpture from Hazor (Yadin, 1960, pl. 197; 1961, pls. 326–330) and Tel Sippor in the Philistine Plain (Biran and Negbi, 1966, pl. 23), from ivory carving in the round from Megiddo (Loud, 1939, pl. 4:3), from an incised ivory plaque from Megiddo (Loud, 1939, pl. 4:2), from a wall painting from Kuntillet 'Ajrud, and from a painted sherd found at Samaria. [See Kuntillet 'Ajrud.] A variety of stool types are well-known from Egypt, where the folding stools frequently ended in ducks' feet. Remains of stools have been found at MB tombs at Jericho; stools are also depicted on LB ivories from Megiddo (Loud, 1939, pl. 32) and Tell el-Far'ah (South). Both Egyptian statuary and reliefs and Palestinian ivories (Loud, 1939, pls. 4, 32) provide evidence of footstools. Beds are best represented in Egypt, where they are known from Old Kingdom times onward. Though beds are known from biblical literature, terra-cotta models found at several Palestinian Iron Age sites are the only evidence. A variety of chests to hold clothing and boxes for wigs and cosmetics are well known in Egypt, but are not represented in Syria and Palestine. However, cosmetic or jewelry boxes inlaid with bone strips and silhouettes are well known from Palestine in the MB (and continue into the very beginning of the LB). The existence of plaited straw mats has been demonstrated by impressions on the bases of EB ceramic vessels.

Materials, Tools, and Techniques. Wood was the primary material used to produce furniture. Local woods used in Egypt include acacia, almond, fig, date palm, dom-palm, persea, sidder, sycamore, tamarisk, and poplar. Imported woods included ash, beech, box, carob, cedar, cypress, ebony, elm, fir, and juniper. Sycamore, pine, and oak, in addition to well-known fruit trees, were available locally in Palestine. More expensive furniture was made from a combination of wood and ivory, or overlaid with gold foil. In Egypt copper was sometimes used to raise the carved animal legs off the ground. Stools were frequently plaited with rushes; however, in Egypt there is also evidence for the use of leopard skin. This must have been viewed as a major luxury item because in some instances leopard skin is imitated in painted wood. [See Wood.]

The repertoire of carpenter's tools, reconstructed on the basis of recovered Egyptian tools (fine examples of which were found in a foundation deposit in the tomb of Hatshepsut at Deir el-Bahari), model tools and wall paintings and reliefs, included ripping saws, bow drills, axes, adzes, mallets, mortising chisels, squares, and awls (Hayes, 1953, figs.

189, 190; 1959, fig. 47). Excavations in Palestine yielded saws, adzes, chisels, and awls. Methods of joinery were sophisticated; Jericho provides several examples, including evidence of the mitred bridle joint and tongues (mortising). Ancient carpenters bored holes through the frames of stools with bow drills in order to plait rushes. However, although veneering was common in Egypt, no evidence exists for its use in Syria and Palestine. Several Egyptian wall paintings and reliefs depict carpenter shops, tools, and carpenters at work.

Furnishings. Like furniture, furnishing varied both diachronically and synchronically. Moreover, it is difficult to determine the nature of Syro-Palestinian objects in their role of furnishings in particular since excavation reports rarely describe finds in the context of the rooms in which they were found, and there are no supporting artistic renditions of interiors. Yet, general observations can provide initial approaches to the topic: in palaces and in the homes of the wealthy, sitting or reception rooms would have been furnished with stools and high-back chairs, tables and stands, mixing bowls (kraters) and drinking cups, lamps, gameboards, and possibly musical instruments. Areas serving as offices in all likelihood contained shelves for papyrus and parchment scrolls. Fixed stone benches along walls, upper and lower millstones, grinding stones, ovens, cooking pots, and baking trays would have furnished courtyards, and were in most cases placed against or near the benches. In exceptional cases where bedrooms existed, they would have been furnished with beds, small tables, chests, lamps, and boxes containing toilet items. Sleeping areas for children most likely contained mats, toys, and chests. Humbler homes would have been more sparsely furnished with perhaps a few stools, mats, small tables, ceramic vessels, and millstones. Though no archaeological evidence for rugs exists, geometric patterns on Egyptian wall paintings suggest representations of rugs, which would corroborate biblical references to rugs. Shields and quivers may have adorned the walls of homes of fighting men, as finer pottery set out on shelves may have adorned the walls of the more peaceful.

BIBLIOGRAPHY

Biran, Avraham, and Ora Negbi. "The Stratigraphic Sequence of Tel Sippor," *Israel Exploration Journal* (1966): 160–173.
Frankfort, Henri. *The Art and Architecture of the Ancient Orient.* 3d ed. Baltimore, 1963.
Hayes, William C. *The Scepter of Egypt: A Background for the Study of the Egyptian Antiquities in the Metropolitan Museum of Art.* Part I: *From the Earliest Times to the End of the Middle Kingdom.* New York, 1953.
Hayes, William C. *The Scepter of Egypt: A Background for the Study of the Egyptian Antiquities in the Metropolitan Museum of Art.* Part II: *The Hyksos Period and the New Kingdom (1675–1080 B.C.).* New York, 1959.
Loud, Gordon. *The Megiddo Ivories.* Oriental Institute Publications, vol. 52. Chicago, 1939.
Manuelin, Peter der. "Furniture." In *Egypt's Golden Age: The Art of Living in the New Kingdom 1558–1085 B.C.* Boston, 1982.
Mallowan, Max. *Nimrud and its Remains.* Vol. 2. London, 1966.
Strommenger, Eva, and Max Hirmer. *5000 Years of the Art of Mesopotamia.* New York, 1964.
Yadin, Yigael. *Hazor II: An Account of the Second Season of Excavations, 1956.* Jerusalem, 1960.
Yadin, Yigael. *Hazor II: An Account of the Third and Fourth Seasons of Excavations, 1957–1958.* Jerusalem, 1961.

HAROLD A. LIEBOWITZ

Furnishings of the Bronze and Iron Ages

A discussion of the furniture and furnishings of Bronze Age Canaan and Iron Age Israel requires familiarity not only with the artifacts themselves, but also with the types of activities that took place in the Canaanite and Israelite home. The primary purpose of housing was to supply a safe venue for sleeping and eating, but houses in antiquity were also the locus of other important activities that varied according to geographic and social setting. Rural and urban dwellers, pastoralists, farmers, and merchants, nuclear and extended families all required different configurations of domestic quarters and different furniture and furnishings to support their requisite specialized activities. Financial well-being and social class also affected the ability of Canaanites and Israelites to furnish their houses with both utilitarian objects and objects of beauty.

Canaanite and Israelite houses incorporated many standard features. They were typically one or two stories high, with access to the second story provided by stairs or a ladder. The roof, reached by a ladder, often functioned as a terrace. A large central space in which multiple activities took place was common in Bronze and Iron Age housing. It is often difficult, however, to determine whether this space was roofed (living room) or unroofed (courtyard).

Even small, one-storied houses provided multiple locations for various domestic activities. A room used for food-related chores and other tasks during the day often served as a sleeping area at night. Domestic activities also took place in the courtyard and other outdoor areas. In many houses, the roof provided an additional venue for daytime chores, socializing, and sleeping.

Because garment production was often a domestic activity, a number of specialized tasks, including carding, spinning, weaving, and sewing, took place in Canaanite and Israelite homes. There is little evidence for where in a home a loom would have been located, but other tools for textile production—ceramic spinning bowls, whorls and loom weights; bone picks/shuttles, needles, spindles, and awls—are commonly found.

Roof maintenance required roof rollers: large cylindrical stones used to flatten rooftops and make roofing materials compact. Rollers were left on the rooftops, along with tools for other rooftop projects. Additional tools for housecleaning and maintenance, as well as for agricultural and live-stock-related activities, were sometimes stored in small first-

FURNITURE AND FURNISHINGS: Bronze and Iron Ages. *Carbonized wood armrest of an Assyrian chair from Ebla, with shell decoration.* Dated from 2400 to 2250 BCE. National Museum, Aleppo, Syria. (Erich Lessing/Art Resource, NY)

tombs. A wooden bed was found in one Jericho tomb, but in homes rush mats more commonly provided the sleeping surface. Stools have also been found, but only rarely. Tabletops were made of wood; the seats of stools and the large horizontal surfaces of beds were of woven materials.

Stone and metal sculpture, remnants of furniture, and pieces of ivory inlay were found at LB Megiddo, Tell el-Farʿah (South), and Hazor and at Iron Age Samaria. Sennacherib's reliefs of the plunder of Lachish include depictions of furniture. Because the context of most of these pieces is either sacred or royal, and most of the representations are of thrones, this furniture cannot be considered typical for the average Canaanite or Israelite house.

Additional evidence for furniture has been excavated in Iron Age tombs at Beth-Shemesh, Lachish, and Tekoa, as well as at Samaria trench E207 and in Jerusalem Cave 1 (Holland, 1977; Tufnell, 1953). At these sites, Iron Age clay models of furniture (chairs, beds, and couches) imitate the simple forms of the full-sized originals.

Kitchen Furnishings. Other than sleeping, the most basic activities that took place in the Canaanite and Israelite house were food storage, preparation, and consumption. Archaeological remains of indoor food-centered activities from the Middle and Late Bronze Ages account for more than 90 percent of the artifacts excavated for those periods. There is no evidence to suggest that this is significantly different for the Iron Age.

Installations associated with food preparation, consumption, and storage included ovens and/or hearths, benches and/or shelves and bins, storage jars fixed in place, silos,

floor "closets" that opened into the central living space or the courtyard.

Certain of the furnishings of Bronze and Iron Age houses were constructed as part of the houses themselves. Such furnishings were permanent fixtures, reused over decades and longer. They include benches and shelves raised above floors, niches cut into walls, depressions or rings of stones set into floors to support storage jars, and cooking pots and storejars partially sunk into floors.

Furniture. In antiquity, furniture was not considered indispensable to domestic comfort. What furniture there was was most often constructed of a combination of organic materials such as wood, rush, ivory, and leather. In consequence, few examples of domestic furniture are available for study; those that are preserved come primarily from tombs.

Many well-preserved pieces of furniture were found in the late MB tombs at Jericho. Economic status determined tomb contents, but most contained a limited assortment of furnishings. Included were low rectangular tables with three legs, beds, stools, and small tables. The legs varied in form from simple to decorated; most were geometrical in shape. Wooden tables were the most typical furniture in the Jericho

FURNITURE AND FURNISHINGS: Bronze and Iron Ages. *Drawing of a Phoenician ivory throne from tomb 79 in Salamis, Cyprus.* The ivory was set directly onto a wooden frame. Dated to the late eighth century BCE. (After Karageorghis, 1969: plate 6)

cisterns, and/or pits. Because most of these installations had multiple functions, the best identifier for the location of food-related activities is the oven. In the Middle Bronze Age, less than 5 percent of courtyards contained ovens, indicating that most cooking took place indoors. At the same time, seasonal considerations undoubtedly influenced the locus of food-related activities.

Tools for processing foodstuffs were permanent domestic features and include querns and grinding stones, mortar and pestles, pounders, and blades. The ceramic assemblage included cookware such as baking trays, mixing bowls, and cooking pots; serving vessels such as kraters, jugs, and juglets; and shallow bowls from which food was eaten.

Food products, including grains, were commonly stored indoors in covered or lidless storage jars placed in stands on the floor or set into depressions in it. Bins were built above ground, in corners of rooms, or against walls. Silos, cylindrical or bell-shaped, lined with plaster-coated stone or brick, were also used to store food products. Crudely excavated pits were occasionally used for storage and for refuse. The ceramic assemblage associated with food and water storage (in in-house cisterns) included small jars and juglets for dipping, scoops and small bowls for scooping, and funnels and strainers.

Various aspects of wine making and milk processing took place in houses or in courtyard areas. Other food preparation, including the slaughtering of animals and the initial processing of grains, took place outdoors, often in venues other than the family courtyard.

It is often assumed that animals were kept in or around houses, although little evidence from the Middle and Late Bronze Ages supports this idea. Animal care required storage bins for feed and troughs and mangers in which to place water and food.

Containers. Containers of various sorts were commonly found in Bronze and Iron Age houses. They were used to hold cosmetics, jewelry, combs, mirrors, and other personal items, as well as hand tools and other small items. Baskets and decorative pottery and wood, ivory, and leather containers have all been found in domestic settings.

Lamps and Hearths. In Bronze and Iron Age houses hearths were used for indoor heating. In the Iron Age, the houses of the wealthy often contained braziers (firepans of metal or clay). In both periods artificial lighting was obtained from ceramic lamps. Sometimes lamps were placed in niches built into the walls; alternatively, they stood on shelves, benches, tables and stools, or on the floor. [*See* Lamps.]

Business transactions often took place in Canaanite and Israelite houses. Furniture used for these transactions included tables, stools and benches used for seating and writing, and shelves and special containers for storing documents and materials. Artifactual evidence of business dealings includes weights, cylinder seals, and scarabs.

The primary biblical source for the discussion of furniture from ancient Israel is *2 Kings* 4:10. In this passage, an unnamed Shunammite woman fitted out an upper-story chamber for the prophet Elisha. In it she placed a bed (*mittâ*), a table (*šulḥān*), a seat (*kisē*), and a lamp (*měnôrâ*). The Bible also documents Hebrew terminology for several additional parts of houses and items of furniture.

[*Most of the individual sites mentioned are the subject of independent entries.*]

BIBLIOGRAPHY

Beebe, H. Keith. "Ancient Palestinian Dwellings." *Biblical Archaeologist* 31.2 (1968): 38–58.
Bloch-Smith, Elizabeth. *Judahite Burial Practices and Beliefs about the Dead.* Journal for the Study of the Old Testament, Supplement 123. Sheffield, 1992.
Daviau, Paulette M. Michele. *Houses and Their Furnishings in Bronze Age Palestine: Domestic Activity Areas and Artifact Distribution in the Middle and Late Bronze Ages.* Sheffield, 1993.
Holladay, John S., Jr. "House, Israelite." In the *Anchor Bible Dictionary*, edited by David Noel Freedman, vol. 3, pp. 308–318. New York, 1992.
Holland, Thomas A. "A Study of Palestinian Iron Age Baked Clay Figurines, with Special Reference to Jerusalem: Cave 1." *Levant* 9 (1977): 121–155.
Kenyon, Kathleen M. *Excavations at Jericho*, vol. 1, *The Tombs Excavated in 1952–54.* London, 1960.
Kenyon, Kathleen M. *Archaeology in the Holy Land.* 3d ed. New York, 1970.
Tufnell, Olga. *Lachish III: The Iron Age.* London, 1953.

BETH ALPERT NAKHAI

Furnishings of the Persian Period

Some remains of furniture and large assemblages of metalware, alabaster, faience, and glass have been found in occupational strata and in tombs of the Persian period in Palestine (sixth–fourth century BCE). Favorable trade conditions seem to have been the stimulus for the sudden increase in luxury articles during that period. The objects reflect the society's standard of living, technical capability, and artistic level, as well as the foreign influences current in Palestine.

Of these objects, most were imported—from Persia, Phoenicia, Egypt, and Greece—and are examples of the crafts in which a high level of skill and production had been achieved in their country of origin: alabaster, faience, mirrors, and cosmetic utensils from Egypt; weapons and gold jewelry from Cyprus; weapons and cosmetic articles from Greece; and furniture, decorated metal bowls, and jewelry from Phoenicia. The importation of luxury items seems to have inhibited local production and stifled its growth. The small number of objects that can be attributed to a Palestinian source are generally inferior in quality and workmanship and are imitations of foreign (Persian or Greek) models.

In a tomb (no. 650) at Tell el-Farʿah (South), a great deal of metalware was discovered, including the bronze joints of

FURNITURE AND FURNISHINGS: Persian Period. Figure 1. *Stool, reconstructed after its bronze joints.* From a Persian-period tomb (no. 650) at Tell el-Far'ah (South). (Courtesy Israel Museum; provided by E. Stern)

A clay mold discovered by the Harvard expeditions to Samaria may be further proof that this material originated in Samaria. The mold, in two parts, is strikingly similar to the bronze cylinder mentioned above. It might also have been used to cast the cylindrical sections of a throne's legs.

A pair of bronze candelabra were found on the floor of the tomb of the Sidonian king Tabnit, from the beginning of the Persian period. The candelabra are some 1.5 m high and are entirely Phoenician in style since their design and technique continue the type, in bronze and ivory, found in late Iron Age graves in the Phoenician cemetery at Salamis on Cyprus. Two other large bronze candelabra, one of distinctly Phoenician manufacture and the other of Persian origin, were found side by side in a fifth-century BCE tomb at Shechem.

Many household utensils from the Persian period made of metal, alabaster, and faience have been uncovered. They mainly include bronze and silver bowls, but a small, three-legged bronze pot (about 15 cm high) was found in a tomb in Gaza that resembles larger examples of much finer workmanship also known from Iron Age Phoenician graves at

a couch and stool (see figure 1); the furniture's wooden parts were not preserved. Following cleaning and restoration, the bronze was studied by J. H. Iliffe, who recognized the style of the furniture—and in particular the pairing of a stool and couch—from its frequent depiction on Greek pottery, suggesting a Greek origin. Cleaning revealed several Phoenician letters incised on some of the joints, one letter in each corner. The marks were apparently intended to implement the assembly of the parts (like the use made of masons' marks). The Phoenician letters in turn suggest that the furniture was produced in a Phoenician workshop that may have specialized in imitations of luxury imports.

Fragments of an Achaemenid throne from Samaria were studied by Tadmor (1974), who concluded that, despite its Achaemenid style, it had been produced in Samaria. Three of its components—two bronze lion's paws 13.7 cm high (see figure 2) and a bronze cylinder 22 cm high—are now in the Israel Museum in Jerusalem. They were acquired in Samaria, where they allegedly had been found. These bronzes were probably also manufactured in Samaria, a Persian province and the seat of its governors and therefore a likely location for objects that reflect Persian imperial art. A throne so similar to that used by the Achaemenid kings might have belonged to their representative, the governor of Samaria, with close connections to the Persian court. Similar bronze paws found in other parts of the Persian Empire such as Egypt and southern Russia strengthen this assumption.

FURNITURE AND FURNISHINGS: Persian Period. Figure 2. *Bronze leg of a governor's throne.* From Samaria. Note the end in the shape of a lion's paw. (Courtesy Israel Antiquities Authority)

Salamis. The vessels discovered in Palestine date mainly to the first part of the Persian period (end of the sixth and the fifth centuries BCE) and bear a strong resemblance to contemporary bowls found in Persia proper—at Persepolis, Susa, and Ecbatana. Some of these bowls may have been imported from manufacturing centers in Persia (which excelled in the production of metalware), but there is no doubt that the majority came from Phoenician centers of production on the Syrian coast. It appears that in the Persian period the Phoenicians primarily copied Achaemenid designs, rather than the Assyrian or Egyptian motifs that had served them as prototypes in earlier periods. Phoenicia was also the source of other metal vessels in Palestine, such as jugs, chalices, ladles, and strainers, which were rendered in a similar Achaemenid style.

The most common cosmetic article found was the mirror, of which two types have been distinguished: one of Egyptian origin and the other Cypriot. Kohl utensils, imported from Egypt, are frequently found in women's graves. The mirrors are of bronze, bone, wood, or paste. Only kohl sticks have been preserved, for the most part; kohl tubes are rarely found. Persian period tombs also contained many scores of alabaster vessels of two types: alabastra, or bottles, and flat-based, small bowls. The alabastra vary in shape from long and narrow to broad and squat and apparently held different amounts of oil or perfume. On several, probably containers for spices or bath oils, the amounts are designated on the outside. Small alabaster bowls appear less frequently and may have been used for grinding spices. In this period they seem to have replaced the well-attested Iron Age limestone bowls decorated with incised geometric motifs. The general consensus among archaeologists is that the alabaster vessels originated in Egypt, which possessed a long tradition of expert craftsmen in this field. After what had been an extended period of decline, the manufacture of alabaster objects was revived in Egypt at the end of the Babylonian period. I. Ben-Dor's study of these vessels revealed that the majority were imported; only a small group of crude examples was made out of the local alabaster. Similar vessels in other materials—such as glass, pottery, and bone—may also have been produced locally. It can be assumed that the Palestinian manufacture of these vessels was renewed as a result of its resumption in Egypt because they generally imitate the Egyptian prototypes of the time.

[*See also* Ecbatana; Far'ah, Tell el- (South); Persepolis; Persians; Salamis; Shechem; *and* Susa.]

BIBLIOGRAPHY

Ben-Dor, I. "Palestinian Alabaster Vases." *Quarterly of the Department of Antiquities, Palestine* 11 (1945). Discussion of the alabaster finds in Palestine.

Gubel, Eric. *Phoenician Furniture.* Studia Phoenicia, 7. Louvain, 1987. Essay on the development of furniture in the Levant.

Iliffe, J. H. "A Tell el Far'a Tomb Group Reconsidered." *Quarterly of the Department of Antiquities, Palestine* 4: 182–186. Discussion of the furniture finds at Tell el-Far'ah (South).

Tadmor, Miriam. "Fragments of an Achaemenid Throne from Samaria." *Israel Exploration Journal* 24 (1974): 37–43. Publication of the unique throne found in Samaria.

EPHRAIM STERN

Furnishings of the Hellenistic, Roman, and Byzantine Periods

The furniture of the Hellenistic, Roman, and Byzantine periods developed directly out of earlier classical Greek traditions. The major types of furniture include the throne *(solium)*, chair with a curved back *(cathedra)*, stool or bench *(subsellium)*, couch *(lectus)*, footstool *(scamnum; suppedarium)*, table *(mensa)*, chest *(arca, arcula, cista, capsa, scrinium, loculus)*, shelf *(pegma, loculamentum, pluteus)*, cupboard *(armarium)*, and sideboard *(abacus)*. These types occur throughout the hellenized world and in the later Roman Empire, well into the Early Islamic periods in the ancient Near East. Furniture and its components are uniform in widely separated parts of the Roman world, from Britain in the west, to North Africa in the south, and Asia Minor and Syria-Palestine in the east. Furniture was crafted out of various types of wood, stone (especially marble), and bronze. The wealthy often had furniture, especially beds, out of more precious metals, such as silver or even gold, and prided themselves on pieces inlaid with ivory or gems. Furnishings such as mattresses, pillows, covers, curtains, draperies, and canopies were decorative accessories for couches and chairs, adding to their comfort.

What is known of ancient furniture and furnishings in the Hellenistic, Roman, and Byzantine periods comes from three principal sources. Occasionally, pieces have been recovered from excavations, mostly from Pompeii and Herculaneum in Italy, but less frequently from sites in North Africa, Egypt, Asia Minor, and Syria-Palestine. More numerous are Roman and Byzantine reliefs, wall paintings, sculpture, and mosaics that depict furniture, albeit mainly of the wealthy classes. [*See* Wall Paintings; Mosaics.] The largest collection of reliefs and wall paintings depicting furniture and furnishings in the Near East comes from the eastern Roman cities of Palmyra and Dura-Europos in Syria. [*See* Palmyra; Dura-Europos.] Lastly, contemporary authors, especially Pliny and Pollux, provide detailed descriptions of furniture. Later rabbinic writings, such as the Mishnah and Talmud also are an important source of information on the furniture in use during the Late Roman and Byzantine periods in Roman Palestine.

Chairs. Several different types of chairs are known. The throne, with four turned or rectangular legs and solid sides, and the armchair, popular in the Roman period, were used mainly for official or public occasions. This type of seat did not usually appear in a domestic context. Latin authors, such as Martial (3.63.7) in the first-century CE describe the *cathedra*, a chair with a curved back, as essentially a woman's chair. Depictions of banqueting scenes confirm this description, portraying men reclined on couches and women often seated on chairs or stools. In a funerary plaque of the mid-second century CE depicting a banqueting scene from Palmyra, Malku's wife (Malku was an important Palmyrene) sits on a *cathedra*. From the end of the second century CE, a Palmyran relief shows the goddess Leto seated on a similar basket chair. The *cathedra* was also used as a litter for the wealthy.

Two types of stools, one with perpendicular legs and a second with folding legs, are known from the classical Greek world and continued to be used commonly in the Roman period. One of the few existing examples of a Roman-period stool is represented by a wooden leg excavated at Rifeh, Egypt. A cross-legged stool with a seated woman appears on a wall painting depicting a banquet in a private house at Dura-Europos; a similar stool appears in the third-century CE scene of Solomon and the Queen of Sheba from the Dura-Europos synagogue. On a Palmyran second-century CE tessera (a small token issued for ritual banquets for the distribution of food stuffs), an artisan is shown seated on a folding stool. Often, stools were elaborately decorated with carved animal-head finials and terminated with animal feet, such as in the early third-century CE honorific statue of Ogeilu from Palmyra.

Benches were the most common form of seating in antiquity. The third–second-century BCE Roman writer Plautus (*Stichus* 2.36) describes benches as the seats of the "humble." Later rabbinic sources mention benches on many occasions in different contexts, including benches in private houses (Tosefta, *Ber.* 4.8; see also Tosefta, *B. Q.* 2.9 for a legal discussion regarding a broken bench). Erwin R. Goodenough (1953–1968, vol. 1, p. 106) even suggests that most Jews of this period preferred eating on benches rather than couches, although rabbinic sources refer to dining on couches (Tosefta *Ber.* 4.8).

Couches. The couch was used for reclining at meals *(lectus tricliniaris)*, for sleeping *(lectus cubicularis)*, and for reading or writing *(lecticula lucubratoria)*. An additional non-domestic function of the couch was at funerary banquets. During the classical Greek period, beds had either rectangular or turned legs. In the Roman period, turned legs appeared more commonly, probably on couches of the more well-to-do. Simple couches, or beds, included legs on which a rectangular frame and flat surface, probably of interlaced leather cording, was constructed; bedding was placed on top. Later, head- and footboards were added that became higher and more elaborate in the Roman period. Occasionally, a couch with a back appears. Couches varied in height, from those that are lower than modern beds to those that are much higher, even requiring a footstool to reach the surface. Though most of what is known about couches depicts

and describes the dining couch, it should be noted that the bed is mentioned in rabbinic sources as an essential piece of furniture in all households—not just for the wealthy (see, e.g., Tosefta *Ket.* 6.8, which states that the community had to provide a bed to an orphan setting up his household).

The dining couch was usually arranged in groups of three, as indicated by the Greek word for the dining room, triclinium (from the Gk., *kline*, "couch"). Couches were often arranged in a horseshoe-shaped or semicircular arrangement, with shared tables or one placed next to each couch. Tosefta *Ber.* 5.5–7 describes the appropriate seating arrangement where the middle couch, the *lectus medius*, was reserved for the most honored guest. The placement of the couches themselves is sometimes indicated in the mosaic pavement of the triclinium, as in the recently excavated Dionysos mosaic in an atrium building from Sepphoris, Israel, dating to the third century CE. [*See* Sepphoris.] Contemporary depictions demonstrate that a mattress was placed on top of the couch with one or two pillows to support the reclining diners.

No complete couch used in a domestic setting has survived. A few fragments of wooden couches have been preserved in Egypt's dry climate, including two pairs of legs and parts of three top rails on display in the Berlin Museum (incorrectly restored as a stool). A pair of lion-headed couch legs (originally belonging to a funerary couch?) from Illahun, Egypt, and several others, whose provenance is unknown, have also been preserved (Petrie, 1927). A few more pairs of legs from Roman Egypt are the only lathe-turned couch legs of the kind imitated in other materials and appearing in reliefs, wall paintings, and sculpture of the period. Pieces of a marble couch (second century BCE) were found at Pergamon in Turkey. [*See* Pergamon.] In contrast, a relatively large number of bronze couch fittings, including fulcra (head- and footboards), turned legs, and parts of sheathing for rails, have been found in North Africa and Asia Minor. [*See* North Africa.] The central part of the couch, which was originally constructed of wood, has not been preserved. One of the richest collections of bronze components from couches was discovered in Volubilis, Morocco (Boube-Picot, 1960). These Roman couches are similar to those found at first-century CE Pompeii and Herculaneum. Other parts of bronze couches, dating to the Hellenistic-Roman periods, have been found at Lixus (Morocco), Mahdiyya (Tunisia), Alexandria (Egypt), and Pergamon and Priene (Turkey). [*See* Alexandria; Priene.]

Popular motifs for the finials of the fulcra belonging to these couches include the heads of mules, horses, satyrs, maenads, swans, ducks, geese, lions, elephants, and dogs and figures of Aphrodite. Heads of mules, often with garlands, were especially common; Latin authors, such as Juvenal (11.96.98), refer to ornamental garlanded asses' heads on dining couches. Decorations typically incised on the frame of a couch include floral and geometric patterns.

Couches are seen usually in banqueting scenes and on tombstones depicting funerary banquet motifs. The scenes reached their peak in popularity in the second and third centuries CE. From Palmyra, one very detailed and monumental depiction from a foundation relief for Kitot (40 CE) shows a couch with turned legs and a very thick, richly decorated mattress and pillow. In the third century CE entire banqueting scenes of groups of diners appeared on Palmyran tombs. One well-preserved example is the banqueting scene from the tomb of Malku (c. 200 CE). In one of the private houses at Dura-Europos, a banqueting scene shows three guests with garlands above them reclining on a couch and propped on pillows. Several beds appear in the third-century CE Dura-Europos synagogue wall paintings—beds with turned legs, upon which Jacob is propped with large pillows, are illustrated in two scenes of Jacob's Blessing; a canopied bed with animal legs appears in the scene of Elijah reviving the widow's son.

Footstools. In order to mount couches and some types of chairs, footstools were necessary. Often the stools ended in animal paws or were even whole figures. A second type of footstool was rectangular and box shaped. Footstools are often shown in Roman- and Byzantine-period depictions, either with beds, as in Jacob's Blessing (see above) or with thrones, as in David, "king over all Israel," both scenes from the Dura-Europos synagogue wall paintings.

Tables. The Roman-period table had many more functions than it did in the preceding Greek period, where the most common three-legged rectangular table was used chiefly for dining. Many types of tables are known, including altar tables, honorary tables, funerary tables, domestic cult tables, apotropaic tables, dining tables, bedroom tables, tables as statue bases, tables for drinking vessels, and tables in shops. However, in the domestic context, tables were still used mostly for eating and serving meals. G. M. A. Richter (1906) distinguishes five main categories of tables: rectangular tables with three legs; rectangular tables with four legs; rounded tables with three legs; rounded or rectangular tables on a single support; and rectangular tables on two solid supports. All five types are known from contemporary depictions. Tables were often constructed of wood or stone, including marble, or a combination of the two, as mentioned in the Tosefta (*Kel., B. B.* 1.10). Rabbinic sources (Mishnah, *Shab.* 21.3) also speak of portable tables that could be dismantled.

A few wooden tables are known from Egypt. The best-preserved example is an elegant wooden round tabletop with three legs, dated to the Hellenistic period, from Luxor, Egypt. The legs of the table are in the shape of water birds at the top, with canine three-clawed feet at the base. A second circular turned wooden tabletop was recovered from Faiyum, Egypt.

Stone tables, mainly out of marble, are found in large numbers throughout the Roman Empire, especially from Pompeii and Herculaneum. Marble tables—and marble furniture and sculpture in general—begin to appear in second-century BCE domestic contexts and coincide with the rise of the more materialistic society of imperial Rome. Colored marble was especially prized by the upper classes of Roman society.

Several stone tables from domestic contexts were discovered in first-century BCE–first century CE contexts in excavations in the Jewish Quarter in Jerusalem's Old City (Avigad, 1983). [*See* Jerusalem.] The tabletops and supports were locally produced out of soft limestone, hard reddish Jerusalem limestone, a black bituminous stone, or imported black granite—similar to contemporary marble tables found at Pompeii and Herculaneum. The two types of stone tables found in Jerusalem are a round table on three low legs and a rectangular table on a high central support.

The round tables from the Jewish Quarter measure about 50 cm in diameter. Three depressions are visible on the underside of the tabletops, where three wooden legs had been attached (Avigad, 1983). Based on Hellenistic and Roman paintings and reliefs, the legs most likely were in the form of animal legs, such as are depicted in a Hellenistic tomb at Mareshah/Marisa in Israel and on several Herodian coins. [*See* Mareshah.] In contemporary depictions, these round tables with three legs are usually shown used at meals, surrounded by guests reclining on couches. However, it is noteworthy that in reliefs from Palmyra, three-legged tables appear only rarely in banqueting scenes.

The rectangular table on a single support, corresponding to Richter's fourth type, was extremely rare in classical and Hellenistic Greece (Richter, 1906). According to the first-century BCE Roman military historian Livy (39.6), the table with one leg was one of the types of furniture among the booty brought from Asia Minor and first introduced to Rome during Roman campaigns in the second century BCE. The first-century BCE Roman scholar Varro describes a tabletop resting on a single small column upon which bronze vessels were placed. Rabbinic sources (Tosefta, *Kel., B. B.* 3.4) also mention tables with one support in the context of a halakhic ruling regarding the contamination of tables by unclean liquids.

The rectangular tabletops excavated in the Jewish Quarter measure about 45×85 cm and rested on a single leg that was shaped like a column. The edges of these tables often were decorated in relief on three sides. The motifs include stylized wreath, meander and rosette, laurel sprig, and other geometric and floral decorations, similar to those designs on furniture depicted in the Palmyran reliefs (see above). A fish with meander and floral decorations is the only faunal motif found in Herodian-period Jerusalem. The rectangular tables with a single leg were used as serving tables to hold drinking vessels, as is illustrated in a relief decoration on the edge of a stone tabletop purchased on the Jerusalem antiquities market (Avigad, 1983).

Marble rectangular tabletops resting on two solid transverse supports are known in large numbers from Italy. This table, used primarily for outdoor functions, corresponds to Richter's fifth type (Richter, 1906). It had Hellenistic antecedents, as is indicated by its occurrence at Pergamon, and elsewhere in the second century BCE.

Containers and Shelves. Several different furniture types were used for storage and display: chests, cupboards, sideboards, and wall shelving. The cupboard probably appears for the first time in the Hellenistic period. Cupboards were usually rectangular, with either a gabled or flat top two doors that reached from top to bottom. The interior had shelving, on which items were placed. The Torah shrine, a type of ceremonial cupboard used for the storage of scrolls in synagogues, is shown in numerous depictions, including mosaic pavements and the Dura-Europos synagogue wall paintings. [*See* Synagogues.] The sideboard was in two parts: the lower section was a table on which shelving was constructed. It was another type of furniture that, according to Latin authors Livy (39.6.7) and Pliny (36.8.14), was brought to Rome following the Roman conquest of Asia Minor in 187 BCE.

Furnishings. By modern standards, ancient furniture and furnishings in their domestic setting would be considered scanty. The interiors of large mansions were decorated with wall paintings, stucco, and mosaics. The walls of simpler domiciles were covered with mud plaster.

Wall paintings were designed to be decorative and often were related to a room's function. Frescoes from Pompeii, Herculaneum, and Rome are the most important source of information about this kind of decor. The four "styles" of Pompeian wall paintings still provide the framework for the classification of all Roman-period frescoes. From Roman Palestine, numerous wall paintings and fresco fragments in the Pompeian "architectural" or Second Style have been uncovered in late first-century BCE Herodian-period buildings at Jerusalem, Masada, Jericho, Herodium, and Samaria. At Jericho, ceramic vessels containing remains of the ground pigment powders used in the wall paintings indicate that the Jericho artist was familiar with Roman techniques and materials.

Stucco refers to a slow-setting lime plaster used for producing a hard, durable surface or a quick-setting gypsum plaster used for producing sharp impressions. Stucco decoration originated in the Hellenistic cities of Asia Minor and reached Rome late in the Hellenistic period. Molded stucco was applied for ornamental purposes to the walls and ceilings of the mansions and palaces of the wealthy, reaching its peak in popularity during Late Republican times. Decoration in stucco appears throughout the Roman Empire. In Judea (Judah) in the late Second Temple period (first century BCE–70 CE), the walls of several mansions and palaces in Jerusalem, on Masada, and at Herodium were decorated with white-stucco ornamentation, imitating ashlar

masonry. Pieces of stucco from a coffered ceiling with geometric ornamentation were recovered from the Herodian mansion in the Jewish Quarter of Jerusalem (Avigad, 1983).

Other types of furnishings, being of perishable organic materials, are rarely preserved in the archaeological record. The main sources of information about them are from several ancient lexicographers (Hesychios, Suidas, Pollux), who mention mattresses, pillows, mats, covers, curtains, and draperies, supplemented by contemporary depictions of these objects. Couches are usually shown with a mattress covered with a richly decorated fabric and one or two pillows, on which the guest reclines. A leather mattress, probably similar to those on beds and couches, was excavated in association with Hellenistic coffins in the Jericho cemetery from the Second Temple period (Killebrew and Hachlili, 1983). Valances and loose draperies and, occasionally, canopies over the couch are portrayed in sculpture, wall reliefs, and wall paintings.

From fragments of textiles that have been recovered at Palmyra, Dura-Europos, and several sites in Egypt, it is possible to reconstruct many aspects of these furnishings. [*See* Textiles, *article on* Textiles in the Classical Period.] The main materials used to manufacture these furnishings include wool, linen, camel hair, cotton, silk, leather, and sheepskin. Wool was the material used most commonly for mattress and cushion covers. Many of the second- and third-century CE fabrics from Palmyra and Dura-Europos were probably woven and embroidered in Roman Syria. The largest collection of textiles dates to Roman and Islamic Egypt, or to what are referred to as Coptic textiles. Among these preserved pieces are fabrics used for cushion and mattress covers, draperies, and wall hangings. Popular designs included floral, geometric, and figurative motifs, sometimes in a medallion pattern. They resemble the patterns used in other media, such as in contemporary mosaic pavements and in stucco, the ornamentation of walls and ceiling coffers.

BIBLIOGRAPHY

Avigad, Nahman. *Discovering Jerusalem*. Nashville, 1983. Popular account of the excavations in the Jewish Quarter, Jerusalem, including a description of the furniture and furnishings discovered in the Herodian mansions.

Boube-Piccot, Christiane. "Les lits de bronze de Maurétaine tingitane." *Bulletin d'Archéologie Marocaine* 4 (1960): 189–286. Extensive discussion of bronze couches from Volubilis, Morocco.

Colledge, Malcolm A. R. *The Art of Palmyra*. Boulder, Colo., 1976. General volume, including numerous depictions of furniture of the Roman period.

Goodenough, Erwin R. *Jewish Symbols in the Greco-Roman Period*. 13 vols. New York, 1953–1968. Basic reference work for Jewish art during the Greco-Roman period; volumes 1–9, dealing with Dura-Europos, are especially relevant.

Hill, D. K. "Ivory Ornaments of Hellenistic Couches." *Hesperia* 32 (1963): 293–300. Description of elements of Hellenistic- and Roman-period couches.

Killebrew, Ann, and Rachel Hachlili. "Jewish Funerary Customs during the Second Temple Period, in Light of the Excavations at the Jericho Necropolis." *Palestine Exploration Quarterly* 115 (1983): 109–132.

Moss, Christopher F. "Roman Marble Tables." 4 vols. Ph.D. diss., Princeton University, 1988. Detailed discussion, typology, and catalog of Roman-period marble tables.

Perkins, Ann. *The Art of Dura-Europos.* Oxford, 1973. General survey.

Petrie, W. M. Flinders. *Objects of Daily Use.* London, 1927. Catalog of objects from ancient Egypt, including furniture and furniture fittings.

Ransom, Caroline L. *Studies in Ancient Furniture: Couches and Beds of the Greeks, Etruscans, and Romans.* Chicago, 1905. Extremely useful but somewhat dated.

Richter, Gisela M. A. *The Furniture of the Greeks, Etruscans, and Romans.* London, 1906. Still the standard work.

Thompson, Deborah. *Coptic Textiles in the Brooklyn Museum.* Brooklyn, 1971. Good introductory book.

Vermeule, Cornelius C. "Bench and Table Supports: Roman Egypt and Beyond." In *Studies in Ancient Egypt, the Aegean, and the Sudan: Essays in Honor of Dows Dunham on the Occasion of His 90th Birthday,* edited by William Kelly Simpson and Whitney M. Davis, pp. 180–192. Boston, 1981. Discussion focuses on depictions from Italy.

Veyne, Paul, ed. *A History of Private Life,* vol. 1, *From Pagan Rome to Byzantium.* Translated by Arthur Goldhammer. Cambridge, Mass., 1987. General work on different aspects of daily life.

Weitzmann, Kurt, and Herbert L. Kessler. *The Frescoes of the Dura Synagogue and Christian Art.* Washington, D.C., 1990. In-depth discussion.

Zevulun, Uzah, and Yael Olnik. *Function and Design in the Talmudic Period.* Tel Aviv, 1979. Catalog of an exhibition at Haaretz Museum, Tel Aviv, on daily life in the Talmudic period, based on archaeological evidence and rabbinic sources.

ANN KILLEBREW

Furnishings of the Islamic Period

As a general rule, the interior of houses in the Islamic world contained very little furniture but plenty of furnishings. The most dominant feature apparent at a glance on entering a home—be it in the Maghrib or the Mashriq—was a profusion of multicolored fabrics scattered on the floors or hanging from the ceiling. The best carpet took pride of place on the ṣadr (the wall opposite the main entrance of a room and its most prestigious side), either covering it or spread in front of it. Placed against the ṣadr was the *martaba* (lit., "step"), a sort of sofa for seating during the day, composed of piles of fabrics and cushions and bolsters of diverse types arranged to enhance comfort. In more modest households, the *martaba* was replaced by a single piece of furnishing, the *maṭraḥ*, a word from which the English mattress is derived together with its Italian, French, and German equivalents.

The most expensive furnishing, for the quality of its fabrics, usually silk produced in Tabaristan, was the *majlis* ("seat," also the name for the sitting or living room) that replaced the *martaba* in the houses of wealthy families. The interior of the home was very much enlivened by the colorful cushions and bolsters on sofas and divans and on the floors, which were covered with simple mats. The cushions, usually quadrangular or oblong rather than round, were covered with fabrics with motifs of flowers, animals, and birds. The

function of the cushions, apart from providing comfort to those who used them, was probably to introduce color to the interior, to contrast with the surrounding monochromatic desert landscape found in many countries in the Islamic world. The proper bed *(firāsh)* was a single piece of furnishing that was long enough to stretch out on and was usually kept apart from a family's daytime quarters. Sometimes the *firāsh* was made of costly materials, such as imported silks; in many cases a less expensive local fabric was used. The covers for the bed included a padlike collection of fabric called *bardaʿa.* The proper blanket was the *liḥāf,* which was stored in a chest during the day (it also carried a symbolic meaning of "conjugal blanket," and for this reason was the most precious item of furnishing). The *liḥāf* was usually made of Byzantine or Maghribi brocade or of a special type of damask called *siqlāṭun.* A multicolored *killa* (a "canopy" or "mosquito net") made of fine linen completed the bed's nighttime outfit.

FURNITURE AND FURNISHINGS: Islamic Period. Figure 1. *Wool textile fragment.* Possibly a curtain from eighth-century Iran or Iraq, 18.75 × 12 in. (Metropolitan Museum of Art, Rogers Fund, 1950, 50.83)

In the house there were many curtains (Ar., *sutūr*) and hangings, also expensive furnishings (see figure 1). They were not used to prevent too much light from filtering through windows, however: in the Islamic world, pierced screens performed that function and also allowed ventilation. Where wood was scarce, though, such as in Egypt and in the Maghrib, curtains replaced doors, serving as portieres, and probably covered open bookcases and multiple recesses in walls. In Anatolia and in the eastern Islamic countries, where wood was more abundant and less expensive, doors were certainly more common than curtains. In private homes, curtains were hung across a room to allow privacy, when needed; otherwise they were raised, to make a room more spacious. The sources have transmitted many stories in which curtains are mentioned, among which the most famous is that concerning the palaces of the 'Abbasid caliph al-Muqtadir (r. 908–932 CE): the palaces were covered with thirty-eight thousand curtains made of gold brocade embroidered with gold and adorned with representations of elephants, horses, camels, lions, and birds (Khātib al-Baghdādī, b. 1071 CE, quoted in Lassner, 1970, pp. 88–89). Umayyad princes had a curtain drawn between them and their audience (Grabar, 1987, p. 149). One of them, the future caliph al-Walīd II (from 743 CE), had a curtain drawn across a pool filled with wine, into which he would dive after each song performed by a singer on the other side of the curtain (Serjeant, 1972, p. 203). The best curtains were produced at Basinna in Khuzistan; Bahnasa in Egypt; Mawsil in northern Jazira; Wasit in Iraq; and Tirmah in Transoxiana, among other places. The curtains were usually inscribed with an embroidered *ṭirāz* (calligraphic decorative band) attesting to their place of manufacture (Gervers, 1977, pp. 74–75).

Carpets *(namaṭ, ṭunfusa, bisāṭ)* were also commonly found in houses, especially in the eastern Islamic countries, where they were produced in great number. The best were as prized as the most expensive textiles; carpets, like textiles, were placed over mats to cover the floor almost entirely. A room's carpet arrangements were completed by long, small rugs laid between the entrance door and the central carpet (the best of the house, placed in front of the *ṣadr*) in order to protect its edge; such small carpets were called *'atabas* (lit., "doorsill" or "threshold"). A special function of the carpet was religious. Ernst Herzfeld's reconstruction of the arrangement of carpets in the audience hall of the 'Abbasid caliphs shows a large frontal carpet (the *ṣadr*) bordered on its sides by two runners called *muṣallās* ("prayer carpets") that show an arched pattern symbolizing multiple prayer niches (Herzfeld, 1948, p. 222). A similar arrangement, composed of small, single prayer rugs, must also have been present in private homes because a Muslim is not compelled to go to the mosque five times a day for the prayer but may pray at home in a sacred space (a carpet with a prayer niche). However, not all floor coverings were textiles, es-

pecially in hot regions, where mats made of reeds or rushes were preferred. These usually covered rooms wall to wall and were made to order in a single piece. The most renowned center of production was Alexandria, Egypt, which exported its mats all over North Africa. Many other places in Egypt provided this commodity, as did Abbadan in Iran. In the Early Islamic period, the floors of both large congregational mosques and of smaller ones were covered, as a rule, by mats rather than carpets. Two small mats, probably for religious buildings, have survived in exceptionally good condition: one was made in Tiberias in Palestine and the other, very close in date (tenth century CE), in Greater Syria (see figure 2). Hides or leather mats (*anṭāʿ*, sg. *naṭʿ*) were

FURNITURE AND FURNISHINGS: Islamic Period. Figure 2. *Hemp and straw mat.* Dyed brown and black with two inscriptional bands containing blessings to the owner. From Greater Syria (Palestine?), first half of the tenth century, 63.375 × 33.875 in. (Metropolitan Museum of Art, Pulitzer Fund, 1939, 39.113)

also used as spreads beneath a dining tray or for other uses, although rarely.

This information represents a reconstruction of the furnishings in homes in the first centuries of Islam. It is information that relies exclusively on written sources (by far the most informative of which are the documents that were found in the Cairo Geniza [Goitein, 1967–1983, esp. vol. 4, pp. 105–129]) because textiles, wood, and leather are among the most perishable materials. They rarely survive intact even in the driest climates. For this reason, only fragments of textiles are preserved in any number, in particular from Egypt (Fustat, i.e., Old Cairo, and Bahnasa); none can be identified positively as part of a curtain, a bed, a hanging, or of a garment, however. In only one case can a multicolored wool fragment showing a human head surrounded by running hares and bearing an inscription stating that it was made at Bahnasa perhaps be considered part of a curtain because Bahnasa was famous for this particular commodity. In general, the thickness of the fabric could be of some help in identifying its function—although many outer garments were probably as thick as draperies and curtains.

Fragments of carved and painted wood have also been found in good number, some at excavated sites (e.g., from Samarra, north of Baghdad, the capital of the 'Abbasids for a few decades in the tenth century) and others still in situ when discovered (e.g., ornamental wooden beams from one of the Fatimid palaces in Cairo). However, ordinary domestic furnishings were probably undecorated.

Among the objects found in houses were baskets (*qafaṣ*) of different vegetal materials with covers made of palm fronds or decorative lacing. Baskets were used to store earthenware and glass vessels and writing materials. Light and heat were certainly among a household's first necessities. Hundreds of small oil lamps (usually called *sirāj*) made of clay, metal, stone, or glass have been collected in excavations all over the Islamic world (e.g., Nishapur in eastern Iran). Hanging glass lamps as well as lanterns made of metal or glass *(miṣbāḥ),* inside of which a small glass vessel containing oil was suspended, were also used (sometimes they were hung for votive purposes). Pottery or stucco portable lanterns, also found at Nishapur, were used to circulate light inside and outside the house at night. Bronze or copper candleholders in various shapes, sometimes decorated, completed the lighting system and were provided with beeswax candles. Candleholders were less common than lamps and lanterns because wax candles were quite expensive. Although almost nothing for heating purposes has survived from before the thirteenth century, metal braziers, firepots, and coal pots have been found in houses, even in countries with the hottest climate.

Finally, fumigators were common pieces of furnishing in the houses of the middle and upper classes: square or cylindrical, surmounted by a domical cover and standing on four legs, or animal-shaped (usually birds or felines) with a hinged opening on the chest or with a detachable head and standing on their legs (see figure 3). Pierced incense burners or censers (*mijmara*, possibly made only of silver; *mibkhara*, of bronze; and *midkhana,* of bronze or other materials) could be of any size and range from undecorated to sumptuously ornamented. A large number of them, sometimes with provenience, can be seen in museums all around the world.

[*Many of the sites mentioned are the subject of independent entries.*]

FURNITURE AND FURNISHINGS: Islamic Period. Figure 3. *Incense burner in the shape of a feline.* Cast bronze with openwork decoration, from Khurasan, Iran, dated to AH 577/1181-82 CE, height 33.5 in., length 31.5 in. (Metropolitan Museum of Art, Rogers Fund, 1951, 51.56)

BIBLIOGRAPHY

Ashtor, Eliyahu. *A Social and Economic History of the Near East in the Middle Ages.* Berkeley, 1976.

Briggs, M. S. "The Saracenic House." *Burlington Magazine* 38 (1921): 228–238, 289–301.

David-Weill, Jean. *Catalogue général du Musée Arabe du Caire: Les bois à épigraphes jusqu'à l'époque mamlouke.* Cairo, 1931.

Ettinghausen, Richard. "The 'Beveled Style' in the Post-Samarra Period." In *Archaeologica Orientalia in Memoriam Ernst Herzfeld,* edited by George Carpenter Miles, pp. 72–83. Locust Valley, N.Y., 1952.

Gervers, Veronika, ed. *Studies in Textile History in Memory of Harold B. Burnham.* Toronto, 1977.

Goitein, S. D. *A Mediterranean Society: The Jewish Communities of the Arab World as Portrayed in the Documents of the Cairo Geniza.* 4 vols. Berkeley, 1967–1983.

Grabar, Oleg. *The Formation of Islamic Art.* Rev. and enl. ed. New Haven, 1987.

Herzfeld, Ernst. *Ausgrabungen von Samarra,* vol. 6, *Geschichte der Stadt Samarra.* Berlin and Hamburg, 1948.

Kühnel, Ernst. *Islamische Stoffe aus ägyptische Gräbern.* Berlin, 1927.

Kühnel, Ernst, and Louisa Bellinger. *Catalogue of Dated Tiraz Fabrics: Ummayad, Abbasid, Fatimid.* Washington, D.C., 1952.

Lassner, Jacob. *The Topography of Baghdad in the Early Middle Ages: Text and Studies.* Detroit, 1970.

Marzūk, Muhammad ʿAbd al-ʿAzīz. *History of the Textile Industry in Alexandria, 331 B.C.–1517 A.D.* Alexandria, 1955.

Pauty, Edmond. *Les bois sculptés jusqu'à l'époque ayyoubide.* Cairo, 1931.

Serjeant, R. B. *Islamic Textiles: Material for a History Up to the Mongol Conquest.* Beirut, 1972.

Stillman, Yedida K. "Female Attire of Medieval Egypt: According to the Trousseau Lists and Cognate Material from the Cairo Geniza." Ph.D. diss., University of Pennsylvania, 1972.

Weibel, Adèle C. *Two Thousand Years of Textiles: The Figured Textiles of Europe and the Near East.* New York, 1952.

STEFANO CARBONI

FURTWÄNGLER, ADOLF (1853–1907), German

historian of ancient art and field archaeologist. In 1874, Furtwängler completed his doctorate at Munich and soon after spent three years (1876–1879) traveling and excavating in Italy and Greece. These laid the foundations for a remarkably varied series of studies of prehistoric Greek, Etruscan, classical Greek, and Roman art that demonstrated his particular talent for the stylistic and historical organization of enormous corpora of artifacts. In Greece, Furtwängler collaborated with Georg Löschcke in publishing Heinrich Schliemann's pottery from Mycenae (1879) and in constructing a typology for Mycenaean ceramics (1886). Furtwängler published (1890) the more than fourteen thousand, mostly fragmentary bronze votives and other small finds of Geometric, orientalizing, and later styles from the Olympia excavations in Greece in which he had participated (1878–1879). Beginning in 1881, he devoted himself to organizing museum collections in Berlin, producing inter alia a comprehensive study of the development of Greek vase painting (1885), as represented by examples in the Antiquarium at the Royal Museum in Berlin, and an encyclopedic study of Greek and Roman gems in relation to the art of the Near East and Etruria (1900). His justifiably famous *Meisterwerken der griechischen Plastik* followed in 1893 (1895 in English translation). In 1894, Furtwängler assumed the chair of classical archaeology at the University of Munich. In 1901, he began new archaeological investigations at the Temple of Aphaia on Aigina, at the center of the classical city-state, and at the sanctuary of Zeus Hellenios on Mt. Oros. The excavations of the Temple of Aphaia, published promptly in 1906, allowed a more accurate sculptural history of its pediments and produced the first evidence for a Mycenaean presence on Aigina. Among the many projects underway at the time of his death was his monumental publication of select Greek vases, *Griechische Vasenmalerei*.

BIBLIOGRAPHY

Church, J. E., Jr. "Adolf Furtwängler: Artist, Archaeologist, Professor." *University of Nevada Studies* 1–3 (1908–1911): 61–66. Affectionate appraisal by an American acquaintance.

Furtwängler, Adolf. *Masterpieces of Greek Sculpture: A Series of Essays on the History of Art.* London, 1895. Translation of Furtwängler's masterwork.

Furtwängler, Adolf, and K. Reichhold. *Griechische Vasenmalerei: Auswahl hervorragender Vasenbilder.* Munich, 1900–1932.

Furtwängler, Andreas E. "Adolf Furtwängler, 30 June 1853–11 October 1907." In *Classical Scholarship: A Biographical Encyclopedia,* edited by Ward W. Briggs and William M. Calder III, pp. 84–92. New York, 1990. Frank assessment of Furtwängler's contributions as a scholar and teacher, including a bibliography of his principal scholarly works, biographies, and necrologies.

Lullies, Reinhard. "Adolf Furtwängler." In *Archäologenbildnisse,* edited by Reinhard Lullies and Wolfgang Schiering, pp. 110–111. Mainz, 1988. Brief study of Furtwängler's career.

Schuchhardt, Walter H. *Adolf Furtwängler.* Freiburg, 1956. Assessment of Furtwängler's contributions to the development of an art historically oriented classical archaeology.

JACK L. DAVIS

FUSTAT, original site from which Cairo grew. When

Amr ibn al-ʿAṣ led an army into Egypt in AH 18–19/639 CE after the quick and spectacular Muslim victories in Greater Syria, the first objective was the capture or reduction of the Byzantine fortress of Bab al-Lun (Babylon) just opposite the Nile island of Roda. Not only was this locus the clear access point to the Delta and, therefore, the land route to Alexandria (the second and supreme objective of the campaign), it also formed the terminus of the river traffic coming from Upper Egypt. Because Amr found it impossible to take the fort or the island by storm, he sustained its slow reduction. To accomplish this attrition he established a campsite to the north of the fortress, arranged his troops relative to tribal origins, and built a ditch around the encampment complete with caltrops (pronged ground-lying weapons) to repel cavalry sorties. This trench configuration is known as *fustat* in Arabic, no doubt deriving from the Latin *fossatum*. (In later European fortifications it is termed a *fosse*.)

Bab al-Lun capitulated. Amr led his army up the Delta, attacked Alexandria, and arranged its surrender. It was assumed that Alexandria, with its unrivaled position relative to the trade and culture of the Mediterranean, would become the capital of the newest Islamic province. The caliph in Medina, ʿUmar ibn al-Khattab, however, ordered Amr to return to Fustat and make it the capital and base for further conquests westward. He acquiesced, returned to the campsite, removed the palisade and ditch, and assigned land grants to the various tribes represented in his army. These grants ensured settlement north to the present aqueduct, east to the edge of the Muqattam quarries, and south to the area known as Stabl Antar in the early sources. Sensing the riches to be gained in Egypt, many Syrians and Arabs from the peninsula migrated throughout the seventh and eighth centuries CE, as well as a continuous movement of craftsmen and artists from Alexandria, to serve and seek the patronage of the new governing class centered now at Fustat.

The growth of the original Fustat was agglutinative because each new set of rulers founded new quarters and the old city grafted onto them. In AH 132/750 CE the 'Abbasids went to the north to establish al-Askar while Ahmad ibn Tulun went in 254/868 to the northeast to found yet another capital at al-Qata'i, which contained his famous mosque on the height of Jabal Yashkur. From this elevation eastward to the Muqattam hills he not only gave a northern boundary to the sprawling metropolis, but he also connected it with the old foundation area and the cemetery area to the east and farther southeast to the settlement around Stabl Antar. All the intervening area filled up gradually (but never totally) along three axes: one continued along the eastern bank of the Nile eventually reaching to Helwan, another went roughly from the mosque of Amr towards the mosque of Ibn Tulun, and a third went from the latter mosque east and southeast to the cemetery areas culminating in Stabl Antar.

This somewhat compact urban mass reached its apogee with the founding of the Fatimid quarter of al-Qahira (Cairo) in 969 CE. This was a fully planned and walled city replete with administrative, military, and religious personnel presided over by an Ismaili caliph, who promptly arrived from Mahdiyya in Tunisia. The compact earlier city did not disappear although it was more often called Misr or Masr than Fustat. At first it remained distinct from Cairo; but eventually the heretofore stable border of al-Qata'i moved north to attend the southern wall. The older axial arrangement continued, but an exact emphasis became visible when the Qarafa road connected the Bab al-Zawayla to the shrine of Sayyida Nafisa. A secondary route also now connected the mosque of Amr with the Fatimid city. Thus, old Fustat was reenergized and experienced its apex of prosperity in the Fatimid period.

This new and most profitable dispensation was shattered in 564/1169. To prevent its falling into the hands of an army of Crusaders poised to the south of Stabl Antar, the grand vizier, Shawar, put all the southern unwalled portions to the flames and the entire population fled to the north toward al-Qahira. Salah ad-Din (Saladin) ordered the resettlement of the old quarters after his seizure of power in 567/1171, and built a girdling wall to protect the much-contracted area of settlement. There are also records of industries during the Mamluk era. Otherwise, Fustat simply decayed and was abandoned, except for the area around the mosque of Amr. Potters from Ballas farther south arrived in the latter half of the eighteenth century. With riverine commerce, Old Cairo (now termed Misr 'Atiqa and not Fustat) presented a sizable habitation strung out along the Nile. Behind this bustling

facade, however, the mounds of the former chief emporium of the country stretched to the Muqattam Hills and abutted the cemetery areas to the south.

These mounds were ransacked by searchers for *sibakh*, the nitrogenous layer above the architectural remains, and became the haunts of free-lance excavators in search of antiquities. A more rational approach toward the tumuli was instituted by Ali Bey Bahgat in 1912 when a concession was granted to the Museum of Arab Art (now the Islamic Museum). He probed over a wide area and by 1924 had uncovered a substantial area to the east of the mosque of Amr. By modern standards Bahgat's excavations were wanting in chronological precision, but they did reveal the general configuration of the urban fabric of the Fatimid period. His work was continued and expanded after World War II by Cairo University (much further to the east of Bahgat's revelations and among the building remains of the more southerly cemetery) and by the Egyptian Antiquities Organization, excavations which stretched out from Bahgat's perimeters. Although very little of this latter work has been published, it did confirm the street context and housing modules revealed by Bahgat. In 1965–1966 a house with an upper story intact was uncovered under the direction of Gamal Mehrez; this has been preserved but only partially published.

After the 1952 revolution a four-lane highway was thrust through the mounds to connect Giza with the back route to Heliopolis and the Cairo airport. The land between this road (now known as Sharia Salah Salem) and the standing remains of the aqueduct became available for low-income housing. Apart from some emergency probes there was no archaeological investigation of this huge area. By 1963 the Cairo Governorate announced plans for further housing developments south of Sharia Salah Salem, which alerted the Antiquities Organization to seek outside assistance toward a rapid investigation of the threatened area. Three concession areas were granted to the American Research Center in Egypt, which began its excavations in 1964. [See American Research Center in Egypt.] The 1967 war diverted attention from the scene, but by 1973 it was clear that the Governorate had again turned its attention to the open spaces of Fustat and large-scale commercial, industrial, and domestic projects (generally unlicensed) ensued. These latter activities resulted in two new problems: the cemetery areas were no longer sacrosanct and large parts of the unexcavated reaches had become the dumping ground of the Cairo Governorate in a move to achieve an all-over level for building and street projects.

The American concessions were worked between 1964 and 1981. They achieved the chronological profile lacking in earlier excavations, more particularly through the stratification of the ganglia of streets. They confirmed the same profile when cuts were allowed into the streets revealed by Bahgat. Because there was no grid plan, the narrow, curling streets dictated the plans of the housing units, which were quite asymmetrical externally and variations of the Tulunid Samarra module internally, centering on one, two, or even three courtyards. Some housing units reached five stories, each in essence a series of flats as described in the Geniza documents or combinations of domestic housing and commercial units in the huge conglomerations of the Geniza merchants. (The Geniza, which means "synagogue" in Arabic, was the place where Jewish merchants deposited their commercial archives.) This endeavor also corrected the impression left by Nasir-i Khusrau that the Fustat houses reached heights of ten and twelve stories. He had not taken into account the upward slope of the *jebel* (hill), which was about 12 m (39 ft.) between the mosque of Amr and the present mosque of Abu Su'ud.

Sections of the main funerary route, the Darb al-Ma'asir, the widest street in the medieval settlement, now stand clear as well as a *serdab* (underground hot-weather living space) dating from the early eighth century CE, the earliest Islamic instance of the phenomenon so far recorded, along its northern edge. Over 200 m (656 ft.) of a rough aqueduct came forth in the area directly adjacent to Bahgat's work, a monument that he overlooked. It is not mentioned in any of the known texts. This aqueduct served the bourgeois area attending the Darb al-Ma'asir, an area that contained one Fatimid complex complete with a small bath *(hammam)*. This combination had been associated heretofore only with Mamluk palaces. Of more interest to the social historian is the workers' quarter revealed in 1980. Their dwellings were built not on the *jebel* but on accumulated rubble, making them extremely unstable. The presence of such a quarter, which is associated with the huge pottery kilns uncovered by the Antiquities Organization in an adjoining mound, contradicts S. D. Goitein's theory of class homogenization as deduced from the Geniza documents.

The pottery yields from the subsequent excavations generally paralleled Bahgat's but showed a greater variety of imports. It is now clear that Chinese pottery first entered the Egyptian markets in the ninth century CE and was preferred (as proved by their imitation) through the seventeenth century. There was substantial representation of the wares of Spain and North Africa; Greater Syria, Iraq, and Iran; the Crusader states and Cyprus; and the excellent slip-painted (but unglazed) wares of Christian Nubia. Very few ceramics from Ottoman Turkey have been found.

Glass finds were plentiful, and it is now reasonable to assume that lustering began on glass in Egypt probably in the early seventh century. The bowl of a stemmed goblet lustered on both sides carried the name of 'Abd al-Samad ibn 'Ali, granduncle of Harun al-Rashid and governor of Egypt in 155/771–72. Only in the 1980 season were discoveries of textile fragments plentiful. Among them was an example of resist-dye decoration of the eleventh century, probably earlier than any reported from India, the natural home of the

technique. That same season yielded substantial paper and parchment fragments among which were a complete wedding contract dated to 348/959, a rare rental receipt dated 432–433/1041, and a block-printed amulet text dated to the eleventh century.

Two other sets of excavations have begun at Fustat. One, begun in the 1970s under the aegis of Waseda University and directed by Dr. Kawatoko, has limited itself to the area between the southwest limit of Bahgat's excavation and the mosque of Amr. The purpose has been to discover the position and extent of the area known from the sources as *ahl al-raya*, that area taken by Amr ibn al-'As and his tribal commanders and directly contingent to the early mosque. To date the publications (in Japanese) have produced little toward attaining the stated goal; rather the finds and most of the plans echo the work of Bahgat and of the Fustat Expedition/American Research Center in Egypt. The other, ongoing excavation, which was begun in 1984 under the aegis of the Institut Français d'Archéologie Orientale du Caire is concentrated in an area connected with the ancient cemetery at Stabl Antar. [*See* Institut Français d'Archéologie Orientale.] Menaced on all sides by an ever-growing settlement of permanent housing, the French have been most fortunate in their small area. Approximately 230 m (754 ft.) of the Atfih Aqueduct running from the Birket al-Habash and servicing the cemetery have now been revealed, providing an earlier parallel to the Aqueduct of Ibn Tulun in the Basatin area. Very early (late seventh- and early eighth-century CE) remains of habitation, which were never subsequently built upon, provide a sharper chronological gauge than has been hitherto realized in areas with more complex patterns of reuse and amalgamation. Ancillary structures including a *hammam* of what might be Fatimid family royal funerary establishments have recently come to light along with some tombs of the tenth and eleventh centuries. If the work is unhampered by further building projects, these excavations will provide unrivaled insights into the social and religious contexts of the Stabl Antar section far to the southeast of Bab al-Lun and the mosque of Amr and add significant tesserae to the mosaic of what we are getting to know of Fustat.

[*See also* Cairo; Fatimid Dynasty.]

BIBLIOGRAPHY

The original Arabic sources have been analyzed in three important publications: A. R. Guest, "The Foundation of Fustât and the Khiṭṭahs of That Town," *Journal of the Royal Asiatic Society* (1907): 49–82 plus map; Paul Casanova, *Essai de reconstitution topographique de la ville d'al-Foustat ou Misr*, Institut Français d'Archéologie Orientale, Mémoire 35 (Cairo, 1919); and Ali Bey Bahgat and Albert Gabriel, *Fouilles d'al-Foustat* (Paris, 1921). These sources are again analyzed in the light of archaeological discoveries by Wladyslaw B. Kubiak, *Al-Fustat: Its Foundation and Early Urban Development* (Cairo, 1987). For a reworking of Casanova's reification of Fustat from these sources, see Sylvie Denoix, *Décrire le Caire Fustat-Misr d'après ibn Duqmaq et Maqrizi* (Cairo, 1992). For a general introductory essay, but one which does not incorporate any archaeological findings post-Bahgat, see Jacques Jomier, "Al-Fusṭāṭ," in *Encyclopaedia of Islam,* new ed., vol. 2, pp. 957–959 (Leiden, 1960–). André Raymond, *Le Caire* (Paris, 1993), surveys the results of excavations subsequent to Bahgat's findings (see pp. 18–55).

To supplement these views of Fustat, it is now mandatory to consult research based on the reports and letters of the *soi-disant* Geniza merchants who either lived in or passed through Fustat from the mid-tenth century CE to the burning of Fustat in the late twelfth century CE. Though rather lean for the period of Fustat's economic dominance (eleventh century CE), these original sources complement, correct, or extend the results garnered from archaeology and the standard Arabic sources. S. D. Goitein has published the material in five volumes as *A Mediterranean Society: The Jewish Communities of the Arab World as Portrayed in the Documents of the Cairo Geniza.* Volume 4, *Daily Life* (Berkeley, 1983), is particularly important.

The results of the Fustat Expedition/ARCE excavations are best gleaned *seriatim* from the preliminary reports published in the *Journal of the American Research Center in Egypt* 4 (1965), 5 (1966), 6 (1967), 10 (1973), 11 (1974), 13 (1976), 16 (1979), 17 (1980), 18 (1981), 19 (1982), and 21 (1984). For the short season in 1973, see George T. Scanlon, "Fustat Expedition, Preliminary Report 1973: Back to Fustat-A," *Annales Islamologiques* 16 (1981): 407–436. For a full analysis of the "workers' quarters," now inundated by the Governorate's dumping process, see Wladyslaw B. Kubiak and George T. Scanlon, *Fustat Expedition: Final Report* vol. 2, *Fustat-C* (Lake Winona, Ind., 1988). For consideration of some unique discoveries, see George T. Scanlon, "The Archaeology of al-Fustat: Some Novelties," *Bulletin de l'Institut d'Égypte* 68–69 (1990): 1–16. For an appendage to Kubiak's version of the early site, see George T. Scanlon, "Al-Fustat: The Riddle of the Earliest Settlement," in *The Byzantine and Early Islamic Middle East,* vol. 2, *Land Use and Settlement Patterns,* edited by G. R. D. King and Averil Cameron, pp. 171–180 (London, 1994). For a synoptic coverage of Fustat housing types up through 1977, see Antoni A. Ostrasz, "The Archaeological Material for the Study of the Domestic Architecture of Fustat," *Africana Bulletin* 26 (1977): 57–86.

To date, the French excavations have been published as preliminary reports by Roland Gayraud in *Annales Islamologiques* 22 (1986): 1–26; 23 (1987): 55–72; and 25 (1989): 57–87. The preliminary reports by Dr. Kawatoko can be found in *Bulletin of the University Museum* (University of Tokyo), nos. 341 *et seq.* (coauthored with K. Sakurai, in Japanese). The house with an intact upper story has been partially published (in Arabic with French abstract) by Gamal Mehrez, "Les habitations d'al-Fustat," in *Colloque international sur l'histoire du Caire,* pp. 321–322 (Cairo, 1972). A short report has been published about the excavations carried out by the University of Cairo: S. Maher, "Hafa'ir Kulliyat al-Athar be jahir madinat al-Fustat," *Majallat Kulliyat al-Athar* 1 (1976): 95–126.

GEORGE T. SCANLON

G

GADARA. *See* Umm Qeis.

GALILEE. [*To survey the archaeological history of the Galilee region, this entry is chronologically divided into two articles:* Galilee in the Bronze and Iron Ages *and* Galilee in the Hellenistic through Byzantine Periods.]

Galilee in the Bronze and Iron Ages

The Galilee region in northern Israel consists of the Upper and Lower Galilee and the upper Jordan Valley, thus incorporating both the hill country and the surrounding plains. The diverse nature of the subregions is reflected in the number and scale of their tells and in their settlement history.

Only a few tells have been excavated in the Galilee, none of which are in the hill country. Most of our information about the region has been gained from the excavations carried out at Hazor and Dan and from the periodic surveys conducted in the twentieth century—from the early 1920s (by William Foxwell Albright, John Garstang, Appaly Saarisalo, and others) through the 1950s (Ruth Amiran, Yohanan Aharoni, and Nehemyah Zori). Since the 1970s, systematic surveys have been carried out on behalf of the Israel Archaeological Survey (Yaaqov Olami, Raphael Frankel, Avner Raban, Zvi Gal, and others).

In the Chalcolithic period (fourth millennium), a few subregional pastoral cultures dominated the Galilee. The first settlements in the area, small rural sites, appeared in the Early Bronze I period (3100–2800 BCE). These were replaced in the Early Bronze II–III period (2800–2200 BCE) by large, flourishing urban centers. A dense occupation is indicated by a network of large sites, all of which were fortified cities. Among the main sites are Tel ʿAlil, Tel Gat-Hepher, Tel Hannaton, Nahaf, and Tel Rechesh in the Lower Galilee; Jish, Meʿona, Tel Qedesh, and Tel Rosh in the Upper Galilee; and Dan, Hazor, and Tel Naʿamah in the upper Jordan Valley. The limited evidence gathered from the excavations at Hazor, Dan, Tel Naʿamah, Tel Qedesh, and Meʿona focuses on the enormous scale of their fortifications. These sites represent the well-developed urban life that existed in the region throughout the Early Bronze II–III period.

The enclosures at Horvat Shahal and at Farod are unusual and are known mostly in the neighboring Golan; they apparently were fortified camps for large herds of cattle.

In the Intermediate Bronze Age (2200–2000 BCE), the Galilee's population was seminomadic, as is evident from the burial caves that comprise most of the archaeological data. On the basis of the pottery, it seems that the region was dominated by a single cultural group. Only a few settlement sites have been found, including that of Murhan on the southern margins of the eastern Lower Galilee, the dwelling caves at Tel Harashim, and the cultic cave near Tel Qedesh.

An elaborate settlement hierarchy developed during the Middle Bronze II (2000–1550 BCE) that is characterized by major cities and many small rural sites. The main sites in the hill country include Tel Gat-Hepher, Tel Hannaton, Tel Qedesh, Tel Rechesh, and Tel Rosh. However, in the upper Jordan Valley, some of the finds from the large cities of Dan and Hazor, such as the former's mud-brick gate and the latter's liver model and cuneiform tablets, suggest that these cities were culturally associated with northern Syria, or even Mesopotamia. This view is also supported by a few of the Mari texts, which mention commercial and political connections between Mari and Hazor and Mari and Laish (Dan).

During the Late Bronze Age (1550–1200 BCE), while the cities of the upper Jordan Valley (Hazor and Dan) flourished, the Galilean hill country was poorly settled. It is this period to which the Bible refers when it describes Hazor as "the head of all those kingdoms" (*Jos.* 11:10). The interpretation of the Egyptian texts, especially the list of Thutmose III (fifteenth century BCE), by some scholars as support for a major occupation of the hill country in this period is not borne out by field surveys, which postulate on the contrary, a distinctly sparse occupation. Only a few large sites were settled in the Lower Galilee, of which Tel Hannaton was the largest. The Upper Galilee was even more sparsely occupied, the main site being Tel Rosh (equated with biblical Beth-ʿAnat). One of the el-Amarna texts confirms this situation: it describes the region between Hazor and Tyre as settled by the Apiru and under dispute between the two cities. The settlement process in the Iron Age I (1200–1000 BCE) should be understood in the light of this reality.

Toward the close of the thirteenth century BCE, the large Canaanite cities were destroyed, as is evident from the excavations at Hazor, Dan, and Tel Qarnei-Ḥittin. Either simultaneously, or just a short while later, a network of rural sites in the Galilee was settled, of which Tel Ḥarashim, Har-Adir, and Horvat 'Avot, as well as Hazor and Dan, have been excavated. The pottery found at these sites exhibits Phoenician as well as local characteristics, suggesting that they were occupied by both Israelites and Phoenicians. The Bible describes the battle at Merom (*Jos.* 11) as a major episode in this period; its location should be looked for at Tel Qarnei-Ḥittin. The finds at Dan may illustrate the migration of the Danites into the Galilee (*Jgs.* 18:28).

During the period of the United Kingdom (tenth century BCE), the Galilee reached its settlement peak. An elaborate settlement pattern consisting of fortified cities, villages, farms, and other small sites sprang up. The fortifications, fortress, storehouses, water system, and domestic structures at Hazor and the gate and the cultic *bāmâ* at Dan demonstrate that development.

Political, commercial, and cultural relations were established between Israel and other nations—with Phoenicia in particular. The result of King Solomon's exchange of the "Land of Cabul" (equated with parts of the Akko plain) for Phoenician supplies (*1 Kgs.* 9:10) is represented by the Phoenician fortress excavated at Ḥorvat Rosh Zayit, in western Galilee.

The ninth century BCE was marked by military clashes between Israel and the Aramaeans (*1 Kgs.* 20) and in the campaign of the Assyrian king Shalmaneser III in 841 BCE. There is evidence of these events in the archaeological record at various sites such as Rosh Zayit. The campaign of Tiglath-Pileser III in 732 BCE brought an end to Iron Age settlement in the Galilean hill country. This end is described both in the Bible (*2 Kgs.* 15) and in Assyrian sources and is evident at excavated sites such as Hazor, Dan, and Megiddo. The valley settlements survived, however, and became a part of the new Assyrian administrative system. According to the archaeological evidence, the Galilean hills were almost completely deserted for more than a century. They were reoccupied only in the late sixth century BCE, a harbinger of the Galilee's dense postbiblical settlement.

[*See also* Amarna Tablets; Dan; Fortifications, *article on* Fortifications of the Bronze and Iron Ages; Hazor; Jordan Valley; Mari Texts; *and* Settlement Patterns.]

BIBLIOGRAPHY

The Galilee has been somewhat neglected in archaeological research, therefore published material is lacking, especially in English. The reader may consult the following:

Aharoni, Yohanan. *The Settlement of the Israelite Tribes in the Upper Galilee* (in Hebrew). Jerusalem, 1957. One of the first modern works conducted in the Galilee. Although some of its conclusions are no longer valid, its importance lies in a close acquaintance with the region and the use of new research methods.

Aharoni, Yohanan. *The Land of the Bible: A Historical Geography*. Rev. ed. Translated and edited by Anson F. Rainey. Philadelphia, 1979. Provides a summary outline of the history of the Galilee based on Aharoni's book above.

Biran, Avraham. *Dan: 25 shenot nafirot be-Tel Dan* (Dan: 25 Years of Excavations at Tell Dan). Tel Aviv, 1992. The only comprehensive study of the history of this important site, based on the results of the excavations carried out there.

Frankel, Rafael. "The Upper Galilee in the Transition from the Late Bronze to Iron Age." In *From Nomadism to Monarchy*, edited by Israel Finkelstein and Na'aman Nadav. Jerusalem and Washington, D.C., 1994. Updated study of the Iron Age I in the hill-country, based on new evidence from field surveys.

Gal, Zvi. *Ramat Issachar: Ancient Settlement in a Peripheral Region* (in Hebrew with English summary). Tel Aviv, 1980. Study of the settlement history of the eastern lower Galilee, from the Chalcolithic period to the Iron Age, based on field surveys.

Gal, Zvi. *Lower Galilee during the Iron Age*. American Schools of Oriental Research, Dissertation Series, vol. 8. Winona Lake, Ind., 1992. The only comprehensive study of the historical geography of the lower Galilee, based on new evidence from field surveys and archaeological excavations.

Gal, Zvi. "The Iron I in the Lower Galilee and the Margins of the Jezreel Valley." In *From Nomadism to Monarchy*, edited by Israel Finkelstein and Na'aman Nadav. Jerusalem and Washington, D.C., 1994. Study of the Iron Age I, combining new evidence from both field surveys and excavations with the written sources.

Yadin, Yigael. *Hazor*. London, 1972. Study of the results of the excavations at Hazor and its history, in relation to some major case studies on the MB II and IA I periods.

ZVI GAL

Galilee in the Hellenistic through Byzantine Periods

There are hints in the literary sources of a greater Galilee than the territory entrusted to Josephus at the outbreak of the first revolt (cf. *Antiquities* 18.4; *War* 2.218, 3.35–39). Archaeological remains can confirm such a picture, since architectural forms, ceramic styles, and language patterns do not recognise the boundaries that political expediency imposes. Other factors such as climate, natural resources, and access in terms of travel also determine human habitation. In this regard it is worthwhile to recall the Mishnah's divisions of the region into Upper and Lower Galilee and the valley and Josephus's description of the fertility of the Plain of Gennesar (Mishnah, *Shev.* 9.2; *War* 3.516–521).

The results of the limited survey of some nineteen sites where synagogue remains existed convinced the members of the Meiron Excavation Project of a cultural continuum between Upper Galilee and western (Lower) Golan (Meyers, Strange, and Groh, 1978). [*See* Golan.] They based their conclusion on the obvious similarities in architectural styles for synagogues, including the absence of representational art; the predominance of Hebrew and Aramaic inscriptions, and the similar pottery types. The sites were technically villages rather than cities, and therefore, might be thought to have lacked a broader cultural horizon, especially because the area's mountainous terrain makes Upper Galilee relatively remote. Even in Late Roman times, Upper Galilee was known as Tetracomia (lit., "the four villages"), despite the fact that a policy of urbanization prevailed elsewhere in Palestine for administrative reasons, especially from the second century CE onward.

The distinctive profile this region presents on both sides of the Jordan River is not one of cultural isolation, however, but that of strong group identity in terms of adherence to the Jewish way of life despite participation in other aspects of the surrounding culture. Undoubtedly, the migration to the north that was the direct result of the Bar Kokhba revolt, meant an increase in Jewish presence. [See Bar Kokhba Revolt.] The archaeological data suggest that this area was chosen because of an earlier well-established Jewish presence there, at least in Upper Galilee (Aviam, 1993), and to a lesser extent in the Golan, which was sparsely populated until the Late Hellenistic/Early Roman period (i.e., second–first century BCE; Urman, 1985). A study of the pottery has established the presence of household ware originating in Galilee competing at various sites with local Golan ware from the early Roman period onward (Adan-Bayewitz, 1993). This would seem to suggest that from the very beginning of Jewish expansion in the north under the Hasmoneans the Upper Galilee/Lower Golan formed a continuous region as far as the population of the north was concerned.

On the basis of the Meiron Survey it was concluded that the cultural continuum between Upper Galilee and the Golan was not maintained in respect of Lower Galilee (Meyers, 1976 and 1985; Meyers, Strange, and Groh, 1978). There, different influences could be discerned that brought the area more into line with the cultural life of the Greek cities of the Decapolis and the coast. [See Decapolis.] The results of ongoing excavations at Sepphoris in Lower Galilee seem to support this view (Meyers, 1986 and 1992; Strange, 1992), provided the overall perspective is maintained that Jewish identity was well-established in both Upper and Lower Galilee, certainly from the early Roman period onward. Despite the emergence of Sepphoris and Tiberias as important administrative and market centers in Lower Galilee in the first century CE, introducing such trappings of Greco-Roman life as the theater, it is noteworthy that neither of these centers has so far yielded evidence of pagan worship such as statues, dedicatory inscriptions and temples that are found, for example, nearby Scythopolis/Beth-Shean or in the Phoenician coastal cities. [See Sepphoris; Tiberias.] Even when the material culture shows far greater signs of a non-Jewish presence at Sepphoris, as witnessed, for example, by the third-century CE Dionysiac mosaic and the Byzantine Nile mosaic, there was at the same time a thriving Jewish intellectual presence at these centers corresponding to that which has left its traces in the great synagogue remains of Upper Galilee and the Golan (Miller, 1984; Meyers, Meyers, and Netzer, 1992;

Netzer and Weiss, 1994). Synagogue remains in Lower Galilee, such as Hammath Tiberias, Horvat ha-'Amudim, and Sepphoris with mosaic floors do appear to adopt a different attitude to the question of representational art (Levine, 1981 and 1987) to those in Upper Galilee, except for the Ark of Nabratein with the two lions and the decorated mosaic floor that has been overlain on the original stone one in the fifth-century CE Meroth synagogue (Meyers, 1993; Ilan, 1993). When all differences are allowed for, including climatic and geophysical realities, the material remains do not support a completely different profile for Upper and Lower Galilee in terms of lifestyle, openness to wider cultural influences, and opportunities (Edwards, 1988 and 1992; Overman, 1988 and 1993).

Population. Some of the most pressing problems in regard to Galilean history are those concerned with the issues of demography and ethnography. Archaeology contributes greatly to clarifying the changes from one period to another, and surveys have not only produced relative figures for settlement densities, but in some instances have identified their ethnic affiliations from the material remains. Pottery analysis, utilizing the most up-to-date methods—neutron activation analysis, binocular microscopy, xeroradiography, and thin-section analysis—has made it possible to draw much more precise conclusions about the provenience, manufacture, and distribution of those goods (Adan-Bayewitz and Wieder, 1992).

The findings of Zvi Gal's survey of Iron Age III sites (i.e., seventh–sixth centuries BCE) challenge Albrecht Alt's contention, argued from the literary sources for the most part, that the Israelite population in the Galilee was relatively undisturbed throughout centuries, thus providing the framework for the incorporation of the region into the *ethnos ton Ioudaion* by the Hasmoneans in the second century BCE (Gal, 1992; Alt, 1953). Alt believed that Galilee had fared better in the first Assyrian onslaught in 732 BCE than Samaria did in 721, when the native population was replaced by people of non-Israelite stock (*2 Kgs.* 15:29; 17:6, 24). The absence from eighty-three surveyed sites in lower Galilee of four different pottery types, dated to that particular period on the basis of stratified digs at Hazor and Samaria, has convinced Gal that there was a major depopulation of the area in the century after the fall of Samaria. Only additional stratified digs will decide whether this population gap was the result of the Assyrian aggression or was due to the migration of the country people to larger settlements.

It was only in the Persian and Early Hellenistic periods that signs of new settlements began to appear in this area once more. Preliminary results from the Archaeological Survey of Israel for Upper Galilee show an upward curve from 93 sites in the Hellenistic period to 138 for the Roman and 162 for the Byzantine periods, respectively (Aviam, 1993). This trend corresponds to the results of Dan Urman's survey of the Golan carried out for the Association for the Archaeological Survey of Israel and the Israel Antiquities Authority (Urman, 1985). It is best explained in terms of the incorporation of the whole Galilee/Golan region into the Jewish state and the need for new settlements and military outposts on both sides of the Jordan. The further increase of settlements in the Roman and Byzantine periods is directly attributable to internal Jewish migration for the most part, both in the wake of the second revolt and as a result of the increased Christian presence in the south from the fourth century CE onward.

These suggestions raise more acutely the issue of the ethnic mix of Galilee. Josephus reports (*Antiq.* 13.318ff.) on the enforced judaization by Judah Aristobulus I (in 105 BCE) of the Itureans, a semi-nomadic Arab people who became sedentarized in the Hellenistic period and who are associated with the Hermon region (Dar, 1988). The claim is that with the breakup of the Seleucid empire during the second century BCE, the Itureans infiltrated Upper Galilee—according to some (Schürer, rev. ed., 1973–1987, vol. 2, pp. 7–10, e.g.), almost all of Galilee—which was hitherto sparsely populated. Archaeological considerations give rise to a number of difficulties with this scenario, however. First, Upper Galilee was not as sparsely populated in the early Hellenistic period as the results of the Archaeological Survey already alluded to make clear (Aviam, 1993). Nor is the character of the settlements similar to those confidently identified as Iturean in the Golan (e.g., Khirbet Zemel), since the Upper Galilean settlements reflect an agricultural rather than a pastoral milieu, so obvious in the Golan remains (Hartel, 1987). According to Mordechai Aviam (1993) many of these settlements were abandoned in the Hellenistic period, only to have been replaced by others (regarded as Jewish from the period of the expansion in the second century BCE, based on the preponderance of Hasmonean coins). To complicate the matter further, sherds which, in terms of clay composition (pinkish brown with coarse grits) and style (from large storage jars, poorly finished) are not dissimilar to so-called Iturean ware from Hermon/Golan (Epstein and Gutman, 1972; Urman, 1985, pp. 162–164; Hartel, 1989, pp. 124–126), have also been found in Upper Galilee. The current political situation has prevented surveying the western Hermon region, which might reveal a greater Iturean presence that can be postulated at present. In any event the notion that most of the Galileans who appear in the first-century CE literary sources were forcibly converted Itureans receives no support from the archaeological data. The evidence indicates rather that if there were Itureans in Upper Galilee in the Early Hellenistic period, they left with the advance of the Hasmonean armies of conquest, an option which they were given according to Josephus (*Antiq.* 13.318ff.).

As already indicated, the marked upsurge in settlements from the Hellenistic to the Byzantine period is understandable in light of Jewish history. In some instances the synagogue remains alone, with their distinctively Jewish iconog-

raphy, inscriptions, and liturgical architecture leave no doubt about the strength of the Jewish presence, especially in Upper Galilee/Golan from the Middle Roman to the Early Arab period at least. Architectural remains of synagogues from Lower Galilee are less well preserved, with a few notable exceptions (Chorazin, Capernaum, Hammath Tiberias), nonetheless a recent survey of some seventy sites shows almost as many remains for Lower as for Upper Galilee (Ilan et al., 1986–1987). [See Chorazin; Capernaum.] Based on stratigraphic evidence and literary sources, it can confidently be asserted that several of these later sites in both Galilees were Jewish settlements beginning in at least the Late Hellenistic period. It is surprising, therefore, that with the exception of Gamla and possibly Magdala, no remains of pre-70 CE synagogues have been identified [See Gamla; Magdala.] This may merely mean that in some instances at least they were insignificant edifices, and possibly smaller settlements had no communal building before the destruction of the Temple (Ma'oz, 1992). On the other hand the presence of *miqva'ot* (ritual baths) at such sites as Sepphoris, Jotapata, Gamla, and Khirbet Shema' from the Middle Roman period are clear indications that a sizable number of the population of such places were concerned with issues to do with ritual purity and its attendant way of life. [See Jotapata; Shema', Khirbet; Ritual Baths.] Presumably, the pattern did not differ greatly in the many other Jewish or predominantly Jewish settlements in the Galilee in the same period. The absence of any human or animal representations on the coins of Herod Antipas, the first to be struck in Galilee itself, would appear to support strongly such a conclusion.

The map of known Jewish settlements, especially where synagogue remains have been claimed, shows a concentration of sites in certain areas of both Galilees. In those districts there are few or no remains of a non-Jewish presence, whereas outside those subregions the evidence is unmistakable. The situation is most obvious in Upper Galilee where a Roman temple from the second century CE at Qedesh points to a thriving pagan culture (Aviam, 1985; Fischer et al., 1984). Farther north the bilingual inscription from Dan ("To the God who is in Dan"), as well as the grotto of Pan at Banias from Seleucid times at least, show that the region south of Hermon was thoroughly hellenized from an early period (Biran, 1981; Tzaferis, 1992b). [See Dan; Banias.] Herod the Great dedicated a temple to Augustus at Caesarea Phillipi (*War* 1.404–406; *Antiq.* 15.360). No material remains of Jewish presence have been found above a line that runs just north of Sasa, Bar'am, and Qazyon, all of which show unmistakable signs of having been Jewish communities. [See Bar'am.] To the west-southwest no synagogal remains have been found west of the line from Peqi'in to Rama in Upper Galilee, and a similar situation obtains in Lower Galilee west of the line running from Rama through I'billin to Tiv'on (Ilan et al., 1986–1987; Aviam, 1993). In the south no clear evidence of Jewish communities have been found south of the Nazareth ridge. Outside these lines one is moving in the orbit of the Greek cities, especially Beth-Shean/ Scythopolis and Akko/Ptolemais, while to the north Tyre was the dominant urban influence, even on Jewish Galilee. [See Akko; Beth-Shean; Tyre].

It is noteworthy that as well as the absence of synagogues, dedicatory inscriptions to pagan gods have so far been found only on the fringes of Galilee, such as the third-century CE inscription addressed in Greek to the Syrian gods Hadad and Atargatis from the region of Akko/Ptolemais, or the one addressed to the Heliopolitan Zeus on Mt. Carmel (Avi-Yonah, 1951 and 1959). On the other hand, the only remains of pagan worship from Jewish Galilee (apart from some personal votive objects from Sepphoris) is the Syro-Egyptian shrine at Har Miṣpe Yamim in the Hermon massif, a site which was abandoned already in the second century BCE (Frankel, 1992). The Jewish and non-Jewish areas were not hermetically sealed from one another, however. The evidence points only to the predominant ethnic identities being localized. The literary evidence that there were Jews living in the city territories of Palestine and that some non-Jews were also to be found in Jewish areas, is not negated. In both instances they would have constituted minorities that were more or less influential on their immediate environment at different periods.

This distinction between Jewish and non-Jewish elements in Galilee is strikingly confirmed by Christian remains. Early archaeological work concentrated on the important Christian sites associated with the life of Jesus, such as Nazareth, Mt. Tabor, Capernaum, and Tabgha. [See Nazareth; Tabgha; Tabor, Mount.] In these areas it would seem that Jews and Christians lived side by side from the Middle Roman period (i.e., second century CE onward) until the Persian conquest in 614 CE (Bagatti, 1971). In western Galilee Aviam (1993) has found many Christian settlements, identified by the number of crosses as well as dedicatory inscriptions on remains of tombs and churches, however. Some of the inscriptions are in Syriac and others are in Greek, suggesting that some of the local Semitic, non-Jewish population may have converted to Christianity. This concentration of a Christian presence in western Galilee seems to corroborate the fact that in that area at least, bordering on the territories of the Phoenician cities, the non-Jewish element continued to predominate from pre-Christian to Christian times.

Trade and Commerce. The literary sources presuppose a rural Galilee thickly populated with towns and villages, and well endowed with natural resources, not least the lake of Gennesar, with its thriving fish industry (Freyne, 1988, 1995a). This has been dramatically corroborated, not just by the discovery of the Galilean boat, but also by the survey of the many anchorages, breakwaters, harbors, and fish pools, often Roman in date, discovered around the lake

when the water levels were very low in 1985 and 1986. (Nun, 1988; Wachsmann, 1990). [See Galilee Boat.] The names of two settlements on or near the lake, Tarichaea (Gk., "salted fish")/Magdala and Bethsaida, are directly associated with the fishing industry, the former in particular alluding to the practice of salting fish for export, introduced in Hellenistic times. [See Bethsaida.] The boat's discovery and the analysis of its construction underline the ancillary industry of boat-building which must have been considerable, especially if Josephus's figures are anything to go by (War 3. 522–531).

In light of recent analysis of the pottery (see above), it seems that the interior of Galilee also could boast of a thriving industry from the Early Roman to the Byzantine periods. Three important centers of pottery manufacture, both known in Talmudic sources for their wares, have been identified: Kefar Ḥananyah, on the borders of Upper Galilee overlooking the Beth-ha-Kerem valley (where a large, fourth-century CE kiln has been excavated; see Adan-Bayewitz, 1986 and 1989); Shikhin, tentatively identified with a site close to Sepphoris (Strange et al., 1994), and Nahf in western Galilee where two kilns have been uncovered (Vitto, 1983–1984). [See Kefar Ḥananyah.] Adan-Bayewitz's (1993) study of the pottery of Galilee not only distinguishes typologies as in previous studies (Díez Fernández, 1983), but also traces provenience and distribution patterns in order to determine local (intra- and interregional) trade. Pottery sherds from seventeen excavated and one surveyed site in Galilee and the Golan were subjected to a chemical analysis of the clay, enabling three separate provenience groups to be determined: Kefar Ḥananyah, Shikhin, and Golan wares. It was concluded that the two Galilean centers provided the majority of the household wares for all of Galilee in addition to a sizable minority of the Golan wares over a considerable period of time. The wares from Kefar Ḥananyah and Shikhin are distinguishable from each other by both form and clay components. Thus, two local manufacturing centers emerge in what would technically be described as Galilean villages (and no doubt there were others like Nahf), each with its own specialization and use of local resources. This points to a rapidly developing market economy, that is interested in supplying surplus goods within a regional trading network of some significance for Galilee as a whole (Adan-Bayewitz and Perlman, 1990).

Kefar Ḥananyah provided 10–20 percent of household wares in the Golan from the Early to Late Roman periods, but no Golan ware has so far been found in Galilee, according to David Adan-Bayewitz's (1993) findings. The fact that the Galilean wares are found not just at Jewish Golan sites such as 'Ein-Nashut and Dabiye but also at Tel Anafa and Hippos/Susita, both Hellenistic foundations, shows that the trade was not just interregional but also interethnic, something that is confirmed by the presence of the Kefar Ḥananyah ware at Akko/Ptolemais also. [See Anafa, Tel.] The fact that no Galilean ware was found among the pottery remains of sites south of the Nazareth ridge, such as Samaria and Beth-Shean/Scythopolis, as well as at the more southerly sites in Transjordan, is surely significant in terms of the extent of the trade. This may be due to several factors: transportation difficulties, ritual concerns to do with vessels, interregional—or, in the case of Samaria, interethnic and religious—rivalries, or competing local ware (as in the case of the Golan, where a local pottery trade could be identified, but which clearly was not sufficient to meet all the local needs).

The pattern of local trade emerging from this study of the pottery is also substantiated by a consideration of the coins to be found at Galilean sites. Money played an important role in the development of more sophisticated modes of exchange in ancient economies (Freyne, 1995b). Galilee had its own coinage, albeit of modest proportions, under Herod Antipas, for whom three strikings of bronze coins have so far been identified. In addition, the cities of Sepphoris/Diocaesarea (from 67 CE) and Tiberias (from 100 CE) struck coins, but the scale appears to be limited by contrast with such important trading centers as Tyre (Meshorer, 1985). The coinage of Tyre (both autonomous city coins and Roman imperial ones struck there) predominates at both Upper and Lower Galilean sites, as well as in the various hoards of coins that have been unearthed. No coins from Lower Galilee occur at any of the Upper Galilean sites, however (Ben-David, 1969; Barag, 1982–1983; Hanson, 1980; Raynor and Meshorer, 1988). Thus a pattern emerges in which Tyre continued to be the predominant outlet for Galilean produce, as suggested by the prophet Ezekiel (chap. 27) already in the sixth century BCE (Diakonoff, 1992). In turn, it depended on the hinterland for its own needs, grain and oil in particular, as well as benefiting from the export trade. The identification of olive and wine presses from western Galilee in particular conforming to a typology found in the Syro-Phoenician region generally, confirms this network of everyday influences that transcends ethnic and cultural affiliations (Frankel, 1992). It is probable that there were regional exchange centers within Galilee also, such as the sites excavated by the Meiron Expedition (Khirbet Shemaʿ, Meiron, Gush Ḥalav) and equally Sepphoris for Lower Galilee, where storage cisterns as well as a weight inscribed with the word *agoranomos* (a Greek magistrate who oversaw transactions in the marketplace) has been discovered (Meyers et al., 1986).

Of the excavated Galilean sites in Upper Galilee, only Nabratein does not seem to conform fully to this pattern. The coin profile there is quite different from the other sites excavated by the Meiron Expedition, with Tyrian coins poorly represented. At the same time the evidence from many plastered storage pits is that it, too, served as a collection center for local produce, wine, and oil. This suggests that its location pointed Nabratein in a more easterly orientation, toward the Hulah valley and beyond for its trading contacts.

This conclusion underlines the adaptability of the Jewish population to its larger environment, and in the case of Nabratein, animal representation in the synagogue shows how this diversification is echoed in religious expressions also, but within a thoroughly Jewish framework. Even at the other Upper Galilean sites that might be labeled conservative in terms of their religious observance, the detailed excavation reports of the Meiron team note the presence of imported fine ware from Cyprus, North Africa, and the East in the late Roman period. This shows that these places were thriving economically, and suggests that their religious views did not isolate them from the trappings of affluence, as expressed in luxury household wares in the region generally (Meyers, Strange, and Groh, 1978).

Charting of the road systems contributes greatly to an understanding of Galilean trading patterns, even when developments in this regard for the Roman period are associated with the greater military presence in Palestine rather than with trading, after the two revolts, especially that under Hadrian (132–135 CE). The presence of milestones and paving, often on top of older tracks from the Hellenistic period, can help in the dating of this process (Roll, 1983 and 1994; Strange, 1994). Earlier discussions of the road systems tended to concentrate on the through roads, particularly the Via Maris, which was believed to bifurcate on crossing the Jordan below the Sea of Galilee, one branch traveling south via Beth-Shean/Scythopolis to Jerusalem and the other heading for the coast through the Great Plain. In addition a road linking Tyre with Damascus through Banias is also suggested (Avi-Yonah, 1966). The more recent archaeological evidence fills out this picture considerably for Lower Galilee through the discovery of milestones: a road from Akko/Ptolemais to Sepphoris and on to Tiberias (nine milestones, seven before and two after Sepphoris, going west); a road from Tiberias, south to Beth-Shean/Scythopolis (nine milestones); a second-century road from Beth-Shean/Scythopolis to Legio in the Jezreel Plain (fifteen milestones); another second-century road from Legio to Akko/Ptolemais (five milestones); a road from Legio to Sepphoris (thirteen milestones), and a road from Bethsaida-Julias northwest past Chorazin, possibly linking to Akko/Ptolemais (Roll, 1983 and 1994). Further exploration will undoubtedly uncover a much more complex network of local roads than is possible to document at present, especially around the larger settlements, such as those reported for the Sepphoris region by Strange (1994).

Language. Language is a general indicator of a wider pattern of cultural affiliation. Inscriptions alone, therefore, are of only limited value in determining everyday language patterns. They may be stylized and atypical, depending on the circumstances in which they occur, as well as on other, more far-reaching factors to do with language, such as its use for administrative or commercial purposes and the possibility of bi- or trilingualism in mixed ethnic contexts. In the Galilee setting the foremost archaeological data for language patterns are the many inscriptions from the necropolis of Beth-She'arim in western Lower Galilee. These are normally dated from the period of Rabbi Judah the Prince (c. 200 CE). [See Beth-She'arim]. The site continued as a necropolis until after the Gallus Revolt in the mid-fourth century CE. Some have suggested that chambers 6 and 11 where only Greek is found should be dated to the first century CE (Lifshitz, 1965). Even then, however, the question is raised about how representative this evidence is of the linguistic habits of Galileans. The Greek is, in many cases, "vulgar" rather than cultured in style, which may point to its being rooted in the region's colloquial practices. The location of Beth-She'arim, however, on the borders of the district of Akko/Ptolemais might be seen as making it unrepresentative, even for Lower Galilee. The practice of secondary burials from the Diaspora also needs to be borne in mind in evaluating the significance of the language of burial inscriptions.

In Upper Galilee, where it might be expected that Greek would be well represented at sites as a result of trade links, Hebrew and Aramaic were found to dominate. A few scattered examples of Greek have emerged—an ostracon and ring from Gush Ḥalav, an inscribed storage jar from Meiron, and a bilingual inscription from Firim (modern Rosh Pinah), and the well-known inscription from Qatsyon (possibly from a Jewish site) honoring Emperor Septimius Severus (Meyers and Strange, 1981; Meyers, 1985, p. 120). [See Gush Ḥalav.] This is in sharp contrast to the linguistic picture emerging further north in the non-Jewish areas from sites such as Qedesh, Banias, and the Hermon region generally (Fischer et al., 1986; Tzaferis, 1992; Dar, 1992). It seems that in Upper Galilee, a conservative linguistic pattern corresponded to an equally conservative attitude toward religious art, despite the readiness of the Jewish inhabitants to trade with the most influential commercial center in the area, Tyre, with its pagan associations.

In Lower Galilee the regional differences in terms of ethnic mix and openness to the surrounding culture (see above) come into play. In addition to the possibly exceptional site of Beth-She'arim, Greek appears at sites along the western shores of the lake and in the lower part of central Lower Galilee, the very areas where, on the basis of both the literary and architectural remains, the Jewish population was located. Yet those Hebrew and Aramaic inscriptions that are found in lower Galilee also occur in these regions. This suggests a pattern of bi- or even trilingualism for Jews in Lower Galilee (Greek, Aramaic, and Hebrew), as distinct from Upper Galilee, where the pattern is Aramaic/Hebrew. However, several factors urge caution: the majority of Greek inscriptions are at Christian sites and date from the Byzantine period; there is a relative paucity of Hebrew/Aramaic inscriptions, which may not reflect the actual picture, but may simply be the result of the poorly preserved state of syna-

gogue remains in Lower Galilee; and the rabbinic sources, though written in Aramaic and Hebrew, show a high incidence of Greek loan words, pointing to a situation in which Aramaic was the lingua franca, but with a gradual infiltration of Greek.

The attempt to produce a comprehensive picture of Galilean society on the basis of the archaeological evidence alone, highlighted by this discussion of the epigraphic evidence for linguistic practices, inevitably must be tentative and open to constant revision. New discoveries are made yearly and more and more sophisticated methods are applied to examine the data from the region from which two world religions have emerged. Archaeological evidence and literary descriptions must be critically correlated, a task that calls for considerable methodological sophistication in several disciplines. Literary theorists have made us aware that all texts are tellings rather than showings; archaeology provides a showing in need of a critical telling.

BIBLIOGRAPHY

Adan-Bayewitz, David. "Kefar Hananya." *Israel Exploration Journal* 37 (1986): 178ff.; 39 (1989): 87ff.

Adan-Bayewitz, David, and Isadore Perlman. "The Local Trade of Sepphoris in the Roman Period." *Israel Exploration Journal* 19 (1990): 153–172.

Adan-Bayewitz, David, and Moshe Wieder. "Ceramics from Galilee: A Comparison of Several Techniques for Fabric Characterization." *Journal of Field Archaeology* 19 (1992): 189–205.

Adan-Bayewitz, David. *Common Pottery in Roman Galilee: A Study of Local Trade.* Ramat Gan, 1993.

Alt, Albrecht. "Galilaische Problemen." In Alt's *Kleine Schriften zur Geschichte des Volkes Israel*, vol. 2, pp. 363–435. Munich, 1953.

Aviam, Mordechai. "The Roman Temple in Kedesh in the Light of Certain Northern Syrian City Coins." *Tel Aviv* 12 (1985): 212–214.

Aviam, Mordechai. "Galilee: The Hellenistic to Byzantine Periods." In *The New Encyclopedia of Archaeological Excavations in the Holy Land*, vol. 2, pp. 452–458. Jerusalem and New York, 1993.

Avi-Yonah, Michael. "Mount Carmel and the God of Baalbeck." *Israel Exploration Journal* 2 (1951): 118–124.

Avi-Yonah, Michael. "Syrian Gods at Ptolemais-Acho." *Israel Exploration Journal* 9 (1959): 1–12.

Avi-Yonah, Michael. *The Holy Land from the Persian to the Arab Conquests, 536 B.C.–A.D. 640: A Historical Geography.* Grand Rapids, Mich., 1966.

Biran, Avraham. "To the God Who Is in Dan." In *Temples and High Places in Biblical Times*, edited by Avraham Biran, pp. 142–151. Jerusalem, 1981.

Bagatti, Bellarmino. *Antichi villaggi cristiani di Galilea.* Studium Biblicum Franciscanum, Collectio Minor, no. 13. Jerusalem, 1971.

Barag, Dan. "Tyrian Currency in Galilee." *Israel Numismatic Journal* 6–7 (1982–1983): 7–13.

Ben-David, Arye. *Jerusalem und Tyros: Ein Beitrag zur Palästinenischen Münz- und Wirtschaftsgeschichte.* Basel, 1969.

Dar, Shim'on. "The History of the Hermon Settlements." *Palestine Exploration Quarterly* 120 (1988): 26–44.

Dar, Shim'on. "The Greek Inscriptions from Senaim on Mount Hermon." *Palestine Exploration Quarterly* 124 (1992): 9–25.

Diakonoff, Igor M. "The Naval Power and Trade of Tyre." *Israel Exploration Journal* 42 (1992): 168–193.

Diez Fernández, Florentino. *Cerámica común romana de la Galilea: Ap-*

proximaciones y diferencias con la cerámica del resto de Palestina y regiones circundantes. Jerusalem and Madrid, 1983.

Edwards, Douglas "First-Century Rural/Urban Relations in Lower Galilee: Exploring the Archaeological Evidence." In *Society of Biblical Literature Seminar Papers,* edited by David J. Lull, pp. 169–182. Atlanta, 1988.

Edwards, Douglas. "The Socio-Economic and Cultural Ethos of the Lower Galilee in the First Century: Implications for the Nascent Jesus Movement." In *The Galilee in Late Antiquity,* edited by Lee I. Levine, pp. 53–73. New York, 1992.

Epstein, Claire, and Shmaryahu Gutman. "The Golan" (in Hebrew). In *Judea, Samaria, and the Golan: Archaeological Survey, 1967–1968,* edited by Moshe Kochavi, pp. 243–298. Jerusalem, 1972.

Fischer, Moshe, et al. "The Roman Temple at Kedesh, Upper Galilee: A Preliminary Study." *Tel Aviv* 11 (1984): 147–172.

Fischer, Moshe, et al. "The Epigraphic Finds from the Roman Temple at Kedesh in the Upper Galilee." *Tel Aviv* 13 (1986): 60–66.

Frankel, Rafael. "Har Mizpe Yamim, 1988/89." *Excavations and Surveys in Israel* 9 (1989–1990): 100–102.

Frankel, Rafael, "Some Oil-Presses from Western Galilee." *Bulletin of the American Schools of Oriental Research,* no. 286 (1992): 39–71.

Freyne, Sean. *Galilee from Alexander the Great to Hadrian, 323 B.C.E. to 135 C.E.: A Study of Second Temple Judaism.* Wilmington, Dela., and Notre Dame, 1980.

Freyne, Sean. *Galilee, Jesus, and the Gospels: Literary Approaches and Historical Investigations.* Dublin and Minneapolis, 1988.

Freyne, Sean. "Jesus and the Urban Culture of Galilee." In *Texts and Contexts: Texts in Their Textual and Situational Contexts; Essays in Honor of Lars Hartman,* edited by Tord Fornberg and David Hellholm, pp. 597–622. Oslo, 1995a.

Freyne, Sean. "Herodian Economics in Galilee: Searching for a Suitable Model." In *Modelling Early Christianity: Social-Scientific Studies of the New Testament in Its Context,* edited by Philip F. Esler, pp. 23–46. London, 1995b.

Gal, Zvi. *Lower Galilee during the Iron Age.* American Schools of Oriental Research, Dissertation Series, no. 8. Winona Lake, Ind., 1992.

Goodman, Martin D. *State and Society in Roman Galilee, A.D. 132–212.* Totowa, N.J., 1982.

Hanson, Richard S. *Tyrian Influence in the Upper Galilee.* Cambridge, Mass., 1980.

Hartal, Mosheh. "Khirbet Zemel, 1985/86." *Israel Exploration Journal* 37 (1987): 270–272.

Hartal, Mosheh. *Northern Golan Heights: The Archaeological Survey as a Source of Local History* (in Hebrew). Qasrin, Israel, 1989.

Ilan, Zvi, et al. "Galilee: Survey of Synagogues." *Excavations and Surveys in Israel* 5 (1986–1987): 35–37.

Ilan, Zvi. "Meroth." In *The New Encyclopedia of Archaeological Excavations in the Holy Land,* vol. 3, pp. 1028–1031. Jerusalem and New York, 1993.

Levine, Lee I., ed. *Ancient Synagogues Revealed.* Jerusalem, 1981.

Levine, Lee I., ed. *The Synagogue in Late Antiquity.* Philadelphia, 1987.

Levine, Lee I., ed. *The Galilee in Late Antiquity.* New York, 1992.

Lifshitz, Baruch. "L'hellénisation des juifs de Palestine à propos des inscriptions de Beshara (Beth She'arim)." *Revue Biblique* 72 (1965): 520–538.

Ma'oz, Zvi. "The Synagogue in the Second Temple Period: Architectural and Social Interpretation." *Eretz-Israel* 22 (1992): 331*–344.*.

Meshorer, Ya'acov. *City-Coins of Eretz-Israel and the Decapolis in the Roman Period.* Jerusalem, 1985.

Meyers, Eric M., "Galilean Regionalism as a Factor in Historical Reconstruction." *Bulletin of the American Schools of Oriental Research,* no. 221 (1976): 93–101.

Meyers, Eric M., James F. Strange, and Dennis E. Groh. "The Meiron Excavation Project: Archaeological Survey in Galilee and Golan,

1976." *Bulletin of the American Schools of Oriental Research,* no. 230 (1978): 1–24.

Meyers, Eric M., and James F. Strange. *Archaeology, the Rabbis, and Early Christianity.* Nashville and London, 1981.

Meyers, Eric M. "Galilean Regionalism: A Reappraisal." In *Approaches to Ancient Judaism,* vol. 5, *Studies in Judaism and Its Greco-Roman Context,* edited by William Scott Green, pp. 115–131. Atlanta, 1985.

Meyers, Eric M., et al. "Sepphoris, 'Ornament of All Galilee.'" *Biblical Archaeologist* 49 (1986): 4–19.

Meyers, Eric M. "Roman Sepphoris in Light of New Archaeological Evidence and Recent Research." In *The Galilee in Late Antiquity,* edited by Lee I. Levine, pp. 321–338. New York, 1992.

Meyers, Eric M., Carol L. Meyers, and Ehud Netzer. *Sepphoris.* Winona Lake, Ind., 1992.

Meyers, Eric M. "Nabratein." In *The New Encyclopedia of Archaeological Excavations in the Holy Land,* vol. 3, pp. 1077–1079. Jerusalem and New York, 1993.

Miller, Stuart S. *Studies in the History and Traditions of Sepphoris.* Studies in Judaism and Late Antiquity, vol. 37. Leiden, 1984.

Netzer, Ehud, and Zeev Weiss. *Zippori.* Jerusalem, 1994.

Nun, Mendel. *Ancient Anchorages and Harbours around the Sea of Galilee.* Ein Gev, 1988.

Overman, J. Andrew. "Who Were the First Urban Christians?" In *Society of Biblical Literature Seminar Papers,* edited by David J. Lull, pp. 160–168. Atlanta, 1988.

Overman, J. Andrew. "Recent Advances in the Archaeology of the Galilee in the Roman Period." In *Current Research in Biblical Studies,* edited by Alan J. Hauser and Philip H. Sellew, pp. 35–58. Sheffield, 1993.

Raynor, Joyce, and Ya'acov Meshorer. *The Coins of Ancient Meiron.* Winona Lake, Ind., 1988.

Roll, Israel. "The Roman Road System in Judea." *Jerusalem Cathedra* 3 (1983): 136–181.

Roll, Israel. "Roman Roads." In *Tabula imperii romani: Iudaea-Palaestina,* edited by Yoram Tsafrir et al., pp. 21–22. Jerusalem, 1994. Includes a detailed map.

Schürer, Emil. *The History of the Jewish People in the Age of Jesus Christ, 175 B.C.–A.D. 135.* 4 vols. Revised and edited by Géza Vermès et al. Edinburgh, 1973–1987.

Strange, James F. "Six Campaigns at Sepphoris: The University of South Florida Excavations, 1983–1989." In *The Galilee in Late Antiquity,* edited by Lee I. Levine, pp. 339–356. New York, 1992.

Strange, James F., et al. "Excavations at Sepphoris: The Location and Identification of Shikhin, Part 1." *Israel Exploration Journal* 44 (1994): 216–227.

Strange, James F. "First-Century Galilee from Archaeology and from Texts." In *Society of Biblical Literature Seminar Papers,* edited by David J. Lull, pp. 81–90. Atlanta, 1994.

Tzaferis, Vassilios. "Cults and Deities Worshipped at Caesarea Philippi–Banias." In *Priests, Prophets, and Scribes: Essays in Second Temple Judaism in Honour of Joseph Blenkinsopp,* edited by Eugene Ulrich, pp. 190–203. Sheffield, 1992a.

Tzaferis, Vassilios. "The 'God Who Is in Dan' and the Cult of Pan at Banias in the Hellenistic and Roman Periods." *Eretz-Israel* 23 (1992b): 128*–135*.

Urman, Dan. *The Golan: A Profile of a Region during the Roman and Byzantine Periods.* British Archaeological Reports, International Series, no. 269. Oxford, 1985.

Vitto, Fanny. "A Look into the Workshop of a Late Roman Galilean Potter." *Bulletin of the Anglo-Israel Archaeological Society* (1983–1984): 19–22.

Wachsmann, Shelley. *The Excavations of an Ancient Boat in the Sea of Galilee.* 'Atiqot, vol. 19. Jerusalem, 1990.

SEÁN FREYNE

GALILEE BOAT. A two-thousand-year-old vessel was discovered in the Sea of Galilee in 1986, south of Kibbutz Ginosar. Found by Moshe and Yuval Lufan, the boat was entirely buried in sediment on an expanse of exposed lake bed. A severe drought had lowered the lake's water level.

The Israel Department of Antiquities carried out a probe that indicated that much of the lower portion of the hull had survived in good condition. Initial investigation revealed that its strakes (planking) had been edge-joined one to the other with pegged mortise-and-tenon joints. This method is known to have been used in the construction of Mediterranean seacraft at least by the Late Bronze Age; it continued in use at least until the end of the Roman period.

Upon the vessel's discovery, the media termed it the Jesus Boat, causing a great stir and initiating a chain of events that threatened the hull's well-being. To prevent any danger to it, the Department of Antiquities carried out an unusual salvage excavation, assisted by volunteers from the Yigal Allon Center, Kibbutz Ginosar, and Moshav Migdal. During the excavation the project's conservator, Orna Cohen, invented a novel method for packaging the hull for transport using fiberglass frames and polyurethane. Once excavated, the boat was sailed out onto the lake and brought to the Allon Center, where a specially built conservation pool was built to conserve it (see figure 1).

The boat's dating was determined by the techniques used in its construction, by pottery found in its proximity, by a battery of carbon-14 tests, and by historical considerations. While no one of these methods is sufficient by itself, together they strongly suggest that the boat was in use on the Sea of Galilee between 100 BCE and 67 CE.

During the excavation, noted ship reconstructor J. Richard Steffy carried out a preliminary study of the hull (see figure 2). Its method of construction was typical in the Mediterranean basin at the time, when it was the practice to build the shell first: after laying the keel and posts, the builder(s) edge-joined the planking one to the other with mortise-and-tenon joints. Only after the hull was raised to a sufficient height were frames inserted into it. [*See* Seafaring.] The boat's preserved length is 8.2 m; its maximum width is 2.3 m. At the stern, where it is best preserved, it is 1.2 m high.

Two timbers were joined with a scarf to form the keel, which is rectangular in section and rockered (curved so that it is deeper amidships than at the boat's extremities). It has no rabbets (grooves). Instead, the abutting garboard strakes are attached horizontally to the keel with mortise-and-tenon joints into which pegs were driven from above. The forward part of the keel contained a row of mortise scars indicating that it had seen previous use.

The hull's planking is somewhat unusual. In many cases the strakes are peculiarly narrow, apparently the result of at least some of the planks also having been recycled from earlier vessels. This would have required the removal of the mortise-and-tenon scars on the lateral and dorsal edges,

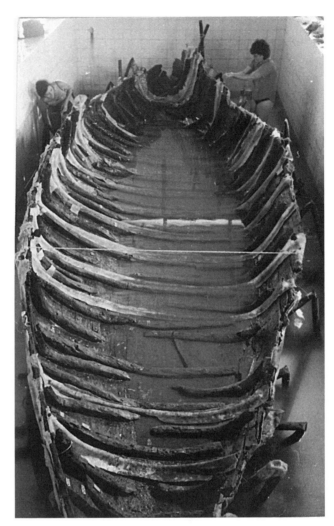

GALILEE BOAT. Figure 1. *The Galilee Boat in its conservation pool.* (Photograph by D. Syon, courtesy Israel Antiquities Authority)

which resulted in the narrowing of the planks. The mortise-and-tenon joints are placed at 12-cm intervals and locked with tapered pegs driven from inside the hull.

The "floor and half-frame" framing pattern is also typical of contemporary Mediterranean ships. Frames were fashioned from timbers poorly suited to their purpose, so that at times they spring significantly from the planking. Some frames still have their bark attached. The boat's construction suggests that it was built by someone familiar with the shipbuilding techniques prevalent on the Mediterranean coast. However, the boatwright used timber of inferior quality to that normally in use on the Mediterranean.

Forty-one of the boat's timbers have been identified by E. Werker. The majority of the strakes studied were fashioned from Lebanese cedar *(Cedrus);* most of the frames were made of oak *(Quercus)* branches. Five additional types of wood have been identified in the boat's construction: sidder (*Ziziphus spina-christi*, also known as christ-thorn or jujube)

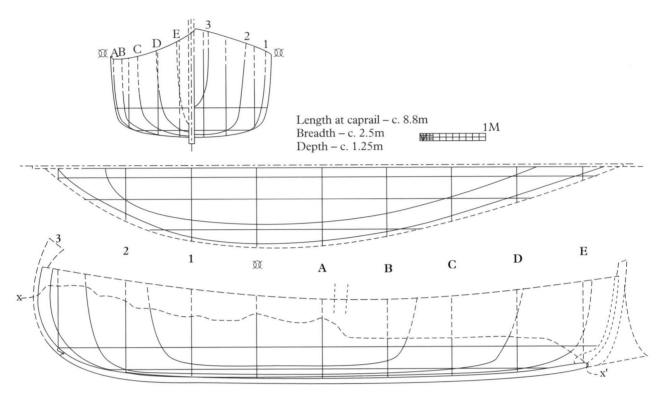

Length at caprail – c. 8.8m
Breadth – c. 2.5m
Depth – c. 1.25m

GALILEE BOAT. Figure 2. *Preliminary line drawings of the boat.* (Drawing by J. R. Steffy, courtesy Institute of Nautical Archaeology)

for the aft part of the keel; Aleppo pine *(Pinus halepensis)* for one of the planks; and single examples of frames from hawthorn *(Crataegus),* willow *(Salix),* and redbud *(Cercis siliquastrum).* With the exception of the cedar, all these trees grow, or grew, in the vicinity of the Sea of Galilee and its environs. The use of a variety of different woods (some of which are inappropriate for naval construction) is highly unusual. Taken together with the evidence for the recycling of wood, this suggests either a deficit of wood or that the boat's owner could not afford better timber.

The boat could have been propelled by oar or sail. It had had a long work life, as evidenced by numerous repairs to the hull. Some repairs had been made by strengthening the planking with large iron staplelike fastenings where the mortise-and-tenon joints had given way.

This type of boat appears to have been built specifically for use with the large seine net (Gk., *segena*) by means of which fish were caught near the shore (*Mt.* 13:47–50). [*See* Fishing.] It was probably the largest type of boat on the lake. Boats of similar size, termed *Arabiye* in Arabic, were used for fishing with the seine net on the Sea of Galilee into the twentieth century. In addition to fishing, the boat probably served a variety of other purposes, including transporting passengers and supplies around the Sea of Galilee.

Some parts of the hull had been intentionally removed in

antiquity, among them the stem construction, the sternpost, the mast step, and several of the frames.

Some of the most memorable Gospel stories deal with voyages and fishing on the lake. The Sea of Galilee and its fishermen and sailors serve as the backdrop to Jesus' ministry. Until the discovery of the Galilee boat, however, virtually nothing concrete was known concerning the boats used on the lake then.

A boat depicted in a first-century CE mosaic from Migdal carries two oars and a quarter rudder on its port side, thus requiring a minimum crew of five: four oarsmen and a helmsman/captain. [*See* Mosaics.] Steffy postulates that a similar number of crew would have been required for the Galilee boat. Furthermore, references to the boats of Zebedee and Simon/Peter—the only two boats specified in the Gospels—indicate that they also had crews of five or more men (*Mk.* 1:20; *Jn.* 21:2–3). Thus, all these sources refer to the same type of boat. Similarly, Josephus, in describing a "sham" fleet he brought against the citizens of Tiberias during the first Jewish Revolt against Rome, mentions placing skeleton crews of four sailors in each of the (fishing) boats in his fleet; elsewhere he refers to helmsmen, indicating that his boats were manned by crews of five men (*Life* 32.163; *War* 2.635, 641). [*See* First Jewish Revolt.]

Despite popular belief, it is not possible to determine how

many individuals took part in any of the boat trips recorded in the Gospels. Josephus, however, indicates that a boat of this type could hold up to fifteen men (*Life* 32.164; 33.168; *War* 2.639).

The boats used by Josephus in his sham fleet are apparently the same ones later used by Jewish forces in their naval battle against Vespasian's troops, following the fall of Migdal, in fall 67 (*War* 3.522–531). During the Roman investiture of the city, some Jews managed to escape in a fleet of fishing boats that had been prepared in anticipation of the Roman advance. Against this fleet Vespasian's forces built makeshift vessels, perhaps catamarans constructed from Jewish boats that had been left behind—and vanquished the Jews.

A pyramidal iron arrowhead found in the sediment inside the Galilee boat is apparently of foreign origin and may have been fired by a Roman *auxilia* archer during the battle. Fourteen similar arrowheads were found at Gamla, the next Jewish city conquered by Vespasian after Migdal. [*See* Gamla.] The arrowhead was not found in an archaeological context, however, and therefore does not indicate that this particular boat participated in the battle. Rather, the evidence suggests that, at the end of a long work life, the boat was brought ashore to have all its reusable parts cannibalized. What remained of the hull was then pushed into the lake, there soon to be buried under sediment.

During the excavation portions of two additional hulls were found in the immediate vicinity of the Galilee boat, suggesting that the boat's find site was an area of boat-building activity in antiquity.

The Galilee boat has provided valuable information about a type of large boat in use on the Sea of Galilee during the first centuries BCE and CE. However, there presently is no evidence to suggest that this vessel took part in any of the events mentioned in contemporary literary sources.

[*See also* Anchors; *and* Ships and Boats.]

BIBLIOGRAPHY

Steffy, J. Richard. "The Kinneret Boat Project, Part II: Notes on the Construction of the Kinneret Boat." *International Journal of Nautical Archaeology and Underwater Exploration* 16 (1987): 325–329. Preliminary report on the Galilee boat's construction.

Steffy, J. Richard. *Wooden Ship Building and the Interpretation of Shipwrecks.* College Station, Tex., 1994. Includes a summary description of the Galilee boat's construction (see pp. 65–67).

Wachsmann, Shelley, et al. "The Kinneret Boat Project, Part I: The Excavation and the Conservation of the Kinneret Boat." *International Journal of Nautical Archaeology and Underwater Exploration* 16 (1987): 233–245. Preliminary report on the discovery, excavation, and transportation of the boat.

Wachsmann, Shelley, et al. *The Excavations of an Ancient Boat in the Sea of Galilee (Lake Kinneret).* 'Atiqot, vol. 19. Jerusalem, 1990. Excavation report.

Wachsmann, Shelley. *The Sea of Galilee Boat: An Extraordinary 2000-Year-Old Discovery.* New York, 1995. Popular account of the discovery, excavation, and research.

SHELLEY WACHSMANN

GALLING, KURT (1900–1987), Hebrew Bible scholar and archaeologist. Born in Wilhelmshaven, Germany, Galling, after completing his gymnasium studies in Berlin in 1917, joined the army, in which he served until the end of World War I. He went on to study theology and oriental studies at the universities of Berlin and Jena. He completed his thesis "Licht und Beleuchtung in Vorstellung und Darstellung israelitisch-jüdischer Kultur" in 1921 and was promoted to doctor of theology. Continuing his studies in classical archaeology, Galling received a Ph.D. with the thesis "Der Altar in den Kulturen des Vorderen Orients." In 1925, having written a third thesis, "Die Erwählungstraditionen Israels," he was promoted to lecturer for Old Testament and biblical archaeology at Berlin's Humboldt University. Between 1928 and 1946 he taught at the university in Halle, where he was an associate professor. From 1946 to 1955, as a full professor, he held an Old Testament chair at the University of Mainz and then, from 1955 to 1962, at the University of Göttingen. He served as director of the Institute of Biblical Archaeology at Tübingen University from 1962 to 1969. He lived in Tübingen until his death.

Galling combined the philological and archaeological aspects of Old Testament studies. Although he had participated in the excavations at Shechem and Tell Beit Mirsim, he never took an active part in fieldwork. Nonetheless, he wrote numerous articles on archaeological subjects and in 1937 published the *Biblisches Reallexikon,* with the intention of illustrating biblical terms, texts, with information about the archaeology of Palestine and other lands of the Bible (a second edition appeared in 1977). Galling's primary area of research was the history and archaeology of the Persian period. As editor in chief he succeeded in publishing the third edition of the theological encyclopedia *Die Religion in Geschichte und Gegenwart.* At the end of his academic career, in 1970, he was honored with a Festschrift, *Archäologie und Altes Testament,* that includes articles written by his colleagues and pupils from all over the world as well as a comprehensive bibliography of his work.

BIBLIOGRAPHY

Weippert, Manfred. "Kurt Galling." *Zeitschrift des Deutschen Palästina-Vereins* 104 (1988): 190–194.

VOLKMAR FRITZ

GAMES. Play is one of the central human expressions. Although anthropologists suggest that human beings have always played games, they have not always produced playthings for use in their games. Objects that are clearly identifiable as toys do not appear in the ancient Near East until the Neolithic period. In general, games and toys can be reconstructed using literary, epigraphic, archaeological, and iconographic sources. Ethnological findings complement and secure the overall picture. The legitimacy of such process of reconstruction is greatly strengthened by the essentially conservative character of most games: a majority of the games played in the various cultures of the ancient Near East were played in the same or a similar manner. Many games have preserved their continuity over centuries and millennia into the modern period. As a whole, however, the historical reality can only be partially recaptured. Because an appreciable portion of ancient playthings was produced of perishable materials such as leather, wood, and unburnt clay or consisted of living animals or were the spontaneous inventions of children, it is clear how little the evidence for the reconstruction approaches historical reality. In addition, the lack of evidence for a game does not necessarily mean that it was unknown in the region under consideration. For example, neither swings nor seesaws are evidenced in ancient Palestine, yet they are well attested among various other pre- and post-Hellenistic cultures in the Near East. Thus, it can be deduced, with probability bordering on certitude, that Palestinian children of the first millennium BCE played with swings and seesaws, even without direct material evidence. From both a phenomenological and an empirical perspective, practically anything can become a toy. Therefore, definitions of playing and playthings are deliberately avoided here (Vandenberg, 1982).

The first toy played with by young children was probably the archaeologically well-attested rattle. Older children enjoyed playing with live birds (cf. *Jb.* 40:29) and turtles, as the votive statues from the Eshmun sanctuary in Bustan esh-Sheikh near Sidon (fourth century, BCE) indicate. Other archaeologically and literarily attested toys include terracotta model wagons, miniature dishes, and beds and animals made of clay, wood, and other materials (cf. Lucian, somn. 2; *Arabic Infancy Gospel* 26:1f). Indirect evidence for playing in the sand is found in *Ezekiel* 4–5. *Isaiah* 22:18 attests to play with balls made of scraps of wool and cloth; they also appear iconographically in Mesopotamia and archaeologically in Egypt. Boys probably liked to play hunting and war games with various weapons, while girls enjoyed playing house with dolls. Together they probably played hide-and-seek (cf. *Arabic Infancy Gospel* 40:1), the "royal game" of *basilinda* (cf. Philo of Alexandria, *In Flacc.* 36–129; *Arabic Infancy Gospel* 42:2) and even *kollabismos* (Gk., a game of teasing; Pollux 9.129). Children in the ancient Near East often played with tops. A series of tops made of wood and other materials is preserved from pharaonic and postpharaonic Egypt. On an eighth-century BCE relief from Carchemish, youths are depicted rotating tops by means of straps. Small (clay) disks in which holes are bored are widely attested in Bronze and Iron Age Palestine, Phoenicia, Syria, and Mesopotamia: a string run through two holes would be by stretched and then relaxed, making the disk whirl, jump, and emit a buzzing or humming sound. This type of disk, known as a buzz or a bull-roarer in English, was called an *iygx* in the Greek world and an *iunx (iynx)* in Latin (Van Beek, 1989).

Both children and adults played with astragali, or animal knucklebones. Astragali are not only the most widely attested but also among the earliest evidenced toys in the ancient Near East. Owing to their four long sides, they were used as four-sided dice. Astragali could be reproduced in other materials, such as stone, metal, and glass. Games employing astragali were played until modern times. Astragali could also be used as dice for board games or as lots for divination. In addition, a number of games were played solely with astragali, including *pentelitha* ("five stones," a game of skill); *ludere par impar* ("to play odds and evens," a guessing game); and *tropa* (also called *orca*) and *ōmilla* (two types of "marbles" games; see the Carchemish relief). In the Middle Bronze Age, six-sided dice in the shape of cubes or truncated pyramids were also used. In the centuries that followed, astragali and dice were used concurrently. Dice, which can be manufactured from a wide range of materials, have, like astragali, been used by children and adults in dice and board games and as lots. In the Roman and Byzantine Near East, playing (throwing) dice is evidenced both iconographically and literarily (Nonnos, *metaphrasis Evangelii Ioannis* 19:23–24; Gk., *morra*, and Lat., *digitis micare*).

Among the various board games attested archaeologically in the Near East, the most popular was the thirty-field game called Senet in Egypt. Evidence for the game has been found from the prehistoric through the Ptolemaic periods (Pusch, 1979). The board consisted of three parallel rows of ten square fields each. The rules are largely unknown, although it is clear that the pieces were advanced by two players by throwing dice. The game was known in Palestine as early as the Neolithic period; in the Bronze and Iron Ages, evidence of the game has been found in Syria, Phoenicia, Mesopotamia, Iran, and on Cyprus. Varieties of the game were played into the Hellenistic-Roman period. Of equal popularity was a game that consisted of a board with 4 + 4 + 12 (= 20) fields (and variations; see, e.g., *ANEP*, 2d ed., no. 212). It was played as of the Middle Bronze Age in Palestine, Syria, Mesopotamia, Egypt, and on Cyprus (*ANEP*, 2d ed., no. 214). In addition, board games usually evidencing about fifty-eight holes were widespread in Egypt, Palestine, Syria, Mesopotamia, Iran, and Anatolia in the Bronze and Iron Ages (*ANEP*, 2d ed., nos. 213, 215). Nine Men's Morris (merels), checkers (draughts), and mancala are board games that are still being played. The first appeared in the Near East in the Roman-Byzantine period, as did a twelve-line dot game (Lat., *ludus duodecim scripta* or *tabula*; Ar.,

GAMES. *Middle Bronze Age gaming stone found at Episkopi-Phaneromeni, Cyprus.* (Courtesy ASOR Archives)

ṭāwila or *nard*) that is similar to modern backgammon. The gaming pieces used vary widely in form and material. Board games, like other games, could be played not only by the living, but by the dead (cf. grave inventories) and by the gods (cf. *Is.* 22:18; *Jb.* 40:29; *Ps.* 104:26; and Plutarch, *De Iside et Osiride* 12).

The inhabitants of both cities and villages were entertained by jugglers, jesters, fire (Jerome, *Apol. contra Rufin* 3:31) and sword swallowers, wandering musicians, and acrobats, as indicated, for example, on reliefs in Turkey at Alaca Höyük (fourteenth century BCE) and Zincirli (eighth century BCE), and by later literary sources (Jerome, epistle 58:4; Tosefta, *San.* 67b; B.T. *Suk.* 53a; see Blocher, 1992). Exhibitions of strength, such as weightlifting (Jerome, *In Zaccharaim* 12:3; *vita Hilarionis* 17), wrestling, and boxing, were also included (cf. *ANEP*, 2d ed., nos. 218, 219; *Testament of Job* 4:10; 27:3–4; *Armenian Infancy Gospel* 21:6–7).

Traditional games that belonged to the private sphere (e.g., tops, astragali, board games) continued to be played in the Hellenistic-Roman period. Hellenization and its cultural and economic opportunities brought with them a gaming culture that had hitherto been largely unknown in the Near East. It was a culture in which the indigenous inhabitants were passive onlookers, rather than participants. If at first these games consisted of athletic and musical contests in the Greek tradition (cf. Plutarch, *Alexander* 72), in the Roman period the most popular ones were horse and chariot races, wrestling and boxing matches, gladiatorial contests, animal hunts, and naval battles. In order to organize these mass entertainments, most large cities in the Roman Empire built theaters and odeums (odeons); gymnasiums, or palestras; and amphitheaters and hippodromes. (The latter often cannot be distinguished because they were erected as multipurpose structures.) The level of distribution of these archaeologically well-attested structures decreased from west to east. Nonetheless, theaters (or odeums) are to be found in Syria at Palmyra and Dura-Europos, and gymnasiums are found in Babylon and at Ai Khanum on the Oxus in Afghanistan. The new gaming culture also left behind many traces in the native languages of the Near East: in Aramaic and in Syriac, for example, many Greek and Latin loanwords appear, among them theater, stadium, and circus.

[*See also* Odeum; *and* Theaters.]

BIBLIOGRAPHY

Blocher, Felix. "Gaukler im Alten Orient." In *Außenseiter und Randgruppen,* edited by Volkert Haas, pp. 79–111. Constance, Germany, 1992.

Decker, Wolfgang. *Sports and Games in Ancient Egypt.* Translated by Allen Guttmann. New Haven, 1992. The authoritative work on sports, games, and toys in pharaonic Egypt.

Decker, Wolfgang, and Michael Herb. *Bildatlas zum Sport im Alten Ägypten: Corpus der bildlichen Quellen zu Leibesübungen, Spiel, Jagd, Tanz und verwandten Themen in pharaonischer Zeit.* 2 vols. Leiden, 1993.

Frézouls, Édmond. "Les édifices des spectacles en Syrie." In *Archéologie et histoire de la Syrie,* vol. 2, *La Syrie de l'époque achéménide à l'avènement de l'Islam,* edited by Jean-Marie Dentzer and Winfried Orthmann, pp. 385–406. Saarbrücken, 1989.

Hübner, Ulrich. *Spiel und Spielzeug im antiken Palästina.* Göttingen,

1992. The first monographical treatment of games, toys, and sports in ancient Palestine from prehistoric times to the Middle Ages, including all important archaeological parallels and literary, epigraphic, iconographic, and ethnological sources in the ancient Near East and an exhaustive bibliography (pp. 149–200).

Jouer dans l'antiquité. Marseilles, 1991. Fine catalog of an exhibition held at the Musée d'Archéologie Méditerranéenne, Marseilles, containing short essays and summaries of different aspects of games and toys in the ancient Mediterranean world.

Laser, Siegfried. *Sport und Spiel.* Göttingen, 1987. Authoritative work on sports, games, and toys in early Greek regions.

Pusch, Edgar B. *Das Senet-Brettspiel im Alten Ägypten.* Berlin, 1979. Authoritative work on Senet, an ancient Egyptian game.

Van Beek, Gus W. "The Buzz: A Simple Toy from Antiquity." *Bulletin of the American Schools of Oriental Research,* no. 275 (1989): 53–58.

Vandenberg, B. "Play: A Concept in Need of a Definition?" In *The Play of Children,* edited by D. J. Pepler and K. H. Rubin, pp. 15–20. Basel, 1982.

ULRICH HÜBNER
Translated from German by Carl S. Ehrlich

GAMLA, Jewish town in the southern Golan Heights at the time of the First Jewish Revolt against Rome (map reference 219 × 256). It is first mentioned by the Jewish historian Josephus Flavius in connection with Alexander Jannaeus's military campaign in the region in about 83–80 BCE (*War* 1.105; *Antiq.* 13.394). The town was conquered by the Roman legion and destroyed in the fall of 67 CE. Josephus describes in some detail the city and the topography of the hill on which the town was constructed (*War* 4.1–83). Based on this description, Y. Gal first identified a rocky spur between the branches of Naḥal Daliyyot near the village of Deir Qeruḥ in the southern Golan at Gamla. The site, called es-Sunas in Arabic, was surveyed by Shmaryahu Gutman in 1970. The lower flank of the spur was excavated under his direction beginning in 1976 on behalf of the Israel Department of Antiquities and Museums. The excavations confirmed Gal's hypothesis.

Remains recovered at Gamla date mainly to the Late Second Temple period through the Jewish Revolt of 66–74. The earliest numismatic remains date to the reign of Antiochus I Soter (280 BCE); the latest are a coin of Akko from the time of Vespasian and six Jewish coins of the First Revolt with the legend "For the redemption of h[oly] Jerusalem," a coin type found only at Gamla.

During the first century, Gamla had a fortification wall that extended for about 350 m to the east of the settlement. Gutman excavated along the wall for its entire length, both within and outside the city. The excavations revealed residential areas and an olive press. On its other sides the town was protected by the hill's steep cliffs. On the east, a large public building identified as a synagogue was discovered adjacent to the town in the first season of excavation. During the Roman siege, the wall was breached at this place. It was repaired once by the defenders and reopened by the Romans.

The synagogue building was constructed of local basalt. It was a rectangular structure (25.5 × 17 m) situated on a northeast–southwest axis. The main entrance was on the west, with an exedra and an open court in front of it. A ritual bath *(miqveh)* was uncovered to the right of the court. The center of the hall (13.4 × 9.3 m) is unpaved and surrounded (except for the main entrance) by stepped benches. Columns divided the unpaved area into two sections: the section on the west is aproximately 7.0 × 6.5 m, and the one on the east 4.0 × 6.5 m. Above the benches is a broad, paved platform with benches that adjoin the exterior walls. The hall is surrounded by four raised platforms. A small basin that the excavator believes was used for hand washing was uncovered (Gutman, 1993). It was fed by a water channel that passed through the wall at the northern part of the basalt paved platform above the four benches on the east. The lintels and capitals of this building, also of basalt, were carved with ornamentation.

Several rooms were discovered to the east of the synagogue, within the first section of the city wall. Gutman suggests that during the siege the room adjacent to the synagogue was filled in to strengthen the wall. Benches on the sides of this room, and what apparently is a window through to the synagogue, were uncovered there. Gutman identifies this as a study room. He suggests that the synagogue, adjoined by a study room, a ritual bath, and a courtyard constituted a community center of sorts for study and prayer. His model for this interpretation is the medieval European synagogue complex, a form that (like synagogue prayer) is presently still unattested. The function of this study room is unknown.

[*See also* First Jewish Revolt; Golan; *and* Synagogues.]

BIBLIOGRAPHY

Gutman, Shmaryahu. "The Synagogue at Gamla." In *Ancient Synagogues Revealed,* edited by Lee I. Levine, pp. 30–34. Jerusalem, 1981. Early report of the synagogue excavation.

Gutman, Shmaryahu. "Gamala." In *The New Encyclopedia of Archaeological Excavations in the Holy Land,* vol. 2, pp. 459–463. Jerusalem and New York, 1993. The most complete report of the excavation available.

Ma'oz, Zvi. "The Synagogue of Gamla and the Typology of Second-Temple Synagogues." In *Ancient Synagogues Revealed,* edited by Lee I. Levine, pp. 35–41. Jerusalem, 1981. The synagogue in the context of other Second Temple period synagogues in Israel.

STEVEN FINE

GARDENS. [*To provide a general typology and morphology of gardens, this entry comprises three articles:*

Gardens in Preclassical Times
Gardens of the Hellenistic and Roman Periods
Gardens of the Islamic Period

Each article surveys the historical development, forms, and functions of gardens during the periods in question.]

Gardens in Preclassical Times

In Mesopotamia, Persia, and Egypt, gardens and parks were generally irrigated land enclosed for collections of cultivated plants and animals; in Lebanon and in temperate areas, managed native habitats or reserves are attested. Gardens are differentiated from other cultivated areas by the water supply and labor regime needed to maintain them, by the language and images used to describe them, and often by their association with architecture. Few gardens have been excavated, but landscape archaeology is an emerging subdiscipline; as cultivated sites are excavated, the textual and art historical evidence will grow.

Mesopotamia. Gardens in Mesopotamia existed in parks, palaces and estates, and temples.

Parks. Gardens first appear in the texts of the third millennium (Postgate, 1994, p. 174). The Epic of Gilgamesh describes a park. Gilgamesh and his companion enter a bounded wood in the Amanus Mountains. The fearsome Humbaba guards its straight paths and tends the cedars. The story raises themes constant in Near Eastern garden history: fascination with foreign landscapes and plants; the admirable, essentially human order of the straight path and plantings; and the violent act of cutting down the trees of one's vanquished enemy.

Stephanie Dalley (1986) points out that in the Sumerian language no distinction is made between an orchard of trees and a garden. Kings boast of large parts of cities devoted to these parks, of the great irrigation works that feed them, and of the distant lands from which the plants and animals are gathered. Tiglath-Pileser I (1114–1076 BCE) created a combined zoological park and arboretum of exotic animals and trees. Ashurnasirpal II (883–859 BCE) created a garden/park at Nimrud (Kalḥu) by diverting water from the Upper Zab River through a rock-cut channel for his impressive collection of foreign plants and animals. [*See* Nimrud.] Sennacherib (704–681 BCE) makes a similar claim for Nineveh. [*See* Nineveh.] Parks are beautifully represented on the reliefs from Sargon II's (721–705 BCE) palace at Khorsabad, in which a variety of trees and a small pavilion with proto-Doric columns are depicted. [*See* Khorsabad.] Other reliefs depict lion hunts and facolnry in the parks. A clay tablet from Babylon names and locates vegetables and herbs in the garden of Merodach-Baladan II (721–710 BCE). [*See* Babylon.] In the palace reliefs of Ashurbanipal, the garden symbolizes the abundance and pleasures of peace after bravery in battle (Albenda, 1977).

Not only are plants collected, but so are entire landscapes. One of Sennacherib's parks is rare in garden history: a recreated marsh of the southern Euphrates River, with canebrakes, wild boar, and roosting herons. [*See* Euphrates.] Elsewhere, terracing provided the three-dimensional evocation of mountains. The famous Hanging Gardens of Babylon of Nebuchadrezzar II (605–562 BCE) were described as being in imitation of the alpine landscape of Media. An archaeological identification of their location on the Euphrates has been rejected, however (Dalley, 1986, p. 370).

Palace and estate gardens. Gardens also formed part of the architecture of the ancient Near East. Texts locate a garden in the internal courtyard of the royal palace at Mari (nineteenth century BCE), featuring palm trees and an ornamental pool. [*See* Mari.] In fifteenth century BCE Ugarit, texts speak of a court with a large stone pond and another with plants and walkways, a pavilion, and a large trough. [*See* Ugarit.] Other texts range from fables that take place in gardens to ration lists, indicating that gardeners were members of a palace's staff (Pritchard, 1950). Most known palace courtyards still await excavation. [*See* Palace.] First-millennium BCE estate records indicate that nonroyal residences of the wealthy in northern Mesopotamia featured gardens with vines, fruit trees, vegetables, pools, ponds, and gardeners' cottages.

Temple gardens. Temple gardens for the provision of fresh offerings are attested but poorly known. According to the excavator of the ziggurat at Ur, trees and shrubs were planted on its tiers, but there is no physical evidence. [*See* Ziggurat; Ur.] At the Temple of the New Year Festival at Aššur, rows of planting pits for shrubs and trees are cut into the rock of the inner courtyard and surrounding area. [*See* Aššur.] Esarhaddon's records describe a temple garden with water channels and vegetable beds. Nebuchadrezzar's temple (see above) included cypress and juniper groves, as well as gardens that supplied offerings for Marduk.

Persian Gardens. The Persian *pairidaeza* are first attested in the works of the Greek Xenophon, who saw these enclosed gardens in Anatolia and Persia. The source of the *paradeisos*, paradise, *pardēs* (Heb.), parcus, and park—monumental, geometric gardens—are the Achaemenid Empire's most enduring cultural contribution. They are known from texts, reliefs, and archaeological remains at Pasargadae, Persepolis, and Susa. [*See* Pasargadae; Persepolis; Susa.] A recent field survey on the Persepolis plain, compared with textual evidence, gives the first regional sketch of Achaemenid royal and nonroyal estates.

There is no clear distinction between parks and palace gardens; in fact, at Pasargadae tombs are part of the complex as well (Strabo 15.3.7). [*See* Tombs.] The palaces are pavilions set into shady, irrigated parks laid out orthogonally. Excavations at Pasargadae revealed the first-known quadripartite, or *chaharbagh* garden (Cyrus is referred to in Babylonian texts as "king of the four quarters"). The axial "vista of power" down the center from the main pavilion allows a glimpse into the political role gardens played (Stronach, 1994). From the throne in his pavillion, Cyrus could view his *paradeisos* in the heat or the day, or festivals and recreation at other times.

The Achemaenid *paradeisoi* may have been influenced by gardens of palaces taken over by the Persian satraps throughout the empire. *Paradesoi* are found at Sardis, Daskyleion, and Kelainai in Anatolia and at Sidon and Lachish in Syria/Palestine, as well as at the unlocated palace of Belyses, satrap of northern Syria. [*See* Sardis; Sidon; Lachish.] Xenophon's description of Cyrus the Younger's garden at Sardis (c. 407 BCE), is definitive: fine trees set in even rows with clean angles, a place rich in fruit and pleasant scents—and cultivated by the satrap himself (*Oeconomicus* 4.20–24). Lydian gardens are later a part of the classical topos for luxury (cf. Athenaeus, *Deipnosophists*). The remains of a Lydian stone pavilion have been found on the terraced site presumed to be the palace of Croesus. The Achaemenid kings rebuilt the Median capitol of Ecbatana in the Zagros Mountains as a summer residence. [*See* Ecbatana.] With its terraced gardens, orchards and vineyard, natural streams, and high altitude, it is the place the Median wife of Nebuchadrezzar II sought to recreate in the Hanging Gardens of Babylon. Diodorus, however, attributes the gardens to an Achaemenid king. Archaeological evidence suggests that a change in the course of the Euphrates destroyed the earlier gardens, and the Achaemenids rebuilt them on a new site (Dalley, 1986).

Egypt. The Egyptians probably cultivated gardens in the Nile Valley as early as the fourth millennium. However, evidence from texts, images, and archaeological excavation begins in the second millenium BCE. The regular flooding of the Nile and the annual need to re-mark the boundaries of fields and gardens is cited by Herodotus as the origin of geometry—"land measurement." The rectilinear order of irrigation channels structures the overall design of Egyptian gardens and fields south of the Delta throughout antiquity. [*See* Delta.]

Palace and house gardens. Palace gardens are known from excavations at Tell ed-Dab'a in the eastern Delta (1782–1650 BCE), which have revealed walled vineyards, flowerbeds, and tree pits (Wilkinson, 1990). The pharaonic palaces at Amarna (Akhenaten) and the Malkata palace (Amenhotep III) at Thebes contained zoological gardens, parks, lakes, and pavillions. [*See* Amarna, Tell el-.] The palace of Apries (588–563 BCE) continued this long tradition, including an impressive approach avenue and grand forecourt (Nielsen, 1994). Information about walls, planting design, and details of life and horticulture is available from tomb paintings. [*See* Wall Paintings.]

The large gardens of rich officials usually featured pools, shade-tree plantings, and shrines. The great abundance of paintings in tombs attests to the variety and vivacity of royal and official estate gardens. Even those who had just a small strip beside their house planted trees in pots. In the workers' village at Amarna, where conditions were crowded, gardens were located outside the housing quarters (Kemp, 1987, pp. 36–41).

Temple and tomb gardens. "The garden was the place of creation from which grew the temple with its vegetal architecture and the habitable world. The pool represents the water of Nun from which life originally sprang" (Wilkinson, 1990, p. 202). Gardens are associated with many types of religious buildings, from the small chapel courtyards in the workers' village at Amarna to the great mortuary temples of the pharaohs. They provided offerings during life and after. The earliest archaeological remains are from Amun's temple at Karnak; they are illustrated further in the tombs of eighteenth-dynasty officials and in texts that describe the trees later brought back from Punt, Palestine, and Syria by Rameses III (1182–1151 BCE). Sycamore fig, tamarisk, and palm trees had particular significance. Queen Hatshepsut, whose paintings at Deir el-Baḥari also indicate journeys made to collect plants for Amun, created gardens between Karnak and Luxor for the Feast of Opet, confirming her right to rule. Like that of Mentuhotep (for which there is a stone plan), Hatshepsut's mortuary temple was reached by a long avenue lined with T-shaped pools for papyrus and sycamore figs found by the excavators to have been cut down, perhaps in *damnaio memoriae* by her son. A similar processional alley was found in the temple at Hermopolis, its flanking trees set into brick-ringed pits. Even the most modest of sacred gardens possessed T-shaped or rectangular pools, and those at the main chapel at Amarna seem to have been rotated in their use, some filled with water, others with soil.

Generally, the gardens provided for the pleasure of the deceased were not planted but painted in the tomb chamber: representations of water and fruit provided nourishment, while the trees allowed the soul to perch. Many garden paintings are quite elaborate, and it can be difficult to distinguish the fictional from the actual. Archaeological remains of tomb gardens are known from Amarna, Abydos, and Thebes. [*See* Abydos.]

BIBLIOGRAPHY

Albenda, Pauline. "Landscape Bas-Reliefs in the *Bīt-Hilāni* of Ashurbanipal." *Bulletin of the American Schools of Oriental Research,* no. 224 (1976): 49–72; no. 225 (1977): 29–48. Important attempt to understand the overall landscape significance of these reliefs, though somewhat controversial.

Badawy, Alexander. *A History of Egyptian Architecture,* vol. 2, *The First Intermediate Period, the Middle Kingdom, and the Second Intermediate Period.* Berkeley, 1966. The best collection of illustrations of ancient gardens.

Brown, John Pairman. *The Lebanon and Phoenicia: Ancient Texts Illustrating Their Physical Geography and Native Industries,* vol. 1, *The Physical Setting and the Forest.* Beirut, 1969.

Buckler, W. H., and D. M. Robinson. *Sardis VII: Greek and Latin Inscriptions,* Part 1. Leiden, 1932.

Dalley, Stephanie. "Mesopotamia, Ancient." In *The Oxford Companion to Gardens,* edited by Geoffrey Jellicoe et al., pp. 368–370. Oxford, 1986. The most authoritative summary, until older assessments are reevaluated in light of advances in translations of Akkadian and Sumerian texts.

Kemp, Barry J. "The Amarna Workmen's Village." *Journal of Egyptian Archaeology* 73 (1987): 21–50. See especially pages 36–41, for the evidence for farming.

Moynihan, Elizabeth. *Paradise as a Garden: In Persia and Mughal India.* New York, 1979. Readable, well-illustrated work with important chapters on pre-Islamic gardens.

Nielsen, Inge. *Hellenistic Palaces: Tradition and Renewal.* Aarhus, 1994.

Peterman, Glen L. "Conservation of the Petra Papyri." *Biblical Archaeologist* 57 (1994): 242–243.

Postgate, J. N. *Early Mesopotamia: Society and Economy at the Dawn of History.* Rev. ed. London, 1994. Discusses gardens within the larger agricultural structure of the landscape.

Pritchard, James B., ed. *Ancient Near Eastern Texts Relating to the Old Testament.* Princeton, 1950.

Stronach, David B. "Parterres and Stone Watercourses at Pasargadae: Notes on the Achaemenid Contribution to the Evolution of Garden Design." *Journal of Garden History* 14 (1994): 3–12. One of several important articles on ancient gardens to appear in this journal recently.

Wilkinson, Alix. "Gardens in Ancient Egypt: Their Locations and Symbolism." *Journal of Garden History* 10 (1990): 199–208. Useful synthesis and bibliography.

KATHRYN L. GLEASON

Gardens of the Hellenistic and Roman Periods

Gardens of the Hellenistic, Roman, and Sasanian periods draw heavily on the Persian *paradeisos,* as interpreted by Alexander the Great at Alexandria. However, in this period, *paradeisos* also refers to any land with trees or orchards interspersed with crops, even grain. Gardens are frequently mentioned in texts and depicted in wall paintings and mosaics throughout the classical and Byzantine eras. Evidence for common domestic gardens and garden practice is abundant in Egyptian and Palestinian papyri, the Hebrew Talmud and Mishna, and the Hebrew and Christian Bibles, as well as in the archaeological remains of intensive agriculture practiced by the Nabateans and other cultures in the arid countryside. The writings of Theophrastus outline botanical knowledge gained during Alexander's campaigns, while Pliny the Elder provides important knowledge of gardens and plants of the Roman Empire.

Egypt. The *basileia* of Alexandria, a great built landscape of palaces, theaters, temples, sanctuaries, and tombs interspersed among groves and parks, provided the model of the garden for the entire Hellenistic and Roman world. Inge Nielsen (1994) demonstrates that the palaces in which Alexander stayed during the course of his campaigns influenced the creation of the city of Alexandria. [*See* Alexandria.] Although little remains archaeologically, the city's plan has been approximated, and Strabo (*Geog.* 17.1.9–10) provides a detailed description of the *basileia,* which occupied one third of Alexandria. Ptolemy VIII *Physcon* wrote a treatise on the birds of the palace area, so that zoological and botanical gardens are perhaps a pharaonic rather than a Persian legacy (Nielsen, 1994, p. 133).

The *Thalamegos,* a Nile festival barge of Ptolemy IV, featured a pavilion and grottoes with statuary, set against the cultivated shoreline of the Nile (Nielsen, 1994, p. 136). Nilotic landscapes inspired gardens, mosaics, and paintings throughout the Roman and Byzantine periods, from Rome to Palestine.

The abundant letters, daybooks, and official documents written on papyrus dealing with gardens and agriculture contribute another view of the estate garden: the logistics of its upkeep. *The Paradise or Garden of the Holy Fathers* (Budge, 1907) gives a similarly detailed view of gardens in the Christian monasteries on the Nile from 250–400 CE. [*See* Papyrus; Monasteries.]

Judea/Palestine/Nabatea. The gardens of ancient Palestine mixed Babylonian and Alexandrian influences. In Ptolemaic Palestine, the palace of Hyrcanus the Tobiad (d. 168/69 BCE), the Qaṣr el-'Abd near 'Iraq el-Amir (Tyros), has a preserved, extensive wadi-based irrigation system that served a large park and lake set within an estate described by Josephus (*Antiq.* 12.4.1). [*See* 'Iraq el-Amir; Irrigation.]

The Hasmonean royal palace in the dynasty's capital, Jerusalem, is not preserved; however, the Hasmoneans (168–38 BCE) built a series of palaces in Wadi Qelt, near Jericho, that featured swimming pools and dining rooms, amid balsam and palm groves watered from springs in the surrounding Judean hills. [*See* Hasmoneans.] The buildings for public entertainment and sacred buildings characteristic of other Hellenistic palace complexes are notably absent in this recreational palace of the Jewish priestly class. [*See* Palace.]

Herod the Great played an important role in Roman garden history, as a friend of the emperors Augustus and Agrippa, who brought eastern elements into their culture; in turn, Herod drew upon Italic traditions, integrating them with Hasmonean and Alexandrian precedents. Josephus gives a detailed description of the gardens of Herod's palace in Jerusalem (*War* 5.177–183), of which only the platform remains. His palaces at Masada, Herodium, and Caesarea bear traces of gardens, but the best-preserved examples are at Jericho. [*See* Jerusalem; Masada; Herodium; Caesarea; Jericho.] In addition to the Hasmonean gardens, Herod built a Roman-style entertainment complex spanning Wadi Qelt. Archaeologists have found the locations of its peristyle gardens, ambulatory walks, and great sunken garden (see figure 1). In many areas flower plots used for propagation and transport were planted with shrubs (perhaps balsam), thus giving a configuration to the general design. An artificial tell with a pavilion on top permitted visitors to admire the great estate of balsam groves and rare palms.

Gardens figure in Hebrew halakhic and aggadic literature. Halakhic discussions give valuable information about cultivation, including such specific features as flowerpots. Aggadic descriptions portray distinctly Hellenistic houses with their gardens (*Ta'an.* 9b; B. T. *Meg.* 12a). Gardens are used in veiled political commentaries by rabbis and sages in rejecting Persian and Hellenistic influences. Gardens and groves are also mentioned in the official documents among the Dead Sea Scrolls.

The Nabateans, described as a nomadic people who cultivated nothing (Diodorus Siculus 19.94.1–6), are in fact known for their intensive cultivation of the desert. [*See* Nabateans.] Their capital at Petra, as described by Strabo (*Geog.* 7.353), possessed irrigated gardens, probably for cen-

GARDENS: Hellenistic and Roman Period. Figure 1. *Reconstructed view of a Herodian Ionic peristyle garden.* (Drawing by Chang Shan Huang; courtesy K. L. Gleason)

turies—as attested in recently discovered Byzantine papyri. [*See* Petra.] The papyri cite the names of owners, the locations and sizes of gardens, and the houses and agricultural land south of the city (Glen L. Peterman, "Conservation of the Petra Papyri," *Biblical Archaeologist* 57 [1994]: 243.)

Syria. The Seleucids continued the Persian tradition of building *paradeisoi* at their new capitals of Antioch and Seleucia. [*See* Seleucids; Antioch, Seleucia on the Tigris.] The royal sanctuary at Daphne, south of Antioch, featured large groves of trees, fountains, and streams that served as a place of festivals (Strabo 16.2.4–5). The site was recaptured in the fine mosaics of the Roman and Byzantine eras. The Alexandrian novelist Achilles Tatius (second century CE) sets *Clitophon and Leukippe* in Sidon (1.15–17), with a vivid description of a villa garden. Theophrastus (*Inquiry* 5.8.1, 3) describes *paradeisoi*, royal parks of managed cedar forest, in the mountains of Syria. [*See* Sidon.] At Tyre the remains of an enclosed Roman funerary garden include niches, irrigation channels, basins, and planting beds for produce; the latter provided a subvention for the upkeep of the monument. [*See* Tyre.]

Asia Minor. The kings of Pergamon drew less from Persian examples than from Macedonian ones, which strongly influenced the gardens in Rome. [*See* Pergamon.] The palaces of the Pergamon kings were tightly grouped alongside the temples and theater on the terraced acropolis. The courtyards typically were paved, except for the garden peristyle in palace V of Eumenes II (d. 160), the most monumental palace in the group. His brother and heir, Attlalus II (220–138 BCE), had a well-known garden in which he culti-

vated poisonous plants (Nicander of Colophon wrote poems on vegetable poisons and their antidotes).

The writings of Athenaeus (*Deipnosophistae* 12) give a fanciful picture of garden luxury in coastal Asia Minor, while a rather different picture emerges from Hellenistic and Roman inscriptions at Sardis (*Sardis* 8:1, 1932, no. 12.6). [*See* Sardis.] The sacred grove of the Greeks is seen in the verdant temple garden of Aphrodite at Knidos. A wall painting in the "hanging houses" at Ephesus, dated to the second century CE, depicts a lush garden in the manner of paintings from Pompeii. [*See* Ephesus.]

Parthian and Sasanian Gardens. During the second and third centuries CE, Persia was held by the Parthians, who received embassies from China bearing new garden plants such as peaches and apricots. [*See* Parthians.] Sasanian rulers adopted the Achaemenid *paradeisoi* as hunting parks and as settings for their palaces. [*See* Sasanians.] Pools have been found within the palace of Ardashir (226–240 CE) in Fars. Khusrau I (531–579 BCE) built a palace at Ctesiphon on the Tigris River. [*See* Ctesiphon; Tigris.] The palace was known for its 30-meter-long Winter Carpet, the legendary model for all Persian garden carpets. Khusrau II built an extensive terraced garden at Taq-i Bostan, of which only the grottoes remain. Its reliefs depict royal ceremonies, vegetation, and hunting scenes. Another *paradeisos* of Khusrau II and his lover Shirin, on the slopes of the Zagros Mountains at Qasr-i Shirin, is known from an aqueduct, a 900-meter pool, and the terraces of a 300-acre estate. [*See* Aqueducts; Pools.] Shabusti (ninth century CE) tells of a fourth-century Christian monastery at Marmi in which gardens adjoined each monk's cell, watered by canals and shaded with fruit trees. [*See* Monasteries.] Other Early Arab sources note the gardens and parks of the settlements they first encountered throughout Iran.

BIBLIOGRAPHY

Buckler, William H., and David M. Robinson. "Greek Inscriptions from Sardes I." *American Journal of Archaeology* 16 (1912): 11–82. Important but little known discussion of textual evidence for *paradeisoi* in Hellenistic Asia Minor (see pp. 78–79).

Budge, E. A. Wallis, trans. and ed. *The Paradise or Garden of the Holy Fathers: Being Histories of the Anchorites, Recluses, Monks, Coenobites, and Ascetic Fathers of the Deserts of Egypt.* 2 vols. London, 1907.

Chéhab, Maurice. *Fouilles de Tyr: La Nécropole.* Vol. 1. Bulletin du Musée de Beyrouth, vol. 33. Paris, 1983. Excavation of tomb gardens.

Gleason, Kathryn L. "A Garden Excavation in the Oasis Palace of Herod the Great at Jericho." *Landscape Journal* 12 (1993): 156–167. Account of the excavation of a peristyle garden, with additional references to Jericho's gardens and a general bibliography.

Grimal, Pierre. *Les jardins romains.* 3d ed. Paris, 1984. Still the best assessment of eastern Mediterranean influences on Roman garden development.

Levi, Doro. *Antioch Mosaic Pavements.* 2 vols. Princeton, 1947. Beautifully reproduced images of mosaics with landscape elements.

Miller, Naomi F., and Kathryn L. Gleason. *The Archaeology of Garden and Field.* Philadelphia, 1994. Overview of current techniques used in excavating garden sites.

Moe, Dagfinn, et al. *Garden History: Garden Plants, Species, Forms and Varieties from Pompeii to 1800.* PACT, vol. 42. Rixensart, Belg., 1994.

Moynihan, Elizabeth. *Paradise as a Garden: In Persia and Mughal India.* New York, 1979. Chapter 2 is devoted to the Sasanian garden.

Netzer, Ehud. "The Winter Palaces of the Judean Kings at Jericho at the End of the Second Temple Period." *Bulletin of the American Schools of Oriental Research,* no. 228 (1977): 1–13.

Newman, Julius. *The Agricultural Life of the Jews in Babylonia between the Years 200 CE and 500 CE.* Oxford, 1932. Although poorly indexed for gardens, they are discussed within the context of agricultural life as described in the Talmud.

Nielsen, Inge. *Hellenistic Palaces: Tradition and Renewal.* Aarhus, 1994. The most recent work on palaces, with exhaustive treatment of Near Eastern cultures; the only overview avaiable on gardens.

Shimoff, Sandra R. "Gardens from Eden to Jerusalem." *Journal for the Study of Judaism in the Persian, Hellenistic, and Roman Periods* 26 (1995): 145–155.

KATHRYN L. GLEASON

Gardens of the Islamic Period

A number of Arabic and Persian terms (*djanna, rawḍa, bāgh, bustān, gulistān*) are included under the English designation *garden*. Gardens in Islamic times rested on historical and sacred foundations. Eastern Roman gardens, particularly in association with country villas, established a tradition of sheltered, irrigated, and agriculturally productive retreats in Palestine and Syria that continued in early Islamic times, especially under the patronage of Umayyad caliphs (661–750 CE), but it is likely that pre-Islamic Iranian prototypes exercised the greatest influence on the development of royal and aristocratic gardens in Islam. The Achaemenid ruler,

Cyrus the Great (550–529 BCE), constructed numerous walled gardens: at Pasargadae the garden had two pavilions with pillared porches *(tālār)* that served as transitional spaces between building and garden. The best-known site in pre-Islamic Iran, the 'Imarat-i Khusrau at Qaṣr-i Shirin built for Shah Khusrau II Parviz (591–628 CE), was a vast walled garden *(pairidaeza)* with an eastern entrance leading to a long rectangular pool and palace from which the garden could be viewed. Subsequently, a pool or pools, watercourses, viewing platform, and pavilion or palace, often sited on an axis with the main gate, became central elements in most Islamic gardens.

The Muslim conquerors of Iran found not only walled gardens, but also works of art replete with garden references. Sasanian (224–651 CE) silver dishes showed emperors reclining, drinking, and listening to music in garden settings, and early Arab writers referred to a carpet made for Shah Khusrau Anushirvan (531–579) that was intended for the audience hall at Ctesiphon near Baghdad: destroyed when this palace was captured in 637, the *Spring of Khusrau* carpet is said to have measured 30 × 150 m (98.5 × 492 ft.) and to have had a garden design with tree branches shown in silver thread; earth rendered in gold thread; watercourses limned with crystals; and leaves, petals, and roots made of colored silk and jewels.

References to springtime meadows, gardens, and water abound in pre-Islamic Arabic poetry, reflecting the importance of water and verdure in an arid environment and indicating that gardens were probably accessible to the well born and wealthy of the Hijaz: the Qur'an's description of the garden of Eden *(djannāt 'adn)* and of paradise *(djanna)* as "gardens underneath which rivers flow" (surah 2:25 and many times thereafter) was connected to a long-established upper-class ideal. Paradise is the most sensually developed image in the Qur'an: it has four rivers (surah 47:15), fountains, cool pavilions, cushions, couches, brocades, beautiful youths, green pastures, palm trees, pomegranates, and two kinds of every fruit. Subsequent worldly gardens thus presented immediate sacred references and provided a pervasive language of garden imagery in Islamic mystical poetry, such as the legend of Shaddad, the pre-Islamic king of South Arabia, whose garden of Iram, built to rival paradise in splendor, brought divine retribution on the patron. Surah 55:46–75 mention a total of four gardens in paradise and may be the source for the predilection that Islamic patrons and builders had for the *chahar-bāgh*, four-part gardens divided by cruciform water courses and walkways. Paradise also had multiple levels, and growing there are the *ṭūbā* tree, more slender than the cypress but providing great shade, and the *sidra* tree (lote-tree). Metaphors for the loveliness of gardens came from both pagan and pious sources: the eleventh-century Iranian poet Manuchihri Damghani could compare a springtime orchard to the idol temple at Farkhar, its birds to the priest, and its rose bushes to the idols but could also liken an orchard to a mosque, for the trees' branches bent down in prayer, and a dove issued the call to prayer. A self-contained architecture within its walls that allowed few references from the outside world, the garden supplied an internal, moderate, and distinctive nature protected from wild and threatening nature outside. A place of coolness, calm, peace, and plenty, as well as an ordered landscape under the direction and control of the owner, the garden supplied valued and repeated metaphors: the rose was compared to the beloved's face or cheeks, her figure to the slender cypress, the jasmine to her hair.

Although no gardens from the Umayyad period (661–750) have survived intact, the pre-Islamic or early Islamic gardens in or around Damascus were likely the inspiration for the mosaics of the Umayyad Great Mosque of Damascus, and the Rusafa garden in the same city was memorable enough so that the first Umayyad ruler of al-Andalus, 'Abd al-Rahman I (755–788), tried to replicate it in exile in Cordoba. In his *Lata'if al-Ma'arif* the Iranian scholar al-Tha'alibi (961–1038) elaborately praises the Ghuta of Damascus as one of the four wonders of the world and an earthly likeness of paradise. The late Umayyad palace at Khirbat al-Mafjar had a garden pavilion, and country villas, like Qasr al-Hayr East, were centers of agricultural estates and must have had gardens, both for entertainment and food. The widespread use of medieval Arabic manuscripts based on translations of the *Materia Medica* of Dioscorides suggests that such estates, as well as smaller households, nurtured herbal and medicinal gardens, like their monastic counterparts in Europe.

With the 'Abbasid (750–1258) dynasty's predilection for pre-Islamic Iranian models of kingship and culture, and its vigorous promotion of imperial culture, the form of the Iranian garden was spread to other parts of the Islamic world. Al-Khatib describes Baghdad in 917 as having one royal garden that served as a wild animal park and another so extensive that it contained four hundred palm trees, as well as citrus and other fruit trees. Most amazing of all was the garden around the Palace of the Tree, for it contained a great circular pool that had in its center an artificial tree with gold and silver branches on which sat gold and silver birds that sang when the wind moved the branches: the entire construct may have been intended to replicate the design of the Sasanian *Spring of Khusrau* carpet.

In the Jawsaq al-Khaqani palace (836) in the 'Abbasid capital of Samarra there were 69.6 ha (171.9 acres) of walled gardens with reception halls and pavilions, and the palace was approached on the east through a vast garden reminiscent of the 'Imarat-i Khusrau. Samarra's Balkuwara Palace (849–859) contained three successive four-part courtyards at the end of which was a four-part garden, flanked by pavilions overlooking the Tigris. They indicate the continuance of two basic palace-garden types from pre-Islamic Iran, namely the large walled garden that contained the palace

within it, and the inner court garden (generally referred to as a *bustan*) that was contained within the palace. Aristocratic houses also had interior gardens. Agriculture expanded vigorously thanks to capital investments in irrigation made possible by the empire's wealth and to a commercial market stretching from India to Spain. Royal and aristocratic gardens and orchards were sometimes experimental grounds for new fruits and vegetables, as well as for innovations in farming techniques; instead of growing staples, they cultivated new and exotic produce that underscored sharp distinctions between the diets of the urban ruling classes and the agricultural lower class. Likewise, an abundance of water, particularly when its principal purposes were to create a cool and pleasant ambience and to sustain luxury produce, was a sign of wealth, and the ordered layout of water channels, pools, and fountains was an expression of control and power over this vital resource: mausolea situated within geometric gardens continued this imagery of power by the expectation that the deceased, buried in an earthly paradise, would eventually be lodged in the paradise described in the Qur'an. The widespread use of garden imagery in poetry, ceramics, manuscripts, ivories, metalworks, carpets, and other arts also implies that enclosed gardens were maintained by those who had power and could afford them and that their wealth enabled them to create tomb gardens for their dead. Religious establishments maintained gardens too as expressions and producers of wealth and as places of contemplation that prefigured paradise.

Although Muslim Spain is outside the area of the Near East, it provides invaluable evidence for the structure and function of the gardens that served as models and that are no longer extant in the central Islamic lands. Designed to emulate the eighth-century Rusafa garden in Damascus, the Rusafa garden in Cordoba was praised by Ibn Sa'id, the thirteenth-century Andalusian historian and man of letters, for its irrigated gardens. It was also famous for plants and animals brought from all over the Islamic world, Turkestan, and India. Most of Cordoba's considerable area was taken up by gardens and orchards that belonged to the city's mosques and palaces, and the courtyard of the Great Mosque was occupied by neat rows of orange trees fed by stone-edged water channels. The most elaborate gardens, however, were in the royal precinct of Medina al-Zahra. The Upper Garden was divided into four parts, and at the crossing of the channels was a pillared rectangular pavilion bordered on each side by a pool, and the Prince's Garden was centered on a rectangular pool with a raised viewing platform on its north side. Observation points such as this one underscored royal perspective and the central authority of the caliph: gardens functioned not only as places of beauty and refuge but also as focused demonstrations of power and prestige.

Evidence indicates that rather than being in massed beds, plantings were individual or in small groups. Flower and orchard beds were frequently sunk below the level of the walkways, so that a visitor strolling on the paths would have had the sensation of walking on a living and luxurious floral carpet. Gardens in Spain functioned also as grave sites: the eleventh-century poet Ibn Shuhai'd was buried in a garden in Cordoba that was described by Ibn Khaqan as having symmetrically rowed trees and a white marble courtyard with a curving water channel and a lower basin into which the water fell, presumably down a waterslide. Luxury objects carried garden themes as well: an ivory pyxis made in 1004–1008 for the Cordoban royal chamberlain Sayf al-Dawlah clearly shows a walled garden with arcades along its sides. Because ivories were originally painted, it would have offered an even more vivid resemblance to a garden.

The Arab historian Muqaddisi (d. 1000) reported that the Buyid ruler of Iran and Iraq, 'Adud ad-Daulah (949–983), built a two-story, 360-room palace in Shiraz with orchards around it and water channels flowing through its ground floor rooms and arcades. Their successors, the Seljuks (1038–1194), further developed the concept of the *bāgh*, or garden with a pavilion or palace, and fourteenth-century manuscript paintings indicate that these buildings were multi-colored and multi-storied: Malik Shah (1072–1092) is credited with constructing four gardens of this type in late eleventh-century Isfahan. The metaphoric content of garden imagery continued to be exploited. The tulip (*lāleh*) had all the same letters of the symbol of Islamic power, the crescent (*hilāl*), and the name of the God (Allāh), and the rose (*gul*) was considered the most perfect manifestation of divine beauty on earth. A ruler like the Seljuk sultan Malik Shah (1072–1092) may even be compared to a doorkeeper (*ridwān*) guarding a garden containing streams, fruits, trees, and flowers of paradise; elaborating the metaphoric link between the ordered garden and the ordered universe, the Seljuk court poet Mu'izzi (d. 1147) described a royal garden filled with streams, herbs, fruits, trees, and flowers like those of paradise, and compared the sultan to the sun and his throne to the seventh heaven.

[*See also* 'Abbasid Caliphate; Baghdad; Ctesiphon; Damascus; Mafjar, Khirbat al-; Pasargadae; Qaṣr al-Hayr ash-Sharqi; Samarra, *article on* Islamic Period; *and* Umayyad Caliphate.]

BIBLIOGRAPHY

Ansari, A. S. Bazmee. "Bustān." In *Encyclopaedia of Islam*, new ed., vol. 1, pp. 1345–1348. Leiden, 1960–.
Brookes, John. *Gardens of Paradise: The History and Design of the Great Islamic Gardens*. London, 1987.
Environmental Design 2 (1986). Special issue entitled "The City as a Garden."
Gardet, Louis. "Djanna." In *Encyclopaedia of Islam*, new ed., vol. 2, pp. 447–452. Leiden, 1960–.
Golombek, Lisa, and Donald Wilber. *The Timurid Architecture of Iran and Turan*. Princeton, 1988.
Lehrman, Jonas. *Earthly Paradise: Garden and Courtyard in Islam*. Berkeley, 1980.
MacDougall, Elisabeth B., and Richard Ettinghausen. *The Islamic Garden*. Dumbarton Oaks Colloquium on the History of Landscape Architecture, 4. Washington, D.C., 1976.
O'Kane, Bernard. *Timurid Architecture in Khurasan*. Costa Mesa, Calif., 1987.
Ruggles, D. F. "The Mirador in Abbasid and Hispano-Umayyad Garden Typology." *Muqarnas* 7 (1990): 73–82.
Ruggles, D. F. "Madīnat al-Zahrā"s Constructed Landscape: A Case Study in Islamic Garden and Architectural History." Ph.D. diss., University of Pennsylvania, 1991.
Schimmel, Annemarie. "The Celestial Garden in Islam." In *The Islamic Garden*, edited by Elisabeth B. MacDougall and Richard Ettinghausen, pp. 11–39. Washington, D.C., 1976.
Watson, Andrew M. *Agricultural Innovation in the Early Islamic World: The Diffusion of Crops and Farming Techniques, 700–1100*. Cambridge, 1983.
Wilber, Donald. *Persian Gardens and Garden Pavilions*. Rutland, Vt., 1962.

ANTHONY WELCH

GARROD, DOROTHY ANNIE ELIZABETH

(1892–1968), prehistorian whose work at the Tabun, Skhul, and el-Wad caves in the Carmel range in Israel provided what became a standard chronological and cultural scale for the region, beginning with the Upper Acheulean and ending with the Natufian culture. Garrod studied at Newnham College at Cambridge (1913–1916). In 1921 she enrolled in the archaeology-anthropology program under R. Marrett at Oxford, and in 1922 she became a student of Abbé Breuil at the Institut de Paléontologie Humaine in Paris. She worked at the site of La Quina in southwest France under Henri Martin and published a summary volume on the British Upper Paleolithic in 1926. Following Breuil's suggestion, she excavated Devil's Tower, a Mousterian rock-shelter on Gibraltar (1925–1927), where a broken juvenile skull cap was uncovered. In 1927 she was invited to participate on the European committee that examined the Glozel figurines, which turned out to be forgeries. In 1928 she excavated the Shukbah cave in Palestine and named its previously unknown microlithic and bone industry the Natufian culture, after the wadi by that name. She later dug two small caves in northeastern Iraq: Hazar Nerd, a Mousterian site, and Zarzi, where the microlithic assemblage was named Zarzian. In 1929 she began, as a salvage project, excavations in the caves at the outlet of Naḥal ha-Me'arot (Wadi Mughara) in the Carmel range. Upon completing the fieldwork there in 1934, she published, in 1937, together with Dorothea Bate, who did the faunal analysis, the seminal volume *The Stone Age of Mount Carmel*. In 1938, after a survey in Anatolia, Garrod excavated the cave of Bacho Kiro in Bulgaria and uncovered an early Aurignacian industry. From 1939 to 1952 she was Disney Professor at Cambridge University, a position interrupted during World War II, when she served in the army (1942–1945). From 1948 to 1963 she participated in the excavations of Suzanne de Saint Mathurin in Anglees sur l'Anglin, a Magdalenian rock-shelter rich in relief representations of animals and humans. From 1958 to 1963 Garrod conducted excavations in the Bezez, Zumoffen, and Ras el-Kelb caves in Lebanon, where Acheulo-Yabrudian and Mousterian layers were exposed. These led her to provide a new synthesis of the Near Eastern Middle Paleolithic that was published in 1962.

[See also Carmel Caves.]

BIBLIOGRAPHY

Caton-Thompson, Gertrude. "Dorothy Annie Elizabeth Garrod." *Proceedings of the British Academy* 55 (1969): 339–361.

Garrod, Dorothy A. E. *The Upper Palaeolithic Age in Britain* (1926). New York, 1979.

Garrod, Dorothy A. E., and Dorothea M. A. Bate. *The Stone Age of Mount Carmel: Excavations at the Wady al-Mughara.* Report of the Joint Expedition of the British School of Archaeology in Jerusalem and the American School of Prehistoric Research, 1929–1934, vol. 1. Oxford, 1937.

Roe, Derek A., ed. *Adlun in the Stone Age: The Excavations of D. A. E. Garrod in the Lebanon, 1958–1963.* 2 vols. British Archaeological Reports, International Series, no. 159. Oxford, 1983.

Ronen, Avraham, ed.. *The Transition from Lower to Middle Palaeolithic and the Origin of Modern Man: International Symposium to Commemorate the Fiftieth Anniversary of Excavations in the Mount Carmel Caves by D. A. E. Garrod.* British Archaeological Reports, International Series, no. 15. Oxford, 1982.

OFER BAR-YOSEF

GARSTANG, JOHN (1876–1956), British archaeologist who began his academic career in mathematics at Jesus College, Oxford University, but while still an undergraduate turned his attention to archaeology. His first fieldwork was done in Egypt, where, at the age of twenty-three, he joined Flinders Petrie. He then worked in Anatolia (1904–1909), returning for a final season of excavations at Sakçagözü in 1911. His influential work, *The Land of the Hittites,* was published in 1910. While still very young (he was twenty-six), he was appointed honorary reader in Egyptian archaeology at Liverpool University. Five years later (in 1907) he became professor of the methods and practice of archaeology, a post he held until his retirement in 1941. From 1909 until 1914 he excavated in the Sudan, at Meroë, capital of an ancient Nubian kingdom.

Garstang was the founding director of the British School of Archaeology in Jerusalem in 1920. In that same year, he made what is probably his most lasting contribution to archaeology by becoming the founding director of the British Mandatory Department of Antiquities of Palestine, a post he held until 1926. In that capacity he drafted the country's antiquities laws, which were notably liberal, enlightened, and practical. Garstang used the material belonging to the Ottoman Palestine Museum as the basis of the collection for the Palestine Museum in Jerusalem, now the Rockefeller Museum. Garstang carried out the first post–World War I excavations in Palestine at Ashkelon, followed by a series of soundings at sites across the country. In 1922, at a historic meeting with William Foxwell Albright of the American School of Oriental Research in Jerusalem and Louis-Hugues Vincent of the École Biblique et Archéologique Française, Garstang formulated the terminology still used for the classification of the archaeological material of the southern Levant. From 1930 to 1936 he carried out a major excavation at Jericho, funded by Charles Marston. Although this excavation was poorly published, and although Garstang's views of Jericho regarding the accounts in *Exodus* and regarding the Israelite conquest are no longer accepted, his work there provided the first information about the existence of an aceramic Neolithic culture.

Following World War II, Garstang returned to Anatolia, where he became the founding director of the British Institute of Archaeology at Ankara (1947). His final excavation was at the site of Mersin, in Cilicia, where he discovered important remains of the Neolithic and Early Bronze Ages. Two days before his death, though very ill and weak, he was able to realize his wish to revisit this site, coming ashore from the boat on which he was enjoying a last cruise.

[See also Ashkelon; British Institute of Archaeology at Ankara; British School of Archaeology in Jerusalem; Cilicia; Jericho; Meroë; and the biographies of Albright, Petrie, and Vincent.]

BIBLIOGRAPHY

FitzGerald, G. M., et al. "John Garstang." *Anatolian Studies* 6 (1956): 27–34. Brief remembrances from several colleagues and a photograph portrait.

Garstang, John. *Land of the Philistines.* New York, 1910.

Garstang, John. *Joshua-Judges.* New York, 1931.

Garstang, John. *Heritage of Solomon: An Historical Introduction to the Sociology of Ancient Palestine.* London, 1934.

Garstang, John. *Prehistoric Mersin, Yumuk Tepe in Southern Turkey.* Oxford, 1953.

Parrot, André. "John Garstang." *Syria* 34 (1957): 401–402. Obituary.

Weidner, E. "John Garstang." *Archiv für Orientforschung* 18 (1958): 228–229. Obituary.

RUPERT CHAPMAN

GAULANITIS. *See* Golan.

GAZA (site). *See* 'Ajjul, Tell el-.

GENESIS APOCRYPHON. One of the seven scrolls found by bedouin in Cave 1 at Qumran in spring 1947 is the *Genesis Apocryphon* (1QApGen). Together with three other scrolls from that cave, it was sold to Mar Athanasius Yeshue Samuel, the Syrian Metropolitan attached to

St. Mark's Monastery in Jerusalem. Unlike the other scrolls, the *Genesis Apocryphon* was not opened until it was sold—to the State of Israel, in June 1954. After the sale, authorities turned the scroll over to J. Biberkraut for unrolling. The scroll's beginning and end were missing and, of the twenty-two columns that survived, only the last three—the scroll's innermost portions, as it was rolled—were more or less completely preserved. The opening portions had suffered greatly from exposure to the elements and from the mordant ink with which the scroll was inscribed. The ink had eaten into the leather, so that many of the words are blurred.

Yigael Yadin and Nahman Avigad published a preliminary edition of the scroll in 1956—only the five columns (2, 19–22) that could readily be deciphered. They never published the other columns, a project that recently was turned over to two Israeli scholars, Jonas Greenfield and Elisha Qimron. They have, to date, published an additional column of the scroll, column 12. In addition, J. T. Milik published fragments belonging to the missing beginning of the scroll as 1Q20. He did not succeed in reading much of the text on what are very badly darkened fragments, but recently new photographs enabled Michael Wise and Bruce Zuckerman to read and reconstruct the 1Q20 fragments as "column 0." Moreover, Zuckerman has brought to light a previously unknown portion of column 1, dubbed the Trever fragment.

The importance of the *Genesis Apocryphon* lies in two principal spheres: language and interpretation. The scroll is written in Aramaic; as a fair amount of text has been preserved, it constitutes one of the primary witnesses to the literary use of that language in late Second Temple period Palestine (200 BCE–70 CE). The interpretive method of the scroll belongs to the category designated "rewritten Bible," in which biblical stories are retold with explanatory changes and additions. The *Genesis Apocryphon* is an early and significant witness to this method of biblical interpretation, with important connections to the pseudepigraphic *Jubilees.*

Largely following the analysis by Joseph A. Fitzmyer, the contents of the scroll can be broken down as follows: columns 0–2, the birth of Noah; 6–10, Noah and the Flood; 11, Noah's covenant; 12–?, Noah's division of the earth among his sons; 18, Abram in Ur and Haran; 18–19:10, Abram in Canaan; 19:10–20:33, Abram in Egypt; 20:33–21:22, Abram in the Promised Land; 21:23–22:26, Abram defeats the four kings; and 22:27–?, Abram's vision of an heir.

[*See also* Dead Sea Scrolls.]

BIBLIOGRAPHY

Avigad, Nahman, and Yigael Yadin. *A Genesis Apocryphon.* Jerusalem, 1956. *Editio princeps;* it includes a descriptive narrative, photographs, a transcription, and an English translation of columns 2, 19–22.
Barthélemy, Dominique, and J. T. Milik. *Qumran Cave I.* Oxford, 1955. Includes Milik's treatment of the 1Q20 fragments (pp. 86–87 and pl. 17) which, even under infrared light, were extremely dark and thus difficult to read.
Fitzmyer, Joseph A. *The Genesis Apocryphon of Qumran Cave I.* 2d rev. ed. Rome, 1971. Contains the Aramaic text, English translation, and line-by-line commentary, with an introduction to the issues raised by the scroll. Excellent treatment, but rapidly becoming outdated.
Greenfield, Jonas C., and Elisha Qimron. "The Genesis Apocryphon Col. XII." In *Studies in Qumran Aramaic,* edited by Takamitsu Muraoka, pp. 70–77. *Abr-Nahrain,* Supplement Series, vol. 3. Leiden, 1992. Includes photograph, transcription, and English translation, with philological analysis. Only about ten new lines are clearly legible.

MICHAEL O. WISE

GEOGRAPHIC INFORMATION SYSTEMS. *See* Computer Mapping.

GEOLOGY. The consulting relationship between geologists and archaeologists/historians is designed to achieve a fuller understanding of a site's occupational and socioeconomic story, ideally as excavation is taking place. Another term for archaeological geology is *geoarchaeology,* the activity in which a geological scientist engages in historical/archaeological analyses and diagnoses from an empirical base.

The locus, a fundamental unit of archaeological stratigraphy, has discrete geological analogues in the bed, tongue, or layer units of a sequence of rock strata in any exposure/outcrop of unconsolidated sediments anywhere on earth. Sedimentary analytic techniques can be applied to a locus to determine its geological makeup: texture, fabric, particle size, micro/macrobedding, mineral/lithic, and material science diagnosis. (the identification of any artifact and its chemical composition and its function in human applications). [*See* Locus.] Studies propose multiple working hypotheses, which set forth probable agencies/events of origin and form the operational archaeological geological research basis.

Geological investigations in historical environmental remains may draw from various subsciences to address the action and interaction of human and natural depositional and erosional activities in, about, and regionally near a site: mineralogy (elements, salts, compounds), sedimentology (origin, movement, accumulation of particles), stratigraphy (forms of layering), structure (spacial geometry of any lithic body), petrology (igneous, sedimentary, and metamorphic rock origin and description), geomorphology (genesis and shape of the earth's surface), aerial photography (database for mapping), geohydrology (presence and behavior of groundwater), pedology (soil science), and especially soil-clay mineralogy, geophysical survey (archaeomagnetism with magnetic- and resistivity-force mapping), tephra (volcanitic ejecta—ash, shards), chronology, radiometric dating (radioactive elements and their isotopes, especially carbon), geochemical analyses (including trace element and isotope, useful for provenance), palynology (pollen and spore identity), and floral or plant inventories (including phytoliths), and coastal paleogeography (ancient shore-zone environments and locations). These and other disciplines form the geological framework through which the depositional record of natural and human agencies are interpreted.

Agents of earth sculpture that are active on/or in terrestrial and submarine surfaces include weathering; erosion; movement and deposition of earth materials by means of atmospheric interaction with mineral, rock, and plant material; gravity-slope kinetics; streams; underground water; waves and currents; wind; ice; and even volcanic activity. Vertical land movement and sea-basin volume changes may need to be considered (site elevation, submergence with associated effects). Physiographic surface environments express socioeconomic settlement-opportunity options often governed by the demands that specific cultures require.

The topographic configuration of a specific site locale is a function of rock and sediment body resistance to forces of degradation (removal) and aggradation (surface buildup), whose rates of progress determine how quickly human presence alters a surface. The difference between the highest and lowest elevations is mapped as a contour (the interval is determined by the steepness of slope and the amount of detail required). An overlay of geologic rock outcrops affords a convenient means of illustrating those formations that were affected by a site's occupants in construction phases. Other surface environments to be understood in archaeohistorical research include plains, plateaus, mesas, hills, mountains (volcanic, folded, fault-block), canyons, basins (graben or rift valleys), alluvial fans, valleys (stream and glacial), alluvial terraces, floodplains, deltas, beach/shore zones, glacial moraines, till plains, and outwash terrains. Historically, these natural depositions formed human-site contexts in temperate, tropical, arid, and polar settings in which settlers would need to control terrain, water, food acquisition/production, trade, roads, and defensible shelter.

Geologic activities that affect human-settlement decisions include water supply—springs, streams, water tables, and even artesian flow. Geothermal (heated) waters find expression as hot springs. Other water-bearing geochemical activities in the earth's crust generate mineral (ore) deposits (ion concentrations) yielding metals such as copper, tin, iron, lead, and zinc. Certain igneous reactions yield other ore deposits. The earliest metal acquisition by humans involved mining naturally occurring elements. As smelting/refining extraction techniques from the ores of those metalic compounds were discovered, the metals were incorporated into tool and weapon economies, recording the historical results of metallurgy. [See Metals.] Precious metals and stones also occur because of geologic concentration conditions. Such utilitarian metal ores were mined for noble and royal use: jewelry, tableware, and (by the end of the seventh century BCE) coins. The geochemical generation of petroleum and its by-products—bitumin, naptha, and sulfur and

the organogenesis of woods, fibers, amber, spices (fragrances), foods, and shell remains—has heavily influenced human behaviors, as recorded in archaeological remains.

Knowledge of the local and regional bedrock—its stratigraphy and structure—gave ancient masons of both stone and mud brick and quarrymen construction resources with which to erect, pave, wall, arch, and bridge for human requirements in urban, domestic, and defensive structures. Some rock types exhibit cutting properties that would produce poor to excellent architectural and sculptural results—cemented beach sands, rock and shell fragments (imprecisely termed poros), versus the finely crystalline limestones employed for Herodian structures in Roman Palestine and white marble for sculpture.

A brief inventory of common construction, building, and sculptural stone utilized throughout the Mediterranean and the Near East consists mainly of limestones, chalks, caliche (such as *nari*), coquina, travertines, quartz and bioclastic sandstones/conglomerates, quartz (and other lithic) sandstones, chert, various lithic-type conglomerates (such as *kurkar*), siltstones, marls, shales, alabasters, halites (from Mt. Sedom, a salt-block feature near the southwestern shore of the Dead Sea), granites, diorites, gabbros, lavas (basalt, from which Levantine and Mediterranean millstones were often crafted), and porphyrys, tuffs, slates, schists, gneiss, marbles, quartzites, and greenstones.

No less vital in human history has been the function of clays, formed mostly in the soil-genesis process, in grazing grasses and food crops. The mineralogical agricultural fertility of floodplain environments (river-valley sediments forming terraces) is well known. These clays and clay minerals have historical significance because they were utilized as tokens, tablets, and letters, mud bricks and mortars, terra cottas (sculptures and ovens), tiles (roofing, flooring, water and drainpipes), and, finally, as pottery.

Commonly, analytic studies and procedures in archaeological geology include, sediment-body (locus) identification, working hypotheses as to origin (source and agent), and sediment surface recognition; architectural building-stone type and source; historical geological/geographic site area-surface morphology; water source and management; pottery composition and provenance; evidence of the presence/absence of bedrock soil-cover depth and extent; stone and ore sources and their proximity to a site; clay/mud sources and their employment throughout the site's cultural history; the encouragement of multidisciplinary site and environmental studies (botany, entomology, zoology, and ecology).

Some of the most important geoscientific methods in archaeological research are petrology (e.g., study of rocks, pottery, bricks, roofing, tiles) in hand specimens and microscopic thin-sections to ascertain mineral makeup, texture, and ultimately, provenance; sedimentology (mineral com-

GEOLOGY. *Scored basalt slabs paving a Roman/Byzantine decumanus at Abila, northern Jordan.* Observe the stratified sediment showing the evidence of disoccupation. Both colluvial slope deposits and architectural fragments have covered the street and its sidewalks. Slumping drain cover blocks reveal the drain path. (Courtesy R. G. Bullard)

GEOLOGY. *Calicheated chalk bedrock used as the foundation level for a wall constructed of the same material.* Step-ledge quarrying techniques are evident. This quarrying method was employed by the Romans all over the Mediterranean. (Courtesy R. G. Bullard)

position and particle size—from clays to boulders), along with hypotheses concerning agency of deposition; ore and gemstone identification and qualitative analysis from wet chemical to X-ray spectroscopy; laser-probe spectroscopy of metals and gems; and core drilling in sediment strata, in- and off-site, to determine shore/harbor boundaries. [*See* Spectroscopy.] Typical field-geology research tools and equipment serve most of the study requirements. A binocular stereo-zoom microscope of 10–45× has been found indispensable in the dig house.

BIBLIOGRAPHY

Bar-Yosef, Ofer, and James L. Phillips, eds. *Prehistoric Investigations in Gebel Maghara, Northern Sinai.* Qedem, vol. 7. Jerusalem, 1977.

Bullard, Reuben G. "Geological Studies in Field Archaeology." *Biblical Archaeologist* 33 (1970): 98–132.

Butzer, Karl W. "The Ecological Approach to Prehistory: Are We Really Trying?" *American Antiquity* 40 (1975): 106–111.

Gladfelter, Bruce G. "Geoarchaeology: The Geomorphologist and Archaeology." *American Antiquity* 42 (1977): 519–538.

Gladfelter, Bruce G. "Developments and Directions in Geoarchaeology." In *Advances in Archaeological Method and Theory*, vol. 4, edited by Michael B. Schiffer, pp. 343–364. New York, 1981.

Goldberg, Paul. "The Archaeologist as Viewed by the Geologist." *Biblical Archaeologist* 51 (December 1988): 197–202.

Hassan, Fekri A. "Sediments in Archaeology: Methods and Implications for Palaeoenvironmental and Cultural Analysis." *Journal of Field Archaeology* 5 (1978): 197–213.

Levy, Thomas E., ed. *Shiqmim*, vol. 1, *Studies Concerning Chalcolithic Societies in the Northern Negev Desert, Israel, 1982–1984.* British Archaeological Reports, International Series, no. 356 Oxford, 1987.

Liebowitz, Harold, and Robert L. Folk. "Archaeological Geology of Tel Yin'am, Galilee, Israel." *Journal of Field Archaeology* 7 (1980): 23–42.

Limbrey, Susan. *Soil Science and Archaeology.* New York, 1975.

Marks, A. E., ed. *Prehistory and Paleoenvironments in the Central Negev, Israel.* Vols. 1 and 3. Dallas, 1976–1983.

Piperno, Dolores R. *Phytolith Analysis: An Archaeological and Geological Perspective.* San Diego, 1988.

Rapp, George, Jr. "The Archaeological Field Staff: The Geologist." *Journal of Field Archaeology* 2 (1975): 229–237.

Rapp, George, Jr., and Stanley E. Aschenbrenner, eds. *Excavations at Nichoria in Southwest Greece*, vol. 1, *Site, Environs, and Techniques.* Minneapolis, 1978.

Rapp, George, Jr., and John A. Gifford, eds. *Archaeological Geology.* New Haven, 1985.

Rosen, Arlene Miller. *Cities of Clay: The Geoarchaeology of Tells.* Chicago, 1986.

REUBEN G. BULLARD

GERASA. *See* Jerash.

GERISA, TEL (Ar., Tell Jerishe), a medium-sized mound (2.6 ha or 6.5 acres) located in the Yarkon valley at the fork of the Yarkon and Ayalon Rivers (32° 05′ N, 34° 48′ E). This location suggests that the site served as a main harbor city during the Middle and Late Bronze Ages. The modern Hebrew name of the site is adapted from the Arabic name of a small nearby village. It is also known by the local population as Napoleon's Hill, a name confirmed by Jacotin's map (prepared by Napoleon's engineer during their campaign to Palestine in 1799). The site is marked as the location of a military camp under the command of one of Napoleon's generals. Topographically, the mound forms a saddle, with the southern summit higher than the northern one. A deep depression on its western side is undoubtedly the location of the city gate. On the opposite side, on the east, the *kurkar* bedrock is exposed, apparently the result of continuous quarrying for building material. Benjamin Mazar identified the site with the Levitical city of Gat-Rimon (Maisler [Mazar], 1950–1951), but this identification is negated by geographic considerations and because the only find for the tenth century BCE was a small farmstead (Rainey, 1987–1989). [*See* Farmsteads.]

The site was excavated by an expedition from the Hebrew University of Jerusalem, directed by Eleazar L. Sukenik for five seasons spread over twenty-five years (1927–1951). No excavation report was published, but a short summary of the work, written by Nahman Avigad (1976), is available. In 1976 Yigael Yadin and Shulamit Geva cut a small probe into the remains exposed in the 1951 season and concluded that the city wall and its glacis had been erected during Middle Bronze IIB period (Geva, 1982). Exploration of the site was renewed in 1981 by a Tel Aviv University expedition directed by Ze'ev Herzog. By 1993, nine seasons had been conducted in four areas, A–D (Herzog, 1993). The eleventh season was scheduled to begin in June 1995.

Bronze Age. The earliest occupation of the site took place in the Early Bronze Age, remains of which were found in the stratigraphic trench cut at the southern end of the mound (area A) and in area C. In both cases shallow depressions in the *kurkar* contained EB III pottery sherds in an ashy debris, pointing to an agricultural settlement. An unfortified village was also erected early in Middle Bronze IIA, whose remains consist of walls belonging to residential units and a circular clay silo. The first fortified city was erected in the second occupational phase of this period. The earliest city wall (1.70 m wide) was made of mud bricks laid on a single course of stone foundations. Two floors, the lowest covered by a thick layer of burnt debris, join this wall inside the city, and a sloped glacis is laid against its outer face. A second MB IIA city wall (2.20 m wide), made solely of clay bricks, was erected about 90 cm farther into the city. Two floors were also laid against this wall; the upper one contained pottery typical of the period's latest phase. On its outer side a new and formidable glacis was erected out of sloping brick layers, with a coating of crushed *kurkar*. Area A's high elevation, the thick walls found there, and some luxurious pottery vessels all suggest that this was the location of the ruler's palace.

During MB IIB, a third fortification system was constructed. A 3-meter-wide brick wall was built above the earlier remains, and a third glacis was laid over the solid remains of the former ones. Inside the city a large building abutted the city wall, which contained four square rooms and a long corridor. Many large storage jars were found smashed on the floors of the rooms, indicating that the rooms had been used as storehouses. The city wall was reused in the Late Bronze Age I, but then only small rooms of a domestic nature were built against it. The ruler's palace was apparently moved to the lower part of the city.

During one of the MB subphases—the only period in which the city was fortified—a water system was constructed at Tel Gerisa. The project's impressive remains consist of a circular shaft (6 m in diameter) hewn into the *kurkar* (see figure 1). Narrow stairs were carved out of the rock along the side of the shaft that descend to the water source, about 22 m below the top of the shaft. So far only the upper 5 m have been exposed. The shaft was converted into a stone-lined well, with space between the well and the original hewn shafted filled in, in the Iron Age I (see below).

Excavation exposed widespread LB remains at the center of the mound (area C), in an area unoccupied in later periods. Its main feature is a large (17 × 16 m), square building located in the center of the tell, directly in front of the city-gate area. The building features a stone-paved courtyard of similar size adjacent to it on the north. The building, whose outer walls are 1.90 m thick is divided into three rows of rooms. The large room in the central row might have been a throne room. The building was artificially elevated by a fill

of sandy red soil and retained by a stone revetment. To the west of the palace, immediately south of the presumed location of the city gate, a large open space was covered with thick white plaster. This area and the structure around it are interpreted as the local marketplace, a function supported by the large quantities of Mycenaean and Cypriot imported vessels, Egyptian scarabs and pottery, and several weights found on and around the plastered floor.

There was no LB city wall at Tel Gerisa. The easternmost walls in area C were constructed over the remains of the MB IIB city wall. Most of the site, except for the palace, was covered by domestic buildings in the LB IIB period, as revealed by the small probes cut into those levels (under the Iron Age I remains) in areas B and D. A large refuse pit, found full of ashy debris, had been dug into the debris of the older acropolis (area A).

Iron Age. During the Iron Age the size of the settlement at Tel Gerisa was considerably reduced. The remains of the Iron I settlement consist of dwellings and storage pits at both the southern and the northern summits of the mound. The center of the mound was not settled and may have been used for horticulture. It has been suggested by Tsvika Tsuk, excavator of the water system, that the well built into the old water system was constructed to irrigate the cultivated plots. The settlements belonged to two separate small villages or farmsteads, each rebuilt several times during the period. Philistine sherds of monochrome (Late Mycenaean III:C$_{1b}$) ware, bichrome pottery, and late red-slipped wares indicate occupation of the site during Iron IB. The central site of

GERISA, TEL.   Figure 1.   *Hewn shaft of a water system.* (Courtesy Z. Herzog)

Philistine occupation in the region was at Tell Qasile, located 1.5 km across the Yarkon River. [*See* Philistines, *article on* Early Philistines; Qasile, Tell.]

Sukenik's expedition cleared a large part of the settlement at the southern end of the site. Remains exposed by the renewed excavations consisted of two houses with stone bases that had held wooden columns as internal partitions. One of the houses had been destroyed by fire. In the destruction layer among the finds recorded were ceremonial pottery vessels and a pair of small bronze cymbals. Nearby a carved five-sided pyramidal seal and a female pillar figurine were found. The occupation on the northern end had been poorer, and in its final stage contained mainly deep storage pits, eventually reused for garbage.

In Iron IIA the occupation at Tel Gerisa was even more limited and was restricted to the southern summit. Remains of a single domestic building were exposed right under the surface. The house had been used in two phases, both dated to the tenth century BCE. Following the destruction of the last phase, the site was deserted for two millennia. Habitation was renewed at the northern end of mound for a short time in the Early Arab period (tenth century CE).

BIBLIOGRAPHY

Avigad, Nahman. "Jerishe Tell." In *Encyclopedia of Archaeological Excavations in the Holy Land*, vol. 2, pp. 575–578. Engelwood Cliffs, N.J., 1976.

Geva, Shulamit. *Tell Jerishe: The Sukenik Excavations of the Middle Bronze Age Fortifications*. Qedem, vol. 15. Jerusalem, 1982.

Herzog, Ze'ev. "Gerisa, Tel." In *The New Encyclopedia of Archaeological Excavations in the Holy Land*, vol. 2, pp. 480–484. Jerusalem and New York, 1993.

Maisler [Mazar], Benjamin. "The Excavations at Tell Qasîle: Preliminary Report." *Israel Exploration Journal* 1.2 (1950–1951): 61–76.

Rainey, Anson F. "Tel Gerisa and the Danite Inheritance" (in Hebrew). *Eretz-Israel Museum Yearbook: Israel—People and Land* 5–6 (1987–1989): 59–72.

ZE'EV HERZOG

GERMAN SCHOOL (Jerusalem). *See* Deutsches Evangelisches Institut für Altertumswissenschaft des Heiligen Landes.

GEZER, ancient site identified with modern Tell el-Jezer in Israel (35°51′ N, 34°55′ E; map reference 142.5 × 140.7), 8 km (5 mi.) southeast of modern Ramla. The prominent 33-acre mound, about 650 yards long and 240 yards wide, is about 225 m above sea level (see figure 1). It is the last of the foothills of the Central Hills where they slope down to join the northern Shephelah, guarding the western end of the Valley of Ayalon. Gezer is thus at the crossroads of the Via Maris and the trunk road leading up to Jerusalem and beyond.

Gezer was correctly identified in 1871 by Charles Clermont-Ganneau, on the basis of several of the now well-known bedrock inscriptions reading "boundary of Gezer" (see below). It was excavated by Robert Alexander Stewart Macalister in 1902–1909 for the Palestine Exploration Fund, in one of the first large-scale modern projects, published as *The Excavation of Gezer* (3 vols., 1912). Alan Rowe conducted brief soundings in 1934, again for the PEF. The Hebrew Union College–Jewish Institute of Religion in Jerusalem, with the Harvard Semitic Museum, carried out major excavations in 1964–1974, directed by G. Ernest Wright, William G. Dever, and Joe D. Seger (again in 1984 and 1990 by Dever, sponsored by the University of Arizona).

History. The excavations have brought to light twenty-six strata, from the Late Chalcolithic to the Roman era.

Stratum XXVI. Gezer was founded in the Late Chalcolithic period, about 3500 BCE. Most of the material (including some of Macalister's "Pre-Semitic") comes from flimsy dwellings on bedrock. The pottery and other material overlaps with both the Beersheba and coastal cultures.

Stratum XXV. The Early Bronze I material from Field I (including some of Macalister's "Pre-Semitic," "First Semitic," and "Troglodyte" cave materials) suggests an expanded settlement, about 3200–3100 BCE. In addition to fragmentary house walls, there are natural and enlarged caves in the bedrock that were used extensively for dwellings and storage. One of them, Cave I.3A, produced an assemblage of storejars and other vessels, as well as stone implements. The scant pottery of Stratum XXV is typical of Early Bronze I, including some red-slipped and "trickle-painted" wares.

Strata XXIV–XXIII. During Early Bronze II, roughly 3100–2600 BCE, Gezer expanded considerably, but it still did not boast city walls such as many other sites had. House walls in Field I were well constructed and had several phases of continuous occupation. The pottery repertoire includes typical red-burnished vessels, Abydos-style pitchers, and a few Egyptian imports. Gezer was abandoned from the end of the Early Bronze II period through Early Bronze IV, during which time a deep layer of humus-like soil formed at the surface (now deeply buried, of course).

Stratum XXII. After a long gap, Gezer was reoccupied sometime in the late Middle Bronze I period, about 1900 BCE. Some of Macalister's "Second Semitic" and several of his tombs, including one typical cist-tomb (III.3) belong to this horizon. A small statuette of Heqab, probably a twelfth-dynasty Egyptian official, also belongs here. Our material, which comes only from Field VI, consists of a partly subterranean plastered granary; a few domestic dwellings; and several infant jar burials. The pottery includes fine red-slipped and burnished carinated bowls.

Strata XXI–XX. Gezer appears to have grown into a relatively large urban site in Middle Bronze II. Much of Ma-

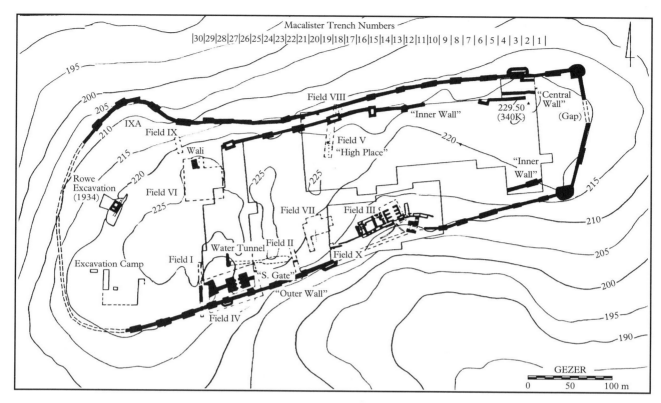

GEZER. Figure 1. *Plan of the site.* (Courtesy W. G. Dever)

calister's "Second Semitic" belongs here. In Field VI there is a continuous development of domestic dwellings; houses are now constructed along terraced slopes and share large courtyards and cisterns fed by runoff water conducted through well-built drains. The pottery is unexceptional but typical of Middle Bronze II, about 1750–1650 BCE.

Stratum XIX. Late in Middle Bronze II or early in Middle III, around 1650 BCE, Gezer was first fortified. Macalister's "Inner Wall" and "South Gate" belong here. In Field I Dever's team reexcavated the "Outer Wall" and its adjoining "Tower 5017." Macalister's plans show the wall encircling the entire site, a length of perhaps 1,300 yards, and incorporating many rectangular towers. The walls of the tower, constructed of dressed cyclopean masonry, are 53 feet wide and still stand to a height of 15 feet. The superstructure is entirely missing today, but the building, probably a citadel, must have stood originally three or four stories high. In Field IV to the west, Macalister's "South Gate," a typical three-entryway monumental gateway, was reexcavated. Its mud-brick superstructure still stands more than 25 feet high, and the springers of the arches are still visible. Late in this stratum, or early in the next, "Glaçis 8012" was added to the "Inner Wall." It was carefully constructed of alternating layers of tamped chalk and occupational debris, rising at a slope of 45 degrees to a preserved height of nearly 20 feet.

Also to be attributed to Stratum XIX is Macalister's "High Place," reexcavated by Dever's team in Field V (see figure 2). It consists of a north–south alignment of ten large standing stones (the biblical *maṣṣēbôt*), some nearly 10 feet high, surrounded by a plastered pavement and a low stone curb. Quantities of burned animal bones and teeth associated with the pavement suggest animal sacrifice at an outdoor cultic installation, perhaps a covenant-renewal sanctuary.

In Field VI on the acropolis, remains of a massive citadel adjoining a cobbled street were found, as well as established houses, courtyards, and cisterns, continuing the strata XXI–XX tradition.

Stratum XVIII. Middle Bronze Age Gezer was brought to a violent end by a fire that was evident in several fields. This may have been the work of Pharaoh Thutmose III, who mentions Gezer in his Karnak inscription, among sites conquered on his first Asiatic campaign about 1468 BCE. Just inside the connector wall between "Tower 5017" and the "South Gate," several destroyed houses yielded almost two hundred pieces of pottery. There was also a cache of gold jewelry, including two foil female figurines, found under the skeleton of a young women who had been crushed by roof-fall.

Stratum XVII. Gezer was probably abandoned for a time following the massive destruction of Stratum XVIII, through most of Late Bronze IA–B. The only evidence of occupation consists of the earliest burials in Cave I.10A (below). The scant Bichrome ware found by Macalister may belong early in this or the preceding phase.

Stratum XVI. By Late Bronze IIA, around 1400–1300 BCE, Gezer is flourishing again. In Field VI, "Palace 14120," although badly ruined later, was a splendid, multistoried building, its few remaining contents speaking of considerable wealth and sophistication. Like Macalister's "Canaanite Castle" in Field XI, it may have been an Egyptian-style "residency" of the Amarna Age. From Amarna itself there are ten letters from Gezer, from three different kings. To this general horizon belongs one of Macalister's cuneiform tablets, apparently from an Egyptian official who is summoning someone or something to Kiddimu, perhaps nearby Tell Ras Abu Hamid (biblical "Gittaim"?). A number of Macalister's tombs and parts of his "Second" and "Third Semitic" belong to this horizon.

Macalister's "Outer Wall" is now dated to the stratum XVI horizon. This wall, built on bedrock, is about 15 feet wide and is preserved in places some 12–14 feet high. It runs some 1,400 yards around the site outside the perimeter of the "Inner Wall." The excavators have dated this wall to the Amarna Age, both on stratigraphic and pragmatic grounds, although others date it to the Iron Age, largely because of the ashlar towers built into it (see below).

Some of the most spectacular finds came from the major period of burials in Cave I.10A in Field I, just outside the "Outer Wall." There were sixty-eight individuals—adults, juveniles, and children—interred in this cave from around 1450 to 1300 BCE. Many suffered from advanced artereosclerosis. Yet in addition to dozens of ordinary local pots and bronzes, there were imported luxury items such as Cypriot vessels, and Egyptian alabasters, scarabs, ivory pieces, and a fine cast sand-core glass vase.

Stratum XV–XIV. During the Late Bronze IIB period, about 1300–1200 BCE, Gezer gradually declined. The end may have come around 1207 BCE in the campaign of Pharaoh Merneptah, whose famous "Victory Stela" names Gezer among conquered cities and peoples in Canaan. In Field II there is a major late thirteenth-century BCE destruction; in Field VI a period of disruption and abandonment is followed by deep pitting and trenching operations. Among Macalister's finds is a carved stone sundial bearing the cartouche of Merneptah.

Stratum XIII–XII. At the transition from the Late Bronze to the Iron Age, about 1200 BCE, Gezer shows both continuity and discontinuity. The disruptions in Fields II and VI have already been noted. In Field I, however, there are new structures in the early twelfth century BCE but no fundamental changes. Also, the ceramic repertoire in all areas shows marked continuity from the mid-thirteenth until at least the mid-twelfth century BCE.

The major changes are in Field VI, where above the filled-in trenches noted above a large, multiroomed public granary

GEZER. Figure 2. *The "High Place."* Middle Bronze III period, c. 1600 BCE. (Courtesy W. G. Dever)

was constructed, surrounded by an extensive threshing floor with many burn-layers. The first typical Philistine Bichrome pottery appears precisely with the earliest floors of this building. The building goes through three building phases interspersed by disruptions, with a massive destruction at the end, about 1150 BCE. The debris produced many restorable vessels, numerous miscellaneous objects, and three contemporary Egyptian scarabs.

Stratum XI. By the late twelfth century BCE the granary had been replaced by two large, well-constructed courtyard houses flanking a lane. Both were violently destroyed in a fire after the first phase; partially rebuilt and destroyed again; and finally abandoned after a third, poorer phase. By the last phase, in the mid-eleventh century BCE, Philistine wares are disappearing, and a few red-slipped wares appear. From the destruction layers came two ceramic swan's heads and a terra-cotta circumcised phallus. Structures of this horizon were also brought to light in Fields I and II, but they were unexceptional.

Stratum X–IX. The late eleventh–early tenth-century BCE horizon is represented mainly by several poor structures and a distinctive "post-Philistine/pre-Solomonic" pottery covered with a thin, streaky red wash.

Stratum VIII. This stratum, spanning the mid- to late tenth century BCE, sees major changes, especially in Fields II and III. In Field III, Macalister's "Maccabean Castle" was reexcavated; Yigael Yadin had already interpreted it, sight unseen, as a four-entryway city gate and stretch of casemate wall, like those at Hazor and Megiddo. He cited the reference in *1 Kings* 9:15–17 to Solomonic defenses at all three sites. Yadin turned out to be correct, the Gezer date confirmed by red-slipped and hand-burnished pottery in the deep constructional fills underlying the walls and first roadway. Low benches ran around the walls of each chamber, and a large stone basin was in one chamber. At the two jambs the masonry was fine ashlar, but elsewhere large boulders were used in the construction. After the first two resurfacings of the roadway, a deep drain was cut into the roadway and downslope that was incorporated into a two-entryway lower gatehouse. At this time "Palace 10,000" was also added, to the west of the gate.

The upper gate was connected on both sides to a short stretch of casemate wall. This wall continued west to Field II, where it was ceramically dated to the late tenth century BCE by hand-burnished wares. Downslope from the gate, the gatehouse was connected on both sides to the "Outer Wall," which was now rebuilt with the addition of several courses of somewhat different masonry, a much higher roadway, and an ashlar tower. In the excavators' opinion, this tower would go with the twenty-five or more ashlar towers that Macalister says were "inserted" in the "Outer Wall" that is now dated to the Late Bronze Age. In Field VI, on the north side of the mound, we also found two markedly different

phases of the "Outer Wall," although the one ashlar tower excavated there seems to go with a third phase of the wall, probably ninth century BCE in date. Both the upper gate and portions of the casemate wall were destroyed by a fire that left the structures severely damaged, probably to be associated with the well known raid of Pharaoh Shishak (Sheshonq) about 920 BCE.

Stratum VII. The ninth century BCE is not well represented at Gezer. The Field III upper gate, badly damaged, was reinforced and rebuilt as a three-entryway gate (see figure 3). Either in the late ninth or early eighth century BCE, "Palace 8,000" replaced "Palace 10,000" west of the gate. In Field VI, the third phase of the "Outer wall" and some of the ashlar towers probably belong to Stratum VII.

Stratum VI. Stratum VI belongs broadly to the eighth century BCE. In Fields II, III, and VI the casemate wall and "Outer Wall" and towers continue, the Field III gate being rebuilt as a two-entryway gate. In Field VII, several fine courtyard houses belong to this horizon (although some may have been built first in the tenth–ninth century BCE).

Stratum VI ends in a violent conflagration. In Field VII the houses are partially destroyed. In Field III the upper gate, the casemate wall, "Palace 8,000," and the lower gatehouse all show dramatic signs of this destruction. Within the casemate walls there is a heavy burn-layer, which produced mid- to late eighth-century BCE pottery encrusted with molten lime, more than 100 fire-baked loom weights, and several unique ceramic inkwells. The lower gate was fired, cracking some of the ashlar stones; and the "Outer Wall" was partially breached, hastily repaired, then finally heavily burned. This destruction is certainly that of Tiglath-Pileser III in his early Asiatic campaigns, about 733 BCE. A relief found by Austen Henry Layard in the Palace of this Assyrian king at Nimrud depicts a siege machine battering the city wall and gate of a Palestinian town, with the name *gaz (ru)*, "Gezer," written at the top in cuneiform characters.

Stratum V. Gezer never really recovered from the Assyrian destruction. Stratum V spans the late eighth–early sixth century BCE, but the remains are unimpressive. The city gate and walls in Fields II and III seem not to have been rebuilt. The Field VII private houses do continue, but in decline. That Gezer was now reckoned with Judah, not Israel, is indicated by a few royal stamped jar handles and shekel-weights found both by Macalister and the later excavators, and two Neo-Assyrian tablets. The end came with the Babylonian destruction of Judah in 598–586 BCE, evidence of which is clear in the Field VII houses.

Stratum IV. The Persian period, the sixth–fourth centuries BCE, is poorly represented at Gezer. There are ephemeral remains of domestic structures in Fields II and VI. Among Macalister's Persian materials, however, are several rich tombs (his "Philistine Tombs"), a few *yehûd* seal impressions, and some small limestone incense altars.

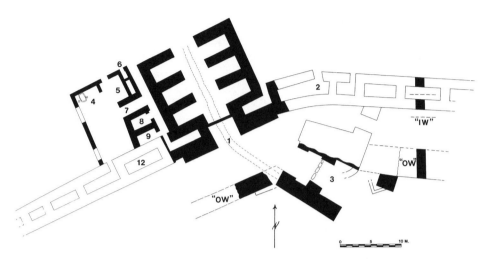

GEZER. Figure 3. *Plan of field III gateway, showing outer and inner city walls.* (1) drain; (2, 12) casemate walls; (3) outer gatehouse; (4-9) palace 10,000. (Courtesy W. G. Dever)

Stratum III. The early Hellenistic period, the late fourth–third century BCE, sees Gezer recover slightly, although few remains have been found in any of the excavations.

Stratum II. The second-century BCE witnesses a last revival of Gezer, especially during the Maccabean period, after about 170 BCE. The Iron Age gate in Field III was partially rebuilt as a single-entryway gate, with repairs made in bossed, marginally drafted masonry. Macalister's "Building H" over the eastern half of the gate dates to this period. Many of the ashlar towers of the "Outer Wall" were now surrounded by semicircular bastions, and upper courses were added to the wall here and there. In Fields II, VI, and VII domestic houses are in evidence, particularly in the latter field. Here a large house produced a horde of iron tools; an inscribed lead weight; stamped amphorae handles, and a coin of Antiochus VII, about 133 BCE.

Stratum I. From the early–mid-Roman period, there is little evidence, except for some domestic remains in Field II. However, the several "boundary inscriptions" found by Macalister and by the later excavators belong to this period and suggest that Gezer was now part of a private estate. These inscriptions, cut into the bedrock, read in Hebrew, *tehûm gezer,* "boundary of Gezer"; and in Greek, *Alkiou,* "belonging to Alkios," presumably the owner of the estate.

After that, Gezer was virtually abandoned, the only later material being Macalister's several Byzantine tombs and a few medieval and Crusader remains in the vicinity.

[*See also the biography of Macalister.*]

BIBLIOGRAPHY

Dever, William G. "Excavations at Gezer." *Biblical Archaeologist* 30.2 (1967): 47–62.

Dever, William G., et al. *Gezer I: Preliminary Report of the 1964–66 Seasons.* Jerusalem, 1970.

Dever, William G., et al. "Further Excavations at Gezer." *Biblical Archaeologist* 34.4 (1971): 94–132.

Dever, William G., et al. *Gezer II: Preliminary Report of the 1967–70 Seasons in Fields I and II.* Jerusalem, 1974.

Dever, William G. "Solomonic and Assyrian 'Palaces' at Gezer." *Israel Exploration Journal* 35 (1985): 217–230.

Dever, William G., et al. *Gezer IV: The 1969–71 Seasons in Field VI, the "Acropolis."* Jerusalem, 1986.

Dever, William G. "Late Bronze Age and Solomonic Defenses at Gezer: New Evidence." *Bulletin of the American Schools of Oriental Research,* no. 262 (May 1986): 9–34.

Dever, William G. "Further Evidence on the Date of the Outer Wall at Gezer." *Bulletin of the American Schools of Oriental Research,* no. 289 (1993): 33–54.

Gitin, Seymour. *Gezer III: A Ceramic Typology of the Late Iron II, Persian, and Hellenistic Periods at Tell Gezer.* Jerusalem, 1990.

Lance, H. Darrell. "Gezer in the Land and in History." *Biblical Archaeologist* 30.2 (1967): 34–47.

Macalister, R. A. S. *The Excavation of Gezer, 1902–1905 and 1907–1909.* 3 vols. London, 1912.

Reich, Ronny, and Baruch Brandl. "Gezer under Assyrian Rule." *Palestine Exploration Quarterly* 117 (January–June 1985): 41–54.

Schwartz, Joshua. "Once More on the 'Boundary of Gezer' Inscriptions and the History of Gezer and Lydda at the End of the Second Temple Period." *Israel Exploration Journal* 40.1 (1990): 47–57.

Seger, Joe D. *Gezer V: The Field I Caves.* Jerusalem, 1988.

WILLIAM G. DEVER

GEZER CALENDAR. The so-called calendar text, discovered at Tel Gezer in 1908, is a showpiece of early Hebrew inscriptions, in spite of various linguistic problems. The text does constitute a "calendar," in the sense that it outlines the principal agricultural activities over a twelve-month period; however, it names the months only by their characteristic activities and presents some activities as spanning two months.

This brief text, inscribed rather roughly on a limestone plaque (see figure 1), may be translated as follows: "Two months of ingathering [lit., its two months are ingathering], two months of sowing, two months of late sowing, one lean more positively in the direction of a Phoenician classification: the forms {w} (*yrḥw*) and {ø} (*yrḥ*) for the third-person masculine dual(/plural); third-person masculine singular pronominal suffixes are characteristic of early Byblian (the feature is as yet unattested in Northern Hebrew), while the proleptic use of these suffixes is more characteristic of Phoenician than of Hebrew (Pardee, 1987, p. 139, n. 20; add to the bibliography cited there Honeyman, 1953, and Rainey, 1983, p. 630).

On the lower left corner of the calendar is a partially preserved word generally taken as a personal name, perhaps that of the author/scribe: {'*by* [. . .]}. Some reconstruct the name as Yahwistic (e.g., Albright, 1943, p. 22), but the elements {'b} and {-y-} also appear in Phoenician names; the correct reconstruction of the name and the ethnic identification of its bearer are thus unknown.

[*See also* Gezer; Hebrew Language and Literature; *and* Phoenician-Punic.]

BIBLIOGRAPHY

Albright, William F. "The Gezer Calendar." *Bulletin of the American Schools of Oriental Research*, no. 92 (1943): 16–26. Cogent remarks on archaeological and paleographic dating, with bibliography. One cannot, however, accept that the inscription "is good biblical Hebrew" (p. 22).

Borowski, Oded. *Agriculture in Iron Age Israel.* Winona Lake, Ind., 1987. Gezer text discussed in the broader context of the agriculture of the time, drawing parallels with the Bible, archaeological finds in Syria-Palestine, and Egyptian representations of agricultural activities.

Dahood, Mitchell. "Some Eblaite and Phoenician Month Names." In *Atti del I Congresso internazionale di studi fenici e punici, Roma, 5–10 Novembre 1979*, vol. 2, pp. 595–598. Rome, 1983.

Dalman, Gustaf. "Notes on the Old Hebrew Calendar-Inscription from Gezer." *Palestine Exploration Fund Quarterly Statement* (1909): 118–119. Parallel with agricultural practices and Arabic terms in use at Dalman's time.

Gray, G. B., Mark Lidzbarski, and E. J. Pilcher. "An Old Hebrew Calendar-Inscription from Gezer." *Palestine Exploration Fund Quarterly Statement* (1909): 26–34. The excavator, R. A. S. Macalister, entrusted the *editio princeps* to three scholars, each of whom produced an independent reading and interpretation.

Honeyman, A. M. "The Syntax of the Gezer Calendar." *Journal of the Royal Asiatic Society* (1953): 53–58. Correct analysis of the forms *yrḥw* and *yrḥ*.

Naveh, Joseph. *An Early History of the Alphabet.* Jerusalem, 1982.

Pardee, Dennis. "Review of John C. L. Gibson, *Textbook of Syrian Semitic Inscriptions*." *Journal of Near Eastern Studies* 46 (1987): 137–142.

Rainey, Anson F. "Review of Ziony Zevit, *Ancient Hebrew Epigraphs*." *Journal of Biblical Literature* 102 (1983): 629–634.

Ronzevalle, Sébastien. "La tablette hébraïque de Gézer." *Mélanges de la Faculté Orientale de l'Université St. Joseph* 5 (1911): 90*–104*. Contains two excellent new photographs (pl. 16), each from a different lighting angle, and a photograph of the reverse (pl. 17).

DENNIS PARDEE

GEZER CALENDAR. Figure 1. *The Gezer Calendar*. (Courtesy ASOR Archives)

month of chopping flax, one month of barley harvest, one month of harvest and completion [i.e., the wheat harvest ends the grain-harvesting season], two months of grape cutting, one month of summer fruits." The precise meaning of some of the terms is uncertain, but it is clear that the text refers to a sequence of twelve months, beginning with the fall equinox.

In spite of imprecise stratigraphic results from the early excavations at Gezer, the archaeological and paleographic indicators agree on a date for this text of roughly 900 BCE (Albright, 1943). The script, however, as many scholars have remarked, shows no features characteristic of Hebrew (cf. Naveh, 1982, p. 65); the linguistic identification is therefore dependent on internal analysis. The text is generally classified with the Hebrew inscriptions, with one feature indicating a Northern Hebrew or Phoenician classification: the writing {qṣ}, "summer fruits," is unusual for Judean inscriptions, where {qyṣ} is expected, but it is characteristic of both Northern Hebrew (Borowski, 1987, pp. 43–44) and Phoenician (Dahood, 1983, pp. 597–598). Two other features

GHIRSHMAN, ROMAN (1895–1979), archaeologist who devoted his career to research in Afghanistan and Iran.

Born in Karkhov, Russia, Ghirshman left his country during the revolution and arrived in Paris in 1923, where he studied history and Orientalism at the Sorbonne and the École du Louvre.

Ghirshman worked at Tello in Iraq in 1930, and in 1931 was made director of the Louvre's new mission to Iran. There he worked at Tepe Giyan, near Nehavend, accompanied by his wife Tania, a dental surgeon, who became his collaborator as an illustrator and restorer. Between 1933 and 1937, Ghirshman explored two necropoleis from the second and first millennia BCE at Tepe Sialk, near Kachan.

His main research began after World War II, as director of the French archeological delegation in Iran. He excavated at Susa for twenty-one seasons, until 1967, establishing its stratigraphy from Islamic times until the end of the third millennium and contributing greatly to what is known of the Elamites and their culture. [See Susa; Elamites.] He simultaneously explored a temple city of the fourteenth century BCE at Chogha Zanbil, near Susa, with its ziggurat, a huge five-story tower of which only two stories remain. [See Chogha Zanbil.] In 1959–1960, the Iranian National Petroleum Company invited Ghirshman to dig at Kharg Island in the Persian Gulf, where he cleared a Greek temple, a Nestorian church, a Sasanian fire temple, and a mosque. Until the age of seventy-seven, Ghirshman excavated in the Bakhtiari Mountains, at Bard-i Nishandeh and Masjid-i Suleiman, Parthian and Sasanian period sites, respectively.

Ghirshman published the results of his excavations as well as other scholarly works, including twenty-three volumes and more than two hundred articles in scientific reviews. He was a member of the Institut de France and of several international academies and received many honors. He exhibited great energy and enthusiasm up until his death, in Budapest, during an international congress.

BIBLIOGRAPHY

Ghirshman, Roman. *Iran from the Earliest Times to the Islamic Conquest.* Harmondsworth, 1954.

Ghirshman, Roman. *Persian Art, 249 B.C.–A.D. 651: The Parthian and Sassanian Dynasties.* New York, 1962.

Ghirshman, Roman. *Ancient Persia: From the Origins to Alexander the Great.* London and New York, 1964. This and the 1962 publication, first published in French, are fully illustrated and include many previously unpublished documents.

Ghirshman, Roman. *Tchoga-Zanbil (Dur Untash).* Vol. 1, *La Ziggourat;* vol. 2, *Temenos, Temples, Palais, Tombes.* Mémoires de la délégation archéologique en Iran, vols. 39 and 40. Paris, 1966–1968.

Ghirshman, Roman. *Terrasses sacrées de Bard-è-Néchandeh et Masjid-i-Sülaiman.* Mémoires de la délégation archéologique en Iran, vol. 45. Paris, 1976.

Ghirshman, Tania. *Archéologue malgré moi: Vie quotidienne d'une Mission Archéologique en Iran.* Neuchâtel and Paris, 1970. Daily life of an archaeological expedition as recorded by Ghirshman's wife between 1932 and 1967; includes a preface by the Sumerologist Samuel Noah Kramer.

AGNÈS SPYCKET

GHRUBBA, site located on the southern side of Wadi Nimrin in Jordan, about 2 km (1 mi.) west of the police station in the village of Shunah (South), on the main Amman-Jerusalem road (31°53′43″ N, 35°34′54″ E). The extent of the site has not been determined, but it is estimated to be about one meter high.

Soundings were made at the site in 1953 by James Mellaart (1956, pp. 14–40). In 1976 the site was resurveyed by Moawiyah Ibrahim, James Sauer, and Khair Yassine under auspices of the Department of Antiquities of Jordan, the University of Jordan, and the American Center of Oriental Research (Yassine et al., 1988, pp. 191, 194) and the collected material studied by Zeidan Kafafi (Kafafi, 1982). In his soundings Mellaart observed sixteen layers. Layers 1–4 had been partially disturbed by a modern burial and produced pottery sherds related to the Ghassulain culture. Sealed by these layers was a pit dug through a layer of unstable gravel down to the underlying soft limestone. The pit appeared oval in shape, measured about 5 × 3 m, and is 1.80 m deep. Inside this pit twelve layers (5–16) of ash and gravel were registered. Only one floor (layer 15a) was recorded.

The pottery from layers 5–16 was mostly handmade. Mellaart distinguished four categories: plain or coarse ware; painted and incised ware; burnished ware; and painted ware. In the plain and coarse ware collection, bowls with knobs and with flaring sides, as well as small jars with lug handles, were noted. Straw temper was visible only in the case of a few coarse white bowls (Mellaart, 1956, p. 30). Bow-rim jars similar to those from Jericho VIII were found in layers 12, 14, and 16 at Ghrubba (Mellaart, 1956, fig. 4, pp. 40–42). The second group was characterized by a red or brown paint or wash covering the vessels, as well as incised decoration—a horizontal band below the rim of the bowls or at the base of the neck of the jars. In the case of jugs the decoration passed through the opening of the loop handles. Below the horizontal band were usually zigzag or herringbone decorations. The painted ware is the most common at Ghrubba. It was handmade and well fired. The surface of the vessels is buff, pink, or whitish, and evidently no slip was used. The decoration consists mostly of triangles, chevrons, diagonal parallel lines, and dots. Mellaart argued that Ghrubba represented a different painted pottery tradition than that at Jericho, comparing it with Hassunian Archaic painted ware (Mellaart, 1956, p. 31).

Because Ghrubba yielded some pottery forms distinct from those of Jericho IX and at Sha'ar ha-Golan and that reflect contact with the earliest painted pottery at Mersin and 'Amuq B, Mellaart placed Ghrubba in the later phase of the Hassuna period and earlier than Jericho IX and the Yarmukian (Mellaart, 1956, pp. 31–33). While Ghrubba has its own characteristics, it may not be earlier than Jericho IX and Sha'ar ha-Golan, however. For instance, bow-rim jars like those from Jericho VIII have been found at Ghrubba. However, when Mellaart excavated at Ghrubba in 1953, no other sites related to the Neolithic and Chalcolithic periods except Shaʿar ha-Golan, Jericho, and Ghassul had been excavated in the Jordan Valley. A. M. T. Moore, on the other hand, has suggested that Ghrubba should be related to the Early Chalcolithic period and not the Neolithic, stressing that the pottery Mellaart published strongly resembles the Ghassulian (Moore, 1973, p. 60). This argument was not confirmed by the pottery collected during the 1976 survey (see above), which resembled the pottery of Late Neolithic (Kafafi, 1982, p. 200).

Based on the results of the excavations in the Jordan Valley at Munhata (Perrot, 1964, 1966), Tell Tsaf, and Abu Hamid (Dollfus and Kafafi, 1993) and in Jordan's hill country, at Abu Thawwab, Ghrubba is either a Yarmukian site or, like Abu Hamid, it is postclassical Yarmukian. Its painted pottery resembles that found at Abu Thawwab (Kafafi, unpublished), except that no "classical" incised or painted pottery was evident.

[*See also* Jordan Valley. *In addition, many of the sites mentioned are the subject of independent entries.*]

BIBLIOGRAPHY

Dollfus, Geneviève, and Zeidan A. Kafafi. "Recent Researches at Abu Hamid." *Annual of the Department of Antiquities of Jordan* 37 (1993): 241–262.

Kafafi, Zeidan A. "The Neolithic of Jordan (East Bank)." Ph.D. diss., Freie Universität, 1982.

Kafafi, Zeidan A. "Jebel Abu Thawwab (Er-Rumman) Excavations." Unpublished manuscript.

Mellaart, James. "The Neolithic Site of Ghrubba." *Annual of the Department of Antiquities of Jordan* 3 (1956): 24–40.

Moore, A. M. T. "The Late Neolithic in Palestine." *Levant* 5 (1973): 36–69.

Perrot, Jean. "Les deux premières campagnes de fouilles à Munhata, 1962–1963: Premiers résultats." *Syria* 41 (1964): 323–345.

Perrot, Jean. "La troisième campagne de fouilles à Munhata (1964)." *Syria* 43 (1966): 49–63.

Yassine, Khair, et al. "The East Jordan Valley Survey, 1976." In *Archaeology of Jordan: Essays and Reports,* edited by Khair Yassine, pp. 189–207. Amman, 1988.

ZEIDAN A. KAFAFI

GIBEAH. *See* Ful, Tell el-.

GIBEON. A site of some importance in the Bible, located approximately 9 km (5 mi) north of Jerusalem (35°11′ N, 31°51′ E; map reference 167.6 × 139.7). The best-known biblical references to Gibeon describe a battle there between the Israelites and the Amorites. The Israelites, led by Joshua and newly allied with the people of Gibeon, protected the city from an Amorite attack led by Adonizedek of Jerusalem. In the battle, Joshua drove back the Amorites and asked God to make the sun stand still at Gibeon until the Israelites were fully victorious (*Jos.* 10:9–14). Gibeon was first identified by the American explorer Edward Robinson in 1838, although two traveler's accounts had suggested the identification as early as 1666 and 1738. Robinson saw the modern Arabic name el-Jib as a corruption of the ancient town name of Gibeon. The identification was confirmed by the excavations carried out by James B. Pritchard for the University Museum of the University of Pennsylvania, between 1956 and 1962. During those excavations, thirty-one Iron Age jar handles were found, inscribed with the name *gbʿn* (Gibeon). A survey of the site carried out by the Palestine Exploration Fund was published in 1870, a plan of the water tunnel was published in 1889 by Conrad Schick of the PEF, and an Iron Age tomb was discovered and published in 1950 by Awni Dajani of the Jordanian Department of Antiquities. A recent survey, done by Hanan Eshel of the Hebrew University of Jerusalem in 1983–1984, documented additional Iron Age burial caves.

The University of Pennsylvania excavations at Gibeon revealed several periods of occupation. The earliest, on the top of the tell, dates to the Early Bronze Age. Unfortunately, much of this level was disturbed in both ancient and modern times, and little can be said about it. There are few occupational deposits but many tombs from the EB IV. The tombs consist of shafts cut into the limestone slope of the tell that lead to circular chambers containing the inhumation. Burial goods include ceramic vessels for food and drink, metal tools, and adornments for the deceased. Some of these tombs were reused for burials in the Middle Bronze II period and in the Late Bronze Age, when additional tombs were cut. A few remains of MB domestic architecture were found, but the main excavations on the tell concentrated on the Iron Age occupation. [*See* Shaft Tombs.]

Gibeon has a large and impressive water system that was built in two stages, both within the Iron Age. The first part of the system was probably begun in the Iron I period. It consists of a long spiral staircase dug to reach a deep pool of groundwater within the city walls. The second system was designed slightly later, perhaps to enhance the pool's water supply. This system involves a stepped tunnel whose mouth is inside the city. The tunnel was cut down to a water chamber that, in turn, had a feeder tunnel connecting it to an underground spring. The water chamber had another point of access in addition to the tunnels, in the form of a door that led outside the city walls and could be sealed in times of siege. [*See* Water Tunnels.]

A winery was discovered that belongs to the eighth and seventh centuries BCE. It contained many wine presses, channels, and basins, as well as sixty-three large vats, cut deep into the limestone. The vats were used as wine cellars for temperature control and once contained hundreds of storage jars as evidenced by the broken jar fragments as well as one complete jar that were found. Much of the wine produced at Gibeon was probably exported; many jar handles inscribed with the name *gbʿn* were found in this industrial area.

There is very little evidence for occupation at Gibeon between the end of the Iron Age and the Roman period. In the Roman period, however, although the site was reoccupied it was not fortified. Excavation of the later remains revealed baths and an elaborate columbarium tomb.

BIBLIOGRAPHY

Eshel, Hanan. "The Late Iron Age Cemetery of Gibeon." *Israel Exploration Journal* 37 (1987): 1–17.
Pritchard, James B. *The Water System of Gibeon.* Philadelphia, 1961.
Pritchard, James B. *Gibeon Where the Sun Stood Still.* Princeton, 1962.
Pritchard, James B. *The Bronze Age Cemetery at Gibeon.* Philadelphia, 1963.
Pritchard, James B. *Winery, Defenses, and Soundings at Gibeon.* Philadelphia, 1964.
Pritchard, James B. "Gibeon." In *The New Encyclopedia of Archaeological Excavations in the Holy Land,* vol. 2, pp. 511–514. Jerusalem and New York, 1993.

RACHEL S. HALLOTE

GILAT, a Chalcolithic commercial and cultic center located in the northern Negev desert, along the eastern bank of Naḥal Patish, about 20 km (12 mi.) northwest of Beersheba. The site (about 10 ha, or 25 acres) is comprised of a large mound (about 8 acres) that rises more than 2.5 m above some 7 ha (17 acres) of surrounding plain.

Gilat was discovered in the early 1950s by David Alon, who, based on the surface discovery of hundreds of artifacts characteristic of the Chalcolithic period (c. 4500–3700 BCE), first recognized the site's archaeological significance. Under the sponsorship of the Israel Antiquities Authority, Alon conducted three seasons of excavations between 1975 and 1977. More recently, in 1987 and from 1990 to 1992, excavations were carried out on behalf of the Hebrew Union College (HUC) in Jerusalem under the direction of Thomas E. Levy and Alon. Largely as a result of its proximity to both the coastal plain and the inland foothills, Gilat served as one of the earliest ritual centers in western Palestine. Similarly, its development as a regional center of exchange can be explained by its central location among the area's large Chalcolithic village sites—south of Gerar, west of Abu Hof, east of the Naḥal Besor sites, and north of the Beersheba valley sites, among them, Shiqmim, Abu Maṭar, Ḥorvat Beṭer, and Bir es-Safadi. Because of this commercial and ritual importance, Gilat held a special status in Israel's protohistory.

In the 1970s, working in the eastern portion of the site, the excavators uncovered an area of approximately 450 sq m and delineated four main strata. The HUC excavations uncovered an area of about 800 sq m, with seven occupa-

tional phases distinguished. All architectural remains from the latest occupational level (stratum I) were destroyed by plowing (the site is in the field of Moshav Gilat), as was stratum II in the east; in the west, however, this stratum was subdivided into subphases IIa, IIb, and IIc (the last labeled stratum III in the first published reports). Remains from stratum III were found all over the site, whereas those from stratum IV, the earliest occupational level, were uncovered in only a few places, in probes dug into a small Pleistocene hill rising above the plain.

An unusually large number of exotic artifacts made of nonlocal materials were uncovered during the HUC excavations. Among these finds were 58 violin-shaped figurines—more than at any other site in the eastern Mediterranean—54 enigmatic tokens, 82 stone palettes, 54 pendants, some 200 fenestrated stands (incense burners) made of ceramic and basalt, 150 spindle whorls, 28 mace heads, and a host of additional objects made of obsidian, green stone, and other materials. Intrasite spatial analysis has not revealed a statistical correlation between the finished stone objects and the raw materials found on site, an indication that the violin-shaped figurines, palettes, fenestrated stands, and other exotica were manufactured elsewhere and brought to the site in finished form. Petrographic studies of the unique Gilat "torpedo" jars also confirmed nonlocal production. These findings, viewed in conjunction with the site's location, indicate that Gilat controlled access to grazing lands on the Negev coastal plain, access that seasonal herders gained by bringing offerings to the sanctuary. Objects found in connection with the architectural remains in stratum IIc suggest a variety of cultic activities. About seventy of the cult objects were discovered in the stratum's main cult room, designated room A (about 3 × 4.5 m). The most important of these finds were the Gilat Ram and Lady. The other finds with cultic significance were recovered in the courtyards linked to this room.

Well-preserved architecture was excavated in the western part of stratum IIb: the remains of three broadroom buildings; three circular, mud-brick and stone platforms; and a large, mud-brick lined silo. A building complex from stratum IIc was exposed in the eastern sector. The stratum IIb structures, which also produced many ritual objects, were connected by a hard mud-brick floor about 10 cm thick. After stratum IIb was abandoned, much of the area was prepared for new construction (stratum IIa)—numerous structures that were short-lived.

BIBLIOGRAPHY

Alon, David. "Two Cult Vessels from Gilat." *'Atiqot* 11 (1976): 116–118.
Alon, David. "A Chalcolithic Temple at Gilath." *Biblical Archaeologist* 40 (1977): 63–65.
Alon, David, and Thomas E. Levy. "Gilat." *Israel Exploration Journal* 37 (1987): 283–84.

Alon, David, and Thomas E. Levy. "Gilat—1987." *Excavations and Surveys in Israel* 7–8 (1988–1989): 63–64.

Alon, David and Thomas E. Levy. "The Archaeology of Cult and the Chalcolithic Sanctuary at Gilat." *Journal of Mediterranean Archaeology* 2 (1989): 163–221.

Amiran, Ruth. "Note on the Gilat Vessels." *'Atiqot* 11 (1976): 119–120.

Frankel, David. "A Possible Relative of the Gilat Woman." *Israel Exploration Journal* 27 (1977): 38–39.

Gilead, Isaac, and Yuval Goren. "Petrographic Analyses of Fourth Millennium B.C. Pottery and Stone Vessels from the Northern Negev, Israel." *Bulletin of the American Schools of Oriental Research,* no. 275 (1989): 5–14.

Levy, Thomas E. "The Chalcolithic Period: Archaeological Sources for the History of Palestine." *Biblical Archaeologist* 49 (1986): 82–108.

Mozel, Ilana. "A Male Partner for the Gilat Woman." *Tel Aviv* 6 (1979): 26–27.

Rowan, Yorke M., and Thomas E. Levy. "Proto-Canaanean Blades of the Chalcolithic Period." *Levant* 26 (1994): 167–74.

Yadin, Yigael. "Note on the Violin-Shaped Figurine from Gilat." *'Atiqot* 11 (1976): 121.

THOMAS E. LEVY

GILEAD, region named in the Hebrew Bible, located on the rocky, and in those days forested, parts of the eastern side of the Jordan River and the Dead Sea, roughly between the Arnon River (Wadi el-Mujib) in the south and the Yarmuk River in the north. The Jabbok River (Nahr ez-Zerqa) divides the area in two: "half the Gilead" is used to cite both (*Dt.* 3:12; *Jos.* 12:2–5). The inhabitants are called Gileadites (*Nm.* 26:30, 36:1; *1 Chr.* 7:17) and belonged to the Israelite tribes of Reuben, Gad, and half of Manasseh. Machir, a son of Manasseh, is the "father of Gilead" (*Jos.* 17:1). The word-stem *gl'd* is to be found in Ugaritic (Gordon, Texts 170 and 301), but the geographic connection is not well defined. In Akkadian, *ga-al'a-⌈a⌉-(za)* (III R 10.2; K 2649) is bordering Aram, possibly Ramoth Gilead, during the reign of Tiglath-Pileser III. The name Gilead is certainly preserved in the Arabic Khirbet Ǧel'ad (or Jel'ad), a site in the area of es-Salt.

Culturally, Gilead is related to Cisjordan. There is evidence of *homo sapiens* in the area about two million years ago (at Abu el-Khas, Wadi Ḥammeh, and Pella). The prehistoric finds are comparable with those at 'Ubeidiya for the Early Paleolithic period. In Mesolithic times, nomadic hunters became sedentary and food producing and were influenced by the Natufian culture.

In the Pottery Neolithic period (5500–4500 BCE), climatic conditions changed in Palestine. Transjordan gradually dried out and became desertic and settlers moved to new agricultural communities. They built circular, and then later, rectangular, houses arranged in communities, such as at 'Ain Ghazal in Amman. In their burial practices they prepared the skulls of the dead with plaster and shells as at Jericho. The following period, the Chalcolithic (4000–3200 BCE), is substantiated at Teleilat el-Ghassul and in the Go-

lan. Ghassul is then a fortified village with dwellings clustered around courtyards measuring 15 × 5 m, made of hand-modeled, sun-dried mud bricks. Of special interest are the buildings' geometric wall paintings in white, black, red, and brown.

The beginning of city life appears in the Early Bronze Age (3200–2100 BCE). On the Bab edh-Dhra' plain and in Khirbet Iskander, Pella, and Khirbet ez-Zeraqun, fortified cities with irrigation systems were founded. More than 200,000 graves have been discovered at Bab edh-Dhra', and at Zeraqun a cultic area with the same layout as the one at contemporary Megiddo was found. Parts of central and northern Gilead were populated in the Middle Bronze Age (1900–1550 BCE), during which time Pella was heavily fortified. The Late Bronze Age (1550–1200 BCE) has been regarded as a dark age in Transjordan. However, at Irbid and Tell el-Fukhar prosperous towns existed with defense walls built with large boulders and cobble chinking. Temple architecture is known from Umm ed-Dananir and Amman, and there was a citadel at Lehun in the south.

The transitional period into the Iron Age is represented at Tell el-Fukhar, which was then transformed into an unfortified settlement on large stone pavements. Remains of pillared buildings and sherds of collar-rim jars belong to this period. In the Iron Age (1200–600 BCE), according to the Bible, many dramatic events took place in Gilead: King Saul rescued Jabesh Gilead (*1 Sm.* 11), and his son Ishba'al governed his kingdom from Maḥanaim (*2 Sm.* 2:8), a town at Wadi Zerqa, in an area densely settled throughout the period; King David besieged his son Absalom in the forest of Ephraim (*2 Sm.* 18:6); and King Solomon cast the pillars for the Jerusalem Temple in the Jordan Valley (*1 Kgs.* 18:6). There are, however, no Iron II A–B remains at Tell el-Fukhar. Surveys in the Ḥesban and Madaba regions show that there was an agricultural expansion throughout the Iron Age, using land belonging to the former LB towns along the King's Highway. The "balm of Gilead" was famous (*Jer.* 8:22; 46:11). Inscriptions in Moabite, Ammonite, and Aramaic dialects are found at Dibon/Dhiban (the Mesha Stone) at Tell Deir 'Alla (the Balaam texts), Amman (the Siran bottle), and Tell el-Mazar and Tell es-Sa'idiyeh (ostraca).

The Persian period is represented by a square building at Tell es-Sa'idiyeh in the Jordan Valley. The same architectural style appears in the Hellenistic period at some sites. At 'Iraq el-Amir the Tobiad Hyrcanus built a fortress he called Tyros, and there is evidence of a Hellenistic villa at Tell el-Fukhar. Gilead may not have been ruled by the Nabateans, whose culture straddled the Hellenistic and Roman periods, but their main caravan roads passed it. During the Roman period some towns of the Decapolis were situated in Gilead (Gadara, Pella, and perhaps Tell el-Ḥusn). Well-built bridges and roads can still be seen, and the Via Nova Trajana was not far away. Many graffiti written in Safaitic script have been found, especially to the east. In the Byzantine period, the population increased and the towns prospered. Gadara's mosaics and the churches in the Madaba region with their mosaic floors and original motifs (including the mosaic map of ancient Palestine) reflect their great wealth.

The Crusaders seem not to have been interested in Gilead. However, in the Ayyubid period (1174–1263 CE), castles were built at Rabadh and es-Salt. Iron was mined and smelted at Mugharat el-Warda.

[*Many of the sites mentioned are the subject of independent entries.*]

BIBLIOGRAPHY

Boling, Robert G. *The Early Biblical Community in Transjordan.* Sheffield, 1988.

Hadidi, Adnan, and Ghazi Bisheh, eds. *Studies in the History and Archaeology of Jordan.* 4 vols. Amman, 1982–1992.

Homès-Fredericq, Denys, and J. Basil Hennessy, eds. *Archaeology of Jordan.* 2 vols. Louvain, 1986–1989.

Homès-Fredericq, Denys, and H. J. Franken, eds. *Pottery and Potters, Past and Present: 7000 Years of Ceramic Art in Jordan.* Tübingen, 1986.

McGovern, Patrick E. *The Late Bronze and Early Iron Ages of Central Transjordan: The Baqʿah Valley Project, 1977–1981.* University Museum, Monograph 65. Philadelphia, 1986.

Ottosson, Magnus. *Gilead: Tradition and History.* Lund, 1969.

Specific citations of original texts and inscriptions refer to the following works: C. H. Gordon, *Ugaritic Textbook: Grammar, Texts in Transliteration, Cuneiform Selections, Glossary, Indices* (Analecta Orientalia, 38; Rome, 1965); III R 10.2 refers to H. C. Rawlinson, *The Cuneiform Inscriptions of Western Asia* (London, 1870), vol. 3, pl. 10, no. 2; K 2649 refers to *Cuneiform Texts from Babylonian Tablets in the British Museum* (London, 1918), pt. 35, pl. 39, K 2649, rev. 1. 3.

MAGNUS OTTOSSON

GILOH (map reference 165 × 125), Iron Age site approximately 2 acres in area located in a southern suburb of modern Jerusalem that bears the same name. Giloh is located on a high ridge 830 m above sea level, overlooking the entire Jerusalem and Bethlehem area. Small-scale salvage excavations were directed here between 1978 and 1982 by Amihai Mazar, on behalf of the Institute of Archaeology of the Hebrew University of Jerusalem and the Israel Department of Antiquities. The ancient name of the site is unknown; it should not be confused with biblical Giloh, which must be located south of Hebron (*Jos.* 15:51). It may be the Baʿal-Perasim mentioned in *2 Samuel* 5:20 or the Har-Perasim in *Isaiah* 28:21.

Giloh is one of the few Iron Age I sites excavated in the central hill country. It was abandoned after the Iron Age and subsequently destroyed by erosion and human activity. A shallow defensive wall surrounded at least its southern part. A solid square stone structure (11.58 × 11.15 m) at its northern part may be the foundation of a building, perhaps a fortified tower.

The site was divided by long walls into large, subsidiary areas that may be animal pens. Dwellings were constructed along the defense wall and near some of the inner dividing walls. It thus appears that the settlement was divided into family units consisting of dwellings attached to animal pens. The one house that was excavated appears to be an early version of the pillared houses that are typical of the Iron Age in Palestine—an early example of a four-room house. [*See* Four-room House.] No cisterns were found at the site, so that water was probably transported from springs located in the Sorek Valley farther to the north. It is estimated that about a dozen families settled here, living on stock breeding and some agriculture. The enclosure wall and the solid tower suggest that the settlement faced challenges to its security, which its proximity to Jebusite Jerusalem may have created.

Giloh's Iron I material culture resembles that at other central hill country sites. Collared-rim store jars, small storage jars, and cooking pots comprise most of the rather limited ceramic assemblage. The pottery is made in a local Canaanite tradition, but no decorated pottery was found. The site appears to have been settled in the twelfth century BCE and may have been abandoned in the eleventh.

The inhabitants' socioeconomic status is similar to that apparent at many other Iron I sites in the hill country. It has been suggested that these settlers were part of an Iron I wave of settlement in the hill country that is commonly identified with the appearance of the Israelites in this region.

In the Iron II (8th–7th centuries BCE), an isolated, large (10 × 10 m) tower was constructed at the summit of the site. Its massive stone walls created a podium on which an unpreserved superstructure would have been constructed. The tower was probably part of Jerusalem's defense system. It would have been used for observation and to give warning to the city by fire signals.

BIBLIOGRAPHY

Mazar, Amihai. "An Early Israelite Settlement Site Near Jerusalem." *Israel Exploration Journal* 31 (1981): 1–36.

Mazar, Amihai. "Iron Age I and II Towers at Giloh and the Israelite Settlement." *Israel Exploration Journal* 40 (1990): 77–101.

AMIHAI MAZAR

GIRSU AND LAGASH, urban centers, along with Nina-Sirara, in the Sumerian city-state of Lagash in ancient Mesopotamia that also comprised several smaller settlements. Girsu (modern Telloh) was located at 31°31′ N, 46°12′ E; Lagash city (modern al-Hiba) at 31°25′ N, 46°24′ E; and Nina-Sirara (modern Zurghul) at 31°21′ N, 46°35′ E. Inscriptions from Telloh identify the site as the ancient city of Girsu in the state of Lagash, while excavation and survey have enabled identification of al-Hiba as Lagash City and Zurghul as Nina-Sirara. Inscriptions and other archaeological evidence have demonstrated the great importance of Lagash, particularly during the later Early Dynastic and immediately post-Akkadian periods. The three main cities of Lagash have received varying amounts of archaeological investigation.

Girsu (Modern Telloh). The mounds of Telloh, ancient Girsu, cover an area of more than 100 ha (247 acres), rising to a height of 15 m. They are located approximately halfway between the Tigris and Euphrates Rivers. The site is made up of a series of adjacent mounds that in ancient times were connected by a substantial waterway to al-Hiba and Zurghul to the south. Telloh was the first Sumerian site ever to undergo archaeological investigation. Encouraged by local reports of inscribed statuary, the French vice-consul at Basra, Ernest de Sarzec, conducted a series of campaigns at Telloh from 1877 to 1900. His spectacular discoveries, the first excavated evidence of Sumerian art and culture, caused a sensation when exhibited in Paris in the 1880s. In 1879, Hormuzd Rassam excavated at Telloh for three days in de Sarzec's absence. Subsequent excavations at Telloh, all French, were undertaken by Gaston Cros (1903–1909), Henri de Genouillac (1929–1931), and André Parrot (1931–1933), amounting to a total of twenty field seasons. Between legitimate field seasons Telloh suffered badly from illicit excavations, especially prior to 1900, which produced up to forty thousand cuneiform texts from tell V, principally of the Ur III period. There have been no excavations at Telloh since 1933.

Little is known of Telloh's prehistory, beyond the presence of Ubaid period pottery and other artifacts in the lower levels of de Genouillac's large sounding on tell K. Many objects appeared higher up in this sounding, including cylinder and stamp seals, metalwork, and pottery of both the Uruk and Jemdet Nasr periods, often as deliberate deposits within graves. Very few remains dated to Early Dynastic I and II have been identified at Telloh. It is not until the Early Dynastic III period that the importance of the site comes into focus, helped by significant finds of inscribed material. Many details, however, remain obscure, partly because of poor excavation standards. The Early Dynastic III texts from Telloh survive principally in the form of royal inscriptions giving details of building projects, irrigation works, and warfare. From these texts something of the political history of the state of Lagash and its neighbors can be reconstructed from roughly 2550–2350 BCE, during which time, at least, the city of Girsu was the capital city of Lagash State.

Lagash. The earliest attested rulers of Lagash state are Lugalsha-engur, a contemporary of Mesalim, king of Kish, and Enhegal, both of whom date to the early part of the Early Dynastic III period. Royal inscriptions at Telloh from about 2500 BCE attest the existence of nine successive rulers, constituting the first dynasty of Lagash. Surprisingly, this dynasty does not feature in the Sumerian king list, despite its considerable achievements in the late Early Dynastic period. The first of these rulers, Ur-Nanshe, tells of his many building projects in Lagash, some involving the transport of tim-

ber by ships of Dilmun (the modern island of Bahrain) from distant foreign lands. Ur-Nanshe also provides accounts of his wars against other Sumerian city-states, such as Ur and Umma. Conflict with Umma, in particular, was to continue more or less unabated for centuries thereafter, caused by dispute over territory located between the two city-states. Few texts survive from the time of the next ruler, Akurgal, but his successor, Eanatum, has left a substantial record of his activities. Again the Lagash-Umma border conflict figures large in Eanatum's inscriptions, most spectacularly on the Stela of the Vultures monument. Other texts tell of his defeat of Elam, Uruk, Ur, Akshak, Subartu, and Mari, an indication of far-ranging military achievements that to some extent presage those of Sargon of Akkad some 150 years later. More building activities are attested in the inscriptions of Enanatum I, while his successor, Enmetena, tells of continued conflict with Umma. At the same time, the inscriptions of Enmetena mention interstate relations, including "establishing brotherhood," between Lagash and Uruk, Larsa and Badtabira, rare hints of the pattern of shifting alliances that is likely to have characterized Sumerian city-state politics at that time. Inscriptions of the next three rulers, Enanatum II, Enentarzi, and Lugalanda, relate to temple construction. The last ruler of the first dynasty of Lagash, Uruinimgina (also known as Urukagina), left many interesting inscriptions, not only relating to his prodigious building feats and strife with Umma, but also telling of his social and religious reforms, implemented, he asserts, at the command of the chief god of Lagash, Ningirsu. Contemporary texts from the Bau Temple at Girsu indicate the wide range of economic activities engaged in by a Sumerian temple. In about 2,350 BCE, Uruinimgina was defeated by Lugalzagesi of Umma, immediately prior to the conquest of all Sumer by Sargon of Akkad.

In spite of the wealth of historical information about the Early Dynastic III period from excavations at Telloh, much less is known of this period than might have been the case: inadequate excavation techniques failed to place the inscribed material within any meaningful architectural contexts. Indeed, the excavators of Telloh identified very few Early Dynastic III buildings. Two small structures, the Construction Inférieure and the Maison des Fruits, are probably religious buildings dating to Ur-Nanshe and earlier. Of the artifacts from this period, the inscribed Stela of the Vultures is an unquestioned masterpiece of Sumerian art, showing on one face a scene of battle and conquest, with the king in a chariot, and on the other face a more mythological scene of the king with a lion-headed eagle. Inscribed stone wall plaques of Ur-Nanshe also display scenes of royal activities. Other important artifacts include inscribed copper foundation figurines, copper daggers and animal heads, and an impressive silver vase of Enmetena engraved with cultic scenes and dedicated by him to Ningirsu.

Of the subsequent Akkadian period (c. 2350–2230 BCE)

GIRSU AND LAGASH. *Shepherd carrying a lamb.* Sumerian terracotta figure; early second millennium. Musée du Louvre, Paris. (Erich Lessing/Art Resource, NY)

numbers of economic texts show that the city was active, while respecting the suzerainty of the city of Ur. A few texts indicate a low level of activity at the site in the subsequent Isin-Larsa and Old Babylonian periods, with scattered evidence of occupation through the late second and early first millennia BCE. In the second century BCE, during the Parthian period, Telloh enjoyed a brief revival. A ruler called Adadnadinahe constructed an impressive palace on tell A, whose inscribed bricks give his very Mesopotamian name in both Aramaic and Greek. The latest evidence of occupation at Telloh is in the form of Sasanian seals.

Al-Hiba. Located 25 km (16 mi.) southeast of Telloh is the mound of al-Hiba, ancient Lagash City. In area, al-Hiba is one of the largest mounds in the ancient Near East, reaching up to 600 hectares (1,482 acres) at its greatest extent, but with a maximum height of only 6 m. Study of inscriptions from al-Hiba and Telloh has established that al-Hiba's ancient name was Lagash City, at some time the capital of Lagash State, in a manner analogous to New York City, the capital of New York State. It is not known when al-Hiba was the capital of Lagash State, but it may have been during the earlier part of the Early Dynastic period, when al-Hiba reached its maximum size and before Telloh/Girsu assumed

there is almost no direct evidence from Telloh, apart from some inscriptions of Rimush, son of Sargon, and of Naram-Sin. For the century or so after the Akkadian period, artifacts and inscriptions from Telloh once more thrust the site into the historical limelight. At that time the city of Girsu appears to have attained its maximum extent. The most famous objects from this period are the statues of Gudea, many examples of which now grace the Louvre Museum in Paris. These statues consist of standing and seated representations, carved in diorite, of Gudea, ruler of Lagash. Inscriptions detail his achievements, largely in terms of building projects at Girsu, Lagash City, and Nina-Sirara, involving the procurement of raw materials from far-flung areas of the ancient Near East. During this period Lagash was clearly once more a city-state of major significance within Mesopotamia, but again the architectural remains at Telloh are disappointing. Little has been identified beyond platform structures, a series of circular brick pillars, and a large baked-brick structure that almost certainly functioned as a water regulator within the city.

Following the Akkadian period, the city of Girsu settled into a long, gentle decline. During the Ur III period large

GIRSU AND LAGASH. *Seated diorite figure of Gudea, king of Lagash.* Dated to 2120 BCE. Musée du Louvre, Paris. (Erich Lessing/Art Resource, NY)

the role of capital in Early Dynastic III times. The earliest excavations at al-Hiba were conducted in 1887 by a German expedition led by Robert Koldewey. Houses and streets were uncovered, but the abundance of intramural burials led Koldewey to conclude mistakenly that the entire site was a necropolis. Brief archaeological surveys in the region of al-Hiba were carried out in 1953 and 1965. A new program of excavations was initiated in 1968 by Donald P. Hansen for the Institute of Fine Arts of New York University and the Metropolitan Museum of Art. Six field seasons have been conducted.

As with Telloh, little is known of al-Hiba's prehistory, although there is some slight evidence for Ubaid and Uruk period occupation. The recent excavations have uncovered buildings, including a large oval precinct probably belonging to a temple, dating to the Early Dynastic I. Substantial deposits from this period remain to be excavated. Most of the excavated remains at al-Hiba date to the Early Dynastic III period, when much of the city was devoted to religious buildings: indeed, one ancient epithet of al-Hiba was Uruku, "holy city." The chief god of Lagash was Ningirsu, whose temple precinct was called the Bagara. Part of this complex has been located and excavated in the central western part of the mound. A building with a buttressed facade and baked-brick pavements contained within a curtain wall yielded inscribed objects dating to Eanatum, in the Early Dynastic III period, indicating that the building was part of the Bagara of Ningirsu. A nearby building contained features and texts that have led to its interpretation as a brewery for the Bagara complex. At the city's southwestern limit, another temple complex has been excavated: the Ibgal of Inanna. This complex takes the form of a building with elaborate foundations set within an oval precinct wall. Inscribed foundation figures identify the builders of the Ibgal as Urnanshe and Enanatum I, successor to Enantum. These temple structures are the earliest known Mesopotamian buildings that can with certainty be associated with historically known figures. Elsewhere on the mound a large administrative building was excavated that provided tablets and sealings dating to Eanatum and Enanatum I and an extremely early example of a die.

There appears to have been a widespread abandonment of al-Hiba at the end of the Early Dynastic III period, perhaps as a consequence of the conquest of Lagash state by Lugalzagesi of Umma. A few Akkadian texts have been found. On the highest central part of the mound there is evidence for the rebuilding of the Bagara by Gudea; an Ur III king, Amar-Sin, is also textually attested. There are traces of further rebuilding in the Isin-Larsa and Old Babylonian periods, with tablets dating to the ruler Sin-iddinam of Larsa (1849–1843 BCE). There is no evidence of any later occupation at al-Hiba.

Ten kilometers (6 mi.) southeast of al-Hiba is the smaller mound of Zurghul, ancient Nina-Sirara, which is 15 m high and covers some 65 hectares (161 acres). Koldewey carried out the only excavations at Zurghul, in 1887, prior to his work at al-Hiba. He also mistakenly concluded that Zurghul was an ancient necropolis. As at Telloh and al-Hiba, there is some evidence for the Ubaid and Uruk periods at Zurghul. The main occupation belongs to the Early Dynastic and immediately post-Akkadian periods, however, as indicated by finds of inscribed bricks and cones relating the construction undertaken by Enanatum I and Gudea, including the a temple for Nanshe.

[See also Isin; Larsa; and Ur.]

BIBLIOGRAPHY

Bauer, J., and Donald P. Hansen. "Lagaš." In *Reallexikon der Assyriologie*, vol. 6, pp. 419–430. Berlin, 1928–. Excellent account of textual (in German) and archaeological (in English) discoveries at al-Hiba–Lagash.

Biggs, Robert D. *Inscriptions from al-Hiba–Lagash: The First and Second Seasons*. Bibliotheca Mesopotamica, vol. 3. Malibu, 1976. Thorough account of inscriptions from al-Hiba discussed in their architectural contexts.

Buchanan, Briggs. "The Prehistoric Stamp Seal: A Reconsideration of Some Old Excavations." *Journal of the American Oriental Society* 87 (1967): 525–540. Detailed and critical reappraisal of H. de Genouillac's prehistoric sounding on tell K at Telloh, including, in particular, much information on the prehistoric burials.

Cooper, Jerrold S. *Reconstructing History from Ancient Inscriptions: The Lagash-Umma Border Conflict*. Sources from the Ancient Near East, vol. 2.1. Malibu, 1983. Sound historical analysis of an extended episode in the history of Lagash State.

Cooper, Jerrold S. *Presargonic Inscriptions*. Sumerian and Akkadian Royal Inscriptions, vol. 1. New Haven, 1986. Excellent English translations and discussion of all Pre-Sargonic royal inscriptions from Mesopotamia, with special focus on the Lagash evidence.

Crawford, Vaughn E. "Excavations in the Swamps of Sumer." *Expedition* 14.2 (1972): 12–20. Entertaining, general article on work at al-Hiba from 1968 and 1971.

Crawford, Vaughn E. "Lagash." *Iraq* 36 (1974): 29–35. Short, pithy account of the identification of al-Hiba as ancient Lagash City.

Falkenstein, A., and R. Opificius. "Girsu." In *Reallexikon der Assyriologie*, vol. 3, pp. 385–401. Berlin, 1928–. Good summary in German of textual and archaeological information from Telloh Girsu.

Hansen, Donald P. "Royal Building Activity at Sumerian Lagash in the Early Dynastic Period." *Biblical Archaeologist* 55 (1992): 206–211. Excellent firsthand account of archaeological results from al-Hiba, written by the site's most recent excavator.

Parrot, André. *Tello: Vingt campagnes de fouilles, 1877–1933*. Paris, 1948. Adequate survey of work by the French at Telloh, now complemented by the excavations at al-Hiba.

R. J. MATTHEWS

GISCHALA. *See* Gush Ḥalav.

GIZA, originally a village (30°00′ N, 31°13′ E) established in 642 CE on the west bank of the Nile opposite Fustat-Masr, has also come to designate the much larger ancient site of the fourth-dynasty (c. 2575–2134 BCE) Sphinx; the pyramids of Cheops, Chephren, and Mycerinus; and the adjacent cemeteries of nonroyal persons (see figure 1). Giza lies on a plateau, which is part of the Libyan mountain range in Egypt's western desert, and stretches approximately 1,000 m (3,280 ft.) from north to south and 2,000 m (6,562 ft.) from east to west. Bounded by two wadis (dried-up riverbeds) and dominating the surrounding plain from a height of some 40 m (131 ft.), Giza is one of the cemeteries of the Memphite region that forms an unbroken line from north to south between Abu Roash and Dahshur.

The site was already famous in antiquity, first in Greece and then in Rome. The pyramids were ranked as one of the wonders of the world. Arab historians and Western travelers had mentioned Giza in their writings since the Middle Ages, but more systematic explorations did not begin until the first half of the nineteenth century. Giovanni B. Caviglia, Henry

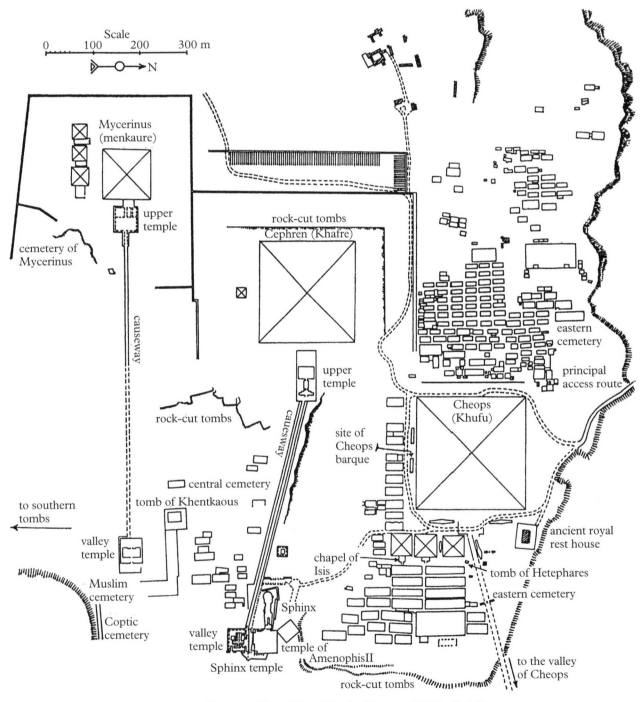

GIZA. Figure 1. *General plan of the site.* (Courtesy C. Zivie-Coche)

Salt, Giovanni B. Belzoni, R. W. Howard Vyse, John S. Perring, and Patrick Campbell uncovered and explored the pyramids' mortuary chambers, which had been ransacked in antiquity. Later C. Richard Lepsius, Auguste Mariette, W. M. Flinders Petrie, and Gaston Maspero excavated the royal complexes and *mastaba*s (tombs). In the earlier twentieth century, the plateau was divided into large concessions that were excavated by Austrians (Hermann Junker), Americans (George A. Reisner), and the Egyptian Antiquities Service (Pierre Lacau and Selim Hassan). Excavations continue and have yielded discoveries of a "satellite" pyramid next to the great pyramid of Cheops, even more *mastaba*s in the western cemeteries, and other tombs belonging to the workers and overseers who built the various pyramids at Giza. [*See the biographies of Mariette, Petrie, Maspero, and Reisner.*]

Although the most spectacular monuments belong to the fourth dynasty, Giza had a very long history, extending practically without interruption from predynastic times up to the Roman period. Located in southern Giza, the earliest monumental remains are the *mastaba*s from the first three dynasties. As evidenced by lithic objects and ceramics, however, the site had been occupied already in predynastic times. The toponym Ra-setau ("entrance to the underworld") probably dates to these initial periods of settlement. Mentioned in the *Pyramid Texts*, ancient Egypt's oldest extant funerary literature, Ra-setau was associated with a cult of Osiris that was maintained until the Late Period.

During the fourth dynasty the three pyramids of Cheops, Chephren, and Mycerinus and their families were erected rather rapidly, using methods of transportation and construction that remain uncertain. These architecturally flawless constructions, which served as royal tombs, had different plans for the burial chambers, which were uninscribed. (Not until the end of the fifth dynasty did the *Pyramid Texts* appear on the walls of royal burials.) Each of the three prominent pyramids at Giza comprises only parts of four elements in a complete royal funerary complex; the others, often drastically destroyed, were a "high" mortuary temple adjacent to the pyramid, a "low" temple in the valley, and an avenue or causeway connecting the two. Almost nothing remains of these temples at the Cheops complex, but the Chephren structures are relatively well preserved. The low temple in the valley was associated with rituals connected to the actual royal burials, whereas the high temple functioned as the site for the postmortem cult of the king. Large disassembled boats, which are known as "solar barques" because the king supposedly traveled in them across the sky in his role as sun god, were buried in hull-shaped pits cut in the rocky plateau. One of them was reassembled and housed in its own museum near its place of discovery.

Chephren added an important element to his pyramid complex by erecting a monumental sphinx with his own image for the head and the body of a lion. The Sphinx was carved from a single knoll of rock north of the pyramid causeway. It was preceded by granite temple, no doubt used for a solar cult. Impressive statues of Chephren were found in his valley temple.

Close family members of the pharaohs—children, mothers, and wives—were also buried on the Giza plateau. The royal wives were sometimes honored with small "satellite" pyramids but more often with decorated *mastaba*s. Hetepheres, wife of Snefru and mother of Cheops, was buried not far from her son's pyramid in an underground tomb that had no superstructure. In 1925 Reisner, director of a joint expedition sponsored by Harvard University and the Museum of Fine Arts, Boston, discovered Hetepheres' remarkable funerary furniture and jewelry that had escaped the depredations of ancient tomb robbers. Another queen, Khentkaues, had a mortuary complex including a vast tomb, albeit a commemorative pyramid was erected for her farther south at Abu Sir.

Cemeteries for private persons were carefully planned and built by royal decree around the royal pyramids. The large necropoleis to the east and west of the Cheops pyramid are particularly significant for their gridlike arrangement; the "streets" formed by the rectilinear plan of the tombs are especially visible in the eastern cemetery. The *mastaba*s found in all the private cemeteries are so named for the Arabic word for "bench." The elaborate design features a large rectangular superstructure covering rock-cut underground rooms, including cult chapels and burial chambers. The walls of these tombs were originally built for the kings' relatives or prominent members of the royal court and, like the tombs at Saqqara, were decorated with reliefs (usually painted) of remarkable quality, featuring scenes of daily life and practically devoid of religious symbols. Placed in the tombs were admirable statues of the deceased, such as the famous bust of Ankhkhaef, now in the Museum of Fine Arts, Boston, as well as the so-called reserve heads, which probably served as spares in case the real head of the mummy was damaged.

After the fourth dynasty, the pharaohs were buried elsewhere, but the private cemeteries continued to grow. Indeed some of the "reserve heads" from Giza burials date to the fifth or sixth dynasty or even a little later. After the end of the Old Kingdom, however, when burials were no longer assured by the king, the site was gradually abandoned. It was forgotten for several centuries; no documents from the Middle Kingdom have been found there.

With the rise of the New Kingdom (eighteenth–twentieth dynasties, c. 1550–1070), Giza benefited from the growth of the nearby city of Memphis, which was Egypt's administrative center. Residence of kings and princes, Memphis was of great economic, military, and artistic importance. Moreover, Heliopolitan religious traditions returned to favor with the growth of the cult of the sun god Amun at Thebes. For these two reasons, Giza became an important pilgrimage site, both for kings and crown princes (as revealed by the stelae or commemorative tablets of the pharaohs Amenophis II, Thutmosis IV, Seti I, and Rameses II) and for individuals, who left votive offerings. The focus of worship was the great Sphinx of Chephren, uncovered and protected from the desert sands by Thutmosis IV and known by the names Horemakhet ("Horus-in-the-Horizon") in Egyptian and, later, Harmachis in Greek. Chephren's image was reinterpreted as a form of the sun god, guarantor of royalty and divine protector, but also accessible to mere mortals. The Sphinx was also linked to a Syro-Palestinian deity, Hauron, worshiped in Egypt since the beginning of the eighteenth dynasty, along with Reshep and Astarte. Hauron appeared on stelae and in sculpture as a sphinx or hawk. At the same time, several texts indicate the continuation of the Osiris cult at Ra-setau, which had a chapel at least in the nineteenth and twentieth dynasties. Beginning in the eighteenth dynasty, the goddess Isis was also worshiped at Giza at her chapel not far from the pyramid of Cheops.

During the Third Intermediate period (twenty-first–twenty-fifth dynasties, c. 1070–712), under the reigns of Psusennes and Amenemope, the chapel of Isis, who was known thereafter as "the lady of the pyramids" and was thus the tutelary deity of Giza, was rebuilt and enlarged. There were several subsequent additions and reconstructions, particularly during the twenty-sixth dynasty (c. 664–525). A document of that time, an inscription, the so-called stela of the daughter of Cheops, names precisely the deities worshiped at Giza: Isis, lady of the pyramids; Hauron-Harmachis; and Osiris of Ra-setau. The cults of the ancient kings regained their prominence, the plateau of Giza being considered by the Egyptians as a historical site with a long and never-forgotten tradition. At the same time, Giza was once again used as a private cemetery. Ancient *mastabas* were reused and new tombs were built, particularly near the Chephren causeway. On such tomb contained the sarcophagi of the wife and a son of the twenty-sixth dynasty pharaoh Amasis (c. 570–526). The discovery of numerous inscribed *shawabti*s (small magical funerary figurines) provides a partial index of the persons buried in the necropolis. In Greek and Roman times, Giza was a prestigious destination for both tourists and religious pilgrims, who inscribed prayers on the paws of the Sphinx.

[*See also* Pyramids.]

BIBLIOGRAPHY

Edwards, I. E. S. *The Pyramids of Egypt.* Rev. ed. London, 1991.
Hassan, Selim. *Excavations at Giza.* 10 vols. Cairo, 1932–1960.
Hassan, Selim. *The Sphinx: Its History in the Light of Recent Excavations.* Cairo, 1949.
Jenkins, N. *The Boat beneath the Pyramid: King Cheops's Royal Ship.* London, 1980.
Junker, Hermann. *Giza: Grabungen auf dem Friedhof des Alten Reiches bei den Pyramiden von Giza.* 12 vols. Leipzig, 1929–1955.
Lauer, Jean-Philippe. *Les mystères des Pyramides.* New ed. Paris, 1989.
Lehner, Mark. *The Pyramid Tomb of Hetep-heres and the Satellite Pyramid of Khufu.* Mainz am Rhein, 1985.
Reisner, George A. *A History of the Giza Necropolis.* Vol. 1. Cambridge, Mass., 1942.
Reisner, George A., and William Stevenson Smith. *A History of the Giza Necropolis,* vol. 2, *The Tomb of Hetep-heres, the Mother of Cheops.* Cambridge, Mass., 1955.
Simpson, William Kelly, ed. *Giza Mastabas.* 5 vols. to date. Boston, 1974–1994.
Zivie-Coche, Christiane. *Giza au deuxième millénaire.* Cairo, 1976.
Zivie, Christiane M. "Gisa." In *Lexikon der Ägyptologie,* edited by Wolfgang Helck and Wolfhart Westendorf, vol. 2, cols. 602–613. Wiesbaden, 1977.
Zivie, Christiane M. "Sphinx." In *Lexikon der Ägyptologie,* edited by Wolfgang Helck and Wolfhart Westendorf, vol. 5, cols. 1139–1147. Wiesbaden, 1984.
Zivie-Coche, Christiane. *Giza au premier millénaire: Autour du temple d'Isis, dame des Pyramides.* Boston, 1991.

CHRISTIANE ZIVIE-COCHE
Translated from French by Monique Fecteau

GJERSTAD, EINAR (1897–1988), Swedish historian and classical archaeologist; father of Cypriot archaeology. Having first excavated in Cyprus from 1923 to 1924, Gjerstad published his results in his Ph.D. dissertation entitled *Studies on Prehistoric Cyprus* (1926). Here he presented a fundamental account of the prehistory of the island.

Gjerstad was leader of a Swedish expedition to Cyprus from 1927 to 1931 and excavated together with Alfred Westholm and Erik Sjöqvist at nearly twenty different sites covering the periods from Aceramic Neolithic to Late Roman. The greatest finds consisted of two thousand terra-cotta figures of the sixth century BCE at the cult center Ajia Irini and the Vouni palace, which dates to the fifth century BCE. The excavated material was published in the three-volume *Swedish Cyprus Expedition* (*SCE*, 1934–1937). The six volumes of conclusions, published together as *SCE* volume 4, appeared between 1948 and 1972. The finds were divided between the Medelhavsmuseet in Stockholm and the Cyprus Museum in Nicosia.

Gjerstad was director of the Swedish Institute in Rome from 1935 to 1940 and professor from 1940 to 1957 and research professor from 1957 to 1972 at the University of Lund. Having devoted twenty-five years (1923–1948) mostly to Cypriot archaeology, Gjerstad spent the same amount of time (1948–1973) to research on early Rome. In 1949 he presented his sensational theory that Rome was not founded in 753 BCE, the traditional date, but around 575, when the first floor was laid on the Roman forum. Therefore, according to Gjerstad, the period of the Roman kings lasted from 575 to 450, instead of the commonly accepted 753–509, and the Roman Republic thus started around 450. Gjerstad published the material from the Roman forum and its vicinity in *Early Rome* (1953–1973).

Although Gjerstad's hypotheses about Cyprus were widely accepted, his theories about early Rome are controversial. Recent studies have lowered the date of the first floor of the Roman forum from 575 to 625. Gjerstad's importance lies in his development of the stratigraphical method of excavation, his formulation of the typology of Cypriot pottery and sculpture, and his brilliant synthesis of historical and archaeological evidence from both ancient Cyprus and early Rome.

[*See also* Cyprus; Vouni; *and* History of the Field, *article on* Archaeology in Cyprus.]

BIBLIOGRAPHY

Callmer, Maj. "The Published Writings of Einar Gjerstad." In *Opuscula Atheniensia IV*, pp. 305–310. Lund, 1962.

Callmer, Maj, and Christian Callmer. "The Published Writings of Einar Gjerstad, 1962–1977." In *Scripta Minora 1977–1978, in honorem Einari Gjerstad*, pp. 3–8. Lund, 1977.

Gjerstad, Einar. *Studies on Prehistoric Cyprus*. Uppsala, 1926.

Gjerstad, Einar, et al. *The Swedish Cyprus Expedition: Finds and Results of the Excavations in Cyprus, 1927–1931.* 4 vols. Stockholm, 1934–1972. The fundamental work on Cypriot archaeology.

Gjerstad, Einar. *The Cypro-Geometric, Cypro-Archaic, and Cypro-Classical Periods.* Swedish Cyprus Expedition, vol. 4.2. Stockholm, 1948. Considered the bible of Cypriot archaeology.

Gjerstad, Einar. "Scavi stratigrafici nel Foro Romano e problemi ad essi relativi." *Bullettino della Commissione Archeologica Communale di Roma* 73 (1949–1950): 13–29. Presentation of sensational theories on Early Rome.

Gjerstad, Einar. *Early Rome*. 6 vols. Lund, 1953–1973. The fundamental work.

CARL-GUSTAF STYRENIUS

GLASS. Glassmaking emerged from a long period of experimenting with glasslike materials. Craftsmen had discovered faience prior to 4000 BCE by heating granules of crushed quartz until their surfaces melted, so that, upon cooling, they fused into a solid mass. By 2000 BCE, beads and other small objects were being manufactured out of glass—that is, out of silica (crushed quartz or sand) and plant ash or the mineral natron (alkalis that act as fluxes). Small amounts of lime, probably introduced unintentionally, made the glass chemically stable.

The first glass vessels were made in western Asia in about 1550 BCE and in Egypt shortly afterward. Their manufacturers used a variety of techniques, including casting in open molds; making "mosaic glass" (in which preformed elements were fused); and, most frequently, core forming (in which the hot glass was formed around a removable clay core). Far more ancient Egyptian glass has been recovered than glass from Mesopotamia. The great majority of the vessels were core formed and decorated with brightly colored trails with featherlike, polychrome designs. Egyptian glassmakers created a number of different forms to contain cosmetic preparations and liquids for drinking. All of these objects are small because there was a limit to the size of the vessel that could be formed around a core, and perhaps also

a limit to the quantity of glass that could be melted in primitive furnaces.

Between 1500 and 1150 BCE, the Egyptians produced some of the world's first glass masterpieces. At the same time, craftsmen in parts of the eastern Mediterranean made rather simpler objects. On Cyprus, they imitated Egyptian core-formed vessels shaped like pomegranates. In southern Greece, Mycenaeans cast beads and pendants in molds made of stone, using raw glass imported in the form of ingots. In the twelfth century BCE, the civilizations of Egypt, Mesopotamia, and the eastern Mediterranean collapsed, and technology (glassmaking included) declined.

Glassmaking was revived in the eighth century BCE in two regions where civilization itself revived: in Mesopotamia and on the Syro-Palestinian coast. In Mesopotamia, the Assyrians produced core-formed containers for perfumes and other cosmetics, as well as objects that were cast and finished by the lapidary techniques of cutting, grinding, and polishing. On the Mediterranean coast, Phoenician glassmakers produced colorful beads and pendants in the form of human and animal heads (see figure 1).

The Phoenicians created one of the leading cultures in the eastern Mediterranean between 800 and 300 BCE; another such culture was created by the Greeks. In parts of the Greek-speaking world (most probably, the islands in the eastern Aegean), craftsmen produced large numbers of small, core-formed perfume bottles, using techniques borrowed from the Near East. The Greeks also experimented with the use of glass as architectural ornament, and the fifth-century BCE sculptor Pheidias created statues with drapery made of cast-glass panels.

Iran emerged as a new world power in the sixth century BCE, under the Achaemenid dynasty. The finest glass of the Achaemenid period consisted of cast, cut, ground, and polished vessels. Careful selection of the raw materials resulted in glass that was almost colorless, like rock crystal; the ex-

GLASS. Figure 1. *Phoenician glass beads, c. 500 BCE.* (Courtesy Pictoral Archive)

pertise of glassmakers enabled them to produce the most accomplished cold-worked glass that had ever been made.

Between 334 and 323 BCE, Alexander the Great conquered the Persian Empire. Following Alexander's death, the empire was divided among his generals, who established independent kingdoms. The Ptolemys became the kings of Egypt, creating a culture that combined Greek and Egyptian elements. In this Hellenistic culture, glassmakers exploited old and new techniques to manufacture exotic luxury objects. Between the fourth and the first centuries BCE, Hellenistic workshops were producing a dazzling array of tableware and perfume bottles out of mosaic glass; *reticelli*, or lace-mosaic glass (with twisted canes of colorless and white glass); and gold sandwich glass (with designs cut out of gold foil sandwiched between two closely fitting vessels fused to form a single object).

In the first century BCE, Rome's leader, Octavian (the future emperor Augustus), annexed Egypt, and emerged as the ruler of an empire. At its greatest extent, the Roman Empire stretched from the Atlantic Ocean to the Persian Gulf and from the Rhine River to the Sahara. The Romans were the last great glassmakers in the ancient world; they inherited the Hellenistic tradition and adapted it to create stunning luxury glass. Some of the finest examples were made between about 30 BCE and 70 CE. Wealthy Romans could purchase multicolored ribbon mosaic glass (made from ribbonlike canes arranged in geometric patterns); gold-band glass (a variation of ribbon mosaic glass that includes strips of gold leaf); and cameo glass (overlays of one or more different colors in which the upper layers are carved, ground, and polished; at the end of the process, the object has an ornament in low relief on a background of a different color). The most popular Roman combination was white on dark blue. Cameos were the most costly glass objects made in the Early Roman Empire. The least expensive objects were made by blowing, a technique discovered in the region of Syrian-Palestine between about 75 and 50 BCE. In the next hundred years, glass vessels took their place beside earthenware in all but the poorest households in the Mediterranean. By 50 CE, glass manufacturers were also operating in several European provinces.

It was a short step from discovering that glass could be blown to discovering that it could be blown into molds. Blowing into decorated molds enabled glassmakers to produce large numbers of identical, often highly ornate objects quickly and inexpensively.

Blown glass can be decorated in a number of other ways while it is hot. One of the techniques used by the Romans was to roll the hot glass on a surface strewn with chips of colored glass, to give a vessel a multicolored appearance. Another, more common technique was to make patterns by trailing molten glass over the surface. Glass can also be decorated when it is cold, by painting, cutting, or engraving. Roman wheel-cutting varied in complexity from simple horizontal lines to faceting and pictorial designs with figures, landscapes, and inscriptions. In late third- and fourth-century workshops, for example, vessels were produced with hunting scenes, episodes from pagan mythology, and scenes from the Hebrew Bible and New Testament.

Hellenistic glassware had included vessels with gold foil sandwiched between two fused layers of glass. A similar technique was practiced in the third and fourth centuries, with glassmakers producing medallions decorated with portraits and roundels forming the centerpieces of dishes or bowls.

The rarest of all Late Roman luxury glass consisted of objects with "cages" made by cutting and grinding the glass when it was cold. The best known of these open-work vessels are cage cups: bowl- and beaker-shaped vessels whose bases and sides are enclosed by open-work cages attached to the wall by posts. The entire object—bowl, cage, and posts—was cut from a single piece of glass.

The Roman Empire disintegrated in the fifth century. In western Europe, Roman rule was replaced by the kingdoms of the Franks and other Germanic nations; in the eastern Mediterranean, the Byzantine Empire was taking shape. In the west, the Franks and their neighbors used basic glassworking techniques to fashion a variety of drinking vessels. In the Byzantine Empire, sixth- and early-seventh-century glass included mold-blown vessels with Christian or Jewish symbols. In both regions, however, glassmakers' skills had declined and elaborate objects ceased to be made. When, centuries later, glassmaking was revived in Europe, the greatest achievements were not luxury tablewares, but stained-glass windows for churches.

Meanwhile, in Iran, the Sasanians made vessels that included cups with wheel-cut facets or bosses. Sasanian glass never achieved the technical mastery of the finest Roman products, but it was prized all over Asia; examples have been found in fourth- to seventh-century tombs and treasuries in China, Korea, and Japan.

In 622 CE, the prophet Muhammad proclaimed a new religion: Islam. Within the next one hundred years, Arab armies carried Islam from the Arabian Peninsula to the Indus Valley in the east to Morocco in the west. The Byzantine Empire was reduced to a fraction of its former extent, and the Sasanian Empire was swept away. Islam's expansion created a multinational community in which styles and techniques spread rapidly, with the result that similar products appeared almost simultaneously in widely separated areas. Early Islamic glassmakers continued to make traditional products. Indeed, it is often impossible to decided whether objects from Syria, Egypt, and Iran were made just before or just after the Islamic conquest. At the same time, Islamic glassmakers were responsible for important innovations, such as the development of luster. This shiny effect was achieved by painting copper or silver oxide on the object, which was then fired at a relatively low temperature in oxygen-free conditions that fixed a film of metallic oxide on the surface.

The first dynasty of Islamic rulers, the Umayyads, lived in Damascus, Syria. In 750, they were overthrown by the 'Abbasids, who founded a new capital at Baghdad, Iraq. There, the presence of the court attracted artists and craftsmen who developed a distinctive decorative style, in which Iranian elements came to the fore. Sasanian glassworkers had finished vessels by cutting and grinding, techniques revived under the 'Abbasids. 'Abbasid wheel-cut objects are among the finest achievements of Islamic glassmaking. Vessels were decorated by relief cutting, in which the entire background was removed, leaving the ornament in relief. Hundreds of relief-cut glass objects have been found in northern Iran. Many scholars associate this style with the city of Nishapur in Khurasan. [See Nishapur.]

By far the rarest variety of Islamic cut glass is cameo glass. Islamic cameo glass almost invariably consists of colorless objects cased with another color (usually blue or green) and cut, ground, and polished so that the design is outlined in color on a colorless background. The latest major group of Islamic glass was decorated with gilding and colored enamels made from powdered glass mixed with an organic medium, painted on the surface, and fixed by firing at a low temperature. Usually, the decorative elements are outlined in red and filled with gilding or enamel. A high proportion of Islamic gilded and enameled glass was made in Syria, the only other known center of production being in Egypt.

The Mongol ruler Timur (Tamerlane) is said to have deported the glassmakers of Damascus to Samarkand in central Asia in 1400, which may have put an end to the manufacture of fine Islamic glass in Syria. The Venetians seized the opportunity and invaded the market. A number of fifteenth-century enameled beakers from Syria are believed to be Venetian, as are Islamic-style enameled lamps from Egypt. Brascha of Milan, a traveler who visited the Holy Land in 1480, tells how the captain of his ship "sent . . . to Damascus glass vessels from Murano" (quoted in Carl Johann Lammu, *Mittelalterliche Gläser und Steinschnittarbeiten aus dem Nahen Osten*, Berlin, 1930, vol. 1, p. 494). The golden age of Islamic glassmaking was over and Venice was about to set new standards for glassmakers all over the world.

[See also Vitreous Materials.]

BIBLIOGRAPHY

Barag, Dan. *Catalogue of Western Asiatic Glass in the British Museum*, vol. 1. London, 1985. Contains discussions of the chronology and provenance of glass made between about 1500 BCE and 200 CE.

Foy, Danièle, ed. *Le Verre de l'Antiquité tardive et du haut Moyen Age*. Guiry-en-Vexin, 1995. Nineteen papers, in French and other languages, on glass of the period between 300 and 700 CE in Europe and the Mediterranean. Contains a great deal of information on recent excavations.

Grose, David Frederick. *Early Ancient Glass*. New York, 1989. Catalog

of Late Bronze Age to early Roman glass in the Toledo Museum of Art, with an authoritative survey of the glass produced in this period.

Harden, Donald B., Hansgerd Hellenkemper, Kenneth Painter, and David Whitehouse. *Glass of the Caesars*. Milan, 1987. Catalog of a major exhibition, with extensive introductions to the main types of glass produced by the Romans.

Jenkins, Marilyn. *Islamic Glass: A Brief History*. New York, 1986. Based on objects in the Metropolitan Museum of Art, this appeared as *The Metropolitan Museum of Art Bulletin* 44, no. 2.

Journal of Glass Studies. Has appeared annually since 1959. The journal contains papers on glass and glassmaking of all periods and regions. Volume 32 (1990) contained a monograph on the Portland Vase.

Naumann-Steckner, Friedericke, ed. "Römisches Glas des 2. bis 6. Jahrhunderts." *Kölner Jahrbuch für Vor- und Frühgeschichte* 22 (1989): 5–203. Twenty-seven papers on Roman glass from archaeological contexts.

Newby, Martine and Kenneth Painter, ed. *Roman Glass: Two Centuries of Art and Innovation*. London, 1991. Twelve studies of Roman glass made between about 50 BCE and 100 CE.

Salden, Axel von, A. Leo Oppenheim, Robert H. Brill, and Dan Barag. *Glass and Glassmaking in Ancient Mesopotamia*. Corning, 1970; reprint, 1988. Edition of the cuneiform texts that contain instructions for glassmakers, with a catalog of surviving objects.

Stern, E. Marianne and Birgit Schlick-Nolte. *Early Glass of the Ancient World 1600 B.C.–A.D. 50*. Ostfildern, 1994. Contains a long (in places, controversial) section on techniques that may have been employed by early glassmakers.

Tait, Hugh, ed. *Five Thousand Years of Glass*. London, 1991; rev. ed., 1995. Includes chapters on Pre-Roman, Roman, and Islamic glass, and a section on techniques by William Gudenrath, which should be compared with Stern and Schlick-Nolte (see above).

Whitehouse, David. "La verrerie." In *Splendeur des Sassanides*, edited by B. Overlaet, pp. 109–113 and 257–270. Brussels, 1993. Introduction to Sassanian glass, with examples from the Corning Museum of Glass and other collections.

DAVID WHITEHOUSE

GLUECK, NELSON (1900–1971), pioneer of the archaeology of ancient Israel and a leading figure in the development of Reform Judaism in the United States. Born in Cincinnati, Ohio, Glueck was ordained in 1923 at the Hebrew Union College (HUC) there. In 1927, he earned his Ph.D. at the University in Jena, Germany, writing on the biblical concept of *ḥesed* (Heb., "goodness," "divine kindness"). That year, he also became a student of William Foxwell Albright's at the American Schools of Oriental Research (ASOR) in Jerusalem (now the Albright Institute); in 1930 and 1932, he worked with Albright in the excavations at Tell Beit Mirsim. While holding a faculty position at HUC, Glueck also served as director of ASOR in Jerusalem (1932–1933, 1936–1940, and 1942–1947) and as field director of ASOR's Baghdad school (1942–1947). During World War II, Glueck worked with the U.S. Office of Strategic Services. In 1947, he was elected president of HUC and in 1949 became president of the combined Hebrew Union College–Jewish Institute of Religion, a position he held until his death. In 1963, under Glueck's leadership, the HUC Biblical and Archaeological School was opened in Jerusalem. In

1972, its archaeological component was renamed the Nelson Glueck School of Biblical Archaeology.

Between 1932 and 1947, Glueck explored Transjordan, surveying more than one thousand sites (for the most part previously unknown) in Moab, Ammon, and Edom. In 1937 he excavated the Nabatean temple at Khirbet et-Tannur, and in 1938 he dug at Tell el-Kheleifeh, which he believed to be Solomon's seaport at Ezion-Geber. [*See* Tannur, Khirbet et-; Kheleifeh, Tell el-.] Between 1952 and 1964, he identified more than five hundred archaeological sites in Israel's Negev desert.

Among Glueck's seminal publications are his four-volume report, *Explorations in Eastern Palestine* (1934–1951); *The Other Side of the Jordan* (1940); *Rivers in the Desert* (1959); and *Deities and Dolphins* (1966). A festschrift in his honor was published on his seventieth birthday (Sanders, 1970).

Glueck's major achievement, a demographic synthesis of the history of Transjordan, was best summarized by G. Ernest Wright in 1959: "Glueck's work is to be rated as one of the two most important individual contributions to the field of Palestinian archaeology in our generation" (*Biblical Archaeologist* 22.4 [1959], p. 98). Later, Albright wrote that "Glueck's most important contribution to general history is his work on the history of the Nabateans and on the economy and ecology of the most important north Arab nation of pre-Islamic times" (*Bulletin of the American Schools of Oriental Research* 202 [1971], p. 5).

While Glueck's theories on Bronze and Iron Age settlement patterns in Jordan and in the Negev are currently being reevaluated, his work remains a textbook for contemporary scholars. The first project Glueck initiated at HUC's new archaeological school in 1964, the watershed excavations at Tell Gezer, also continues to have an enduring effect on archaeological research in the Middle East. Gezer was the training ground for almost the entire current generation of senior American archaeologists working in the eastern Mediterranean basin. [*See* Gezer.]

As a proponent of biblical archaeology, Glueck believed that the biblical tradition reflects historical memory. He also held, however, that no one could "prove the Bible, for it is primarily a theological document" (*Biblical Archaeologist* 22.4 [1959], p. 106). Glueck, the indefatigable scholar, the man of rare imagination, vision and insight, was one of the most renowned and productive archaeologists of his time.

[*See also* Nelson Glueck School of Biblical Archaeology.]

BIBLIOGRAPHY

Glueck, Nelson. *Explorations in Eastern Palestine.* 4 vols. Annual of the American Schools of Oriental Research, 14, 15, 18/19, 25/28. New Haven, 1934–1951.
Glueck, Nelson. *The Other Side of the Jordan.* New Haven, 1940. Rev. ed. Cambridge, Mass., 1970.
Glueck, Nelson. *Rivers in the Desert: A History of the Negev.* New York, 1959.
Glueck, Nelson. *Deities and Dolphins: The Story of the Nabataeans.* London, 1966.
Sanders, James A., ed. *Near Eastern Archaeology in the Twentieth Century: Essays in Honor of Nelson Glueck.* Garden City, N.Y., 1970.

SEYMOUR GITIN

GOATS. *See* Sheep and Goats.

GODIN TEPE, site located in the Kangavar Valley of central western Iran (34°31′ N, 48°04′ E). Found on survey in 1961, a test sounding was made in 1965, and large-scale excavations directed by T. Cuyler Young, Jr., were conducted in the summers of 1967, 1969, 1971, and 1973, sponsored by the Royal Ontario Museum, Canada. Eleven distinct cultural phases were identified. Periods VI–XI were excavated in only a small test trench; except for period XI, they are much more widely exposed at the neighboring site of Seh Gabi. Period I is recent Islamic. Excavations at Godin concentrated on periods II–V.

Period V (c. 3500–3200 BCE) was exposed over an area of about 500 sq m, in an oval enclosure containing a central courtyard, three major structures, a gatehouse, and storage rooms (see figure 1). Pottery and small finds have close parallels in Uruk IV and Susa Acropole 17 (Late Uruk period). The oval is at the summit of the mound, the remainder of which was contemporaneously occupied by a local Chalcolithic Zagros culture, Godin VI. It is assumed that the Oval Enclosure was occupied by Sumerian or Elamite traders. [*See* Sumerians; Elamites.]

Period IV (c. 3100–2650 BCE) was also exposed over an area of about 500 sq m. It reflects a major incursion from the north into the central western Zagros Mountains of the Transcaucasian Early Bronze I culture. At Godin this phase yielded village houses, elaborate ceremonial open air-structures on the summit of the mound, and an industrial area (metalworking?). The "invasion" of this culture from the north is probably responsible for the abandonment of the period-V Oval Enclosure.

Period III (c. 2600–1500/1400 BCE) was exposed over an average area of 700 sq m; it is an uninterrupted sequence for some 11 m of Bronze Age occupation. Six subperiods were identified stratigraphically and by distinct changes in both painted and plain ceramics. The period's strong initial connections with Susa D and Late Banesh Malayan and its continuing connections with most of Luristan suggest that Godin was, throughout period III, within the Elamite confederacy (perhaps Shimashki). At this time Godin was the largest site in the valley. It can be called a town in this period because its pottery was manufactured in centralized workshops and meat was sold from butcher shops. Godin was abandoned between 1400 and about 750 BCE, at which time

GODIN TEPE.   Figure 1.   *Oval enclosure, period V.* (Courtesy T. C. Young)

the north side of the mound was considerably eroded by the Khorramrud River.

Period II is a single structure: a fortified palace of a Median khan (about 133 × 55 m). The structure contains three major columned halls, magazines (with a second story for living quarters), and a kitchen. It has ceramic and architecteial parallels with Hasanlu III, Ziweye, the Zendan-i Suleiman, Nush-i Jan, Baba Jan, and Pasargadae. [*See* Hasanlu; Pasagardae; Medes.] The building was abandoned at an unknown date and subsequently occupied by squatters. Founded in the Iron Age III period (c. 750/700 BCE), it may well have been occupied into Achaemenid times (c. 500 BCE). Period I is represented by an Islamic shrine (c. fifteenth century CE) and by an associated modern cemetery.

BIBLIOGRAPHY

Henrickson, Robert C. "Godin III and Chronology of Central Western Iran circa 2600–1400 B.C." In *The Archaeology of Western Iran,* edited by Frank Hole, pp. 205–227. Washington, D.C., 1987. Good summary of period III.
Weiss, Harvey, and T. Cuyler Young, Jr. "The Merchants of Susa: Godin V and Plateau-Lowland Relations in the Late Fourth Millennium B.C." *Iran* 13 (1975): 1–17. Presentation and discussion of the Late Uruk period trading post of Godin V.
Young, T. Cuyler, Jr., and Louis D. Levine. *Excavations at the Godin Project: Second Progress Report.* Toronto, 1974. Summary of the excavations as they stood at the end of the fourth season.

T. CUYLER YOUNG, JR.

GOLAN. The region east and northeast of the Sea of Galilee, the Golan (Heb., Ramat Ha-Golan; Ar., el-Jaulan) extends from the Yarmuk River in the south to the slopes of Mt. Hermon in the north and from the Jordan Rift Valley and the Sea of Galilee on the west to the Raqqad River on the east (1200 sq km, or 744 sq. mi.). This volcanic plateau rises from 250 m above sea level in the south to 900 m above sea level in the northeast; because of geological faults, it breaks sharply on the west, toward the Rift Valley. The streams that flow on the plateau are shallow, but nearing the Jordan Rift they rapidly descend through waterfalls into deep canyons or wide basins. The basalt rock covering most of the surface of the Golan Heights originated in a series of volcanic eruptions dating from 3.7 to 0.14 million years BP (Mor, 1986). Four main routes cross the region from east to west connecting Damascus and the Bashan to the Mediterranean: Banias—Damascus, Gesher Benot Ya'aqob ("daughters of Jacob bridge")–Quneitra (Via Maris), Beth-saida–Khushniye, and Zemah–Rafid.

The Golan is divided into three subunits, the south, the center, and the north:

1. *South.* A level, fertile plain ranges from the yarmuk gorge to Wadi Samakh in the north. It is the region's main agricultural zone and was densely occupied throughout all archaeological periods.

2. *Center.* A rough area suitable mainly for grazing and limited agriculture, especially olive groves, the center of the Golan extends from Naḥal Samakh to the Naḥal Shelef–Tell Khariʿa line (8 km, or 5 mi., south of Quneitra). The area was inhabited in most archaeological periods, although with many gaps in the sequence. It was densely settled in the Byzantine period.

3. *North.* The northern Golan, from Naḥal Shelef to Naḥal Saʿar is mostly covered with thick oak forests; it has limited arable land and a few springs. Sparsely settled in the Early Bronze and Iron I periods, it was, however, densely occupied in the Hellenistic period by a settlement of Iturean Arabs.

Paleolithic–Neolithic Periods. The earliest human remains unearthed in the Golan date to the Upper Paleolithic period. At Berekat Ram (east of Masʿada), a paleosol layer containing flints and basalt implements from the Acheulean culture indicates habitation over a quarter of a million years ago (Goren-Inbar, 1985; Davies et. al., 1988). The Mousterian culture is represented by an open-air site at Biqʿat Quneitra (Goren-Inbar, 1989) and by a few industrial sites (approximately 50,000 BP). The large site of Mjhiyye in the southern Golan belongs to the Pre-Pottery Neolithic period (Gopher, 1990).

Chalcolithic Period. Some thirty Chalcolithic sites have so far been found in the central Golan, fifteen of which have been excavated or probed (Epstein, 1986). Extensive pasturelands and moist tracts were exploited for sheep and goat rearing and the seasonal cultivation of wheat, barley, and legumes. [*See* Sheep and Goats; Cereals.] The sites are unwalled and spread over a large area. There are villages of between fifteen and forty houses, as well as smaller hamlets and individual farms. The houses are built in parallel rows in chain formation, with neighboring houses sharing a joint side wall. They have a broadhouse plan with basalt walls constructed in dry masonry and an average size of 15 × 6 m. They were entered from the south, are characterized by a bench at the base of the walls, and, in a few cases, have grain silos. [*See* Granaries and Silos.] The internal partition walls form either a long narrow back room or smaller side rooms.

At all the sites a wide range of ceramic, basalt, and flint vessels was found. They show affinities to assemblages in other regions but with many features unique to the Golan. Many vessels are decorated with bands of impressed rope ornament, while others are ornamented with incised and punctured designs. Particularly noteworthy is the large number of pithoi for storing grain. Other vessels include jugs, bowls, holemouth jars, spouted jars, bowls with a fenestrated foot ("incense burners"), and spindle whorls. Few vessels for everyday use, such as cups and cooking pots, have come to light. The repertoire of basalt vessels includes bowls, basins, querns, and grinding and pounding stones, and such tools as hammers, hoes, and digging sticks. The flint implements include axes, adzes, scrapers, awls, fan scrapers, and a large number of sickle blades. In addition, there are circular or ovoid perforated tools made of tabular flint, some with peripheral denticulations. They are found mostly in the northern Golan (Epstein and Noy, 1988).

A unique feature of the Golan culture are cylindrical basalt pillar figures: they display a shallow offering bowl above, with a protruding nose and, in some cases, horns and a goatee (Epstein, 1982, 1988). The horned and bearded figures were associated with fertility for the flocks and the hornless ones with the general concept of life, fertility, and abundance for humans and their crops.

The Chalcolithic culture of the Golan represents a single phase that lasted from between two hundred to three hundred years. Calibrated carbon-14 dates of charred wood fragments provide a date of 4140 ± 150 BCE; burned wheat grains provide a calibrated date of 3800 ± 100 BCE.

Early Bronze Age. The EB I is found so far only at three sites adjacent to the Yarmuk River and Naḥal Meizar, in the southern Golan (Epstein 1985c). In the rest of the region there seems to be a gap in occupation in this period. In contrast, surveys located forty-two sites inhabited in EB II throughout the Golan (Epstein and Gutman, 1972; Hartal, 1989): seven in the south, twelve in the center, seventeen in the north, and six more at the foot of Mt. Hermon. [*See* Hermon, Mount.] The sites include settlements and large fortified enclosures. At Zaʿarta, Zalabeh, and Gamla, sections of fortification walls have been identified together with building remains. [*See* Gamla.] The enclosure sites are surrounded by massive fortifications that sometimes incorporate natural elements such as rocks, cliffs, and abysses overhanging wadis (Mitham Yitzhaki, Mitham Leviah, Mitham Bardawil). Other enclosures, erected in areas without natural fortifications, are surrounded on all four sides by huge stone-heaped walls (Shaʿabniah, Es-Sur.) Excavations at Mitham Leviah (Kochavi, 1989) revealed three parallel walls (up to 4 m thick) crossing the narrow spur that are otherwise protected by steep precipices on the north, south, and west. On the west of the site EB III rectangular stone-built houses were discovered together with Khirbet Kerak ware in situ. EB IA, EB IB, EB II and EB IV/MB I pottery, also found in this area, indicate habitational continuity at the site. It is clear that the enclosures sometimes incorporated buildings, such as at Mitham Leviah and es-Sur, but the function of the enclosures has yet to be clarified. They may either be fortified areas, occupied by an unsettled local pastoralist population and their flocks in times of danger, or walled cities.

An unusual and unique site, perhaps dating to EB II is Rujm el-Hiri (Zohar, 1989; Kochavi, 1989). It contains a huge central tumulus (20–25 m in diameter, 7 m high) surrounded by four concentric walls; the outer walls, in which there are two entryways, is 155 m in diameter. The central tumulus, recently excavated by Yonathan Mizrachi and Moshe Kochavi for Tel Aviv University, housed an oval burial chamber entered through a dromos. It was robbed in antiquity, but the few remaining earnings, arrowheads, and sherds date the burial to the Late Bronze Age. Stone-paved courts surrounded the tumulus, on top of which a few Iron I and Byzantine sherds were found. The site's original function and date have not yet been established, but it may have been a ceremonial center with symbolic significance for the contemporary population. [See Rujm el-Hiri.]

Early Bronze Age IV/Middle Bronze Age I (2350–1950 BCE). At the end of the third millennium a significant change occurred in the pattern of settlement in the Golan. No occupation sites have been located in the north and central Golan. In the south eight sites have been identified, of which three are burial sites. The indications are that during this period pastoralists, whose origins have not yet been fully established, moved through the north and central Golan but did not construct any permanent settlements. [See Pastoral Nomadism.] On the other hand, they erected hundreds of dolmens in standing groups and sometimes concentrated in dolmen "fields" (Epstein, 1985a. [See Dolmen.] The type of dolmen most frequently found is a rectangular, or sometimes trapezoidal (about 3.5 × 1.5 m), construction with an entrance on one of its short sides. Built of monolithic basalt blocks, upright slabs served as walls and the floors were paved. In one type of dolmen the roof is constructed of large stone slabs that rise toward the center in a steplike formation. A huge capstone creates a corbeled ceiling within the chamber. The Golan dolmens are frequently covered by a surrounding oval stone heap, or tumulus, supported at the bottom by a circular wall; in many cases only the top roof stone is visible.

The earliest finds from the dolmens date to EB IV/MB I and include jars, "teapots," a bottle, pedestal lamps, and round, handleless cooking pots. The metal finds are of copper and include a long pin with a bent head, pins with points at each end, a bracelet and ring, and weapons, including a dagger, a socketed spearhead, and leaf-shaped blades. [See Jewelry; Weapons.] These ceramic and metal types have clear parallels in assemblages from burials from this period in northern Israel and Syria (e.g., Megiddo, Ugarit). [See Burial Sites; Grave Goods; Megiddo; Ugarit.]

Middle Bronze Age II–Late Bronze Age (2950–1200 BCE). Following the EB IV/MB I period there was probably an occupation gap in the Golan of about 150 years as no sites that can be dated to the MB IIA have been found. The only finds are a few pottery vessels from a dolmen in secondary use. The vessels are characteristic of the transition between MB IIA and MB IIB, with parallels in graves at Ginossar, Hazor, Dan, and other northern sites (Epstein 1985a). [See Hazor; Dan.]

The beginning of MB IIB saw the resettlement of the Golan. About forty sites, including cemeteries, have been identified in surveys (Epstein and Gutman, 1972; Hartal, 1989): eleven in the north, only four in the center, and twenty-five concentrated in the southern Golan. Many settlements, often fortified, were established in MB IIB at strategic locations for defense and for control of roads and territories, with a particularly strong concentration on the slopes overlying Nahal Samakh and its tributaries. The main tells include Ai/et-Tell in the Bethsaida valley, Masharfawi in Nahal Kanaf (surrounded by a cyclopean wall), Fakhuri, el-Mudowarah, Hutiyye in the Samakh basin, and Tell ed-Dahab (wall remains). [See Ai.] Only fourteen of these sites continued to be occupied in the LB period. In addition to the tell sites there are small forts, such as site 151 in Nahal Samakh: a rectangular fort (20 × 24 m) whose fortification wall incorporates small rooms and two square towers. Other sites are burial caves rich in funerary goods. Noteworthy in the ceramic repertoire from surveys are large storage jars of coarse clay, decorated with applied bands of incised herringbone or zigzag patterns, with parallels at Hazor and other sites in the northern part of the country.

Late Bronze Age. The number of sites in the Golan decreased by more than a half in the Late Bronze Age. Most overlie MB II sites and continued into the Israelite period (tenth–ninth centuries BCE). No LB sherds were found on the surface at Tell el-Mudowarah indicating a gap in the settlement there. However, a burial cave with complete LB vessels was found at the foot of the site, indicating, perhaps, the existence of pastoralists in the area. Another burial cave has been found at the foot of Tel Soreg, a small tell in Nahal 'Ein-Gev (Kochavi, 1989, p. 7). Tel Soreg itself indicates settlement continuity from EB IV/MB I through MB IIB and LB II to the Israelite period.

Characteristic of LB pottery in the Golan are storage jars of coarse, light-colored clay decorated with red-painted geometric motifs. Noteworthy is a bichrome fragment decorated with a bird eating a fish. In some dolmens imported Cypriot ware was found; and the figurine of a woman wearing a Hathor wig was also recovered.

Egyptian records from Amarna relate directly to the area of the Golan. [See Amarna Tablets.] In EA364 a dispute over three cities between the kingdoms of 'Ashtartu and Hazor is reported, and it is likely that the area of controversy was the central Golan. Another letter (EA256) describes a conflict between Pihilu (Pella) and 'Ashtartu on the one hand, and the land of Ga-ri on the other (Pritchard, 1955, p. 486). It appears that the two cities of URU Ha-iu-ni and URU Ia-bi-li-ma were captured from the prince of Pihilu by the cities (a league?) of the land of Ga-ri. [*See* Pella.] William F. Albright (1943) identified the former city with Khirbet el-Ayun, in the southern Golan, and the latter with Tell Abil in the Yarmuk riverbed. Other cities in the letter have also been identified in the southern Golan. Subsequently, Benjamin Mazar argued that the reading *Ga-ri* in EA256:23 should be emended to *Ga-⟨su⟩-ri*—that is, biblical Geshur (Mazar, 1986a). It may thus be deduced that the land of Geshur existed as a political unit in the southern Golan at least as early the fourteenth century BCE.

Ma'acha, the entity bordering Geshur (*Jos.* 12:5, 13:11), is alluded to even earlier, in the Egyptian Execration texts, as a tribal name (E62) and a place name (E37; Ahituv, 1984, p. 132). It is presumed to lie north of Geshur, in the northern Golan, extending to the Hula Valley and southern Biqa' Valley.

Iron Age (1200–732 BCE). Following the decline in settlements in the Late Bronze Age, a renewed spread of sedentarization took place in the Iron Age, in which many MB II settlements were reoccupied. Surveys reveal more than fifty-two sites (twenty-two in the north, ten in the center, and twenty in the south). They include small settlements, forts, and dolmens in secondary use for burials (see above). Among the sites established for the first time in this period are fortresses and fortified settlements, erected at strategic locations: Tel Dover at the western entrance to the Yarmuk valley; Khirbet Dajajiyye at the western entrance to Nahal Samakh; 'Ein-Gev and Tel Hadar (Sheikh Khadr), both on the east bank of the Sea of Galilee; and Tell Abu Zeitun and "Mezad Yehonatan" (Tannuriyye) on the Golan plateau. [*See* Hadar, Tel.] Strata of this period have been exposed at the following excavated sites: 'Ein-Gev, Tel Soreg, Tel Hadar, Mezad Yehonatan, Tell Abu Zeitun, Bab el-Hawa, Horvat Kanaf, and Qasrin. [*See* Qasrin.] At 'Ein-Gev, five Iron Age strata were exposed (Mazar et al., 1964). Limited probes at the southern and northern edges of the mound (about 250 × 120 m) revealed a sequence of fortifications, the earliest (stratum V) of which was a solid wall (1.85 m wide) followed by a casemate wall (stratum IV). These fortifications are similar to those unearthed at Hazor and Megiddo. The probes also detected a citadel (about 60 × 60 m) erected at the northern end of the site. The construction of stratum IV is attributed to King Solomon. In stratum III (ninth century BCE), which was destroyed in a conflagration, an offset/inset wall (5 m thick) was erected, beyond which was an alley and a courtyard building. Stratum II (838–790 BCE) continued the same building plan. Stratum I (790–732 BCE) was unfortified, but a public building (perhaps a fort) was located in the north. The ceramic repertoire includes red-slipped burnished bowls similar to the Samaria type, cooking pots with triangular rims, jugs, storage jars, holemouth jars, and lamps. The stone objects include basalt pestles, a tripod bowl, an "incense bowl," and a votive axe out of nephrite. Especially important is an ostracon inscribed in

Aramaic: *lsqy'* (c. 850 BCE), probably a dignitary title such as "cupbearer" for an official at the site. [*See* Ostracon.]

At Tel Hadar a substantial round fort, surrounded by two fortification walls some 70 m across and a gate, was exposed that dates to Iron I (and perhaps before MB II) (Kochavi, 1989, pp. 9–11). Inside the fort were granary rooms containing quantities of charred grain and four-room houses. [*See* Four-room House.] This stratum was destroyed in a fire at the end of the eleventh century BCE. After a gap, the site was reoccupied in the ninth–eighth centuries BCE. The floors of the houses overlie the old walls.

A similar round or ovoid fort (some 70 m in diameter) was partially exposed at Tell Abu Zeitun, on the upper plateau of the southern Golan. Part of the outer face of a well-preserved fortification wall came to light there, with pottery dated to Iron I. At Tel Soreg, a fortified settlement from the ninth to eighth centuries BCE was exposed, including a fortification wall, a large building, and a series of dwellings (Kochavi, 1989, pp. 6–9).

At Mezad Yehonatan, on the upper tributary of Wadi Tannuriyye in east-central Golan another fort (26 sq m) dating to Iron I was probed (Epstein, 1984, p. 77). Its walls, preserved to a height of about 3 m in three–seven courses, were built with an inner vertical wall (1.7 m thick) abutted on the outside by a sloping stone glacis. The gate (2.45 m wide, 1.65 m deep), set in the east, was narrowed on the inside by a pair of pilasters.

According to the Bible, the area to the east of the Golan—the southern Bashan—was occupied by the Israelite tribe of half-Manasseh, while the Golan itself remained in the domain of the tribes of Geshur and Ma'acah (*Jos.* 12:5).

According to 2 *Samuel* 8:3–6, David smote Hadadezer, the king of Zobah, and his ally Aram-Damascus and set up garrisons in Damascus. [*See* Damascus.] The area under the control of Solomon (*1 Kgs.* 9:18) reached Tadmor and Hamath and would have included Geshur and Ma'acah probably as vassal states. Geshur became David's political ally, as is indicated by the marriage pact between David and the daughter of Talmai, king of Geshur. Ma'acah, on the other hand, took part in a coalition led by Hadadezer of Damascus against David (2 *Sm.* 10:6–19). Ben-Hadad (Bir-Hadad I), campaigned against Baasha, the king of Israel in about 886 BCE (Mazar, 1986b; Pitard, 1987, pp. 107–114), "and smote Ijon, and Dan, and Abel-Beth-Ma'acah and all of Kinneroth, over all the land of Naphtali" (*1 Kgs.* 16:20). This campaign led, according to Mazar, to the destruction of several cities, including the Israelite stratum IV at 'Ein-Gev and the establishment of an Aramean fort at the site (Mazar et al., 1964, pp. 29, 32; Mazar, 1986b). [*See* Arameans.] Another series of clashes between Israel and Aram Damascus, with a decisive battle at Aphek in the southern Golan, is recorded in *1 Kings* 20:1–43. [*See* Aphek.] Though the name of the king of Israel mentioned in this cycle of stories (*Kgs.* 20, 22) is Ahab, it has been suggested that the event took place later, in the days of Joash of the dynasty of Jehu (Pitard, 1987, pp. 114–125). 2 Kings 10:32–33 records: "In those days, Yahweh began to cut off parts of Israel, and Hazael smote them in all the territory of Israel from the Jordan eastward, all the land of Gilead, the Gadites, the Reubenites, the Manassites, from ʿAroʿer, which is in the Arnon Valley, Gilead, and Bashan." Revival seems to have come only in the reign of Joash, after the death of Hazael, at the beginning of the eighth century BCE (Pitard, 1987, pp. 161–170). In a series of battles lasting some five years, Hazael's son, Ben-Hadad (Bir-Hadad III), was first repulsed in battle close to Samaria (2 Kgs. 6:24–27) and then defeated near Succoth in Transjordan (1 Kgs. 20:1–21). [See Samaria.] The third, and final, battle was fought near Aphek (1 Kgs. 20:24–43). This site has been identified recently with Tel Soreg, in the southern Golan (see above). In the ensuing period, the territory of the Golan probably remained in Israel's hands (2 Kgs. 14:25) and was only finally annexed to the Assyrian Empire, together with the rest of northern Israel, by Tiglath-Pileser III, following his conquest in 732 BCE (1 Kgs. 15:29; Pitard, 1987, pp. 186–189). [See Assyrians.]

The Golan Heights was probably not settled during the Babylonian, Persian, and Early Hellenistic periods (sixth–third century BCE). From the time Palestine was conquered by the Seleucids in 200 BCE until the Byzantine period, there is an impressive growth in the number of sites in the Golan (more than 173 sites in the sixth century CE). The number of sites and settlements in the Byzantine period amounts to six times the figure for the Middle Bronze Age. Settlements are particularly prominent in the central and northern Golan, which had almost no permanent agricultural settlements during the earlier periods.

Hellenistic Period (200–64 BCE). The earliest settlements in the Hellenistic period were established at the beginning of the second century BCE, mainly in the southern Golan, where they were situated at the edges of the fertile plains, above the rich springs, and in the nearby river valleys. In addition to the agricultural villages, a system of fortresses and towers were built to defend and control the region and its roads, chief among them Hippos/Susita. Toward the end of the second century BCE their number was reinforced by the addition of Gamala/Gamla. These fortresses are typical products of Hellenistic military doctrines—strongholds built on high hills, isolated from their surroundings, and out of range of artillery fire—controlling the main highways, while ascents and secondary roads were defended by towers.

The Itureans, a tribe probably of Aramean stock, established settlements in the northeastern Golan in the middle of the second century BCE. Their distinctive pottery, "Golan ware," has been found at sixty-seven sites from this period. Fifty of these Iturean sites remained populated through the Late Roman and Byzantine periods. Excavations have been conducted at three Iturean sites in Golan: Horvat Zemel, where there were remains of five houses, and a large quantity of pottery, some with Greek inscriptions; Horvat Namra, which had one building and courtyard, with a great deal of pottery; and Bab el-Hawa, where there were a street and a building with two or three apartments.

Early Roman Period (64 BCE–67 CE). Excavations at Gamla and Horvat Kanaf, together with remains from about 141 surveyed sites throughout the Golan, indicate the magnitude of the settlement in the Early Roman period. At Gamla—an example of a planned city—the construction is of an exceptionally fine quality with a magnificent synagogue, private houses, streets, and an oil extraction installation. Fragments of stone vessels made of chalk, attest to socioeconomic contacts with the metropolis of Jerusalem. The town was destroyed by the Roman army in 67 CE and abandoned. [See Gamla.]

Excavations at Gamla and Horvat Kanaf and surveys of other sites testify to an archaeological gap from the late first to the early fourth centuries CE. Moreover, as there is almost no mention of places in the Golan in the Mishnah or the Talmud, it would seem that the Jewish population was obliterated in the First Revolt, following which there was a drastic decline of Jewish settlement in the region. [See First Jewish Revolt.]

Middle and Late Roman Periods (67–365 CE). Excavations have exposed occupation levels from the Middle Roman period, with the most impressive finds coming from the cities of Hippos, where a *cardo maximus,* an imposing east gate, sections of a stonepipe siphon, a nymphaeum of basalt stone, a subterranean stone-vaulted reservoir, monumental basalt buildings, and ornate Corinthian capitals attest to the wealth and magnificence of this city in the Middle Roman period; and Banias, which had a sanctuary to the god Pan above the spring, including an Augusteum, a Cult Court to Pan and the Nymphs with niches hewn in the rock escarpment, a Temple of Zeus, a Court of Nemesis, a Tomb-Temple of the Sacred Goats, and a Temple for Pan and the Goats. In the city center there were monumental public buildings and a gigantic late third-century CE palace with horrea, circular halls, and vaulted passages. [See Banias.]

In some Golan villages, private houses built of basalt ashlars with stone ceilings have been preserved. In some sites in the southern and eastern Golan, finds associated with cults from the Roman period have also been discovered, like statues of Tyche, altars, and architectural fragments from temples.

Remains of pavements, milestones, and watchtowers characteristic of Roman roads attest to the existence of several roads: A Roman road from Banias toward Damascus; possible remains of the Scythopolis–Hippos road; remains of a branch of a road linking the road to Hippos with the road coming from Bethsaida; and impressive remains of a paved road from the Lawiyye spur eastward to Nawa in Syria.

Byzantine Period (365–636 CE). The Byzantine period was a time of great prosperity in the Golan, as in other parts of the country, proved by the increase in the number of sites and in the extent of the built-up area. The southern Golan, including the city of Hippos and a chain of small towns, was the most densely populated area, while central Golan only had one town, Dabura. To the north, the city of Banias enjoyed great prosperity at this time, in part because of its abundant water sources and its location on the road from Tyre and Sidon to Damascus.

Village and house plans. The village plan followed one of three basic patterns: (1) orthogonal, where narrow streets and parallel lanes run between the buildings, crossing one another at right angles, with buildings of different sizes; (2) streets like the spokes of a wheel, with the streets converging toward the center of the village; and (3) no regular plan, with houses dispersed according to the topography. Village streets were unpaved and houses were built of local basalt, with stone ceilings. The pottery repertoire of this period in the southern and central Golan is basically similar to that common in the country as a whole, the most common household vessels being storage jars, cooking pots, kraters and bowls, as well as jugs, juglets and a variety of lamps. Most of this pottery was produced in Golan itself with only a small amount imported from the Galilee.

Ethnic makeup. Excavations of public buildings such as synagogues and churches provide clear guidelines to the ethno-religious map of the Golan in this period. Remains of synagogues have been found at twenty-five sites. Numerous remains of churches and Christian symbols have been found in the eastern and southern Golan, but only in a few villages in the Iturean territory of the northern Golan.

Churches. Two main architectural types of churches have been found. The first was most common in the coastal and valley regions of Palestine, and consisted of basilicas with walls built of stones and mortar, two rows of arcades on columns that divide the building into a nave and two aisles, a semicircular apse, mosaic floors, and tiled roofs (Hippos, Kursi, and Khisfin). The second type was common at the time in the Hauran, with the apse sometimes being square, the ceilings of basalt slabs resting on large arches supported by square pillars, and the floors generally paved with stone slabs and, rarely, mosaics (er-Ramthaniyye, Deir Qeruh, Duer el-Loz, and Deir Sras). [*See* Churches; Basilicas; Kursi.]

Synagogues. Remains of seventeen synagogues were found in the western part of the central Golan, at eight other sites architectural fragments were found from synagogues whose exact locations are unknown. The synagogue was generally the only public building in the typical Jewish village in the Golan. They were built on the best location available, often on the highest point on a slope or near a spring. These synagogues constitute a regional architectural group, sharing certain common features: basalt ashlar masonry, thick dry-stone walls, a single entrance in an ornamented facade, columns and stone architraves, an internal division by two rows of columns, galleries, and gabled roofs made of tiles. At the same time different "schools" of masons each had its own distinctive plan, elevation and carved decorations:

1. *Chorazin–'Ein-Nashut "School."* Features of this school, assigned to the mid-fifth century, include richly decorated facades, columns on pedestals, and an abundance of sculptures in relief. Among the finds are decorations with lions, eagles, vine branches, the Ark of the Law, a seven-branched menorah, Ionic, Corinthian, and Doric capitals, and Aramaic and Hebrew inscriptions. Examples of this school are: Chorazin, on the west bank of the Jordan River; 'Ein-Nashut, on the banks of Nahal Meshushim; and ed-Dikkeh, situated on the east bank of the Jordan River. [*See* Chorazin.] Some of the synagogues of this school have been surveyed, but not yet excavated: Khirbet er-Rafid, overlooking the east bank of the Jordan River; Khirbet Khawkha, on the southern bank of Nahal Daliyyot; Horvat Beth-Lavi (Wakhshara), northeast of the peak of Qubbat Qar'a; Khirbet Zumeimira, north of Nahal Zavitan; and Jarabeh, west of Nahal Meshushim.

2. *Kanaf "School."* Assigned to the beginning of the sixth century, the Kanaf school is notable for its meager decoration in a simple style concentrated on the outer facade and columns without pedestals. Among the finds are reliefs of lions, Hercules knots, vine branches, Doric capitals, and an Aramaic inscription. The group includes Horvat Kanaf, in south Golan, between Nahal Kanaf and Nahal Sfamnun; Deir 'Aziz, on the southern bank of Nahal Kanaf; and probably Taibeh, on the banks of Nahal Yahudiyye.

3. *Qasrin "School."* Also dated to the beginning of the sixth century, the Qasrin school features decoration concentrated on the entrance of the synagogues, all of them with the same type of portal frame; in the hall two rows of columns stand on Attic bases with Ionic capitals; there is an elevated clerestory rather than galleries. Among the finds are decorations with seven-, nine-, and eleven-branched menorahs, the Ark of the Law, shofars, incense shovels, eagles, vines and grapes, and an Aramaic inscription. Some of these synagogues are: Qasrin, in central Golan; Assaliyye, a large ruin west of Qasrin; Yahudiyye, a village north of Nahal Yahudiyye; Khirbet Qusbiyye, a small abandoned village on a hill west of the Yahudiyye–Khusniyye road. [*See* Qasrin.]

In some Golan synagogues the main entrance in the facade of the building was displaced from the center. This was done in order to make place for the Torah shrine on the inside. The orientation of these synagogues and the direction of prayer are still open questions. Some are built along an east–west axis, with the facade oriented west. However, other Golan synagogues were aligned north–south, with their facades facing south; the facade of the Qasrin synagogue is in the north, but the Ark of the Law was installed in the southern wall, so that there too, the congregation faced south. A common Jewish symbol in synagogue art in the Golan is the menorah with varying numbers of branches, generally carved on the lintels of side entrances or windows, on capitals, and on arch stones. Another Jewish symbol is the Ark of the Law, featured on lintels. [*See* Synagogues.]

The literary sources do not attest to a Jewish population in the Golan Heights during the Late Roman and Byzantine periods. Only archaeological data enable a reconstruction of its size, history, material culture, and artistic achievements. It seems that after the destruction of most of the settlements during the First Revolt and their subsequent abandonment, Jewish settlement in the Lower Golan was interrupted until the end of the third century CE. It was only in Dabura that a Jewish village survived up to the time of the Mishnah and the Talmud. Jews returned to the Golan in the fourth century CE, migrating from the Galilee. The economy of the region based on agriculture, particularly the production of olive oil. Villages were generally small, not more than twenty to fifty buildings, owing to the scarcity of water. It appears that the first synagogues were built in the second half of the fifth century CE, and a few buildings were added in the sixth century. Some of these synagogues were damaged by earthquakes in the sixth century and repaired in the sixth and seventh century. The architectural and artistic level of the Golan synagogues is high, revealing influences from the Galilee, as well as the culture of the eastern Mediterranean coastal region. The Aramaic and Hebrew inscriptions point to the congregants' familiarity with the Torah. Excavations reveal that many of the villages were abandoned as early as the end of the sixth and beginning of the seventh century CE, probably because of the continuing state of war between the Persians and the Byzantines, a possibly frequent Bedouin raids. In Qasrin, however, the Jewish community persisted until the Early Arab period, probably coming to an end only with the earthquake of 749 CE, at the end of the Umayyad period.

BIBLIOGRAPHY

Ahituv, Shmuel. *Canaanite Toponyms in Ancient Egyptian Documents.* Jerusalem, 1984.

Albright, William Foxwell. "The Land of Damascus between 1850 and 1750 B.C." *Bulletin of the American Schools of Oriental Research,* no. 83 (1941): 30–36.

Albright, William Foxwell. "Two Little Understood Amarna Letters from the Middle Jordan Valley." *Bulletin of the American Schools of Oriental Research,* no. 89 (1943): 7–17.

Albright, William Foxwell. "The List of Levitic Cities." In *Louis Ginzberg Jubilee Volume,* edited by Alexander Marx et al., pp. 49–73. New York, 1945.

Bar-Kochva, Bezalel. "Gamala in Gaulanitis." *Zeitschrift des Deutschen Palästina-Vereins* 92 (1976): 54–71.

Davies, Simon J. M., et al. "The Animal Remains from Biq'at Quneitra." *Paléorient* 14.1 (1988): 95–105.

Epstein, Claire, and Shmaryahu Gutman. "The Golan." In *Judea, Samaria, and the Golan: Archaeological Survey, 1967–1968* (in Hebrew), edited by Moshe Kochavi, pp. 243–298. Jerusalem, 1972.

Epstein, Claire. "Basalt Pillar Figures from the Golan." *Israel Exploration Journal* 25 (1975): 193–201.

Epstein, Claire. "The Chalcolithic Culture of the Golan." *Biblical Archaeologist* 40 (1977): 57–62.

Epstein, Claire. "Aspects of Symbolism in Chalcolithic Palestine." In *Archaeology in the Levant: Essays for Kathleen Kenyon,* edited by P. R. S. Moorey and Peter J. Parr, pp. 22–35. Warminster, 1978a.

Epstein, Claire. "A New Aspect of Chalcolithic Culture." *Bulletin of the American Schools of Oriental Research,* no. 229 (1978b): 27–45.

Epstein, Claire. "More on the Chalcolithic Culture of the Golan" (in Hebrew). *Eretz-Israel* 15 (1981): 15–20.

Epstein, Claire. "Cult Symbols in Chalcolithic Palestine." *Bollettino del Centro Camuno di Studi Preistorici* 19 (1982): 63–82.

Epstein, Claire. "Meṣad Tannuriye." *Excavations and Surveys in Israel* 3 (1984): 77.

Epstein, Claire. "Dolmens Excavated in the Golan." *'Atiqot* 17 (1985a): 20–58.

Epstein, Claire. "Laden Animal Figurines from the Chalcolithic Period in Palestine." *Bulletin of the American Schools of Oriental Research,* no. 258 (1985b): 53–62.

Epstein, Claire. "Notes and News: Golan." *Israel Exploration Journal* 35 (1985c): 53–56.

Epstein, Claire. "Chalcolithic Settlement Patterns and House Plans in the Golan" (in Hebrew). *Michmanim* 3 (1986): 34–35.

Epstein, Claire. "Basalt Pillar Figurines from the Golan and the Huleh Region." *Israel Exploration Journal* 38 (1988): 205–223.

Epstein, Claire, and Tamar Noy. "Observations Concerning Perforated Flint Tools from Chalcolithic Palestine." *Paléorient* 14.1 (1988): 133–141.

Gopher, Avi. "An Early Pre-Pottery Neolithic B Site in the Golan Heights." *Tel Aviv* 17 (1990): 115–143.

Goren-Inbar, Na'ama. "The Lithic Assemblage of the Berekhat Ram Acheulian Site, Golan Heights." *Paléorient* 11.1 (1985): 7–28.

Goren-Inbar, Na'ama. "Typological Characteristics of the Mousterian Assemblage from Biquat Quneitra." In *Investigations in South Levantine Prehistory,* edited by Ofer Bar-Yosef and Bernard Vandermeersch, pp. 125–146. British Archaeological Reports, International Series, no. 497. Oxford, 1989.

Goren-Inbar, Na'ama. *Quneitra: A Mousterian Site on the Golan Heights.* Qedem, vol. 31. Jerusalem, 1990.

Hartal, Mosheh. *Northern Golan Heights: The Archaeological Survey as a Source of Local History* (in Hebrew). Qazrin, Israel, 1989.

Kochavi, Moshe. "The Land of Geshur Project: Regional Archaeology of the Southern Golan, 1987–1988 Seasons." *Israel Exploration Journal* 39 (1989): 1–17.

Kochavi, Moshe. "The Land of Geshur Project, 1989–1990." *Israel Exploration Journal* 41 (1991): 180–184.

Loewenstam, Shmuel. "Geshur" (in Hebrew). In *Encyclopaedia Biblica,* vol. 2, col. 568. Jerusalem, 1954.

Ma'oz, Zvi, and Ann Killebrew. "Qaṣrin, 1983–1984." *Israel Exploration Journal* 35 (1985): 289–293.

Ma'oz, Zvi. *The Golan Heights in the Ancient Period: Historical-Geographical Research* (in Hebrew). Qazrin, Israel, 1986.

Mazar, Benjamin, et al. "'Ein-Gev Excavations in 1961." *Israel Exploration Journal* 14 (1964): 1–49.

Mazar, Benjamin. "Geshur and Maachah." In Mazar's *The Early Biblical Period.* Edited by Shmuel Ahituv and Baruch Levine. Jerusalem, 1986a.

Mazar, Benjamin. "The Aramaean Empire and Its Relations with Israel." In Mazar's *The Early Biblical Period.* Edited by Shmuel Ahituv and Baruch Levine. Jerusalem, 1986b.

Mor, Doron. *The Volcanism of the Golan Heights* (in Hebrew). Geological Survey of Israel, Report no. GSI/5/86. Jerusalem, 1986.

Oded, Bustanay. *The Political Status of Israelite Transjordan during the*

Period of the Monarchy to the Fall of Samaria (in Hebrew). Jerusalem, 1968.

Pitard, Wayne T. *Ancient Damascus*. Winona Lake, Ind., 1987.

Pritchard, James B., ed. *Ancient Near Eastern Texts Relating to the Old Testament*. Princeton, 1955.

Schumacher, Gottlieb. *The Jaulân*. London, 1888.

Urman, Dan. *The Golan: A Profile of a Region during the Roman and Byzantine Periods*. British Archaeological Reports, International Series, no. 269. Oxford, 1985.

Zohar, Mattanyah. "Rogem Hiri: A Megalithic Monument in the Golan." *Israel Exploration Journal* 39 (1989): 18–31.

ZVI URI MA'OZ

GOLD. *See* Coins; Jewelry; Metals.

GOLDMAN, HETTY (1881–1972), member of the Institute for Advanced Study, Princeton, New Jersey, and excavator of Tarsus, in southern Turkey. Born in New York City, Goldman received a bachelor's degree from Bryn Mawr College in 1903 and a master's degree in classical language and archaeology from Radcliffe in 1910. From 1910 to 1912 she attended the American School of Classical Studies in Athens, which sponsored her excavations at Halae, a small classical and prehistoric village in central Greece. During the excavation her interests shifted to prehistory and she made the necropolis at Halae the subject of her Ph.D. dissertation, also from Radcliffe (1916). In 1922 Goldman began excavating Colophon in Ionia, western Greece, sponsored by the Fogg Museum of Harvard University; and from 1924 to 1927 she excavated at Eutresis in Boeotia, also in central Greece. She was appointed a professor at the Institute for Advanced Study in 1936.

Goldman's most important contribution to Near Eastern archaeology was the result of her last excavation, Gözlü Kule, in Tarsus, carried out under the auspices of Bryn Mawr College, Harvard University, and the Archaeological Institute of America. She directed the excavations between 1934 and 1939 and resumed them after World War II from 1947 to 1948. Having selected Tarsus for its potential as a link between east and west, Goldman identified interconnections with Troy and the Aegean region in pottery as early as Early Bronze Age III (c. 2500 BCE). She also identified evidence for interaction with Mycenaeans or "Sea Peoples" in the pottery of the end of the Late Bronze Age (c. 1200 BCE). The recovery of tablets, inscribed seal impressions, and seals dating to the Hittite period revealed the historical importance of Tarsus and its interaction with the Hittite Empire. The meticulous care she gave to excavation, recording, analysis, and publication of finds and architecture allowed Goldman and later scholars to produce the only reliable stratigraphic sequence for Cilicia from the Neolithic to the Roman period (Goldman, 1956–1963). The Tarsus volumes are still used as a standard reference in comparative dating of Anatolian and North Syrian sites, particularly for the Bronze and Iron Ages.

BIBLIOGRAPHY

Goldman, Hetty, and John Garstang. "A Conspectus of Early Cilician Pottery." *American Journal of Archaeology* 51 (1947): 370–388.

Goldman, Hetty, ed. *Excavations at Gözlü Kule, Tarsus*, vol. 1, *The Hellenistic and Roman Periods*; vol. 2, *From the Neolithic Period through the Bronze Age*; vol. 3, *The Iron Age*. Princeton, 1950–1963.

Mellink, Machteld J. "Goldman, Hetty." In *Notable American Woman*, edited by Barbara Sicherman and Carol Hurd Green, pp. 280–282. Cambridge, 1980.

BONNIE MAGNESS-GARDINER

GÖLTEPE, site located 2 km from the Kestel mine on top of a large natural hill 4 km (2 mi.) from Çamardı, a town in the Taurus Mountains of south-central Turkey (37°50′ N, 34°58′ E). The natural hill measures close to 60 ha (148 acres) and is fortified at the summit, with cultural deposition covering its surface. Göltepe is located 1,767 m above sea level.

In 1988, intensive surface surveys revealed multifaceted molds, tin-rich slagged crucibles, ores, and an estimated fifty thousand ground-stone tools for ore dressing on the site's surface. A total of 698 sq m was excavated at Göltepe in 1990 and 1991 (see below); 2,500 sq m were tested through magnetic resistivity, which indicated anomalies where underground structures may exist. A total of 858 sq m was excavated at Göltepe in 1993. The excavations aimed at horizontally exposing as much of an area as possible to obtain settlement layout and densities and differential quarters with special functions and to understand the use of space and the distribution of artifacts. The extent of the settlement has now been estimated to be 8–10 ha (148 acres) between the mine and processing and habitation areas. C14 uncalibrated dates from the 1990 season at the Göltepe site range from 3290 to 1840 BCE. A dendrochronological date of 1978 ±37 years was obtained for a piece of charcoal from a pit fill context. [*See* Resistivity; Dating Techniques.]

The excavations at Göltepe, which began in 1990 and were continued in 1991 and 1993 under the direction of K. Aslıhan Yener under the auspices of the Niğde Archaeological Museum (1990–1991) and the Oriental Institute of the University of Chicago (1993), were designed to illuminate the origins, formation, and organization of a tin-production/habitation site and its contemporary tin mine. Parallel excavations proceeded at the Kestel mine in 1987, 1988, 1990, and 1992. These sites were discovered during ten years of archaeological and mineralogical surveying in Turkey's metal-rich zones. A result of these surveys was the solution of an enigma that had puzzled scholars for decades: a source of the elusive tin of antiquity. It is tin, when alloyed up to 5–10 percent with copper, that produces bronze. Its economic role in metal technology, prior to the introduction of iron, is perhaps akin to that of oil in industry today—that is, it was the most important additive to the then high-tech metal of its age, bronze. The alternative form of alloy, made with arsenic (1–5 percent), was widespread in Anatolia in the fourth millennium but diminished with the use of tin alloys.

The project focused on a search for the sources of these vital raw materials in Turkey, the birthplace of some of the earliest pyrotechnological innovations. The primary intent was to track down the direction and magnitude of the traffic in metals and the impact of this trade on the producers of metals. The second goal was to understand the technological processes involved in the manufacture of tools, weapons, and ornaments in the Taurus area, a major source zone accessible to neighboring Syria, Mesopotamia, and the coastal Mediterranean. The objectives were multidimensional: where the sources of metals were, how they were made, and the socioeconomic and political systems that impacted on and in turn were changed by this industry.

Göltepe is architecturally unlike any site in Turkey. The workshop/habitation units are semisubterranean and fully subterranean pit houses. Apart from its location and time span, the site's relatively unique morphology was created by carving the clays for habitation. Subterranean structural units were cut into the underlying basal clays using the outcroppings as walls—that is, the cultural deposition consisted of the accumulation of strata all cut into underlying geologic sediments, a highly unusual architectural feature in Anatolia during this period. Göltepe yielded several neighborhoods of subterranean and semisubterranean pit houses that may have functioned as combined workshop/habitation units. The pit-house structures are cut into the graywacke bedrock and associated with smaller subsidiary pits. The smaller houses measure 4–6 m in diameter. Larger units are 9 × 7 m and are terraced off the slope, much like the present-day neighboring mountain village, Celaller. The superstructure of these units is wattle and daub, great numbers of branch impressions on mud, structural daub, as well as postholes have been found that may enable a reconstruction of the architecture of the site. In some instances a dry-laid stone wall served to buttress the crumbling bedrock. Although very few postholes were identified, a superstructure of wattle and daub is inferred by the branch impressions on vitrified mud lumps in the collapse levels. The units were repeatedly plastered, and up to twenty-five layers of plaster could be identified. Additional smaller pits cut into the bedrock probably served storage functions. The pits ranged in size from under one meter in diameter and less than 0.5 m in depth to several meters. All of the pits were filled with a similar debris: small to medium stones, ground-stone tools, relief-decorated slabs, crucible fragments, powdered ore and ore fragments, and ceramic sherds. Some storage pits were identified by pot rests on the bottom for large pithos vessels. Unique also are what appear to be structural features: geo-

metrically designed clay panels may have decorated the interior of the pit houses, providing decorative borders for doors, bins, and altars.

The earliest phase at the site is phase V, basal pits. Phases III and IV are characterized by subterranean pit structures and storage/refuse pits. Tentatively, they correspond to the Early Bronze II period on the basis of pottery parallels with Tarsus. Phase II, which overlies them, represents a stratigraphic break and an architectural reorientation. The phase is characterized by the construction of above-surface structures and represents a period of expansion. The walls of the phase II buildings were often built over the underlying pit houses, which were filled in with industrial and domestic debris. Although pit houses continued to be built, large walled structures were erected on top of massive terraces constructed of colluvial stones. In area E, only the terrace is preserved; the architectural plans of the structure are lost to erosion. The circuit wall dates to this phase and corresponds roughly to EB III at Tarsus. At Tarsus there is an architectural break between EB II and EB III as well, when megaron-related structures appear. The uppermost levels are dated to phase I. These are topsoil and transitional levels and represent collapse and site abandonment at the end of the third millennium. In one restricted sector on the eastern slope, an Iron Age reuse of EB pit houses was also identified.

Some of the most important finds relating to the processing of tin have been the hundreds of vitrified earthenware crucibles with a glassy slag accretion rich in tin. Constructed with a coarse straw-and-grit-tempered ware, they have slagged surfaces measuring between 30–90 percent tin content; they range from a rim size of 6 cm in diameter to one of 50 cm. In some instances, tin particles were entrapped in the slag and identified by microprobe, scanning electron microscopy, and X-ray diffraction as the product of the smelt. [See Spectroscopy; Microscopy; X-ray Diffraction Analysis.] The activities demonstrated by analysis at the Conservation Analytical Laboratory of the Smithsonian Institution in Washington, D.C., include a labor-intensive, multistep, low-temperature process carried out between 800° and 950° C. Processing involved intentionally producing tin metal by reduction firing tin oxide in crucibles—with repeated grinding, washing, panning, and resmelting. The raw materials being processed in the crucibles consisted of tin oxide (cassiterite) with no copper ores present, along with calcium carbonate, iron oxide with minor amounts of magnesia and titania, an alumino-silicate containing more than 12 percent potassia, and soda and charcoal as the reduction agent. This recent evidence put to rest initial skepticism over the concentrations of tin in the Taurus and reveals it to be an important tin processing center (Yener et al., 1993a; Yener and Vandiver, 1993b).

Large numbers of crucibles came from multicelled structures at Göltepe. Along with the crucibles, the pithouse structures contained pyrotechnological installations, many ore-processing ground stones, and tin-ore nodules. One pit-house structure revealed an unusual crucible, possibly in situ. Pulverized ore of the consistency of fine powder, containing from 0.3–1.8 percent tin was discovered in cups in sealed deposits on the floors of these pit houses. Other indicators of ore processing and metal production came from the more interesting ore-dressing equipment—large mortars and pestles (weighing 26.3 kg and 6.5 kg)—used for crushing the ore. Querns, grinding stones with multiple flat facets, polishing stones, and large ground-stone axes weighing 2.9 kg, as well as bucking stones with multiple hollows, also indicate an important commitment to industry. A number of sandstone and clay molds with beds carved on several surfaces with bar-shaped forms suggest that tin metal was being produced and poured into ingot forms before transshipment to locations for bronze alloying. Tin-bronze pins, awls, rings and other fragments containing 4.75–12.3 percent tin were also found in several of the pit houses.

The EB ceramic assemblage at Göltepe is similar to the finds from Kestel mine. Important parallels with Tarsus, Mersin, and Kültepe give comparable chronological spans for both sites. Cups with a single handle and miniature vases, both plain and painted, are dated to roughly the end of the third millennium. Also called Anatolian metallic ware, this pottery was surveyed in the same regions; Machteld Mellink (1989) describes it as an import to Tarsus from the Taurus Mountains and adjoining plateau and suggests connections with the metal sources. To prevent confusing it with Syrian metallic wares, this pottery is called Anatolian metallic ware at Göltepe and at Kestel mine. The dark-burnished wares come in red and black, as well as in a related unburnished variant. Tempered with fine grit and with some chaff, the pottery is handmade and is often slipped. Simple bowls and single-handled cups are some of the more predominant shapes. The closest parallels for this pottery come from EB I and II at Tarsus for the plain black-burnished and red-burnished types.

The work done at Göltepe has gone a long way toward couching intelligent questions regarding the context and organization of tin production in the region: were specialist laborers operating out of a larger site, was it part of a more complex system, was it a cottage industry? The possibilities are interesting and quite varied. Clearly, tin processing occurred at Göltepe and, to judge from the quantities, on a large scale.

[*See also* Kestel; Taurus Mountains.]

BIBLIOGRAPHY

Mellink, Machteld. "Anatolian and Foreign Relations of Tarsus." In *Anatolia and the Ancient Near East: Studies in Honor of Tahsin Özgüç*, edited by K. Emre et al., pp. 319–331. Ankara, 1989.

Vandiver, Pamela B. et al., "Third Millennium B.C. Tin Processing Debris from Göltepe (Anatolia)." In *Materials Issues in Art and Archaeology*, vol. 3, edited by Pamela B. Vandiver et al., pp. 545–569. Pittsburgh, 1992.

Vandiver, Pamela B. et al., "Thermoluminescence Dating of a Crucible Fragment from an Early Tin Processing Site in Turkey." *Archaeometry* 35 (1993): 295–298.

Yener, K. Aslıhan et al., "Reply to J. D. Muhly, 'Early Bronze Age Tin and the Taurus.'" *American Journal of Archaeology* 97 (1993a): 255–264.

Yener, K. Aslıhan, and Pamela B. Vandiver. "Tin Processing at Göltepe, an Early Bronze Age Site in Anatolia." *American Journal of Archaeology* 97 (1993b): 207–238.

Yener, K. Aslıhan. "Managing Metals: An Early Bronze Age Tin Production Site at Göltepe, Turkey." *Oriental Institute News and Notes* 140 (1994): 1–4.

K. ASLIHAN YENER

GORDION. Near the juncture of the Porsuk and Sakarya rivers in central Turkey lies a large, flat-topped mound called Yassıhöyük (39°39′ N, 32°00′ E). The form of the site, typical of large, long-term settlements in this region, plus the presence of small, conical burial mounds on nearby slopes, suggest a place of some importance. In 1900 two German scholars, Gustav and August Körte, began to investigate the site convinced that their trenches would reveal Gordion, capital of the Phrygian kingdom of the first millennium BCE (Körte and Körte, 1904). They selected Yassıhöyük because it alone conformed to an ancient historian's descriptions, which placed Gordion on the Sangarios (Sakarya) River, at a point "equally distant from the Pontic and Cilician Seas" (Quintus Curtius, *Historiae Alexandri Magni Macedonis* 3.1.11). Today this identification is supported by excavated remains of appropriate scale and date and by associated inscriptions in the Phrygian language; the site has not, however, yielded inscribed material attesting either the place name Gordion or the name of its most famous king, Midas. In fact, with the exception of a few references to well-known historical figures and pivotal events, most of our information about Gordion and the Phrygians comes from archaeology rather than texts.

The ancient settlement is actually composed of three distinct topographic units (see figure 1). Yassıhöyük itself rises 16 m (52.5 ft.) above plain level, and measures 500 × 350 m (1,640 × 1148 ft.). At least 4 m (13 ft.) more of archaeological deposit lie beneath the modern land surface; thus, the mound consists of more than 20 m (65.6 ft.) of occupation debris dating from the Early Bronze Age to medieval times. Heavily fortified during much of its history, this area is referred to here as "the Citadel Mound" (formerly the "City Mound"). A fortified lower town lies adjacent to the Citadel to the south and west, and to the north and northwest a large, unwalled outer town extends over an area of nearly 1 sq km. Surface survey and excavation conducted between 1987 and 1994 have provided some information on fluctuations in the size and topography of ancient Gordion. We now know that the lower and outer towns were settled by the seventh century BCE if not earlier; by the third century the lower town had been abandoned, but parts of the outer

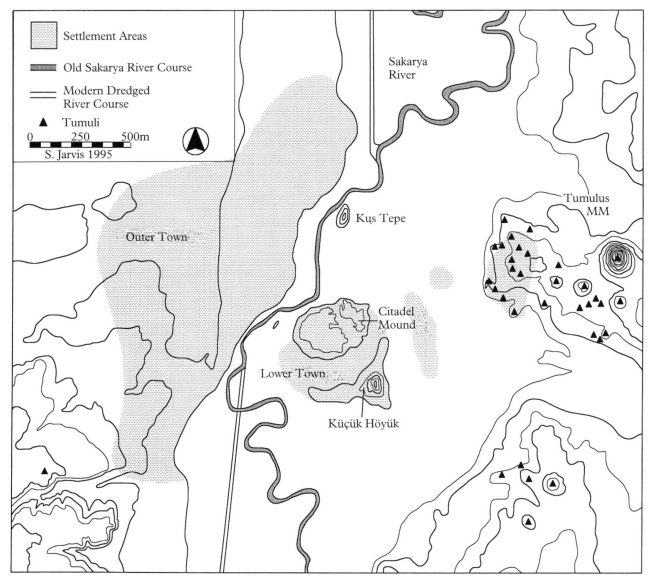

GORDION.   Figure 1.   *Map of the Gordion area.* (Courtesy of the Gordion Project)

town were occupied into the Roman period. It is worth noting that estimates of site size are more likely to be too small than too large because the land surface of ancient times lies buried beneath about 4 m (13 ft.) of alluvium; parts of the site have also been eroded by the meandering Sakarya River, which flowed to the south and east of the site until relatively recently.

Scattered along the slopes and ridge tops surrounding Gordion are about one hundred burial mounds or tumuli, of which nearly forty have been investigated by archaeologists. The greatest number lie to the east, where a linear distribution suggests that they may have lined an ancient road or ceremonial way. The mounds vary considerably in size. The largest (Tumulus MM) is about 50 m (164 ft.) in height with a diameter of nearly 300 m (984 ft.) and some

of the smaller mounds have been so reduced by erosion and plowing (not to mention robber trenches) that they are barely visible. The excavated tombs range in date from the eighth to first century.

Previous Excavations at Gordion. Alfred and Gustav Körte placed three trenches on the Citadel Mound and excavated five tumuli, two of which produced burials dated to the Early Phrygian period. Far more extensive in scope and duration was the research carried out by the University of Pennsylvania Museum's Gordion Project, directed by Rodney S. Young. Working with Machteld Mellink and G. Roger Edwards, Young excavated for sixteen seasons between 1950 and 1973. On the Citadel, much of a burned settlement destroyed by fire was cleared, providing a rich and unique picture of the Early Phrygian capital. Young's team also explored the lower-town fortifications and excavated thirty-one burial mounds. To document earlier periods Young and Mellink dug below the destruction level until they were stopped by ground water rising in their trenches. This phase of fieldwork ended with Young's accidental death in 1974.

In 1988 a new cycle of excavation and regional surface survey began, directed by Mary M. Voigt in cooperation with G. Kenneth Sams. The initial goals of Voigt's research were to record a detailed stratigraphic sequence for all periods of occupation on the Citadel Mound and to recover information on the economy of the settlement including the subsistence system, land use, and manufacturing. Attention was also focused on the documentation of domestic architecture and on variation in material culture between areas within the city.

Archaeological Sequence. The earliest-known occupation at Gordion dates to the mid-third millennium, when the settlement consisted of small mud-walled houses surrounded by an embankment and fortification wall. Material dating to the first half of the second millennium consists primarily of ceramics obtained from the citadel soundings, supplemented by more complete vessels from extramural cemeteries.

Better known are the Late Bronze and Early Iron Age settlements. The final Late Bronze Age level (c. 1200) includes a house with nearby storage pits, which eventually filled with domestic trash. The house was constructed by cutting a rectangular cellar more than a meter deep and lining the walls with large stones; this preparation served as the foundation for a wooden superstructure, with a porch on one end. The settlement is linked to the Hittite Empire by similarities in architecture, ceramics, metal artifacts, and glyptic material. Mass production of ceramics points to an economy based on specialization and exchange. We cannot estimate the size of Gordion at this time, but it appears to be part of a small polity in contact with the Hittites and affiliated with them to some degree.

Built directly above and partially into the ruins of the Late Hittite building was an Early Iron Age architectural complex. Small houses, sometimes consisting of a single room, were set in shallow rectilinear pits that were lined with mud plaster or stone slabs. Around the edge of the house pit were built walls of reeds or other lightweight material covered with mud; characteristic domestic features include ovens and bins built of stone slabs plastered with mud. Found on the floors of these houses were handmade pots fired at low temperatures; these vessels are extremely variable in form and decoration, attributes of a household ceramic industry. Architecture, artifacts, and a preliminary assessment of household economy suggest a relatively small and isolated community.

This archaeological sequence can be used to address a question raised by historians: What was the relationship between the migration of Phrygian speakers from Thrace into Anatolia, and the fall of the Hittite Empire? Gordion provides no evidence for a significant hiatus in settlement between the Late Bronze Age and Early Iron Age occupations; nevertheless, there are changes in virtually every aspect of material culture between these periods. Thus the archaeological remains suggest that the Late Bronze Age/Hittite affiliated population moved out of the area or at least away from Gordion and that a new group settled there at near the beginning of the first millennium. Based on admittedly vague similarities between the Early Iron Age pottery at Gordion and roughly contemporary pottery from Thrace, it is reasonable to identify the archaeological remains of this period with the immigration of Phrygian speakers into central Anatolia.

The Phrygians' growing political power was soon reflected by new construction on the Citadel Mound. A visitor to the heart of Gordion around 800 would have passed through massive fortifications into a small gate building constructed of red, white, and gray stone. Inside, red and white stone paving led to a large court with a packed earth floor; bordering the court were at least two rectangular buildings constructed of soft white stone and wood. One or more of the structures was decorated with stone sculptures in a style related to Syro-Hittite reliefs of the ninth century. With the exception of the fortification system, all of these structures were demolished as part of a rebuilding of the elite quarter during the eighth century, and it is the latter architectural phase that was preserved by fire and explored by Rodney Young.

In 700 the kingdom of Phrygia was ruled by a king known as Midas to the Greeks, and Mita of Muški to the Assyrians. By this time Gordion had grown and may have covered much of the area now lying beneath Yassıhöyük. There were now two distinct zones within the city: the walled elite quarter to the east, and an area to the west, which was presumably occupied by ordinary people. Although only 2 sq m (2.4 sq. ft.) of the western zone has been excavated, the elite quarter has been exposed over an area of more than 2 ha (5 acres). Inside its walls were three functionally differentiated zones that were physically separated by walls and changes in level: a palace complex divided into two courts; two long service buildings; and a large building composed of small cell-like rooms (see figure 2). The stone-paved outer court of the palace complex was bordered to both east and west by large megarons (halls) built of stone or mud brick with timber elements, and possibly gabled roofs made of reeds covered with clay. Because the outer-court buildings were empty when discovered, there is little direct evidence of their precise function, but from their location we may surmise that they housed reception and storage areas, and one building may have been a temple. The most elaborate structure (Megaron 2) had a multicolored pebble mosaic floor set in geometric motifs; incised on the soft-stone walls of this building were many graffiti, showing gable-roofed buildings, birds, animals, and (occasionally) people. Although these "doodles" may simply be the work of people waiting to see officials or members of the royal household, some scholars see hawk and lion graffiti as evidence that Megaron 2 was a cult building dedicated to Matar or Cybele—the primary Phrygian goddess, who is often depicted with raptors and lions.

A thick wall separated the outer court from an inner court, which was again bordered by megarons. The largest of these (Megaron 3) contained large quantities of smashed and charred artifacts including metal and ceramic storage and serving vessels, foodstuffs, carved wooden furniture, ivory inlays, and textiles. Either this building or the adjacent Megaron 4 (which was disturbed after the fire and so presumed to have contained things worth salvaging) probably served as the royal residence. Another partition wall separated the inner court from a structure made up of small rectangular rooms; this structure was used for many years after the fire. Artifacts provide no clue to its function during the Early Phrygian period.

To the west of the palace complex was a high terrace with two long service buildings facing each other across a broad street. Each building is divided into a series of megaron units consisting of a large inner room with central hearth and a smaller anteroom. The rooms often contained ovens, and most had rows of grinding stones set on mud platforms. Their function as cooking and storage areas is also indicated by charred grain and other seeds and masses of pottery. Other evidence for domestic production includes spindle whorls, loomweights, and partially woven textile fragments. Two rooms stored more valuable items such as imported ivory horse trappings, bronze vessels, and animal figurines, and gold and electrum jewelry.

The wealth and craftsmanship of the Phrygians suggested by charred and broken fragments within the Citadel are clearly documented by tombs, especially Tumulus MM and P. Huge conical mounds of clay and stone were laid over wooden chambers containing elaborately inlaid wooden furniture, local and imported pottery of high quality, bronze and brass vessels, and jewelry such as belts and fibulae

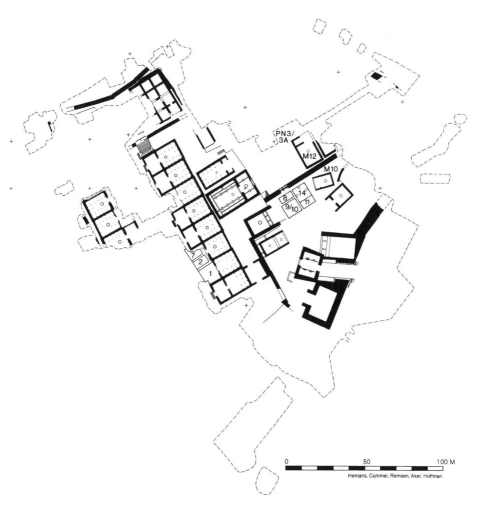

GORDION.   Figure 2.   *Plan of the Early Phrygian period.* (Courtesy of the Gordion Project)

(brooches). The largest tumulus (MM) is interpreted by many as the tomb of Midas, who supposedly committed suicide when his kingdom was destroyed by the Cimmerians shortly after 700. Other scholars prefer a late eighth-century date for the log tomb chamber and/or its contents and suggest that an earlier ruler was interred there—perhaps Midas's father.

Lying above the ruins of the destruction level on the Citadel is a 3–5-meter-thick layer of clay supporting new stone buildings that had rubble foundations set deeply into the clay. In plan, the elite quarter of the rebuilt or Middle Phrygian settlement replicates key elements of the Early Phrygian settlement lying directly below. There are differences, however, in construction methods and in the plan of individual structures, especially the gate building. With its increased height and massive polychrome walls, the settlement dominated the surrounding countryside. Its topography was relatively complex. The walled elite quarter and the western residential zone (also built on a 5–6-meter-thick layer of clay) were distinct mounds, separated by a broad, paved avenue, which led south, presumably into the lower town. It is not clear whether the western mound was fortified, but protected by its own height it contained well-built houses, which probably belonged to merchants or minor officials. In the lower town, stone and mud buildings were protected by 3.5-meter-thick fortification walls with square towers set at regular intervals; the walls were anchored by a mud-brick fortress (the Küçük Höyük). On the slopes to the north and west of the twin mounds lay the unfortified outer town where houses may have been interspersed with gardens or small fields.

The absolute date of the Middle Phrygian rebuilding, and therefore its historical significance, has been the subject of considerable discussion, debate, and revision. Although Rodney Young had long thought that Gordion was rebuilt during the second half of the sixth century, after the Persians gained power in central Anatolia, during the last years of his life he placed the rebuilding in the first half of the sixth century. This dating has been accepted by other scholars, some of whom credit the Lydians with support for this project if not direct sponsorship (see, e.g., DeVries, 1990, pp. 391–392). New evidence challenges this view, suggesting that the rebuilding process began almost immediately after the fire and was completed by the middle of the seventh century, if not earlier (Voight, 1994; see also Henrickson, 1994). If this dating is correct, the Phrygian political system was not destroyed in 700, and the ruling elite was able to mobilize a substantial labor force to recreate and enhance a citadel that was both product and symbol of their right to collect tribute or taxes.

By the early sixth century, Phrygian Gordion was certainly under strong Lydian influence, incorporated into the kingdom of Alyattes and Croesus. This situation ended when Cyrus the Great took the city in 547, an event documented in the archaeological record by the destruction of the Küçük Höyük fortress. Under the Persians, Gordion was reduced in importance as a political center, but its role as an economic center continued or was perhaps enhanced by the unification of Anatolia within the Persian Empire. One source of prosperity seems to be manufacturing, with evidence for the production of stone, bone, ivory, and metal artifacts. The items received in exchange for such goods included Attic and Lydian fine wares and Greek wines. Gordion under the Achaemenids was in fact a fascinating place: juxtaposed with elements of indigenous Phrygian material culture were new Iranian ceramic forms and horse harness, a building decorated with painted tiles in Lydian style, and a room decorated with polychrome murals painted in Greek style.

No archaeological remains testify to the visit of Alexander the Great in 334/33, but its effect is clear. Gordion became thoroughly hellenized, as evidenced by Greek inscriptions and graffiti, Greek style house plans and grain mills, and the importation of masses of black-glazed pottery. The settlement appears to have been reduced in size, but ashlar (dressed masonry) walls indicate the presence of one or more monumental structures, this time in the northwest quadrant of the citadel. The low street between the two mounds was filled, and houses were built above the former palace quarter and its walls. The best known phase of the Hellenistic occupation is also the latest. Early in the second century, houses on the Citadel caught fire and were abandoned with their contents left in situ. The Roman historian Livy provides an explanation for this catastrophe (*History of Rome* 38.12.1–27.9). At the end of the third century Gordion was an *oppidum* or hill fort occupied by immigrant Galatian mercenaries. In 189 the Roman consul and general Manlius Vulso campaigned against the Galatians in Anatolia. When he came to Gordion, its inhabitants had fled, and he found an empty settlement, which he presumably looted of its more valuable items before setting it afire.

Nearly two centuries later, Roman settlers reestablished Gordion, which was known in Latin as Gordium. Although the settlement was small (Strabo refers to it as a "village" in *Geog.* 12.5.3, 568), it may have been important as a market and source of agricultural products. This function is suggested by the location of Gordion along the road between Pessinus and Ancyra, cities founded by the Romans after the annexation of Galatia into the empire in 27. Gordion's prosperity is indicated by imported red-glazed ceramics from the settlement and by grave goods deposited in cemeteries located in the lower town and on the east slopes of the valley. Cremations and inhumations were sometimes accompanied by glass or pottery vessels as well as jewelry incorporating carved stone signets. When Roman prosperity declined in Asia Minor during the initial phase of warfare with the Sasanian Empire in the second half of the third century CE, Gordion was again abandoned. It was briefly occupied during medieval times, but excavated material from graves and houses has not been analyzed or precisely dated.

BIBLIOGRAPHY

DeVries, Keith. "The Gordion Excavation Seasons of 1969–1973 and Subsequent Research." *American Journal of Archaeology* 94 (1990): 371–406. The most recent summary of chronology and architecture from Young's excavations, especially important for its well-illustrated discussion of a construction project underway when the Early Phrygian citadel was destroyed. DeVries's definition of the Middle and Late Phrygian periods still stands, but chronology and details have been revised as a result of more recent excavation.

Gunter, Ann C. *The Gordion Excavations, 1950–1973: Final Reports,* vol. 3, *The Bronze Age.* Philadelphia, 1991. Catalogue of the Bronze Age pottery and a discussion of the place of Gordion within Bronze Age Anatolia.

Henrickson, Robert C. "Continuity and Discontinuity in the Ceramic Tradition at Gordion during the Iron Age." In *Anatolian Iron Ages 3: The Proceedings of the Third International Anatolian Iron Ages Symposium Held at Van, 6–12 August 1990,* edited by David H. French and Altan Çilingiroğlu, pp. 95–129. London, 1994. Presents the first comprehensive ceramic typology for Gordion, as well as evidence critical for an understanding of the Early Iron Age and the arrival of the Phrygians.

Körte, Gustav, and Alfred Körte. *Gordion: Ergebnisse der Ausgrabung im Jahre 1900.* Berlin, 1904. While difficult to obtain, this volume contains a full discussion of the historical sources related to Gordion, and the argument for the identification of Yassıhöyük as Gordion.

Mellink, Machteld J. "The Native Kingdoms of Anatolia." In *The Cambridge Ancient History,* vol. 3, pp. 619–665. New York, 1991. Excellent summary of the archaeology and history of Phrygians and Lydians, providing additional information on the Early Phrygian period and a context for events at Gordion.

Mitchell, Stephen. *Anatolia: Land, Men, and Gods in Asia Minor,* vol. 1, *The Celts in Anatolia and the Impact of Roman Rule.* New York, 1993. Comprehensive and lucid account of historical and archaeological evidence for the emigration of the Celts, their roles as mercenaries and settlers, and their incorporation in the Roman empire.

Muscarella, Oscar White. *Bronze and Iron: Ancient Near Eastern Artifacts in the Metropolitan Museum of Art.* New York, 1988. Excellent introduction to the material culture of the Near East, including the Phrygians and their contemporaries, with summary sections providing overviews as well as a guide to key sources.

Sams, G. Kenneth. *The Gordion Excavations, 1950–1973: Final Reports,* vol. 4, *The Early Phrygian Pottery.* Philadelphia, 1994. Contains a detailed description of Early Phrygian ceramics and their distribution of types within architectural units on the Citadel Mound and in contemporary tumuli.

Source: Notes in the History of Art 7.3–4 (1988). Collection of essays on Phrygian art and archaeology written in 1987, with useful discussions on Phrygian religion (Buluç and Roller) and Early Phrygian furniture (Simpson), as well as the only published summary on Hellenistic Gordion (Winter). G. Kenneth Sams presents his view of the development of Phrygian material culture as a merging of European and Anatolian elements.

Voigt, Mary M. "Excavations at Gordion, 1988–89: The Yassihoyuk Stratigraphic Sequence." In *Anatolian Iron Ages 3: The Proceedings of the Third International Anatolian Iron Ages Symposium Held at Van, 6–12 August 1990,* edited by David H. French and Altan Çilingiroğlu, pp. 265–291. London, 1994. Summary of the stratigraphy and chronology of Gordion from the Late Bronze Age through the Late Phrygian period as understood from excavations in 1988–1989.

Young, Rodney S., et al. *The Gordion Excavations, 1950–1973: Final Reports,* vol. 1, *Three Great Early Tumuli.* Philadelphia, 1981. Completed by Young's colleagues after his death, this volume provides a complete description of tomb architecture and the spectacular wooden and metal finds within them. The introduction contains a list of major preliminary reports on the Young excavations, including dissertations.

MARY M. VOIGT

GRAINS. *See* Cereals.

GRANARIES AND SILOS. The beginning of grain storage can be attributed to surplus production associated with the domestication of cereals and other crops at the beginning of the Neolithic period. As social structures developed, so did different types of grain-storage facilities that were either publicly or privately owned. Such facilities were subterranean or above ground; the grain was deposited in bulk or in containers.

Most above-ground facilities seem to have been publicly owned. Some of the earliest have been found in the Ubaid 4 level at Tell el-'Oueili in Iraq (Huot, 1992, p. 192); however, the shape of the superstructure is unknown. The development of beehive-shaped granaries for storage in bulk probably originated in Egypt in the Early Bronze Age (Borowski, 1987, p. 76) and spread to Palestine. Remains of similar structures dating to the EB II and EB III were discovered at Arad (Currid, 1986) and Beth-Yeraḥ (Mazar, 1990), respectively. The latter, which could hold 2,250 cubic meters of grain, was made of nine circular structures connected to what appears to be a temple (Mazar, 1990, pp. 129–130). Similar buildings were discovered in Anatolia and on Crete. Artistic representations show that this type of granary also continued in use during the New Kingdom (Gressmann, 1927, pl. 177). These structures were filled through windows at the top by ladder-climbing, grain-carrying workers and emptied through doors at the bottom. Remains of Late Bronze Age beehive granaries were found at Bir el-'Abd in northern Sinai, where a fort from the time of Seti I was maintained (Oren, 1973). Similar structures dating to the Hellenistic period were discovered at Tell Jemmeh by Sir William Flinders Petrie (1928, pp. 8–9, pl. 14) and more recently by Gus Van Beek (1986). The absence of remains of beehive granaries during the Iron Age gives credence to Petrie's suggestion that the structures at Tell Jemmeh were constructed under foreign influence, possibly from Mesopotamia.

During the Iron Age, the main publicly owned storage facilities were the tripartite, pillared buildings uncovered at Tell el-Ḥesi, Tell Qasile, Tell Abu Hawam, Megiddo, Hazor, and Beersheba. At Tel Hadar (Kochavi et al., 1992, pp. 36–41) the only above-ground, rectangular grain-storage complex known from the Iron Age Levant was recently discovered, attached to a tripartite building. The function of the tripartite buildings is controversial; some consider them stables. Another common type of Iron Age storehouse, with long rooms and thick walls, has been discovered at Jericho, Lachish, Megiddo, Beth-Shemesh, Tell Jemmeh, Tell en-Naṣbeh, and Tell Beit Mirsim (Borowski, 1987; pp. 78–79), in which jars and other vessels such as jugs and bowls held commodities. In the Bible, storehouses are called *miskĕnôt*, from the Akkadian *maškanâti*.

During the Roman Empire, granary construction was standardized. Whether for civilian or military use, granary buildings were long and narrow with thick walls, raised floors, and proper ventilation. Examples can be found throughout the former Roman Empire in cities, at harbors, and at military installations (Rickman, 1980).

Subterranean facilities were publicly and privately owned. This type of storage facility dates back to the time of the Neolithic revolution. Some of the earliest grain-storage pits have been discovered at Maghzaliyeh (Iraq) dating to the seventh millennium BCE (Huot, 1992, p. 189). Plastered subterranean granaries have been found at Gezer in Iron Age I and Middle Bronze IIA levels. The stone-lined, sometimes plastered, storage pit was a very common feature in the Late Bronze and Iron Ages, in both large and small communities. Privately owned storage pits have been discovered near

dwellings and in courtyards at Tell Beit Mirsim, 'Izbet Sarṭah, Beersheba, Tell Ḥalif, and many other sites. One of the best examples of publicly owned storage pits, or silos, was found at Megiddo. There, a round pit has two sets of stairs along the wall to facilitate the heavy traffic of workers bringing in or taking away grain. Storage pits at Beersheba had mortars and grinding stones set next to their rim to enable more efficient grinding of grain. Tell Beit Mirsim and Beersheba may be the only sites where an Iron Age cellar was used for storage in jars. The biblical term for a privately owned storage pit is *'āsām**.

Publicly owned grain-storage facilities were mostly used for the collection and disbursement of revenues to functionaries, such as the civic and religious bureaucracy and the military. Private facilities were located close to or in dwellings, to facilitate the use of grain in daily food preparation and to store seeds.

[*See also* Agriculture; Cereals; *and* Food Storage. *In addition, most of the sites mentioned are the subject of independent entries.*]

BIBLIOGRAPHY

Borowski, Oded. *Agriculture in Iron Age Israel.* Winona Lake, Ind., 1987. The most recent work combining biblical and archaeological information about Israelite agriculture.

GRANARIES AND SILOS. *Stone-lined (storage?) bin from stratum VII at Tel Ḥalif.* (Courtesy ASOR Archives)

Currid, John D. "The Beehive Building of Ancient Palestine." *Biblical Archaeologist* 49 (1986): 20–24. Recent treatment of this and other types of granaries.

Gressmann, Hugo. *Altorientalische Texte und Bilder zum Alten Testament*. Berlin, 1927. A very good collection of artistic representations related to biblical topics from the ancient Near East.

Huot, Jean-Louis. "The First Farmers at Oueili." *Biblical Archaeologist* 55 (1992): 188–195. Coverage of early Mesopotamian settlements, in an issue devoted to the region.

Kochavi, Moshe et al., "The Land of Geshur." *Biblical Archaeology Review* 18 (July–August 1992): 30–44, 84–85. First English-language report of this excavation.

Mazar, Amihai. "On the Significance of the Early Bronze III 'Circles Building' at Beth-Yerah" (in Hebrew). *Shenaton le-Mikra ule-heker ha-mizrah ha-Kadum* (Annual for Biblical and Ancient Near Eastern Studies) 10 (1990): 123–135. The most recent treatment of this structure and its possible function.

Oren, Eliezer D. "Notes and News: Bir el-'Abd (Northern Sinai)." *Israel Exploration Journal* 23 (1973): 112–113. Report of this discovery.

Petrie, W. M. Flinders. *Gerar*. London, 1928. Final report on the excavations and discoveries.

Rickman, Geoffrey. *Roman Granaries and Store Building*. Cambridge, 1980. Important work on the design and construction of civil and military granaries and storehouses throughout the Roman Empire.

Van Beek, Gus W. "Are There Beehive Granaries at Tell Jemmeh? A Rejoinder." *Biblical Archaeologist* 49 (1986): 245–247. Important treatment of the beehive granary.

ODED BOROWSKI

GRAPES. *See* Viticulture.

GRAVE GOODS. The objects that accompany the dead in mortuary contexts are widely interpreted as part of the sustenance required in a postmortem existence (the netherworld or afterlife). The repertoire of grave goods is usually similar but not identical to that of domestic contexts; particular shapes or types of decoration are sometimes reserved for burial alone. Tombs also tend to contain richer assemblages per square meter than living contexts. While in some cases this wealth may actually reflect the elite status of the dead or the cultic nature of mortuary rites, it more often seems to mirror the perceived importance of wealth in the hereafter, using a fairly standardized format and inventory. Food and drink were ubiquitous provisions, preserved in the form of animal bones (cuts of meat), open vessels (for perishable produce), and closed vessels (liquids: wine, oil, water and perhaps milk for infants). Other containers, fashioned of exotic materials—alabaster, faience, and glass—may have contained cosmetics, ointments, or processed, scented oils.

A grave good inventory can reflect social status. Warrior status is inferred by the presence of weapons in certain burials, generally of adult males. Equid (usually donkey) burials in Middle Bronze Age tombs at Jericho, Tell el-'Ajjul, and Tell ed-Dab'a, for example, probably imply status distinction as well—perhaps that of a merchant. [*See* Jericho; 'Ajjul,

Tell el-; Dab'a, Tell ed-.] Some Mesopotamian necropoli show a disparity in grave good affluence that may betoken social stratification (e.g., Tepe Gawra, Ur, and Aššur). [*See* Tepe Gawra; Ur; Aššur.] The same was true for Egypt, albeit to a lesser extent, because it is probable that only the upper classes are represented in the archaeological record. Certain tombs or burial sites whose contents are several degrees more profligate than other contemporary burials may be interpreted as elite tombs (e.g., the Royal Cemetery of Ur, the royal necropoli on the west bank of the Nile in Egypt, and, probably, the Chalcolithic Naḥal Mishmar "hoard" in Israel). [*See* Judean Desert Caves; Cave Tombs.] Subsidiary, "servant" burials appended to larger, more extravagant ones have been discerned at the Royal Cemetery of Ur in southern Mesopotamia and at Tell ed-Dab'a in the Egyptian Delta. Graves of the southern Levant show less class division based on wealth, though the sample may not be completely representative if, in certain periods, only the elite adopted enduring tomb types.

In the southern Levant, the Middle Bronze Age cemeteries show the greatest variety of offerings and status categories. Infants are found buried without offerings or with just a few—a juglet near the mouth and a talismanic scarab are the most common. Tombs of children tend to contain an equally modest array, though they rarely lack offerings completely. Adult interments are generally the most affluent, each corpse typically being accompanied by a number of objects of the kind described above.

The Middle Bronze and Roman period tombs at Jericho have been especially instrumental in permitting an understanding of the nature of grave goods because of the remarkable preservation of their organic contents. The many wooden objects—beds, stools, headrests, bowls, boxes, and combs—and the remains of foodstuffs—cuts of meat, pomegranates, and grapes—reveal that such organic materials were used more frequently than the remains of other tomb assemblages suggest.

Subtle changes occurred during that time: in the southern Levant, cooking pots, for example, only became statistically significant as a grave good in the Iron Age and truly common in the Hellenistic–Roman period. In the grave good assemblages of the Hellenistic, Roman, and Byzantine periods glass vessels, lamps, unguentaria, and various personal possessions are commonly found. In coffin burials these offerings were placed inside the coffin. In ossuary burials, the presents were most often found next to, but not inside, the box. [*See* Ossuary.] A new custom of the period, introduced by Hellenistic culture, was the placing of coins on the eyes or in the mouth of the deceased for paying ferry charges to Charon to cross the river Styx. This was a common practice among Gentiles but is rarely found in Jewish tombs.

The placement of grave goods was a normal, if not universal, practice until the Islamic period. Theological developments in the classical periods were paralleled first by changes in the way burial offerings were perceived and later by the gradual cessation of the practice. The frequent occurrence of defective goods and Mishnaic writings decrying the wasteful disposal of wealth in Jewish burials suggest that burial offerings came to be considered nonessential or purely symbolic, and eventually as superfluous and downright sinful.

[*See also* Burial Sites; *and* Burial Techniques.]

BIBLIOGRAPHY

Bloch-Smith, Elizabeth. *Judahite Burial Practices and Beliefs about the Dead.* Journal for the Study of the Old Testament, Supplement 123. Sheffield, 1992. Comprehensive study of Iron Age burial practices in Judah from both an archaeological and biblical point of view. Chapter 2 deals with burial contents.

Campbell, Stuart, and Anthony Green, eds. *The Archaeology of Death in the Ancient Near East.* Oxford, 1995. Collection of articles dealing with mortuary practices from prehistory to the modern era, including a trove of new data.

Hachlili, Rachel. *Ancient Jewish Art and Archaeology in the Land of Israel.* Leiden, 1988. See chapter 4, "Funerary Customs and Art," for a good synopsis of Late Second Temple period burial practices; weak on Jewish mortuary behavior of the later Roman and Byzantine period.

Kenyon, Kathleen M. *Digging Up Jericho.* London, 1957. Lively account of the Jericho excavations containing detailed descriptions of tombs and their contents from the Natufian period through the Iron Age. Still the site with the longest, best-excavated, and best-reported burial sequence available for the southern Levant.

Palumbo, Gaetano. "'Egalitarian' or 'Stratified' Society? Some Notes on Mortuary Practices and Social Structure at Jericho in EB IV." *Bulletin of the American Schools of Oriental Research,* no. 267 (1987): 43–59. Good example of the criteria and statistical techniques that can be used (and abused) to infer social structure.

Rahmani, L. Y. "Ancient Jerusalem's Funerary Customs and Tombs." *Biblical Archaeologist* 45 (1982): 43–53, 109–119. Deals with, among other things, the religious beliefs and the social and psychological motivations behind burial offerings or the lack thereof.

Woolley, C. Leonard, et al. *Ur Excavations.* Vols. 2–9. Publications of the Joint Expedition of the British Museum and of the Museum of the University of Pennsylvania to Mesopotamia. London, 1934–1962. Excavation reports containing a wealth of mortuary data encompassing approximately 3,500 years, with a range of social strata represented for some periods.

DAVID ILAN

GREEK. A highly inflected language, Greek encodes the syntactical structure of the sentence by accentuation of words rather than by word order. Verbs are typically marked to express tense, mood, voice, person, and number, and adjectives, articles, pronouns and nouns can be marked to reflect gender, number, and case. Greek, like Latin, Sanskrit, and German, has three genders: masculine, feminine, and neuter. In addition to singular and plural, classical Greek (like Sanskrit) has a dual. The eight Indo-European cases were reduced to five in Greek: nominative, vocative, accusative, genitive, and dative. Greek (again like Sanskrit), has three voice distinctions: active, passive, and middle (which

has a generally reflexive meaning). In classical Attic prose, accent was based on differences in pitch (i.e., the high tone is *the* accent of a word), and duration. Poetry, however, had duration only. Unlike Latin, the rules of accent involve primarily the vowel elements. During the fifth and fourth centuries BCE, Attic developed two phonemic subsystems revealed through orthographical variations in inscriptional evidence, a conservative subsystem with six vocalic phonemes /i, e, a, o, u, y/, and sixteen consonantal phonemes /p, t, k, b, d, g, ph, th, kh, s, z, h, l, r, m, n/, and an innovative subsystem consisting of eight vocalic phonemes /i, e, ɛ, a, ɔ, o, u, y/, though retaining the same sixteen consonantal phonemes (Teodorsson 1978, pp. 94–98).

History of Greek. Included under the generic linguistic term *Greek* are several related dialects that can be traced back to a reconstructed Proto-Greek language, which in turn derives from the Indo-European family of languages. The Greeks called themselves *Hellenes,* recognizing mutual ties of history, language, and culture. They labeled everyone else as *barbaroi* (i.e., non-Greeks). It is uncertain just how the Romans came to call the Hellenes *Graeci* (a latinized form of the Greek term *Graikoi,* of uncertain etymology) and their language as *Graecum* (Apollodorus, 1.7.3; Aristotle, *Meteorologica* 1.352a), perhaps because the first Hellenes whom the Romans encountered were the settlers in Cyme north of the Bay of Naples called *Graii* after their place of origin, Graia in Euboea (Homer, *Iliad* 2.498). During the late republic and early empire many Romans used a diminutive to refer disparagingly to Greeks as *Graeculi* (Cicero, *De oratore* 1.47; Pliny, *Epistula* 10.40.2). Some Romans even described the philhellene emperor Hadrian disparagingly as a *graeculus* (*Historia Augusta Hadrian* 1.5). The Indo-European family of languages includes most European languages as well as Sanskrit. Basque, the Finno-Ugric languages, and ancient Etruscan are major exceptions. The two major divisions of Indo-European are the eastern *satem* languages (Indo-Iranian, Balto-Slavic, Armenian, Albanian, Tocharian) and the western *centum* languages (Celtic, Italic, Germanic, Greek, Hittite), though this division is not without difficulties. The comparison of numerals from one through ten in a selection of these languages in table 1 reveals a genetic relationship still recognizable despite various vocalic and consonantal shifts and transformations.

Linear B syllabary. Speakers of Proto-Greek very probably arrived in the Greek peninsula about the beginning of the second millennium BCE. The earliest written Greek is found in the syllabic inscriptions on clay tablets of Linear B, now called Mycenaean Greek. It is found on Crete at Knossos and on mainland Greece at Pylos, Mycenae, and Thebes. This syllabary originated in the Mycenaean and Minoan periods (1450–1200) and served the needs of the royal administration, particularly the scribes. The syllabary consisted of eighty-seven signs representing a consonant-vowel combination (e.g., *da, do, de, du*) and did not distin-

TABLE I. *Numerals in Selected Indo-European Languages*

English	Sanskrit	Greek	Latin	Gothic	Indo-European[1]
one	ekas	heis	unus	ains	*sem
two	duvâ, dvê	duo	duo	twai	*duwô
three	tráyas	treis	tres	trija	*trejes
four	čatvâras	tettares	quattuor	fidwor	*q^we-twores
five	páñca	pente	quînque	fimf	*penq^{w}e
six	sas-	hex	sex	saihs	*s(w)eks
seven	sapta	hepta	septem	sibun	*septm
eight	astâ	oktō	octo	ahtau	*oktô
nine	náva	ennea	novem	niun	*newn
ten	dáśa	deka	decem	taihun	*dekm(t)

[1] All items in this column (marked with an asterisk) are reconstructed, nonattested forms in Proto-Indo-European.

guish between *r* and *l*. The decipherment of the syllabic script of Linear B shows a close relationship with later Greek dialects, particularly Arcado-Cypriot, which was located in the central Peloponnesus and Cyprus. The comparison in table 2 of some common Greek words with transliterated Mycenaean syllabic symbols suggests that Linear B is in fact an earlier form of Greek.

Adoption of the Alphabet. Mycenaean civilization disintegrated about 1200 BCE approximately the same time as the fall of Troy. The collapse of Mycenaean civilization was closely followed by the Dorian migrations into Greece, but there are no distinctive material features that allow archaeologists to identify this invasion. Survivors of the various conflicts at this time, the so-called Sea Peoples (i.e., Philistines, Sicilians, Tyrrhenians, Etruscans, and Sardinians), moved along the Mediterranean coast and settled in different places. This cultural collapse was followed by the Dark Age (c. 1100–950), an era of illiteracy in which earlier writing was only a dim memory. A written form of the Greek language appears again toward the end of the eighth century in an alphabetic script borrowed from North Semitic (see figure 1). The earliest evidence for Greek alphabetic writing is found on the Dipylon Jug (c. 724), a few decades after Greek trade with the eastern Mediterranean had resumed. The Greeks called their alphabet *grammata phoinikēia*, "Phoenician letters" (Herodotus, 5.58; *Sylloge Inscriptionum Graecarum*, ed. W. Dittenberger, Hildesheim, 1960 38.37; Diodorus, 5.74.1) and believed that the alphabet was introduced by the Phoenicians accompanying Cadmus, king of Tyre, who settled in Thebes (Herodotus, 5.58; Diodorus, 3.67.1; see Tacitus, *Annals* 11.14). Rhys Carpenter has argued persuasively that the Greek alphabet was taken over and modified only shortly before the first extant written inscriptions, that is, in the latter half of the eighth century BCE (Carpenter, 1933). This alphabet existed in a large number of local variations (see Jeffery, 1967), though the Ionic form eventually predominated over the many epichoric alphabets.

Major dialects. By the fifth century, two major groups of Greek dialects appeared. West Greek included "strict" Doric dialects (Laconian, Messenian, Cretan, Cyrenaean), "middle" Doric dialects (West Argolic, East Aegean Doric), and "mild" Doric dialects (Megarian, Corinthian, East Argolic, Northwest dialects). East Greek (or non-West Greek) included Attic-Ionic (Attica, Euboea, the Cycladic islands and the coast of Asia Minor), Aeolic (island of Lesbos, Thessalia, Boeotia), and Arcado-Cypriot or Achaean (spoken in central Peloponnesus and Cyprus). The Greeks themselves distinguished four dialects—Attic, Ionic, Doric, and Aeolic (Strabo, 8.1.2; 14.5.26).

Following the Dark Age, a period of Greek colonial expansion began during the mid-eighth century, motivated both by merchants seeking profit and by hunger for land. Various groups of Greeks from the mainland, the Peloponnesus, and the coast of Asia Minor founded colonies and established trade throughout much of the Mediterranean world. Two of the earliest trading centers were founded by traders from Chalcis and Eretria in Euboea, Al Mina at the mouth of the Orontes River in northern Syria in the east, and the island of Ischia (Pithecusae) north of the Bay of Naples in the west. Among the earliest Greek inscriptions extant is the longest eighth-century inscription, a graffito on a Geometric-period cup from Ischia in Euboean Greek (*Supplementum Epigraphicum Graecum*, vol. 14, edited by A. G. Woodhead, 1957, p. 604). Later colonies were founded on the coast of the Black Sea, the Propontis (the narrow

TABLE 2. *Comparison of Equivalent Greek and Mycenaean Words*

English	Greek	Mycenaean Greek
king	basileus	pa-si-re-u
priest	hiereus	i-je-re-u
fuller	knapheus	ka-na-pe-u

PHOENICIAN		GREEK		
Name	c. 900 BCE	800–600 Attic (400)		Name
ʾalef	K K X	Δ Δ A	A	alpha
bet	2 9	₵ ℬ B	B	beta
gimel	⌐ ⌐	Γ Γ C	Γ	gamma
dalet	Δ Δ Δ	D Δ D	Δ	delta
he	ⴽ Ⴝ	� E E	E	epsilon
waw	Y Y Y	F F C		(digamma)
zayin	I ㅍ I	I ㅍ I	I	zeta
ḥet	B B B	B Ⴙ H	H	eta
ṭet	⊗ ⊕	⊗ ⊗ ⊙	⊙	theta
yod	⟨ Ⅎ Ⅎ	⟨ ⟨ I	I	iota
kaf	⋃ ⋎ ⋎	K K K	K	kappa
lamed	⌐ ⌐ ⌐	L ⌐ Λ	Λ	lamda
mem	⟩ ⟩ ⟩	⟩ ⟩ M	M	mu
nun	⟩ ⟩ ⟩	⟩ ⟩ N	N	nu
samek	≠	≠ ⵣ ≡	Ξ	ksi
ʿayin	O	O	O	omikron
pe	⟩ ⟩	⌐ ⌐	⌐	pi
ṣade	⌐ ⟨	M		(san)
qof	⟨ ⟨ φ	φ φ		(qoppa)
reš	⟨ 4	P D ℝ	P	rho
śin/šin	W	⟨ ⟨ ⟨	Σ	sigma
taw	+ X	T	T	tau
		⟨ Y V	Y	upsilon
		φ ⊕ φ	φ	phi
		X +	X	chi
		⟨ V	Ψ	psi
		⟨ Ω Ω	Ω	omega

GREEK. Figure 1. *Comparison of the Phoenician consonantal signs and the letters of the Greek alphabet.* (After Peter T. Daniels and William Bright, eds., *The World's Writing Systems,* New York, 1996; courtesy Oxford University Press)

passage between the Aegean and the Black Sea), the northern shores of the Aegean, Sicily (by the Euboeans and Dorian groups), the southern coasts of Italy, Magna Grecia (by the Euboeans and Achaeans), the southern coast of France, and the northern coast of Africa at Cyrene, all linked by sea routes which carried their trade. In Italy the Greeks had important cultural and commercial contacts with the Etruscans, which in turn affected the Romans.

From Imperial Attic to Koine. The common Greek of the Hellenistic period (325–150) and the Roman period (150 BCE–300 CE) is called Koine, following the ancient designation *hē koinē (dialektos),* "the common (dialect)." This common dialect was based on fourth-century Attic Greek and was in use from the late fourth century BCE to the mid-sixth century CE, when it developed into Byzantine Greek. The

independence and isolation of the Greek city-states had encouraged the preservation of local dialects, but the formation of political leagues tended to foster linguistic homogenization. The key role Athens had played in resisting and defeating the Persians in the early fifth century (490–479) was parlayed into political power through the formation of the First Maritime League. The linguistic corollary of the ensuing sociopolitical developments was that Attic replaced Ionic as the most prestigious Greek dialect; mercenaries in the Athenian army and fleet had to learn Attic, the language of command. After unifying Macedonia, Philip II of Macedon (372–336) defeated the Athenians and the Thebans at the battle of Chaeronea, thereby forming an extensive Greco-Macedonian empire. Philip adopted Greek culture to provide cohesion to his empire, and made Attic Greek, the dialect of Athens, the official language of his court and his diplomatic correspondence, transforming what was primarily a local dialect in the fifth century into Imperial Attic, a new common dialect. This policy was continued by Alexander III (356–323), better known as Alexander the Great, who succeeded Philip in 336 and immediately planned and expedited the invasion and conquest of the Persian Empire, whose official lingua franca was Aramaic. As he marched through Asia Minor, Syria-Palestine, and Egypt, and then proceeded east by means of the Fertile Crescent through Mesopotamia to India, Alexander established numerous city-states and military garrisons that were populated with Greek-speaking Macedonian soldiers, veterans, and thousands of Greek settlers including artisans and merchants from Macedonia and all other parts of the Greek world. They brought with them their native dialects, but Koine was the language of the army and the common speech of settlers; therefore, these other dialects disappeared by the third generation. Koine became the language of government, diplomacy, commerce, and education, the spoken and written language of the ruling elite and upper-class natives because Greek language and culture was tacitly considered superior to other languages and cultures. In much of the Near East, literacy meant literacy in Greek, and the native languages were spoken by those who did not read or write. Aramaic, however, was never completely displaced. Greeks who settled throughout the Near East, however, tended to be monolingual because of the high status of their own language and culture. Indigenous languages were regarded as culturally inferior by both Greek immigrants and upper-class natives. After the death of Alexander in 323, his successors consolidated power in three great Hellenistic monarchies—Antigonid Macedonia, Seleucid Syria, and Ptolemaic Egypt—in addition to many petty kingdoms. Koine was the official language of all these Hellenistic kingdoms.

Written Koine was a uniform language that had no local dialects but exhibited only stylistic, lexical, and phonological variation. Hellenistic Koine became the standard language of Greece and was realized in many regional phonological substandards, that is, Attic-Ionic, Aegean-Doric, Achaean-Doric, Northwest-Doric, South-East Aegean, Egyptian, Syro-Palestinian, and Asia Minor (Bubeník, 1989, pp. 175–255). The uniform character of the written language appears to have contributed to the standardization of the spoken language. The transformation from Attic to Koine was characterized by a variety of linguistic developments that occurred throughout the Hellenistic and Roman periods: (1) The Attic preference for the double consonant -tt- (as in thalatta, "sea") was bypassed by the Koine preference for -ss- (as in thalassa); -ss- was actually an earlier preference of the Athenian tragedians and Thucydides; (2) in Koine there was an increasing tendency to ignore the Attic distinction between long and short vowels; (3) the athematic aorist disappeared; (4) the optative became obsolete; (5) the dative was gradually phased out; (6) prepositions were increasingly used to indicate case relations; (7) the Greek vowels or diphthongs i, ei, ê, oi, and u were pronounced so similarly that they were frequently interchanged in orthography during the Roman period; (8) the sounds of o and ô, e and ai, ei and i, ou, and u were confused orthographically.

Greek in the Near East. During the Mycenaean and Minoan periods, mainland Greece and Crete had extensive commercial contacts with the Near East. The Mycenaeans apparently brought their language to Cyprus. The Arcado-Cypriot dialect is known exclusively from inscriptions in the Cypriot syllabary (related to Linear A), used from the seventh to the third century) Pottery from Mycenaean Greece and Cyprus were discovered at Ugarit (modern Ras Shamra) in northern Syria as well as tablets in the still-undeciphered Cypro-Minoan script. Although interrupted by the dissolution of Mycenaean-Minoan civilization, commercial contacts were renewed and extended when Greek city-states began extensive colonization in the eighth century. Throughout the Hellenistic cities of Egypt and Syria-Palestine, the middle- and upper-class Greeks lived in relative isolation from the natives; consequently, the influence of indigenous languages (e.g., ancient Egyptian, Aramaic, Phoenician, Hebrew, and Arabic) was not strong. Greek was still spoken in the Hellenistic cities in the former Persian Empire, such as Seleucia on the Tigris and Susa.

In the sixteen Roman provinces of the Greek East, the use of the Greek language was dominant and was the language of local Roman administration. Many Greeks, however, disregarding the existence of the Roman Empire, continued to divide humanity into two categories, Greeks and barbarians (Strabo, 6.1.2; Dio Chrysostom, Orations 1.14; Josephus, Antiquities 18.20; Philo, Legatio 8, 83, 145, 292), and Apollonius of Tyana supposedly divided the Roman world up into Greek-speaking and Latin-speaking provinces (Philostratus, Vita Apollonii 5.36), and Aelius Aristides even wanted to modernize the Greek-barbarian division into a Roman vs. non-Roman one (Orations 26.63). Others wanted to expand

the categories to Greeks, Romans and barbarians (Cicero, De finibus 2.49; Plutarch, On the Fortune of the Romans 324B).

In the Greek-speaking provinces, even official Roman decrees, letters and edicts, and honorary inscriptions to Roman magistrates, emperors, and members of the imperial family were routinely promulgated in Greek. Most inscriptions on public works, however, are in Latin, and about 30 percent are bilingual. Milestones are often bilingual, but in Syria and Arabia they are almost always in Latin. In Asia Minor and Thrace there are many written only in Greek. Latin and Greek were used in the administration of eastern Roman provinces. Latin was the language of administration used for communication between the central government and Roman magistrates, between Roman magistrates and Roman colonies (as well as within Roman colonies), and sometimes between Roman citizens. The language of the native population was nearly always Greek.

Egypt. Although Minoans had visited Egypt sporadically since the seventeenth century, the first significant Greek presence in Egypt did not occur until the seventh century when a trading colony was established in the northwest Delta. Greek domination of Egypt was established in 332 and lasted until 30. In Ptolemaic Egypt, Greco-Macedonian immigrants settled in two new urban centers of Hellenism, Alexandria in the north and Ptolemais in the south.

The preservation of non-literary Greek papyri in Egypt from the third century BCE through the third century CE provides an important avenue into the written Koine of this period, but the absence of comparable documentary material from other Mediterranean lands makes it impossible to detect the presence of a distinctive dialect. Papyrus letters in Greek begin to appear in the third century BCE. Evidence for Egyptian Koine is found in documents written by bilingual Egyptians (primarily those in the inferior local administration). These documents exhibit linguistic interference. An example consists of the Egyptian-Greek contracts from Soknopaiou Nesos in the northern Faiyum (Papyrus Rylands 160–160D), which reveal the interchange of voiced stops (b, d, g) with voiceless stops (p, t, k), and the interchange of the liquids (l, r). Some letters written by Greeks also exhibit a high degree of interference. Such orthographic confusion, however, reflects differences in phonology or accent rather than differences in dialect.

The evidence from inscriptions indicates little dialectal difference between the Koine of Egypt, Asia Minor, Italy, and Syria-Palestine. Low-status Egyptian natives continued to speak Egyptian until the third century CE. In the second century CE, the Egyptian language, at this stage known as Coptic, was increasingly written using Greek characters and was heavily dependent on other aspects of Greek. As much as 20 percent of the Coptic lexicon, for example, consists of Greek loanwords, and some Greek verbs were adapted to Coptic morphology. Upper-class administrators and aristocrats as well as the lower social classes (especially in Upper Egypt), were generally monolingual.

Syria-Palestine. The earliest Greek loanword in Hebrew is the name *Yāwān* (*Gn.* 10:2; *1 Chr.* 1:5). It was borrowed before the seventh century BCE because *Yāwān* reflects the reconstructed archaic form *Iawones* with the phoneme [w], which became generally obsolete by the sixth century. Elsewhere in the Hebrew Bible, *Yāwān* is used as a generic term for the Greeks (*Jl.* 4:6; *Zec.* 9:13; *Dn.* 8:21; 10:20; 11:2), and in some Qumran texts it refers to Seleucid Greeks (4Q *Pesher Nahum* frags. 3–4 i 2, 3; *Damascus Document* [CD] 8.11). This occurrence suggests that the first Greeks whom the Hebrews contacted were the Ionians. Similarly, Akkadian records from the reign of Sargon II (eighth century) designated western Asia Minor as *Jawan* or *Jaman*, again with the archaic phoneme [w], and the Persians of the sixth century referred to their satrapy of Ionia as *Yauna*, a form already missing the phoneme [w] (Aeschylus, *Persians* 178, 563). Ten of the Arad ostraca (605–595) mention the *Ktyym* (from *Kition*, a Phoenician city on Cyprus), referring to Greek or Cypriot mercenaries in the Judean army. *Ktyym* in the Hebrew Bible refers to Greeks (*Is.* 23:1; *Jer.* 2:10; *Ez.* 27:6; see also *1 Mc.* 1:1; 8:5), but later to the Romans (1Q *Pesher Habakkuk* 2.12–13; 4.5–6; 6.1–4; 4Q *Pesher Nahum* frags. 3–4. i. 3).

After the death of Alexander in 323, Coele-Syria, Syria, Phoenicia, and Palestine were controlled by Ptolemaic Egypt until these lands were conquered by the Seleucids in 201. From the third century, most of the inscriptions found in Syria-Palestine are in Greek. Among the earliest Greek documents from Palestine are two of a cache of six ostraca, four in Aramaic, one in Greek, and one an Aramaic-Greek bilingual, found at Khirbet el-Qom (12 km [7 min] west of Hebron). They are dated to 12 Tammuz, year 6, probably the sixth year of Ptolemy II Philadelphus (277). From 259 to 257 the Zenon papyri reflect the relationship between the Jew Tobias and Egyptian authorities.

The Phoenician coastal cities of Aradus, Byblos, Berytus (Beirut), Sidon, Tyre, and Akko, were most affected by Hellenistic culture and were in effect Greek cities. Many Greek settlers had arrived during the third century BCE. The traditional bilingualism of these cities was replaced by a Hellenistic Koine monolingualism, but inscriptions in Phoenician occur as late as the first century CE. Palmyra, an oasis in the Syrian desert midway between the Phoenician coast and the Euphrates, was multilingual in the Greco-Roman period. The educated class was bilingual, speaking both Palmyrene Aramaic and Hellenistic Koine.

The role of Greek in Palestine during the Roman period has been intensely investigated because of the problem of the language(s) of Jesus and the more general problem of the degree to which Palestinian Judaism was hellenized. It now seems clear that Hebrew was a spoken language in Palestine until the Mishnaic period, but it is not clear how widely it was spoken. In reference to Palestine, instead of the terms *bilingual* or *trilingual*, it is more useful to use the sociolinguistic designations *diglossic* and *triglossic*, that is, the use of two or three languages for different kinds of social communication in a variety of social contexts. From this perspective, it is probable that both Hebrew and Greek were *both* regarded as prestige languages *in different social contexts*. During the second and first centuries BCE, Hebrew was used at least as a literary language. Compositions such as *Daniel*, *Ben Sira*, and much of the Qumran literature were written in Hebrew. Hellenistic and Roman Palestine was a bilingual speech community. Hellenistic Koine was used by all social classes, not just the educated elite. Oddly, public and private Hellenistic Koine inscriptions do not display any Semitisms. Among the Dead Sea scrolls are a number of Greek manuscripts dating from the mid-second century BCE to as late as the mid-first century CE, including fragments of four Septuagint scrolls from Cave 4 (two of *Leviticus* and one each of *Numbers* and *Deuteronomy*) and two other fragmentary Greek scrolls closely related to the Bible. A scroll of the minor prophets in Greek was discovered at Naḥal Ḥever (perhaps late first century BCE).

Two of the fifteen Bar Kochba letters (written 132–35 CE) from Naḥal Ḥever are written in Greek, and the other thirteen together with nine Bar Kochba letters from Wadi Murabbaʿat are in Hebrew and Aramaic. In addition there is the Babatha archive from Naḥal Ḥever, consisting of thirty-six or thirty-seven documents written around 93 to 132 CE in Nabatean, Aramaic, and Greek. The 221 Greek inscriptions from the third and fourth centuries CE discovered in the necropolis of Besara or Beth-Sheʿarim in Galilee far outnumber those in Hebrew and Aramaic and reveal the extent to which the Greek language had penetrated Palestinian Jewish culture. In the case of epitaphs, however, there are sociolinguistic differences between the language(s) of the deceased (as formulated by family and friends), usually Hebrew or Aramaic, and inscriptions formulated by family and friends for the consumption of visitors and pilgrims, frequently Greek. More than 60 percent of all Jewish funerary inscriptions in Palestine are written in Greek, and even in Jerusalem the ratio of epitaphs in Greek is approximately 40 percent. The fact that there are approximately 1500 Greek loanwords in Talmudic literature underlines the widespread use of Greek in the first centuries CE.

Writing Systems. The twenty-two-character Semitic syllabic alphabet was borrowed and modified by Greeks into a twenty-six-character alphabet toward the end of the eighth century BCE. The Greeks required fewer consonants than the Phoenicians. An important innovation was the transformation of some Semitic consonantal symbols to represent vowels (i.e., the Semitic consonantal glottal stops *aleph* and *ayin* were used to represent the vowels *a* and *o*, and the consonants *he* and *yod* were used for the vowels *e* and *i*. Although Greek required fewer sibilants than the Phoenicians (*śin*, *shin, ṣade, samekh)*, they introduced five additional characters to the Semitic alphabet: *upsilon*, representing the vowel *u*, the *digamma* (both from the Phoenician letter *waw*), and the double consonants *phi, chi*, and *psi* (combinations of two phonemes). The sources for these letters remain unknown. The consonant *s* was represented in some Greek alphabets by the letter *san*, which was eventually dropped, modeled on the Semitic *ṣade* or the *sigma*, which was adapted from the *shin*, but never both (Herodotus, 1.139). Later the *omega* was added to represent long *o*. The *omicron* was restricted to the short *o*. Earlier inscriptions, following the Semitic pattern, were written right-to-left (retrograde), or left-to-right, the style that came to predominate. Some texts were even written in the previously mentioned *boustrophedon* style (Pausanias, 5.17.6), which lasted into the fifth century. Another inscriptional style called *stoichedon* aligned letters both horizontally and vertically.

Genre and Text. Modern knowledge of ancient Greek is derived from three kinds of sources: (1) Byzantine-period copies of earlier Greek texts (2) literary and nonliterary papyri preserved primarily in Egypt and dating from 300 BCE to 300 CE and even later; and (3) public and private inscriptions from all over the Greek world.

Literature. Greek literature consists of an enormous number of texts beginning with the *Iliad* and *Odyssey* of Homer through to late antiquity (survey in Easterling and Knox, 1985). The language of the *Iliad* and *Odyssey* is an artificial amalgam (including archaisms and new coinages), constructions, and dialect-forms from the Late Bronze Age (i.e., the Late Minoan and Late Helladic periods, c. 1600–c. 700 BCE), which based on a spoken form of Ionic. The language of Homer was formed and transmitted in a nonliterate environment (Kirk, 1976). It was the invention of writing that froze the ordinarily varied oral performances of the Homeric poems into their final, authoritative form in the late seventh century.

The dissemination of epic poetry throughout the Greek world resulted in the literary imitation of Homeric language by Hesiod of Boeotia for his didactic, moralizing poems including the *Theogony* and *Works and Days*. Elegaic, iambic, and solo lyric poetry developed in the seventh century by Ionian poets writing in Ionic in a modified form of epic hexameter and spread from there to the mainland. Important elegaic poets, who are known from references by later writers, include Callinus of Smyrna, Tyrtaeus of Sparta, Mimnermus of Colophon, Solon of Athena, and Theognis of Megara (the only author whose work has survived). Elegiac epitaphs became popular in the sixth century and were written until the fourth century. Archilocus of Paros was a seventh-century iambic poet, and Sappho of Lesbos was a solo lyric poet who wrote in Aeolic. Choral lyric poetry, which was written in the Doric dialect, arose in the Peloponnesus, Sicily, and Boeotia, where Pindar, its most famous exponent, lived. Fifth-century Athenian tragedy, which was written in Attic, developed during the zenith of the Athenian Empire, was an extremely popular form of entertainment. The important tragedians include Aeschylus, Sophocles, and Euripides. Old Comedy, which emphasized satire and fantasy, consists primarily of works by Aristophanes, who wrote in an educated form of Attic. The development of Middle Comedy (c. 404–321 BCE), represented by Aristophanes' *Ecclesiazusae* and *Plutus*, served as a transition to the development of the realism of New Comedy (after 321 BCE), represented by Menander.

Greek prose literature first appeared during the fifth century in Ionia with the work of the Ionian philosophers (Heracleitus, Democritus, Hippocrates). The greatest philosophical and scientific writers, Plato and Aristotle, were Athenians. The first significant historian was Herodotus (c. 485–425), who was born in Asia Minor but wrote in the Ionic dialect for a largely Athenian audience. He narrated the wars between Greeks and the Persians and is considered the father of history. Thucydides, the author of an incomplete account of the Peloponnesian War, was the first genuinely Athenian historian. Historiography became one of most important literary genres in the following centuries and spawned many subgenres including local history, geography, and antiquarian history. Some of the more important later historians include Xenophon (fourth century), Polybius (second century), Diodorus Siculus (late first century BCE–early first century CE), his contemporary Dionysius of Halikarnassos, and his imitator Flavius Josephus (late first–early second century CE).

After the conquests of Alexander the Great and the division of his empire into the various Hellenistic kingdoms, the earlier literary hegemony that Athens had in the Greek world ended. The new Hellenistic capitals, particularly Alexandria, were not Greek city-states but centers of great imperial governments. Hellenistic poetry flourished particularly in Alexandria under the patronage of the Ptolemies. Callimachus and later Apollonius of Rhodes were poets who were also librarians at the royal Ptolemaic library at Alexandria. One of the influential literary monuments of Hellenistic Koine was the translation of the Jewish Bible into the Greek translation known as the Septuagint beginning in the early Ptolemaic period (c. 300 BCE).

Papyri. The Greek term *byblos* or *biblos*, meaning "papyrus" (Strabo, 17.1.15) and connoting "papyrus roll, book," may have been derived from Byblos, the hellenized name of the Phoenician port Gubal, an important trading center from which Greeks obtained Egyptian papyrus, though by the mid-seventh century they must certainly have imported it directly from Egypt. With few exceptions most of the extant literary and nonliterary papyrus documents come from Egypt and parts of Palestine and Mesopotamia, primarily because of the dry climate. Major exceptions are the fourth-century BCE Derveni papyrus, preserved through carbonization and the approximately eight hundred papyrus rolls discovered at Herculaneum (destroyed by Vesuvius in 79 CE). [*See* Papyrus.]

Inscriptions. Two categories cover the vast range of inscriptions. "Public" inscriptions are determined by a magistrate or official body and consist of such texts as decrees, dedications, honorary inscriptions, epitaphs, manumissions, and milestones. "Private" inscriptions are formulated by an individual. Among the many types of private texts are funerary inscriptions, private dedications, manumissions, and curses. Our knowledge of "vulgar" Attic is based primarily on curses epitaphs. The survival of local inscriptions and the use of dialect in comedies provides the primary basis for our knowledge of dialects other than Attic and Ionic. The earliest Ionic inscription known is a graffito on a *kylix* (shallow drinking cup) from the seventh century BCE found at Smyrna (*SEG* 12.480).

BIBLIOGRAPHY

Aharoni, Yohanan, with contributions by Joseph Naveh. *Arad Inscriptions.* Translated by Judith Ben-Or. Jerusalem, 1981.

Allen, W. Sidney. *Vox Graeca: A Guide to the Pronunciation of Classical Greek.* 2d ed. London, 1974.

Altheim, Franz, and Ruth Stiehl. *Die aramäische Sprache unter den Achaimeniden.* Frankfurt am Main, 1963.

Barr, James. "Hebrew, Aramaic, and Greek in the Hellenistic Age." In *The Cambridge History of Jerusalem,* vol. 2, edited by W. D. Davies and Louis Finkelstein, pp. 79–114. Cambridge, 1989.

Bubeník, Vit. *Hellenistic and Roman Greece as a Sociolinguistic Area.* Amsterdam, 1989. Important discussion of the social factors influencing linguistic development and usage.

Carpenter, Rhys. "The Antiquity of the Greek Alphabet." *American Journal of Archaeology* 37 (1933): 8–29. In this article, Carpenter argues convincingly that the Greek alphabet was not invented until the late eighth century BCE.

Easterling, P. E., and B. M. W. Knox. *The Cambridge History of Classical Literature,* vol. 1, *Greek Literature.* Cambridge, 1985. Standard English-language survey of the history of Greek literature.

Fitzmyer, Joseph A. "The Languages of Palestine in the First Century A.D." In Fitzmyer's *A Wandering Aramean: Collected Aramaic Essays,* pp. 29–56. Missoula, 1979. Slightly updated version of the important article originally published in *Catholic Biblical Quarterly* 32 (1970): 501–531.

Gignac, Francis T. *A Grammar of the Greek Papyri of the Roman and Byzantine Periods,* vol. 1, *Phonology;* vol. 2, *Morphology.* Milan, 1976–1981.

Hengel, Martin. *Judaism and Hellenism: Studies in Their Encounter in Palestine during the Early Hellenistic Period.* 2 vols. Translated by John Bowden. Philadelphia, 1974. Indispensable study of the influence of Hellenism on Palestinian Judaism during the second century BCE.

Horbury, William, and David Noy. *Jewish Inscriptions of Graeco-Roman Egypt.* Cambridge, 1992.

Horsley, G. H. R. "The Fiction of 'Jewish Greek.'" In *New Documents Illustrating Early Christianity,* vol. 5, pp. 5–40. New South Wales, 1989.

Jeffery, Lilian H. *The Local Scripts of Archaic Greece.* Oxford, 1961. Detailed discussion of the various early Greek alphabets.

Kaimio, Jorma. *The Romans and the Greek Language.* Helsinki, 1979.

Kirk, G. S. *Homer and the Oral Tradition.* Cambridge, 1976.

Lewis, Naphtali, et al., *The Documents from the Bar Kokhba Period in the Cave of Letters: Greek Papyri, Aramaic and Nabatean Signatures and Subscriptions.* Jerusalem, 1989.

Lieberman, Saul. *Greek in Jewish Palestine.* 2d ed. New York, 1965. Deals with the second through fourth centuries CE.

Lüddeckens, Erich. "Ägypten." In *Die Sprachen im römischen Reich der Kaiserzeit,* edited by Günter Neumann and Jürgen Untermann, pp. 241–265. Beihefte der Bonner Jahrbücher, 40. Cologne, 1980.

Meiggs, Russell, and David Lewis. *A Selection of Greek Historical Inscriptions to the End of the Fifth Century B.C.* Oxford, 1969. Critical texts and discussions of important early inscriptions.

Millar, Fergus. *The Roman Near East, 31 BC–AD 337.* Cambridge, Mass., 1993.

Mussies, Gerard. "Greek in Palestine and the Diaspora." In *The Jewish People in the First Century,* vol. 2, edited by D. Flusser and W. C. van Unnik, pp. 1040–1064. Compendia Rerum Iudaicarum ad Novum Testamentum, section 1. Amsterdam, 1976.

Palmer, Leonard R. *The Greek Language.* Atlantic Highlands, N.J., 1980. The most important discussion in English of the history and structure of the Greek language.

Prentice, William K. *Greek and Latin Inscriptions: Northern Syria.* 2 vols. Leiden, 1908–1922.

Rey-Coquais, Jean-Paul. *Inscriptions grecques et latines de la Syrie,* vol. 6, *Baalbek et Béqa.* Institute Français d'Archéologie de Beyrouth, Bibliothèque Archéologique et Historique, 78. Paris, 1967.

Rosén, Haiim B. "Die Sprachsituation im römischen Palästina." In *Die Sprachen im römischen Reich der Kaiserzeit,* edited by Günter Neumann and Jürgen Untermann, pp. 215–239. Beihefte der Bonner Jahrbücher, 40. Cologne, 1980.

Schwabe, Moshe, and Baruch Lifshitz. *Beth She'arim,* vol. 2, *The Greek Inscriptions.* New Brunswick, N.J., 1974.

Sevenster, Jan N. *Do You Know Greek? How Much Greek Could the First Jewish Christians Have Known?* Supplement to Novum Testamentum, 19. Leiden, 1968. Important discussion of the use of Greek in first-century Palestine.

Sherk, Robert K. *Roman Documents from the Greek East.* Baltimore, 1969. Collection of epigraphical texts of Roman legal documents, *senatus consulta* (senatorial decrees), and *epistulae* (official Roman correspondence) written primarily in Greek.

Spolsky, Bernard. "Triglossia and Literacy in Jewish Palestine of the First Century." *International Journal of the Sociology of Language* 42 (1983): 95–109.

Teodorsson, Sven-Tage. *The Phonology of Ptolemaic Koine.* Göteborg, 1977.

Teodorsson, Sven-Tage. *The Phonology of Attic in the Hellenistic Period.* Göteborg, 1978.

Turner, Eric G. *Greek Papyri: An Introduction.* Oxford, 1968.

Wachsmann, Shelley. *Aegeans in the Theban Tombs.* Orientalia Lovaniensia Analecta, vol. 20. Louvain, 1987.

Welles, Charles Bradford. *Royal Correspondence in the Hellenistic Period.* New Haven, 1934. Collection of Greek epigraphical texts issued by the chanceries of the Hellenistic kingdoms.

Woodhead, Arthur G. *The Study of Greek Inscriptions.* 2d ed. Cambridge, 1981. The basic textbook on Greek inscriptions.

DAVID E. AUNE

GREENFIELD, JONAS CARL (1926–1995), American scholar of ancient Semitic languages. Born in New York City, Greenfield, like many of his generation, received a parochial education that included a traditional American as well as a traditional Jewish curriculum. By the time he was thirteen, he was fluent in both Hebrew and Aramaic, which he had studied in texts at school; at the age of fourteen he studied Aramaic grammar from a copy of Casper Levias's grammar of Babylonian Aramaic and taught himself Arabic, as well.

While majoring in English at the City College of New York, he was simultaneously studying Arabic and comparative Semitics at the New School for Social Research. After receiving his bachelor's degree in 1949, he went to Yale University, where he planned to do advanced work in English; however, under the influence of the cuneiform scholar Albrecht Goetze, he switched to ancient Near Eastern studies. He received his Ph.D. in 1956, with his dissertation "The Lexical Status of Mishnaic Hebrew." The legacy of his work in English to his Semitic scholarship was a finely honed instinct for semantic nuances and stylistic subtleties. He began his teaching career at Brandeis University in 1954 and went on from there, in 1956, to teach at UCLA and, in 1965, at the University of California at Berkeley. In 1971 he joined the Hebrew University of Jerusalem, where he became the Casper Levias Professor of Ancient Semitic Languages, a position he held until his death.

Greenfield was interested in almost everything that had to do with the ancient Near East. A voluminous reader who could recall with ease much of what he had read, he was conversant with most of the scholarly literature. A convivial person, notorious punster, and excellent raconteur who enjoyed attending scholarly meetings, he was familiar both with most living scholars and with the history of scholarship. Because of his knowledge, diligence as a scholar, and generally easy bearing, he was in constant demand as a referee, adviser, mentor, and colleague. Students commented that after introducing them to scholarly articles in his seminars, he introduced them to the scholars in his living room.

He edited the *Israel Exploration Journal* (1976–1995) and was on the editorial staff of the *Bulletin of the American Schools of Oriental Research* (1969–1971; 1991–1995). In addition, he coedited nine books; wrote 150 scholarly articles; was part of the New Jewish Publication Society's (NJPS) translation committee for the Writings; was a trustee of the Albright Institute of Archaeological Research in Jerusalem; was a member of the Dead Sea Scrolls Supervisory Committee; and advised on countless dissertations in Israel, the United States, and Europe.

His own publications focused primarily on Hebrew and Aramaic lexicographic matters, but by the 1970s his interests expanded to include Qumranica and other documents discovered in the region. His studies were characterized by the juxtaposition of diverse elements from the ancient Near East to the issue at hand—be they legal, historical, religious, literary, etymological, or lexicographic—by a wealth of ancillary details and by the latest literature on each subject from even the most obscure sources.

Greenfield was an honorary member of the Royal Danish Academy of Sciences and Letters and a member of the Royal Asiatic Society, the Israel Academy of Sciences and Humanities, and the American Academy of Arts and Sciences.

[*See also* Dead Sea Scrolls.]

BIBLIOGRAPHY

For a complete bibliography of Greenfield's work, see Ziony Zevit et al., eds., *Solving Riddles and Untying Knots: Biblical, Epigraphic, and Semitic Studies in Honor of Jonas C. Greenfield,* pp. xiii–xxvii (Winona Lake, Ind., 1995). The following are some of Greenfield's more notable publications.

"Lexicographical Notes." *Hebrew Union College Annual* 29 (1958): 203–228; 30 (1959): 141–151.

"The Zakir Inscription and the Danklied." In *Proceedings of the Fifth World Congress of Jewish Studies, 1969,* vol. 1, pp. 174–191. Jerusalem, 1971.

"Aramaic and Its Dialects." In *Jewish Languages: Theme and Variations,* edited by Herbert H. Paper, pp. 29–43. Cambridge, 1978.

"Notes on the Early Aramaic Lexicon." *Orientalia Suecana* 33–35 (1984–1986): 149–156.

"The 'Cluster' in Biblical Poetry." *Maarav* 5–6 (1990): 159–168.

"The Wisdom of Ahiqar." In *Wisdom in Ancient Israel: Essays in Honor of J. A. Emerton,* edited by John Day et al., pp. 43–52. Cambridge, 1995.

ZIONY ZEVIT

GRID PLAN. A common way for excavators to make easy reference to a specific location on an archaeological site is by using a grid. The meaning of any archaeological information, such as an excavated object or architectural remain, is derived largely from its context, and a grid helps to identify that location and context. To form a grid, an arbitrary system of intersecting perpendicular lines is imposed on a site. The lines are usually established according to magnetic directions, running north–south and east–west. A midpoint for the grid is often set at the center of the excavation area. However, at complex urban sites or at sites with visible surface remains or important topographic features, it may make more sense to center the grid on those elements. The size of the resulting square areas and the means used to refer to them may be determined by an excavator's goals and the kind of site being investigated. On large urban tells in the Near East, areas of 50 × 50 m or 100 × 100 m are given designations, and smaller grids are established for excavation purposes within them. A surveyor or an expedition's architect usually determines the boundaries of the areas, where permanent markers are established at a corner. Selected portions of the grid are conventionally excavated within squares of 5 × 5 or 10 × 10 m.

The use of the same site grid over the entirety of a complex tell allows for the easy correlation of the locations of recovered features, such as wall lines or roadways, from widely spaced portions of the site. In recording archaeological data, some form of grid or area designation accompanies all aspects of the excavation of specific structures and artifacts.

[*See also* Architectural Drafting and Drawing; Recording Techniques; *and* Site Survey.]

BIBLIOGRAPHY

Blakely, Jeffrey A., and Lawrence E. Toombs. *The Tell el-Hesi Field Manual.* Joint Archaeological Expedition to Tell el-Hesi, vol. 1. Winona Lake, Ind., 1980. Basic conceptual and terminological introduction to the spatial concepts in excavation (see pp. 6–13).
Dever, William G., and H. Darrell Lance, eds. *A Manual of Field Excavation: Handbook for Field Archaeologists.* Cincinnati, 1978. Brief but very comprehensive description of the goals and processes used in laying out a site grid and establishing excavation areas within the grid (see pp. 141–149).

KENNETH G. HOGLUND

GUÉRIN, VICTOR HONORÉ (1821–1890),

French Palestinologist. Born in Paris, Guérin studied classical philology at the École Normale Supérieure, Paris, and then taught in several *lycées.* He joined the École Française d'Athènes in 1852 and spent two years traveling and doing research in Greece, the Aegean, Turkey, Syria, and Palestine. He thus inaugurated a lifetime of scientific travel that also took him to Malta, Tunisia, Libya, Egypt, and Nubia.

Most of Guérin's time and energy from 1863 onward were devoted to the study of ancient Palestine. He carried out three major surveys: a detailed exploration of Judea (Judah) in 1863, of Samaria and the Jordan Valley in 1870, and of Galilee and Phoenicia in 1875. His subsequent travels to Palestine and Lebanon (in 1882, 1884, and 1888) were to prepare his last major publications, *La Terre Sainte* and *Jérusalem,* which were geared to the general public.

Guérin's major contribution to archaeology and Near Eastern studies is the seven volumes of his *Description géographique, historique et archéologique de la Palestine,* an admirable achievement for one person and comparable to the scope and teamwork of the publications of the Palestine Exploration Fund. Nobody before him had conducted such a systematic exploration of the country. Traveling on horseback, he visited and recorded in detail and with scrupulous exactitude every ruin and village in Judea, Samaria, and Galilee, discovering numerous sites in the process. His method was to identify biblical sites from the landscape, analyze their mutual relationship, and combine his observations with the biblical evidence. His work greatly advanced what was known about the historical geography of Palestine. Guérin's surveys belong to the prearchaeological phase of exploration in Palestine, when it was not yet recognized that the country's many tells covered the sites of ancient cities and "progress" had not yet destroyed so many ancient remains.

BIBLIOGRAPHY

The list below includes some of Guérin's most important contributions to the field.
De ora Palaestinae a promontorio Carmelo usque ad urbem Joppen pertinente. Paris, 1856.
Description géographique, historique et archéologique de la Palestine, première partie: Judée. 3 vols. Paris, 1868.
Description géographique, historique et archéologique de la Palestine, seconde partie: Samarie. 2 vols. Paris, 1874–1875.
Description géographique, historique et archéologique de la Palestine, troisième partie: Galilée. 2 vols. Paris, 1880.
La Terre Sainte: Son histoire, ses souvenirs, ses sites, ses monuments. Paris, 1882.
La Terre Sainte, deuxième partie: Liban, Phénicie, Palestine occidentale et méridionale, Pétra, Sinaï, Égypte. Paris, 1884.
Jérusalem: Son histoire, sa description, ses établissements religieux. Paris, 1889.

PIERRE DE MIROSCHEDJI

GUSH ḤALAV (Ar., el-Jish; Gk., Gischala/Giscala),

site located on the western flank of a deep wadi (Wadi Gush Ḥalav) several miles northwest of Safed in Upper Galilee (map reference 191 × 270). The Greek name is probably a corruption of the Hebrew *gush ḥalav,* (lit., "block of white"), perhaps in reference to the towering white cliffs on the east side of the wadi. Another possibility is that the name means "fat ground," a derivation reflecting the area's flourishing olive oil trade in antiquity.

Josephus, the first-century Jewish historian, presents the activities of an individual named John of Giscala, whose economic dealings are viewed harshly in both *Life* (70–76) and *War* (2.590–592; 4.92–120). The site is also mentioned in *Ecclesiates Rabba* (2.8), in a document from Wadi Murabba'at, on a sixth-century marble plaque from Beersheba, and in the Mishnah (*Arakh.* 9.6). The church father Jerome (in *Lives of Illustrious Men* and in his commentary on the Epistle to Philemon) reports, enigmatically, that the apostle Paul came from "Giscalis in Judea."

The full extent of the ancient settlement, which was an important trading center in the Roman and Byzantine periods, cannot be determined. It surely included the top of the prominent hill now occupied by the Arab village of el-Jish; an ancient synagogue may have existed at the top of the hill, where a Maronite church now stands. A number of chamber tombs in the vicinity, which were the focus of medieval Jewish pilgrims, were excavated in 1937 (Makhouly, 1938); and a monumental tomb on the western side of the modern village was discovered and excavated in 1973 (Vitto and Edelstein, 1974). A hoard of 237 coins was discovered some time prior to 1948 (Hamburger, 1954). The tombs and coins date to the Roman and Byzantine periods.

Sustained excavations at Gush Ḥalav have concentrated on a monumental building on the eastern slope of the Jish hill. Early in the twentieth century, the German team of

Heinrich Kohl and Carl Watzinger (1916) spent several days clearing and recording this building, identified as a synagogue, as part of their investigation (1905–1907) of Galilean synagogues. [*See* Synagogues.] Two seasons of excavation at this lower synagogue site were carried out by a Duke University team, as a project of the American Schools of Oriental Research in 1977 and 1978 (Meyers, Strange, and Meyers, 1979; Meyers, Meyers, and Strange, 1990). Additional support for both seasons came from Garrett Evangelical Seminary at Northwestern University; the University of the Orange Free State in Bloemfontein, South Africa, supported the 1977 season. Eric M. Meyers served as project director; James F. Strange and Carol L. Meyers were associate directors.

To the surprise of the excavation team, the synagogue was found to be built on a considerable depth of debris, attesting to a long history of occupation at the site. In addition to a scattering of Late Bronze II/Iron I sherds, the ceramic horizon includes some Iron II, Persian, Hellenistic, and Early Roman material; however, no structural remains from those periods could be discerned in the very limited area in which the excavation team was permitted to dig. The synagogue itself had stood for some three centuries; its history spans the Middle to Late Roman (250–306 CE), Late Roman (306–363), Byzantine I (363–460), and Byzantine IIA (460–551) periods. After the collapse and abandonment of the synagogue in the mid-sixth century, some sporadic occupation continued in the Byzantine IIB and the Early and Late Arab periods.

Although the synagogue appeared almost square to its earliest investigators, the work of the 1978–1979 expedition established that it is a small basilical building with two rows of four columns. [*See* Basilicas.] The interior dimensions of its main room, which is bounded on three sides by corridors or rooms, are 13.75 × 10.6–11.0 m. Only its southern, Jerusalem-oriented wall borders directly on exterior space. That facade wall is also the only one constructed with well-dressed ashlar masonry. The single major entry is in the center of that wall, and the building's bema is situated against the inside of the southern wall to the west of the entrance. Benches were recovered on the west and north. Remnants of heart-shaped columns and other architectural fragments, as well as a hoard of 1,953 coins dating mainly to the fourth–sixth centuries, were found in the debris in or adjacent to the building. Perhaps the most notable architectural fragment is a lintel with an eagle and a garland finely carved on its underside. Anyone entering the building would have to look directly overhead to see this decorative element. An Aramaic dedicatory inscription on one of the columns, first published in the nineteenth century, reads "Jose bar Nahum/made this (column?)/may it be for him/a blessing."

The paucity of decorative elements suggests religious conservatism; yet, the adaptive use of space, the high quality of the prominent masonry, and the idiosyncratic placement of the essential features of a synagogue building reflect authentic independence and technological expertise. The flourishing of Gush Ḥalav in the Late Roman and Byzantine periods is reflected in the sophisticated simplicity of its lower synagogue.

BIBLIOGRAPHY

Hamburger, H. "A Hoard of Syrian Tetradrachms and Tyrian Bronze Coins from Gush Ḥalav." *Israel Exploration Journal* 4 (1954): 201–226.
Kohl, Heinrich, and Carl Watzinger. *Antike Synagogen in Galilaea.* Leipzig, 1916.
Makhouly, Na'im. "Rock-Cut Tombs at el-Jīsh." *Quarterly of the Department of Antiquities in Palestine* 8 (1938): 45–50.
Meyers, Eric M., James F. Strange, and Carol L. Meyers. "Preliminary Report on the 1977 and 1978 Seasons at Gush Halav (el-Jish)." *Bulletin of the American Schools of Oriental Research,* no. 233 (1979): 33–58.
Meyers, Eric M., and Carol L. Meyers, with James F. Strange. *Excavations at the Ancient Synagogue of Gush Ḥalav.* Meiron Excavation Project, vol. 5. Winona Lake, Ind., 1990.
Vitto, Fanny, and Gershon Edelstein. "The Mausoleum at Gush Ḥalav" (in Hebrew). *Qadmoniot* 7 (1974): 49–55.

CAROL L. MEYERS

GUY, PHILIP LANGSTAFFE ORDE

GUY, PHILIP LANGSTAFFE ORDE (1885–1952), British archaeologist and administrator, instrumental in the establishment of both the Palestine and Israel departments of antiquities. Born in Lanarkshire, Scotland, Guy was educated at the universities of Glasgow and Oxford. After active service in World War I, he joined Leonard Woolley's expeditions to Carchemish and Amarna, where he served as ceramic specialist. In 1922, he was appointed chief inspector of the newly established Palestine Department of Antiquities and in that position was called upon to undertake salvage excavations and surveys throughout the country. In 1927 Guy succeeded Clarence Fisher as director of the Megiddo excavations of the Oriental Institute of the University of Chicago. There, in addition to supervising the excavation of the Megiddo tombs, Guy introduced the extensive use of aerial photography from helium balloons to aid in mapping and analyzing the excavated architecture. As a result of professional disagreements with the authorities of the Oriental Institute, however, Guy ended his association with the Megiddo expedition in 1935.

As director of the British School of Archaeology in Jerusalem in 1938–1939, Guy planned a comprehensive archaeological survey of Palestine. He personally undertook initial explorations for this survey in the Negev desert and on the coastal plain. During World War II, Guy served in the British army as military governor of Benghazi and Asmara and as a member of the Allied Supply Mission to Syria. After the war, he returned to the civil service in Palestine, as director of the Government Stud Farm in Akko for the Department of Agriculture (1945–1947). He subsequently renewed his professional connection to the Palestine Department of Antiquities (1947–1948).

As one of the few British administrators to remain in the newly created State of Israel, Guy was appointed chief of the Division of Surveys and Excavation of the Israel Department of Antiquities in 1948. In that position, he carried out important salvage excavations at Jaffa, Beth-Yeraḥ, and Ayyelet ha-Shaḥar. He also established the department's system of regional inspectors and revived his earlier plans for a comprehensive national archaeological survey.

[*See also* Beth-Yeraḥ; British School of Archaeology in Jerusalem; Jaffa; Megiddo; *and the biographies of Fisher and Woolley.*]

BIBLIOGRAPHY

Avi-Yonah, Michael. "P. L. O. Guy, 1885–1922: In Memoriam." *Israel Exploration Journal* 3 (1953): 1–3. Includes a bibliography of Guy's work.

Guy, P. L. O. "Balloon Photography and Archaeological Excavation." *Antiquity* 6 (1932): 148–155, plus 4 pls.

Guy, P. L. O. *Megiddo Tombs.* Chicago, 1938.

NEIL ASHER SILBERMAN

H

HABAKKUK COMMENTARY. The scroll known as the *Habakkuk Commentary,* or *Pesher Habakkuk,* was discovered in 1947 at Qumran in Cave 1. In the corpus of Dead Sea Scrolls it is designated 1QpHab. W. H. Brownlee prepared the *editio princeps* (Burrows, ed., 1950). The scroll contains thirteen columns (originally the first twelve columns with seventeen lines each, and the last column with four lines). It is preserved almost intact, except that in the first column only the ends of the lines remain, and, because the bottom of the scroll deteriorated, that the last two or three lines of every column are lost. The scroll was written by two scribes, A and B: scribe A wrote col. i–col. xii, l. 13a, and scribe B col. xii, l. 13b–col. xiii, l. 4. The script of both hands is Herodian, characteristic of the second part of the first century BCE.

This scroll, like other scrolls of its type from Qumran, incorporates a commentary of the prophetic words (Heb., *pesher*), which is placed between the lemmas, or verses, in the scroll. In 1QpHab column ii, lines 6–10, and in column vii, lines 4–5, the *pesher* interprets mysterious presages contained in the words of the prophets concerning their actual fulfillment in historical events leading to the eschatological era. The man inspired by God to unravel the prophetic mysteries is the Teacher of Righteousness (see below).

The relationship between the prophetic words and the *pesher* is formally carried out in a lemmatic pattern—namely, citations of the biblical text of the first two chapters of *Habakkuk,* verse by verse—followed by *pesher* sections. The sections of the *pesher* follow the biblical lemmas by means of an introductory formula such as *pšrw ʿl* ("its interpretation concerns . . .") and *pšr hdbr ʿl* ("the interpretation of the quoted text concerns . . ."), applied to persons, and *pšrw ʾšr* ("its interpretation is that . . .") and *pšr hdbr ʾšr* ("the interpretation of the quoted text is that . . ."), applied to events. The phraseology of the *pesher* sections is related to the biblical text principally by paronomasia (a punning of its words and letters in variegated forms). The adaptation of the biblical content into new historical circumstances is achieved by means of exegetical techniques such as analogy, allegory, and double meanings. Through such techniques, the content of the *Book of Habakkuk* became typological and was adapted to specific historical situations in the Second Temple period. For example, the Chaldeans of *Habakkuk* became the Kittim, in all probability the Romans, the imperialistic power since the second century BCE. Other figures in the *Book of Habakkuk* became typological for figures who took part in the internecine struggles in Judea (Judah) in that period. *Pesher Habakkuk* hints at the halakhic controversy between the Teacher of Righteousness, the first leader of the Qumran community (see Cairo Damascus [CD], col. i, l. 11; *Pesher Psalms,* manuscript a [4QpPsᵃ], col. iii, ll. 14–17), and the Man of Lie (1QpHab col. v, ll. 8–11; col. x, ll. 9–13), a leader of an opposing community, probably the Pharisees, who was supported by those who had left the Qumran community (col. i, l. 16–col. ii, l. 6; col. v, ll. 8–11). It also depicts the political and cultic struggle between the Wicked Priest, probably the Hasmonean king who was also the high priest, and the Teacher of Righteousness, who criticized his politics (col. viii, l. 3–col. ix, l. 3; col. xi, ll. 2–10). As these figures are not called by their names but are referred to cryptically, scholars disagree on their identification—particularly about whether the Wicked Priest was Jonathan, the first Hasmonean high priest (161–142 BCE), during whose rule the Teacher of Righteousness would have established the Qumran community, or Alexander Jannaeus (103–76 BCE), who ruled when the internal political and religious struggle in Judea was most critical. (These are the two principal interpretations; others exist.) However, the symbolic presentation of figures and events is typological within the apocalyptic concept held by the Qumran community. It places their destiny in the universal struggle between righteousness and wickedness at the end of days, when wickedness is to be destroyed forever (col. vii, l. 1–col. viii, l. 3; col. xii, l. 10–col. xiii, l. 4).

[*See also* Dead Sea Scrolls.]

BIBLIOGRAPHY

Brownlee, William H. *The Midrash Pesher of Habakkuk.* Society of Biblical Literature, Monograph Series, no. 24. Missoula, 1979.

Burrows, Millar, ed., with John C. Trevor and William H. Brownlee. *The Dead Sea Scrolls of St. Mark's Monastery,* vol. 1, *The Isaiah Manuscript and the Habakkuk Commentary.* New Haven, 1950.

Dimant, Devorah. "Pesharim, Qumran." In *The Anchor Bible Dictionary,* vol. 5, pp. 244–251. New York, 1992.

Elliger, Karl. *Studien zum Habakuk-Kommentar vom Toten Meer*. Bei-
träge zur historischen Theologie, 15. Tübingen, 1953.
Horgan, Maurya P. *Pesharim*. Catholic Biblical Quarterly, Monograph
Series 8. Washington, D.C., 1979.
Nitzan, Bilhah. *Pesher Habakkuk: A Scroll from the Wilderness of Judaea
(1QpHab)* (in Hebrew). Jerusalem, 1986.

BILHAH NITZAN

HABUBA KABIRA, site of two ancient settlements, located on the western edge of the Euphrates River's Tabqa dam reservoir in Syria (36°10′ N, 38°4′ E). One of the settlements was a mound of medium size, Tell Habuba Kabira; the other was a large settlement, about 900 m long, Habuba Kabira South, whose size could only be ascertained from the extent to which sherds were scattered and within which lay a smaller mound (Tell Qannas).

The site was noted in surveys carried out by American and Syrian teams directed by Abdel Kader Rihaoui and Maurits N. van Loon in 1963 and 1964. Tell Habuba Kabira and Habuba Kabira (South) were investigated from 1969 to 1975 by the Deutsche Orient-Gesellschaft, under the direction of Ernst Heinrich and Eva Strommenger; Tell Qannas was excavated by a Belgian mission headed by André Finet. [*See* Deutsche Orient-Gesellschaft.]

Habuba Kabira (South) is the only large-scale example of Late Uruk residential architecture. [*See* Uruk-Warka.] The administrative-religious center of the city was hidden in the lower layers of Tell Qannas. The regional administrative center was not in this town, but on a slope of the Jebel ʿAruda Mountain to the north. There were other contemporary settlements in the vicinity, at Tell Hajj, Tell Hadidi, and Tell Sheikh Ḥassan, the latter on the east bank of the Euphrates and certainly dating back to the Middle Uruk period. [*See* Hadidi, Tell.] Habuba Kabira (South) existed only for a short time, as is indicated by a maximum of three building levels. Tablets, clay balls with tokens inside, and clay bullae,

HABUBA KABIRA. *Plan of the southern gate and houses.* (Courtesy Habuba Kabira Expedition, Deutsche Orient-Gesellschaft)

HABUBA KABIRA. *Room with pottery in situ.* (Courtesy Habuba Kabira Expedition, Deutsche Orient-Gesellschaft)

all with numerical signs, as well as the pottery, point to a date that corresponds to Uruk-Eanna, archaic levels VI–V. The later level of Habuba Kabira (South) has been carbon dated to 3290–2920 BCE and 3030–2910 BCE (calibrated; all dates according to Günter Kohl and Jochen Görsdorf).

The settlement was a station along the routes from Anatolia and northern Syria to Mesopotamia. It was involved mainly in a long-distance trade. Its role in the local exchange system is not yet clear. The town was obviously deserted peacefully, presumably as the result of a blockade of the trade routes to the south. The main roads in Habuba Kabira (South) followed the contour lines of the bank terrace or were at right angles to them and were equipped with drains. The development of peripheral areas and the subdivision of courtyards indicate that some of the site's residential quarters became densely built up.

The buildings vary in type. Most common are houses with a large hall flanked by small rooms along both long walls (tripartite houses) or along one of them. Rooms sometimes were added to the short wall. These houses were used for all daily activities and domestic duties, except for preparing meals. The main room was lived in or sometimes also used for storage, along with small chambers. Less common are large halls that open onto inner courtyards through two or three doors in one long wall (one-hall buildings). This long wall was usually remarkably thick. Rooms with one entrance on the long wall near the corner were probably used as workshops or food preparation or storage areas. They are monocellular or surround a courtyard. Multicellular buildings without a main room are scarce. Sometimes several buildings formed a domestic unit. The most important estates consisted of one tripartite house and two one-hall buildings. Sometimes the outline of buildings has the 3:4:5 proportion of the Pythagorean triangle. The settlement was at first unfortified but later was surrounded by a city wall. Parts of this 3-meter-thick wall were uncovered to the north and to the west. Eight towers or bastions protect the northern front, twenty-nine are still preserved on the western front, as well as two gates. The central buildings at Tell Qannas were, next to the large storage areas, two tripartite houses and a one-hall building whose dimensions (approximately 13.6–17.2 × 9.6–15.7 m) are greater than comparable buildings in the settlement.

Handicrafts in Habuba Kabira (South) included a recycling workshop for stone objects and a metal workshop. There was, in particular, evidence of lead processing—along with copper—pieces of oxide, which are residuals of cupellation for separating silver from lead ores. Kilns for pottery were outside the settlement. Apart from ceramics, the small finds include a wide spectrum of stone, terra-cotta, and copper objects. Worthy of mention are large stone vessels, amulets and cylinder seals, copper axes, pins and fishhooks, tokens and sealed clay tablets, bullae, and door locks.

The principle source of meat was domesticated animals and, to a lesser extent, wild animals and fish. It is difficult to prove this on the basis of the fish bones because they may be poorly preserved. Much more beef was consumed than smaller ruminants (according to Angela von den Driesch et al.).

Tell Habuba Kabira is an irregular, oval mound approximately 230 m in diameter and with 9 m of settlement debris. Its stratigraphy is numbered according to the largest excavation area, which is in the east. The lowest level, East 1, yielded only Late Uruk sherds. The corresponding building structures must have been placed in the unexcavated center of the mound. Level East 2, which belongs to an earlier phase of the Early Bronze Age, revealed a small settlement with living areas and workshops near each other and a unified outer boundary. Four radiocarbon dates for the burnt level in level East 3 range from 2900–2690 BCE to 2860–2520 BCE (calibrated). The settlement's exterior, with a gate in the east, was continuously reinforced so as to serve as a protective wall. In level East 8, a protective forecourt with a well was built in front of this gate. The courtyard was enclosed in level East 9 with a building, in all probability a temple, consisting of two broad rooms with gates in the central axes. A road paved with stones led to the entrance from the river. Fire and flood brought about the end of the East 9 level. One radiocarbon dating indicates the period from 2870 to 2510 BCE (calibrated).

In level East 10, a long temple with an open porch was erected in the northeast. In the following level, the temple was reinforced and an entrance was installed in one of the antae. Carbonized beams from the temple (level East 12) were dated to 2290–2040 BCE (calibrated). In level East 13, the settlement was extended east with a wall 2.8 m thick. The wall had been rebuilt several times in East 15 and reached a thickness of 3 m and a minimum height of 6 m. The buildings within, apart from the temple, were residential in character. The temple can be followed as far as level East 17, in which small houses covered the summit of the mound. This level and the following ones, up to the most recent Middle Bronze Age level, East 20, were badly disturbed by Islamic period graves.

From the small finds, it seems as if the economy of Tell Habuba Kabira was based on stone and metal processing. Molds and a hoard of bronze objects including fragments of plano-convex ingots are worthy of mention. In addition jewelry and ceramics were produced. The inhabitants kept cattle, sheep, and goats. Over time, the percentage of cattle diminished; in the Middle Bronze Age, sheep and goats predominated, which can be taken as evidence of the impoverishment of the grazing land. Game included onagers and gazelles. Donkeys have been shown to have existed at the site in the Early Bronze Age and horses in the Middle Bronze Age (according to Reinhard Ziegler).

BIBLIOGRAPHY

Finet, André, ed. *"Lorsque la royauté descendit du ciel . . ."* Les fouilles belges du Tell Kannâs sur l'Euphrate en Syrie. Morlanwelz, 1982. Excavations at Tell Qannas.

Strommenger, Eva. "Ausgrabungen der Deutschen Orient-Gesellschaft in Habuba Kabira." In *Archeological Reports from the Tabqa Dam Project—Euphrates Valley, Syria,* edited by David Noel Freedman, pp. 63–78. Annual of the American Schools of Oriental Research, 44. Ann Arbor, Mich., 1979. Preliminary report; some results need revision.

Strommenger, Eva. "The Chronological Division of the Archaic Levels of Uruk-Eanna VI to III/II: Past and Present." *American Journal of Archaeology* 84 (1980): 479–487. Habuba Kabira (South) and chronological problems.

Strommenger, Eva. *Habuba Kabira, eine Stadt vor 5000 Jahren: Ausgrabungen der Deutschen Orient-Gesellschaft am Euphrat in Habuba Kabira, Syrien.* Sendschrift der Deutschen Orient-Gesellschaft, 12 Mainz, 1980. Preliminary report, in need of revision.

Strommenger, Eva, and Kay Kohlmeyer, eds. *Ausgrabungen in Habuba Kabira,* vol. 1, *Habuba-Tall, Architektur* (Kohlmeyer); vol. 2, *Habuba-Tall, Kleinfunde* (Strommenger et al.); vol. 3, *Habuba-Süd, Architektur* (Kohlmeyer and Wido Ludwig); vol. 4, *Habuba-Süd, Kleinfunde* (Strommenger et al.). Final reports, including the quoted results of researches on radiocarbon dates by Günter Kohl and Jochen Görsdorf, animals at Habuba Kabira (South) by Angela von den Driesch et al., and animals at Tell Habuba Kabira by Reinhard Ziegler.

van Loon, Maurits N. *The Tabqa Reservoir Survey, 1964.* Damas, 1967.

KAY KOHLMEYER

HACILAR, prehistoric mound (37°17′ N, 30°32′ E) situated 1.5 km west of the village of Hacılar, about 26 km (16 mi.) southwest of Burdur on the southwest Anatolian plateau, on the main road from Burdur to Yeşilova and Denizli. This small and rather inconspicuous mound is about 150 m in diameter and fewer than 5 m high. It lies in an intermontane valley at an elevation of approximately 940 m above sea level and 100 m above the level of Lake Burdur. Steep rocks overlook the village from a height of 560 m. At the foot of this great limestone crag is a perennial spring, known as Koca Çay. In this region of the plateau (Pisidia), also known as the Lake District, the proximity of the coast provides for a rather mild Aegean climate. Rainfall is abundant, with a current average of 30–50 cm; an occasional snowfall between December and February is not unusual.

The prehistoric mound of Hacılar was excavated by James Mellaart from 1957–1960, on behalf of the British Institute of Archaeology at Ankara. Mellaart had first visited the site, already known to the villagers of Hacılar, in 1956. He had been informed that painted wares similar to the sherds he found in the provinces of Burdur, Afyon, and Antalya in his southwestern Anatolia survey in 1951 and 1952 were being illegally excavated at Hacılar. Mellaart considered the discovery of a prehistoric mound with no overlying late deposits to be a unique opportunity to investigate the Neolithic and Chalcolithic periods in this part of the plateau. The stratigraphic sequence he published suggests that the site was first inhabited during the Aceramic Neolithic period. He briefly investigated seven phases of occupation from the period in an area of 150 sq m with a cultural deposit 1.5 m deep. It was impossible to determine the size of the village, but he did establish that its occupants had been farmers living in permanent mud-brick houses. The houses had plastered floors and walls and were comprised of small rectangular rooms, possibly including a courtyard. Some of the floors and lower inner walls were painted with red ocher. This village was abandoned for unknown reasons, and the site remained uninhabited for an unspecified period of time.

Following a considerable gap in occupation, architectural levels IX–VI revealed evidence of renewed occupation in the sixth millennium BCE. Of these four levels representing a Late Neolithic village, the earliest three were poorly preserved. The last level, VI, produced important data concerning socioeconomic aspects of the Late Neolithic community. The villagers lived in mud-brick houses built on stone foundations. These domestic units, with plastered floors, had a central courtyard and perhaps a second story constructed of wood. The units were no doubt occupied by fully sedentarized farmers. Unlike the mostly single-room houses at the Early Neolithic village of Çatal Höyük (with entrances through the roof), the dwellings at Hacılar were large, about 60 sq. m. They contained built-in features such as ovens, hearths, benches, and small storage bins; access was through a doorway along one of the long walls. The handmade and well-burnished monochrome pottery of the period has its roots in the Early Neolithic pottery of the southern Anatolian plateau. Light and cream wares from Hacılar levels IX–VIII were gradually replaced by the brown- and red-slipped and burnished wares of levels VII–VI. The pottery repertoire of this period consisted of cups, bowls, and jars. In level VI, carved and polished white-marble vessels were produced in small numbers. They disappear in level I. The chipped-stone industry consisted of flint and obsidian flakes, scrapers, angular knives, blades (including sickle blades), and micropoints.

The Late Neolithic village produced a large quantity of terra-cotta female statuettes in standing, resting, and seated positions that vary in height from 7 to 24 cm. Some of these figures wear some sort of a skirt and are sometimes depicted holding an infant, a young child, or a leopard cub in their arms. The community's economy was based on agriculture, supplemented by hunting, fishing, and cattle, sheep, and goat herding. Farmers grew einkorn and emmerwheat, barley, lentil, purple pea, and bitter vetch. Red and roe deer, aurochs, wild sheep, goat, and probably leopard were hunted.

After the destruction of Hacılar VI, by the mid-sixth millennium, the village was rebuilt (level V) and the Late Neolithic culture developed into the Early Chalcolithic. The most characteristic feature of this period (levels V–I) is the popularity of red-on-cream painted wares. The decorative patterns show a preference for geometric and curvilinear motifs. The pottery repertoire includes—in addition to simple cups, bowls, and jars—new shapes, such as collar-neck jars and oval cups.

Building remains from levels V–III are not well preserved at Hacılar. The level II remains suggest that the small walled village was composed of a few mud-brick units built on stone foundations. These units, which included a number of domestic facilities and pottery workshops, were grouped around several courtyards within the village.

Hacılar II was destroyed in a conflagration in the last quarter of the sixth millennium and rebuilt shortly afterward with fortresslike characteristics. The new village, Hacılar I, was much larger and roughly circular. It had a generous central courtyard surrounded by large blocks of rooms built in mud brick and forming the inner part of the casematelike fortification wall. During this period of occupation, Hacılar potters produced wares that differed from those of level II: in addition to red-and-cream monochrome wares, they produced large quantities of linear-style red-on-white painted ceramics. The repertoire of this period includes cups, shallow bowls, deep bowls, and collar-neck jars with square, oval, ovoid, and basket shapes. The female statuettes of this period are rather crude, compared to those from the Late Neolithic levels.

Evidence for the economic activities of the villagers is not abundant, but it can be postulated that farming still constituted the main subsistence economy of the village. This Early Chalcolithic village was abandoned at the end of the sixth or early fifth millennium.

BIBLIOGRAPHY

Mellaart, James. *Çatal Hüyük: A Neolithic Town in Anatolia.* London, 1967.
Mellaart, James. *Excavations at Hacılar.* 2 vols. Edinburgh, 1970.
Mellaart, James. *The Neolithic of the Near East.* London, 1975.
Singh, Purushottam. *The Neolithic Cultures of Western Asia.* London, 1974.
Yakar, Jak. *Prehistoric Anatolia: The Neolithic Transformation and the Early Chalcolithic Period.* Tel Aviv, 1991.

JAK YAKAR

HADAR, one of the most productive hominid fossil-bearing sites in Africa. Roughly 300 km (186 mi.) northeast of Addis Ababa and situated in the west-central Afar Depression of Ethiopia (11°10′ N, 40°35′ E), the mid-Pliocene site of Hadar takes its name from a large wadi known by the local Afar tribesmen as the Kada Hadar. Paleontological field investigations at Hadar during 1973–1977, 1980, 1990, and 1992–1994 have produced more than 300 hominid fossil specimens. Most noteworthy is nearly 40 percent of a single skeleton (nicknamed Lucy) and the partial remains of at least thirteen individuals (the so-called First Family) from a single geological stratum at.

The fossiliferous deposits, extending over roughly 100 sq

km (39 sq. mi.) and known as the Hadar Formation, consist of 160 to 270 m (525–886 ft.) of lacustrine, lake-margin, and fluvial sediments. Widespread and distinctive volcanic-marker beds permit the subdivision of the formation into four stratigraphic members (from bottom to top): Basal, Sidi Hakoma, Denen Dora, and Kada Hadar.

In 1968 Maurice Taieb first visited Hadar and recognized its great potential for paleoanthropological research. Following a regional survey of sites in the Afar Depression in 1972, Taieb established the International Afar Research Expedition with his coworkers Donald C. Johanson, Yves Coppens, and John E. Kalb. Based on geological considerations as well as the superb preservation of faunal remains, the team initiated intensive study of Hadar in 1973. It was then that the first fossil hominid, a knee joint, confirmed the presence of human ancestors within the Hadar Formation.

The sparsely vegetated and heavily eroded outcrops at Hadar permitted the recovery of close to seven thousand fossil specimens of a wide variety of carnivora, poboscidea, perissodactyla, artiodactlya, rodents, birds, reptiles, fish, nonhominid primates, and other mammalian taxa. The faunal picture is characteristically African (Ethiopian faunal region) and indicates a mosaic of habitats, ranging from closed and open woodland bush and grassland conditions. Fossil pollen and microfauna indicate that the elevation of site was considerably higher than the present day altitude of 500 m (1,640 ft.).

Age calibration of the Hadar Formation is now firmly established on the basis of vertebrate biostratigraphy (correlation to other sites of known absolute age), paleomagnetism, and fission track dating as well as K-Ar and ^{40}Ar/^{39}Ar dating of the volcanic horizons. The hominid fossil-bearing strata at Hadar span a time range from at least 3.4 million years to approximately 3.0 million years ago. The best age estimate for the Lucy skeleton is 3.2 million years old.

Detailed anatomical study of the Hadar hominid collection led to the recognition that they were morphologically identical with those from the 3.5-million-year-old site in northern Tanzania known as Laetoli. In 1978, because of the recognition of a number of primitive cranial, mandibular, and dental characteristics these hominid fossils were distinguished from other known hominids, and placed in a new species, *Australopithecus afarensis* (Johanson et al., 1978). Although individual anatomical features are seen in other species of *Australopithecus* it is the constellation of features in *A. afarensis* that makes this species distinct.

A. afarensis is sexually quite dimorphic, and males are considerably larger than females. The locomotor skeleton, represented in the Hadar collection including the lower limb, the pelvis, and the foot, as well as the remarkably well preserved hominid footprints from Laetoli indicate that *A. afarensis* was fully bipedal. Some investigators have pointed out that primitive features in the pelvis, ankle, and foot suggest a more arboreal lifestyle for this species. However, it is more likely that these features are merely "evolutionary baggage" from an arboreal ancestry.

Now widely recognized as a distinct hominid species, *Australopithecus afarensis* with its amalgam of primitive and advanced features is currently the best link between an ancient ape ancestor and more recent hominids. Although the precise geometry of the human family tree is widely debated, this primitive species of *Australopithecus* is considered to be an ancestor to all later hominids, including the lineage which ultimately led to modern *Homo sapiens*.

No archaeological traces have been found in association with the Hadar fossil hominids. However, during survey and limited excavation in the Gona area, west of the hominid bearing deposits at Hadar, lithic artifacts were found. The flakes and cores are broadly assigned to the Oldowan industry. They are stratigraphically above the hominid bearing deposits and have been estimated to be approximately 2.5 million years old, making them among the oldest stone tools in Africa.

BIBLIOGRAPHY

Aronson, James L., and Maurice Taieb. "Geology and Paleogeography of the Hadar Hominid Site, Ethiopia." In *Hominid Sites: Their Geologic Settings*, edited by George Rapp and Carl Vondra, pp. 165–195. Washington, D.C., 1981.

Johanson, Donald C., et al. "A New Species of the Genus *Australopithecus* (Primates: Hominidae) from the Pliocene of Eastern Africa." *Kirtlandia* 28 (1978): 1–14.

Johanson, Donald C., and T. D. White. "A Systematic Assessment of Early African Hominids." *Science* 203 (1979): 321–330.

Johanson, Donald C., and Maitland A. Edey. *Lucy: The Beginnings of Humankind*. New York, 1981.

Walter, Robert C. "Age of Lucy and the First Family: Single-Crystal ^{40}Ar/^{39}Ar Dating of the Denen Dora and Lower Kada Hadar Members of the Hadar Formation, Ethiopia." *Geology* 22 (1994): 6–10.

DONALD C. JOHANSON

HADAR, TEL (Ar., Sheikh Khadhr), site situated on the eastern bank of the Sea of Galilee, 1.6 km (about 1 mi.) north of the estuary of Naḥal Samakh, which was, and still is, the main ascent to the Golan Heights (32°53′ N, 35°24′ E; map reference 2112 × 2507). Two of the site's concentric defense walls can be seen aboveground, enclosing an area of about 2 ha (5 acres). Tel Hadar was discovered by the Golan Survey Team of 1967–1968 (site 140) and was excavated from 1987 to 1995 by the Land of Geshur Project of Tel Aviv University, under the direction of Pirhiya Beck and Moshe Kochavi; Esther Yadin was field director.

The site's final stratigraphy was established only after virgin soil was reached in 1992. The site was founded in the Late Bronze Age I (stratum VI). The inner city wall, about 2.5 m wide, was built of large basalt boulders in this stratum; the outer wall was not yet built. A round tower with a diameter of 19 m adjoining the inner wall crowned the site. The excavation of one of its rooms revealed a floor of leveled bedrock. Of the two doors that gave access to a room, one was found with its lintel in situ. The site was destroyed and deserted during the LB I. No later Bronze Age occupation was attested.

The site was resettled in the Iron Age I (stratum V), when some stone-lined silos were constructed adjacent to the inner wall amid the debris of the tower. The site's most important stratum (stratum IV), is dated to the eleventh century BCE. During that period, the southern part of the area within the inner wall was leveled, and two large public buildings were constructed on two terraces. The first, a storehouse comprised of three long, narrow halls, was built parallel to the inner city wall on the upper terrace; the second, a tripartite pillared building with a unique granary, was built perpendicular to the wall, on the lower terrace. The storehouse had solid stone walls and beaten-earth floors. Portions of its halls were used for grinding flour and similar activities. A door led to the two wings of the second building. Some of the pillars in the building on the lower terrace were monoliths; others were built of several stones (see figure 1). Its outer halls were paved, but the central one was not. There were no troughs or holes in the pillars. The granary had six rooms (3 × 3 m) connected by doors raised 0.80 m from the floor. It was completely plastered and found full of carbonized wheat grains. More than one hundred complete vessels were found in the destruction level of this building, most of them in the tripartite wing. Besides the usual eleventh-century BCE assemblage, there were three-handled storage jars, jars with handles drawn from their lip, "Phoenician" decorated flasks and jugs, bowls previously found only at Gilead, a unique model of a shrine, a juglet full of astragali, a cup-and-lamp vessel, and a Greek Proto-Geometric bowl.

Following the total destruction of stratum IV, there was a long gap in occupation at the site. When it was resettled, in strata III–I, its plan and function were entirely different. Only private buildings, dated to the ninth–eighth centuries BCE, were attested in these strata. The 4-meter-wide outer wall was the settlement's only defensive wall. The broadroom plans of most of the private buildings were uncommon for the Iron Age, and the use of pillars was restricted to stratum III. Among the finds are the Gileadite bowls, small basalt anchors, and an incised enigmatic Aramaic inscription on the shoulder of a jar: LSD'L. The site was abandoned forever at the end of stratum I.

In summary, Tel Hadar's *raison d'être* stemmed from its location near the Sea of Galilee and the main highway leading from Bashan to the Galilee and beyond. The site's heyday was in the eleventh century BCE, when it probably played a major role in the Kingdom of Geshur. In the ninth century BCE, after Geshur was integrated into the Kingdom of Aram-Damascus and 'Ein-Gev was built as the main Aramean stronghold in the area, Tel Hadar became a small village inhabited by fishermen and peasants. [*See* 'Ein-Gev; Arameans.] The destruction of both Aram-Damascus and Israel

HADAR, TEL. Figure 1. *General view of the site.* Note the various stone pillars along two of the walls. (Courtesy M. Kochavi)

by Tiglath-Pileser III in 732 BCE brought an end to settlement at Tel Hadar.

BIBLIOGRAPHY

Epstein, Claire, and Shmaryahu Gutman. "The Golan." In *Judea, Samaria, and the Golan: Archaeological Survey, 1967–1968* (in Hebrew), edited by Moshe Kochavi, p. 282. Jerusalem, 1972. The first survey of the site.

Kochavi, Moshe. "The Land of Geshur Project: Regional Archaeology of the Southern Golan, 1987–1988 Seasons." *Israel Exploration Journal* 39 (1989): 1–17. Preliminary report of the first two seasons of excavation.

Kochavi, Moshe, et al. "Rediscovered! The Land of Geshur." *Biblical Archaeology Review* 18.4 (1992): 30–44, 84–85. Popular updated report of the first four seasons of excavation.

Kochavi, Moshe. "The Land of Geshur Regional Project: Attempting a New Approach in Biblical Archaeology." In *Biblical Archaeology Today, 1990: Proceedings of the Second International Congress on Biblical Archaeology, Jerusalem, June–July 1990*, edited by Avraham Biran and Joseph Aviram, pp. 725–737. Jerusalem, 1993. Lecture based on the first three excavation seasons.

Shoval, S., et al. "Rehydroxylation of Clay Minerals and Hydration in Ancient Pottery from the 'Land of Geshur.'" *Journal of Thermal Analysis* 37 (1991): 1579–1592. Fixes the temperature of the fire that destroyed Tel Hadar stratum IV to 1200°C.

MOSHE KOCHAVI

ḤADHRAMAUT (Heb., Ḥazermawet, probably "the court of death,"), one of the largest wadis on the Arabian Peninsula, stretches about 465 km (288 mi.) parallel to the south coast and descends from west to southeast to the Indian Ocean. The wadi bed, about 308 m deep, cuts through the Eocene limestone tableland (the Jol), and varies in width from 15 km (9 mi.) on the west to about 92 m in Wadi Maseila. Its bed has an elevation of about 920 m above sea level. The Ḥadhramaut receives less than 200 mm of rainfall annually and is dry except during April–May when flash flooding, fed by numerous tributaries on both its north and south sides, inundates groves of date palms and fields for cereals. During the remainder of the year, wells, ranging from 15 to 20 deep, provide water for garden plots. The major section of the Ḥadhramaut boasts of three cities, built entirely of mud brick and featuring some of the world's most exotic architecture: Shibam, Seiyun, and Tarim. Although neither environment nor known historical events justifies or explains the name *Hadhramaut,* it is used for both a wadi and a pre-Islamic kingdom.

The kingdom of Ḥadhramaut was centered in the main wadi and extended eastward and southward to the ocean. Its capital, Shabwa, was located in the westernmost part of the valley. It is one of six pre-Islamic kingdoms; the others are Sheba, Ma'in, Qataban, Ḥimyar, and Ausan. [*See* Sheba; Qataban; Ḥimyar.] Hadhramaut is the easternmost state. Names of Ḥadhrami kings are known as early as the fifth century BCE, and they, with later rulers, can be correlated in a chronological framework with kings of the other South Arabian states.

In the Table of Nations (*Gn.* 10:26; *1 Chr.* 1:20), Ḥadhramaut belongs to the fifth generation descended from Shem via Eber and is one of the thirteen sons of Joktan. Among classical authors, Strabo (16.4.4) mentions Chatramotitis (Ḥadhramaut) as the beginning of an incense route crossing Arabia to Gerrha on the Arabian Gulf. Pliny the Elder (12.35.64) refers to Astramitica (Hadhramautic) as a variety of myrrh. He also notes (12.32.63–64) that Shabwa marks the beginning of the major incense route along the western fringe of the Arabian desert to the Mediterranean port of Gaza.

Theodore Bent and his wife were the first Western visitors to the Ḥadhramaut in 1893–1894, but the beginning of major exploration began in the 1930s. Daniel Van der Meulen and Hermann von Wissmann conducted research in historical geography in 1931 and 1939. A number of British political officers, notably Harold and Doreen Ingrams, published information gleaned during their extensive travels throughout the region. Freya Stark conducted explorations in 1935 and in 1937. The first excavation occurred in 1937–1938 at Ḥureidha, undertaken by Gertrude Caton-Thompson, Elinor Gardner, and Stark. [*See* Ḥureidha.] The following year, R. A. B. Hamilton (Master of Belhaven) undertook exploratory excavations at Shabwa. [*See the biography of Caton-Thompson.*]

Following World War II, G. Lankester Harding visited sites in the Ḥadhramaut and elsewhere in the Aden Protectorates (1959–1960). [*See the biography of Harding.*] During 1961–1962, Gus Van Beek, Glen Cole, and Albert Jamme, under the auspices of the Smithsonian Institution, conducted an intensive archaeological survey between Tarim and Qarn Qaimah, along tributaries, and the Jol. The French Archaeological Mission, directed by Jean-François Breton, excavated Shabwa from 1975–1987. During this period, Russian scholar Mikhail Piotrovski and his colleagues conducted excavations and historical research at Raybun.

The earliest prehistoric evidence stems from the Middle Paleolithic, characterized by a Levallois technique of flake preparation. This phase continued without obvious development until tools produced by a preagriculture, desert Neolithic technology appeared. To this or the succeeding period belong numerous megalithic structures, large stone circles, and a unique complex of four dolmenlike structures whose inner surfaces are decorated with repeated rows of a pecked meander or crenellated design.

The excavation of pre-Islamic town sites shows that Ḥadhramaut culture developed with mainstream South Arabian culture, as at Qataban, Sheba, Ma'in, and Ḥimyar, with only a few minor differences. It shared the same language, with characteristics like those at Qataban and Ma'in. Identical methods of flash-flood and well irrigation were used. A similar religious pantheon featuring the moon god, known there as Sin, and cult paraphernalia prevailed. The architectural forms and designs are identical, except for the discovery at Shabwa of "skyscrapers," or tall buildings. One of these, reaching six stories, preserves a post-and-beam skeleton, not unlike structural steel frameworks used today, featuring massive *'ilb* (jujube) wooden beams, rigidly assembled with tongue-and-groove, pegs, and with brick curtain walls. This building, a palace, probably dates to the second century CE and was destroyed by fire in the fifth century.

[*See also* Shabwa.]

BIBLIOGRAPHY

Albright, William Foxwell. "The Chronology of Ancient South Arabia in the Light of the First Campaign of Excavation in Qataban." *Bulletin of the American Schools of Oriental Research*, no. 119 (1950): 5–15. Useful correlation of the royal chronologies of Qataban, Ma'in, Sheba, and Hadhramaut with historical events.

Harding, G. Lankester. *Archaeology in the Aden Protectorates*. London, 1964. Outdated but useful book, primarily for its photographs of sites and objects as well as pottery drawings.

Van Beek, Gus W. "South Arabian History and Archaeology." In *The Bible and the Ancient Near East*, edited by G. Ernest Wright, pp. 229–248. New York, 1961. Succinct summary of sources, exploration, and excavation from the eighteenth century to 1958.

Van Beek, Gus W. et al., "An Archeological Reconnaissance in Hadhramaut, South Arabia: A Preliminary Report." In *Annual Report of the Board of Regents of the Smithsonian Institution: General Appendix*, pp. 521–545. Washington, D.C., 1963. Account of sites, artifacts, and pre-Islamic inscriptions discovered during a walking survey, with tentative general interpretations of the cultural history of the wadi from the prehistoric to the recent Islamic period.

Western Arabia and the Red Sea. Geographical Handbook Series, Great Britain Naval Intelligence Division. London, 1946. The best available description of the geography, environment, agriculture, and tribal history of southern Arabia as of 1946.

GUS W. VAN BEEK

HADIDI, TELL, site located near the now-submerged village at Hadidi, situated on the west bank of the Euphrates River in Syria, about 110 km (68 mi.) east of Aleppo (36°15'54" N, 38°8'56" E). The site was excavated between 1972 and 1978 by the Milwaukee Public Museum, in cooperation with the University of Wisconsin, Milwaukee, and the University of Michigan, under the direction of Rudolph H. Dornemann, and from 1972 to 1974 by a Dutch expedition from the University of Leiden under the direction of Henk Franken. Tell Hadidi was one of many sites affected by the construction of the hydroelectric dam at Tabqa and the creation of Lake Assad. It was noted in the 1964 survey of the region conducted by Maurits van Loon of the University of Chicago. The occupation sequence is primarily Bronze Age (3050–1400 BCE), with areas of Early Roman and Early Islamic remains. At its greatest extent, the site occupied 135 acres along the terrace overlooking the Euphrates. Its basic outline is semicircular, with a diameter of 500 m. A smaller, higher portion of the tell, 55 acres in extent, is situated on the western side of the site.

Despite the large number of areas excavated—several with sizable exposures—only a small portion of the site has been exposed. The sequences of occupation are clear, and at least a basic assemblage of artifacts is represented for each. An excellent pottery sequence, a good representation of small finds, and a some of tablets have been excavated.

The earliest occupational remains date to the beginning of the Bronze Age. A series of buildings excavated in area RII and sherds found in the earliest fills in many areas indicate settlement over the entire 135 acres. The most abundant remains date to the Early Bronze III and IV periods, with buildings in most areas cutting through earlier occupation to virgin gravel. A large number of EB tombs were encountered, many of which were examined. The tomb assemblages, for the most part, had to be reconstructed from sherds because most of the tombs had been disturbed. A large quantity of reconstructed vessels from the tombs complemented the stratified materials, however. The tombs illustrate a variety of construction methods, including both stone-built chambers and simple shaft tombs excavated into the virgin gravel. Scanty remains of a mud-brick fortification wall were preserved.

Occupation seems to have been continuous from the Early to the Middle Bronze Ages, but the size of the settlement was reduced significantly and shifted to the western part of the tell. Excavation exposed a good sample of MB domestic occupation and sections of the fortification system. One excavated tomb showed evidence of reuse in the Middle Bronze Age, and a number of infant burials were recovered from under floors inside buildings.

Occupation was again continuous through the transition from the Middle to the Late Bronze Ages. The major exposure in area B showed a Middle Bronze fortification wall that was rebuilt at the beginning of the Late Bronze Age in an extension of the city. The pattern of fortification wall with moat was repeated. The lower eastern portion of the tell was apparently reoccupied when the city was rebuilt. In area H, two adjacent houses were excavated that had been constructed when the city was expanded in the Late Bronze Age. These two adjacent but successive houses had similar plans, organized around large, rectangular central rooms. The southernmost house, excavated by the American expedition in area H, was well preserved, to heights of more than 2 m and with its inventory basically intact.

A small but important collection of tablets from private archives was discovered in this building and provided dating evidence as well as a name for the site: two tablets attest that in antiquity it was the city of Azu. A number of houses with similar plans and inventory have been excavated at Tell Mumbaqat/Ekalte, not too far across the Euphrates. The remains of two LB tombs were excavated at Tell Hadidi; several others showed signs of reuse at this time. The Bronze

HADIDI, TELL. *Clay tablet depicting a beer-drinking ceremony.* Middle Bronze II period. (Courtesy R. Dornemann)

Age occupation came to an end with the decline of the kingdom of Mitanni at the end of the fifteenth century BCE.

Later occupation was preserved on the southern, river side of the tell. A large shallow area of Roman occupation was excavated on the lower, eastern side of the tell and on the southeastern side of the high tell. The Umayyad through 'Abbasid occupation was confined primarily to the river side of the high tell, and an extensive 'Abbasid cemetery stretched from the southwest corner of the tell toward its center.

BIBLIOGRAPHY

Dornemann, Rudolph H. "MPM Euphrates Valley Expedition, 1974: Excavations at Tell Hadidi." *Lore* 25 (1975): 2–23. Initial general report on the Tell Hadidi excavations.

Dornemann, Rudolph H. "Tell Hadidi: A Bronze Age City on the Euphrates." *Archaeology* 31 (1978): 20–26. Summary of the results of the excavation for a general audience.

Dornemann, Rudolph H. "Tell Hadidi: A Millennium of Bronze Age City Occupation." *Annual of the American Schools of Oriental Research* 44 (1979): 113–151. First substantive preliminary report on the Tell Hadidi excavations.

Dornemann, Rudolph H. "The Late Bronze Age Pottery Tradition at Tell Hadidi, Syria." *Bulletin of the American Schools of Oriental Research,* no. 241 (1981): 29–47. Basic representation of the LB materials, particularly the "tablet building."

Dornemann, Rudolph H. "Salvage Excavations at Tell Hadidi in the Euphrates River Valley." *Biblical Archaeologist* 48 (1985): 49–59. Updated general summary of excavation results at Tell Hadidi.

Dornemann, Rudolph H. "The Syrian Euphrates Valley as a Bronze Age Cultural Unit Seen from the Point of View of Mari and Tell Hadidi." *Annales Archéologiques Arabes Syriennes* 34 (1987): 63ff.

Dornemann, Rudolph H. "Tell Hadidi: One Bronze Age Site among Many in the Tabqa Dam Salvage Area." *Bulletin of the American Schools of Oriental Research,* no. 270 (1988): 13–42. Primary update of materials from Tell Hadidi.

Dornemann, Rudolph H. "Comments on Small Finds and Items of Artistic Significance from Tell Hadidi and Nearby Sites in the Euphrates Valley, Syria." In *Essays in Ancient Civilization Presented to Helene J. Kantor,* edited by Albert Leonard, Jr., and Bruce B. Williams, pp. 59–75. Chicago, 1989. Preliminary review of small finds from Tell Hadidi and their comparative setting.

Dornemann, Rudolph H. "The Beginning of the Bronze Age in Syria in Light of Recent Excavations." In *Resurrecting the Past: A Joint Tribute to Adnan Bounni,* edited by Paolo Matthiae, et al., pp. 85–100. Istanbul, 1990. Primary preliminary study of the EB ceramics from Tell Hadidi.

van Loon, Maurits N. "The Tabqa Reservoir Survey, 1964." *Annales Archéologiques Arabes Syriennes* 17 (1967): 1–27. Primary reconnaissance of the Euphrates Valley prior to the commencement of salvage excavations.

RUDOLPH H. DORNEMANN

HAFT TEPE (Pers., seven mounds), site located in Khuzistan province, on Iran's southwestern alluvial plain, about 10 km (6 mi.) southeast of Susa and 50 km (31 mi.) south of Andimeshk (at approx. 32° N, 48° E). This large Elamite site, composed of many individual mounds, forms an imposing and prominent mass rising above the surrounding plain. As early as the late nineteenth century, Jean Jacques de Morgan of the French Archaeological Mission in Iran described its ancient remains, referring to them as Haft Shogal (lit., "seven jackals"), apparently a misunderstanding of the name in the local dialect in which it is called Haft Chogha, with *chogha* being the local word for an artificial mound, or tell. In Persian, seven is a term often used to indicate any large number, a reference to the multiple mounds of the complex. [*see* Susa; Elamites.]

The site's ancient name remains in question. Some scholars have suggested that it may have been Tikni, which is described in early documents as a religious center located between Susa and Chogha Zanbil. While no evidence has yet appeared at Haft Tepe itself to support this theory, several seal impressions and clay tablets found there contain the name *Ka-ap-nak,* which may have been the site's original name (Herrero, 1976).

In the 1950s and 1960s, Haft Tepe became the center of a large sugar cane plantation. In leveling land for planting, some archaeological remains were destroyed and others exposed. During construction of the main road to the plantation, a baked-brick wall was uncovered that the project's managers reported to the Iranian Archaeological Service.

In 1965 an expedition was organized to excavate the site, sponsored by the Ministry of Culture and Art. From the fourth season onward, a program of field training in excavation techniques was instituted for graduate students of the Institute of Archaeology of the University of Tehran. Eventually, a site museum was built, along with permanent headquarters for the excavation team. Although the expedition worked for fourteen seasons, until political conditions in Iran made it impossible to carry on, only a small fraction of this large site has yet been uncovered.

The archaeological complex contains fourteen major visible mounds, the largest of which rises about 17 m above the surrounding plain, with extensions covering an area about 1,500 m long and 800 m wide. This is a single-level site with almost no evidence of occupation before its major period of construction and very minimal evidence afterward. The massive sun-dried and baked-brick buildings of Haft Tepe, which seem to be of a religious or other public nature, were constructed during a single period that lasted for one or at the most two centuries in the mid-second millennium BCE, at which time Haft Tepe was a major Elamite city.

Most of the construction is of sun-dried brick, with baked brick used only for very important buildings and in areas particularly exposed to weather. Between sun-dried bricks is simple clay mortar; and between the baked brick is an extremely strong gypsum mortar. Gypsum was also used as a covering for the baked-brick pavements and for plastering walls and the inner surfaces of vaulted roofs. Natural bitumen was used to seal basins and water channels and as a mortar and surface covering.

The architectural remains thus far uncovered include a royal tomb of baked brick with a barrel-vaulted roof (see figure 1) and another subsidiary baked-brick tomb, also with a vaulted roof, now collapsed. Both were attached to a large temple of sun-dried brick with two parallel halls opening onto a long portico that in turn opened onto a large courtyard paved with several layers of baked brick. The courtyard contained two broken stone stelae inscribed with the name of the Elamite king Tepti-ahar. It is believed that he built the Haft Tepe complex in the mid-second millennium BCE.

A massive wall of sun-dried brick surrounds the temple complex. Large architectural remains, with a massive wall at least 60 m long, extend in an easterly direction from the outside wall of the courtyard. About 100 m southeast of the temple complex, connected by this massive wall, is a large, solid, sun-dried brick construction that forms a many-sided terrace (Terrace Complex 1), built in sections. It may have served as the foundation of a much taller structure, a ziggurat palace or temple, whose plan can no longer be distinguished. [See Ziggurat.] Around this massive terrace are numerous halls, many of whose walls had been covered with polychrome paintings on gypsum surfaces. The halls had had flat roofs supported by large slats of palm tree fiber covered with reed and matting.

On the eastern side of the massive terrace, a particularly interesting large hall, apparently an artist's workshop, was

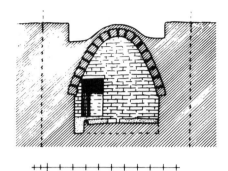

HAFT TEPE. Figure 1. *Tomb-temple complex of Tepti-ahar.* (Courtesy E. O. Negahban)

partitioned into several sections, in which various crafts had been produced. Bowls with dried paint, a sawn elephant skeleton, a solidified cluster of several hundred oxidized bronze arrowheads and small bronze tools, fragments of colored-stone mosaic framed in bronze, and a butterfly pin of gold and carnelian were found there. The most unusual objects recovered are two life-sized painted portrait heads of an Elamite king and queen (see figure 2), together with a clay mask. Directly in front of this workshop was a very large kiln, composed of two long, partitioned wings with a fire chamber in the center, in which apparently pottery was fired and bronze was smelted. South of Terrace Complex 1 another massive solid brick terrace was only partially excavated. Altogether, during the fourteen seasons of work, one

HAFT TEPE. Figure 2. *Portrait head of an Elamite queen.* (Courtesy E. O. Negahban)

hundred and fifty trenches (10 × 10 m), concentrated for the most part and covering an area of 15,000 sq m, were opened.

Among the most important remains are the written records, which include several stone stelae and many hundreds of inscribed clay tablets. The tablets were almost all Elamite tablets written in Babylonian; they include letters, accounts, scholarly treatises, and works of divination. The name *Kadashman Enlil* is inscribed on one, with an impression of the seal of Tepti-ahar. It seems that Tepti-ahar, king of Elam, was a contemporary of Kadashman Enlil I, the Kassite king of Mesopotamia. The Kassite king reigned before Burna-Buriash III, whose rule began in about 1375 BCE (Negahban, 1991). Many cylinder seals and seal impressions belonging to the middle of the second millennium BCE were also found, some with specific design details unique to Haft Tepe. [*See* Kassites; Seals.]

The bulk of the Haft Tepe pottery is comparable to that of the Late Kassite period. Most of the vessels, including jars and bowls, are of plain, unpainted pottery in various shades of buff; a very limited amount is plain gray pottery. Some stone vessels and mace heads were also found. Other objects from the site include many broken figurines of Ishtar,

in a wide variety of costumes and headdresses (see figure 3); male figurines, including musicians holding stringed instruments; animal figurines in different materials, and, among the bronze objects, arrowheads, axes, daggers, and tools, including a wide variety of chisels.

Evidence indicates that the complex had been sacked and burned at some time. In the courtyard of the Tomb Temple Complex, a solidly built platform formed of nine layers of baked brick with gypsum mortar had been completely cut into. Scattered over this platform were pieces of stone inscribed in cuneiform writing. They apparently belonged to stone stelae originally installed on the platform but were found lying elsewhere in the courtyard. It seems that after the stelae were dismantled, they proved to be too heavy to carry away and so were abandoned. In many of the halls of Terrace Complex 1, traces of roofing slats were found on the floor, indicating that the rooms had been set on fire. Nothing was found to show when this destruction took place, but the material uncovered in the Tomb Temple

HAFT TEPE. Figure 3. *Figurine of Ishtar.* (Courtesy E. O. Negahban)

Complex and Terrace Complex 1 points to a major occupation of the site for, at most, two to three centuries during the second half of the second millennium BCE.

Because Haft Tepe itself is a single-level site, during the first season of excavation a step trench was dug into the large mound of Abu Fandowa, about 1 km northwest of Haft Tepe, in order to obtain background material on the area's prehistory. This step trench revealed twelve archaeological levels, from the sixth millennium through the protoliterate and Elamite periods. During the last two seasons of the Haft Tepe excavation, work was reopened at Abu Fandowa. On its northwestern and northeastern slopes, kilns from the protoliterate period were uncovered and remains of the early first millennium BCE, including some inscribed cuneiform tablets of the Neo-Elamite period, were found in the mound's topmost levels.

[See also Chogha Zanbil; Elamites; and Susa.]

BIBLIOGRAPHY

Beckman, Gary. "A Stray Tablet from Haft Tepe." *Iranica Antiqua* 26 (1991): 81–83.

Glassner, J.-J. "Les textes de Haft Tepe: La Susiane et l'Elam en deuxième millénaire." In *Mésopotamie et Elam: Actes de la XXXVIème rencontre assyriologique internationale, Gand, 10–14 juillet 1989*. 1991.

Herrero, Pablo. "Tablettes administratives de Haft Tepe." *Cahiers de la Délégation Archéologique Française en Iran* 6 (1976): 93–116.

Herrero, Pablo, and J.-J. Glassner. "Haft Tepe: Choix de textes." *Iranica Antiqua* 25 (1990): 1–45; 26 (1991): 39–80.

Negahban, Ezat O. "Excavation of Marlik." In *Actes du VIIe congrès international des sciences préhistoriques et protohistoriques*, pp. 220–222. Prague, 1971.

Negahban, Ezat O. "Brief General Report of Third Season of Excavation of Haft Tepe." In *Memorial Volume of the Fifth International Congress for Iranian Art and Archaeology, Tehran, Isfahan, Shiraz, 11th–18th April 1968*, vol. 1, pp. 153–163. Tehran, 1972.

Negahban, Ezat O. "Brief Report of the Haft Tepe Excavation, 1974." In *Proceedings of the Third Annual Symposium on Archaeological Research in Iran*, pp. 171–178. Tehran, 1975.

Negahban, Ezat O. "Haft Tepe." *Iran* 13 (1975).

Negahban, Ezat O. "Die elamische Siealung Haft Tepe." *Antike Welt* 2 (1977): 42–48.

Negahban, Ezat O. *A Guide to the Haft Tepe Excavation and Museum*. Tehran, 1977.

Negahban, Ezat O. "Architecture of Haft Tepe." *Archäologische Mitteilungen aus Iran* 6 (1979): 9–29.

Negahban, Ezat O. "Haft Tepe Roundels: An Example of Middle Elamite Art." *American Journal of Archaeology* 88 (January 1984): 3–10.

Negahban, Ezat O. "The Haft Tepe Bronze Plaque." In *Contributions à l'histoire de l'Iran: Mélanges Jean Perrot*, pp. 137–142. Paris, 1990.

Negahban, Ezat O. *Excavations at Haft Tepe, Iran*. Philadelphia, 1991.

Negahban, Ezat O. "Seal Impressions on a Jar Stopper from Haft Tepe." In *South Asian Archaeology Studies*, edited by Gregory L. Possehl, pp. 87–99. New Delhi, 1992.

EZAT O. NEGAHBAN

HAJAR BIN ḤUMEID, site located about 255 km (158 mi.) north–northeast of Aden and about 82 km (51 mi)

south–southeast of Marib (14°54′0″ N, 45°45′45″ E). It occupies the east bank of Wadi Beihan opposite the strategic Mablaqah Pass. This major caravan route led to Wadi Ḥarib, Marib, and northward to Gaza, the primary Mediterranean incense port. The site probably served as a control point under the aegis of Timnaʿ, the capital of the kingdom of Qataban.

Hajar Bin Ḥumeid is an oval-shaped mound with almost 15 m of debris. In area, the site measures 9.79 acres at the 10-m contour; 5.05 acres at the 14-m contour; and 2.67 acres at the 20-m contour. Flash floods have partially destroyed the site's long west side, and a modern irrigation canal was dug through the talus on this side.

The site was discovered by Nigel Groom, a British political officer, in 1948. Two years later, the American Foundation for the Study of Man, with Wendell Phillips, who was its president, and William Foxwill Albright, its archaeological director, excavated an area of 392 sq m on the west side, along the escarpment, through the upper four strata. In 1951, under Albright's direction, Don Dragoo and Gus Van Beek were in charge of excavation. To reach virgin soil during the field season and to protect excavators from sloughing debris, the digging area was reduced by a series of broad steps, making the area of stratum S one-tenth that of stratum A, or 39.2 sq m.

The excavations disclosed eighteen strata, spanning from about the eleventh century BCE to the second–fourth centuries CE. Two strata—D and F—had two phases each. From strata S through D, buildings were built entirely of sun-dried mud brick, with or without coursed rubble foundations; strata C–A featured fine ashlar buildings; this change in architecture corresponds to a change in pottery type frequencies, indicating a break with traditions in the late second–early first centuries BCE, when Qataban reached the zenith of its prosperity and power.

The site was a small town with a population of from six hundred to twelve hundred. It was an agricultural community utilizing both flash-flood irrigation and well irrigation. U-shaped, fired clay spouts were efficiently used to break the dikes surrounding garden plots to admit water during well irrigation. Among the crops cultivated were barley, tef grass, millet, cumin, sesame, flax, sorrel, grapes, possibly oats, and probably other crops for which evidence is lacking. Bovines, sheep, goats, and game, probably including fowl, provided protein; sheep, goats, and camels yielded wool; camels and asses were used for transport; bovines, camels, asses, and people served in draft work.

The economy of Hajar Bin Ḥumeid must have been greatly enhanced by the customs collected from caravan traffic through the Mablaqah Pass. Imported artifacts indicate wide-ranging international trade: a small brass chalice with delicately tapped designs was probably imported from Egypt; a lead glazed crater, made with a molded exterior and turned interior, may have come from Asia Minor, per-

HAJAR BIN HUMEID. *Bowl.* Note molded ibex head and recumbent bulls on rim, eighth century BCE. (Courtesy G. W. Van Beek)

haps Tarsus; and an unusual green-and-white glass base probably came from Mesopotamia. Cultural influences were wide ranging as well: a calcite (alabaster) stela showing a man holding a staff imitates a Syro-Hittite prototype, and pottery-finishing techniques were borrowed from southern Palestine and some shapes from Ethiopia. Local craftsmen plied their trades: metallurgy; ceramics; and stone-working, including carving inscriptions, sculpture, and vessels; and mud and stone construction. There is no evidence of fortifications or of destruction by warfare, suggesting a peaceful life isolated from potential predators.

The most significant of the results of the Hajar Bin Humeid excavations was Van Beek's development of the first pottery chronology for pre-Islamic South Arabia, covering the period from about 1100 BCE to 200 CE. Owing to the paucity of pottery and restorable pots in ancient Arabia, it relies on a typological method developed by James Ford (1962) that quantitatively measures the frequencies of all possible pottery traits (e.g., tempers, forming techniques, and types of decoration). These categories serve as the principal typological criteria, with shape relegated to secondary status.

The ubiquitous remains in every wadi of diversion dams and sluices, together with silt deposition and rectangular erosion patterns, led Richard Bowen (1958) to the first comprehensive reconstruction of techniques for pre-Islamic flash-flood and well irrigation. For environmental reconstruction, a technique borrowed from paleontology enabled Thomas R. Soderstrom (1969), Elizabeth F. Wiseman, and Van Beek to identify both wild and domestic plants from seed impressions in plant-tempered pottery. Hajar Bin Humeid was the site of the first successful use of X-rays to identify joints in pots assembled from multiple sections.

With subsequent technological development, the technique become standard procedure.

[*See also* Qataban; *and the biographies of Albright and Phillips.*]

BIBLIOGRAPHY

Bowen, Richard Le Baron. "Irrigation in Ancient Qatabân (Beihân)." In *Archaeological Discoveries in South Arabia,* edited by Richard Le Baron Bowen and Frank P. Albright, pp. 43–131. Publications of the American Foundation for the Study of Man, vol. 2. Baltimore, 1958. The most comprehensive treatise on ancient and contemporary flash-flood and well irrigation methods in southern Arabia.
Ford, James A. *A Quantitative Method for Deriving Cultural Chronology.* Washington, D.C., 1962. An excellent method of classifying potsherds at sites where there are not enough whole or restored pots or painted designs to construct a conventional, Near Eastern ceramic typology.
Soderstrom, T. R. "Appendix III: Impressions of Cereals and Other Plants in the Pottery of Hajar Bin Humeid." In *Hajar Bin Humeid: Investigations at a Pre-Islamic Site in South Arabia,* by Gus W. Van Beek, pp. 399–407. Publications of the American Foundation for the Study of Man, vol. 5. Baltimore, 1969. Discusses a technique for recovering environmental information on plants in antiquity from pottery tampered with grasses and plant seed.
Van Beek, Gus W. *Hajar Bin Humeid: Investigations at a Pre-Islamic Site in South Arabia.* Publications of the American Foundation for the Study of Man, vol. 5. Baltimore, 1969. Scholarly study of a pre-Islamic archaeological site in southern Arabia spanning more than a thousand years, with the only lengthy pottery chronology to date and several innovative research techniques.

GUS W. VAN BEEK

HAJJI FIRUZ, a small, mounded site in the Solduz valley of northwestern Iran (37°01'06" N, 45°28' E). The site was first recorded in 1936 by Aurel Stein and named after a nearby village (Stein, 1940). In 1956, Robert H. Dyson, Jr., of the University of Pennsylvania Museum began a long-term program of archaeological research in Solduz, focused on the large site of Hasanlu with its well-preserved Iron Age citadel. [*See* Hasanlu.] One of Dyson's goals was to document the history of settlement in the region; to achieve this goal, soundings were made at several sites with limited periods of occupation. Located only 2 km from Hasanlu, Hajji Firuz was tested in 1958 by Charles Burney and in 1961 by T. Cuyler Young, Jr. More extensive excavations were carried out by Mary M. Voigt in 1968.

The site can be divided into two topographic areas: a high, relatively steeply sloping central mound and a low, gently sloping outer flat. Burney's small sounding near the center of the mound defined three distinctive ceramic assemblages dated to early prehistoric times. All absolute dates for these assemblages are based on calibrated radiocarbon determinations. Resting on virgin soil are deposits assigned to the Hajji Firuz period (Hasanlu X, c. 6500–5500 BCE); stratified above were occupations designated as the Dalma (Hasanlu IX, c. 5100–4800 BCE) and Pisdeli (Hasanlu VIII, c. 4800–

3800 BCE) assemblages. Subsequent excavation was focused on the Hajji Firuz, or Neolithic, period and was carried out on the lower slope of the mound, where the sixth-millennium settlement lay near the site's modern surface. Young defined a sequence of building levels spanning about five hundred years (6000–5500 BCE), but did not reach virgin soil, which lay under the water table near the edge of the mound. Voigt's principal goal was to understand better the architecture and settlement plan of the village. She therefore cleared a broad area of the latest well-preserved Hajji Firuz occupation. Additional information was obtained from a regional surface survey that showed that Hajji Firuz Tepe was one of (at least) six Neolithic villages clustered in a well-watered zone in the Solduz valley. One additional site was located on the Gadar River in the Ushnu valley to the west.

The Ushnu-Solduz valley was initially occupied in about 6500 BCE by farmers who migrated across the Zagros Mountains from northern Mesopotamia, carrying with them a material culture similar in many ways to that of such Hassuna sites as Umm Dabaghiyeh and Tell Hassuna. [*See* Hassuna.] Floral and faunal evidence from Hajji Firuz indicates that these people cultivated wheat, barley, and lentils and herded sheep, goats, and pigs. Although domesticates provided the bulk of their food supply, they also gathered wild plants and hunted both large and small game (aurochs, red deer, wild boar, hare, and a variety of birds). The restriction of settlements to areas with relatively rich pasture suggests that herding played a significant and perhaps crucial role in the subsistence system of these frontier farmers; it provided a buffer against serious crop shortages caused by drought, as well as a means of avoiding minor (seasonal) shortages.

The village at Hajji Firuz was made up of small rectangular houses built of mud bricks covered with mud plaster and roofed with a layer of reed and mud resting on short wooden beams (figure 1). Each house was oriented along the cardinal points of the compass and was divided into two rooms. The rooms differed in details of construction and contents: a cleaner and more elaborately finished "living room" and a "utility room" with uneven floors covered with trash and evidence of food storage (pottery storage jars, bins) as well as cooking (hearths, ovens).

The small size of the Hajji Firuz houses (about 30 sq m of roofed space) suggests that each served as the domicile of a single nuclear family. The archaeological distribution of artifacts and manufacturing debris indicates that each family controlled its own food supply and manufactured such commonly used items as flint, obsidian, and bone tools. The pottery was handmade; the variation in form, finish, and painted decoration suggests a large number of potters and probably manufacture within each domestic unit. Thus, at Hajji Firuz the household was the unit of consumption and the basic (if not sole) unit of production.

That village households were homogeneous with regard to wealth and status can be inferred from the houses (similar in both size and contents) and from burial patterns. Clay bins used as ossuaries were built inside most of the excavated houses, usually in the living room. [*See* Ossuary.] The bones of males, females, and children apparently remained exposed for some time, but eventually the bins were sealed with clean clay to form platforms. In some cases human bone was scattered in a layer between house floors, and children were sometimes placed in jars or pits beneath the lowest floor. The bones were almost always disarticulated before interment, so that there must have been an area outside the village where bodies were exposed until scavengers had picked the bones clean. In one case a bone was intensely burned, an early example of cremation. Items commonly deposited as grave goods included small pots, clay spindle whorls, and grindstones.

Hajji Firuz (c. 6000 BCE) can be described as an egalitarian society, similar to the model of the "early farming community" proposed by anthropologist and archaeologist Robert Braidwood in the 1950s, and typical of the earliest food-producing villages in the Near East. [*See* Jarmo.] Ironically, recent evidence suggests that most seventh-millennium villages had more complex social and economic systems, and that Hajji Firuz may represent a conservative group that chose to move into a new area rather than participate in the changes taking place on the plains of northern Mesopotamia.

BIBLIOGRAPHY

Braidwood, Linda S., Robert J. Braidwood, Bruce Howe, Charles A. Reed, and Patty Jo Watson. *Prehistoric Archeology along the Zagros Flanks.* Oriental Institute Publications, vol. 105. Chicago, 1983. Description of the work of the Iraq-Jarmo prehistoric project, which sought to document Robert Braidwood's model for the development of agriculture and social systems in the prehistoric Near East.

Dyson, Robert H., Jr. "The Genesis of the Hasanlu Project." Introduction to *Hajji Firuz Tepe, Iran: The Neolithic Settlement*, by Mary

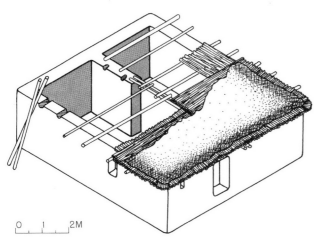

HAJJI FIRUZ. Figure 1. *Reconstruction of a mud-brick house.* C. 5500 BCE. (Courtesy M. M. Voigt)

M. Voigt. Hasanlu Excavation Reports, vol. 1. University Museum Monograph, no. 50. Philadelphia, 1983. History of work in the Ushnu-Solduz valley, including a summary of the archaeological sequence with key references.

Stein, Aurel. *Old Routes of Western Iran*. New York, 1940. Account of Stein's survey of major sites in the Zagros mountains, including the initial description of Hajji Firuz Tepe.

Voigt, Mary M. *Hajji Firuz Tepe, Iran: The Neolithic Settlement*. Hasanlu Excavation Reports, vol. 1. University Museum Monograph, no. 50. Philadelphia, 1983. Presents all material excavated by Burney, Young, and Voigt; suggests a reconstruction of village economic and social organization, and places the site within the culture history of the Zagros and adjacent regions. Includes a general discussion of clay figurines and their interpretation.

Voigt, Mary M. "Relative and Absolute Chronologies for Iran between 6500 and 3500 cal BC." In *Chronologies in the Near East*, edited by Olivier Aurenche et al., pp. 615–646. British Archaeological Reports, International Series, no. 379. Oxford, 1987. Summarizes information on stratigraphy and chronology of the Neolithic and Chalcolithic periods in the Solduz valley; lists radiocarbon dates for Neolithic and Chalcolithic Iran.

Voigt, Mary M. "Reconstructing Neolithic Societies and Economies in the Middle East." *Archaeomaterials* 4 (1990): 1–14. Discussion of the social and economic organization of early agricultural communities of the Near East (c. 7500–5500 BCE); suggests relatively rapid change in social forms and significant economic specialization by 6000 BCE.

MARY M. VOIGT

ḤALAF, TELL, site located at Ras al-ʿAin, at the headwaters of the Khabur River, at the Syrian/Turkish border, about 60 km (38 mi.) south of the foothills of the Taurus Mountains (36°48′ N, 40°02′ E). It is about 70 km (43 mi.) northwest of Hasseke and about 130 km (81 mi.) southwest of the Qamishli/Nisibin area. It is 330 km (205 mi.) northeast of Aleppo, Syria. The fertile North Syrian plain there supports excellent rainfall agricultural production. The closest major ancient archaeological site is Tell Fakhariyah, about 3 km (2 mi.) to the east, on the other side of the Khabur. The archaeological sequences at Ḥalaf and Fakhariyah complement each other and sometimes seem to overlap. Tell Ḥalaf is associated with the name *Guzana* in both the Bronze and Iron Ages, while the name for Fakhariyah is uncertain in the Bronze Age and is documented as Sikanu in the Iron Age (Abou Assaf et al., 1982). Guzana was the capital city of the Aramean state of Bit-Baḫiani. [*See* Fakhariyah, Tell.]

Tell Ḥalaf was first explored by the German diplomat Max Frieherr von Oppenheim with soundings in 1899 and excavations between 1911 and 1913 and again in 1927 and 1929 (von Oppenheim, 1931). Two major periods of occupation were encountered. The first was a sixth-millennium BCE occupation with a distinctive ceramic assemblage that has given the site name to this period for North Syria and northern Iraq. The stratum was excavated at a depth of 22 m, primarily under the acropolis area and near the spring that issues from the ground at the foot of the mound on the north side and feeds into the Khabur. The present-day contours of the site reflect its Iron Age plan. A large, basically

rectangular area about 600 × 360 m was framed by a fortification system of straight stretches of walls with regularly spaced rectangular towers. This lower town surrounded the rectangular acropolis (about 150 × 200 m) in the north-central area, backing up to the banks of the Khabur.

Ḥalaf and Earlier Material. The earliest ceramic material from the lowest levels at the bottom of deep test pits is coarse, unpainted pottery, apparently dating to the earliest phases of the Pottery Neolithic (early in the sixth millennium BCE). Red, gray, and plain burnished wares occur at this time and then continue side by side with more elaborate painted wares followed by the deposits of the Ḥalaf period itself (mid-sixth–fifth millennium). The Ḥalaf-period assemblage is characterized by beautifully decorated polychrome vessels. A large repertoire of decorative motifs is executed in a fine, lustrous paint that appears to be almost a glaze. It was applied primarily on jars and bowls in a number of quite distinctive forms. Copper objects, flint tools, handmade figurines, and stone vessels are among the categories of objects that comprise this rich assemblage, but they are summarily represented because of the limited soundings (von Oppenheim, 1943). The Ḥalaf culture has now been investigated or recovered from a range of sites that covers a wide band across northern Mesopotamia, from the Khabur area west to the Euphrates River and east to the Zagros Mountains.

Aramean and Assyrian Occupations. The excavators do not mention any occupation between the earliest levels of the Pottery Neolithic through the Chalcolithic and the earliest occupation in the Iron Age. Several levels of Iron Age settlement were blocked out from at least the tenth through the seventh centuries BCE. The *altbau* (early building) period was encountered in soundings that provided earlier phases of fortification, a gateway, and major building construction underlying the extensive remains of the Kapara period (von Oppenheim, 1950; see below).

The name of the Iron Age city at Tell Ḥalaf is known as Guzana from Assyrian sources and materials found at the site. The literary references date from the time of Adad-Nirari II (911–891 BCE). He is said to have received tribute from Abisalamu of Bit-Baḫiani, where Guzana is the capital city, to the time of Sargon II (721–705 BCE), when the latest of many governors is mentioned. The Assyrian rulers Tukulti-Ninurta II and Ashurbanipal II mention the site in their inscriptions. Among a long list of governors mentioned in the Assyrian eponym lists, down through 706 BCE, are Mannukiaššur (793 BCE) and Pursagale (763 BCE). The seventh-century BCE site is considered to have been fully assyrianized on the basis of letters and legal documents recovered there. At what point in the eighth century BCE the Assyrian governors replaced the local Aramean rulers is not clear. Many inscriptions were found from the ruler Kapara; his father Handianu is also mentioned, but it has not been possible to fix precisely the years in which they lived, though a tenth–

HALAF, TELL. Figure 1. *Basalt orthostat.* Aleppo Museum. (Courtesy J. S. Jorgensen)

ninth-century date is probable. At nearby Tell Fakhariyah, ancient Sikanu, a statue with a bilingual inscription in Aramaic and Akkadian, possibly dating to the end of the ninth century BCE, was dedicated to the god Hadad by Hadadyis'a, son of Shamash-Nuri. [*See* Fakariyah Aramaic Inscription.] In the Assyrian version he is referred to as the governor of Guzana, and in the Aramaic version he is king of Guzana. Tukultisharru, the son of Hadadyis'a, may have been one of the last of the Aramaic rulers of Guzana.

Assigned to the ninth century BCE, though possibly earlier in date, is the later palace structure, the northwestern palace, with its many sculptural embellishments and inscriptions of the ruler Kapara. A two-chambered gateway on the western side of the south wall gives access to the acropolis. A large mass of brickwork was encountered west of the gateway, covering an area of about 3600 sq m, whose function is unclear. A street runs directly north of this citadel gateway, through a gateway on the eastern side of the northwest palace, that connects to the courtyard north of the palace.

Alternating small basalt and limestone orthostats (see figure 1), each with a separate carved scene, decorate the southern facade of the building from its western corner, around its eastern corner, and continuing up to the palace gateway. The orthostats were carved in a variety of styles that include representations of soldiers standing with their weapons, engaged in combat, or hunting. The animals represented include horses, bulls, lions, a panther, reindeer, gazelles, an ostrich, birds, fish, and snakes; mixed creatures include a scorpion man, a fish man, bull men, sphinxes, griffins, and a human figure with two lion heads; and even a camel rider and a boat are included. There is also a variety of ritual scenes. Evidence of rebuilding indicates that this row of sculptures belonged to an early phase of the palace, but it contains inscriptions of Kapara, to whom other inscriptions attribute the palace. Two inscriptions appear over erasures of earlier inscriptions. They refer to the building both as a temple and as a palace. The early phase of occupation in the citadel area is best represented in the gateway. It was a complex structure with an indirect-access plan. [*See* Palace; Temples, *article on* Mesopotamian Temples.]

At the palace gateway, the entrance to the first chamber

HALAF, TELL. Figure 2. *Orthostat of a lion.* Aleppo Museum. (Courtesy J. S. Jorgensen)

HALAF, TELL. Figure 3. *Entrance support from the Palace of Kapara.* Aleppo Museum. (Courtesy J. S. Jorgensen)

is flanked by large, elaborate orthostats carved in the form of human-headed birds with scorpion stingers. The palace's main entrance is located on the north. Raised on a terrace reached by a flight of stairs from the northern courtyard, its decoration is innovative and unique. The doorway is flanked by sphinxes and the base of the front wall is decorated with a basically symmetrical arrangement of carved orthostats of lions, (see figure 2), bull and lion hunts, and other scenes. Most of the action in these scenes is directed toward the entrance. The portico's wide entrance is supported by three elaborately decorated columns representing two men standing on lion and bull figures in the round (see figure 3) and a woman standing on a lion, similarly sculpted in the round. The style of the figures and the orthostats combines elements from different artistic traditions into the distinctive style of these locally produced works. The interior door leading from the portico is flanked by griffins. Other sculpture in the round is scattered at a number of locations. (The sculpture is published in von Oppenheim et al., 1955; stylistic analysis is included in Orthmann, 1971, pp. 119–129,

178–181, and 233–474.) A freestanding griffin is notable, as is a group of human figures that was associated with a rich royal tomb.

At the front of the palace, green and yellow glazed bricks were used in the elaborate geometric decoration of a structure that may have been a freestanding altar. A number of decorated gold items and silver and bronze vessels were part of the inventory of the royal tomb, but they represent only a small part of the site's rich inventory: carved stone stands; decorated ivory fragments, primarily for inlays; cylinder and stamp seals; scaraboids; small relief plaques; and beads. Only a very basic and general inventory of the pottery vessels is published (Hrouda, 1962, tafeln 56–85).

The northern palace was not nearly as well preserved as Kapara's palace, but a basic plan of a portion of the building identified as the governor's residence was cleared. It and a number of smaller, probably private, buildings were excavated close to the surface of the site and attributed to the Assyrian phase of occupation, primarily to the late ninth–seventh centuries BCE.

Hellenistic, Roman, and Islamic remains were encountered in the upper 1.5 m of deposit. Very little of this material is published besides fragments of Hellenistic and Roman mold-made figurines.

BIBLIOGRAPHY

Abou Assaf, Ali, et al. *La statue de Tell Fekheryé et son inscription bilingue assyro-araméenne.* Paris, 1982. Primary publication of the Tell Fakhariyah statue with a bilingual inscription.

Hrouda, Barthel. *Tell Halaf IV: Die Kleinfunde aus historischer Zeit.* Berlin, 1962. Final publication of the report series, covering the small finds.

Orthmann, Winfried. *Untersuchungen zur späthethitischen Kunst.* Saarbrücker Beiträge zur Altertumskunde, vol. 8. Bonn, 1971. Detailed discussion of Tell Ḥalaf sculpture and similar contemporary sculpture.

von Oppenheim, Max Freiherr. *Der Tell Halaf: Eine neue Kulture im ältesten Mesopotamien.* Leipzig, 1931. First general book about the finds of the Tell Ḥalaf expedition.

von Oppenheim, Max Freiherr. *Der Tell Halaf I: Die prähistorischen Funde.* Berlin, 1943. Publication of the early materials from Ḥalaf, primarily the painted wares.

von Oppenheim, Max Freiherr. *Der Tell Halaf II: Die Bauwerke.* Berlin, 1950. Detailed publication of the architecture excavated at Tell Ḥalaf, with many reconstructions of buildings and building techniques.

von Oppenheim, Max Freiherr, et al. *Tell Halaf III: Die Bildwerke.* Berlin, 1955. Primary publication of the sculptures.

RUDOLPH H. DORNEMANN

HALA SULTAN TEKKE,

Cypriot Bronze Age town situated in a field west of the mosque of Hala Sultan Tekke and the Larnaca Salt Lake, south of Laxia tou Riou and Kition, and east of Klavdhia. The site's ancient name is unknown.

Hala Sultan Tekke has been excavated by two missions

sponsored by the British Museum (1897 and 1898) and by the Department of Antiquities of Cyprus (1948, 1968, 1983). Since 1971 a Swedish expedition there has been directed by Paul Åström of Göteborg University. The British excavators emptied many tombs containing a wealth of precious objects of gold, silver, bronze, ivory, and faience and imported pottery, all dating to the Late Bronze Age before 1200 BCE. In 1948 the Department of Antiquities recovered a huge pithos and two so-called chimney tombs in 1968 dating to about 1200 BCE. Although the British Museum excavations produced material earlier than 1200 BCE, the Swedish excavations, conducted in various parts of the site, have revealed a later town, mainly from the Late Cypriot IIIA period.

The site was founded in the Middle Cypriot III (c. 1600 BCE) and flourished until the end of the Late Cypriot IIC (c. 1190 BCE). Like the town of Sinda in eastern Cyprus, it was probably destroyed twice, in 1190 and 1175 BCE; it experienced a scant reoccupation until about 1100 BCE and was partially resettled in the Hellenistic period.

In the central part of the town, a street 4–5 m wide stretches in an approximately north–south direction. Three domestic complexes there consist of a courtyard surrounded by rooms similar in plan to houses at Pyla near Dhekelia in eastern Cyprus. Another large rectangular building with two interior stone bases for pillars and an inner room may be a sanctuary. Some of the walls in two well-cut, luxurious bathrooms were built of ashlars. The houses were, as a rule, built on a foundation of fieldstones, sometimes of ashlar blocks, with a superstructure of terre pisée and walls plastered with crushed lime.

The finds reveal various activities: copper working (copper slag, a mold for making arrowheads, and bronze tools such as a pruning hook, trident, shepherd's crook, and a charcoal shovel); jewelry making (gold- and silverwork); fishing (fish bones and net weights of lead and beach stones); and ivory working (carved pieces of elephant tusk). They testify to widespread connections with eastern Mediterranean countries. Mycenaean and Minoan pottery were imported from Greece and Crete, gray Minyan vases from Asia Minor, and so-called Canaanite jars and a silver bowl with a West Semitic cuneiform inscription from Syria-Palestine. Fragments of bones of Nile perch throw light on the Story of Wenamun, who received baskets of fish from Egypt during his stay at Byblos. Wine jars and cartouches of Horemheb, Seti I, and Rameses II are among the witnesses to contact with Egypt.

BIBLIOGRAPHY

Åström, Paul, et al., *Hala Sultan Tekke.* 9 vols. Studies in Mediterranean Archaeology, vol. 45:1–9. Göteborg, 1975–1989.
Åström, Paul. "Hala Sultan Tekke and Its Foreign Relations." In *Acts of the International Archaeological Symposium, "Cyprus between the Orient and the Occident," 8–14 September 1985,* edited by Vassos Karageorghis et al., pp. 63–68, pls. 4–5. Nicosia, 1986.
Åström, Paul. "Hala Sultan Tekke: An International Harbour Town of the Late Cypriote Bronze Age." *Opuscula Atheniensia* 16 (1986): 7–17.

PAUL ÅSTRÖM

HALIKARNASSOS (Lat., Halicarnassus; mod. Bodrum), city founded by Greek colonists from the northeastern Peloponnesos on the western coast of what is now Turkey around 1000 BCE, but always populated by a large number of Carians (37°03′ N, 27°28′ E). Little is known of the city prior to the classical period and Halikarnassos seems to have experienced its first flourishing during the early and middle part of the fifth century. At that time it was politically dominated by a dynasty whose most famous representative, Artemisia the Elder, fought at Salamis in 480 on the side of the Persian king Xerxes (Herodotus, 7.99). The dynasty was removed from power toward the middle of the century after civil strife in which both the historian Herodotus and his uncle (or cousin) the epic poet Panyasis were involved (Suidas, S. V. Panyasis and Herodotus).

In the fourth century the Hecatomnid dynast Mausolus and his sisters and brothers ruled Halikarnassos in turn as Persian satraps (provincial governors) from 377 to 334, when the city was conquered by Alexander the Great. These decades constitute the most important epoch in the history of Halikarnassos. The Hecatomnids initiated rich building activity both in Halikarnassos and on other sites of the Carian satrapy, thereby giving an impetus to the fourth-century "Ionian renaissance," which can also be studied in Labraunda, Priene, and in the new temple of Artemis at Ephesus. After Alexander (r. 332–323), the city entered the epoch of the great Hellenistic monarchies. During the succeeding centuries Halikarnassos received the buildings and monuments characteristic of a provincial Hellenistic-Roman city, but generally it seems to have played a less important role. A certain flourishing in late antiquity is indicated by important archaeological discoveries. In 1404 CE the knights of the Order of St. John started building the impressive castle of St. Peter, and these constructions, which utilized ancient material from the Mausoleum (tomb of Mausolus) and other monuments, were carried on until the castle was ceded to the Turkish sultan in 1522.

An extant eyewitness report of the demolishing of the Mausoleum by the Crusaders forms the beginning of modern investigation of ancient Halikarnassos. Travelers of the eighteenth and nineteenth century have reported on its topography and monuments, but the first comprehensive investigations were carried out by an English expedition directed by Charles T. Newton in 1856–1858. In 1921–1922 Amadeo Maiuri published studies in Halikarnassos, and an important report was given by George E. Bean and John M.

Cook in 1950. New excavations on the Mausoleum site were carried out by a Danish expedition directed by Kristian Jeppesen in 1966–1977 and in the 1970s a Turkish team directed by Ümit Serdaroğlu excavated the theater. Since then, excavations have been carried out by the Museum of Bodrum (Oğuz Alpözen, Akyut Özet) occasionally in cooperation with the Danish Halikarnassos Expedition (Poul Pedersen, Birte Poulsen).

Although Late Mycenaean and Protogeometric tombs have been found in the surroundings of Halikarnassos, only very few finds from before the classical period are known from the city itself. In the fifth century the central area of the city had a cemetery with large rock-cut tombs, possibly of the local nobility. This probably indicates that the city was divided into a western part, Salmakis, and an eastern part on the mainland opposite the Zephyrion Peninsula, where the Greek colonists probably first settled down. Some ornamented column drums of exquisite workmanship could perhaps originate from an early classical temple of Apollo on the Zephyrion Peninsula.

When Mausolus made Halikarnassos capital of the Carian satrapy around 370, the city was refounded on a large scale, obliterating most traces of the earlier city. The inhabitants of six neighboring towns were transferred to Halikarnassos to populate the new city.

The Roman writer Vitruvius gives an important description of the topography of the new city, the configuration of which he compares to that of a theater (2.8.10–15). The city was surrounded by a city wall, almost 7 km long, which ended in the Salmakis fortress on the west side of the well-sheltered harbor and the Zephyrion fortress on the east. The latter probably still contained the old temple of Apollo and in addition the palace of Mausolus, of which a large terrace wall as well as other remains have been discovered (see Pedersen, 1994b, 1995, 1996). The city received an orthogonal street-plan with a 15-meter-wide main avenue running west–east from the Myndos city gate past the north side of the Mausoleum terrace and probably continuing all the way to the Mylasa gate on the east. Outside these two gates were the cemeteries, of which the eastern was partly investigated by the English in the nineteenth century. In 1989 a rich tomb of the late fourth century, possibly belonging to a woman of the satrapal family was excavated in the eastern necropolis (see articles by Özet, Prag and Neave, and Alpözen in Isager, 1994, pp. 88–114). On the site of the earlier cemetery in the center of the city Mausolus built his monumental tomb on a very large terrace. The Mausoleum is described by Pliny (*Natural History* 36.30–31), and although it was demolished by the Crusaders, it has now been reconstructed (see figure 1) in most details by Jeppesen (1992). The foundations are 32.5 m (106.6 ft.) wide and 38.25 m (125.5 ft.) long. The lower part consisted of a podium, perhaps 25.2 m (82.6 ft.) high surrounded by two high bases carrying large groups of sculpture. On top of the podium was a per-

HALIKARNASSOS. Figure 1. *Reconstruction of the mausoleum.* (Courtesy Kristian Jeppesen)

istyle (colonnade) of 9 × 11 Ionic columns and then followed a pyramidal roof of twenty-four steps of marble. The height of the monument has been calculated to approximately 49.6 m (162.7 ft) including the quadriga (statue of chariot drawn by four horses), on the top. The monument was unusually rich in sculptures, which no doubt added much to its reputation as one of the Seven Wonders of the ancient world. The actual tomb chamber was placed off axis in the rock below the building and may already have been robbed long before the arrival of the Crusaders. The location of the Mausoleum in the center of the city, fronting the marketplace probably indicates Mausolus's wish to be regarded as new founder hero of Halikarnassos.

Prominent among the other fourth-century buildings of Halikarnassos are the temple of Ares situated on a large terrace in the northern part of the city and a fine, but smaller Ionic temple, from which several architectural members have been found a few hundred meters further to the southeast in the Türkkuyusu district.

The "Doric stoa," which is illustrated on eighteenth-century engravings may be part of the gymnasium and is probably of early Roman date. In 1987 well-preserved parts of the ancient stadium were temporarily unearthed during modern construction works in the eastern part of the city.

The theater is about 110 m (361 ft.) in diameter and has fifty-three tiers of stone seats. It is of the Hellenistic type and was originally constructed in the fourth century (Ümit Serdaroğlu, "Bautätigkeit in Anatolien unter der Persischen Herrschaft," *Palast und Hütte*, 1982, p. 347ff.).

Mosaics and other remains of the Late Roman period have turned up in different parts of the city. Most important among these are the remains of a large villa of the fifth century CE, which was partly excavated by the English in the nineteenth century. Additional parts of this villa have been investigated by Bodrum Museum and the Danish Halikarnassos Expedition in 1990–1993, but the total extent of this large building and its mosaic decorations is unknown (Poulsen, forthcoming).

BIBLIOGRAPHY

Bean, George E., and J. M. Cook. "The Halicarnassus Peninsula." *Annual of the British School at Athens* 50 (1955): 85–108.

Bürchner, Ludwig. "Halikarnassos." In *Paulys Realencyclopädie der classischen Altertumswissenschaft*, vol. 1, cols. 2253–2264. Stuttgart, 1896.

Højlund, Flemming, and Kim Aaris-Sørensen. *The Sacrificial Deposit.* The Maussolleion at Halikarnassos, vol. 1. Copenhagen, 1981.

Hornblower, Simon. *Mausolus.* Oxford, 1982.

Isager, Jacob, ed. *Hekatomnid Caria and the Ionian Renaissance.* Halicarnassian Studies, vol. 1. Odense, 1994. Further volumes in this series are in preparation.

Jeppesen, Kristian. "Zur Gründung und Baugeschichte des Maussolleions von Halikarnassos." *Istanbuler Mitteilungen* 27–28 (1977–1978): 169–211.

Jeppesen, Kristian, and Anthony Luttrell. *The Written Sources and Their Archaeological Background.* The Maussolleion at Halikarnassos, vol. 2. Aarhus, 1986.

Jeppesen, Kristian. "Tot operum opus: Ergebnisse der dänischen Forschungen zum Maussolleion von Halikarnass seit 1966." *Jahrbuch des Deutschen Archäologischen Instituts* 107 (1992): 59–102. Detailed survey of recent work at the site.

Maiuri, Amadeo. *ASAtene IV–V.* Rome, 1921–1922. See in particular "Una nuova scultura del Mausoleo di Alicarnasso" (pp. 271–274), "Il Castello di S. Pietro al Alicarnasso." (pp. 290–343), and "Viaggio di Esplorazione in Caria, parte III—Inscrizioni" (p. 461ff.).

Newton, Charles Thomas. *A History of Discoveries at Halicarnassus, Cnidus, and Branchidae.* 2 vols. in 3. London, 1862–1863.

Pedersen, Poul. *The Maussolleion Terrace and Accessory Structures.* The Maussolleion at Halikarnassos, vol. 3.1–2. Aarhus, 1991.

Pedersen, Poul. "The Fortifications of Halikarnassos." *Revue des Études Anciennes* 96 (1994a): 215–235. Part of a special issue entitled "Fortifications de défense du territoire en Asie Mineure occidentale et méridionale."

Pedersen, Poul. "Excavations in Halikarnassos 1992." *XV Kazi Sonuclari Toplantisi II*, pp. 135–147. Ankara, 1994b.

Pedersen, Poul. "Excavations and Research in Halikarnassos 1993." *XVI Kazi Sonuclari Toplantisi II*, pp. 327–334. Ankara, 1995.

Pedersen, Poul. "Excavations and Research in Halikarnassos 1994." *XVII Kazi Sonuclari Toplantisi.* Ankara, 1996.

Poulsen, Birte. "The Late 'Roman Villa' in Halikarnassos." *Halicarnassian Studies* 3 (forthcoming).

Waywell, Geoffrey B. *The Free-Standing Sculptures of the Mausoleum at Halicarnassus in the British Museum.* London, 1978.

POUL PEDERSEN

HALUṢA (Ar., el-Khalus), a Negev settlement founded by the Nabateans as a trade route site, located about 20 km (12 mi.) southwest of Beersheba (map reference 117 × 056). Translators of the Bible into Aramaic (the targum) joined the site's Hebrew name, Haluṣa, to the name *Shur* in the Jerusalem Targum of *Genesis* 16:7. In the mid-second century CE, Ptolemy included Haluṣa (Gk., Elousa) in his *Geography* (5.16.10) locating it in Idumea (Gk., Edom), west of the Jordan River. The site's ancient Arabic name, as recorded in Greek-Arabic papyri, is retained in the modern Arabic designation el-Khalasa.

Hellenistic pottery dates the earliest settlement to the third century BCE, when Haluṣa developed as a trade station for Nabatean caravans venturing from Petra to Gaza. An Aramaic-Nabatean inscription dedicating a shrine to the "king of NBTW," a reference to Aretas I (c. 168 BCE), and pottery uncovered at the site indicate that the Nabatean settlement continued into the reign of Aretas IV (9 BCE–40 CE). According to an account by the church father Jerome, a temple to Venus was in use at Haluṣa in the fifth century CE, at the time a small Christian community resided there. That bishops from Haluṣa attended the early church councils at Ephesus (421 CE) and Chalcedon (451 CE) further demonstrates that pagans and Christians coexisted at the site. Two sixth-century Byzantine sources, the mosaic Madaba map and the Nessana papyri, describe Haluṣa as a large city; the papyri refer to it as a district capital, a status it apparently retained into the Arab period. [*See* Madaba; Nessana.]

Edward Robinson first identified the site in 1838. His discovery was followed, in 1897, by the first of several visits to the site by Alois Musil, who later concluded, based on the ruins of one large public building, that the entire site had been destroyed. The exploratory excavation conducted in 1938 by the Anglo-American Colt expedition centered on several dumps at the site. These large mounds, made up almost entirely of sand and dust, were probably created by the sweeping of public areas in the Late Roman period. A full-scale survey of the site was undertaken by Avraham Negev in 1973 on behalf of the Hebrew University of Jerusalem. The purpose of the survey was to test Musil's thesis regarding the total destruction of Haluṣa—an extrapolation that proved to be false. Negev investigated the site further in 1979 and 1980, both seasons on behalf of the Hebrew University and in collaboration, respectively, with Ben Gurion University and Mississippi State University. Among the finds from these excavations were two burial grounds, both uncovered east of the town site. One dates to the Nabatean period; the other, to the Late Roman and Byzantine periods.

Haluṣa was most prosperous in the Late Nabatean and Late Roman periods but continued as a major city of the Negev into the Byzantine period. Findings from the 1973 survey, including various suburbs, showed that Middle and Late Nabatean settlements were concentrated on the eastern third of the site, and the Late Roman and Byzantine settlements covered the rest of it. The site was bounded by two wadis, Naḥal Besor, running southeast–northwest, and its tributary, Naḥal Atadim. The main streets of the Late Roman city were laid out parallel to these wadis, and a series of towers—the site's only line of defense—faced them. The remains of a large fortified palace, believed to have been that of the district governor of Palaestina Tertia, were found at the western edge of town. A sophisticated reservoir system, a Nabatean innovation, supplied water to residences as well as to the public bathhouse. In addition, a three-level wine press was discovered about 1 km north of the site. [See Reservoirs; Baths.]

The remains of a small theater, located in the eastern third of the site, were partially excavated in 1979 and 1980. The theater is an Early Roman design with local modifications. For example, the outside corridor surrounding the semicircular cavea (auditorium) did not contain the customary principal entrances (vomitoria) but instead was filled with earth and served as a support for the tiered seating. Access was through two vaulted corridors (parodoi) located at either side of the auditorium. The lower midsection of the cavea held a special box seat, apparently for nobles or priests—one of several indications that the theater was associated with cult activity. A dedicatory inscription on a lintel found in the remains of one of three portals leading from the scaena frons to the orchestra dates the laying of a new floor to the mid-fifth century; however, much earlier Nabatean capitals were found among the remains of another portal in the same area. [See Theaters.]

Also uncovered in the eastern third of the site, immediately northeast of the theater, were the remains of a church that may have been constructed on the ruins of a Nabatean temple. Much larger than most churches in the Negev (29.60 × 77.40 m), it had an expansive, roughly square atrium (28 × 32 m) enclosed by colonnades. The basilica (17.70 × 39.45 m) featured two long rows of columns, ten columns per row, with Corinthian capitals and Attic bases made of imported Proconessian marble. [See Basilicas.] The nave comprised two aisles of slightly unequal widths; the depth of the bema in the sanctuary was two and a half column spaces. The central apse was dominated by a structure with seven steps that at one time had a marble facade with a bronze balustrade. If this structure was in fact the base of the bishop's throne, then the church also served as a cathedral. Originally, the central apse was flanked by two rectangular rooms, but in a later period those rooms were turned into separate apses, situated north and south of the central apse. Excavators estimate the date of the two building phases at 350 and 450 CE, respectively—both toward the end of the church's history. Reliquaries were found in the southern apse.

[See also Churches; Nabatean Inscriptions; Nabateans; and Petra.]

BIBLIOGRAPHY

Mazor, G. "The Wine-Presses of the Negev" (in Hebrew). Qadmoniot 14.1–2 (1981): 51–60.

Negev, Avraham. "L'histoire de l'antique cité d'Élusa." Bible et Terre Sainte 164 (1974): 8–10.

Negev, Avraham. "Nabatean Capitals in the Towns of the Negev." Israel Exploration Journal 24 (1974): 153–159.

Negev, Avraham. "Vingt jours de fouilles à Élusa." Bible et Terre Sainte 164 (1974): 11–18.

Negev, Avraham. "Élusa (Halutza)." Revue Biblique 82 (1975): 109–113.

Negev, Avraham. "Permanence et disparition d'anciens toponymes du Negev central." Revue Biblique 83 (1976): 545–557.

Negev, Avraham. "Survey and Trial Excavations at Haluza (Élusa), 1973." Israel Exploration Journal 26 (1976): 89–95.

Negev, Avraham. "Élusa, 1980." Revue Biblique 88 (1981): 587–591.

Negev, Avraham. The Greek Inscriptions from the Negev. Jerusalem, 1981. See pages 73–76.

Negev, Avraham. "Les Nabatéens au Negev." Le Monde de la Bible 19 (1981): 4–46.

Negev, Avraham. "Christen und Christentum in der Wüste Negev." Antike Welt 13 (1982): 2–33.

Negev, Avraham. Tempel, Kirchen und Zisternen. Stuttgart, 1983.

Negev, Avraham. Nabatean Archaeology Today. New York, 1986.

Negev, Avraham. "The Cathedral of Élusa and the New Typology and Chronology of the Byzantine Churches in the Negev." Studium Biblicum Franciscanum/Liber Annuus 39 (1989): 129–142.

Wenning, Robert. Die Nabatäer: Denkmäler und Geschichte. Göttingen, 1987. Contains a full bibliography (pp. 141–144).

AVRAHAM NEGEV

HAMA, city on the Orontes River, between the barren Syrian steppe to the east and the well-watered western Mediterranean highland zone to the west (35°08′ N, 36°44′ E). The highlands include the Jebel Ansariye, which separates the Orontes Valley from the Mediterranean littoral. Hama is located 146 km (91 mi.) south of Aleppo, about 140 km (87 mi.) to the east of Banias on the Mediterranean coast, about 47 km (29 mi.) north of Homs and 209 km (130 mi.) north of Damascus. The course of the Orontes River moves through Hama in a northwesterly direction from the desert toward the Ghab, an area of exceptionally rich, dark soil from Asharneh to Qarqur that until recently was a marshy area. Hama has a long history, documented for thousands of years by written, cultural, and archaeological remains. The extended modern city, whose emblem is the nouria, or "water wheel," traces its history back to the Early Islamic city. Islamic buildings and building remains are still visible throughout the modern urban configuration, which supports almost 200,000 people and includes the classical city (Epiphaneia Syriae or Epiphaneia ad Orontem) and still earlier ones.

Medieval and classical remains were encountered in the highest levels of the ancient tell excavated by a Danish expedition supported by the Carlsberg Foundation between 1930 and 1938. An Iron Age acropolis, in phases E and F of the site's sequence, contains monumental buildings most likely associated with the capital city of the biblical land of Hamath (*2 Sm.* 8:9). In the Bronze Age, the site is identified with an Ematu mentioned in the Ebla texts and possibly with the Imat or Amata mentioned in Egyptian texts. After the Islamic conquest, the name reverted from its classical name to the earlier form.

Earliest Remains. Scatters of Paleolithic artifacts in the vicinity of Hama attest to a long human history in the area. A long sequence of cultural remains in focused on the ancient tell (45 m high and approximately 400 × 300 m). The earliest documented remains on the tell date to the sixth millennium: an assemblage of Neolithic flint, plaster-vessel fragments, and pottery. These materials, in the earliest levels of phase M, provide the beginning of the long sequence of thirteen phases encompassing forty-two levels, one of the most complete sequences yet excavated on a single site in northwestern Syria. The Hama citadel continues to be one of the main reference points for archaeological sequences excavated in Syria, Palestine, and elsewhere in the Near East.

The earliest phases on the tell were exposed in limited areas at least 27 m below the surface of the mound. Following the Neolithic remains in phase M, Halaf and Ubaid materials are represented in phase L; phase K represents an increasingly developed society at the end of the fourth millennium and the beginning of the third. The potter's wheel is first in evidence at the beginning of the phase in K10 and, like the possible remains of a city fortification wall, demonstrates an important feature of the local culture. Subfloor burials, common since the Neolithic layers, gradually disappear after phase K. Levels K9–2 contained beveled-rim bowls and Mesopotamian-type seals, as well as primitive local sculpture and handmade clay figurines. In levels K7–1, examples of Red and Black-Burnished, or Khirbet Kerak, Ware represent a remarkable tradition of handmade pottery found over an extended area from southeastern Anatolia to the Jordan Valley.

Bronze Age. The remaining Bronze Age sequences in phases J, H, and G on the citadel are much better documented. There is evidence primarily for domestic architecture in densely occupied areas with narrow streets. The occupation remains are rich in artifacts. In addition to the distinctive ceramic inventories, characteristic utilitarian and decorative metal items, pottery figurines, stone tools, decorated stamp and cylinder seals, and ivory and bone inlays were recovered.

Phase J primarily covers the second half of the third millennium with a sequence that is now complimented by excavated remains from the 'Amuq to the north on the Orontes; Tell Mardikh (Ebla) to the northwest; and the Euphrates Valley salvage sites to the east. [*See* 'Amuq; Ebla.] In addition to the artifactual assemblages, botanical and zoological remains document the ecology of the area then. Barley, wheat, horsebean, lentil, a plant resembling peas, grapes, cherries, and olives are represented in the botanical sample, and donkeys, oxen, sheep, goats, and pigs are represented in the zoological sample. [*See* Paleobotany; Paleozoology; Cereals; Olives; Viticulture; Cattle and Oxen; Sheep and Goats; Pigs.]

In phase H, a shift in the ceramic sequence takes place with many new forms for simple, primarily light-brown wares, best represented by vessels with comb-incised decoration and a variety of carinated bowls. Architecturally, the large cylindrical grain silos excavated in the center of the town are the most significant features. [*See* Granaries and Silos.]

Phase G provides a sketchy representation of the final international phase of the Bronze Age, with representations of imported Cypriot and Mycenaean pieces from the fourteenth and thirteenth centuries BCE, as well as earlier Nuzi painted ware. Buildings in this phase were more spacious than earlier.

Iron Age. The Iron Age remains in phases E and F on the citadel and in the cemeteries south and west of it provide important but incomplete documentation of the period. Cremation burials are an important feature of the cemetery remains, and a valuable typological sequence was reconstructed from the pottery and other grave goods. [*See* Tombs; Burial Sites; Grave Goods.] The contemporary stratified remains on the tell do not, however, provide a convincing framework with which to structure these sequences. Some pottery forms and decoration reflect Greek traditions of the twelfth century BCE. Iron tools and weapons became part of the material inventory, as did, in particular, the fibula, which replaced the straight garment pin. [*See* Jewelry.]

Phase E provides a portion of an administrative center of an Aramean state capital and Assyrian administrative center. [*See* Arameans; Assyrians.] It is contemporary with the historical records in Assyrian and biblical texts, but the artifactual and stratigraphic record is not securely tied to the sources. Several monumental buildings ring a courtyard entered through a gateway on the south. A few cuneiform tablets and fragments, including a letter to king Uratamis, were found, as well as some fine ivory carvings, cylinder and stamp seals, and a gold-plated statuette of a seated god. The entrances to several buildings were flanked by lion sculptures, and a decorated stela was reused as a threshold for a building tentatively identified as a temple. A large building (no. II) is considered a palace by the excavators. It has a buttressed facade and on the ground floor its most noteworthy features are an entrance court and a large number of storage rooms. The royal residence is considered to have been located on the second floor. The storerooms contained jars for grain, wine, and oil; among the many other items excavated were tools, weapons, and horse trappings. Bricks with incised Aramaic inscriptions were found in the pavement at the front of the building. [*See* Cuneiform; Weapons; Aramaic.]

Iron Age Textual References. Assyrian texts mention King Urahilina of Hamath as one of the leading figures in a coalition of states that confronted the Assyrian army of Shalmaneser III at Karkara, within the territory of Hamath, when the Assyrians tried to dominate northwestern Syria between 853 and 845 BCE. Urahilina is also mentioned in a Luwian inscription in hieroglyphic script found on the citadel many years before the excavations began. [*See* Luwians.] It also mentions his son Uratamis and his father Paritas, as well as a temple of the goddess Baalat. A later inscription dated to the beginning of the eighth century BCE is written in Aramaic. It is a victory stela of Zakkur, king of Hamath and Lu'ath, and was found at Tell Afis, about 110 km (68 mi.) north of Hama. [*See* Zakkur Inscription.] The last-known Iron Age ruler of Hamath is mentioned both in Assyrian texts and in a local inscription. He is designated as a usurper in the texts of Sargon II dated to 720 BCE. This Iaubi'di was defeated and killed, and his kingdom was incorporated into the Assyrian Empire as a province. Some citizens of Hamath were deported and a contingent of its military forces was incorporated into the Assyrian army. Little evidence is available for the seventh and sixth centuries BCE, though literary sources continue to mention Hamath.

Classical and Medieval Periods. A new settlement was constructed over the Iron Age remains in a rectangular plan across the tell. Its streets were oriented north–south and east–west. Coins from the third and second centuries BCE found under the buildings of this settlement date the new construction securely to the Seleucid era. They connect it with Antiochus II Epiphanes, whose name is undoubtedly reflected in the city's designation as Epiphaneia.

In the subsequent Roman period, the city gradually expanded into the valley. Building remains from this period are limited, but portions of a third-century CE temple are preserved in the present Great Mosque. The temple was transformed into a church in the fourth and fifth centuries and was rebuilt in the sixth century. Remains of other churches from this period have been documented in the city. A reference to a local bishop is known from 325. Occupation was continuous on the ancient tell until the thirteenth century, when it apparently came to an end with the Mongol invasion of Syria in 1260.

BIBLIOGRAPHY

Buhl, Marie-Louise. "Hamath." In *The Anchor Bible Dictionary*, vol. 3, pp. 33–36. New York, 1992. Excellent summary.

Fugmann, Ejnar. *Hama, fouilles et recherches, 1931–1938*, vol. 2.1, *L'architecture des périodes pré-hellénistiques*. Copenhagen, 1958. Standard reference work for the pre-Hellenistic remains.

Modderman, P. J. R. "On a Survey of Palaeolithic Sites near Hama." *Annales Archéologiques de Syrie* 14 (1964): 51–66.

Papanicolaou Christensen, Aristea, and Charlotte Friis Johansen. *Hama, fouilles et recherches, 1931–1938*, vol. 3.2, *Les poteries hellénistiques et les terres sigillées orientales*. Copenhagen, 1971.

Papanicolaou Christensen, Aristea, et al. *Hama, fouilles et recherches, 1931–1938*, vol. 3, *The Graeco-Roman Objects of Clay, the Coins, and the Necropolis*. Copenhagen, 1986.

Ploug, Gunhild, et al. *Hama, fouilles et recherches, 1931–1938*, vol. 4.3, *Les petits objets médiévaux sauf les verreries et poteries*. Copenhagen, 1969.

Ploug, Gunhild. *Hama, fouilles et recherches, 1931–1938*, vol. 3.1, *The Graeco-Roman Town*. Copenhagen, 1985.

Riis, P. J. *Hama, fouilles et recherches, 1931–1938*, vol. 2.3, *Les cimetières à crémation*. Copenhagen, 1948.

Riis, P. J., et al. *Hama, fouilles et recherches, 1931–1938*, vol. 4.2, *Les verreries et poteries médiévales*. Copenhagen, 1957.

Riis, P. J., and Marie-Louise Buhl. *Hama, fouilles et recherches, 1931–1938*, vol. 2.2, *Les objets de la période dite syro-hittite (Âge du Fer)*. Copenhagen, 1987. The Iron Age objects from the citadel at Hama.

Thuesen, Ingolf. *Hama, fouilles et recherches, 1931–1938*, vol. 1, *The Pre- and Protohistoric Periods*. Copenhagen, 1988. Detailed presentation of the earliest remains from the tell at Hama.

Zaqzouq, A. "Fouilles préliminaires à Hama" (in Arabic). *Annales Archéologiques Arabes Syriennes* 33.2 (1983): 141–178. The most recent excavations on the tell at Hama.

RUDOLPH H. DORNEMANN

HAMADAN. *See* Ecbatana.

HAMMATH-GADER (Ar., El-Hammeh), Transjordanian site noted in antiquity for its hot medicinal baths, located on the Yarmuk River, in a valley 7 km (4.5 mi.) east of the Sea of Galilee (map reference 212 × 232). The site is 1,450 m long and 500 m wide (180 acres). The site's ancient name is preserved not only in the modern Arabic place name but also in the name of the mound, Tell Bani ("mound of the bath").

Historical References. The earliest recorded mention of Hammath-Gader was made late in the first century BCE by the Greek geographer Strabo in his description of the hot springs located near Gadara (*Geography* 16.45). Some two and a half centuries later, the early church father Origen mentioned the baths in his commentary on John's gospel. The Greek biographer Eunapius asserted in his *Life of Jamblichus* (late fourth century CE) that only the baths at Baia in the Bay of Naples were more beautiful than those at Hammath-Gader, which apparently attracted a wide variety of visitors (Epiphanius, *Haereses* 30.7). According to Antoninus of Placentia, a pilgrim who visited Hammath-Gader in the second half of the sixth century CE, the baths, called *Thermae Heliae*, had been named for the prophet Elijah and were believed to heal leprosy (*Itineraria Antoninum* 7).

Excavation of the Baths. Much of the Roman bath complex was cleared during seven seasons of excavations, beginning in 1979 (see figure 1). This work, conducted by the Hebrew University, the Israel Exploration Society, and

HAMMATH-GADER. Figure 1. *General view of the Roman baths, looking south.* (Photograph by Zeev Radovan; courtesy Y. Hirschfeld)

the Israel Department of Antiquities and Museums, was led by Yizhar Hirschfeld and Giora Solar. An area of about 5,200 sq m was cleared, including seven bathing pools housed in individual halls of various shapes and sizes. These pools, constructed around the site's hot spring (52° C), were filled via an elevation pool built at the edge of the spring. The water in the pools became increasingly hot, gradually acclimating bathers to the high temperature of the pool closest to the spring.

The bath complex was constructed of coarsely dressed basalt stones. The walls of the long Hall of Fountains and the ceilings of many halls were of finely worked limestone. The floors of the complex were paved with slabs of a buffed clayey limestone. The most impressive construction was carried out between the fifth and seventh centuries CE. The complex was destroyed in the eighth century, probably by the earthquake of 749. It was subsequently abandoned, although people seeking cures continued to visit the site until the modern period.

Other Excavation Work. The earliest excavation work at the site was undertaken in 1932 by Nelson Glueck, in whose soundings at Tell Bani sherds were recovered from the Early Bronze Age. The absence of any Middle Bronze sherds indicated that the site, like others in Transjordan, was abandoned by that time. Hammath-Gader was not resettled until the Roman period.

Also in 1932, Eleazar L. Sukenik, leading a team sponsored by the Institute of Archaeology of the Hebrew University of Jerusalem, made soundings along the artificial mound (11 m high) on which a Roman theater had been built. Excavators determined that the cavea had fifteen rows of seats and held between one thousand five hundred and two thousand spectators. The row farthest from the stage was situated 6.6 m above the orchestra, whose diameter was 13 m. The stage (5.8 m deep and 29.6 m long) was 1.5 m higher than the orchestra.

The Sukenik expedition also uncovered a synagogue hall on the summit of Tell Bani, whose excavation was resumed by the Israel Department of Antiquities and Museums in 1982. Three phases of construction were discerned, with the building Sukenik discovered representing the latest phase. Based on names in the dedicatory inscriptions in the mosaic floors, the excavators dated the synagogue to the first half of the fifth century CE. However, the mixture of architectural elements characteristic of both early and late synagogue types (the transverse row of columns and the square hall are representative of the former; the apse and mosaic pavement, of the latter) suggests an earlier date, in the transitional period between the two synagogue types.

[See also Baths; Synagogues; and the biography of Sukenik.]

BIBLIOGRAPHY

Di Segni, Leah, and Yizhar Hirschfeld. "Four Greek Inscriptions from Hammet Geder from the Reign of Anastasius." *Israel Exploration Journal* 36 (1986): 251–268.

Foerster, Gideon. "Hammat Gader." *Excavations and Surveys in Israel* 2 (1983): 41.

Glueck, Nelson. "The Archaeological Exploration of El-Hammeh on the Yarmuk." *Bulletin of the American Schools of Oriental Research,* no. 49 (1933): 22–23.

Glueck, Nelson. "Tell El-Hammeh." *American Journal of Archaeology* 39 (1935): 321–330.

Glueck, Nelson. "Tell El-Hammeh." In Glueck's *Explorations in Eastern Palestine.* Vol. 4. Annual of the American Schools of Oriental Research, 25/28. New Haven, 1951. See pages 137–140.

Green, Judith, and Yoram Tsafrir. "Greek Inscriptions from Hammet Gader: A Poem by the Empress Eudocia and Two Building Inscriptions." *Israel Exploration Journal* 32 (1982): 77–96.

Hirschfeld, Yizhar, and Giora Solar. "The Roman Thermae at Hammat Gader: Preliminary Reports of Three Seasons of Excavations." *Israel Exploration Journal* 31 (1981): 197–219.

Hirschfeld, Yizhar, and Giora Solar. "Sumptuous Roman Baths Uncovered Near Sea of Galilee." *Biblical Archaeology Review* 10.6 (1984): 22–40.

Hirschfeld, Yizhar. "The History and Town Plan of Ancient Hammat Gader." *Zeitschrift des Deutschen Palästina-Vereins* 103 (1987): 101–116.

Sukenik, Eleazar L. "The Ancient Synagogue of El-Hammeh." *Journal of the Palestine Oriental Society* 15 (1935): 101–180.

Sukenik, Eleazar L. *The Ancient Synagogue of El-Hammeh.* Jerusalem, 1935.

YIZHAR HIRSCHFELD

HAMMATH TIBERIAS, site located on the western shore of the Sea of Galilee, extending from the hots springs (Ar., el-Ḥammam) south of ancient Tiberias (32°47′ N, 35°32′ E). The Talmudic identification (J.T., *Meg.* 1, 70a) with biblical Hammath (*Jos.* 19:35) is questionable, given a survey of the area and excavations that revealed no remains prior to the Hellenistic period. Originally separate, walled cities (J.T., *Meg.* 2:1–2), the Mishnah records that sometime in the first century CE Tiberias and Hammath were united (Tosefta, ʿEruv. 7:2). In the third century CE, Hammath benefited from Tiberias's distinction as Judaism's spiritual center. Hammath fell into decline in about 429 but capitalized on its noted hot springs and continued as a city until about 750.

In 1921 N. Slouschz excavated at the site on behalf of the Palestine Department of Antiquities, about 500 m north of the southern part of the city wall. He uncovered a square, basilica-style synagogue with a double row of columns separating a nave and two aisles. [See Basilicas.] There were three entrances on the north. On the east, a doorway opened to an outer courtyard. At the southern end of the nave four small columns partitioned an enclosed area, perhaps for the Ark of the Law. Multiple levels of pavements, mosaics, and alterations in the building confirm at least two phases of construction, with the first placing the entrance on the south. Slouschz identified the building as the synagogue of Hammath in the Early Roman period, disagreeing with Louis-Hugues Vincent. Comparing the building's small size to other ancient synagogues, Vincent in 1921 had assigned the later phase to the fourth or fifth century CE. Subsequent research identifies the building as a fourth-century synagogue. [See the biography of Vincent.]

Moshe Dothan directed excavations for the Israel Department of Antiquities from 1961 to 1963 near the hot springs, about 150 m west of the Sea of Galilee. He excavated three major construction levels dating from the first century BCE to the eighth century CE. Dothan assigned the primary building in level III to the first century or first half of the second century CE. Consisting of a central court with halls or rooms on three sides, the plan resembled a public building—a gymnasium or possibly a synagogue. Meager finds included a cantharus-shaped glass goblet. Level III was apparently destroyed in the mid-second century.

In level II, the synagogue of phase IIA is a broadhouse building based on the earlier phase IIB. Building IIB is a separate structure with three rows of columns, each with three columns each, creating four halls, the widest being the nave. A mosaic-paved corridor is attached to the building on the south with an entrance on the east. A small room in the northeast corner may have been a stairwell.

In building IIA, the corridor was divided into cells and the entrance on the east was closed. According to Dothan (1983) there were three entrances on the north. The northeast stairwell went out of use and a staircase was placed in one of the cells in the former south corridor. At the nave's south end a step led to a raised niche in the corridor for holding the Ark of the Law. Excavated debris contained remains of brightly painted interior walls. [See Wall Paintings.]

Magnificent mosaics using thirty hues, superbly preserved, paved the nave and aisles. Most significant are three panels in the nave mosaic. The southern panel depicts the Ark of the Law, flanked by a seven-branched menorah with flames, a lulab, ethrog, shofar, and incense shovel. The center panel depicts the zodiac surrounding the figure of the sun god Helios riding in his chariot. A halo is above his head, his right hand is raised in benediction, and he holds a globe of the universe in his left hand. In each corner of the panel a female bust with a Hebrew name beside it symbolizes each of the four seasons of the year. In the north panel a dedicatory inscription in Greek is flanked by two lions. [*See* Mosaics.] The high artistic level, in design and execution, of the mosaics, as well as the various finds, confirm a date of 300–350 CE for level IIA. This unique broadhouse plan remained in use until the fifth century, when it was replaced by a new synagogue in phase IB, built in the basilica style common to the period.

The buildings of level IB–A, also oriented southwest–northeast, were divided by two rows of columns into a nave and two aisles. An entrance hall was formed with a transverse division of the nave by a third row of columns. A second-story gallery running along three sides of the building was supported by all three of the columns' rows. From the nave, three steps led to the apse. In a room east of the apse, a staircase gave access to the second floor; in a room to the west, the synagogue's "treasury" had been hidden in the floor. The three main entrances were on the north. On the west, three doorways opened to a paved courtyard. Tiny colored tesserae formed the hall's mosaic in faunal, floral, and geometric designs. Level IB was destroyed in about 600–650 CE, perhaps by the reconquering Byzantines, and replaced by a very similar structure in level IA.

Rich finds in level IA included pottery of a type found at Khirbat al-Mafjar, Arabic inscriptions on some of the many clay lamps, and a jug inscribed in Aramaic concerning a gift of oil from Sepphoris. [*See* Mafjar, Khirbat al-; Sepphoris.] Numismatic evidence indicates that level IA was destroyed at the beginning of the 'Abbasid period (c. 750), never to be rebuilt. Squatters occupied the site from about 1100 to 1400, using the ruins for habitation and storage.

[*See also* Synagogues; Tiberias.]

BIBLIOGRAPHY

Dothan, Moshe. *Hammath Tiberias: Early Synagogues and the Hellenistic and Roman Remains.* Final Excavation Report, 1. Jerusalem, 1983.

DOUGLAS L. GORDON

HAMRIN DAM SALVAGE PROJECT.

In 1977 the Iraqi State Organization for Antiquities and Heritage invited foreign archaeological teams to join Iraqi teams excavating sites threatened by flooding from a dam built on the Diyala River where it flowed through Jebel Hamrin, about 100 km (60 mi.) northeast of Baghdad (34°07′ N, 44°59′ E). Earlier travelers had noted archaeological sites in the valley and Robert McC. Adams included twelve sites in his survey (*Land behind Baghdad,* Chicago, 1965, pp. 135–136, map section 1B). During the Hamrin Dam Salvage Project about one hundred archaeological sites were identified in the approximately 425 sq km (265 sq. mi.) area to be flooded (below 108 m above mean sea level) and some sixty-five were

excavated as part of the project. Some of the excavations were extensive and others were small soundings. The Iraqi State Organization excavated twenty-three sites and the Universities of Baghdad and Mosul worked at two. In addition, American, Austrian, Belgian, British/Canadian, Danish/American, French, East German, three West German, Italian, Japanese, Lebanese (called Palestinian by the Iraqis), and Polish expeditions each worked on one or more sites. The foreign expeditions paid their own expenses but equipment, accommodations, and labor were paid for by the State Organization. Most of the excavations were completed by March 1980 when the lake first began to fill, but excavations at the sites of Tell Haddad and Tell Suleimeh continued until 1984.

The Diyala River flowed across the plain, and near the site of the dam it was joined by two smaller streams, the Narin, flowing down from the northwest, and the Kurdere, from the southeast, both running along the edge of Jebel Hamrin. Geomorphological investigations showed that in the past a major branch of the Diyala River had flowed farther north, entering the Hamrin basin from the north; it seems probable, however, that both courses remained in use.

The valley lies near the limits of the dry-farming zone, with an average of 250–300 mm of annual rainfall; the surrounding hillsides provide grazing for flocks. The most important route from Iran to Mesopotamia, the Khorasan road, part of the so-called Silk Route, crossed the valley. At right angles to this an important route, perhaps on the course of the so-called Achaemenid Royal Road from Susa to Sardis, ran along the northeast side of the valley. In the Ottoman period, and probably also in certain earlier periods, the main route from southern Iraq went via the Hamrin basin, crossing Jebel Hamrin west of the Diyala, and continuing via Qara Tepe to Kifri and on to Kirkuk, Arbil (Erbil), and Mosul.

The excavations in the Hamrin basin give an outline of the history of settlement in the region, although the picture has gaps that cannot be filled, and the pattern of settlement does not exactly match that derived from a study of historical texts. In addition it does not mirror the settlement pattern adumbrated by Adams for the lowland plains of Iraq (*Heartland of Cities,* Chicago, 1981). The reason for this seems to be that the prosperity of the Hamrin region was extremely sensitive to considerations of political stability: dry farming and irrigation agriculture, as well as the trade routes through the region, were dependent on outside investment which was not normally forthcoming when the region lay on the border between different political powers.

It is also likely that for most periods sites have not been recorded either because they are covered by alluvium (excavations at Tell Madhhur in the northern part of the basin showed that there had been as many as 4 m of silt deposited in the last six thousand years) or have been eroded. Furthermore, settlements that were not marked by substantial mud-brick buildings were probably missed. Thus nomadic settlements, settlements of tents or insubstantial wood or reed structures, and scattered buildings have probably not been observed.

The earliest site recorded was an aceramic settlement at Tell Rihan. Two Samarran sites were investigated, including that at Tell Songor A, where eight buildings with regular grid plans, like those at Chogha Mami, and a possible surrounding wall belong to the late Samarran period. The Hamrin basin lies at the southeastern end of the maximum extent of the Halaf culture and four sites were excavated with late Halaf pottery. On two sites occupation levels containing both Halaf and Ubaid 3 pottery were stratified above Halaf pottery.

Perhaps the greatest surprise of the Hamrin Salvage Project was the number of sites from the Ubaid period. Fourteen sites with Ubaid occupation levels were excavated. Most of these belonged to the later Ubaid (Ubaid 3 and 4) period, but in level III at Tell Abada Samarran, Chogha Mami Transitional, Eridu (Ubaid 1), and Hajji Muhammad (Ubaid 2–3) sherds were found together. [See Eridu.] This unusual combination suggests that either the level was mixed or that the earlier sherds were residual. A complete village consisting of eleven building units was excavated in level II (Ubaid 2–3) at Abada, and some were rebuilt in level I (Ubaid 3). The buildings are mostly tripartite with cruciform central rooms. Some have an intricate arrangement of three interlocking cruciform rooms. A similar plan was found at Kheit Qasim III (Ubaid 3), and a house with a similar but simpler plan was excavated at Tell Madhhur.

The house at Madhhur had been burned and the walls were still standing up to 2 m high and much of its contents was found in the house. [See Ubaid.]

There were no definite Early or Middle Uruk settlements, but four Late Uruk sites were recorded. The following Jemdet Nasr period, or late Protoliterate, was represented at three sites: Tell Suleimeh, Tell Gubba, and Tell Abu Qasim. The architectural remains at Tell Gubba were spectacular, including intact corbeled vaulting. The building (about 70 m in diameter), consisted of a central circular core with seven concentric walls and a surrounding moat. [See Uruk-Warka; Jemdet Nasr.]

In contrast to the Uruk and Jemdet Nasr periods, the Early Dynastic I period, characterized by scarlet ware pottery was a time of prosperity in the valley, with numerous settlements and a variety of substantial architecture and rich cemeteries. The Tell Gubba building remained in use. A second round building (27 m in diameter) of different design was excavated at Tell Razuk: this had a circular courtyard surrounded by curving corbel-vaulted rooms (see figure 1). This appears to have been the citadel of a small settlement. Two further round buildings were excavated at Tell Suleimeh and Tell Madhhur. Extramural cemeteries were excavated at Kheit Qasim and Ahmed al-Hattu. The settlement associated with Kheit Qasim I, Abu Qasim, a small rectangular walled settlement, was also excavated.

The archaeological sequence revealed by the excavations in the Hamrin was very similar to that established by the Oriental Institute of the University of Chicago excavations in the Diyala in the 1930s, but the Early Dynastic II period

HAMRIN DAM SALVAGE PROJECT. Figure 1. *Round fortress at Tell Razuk.* ED I-II period. (Courtesy I. Thuesen)

was not as easily recognized in the Hamrin basin. [*See* Diyala.] There were a number of important sites in the late Early Dynastic and Akkadian periods. At Tell Suleimeh (probably to be identified with ancient Awal or Batir), a temple with a thick oval wall rebuilt many times was in use from the Early Dynastic to the Akkadian period. Cuneiform tablets of the Akkadian period were also found there. At three sites, Tell Madhhur, Tell Gubba, and Tell Razuk, the abandoned mounds were used as burial places and produced large, rich tombs. Among the grave goods were equids (bringing to mind, albeit on a smaller scale, the Royal Tombs of Ur and Kish, except that there was no evidence for chariots in these Hamrin graves). [*See* Ur; Kish.]

The Ur III period was not well-recognized in the valley, but it is likely that some of the sites with Akkadian and Isin-Larsa material were also occupied in the Ur III period. [*See* Isin; Larsa.] The Isin-Larsa period was one of prosperity, during which the Hamrin was under the control of the rulers of Eshnunna. [*See* Eshnunna.] There were a number of important towns in the region with public buildings, such as the palatial building excavated at Tell Suleimeh. At the neighboring mounds of Tell Haddad and Tulul al-Sib, which formed part of the city of Me-Turan, the city wall, various temples, and private houses were investigated. More than eight hundred cuneiform tablets were recovered, some of which came from a temple library and include letters, contracts, omens, and mathematical, literary, and school texts. Another palatial building was excavated at Tell Yelkhi, where some seventy tablets were recovered. At Tell Khallawa an extensive area of an Isin-Larsa period settlement with houses and a small temple was exposed and cuneiform tablets were recovered.

The destruction of Eshnunna by Hammurabi might have been expected to have reduced the region's prosperity and, although in many reports a distinction between Old Babylonian and Isin-Larsa was not made, this does appear to have been the case. Cuneiform tablets from this period were found at Tell Yelkhi, but in general the middle centuries of the second millennium BCE are not well represented in the valley.

Several Kassite sites were investigated. [*See* Kassites.] A small palace was uncovered at Tell Yelkhi and thirteenth-century BCE cuneiform tablets were recovered from Tell Imleihiyeh and Tell Zubaydi.

Surprisingly, there was very little evidence for occupation in the valley in the Neo-Assyrian period. Shalmaneser III and Shamshi-Adad V both captured Me-Turnat (Tell Haddad) and campaigned against Gannanate, which may have been close to Sa'adiyeh. Archaeological evidence for the period is sparse. The most substantial remains are those of a well-preserved temple of Nergal at Tell Haddad which was restored by Ashurbanipal and may be the temple mentioned in the Cyrus Cylinder. Next to the temple traces of other large buildings were discovered. Elsewhere in the valley the only Neo-Assyrian remains are unstratified sherds and a few graves discovered near Tell Yelkhi.

With the fall of the Assyrian Empire, the Hamrin valley lay on the border between the Median and Neo-Babylonian Empires. The small square fortress at Tell Gubba, with parallels at Nush-i Jan and Persepolis, may belong to the early sixth century or perhaps to later in the Achaemenid period. [*See* Persepolis.] Other Achaemenid remains have been noted in the valley, but there is some doubt about the dating. It is possible that they really belong to the following period.

The Seleucid and Parthian periods were not distinguished by most of the excavators, and thus their chronological development is not well known. It is clear, however, that the Parthian period was one of the most important in the valley, with the largest occupation area. A two story fortress with some forty-eight rooms on the ground floor was excavated at Tell Baradan. Other fortified sites of this period were Tell Ababra, Tell Abqa, and Tell Abu Su'ud.

The most outstanding Sasanian site excavated in the valley was the small manor of Abu Shi'afeh. The building was square, with sides 30 m long with attached semicircular towers. It had a central courtyard and iwans *(ayvans)* on the northeast and southwest sides. In a small room on the northwest some eight hundred bullae, each with between one and twenty-five stamp seal impressions, were discovered. There may have been a similar building at Tell Ibn Alwan, but only a small area was excavated there. A large number of sites had superficial eroded remains from the Sasanian period, but the major settlements may have been outside the area to be flooded. The city of Jalawla, near which the decisive battle between the Islamic Arabs and the Sasanian Persians was fought in 637 CE, is to be sought near Sa'adiyeh, rather than in the modern city of Jalawla, which was previously called Qaraghan. Although Islamic remains were found at many sites, it is clear that the Hamrin basin had lost its importance by this period.

The investigations carried out in the Hamrin Dam Salvage Project make the Hamrin basin, "the Land behind the Land behind Baghdad" (T. C. Young and R. Killick in Killick, ed., 1988, p. 5), one of the most intensely investigated areas in the Near East. The slopes of Jebel Hamrin and Jebel Nasaz form natural borders on the southwest and northeast, but the flat alluvium extended with no natural obstacles to the southeast and north, and detailed survey of the sites outside the area of the project might alter our perception of the settlement distribution pattern. Furthermore, because the expeditions operated more or less independently and the standards of excavation and publication varied greatly, it is difficult to give a definitive and comprehensive evaluation of the results.

BIBLIOGRAPHY

Preliminary reports on the sites excavated in the Hamrin Dam Salvage Project from 1977 to 1984 are published in *Iraq* 41 (1979): 141–

181; 43 (1981): 167–198; 45 (1983): 210–211, 220–221; and 47 (1985): 220, 225. Papers from an international symposium on Babylon, Aššur, and Hamrin, held in 1978, are published in *Sumer* 35 (1979), which also devoted a special issue to research on Hamrin presented in two international symposia from 1979 and 1981: *Sumer* 40 (1984). Reports on excavations in the Hamrin project are to be found in other academic journals; final reports are available for several sites. It is likely, however, that many sites, particularly those excavated by the Iraqi teams will not receive the publication they deserve. The reader may also consult the following:

Gibson, McGuire, ed. *Uch Tepe I: Tell Razuk, Tell Ahmed al-Mughir, Tell Ajamat.* Chicago and Copenhagen, 1981. Final report on three sites excavated by the Chicago-Copenhagen Expedition, including an overview of the region's history.

Huot, Jean-Louis, ed. *Préhistoire de la Mésopotamie: La Mésopotamie préhistoire et l'exploration récente du djebel Hamrin, Paris 17–19 décembre 1984.* Paris, 1987. Proceedings of a conference particularly concerned with the Ubaid and Early Dynastic I periods in the Hamrin.

Killick, R. G., ed. *Excavations at Tell Rubeidheh.* Warminster, 1988. Final report on the excavations at the Uruk site of Tell Rubeidheh, including a discussion of the settlement pattern up to the Sasanian period.

Kim, Gwon-Gu. "Diachronic Analysis of Changes in Settlement Patterns of the Hamrin Region." M. Phil. diss., Cambridge University, 1989.

MICHAEL ROAF

HARDING, GERALD LANKESTER (1901–1979), archaeologist who might well be called the father of Jordanian archaeology. Harding served for twenty years (1936–1956) as the director of the Jordanian Department of Antiquities. In 1951 he founded the *Annual of the Department of Antiquities of Jordan (ADAJ)*, which continues to be one of the most important scholarly publications dealing with current archaeological work in Jordan. Born in China, Harding spent his childhood in Singapore and England. His introduction to archaeological fieldwork came in 1926, when he joined the Tell Jemmeh excavation directed by Sir Flinders Petrie. Petrie also served as his mentor on the Tell el-Far'ah North (1927–1928) and Tell el-'Ajjul (1929–1932) excavations. From 1932 through 1936 he worked with James L. Starkey and Olga Tufnell at Tell ed-Duweir (Lachish). [*See* Jemmeh, Tell; Far'ah, Tell el- (North); 'Ajjul, Tell el-; Lachich; *and the biographies of Petrie, Starkey, and Tufnell.*]

Harding is best known for his work at Qumran and his documentation of Safaitic inscriptions from the Jordanian desert. Following the discovery of the Dead Sea Scrolls, he worked with Père Roland de Vaux for several seasons at the excavation at Khirbet Qumran. He was instrumental in assembling an international team of scholars to reconstruct, study, and publish the scrolls. [*See* Qumran; Dead Sea Scrolls; *and the biography of Vaux.*]

In the latter years of his career, Harding focused his attention on pre-Islamic inscriptions. In a series of expeditions to Jordan's northeastern (H5, oil pipeline pumping station) desert region, he collected nearly six thousand Safaitic inscriptions. He published them in numerous books and articles, including *An Index and Concordance of Pre-Islamic Arabian Names and Inscriptions* (1971), which is still considered an authoritative text. Harding concluded his work as a field archaeologist with surveys of the Aden Protectorates (1959–1960) and northwestern Saudi Arabia (1970; 1972).

In addition to his extensive scholarly publications, Harding promoted greater public awareness of Jordan's archaeological heritage through such popular publications as *The Antiquities of Jordan* (1959).

BIBLIOGRAPHY

"A Bibliography of Gerald Lankester Harding." *Annual of the Department of Antiquities of Jordan* 24 (1980): 8–12.

Harding, G. Lankester. *The Antiquities of Jordan.* New York, 1959.

Harding, G. Lankester. *Archaeology in the Aden Protectorates.* London, 1964.

Harding, G. Lankester, with Peter J. Parr and J. E. Dayton. "Preliminary Survey in N.W. Arabia, 1968, Part I: Archaeology." *Bulletin of the Institute of Archaeology* (University of London) 8–9 (1970): 193–242, pls. 1–42.

Harding, G. Lankester. *An Index and Concordance of Pre-Islamic Arabian Names and Inscriptions.* Toronto, 1971.

Harding, G. Lankester, and J. E. Dayton. "Preliminary Survey in N.W. Arabia, 1968, Part I: Archaeology (Continued)." *Bulletin of the Institute of Archaeology* (University of London) 10 (1972): 23–35, pls. 1–18.

Harding, G. Lankester, Peter J. Parr, and J. E. Dayton. "The Thamudic and Lihyanite Texts." In "Preliminary Survey in N.W. Arabia, 1968, Part II: Epigraphy." *Bulletin of the Institute of Archaeology* (University of London) 10 (1972): 36–52, 60; pls. 19–25.

DAVID W. McCREERY

HAROR, TEL (Ar., Tell Abu Ḥureyra), site located in the western Negev desert, on the north bank of Naḥal Gerar (31°23' N, 34°37' E). The site has been identified with Beth-Merkabot (William F. Albright, 1925, p. 6), Gerar (Yohanan Aharoni, 1954, pp. 110–111), Gath (Lawrence Stager, 1995, pp. 342–343), and Sharuhen (Anson F. Rainey, 1993, p. 185*). This 40-acre trapezoidal mound is crowned by an upper tell some 3 acres in size and 10 m high. Excavations conducted between 1982 and 1992 by an expedition from Ben Gurion University, directed by Eliezer D. Oren, indicated that the site had been inhabited only sporadically during the Chalcolithic–Early Bronze Age I, but continuously between the Middle Bronze and Persian periods.

The MB II–III town is represented by a 40-acre compound surrounded by a formidable defense system of earthen ramparts (20 m wide × 8 m high) and a deep fosse (5–7 m deep × 15 m across). Area K, in the southwest corner of the compound, was occupied by the architectural remains of a spacious cult precinct. The two-phased (K4–5) temple complex comprised a massive Syrian-style *migdal*, or "tower," sanctuary; a chamber with benches and niches for offerings; and a mud-brick (offering ?) altar. [*See* Altars.] The *favissae*, or "pits," in the courtyard yielded many bones

HAROR, TEL. Figure 1. *Cult stand from the MB temple courtyard.* (Courtesy E. D. Oren)

of ritually slaughtered animals, including complete skeletons of puppies and birds. Nearby, another pit was uncovered, that contained skeletons of donkeys. The rich store of cult vessels and ex-votos—animal and human figurines, incense stands, vessels applied with figures of horned animals and snakes—supplies details of Canaanite cult and religion during the Middle Bronze Age (see figure 1). [*See* Canaanites; Cult.] In area L, on the upper slope of the rampart, the remains of a large MB III public building were found, apparently a courtyard-style palace, with stone-lined buttressed foundations (L4). [*See* Palace.] In area B, under Iron Age I strata, a stone-lined MB grave with the burials of infants and an adult was recovered. [*See* Burial Techniques.] Although the extent of the succeeding LB I–III settlements at Tel Haror remains undetermined, it was probably considerably smaller than, and restricted to certain areas of, the MB town. A large and well-organized public structure (L2–3), perhaps a patrician house, was explored in area L, directly above the walls of the MB palace. Excavations in area K unearthed various installations from the LB III, notably a well-preserved potter's kiln and associated refuse pits.

The main Iron I settlement is recorded in area B and on the upper slope of the rampart. Excavations yielded a sequence of building phases (B7–1) that span the LB III and the end of the Iron I period. The remains of phases B6–5 of Iron I belong to a spacious structure with a stone-paved courtyard. It is noteworthy that these deposits produced locally manufactured monochrome pottery of Aegean types.

Phases B4–2 are represented by a series of carefully constructed buildings on stone foundations and by stone-lined grain silos that yielded rich assemblages of both monochrome and bichrome painted ceramics as well as nicely cut stone seals. [*See* Granaries and Silos.] To the last phase of Iron I (B1) in the late eleventh century BCE belongs a massive citadel and a building with a cobbled courtyard. Certain activities, industrial and domestic, in this period were also recorded in other areas of the tell (D, K, L).

Excavations in 1982–1986 in areas D, E, and G on the upper tell uncovered exceptionally well-preserved remains of a highly organized Iron II–III fortified citadel at the northeastern corner of the MB rampart (see figure 2). The overall shape of the upper tell was determined by the defense complex, which included a rampart, massive defense wall, glacis, and probably also a corner bastion. The 4-meter-wide enclosure wall is preserved to a height of 4 m; its base is supported by a massive embankment and glacis constructions. A formidable mud-brick tower (about 9 × 7 m) protrudes from the wall; nearby, a mud-brick platform had supported the corner tower.

A cluster of well-planned and exceptionally well-preserved storehouses was explored in area G, including long-halled magazines constructed against the enclosure wall. The magazines were elevated on mud-brick platforms that

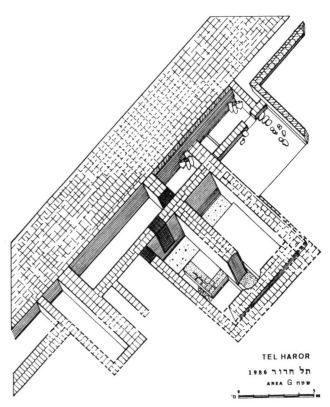

TEL HAROR
תל חרור 1986
AREA G שטח

HAROR, TEL. Figure 2. *Isometric view of the citadel wall and magazine.* (Courtesy E. D. Oren)

consisted of massive foundation walls with stones and fragments of bricks packed tightly in between them. Stratigraphic and artifactual considerations imply a mid- or late eighth-century BCE date for the construction of the citadel and the buildings inside it (G6–5). For some reason (earthquake?), soon after their construction, both the fortification system and the buildings inside underwent a major renovation (G4) that involved the raising of the glacis and floors for some 2 m. The citadel (G3) came to an end in a violent conflagration sometime in the mid- to late seventh century BCE, likely caused by an Egyptian military expedition of the Saite kings. Excavations yielded a rich store of finds, such as Phoenician-style transport amphorae, as well as jars with incised inscriptions, including one inscribed with the word *lbgd* alongside an Egyptian ankh and the hieratic numeral 8 inscribed four times. The results of the excavations on the upper tell suggest that the building of the citadel at Tel Haror may have been part of Assyria's overall military and economic organization in southern Philistia and on the border of Egypt. [*See* Assyrians.] The reoccupation in the Persian period (G, D1) of the upper tell involved a large-scale leveling of the preceeding Iron Age site. The remains in area G consisted of a spacious building with cobbled floors and grain pits; another building, in area D, had a large courtyard paved with stone slabs. The finds included Greek and Cypriot imports, clay figurines, and Aramaic ostraca.

BIBLIOGRAPHY

Albright, William F. "The Fall Trip of the School in Jerusalem: From Jerusalem to Gaza and Back." *Bulletin of the American Schools of Oriental Research*, no. 17 (1925): 4–9.

Aharoni, Yohanan. "The Land of Gerar." *Eretz-Israel* 3 (1954): 108–111 (in Hebrew).

Oren, Eliezer D., et al. "Tel Haror." *Excavations and Surveys in Israel* 2 (1983): 33–35.

Oren, Eliezer D., and M. A. Morrison. "Land of Gerar Expedition: Preliminary Report for the Seasons of 1982 and 1983." In *Preliminary Reports of ASOR-Sponsored Excavations, 1980–84*, edited by Walter E. Rast, pp. 57–87. Bulletin of the American Schools of Oriental Research, Supplement no. 24. Winona Lake, Ind., 1986.

Oren, Eliezer D. "Haror, Tel." In *The New Encyclopedia of Archaeological Excavations in the Holy Land*, vol. 2, pp. 580–584. Jerusalem and New York, 1993.

Rainey, Anson F. "Sharhan/Sharuhen—The Problem of Identification." *Eretz-Israel* 24 (1993): 178*–187*.

Stager, Lawrence E. "The Impact of the Sea Peoples in Canaan (1185–1050 BCE)." In *The Archaeology of Society in the Holy Land*, edited by Thomas E. Levy, pp. 332–348. Leicester, 1993.

ELIEZER D. OREN

HARTUV (Ar., er-Rujum; map reference 149 × 129), Early Bronze I site located near Naḥal Sorek, north of Beth-Shemesh, in Israel's northern Shephelah. Hartuv is the site's modern Hebrew name. The site was discovered during field surveys; small-scale excavations were conducted between 1985 and 1988 under the direction of Pierre de Miroschedji and Amihai Mazar, on behalf of the French Research Center in Jerusalem and the Hebrew University of Jerusalem.

The site is approximately 7.5 acres in area; two strata dated to the EB I were observed, apparently founded on virgin soil. Only a few remains from later periods were found.

A hillock at the center of the site (area A) marks the remains of a public architectural complex, a rare feature in an EB I settlement. The complex, only partially excavated, includes a central courtyard surrounded by rooms on at least three sides. The main room on the south was probably a sanctuary (5.8 × 15 m), with a line of pillar bases along its long axis and an entrance in one of the long walls. The wall opposite the entrance was lined with standing stones, fronted by a narrow bench. Some of the stones were smooth and shaped into rectangles. The excavators identified them as a line of *maṣṣēbôt* ("standing stones"), used in the cult as memorials to tribal ancestors or as symbols of deities. It is possible that in an earlier stage the stones stood in an open cult place and only later were incorporated into the building.

Another broad hall in this complex had a monumental entrance with two monolithic doorjambs made of well-cut stone blocks up to 1.9 m high. These architectural features are unknown from other EB I sites. Two narrow subsidiary chambers formed another part of the complex. The complex may have served as the community's joint religious and secular center.

The pottery assemblage found at the site is homogeneous and can be identified as a southern version of the EB I culture in Palestine. It is characterized by an abundance of incised and painted designs but lacks red slip and burnish. Similar assemblages are known from several sites in southern Palestine. Some of the sherds belong to a group of pottery inspired by Egyptian techniques and forms, though they were produced in southern Palestine. These connect Hartuv with the Egyptian colony at Tel 'Erani to the south, dated to the time of the first dynasty.

Hartuv has important implications for several aspects of EB I culture, such as architectural forms and monumental building techniques; regionality in the material culture; and perhaps also cult practices and the role of religious institutions in the society. The site was abandoned before the end of the EB I, perhaps when nearby Yarmut developed as an urban center.

[*See also* Yarmut, Tel.]

BIBLIOGRAPHY

For brief reports on the excavations at Hartuv, see Amihai Mazar and Pierre de Miroschedji, "Hartuv (Er-Rujum)," *Excavations and Surveys in Israel* 4 (1985): 45, and "Hartuv: Notes and News," *Israel Exploration Journal* 36 (1986): 109; 38 (1988): 84; and 39 (1989): 110–112.

AMIHAI MAZAR and PIERRE DE MIROSCHEDJI

HASA, WADI EL-, one of the main east–west wadis in Jordan; it begins in the eastern Jordan desert and flows in a northwesterly direction to the Southern Ghors at es-Safi at the southeast end of the Dead Sea. Elevations range from about 800 m near its eastern end at Qal'at el-Hasa (2392.5 × 0278) to about −370 m at its western end, just west (194.9 × 49.9) of es-Safi. Elevations to the north and south of the wadi range in excess of 1,200 m, however.

Wadi el-Hasa is situated on the west side of a physiographic province geologists describe as the mountain ridge and northern highlands east of the Great Rift Valley. Immediately west of the wadi is a sharp change in geologic style. The north–south boundary fault of the Dead Sea Rift is located just east of es-Safi. This is marked by a sharp change in elevation with values being in excess of 1,000 m east of the fault and fewer than −200 m to its west.

A number of explorers visited the area south of Wadi el-Hasa in the nineteenth and early twentieth centuries. Among them, Nelson Glueck extensively explored the area (1934–1939), excavating the Nabatean temple at Khirbet et-Tannur (2173 × 0420), immediately south of Wadi el-Hasa, in 1937 and 1938 (Glueck, 1966). Manfred Weippert (1979) surveyed several sites immediately south of Wadi el-Hasa in 1974.

Between 1979 and 1983, Burton MacDonald directed the Wadi el-Hasa Archaeological Survey (WHS), examining 1,074 sites both within and south of the wadi. The survey published a final report in 1988 (MacDonald, 1988). The occupational history north of the wadi is reported on in Miller (1991). Wadi el-Hasa was the WHS's northern boundary. On the east, the survey territory extended to Qal'at el-Hasa, immediately west of the Desert Highway; on the west, it went just beyond the edge of the plateau where the terrain drops off appreciably toward the southeast plain of the Dead Sea. The WHS's southern boundary went from 15 km (9 mi.) in the west to less than 1 km in the east, south of Wadi el-Hasa. The survey territory is cut by a number of impressive and deep wadis flowing south to north.

The WHS found lithic evidence of human occupation in the area beginning as early as the Lower Paleolithic period. This evidence spans all time-strategic units from the Lower Paleolithic through the Pre-Pottery Neolithic periods (PPN). There is little evidence of a Pottery Neolithic presence except in the western segment of the survey territory. The number of Chalcolithic sites seems to indicate an increase in population south of Wadi el-Hasa then. This trend continues into the Early Bronze I period but not into the Early Bronze II–IV. The Middle Bronze and Late Bronze Ages are poorly represented in the WHS territory. There is evidence, however, for the renewal of sedentary occupation in the area at the end of LB II. There are further indications of population increase during the Iron I period, with twelfth–

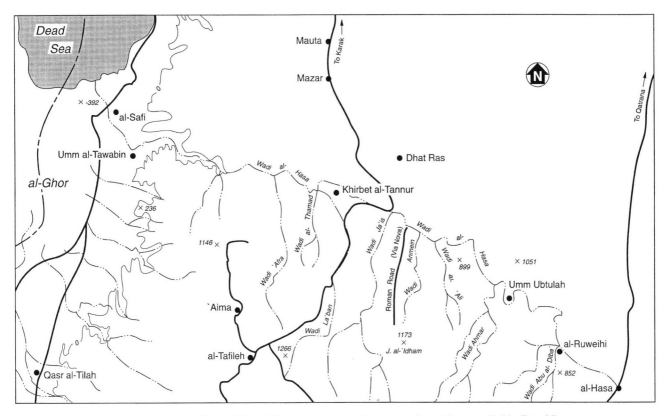

HASA, WADI EL-. *Map of Wadi el-Hasa Archaeological Survey territory.* (Courtesy B. MacDonald)

eleventh-century BCE settlements in the western section. This population increase seems to accelerate during Iron II and possibly is sustained until it begins to wane at the beginning of the Hellenistic period. Nabatean sites are found, especially in the wadis, throughout the WHS territory. Roman period sites are also found throughout the territory and a segment of the Via Nova Traiana is well preserved in the central segment. The Byzantine period seems to be, on the basis of the number of sites, one of significant population. The Early Islamic evidence is sparse, but there are several major sites among those from the Ayyubid/Mamluk period. A number of the Ottoman period sites are probably villages associated with the pilgrimage route to Mecca.

Since the completion of the WHS fieldwork in 1983, a number of archaeologists have worked on sites the WHS surveyed, illuminating human occupation in the area in the Paleolithic period: Gary O. Rollefson and Zeidan A. Kafafi (1985) studied WHS site 149, Khirbet Hammam/Abu Ghrab (2136 × 0437), a PPNB village site; Brian F. Byrd and Rollefson (1984) revisited WHS site 895, Tabaqa (2322.5 × 0342), an Epipaleolithic site; Zeidoun Muheisen and François Villeneuve began excavating the Nabatean-Roman village, temple, and cemetery at Khirbet ed-Darih, WHS sites 253–254 (2172 × 0352), in Wadi La'ban in 1984 (Villeneuve, 1988); and Philippe Bossut, Zeidan Kafafi, and Genevieve Dollfus investigated WHS site 524 (2173 × 0362), a Pottery Neolithic site, more extensively in 1987 (Bossut et al., 1988). In particular, in 1984 Geoffrey A. Clark began excavating a number of WHS sites at the eastern end of Wadi el-Hasa and in Wadi el-'Ali: WHS site 618 (2387.5 × 0278), a series of Upper Paleolithic Ahmarian and Levantine Aurignacian as well as Epipaleolithic Kebaran sites located on the northwest shore of Pleistocene Lake el-Hasa, with a C-14 date of 20,000 years BP from its Kebaran component, and a probable age for the sites at about 25,000–15,000 years BP; WHS site 621 (2380.5 × 0286.5), a slightly later Middle Paleolithic (*tabun* B–C-type Mousterian) open site located on the northwest shore of Lake el-Hasa, that is probably about 60,000 years old; WHS site 623X (2380.5 × 0288), a small (4 sq m) Upper Paleolithic Ahmarian open-air knapping station on the shore of Lake el-Hasa with many reconstructible cores that is undated but whose probable age is about 25,000 years BP; WHS 634, 'Ain Difla, (2274.5 × 0349.1), located in Wadi el-'Ali (one of the main south–north wadis emptying into Wadi el-Hasa), an early Middle Paleolithic (*tabun*-D-type Mousterian) rock-shelter associated with the middle terrace of Wadi el-'Ali, with 7-meter-high stratified deposits (the Oxford thermoluminescence date for burnt flint from the uppermost five levels, of the twenty excavated so far, is 105,000 ± 15,000 years BP); WHS 784X, Yutil el-Hasa (2375 × 0311), a terminal Ahmarian collapsed rock-shelter site with excellent faunal preservation, hearths, features, and a pollen sequence C-14 dated to 19,000 years BP; and WHS 1065, 'Ain el-Buheira (2385.5 × 0276.5), an Epipaleolithic Kebaran and Natufian open-air site associated with Lake el-Hasa and found adjacent to a rock-shelter and a fossil spring (five of its C-14 dates range from 16,900 to 15,600 years BP).

BIBLIOGRAPHY

Bossut, Philippe et al., "Khirbet ed-Dharih (Survey Site 49/WHS 524): Un nouveau gisement néolithique avec céramique du Sud-jordanien." *Paléorient* 14.1 (1988): 127–131.

Byrd, Brian F., and Gary O. Rollefson. "Natufian Occupation in the Wadi el-Hasa, Southern Jordan." *Annual of the Department of Antiquities of Jordan* 28 (1984): 143–150.

Clark, Geoffrey, et al., "Paleolithic Archaeology in the Southern Levant: A Preliminary Report of Excavations at Middle, Upper, and Epipaleolithic Sites in Wadi el-Hasa, West-Central Jordan." *Annual of the Department of Antiquities of Jordan* 31 (1987): 19–78.

Clark, Geoffrey, et al., "Excavations at Middle, Upper, and Epipaleolithic Sites in the Wadi Hasa, West-Central Jordan." In *The Prehistory of Jordan*, vol. 1, edited by Andrew N. Garrard and Hans G. Gebel, pp. 209–285. British Archaeological Reports, International Series, no. 396. Oxford, 1988.

Clark, Geoffrey, et al., "Wadi Hasa Paleolithic Project, 1992: A Preliminary Report." *Annual of the Department of Antiquities of Jordan* 36 (1992): 13–23.

Glueck, Nelson. *Explorations in Eastern Palestine*. Vols. 1–3. Annual of the American Schools of Oriental Research, 14, 15, 18/19. New Haven, 1934–1939. Important for early exploration in the area.

Glueck, Nelson. *Deities and Dolphins: The Story of the Nabataeans*. London, 1966. Important for Glueck's work at Khirbet et-Tannur.

Glueck, Nelson. *The Other Side of the Jordan*. Rev. ed. Cambridge, Mass., 1970.

Lindly, John, and Geoffrey Clark. "A Preliminary Lithic Analysis of the Mousterian Site of 'Ain Difla (WHS Site 634) in the Wadi Ali, West-Central Jordan." *Proceedings of the Prehistoric Society* 53 (1987): 279–292.

MacDonald, Burton. *The Wadi el Hasā Archaeological Survey, 1979–1983, West-Central Jordan*. Waterloo, Ontario, 1988. Main publication on the archaeological history of the south bank of Wadi el-Hasa.

Miller, J. Maxwell, ed. *Archaeological Survey of the Kerak Plateau*. American Schools of Oriental Research, Archaeological Reports, 1. Atlanta, 1991.

Rollefson, Gary O., and Zeidan A. Kafafi. "Khirbet Hammām: A PPNB Village in the Wādī el Hasā, Southern Jordan." *Bulletin of the American Schools of Oriental Research*, no. 258 (1985): 63–69.

Villeneuve, François. "Fouilles à Khirbet edh-Dharīh (Jordanie), 1984–1987: Un village, son sanctuaire et sa nécropole aux époques nabatéenne et romaine (Ier–IVe siècles ap. J.C.)." *Comptes-Rendus des Séances de l'Académie des Inscriptions et Belles-Lettres* (1988): 458–479.

Weippert, Manfred. "The Israelite 'Conquest' and the Evidence from Transjordan." In *Symposia Celebrating the Seventy-Fifth Anniversary of the Founding of the American Schools of Oriental Research, 1900–1975*, edited by Frank Moore Cross, pp. 15–34. Cambridge, Mass., 1979.

BURTON MACDONALD

HASANLU, site located in the northern half of the Solduz valley, just south of the southwestern corner of Lake Urmia in western Azerbaijan province, Iran (37°00′ N, 45°13′ E). The site rises 25 m above the surrounding plain and consists of a central high mound (the Citadel mound),

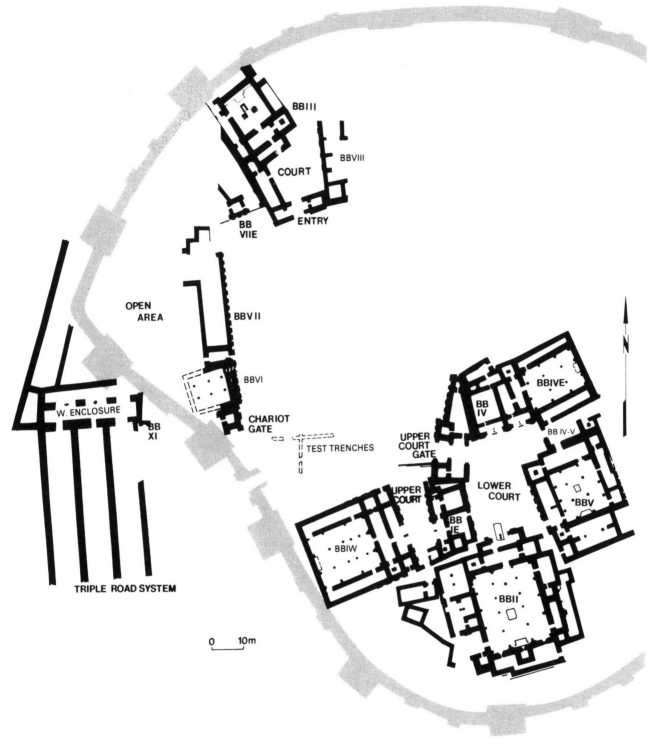

HASANLU.   Figure 1.   *Plan of the site.*   The period IV B structures in black were destroyed c. 800 BCE.
The fortification wall in gray belongs to the Urartian occupation (period III B), c. 750–600 BCE.
(Courtesy University of Pennsylvania Museum, Philadelphia)

about 200 m in diameter (see figure 1), flanked by a low terraced mound about 8 m high and about 600 m in maximum diameter as presently preserved (the Outer Town). The site clearly extended farther in antiquity because archaeological deposits occur in nearby fields and have been found beneath the modern village of Hasanlu. Soundings on the central mound indicate that the total depth of deposit is more than 27.5 m, extending beneath the present water table.

Solduz lies at the eastern end of the Qadar River valley, which runs from the Zagros Mountains on the Iraq frontier on the west to the edge of the grassy plains of Miandoab on the east. The kingdom of Assyria to the west and Urartu to the north vied for control of this region during the early first millennium BCE. In the ninth century BCE, the Qadar valley and Solduz appear to have been under the influence of the Assyrians, to judge from the material culture dating to that period at Hasanlu. Between 800 and 780 BCE the Urartians, who had established settlements and fortresses to the north and west, appear to have pushed south and occupied the Qadar valley. Joint inscriptions of Ishpuini and his son Menua are found at Kel-i Shin near the sources of the Qadar, at Qalatgah (down the Qadar about 27 km [17 mi.] to the west of Hasanlu) and at Tash Tepe to the east, at the edge of the Miandoab plain. In the eighth century BCE the Urartian settlement of Musasir was located to the west of Hasanlu, somewhere near the Kel-i Shin pass. East of Hasanlu, an Urartian inscription at Tash Tepe mentions the name of the Mannean town of Meshta. By general consensus, the kingdom of Mannai (biblical Minni) lay to the southeast of Tash Tepe, in the region of modern Mahabad and Saqqiz—although the details of the historical geography of this area are much disputed as a result of the lack of written records (Levine and Young, 1977; Reade, 1979). In the late eighth century BCE, the well-known eighth campaign of Sargon II passed through some part of this region (Levine and Young, 1977). Archaeological remains show an Urartian occupation of Hasanlu in the late eighth to seventh century BCE.

Archaeologically, the best-known period of occupation at Hasanlu is the Iron Age (periods V–III), but earlier periods have also been documented, extending back to the Late Neolithic (Hasanlu X, or the Hajji Firuz period; see Dyson, 1983). Hasanlu V begins in the second half of the second millennium BCE; period IV, dating from the end of the second millennium to the end of the ninth century BCE is richly documented because it was destroyed by fire sometime around 800 BCE. A short hiatus was followed by an Urartian occupation (IIIB) that in turn was followed by an occupation of the Achaemenid period (IIIA). Period II is poorly known but appears to belong to the end of the fourth or beginning of the third century BCE. After a long abandonment, the site was reoccupied in later Islamic times (period I).

The archaeological remains of Hasanlu Tepe first became known in 1934–1935 as a result of commercial digging in a cemetery along the northeastern edge of the Outer Town. The contents of one of these graves was published by Roman Ghirshman (1939, pp. 78–79, 253–254, pl. C). In 1935–1936, Erich F. Schmidt photographed the site from the air for the first time, although the picture was not included in his volume *Flights over Ancient Cities of Iran* (Chicago, 1940). In 1936 the British excavator Marc Aurel Stein spent six days at the site putting trenches in at the northern Outer Town and at the foot of the northern slope of the Citadel Mound (Stein, 1940, pp. 389–404). These excavations also encountered Early Iron Age burials; some artifacts from these contexts are now housed in the British Museum. In 1947 and again in 1949, the Archaeology Service of Iran undertook further excavation in both the northern and eastern Outer Town cemetery areas (Hakemi and Rad, 1950). They recovered Early Iron Age graves (later designated as Hasanlu V and IV; c. 1500–800 BCE).

The Hasanlu Project of the University Museum of the University of Pennsylvania was directed by Robert H. Dyson, Jr., from 1956 through 1977, when the Iranian Revolution ended fieldwork. After 1958 this research was conducted jointly with the Metropolitan Museum of Art (New York City); the project enjoyed the cooperation of the Archaeological Service of Iran during its early years, and, after 1971, the collaboration of the Iran Center for Archaeological Research (directed by Firouz Bagherzadeh). Excavation included stratigraphic soundings, horizontal clearance of the well-preserved Iron Age levels, and test excavations at smaller, adjacent sites (Hajji Firuz, Dalma, Pisdeli, Dinkha, and Agrab Tepes); general survey of the valley was also carried out. (See Dyson, 1983; for a bibliography of the project through 1976, see Levine and Young, 1977).

Excavation at Hasanlu Tepe focused on the ninth-century BCE level (period IVB), which was uniquely preserved because the site was burned during a military attack, probably by Urartians. Within the surrounding walls of this settlement four major buildings were set around two open courtyards. Each building was characterized by a portico and a large central columned hall surrounded by first- and second-story storerooms. These are the oldest such buildings so far excavated in later Iran and form an architectural link between Bronze Age Anatolia and Iron Age Iran. These large buildings and the smaller structures surrounding them collapsed, burying their contents in piles of debris. As a result, thousands of objects were recovered made of copper, bronze, iron, silver, gold, glass, ceramic, amber, ivory, bone, shell, wood, antler, and other materials. A wide variety of objects was found, including a large quantity of horse trappings (bits, bridles, breastplates), containers, weapons, personal ornaments, and tools (de Schauensee, Muscarella, 1988; Winter, 1980). Cylinder seals and sealings (Marcus, 1988) relate to Assyria and to local traditions, as do carved

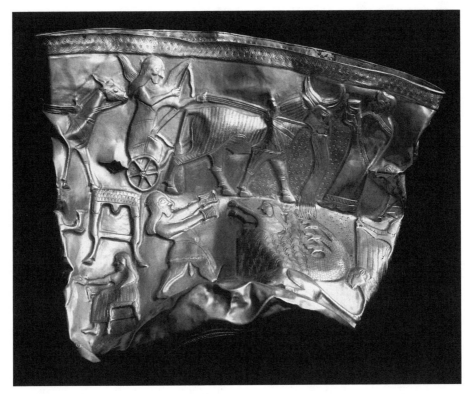

HASANLU.   Figure 2.   *Gold bowl.* Photographed in the Tehran Museum, Iran. (Courtesy University of Pennsylvania Museum, Philadelphia)

ivories (Muscarella, 1980, 1988). No tablets were found, but several fragments of stone artifacts carry names that indicate both Assyrian and Elamite contacts. A unique object, found in 1958, was a large gold bowl (see figure 2) covered with repoussé figures representing religious mythology involving three gods riding in chariots (storm god, sun god, and moon or local god), offerings, heroes in combat, and other elements (Porada, 1967; for detailed color illustrations see *Life* magazine 12 January 1959). These episodes draw on older Mesopotamian and/or Anatolian (Hurrian?) myths and symbols but are executed in a technique of metalwork common to late second and early first millennium BCE Iran (*Expedition*, 1989; Muscarella, 1980, 1988; Winter, 1989).

BIBLIOGRAPHY

de Schauensee, Maude. "Northwest Iran as a Bronze-Working Centre: The View from Hasanlu." In *Bronze Working Centres of Western Asia, ca. 1000–539 B.C.,* edited by John E. Curtis, pp. 45–62. London, 1988.

de Schauensee, Maude. "Horse Gear from Hasanlu." *Expedition* 31.2–3 (1989): 37–52.

Dyson, Robert H., Jr. "The Genesis of the Hasanlu Project." Introduction to *Hajji Firuz Tepe, Iran: The Neolithic Settlement,* by Mary M. Voigt. Hasanlu Excavation Reports, vol. 1. University Museum Monograph, no. 50. Philadelphia, 1983.

Expedition 31.2–3 (1989). Special issue entitled "East of Assyria: The Highland Settlement of Hasanlu," edited by Robert H. Dyson and Mary M. Voigt.

Ghirshman, Roman. *Fouilles de Sialk près de Kashan 1933, 1934, 1937.* Vol. 2. Paris, 1939.

Hakemi, Ali, and Mahoud Rad. "The Description and Results of the Scientific Excavations [of Hasanlu, Solduz]" (in Persian). In *Gazarishha-yi Bastan Shinasi,* vol. 1, pp. 87–103. Tehran, 1950.

Levine, Louis D., and T. Cuyler Young, Jr., eds. *Mountains and Lowlands.* Malibu, 1977. See especially Louis D. Levine, "Sargon's Eighth Campaign" (pp. 135–151).

Marcus, Michelle I. "The Seals and Sealings from Hasanlu IVB." Ph.D. diss., University of Pennsylvania, 1988.

Muscarella, Oscar White. *The Catalogue of Ivories from Hasanlu, Iran.* University Museum Monograph, no. 40. Philadelphia, 1980.

Muscarella, Oscar White. *Bronze and Iron: Ancient Near Eastern Artifacts in the Metropolitan Museum of Art.* New York, 1988.

Porada, Edith. "Notes on the Gold Bowl and Silver Beaker from Hasanlu." In *A Survey of Persian Art,* vol. 4, edited by Arthur Upham Pope, pp. 2971–2978. London and New York, 1967.

Reade, Julian. "Hasanlu, Gilzanu, and Related Considerations." *Archäologische Mitteilungen aus Iran* 12 (1979): 175–182.

Stein, M. Aurel. *Old Routes of Western Iran.* London, 1940.

Winter, Irene J. *A Decorated Breastplate from Hasanlu, Iran: Type, Style, and Context of an Equestrian Ornament.* University Museum Monograph, no. 39. Philadelphia, 1980.

Winter, Irene J. "The 'Hasanlu Gold Bowl': Thirty Years Later." *Expedition* 31.2–3 (1989): 87–106.

ROBERT H. DYSON, JR.

HASMONEANS. The Hasmonean state was created in the second century BCE, following a long struggle with the Seleucids and with some of the peoples settled in Palestine. The house of Mattahias the Maccabee, a priestly family from Modi'in, began a military struggle against the Seleucid

Empire (168 BCE). A struggle was also launched against the hellenizers connected to the Seleucid court, led by the most prominent priestly houses. The struggle started with the limited goal of achieving religious autonomy, which had been taken from the Jews by the restrictions of Antiochus IV Epiphanes. After Mattathias's death in 168, his son Judah (Judas), called the Maccabee, took over the command. After many battles with the Seleucid army and the hellenizers, he managed to take hold of the Temple Mount and purify the Temple (164 BCE). He fell bravely in battle in 161/60 BCE, and his brother Jonathan took over the command. [See Seleucids.]

As soon as the Hasmoneans became more powerful, their goal shifted to the more political one of creating a Jewish state in Palestine. Thus, from the 150s BCE onward, the Hasmonean brothers became preoccupied with fighting the Seleucid princes and strengthening their foothold in Palestine. After 161 BCE they were supported by Rome, which concluded a treaty with them; by Sparta; and by the Ptolemies, who ruled Egypt. After Judah's successor, Jonathan died, their brother Simeon took over. In 143 BCE Simeon officially laid the foundation of an independent Hasmonean state, which became an important political factor in the ancient Near East. The state fell to the Romans in 63 BCE, when the Roman commander Pompeius conquered Palestine. Simeon's successors, John Hyrcanus I (135–104 BCE) and his sons Aristobulus I (104/03 BCE) and Alexander Jannaeus (103–76 BCE), wanted to enlarge the area of the land of Israel and to make it their sovereign territory. Whereas Hyrcanus I mainly subjected the Samaritans and conquered and judaized the Idumeans, Aristobulus I (who ruled for less than one year, dying prematurely in 104/03 BCE) conquered the Galilee and judaized the Itureans (Arab tribes). His successor, Alexander Jannaeus, conquered even more land, and under his rule the territorial dimensions of Palestine were comparable to the Davidic kingdom at its peak. His wife, Salome Alexandra, who ruled the country after his death (76–67 BCE), did not extend the territory further. [See Samaritans; Idumeans.]

The conquering Jewish dynasty based its claims on the historical legitimacies of the biblical period, asserting that the land was theirs because it belonged to their ancestors. However, both during and after their conquest, they had to live alongside the Gentiles in Palestine—the Idumeans, the Arabs, the Greeks in the cities on the coastal plain, as well as the Phoenicians who lived throughout the land. Their most problematic relationships were with the Samaritans, who claimed themselves to be the true Jews, and who were settled in the center of Palestine, in the region around Shechem in the Samarian hills. [See Shechem.] Whereas at the beginning of the Hasmonean era the Jews lived mainly in the hill country of Judea (Judah), toward the period of the Roman conquest Jews were settling in many other regions of the country—in Gezer, Jaffa, the Galilee, and Transjordan.

From the reign of Jonathan in 152 BCE onward, the Hasmoneans, as well as being secular rulers, took upon themselves the high priesthood. The position was vacant between 159 and 152 BCE because Onias III (or IV) had gone to Egypt, where he had founded a new Yahweh temple at Tell el-Yahudiyeh. [See Yahudiyeh, Tell el-.] The high priesthood enhanced the stature of the Hasmoneans in the eyes of their own people and the outside world. Although the Hasmoneans were primarily secular rulers, they did not take the throne until Aristobulus I, who, in 104/03 BCE became the first Hasmonean king. Thus, the last three Hasmoneans to rule before the Roman conquest of Palestine were monarchs of a new Jewish dynasty. The Hasmoneans had some of the attributes of a Hellenistic kingdom—for example, they had a strong army that, since the reign of John Hyrcanus I, employed foreign mercenaries—although the exact proportion of Jews as opposed to foreigners in this army cannot be ascertained. It is, however, thought that the number of mercenaries increased throughout the reigns of Alexander Jannaeus and Salome Alexandra. During that period the army began to adopt techniques of warfare from the armies of the Hellenistic princes in the region (Shatzman, 1991).

The Hasmoneans, like other Hellenistic monarchs, ruled a vast territory that, at the time of Alexander Jannaeus, included almost the whole of Palestine on both sides of the Jordan River. Hyrcanus I was the first ruler to mint Hasmonean coins, and under the later monarchs these coins had a Greek inscription on them, "the king" (basileus), together with a Hebrew inscription. The inscriptions in Greek were probably meant both for foreigners who had settled in Palestine and for use outside the kingdom. No coin of the Hasmonean kings bears any human figure, however, which, in this matter at least, indicate that they were Jewish rulers and resisted Hellenistic influence. (Meshorer, 1982). Although the last monarchs of the Hasmonean dynasty wanted to appear to be like the Hellenistic monarchs elsewhere in the region, the extent of their hellenization remains an enigma.

The hellenization of Jews and of Judaism in Palestine during the Hasmonean era is a subject that has attracted many scholars. They point to the use of Greek as opposed to Aramaic and Hebrew, to archaeological remains showing Greek influence, to Greek motifs in the art and literature of the period, and to the Greek influence on Jewish thought. However, the existing literature that can be dated with any certainty to the Hasmonean era shows very little Greek influence (see below). Even less is known about the Hasmonean institution of kingship at the time, and the archaeological remains are too scant to lead to any definite conclusions as to the degree that Hellenism penetrated Jewish Palestine. Also, although there are sites at which it can be shown that

Jews lived in houses whose architectural motifs were Greek, that is not evidence that those Jews were hellenized (Kuhnen, 1990). There are signs, however, of the hellenization of the pagan population—in, for example, the existence of some syncretistic dieties in the cities on the coastal plain (Ashkelon, Tyre). On the whole, the Jews who were settled in the cities and villages may have been more influenced by Greek architecture and culture than those living in rural areas. Some scholars point to another area of possible influence that infiltrated both Jewish and pagan Palestine long before the Hasmonean period, namely the eastern cultures—Iranian, Aramaic, and Phoenician.

During the Hasmonean era the Temple in Jerusalem was not only a religious center for the Jews throughout Palestine and the Diaspora (Jews in the Diaspora sent contributions to the Holy City), it also had considerable political significance because the Hasmonean kings were also its high priests. Indeed, just because of this, there was some Jewish opposition to the Hasmoneans that even became actively militant during the reign of Alexander Jannaeus. The Pharisees, Josephus relates (*Antiq.* 13. 288–292), told John Hyrcanus I to be content with secular rulership and to abandon the priestly office altogether (there is an echo of these disputes in Jannaeus's time; *Antiq.* 13. 372). Salome Alexandra had to nominate her son Hyrcanus II to become high priest because as a woman she could not hold the office.

The cultural heritage of the Hasmonean kingdom is uneven, inasmuch as a large part of the surviving literature is from the Essenes (see below), most of which was found in the caves surrounding the site of Qumran, near the Dead Sea. [*See* Essenes; Qumran; Dead Sea Scrolls; Judean Desert Caves; Temple Scroll; War Scroll.] For almost half a century many scholars have claimed that this literature has numerous ideas in common with the other Jewish schools of the day, the Pharisees and the Zaddokites. Some writings exist that may have come from these latter circles, although their exact identity is still problematic and their transmission indirect—such as the apocryphal and pseudepigraphic literature excluded by the Jewish Sages (parts of *1 Enoch*, *Jubilees*, the *Testaments of the Twelve Patriarchs*, and perhaps parts of *Judith*).

The sources for the period are archaeological, numismatic, and literary. The latter contain the two books of *Maccabees*, and Josephus's *Antiquities* (books 12–14) and his *Jewish War* (Book 1), which briefly describe the period. There is very little left of pagan Greek and Latin literature that adds to the picture. The two books of *Maccabees* differ considerably from each other: *1 Maccabees* was probably written in Hebrew during the reign of John Hyrcanus I, whereas *2 Maccabees* was written in Greek outside Palestine by a Diaspora Jew called Jason of Cyrene (probably second century BCE). It was a five-volume book covering the period 175–160 BCE (ending with the death of Judas Maccabee). The book was condensed, and only this version is available. In contrast with *1 Maccabees*, which gives a more or less linear history of the period up to the rule of Simeon, *2 Maccabees* is full of Jewish theology and constantly emphasizes the intervention of God in favor of the people of Israel. Josephus remains the only historiographic source for the period from John Hyrcanus I through the fall of the Hasmonean independent state in 63 BCE. His account is too concise to form a very comprehensive picture, however. Numismatic material abounds but adds little to what is known of the nature of the Hasmonean kingdom.

BIBLIOGRAPHY

Avigad, Nahman. *Discovering Jerusalem.* Nashville, 1983.
Bickerman, Elias J. *The God of the Maccabees: Studies in the Meaning and Origin of the Maccabean Revolt.* Leiden, 1979.
Hengel, Martin. *Judaism and Hellenism: Studies in Their Encounter in Palestine during the Early Hellenistic Period.* 2 vols. Translated by John Bowden. Philadelphia, 1974.
Kuhnen, Hans-Peter. *Palästina in griechisch-römischer Zeit.* Munich, 1990.
Mendels, Doron. *The Land of Israel as a Political Concept in Hasmonean Literature.* Tübingen, 1987.
Mendels, Doron. *The Rise and Fall of Jewish Nationalism.* New York, 1992.
Meshorer, Ya'acov. *Ancient Jewish Coinage.* 2 vols. Dix Hills, N.Y., 1982.
Momigliano, Arnaldo. *Alien Wisdom: The Limits of Hellenization.* Cambridge, 1975.
Schürer, Emil. *The History of the Jewish People in the Age of Jesus Christ, 175 B.C.–A.D. 135.* 4 vols. Revised and edited by Géza Vermés et al. Edinburgh, 1973–1987.
Shatzman, Israel. *The Armies of the Hasmonaeans and Herod: From Hellenistic to Roman Frameworks.* Tübingen, 1991.
Stern, Menachem, ed. and trans. *Greek and Latin Authors on Jews and Judaism.* 3 vols. Jerusalem, 1976–1984.
Stern, Menachem. *Studies in Jewish History: The Second Temple Period* (in Hebrew). Edited by M. Amit et al. Jerusalem, 1991.
Tcherikover, Avigdor. *Hellenistic Civilization and the Jews.* Philadelphia, 1966.

DORON MENDELS

HASSUNA, site located in northern Mesopotamia, about 35 km (22 mi.) south of Mosul, between the Tigris River and the western Jezireh (36°10′ N, 43°06′ E). It is a type-site for the Hassuna culture, which represents one of the early farming village cultures of the Near East, dating to the late seventh and early sixth millennia. Hassuna sites are located in the north-central Jezireh, where rainfall agriculture can be practiced.

Hassuna covers a maximum area of 2.5 ha (6 acres). The site was discovered by Fuad Safar in 1942, and excavations, under the direction of Safar and Seton Lloyd, were carried out by the Iraqi Directorate General of Antiquities in 1943–1944. The ceramic sequence at Tell Hassuna is important in reconstructing the relative chronology of the Late Neolithic/Early Chalcolithic painted ceramic traditions of northern Mesopotamia. [*See the biographies of Safar and Lloyd.*]

Fifteen stratigraphic levels were distinguished in two soundings. The main area, sounding 1, was located 20 m southeast of the summit of the mound and comprised an area of about 2,500 sq m. Sounding 2 was located on the summit. The two excavation units were linked by a 2-meter-wide trench. The earlier occupation phases were uncovered in sounding 1, the later in sounding 2. The excavators considered the material from levels XIII–XV unreliable because of the proximity of the surface.

The Hassuna period was divided into two phases on the basis of ceramic developments. The Hassuna Archaic of levels Ia–c, II, and III is characterized by large storage vessels made of coarse, straw-tempered material and by small burnished bowls. A painted variety of the Hassuna Archaic pottery emerged in level Ib. The Hassuna Standard spanned levels Ib–VI and was divided into three general types based on design: incised, painted, and painted and incised. Samarran pottery first appeared in levels III–IV and continued until level IX (level V had the most). The Samarran pottery included the neck of a tall jar. The neck was ornamented with a human face, partly in relief. Many of the Samarran vessels had been repaired with bitumen and riveting, which suggests that the ware was a valued import. Halaf material was found in levels VI–XII and Ubaid material in levels XI–XII. [See Halaf, Tell; Ubaid.]

The earliest level at Hassuna, level Ia, rested on virgin soil. No architectural remains were recovered from it, leading the excavators to interpret it as the site of a series of tent encampments. Level Ia is now generally considered to date to the proto-Hassuna, a developmental phase of the Hassuna period recognizable primarily by its ceramics. As observed, for example, at Yarim Tepe (mound) I, the ceramics are stratigraphically earlier than the Hassuna Archaic and Standard ceramic traditions. In addition to Yarim Tepe I, proto-Hassuna remains have been found in Iraq at Umm Dabaghiyeh, Tell Sotto, Kültepe and Tellul eth-Thalathat, and at Tell Kashkashuk II, 20 km (12 mi.) north of Hasseke, in northeastern Syria.

BIBLIOGRAPHY

Lloyd, Seton, and Fuad Safar. "Tell Hassuna: Excavations by the Iraq Government Directorate General of Antiquities in 1943 and 1944." *Journal of Near Eastern Studies* 4 (1945): 255–289.

MICHAEL D. DANTI

HATRA (mod. al-Hadhr), site located about 90 km (55 mi.) south–southwest of Mosul in Iraq (35°35′ N, 42°44′ E). Hatra was situated just a little to the west of ancient Aššur, along the route from the Euphrates River corridor at Seleucia/Ctesiphon that connected to the northern route from Bactria to the west (running from Arbela to Singara, Nisibis, Carrhae [Harran], Apamea, and Zeugma). The city was first settled in the Late Hellenistic period (second–first centuries BCE) by Aramaic tribes with ties to Adiabene. By the first century CE these semi-independent dynasts developed into a buffer state of the Parthian kingdom (240 BCE–226 CE), against the Romans. [See Parthians.] Hatra was the capital of their kingdom and apparently had close ties to the Parthian capital at Ctesiphon. Both Trajan (116–118) and Septimius Severus (197–198) were unsuccessful in attempts to conquer Hatra (see Dio Cassius 68.31). In about 220–226, with the collapse of the Parthians and the advance of the Sasanians, it allied with Rome and was reinforced as a legionary garrison. [See Sasanians.] It was taken by Ardashir and his son Shapur I in 239–241. The site was deserted by the mid-fourth century, as it was seen by retreating Roman troops in 363, after the death of Julian (Ammianus Marcellinus 25.8.5).

Excavations at Hatra revealed the city of the first–second centuries CE that had developed chiefly under the Parthian sphere, but with (as with other Parthian centers) significant Hellenistic influences. The early inscriptions are predominantly in Aramaic. In the last phase, however, numerous Greek and Latin inscriptions attest to the influence of the Roman garrison. The architecture and art similarly reflect the mixture of Hellenistic, Parthian (Neo-Iranian), and Roman elements. The city was laid out in a large circular plan (c. 320 ha, or 790 acres) with a towered circuit wall and defense ditch, very similar to the plan at Ctesiphon. There is no regular street plan, and houses are grouped around the center of the city. Both the domestic and public architecture are of Late Parthian types.

The city center was dominated by a rectangular walled enclosure subdivided by a partition wall into a large outer court to the east (c. 300 sq m) and a small enclosure to the west (c. 150 × 300 m). The western enclosure served as the precinct of the Temple of Shamash (the Assyrian sun god), but also contained other smaller sanctuaries and likely the administrative center. The temple precinct was entered by two gates flanking the central axis of the inner precinct. Before the temple proper was a series of lateral vaulted chambers (iwans) facing onto the open court. Two large iwans (21 m wide) stood in the center, directly opposite the two gates; each one was flanked by a row of smaller iwans. In contrast to the pitched-brick vaulting used in the grand iwan of Taq Kisra at Ctesiphon (third–sixth centuries CE), the vault construction at Hatra used stone voussoirs. The walls were made of rubble-and-mortar cores with a dressed-stone facing. This type of construction (Romano-Syrian) is highly unusual in the region, especially in connection with architectural forms. One inscription indicates that the Temple of Shamash was under construction in 77 CE, which is likely the period during which the entire complex was built in its present form. Adjacent to the iwan of Shamash is a square platform with vaulted galleries on all sides, usually called a fire temple. Other temples were arranged in the outer courtyard or against the partition wall; a large temple in the northern part of the court was in an Early Hellenistic style, with a double colonnade. Both Ionic and Corinthian orders were found. The moldings may reflect influences from Baalbek, while some artistic elements suggest Achaemenid traditions.

The predominant language used at Hatra was Aramaic, as attested by more than three hundred inscriptions dating to the second century CE. Among other things, these texts indicate that the semi-independent dynasts took such titles as "king of Arab" (MLK' DY 'RB) and "king of the Arabs" (MLK' D'RBY'). If these titles were not used to connote rule over the neighboring region (called Arabia), as appears from similar texts at both Dura-Europos and Edessa, this may be the earliest preserved instance of *Arab* as a self-designation of a group, even though Hatra is quite a distance from the regions usually associated with the term. The Latin inscriptions all date to the 230s and 240s CE, during which time the city served as the easternmost garrison in Upper Mesopotamia. Whether the Roman presence is best understood as an alliance or an occupation is not entirely clear. The tribune of the I Parthica Legion was stationed there and made a dedication to Hercules. The tribune of the IX Maurorum Gordiana Cohort (238–244), also made a dedication to the Deus Sol Invictus ("The God, Unconquered Sun") of Hatra, a blend between the local tradition of Shamash and the romanized cult of Sol Invictus, found prominently in the third century and often in military contexts.

The date of the fall of Hatra is given by a reference from the Cologne Mani Codex, which preserves in a miniature fourth-century Greek codex a life of the Christian "heretic" Mani, the founder of Manichaeism. This document ostensibly preserves Mani's own account of his call to preach at the age of twenty-four, which he dates to the year in which Ardashir defeated Hatra and Shapur assumed the throne: "in the year in which Dariardaxar, the king of Persia, subdued the city of Atra, also in which his son Sapores, the king, crowned himself with the grand diadem" (*P. Colon.* 4780, col. 18.3–7). This yields a date based on the Persian regnal calendar of either 239/40 or 240/41 for the fall of Hatra, the death of Ardashir, and the accession of Shapur. This was also the beginning of the Sasanian encroachment on the eastern limes (border) of the Roman Empire, which would succede eventually in wresting the area from Roman control by the 260s. The Sasanian Empire lasted until 642.

[*See also* Hatra Inscriptions; *and* Persia, *article on* Ancient Persia. *In addition, many of the other sites mentioned are the subject of independent entries.*]

BIBLIOGRAPHY

Andrae, Walter. *Hatra.* 2 vols. Leipzig, 1908–1912.
Drijvers, H. J. W. "Hatra, Palmyra und Edessa: Die Städte der syrisch-mesopotamischen Wüste in politischer, kulturgeschichtlicher und religionsgeschichtlicher Bedeutung." In *Aufstieg und Niedergang der römischen Welt,* vol. II.8, edited by Hildegard Temporini and Wolfgang Haase, pp. 799–830. Berlin and New York, 1977.
Homès-Fredericq, Denyse. *Hatra et ses sculptures Parthes.* Istanbul, 1963.
Ingholt, Harald. *Parthian Sculptures from Hatra.* New Haven, 1954.
Kennedy, David L., and Derrick N. Riley. *Rome's Desert Frontier from the Air.* Austin, 1990. See pages 106–107.
Maricq, André. "Les dernières années d'Hatra: L'alliance romaine." *Syria* 34 (1957): 288–296.
Millar, Fergus. *The Roman Near East, 31 BC–AD 337.* Cambridge, Mass., 1993. See pages 102, 129, and 451–452.
Vattioni, Francesco. *Le iscrizioni di Hatra.* Naples, 1981.

L. MICHAEL WHITE

HATRA INSCRIPTIONS. Hatra lies some 55 km (34 mi.) northwest of ancient Aššur and approximately 80 km (50 mi.) southwest of Mosul in modern Iraq. The site was probably a camping ground used for seasonal occupation by seminomads from the Jezireh in northern Mesopotamia before it became a permanent settlement in the first century BCE. On the periphery of the Parthian Empire, Hatra remained, until the end of the third century CE, an important caravan town on the trade route connecting Seleucia-Ctesiphon with Singara and Nisibis. In wartime, Hatra would have been a crucial halting place for any army marching from Singara to Ctesiphon. The Romans, however, failed to conquer it during the Parthian wars, and only a Roman cohort occupied the town for a short period in the third century CE. The site's religious prestige, always prominent, accounts for the existence of a monumental temple complex and of large number of smaller shrines there.

What is known of Hatra is derived from classical sources, Arab legends, and some four hundred inscriptions of little consequence for the historian and of very uneven value for the linguist. The Hatraean texts are written in an Aramaic dialect of northern Mesopotamia that differs from Syriac especially in the use of performative *l-* for the third-person imperfect. This is the major characteristic feature; other phonological, morphological, or syntactical features cannot be confidently described because a serious study of the epigraphic material has yet to be done. The presence of many local dialects in the whole area, replacing the Imperial Aramaic that had, a few centuries earlier, been its official language, can be explained by the incursion of Greek at the end of the fourth century BCE. The script is, in many respects, close to that of the inscriptions from Aššur, Sari, and Hassan-Kef in the Tur 'Abdin, and from other sites in the Upper Tigris River area. The similarities between some letters of the Hatraean script and those of the inscriptions found at Garni in Armenia and at Armazi in Georgia are not negligible. In the Hatra inscriptions, however, the neat, distinctive handwriting of the *aleph*, the long *nun*, the shape of the *shin*, and the absence of diacritics on *d/r* are noticeable. All of these features distinguish the script of Hatra from that of Palmyra and from Syriac. The Hatrean script, along with some of its orthographic conventions, was taken over from

Arsacids. This borrowing cannot be ignored in an area that was always exposed to cultural influences from the East, if not its direct control.

The studies produced so far are of uneven quality and have not succeeded in placing Hatra in its proper historical context. Thus, in spite of much excavation and reconstruction, the ancient city falls short of being as well known as Palmyra. For example, little is known about the tribes who first settled Hatra. Compared to the dozens of tribal names attested by the Palmyrene inscriptions, the paucity of the Hatraean data is disturbing. Only three tribal names are known: *bny blʿqb, bny rpšmš,* and *bny tymw,* raising the question of why its habitants left their ethnic background unmentioned when writing their names. The forms of the names themselves help to answer that question: they portray a population mostly of Arab origin in which Assyrian and Parthian families merged to create a society the inscriptions reveal as both homogeneous and very religious. Theophorous names of Shamash are frequent at Hatra because the cult of the sun deity was particularly important. Equally so was a trinity of deities whose cult was especially remarkable for its clear definition of the relationships among the three deities: one is "our lord," another "our lady," and the third is "their son." No other community in the West Semitic area worshiped such a group of deities.

[*See also* Hatra.]

BIBLIOGRAPHY

Abbadi, Sabri. *Die Personennamen der Inscriften aus Hatra.* Hildesheim, 1983.

Aggoula, Basile. *Inventaire des inscriptions hatréennes.* Institut Français d'Archéologie du Proche-Orient, vol. 139. Paris, 1991. Contains information necessary to pursue independent study of the texts and their archaeological context.

Beyer, Klaus. *The Aramaic Language: Its Distribution and Subdivisions.* Translated by J. F. Healey. Göttingen, 1986. See pages 30–34.

JAVIER TEIXIDOR

ḤATTUŠA. *See* Boğazköy.

HAYONIM,

cave and terrace located in Naḥal Meged in western Galilee. From 1965 to 1979 the cave was excavated by Ofer Bar-Yosef, Eitan Tchernov, and Baruch Arensburg, under the auspices of the Institute of Archaeology of the Hebrew University of Jerusalem. In 1992 Bar-Yosef, Bernard Vandermeersch, and Arensburg, under the auspices of Harvard, Bordeaux I, and Tel Aviv universities, renewed excavations in the cave to clarify the stratigraphy and chronology of the Early Mousterian phase (see below). In 1974–1975 Donald Henry excavated Natufian remains on the terrace in front of the cave. François Valla of the French

Archaeological Mission in Jerusalem has been excavating on the terrace since 1980.

A Paleolithic sequence (layers A–E) is represented in the cave. Layer A consists of ashy accumulations from the use made of the site by shepherds beginning in the third century CE. This occupation had been preceded by the construction of a glass furnace in the second century CE that leveled the first stratum of Natufian remains.

The Natufian layer (layer B; Epipaleolithic) consists of three major habitation phases: the partial remains of a building with a burial from the early phase and a series of burials from the late phase. The main finds from the middle phase are a series of nine or ten unroofed, well-built, rounded rooms, each with a fireplace. During the time they were occupied, several of the rooms were modified for a new use; in one case, a lime kiln was installed.

The skeletons in the Natufian burials were positioned in various ways: extended, semiflexed, and flexed. Secondary burials were also present in a few graves. On rare occasions, the skulls of an adult had been detached from the body with the mandible left intact, a practice that became widespread in the Early Neolithic period. Bodies were decorated with necklaces and bracelets of dentalium shells and belts and pendants out of bone and teeth. [*See* Skeletal Analysis; Burial Techniques.]

The Natufian lithic assemblage is characterized by burins, Helwan lunates, and elongated picks. Stone implements for grinding consist of basalt and limestone pestles and mortars in various sizes, including a rare, large, gobletlike basalt mortar. Bone objects include gorgets, awls, bone points, spatulae (some decorated with a net pattern), hide burnishers, broken sickle hafts, and rounded objects shaped from bovid bones. The pendants were shaped, polished, and subsequently perforated, as the unfinished or broken pieces found reveal. Three caches were uncovered near the cave wall: one contained a group of basalt pestles, the second burned gazelle horn cores, and the third bovid ribs cut in two, as well as an unfinished sickle haft that lacks a groove.

Gazelle was the main game represented, along with numerous birds and some fish. Radiocarbon-dated legume seeds and a few wild barley grains reflect, although poorly, plant gathering in the Natufian period; better evidence is provided by the rich collection of processing tools such as mortars and pestles. The high frequency of commensals—the house mouse, house sparrow, and rats—indicates that the terrace was occupied almost year-round.

Two circular Natufian houses, a well-built silo of stone slabs, and an abundance of flints and bone tools were uncovered on the terrace by Valla. The graves from the terrace usually contained a single skeleton in a flexed position. It is the joint burials of humans and dogs that are of special interest, however. Again gazelle appears to have been the primary game hunted, one-third of which were juveniles, reflecting year-round hunting. Analysis of the cementum increments of gazelle teeth, which demonstrates that the animals were culled in both summer and winter, supports this conclusion.

A Geometric Kebaran lithic assemblage with characteristic elongated trapeze-rectangle microliths was uncovered under the Natufian layer on the terrace. In the cave, the Kebaran layer (C) contained mainly lithics and rare bone tools. Dominant among the microliths in the upper levels were obliquely truncated backed bladelets (Kebara points); on the lower levels arched micropoints and retouched bladelets dominated. The scarcity of faunal remains indicates that the site was occupied seasonally, probably during late summer and fall.

The Aurignacian layer (D) in the cave was seriously damaged by the Natufian burials. Radiocarbon dates place it between 29,000 and 27,000 BP. The lithics consist mostly of carinated and nosed scrapers, a few blades, and burins; the numerous horn tools include awls, points, double points, a broken split-base point, spatulae, and pendants made of deer teeth with perforated roots. Among the stone objects recovered are slabs colored with red ocher, a shaft straightener, and two stone slabs with intentional engravings—one apparently depicting an animal reminiscent of a horse. The abundant faunal assemblage provided remains of more than 120 gazelles, but only a few fallow deer, red deer, and boar. Three deep hearths in the cave's lowest level were dug into the Mousterian layer, as well as one rounded hearth with many stones. Another hearth, at a higher level, was constructed of two stone slabs.

The partially probed Mousterian layers yielded only meager flint assemblages dominated by Levallois flakes, elongated Levallois points, and some side scrapers. Only a few isolated human bones were found. The study of the rodent bones showed similarities with sites such as Tabun (layer C) and Qafzeh cave, while the deeper levels contained archaic species, as at Tabun D. [See Tabun.] Bedrock was not reached.

[See also Carmel Caves.]

BIBLIOGRAPHY

Bar-Yosef, Ofer, and N. Goren. "Natufian Remains in Hayonim Cave." *Paléorient* 1 (1973): 49–68.
Bar-Yosef, Ofer. "The Archaeology of the Natufian Layer at Hayonim Cave." In *The Natufian Culture in the Levant*, edited by Ofer Bar-Yosef and François R. Valla, pp. 81–92. Ann Arbor, Mich., 1991.
Belfer-Cohen, Anna, and Ofer Bar-Yosef. "The Aurignacian at Hayonim Cave." *Paléorient* 7.2 (1981): 19–42.
Belfer-Cohen, Anna. "The Natufian Graveyard in Hayonim Cave." *Paléorient* 14.2 (1988): 297–308.
Henry, Donald O. et al., "The Excavation at Hayonim Terrace: An Examination of Terminal Pleistocene Climatic and Adaptive Changes." *Journal of Archaeological Science* 8 (1981): 33–58.
Valla, François R. et al., "Les fouilles en cours sur la Terrasse d'Ha-
yonim." In *The Natufian Culture in the Levant*, edited by Ofer Bar-Yosef and François R. Valla, pp. 93–110. Ann Arbor, Mich., 1991.

OFER BAR-YOSEF

ḤAYYAT, TELL EL-, small (approximately 5,000 sq m) Bronze Age village site, located 2 km (1 mi.) east of the Jordan River, 240 m below sea level, on the first terrace above the existing floodplain (map reference 205 × 203). Nelson Glueck's report of his explorations in eastern Palestine between 1939 and 1947 suggests that Tell Abu Hayet (his site no. 154) was occupied during the Middle Bronze, Late Bronze, and Iron Ages (Glueck, 1951, p. 259). James Mellaart's 1953 Jordan Valley survey (1962) preserves this site name (his site no. 24) and notes the EB period, the EB–MB transition, and the Iron Age as possible periods of occupation. The East Jordan Valley Survey (Ibrahim et al., 1976) reports surface pottery from Tell el-Ḥayyat (their site no. 56) dating to the EB–MB transition, Middle Bronze A, B, and C periods, and the Persian era. These authors include Ḥayyat among a large number of sites threatened by agricultural development.

Excavations in 1982, 1983, and 1985 directed by Steven Falconer and Bonnie Magness-Gardiner (1983; 1984; 1989a; 1989b) exposed 400 sq m through 4.5 of cultural deposition. Ḥayyat's stratification, material culture, and four radiocarbon dates show that habitation began late in the EB–MB transition and continued through six stratigraphic/architectural phases to late MB IIC. Phase 6 (late EB–MB) and phase 1 (late MB IIC) deposits, which are limited to the center of the site, contain modest amounts of unmixed pottery and scanty floral and faunal remains. Phase 1 architecture consists of isolated stone wall foundations, whereas phase 6 lacks architecture altogether.

During MB IIA–C (phases 5–2), Tell el-Ḥayyat was a sedentary Canaanite farming hamlet, as demonstrated by abundant fragments of annual cereals and legumes (e.g., wheat, barley, peas, lentils) and perennial fruit-bearing trees and vines (e.g., figs, grapes, olives). Ninety-five percent of the animal bones are from domesticated farm animals (sheep, goats, pigs, and cattle).

This hamlet grew around a stratified series of four mud-brick temples at the tell's center, each of which is characterized by anterior "buttresses" and a surrounding enclosure wall. The temple forecourts in phases 5 (early MB IIA), 4 (MB IIA), and 3 (MB IIB) include small, undecorated standing stones, many with an adjacent stone lying flat at their base. The phase 2 temple (MB IIC) features plastered floors and walls; fragments of the exterior walls bear red paint. Phase 5 apparently lacks domestic architecture, but outside the enclosures of phases 4, 3, and 2 lie mud-brick houses, courtyards, and alleyways.

Copper and bronze artifacts include javelin points and

zoomorphic figurines. Carved limestone molds, a ceramic crucible, and slag indicate that tools and anthropomorphic figurines were cast here. Pottery manufacture is reflected by ceramic wasters and slag and an intact kiln (phase 4). The fill debris within this kiln included the severed head and hands of a young adult male.

The excavation areas at Tell el-Ḥayyat were backfilled after the 1985 season.

BIBLIOGRAPHY

Falconer, Steven E., and Bonnie Magness-Gardiner. "The 1982 Excavations at Tell el-Ḥayyat Project." *Annual of the Department of Antiquities of Jordan* 27 (1983): 87–104.
Falconer, Steven E., and Bonnie Magness-Gardiner. "Preliminary Report of the First Season of the Tell el-Ḥayyat Project." *Bulletin of the American Schools of Oriental Research,* no. 255 (1984): 49–74.
Falconer, Steven E., and Bonnie Magness-Gardiner. "Bronze Age Village Life in the Jordan Valley: Archaeological Investigations at Tell el-Ḥayyat and Tell Abu en-Niʿāj." *National Geographic Research* 5.3 (1989a): 335–347.
Falconer, Steven E., and Bonnie Magness-Gardiner. "Tell el-Ḥayyat." In *Archaeology of Jordan,* vol. 2, *Field Reports,* edited by Denys Homès-Fredericq and J. Basil Hennessy, pp. 254–261. Louvain, 1989b.
Glueck, Nelson. *Explorations in Eastern Palestine.* Vol. 4. Annual of the American Schools of Oriental Research, 25/28. New Haven, 1951.
Ibrahim, Moʿawiyah, et al. "The East Jordan Valley Survey, 1975." *Bulletin of the American Schools of Oriental Research,* no. 222 (1976): 41–66.
Mellaart, James. "Preliminary Report on the Archaeological Survey in the Yarmuk and Jordan Valley for the Point Four Irrigation Scheme." *Annual of the Department of Antiquities of Jordan* 6–7 (1962): 126–157.

STEVEN E. FALCONER
and BONNIE MAGNESS-GARDINER